THE ROUGH GUIDE TO BRAZIL

This ninth edition updated by
Daniel Jacobs, Stephen Keeling, Madelaine Triebe and Chris Wallace

Contents

IGUAÇU FALLS

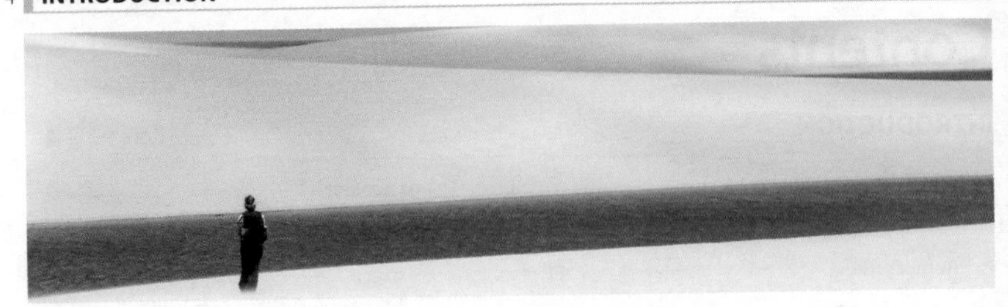

Introduction to **Brazil**

The mighty rivers of the Amazon, the pulsing Carnaval rhythms, bone-white beaches and footballing flair: almost everyone on the planet knows something about Brazil. Yet South America's biggest country still holds plenty of surprises. Though Rio de Janeiro draws by far the most tourists – indeed, for many visitors Rio *is* Brazil – this is a land of stunningly diverse and staggeringly beautiful landscapes, with a kaleidoscope of culture to match. In one, vast nation this up-and-coming superpower encompasses the dry, mythic landscapes of the northeastern sertão; the wildlife-rich plains of the Pantanal; the gorgeous colonial hill towns of Minas Gerais; churning São Paulo's urban chic; the watery labyrinth of Amazonia; and seemingly endless, mesmerizing tropical beaches all along the South Atlantic coast.

The sheer **size** of the country prevents any sort of overarching statement about the typical Brazilian experience, just as the diversity of its people undercuts any notion of the typical Brazilian. Indeed, Brazil often seems isolated in its own vastness, a world apart with apparently little connection to or interest in its seven Spanish-speaking neighbours. Cut off by language (**Portuguese**), culture and especially race, Brazil is proud of its diversity, from its native indigenous population and early Portuguese conquerors, to later waves of Italians, Germans, Spanish, Ukrainians, Polish, Arabs and Japanese migrants. In stark contrast to its neighbours it also has a relatively large **African population** – a legacy of slavery, which was legal here right up until 1888. As a result, Brazil is home to the most varied and dynamic artistic movements on the continent, with **Carnaval** the biggest party season anywhere and a bewildering range of musical styles, festivals and celebrations in evidence all year round.

Perhaps the biggest surprise is that most Brazilians now live in cities (seventeen of them contain over one million people), with seventy percent of the population crammed along the coastal strip; São Paulo alone boasts over twelve million inhabitants. Though vast regions of Brazil are empty or sparsely populated farmland,

BOYS PLAYING FOOTBALL, FAVELA MORRO DA MINEIRA IN RIO DE JANEIRO agriculture only represents a fraction of total GDP today and the nation is primarily an urban, developed society. As a result, though it is still possible to travel on a budget here, prices are much higher than in any other South American country.

Yet even on the shortest visit, Brazil's problems are glaringly obvious. The **economy** went through a devastating recession between 2014 and 2017, and the divide between rich and poor remains a contentious issue, with a mind-bending disparity of wealth – the grinding poverty of the *favela* (the generic name for slums present in every city), ongoing drug wars and high crime rates can be depressing.

While many Brazilians were proud of the nation's role (if not their team's performance) as football World Cup (2014) and Olympic (2016) host, billions were spent on new stadiums while millions of Brazilians still struggle to pay rent and find enough to eat each day – the exposure of a massive government bribery scandal helped spark the latest economic downturn. It's a challenging but fascinating time for Brazil, and a privilege to witness what's happening first hand. There are few places where strangers can feel so confident of a warm welcome – and a really good party.

Where to go

The most heavily populated part of Brazil is the Southeast, where the three largest cities – **São Paulo**, **Rio de Janeiro** and **Belo Horizonte** – form a triangle around which the economy pivots. All are worth visiting, but Rio, which really is as beautiful as it seems in pictures, is an essential stop, while the ravishing colonial relic of **Paraty** lies between here and booming São Paulo. North of here, the city of **Belo Horizonte** sits at the heart of **Minas Gerais**, where the old Portuguese towns of **Ouro Preto**, **Tiradentes** and **Diamantina** drip with colonial history. The **South**, encompassing the states of Paraná, Santa Catarina and Rio Grande do Sul, boasts the spectacular **Iguaçu Falls** on the border with Argentina – one of the great natural wonders

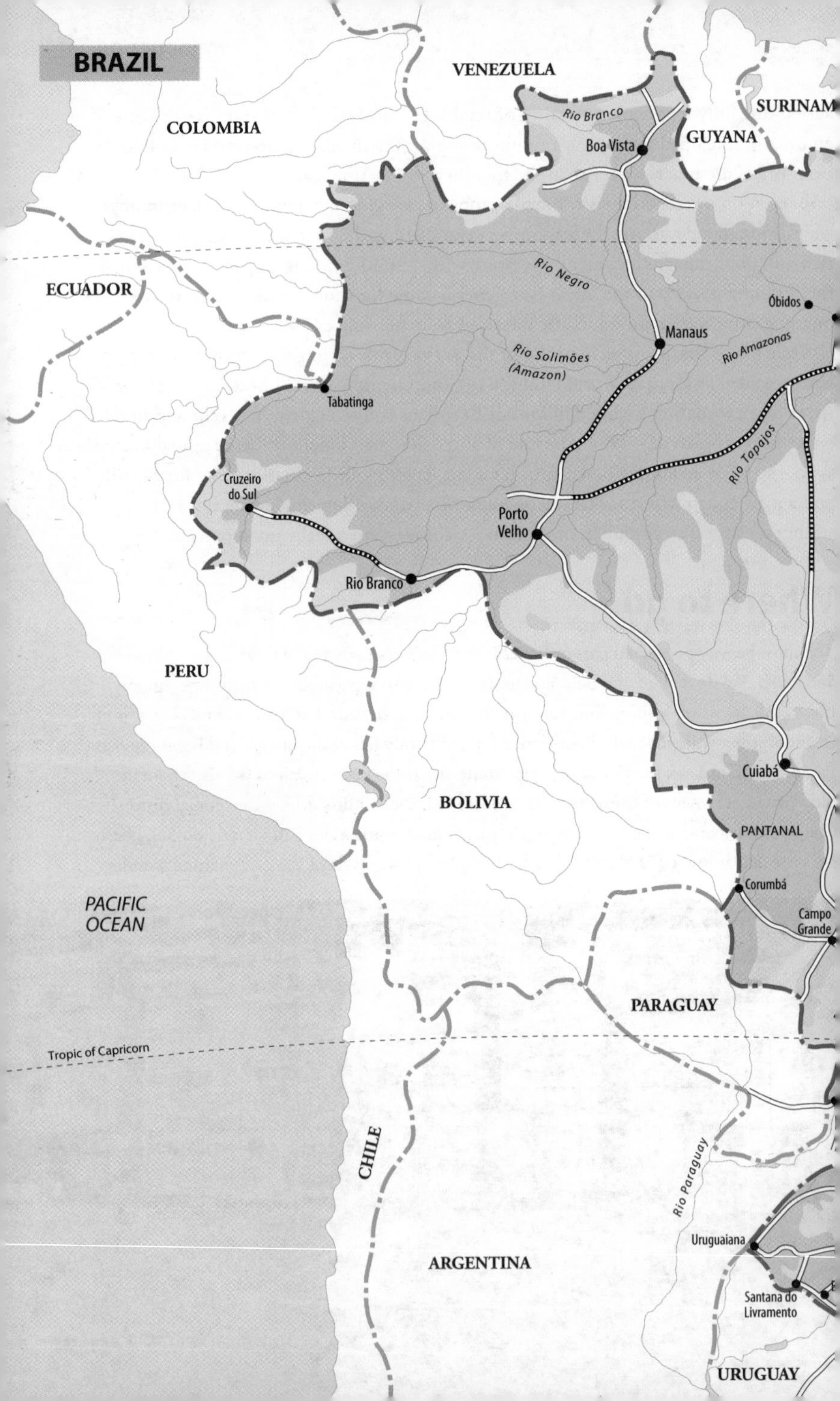

BRAZIL
VENEZUELA
SURINAM
COLOMBIA
Rio Branco
Boa Vista
GUYANA
ECUADOR
Rio Negro
Óbidos
Manaus
Rio Amazonas
Rio Solimões
(Amazon)
Tabatinga
Rio Tapajos
Cruzeiro
do Sul
Porto
Velho
Rio Branco
PERU
Cuiabá
BOLIVIA
PANTANAL
Corumbá
PACIFIC
OCEAN
Campo
Grande
PARAGUAY
Tropic of Capricorn
CHILE
Rio Paraguay
Uruguaiana
ARGENTINA
Santana do
Livramento
URUGUAY

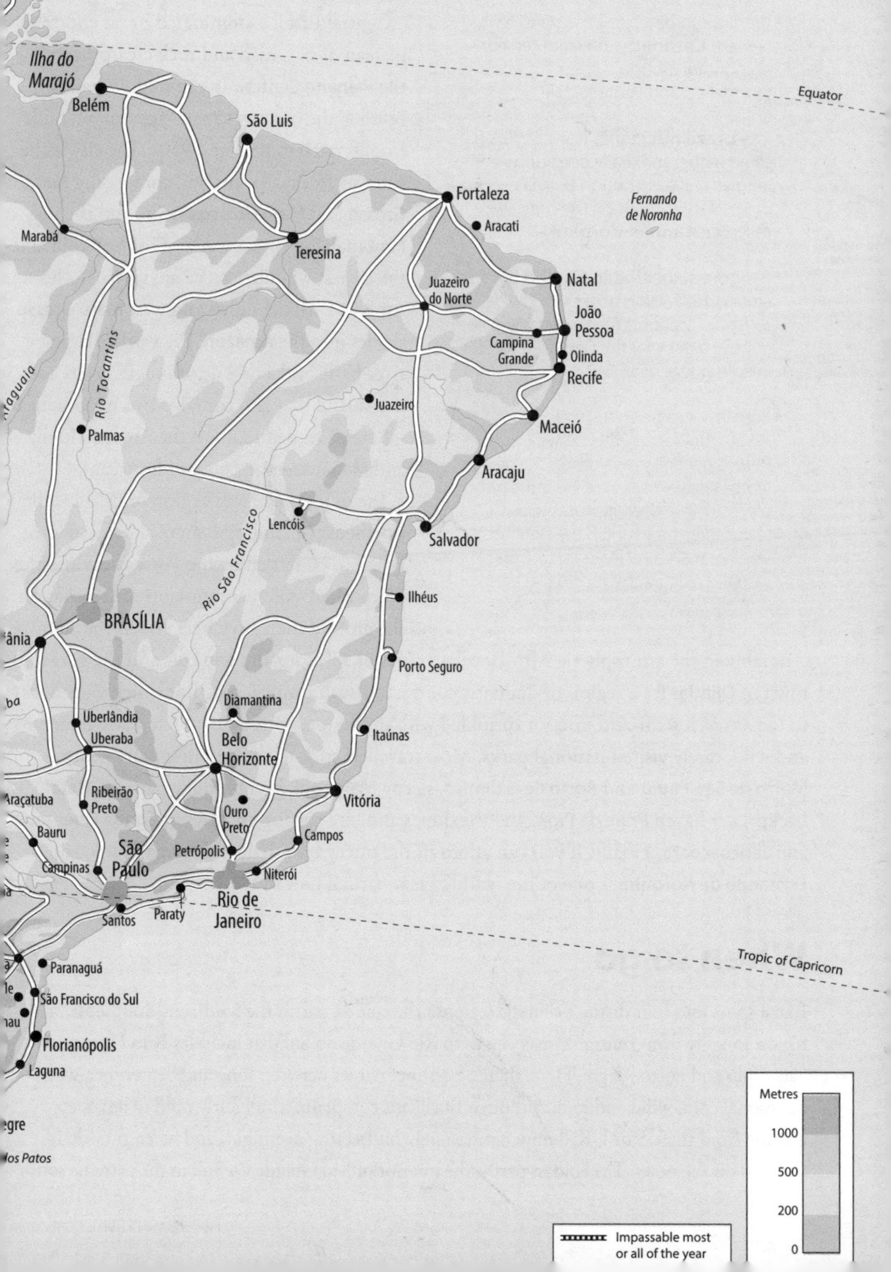
0
500
kilometres
ATLANTIC OCEAN
Ilha do Marajó
Belém
São Luis
Fortaleza
Aracati
Fernando de Noronha
Equator
Marabá
Teresina
Natal
Juazeiro do Norte
João Pessoa
Campina Grande
Olinda
Recife
Rio Tocantins
Juazeiro
Maceió
Palmas
Aracaju
Lencóis
Salvador
Rio São Francisco
Ilhéus
BRASÍLIA
Porto Seguro
Diamantina
Uberlândia
Itaúnas
Uberaba
Belo Horizonte
Ribeirão Preto
Vitória
Ouro Preto
Bauru
Campos
São Paulo
Petrópolis
Campinas
Niterói
Rio de Janeiro
Santos
Paraty
Tropic of Capricorn
Paranaguá
São Francisco do Sul
Florianópolis
Laguna
Metres
1000
500
200
0
Impassable most or all of the year

FACT FILE

- At around 210 million, Brazil has the fifth largest **population** in the world. It's also the fifth largest country.
- Brazil is estimated to be around 65 percent **Catholic**; Protestant religions account for around 22 percent (mostly Evangelical and Pentecostal).
- The **brazil nut** comes from a tree of the same name, and really does grow in the jungles of Brazil, though Bolivia exports more of them. In Brazil the nuts are called **castanhas-do-pará**.
- Rio-born author **Paulo Coelho** has sold around 150 million books worldwide (*The Alchemist* accounts for around 65 million), making him by far the bestselling writer in Portuguese of all time.
- Born in Minas Gerais in 1940, Edson Arantes do Nascimento, better known as **Pelé**, is generally regarded as the greatest football player of all time. He is the only player to have been in World Cup-winning teams three times and is the all-time leading goal scorer for Brazil (77). Brazil has won the World Cup a record five times.

of South America. From **Curitiba** the scenic **Serra Verde Express** snakes down to the coast, where you can chill out on **Ilha do Mel** or beach-hop around **Florianópolis**.

Central Brazil is dominated by an enormous plateau of savannah and rock escarpments, the **Planalto Central**. In the middle stands **Brasília**, the country's space-age capital, built from scratch in the late 1950s. The city is the gateway to Brazil's interior, comprising **Mato Grosso** and **Mato Grosso do Sul**, and the vast **Pantanal**, the largest wetland in the world and the richest wildlife reserve anywhere in the Americas. To the north and west **Mato Grosso** shades into the **Amazon**, the world's largest river basin and a mosaic of jungle, rivers and marshland that also contains two major cities – **Belém**, at the mouth of the Amazon itself, and **Manaus**, some 1600km upstream.

The other major sub-region of Brazil is the **Northeast** (including **Bahia**), the first part of Brazil to be settled by the Portuguese and the place where colonial remnants are thicker on the ground than anywhere else in the country – notably in the atmospheric Afro-Brazilian cities of **Salvador** and **São Luís** and the gorgeous town of **Olinda**. It's a region of dramatic contrasts: a lush tropical coastline quickly gives way to the *sertão*, a semi-arid interior sprinkled with mysterious monoliths, prehistoric remnants and wild, rarely visited national parks. Most travellers stick to the beaches: party centrals **Morro de São Paulo** and **Porto de Galinhas**, sleepy **Maragogi**, beach-buggy paradise **Natal**, backpacker haven **Praia da Pipa**, and the dunes and kite-surfing enclaves of **Canoa Quebrada** and **Jericoacoara**. Finally, if you can afford it, the pricey but idyllic offshore island chain of **Fernando de Noronha** is one of the world's great natural hideaways.

When to go

Brazil splits into four distinct **climatic** regions. The coldest part is the **South** and **Southeast**, the region roughly from central Minas Gerais to Rio Grande do Sul that includes Belo Horizonte, São Paulo and Porto Alegre. Here, there's a distinct winter between June and September, with occasional cold, wind and rain. Although Brazilians complain, it's all fairly mild to anyone coming from the US or UK. Temperatures rarely hit freezing overnight, and when they do it's featured on the news. The coldest part is the interior of Rio Grande do Sul, in the extreme south

CHRISTMAS FESTIVITIES, SALVADOR

of the country, but even here there are many warm, bright days in winter, and the summer (Dec–March) is hot. Only in Santa Catarina's central highlands does it (very occasionally) snow.

The **coastal climate** is exceptionally good. Brazil has been called a "crab civilization" because most of its population lives on or near the coast – and with good reason. Seven thousand kilometres of coastline, from Paraná to near the equator, bask under a warm tropical climate. There is a "winter", when there are cloudy days and sometimes the temperature dips below 25°C (77°F), and a **rainy season**, when tropical downpours are severe enough to kill dozens in flash floods and landslides. In Rio and points south, the rains last from October through to January, but in the Northeast they last about three months from April in Fortaleza and Salvador, and from May in Recife. Even in winter or the rainy season, the weather will be **sunny** much of the time.

The **Northeast** is too hot to have a winter. Nowhere is the average monthly temperature below 25°C (77°F) and the interior often soars beyond that – regularly to as much as 40°C (104°F). Rain is sparse and irregular, although violent. **Amazônia** is stereotyped as steamy jungle with constant rainfall, but much of the region has a distinct dry season – apparently getting longer every year in the most deforested areas. Belém is closest to the image of a humid tropical city: it rains there an awful lot from January to May, and merely quite a lot for the rest of the year. Manaus and central Amazônia, in contrast, have a marked dry season from July to October. The Pantanal has a similar climate to central Amazônia, with a winter dry season from July to October and heavier rains from January to March. It's generally at its hottest between September and November.

AVERAGE TEMPERATURES AND RAINFALL

	Jan	Mar	May	Jul	Sep	Nov
BRASÍLIA						
Max/min (°C)	27/18	28/18	27/15	26/13	30/16	27/18
Max/min (°F)	81/64	82/64	81/59	79/55	86/61	81/64
Rainfall (mm)	155	142	17	3	36	177
MANAUS						
Max/min (°C)	30/23	30/23	31/24	32/23	33/24	32/24
Max/min (°F)	86/73	86/73	88/75	90/73	91/75	90/73
Rainfall (mm)	260	314	256	88	83	183
PORTO ALEGRE						
Max/min (°C)	31/20	29/19	22/13	20/10	22/13	27/17
Max/min (°F)	88/68	84/66	72/55	68/50	72/55	81/63
Rainfall (mm)	78	80	70	129	132	72
RIO DE JANEIRO						
Max/min (°C)	30/23	27/23	26/20	25/18	25/19	28/20
Max/min (°F)	86/73	81/73	79/68	77/64	77/66	82/68
Rainfall (mm)	126	125	78	39	65	100
SALVADOR						
Max/min (°C)	29/23	29/24	27/22	26/21	27/21	28/23
Max/min (°F)	84/73	84/75	81/72	79/70	81/70	82/73
Rainfall (mm)	34	48	161	82	58	61

Author picks

From remote Jesuit missions to São Paulo's rush hour and the vast jungles of Amazonia, our hard-travelling authors have visited every corner of Brazil. Here are their personal highlights:

Best street snack Head to *Acarajé da Cira* in Salvador (see page 224) for sumptuous *acarajé* (deep-fried balls of black-eyed peas stuffed with spicy seafood); grab a tasty hot dog from *Cachorro Quente do R* in Porto Alegre (see page 612); or savour roast leg of pork sandwiches in Belém (see page 343).

Most unusual place to stay Check out *The Maze* in Rio (see page 95), located in the middle of one of the city's safest *favelas*, and famous for its jazz nights and panoramic views (see page 105).

Mesmerizing rides Glide over the Amazon rainforest in Acre by hot-air balloon, spotting geoglyphs and curious geometrical formations as you go (see page 395); or take a wild jet-boat ride right up to and into the Iguaçu Falls (see page 570).

Best beach bar It's hard to beat *Pedra Sobre Pedras* in Morro de São Paulo, perched on a wooden deck with magnificent views and open 24 hours a day (see page 238); *Bar do Arante* lies on the quiet side of Santa Catarina island (see page 584); and *Kanoa* keeps the party going in Maceió (see page 264).

Microbrewing heaven Since the 1990s southern Brazil has been experiencing something of a craft beer revolution, with the German-influenced breweries in Blumenau some of the best (see page 594); there's also *Cervejaria Bierbaum* in Treze Tílias (see page 603); and *Wäls Gastropub* in Belo Horizonte (see page 155).

Natural wonders To see the Brazilian coast at its most raw and beautiful, visit the jaw-dropping sand dunes and lagoons of the Parque Nacional dos Lençóis (see page 325); stand in awe at the vast canyon in the Parque Nacional dos Aparados da Serra (see page 619); and admire the gorgeous Cascata do Caracol in the far south (see page 617).

> Our author recommendations don't end here. We've flagged up our favourite places – a perfectly sited hotel, an atmospheric café, a special restaurant – throughout the Guide, highlighted with the ★ symbol.

ACARAJÉ SELLER, SALVADOR

CASCATA DO CARACOL

25 things not to miss

It's not possible to see everything Brazil has to offer in one trip – and we don't suggest you try. What follows is a selective taste of the country's highlights: vibrant cities, world-class festivals, natural wonders and stunning architecture. All highlights are colour-coded by chapter and have a page reference to take you straight into the Guide, where you can find out more.

1

1 VIEWS FROM THE CORCOVADO

See page 73

Ascend the Corcovado mountain – where the image of Christ the Redeemer stands – for mesmerizing views taking in the whole of Rio and Guanabara Bay.

2 SALVADOR

See page 204

The capital of Afro-Brazilian culture boasts the best live music, capoeira schools, and the most beautiful architecture in Brazil.

3 BRASÍLIA

See page 402

Brazil's rather isolated capital is still best known for Oscar Niemeyer's architectural Modernist masterpieces.

4 PARATY

See page 130

This picturesque spot remains one of Brazil's best-preserved colonial towns, and it's a great base from which to explore the surrounding Costa Verde.

5 CARNAVAL

See pages 105, 226 and 280

For a memorable experience, take in the most important of Brazil's festivals, celebrated in notably grand style in Rio, Salvador and Olinda.

9

6 THE AMAZON

See page 328

Take a slow boat along the Amazon for close-up views of the mighty river and its wildlife.

7 FERNANDO DE NORONHA

See page 287

A gorgeous archipelago off the Northeast coast, blessed with empty beaches that are visited by thousands of dolphins early each morning.

8 SÃO PAULO

See page 482

It's impossible to ignore South America's largest city, the vast, dynamic behemoth of new Brazil, crammed with attractions, bars and restaurants.

9 THE PANTANAL

See page 459

The world's biggest inland swamp teems with wildlife, from capybaras and stealthy jaguars to giant anteaters and caimans.

10 CHURRASCARIAS OF PORTO ALEGRE

See page 612

Sample sumptuously grilled meats – beef, pork, lamb, chicken, duck and more – at these typical *gaúcho* barbecue houses.

10

11 TREKKING IN THE CHAPADA DIAMANTINA

See page 246

Explore the dramatic terrain of this enormous national park, which includes mesas, forest, river beaches, waterfalls and a kilometre-long grotto.

12 OLINDA

See page 278

The cobbled streets of this city's historic centre offer up countless examples of romantic colonial architecture.

13 ILHA SANTA CATARINA BEACHES

See page 577

Head to the island capital of Santa Catarina state, where kilometres of glorious beaches include gnarly surfing breaks and calmer waters for safe swimming.

14 RIO NIGHTLIFE

See page 102

A rather seedy inner-city *bairro* by day, Lapa at night pounds to infectious Brazilian rhythms, its nightclubs and bars teeming with locals and tourists alike.

15 SERRA VERDE EXPRESS

See page 549

One of South America's most scintillating train rides, through a rare, untouched slice of Mata Atlântica.

11

12

13
14
15

16 IGUAÇU FALLS

See page 562

The power and beauty of these massive falls is quite simply astonishing, and only rivalled by the tranquillity of the Mata Atlântica surrounding it.

17 BRAZILIAN FUTEBOL

See pages 89, 147 and 673

The greatest footballing nation on earth has produced Pelé and won five World Cups; see a game at the Maracanã (Rio) or check out Belo Horizonte's top teams.

18 COLONIAL RIO

See page 74

There are more colonial churches in Rio than anywhere else in Brazil – the pretty Igreja de Nossa Senhora da Glória do Outeiro is perhaps the city's finest.

19 MORRO DE SÃO PAULO

See page 235

Bahia's party central is also home to some jaw-dropping stretches of sand.

20 OURO PRETO

See page 168

Check out the truly remarkable Baroque churches and mansions tucked away in the steep, narrow streets of this charming colonial mining town.

18
19
20

21
22

23

21 COPACABANA

See page 80

On weekends you can hang out with locals who escape to Rio's sands to play sports, catch up on gossip or simply people-watch.

22 THE AQUÁRIO NATURAL

See page 451

Snorkel among some thirty-odd species of fish in the crystalline waters of this marine sanctuary, or spy on them from above in a glass-bottomed boat.

23 THE PROPHETS BY ALEIJADINHO (CONGRONHAS)

See page 178

Amazingly, the master sculptor of Brazilian Baroque produced his best work after leprosy deformed his hands.

24 JERICOACOARA

See page 309

With some of the finest beaches and the best surf and wind in Brazil, this is the crown jewel of a long list of sensational Northeastern beach resorts.

25 MANAUS

See page 364

Brazil's Amazon capital boasts an up-and-coming culinary and cultural scene, as well as the famous opera house.

Itineraries

The following itineraries span the entire length of this incredibly diverse country, from the mega cities of the south to the deserts and untrammelled beaches of the northeast. Given the vast distances involved, you may not be able to cover everything, but even picking a few highlights will give you a deeper insight into Brazil's natural and historic wonders.

THE GRAND TOUR

This three-week tour gives a taster of Brazil's most iconic sights and cities from south to north, travelling from Rio to Bahia by bus and by plane.

❶ **Rio de Janeiro** One of the world's truly great cities, with mind-blowing views seemingly at every corner, and legendary beaches at Copacabana and Ipanema. See page 57

❷ **Paraty** Travel along the coast to this picturesque colonial town, crammed with enticing *pousadas* and restaurants. See page 130

❸ **São Paulo** Don't skip Brazil's largest city; it might appear intimidating, but it contains the best restaurants, art galleries and museums in the country. See page 482

❹ **Iguaçu Falls** Stand in awe at the world's largest waterfall, a vast series of cascades plunging along the Rio Iguazu. See page 562

❺ **Ouro Preto** Fly up to Belo Horizonte, gateway to the pretty colonial hill towns of Minas Gerais: if you have time for only one, this is it, a beguiling collection of steep cobbled streets and elegant Baroque churches. See page 168

❻ **Brasília** Take a flight up to Brazil's capital city, a remarkable monument to the vision of iconic architect Oscar Niemeyer. See page 402

❼ **Salvador** Head back to the coast to soak up the sun, rhythms and flavours of the Afro-Brazilian capital of the nation. See page 204

❽ **Morro de São Paulo** End your tour on the beach, at one of Brazil's most fashionable and fun resort towns, just south of Salvador. See page 235

THE NORTHEAST BEACH TRAIL

Hot, sultry, rich in history, culture and some of the greatest music made in Brazil, the Northeast is perhaps the most beguiling part of Brazil; take two or three weeks to see the highlights, travelling by car or by bus from Salvador to São Luís.

❶ **Salvador** It's impossible not to fall in love with this gorgeous city, with its romantic colonial remnants, exotic food, capoeira and famously musical citizens. See page 204

❷ **Praia do Francês** Close to the congenial resort city of Maceió, this is a fabulous, chilled-out beach backed with excellent places to eat and drink. See page 264

❸ **Porto de Galinhas** Transformed from sleepy port town to hip resort in just a few years, with a hypnotic strip of perfect white sand and a party crowd at night. See page 284

❹ **Olinda** Brazil's picture-perfect colonial enclave is a languid, liberal ensemble of Baroque architecture, art galleries and live music. See page 278

❺ **Praia da Pipa** Soak up Brazil's most ashionable beach scene, enhanced by dreamy beaches, pristine lagoons and rich marine life, ncluding dolphins. See page 299

❻ **Natal** From this lively coastal city – a hub for music and dance – you can explore hundreds of kilometres of wide, dune-backed beaches by 4WD or beach buggy. See page 293

❼ **Jericoacoara** This low-key backpacker village n the dunes is far less isolated than it used to be, but just as compelling, with quality surf, wind and lagoons to lounge next to the top draws. See page 309

❽ **Parque Nacional dos Lençóis** It's worth making the effort to reach this spectacular national park, a vast area of untouched sand dunes studded with crystal-clear pools. See page 325

❾ **São Luís** End up at this steamy colonial relic, its opulent *azulejo*-smothered mansions half crumbling but filled with vibrant bars, museums and galleries. See page 316

THE AMAZON

Floating down the Amazon has been a romantic dream of travellers for centuries, and though the journey is a lot easier (and safer) today, it still requires some planning and patience. Take your time and make these stops along the way.

❶ **Belém** The gateway to the Amazon basin is a surprisingly intriguing old city of museums, mango trees, live music and craft beer. See page 334

❷ **Ilha do Marajó** This vast island at the end of the Amazon delta remains well off the beaten track, with wild, untouched beaches and herds of water buffalo. See page 348

❸ **Alter do Chão** This remote Amazon town is the home – bizarrely – of a wonderful white-sand beach and a wildlife-rich lagoon surrounded by jungle. See page 358

❹ **Floresta Nacional do Tapajós** Take a trip from Santarém to this tropical sanctuary along the Rio Tapajós, noted for its jungle trails and mammoth *samaúma* trees. See page 360

❺ **Rio Amazonas** If you haven't done so already, hop on an iconic Amazon riverboat at Santarém for the two-day journey into the heart of the jungle at Manaus. See page 333

❻ **Manaus** The capital of Amazonia is home to the incredibly opulent (and incongruous)

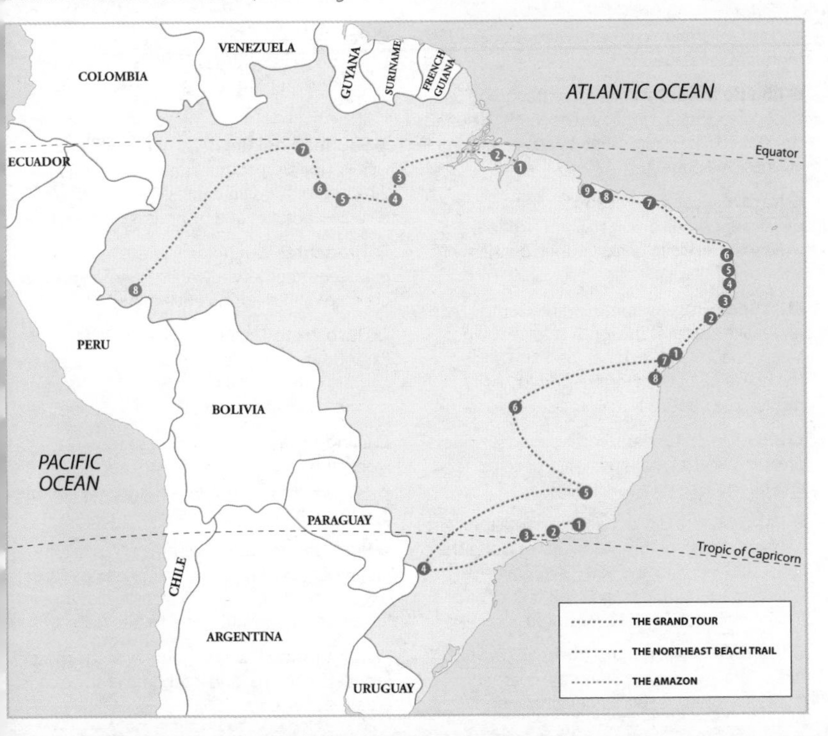

Teatro Amazonas, a host of creative restaurants and numerous jungle tour operators. See page 364

❼ **Jungle-tripping** Manaus is the perfect base from which to organize excursions into the surrounding jungle, with stays in romantic forest lodges or on riverboats. See page 376

❽ **Acre** The wild, untrammelled jungles of Acre, on the Bolivian border, are prime wildlife territory – make sure you take a balloon ride over the forest to soak it all up. See page 395

THE SOUTHERN COASTAL ROUTE

Though the Northeast gets the most attention, you can also travel south from Salvador along the Brazilian coast and see just as many pristine slices of sand, from burgeoning beach resorts to quiet colonial towns. This route can be completed by car or bus in two to three weeks, from Salvador to Florianópolis.

❶ **Salvador** Explore the crumbling colonial churches, samba-soaked lanes and vibrant bar scene of this wonderful, historic city. See page 204

❷ **Morro de São Paulo** A short boat ride from Salvador but another world completely, with exquisite palm-lined beaches and exuberant nightlife. See page 235

❸ **Ilha de Boipeba** For a more tranquil experience, head a little further south to this less developed island of pristine beaches and simple villages. See page 238

❹ **Itacaré** A backpacker and surfer haven south of Salvador, where you can learn to ride the waves, try capoeira or just lounge on the sands. See page 239

❺ **Itaúnas** Cross over into Espírito Santo and make a stop at this small seaside town surrounded by giant dunes, best known as the home of *forró* (a Northeastern style of folk music). See page 195

❻ **Rio** Make some time (and budget) for Brazil's great city and its glorious sights, beaches, food and *futebol*. See page 57

❼ **Paraty** Take a day or two to explore the cobbled streets of this historic town along the coast between Rio and São Paulo, crammed with elegant *pousadas* and remnants of Brazil's Baroque golden age. See page 130

❽ **Ilhabela** Check out this exclusive *Paulista* getaway a little further along the coast from Paraty – an alluring island bursting with tantalizing beaches, untouched jungle, volcanic peaks and waterfalls. See page 528

❾ **Ilha do Mel** Another popular surf and backpacker hangout, just off the coast of Paraná and a great place to rest up, hike or hit the waves for a few days. See page 559

❿ **Florianópolis** The premier resort island in the South, this is a laidback place with traditional Azorean fishing villages, modern beach hotels, untouched surf beaches and a plethora of activities on offer. See page 572

ESTRADA REAL

In the seventeenth century Brazil boomed on the back of vast reserves of gold, feverishly dug out of mines throughout Minas Gerais and beyond. Most of the gold ran out eventually, but the riches funded the construction of magnificent colonial towns that still remain; this route begins at Rio and works north tracing the old "Estrada Real" to the mines.

❶ **Rio** Though Rio is better known for its beaches, the colonial heart of the city is one of the richest historical zones in Brazil, with an elegant ensemble of Baroque churches and handsome mansions. See page 57

❷ **Paraty** The original "Royal Road" – the Caminho Velho – began in this old port city, still one of the prettiest towns in the nation. See page 130

❸ **São João del Rei** Head north in Minas Gerais, stopping at this modern university town, which still retains an impressive collection of colonial churches and museums. See page 179

❹ **Tiradentes** Wonderfully preserved eighteenth-century town, boasting magnificent churches and mansions. See page 183

❺ **Ouro Preto** The richest concentration of Baroque and Rococo art and architecture in the country makes Brazil's eighteenth-century gold-mining centre an essential stop. See page 168

❻ **Congonhas** Make a detour to view *The Prophets* by Aleijadinho, an astounding ensemble of statuary created at the end of the Baroque era. See page 178

❼ **Belo Horizonte** The booming capital of Minas Gerais contains the enlightening Museu das Minas e do Metal, which chronicles the history of mining in the region. See page 145

❽ **Diamantina** End your journey at the most remote, traditional and intriguing of the *cidades históricas*. See page 156

THE NATIONAL PARKS LOOP

Brazil isn't just about beaches – the interior harbours some mind-bending national park scenery too, from the craggy canyons of the south to the jungles of the north. To complete this trip you'll need to fly and have lots of time.

❶ **Parque Nacional dos Aparados da Serra** Hike the plateau rim of one of the continent's most eye-popping canyons – a subtropical gash into the massive ridge that runs along the Atlantic plain. See page 619

❷ **Parque Nacional da Chapada dos Veadeiros** Fly up to Brasília to experience the landscape of Brazil's high-altitude inland plain, studded with waterfalls, cave systems and hiking trails. See page 431

❸ **Parque Nacional da Chapada Diamantina** Serious hikers will find plenty of targets further east in Bahia, where this remote park contains dramatic valleys, peaks and monoliths. See page 246

❹ **Parque Nacional da Serra da Capivara** Head north into Piauí to view the many prehistoric wonders inside this vast, isolated park, including rare cave paintings and petroglyphs. See page 314

❺ **Parque Nacional dos Lençóis** The gem in Brazil's park system – a pristine wilderness of giant sand dunes and crystal-clear lagoons – lies on the north coast. See page 325

❻ **Floresta Nacional do Tapajós** Fly or sail up the Amazon as far as Santarém, where this forest reserve protects hundreds of giant *samaúma* trees. See page 360

❼ **Mamirauá Sustainable Development Reserve** Not a national park but just as spectacular, this private reserve lies in the heart of the Amazon, rich in flooded *várzea* forests and wildlife. See page 378

❽ **Parque Nacional da Chapada dos Guimarães** This major park near Cuiabá, the capital of Mato Grosso, is famed for the 60m-high Véu de Noiva falls and the Cidade de Pedra. See page 474

❾ **Iguaçu Falls** End your odyssey back in the south at the Argentine border, where these mighty falls on the Rio Iguaçu thunder over great ledges of rock. See page 562

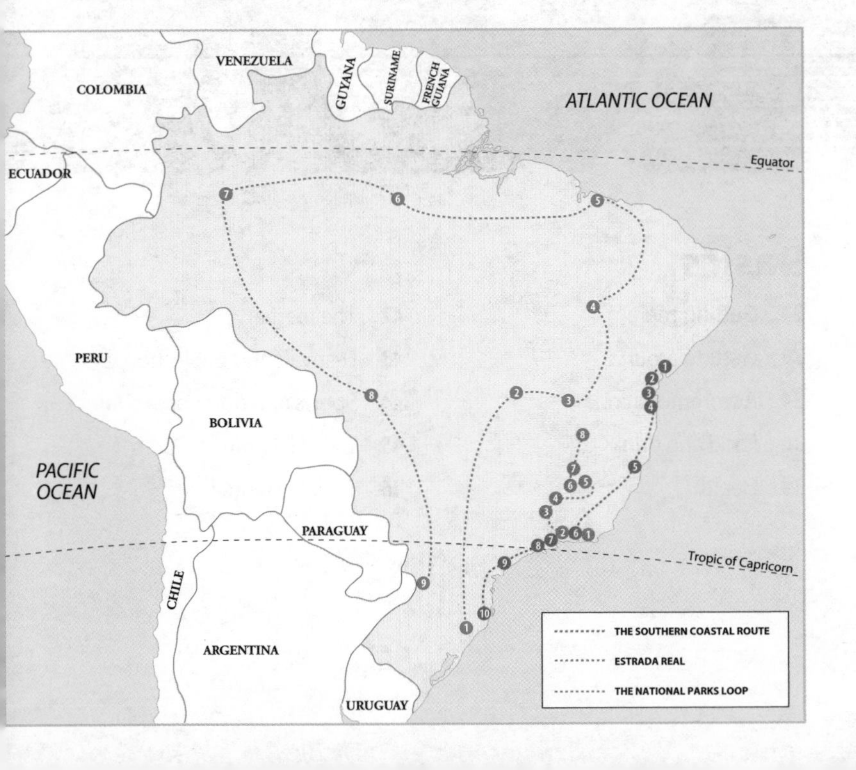

MERCADO MUNICIPAL, SÃO PAULO

Basics

Getting there

Unless you're entering Brazil overland from a neighbouring country (see page 29), you'll almost certainly arrive by air. Airfares always depend on the season: specific dates vary between airlines, but high season is generally July and August, then again mid-December to Christmas Day; low season is any other time. Fares don't normally rise over Carnaval (Feb–March), but getting a seat at this time can be difficult. For flights to Rio and São Paulo airline competition is fierce, however, and offers are often available.

Though most journeys will route through these two main cities, non-stop flights to other destinations such as Salvador, Fortaleza and Manaus are available (especially from the US), potentially saving lots of time and avoiding the long lines at Galeão (Rio) and Guarulhos (São Paulo) airports. On the downside, these services can be more expensive and the planes are often much smaller, even for long-distance flights.

Note that when you fly into any Brazilian airport on an international flight you must **clear immigration** and **claim your luggage**, even if connecting with a domestic flight – you'll have to re-check in once you've cleared customs (even if your airline insisted you were checked-in "all the way"). Once in the terminal there should be a special transfer desk so you can check-in again. Don't be surprised for it to take an hour or more to clear customs and immigration at airports in Rio or São Paulo. If travelling with children, go straight to the front of the lines: pregnant women and seniors also have priority.

Visas and red tape

Citizens of most EU countries, New Zealand and South Africa only need a valid passport and either a return or onward ticket (or evidence of funds to pay for one) to enter Brazil. You fill in an entry form on arrival and get a **tourist stamp** allowing you to stay for ninety days. Citizens from Australia, US and Canada need tourist visas in advance, issued electronically since 2018; application and payment of fees is all handled online at Ⓦformulario-mre.serpro.gov.br. You should receive visa confirmation via email within four to five business days (the visa is valid for two years, but stays in Brazil are limited to ninety days per year). E-visa fees are US$40 (plus US$4.24 service fee) for all three nationalities (payable in US$ only); note that applying for a visa at a Brazilian consulate (which you can still do) will be considerably more expensive.

Try not to lose the carbon copy of the **entry form** the officials hand you back at passport control; you are meant to return it when you leave Brazil, but you are no longer fined if you don't.

Visa extensions

Citizens from the EU, New Zealand and South Africa can extend a tourist permit for an additional ninety days by applying at least fifteen days before their initial one expires, but it will only be extended once. **To extend your visa** you will need to visit the nearest federal police (Polícia Federal) office – such as Rio's airport (see page 111), or in São Paulo (see page 515) – bringing your passport, tourist card, onward flight ticket and proof of funds (a bank statement, for example). You also need to fill in an extended stay application form (*Requerimento de Prorrogação de Estada*), which you can download online Ⓦbit.ly/formcorretoturista, and bring proof of payment; start by completing another form (the *Guia de Recolhimento da União* or GRU) online at Ⓦpf.gov.br/servicos-pf/gru then print it out, taking it to a branch of Banco do Brasil where you can make your visa extension payment (around R$110) and pick up the receipt (you must show this to get an extension).

If you want to stay even longer, you'll have to leave the country and re-enter; there's nothing in the rulebook to stop you re-entering immediately, but it's advisable to wait at least a day.

Flights from the UK and Ireland

There are plenty of choices of carrier to Brazil **from the UK**, though São Paulo and Rio are the only destinations for non-stop flights. If your ultimate desti-

> **A BETTER KIND OF TRAVEL**
>
> At Rough Guides we are passionately committed to travel. We believe it helps us understand the world we live in and the people we share it with – and of course tourism is vital to many developing economies. But the scale of modern tourism has also damaged some places irreparably, and climate change is accelerated by most forms of transport, especially flying. All Rough Guides' flights are carbon-offset.

nation is neither of these cities, it is usually best to connect in Rio, or connect with a TAP flight in Lisbon to Belém, Recife, Salvador, Fortaleza, Natal, Belo Horizonte or Brasília. If you only want to go to the **Amazon**, Manaus via Miami with LATAM (Ⓦlatam.com) is your best bet, but it's unlikely to be cheaper or quicker than a flight to Rio or São Paulo and then a connection north.

British Airways (Ⓦbritishairways.com) and LATAM operate **non-stop flights** to Brazil from London Heathrow; official fares are usually very similar, starting at around £830 return to Rio or São Paulo in low season and £1200 in high season (July, Aug & Dec 14–25). The cheapest fares, however, are often offered on routes **via Europe** – with Alitalia (Ⓦalitalia.com) via Rome, TAP via Lisbon (Ⓦflytap.com), Iberia via Madrid (Ⓦiberia.com), Lufthansa via Frankfurt (Ⓦlufthansa.com) and Swiss Air via Zurich (Ⓦswiss.com) – all to both Rio and São Paulo. Prices tend to be the same whether you begin your journey in London or at one of the UK's **regional airports**.

As Brazil is such a large country, an **open-jaw ticket** – flying into one city and leaving from another – may, according to your itinerary, make sense. Rio and São Paulo offer most airline possibilities, but flying with TAP, for example, broadens your options.

There are no direct flights **from Ireland** to Brazil: you can connect via London or other European capitals, though the cheapest deals often route through the US on Delta and American, with rates around €800 return from Dublin in high season, but with journey times of around 24 hours or more.

RTW ticket options

Combining Brazil with a longer trip in the southern hemisphere, or putting together a **round-the-world (RTW) ticket**, is possible but expensive. The most popular ticket option is a one-way to Sydney via Brazil and Argentina and a separate ticket back to London via Southeast Asia or North America. Another possibility is onward to Johannesburg from São Paulo on South African Airways (Ⓦflysaa.com).

Flights from the US and Canada

There are numerous gateways to Brazil **from the US and Canada**, with direct flights from Atlanta, Chicago, Dallas, Detroit, Houston, Los Angeles, Miami, New York, Orlando, Washington and Toronto – most West Coast flights route through Dallas or Houston. LATAM Airlines Brasil (Ⓦlatam.com) is the major Brazilian carrier serving the US, while Avianca Brazil (Ⓦavianca.com.br) also operates flights from Miami to São Paulo. American (Ⓦaa.com), Air Canada (Ⓦaircanada.com), Delta (Ⓦdelta.com) and United (Ⓦunited.com) also carry passengers between the US/Canada and Brazil.

Almost all flights go to **Rio** or **São Paulo**, but there are several other options; LATAM from Miami to Belém, Fortaleza, Manaus, Recife and Vitória; Azul Brazilian Airlines (Ⓦvoeazul.com.br) from Orlando to Belo Horizonte, Campinas and Recife; Delta from Atlanta to Brasília; and American from Miami to Manaus, Brasília and Belo Horizonte. If your ultimate destination is somewhere other than these cities, it is usually best to connect in Rio or São Paulo.

Ticket **prices** vary considerably depending on how early you book your flight and on your length of stay in Brazil. Fares to Rio and São Paulo are almost always the same. The cheapest return fares typically range from US$1100 to US$1500 out of New York, though these can drop to as low as US$800 for advance bookings in a quiet period (mid-Feb, for example); figure on US$800–1000 from Miami.

Flights via other countries

For slightly cheaper fares (but longer flight times), or if you're tempted to break your journey up, it's worth checking out what the national airlines of Brazil's Latin American neighbours have to offer. Copa Airlines (Ⓦcopaair.com) will fly you to Manaus via Panama City from various airports throughout the US, for example. **Aerolíneas Argentinas** (Ⓦaerolineas.com.ar) flies to Rio and São Paulo from Miami and New York via Buenos Aires. If you do route yourself via another South American country, however, you may need a **vaccination certificate** for yellow fever.

Flights from Australia, New Zealand and South Africa

The best deals and fastest routes to Brazil **from Australasia** are offered by Qantas (Ⓦqantas.com) and LATAM. **Round-the-world** fares that include South America tend to cost more than other RTW options, but can be worthwhile if you have the time to make the most of a few stopovers.

From Australia, the most direct route is with Qantas/LATAM, which involves a twelve-hour forty-minute non-stop flight from Sydney to Santiago followed by a four-hour flight to São Paulo or Rio. Aerolíneas Argentinas also flies non-stop to Buenos Aires, from where there are good connections direct o Florianópolis, Porto Alegre, Rio and São Paulo.

rom New Zealand LATAM and Air New Zealand (airnewzealand.co.nz) also run non-stop flights om Auckland to Santiago (11hr 5min) for connecons to São Paulo or Rio.

Flying via Santiago with Qantas/LATAM, you can xpect to pay around A$1700–2000/NZ$2000. An **pen-jaw ticket** – flying into Rio and out of São aulo (or vice versa) on Aerolíneas Argentinas or ATAM, for example – won't cost you any more than straight through-fare to Rio.

From South Africa, LATAM and South African irlines (flysaa.com) fly non-stop from Johanesburg to São Paulo (10hr 30min), where you can witch to domestic airlines for Rio and other destiations. Prices range from ZAR10,000 to ZAR12,000 or a return ticket, depending on the exchange rate.

Travelling overland to and from neighbouring countries

ou can enter Brazil **by land** from virtually all the ountries with which it shares a border (Suriname rossings are for professional adventurers only): **Argentina, Bolivia, Colombia, French Guiana, Paraguay, Peru, Uruguay** and **Venezuela**.

Crossing the Argentine border

oz do Iguaçu in Paraná is well-connected by bus and taxi to **Puerto Iguazú** in **Argentina** (see page 565), where there are regular flights to Buenos Aires and numerous buses south. There are also several crossings from Rio Grande do Sul, notably **Uruguaiana** (see page 630) and **São Borja** (see page 631).

Crossing the Bolivian border

From Brazil, the main entrance point to **Bolivia** is the city of **Corumbá** in Mato Grosso do Sul, close to the Bolivian city of **Puerto Quijarro** (see page 457). From Quijarro you can travel to Santa Cruz by train or bus. There's another minor land crossing in the far east of Bolivia at **San Matías** (with flights to Santa Cruz), with connections to **Cáceres** in Mato Grosso (see page 466). You can also cross between Bolivia and Brazil at several points in Amazonia, most notably from **Brasiléia** in Acre to **Cobija** (see page 394) and **Guajará-Mirim** in Rondônia (see page 394) across the Rio Mamoré to **Guayaramerín** in Bolivia.

Crossing the Colombian and Peruvian borders

The point in the Amazonas region where Brazil meets **Peru** and **Colombia** is known as the three-way frontier, with access to **Leticia** in Colombia and boats to **Iquitos** in Peru (see page 382). Moto-taxis, lanchas and Colombian moto carros connect the three countries. **Tabatinga** (see page 381) is the place to complete Brazilian exit (or entry) formalities. **Assis Brasil** in the state of Acre also provides access to Peru; a bridge runs across the Rio Acre to **Iñapari** in the Peruvian Amazon, with onward connections by bus to Puerto Maldonado.

Crossing the French Guianan border

The northern Brazilian state of Amapá shares a border with **French Guiana**; boats zip across the river between **Oiapoque** in Brazil, connected to the state capital Macapá by bus (see page 352) and **Saint-Georges** (with bus connections to Cayenne, the capital of French Guiana). French Guiana is actually an overseas department and region of France, which means it's **part of the EU** and uses the **euro** as currency – entry requirements are the same as for France.

Crossing the Guyanese border

The northern Brazilian state of Roraima provides access to **Guyana** via the small border town of **Bonfim**, where a bridge crosses the Rio Tacutu to **Lethem**, with customs and immigration on both sides (see page 389).

Crossing the Paraguayan border

The easiest crossing between Brazil and **Paraguay** is at Foz do Iguaçu in Paraná, where buses and taxis zip across the Rio Paraná to **Ciudad del Este** (see page 565). Both cities are well-connected by bus and plane to destinations in their respective countries.

Crossing the Uruguayan border

Crossing between the Brazilian state of Rio Grande do Sul and **Uruguay** is easy and very casual; the border actually cuts through the town of **Chuí/Chuy** with no sign you've walked between the two (see page 630), though you still need to find immigration offices to have your passport stamped. Other crossing points are at **Quaraí** and **Santana do Livramento**, while direct buses connect Porto Alegre and Montevideo.

Crossing the Venezuelan border

Roraima also borders **Venezuela**, with taxis running between **Pacaraima** in Brazil, connected by bus with the state capital Boa Vista (see page 389) and **Santa Elena de Uairén** in Venezuela (with bus connections to Ciudad Bolívar). Santa Elena has largely avoided the ongoing troubles in

Venezuela's larger cities, though you should always check the current situation. Due to hyper-inflation and currency controls getting **Venezuelan bolivars** can be a tricky business – check the latest rules (and black-market rates), and bring plenty of US dollars.

SPECIALIST TRAVEL AGENTS AND OPERATORS

Birding Mato Grosso Manaus, Brazil **T** 66 3521 1039, **W** **birdingmatogrosso.com.** Specialist birding tours run by experts in the field to the Amazon and Pantanal.

Craft Travel Group US **T** 1800 562 2028, UK **T** 0800 553 9959, **W** **crafttravelgroup.com.** Tours that promise to take you off the beaten track to experience Brazil's cities, the Amazon basin and the Pantanal.

Festival Tours US **T** 1800 225 0117, **W** **festivaltours.com.** An all-encompassing tour operator to Latin America focusing on main tourist sights.

Journey Latin America UK **T** 020 8747 3108, **W** **journeylatinamerica.co.uk.** Flight agents and tour operators offering guided tours of Brazil as well as larger-scale overland options, which also take in Paraguay, Bolivia and Peru, or Chile and Argentina.

Last Frontiers UK **T** 01296 653 000, **W** **lastfrontiers.com.** Tailor-made itineraries to Brazil with a strong wildlife slant. Friendly and knowledgeable staff will point you towards small hotels in destinations throughout the country.

Lost World Adventures US **T** 1800 999 0558, **W** **lostworld.com.** Customized individual and group tours to Brazil, including Amazon River excursions, and multi-country tours.

Peregrine Travel Qld Australia **T** 07 3850 7699, **W** **peregrinetravelqld.com.au.** Independent and group travel specialists.

South America Travel Centre Australia **T** 1300 784 794, **W** **southamericatravelcentre.com.au.** Specializes in tailor-made trips to Brazil.

Steamond Travel UK **T** 020 7730 8646, **W** **steamondtravel.com.** Flight agents and tour operators for Brazil and Latin America.

Tripmasters US **T** 1800 430 0484, **W** **tripmasters.com.** A big operator throughout Latin America, offering cruises, city tours, jungle trips and Carnaval specials.

Veloso Tours UK **T** 020 8762 0616, **W** **veloso.com.** Latin American flight specialist and tour operator with a range of Brazilian options including Rio de Janeiro, the Northeast and the Amazon.

Getting around

Travel within most parts of Brazil is easy. Public transport outside of the Amazon is generally by bus or plane, with services plentiful and relatively cheap. Car rental is possible, but driving in Brazil is not for the faint-hearted. Hitchhiking, over any distance, is not recommended.

By plane

It's hardly surprising that a country the size of Brazil relies on **air travel** a good deal; in some parts of Amazônia air links are more important than roads and rivers. Any town has at least an airstrip, and all major cities have airports, usually some distance from downtown. The airports of Congonhas and Guarulhos in São Paulo tend to be chronically crowded, with long check-in lines, so allow extra time when flying from these locations.

Budget airlines and fares

Budget airlines are well established in Brazil, the biggest being **GOL** (**W** voegol.com.br); its main competitors other than LATAM (**W** latam.com), which has been forced to lower prices on domestic routes and cut business class to compete, are **Avianca Brasil** (**W** avianca.com.br) and **Azul** (**W** voeazul.com.br), launched by the founder of US budget carrier Jet Blue. GOL has an extensive network, cheap seats, is efficient and usually better value than LATAM – though the latter still provides free snacks and drinks on most flights (with GOL you have to pay for anything other than glasses of water). Azul is also very efficient and has a large network, and though its planes are usually small (mostly Embraer aircraft), they generally come with live TV in each headrest. GOL and LATAM are the best equipped to handle English-speakers, though **websites** for all of these carriers have an English option and now take most foreign credit cards (debit cards can be a problem, however).

In Brazilian **holiday periods** (July, around Christmas, and Carnaval) flights are often booked up and you need to book as far in advance as you can – as in other countries, prices for budget flights become more expensive closer to departure. The best deals are typically on well-travelled routes such as the Rio–São Paulo–Belo Horizonte triangle (from just R$150 one-way), and for flights of one hour or less anywhere in Brazil rates can be very reasonable – and still save five to six hours of bus travel. Travelling further afield – Rio to Fortaleza or Manaus for example – starts to get a lot more expensive (from R$800 one-way). Again, book several weeks in advance for the best deals.

Flying within the Northeast or Amazônia can be tiresome, as many long-distance routes are no more than glorified bus runs, stopping everywhere en route. When planning your itinerary, it's a good idea to check carefully how many times a plane stops – for example, between Manaus and São Luis, a flight may stop as many as four times or as few as once.

There are **safety issues** to consider when flying in the Amazon. Where possible, stick to GOL, Azul and LATAM when flying around Amazônia, or regional carrier MAP Linhas Aéreas (voemap.com.br).

Air passes

When buying your international ticket, you should consider the possibility of adding an **air pass**, though note that the presence of budget airlines and cheap direct on-line booking for multi-flight itineraries has made these virtually redundant. In addition, the creation of LATAM (via the merger of TAM and LAN Chile) has meant the end of several TAM air passes – check the latest on the LATAM website. **GOL**, the low-cost Brazilian airline, still offers Brazil and South American air passes, but only through registered travel agencies. The **Brazil Airpass** includes a minimum of four flight coupons (U$505–571) and a maximum of nine (US$1094–1379), with a maximum stay of thirty days – all for flights within Brazil. Your international travel must be flown on GOL flights or any GOL partner flights (Air France, Delta, KLM).

Lastly, if you have an air pass and change the time or date of your flight, always remember to **cancel the original flight**. If you don't, the computer flags you as a no-show, and all your other air-pass reservations will also be cancelled.

By train

You probably won't be taking many **trains** in Brazil. Although there's an extensive rail network, most of it is for cargo only, and even where there are passenger trains they're almost invariably slower and less convenient than the buses. Exceptions are the *metrô* rail systems in Porto Alegre, Rio, São Paulo and Brasília and a few **tourist journeys** worth making for themselves, especially in the South and Minas Gerais.

By bus

The **bus system** in Brazil is excellent and makes travelling around the country easy, comfortable and economical, despite the distances involved. Inter-city buses leave from a station called a **rodoviária**, usually built on city outskirts.

Buses are operated by hundreds of private companies, but **prices** tend to be similar (though faster or all-night services may be more expensive), and are reasonable: Rio to São Paulo is around R$110, to Belo Horizonte R$70–115, to Foz do Iguaçu R$275–350 and to Salvador R$300, while São Paulo to Brasília is around R$225. **Long-distance buses** are comfortable enough to sleep on, and have on-board toilets (which can get smelly on long journeys): the lower your seat number, the further away from them you'll be. Buses stop every two or three hours at well-supplied *postos* (highway rest stops with restaurants and toilets), but as prices at these are relatively high it's not a bad idea to bring along water and some food. Some bus companies will supply meal vouchers for use at the *postos* on long journeys.

There are luxury buses, too, called **leitos**, which do overnight runs between the major cities – worth taking once for the experience, with fully reclining seats in curtained partitions, freshly ironed sheets and an attendant plying insomniacs with coffee and conversation. They cost about a third of the price of an air ticket, and twice as much as a normal long-distance bus; they're also less frequent and need to be booked a few days in advance. No matter what kind of bus, it's a good idea to have a **light sweater** or **blanket** during night journeys, as the air conditioning is often uncomfortably cold.

For **route planning**, websites such as buscaonibus.com.br and clickbus.com.br maintain fairly accurate long-distance bus timetables for much of the country. Going any distance, it's best to **buy your ticket** at least a day in advance, from the rodoviária or, in some cities, from travel agents.

ADDRESSES

Trying to find an **address** in Brazil can be confusing: streets often have two names, numbers don't always follow a logical sequence, and parts of the address are often abbreviated – Brasília is a special case (see page 413). The street name and number will often have a floor (*andar*), apartment or room (*sala*; "*s*" for short) number tacked on: thus R. Afonso Pena 111-3° s.234 means third floor, room 234 at 111 Rua Alfonso Pena. You may also come across *Ed.* (*edifício*, or building) or *s/n* (*sem número*, no number), very common in rural areas and small towns. All addresses in Brazil also have an eight-digit **postcode**, or *CEP*, often followed by two capital letters for the state; leaving it out causes delay in delivery. So a full address might read:
Rua do Sol 132-3° andar, s.12
65000-100 São Luís – MA

An exception is the Rio–São Paulo route, where a frequent shuttle service means you can always turn up without a ticket and never have to wait more than fifteen minutes.

Numbered seats are provided on all routes: if you want a window, ask for *janela*. If the bus is going to cross a state line, you may be asked for proof of ID when buying the ticket (your passport is best). Buses have **luggage** compartments, which are safe: you check pieces at the side of the bus and get a ticket for them. Keep an eye on your hand luggage, and take anything valuable with you when you get off for a halt.

By car

Driving standards in Brazil hover between abysmal and appalling. The country has one of the highest death tolls from driving-related accidents in the world, and on any journey you can see why, with thundering trucks and drivers treating the road as if it were a Grand Prix racetrack. Fortunately, inter-city bus drivers are the exception to the rule: they are usually very good, and their buses usually have devices fitted that make it impossible for them to exceed the speed limit. Electronic speed traps are widely used everywhere, and if you get caught by one in a rental car, the fine will simply be added to your credit card. Since 2008, a zero-tolerance law has made it strictly illegal to drive after consuming any amount of **alcohol**, a response to the enormous death toll caused by drunk drivers. Offenders risk severe punishments if tests detect any alcohol in their blood – expect at least a hefty fine and the threat of imprisonment.

Rules of the road

Standards have improved in recent years (especial in the South), but driving in Brazil remains ver different from northern Europe and the US. Do nc expect Brazilians to pay much attention to lan markings, use indicators or worry about cuttin you off or overtaking you on the inside. Make sur that you use your rear and wing mirrors constant when city driving. At night, you should cautious roll through red lights in city centres or desert ed-looking streets, to avoid *assaltantes* (muggers And a crucial thing to know is that **flashing light** from an oncoming car mean "I'm coming throug – get out of the way" and NOT "please go ahead as in the UK and US. It sounds intimidating, and is for the first couple of days, but it is surprising hov quickly you get used to it.

Road quality varies according to region: th South and Southeast have a good paved network the Northeast has a good network on the coast bu is poor in the interior; and roads in Amazônia are b far the worst, with even major highways closed fc weeks or months at a time as they are washed awa by the rains. Most cities are fairly well signposted, sc getting out of town shouldn't be too difficult; if cit traffic is daunting, try to arrange to collect your ca on a Sunday when traffic is light.

If at all possible, avoid driving at night becaus potholes (even on main roads) and *lombadas* (speec bumps) may not be obvious, and breaking dowr after dark could be dangerous. Outside the big cities Brazilian roads are death traps at night, poorly lit, ir bad condition and lightly policed. Especially wortl avoiding at night are the **Via Dutra**, linking Rio anc São Paulo, because of the huge numbers of trucks and the treacherous ascent and descent of the

AMAZON RIVERBOATS

In Amazônia, rivers have been the main highways for centuries, and the Amazon itself is navigable to ocean-going ships as far west as Iquitos in Peru, nearly 3000km upstream from Belém.

In all the large riverside cities of the Amazon – notably Belém, Manaus and Santarém – there are *hidroviárias*, ferry terminals for waterborne bus services. **Amazon river travel** is slow and can be tough going, but it's a fascinating experience. On bigger boats, there are a number of classes; in general, it's better to avoid *cabine*, where you swelter in a cabin, and choose *primeiro* (first class) instead, sleeping in a hammock on deck. *Segundo* (second class) is usually hammock space in the lower deck or engine room. Wooden boats are much more comfortable than metal, but usually slower. Take plenty of provisions, and expect to practise your Portuguese.

The range of **boat transport** in the Amazon runs from luxury tourist boats and large three-level riverboats to smaller one- or two-level boats (the latter normally confining their routes to main tributaries and local runs) and covered launches operated by tour companies. The most popular route is the **Belém–Manaus trip**, which takes four to six days.

Serra do Mar, and the **Belém–Brasília highway**, whose potholes and uneven asphalt make it difficult enough to drive even in daylight. Where possible, avoid driving after dark in the Mato Grosso and Amazon regions as well; though rare, armed roadside robberies have been known to happen there.

An **international driving licence** is useful: although foreign licences are accepted for visits of up to six months, you may have a hard time convincing a police officer of this.

Petrol and ethanol

Outside of the towns and cities, **service stations** can be few and far between, so keep a careful eye on the fuel gauge. Service stations sell both petrol (*gasolina*) and ethanol (*etanol* or *álcool*), with new cars (including rentals) usually capable of running on either fuel. *Etanol* is considerably cheaper than *gasolina*, and there's no longer a noticeable difference in terms of performance. Service stations in rural areas do not always accept international credit cards, so make sure you have sufficient cash on a long trip. In urban areas, plastic is universally accepted at petrol stations, although a common scam is to charge around twenty percent more per litre when payment is made by credit card rather than cash: always check in advance whether there is a price difference if you intend to pay by credit card.

Parking

Parking, especially in Brazil's cities, can be tricky due to security and finding a space, and it's worth paying extra for a hotel with some kind of lock-up garage. A universal feature of city driving in Brazil is the *flanelinha*, named for the flannel that informal parking attendants wave at approaching cars; these attendants will help you into and out of parking spaces and guard your car, in return for a *real* or two. Brazilians will go to almost any lengths to avoid paying them, but they're making a living and providing a service, so do the decent thing. In any event, never leave anything valuable inside the car.

Renting a car

Renting a car in Brazil is straightforward. Of the big-name international companies, Avis/Budget is the most widely represented. There are also plenty of reliable Brazilian alternatives, such as Unidas (Ⓦunidas.com.br), Interlocadora (Ⓦinterlocadora.com.br), Movida (Ⓦmovida.com.br) and Localiza Hertz (Ⓦlocalizahertz.com). Car-rental offices (*locadoras*) can be found at every airport and in most towns regardless of size, although you will pay slightly more for airport pick-up and drop-off. Almost all cars in Brazil have manual gears; automatics are rare.

Rates start from around R$130 a day for a compact car (Fiat Punto or similar) including unlimited mileage; a basic air-conditioned model will start at around R$150, also including unlimited mileage. Four-wheel-drive vehicles are rare and extremely expensive. Prices don't always include **insurance** – a comprehensive policy will cost an additional R$25 per day or so with an excess of R$500. If you have a US credit card, you may find that it can be used to cover the additional liability – check before leaving home. In any case, a credit card is essential for making a deposit when renting a car. It's not a bad idea to reserve a car before you arrive in Brazil, as you can be sure to get the best available rate.

As you would anywhere, carefully check the condition of the car before accepting it and pay special attention to the state of the tyres (including the spare), and make sure there's a jack, warning triangle and fire extinguisher: the police will check for these if you get pulled over. All cars have front and back seatbelts; their use is compulsory, and stiff on-the-spot fines are imposed on drivers and front-seat passengers found not to be wearing them.

Taxis

There are enormous numbers of **taxis** in Brazilian cities, and depending on where you are, they are relatively cheap, though rates have risen a lot in recent years. City cabs are metered, and usually have **two rates**: 1 is cheaper, 2 more expensive. The rate the taxi is using is indicated on the taximeter, after the fare. Rate 2 is usually automatic on trips to and from airports and bus stations in big cities, after 8pm, and all-day Sunday and on public holidays. Many cities give taxi drivers a Christmas bonus by allowing them to charge Rate 2 for the whole of **December**. Occasionally, drivers will refer to a sheet and revise the fare slightly upwards – they are not ripping you off, but referring to price updating tables that fill the gap until taximeters can be readjusted to reflect the official annual increases.

Taxis in small towns and rural areas do not often have meters, so it's best to agree on the fare in advance – they'll be more expensive than in the cities. Most airports and some bus stations are covered by taxi **cooperatives**, which operate under a slightly different system: attendants give you a **coupon** with fares to various destinations printed on it – you pay either at a kiosk in advance, or the driver. These are more expensive than regular taxis, but they're reliable and often more comfortable. **Tipping** is not obligatory, but appreciated.

Uber (and other apps) in Brazil

The app-based taxi service **Uber** is widely available in major cities across Brazil and is generally safe to use, though there have been cases of **express kidnappings** (where muggers will drive you from ATM to ATM demanding you withdraw money before releasing you) in the biggest cities – don't get into a car alone to be safe. It's the Uber drivers that have been most at risk, with several murdered by robbers posing as passengers in São Paulo in 2017. Part of the problem is that in Brazil you can pay for Uber with cash; new regulations now mean you must register a CPF number to pay cash (meaning foreigners must stick to credit card payments). For a full list of cities where Uber is available consult Ⓦuber.com/cities. Other local transport-sharing apps in Brazil include **Cabify** (Ⓦcabify.com), **99** (Ⓦ99app.com) and **LadyDriver** (Ⓦladydriver.com.br).

By ferry and boat

Boats and ferries are important forms of transport in parts of Brazil. Look out for the ferry to Niterói, without which no journey to **Rio** would be complete; **Salvador**, where there are regular services to islands and towns in the huge bay on which the city is built; in the **South** between the islands of the Bay of Paranaguá; and most of all in **Amazônia** (see page 32).

Accommodation

Accommodation in Brazil covers the full range, from hostels and basic lodgings clustered around bus stations to luxury resort hotels. You can sometimes find places to sleep for as little as R$35 a night, but, more realistically, a clean double room in a basic option will set you back upwards of R$50–60. A good, comfortable hotel varies according to the city – Rio being one of the most expensive in the world when it comes to hotels – but R$200 a night will get you better accommodation than you'd expect for that price in Europe. As is so often the case, single travellers get a bad deal, usually paying almost as much as the cost of a double room. In whatever category of place you stay, in tourist spots – both large and small – over New Year and Carnaval you'll be expected to book a room for a minimum of four or five days.

Hotels

Hotels proper run the gamut from dives to luxury apartments. There is a Brazilian **classification system**, from one to five stars, but the absence of stars doesn't necessarily mean a bad hotel: they depend on bureaucratic requirements such as the width of lift shafts and kitchen floor space as much as on the standard of accommodation – many perfectly good hotels don't have stars.

A **quarto** is a room without a bathroom, an **apartamento** is a room with a shower (Brazilians don't use baths); an *apartamento de luxo* is normally just an *apartamento* with a fridge full of (marked-up) drinks; a **casal** is a double room; and a **solteiro** a single. In a starred hotel, an *apartamento* upwards would come with telephone, air-conditioning (*ar condicionado*) and cable TV; a *ventilador* is a fan. Even cheaper hotels now have wi-fi (*sem fio*), and three-star hotels upwards have wi-fi and/or cable TV (*cabo*) in rooms as standard (though English-language channels are rare). Throughout this guide, the availability of free **wi-fi** has been denoted by a ᯤ sign at the end of each review.

Most hotels will usually include a breakfast buffet with fruit, lots of cheese, ham/chorizo bread, eggs, cakes and coffee (this line-up is

AIRBNB AND COUCHSURFING IN BRAZIL

Airbnb (Ⓦairbnb.com) is booming in Brazil as a way to rent rooms in private houses or apartments and other private accommodation and can be a great way to lower your accommodation costs – as always, read reviews carefully (avoid places with no reviews just to be safe) and research the area in which the property is located, especially in Rio and São Paulo. **CouchSurfing** (Ⓦcouchsurfing.org) is just as popular with over 40,000 hosts in Rio, over 80,000 in São Paulo, over 8,000 in Salvador and over 15,000 in Brasília – remember that very few hosts will speak English. Another useful website is Ⓦhiddenpousadasbrazil.com.

remarkably similar throughout the country), but no other meals, although there will often be a restaurant on-site. Hotels usually have a **safe deposit box**, a *caixa*, which is worth asking about when you check in; they are free for you to use and, although they're not invulnerable, anything left in a *caixa* is safer than on your person or unguarded in your room. Many hotels also offer a safe deposit box in your room, which is the safest option of all.

Brazilian "motels"

In Brazil, a **motel**, as you'll gather from the names and decor, is strictly for couples. This is not to say that it's not possible to stay in one if you can't find anything else – since they're used by locals, they're rarely too expensive – but you should be aware that most of the other rooms will be rented by the hour.

Pensões, postos and pousadas

Small, family-run hotels are called either a **pensão** (*pensões* in the plural) or a *hotel familiar*. These vary a great deal: some are no more appealing than a hostel, while others are friendlier and better value than many hotels and can be places of considerable character and luxury. *Pensões* tend to be better in small towns than in large cities, but are also usefully thick on the ground in some of the main tourist destinations. In southern Brazil, many of the **postos**, highway service stations on town outskirts, have cheap rooms and showers too, and are usually well kept and clean.

You will also come across the **pousada**, which can just be another name for a *pensão*, but can also be a small hotel, running up to luxury class but usually less expensive than a hotel proper. In some small towns – such as Ouro Preto and Paraty – *pousadas* form the bulk of mid- and upper-level accommodation options. In the Amazon and Mato Grosso in particular, *pousadas* tend to be purpose-built *fazenda* lodges geared towards the growing ecotourist markets.

Dormitórios and hostels

At the bottom end of the scale, in terms of both quality and price, are **dormitórios**, small and very basic (to put it mildly) hotels, situated close to bus stations and in the poorer parts of town. They are extremely cheap (just a few dollars a night), but usually unsavoury and sometimes downright dangerous. They should be avoided unless you have no choice.

ACCOMMODATION PRICES

Accommodation prices given in our listings are the minimum you can expect to pay for a **double room** (with bathroom, unless stated otherwise) in high season, and include all **taxes** and **service charges**. Rates can be cheaper if you book well in advance, and hotels usually offer a range of different rooms, with significant price differences. For hostels we have also included the price of a **dorm bed** (for nonmembers in HI hostels) and for **campsites** prices are listed per person or per pitch.

You could stay for not much more, in far better conditions, in a **youth hostel**, an *albergue de juventude*, also sometimes called a *casa de estudante*, where the cost of a dorm bed is usually between R$35 and R$70 a night. There's an extensive network of these hostels, with at least one in every state capital, and they are very well maintained, often in restored buildings. It helps to have an IYHF card (available from your national youth hostel association) with a recent photograph – you're not usually asked for one, but every so often you'll find an *albergue* that refuses entry unless it's produced, and prices are generally a little cheaper for members. The **Federação Brasileira dos Albergues de Juventude** (ⓦ hihostelbrasil.com.br) in Rio publishes an excellent illustrated guide to Brazil's official hostels – and there's a growing number of hostels that aren't affiliated with the IYHF, many of which are very good.

Demand for places far outstrips supply at certain times of year – July, and December to Carnaval – but if you travel with a **hammock** you can often hook it up in a corridor or patio. A major advantage that hostels have is to throw you together with young Brazilians, who are the main users of the network.

Camping

There are numerous **campsites** in Brazil and almost all of them are on the coast near the bigger beaches – mostly, they're near cities rather than in out-of-the-way places. They will usually have basic facilities – running water and toilets, perhaps a simple restaurant – and are popular with young Argentines and Brazilians. A few fancier sites are designed for people with camper vans or big tents in the back of their cars. Having your own tent, or renting one, is also particularly useful in ecotourism regions such as the Amazon and the Pantanal, where it can really open up the wilderness to you. In all cases, however, the problem is **security**, partly of your person, but more significantly of your possessions, which can never really be made safe. Great caution should be exercised before camping off-site – only do so if you're part of a group and you've received assurances locally as to safety.

Food and drink

It's hard to generalize about Brazilian food, largely because there is no single national cuisine but numerous very distinct regional ones. Nature dealt Brazil a full hand for these: there's an abundant variety of fruit, vegetables and spices, as you can see for yourself walking through any food market.

Regional cuisine

There are five main **regional cuisines** in Brazil: *comida mineira* from Minas Gerais, based on pork, vegetables (especially *couve*, collard greens) and *tutu*, a kind of refried bean cooked with manioc flour and used as a thick sauce; *comida baiana* from the Salvador coast, the most exotic to gringo palates, using fresh fish and shellfish, hot peppers, palm oil, coconut milk and fresh coriander; *comida do sertão* from the interior of the Northeast, which relies on rehydrated, dried or salted meat and the fruit, beans and tubers of the region; *comida gaúcha* from Rio Grande do Sul, the most carnivorous diet in the world, revolving around every imaginable kind of meat grilled over charcoal; and *comida amazônica*, based on river fish, manioc sauces and the many fruits and palm products of northern Brazil. *Comida do sertão* is rarely served outside its homeland, but you'll find restaurants serving the others throughout Brazil, although – naturally – they're at their best in their region of origin.

The staples

Alongside the regional restaurants, there are **standard foods** available everywhere that can soon get dull unless you cast around: steak (*bife*) or chicken (*frango*), served with *arroz e feijão* (rice and beans), and often with salad, fries and *farinha* (dried manioc/cassava flour that you sprinkle over everything). *Farofa* is toasted *farinha*, and usually comes with onions and bits of bacon mixed in. In cheaper restaurants, all this would come on a single large plate: look for the words "*prato feito*", "*prato comercial*" or "*refeição completa*" if you want to fill up without spending too much. Hotel breakfast buffets can be disappointingly uniform around the country: slices of cheese, the ubiquitous *pão de queijo* (a savoury cheese ball made with manioc flour), lots of breads and cakes, fruits, coffee, cold cuts and some variation of chorizo and scrambled eggs. "**Tapioca**" is ubiquitous in Brazil, though it usually refers to manioc/cassava flour products (typically grainy pancakes with sweet or savoury fillings) rather than the sweet tapioca pudding familiar to foreigners.

Feijoada is the closest Brazil comes to a national dish. It is a stew of pork leftovers (ear, pizzle and other unmentionables that fortunately can be fished out), sausage, smoked ribs and beef jerky cooked slowly for hours with black beans and garlic until mouth-wateringly tender, served garnished with slices of orange and pork crackling and accompanied by shots of cachaça. It is a national ritual for Saturday lunch, when restaurants serve *feijoada* all day.

Some of the **fruit** is familiar – *manga* (mango), *maracujá* (passion fruit), *goiaba* (guava), *limão* (lime) – but most of it has only Brazilian names: *jaboticaba*, *fruta do conde*, *sapoti* and *jaca*. The most exotic fruits are Amazonian: try *bacuri*, *açaí* – increasingly seen in Europe and the US as a health food or juice – and the extraordinary *cupuaçú*, the most delicious of all. These all serve as the basis for juices and **ice cream** (*sorvete*), which can be excellent; keep an eye out for *sorvetarias* (ice-cream parlours). Our Language section has a list of **common menu terms** (see page 680).

Snacks and street food

On every street corner in Brazil you will find a **lanchonete**, a mixture of café and bar that sells beer and cachaça, snacks, cigarettes, soft drinks, coffee and sometimes small meals. **Bakeries** – *padarias* – often have a *lanchonete* attached, and they're good places for cheap snacks: an *empada* or *empadinha* is a small pie, which has various fillings – *carne* (meat), *palmito* (palm heart), *frango* (chicken) and *camarão* (shrimp) being the best (*misto* is "mixed"); a *pastel* is a fried filled pasty; an *esfiha* is a savoury pastry stuffed with spiced meat; and a *coxinha* is spiced chicken rolled in manioc dough and then fried; in the Amazon

THE CAIPIRINHA – BRAZIL'S NATIONAL COCKTAIL

By far the best way to drink the national spirit cachaça is in a **caipirinha**, which is, along with football and samba, one of Brazil's great gifts to world civilization – cachaça mixed with fresh lime, sugar and crushed ice. It may not sound like much, but it is the best cocktail you're ever likely to drink. Be sure to stir it regularly while drinking, and treat it with healthy respect – it is much more powerful than it tastes. Variants are the *caipirosca* or *caipiríssima*, the same made with vodka. Waiters will often assume foreigners want vodka, so make sure you say *caipirinha de cachaça*. You can also get *batidas*, cachaça mixed with fruit juice and ice, which flow like water during Carnaval: they also pack quite a punch, despite tasting like a soft drink.

keep an eye out for a *tapioquinha*, a tapioca pancake folded with cheese, ham or whatever else you want to start the day with. All these savoury snacks fall under the generic heading *salgados*.

Food sold by **street vendors** should be treated with caution, but not dismissed out of hand. Some of the food they sell has the advantage of being cooked a long time, which reduces the chance of picking anything up, and in some places – Salvador and Belém especially – you can get good food cheaply in the street; just choose your vendor sensibly. A good example in Salvador is *acarajé*, only available from street vendors – a delicious fried bean mix with shrimp and hot pepper.

Restaurants

Restaurants are ubiquitous, portions are very large and prices extremely reasonable. A *prato comercial* is often no more than R$14, while a good full meal can usually be had for about R$40 in cheaper restaurants. Cheaper places, though, tend only to be open for lunch. One of the best options offered by many restaurants, typically at lunchtime only, is self-service *comida por quilo*, where a wide choice of food is priced according to the weight of the food on your plate. Specialist restaurants to look out for include a *rodizio*, where you pay a fixed charge and eat as much as you want; most *churrascarias* – restaurants specializing in charcoal-grilled meat of all kinds, especially beef – operate this system, too, bringing a constant supply of meat on huge spits to the tables.

Many restaurants will present unsolicited food the moment you sit down – the **couvert**, which can consist of anything from a couple of bits of raw carrot and an olive to quite an elaborate and substantial plate. Although the price is generally modest, it still has to be paid for. If you don't want it, ask the waiter to take it away.

Brazil's restaurant scene also includes cuisines from around the globe, thanks to the generations of Portuguese, Arab, Italian, Japanese, German and other immigrants who have made the country their home. The widest selection is in São Paulo, with the best Italian, Lebanese and Japanese food in Brazil, but almost anywhere of any size will have a good spread of international restaurants.

In almost all restaurants the bill comes with a ten percent service charge; whatever you may be told, this is not a mandatory charge, but to not pay it is considered very bad form. Most locals tend not to leave an additional tip, but unless you've had bad service it's a good idea to leave some change, as waiters rely on this to supplement their very low wages (and many restaurants simply pocket the ten percent).

Vegetarian food

Being a **vegetarian** – or at least a strict one – is no easy matter in Brazil. If you eat fish, there's no problem, especially in the Northeast and Amazônia, where seafood forms the basis of many meals. You can usually get a fair choice of vegetarian food at a *comida por quilo* restaurant, which offers a range of salads and vegetables, as well as rice, manioc and potatoes. However, they are often only open during the day, as are the occasional vegetarian restaurants (usually described as *restaurante natural*) that can be found in the larger cities. Otherwise, you're up against one of the world's most carnivorous cultures. At most restaurants – even *churrascarias* – huge salads are available but, if you're a vegan, always enquire whether eggs or cheese are included. If you get fed up with rice, beans and salad, there are always pizzerias around.

Drinks

Coffee is the great national drink, served strong, hot and sweet in small cups and drunk quickly. However, coffee is often a great disappointment in Brazil: most of the good stuff is exported, and what's available tends to come so stiff with sugar that it's almost undrinkable unless you order an *espresso*. By far the best coffee is found in São Paulo and points

ALCOHOLIC DRINKS – THE RULES

There are no **licensing laws** in Brazil, so you can get a drink at any time of day or night – though **driving** after consuming even a small amount of alcohol is strictly forbidden. Drinking is allowed in **public places** (and on the beach), though it is banned in many football stadiums. Officially, the **legal drinking age** in Brazil is 18.

south. You are never far from a *cafézinho* (as these small cups of coffee are known; *café* refers to coffee in its raw state). The best way to start your day is with *café com leite*, hot milk with coffee added to taste. Decaffeinated coffee is almost impossible to find in restaurants, and difficult even in delicatessens.

Brazil's herbal teas are surprisingly good. Try *chá mate*, a strong green infusion with a noticeable caffeine hit, or one of the wide variety of herbal teas, most notably that made from *guaraná* berries. One highly recommended way to drink *mate* is using the *chimarrão*, very common in Rio Grande do Sul: a gourd filled with *chá mate* and boiling water, sucked through a silver straw. You will need some practice to avoid burning your lips, but once you get used to it, it is a wonderfully refreshing way to take *mate*.

Fruit drinks

The great variety of **fruit** in Brazil is put to excellent use in *sucos*: fruit is popped into a liquidizer with sugar and crushed ice to make a delicious drink. Made with milk rather than water, it becomes a *vitamina*. Most *lanchonetes* and bars sell *sucos* and *vitaminas*, but for the full variety you should visit a specialist *casa de sucos*, which are found in most town centres. Widely available, and the best option to quench a thirst, are *suco de maracujá* (passion fruit) and *suco de limão* (lime). In the North and Northeast, try *graviola*, *bacuri* and *cupuaçu*. Sugar will always be added to a *suco* unless you ask for it *sem açúcar* or *natural*; some, notably *maracujá* and *limão*, are undrinkable without it.

Soft drinks

All the usual brands of **soft drinks** are available in Brazil, but outshining them all is a local variety, *guaraná*, a fizzy and very sweet drink made out of Amazonian berries. An energy-loaded powder is made from the same berries and sold in health stores in the developed world – basically, the effect is like a smooth release of caffeine without the jitters.

Beer

Beer is mainly of the lager type, though craft beers made in microbreweries are becoming increasingly popular in the South, São Paulo and Minas Gerais. Brazilians drink beer ice-cold, mostly in 600ml bottles or cans: ask for a *cerveja*. Many places only serve beer on draught – called *chopp*. The best brands are the regional beers of Pará and Maranhão, Cerma and Cerpa, the latter available in good restaurants nationwide and called a *cerpinha*. The best nationally available beers are Antárctica, Bohêmia and Brahma.

Wine

Brazilian wine (*vinho*) is mostly mediocre and sweet, though some of the wines produced in areas of Italian settlement in the South are pretty good, while sparkling wines can be excellent. The most reliable, widely available Brazilian label is Miolo, a smallish producer whose wines are found in good supermarkets throughout Brazil. Keep an eye out for the wines of the Casa Valduga and Don Laurindo, as well as the truly outstanding Villa Francioni label, a fragrant white produced near São Joaquim in the highlands of Santa Catarina. Commercial wine production has recently started in Bahia's São Francisco valley, with some surprisingly good results: the Miolo Shiraz can be found in many supermarkets. Despite the undoubted improvement in the quality of Brazilian wines in recent years, however, imported wines from Chile and Argentina (or Europe) remain more reliable, though even the cheapest bottles are around R$35–40.

Spirits and cachaça

As for **spirits**, you can buy **Scotch** (*uisque*), either *nacional*, made up from imported whisky essence and not worth drinking, or *internacional*, imported and extremely expensive. Far better to stick to what Brazilians drink, **cachaça** (also called *pinga* or, in Rio, *paraty*). Cachaça is similar to rum, but it's made from fresh sugarcane juice (fermented and distilled) rather than the molasses used to make conventional rum (the *rhum agricole* produced in Martinique, Haiti and Guadeloupe is basically cachaça). The best cachaça is produced in stills on country farms: it is called *cachaça da terra* and, when produced with care, has a smoothness and taste the larger commercially produced brands lack; look out for cachaça from Minas Gerais particularly. Alternatively, there are scores of national brands: some of the commonest ones are Velho Barreiro, Pitu and 51, but they are best drunk mixed in a **caipirinha** (see page 37) than neat.

Health

There are no compulsory vaccinations required to enter Brazil from Europe or North America, but a list of recommended jabs and health recommendations can be found at Ⓦfitfortravel.nhs.uk. A yellow fever certificate may be a requirement if you are entering from another South American country, and you should take your vaccination records with you. Certain health precautions should be taken on your travels, especially if you're staying for any length of time or visiting more remote regions: in this case it is wise to travel with your own medical supplies. Taking out travel insurance is vital (see page 48), and you should be especially aware of dengue fever, a significant problem in Rio and other cities during the Brazilian summer (Dec–April). But you should not let health issues make you unduly paranoid – if you need it, good medical care is available cheaply for all but the most serious of problems.

Pharmacies and medical treatment

Most standard drugs are available in **pharmacies** (*farmácias*), which you'll find everywhere – no prescriptions are necessary. A pharmacy will also give free medical advice, and they're a good first line of defence if you fall ill.

If you are unlucky enough to need **medical treatment** in Brazil, forget about the public hospitals – as a foreigner, you have virtually no chance of getting a bed unless you have an infectious disease, and the level of health care offered by most is poor. You can get good medical and dental care in **private hospitals** and clinics: North Americans will think it fairly inexpensive, but Europeans used to state-subsidized health care may not. A doctor's visit will cost on average R$120–160, and drugs are relatively cheap. Hotels in big cities will have lists of English-speaking **doctors**; ask for a *médico*. Outside the larger centres, you will probably have to try out your Portuguese. Any Brazilian doctor will usually understand – although not necessarily speak – Spanish.

Chagas' disease

Chagas' disease is endemic in parts of the **Northeast** and **the Amazon**. Although it is difficult to catch, it can lead to serious heart and kidney problems that appear up to twenty years after infection. The disease is carried in the faeces of beetles that live in the cracks of adobe walls, so if sleeping in an adobe hut, make sure nothing can crawl into your hammock; either use a mosquito net or sling the hammock as far from walls as you can. The beetle bites and then defecates next to the spot: scratching of the bite will rub in the infected faeces, so before scratching a bite that you know wasn't caused by a mosquito, **bathe it in alcohol**. If you are infected, you will have a fever for a few days that will then clear up as if nothing untoward happened. Though the disease can be treated in its early stages, it becomes incurable once established. If you travel through a Chagas area and get an undiagnosed fever, have a blood test as soon as possible afterwards.

Dengue fever, chikungunya and zika

Dengue fever, a viral disease transmitted by mosquito bites, is increasingly common in all Brazilian cities (especially in the southeast), though the number of deaths caused by the disease dropped dramatically in 2017. It is highly seasonal, peaking in the southern hemisphere summer (Dec–April). The symptoms are debilitating: light but persistent fever, tiredness, muscle and joint pains (especially in the fingers), and nausea and vomiting. There is currently no cure for dengue, so it is likely that you will feel pretty grim for a week or so even with treatment, and you should be aware that some of its complications can be dangerous. The same precautions against mosquito bites that should be undertaken to protect against malaria (see page 41) apply here too; the difference is that the dengue mosquito comes out **during the day** rather than at night.

There is one dangerous form of dengue, **hemorrhagic dengue**, which can be fatal. Tourists tend not to get it, since you almost always need to have had a previous attack of dengue to be vulnerable to it. It is particularly dangerous to children. If dengue-like symptoms are accompanied by bleeding from the nose, ears or gums, highly bloodshot eyes, blood in your vomit or urine or a pin-prick red rash, get yourself to a private hospital fast.

Chikungunya is another viral disease transmitted by infected mosquitoes during the day, causing fever and severe joint pain – there is no cure but it is rarely fatal. There were over 60,000 reported cases in Brazil in 2017 (Bahia is especially prone to outbreaks). Since a major outbreak in 2015/2016, the risk of **Zika** (ZIKV) infection (also mosquito born) is now much lower in Brazil – cases were down over 90 percent by 2017. The illness itself is usually mild but there is a link between infection during pregnancy and babies being born with birth defects. Note that dengue, chikungunya and zika present similar symptoms and misdiagnosis is common.

Diarrhoea, dysentery and giardia

Diarrhoea is something everybody is likely to get at some stage, and there's little to be done except drink a lot (not alcohol) and bide your time. You should also replace salts, preferably by taking oral rehydration salts (one after each episode), or by mixing a teaspoon of salt and eight of sugar in a litre of purified water. You should seek help if you can't keep any fluids down at all (sucking ice cubes can be a good way to stay hydrated).

If your diarrhoea contains blood or mucus, the cause may be dysentery or giardia. With a fever, it could well be caused by **bacillic dysentery** and may clear up without treatment. Nevertheless, a course of antibiotics such as ciprofloxacin is advised. It is best to consult a doctor or pharmacist about which antibiotic to take as different bugs may be resistant locally, and you should avoid taking Loperamide (Imodium) if at all possible. Note that these drugs also destroy "gut flora" that help protect you. Once your symptoms have disappeared you may be a bit intolerant to milk, spicy food and alcohol, and it is a good idea to stick to small, bland meals.

Similar symptoms without fever indicate **amoebic dysentery**, which is much more serious, and can damage your gut if untreated. The usual cure is a course of metronidazole (Flagyl), an anti-biotic that may itself make you feel ill, and should not be taken with alcohol. Similar symptoms, plus rotten-egg belches and farts, indicate **giardia**, for which the treatment is again metronidazole. If you suspect you have any of these, seek medical help. It would be wise to travel with a supply of antibiotics if you are going off the beaten track for several weeks, but you should only take them if there is definitely blood in your diarrhoea and it is impossible to see a doctor.

Food and water

Many diseases are directly or indirectly related to **impure water** and **contaminated food**, and care should be taken in choosing what to eat and drink. You should, of course, take particular care with seafood, especially **shellfish** – don't eat anything that's at all suspicious. Fruit and salad ingredients should be washed in bottled or purified water or, preferably, peeled. Ultimately, you are going to run some risks with all food, so if you're going to enjoy your stay to the full, you can't be too paranoid.

Even in the most remote towns and villages **mineral water** (*água mineral*), either sparkling (*com gás*) or still (*sem gás*), is easily available and cheap. As with food, it's difficult to be on guard all the time while drinking; be aware that fruit juices are often diluted with water, and ice is rarely made with filtered water outside a smart hotel.

In many Brazilian cities **tap water** is clean enough to drink (and locals do so all the time); though it will be free of diseases, you may still get mildly sick from any bacteria in the water supply that your body is not used to. If you are travelling in remote areas, consider taking a water purification agent, such as iodine, with you. To avoid dehydration be sure to drink plenty of non-alcoholic liquids, always carry a bottle of water on long trips and check that the seal on any bottled water you use is intact.

Hepatitis A

Wherever you go in Brazil, protection against **hepatitis A** is a sensible precaution. The disease is transmitted through contaminated water and food, resulting in fever and diarrhoea, and it can also cause jaundice and liver damage; good food and hand hygiene are the best preventatives. Gammaglobulin injections are the traditional protection but require regular boosters. A newer vaccine – Havrix – is very effective and lasts for up to ten years if you have a booster jab after six months.

HIV and AIDS

Brazil has a relatively high number of people with **AIDS** and **HIV**, though the number has declined significantly since the 1990s when it seemed that the epidemic was getting out of control. Indeed, the Brazilian anti-AIDS programme is considered by the UN to be the most successful in the developing world. There are many reasons for this: free, universal provision of anti-retroviral drugs (ARVs); a dramatic increase in the awareness of, and availability of, condoms, spurred by government programmes (especially and controversially within the sex worker community); and needle exchange programmes.

Brazil also has some of the funniest and most imaginative safe-sex campaigns anywhere, particularly in evidence during Carnaval.

The best preventative for transmission is to **use a condom**, which is also a sensible way to avoid catching other STDs. They are widely available in pharmacies, where you should ask for a *camisinha*. A majority of Brazil's HIV carriers are concentrated in the big cities, and the gay community is the highest risk group. As anywhere else, anal sex or sex with a prostitute are high-risk activities. The situation with blood and blood products has now improved enormously, but in more remote parts of the country, especially the Amazon, make sure that if you have an injection it is with a needle you see being removed from its packaging, or carry your own needles with you.

Malaria

Malaria is endemic in northern Brazil: **Amazônia**, **Southern Pará** and much of rural **Rondônia** are the riskiest areas. It may be advisable to avoid some areas entirely if you are travelling with **children** as malaria can be a much more serious issue for them. In recent years rates have climbed as mosquitoes have become more resistant to insecticides and drugs, and a small number of tourists die avoidably every year. However, with simple precautions you can minimize the chances of catching it, even in highly malarial areas. Make no mistake, though, without the correct **precautions** and **prophylaxis**, malaria can kill.

There are two kinds of malaria in Brazil: **falciparum**, which is more serious but less common, and **vivax**. Both are transmitted by anopheles mosquitoes, which are most active at sunrise and for an hour or so before sunset. Even in very malarial areas, only around five percent of anopheles are infected with malarial parasites, so the more you minimize mosquito bites, the less likely you are to catch it.

Make sure that you use **insect repellent**: the most commonly used in Brazil is **Autan**, often in combination with Johnson's Baby Oil to minimize skin irritation. The most effective mosquito repellents – worth looking out for before you leave home – contain **DEET** (diethyl toluamide). DEET is strong stuff, so follow the manufacturers' instructions, particularly with use on children. If you have sensitive skin, a natural alternative is citronella or, in the UK, **Mosi-guard Natural**, made from a blend of eucalyptus oils (though still use DEET on clothes and nets). Wear long-sleeved shirts and trousers, shoes and socks during the times of day when mosquitoes are most active. You should also sleep under a sheet and, crucially, use a **mosquito net**. Nets for hammocks (*mosqueteiro para rede*) are reasonable and easily available in Amazonian cities and towns. Mosquito coils also help keep the insects at bay.

Prevention and treatment

When taking **preventive tablets** it's important to keep a routine and cover the period before and after your trip with doses; doctors can advise on which kind to take. As resistance to chloroquin-based drugs increases, mefloquin, which goes under the brand name of Lariam, has become one of the most recommended prophylactics for travellers to Brazil. This can have very strong psychiatric side effects, though, and its use is controversial. The websites Ⓦ cdc.gov/travel/regionalmalaria and Ⓦ www.fitfortravel.nhs.uk are useful resources, giving advice on risk areas in Brazil and the best methods of protection.

Malaria has an incubation period of around two weeks. The first **signs of malaria** are remarkably similar to flu – muscle and joint pains and weakness that last for a day or two before the onset of malaria fever proper – and may take months to appear: if you suspect anything, go to a hospital or clinic immediately. You will need immediate treatment and a blood test to identify the strain.

Malaria treatment is one public-health area where Brazil can take some credit. Dotted in malarial parts of the Amazon are small malaria control posts and **clinics**, run by the anti-malaria agency SUCAM – ask for the *posto da SUCAM*. They may not look like much, but the people who staff them are very experienced and know their local strains better than any city specialist. Treatment in a *posto* is free, and if you do catch malaria you should get yourself taken to one as quickly as possible; don't shiver in your hammock and wait for it to pass. If in a city and you get the same symptoms (a fever and the shakes), make sure you get a blood test right away; you'll get your results in a few hours and quick diagnosis is vital. Remember that the **incubation period** means that the symptoms may only appear after you return home – make sure to tell your doctor where you've been if you get a fever shortly after your return home.

Rabies

Though the government has had great success in containing the disease in recent years, **rabies** does exist in Brazil – feral dogs (which should not be petted) in the cities and bats in the Amazon are the biggest dangers. If you are bitten or scratched, wash the wound immediately with soap and running water for five minutes and apply alcohol or iodine. If possible try to see whether the animal itself has any rabies symptoms. Seek treatment immediately

– rabies is fatal once symptoms appear, and you may also need to get a tetanus jab. If you're going to be working with animals or planning a long stay, especially in rural areas, you should consider a rabies **vaccination** beforehand. Although this won't give you complete immunity, it will give you a window of 24–48 hours to seek treatment and reduce the amount of post-exposure vaccine you'll need if bitten.

Yellow fever

Getting a **yellow fever vaccination**, which offers protection for ten years, is recommended for most regions outside of Fortaleza, Recife, Rio de Janeiro, Salvador and São Paulo (see cdc.gov/travel for more details). This viral disease is transmitted by mosquitoes and can be fatal, but is extremely rare even in places where it is endemic. Symptoms include headache, fever, abdominal pain and vomiting, and though victims may appear to recover, without medical help they may suffer from bleeding, shock and kidney and liver failure. While you're waiting for help, it is important to keep the fever as low as possible and prevent dehydration.

In the Amazon

Given the remoteness of many parts of the **Amazon** and the prevalence of insects and snakes, health care takes on a special significance. If you are trekking through forest or savannah, long trousers are a good idea, and it is vital to wear good boots that protect your ankles from snake bites, chiggers (mites) and scorpions. You should never trek alone.

Snakes are timid and, unless you're unlucky, only attack if you step on them. Many of the most venomous snakes are tiny, easily able to snuggle inside a shoe or a rucksack pocket. Always shake out your hammock and clothes, keep rucksack pockets tightly closed and take special care when it rains, as snakes, scorpions and other nasty beasties quite sensibly head for shelter in huts.

If you do get bitten by a snake, try to kill it for identification – but only if this can easily be done. Contrary to popular belief, cutting yourself and sucking out blood will do you more harm than good. It goes without saying that you should get yourself to a doctor as soon as possible. Health posts in the nearest town may have serum, but you must know the type of snake involved.

Due to the humidity, any **cut** or **wound** gets infected very easily. Always clean cuts or bites with alcohol or purified water before dressing. As a general rule, leave all **insects** alone and never handle them. Even the smallest ants, caterpillars and bees can give you nasty stings and bites, and scorpions, large soldier ants and some species of bee will give you a fever for a day or two as well.

The media

Brazil has a vibrant, free regional press rather than a national one. Even the top Rio and São Paulo papers, available throughout the country, are a little parochial; elsewhere, newspapers are at best mediocre but are always valuable for listings of local events. Brazil also boasts a lurid but entertaining tabloid press, specializing in gruesome murders, political scandals and football.

Newspapers and magazines

The top **newspapers** are the slightly left-of-centre *Folha de São Paulo* (folha.uol.com.br) and the Rio-based, right-of-centre *O Globo* (oglobo.globo.com), usually available a day late in large cities throughout the country. Both are independent and have extensive international news, cultural coverage and entertainment listings. Even stodgier but reasonable is the right-wing *Estado de São Paulo* (estadao.com.br), while the *Valor Econômico* (valor.com.br) is a high-quality equivalent of the *Financial Times* or *Wall Street Journal*.

There are also two good weekly current-affairs **magazines**: *Veja* (veja.abril.com.br) and *ISTOÉ* (istoe.com.br). You will find Brazilian editions of most major fashion and women's magazines: *Vogue Brasil* (vogue.globo.com) is a quality monthly magazine offering great insight into the style of the Brazilian elite. The monthly *Placar* (placar.abril.com.br) is essential for anyone wanting to get to serious grips with Brazilian football.

Apart from in airports, Rio and São Paulo, where you can find the *International New York Times* and *The Economist*, **English-language newspapers** and magazines are very difficult to find in Brazil.

Television

Cable and satellite TV is now extremely common in Brazil (especially in hotels), meaning access to the main US channels (though with programmes mostly dubbed into Portuguese), and a handful of channels from the rest of the world. Don't expect much more than CNN and the odd movie channel in English. Domestic Brazilian programming is poor to say the least, but often compulsive viewing even if you don't understand a word of Portuguese. There are several Brazilian national networks, of which the most dominant is **TV Globo**, the centrepiece of the Globo empire, Latin America's largest media conglomerate. The other major national networks are TV Bandeirantes (aka "Band"), SBT, RecordTV and the non-profit public broadcasting TV Brasil.

Local channels are still dominated by game shows and **telenovelas**, glossy soap operas that have massive audiences in the evenings, though viewing numbers have been in decline in recent years. **Football coverage** is also worth paying attention to, a gabbling, incomprehensible stream of commentary, punctuated by remarkably elongated shouts of "Gooooool" whenever anyone scores.

Festivals and public holidays

Carnaval is the most important festival in Brazil, but there are other parties, too, from religious anniversaries to celebrations based around elections. In towns and rural areas, you may well stumble across a *dia de festa*, the day of the local patron saint, a very simple event in which the image of the saint is paraded through the town with a band and firecrackers, a thanksgiving Mass is celebrated, and then everyone turns to the secular pleasures of the fair, the market and the bottle.

On **national public holidays** banks and offices are liable to be closed all day, and shops may reduce their hours. For other festivals, most things will be open as normal, but check with local tourist offices or your hotel.

Carnaval

When **Carnaval** time arrives, Brazil gets down to some of the most serious partying in the world. A Caribbean carnival might prepare you a little, but what happens in Brazil is more spectacular, goes on longer and is on a far larger scale. Every place in Brazil, large or small, has some form of Carnaval, and in three places especially – **Rio** (see page 105), **Salvador** (see page 226) and **Olinda** (see page 280), just outside Recife – Carnaval has become a mass event, involving seemingly the entire populations of the cities and drawing visitors from all over the world. When exactly Carnaval begins depends on the **ecclesiastical calendar**: it starts at midnight of the Friday before Ash Wednesday and ends on the Tuesday night, though effectively people start partying on Friday afternoon – over four days of continuous, determined celebration. It usually happens in February, although very occasionally it can be early March. In effect, the entire period from Christmas is a kind of run-up to Carnaval. People start working on costumes, songs are composed and rehearsals staged in school playgrounds and backyards, so that Carnaval comes as a culmination rather than a sudden burst of excitement and colour.

Festivals and holidays calendar

JANUARY

New Year's Day (Ano Novo) **Jan 1, national public holiday.** Procissão no Mar, the "Sea Procession", takes place in Salvador (see page 217). On New Year's Eve, some two million people (mostly wearing white) gather on Copacabana beach (Rio de Janeiro) to watch the midnight fireworks and then party till dawn.

Festa Pomerana Pomerode, SC. **First half of Jan.** One of the country's best agricultural shows (see page 596).

Lavagem do Bonfim Salvador, BH. **Second Thurs of Jan.** Bahia's major religious festival is also one its most colourful (see page 217).

Torneio dos Repentistas Olinda, PE. **Three days in late Jan.** Biggest festival of duelling *repentistas*, the singer-poets of the Northeast (see page 282).

FEBRUARY

Carnaval Friday before Ash Wednesday to Shrove Tuesday night. Celebrated everywhere, with major events in Rio de Janeiro (see page 105), Ouro Preto (see page 168), Olinda (see page 280) and Salvador (see page 226). Don't expect to find many things open or to get much done in the week before Carnaval, or the week after it. During Carnaval itself, shops open briefly on Monday and Tuesday mornings, but banks and offices stay closed.

MARCH/APRIL

Semana Santa (Easter). **Ouro Preto, MG.** Ouro Preto becomes the focus of a spectacular series of plays and processions lasting for about a month before Easter Sunday itself (see page 168).

Paixão de Cristo ("The Passion of Christ") **Nova Jerusalém, PE. Usually performed nightly over Easter Week.** Huge passion play (re-enacting the events of Holy Week), performed in a specially designed complex with nine stages (see page 286).

Lollapalooza Brasil São Paulo (**most recently at Autódromo de Interlagos). Usually over two or three days in late March.** Brazilian edition of the famous US indie and rock concert festival.

APRIL

Tiradentes Day (Dia de Tiradentes) **April 21, national public holiday.** Commemorates Joaquim José da Silva Xavier, leading member of Inconfidência Mineira, executed by the Portuguese in 1792 (see page **170**).

Skolbeats São Paulo. **April or May.** Latin America's biggest dance music festival.

MAY

Labour Day (Dia do Trabalhador) **May 1, national public holiday.**

Festa do Divino Espírito Santo Alcântara, MA. **Usually in the week running up to the seventh Sun after Easter (Pentecost Sunday).** Exuberant parades that blend Portuguese Catholic and African traditions (see page 324); also celebrations in Pirenópolis, Goiás (see page 425).

JUNE

Brasília International Film Festival Brasília. **Usually one week in early June.** Highlights new South American and international movies (see page 416).

Festas juninas Celebrated all over Brazil. **Third week in June.** Geared mainly towards children, who dress up in straw hats and checked shirts, and release paper balloons with candles attached (to provide the hot air), causing anything from a fright to a major conflagration when they land.

Forró Caju Aracaju, SE. **Usually two weeks in June.** Massive celebration of *forró* music.

Bumba-meu-boi São Luís, MA. Usually starts on Santo Antônio's day, June 13, culminating on São João's day, June 24. Massive celebration of the distinctive Northeastern dance and music, featuring giant papier-mâché bulls (see page 321).

Festival Folclórico de Parintins Parintins, AM. Another major Boi Bumbá festival, with a spectacular parade, feverish dancing and infectious beats (see page 357).

JULY

Festival Nacional de Forró Itaúnas, ES. **Usually one week in mid-July.** Wild celebration of *forró* music (see page 195).

Festival de Dança de Joinville Joinville, SC. **Usually over two weeks in July.** Joinville Dance Festival, reputed to be the world's largest classical dance event (see page 588).

AUGUST

Fiesta Nossa Senhora da Boa Morte Cachoeira, BH. **The first Fri before Aug 15.** Raucous celebration of candomblé (see page 230).

Festival de Cinema Gramado, RS **T 54 3286 1475, W festivaldegramado.net. One week in mid-Aug.** Most important film festival in Brazil (see page 615).

SEPTEMBER

Independence Day (Dia da Independência or "Sete de Setembro") **Sept 7, national public holiday.** Celebrates Brazil's independence from Portugal in 1822. Major festivities/parades in Brasília and all state capitals, especially São Paulo.

Festival do Rio Rio de Janeiro, **late Sept/early Oct T 21 2543 4968, W festivaldorio.com.br.** Major film festival over two weeks (see page 105).

OCTOBER

Círio de Nazaré Belém, PA. **Second Sun of Oct.** Crowds of over a million follow the procession of the image of Nossa Senhora de Nazaré, a beloved incarnation of the Virgin Mary (see page 341).

Feast Day of Our Lady of Aparecida Oct 12, **national public holiday.** Celebration of Nossa Senhora Aparecida, a venerated statue of the Virgin Mary (housed in Aparecida, São Paulo) and patron saint of Brazil.

Oktoberfest Blumenau, SC, **18 days in Oct T 47 3326 6901, W oktoberfestblumenau.com.br.** Boisterous version of the Munich beer festival (see page 592).

Mostra São Paulo, **Oct.** Sao Pãulo's international film festival (see page 513).

NOVEMBER

All Souls' Day, or "Day of the Dead" (Dia dos Finados) **Nov 2, national public holiday.**

Republic Day (Proclamação da República) **Nov 15, national public holiday.** Celebrates the creation of the Brazilian republic in 1889 after the removal of Emperor Dom Pedro II.

DECEMBER

Christmas Day (Natal) **Dec 25, national public holiday.**

Sports and outdoor activities

Brazil's national parks, rivers and gorgeous coastline offer the opportunity to indulge in a vast range of outdoor pursuits, everything from surfing, fishing and hiking, to scuba diving, caving and kayaking. When it comes to sport, Brazilian football (*futebol*) is globally revered and a privilege to watch, at its best reminding you why it's known as "the beautiful game". Brazil have been world champions a record five times, and Pelé – born in Minas Gerais – is still regarded as the best player of all time. Indeed, you won't really have experienced Brazil until you've attended a match.

Football

Brazil's major teams have traditionally been concentrated in Rio and São Paulo, though things have been changing in recent years and Série A (the top league) is a lot more competitive. In Rio, **Flamengo** is the best-supported team in the country, and its distinctive shirt of red and black hoops is seen everywhere. Its clashes with perennial Rio rival **Fluminense** (maroon, green and white stripes) at the Maracanã stadium are among the most intense matches in Brazilian club football. **Botafogo** (black and white stripes with the famous white-star badge) and **Vasco da Gama** (white with black diagonal stripe) vie with "Fla-Flu" for dominance.

São Paulo's two leading teams, **São Paulo** (white with red and black hoops) and **Corinthians** (white), champions in 2017, share a similarly bitter rivalry, while **Portuguesa** (red and green), **Palmeiras** (green), champions in 2016, and **Santos** (white) make up the other major teams in the region. Teams that now consistently compete with the best of Rio and São Paulo are **Grêmio** (blue, white and black stripes) from Porto Alegre, and **Atlético Mineiro** (white) and **Cruzeiro** (dark blue) from Belo Horizonte (the latter won Série A in 2013). **Atlético Goianiense in Goiânia, Bahia** and **Vitória** (both in Salvador), **Atlético Paranaense** and **Coritiba** in Curitiba, and **Sport Club do Recife** have been successful in recent years too.

Brazil's top domestic football league, the **Campeonato Brasileiro Série A**, is contested annually by twenty teams (typically May–Dec), with the standard of play usually very high. **Tickets** are very cheap by European standards; good seats at a *clássico* will cost no more than R$75, but an ordinary match will be half that or less – the issue is availability rather than price. For *clássicos*, hotels often have packages that include transport, tickets and a guide for around R$100 all in, an expensive way of doing it but often the only practical option if you can't get a ticket a few days in advance. For ordinary matches, you can almost always turn up half an hour beforehand and look for the *bilheteria*, the ticket office, which usually only takes cash.

Brazilian **stadiums** tend to be enormous and rarely full save for *clássicos*, matches between major teams. All major stadiums are two-deckers, most are now all-seaters but a few still have terracing on the lower deck: upper-deck seats are *arquibancada*, lower-deck *geral*. Some stadiums are worth going out of your way for: the **Maracanã** in Rio, it goes without saying, but also the beautiful Art Deco **Pacaembu** in São Paulo.

There is not as much of a problem with **crowd violence** in Brazil as in many European countries, but don't wear a Brazilian club shirt just to be on the safe side: non-Brazilian shirts are no problem (except for Argentine ones – the two countries don't get on well in footballing terms), and Brazilian fans are extremely friendly to foreigners.

Volleyball

The other major national Brazilian sport is **volleyball** (*volei*), mostly played on the beach, though the hard-court game is also popular and sand is imported inland for beach volleyball championships elsewhere. In Rio especially, beach foot-volleyball (*futevolei*) has gained massive popularity in the last decade.

Outdoor activities

A full range of outdoor activities is available across the country, with regional highlights including **hang-gliding** in Rio (see page 87), **hiking** and waterfall hunting in the coastal forests of the Serra do Mar or Bahia's marvellous Chapada Diamantina (see page 246), river-based pursuits in the Amazon, and snorkelling and **piranha fishing** in the Pantanal (see page 447), and exploration of the lunar-like dune systems of Maranhão's Lençois Maranhenses (see page 324). **Watersports**, from diving to surfing, are a huge part of Brazilian culture, with the offshore archipelago of Fernando de Noronha (see page 287) the country's most pristine destination.

Travelling with children

Travelling with children is relatively easy in Brazil. They are made to feel welcome in hotels and restaurants in a way that's not always so in Europe or North America. In fact, it is also more secure: even thieves and *assaltantes* seem to respect families with children and leave them alone.

Travelling around Brazil takes time, so try not to be too ambitious in terms of how much you aim to cover. Long bus journeys are scheduled overnight and can be exhausting. Children pay full **fare** on buses if they take up a seat, ten percent on planes if under 2 years old, half-fare between 2 and 12 years old, and full fare thereafter. Newer airports have a **nursery** (*berçário*) where you can change or nurse your baby and where an attendant will run your baby a bath, which is great on a hot day or if your plane's delayed. If you plan on **renting a car**, bring your own **child or baby seat** as rental companies rarely supply them and they are very expensive in Brazil. Cars are fitted with three-point shoulder seatbelts in the front, but many only have lap seatbelts in the back.

Accommodation

In **hotels**, kids are generally free up to the age of 5, and double rooms often include both a double and a single bed; a baby's cot may be available, but don't count on it. It's rare that a room will sleep more than three, but larger hotels sometimes have rooms with an interlinking door. Hotels will sometimes offer discounts, especially if children share rooms, and even beds, with siblings or parents; the lower- to mid-range hotels are probably the most flexible in this regard. If you're planning on staying more than a few days in a city, you may find it cheaper and more convenient to stay in an **apartment-hotel**, which will sleep several people and comes with basic cooking facilities.

Many of the mid- and upper-range hotels have swimming pools, gardens and even games rooms, which are often useful in **entertaining** kids. Most large towns also have cinemas, the best often being the new multiplexes found in shopping centres.

Food and health

Food shouldn't be a problem as familiar dishes are always available and there's also the ubiquitous *comida por quilo* option. Portions tend to be huge, often sufficient for two large appetites, and it's perfectly acceptable to request additional plates and cutlery. Most hotels and restaurants provide high chairs (*cadeira alta*) as well. Commercial **baby food** is sold in Brazilian supermarkets. Remember to avoid tap water and use only mineral water when preparing formula and washing out bottles. Mid-range hotels and upwards have a **minibar** (*frigobar*) in the rooms where you can store bottles and baby food, but where there isn't one you will be able to store things in the hotel's refrigerator. A small cool box or insulated bag is a good idea.

Most Brazilian families use disposable **nappies/ diapers** (*fraldas*), and brands such as Pampers are sold in pharmacies and supermarkets – it's worth only bringing the minimum with you until you can make it to a shop.

Health shouldn't be a problem, but before planning your itinerary check which areas entail taking **anti-malarial tablets** (the state of Rondônia other than Porto Velho, rural Acre and Amapá and southern Pará are rife with malaria and should be avoided), and make enquiries as to whether the **vaccines** recommended or required in some parts of Brazil (in particular the Amazon) are likely to have any unpleasant side effects. At the time of writing **zika** had largely been contained in Brazil, but **dengue fever** is a perennial problem (see page 39). For most of Brazil, the only likely problem will be the strength of the tropical sun and the viciousness of the mosquitoes: bring plenty of **sunscreen** and an easy-to-apply **non-toxic insect repellent**.

Travel essentials

Costs

Prices in Brazil have risen considerably in recent years, though the recent economic downturn has tempered this somewhat – hotel prices in particular have dropped overall (along with the cost of car rentals) and most tourist attractions have frozen (or even lowered fees), though the price of food, taxis, local transport and most goods have continued to increase. Indeed, the *custo Brasil* ("Brazil cost") has become one of the most contentious issues of the day, with millions of Brazilians unable to participate in the nation's "middle-class" economy. In most of Brazil you'll still pay relatively **high prices** comparable to the US and Europe for meals in top restaurants and long-distance flights – things like sunblock, good-quality clothing, cameras and anything to do with computers tend to cost even more. Hotels in **São Paulo** and **Rio** are still very expensive.

The good news is that outside of these two big cities, Brazil remains very much a viable destination for the budget traveller. Every town has a range of cheap eats and hostels, and the fact that the best attractions, such as the beaches and many museums, are free, makes it possible to have an enjoyable time on a **budget** of less than R$120 a day. Staying in good hotels, travelling by comfortable buses or planes and not stinting on the extras is likely to cost you a lot more – at least R$400 a day.

Crime and personal safety

Brazil has a reputation as a rather dangerous place, and while it's not entirely undeserved, it is often overblown and you should not let fear overshadow your stay. If you take the precautions outlined below, you are extremely unlikely to come to any harm. The tips in this section apply everywhere, but be particularly alert in Rio, Salvador and São Paulo.

Criminals know that any injury to a foreign tourist is going to mean a heavy clampdown, which in turn means no pickings for a while. So unless you resist during an incident, nothing is likely to happen to you. Needless to say, **avoid favelas** in any city unless you are visiting with locals/tour guides who know the area – drug gang members shot a British tourist when her husband drove into a *favela* near Rio by accident in 2017. **Use GPS/SatNav devices with caution** (double-checking routes with maps), as they can sometimes lead you through shady areas as the "fastest" or "shortest" route to a destination.

Avoiding assaltos

As a rule, *assaltos* (muggings) are most common in the larger cities, and are rare in the countryside and towns. Most *assaltos* take place at night, in backstreets with few people around, so stick to busy, well-lit streets; in a city, it's always a lot safer to take a taxi than walk. Also, prepare for the worst by locking your money and passport in the hotel safe – the one in your room is more secure than the one at reception. If you must carry them, make sure they're in a **moneybelt** or a **concealed internal pocket**. Do not carry your valuables in a pouch hanging from your neck. Only take along as much money as you'll need for the day, but do take at least some money, as the average *assaltante* won't believe a gringo could be out of money, and might get rough. Don't wear an expensive **watch** or **jewellery**: if you need a watch you can always buy a cheap plastic digital one on a street corner. And keep wallets and purses out of sight – pockets with buttons or zips are best. Needless to say, flaunting fancy phones, iPads and other high-tech paraphernalia is not a good idea.

If you are unlucky enough to be the victim of an *assalto*, try to remember that it's your **possessions** rather than you that are the target. Your money and anything you're carrying will be snatched, your watch will get pulled off your wrist, but within a couple of seconds it will be over. On no account resist: it isn't worth the risk. If in a car, and someone taps on the window with a gun, they want your wallet – hand it out through the window. If they want the car, they will signal you out of it; get out immediately and do not delay to pick up anything. If you try to drive off at speed, there's a good chance they will shoot. If in a restaurant or sitting down, make no sudden movements and do not stand up, even if only to get your wallet out – wriggle instead.

Scams

At international **airports**, particularly Rio and São Paulo, certain scams can operate; for instance, well-dressed and official-looking men target tourists arriving off international flights in the arrivals lounge, identify themselves as policemen, often flashing a card, and tell the tourists to go with them. The tourists are then pushed into a car outside and robbed. If anyone, no matter how polite or well dressed they are, or how good their English is, identifies themselves as a policeman to you, be instantly on your guard – real policemen generally leave foreigners well alone. They won't try anything actually inside a terminal building, so go to any airline desk or grab one of the security guards, and on no account leave the terminal building with them or leave any luggage in their hands. Scams involving ATM machines are also common in the big cities (see page 49).

EMERGENCY PHONE NUMBERS

Police ⓣ 190
Ambulance ⓣ 192
Fire department ⓣ 193

Avoiding theft

More common than an *assalto* is a simple theft, a **furto**. Brand-new, designer-label bags are an obvious target, so go for the downmarket look. You're at your most vulnerable when travelling, and though the **luggage compartments** of buses are pretty safe – remember to get a baggage receipt from the person putting them in and don't throw it away – the overhead racks inside are less safe; keep an eye on things you stash there, especially on night journeys. On a **city beach**, never leave things unattended while you take a dip: any beachside bar will stow things for you for free.

Most hotels (even the cheaper ones) will have a **safe** (*caixa*), and unless you have serious doubts about the place you should lock away your most valuable things: the better the hotel, the more secure it's likely to be. In cheaper hotels, where rooms are shared, the risks are obviously greater – some people take along a small padlock for extra security and many wardrobes in cheaper hotels have latches fitted for this very purpose. Finally, take care at **Carnaval** as it's a notorious time for pickpockets and thieves.

Drugs

The drug wars in the *favelas* that you will have heard about and may well see on local TV during your stay are very localized and unlikely to have any impact on foreign tourists. But you should be extremely careful about using drugs in Brazil.

Marijuana – *maconha* – is common, but you are in trouble if the police find any on you. You'll be able to bribe your way out of it, but it will cost you the daily withdrawal limit on whatever plastic you have. Foreigners sometimes get targeted for a shakedown and have drugs planted on them – the area around the Bolivian border has a bad reputation for this – in order to get a bribe out of them. If this happens to you, deny everything, refuse to pay and insist on seeing a superior officer and telephoning the nearest consulate – though this approach is only for the patient.

The police

If you are robbed or held up, it's best to go to the **police** immediately, even though, they're very unlikely to be able to do anything (except with something like a theft from a hotel room) – and reporting a theft can take hours even without the language barrier. You may have to do it for insurance purposes, for which you'll need a local police report: this could take an entire, very frustrating, day, so think first about how badly you want to be reimbursed. If your **passport** is stolen, go to your consulate and they should be able to assist.

There are various types of police. The best are usually the **Polícia de Turismo**, or tourist police, who are used to tourists and their problems and often speak some English, but they're thin on the ground outside Rio. In a city, their number should be displayed on or near the desk of all hotels. The most efficient police by far are the **Polícia Federal**, the Brazilian equivalent of the American FBI, who deal with visas and their extension; they have offices at frontier posts, airports and ports and in state capitals. The ones you see on every street corner are the **Polícia Militar**, with blue or green uniforms and caps. They look mean – and very often are – but, apart from at highway road blocks, they generally leave gringos alone. There is also a plain-clothes **Polícia Civil**, to whom thefts are reported if there is no tourist police post around – they are overworked, underpaid and extremely slow. If you decide to go to the police in a city where there is a **consulate**, get in touch with the consulate first and do as they tell you.

Electricity

Electricity supplies vary – sometimes 110V and sometimes 220V – so check before plugging anything in. Plugs have two round pins, as in Continental Europe.

Insurance

Prior to travelling, you should take out an **insurance policy** to cover against theft, loss and illness or injury. Before paying for a new policy, however, it's worth checking whether you already have some degree of coverage – credit-card companies, home-insurance policies and private medical plans sometimes cover you and your belongings when you're abroad. Remember that when securing baggage insurance, make sure that the per-article limit – typically under £500 equivalent – will cover your most valuable possession.

Internet

Brazil has the highest number of computers with **internet access** in South America and all things online are highly developed, with wi-fi increasingly available; as a result, internet cafés are dwindling in number. Almost every hotel in Brazil (unless in very remote locations) offers free **wi-fi** – noted in the Guide with a symbol – as do many cafés.

Laundry

Even the humblest of hotels has a *lavadeira*, who will wash and iron your clothes. If the rates are not clearly published, agree on a price beforehand.

ATMS – A WARNING

One of the sneakiest financial **scams** in Brazil today is a rather sophisticated one. Cartels across the country rig ATM machines so that they can record the details of your card (and your password); a few weeks later an identical cloned copy of your card will be used to withdraw cash from machines globally. Unless you are in dire financial straits, **DO NOT use third party (non-bank) ATM machines**, especially at airports, bus stations or shopping centres – only use official machines in banks. The problem is most acute in Rio and São Paulo, but it pays to take care throughout the country. And check your card activity regularly, even several weeks after you've returned home. Once notified, your bank will cancel the card and usually refund any money stolen, but check in advance.

Larger hotels always have set prices for laundry services – they are usually surprisingly expensive. Very common in larger cities are *lavandarías*, which operate a very useful *por peso* system – the clothes are weighed at the entrance, you pay per kilo, and pick them up washed and folded the next day for a couple of dollars per kilo. Ironing (*passar*) costs a little more.

LGBT travellers

Gay life in Brazil thrives, especially in the large cities, Rio in particular being one of the great gay cities of the world. In general, the scene benefits from Brazil's hedonistically relaxed attitudes towards sexuality in general, and the divide between gay and straight nightlife is often very blurred. Attitudes vary from region to region. The two most popular gay destinations are Rio and Salvador. Rural areas and small towns, especially in Minas Gerais, the Northeast and the South, are conservative; the medium-sized and larger cities less so.

Maps

We've provided detailed full-colour **maps** throughout the Guide. More detailed maps are surprisingly hard to get hold of outside Brazil and are rarely very good: *Bartholomew, International Travel Maps, Michelin and National Geographic* produce country maps (typically 1:4,200,000), but these are not updated often. Much better are the regional maps in the *Mapa Rodoviário Touring* series (1:2,500,000), which clearly mark all the major routes, although these, even in Brazil, are difficult to find; almost all Brazilians with cars use some sort of GPS navigation system (usually via smartphones).

Money

The Brazilian **currency** is the *real* (pronounced "hey-al"); its plural is *reais* (pronounced "hey-ice"), written R$. The *real* is made up of one hundred *centavos*, written ¢. Notes are for 2, 5, 10, 20, 50 and 100 *reais*; coins are 1, 5, 10, 25, 50 *centavos* and the 1 *real*. Throughout the Guide, all prices are given in Brazilian *reais* unless otherwise noted. However, US dollars and euros are easy enough to change in banks and exchange offices anywhere. **Exchange rates** have stabilized somewhat after the *real* weakened sharply against the dollar in 2015/2016; the currency has been strengthening a little since 2017, but exchange-rate turbulence is unlikely to be a feature of your stay. Rates out of ATMs are usually better than at *câmbios*.

ATMs

Getting cash in Brazil is simple in theory; just take your debit or credit card and use **ATMs** – they are now ubiquitous in Brazil, to be found in most supermarkets, many pharmacies and all airports, as well as banks. The problem is getting them to work for international cards – always plan ahead and make sure you have enough cash to last a day or so in advance.

Increasing numbers of Brazilian banks are linking their cash dispensers to the Cirrus and Maestro networks; the most reliable and widespread is the Banco 24 Horas network, including Banco do Brasil, Citibank and HSBC (Santander and Bradesco also usually have ATMs that are compatible), though don't be surprised if your card is rejected; only try machines which have the "Visa" or "MasterCard" (or Cirrus and Maestro) logos (not all the machines in the same bank do). Another important thing to note is that for security reasons most bank ATMs stop dispensing cash **after 10pm** (or at least, limit the amount you can take out). Airport ATMs are the only ones that dispense cash at all hours.

Credit cards

All major **credit cards** are widely accepted by shops, hotels and restaurants throughout Brazil,

CALLING HOME FROM BRAZIL

Note that the initial zero is omitted from the area code when dialling the UK, Ireland, Australia and New Zealand from abroad.

US and Canada 00 + carrier selection code + 1 + area code.

UK 00 + carrier selection code + 44 + city code.

Republic of Ireland 00 + carrier selection code + 353 + city code.

Australia 00 + carrier selection code + 61 + city code.

New Zealand 00 + carrier selection code + 64 + city code.

South Africa 00 + carrier selection code + 27 + city code.

even in rural areas. MasterCard and Visa are the most prevalent, with Diners Club and American Express also widespread. It's a good idea to inform your credit-card issuer about your trip before you leave so that the card isn't frozen for uncharacteristic use (and Brazil always raises red flags). **Travellers' cheques** are not recommended.

Opening hours

Basic hours for most **stores and businesses** are from Monday to Saturday 8am to noon and 2pm to 6pm (with smaller shops tending to close Saturday afternoons). Shops in **malls** tend to stay open until late Friday and Saturday nights. **Banks** open at 10am, and stay open all day, but usually stop changing money at either 2pm or 3pm; except for those at major airports, they're closed at weekends and on public holidays. **Museums and monuments** more or less follow office hours but most are closed all day on Monday and Sunday afternoons.

Phones

With the explosion of mobile/wireless communications, public phones are now hard to find in Brazil – aim to use a mobile phone if you can. Hostels are also usually happy to call ahead for reservations at your next stop.

Mobile phones

International visitors who want to use their mobile phones in Brazil will need to check with their phone provider to make sure it will work and what the call charges will be. Assuming your phone does work, you'll need to be extra careful about **roaming charges**, especially for data, which can be extortionate; even checking voicemail can result in hefty charges. Many travellers turn off their voicemail and data roaming before they travel.

If you have a compatible (and unlocked) GSM phone and intend to use it a lot, it can be much cheaper to buy a **Brazilian SIM card** (R$10 or less) to use during your stay. Vivo (W vivo.com.br) has the best coverage – foreigners can buy SIM ("chips") or phones but you'll need to show your passport. Currently, TIM Brasil (W tim.com.br) usually offers the best deals for pre-paid SIM cards (look for TIM outlets or visit a branch of the Lojas Americanas chain store). Once the SIM is installed, you should opt for a pre-pay plan (*pré-pago*); to add credit to your phone, just go to TIM shops, newspaper stalls or pharmacies and ask for TIM "cargas".

Carrier selection codes

The privatization of Brazil's telephone system has led to a proliferation of new telephone companies and increased competition. Before making a national or international call you must now select the telephone company you wish to use by inserting a **two-digit carrier selection code** between the zero and the area code or country code of the number you are calling. To call Rio, for example, from anywhere else in the country, you would dial zero + phone company code + city code (21) followed by the eight-digit number. For local calls, you simply dial the seven- or eight-digit number. Assuming you have a choice, it doesn't matter which company you use, as costs are very similar (this goes for international calls too).

The most common codes are 21 (Embratel), 23 (Intelig Telecom), 31 (Oi), 15 (Telefónica), 41 (TIM) and 14 (Brasil Telecom). If you want to reverse the charges for a local call, dial 9090 plus the number. For long-distance collect calls, dial 90 then the number with carrier code as above (90 + carrier code + area code + number).

To reverse the charges on an international call, dial T 0800 703 2111 or T 0800 890 0288 (for the English-speaking AT&T operator, for North American calls) and follow the instructions. The **country code** for Brazil if calling from overseas is T +55.

Post

A **post office** (run by the national postal service Correios; W correios.com.br) is called a *correio*, identifiable by their bright yellow postboxes and signshops An imposing *Correios e Telégrafos* building will always be found in the centre of a city of any size, but there are also small offices and kiosks scattered around that only deal with mail. Queues are often a problem, but you can save time by using one of their franking machines for stamps; the lines move much more quickly. **Stamps** (*selos*) are most commonly available in two varieties, either for mailing within Brazil or abroad. A postage stamp for either a postcard or a letter up to 20g to the USA costs R$1.80; R$2 to the UK, Ireland and most of Europe; and R$2.20 to Australia, New Zealand and South Africa. It is expensive to send parcels abroad.

Mail within Brazil takes three or four days (longer in the North and Northeast), while **airmail** letters to Europe and North America usually take about a week. **Surface mail** takes about a month to North America, and two to Europe. Although the postal system is generally very reliable, it is not advisable to send valuables through the mail.

Time

Most of Brazil is three hours behind GMT/UTC (Fernando de Noronha is two hours behind); during daylight saving (summer) time (Oct–Feb) it's two hours behind, but confusingly, the northern and northeastern states don't change – check timetables carefully. Most of Amazonas, Rondônia, Mato Grosso and Mato Grosso do Sul are four hours behind – that includes the cities of Manaus, Corumbá, Rio Branco, Porto Velho, Cuiabá and Campo Grande.

The far-western tip of the country (Acre and the southwestern portion of Amazonas) is five hours behind.

Tipping

Restaurant bills usually come with ten percent *taxa de serviço* included, in which case you don't have to tip – ten percent is about right if it is not included. Waiters and some hotel employees depend on tips. You don't have to tip taxi drivers (though they won't say no), but you are expected to tip barbers, hairdressers, shoeshine kids, self-appointed guides and porters. It's useful to keep change handy for them – and for beggars.

Tourist information

You'll find tourist information fairly easy to come by once in Brazil, and there are some sources to be tapped before you leave home. Popular destinations such as Rio, Salvador, the Northeast beach resorts, and towns throughout the South have efficient and helpful **tourist offices**, but anywhere off the beaten track has nothing at all.

Most **state capitals** have tourist information offices, which are announced by signs saying "**Informações Turísticas**". Many of these provide free city maps and booklets, but they are usually all in Portuguese. As a rule, only the airport tourist offices have **hotel-booking services**, and none of them is very good on advising about budget accommodation. Tourist offices are run by the different state and municipal governments, so you have to learn a new acronym every time you cross a state line. In Rio, for example, you'll find TurisRio, which advises on the state, and Riotur, which provides information on the city. There's also **EMBRATUR**, the national tourist organization, but it doesn't have direct dealings with the general public apart from via its excellent website, Ⓦ visitbrasil.com.

BRAZIL WEBSITES

Cidade de São Paulo Ⓦ cidadedesaopaulo.com
Riotur Ⓦ rio.rj.gov.br/riotur
Turismo de Minas Gerais Ⓦ minasgerais.com.br
TurisRio Ⓦ www.turisrio.rj.gov.br
Visit Brazil Travel Association UK Ⓦ vbrata.org.uk

Travellers with disabilities

Travelling in Brazil for **people with disabilities** is likely to be difficult if special facilities are required. For example, access even to recently constructed buildings may be impossible, as lifts are often too narrow to accept wheelchairs or there may be no lift at all. In general, though, you'll find that hotel and restaurant staff are helpful and will do their utmost to be of assistance to try to make up for the deficiencies in access and facilities.

Buses in cities are really only suitable for the agile; **taxis**, however, are plentiful, and most can accommodate wheelchairs. Long-distance buses are generally quite comfortable, with the special *leito* services offering fully reclining seats. Internal **airlines** are helpful, and wheelchairs are available at all the main airports.

The IBDD (Ⓦ ibdd.org.br), Centro de Vida Independente (Ⓦ cvi.org.br) and Turismo Adaptado (Ⓦ turismoadaptado.com.br) campaign for disabled rights in Brazil, but with the exception of the latter, their websites are in Portuguese only – English-speakers are better off visiting sites such as Ⓦ disabilitytravel.com for tips on Brazil travel.

Rio de Janeiro

CABLE CAR, SUGAR LOAF MOUNTAIN

Rio de Janeiro

The citizens of the thirteen-million-strong city of Rio de Janeiro call it the Cidade Marvilhosa – and there can't be much argument about that. Although riven by inequality, Rio has style. Its international renown is bolstered by some of the greatest landmarks in the world: the Corcovado mountain supporting the great statue of Christ the Redeemer; the rounded incline of Sugar Loaf mountain, standing at the entrance to the bay; and the famous sweeps of Copacabana and Ipanema beaches, probably the most notable lengths of sand on the planet. It's a setting enhanced annually by the frenetic sensuality of Carnaval, an explosive celebration that – for many people – sums up Rio and its citizens, the cariocas. The major downside in a city given over to conspicuous consumption is the rapacious development that has engulfed Rio. As the rural poor, escaping drought and poverty in other regions of Brazil, swell Rio's population, the city has been squeezed between mountains and sea, pushing its human contents ever further out along the coast.

The **state of Rio de Janeiro**, surrounding the city, is a fairly recent phenomenon, established in 1975 by amalgamating Guanabara state with Rio city, formerly the federal capital. Fairly small by Brazilian standards, the state is both beautiful and accessible, with easy trips either northeast along the **Costa do Sol** or southwest along the **Costa Verde**, taking in unspoilt beaches. Inland routes make an interesting contrast, especially the trip to **Petrópolis**, a mountain retreat for Rio's rich. If you plan on **renting a car** in Rio (see page 93), this is as good a state as any to brave the traffic: the coasts are an easy drive from the city and stopping off at more remote beaches is simple, while having your own wheels lets you get to grips with the extraordinary scenery up in the mountains too.

The **best time to visit**, so far as the climate goes, is between May and August, when the region is cooled by trade winds – the temperature remains at around 22–32°C and the sky tends to be clear. Between December and March (the rainy season) it's more humid, with the temperature hovering around 40°C; even then it's rarely as oppressive as in northern Brazil, and there's a chance of blue sky for at least part of the day.

MUSEU DE ARTE CONTEMPORÂNEA, NITERÓI

Highlights

❶ **The Corcovado** Its giant statue of Christ with outstretched arms is Rio's most famous image and it has the best views across the city. See page 73

❷ **Igreja de Nossa Senhora da Glória do Outeiro** One of the smallest of Rio's colonial churches, but certainly the most beautiful. See page 74

❸ **Ipanema beach** The city's best beach for people watching. See page 82

❹ **Instituto Moreira Salles** This splendid modernist house hosts noteworthy exhibits of nineteenth-century Brazilian art and photography. See page 86

❺ **Parque Nacional da Tijuca** With a variety of trails and a wealth of flora and fauna, this fine city park offers spectacular views of Rio. See page 87

❻ **Lapa nightlife** Samba, *forró* and other Brazilian rhythms pound out of the bars and nightclubs of this central Bohemian district. See page 102

❼ **Museu de Arte Contemporânea** One of Oscar Niemeyer's most stunning creations; on a fine day, its views across the bay to Rio are dazzling. See page 112

❽ **Paraty** Among the prettiest and best-preserved colonial towns in Brazil, Paraty is also a great base to explore the Costa Verde's islands and beaches. See page 130

HIGHLIGHTS ARE MARKED ON THE MAPS ON PAGES 56, 58 AND 75

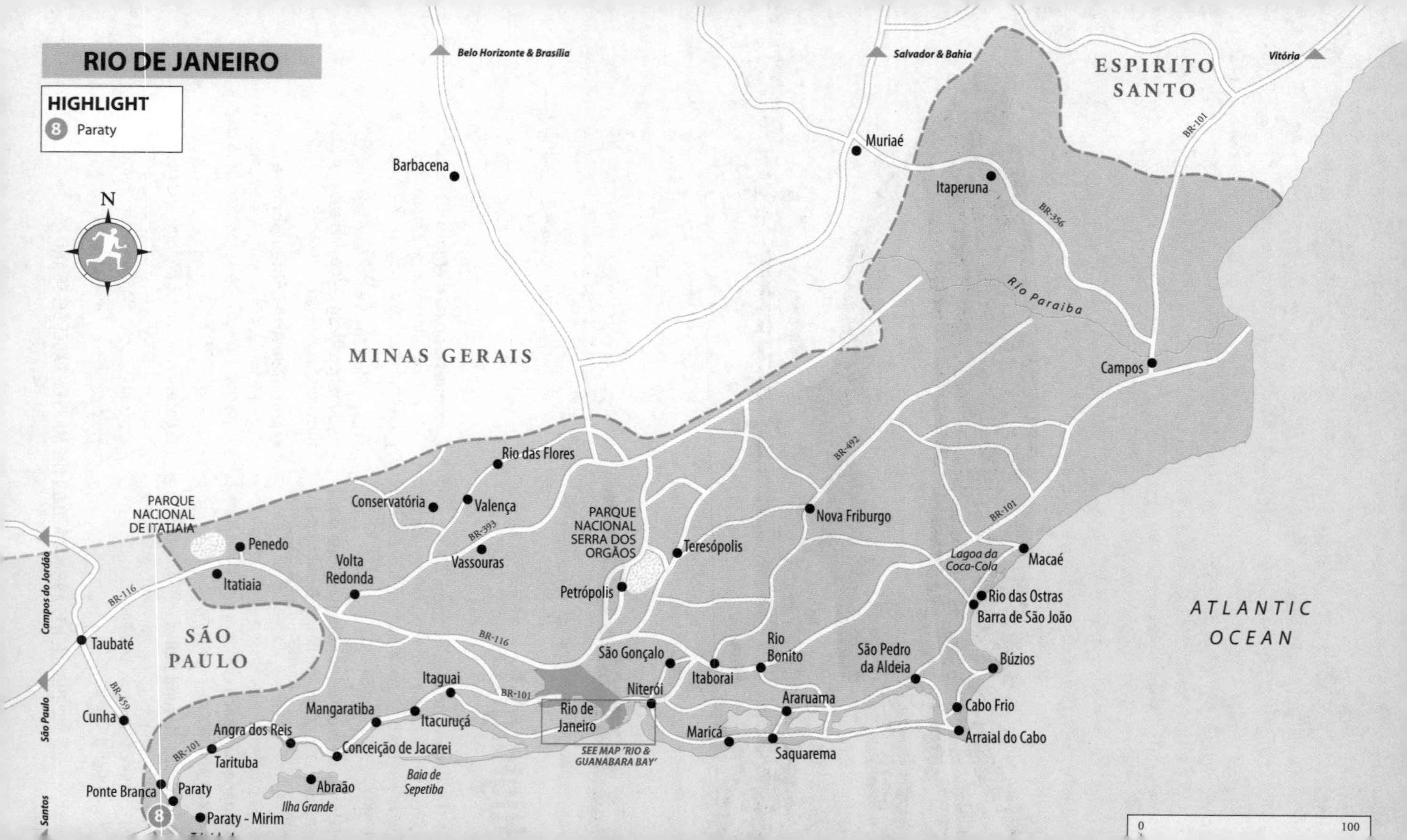
RIO DE JANEIRO
HIGHLIGHT
8 Paraty
N
Belo Horizonte & Brasília
Salvador & Bahia
Vitória
ESPIRITO SANTO
MINAS GERAIS
SÃO PAULO
ATLANTIC OCEAN
Barbacena
Muriaé
Itaperuna
BR-356
BR-101
Rio Paraiba
Campos
BR-492
Rio das Flores
Conservatória
Valença
BR-393
Vassouras
PARQUE NACIONAL DE ITATIAIA
Penedo
Itatiaia
Volta Redonda
PARQUE NACIONAL SERRA DOS ORGÃOS
Teresópolis
Petrópolis
Nova Friburgo
Lagoa da Coca-Cola
Macaé
Rio das Ostras
Barra de São João
Búzios
São Pedro da Aldeia
Cabo Frio
Arraial do Cabo
Rio Bonito
Itaborai
São Gonçalo
Niterói
Araruama
Maricá
Saquarema
Rio de Janeiro
SEE MAP 'RIO & GUANABARA BAY'
BR-116
Itaguai
Itacuruçá
Mangaratiba
Conceição de Jacarei
Baia de Sepetiba
Angra dos Reis
Tarituba
Abraão
Ilha Grande
Paraty
Ponte Branca
Paraty - Mirim
Cunha
BR-459
Taubaté
Campos do Jordão
São Paulo
Santos
0
100

Rio de Janeiro city

Sitting on the southern shore of the magnificent Guanabara Bay, **RIO DE JANEIRO** has, without a shadow of a doubt, one of the most stunning settings in the world. Extending for 20km along an alluvial strip, between an azure sea and forest-clad mountains, the city's streets and buildings have been moulded around the foothills of the mountain range that provides its backdrop, while out in the bay there are many rocky islands fringed with white sand. The aerial views over Rio are breathtaking, and even the concrete skyscrapers that dominate the city's skyline add to the attraction. As the former capital of Brazil and now its second-largest city, Rio has a remarkable architectural heritage, some of the country's best museums and galleries, superb restaurants and a vibrant nightlife – in addition to its legendary beaches. With so much to see and do, Rio can easily occupy a week and you may well find it hard to drag yourself away.

Many people visiting Rio simply scramble their way to Copacabana or Ipanema and go no further, except on an occasional foray by guided tour. The beaches, though, are only one facet of Rio, and there is plenty more to see. The city is divided into three parts – the centre (Centro), north (Norte) and south (Sul). **Centro** is the commercial and historic centre of Rio, whose elegant colonial and Neoclassical architecture has become overshadowed by towering office buildings, although it has by no means yet been swamped. To its northwest, the sprawling **Zona Norte** contains the city's industrial areas – large expanses of *favelas* and other working-class residential *bairros* with little in the way of historic interest or natural beauty, but some sights still worth seeking out. The **Zona Sul**, in principle covering everything south of the city centre, most particularly means the *bairros* shouldering the coastline, including of course Rio's famous sandy **beaches** – some 90km of them.

Brief history

Over five hundred years, Rio has transformed from a fortified outpost on the rim of an unknown continent into one of the world's great cities. Its recorded past is tied exclusively to the legacy of the colonialism on which it was founded. No vestige survives of the civilization of the **Tamoios** people, who inhabited the land before the Europeans arrived, and the city's history effectively begins on January 1, 1502, when a **Portuguese** captain, André Gonçalves, steered his craft into Guanabara Bay, thinking he was heading into the mouth of a great river (Rio de Janeiro means the "River of January"). In 1555, the French, keen to stake a claim on the New World, established a garrison near Sugar Loaf Mountain. Not until 1567 were they expelled by the Portuguese, who soon after gave the settlement around the Morro do Castelo – in front of where Santos Dumont airport now stands – its official name, São Sebastião de Rio de Janeiro, after the infant king of Portugal.

Colonial capital

With Bahia the centre of Portugal's new Brazilian colony, progress in Rio was slow, and only in the 1690s, when gold was discovered in neighbouring Minas Gerais, did the city's fortunes look up, as it became the control and taxation centre for the gold trade. During the seventeenth century, sugar brought new wealth, but despite being a prosperous entrepôt, the city saw little development. However, Rio's strategic importance grew because of Portugal's struggle with Spain over territories to the south, and in 1763 it replaced Bahia (Salvador) as Brazil's capital.

By the eighteenth century, the majority of Rio's inhabitants were **African** slaves. Miscegenation became commonplace, and almost nothing in Rio remained untouched by African customs, beliefs and behaviour – a state of affairs that clearly influences today's city, with its mix of Afro-Brazilian music, spiritualist cults and cuisine.

In March 1808, having fled before the advance of Napoleon Bonaparte's forces during the Peninsular War, **Dom João VI** of Portugal arrived in Rio, bringing with

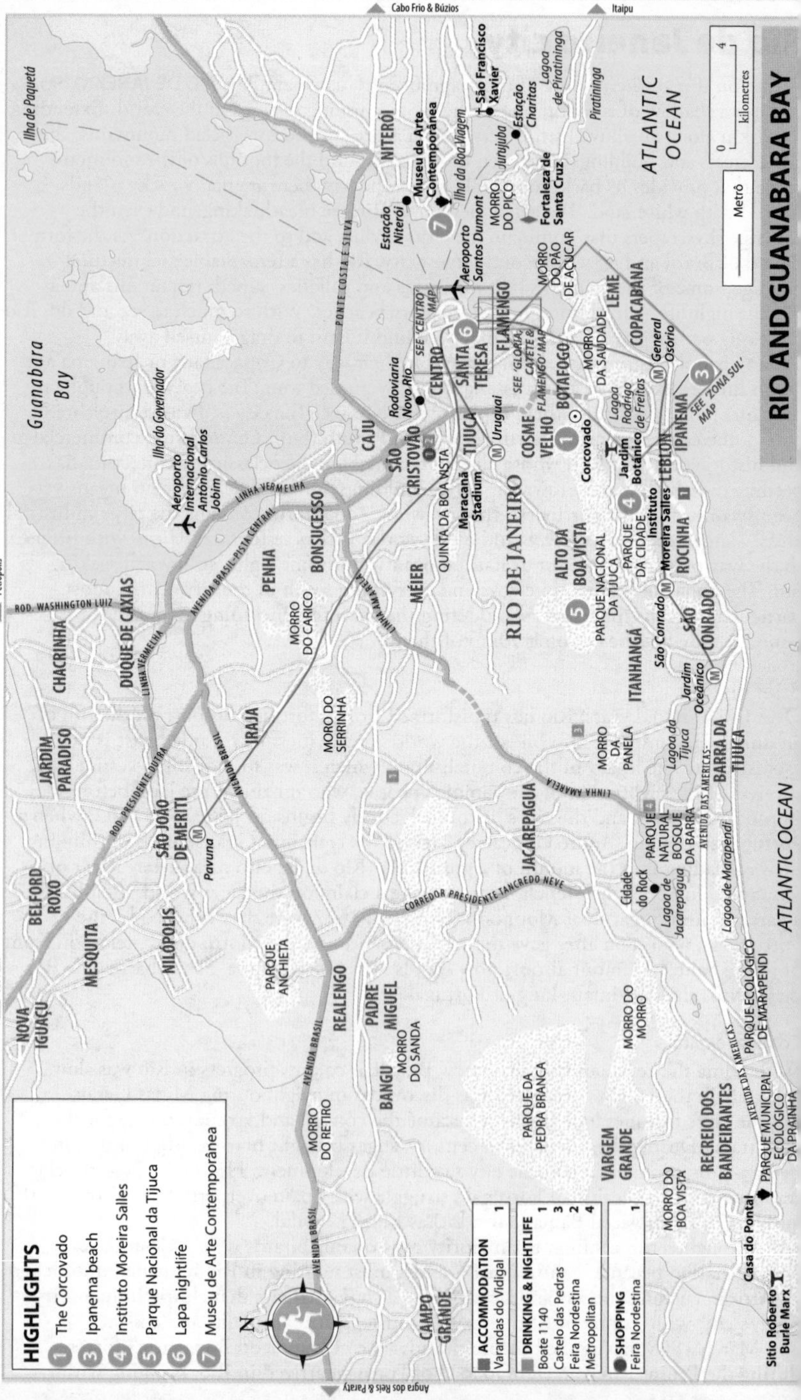

RIO AND GUANABARA BAY
HIGHLIGHTS
1 The Corcovado
3 Ipanema beach
4 Instituto Moreira Salles
5 Parque Nacional da Tijuca
6 Lapa nightlife
7 Museu de Arte Contemporânea
ACCOMMODATION
Varandas do Vidigal 1
DRINKING & NIGHTLIFE
Boate 1140 1
Castelo das Pedras 3
Feira Nordestina 2
Metropolitan 4
SHOPPING
Feira Nordestina 1
Metrô
0 4 kilometres
N
Cabo Frio & Búzios
Itaipu
Petrópolis
São Paulo
Angra dos Reis & Paraty
Guanabara Bay
ATLANTIC OCEAN
Ilha de Paquetá
Ilha do Governador
Aeroporto Internacional Antônio Carlos Jobim
NITERÓI
Museu de Arte Contemporânea
Estação Niterói
Ilha da Boa Viagem
São Francisco Xavier
Jurujuba
Estação Charitas
Lagoa de Piratininga
Piratininga
MORRO DO PIÇO
Fortaleza de Santa Cruz
Aeroporto Santos Dumont
PONTE COSTA E SILVA
SEE 'CENTRO' MAP
SEE 'GLÓRIA, CATETE & FLAMENGO' MAP
SEE 'ZONA SUL' MAP
MORRO DO PÃO DE AÇÚCAR
FLAMENGO
LEME
COPACABANA
MORRO DA SAUDADE
General Osório
SANTA TERESA
CENTRO
Rodoviaria Novo Rio
BOTAFOGO
Lagoa Rodrigo de Freitas
IPANEMA
LEBLON
Jardim Botânico
Corcovado
COSME VELHO
Uruguai
TIJUCA
CAJU
SÃO CRISTOVÃO
Maracanã Stadium
QUINTA DA BOA VISTA
RIO DE JANEIRO
ALTO DA BOA VISTA
PARQUE NACIONAL DA TIJUCA
PARQUE DA CIDADE
Instituto Moreira Salles
ROCINHA
São Conrado
SÃO CONRADO
ITANHANGÁ
Jardim Oceânico
LINHA VERMELHA
BONSUCESSO
PENHA
MORRO DO CARICO
MÉIER
LINHA AMARELA
AVENIDA BRASIL-PISTA CENTRAL
ROD. WASHINGTON LUIZ
DUQUE DE CAXIAS
CHACRINHA
JARDIM PARADISO
ROD. PRESIDENTE DUTRA
SÃO JOÃO DE MERITI
Pavuna
IRAJÁ
AVENIDA BRASIL
MORO DO SERRINHA
MORRO DA PANELA
JACAREPAGUÁ
Lagoa da Tijuca
AVENIDA DAS AMERICAS
BARRA DA TIJUCA
PARQUE NATURAL BOSQUE DA BARRA
Cidade do Rock
Lagoa de Jacarepaguá
Lagoa de Marapendi
CORREDOR PRESIDENTE TANCREDO NEVE
BELFORD ROXO
MESQUITA
NILÓPOLIS
NOVA IGUAÇU
PARQUE ANCHIETA
REALENGO
PADRE MIGUEL
MORRO DO SANDA
BANGU
MORRO DO RETIRO
PARQUE DA PEDRA BRANCA
MORRO DO MORRO
PARQUE ECOLÓGICO DE MARAPENDI
VARGEM GRANDE
RECREIO DOS BANDEIRANTES
MORRO DO BOA VISTA
PARQUE MUNICIPAL ECOLÓGICO DA PRAINHA
Casa do Pontal
Sitio Roberto Burle Marx
CAMPO GRANDE

him an astounding ten thousand nobles, ministers, priests and servants of the royal court. So enamoured of Brazil was he that after Napoleon's defeat in 1815 he declined to return to Portugal, proclaiming Rio, instead of Lisbon, the capital of the greatest **colonial empire** of the age. During Dom João's reign, the Enlightenment came to Rio, the city's streets were paved and lit, and it acquired a new prosperity centred on **coffee production**. Royal patronage allowed the arts and sciences to flourish. Yet behind the imperial gloss, Rio was still mostly a slum of dark, airless habitations, intermittently scourged by outbreaks of yellow fever, and with an economy reliant upon **slavery**.

Modern city

In the late nineteenth century, Rio started to develop as a modern city: trams and trains replaced sedans, the first sewerage system was inaugurated in 1864, a telegraph link to London was established and a tunnel was excavated that opened the way to Copacabana, as people left the crowded centre and looked for new living space. Rio went through a period of **urban reconstruction**, all but destroying the last vestiges of its colonial design. The city was torn apart by a period of frenzied building between 1900 and 1910, its monumental splendour modelled on the *belle époque* of Paris with new public buildings, grand avenues, libraries and parks embellishing the city.

During the 1930s and 1940s, Rio enjoyed international renown, buttressed by Hollywood images presented by the likes of **Carmen Miranda** and the patronage of the first-generation jet-set. It was the nation's commercial centre, and a new wave of modernization swept the city. Even the removal of the country's political administration to the new federal capital of Brasília in 1960 and the economic supremacy of São Paulo did nothing to discourage the developers. Today, with the centre rebuilt so many times, the interest of most visitors lies not in Rio's architectural heritage but firmly in the **beaches** to the south of the city centre, in an area called the Zona Sul. For more than seventy years, these strips of sand have been Rio's heart and soul, providing a constant source of recreation and income for *cariocas*. In stark contrast, Rio's **favelas** (see page 84), clinging precariously to the hillsides of the Zona Sul and across large expanses of the Zona Norte, show another side to the city, saying much about the divisions within it. Although not exclusive to the state capital, these slums seem all the more harsh in Rio because of the abundance and beauty that lie right next to them.

Centro

Much of historical Rio is concentrated in **Centro**, the commercial and historic centre of Rio, and, though the elegance of its colonial and Neoclassical architecture is now overshadowed by towering office buildings, it hasn't yet been swamped. The area's street

STAYING SAFE

Although it sometimes seems that one half of Rio is constantly being robbed by the other, don't let paranoia ruin your stay. It's true that there is quite a lot of **petty theft** in Rio – pockets are picked and bags and cameras swiped – but use a little common sense and you're unlikely to encounter problems. Most of the real violence affecting Rio is drug related and concentrated in the *favelas*, but one or two other areas should also be avoided. In **Centro**, contrary to popular belief, Sunday is not the best time to stroll around – the streets are usually empty, which means you can be more easily identified, stalked and robbed. The area around **Praça Mauá**, just to the north of Centro, should be avoided after nightfall, and even during the day care should be taken. In the Zona Sul's **Parque do Flamengo** it's also inadvisable to wander unaccompanied after nightfall. Similarly, tourists who choose to walk between **Cosme Velho** and the **Corcovado** have been subject to robbery and assault – a danger that can be avoided by taking the train. **Copacabana**'s record has improved since the authorities started to floodlight the beach at night, but it's still not a good idea to remain on the sand after sunset.

grid is cut by two main arteries at right angles to each other: **Avenida Presidente Vargas** and **Avenida Rio Branco**. You'll find you can tour the centre fairly easily on foot, but bear in mind that lots of the old historical squares, streets and buildings disappeared in the twentieth century under a torrent of redevelopment, and fighting your way through the traffic – the reason many of the streets were widened in the first place – can be quite a daunting prospect. However, while much of what remains is decidedly low-key, there are enough points of interest to keep anybody happy for a day or two. The cultural influences that have shaped the city – the austere Catholicism of the city's European founders, the squalor of colonialism and the grandiose design of the Enlightenment – are all reflected in the surviving churches, streets and squares.

Praça XV de Novembro

Ⓜ Carioca or Uruguaiana or Ⓥ Praça XV

Once the hub of Rio's social and political life, **Praça XV de Novembro** takes its name from the day (November 15) in 1899 when Marechal Deodoro da Fonseca, the first president, proclaimed the Republic of Brazil. One of Rio's oldest **markets** is held in the square on Thursdays and Fridays (8am–6pm): the stalls are packed with typical foods, handicrafts and ceramics, and there are paintings and prints, as well as a brisk trade in stamps and coins.

The Paço Imperial

Praça XV de Novembro • Tues–Sun noon–6pm • Free; audioguide free with photo ID, or download as app to your phone • Ⓣ 21 2215 2093, Ⓦ amigosdopacoimperial.org.br • Ⓜ Carioca or Ⓥ Praça XV

Praça XV de Novembro was originally called the Largo do Paço, a name that survives in the imposing **Paço Imperial**. Built in 1743, though tinkered with over the years, until 1791 the building served as the palace of Portugal's colonial governors in Rio. It was here, in 1808, that the Portuguese monarch, Dom João VI, established his Brazilian court (later shifting to the Palácio da Quinta da Boa Vista, now the Museu Nacional), and the building continued to be used for royal receptions and special occasions. On May 13, 1888, Princess Isabel proclaimed the end of slavery in Brazil from here. Today, the Paço Imperial hosts installations and other modern art exhibitions. On the ground floor, there's a café and a restaurant.

Arco de Teles

Ⓜ Carioca and Uruguaiana, or Ⓥ Praça XV

On the northern side of Praça XV de Novembro, the **Arco de Teles** was named after the judge and landowner Francisco Teles de Meneza, who ordered its construction upon the site of the old *pelourinho* (pillory) around 1755. More an arcade than an arch, the *arco* is connected to Rua Ouvidor by the Travessa do Comércio, a narrow cobblestoned alley which still boasts some charming nineteenth-century buildings.

Palácio Tiradentes

Rua Primeiro de Março and Rua da Assembléia • Mon–Sat 10am–5pm, Sun & public holidays noon–5pm • Free • Ⓣ 21 2588 1251, Ⓦ www.palaciotiradentes.rj.gov.br • Ⓜ Carioca

Behind the Paço Imperial, the **Palácio Tiradentes** is a very grand Neoclassical building dating from 1926. In front of it stands a 4.5m-tall statue of Tiradentes, who was slung into a prison on this very spot following the betrayal of the Inconfidência Mineira in 1789 (see page 170) and held here until his execution three years later. Guides escort you round the building, which is now the seat of Rio's state government.

Antiga Sé

Rua Sete de Setembro 14 and Rua Primero de Março • Mon–Fri 7am–4.30pm, Sat 9.30am–12.30pm • Free • Guided tours Sat 9.30am, R$5 • Ⓣ 21 2242 7766, Ⓦ antigase.com.br • Ⓜ Carioca

On the west side of Praça XV de Novembro, the **Igreja de Nossa Senhora do Carmo**, or **Antiga Sé**, served until 1980 as Rio's cathedral. Construction started in 1749 and, to all

TOFFS AND TOUGHS

Families belonging to Rio's wealthy classes originally lived in **luxurious apartments** above street level in what is now Centro, while the street below was traditionally a refuge for "beggars and rogues of the worst type; lepers, thieves, murderers, prostitutes and hoodlums", as Brasil Gerson put it in his 1954 book, *História das Ruas do Rio de Janeiro*.

In the late eighteenth and early nineteenth centuries, one local ex-prostitute, **Bárbara dos Prazeres**, achieved notoriety as a folk devil. It was commonly believed that the blood of a dead dog or cat applied to the body provided a cure for leprosy, and Bárbara is supposed to have enhanced the efficacy of this cure by stealing newborn babies and draining their blood. Sought by the authorities for a spate of child murders, Bárbara mysteriously vanished, but her ghost is said to haunt the Arco de Teles to this day.

ntents and purposes, continued into the twentieth century as structural collapse and inancial difficulties necessitated several restorations and delays. The present tower, for xample, designed by the Italian architect Rebecchi, was built in 1905. Inside, the high ltar is detailed in silver and boasts a beautiful work by the painter Antônio Parreires, epresenting Nossa Senhora do Carmo (an incarnation of the Virgin Mary) seated among he clouds and surrounded by the sainted founders of the Carmelite Order. Below, in the **rypt**, are the supposed mortal remains of Pedro Alvares Cabral, Portuguese discoverer of Brazil; in reality, he was almost certainly laid to rest in Santarém in Portugal.

Igreja da Ordem Terceira do Monte do Carmo

Rua Primeiro de Março, next to the Antiga Sé • Mon–Fri 8am–4pm, Sat 8–11am • Free • 21 2242 4828, igrejanscarmorj.com.br • Carioca and Uruguaiana

Next door to the Antiga Sé, the late eighteenth-century **Igreja da Ordem Terceira do Monte do Carmo** has no fewer than seven altars, all sculpted by Pedro Luiz da Cunha. Each bears an image symbolizing a moment in the Passion of Christ, from Calvary to the Crucifixion. The high altar itself is beautifully worked in silver. The church and adjacent convent are linked by a small public chapel, the Oratório de Nossa Senhora da Boa Esperança, which is dedicated to Our Lady of the Cape of Good Hope and decorated in *azulejo* blue tiling.

Igreja de Santa Cruz dos Militares

Rua Primeiro de Março 36 • Mon–Thurs 9am–4pm, Fri 9am–1pm, Sat 10am–1pm • Free • 21 2506 7600 • Uruguaiana

On the east side of Primeiro de Março, two blocks north of Praça XV de Novembro, the church of **Santa Cruz dos Militares** was founded by a group of army officers in 1628 on the site of an old fort. It was used for funerals of serving officers until taken over in 1716 (against opposition from the army) by the Fathers of the Igreja de São Sebastião, which had become dilapidated. They soon let this one fall into a similar state of ruin, which was only reversed when the army officers took back control in 1780 and put up the granite and marble building that survives today. Inside, the nave, with its stuccoed ceiling, has been skilfully decorated with plaster relief images from Portugal's imperial past. A small **museum** on the ground floor houses a collection of military and religious relics.

Centro Cultural Banco do Brasil

Rua Primeiro de Março 66 • Daily except Tues 9am–9pm • Free • 21 3808 2020, bb.com.br/cultura • Uruguaiana

Opposite the end of Rua da Alfándega, the Rio branch of the **Centro Cultural Banco do Brasil** is housed in the former headquarters of Brazil's oldest bank, a handsome six-storey building designed by Brazilian architect Francisco Joaquim Bethencourt da Silva, which dates from 1880. The Centro is one of Rio's foremost arts centres, with a regular programme of events, and puts on a varied programme of exhibitions, as well as films, music and plays – often free – having several exhibition halls, a cinema, two theatres, a tearoom and a restaurant. On the fourth floor, there's a permanent exhibition of Brazilian coins and banknotes, but labelled only in Portuguese.

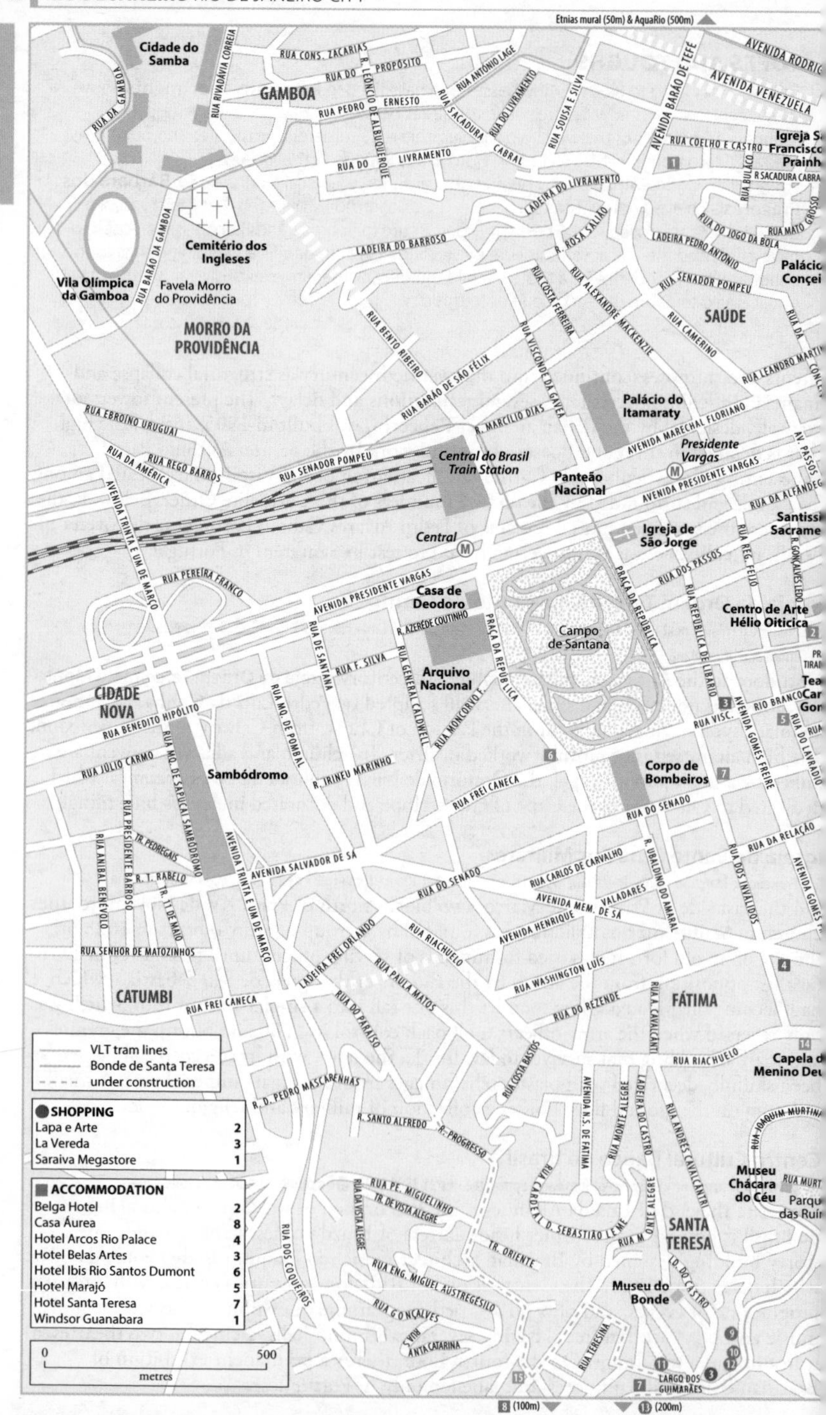
1
Etnias mural (50m) & AquaRio (500m)
Cidade do Samba
GAMBOA
Cemitério dos Ingleses
Vila Olímpica da Gamboa
Favela Morro do Providência
MORRO DA PROVIDÊNCIA
SAÚDE
Palácio do Itamaraty
Presidente Vargas
Central do Brasil Train Station
Panteão Nacional
Central
Igreja de São Jorge
Casa de Deodoro
Campo de Santana
Arquivo Nacional
Centro de Arte Hélio Oiticica
CIDADE NOVA
Sambódromo
Corpo de Bombeiros
CATUMBI
FÁTIMA
SANTA TERESA
Museu do Bonde
Museu Chácara do Céu
LARGO DOS GUIMARÃES
8 (100m)
13 (200m)
VLT tram lines
Bonde de Santa Teresa
under construction
SHOPPING
Lapa e Arte 2
La Vereda 3
Saraiva Megastore 1
ACCOMMODATION
Belga Hotel 2
Casa Áurea 8
Hotel Arcos Rio Palace 4
Hotel Belas Artes 3
Hotel Ibis Rio Santos Dumont 6
Hotel Marajó 5
Hotel Santa Teresa 7
Windsor Guanabara 1
0
500
metres

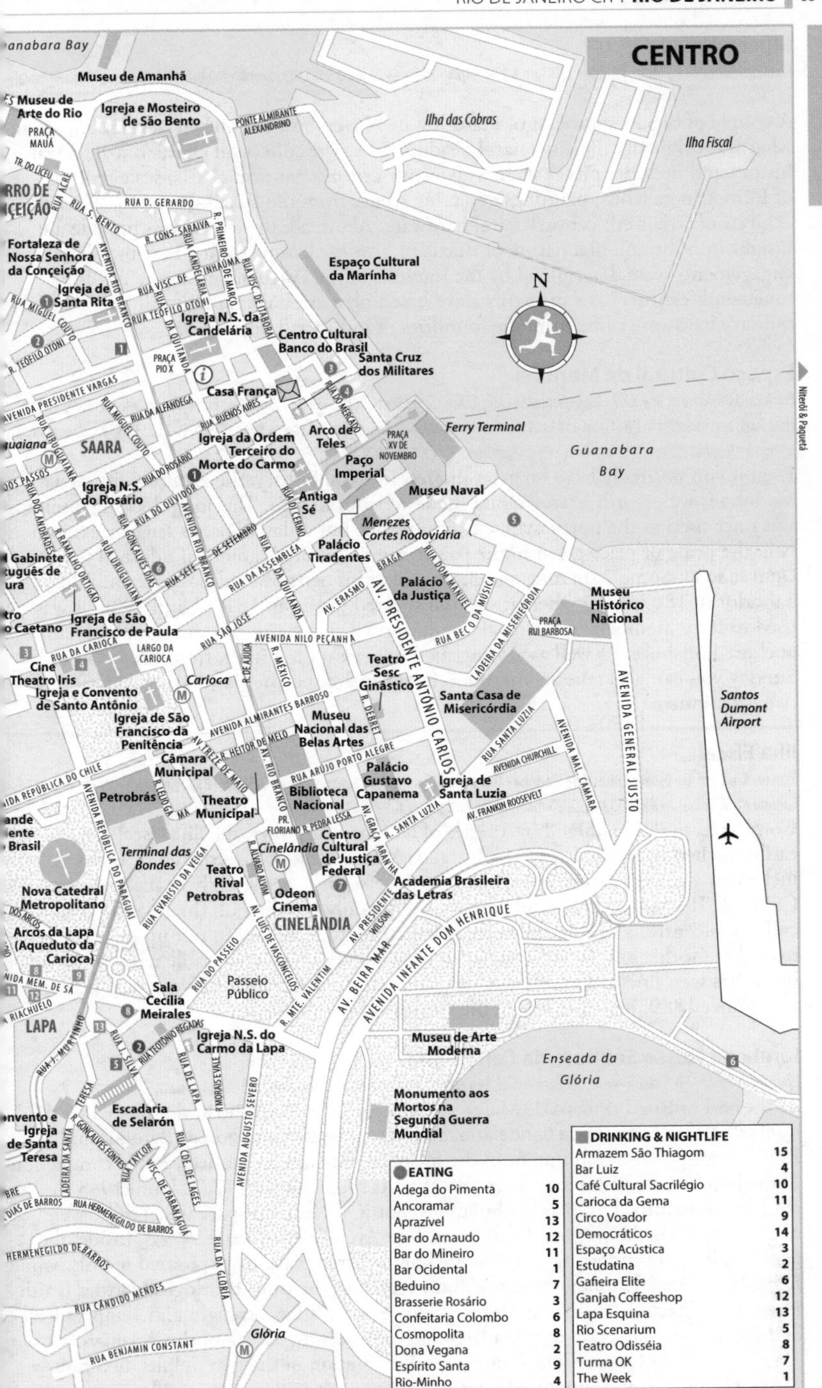
CENTRO
Guanabara Bay
Ilha das Cobras
Ilha Fiscal
Museu de Amanhã
Museu de Arte do Rio
Igreja e Mosteiro de São Bento
Praça Mauá
Ponte Almirante Alexandrino
Fortaleza de Nossa Senhora da Conçeição
Igreja de Santa Rita
Espaço Cultural da Marínha
Igreja N.S. da Candelária
Centro Cultural Banco do Brasil
Santa Cruz dos Militares
Praça Pio X
Casa França
SAARA
Igreja da Ordem Terceiro do Morte do Carmo
Arco de Teles
Praça XV de Novembro
Ferry Terminal
Paço Imperial
Igreja N.S. do Rosário
Antiga Sé
Museu Naval
Menezes Cortes Rodoviária
Palácio Tiradentes
Palácio da Justiça
Museu Histórico Nacional
Praça Rui Barbosa
Igreja de São Francisco de Paula
Largo da Carioca
Cine Theatro Iris
Igreja e Convento de Santo Antônio
Carioca
Teatro Sesc Ginástico
Santa Casa de Misericórdia
Santos Dumont Airport
Igreja de São Francisco da Penitência
Museu Nacional das Belas Artes
Câmara Municipal
Palácio Gustavo Capanema
Igreja de Santa Luzia
Petrobrás
Theatro Municipal
Biblioteca Nacional
Centro Cultural de Justiça Federal
Cinelândia
Terminal das Bondes
Teatro Rival Petrobras
Odeon Cinema
Academia Brasileira das Letras
Nova Catedral Metropolitano
CINELÂNDIA
Arcos da Lapa (Aqueduto da Carioca)
Passeio Público
Sala Cecília Meirales
LAPA
Igreja N.S. do Carmo da Lapa
Museu de Arte Moderna
Enseada da Glória
Escadaria de Selarón
Monumento aos Mortos na Segunda Guerra Mundial
Glória
Niterói & Paquetá
Avenida Presidente Vargas
Avenida Rio Branco
Av. Presidente Antônio Carlos
Avenida General Justo
Avenida Infante Dom Henrique
Av. Beira Mar
Avenida República do Chile
Avenida República do Paraguai
Avenida Almirantes Barroso
Avenida Nilo Peçanha
Rua Primeiro de Março
Rua da Quitanda
Rua do Ouvidor
Rua Sete de Setembro
Rua da Assembléia
Rua São José
Rua da Carioca
Rua Uruguaiana
Rua do Passeio
Rua da Lapa
Rua da Glória
Rua Cândido Mendes
Rua Benjamin Constant
Avenida Augusto Severo

EATING
Adega do Pimenta 10
Ancoramar 5
Aprazível 13
Bar do Arnaudo 12
Bar do Mineiro 11
Bar Ocidental 1
Beduino 7
Brasserie Rosário 3
Confeitaria Colombo 6
Cosmopolita 8
Dona Vegana 2
Espírito Santa 9
Rio-Minho 4

DRINKING & NIGHTLIFE
Armazem São Thiagom 15
Bar Luiz 4
Café Cultural Sacrilégio 10
Carioca da Gema 11
Circo Voador 9
Democráticos 14
Espaço Acústica 3
Estudatina 2
Gafieira Elite 6
Ganjah Coffeeshop 12
Lapa Esquina 13
Rio Scenarium 5
Teatro Odisséia 8
Turma OK 7
The Week 1

Museu Naval

Rua Dom Manuel 15 • Mon–Fri 8.30–11.45am & 1.15–4pm • Free • ⓣ 21 2233 9165, ⓦ marinha.mil.br/dphdm/museus/museu-naval • ⓜ Carioca

A couple of blocks southeast of Praça XV de Novembro, the **Museu Naval** is housed in what was originally the city's naval headquarters. The collection charts Brazil's naval history and includes pieces such as sixteenth-century nautical charts, scale replicas of European galleons, paintings depicting scenes from the Brazil–Paraguay War and exhibits of twentieth-century naval hardware. Above all, the collections provide an insight into the colonial nature of Brazilian history, demonstrating that Brazilian naval engagements were determined by the interests of the Portuguese Empire until the nineteenth century; as a primarily slave-based plantation economy until 1888, Brazil's military hardware came from the foundries of industrialized Europe.

Espaço Cultural da Marinha

Boulevard Olímpico at Praça XV • Tues–Sun: May–Aug 11am–5pm; Sept–April 11am–5.30pm; last entry 30min before closing • R$10 (free Tues, and included in Ilha Fiscal and boat trip tickets) • Boat trips Thurs–Sun 1.15pm & 3pm; R$30 • ⓣ 21 2532 5592, ⓦ marinha.mi br/dphdm/espaco-cultural-da-marinha • ⓜ Uruguaiana

Even if you normally have no great interest in naval history, the **Espaço Cultural da Marinha** is well worth a stroll along the waterfront to visit. This long dockside building was once used as the port's main customs wharf, but today houses a lengthy exhibition hall, the pride of place given to the painstakingly restored, gold-leaf-adorned **Galiota Dom João VI**. Some 24m long and 3.6m wide, this oar-powered boat was built in Salvador in 1807, from where it was transported to Rio in 1817. Until 1920, it was used to ferry members of the royal family and visiting heads of state from their ships anchored offshore. As well as visiting the Espaço Cultural itself, from Thursday to Sunday you can also take an afternoon **boat trip** around the Bay, lasting an hour and twenty minutes.

Ilha Fiscal

1km northeast of the Espaço Cultural da Marinha • Thurs–Sun crossings at 12.30pm, 2pm & 3.30pm • R$30 (includes entry to Espaço Cultural da Marinha) • ⓣ 21 2532 5992, ⓦ marinha.mil.br/dphdm/ilha-fiscal

Connected to the mainland by a series of lengthy causeways, the **Ilha Fiscal** is more easily reached from the Espaço Cultural da Marinha by boat (replaced by buses in inclement weather). To ensure a place on the crossings, arrive early at the Espaço Cultural. The visit lasts around two hours. The only building on the Ilha is a customs collection centre, a wonderfully ornate structure from the 1880s put up in a bizarre hybrid of Gothic and Moorish styles. It now houses an unremarkable naval museum, but it has seen finer times. Indeed, the last ever grand Imperial ball was held here in November 1889, just days before the collapse of the monarchy.

Igreja de Nossa Senhora da Candelária

Praça Pio X • Mon–Fri 7.30am–4pm, Sat 8am–noon, Sun & public holidays 9am–1pm • Free • ⓜ Uruguaiana

At the end of Rua Primeiro de Março you emerge onto **Praça Pio X**, dominated by the **Igreja de Nossa Senhora da Candelária**, an interesting combination of Baroque and Renaissance features resulting from the financial difficulties that delayed the completion of the building for more than a century after its foundation in 1775. Until 1943 the church was hemmed in by other buildings, but it got its own space when those were demolished to make way for the fourteen-lane Avenida Presidente Vargas. Inside, the altars, walls and supporting columns are sculpted from variously coloured marble, while high above, the eight pictures in the dome represent the three theological virtues (Faith, Hope and Charity), the cardinal virtues (Prudence, Justice, Strength and Temperance), and the Virgin Mary – all of them late nineteenth-century work of the Brazilian artist João Zeferino da Costa. There's more grand decoration in the two pulpits, luxuriously worked in bronze and supported by large white angels sculpted in marble.

Museu de Arte do Rio

Praça Mauá 5 • Tues –Sun 10am–5pm • R$20; R$32 combined entry with Museu do Amanhã; Tues free • 21 3031 2741, museudeartedorio.org.br • Uruguaiana

Housed in two adjacent but quite different buildings – an early twentieth-century palace and a more functional 1940s building that was previously a bus station and police hospital – the **Museu de Arte do Rio** unites both under a single wavy roof to create a museum dedicated to the art of Rio. Exhibits include images of the city going back to colonial times, along with nineteenth- and early twentieth-century paintings, posters and postcards, and depictions of Rio on tourist souvenirs, as well as one of Paul Landowski's models for the head of Cristo Redentor. In some ways, with so many images of Rio as it was, it's more a museum about the history of Rio than a museum of art, but either way it's well worth checking out, and the terrace has great views over the port and Guanabara Bay.

Museu do Amanhã

Praça Mauá 1 • Tues –Sun 10am–6pm • R$20; R$32 combined entry with Museu de Arte do Rio; Tues free; tickets for Aug & Sept are available online only • 21 3812 1812, museudoamanha.org.br • Uruguaiana

The **Museu do Amanhã**, or Museum of Tomorrow, is Rio's science museum, and very impressive it is too. Housed in a futuristic building by Spanish architect Santiago Calatrava, it juts out seaward on a pier off Praça Mauá. Inside there are exhibits on physics, cosmology and biology, all intertwined so as to show that these disciplines are interconnected. The cosmology area, for example, is not just about the nature of the universe but also about how life on earth depends on the internal physics of stars. The most important part of the museum, called the Anthropocene area, explores the idea that we, the human race, have now become part of the world's geology, and a natural force in ourselves. The museum is hugely popular, with big queues, especially on Tuesdays and weekends, and in August and September you can't even buy tickets on the door, only online in advance, which is often a good idea anyway, especially at weekends.

Etnias

Av Rodrigues Alves • Parada dos Navios

Fifteen metres high and 170 metres long, street artist Eduardo Kobra's huge mural **Etnias** ("Ethnicities") was painted for the 2016 Olympic Games, and it is undoubtedly one of the most exciting and impressive pieces of art – let alone street art – in the world. Huge, vibrantly colourful and very imposing, its five faces are of indigenous people from five regions of the world, echoing the five rings of the Olympic flag and representing the international diversity of the games. It's also the biggest mural ever painted by one person. The faces on it are of people from Ethiopia, southeast Asia's Golden Triangle, the Brazilian Amazon, Lapland and Papua, and the fact that Kobra has chosen indigenous minorities rather than people from the globalized mainstream is of course a political statement too. But never mind that: it's a fantastic work of art, and one you shouldn't miss.

Igreja e Mosteiro de São Bento

Rua Dom Gereardo 68 • Daily 7am–7pm; Mass with Gregorian chant Sun 10am • Free

Looking down on the run-down (and, at night, not very safe) *bairro* of Saúde, the **Igreja e Mosteiro de São Bento** was founded by Benedictine monks who arrived in Rio in 1586 by way of Bahia; building started in 1633, finishing nine years later. The facade displays a pleasing architectural simplicity, its twin towers culminating in pyramid-shaped spires, while the interior of the church is richly adorned in wonderfully sombre Baroque red and gold. Images of saints cover the altars, and there are statues representing various popes and bishops, work executed by the deft hand of Mestre Valentim. The late seventeenth-century panels and paintings are particularly valuable examples of colonial art.

Igreja da Santa Rita

Rua Visconde de Inhaúma • Mon–Fri 7.30am–4pm, Sat 8am–noon, Sun 9am–1pm • Free • Ⓜ Uruguaiana

On the Largo Santa Rita, the **Igreja da Santa Rita** was built in 1721 on land previously used as a burial ground for slaves. Its bell tower, tucked to one side, gives it a lopsided look. From the outside, it's not one of Rio's more attractive churches, but the interior stonework is a fine example of Rococo style, and it's magnificently decorated with a series of panels, three on the high altar and eight on the ceiling. Painted by Ananias Correia do Amaral, they depict scenes from the life of St Rita, a fifteenth-century Italian nun.

Saara

In the streets between Rua Uruguaiana and Rua Primeiro de Março lies the most interesting concentration of stores in Rio, in the area known as **Saara**. Traditionally the cheapest place to shop, it was originally peopled by Jewish and Arab merchants, who moved into the area after a ban prohibiting their residence within the city limits was lifted in the eighteenth century; in recent years, a new wave of Jewish and Arab business-owners – along with, most recently, Chinese and Koreans – has moved here. The maze of narrow streets is lined with stalls selling trinkets and stores offering everything from basic beachwear and handicraft items to expensive jewellery; additionally, the throngs of street traders and folk musicians make it a lively place to visit. Particularly good buys here include sports equipment, musical instruments and CDs.

Igreja de São Francisco de Paula

Largo de São Francisco de Paula • Mon–Fri 8am–7pm, Sat 8am–5pm, Sun 9am–1pm • Free • Ⓜ Uruguaiana

West of Rua Uruguaiana, on the **Largo de São Francisco de Paula** – a square that was once a lake outside the city walls – the **Igreja de São Francisco de Paula** has hosted some significant moments in Brazil's history. Behind the monumental carved wooden entrance door the *Te Deum* was sung in 1816 to celebrate Brazil's promotion from colony to kingdom, and in 1831, the Mass celebrating the "swearing-in" of the Brazilian Constitution was performed here. The meticulous decoration of the chapel of Nossa Senhora da Vitória (halfway down the north side) is attributed to the great eighteenth-century Brazilian sculptor Mestre Valentim, who spent thirty years working here, while the paintings on the walls were created by a slave called Manoel da Cunha. With the consent of his owner, Manoel travelled to Europe as the assistant of the artist João de Souza, and on his return bought his own freedom with money earned from the sale of his artwork.

Real Gabinete Português de Leitura

Rua Luís de Camões 30 • Mon–Fri 9am–6pm • Free • ⓣ 21 2221 3138, Ⓦ www.realgabinete.com.br • Ⓜ Uruguaiana

A block west of the Largo de São Francisco de Paula, the **Real Gabinete Português de Leitura** is a library dedicated to Portugal and Portuguese literature. The building was completed in 1887 and is immediately identifiable by its magnificently ornate facade, styled after fifteenth-century Portuguese architecture. The reading room is lit by a red, white and blue stained-glass skylight and contains many of the library's 350,000 volumes. Among the rarest is the 1572 first edition of *Os Lusíados* – the Portuguese national epic poem by Luís de Camões, based on Vasco da Gama's voyage of exploration – which is occasionally on view.

Igreja e Convento de Santo Antônio

Largo da Carioca • Mon, Wed, Thurs & Fri 8am–7pm, Tues 6.30am–8pm, Sat 8–11am, Sun 9–11am, closed on public holidays • Free • Ⓦ conventosantoantonio.org.br • Ⓜ Carioca

At the southern end of Rua Uruguaiana, the **Largo da Carioca**, a large square (originally a lake) where street traders sell leather goods, is presided over by the **Igreja e Convento de Santo Antônio**. A tranquil, cloistered refuge, built between 1608 and 1620, this is the oldest church in Rio and was founded by Franciscan monks who arrived in Brazil in 1592. Known as St Anthony of the Rich (to differentiate it from St Anthony of the

Poor, which is located elsewhere in the city), it is dedicated to St Anthony, a popular saint in Brazil. Although he was from Lisbon, and lived in Padua, Italy (where he died in 1231), St Anthony was enlisted during the French invasion of 1710 and made a captain in the Brazilian army. He had, however, to wait until 1814 to be promoted to lieutenant-colonel, a rank he held for a century before retiring from service in 1914.

The interior of the church contains a beautiful **sacristy**, made of Portuguese marble and decorated in blue *azulejo* tiles, which depict St Anthony's miracles. The rich wooden ornamentation, carved from jacaranda, includes the sacristy's great chest. The image of Christ, adorned with a crown of thorns – a remarkable work of great skill – was brought over from Portugal in 1678.

In the church's crypt, the **Tomb of Wild Jock of Skelater** is the last resting place of a Scottish mercenary who entered the service of the Portuguese Crown during the Napoleonic Wars and was later appointed commander-in-chief of the Portuguese army in Brazil.

Praça Tiradentes

Ⓜ Carioca

A couple of blocks northwest of Largo da Carioca on Rua da Carioca, **Praça Tiradentes** is named after the leader of the Inconfidência Mineira (see page 170), who was hanged here on April 21, 1792. On the north side of the square, the **Teatro João Caetano** (box office daily 2–6pm & before shows; Ⓣ 21 2332 9166, Ⓦ cultura.rj.gov.br/espaco/teatro-joao-caetano) is named after João Caetano dos Santos, who based his drama company in the theatre from 1840. His shows starred some of the most famous actors of the day, including Sarah Bernhardt, and Caetano is also honoured by a bust in the square itself. In the second-storey hall of the theatre hang two large panels painted in 1930 by Emiliano di Cavalcanti (one of Brazil's great modernist artists), which, with strong tropical colours, explore the themes of Carnaval and popular religion.

Centro de Arte Hélio Oiticica

Rua Luís de Camões 68 • Mon, Wed & Fri noon–8pm, Tues, Thurs & Sat 10am–6pm • Free • Ⓣ 21 2588 1251, Ⓦ facebook.com/CMA.HelioOiticica • Ⓜ Carioca

In a fine old house in a lively street just north of Praça Tiradentes, the **Centro de Arte Hélio Oiticica** is an art gallery dedicated to the memory of Rio-born minimalist sculptor Hélio Oiticica, who founded the art movement known as Neo-Concretism. Not all the works here are by him, but minimalism and installation art are the order of the day.

West from Centro

From the waterfront and Igreja de Nossa Senhora da Candelária, **Avenida Presidente Vargas** runs west, to Centro do Brasil (Dom Pedro II) **train station** and on to the **Sambódromo**, where the Carnaval procession takes place. The avenue was inaugurated with a military parade in 1944, watched by Vargas himself. Today, it's Rio's widest avenue, running west for almost 3km, and carrying fourteen lanes of traffic. Although not as dense with sights as Centro, the *bairros* north and south of the avenue still boast a few points of interest.

Campo de Santana and around

Praça da República • Daily 7am–5pm • Free • Ⓜ Central

West of the historical centre, between Avenida Presidente Vargas and Rua Visconde do Rio Branco, the **Campo de Santana** is the nearest thing Rio has to a city-centre park. Originally located outside the city limits, which extended only as far as Rua Uruguaiana, its sandy and swampy soils made it unsuitable for cultivation and the only building here was the chapel of St Domingo, sited in the area now covered by Avenida Presidente Vargas and used by the Fraternity of St Anne to celebrate the festivals of their patron saint – hence the name, Campo de Santana (Field of St Anne).

By the end of the eighteenth century, the city had spread to surround the Campo de Santana, and in 1811 an army barracks was built, the soldiers using the field as a parade ground. It was here that Dom Pedro I proclaimed Brazil's independence from the Portuguese Crown in 1822, and after 1889 it took the name **Praça da República**, which is still used to denote the streets east and west of it; the first president of the new republic, Deodoro da Fonsceca, lived at Praça da República no. 197. At the start of the twentieth century, the field was landscaped, and today it's a pleasant place for a walk, with lots of trees and small lakes ruled by swans, while agoutis scurry about on the grassy areas.

Directly across Avenida Presidente Vargas is the Praça Duque de Caxias and the **Panteão Nacional**, on top of which stands the equestrian statue of the Duque de Caxias, military patron and general in the Paraguayan War – his remains lie below in the Pantheon. Nearby, the **Dom Pedro II train station** – known more commonly as the Central do Brasil – is an unmistakeable landmark, its tower rising 110m into the sky and supporting clock-faces measuring 7.5m by 5.5m.

Museu Histórico e Diplomático do Itamaraty

Palácio do Itamaraty, Av Marechal Floriano 196 • Visit by guided tour Mon 1pm, 2pm & 3pm, Tues–Fri 10am, 11am, 1pm, 2pm & 3pm • Free, but photo ID needed • ⓣ 21 2253 2828 • Ⓜ Central

Just beyond the station, the **Palácio do Itamaraty** is one of Rio's best examples of Neoclassical architecture. Completed in 1853 as the pied-à-terre of the great landowner Baron of Itamaraty, it was bought by the government and became home to a number of the republic's presidents. The *palácio* now houses the **Museu Histórico e Diplomático do Itamaraty**, a repository of documents, books and maps relating to Brazil's diplomatic history, its collections primarily of interest to serious researchers. Of wider interest is the section of the building that has been painstakingly restored with period furnishings to show how the upper classes lived in the nineteenth century.

Cemitério dos Ingleses

Rua da Gamboa 181 • Mon–Fri 8am–4pm • Free • ⓣ 21 2286 7899, ⓦ bit.ly/CemiteriodosIngleses • Ⓥ Gamboa

North of Itamaraty is the extremely seedy port area Gamboa, one of the oldest parts of Rio and home to its first *favela*. Right alongside is the strangely beautiful **Cemitério dos Ingleses**, or English Cemetery; it's the oldest Protestant burial site in the country, dating from 1809, when the British community was given permission to establish a cemetery and Anglican church in Rio – essential if English merchants were to be attracted to the newly independent Brazil. Still in use today, the cemetery is set in a dramatic hillside location looking down to Guanabara Bay. The inscriptions on many of the stones make poignant reading, recalling the days when early death was almost expected.

Cidade do Samba

Rua Rivadávia Correia 60, Gamboa • Tues–Sat 10am–5pm with shows at 10am, noon & 3.30pm; Carnaval season parades 8pm • R$10; Carnaval season parades R$150 including buffet dinner • ⓣ 21 2213 2503, ⓦ cidadedosambarj.com.br • Ⓥ Gamboa or Cidade do Samba

There's long been talk about developing Gamboa's dockside area, but until recently little has been done apart from turning some of the *armazéms* (warehouses) into temporary centres for performing-arts events. The one enduring project has been the **Cidade do Samba**, a vast complex where Rio's fourteen top samba schools practise and make their floats for Carnaval. For much of the year, there's little activity in the workshops, but at the very least you'll be able to inspect the previous year's floats. Shows are held three times daily, with a mini-parade in the evening featuring some of Rio's best samba groups and singers in a small version of the annual Sambódromo extravaganza. As Carnaval nears, activity increases and you'll be able to snatch a preview of the big event ahead. The area around the Cidade being rather run-down, the safest way to get here is by taxi: ask for the entrance at warehouse #11 (*barracão onze*) on Rua Rivadávia Correia.

AquaRio

Praça Muhammad Ali, Gambôa • Daily 10am–6pm (last ticket sold at 5pm) • R$80 • ⓣ 21 3613 0700, ⓦ aquariomarinhodorio.com.br • ⓥ Utopia Aquario

Rio's bright, new marine aquarium is pretty impressive, although the entrance fee is a bit steep. It's South America's biggest aquarium, with over 350 different species of fish and other marine animals, and a huge main tank which you walk though in a glass tunnel, seemingly right down there among the sharks, stingrays and other fearsome denizens of the deep, although actually you get a better view of the assorted sea animals in the smaller tanks. The aquarium is also child-friendly, and indeed kids should love it, but for the same reason it tends to get rather crowded, especially at weekends, when local families pack in to see it, so come midweek if possible.

Cinelândia and around

The neighbourhood known as **Cinelândia**, at the southern end of Avenida Rio Branco, takes its name from the 1930s movie houses that once stood here, most of them now long gone. Old photos of Avenida Rio Branco (originally named Avenida Central) show its entire length bordered by Neoclassical-style buildings of no more than three storeys high, its pavements lined with trees, and with a promenade that ran right down the centre. Nowadays, however, the once-graceful avenue has been marred by ugly office buildings and traffic pollution.

Cinelândia centres on **Praça Floriano**, the one section of Avenida Rio Branco that still impresses. Several pavement cafés on the western side of the square serve as popular central meeting points in the evening, when the surrounding buildings are illuminated and at their most elegant. In the centre of the *praça* is a bust of **Getúlio Vargas**, still anonymously decorated with flowers on the anniversary of the ex-dictator's birthday, March 19.

Theatro Municipal

Praça Floriano • Tours Tues–Fri 11.30am, noon, 2pm, 2.30pm, 3pm & 4pm, Sat 11am, noon & 1pm • Tours R$20 • ⓣ 21 2332 9220, ⓦ www.theatromunicipal.rj.gov.br • ⓜ Cinelândia

At the north end of Praça Floriano, the **Theatro Municipal**, opened in 1909 and a dramatic example of Neoclassical architecture, was modelled on the Paris Opéra – all granite, marble and bronze, with a foyer decorated in the white and gold characteristic of Louis XV style. Since opening, the theatre has been Brazil's most prestigious artistic venue, hosting visiting Brazilian and foreign orchestras, opera and theatre companies, and singers. Tours can be booked at the box office at the back of the building.

Museu Nacional das Belas Artes

Av Rio Branco 199, at Praça Floriano • Tues–Fri 10am–6pm, Sat & Sun 1–6pm (last entry 5.30pm) • R$8; Sun free • ⓣ 21 3299 0600, ⓦ mnba.gov.br • ⓜ Cinelândia

On the east side of Praça Floriano, the **Museu Nacional das Belas Artes** is a grandiose Neoclassical pile built in 1908 as the Escola Nacional das Belas Artes, with the museum created in 1937. The modest European collection includes works by Boudin, Tournay and Franz Post among many others, but it's the **Brazilian collection** that's of most interest. Organized in chronological order, each room shows the various stages in the development of Brazilian painting as well as the influences imported from Europe: the years of diversification (1919–28); the movement into modernism (1921–49); and the consolidation of modern forms between 1928 and 1967, especially in the works of Cândido Portinari, Djanira and Francisco Rebolo.

Biblioteca Nacional

Av Rio Branco 219 and Praça Floriano • Mon–Fri 10am–5pm, Sat 10.30am–noon; guided tours in Portuguese hourly, and in English Mon–Fri 2pm • Free but photo ID required • ⓣ 21 3095 3879, ⓦ bn.gov.br • ⓜ Cinelândia

Even if you don't need to consult its tomes and manuscripts, it's worth popping into the **Biblioteca Nacional** (National Library) to check out the stairway, decoratively

1

painted by some of the most important artists of the nineteenth century, including Modesto Brocas, Eliseu Visconti, Rodolfo Amoedo and Henrique Bernadelli.

Igreja de Santa Luzia

Rua Santa Luzia and Praça da Academia • Mon–Fri 8.30am–5pm • Free • Ⓜ Cinelândia

East of Cinelândia, on a tree-shaded square called Praça da Academia, the **Igreja de Santa Luzia** is an attractive eighteenth-century church whose predecessor was built here in 1592, when it was the seashore – hard to believe today, overshadowed as it is by huge downtown office buildings. On December 13 each year, devotees enter the "room of miracles" at the back of the church and bathe their eyes in water from the white marble font, as this is reputedly a miraculous cure for eye defects.

Santa Casa de Misericórdia

Rua Santa Luzia 206 • **Museu da Farmácia** Mon–Fri 8am–noon & 1–4.30pm • Free • Ⓣ 21 2297 6611 **Igreja de Nossa Senhora de Bonsucesso** Mon–Fri 9am–4pm • Free • Ⓣ 21 2260 7341, Ⓦ santacasarj.org.br • Ⓜ Cinelândia

At the intersection of Rua Santa Luzia with the busy Avenida Presidente Antônio Carlos, directly across the road from the imposing **Fazenda Federal** (Federal Treasury building), the **Santa Casa de Misericórdia** is a large colonial structure dating from 1582. It was built for the Sisterhood of Misericordia, a nursing order dedicated to caring for the sick and providing asylum to orphans and invalids, and it was here in 1849 that, for the first time in Rio, a case of yellow fever was diagnosed. From 1856 to 1916 the building was used as Rio's Faculty of Medicine.

The Santa Casa is not open to the public, but you can visit its **Museu da Farmácia** for its curious collection of pharmacological implements. Also attached to the Santa Casa is the **Igreja de Nossa Senhora de Bonsucesso**, which contains finely detailed altars, a collection of Bohemian crystal and an eighteenth-century organ.

Museu Histórico Nacional

Praça Marechal Âncora • Tues–Fri 10am–5.30pm, Sat, Sun & public holidays 1–5pm • R$10; audio guide R$8 • Ⓣ 21 3299 0324, Ⓦ museuhistoriconacional.com.br • Ⓜ Cinelândia

Uncomfortably located in the shadow of the Presidente Kubitschek flyover, the **Museu Histórico Nacional** was built in 1762 as an arsenal, and later served as a military prison where escaped slaves were detained. In 1922, the building was converted into an exhibition centre for the centenary celebrations of Brazil's independence from Portugal and has remained a museum ever since.

The large **collection** contains some pieces of great value, from furniture to nineteenth-century firearms and locomotives, and the display on the second floor, a documentation of **Brazilian history** since 1500, make it a must. Artefacts, charts and written explanations trace the country's development from the moment of discovery to the proclamation of the Republic in 1889 – a fascinating insight into the nature of imperial conquest and subsequent colonial culture. The structure of sixteenth-century Brazilian society is clearly demonstrated, for example, including the system of *sesmarias*, enormous royal land grants which are the basis of Brazil's highly unequal land tenure system to this day. Scale models and imaginative displays illustrate Brazil's economic history up to the nineteenth century, including the slave-labour plantation system that produced – at different times – sugar cane, cattle, cotton, rubber and coffee, as well as the transition from slavery to free labour and the importance of immigration to Brazil. More recent developments are taken up by the **Museu da República** (see page 76).

Passeio Público

Rua do Passeio Público • Daily 9am–5pm • Free • Ⓦ passeiopublico.com • Ⓜ Cinelândia

At the southern end of Cinelândia, where it meets Lapa, the beautifully maintained **Passeio Público** park is an oasis away from the hustle and bustle of the city. Opened in 1783, it was designed in part by Mestre Valentim da Fonseca e Silva, Brazil's most important late eighteenth-century sculptor, its trees providing shade for busts commemorating famous figures from the city's history, including Mestre Valentim himself.

Museu de Arte Moderna

Av Infante Dom Henrique 85, Parque do Flamengo • Tues–Fri noon–6pm, Sat, Sun & public holidays 11am–6pm • R$14 • ⓣ 21 3883 5600, ⓦ mamrio.com.br • Ⓜ Cinelândia

South of the Passeio Público, a larger park, the northern end of the Parque do Flamengo (see page 78) is home to the glass-and-concrete **Museu de Arte Moderna**, designed by the Brazilian architect and urbanist Affonso Reidy and inaugurated in 1958. The museum's collection was devastated by a fire in 1978 and only reopened in 1990 following the building's restoration. The permanent collection is still small and, despite boasting some of the great names of twentieth-century Brazilian art, extremely weak, though visiting exhibitions are occasionally worth checking out.

Monumento aos Mortos na Segunda Guerra Mundial

Avenida Beira Mar, Parque do Flamengo • Museum: Tues–Sun 9am–5pm • Free • ⓣ 21 2240 1283 • Ⓜ Cinelândia

Near Museu de Arte Moderna in the northern section of the Parque do Flamengo, the **Monumento aos Mortos na Segunda Guerra Mundial**, or **Monumento aos Pracinhas**, an elegant tall canopy over the tomb of an unknown soldier, and, set apart, a statue of a soldier, sailor and airman, commemorates the 462 Brazilian troops who died fighting for the Allies in World War II. Their remains were expatriated from Italy, where they were killed, to be buried here when the monument was completed in 1960. The small museum underneath exhibits some soldiers' kit and uniform.

Lapa

West of Cinelândia, **Lapa** is an old *bairro* with a faded charm. *Carioca* historian Brasil Gerson, in his 1954 *História das Ruas do Rio de Janeiro*, describes it as having been an "area of cabarets and bawdy houses, the haunt of scoundrels, gamblers, swashbucklers and inverts, and the walkway of poor, fallen women", but until the mid-seventeenth century, it was just a beach, known as the "Spanish Sands". More recently, things have been looking up, with the area blossoming into Rio's top spot for an evening's drinking, especially at weekends, when all its **bars** (see page 102) spill out onto the street.

Nova Catedral Metropolitana

Av Chile 245 • Daily 7am–5pm • Free • ⓣ 21 2240 2669, ⓦ catedral.com.br • Ⓜ Carioca and Cinelândia

South of Largo da Carioca, the unmistakeable shape of the **Nova Catedral Metropolitana** rises up like some futuristic teepee. Built between 1964 and 1976, it's an impressive piece of engineering, whatever you think of the architecture: the Morro de Santo Antônio was levelled to make way for the cathedral's construction, and the thousands of tonnes of resulting soil were used for the land reclamation project that gave rise to the Parque do Flamengo (see page 78). The cathedral is 83m high with a diameter of 104m and a capacity of 20,000 people. Inside, it feels vast, a remarkable sense of space enhanced by the absence of supporting columns. Filtering the sunlight, four huge stained-glass windows dominate, each measuring 20m by 60m and corresponding to a symbolic colour scheme – ecclesiastical green, saintly red, Catholic blue and apostolic yellow.

Arcos da Lapa (Aqueduto da Carioca)

Ⓜ Cinelândia

South of the Nova Catedral Metropolitana, a monumental Roman-style aqueduct, the mid-eighteenth-century **Aqueduto da Carioca** (more commonly called the **Arcos da Lapa**), was built to bring drinking water into the city, but was converted in 1896 to carry trams up to the hillside *bairro* of Santa Teresa (see page 72). The trams start from the terminal (*terminal dos bondes*) between the cathedral and the Largo da Carioca, behind the glass, steel and concrete **Petrobrás building**, headquarters of the state oil company.

Escadaria de Selarón

Ⓜ Cinelândia ot Glória

Climbing up into Santa Teresa from Rua Joaquim Silva, Rua Manoel Caneiro is a steep stairway better known as the **Escadaria de Selarón** (Selarón's Stairway) for its colourful display of tiles put together by Chilean artist Jorge Selarón. He began making it in 1990, originally in the colours of the Brazilian flag as a tribute to the people of Brazil, but in 1998 he began incorporating old European tiles and then started adding his own ceramic pictures. People sent him tiles from all over the world, and so the stairway kept changing. He refused to pay protection to local gangsters, and unfortunately as a result was brutally murdered in January 2013. On Friday and Saturday nights, you'll find a motley crew gathered here, with caipirinhas on sale, in a slightly downmarket extension of Lapa's street nightlife.

Santa Teresa

South of Lapa, **Santa Teresa**, a leafy *bairro* of labyrinthine, cobbled streets and steps (*ladeiras*), and with stupendous vistas of the city and bay below, makes a refreshing contrast to the city centre. Although it clings to the side of a hill, Santa Teresa is no *favela*: it's a slightly dishevelled residential area dominated by the nineteenth-century mansions and walled gardens of a prosperous community that still enjoys something of a bohemian reputation, with many artists choosing to live and work here. Nonetheless, for all its arty tranquillity, Santa Teresa does have quite a high crime rate, so bear it in mind and keep your wits about you here.

The tramway

Mon–Fri 6am–6.45pm, Sat 10am–6pm, every 20min (a half-hourly 11am–5pm Sunday service may also be introduced) • R$20 round trip

Santa Teresa is traditionally served by ageing trams (*bondes*), providing a bone-rattling ride up and down the hill and across the Arcos da Lapa from the terminal behind the Petrobrás building (see page 71). Unfortunately the tramway was closed after a fatal accident in 2011, and although part of it (up as far as Largo dos Guimarães) has now reopened, with new vehicles, two in number, the price has increased from R$0.60 each way to R$20 for a (compulsory) round-trip ticket – in other words, the tram is now a tourist curiosity rather than a practical piece of public transport. Needless to say, local residents, who had been running a campaign for its reinstatement, were not best pleased (you can't even hang off the sides any more, like people used to). On its way up, it passes the **Carmelite Convento e Igreja Santa Teresa**, on the spot where Rio's inhabitants beat off the French army in 1710. There are plans to extend the service beyond Largo dos Guimarães, but no definite date as yet.

Museu do Bonde

Rua Carlos Brant 14 (but currently in temporary accommodation by Carioca *bonde* station) • Mon–Sat 10am–4pm • Free • ⓣ 21 2222 1003

The **Museu do Bonde**, illustrating the tramway's history, will eventually be housed in the old tram works depot just off Largo dos Guimarães, but is temporarily located in a small room by the Carioca tram station in Lapa. The collection includes photo displays and memorabilia documenting the history of trams in Rio from their nineteenth-century introduction, showing how this means of public transport enabled the city to expand so rapidly along the coast. When it's rehoused, the displays will include old tramcars as well.

Museu Chácara do Céu

Rua Murtinho Nobre 93 • Daily except Tues noon–5pm • R$6; Wed free • ⓣ 21 3970 1093, Ⓦ museuscastromaya.com.br

Located in a modernist stone building erected in 1957, the **Museu Chácara do Céu** made headline news during the 2006 Carnaval when it was raided in broad daylight by armed thieves, who took four paintings by Matisse, Monet, Picasso and Dalí valued at US$50 million, before melting into the crowd outside. Despite these important losses, it remains one of Rio's better museums, holding an eclectic European collection as well as twentieth-century Brazilian works by painters such as Cândido Portinari, Emiliano di Cavalcanti, Heitor dos Prazeres and Djanira. In the upper hall, two screens depict the life of Krishna, and there are twin seventh-century iron-sculptured horses from the Imperial Palace in Beijing.

Parque das Ruínas

Rua Murtinho Nobre 169 • Tues–Sun 8am–6pm • Free

The **Parque das Ruínas** is an attractive public garden that contains the ruins of a mansion, formerly home to Laurinda Santos Lobo, a Brazilian heiress around whom artists and intellectuals gathered in the first half of the twentieth century. After her death in 1946, the mansion was allowed to fall into disrepair, but in the 1990s it was partially renovated as a cultural centre and today houses art exhibitions. There's a pleasant café on site, and a small stage where jazz concerts are often held, usually on Thursday evenings.

The Corcovado

The most famous of all images of Rio is that of the vast statue of Christ the Redeemer gazing across the bay from the **Corcovado** (hunchback) hill, and to visit Rio without making the tourist pilgrimage up the Corcovado is nigh on unthinkable, but do plan ahead, as you need to buy your ticket in advance.

GETTING TO THE CORCOVADO

All major hotels organize **excursions** to the Corcovado, but you can also go independently. Most people go up on a **cog train** (every 30min 8am–7pm) a twenty-minute ride to the top, from where there's an escalator leading to the viewing platform. It's highly advisable to buy **tickets** for the train (R$61–74 including entry) in advance as they are subject to availability, so they may sell out, there are often huge queues, especially at weekends and in August and September, and from time to time they make online purchase compulsory, so check in advance. You can buy tickets online (ⓦ tremdocorcovado.rio), or at post offices, or at the **Riotur information kiosks** (see page 93) on Praça Largo do Machado (map p.75) and on Av Atlântica in Copacabana opposite Rua Hilário de Gouveia (map p.81), or on the first floor of the Rio Sul shopping mall in Botafogo (map p.76) near the Rua Lauro Muller entrance. Tickets include entry to the Cristo Redentor belvedere and a round trip up to it on the cog train. To reach the cog train, unless you're driving or taking a cab, you can take a **bus** (#180 from Centro or Catete, #570 from Ipanema, #583 from Copacabana, or a *metrô* feeder bus from Largo do Machado station) to the **Estação Cosme Velho**, at Rua Cosme Velho 513 in the *bairro* of Cosme Velho. Before buying your ticket, it's wise to check the weather forecast: what ought to be one of Rio's highlights can turn into a great disappointment if the Corcovado is shrouded in clouds.

A cheaper and easier, though less exciting, alternative to the train is to take a **shuttle bus** from one of the two Riotur kiosks (Mon–Fri 8am–4pm, Sat & Sun 8am–5pm; R$51–62 including entry); note however that you may have to change vehcies on the way. You can also drive up to a car park at Paineiras, near the top, from which there are shuttle buses up to the viewing plaform. In principle it is even possible to **hike** up in about three hours from Parque Lage (see page 85), but people frequently get robbed using this path, so it is not a great idea, unless perhaps you do it in a large group; if you do take the hike, or if you drive up to Paineiras, you only need to pay the site entrance fee (R$27–40).

Cristo Redentor

The Corcovado • Daily 8am–7pm • R$61 Mon–Fri during school term; R$74 weekends, public and school holidays; tickets must be purchased in advance (see page 73) • ☎ 21 2558 1329, ⓦ corcovado.com.br

The Art Deco **statue of Cristo Redentor** (Christ the Redeemer), arms outstretched in welcome, or as if preparing for a dive into the waters below, stands 30m high and weighs over 1000 tonnes. It was supposed to be completed for Brazil's centenary independence celebrations in 1922, but wasn't actually finished until 1931. French sculptor Paul Landowski made the head and hands, with the rest put together by local engineers Heitor Silva Costa and Pedro Viana.

In clear weather, fear no anticlimax: climbing to the statue is a stunning experience by day, and nothing short of miraculous in the early evening. In daylight, the whole of Rio and Guanabara Bay is laid out before you; after sunset, the floodlit statue can be seen from everywhere in the Zona Sul, seemingly suspended in the darkness that surrounds it and often shrouded in eerie cloud. Up on the platform at the base of the statue, the effect of the clouds, and the thousands of tiny winged insects clustering round the spotlights, help give the impression that the statue is careering through space out into the blackness that lies beyond the arc of the lights – dramatic, and not a little hypnotic.

The **view** from the statue can also be helpful for **orientation** if you've just arrived in Rio. On a clear day, you can see as far as the outlying districts of the Zona Norte, while on the south side of the viewing platform you're directly over the Lagoa Rodrigo de Freitas, with Ipanema on the left and Leblon on the right. On the near side of the lake, Rua São Clemente is visible, curving its way through Botafogo, towards the Jardim Botânico and the racecourse, and on your left, the small *bairro* of Lagoa can be seen tucked in beneath the Morro dos Cabritos, on the other side of which is Copacabana.

Largo do Boticário

A few hundred metres west (uphill) from the Cosme Velho cog-train station, the much-photographed **Largo do Boticário** is named after royal apothecary Joaquim Luiz da Silva Santo, who lived here in the nineteenth century. With its pebbled streets and fountain set in the small courtyard, this is a particularly picturesque little corner of Rio. However, as old as the *largo* might appear to be, the original mid-nineteenth-century houses were demolished in the 1920s and replaced by colourful Neocolonial-style homes, many with *azulejo*-decorated facades.

Glória, Catete and Flamengo

The nearest beach to the city centre is at **Flamengo**, and although it's not the best in Rio you might end up using it more than you think, since the neighbouring *bairros*, **Catete** and **Glória**, are useful and cheap **places to stay** (see page 94). Until the 1950s, Flamengo and Catete were the principal residential zones of Rio's wealthier middle classes, and although the mantle has now passed to Ipanema and Leblon, the *bairros* still have a relaxed appeal. Busy during the day, the tree-lined streets come alive at night with residents eating in the local restaurants, and it's tranquil enough to encourage sitting out on the pavement at the bars, beneath the palm trees and apartment buildings.

Igreja de Nossa Senhora da Glória do Outeiro

Praça Nossa Senhora da Glória 135 **Igreja de Nossa Senhora da Glória do Outeiro** Mon–Fri 9am–4pm, Sat, Sun & public holidays 9am–noon • Free • **Museum** Tues–Fri 9am–noon & 1–5pm, Sat 9am–noon, Sun 9am–1pm • R$2 **Funicular elevator** Rua do Russel 312 • Tues–Fri 7am–7pm, Sat & Sun 7am–1pm • Free • ☎ 21 2225 2869 • Ⓜ Glória

Across from the Glória *metrô* station, on top of the Morro da Glória, the early eighteenth-century **Igreja de Nossa Senhora da Glória do Outeiro** is notable for its innovative octagonal ground-plan, and for its domed roof decked with lovely seventeenth-century blue-and-white *azulejo* tiles and nineteenth-century marble masonry. Painstakingly renovated, the church, quite simply the prettiest in Rio, is an absolute gem, easily worth a detour to visit. Its small **museum** has a small collection of religious relics, *ex votos* and the personal possessions of Empress Tereza Cristina. You can reach the church from Rua do Russel on a little funicular elevator.

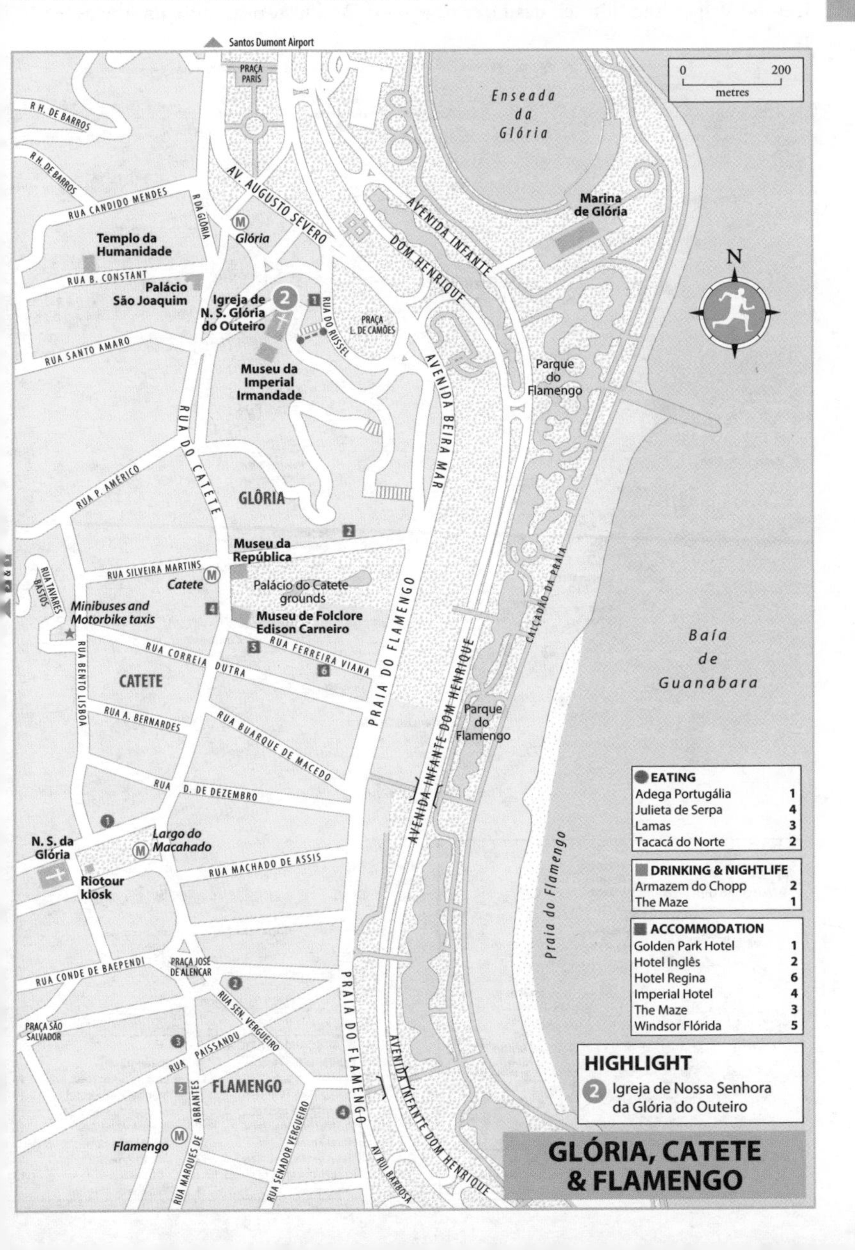

1

Museu da República (Palácio do Catete)

Rua do Catete 153 • **Museu** Tues–Fri 10am–5pm, Sat, Sun & public holidays 11am–6pm • R$6; free Wed & Sun **Grounds** Daily 8am–8pm • Free • 21 2127 0324, museudarepublica.museus.gov.br • Catete

The **Museu da República** is housed in the **Palácio do Catete**, which was the presidential residence from 1897 until 1960. Erected in the 1860s as the Rio home of a wealthy coffee-*fazenda* owner, it was here in 1954 that the country's longest-serving president, Getúlio Vargas, shot himself dead (see page 643). As a historical museum, the *palácio*

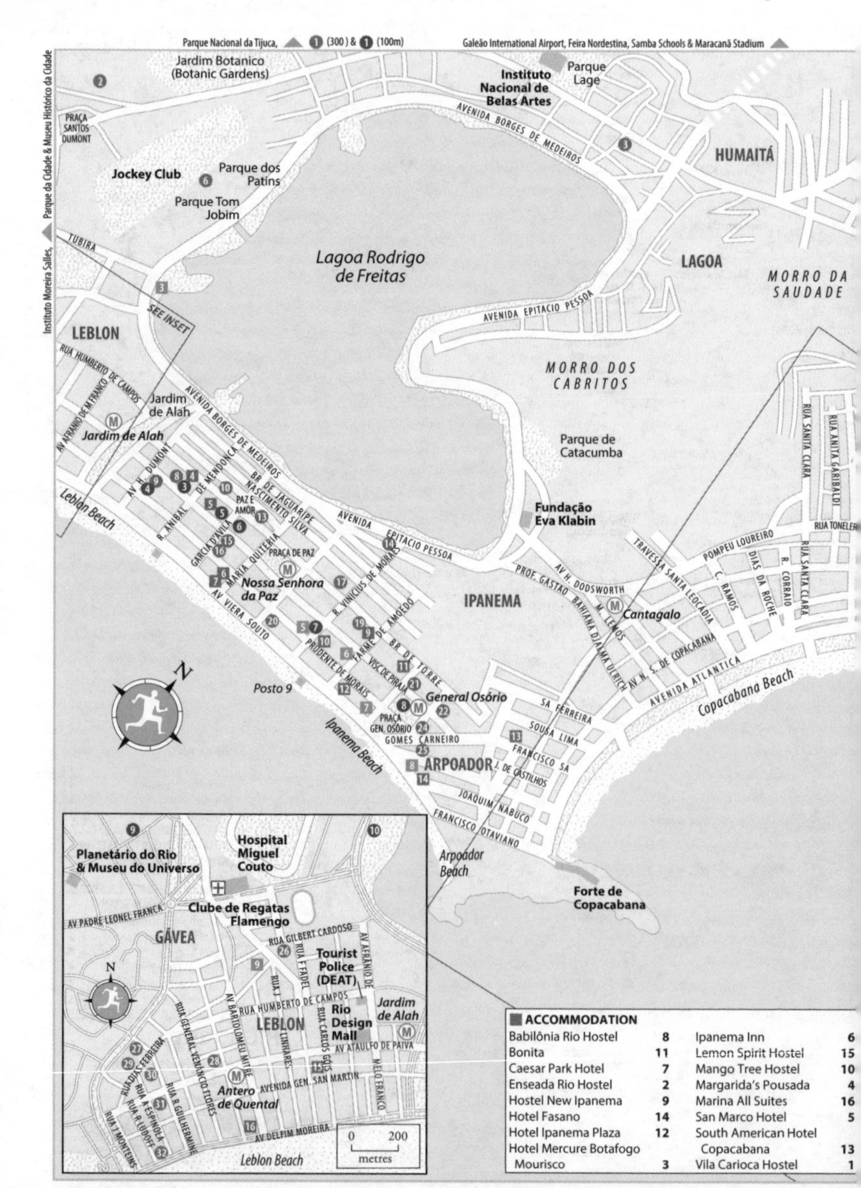

continues where the Museu Histórico Nacional (see page 70) leaves off, with the establishment of the first Republic in 1888. The collection features both period furnishings and presidential memorabilia – including Vargas's bullet-holed pyjamas (and the gun and bullet which killed him) – though it's the opulent marble and stained glass of the building itself that make a visit so worthwhile.

The **grounds** of the palace are effectively a park, where the birdlife, towering palms and quiet walking trails make it a good place for a break from the city. This is also a

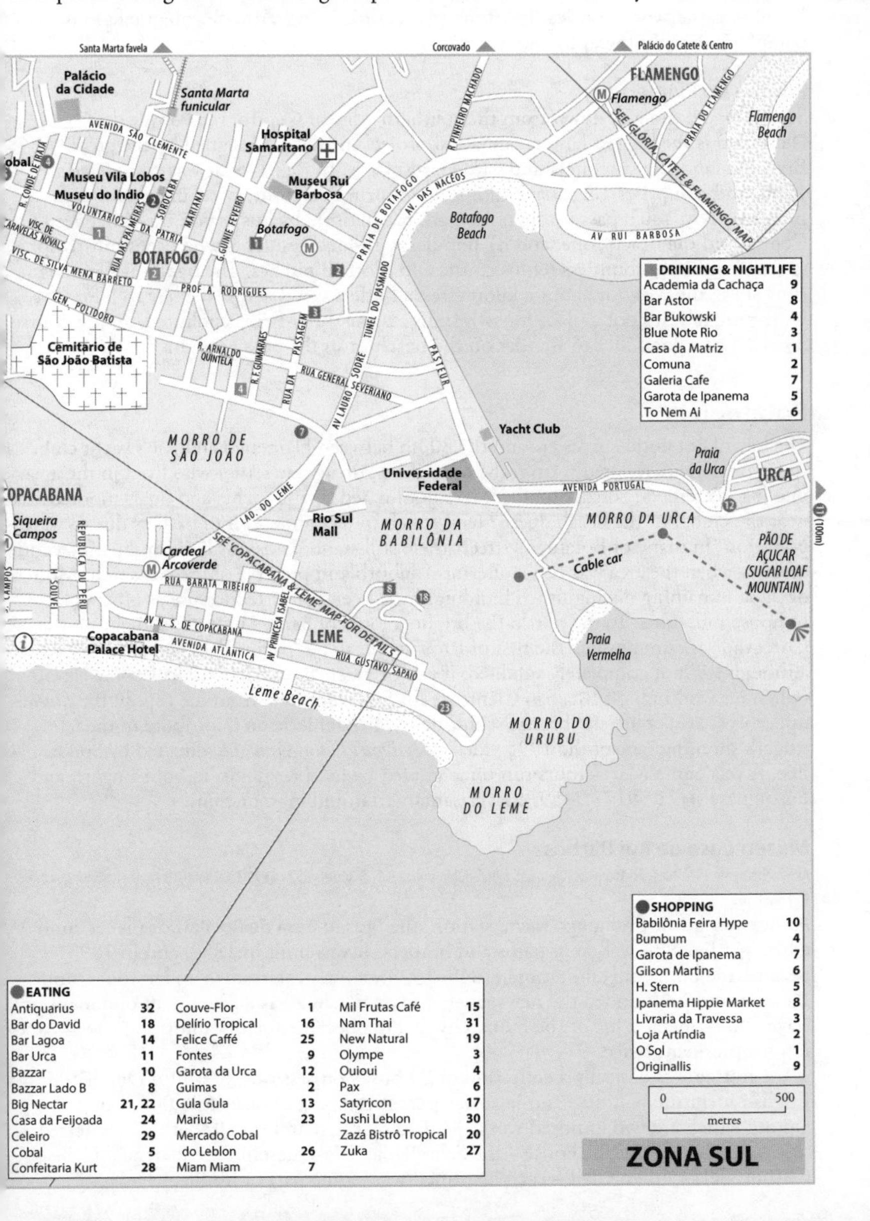

pleasant place to take small children, as it has a pond with ducks and other waterfowl, as well as a playground with tricycles and other toys.

Museu de Folclore Edison Carneiro

Rua do Catete 179 • Tues–Fri 10am–6pm, Sat, Sun & public holidays 3–6pm • Free • ⓣ 21 3826 4325, ⓦ cnfcp.gov.br • Ⓜ Catete

In a house adjacent to the grounds of the Palácio do Catete, the **Museu de Folclore Edison Carneiro** is a fascinating collection that unites pieces from all over Brazil – leatherwork, musical instruments, ceramics, toys, Afro-Brazilian religious paraphernalia, photographs and *ex votos*.

Parque do Flamengo

Stretching all the way down from the southern edge of Centro, the **Parque do Flamengo** is the biggest land reclamation project in Brazil. Designed by the great Brazilian landscape architect and gardener Roberto Burle Marx, it was completed in 1960, and comprises 1.2 square kilometres of prime seafront, sweeping round as far as Botafogo Bay. You'll pass through the park many times by bus as you travel between Centro and the beach zone, and it's popular with local residents who use it mostly for sports – there are countless tennis courts and football pitches. The **beach** at Flamengo runs along the park for about a kilometre and offers views across the bay to Niterói. Unfortunately, it's not a place for swimming as the water here is polluted, and of course it's also not a good idea to wander on the beach or in the park at night.

Botafogo

The bay of **Botafogo** curves around the 800m between Flamengo and Rio's yacht club. Its name derives, reputedly, from the first white Portuguese settler who lived in the area, one João Pereira de Souza Botafogo. It is dominated by the yachts and boats moored near the club, but the beach doesn't have much to recommend it to bathers due to water pollution. In many of Botafogo's streets there still stand mansions built in the nineteenth century when the area was Rio's outermost suburb and preserve of the city's rich. Most of these remaining distinguished buildings have been converted for use as offices or to house museums. To the north, the bright colours of **Santa Marta** *favela* light up the Corcovado mountainside. The first of Rio's *favelas* to be "pacified" by police in 2008, although still not completely subdued, it can be reached on a free funicular-like elevator (when it's working) off Rua São Clemente for fantastic views from the top. In the *favela*'s upper west area, a life-size bronze sculpture of **Michael Jackson** is a tribute to the late singer's shooting here of the 1995 video *They Don't Care About Us*, directed by Spike Lee. Favela Santa Marta Tours run tours guided by local residents, in both English and Portuguese (ⓣ 21 99177 9459, ⓦ favelasantamartatour.blogspot.com).

Museu Casa de Rui Barbosa

Av São Clemente 134 • Tues–Fri 10am–5.30pm, Sat, Sun & public holidays 1–5.30pm • R$2 • ⓣ 21 3289 4600, ⓦ casaruibarbosa.gov.br • Ⓜ Botafogo

A short walk from Botafogo *metrô* station, the **Museu Casa de Rui Barbosa** is set amid a lush garden with well-kept paths and borders. It was built in 1850, and in 1893 became the home of Rui Barbosa (1849–1923), a jurist, statesman and author from Bahia state who founded the newspaper *A Imprensa* and was a prominent opponent of slavery and liberal critic of the monarchy. Babosa became finance minister in 1890, and ran for president twice.

The museum is basically a collection of Barbosa's possessions: beautiful Dutch and English furniture, Chinese and Japanese porcelain and a library of 35,000 volumes, among which are two hundred works penned by the man himself. Barbosa conferred a title on each room in the house – the Sala Bahia, Sala Questão Religiosa, Sala Habeas Corpus, Sala Código Civil – each identified with some part of his life.

Museu Villa-Lobos

Rua Sorocaba 200 • Mon–Fri 10am–5pm • 21 2226 9818, museuvillalobos.org.br • Free • Botafogo

On Rua Sorocaba, a turning off Avenida São Clemente, is the **Museu Villa-Lobos**, established in 1960 to celebrate the work of the great Brazilian composer, Heitor Villa-Lobos (1887–1959). It's largely a display of his personal possessions and original music scores, which will really only be of interest to fans and music enthusiasts, who'll also be pleased to know that you can also buy CDs of his music here.

Museu do Índio

Rua das Palmeiras 55 • Tues–Fri 9am–5.30pm, Sat, Sun & public holidays 1–5pm • Free • 21 3214 8700, museudoindio.gov.br • Botafogo

Closed for refurbishment until 2018, the **Museu do Índio**, dedicated to Brazil's indigenous peoples, is housed in an 1880 mansion and exhibits a broad and interesting collection, including utensils, musical instruments, tribal costumes and ritual devices. There's a good photographic exhibition and an accessible anthropological explanation of many rituals and institutions. Most interesting of all are the full-size shelters of different peoples that are erected on a temporary basis in the museum's grounds. The shop sells a range of carefully sourced original artefacts.

Urca

The best bet for swimming near the city centre is around **Urca**. There are small beaches on each side of the promontory on which this small, wealthy *bairro* stands, its name an acronym of the company that undertook its construction – Urbanizador Construção. Facing Botafogo, the **Praia da Urca**, only 100m long, is frequented almost exclusively by local inhabitants, while in front of the cable-car station, beneath the Sugar Loaf Mountain, **Praia Vermelha** is a cove sheltered from the South Atlantic, whose relatively gentle waters are popular with swimmers.

Sugar Loaf Mountain

Urca • Daily 8am–9pm (ticket office closes 7.50pm) • R$80 • 21 2546 8400, bondinho.com.br • Cable car every 20min from Praça General Tibúrcio, reached on buses marked "Urca" or "Praia Vermelha", including #513 from Botafogo, and #581 from Ipanema and Copacabana (it's best to take #581 coming, #582 going back)

The **Pão de Açúcar** (in English, **Sugar Loaf Mountain**) rises where Guanabara Bay meets the Atlantic Ocean. Its name may simply reflect a resemblance to the moulded loaves in which sugar was once commonly sold. Alternatively, it may be a corruption of the indigenous Tamoya word *Pau-nh-Açuquá*, meaning "high, pointed or isolated hill". The first recorded non-indigenous ascent to the summit was made in 1817 by an English nanny, Henrietta Carstairs. Today, mountaineers scaling the smooth, precipitous slopes are a common sight, but there's a cable-car ride to the summit for the less adventurous.

The **cable-car** system has been in place since 1912, though the present system was installed in 2008. The 1.4km journey to the summit (396m) is made in two stages, first to the summit of **Morro da Urca** (220m), where there is a theatre, restaurant and shops, as well as a helipad, from which helicopter tours depart (see page 93). In fact you can walk up to here but it will not save you any money as you must first buy a ticket for the whole journey from the cable-car station; tickets are not sold at the halfway stage. The cable cars have glass walls, and the view from the top is as glorious as you could wish. Facing inland, you can see right over the city, from Centro and the Santos Dumont airport all the way through Flamengo and Botafogo; face Praia Vermelha and the cable-car terminal, and to the left you'll see the sweep of Copacabana and on into Ipanema, while back from the coast the mountains around which Rio was built rise to the Parque Nacional da Tijuca. Try to avoid the busy times between 10am and 3pm: the ride is best at sunset on a clear day, when the lights of the city are starting to twinkle. Leading down from the summit is a series of wooded trails along which you'll encounter curious small marmosets, and it's easy – and safe – to get away from the crowds.

Copacabana and Leme

Copacabana and Leme are different stretches of the same 4km-long beach: **Leme** extends for 1km, between the Morro do Leme and Avenida Princesa Isabel, by the luxury hotel *Le Meridien*, from where Copacabana runs for a further 3km to the Forte de Copacabana. Leme beach is slightly less packed than Copacabana and tends to attract families, but avoid walking through the **Túnel Novo from Botafogo**, as it's a favourite place for tourists to be relieved of their wallets.

Copacabana is dominated to the east by Sugar Loaf Mountain and circled by a line of hills that stretch out into the bay. The *bairro*'s expansion as a residential area has been

ON THE BEACH

Rio's sophisticated beach culture is entirely a product of the **twentieth century**. The 1930s saw the city's international reputation emerge and "flying down to Rio" became an enduring cliché, celebrated in music, film and literature. Nonetheless, Rio's beaches are first and foremost the preserve of *cariocas*: rich or poor, young or old, everybody descends on the beaches throughout the week, treating them as city parks. They are divided into informal segments, identified by numbered *postos* (marker posts), and in Copacabana and Ipanema in particular, gay men, families, beach-sport aficionados and even intellectuals claim specific segments.

BEACH FASHION

Looking good is important on Rio's beaches, and you'll come across some pretty snappy seaside threads. Fashions change fast, though, so if you're keen to make your mark you should buy your **swimsuits** in Rio. Keep in mind that although women may wear the skimpiest of bikinis, going topless is not acceptable.

BEACH SPORTS

Maintaining an even tan and tight musculature is the principal occupation for most of Rio's beachgoers. Joggers swarm up and down the pavements, bronzed types flex their muscles on parallel bars located at intervals along the beaches, and **beach football** on Copacabana is as strong a tradition as legend would have it. There's lots of **volleyball**, too, as well as the ubiquitous **batball**, a kind of table tennis with a heavy ball, and without the table.

EATING

A lot of people make their living by plying **food** – sweets, nuts, ice cream – and beach equipment along the seashore, while dotted along the sand are makeshift canopies from which you can buy cold drinks. Like bars, most of these have a regular clientele and deliver a very efficient service. Coconut water (*côco verde*), sold everywhere, is supposedly a good hangover cure.

STAYING SAFE

The water off many of the beaches can be **dangerous**. The seabed falls sharply away, the waves are strong, and currents can pull you down the beach. Mark your spot well before entering the water, or you'll find yourself emerging from a paddle twenty or thirty metres from where you started – which, when the beaches are packed at weekends, can cause considerable problems when it comes to relocating your towel. Copacabana is particularly dangerous, even for strong swimmers. However, the beaches are well served by **lifeguards**, whose posts are marked by a white flag with a red cross; a **red flag** indicates that bathing is prohibited. Constant surveillance of the beachfronts from helicopters and support boats means that, if you do get into trouble, help should arrive quickly.

Pollution is another problem to bear in mind. Although much has been done in recent years to clean up Guanabara Bay, it is still not safe to swim in the water from Flamengo or Botafogo beaches. While the water beyond the bay at Copacabana and Ipanema is usually clean, there are times when it – and the beaches themselves – aren't, especially following a prolonged period of heavy summer rain, when the city's strained drainage system overflows with raw sewage.

Natural dangers aside, the beaches hold other unwelcome surprises. Giving your passport, money and **valuables** the chance of a suntan, rather than leaving them in the hotel safe, is madness. Take only the clothes and money you'll need – it's quite acceptable to use public transport while dressed for the beach.

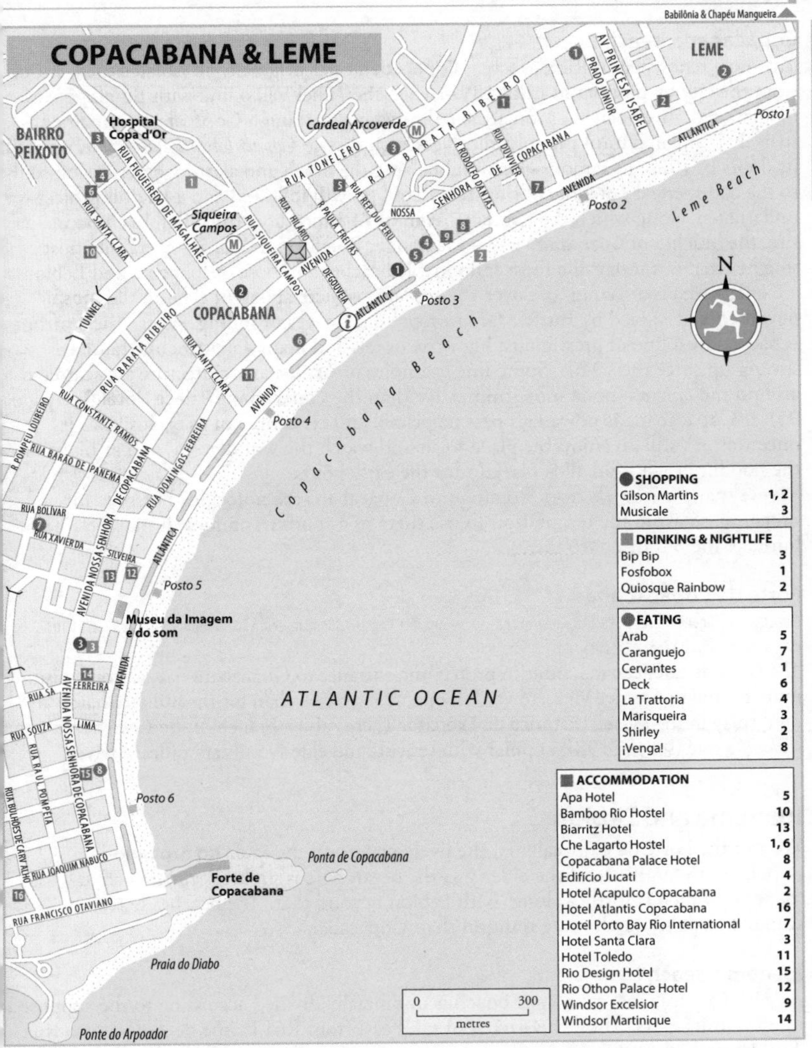

restricted by the Morro de São João, which separates it from Botafogo and the Morro dos Cabritos, a natural barrier to the west. Consequently, Copacabana is one of the world's most densely populated areas as well as a frenzy of sensual activity.

Of course, Copacabana hasn't always been as it is today, and traces remain of the former fishing community that dominated the area until the first decades of the twentieth century. Each morning before dawn, the boats of the *colônia de pescadores* (the descendants of the fishermen) set sail from the **Forte de Copacabana**, returning to the beach by 8am, and you can still buy their their fish at the southern end of the beach, just by the entrance to the fort. The area's latest billed attraction is the **Museu da Imagem e do Som**, with exhibits on the history of film, TV, music and radio in Brazil in a snazzy, though long delayed new building at Avenida Atlântica 3432, which remained under construction at time of research.

Copacabana beach

The most renowned of Rio's beaches, **Copacabana** was originally an isolated area, cut off from the city by mountains until 1892, when the Túnel Velho link with Botafogo was inaugurated. The open sea soon attracted beachgoers, though Copacabana remained sparsely populated until the splendid Neoclassical-style *Copacabana Palace Hotel* opened its doors in 1923, its famous guests publicizing the beach and alerting enterprising souls to the commercial potential of the area. Rapid growth followed and a landfill project was undertaken, along which the two-lane **Avenida Atlântica** now runs. Before Copacabana's rise, the beaches of **Guanabara Bay** – Flamengo, Botafogo and Urca – were the most sought after, but today, the most fashionable beaches are those of Ipanema and Leblon.

Copacabana is amazing, the over-the-top atmosphere apparent even in the **mosaic pavements**, designed by Burle Marx to represent images of rolling waves. The seafront is backed by a line of prestigious, high-rise hotels and luxury apartments that have sprung up since the 1940s. Some fine examples of Art Deco architecture are scattered around the *bairro* – none more impressive than the **Copacabana Palace Hotel** (see page 95). If Copacabana is nowadays past its prime, and certainly not as exclusive as it once was, it's still an enjoyable place to sit and watch the world go by, and at night on the floodlit beach football is played into the early hours.

Note that the tunnels from Botafogo to Copacabana are notorious hotspots for mugging, so avoid the temptation to use them as a shortcut on foot; it may be a pain, but take the bus or metrô instead.

Forte de Copacabana

Praça Coronel Eugênio Franco 1, Posto 6, Copacabana • Tues–Sun: fort 10am–7.30pm; museum 10am–6pm • R$6 • Ⓣ 21 2521 1032, Ⓦ fortedecopacabana.com • Ⓜ Cantagalo

The **Forte de Copacabana**, built to protect the entrance to Guanabara Bay, is worth visiting more for the impressive views towards Copacabana beach than for the military hardware on display in the **Museu Histórico do Exército**. There's also a branch of the *Confeitaria Colombo* café (see page 98), popular with tourists and elderly military officers' wives.

Ipanema and Leblon

West of the Forte de Copacabana, the lively waters off the **Praia do Arpoador** are popular with families and the elderly as the ocean here is slightly calmer than at **Ipanema**, which is further along, with **Leblon** beyond that. The beaches here are stupendous, and much more tranquil than Copacabana.

Ipanema beach

As with Copacabana, Ipanema's **beach** is unofficially divided according to the supposed interest of its users. Thus, the stretch of sand east from Rua Farme de Amoedo to Rua Teixeira de Melo around *posto 8* is where gay men are concentrated, while the nearby *posto 9* is where artists and intellectuals ponder life. On Sunday, the seafront roads – Avenida Vieira Souto in Ipanema and Avenida Delfim in Leblon – are closed to traffic, given over to strollers, skateboarders and rollerbladers.

Since the 1960s, Ipanema has developed a reputation as a **fashion centre** second to none in Latin America. Although many in São Paulo would dispute this, certainly the *bairro* is packed with *bijou* boutiques flogging the very best Brazilian names in fine threads. If you do go shopping here, go on a Friday and take in the large **food and flower market** on the Praça de Paz. For quality clothes, however, prices are quite high compared with their European or North American equivalents.

FOOTBALL ON IPANEMA BEACH

1

Lagoa and Gávea

Inland from Ipanema's plush beaches lies the **Lagoa Rodrigo de Freitas**, a lagoon linked to the ocean by a narrow canal that passes through Ipanema's Jardim de Allah. The lagoon is fringed by apartment buildings, and the *bairro* to its east, home since the 1920s to some of Rio's richest and most status-conscious citizens, is called **Lagoa** after the lagoon. The neighbourhood on the lagoon's western side is called **Gávea**, and is linked to Lagoa by a *bairro* that is known as **Jardim Botânico** thanks to the botanical garden that it surrounds.

Parque Tom Jobim

A programme to clean up the lagoon's water has been remarkably successful and its mangrove swamps are now growing back after years of pollution damage. The shore surrounding the lagoon forms the **Parque Tom Jobim** (named after Rio's famed bossa-nova composer, who died in 1994), and the area comes alive each Sunday as people walk, rollerblade, jog or cycle along the 7.5km perimeter pathway, or just gaze at the passers-by. Summer evenings are especially popular when, on the west side of the lagoon in the area known as the **Parque dos Patins** (Skaters' Park), there are food stalls, live music and *forró* dancing.

Fundação Eva Klabin

Av Epitácio Pessoa 2480 • Tues–Sun 2–6pm • R$10; weekends and public holidays free • T 21 3202 8550, W evaklabin.org.br

One of the few remaining original homes in Lagoa now contains the **Fundação Eva Klabin** cultural centre. The house was built in 1931, in the style of rural Normandy – a popular fashion in house-building at the time – and became the family residence of Eva Klabin, a wealthy art collector of Lithuanian origin. Visitors are taken on a guided tour of the wide-ranging collection of Egyptian, classical Greek and Roman, Italian, French and Flemish works of art, all beautifully displayed in elegant, wood-panelled rooms, and classical music recitals are regularly held here.

RIO'S FAVELAS

In a low-wage economy, and with minimal social services, life is extremely difficult for the majority of Brazilians. During the last forty years, the rural poor have descended upon urban centres in search of a livelihood – often unable to find accommodation, or pay rent, they have established shantytowns, or **favelas**, on any available empty space, which in Rio usually means the slopes of the hills around which the city has grown.

Favelas start off as huddles of cardboard boxes and plastic sheeting, and slowly expand and transform: metal sheeting and bricks provide more solid shelters of often two or more storeys. Clinging to the sides of Rio's hills, and glistening in the sun, they can from a distance appear not unlike a medieval Spanish hamlet, perched securely atop a mountain. It is, however, a spurious beauty. The *favelas* are creations of need, and their inhabitants are engaged in an intense daily struggle for survival, worsened by the prospect of landslides caused by heavy rains, which could tear their dwellings from their tenuous hold on precipitous inclines.

Life for some of Rio's *favela* dwellers is slowly changing for the better, however. Bound together by their shared poverty and exclusion from effective citizenship, the *favelados* display a great resourcefulness and cooperative strength. **Self-help initiatives** – some of which are based around the *escolas de samba* (see page 107) that are mainly *favela*-based – have emerged, and the authorities are finally recognizing the legitimacy of *favelas* by promoting "*favela-bairro*" projects aimed at fully integrating them into city life. Private enterprise, too, is taking an interest as it becomes alert to the fact that the quarter of the city's population that live in *favelas* represents a vast, untapped market. Not all such enterprise is legal, and some *favelas* are controlled by highly organized **drug gangs**. These then become almost no-go areas for police, but every so often the police instigate "pacification" programmes to chase out the gangsters and take control themselves. The latest such initiative took place across the *favelas* in the city's Zona Sul and Zona Oeste in the run-up to the 2016 Olympics – needless to say, it went back to business as usual as soon as the games were over.

Parque da Catacumba

Av Epitácio Pessoa 3000 • Tues–Sun 8am–5pm • Free • parquedacatacumba.com.br

The steep slopes behind Lagoa's apartment buildings are still well forested, and in 1979 a *favela* was cleared away and the **Parque da Catacumba** developed in its place on one of the more accessible hills, by the southeast corner of the lagoon on Avenida Epitácio Pessoa. It's a wonderful, shaded place to relax, and the dense tropical vegetation forms an excellent backdrop for one of Brazil's few **sculpture parks**.

Parque Lage

Rua Jardim Botânico 414 • Daily 8am–5pm • Free • 21 3257 1800

Northwest of the Lagoa, in the *bairro* of **Jardim Botânico**, the **Parque Lage** was designed by English landscape gardener John Tyndale in the 1840s. The mansion overlooking it, now an arts school, was bought in 1920 by the aeronautics entrepreneur Henrique Lage, after whom the park is named. Its 128 acres of foliage includes pristine Atlantic forest on the, with a labyrinthine network of paths, seven small lakes and a good park café. Note however that the paths from here up the Corcovado are not safe to use, as robberies have occurred on them.

Jardim Botânico

Rua Jardim Botânico 1008 • Mon noon–5pm, Tues–Sun 8am–5pm • R$15 • 21 3874 1808 • jbrj.gov.br

About halfway along the Rua Jardim Botânico, the **Jardim Botânico** itself consists largely of natural forest. The rest is laid out in impressive avenues lined with immense imperial palms that date from the garden's inauguration in 1808. Dom João used the gardens to introduce foreign plants into Brazil – tea, cloves, cinnamon and pineapple among them – and they were opened to the public in 1890. One of the world's finest botanic gardens, it now contains five thousand plant species, among which live monkeys, parrots and other assorted wildlife. There are also a number of sculptures to

FAVELA TOURS

Wandering into a *favela* does not, as many middle-class *cariocas* would have you believe, guarantee being robbed or murdered. Some of them, especially the smaller ones, are quiet if poor communities. Even in those controlled by drug gangs, it's not in their interest to create trouble for visitors, as this would only attract the attention of the police, who normally stay clear. Alone however, you're liable to get lost and, as in any isolated spot, may run into opportunistic thieves, but if accompanied by a *favela* resident you'll be perfectly safe and received with friendly curiosity. For most visitors however, the best option is to take a **tour**, with the most insightful and longest-established run by ★ **Marcelo Armstrong**. Marcelo, who speaks excellent English, is widely known and respected in the *favelas* that are visited and has made a point of getting community approval. It is strongly advised to make your own arrangements with Marcelo rather than through a travel agent or hotel front desk, where you may end up with an inferior tour and be charged too much – some operators treat the *favelas* rather as they might an African game park, ferrying groups in open-topped camouflaged jeeps. But if you're worried about voyeurism, you shouldn't be: residents want outsiders to understand that *favelas* are not in fact terrifying and lawless ghettos, but inhabited by people as decent as anywhere else, eager to improve the local quality of life.

Marcelo's highly responsible tours usually take in two *favelas*: **Rocinha** (see page 86), and **Vila Canoas**, which is much smaller, with some 3000 residents. Twice on most days (Mon–Sat 9am & 2pm, Sun 10am; R$95, part of which is donated to community projects in the *favelas*), tourists are picked up from their hotels or pre-arranged spots in the Zona Sul for the three-hour tour, which stops at lookout points, a day-care centre, a bar and other places of interest. Marcelo offers a fascinating commentary, pointing out the achievements of *favelas* and their inhabitants without romanticizing their lives. To reserve a place on a tour, call Marcelo between 8am and 10pm on 21 3322 2727 or (including via WhatsApp) 21 99989 0074, or for more information, check out favelatour.com.br.

Another responsible operator, **Favela Adventures** (21 98221 5572, favelatour.org), offers a variety of tours of Rocinha, including opportunities to party with local residents.

be seen throughout the garden, notably the *Ninfa do Eco* and *Caçador Narciso* (1783) by Mestre Valentim, the first two metal sculptures cast in Brazil.

The Jockey Club

Rua Jardim Botânico • Races Mon 6.15–11pm, Fri 5–9.30pm, Sat & Sun 1.15–8pm • Free • ⊕ 21 3534 9000, ⊕ www.jcb.com.br

On the **Gávea** side of Lagoa, the **Jockey Club**, or Hipódromo da Gávea, can be reached on any bus marked "via Jóquei" – get off at Praça Santos Dumont at the end of Rua Jardim Botânico. Racing in Rio was introduced by the British in 1825, though the Hipódromo wasn't built until 1926. Today, **races** take place four times a week, with the international Grande Prêmio Brasil taking place in mid-June. A night at the races is great fun, especially during the floodlit evening races, when the air is balmy and you can eat or drink as you watch the action, and visitors can get into the palatial members' stand for just a few *reaís* (note that no one in shorts is admitted).

Instituto Moreira Salles

Rua Marquês de São Vicente 476 • Tues–Sun 11am–8pm • Free • ⊕ 21 3284 7400, ⊕ ims.com.br • It's a good 20min walk to the *Instituto* from the Jockey Club; alternatively, take bus #112 or #538, or bus #539 from Copacabana

About 2km west of the Jockey Club, the **Instituto Moreira Salles** is one of Rio's most beautiful private cultural centres. Located in the former home of the Moreira Salles family (the owners of Unibanco, one of the country's most important banks), the house, built in 1951, is one of the finest examples of modernist residential architecture in Brazil. Designed by the Brazilian architect Olavo Redig de Campos – with gardens landscaped by Roberto Burle Marx, who also contributed a tile mural alongside the terrace – the building has been open to the public since 1999. Important exhibitions of nineteenth- and twentieth-century painting and photography are staged here and for refreshment there's a bistro serving light meals.

Museu Histórico da Cidade

Estrada de Santa Marinha • Tues–Sun: winter 10am–5pm; summer 10am–6pm • Free • ⊕ 21 97532 4428, ⊕ museudacidadedorio.com.br • Bus #105 from Centro to Estrada da Gávea

The **Parque da Cidade**, at the top of the rather steep Estrada de Santa Marinha, contains the **Museu Histórico da Cidade**, housed in a two-storey nineteenth-century mansion once owned by the Marquês de São Vicente. Its collection is related to the history of Rio from its founding until the end of the Old Republic in 1930, and includes paintings, weapons, porcelain, medals and the like, arranged in chronological order. The first salon deals with the city's foundation, the rest with the colonial period.

Zona Oeste and western Zona Sul

West of Leblon, the coast runs on into kilometre after kilometre of white sand. The first few are still part, like Copacabana and Ipanema, of Rio's Zona Sul, but those beyond belong to the city's ever-growing **Zona Oeste**, a land of apartment blocks interspersed with lagoons and nature parks. All of these areas will become a whole lot more accessible when construction of *metrô linha 4* is complete.

Rocinha

On the slopes between the Tijuca mountains and the peak of Pedra dos Dois Irmãos sits **Favela Rocinha**, misleadingly picturesque as it glistens in the sun. The largest *favela* in Rio, it's also the oldest, dating back to the 1930s, and swelled in the 1950s with the arrival of migrants from Brazil's northeastern states. Around 200,000 people live here today, and it's still growing. Some local residents have decent jobs and quite large houses, but many families here subsist on a salary of just R$300 a month or less. Rocinha is visited by some of the popular *favela* tours (see page 84), and it isn't otherwise advisable to just come in and wander around on your own.

ᵓarque Nacional da Tijuca

aily: winter 8am–5pm; summer 7am–6pm • Free • ⓣ 21 2491 1700, ⓦ parquedatijuca.com.br

.ooking up from the streets of Zona Sul, you'll see that the mountains running outhwest from the Corcovado are covered with exuberant forest. This is the **Parque Nacional da Tijuca**, an area of some 120 square kilometres. In the seventeenth entury, the forests that originally covered the area were cut down for hardwood, the rees replaced by sugar cane and then coffee plantations. In 1857, however, the city uthorities, alarmed by landslides and a resulting shortage of clean water, began a **eafforestation** project, and by 1870, over 100,000 trees had been planted (all species ative to the area). Today the park serves as a remarkable example of the potential for he regeneration of the Mata Atlântica. **Fauna** have also gradually been reintroduced, naking the forest once again home to insects, reptiles, ocelots, howler monkeys, goutis, three-toed sloths and other animals. Most successful of all has been the return of **birdlife**, making Tijuca a paradise for birdwatchers. At the same time, overstretched ark rangers struggle to keep residents of the neighbouring *favelas* from hunting vildlife for food or trade.

Be sure to come well supplied with drinks and snacks, as vendors are few and far etween. Mosquito repellent is also a good idea, and be aware that robberies of hikers n the park are not unknown. In fact, the safest and easiest way to visit the park if you lon't have your own transport is to join an **organized tour** (see below).

ARRIVAL AND INFORMATION — PARQUE NACIONAL DA TIJUCA

By car Buses don't enter the park, so a car is useful if you lan to do an extensive tour. By car, there are several points of ntry, including the Entrada dos Caboclos in Cosme Velho, on he north side of the Corcovado, and the Entrada dos Macacos n Rua Leão Pacheco, which runs up from the north the side of he Jardim Botânico (see page 85). Both of these entrances ead to different roads that run through the park, but they onverge eventually in the *bairro* of Alta da Boa Vista. If you're ntent on walking from either of these entrances, be warned hat even the shorter trip from the Entrada dos Macacos will nean a hot, dehydrating climb for more than 20km.

By bus It is also possible to reach Alta da Boa Vista by bus (#301 or #345 from Av Presidente Vargas in Centro or from Jardim Oceânico *metrô* station) and get off at Praça Alfonso Viseu near he Entrada da Floresta, with its distinctive stone columns. A few hundred metres after the entrance is a 35m-high waterfall and, further on, the Capela do Mairynk, first constructed in 1860 but almost entirely rebuilt in the 1940s.

By tour Most of the Parque da Tijuca tours offered by hotels and travel agents involve nothing more strenuous than a short walk along a paved road, but more personal – and infinitely more rewarding – are the tours run by ★ **Rio Hiking** (ⓣ 21 2552 9204 or ⓣ 21 99721 0594, ⓦ riohiking.com.br), which take small groups of people on half- or full-day hikes along the park's many trails. The same firm also offers other hikes around Rio and runs a tour to Ilha Grande and Paraty (see page 130) and to Serra dos Orgãos and Petrópolis (see page 120).

Tourist information The Centro de Visitantes at Estrada da Cascatinha 850/590 (about 1km above Plaça Afonso Viseu; daily 8am–5pm; ⓣ 21 2491 1700) has maps and information about the park.

São Conrado

Bus #554 or #557 from Copacabana, Ipanema and Leblon, or from Ⓜ São Conrado (which is about 500m from the eastern end of the beach)

West of Vidigal and Rocinha, the beautiful beach at **São Conrado** is dominated by apartment buildings and high-rise hotels. Frequented by the rich and famous, and packed at weekends with hang-gliders and surfers, it's an area where the upper

HANG-GLIDING ABOVE RIO

For a bird's-eye view of Rio's beaches and forest, take off with an experienced pilot on a tandem **hang-glider** flight from the Pedra Bonita ramp on the western edge of the Parque Nacional da Tijuca (see page 87), 520m above the beach at São Conrado. Depending on conditions, flights last between ten and thirty minutes, flying alongside the mountains and over the forest and ocean before landing on the beach at São Conrado.

The most experienced operator, ★ **Just Fly** ⓣ 21 99985 7540, ⓦ justfly.com.br), offers flights daily (usually 8am–sunset) when weather permits, for R$420.

1

AFTER THE OLYMPICS

Rio hosted, in quick succession, the 2014 World Cup and the **2016 Olympic Games**. The Olympic Village was located in Barra da Tijuca, and most of the events were held in all-new purpose-built stadiums out on the Barra, intended to give the city's **Zona Oeste** a range of world-class sports venues. Unfortunately, most of them have been little used since then and in retrospect have the look of a very pale pachyderm about them. Even before the Cup and the Games, *cariocas* were unimpressed; thousands took to the streets to protest the spending of over US$4bn on what was widely seen as a prestige project of little use to a city that was crying out for money to ease its many social ills. One positive legacy of the Olympics that does remain, however, is the city's improved **transport system**, including the VLT tram and *Linha 4* of the *metrô*, both of which were put in ahead of the games as part of an infrastructure upgrade. For a more in-depth view of post-Olympic Rio check out the excellent websites Ⓦ riorealblog.com and Ⓦ rioonwatch.org.

classes flaunt their wealth without shame, though some are uncomfortable with the encroachment of nearby *favelas*.

Barra da Tijuca

Bus #308 or #345 from Centro, #INT-01, #INT-02 or #INT-09 from Copacabana or Botafogo, or *metrô* to Ⓜ Jardim Oceânico

As Rio expands westward, many of the city's more affluent residents have been moving out of the Zona Sul and into new neighbourhoods in the Zona Oeste such as **Barra da Tijuca**, where property developers have been putting up apartment buildings and shopping malls at breakneck speed. The neighbourhood itself is a car-friendly suburb where you'll see few pedestrians, but what you really come out here for are the clean waters and white sands of its spacious 16km-long **beach**. The **Lagoa de Marapendi**, behind the beach, was once a lagoon full of mangroves, an ecosystem destroyed by development except for its last remaining holdout in the **Parque Municipal Ecológico de Marapendi** at the lagoon's very western end. And just in case the Barra's own beach is not enough for you, there are further beaches to its west at **Prainha** (Rio's best surfing beach) and, beyond that, the still largely undeveloped beach at **Grumari**.

Sítio Roberto Burle Marx

Estrada Roberto Burle Marx 2019, Guaratiba • Tours daily 9.30am & 1.30pm (90–120min), must be booked in advance on Ⓣ 21 2410 1412 • R$10 • Bus #INT-109 from Copacabana, Ipanema, Jardim Oceânico *metrô* station or Barra da Tijuca to Ipiranga petrol station in Guaratiba and then a 15min walk

Some 25km west of Barra da Tijuca, in the quiet and unremarkable village of Guaratiba, the influential landscape gardener **Roberto Burle Marx** (1909–94) bought a 100-acre former coffee plantation – the **Sítio** – in 1949. He then converted it into a nursery for the plants he collected on his travels around the country, moving in permanently in 1973.

Today, the Sítio is used as a botany research and teaching centre, with **tours** of the property and grounds given mostly in Portuguese, but sometimes in English (check when booking). Burle Marx was not only a collector of plants but also of Brazilian folk art and Peruvian ceramics – his vast collection is on display along with his own paintings and textiles inside the house. A small chapel, dating from 1610, and the Sítio's original colonial-era farmhouse are also on the grounds.

Zona Norte

The parts of the **Zona Norte** you'll have seen on the way in from the city's transport terminals aren't very enticing, and they're a fair reflection of the general tenor of northern Rio. Most of the area between the international airport and the city centre is given over to vast *favelas* and other low-income housing, but a few places – Macaranã Stadium, the zoo, the Museu Nacional, the Quinta da Boa Vista and the **Feira Nordestina** (see pages 105 and 108) – are worth making the effort to visit.

Quinta da Boa Vista

Av. Pedro II, São Cristovão • Daily 9am–5pm • Free • 21 3878 4200 • São Cristovão

In the sixteenth and seventeenth centuries, the **Quinta da Boa Vista** was part of a *sesmaria* (royal land grant) held by the Jesuits, who used it as a sugar plantation, but in 1808 it became the royal family's *chácara* (country seat) when Portuguese merchant Elias Antônio Lopes presented the Palácio de São Cristovão (now the Museu Nacional) and surrounding lands to Dom João VI. Today, the park, with its wide-open expanses of greenery, tree-lined avenues, lakes, sports areas and games tables, is an excellent place for a stroll, though at weekends it can get very crowded.

Museu Nacional

Quinta da Boa Vista, São Cristóvão • Winter Mon noon–5pm, Tues–Sun 10am–4pm; summer Mon noon–6pm, Tues–Sun 10am–6pm, last ticket sold an hour before closing • R$6 • 21 3938 1100, museunacional.ufrj.br

In the centre of the Quinta da Boa Vista, on a small hill, the **Museu Nacional** is an imposing Neoclassical structure, and Brazil's oldest scientific institution, containing extensive archeological, zoological and botanic collections, an excellent ethnological section and a good display of artefacts dating from classical antiquity – around a million pieces in total.

The **archeological** section deals with the human history of Latin America, displaying Peruvian ceramics, the craftsmanship of the ancient Aztec, Mayan and Toltec civilizations of Mexico and mummies excavated in the Chiu-Chiu region of Chile. In the Brazilian room, exhibits of Tupi-Guaraní and Marajó ceramics lead on to the indigenous **ethnographical** section, uniting pieces collected from the numerous indigenous peoples who once populated Brazil. The genocidal behaviour of Brazil's European settlers, together with the ravages of disease, reduced the indigenous population from an estimated six million in 1500 to the present-day total of fewer than two hundred thousand. The **ethnological** section has a room dedicated to Brazilian folklore, centred on an exhibition of the ancient Afro- and Indo-Brazilian cults – such as *macumba*, candomblé and *umbanda* – that still play an important role in modern Brazilian society.

The mineral collection's star exhibit is the **Bendigo Meteorite**, which landed in the state of Bahia in 1888 (for sign-seekers, the year slavery was abolished). Its original weight of 5360kg makes it the heaviest metallic mass known to have fallen through the Earth's atmosphere. Elsewhere in the museum, you'll find Etruscan pottery, Greco-Roman ceramics, Egyptian sarcophagi and prehistoric remains – all in all, a good half-day's worth of exploring.

Jardim Zoólogico

Quinta da Boa Vista, São Cristóvão • Tues–Sun 9am–5pm (last ticket sold at 4pm) • R$15 • 21 3878 4200, riozoo.com.br

Founded in 1888, Rio's **zoo** was run-down for decades. Now that it's been spruced up, the animals look happier and the grounds are now kept scrupulously clean by zealous functionaries, but it's still an old-fashioned site where animals are kept in small cages. That said, the zoo serves an important scientific role in Brazil, managing some prominent breeding programmes for endangered native fauna.

The zoo's **Museu da Fauna** has a collection of stuffed birds, mammals and reptiles from throughout Brazil that is worth a passing look at on the way in.

Maracanã Stadium

Rua Professor Eurico Rabelo, Maracanã • Guided tours hourly 9am–4pm, last tour on match days 7hr before kick-off • R$60 • tourmaracana.com.br • Maracanã, or bus #402 and #435 from Leblon, Ipanema, Copacabana and Flamengo

To the west of Quinta da Boa Vista, a short walk across the rail line, over the Viaduto São Cristovão, stands the **Maracanã** or, more formally, the Estádio Jornalista Mário Filho. Built in 1950 for the World Cup, it's the biggest stadium of its kind in the world, holding nearly 200,000 people – in the final match of the 1950 tournament, 199,854 spectators turned up here to watch Brazil lose 1–0 to Uruguay, and well over 100,000 fans attend local derbies, such as the Flamengo v Fluminense fixture. During November and December, games are often played here three times a week, as many

1

GETTING TO THE MARACANÃ AND SEEING A GAME

The easiest way to reach the Maracanã is by **metrô** to Maracanã station (line 2), which has a walkway directly to the stadium; the adjacent stations are also within easy walking distance.

Arrive in plenty of time (at least a couple of hours before kick-off) to buy your ticket at any of the **ticket offices** set in the perimeter wall. The stadium is now all-seater, with tickets costing R$80–240. Things get frantic around the ticket offices before big games and if you're not there early enough you may get stranded outside, as the kiosk attendants leave their positions as soon as the starting whistle blows so as not to miss an early goal. For really big games, it's best to buy your ticket in advance. The *metrô* is pretty efficient at shifting people away fast after matches, but of course all transport is packed, so watch your belongings in the thick crowds and, if travelling both ways by *metrô*, buy a return ticket on the way up to avoid queuing on the way back.

of Rio's teams have followings that exceed the capacity of their own stadiums. The stadium hosted the opening and closing ceremonies of the 2016 Olympic Games.

Attending a **game** is one of the most extraordinary experiences Rio has to offer, even if you don't like football, and it's worth going just for the theatrical spectacle. The stadium looks like a futuristic colosseum, its upper stand (the *arquibancadas*) rising almost vertically from the playing surface. Great silken banners wave across the stand, shrouded by the smoke from fireworks, while support for each team is proclaimed by the insistent rhythm of massed samba drums that drive the game along. *Carioca* supporters are animated to say the least, often near hysterical, but their love of the game is infectious.

The Maracanã is open for **guided tours**, too. You'll be shown through the interesting **Museu dos Esportes**, with its extensive collection of Brazilian sporting memorabilia, and get to see the view from the presidential box (reached by lift), wander through the changing rooms and have a chance to tread on the hallowed turf itself.

ARRIVAL AND DEPARTURE — RIO DE JANEIRO CITY

You're most likely to **fly** into Rio or arrive by **bus**, as the city's train station is now only used for commuter services. Be warned that opportunistic **thieves** are active at all points of arrival, so don't leave baggage unattended or valuables exposed.

BY PLANE

GALEÃO

Rio is served by two airports. The Aeroporto Galeão, now officially called Aeroporto Internacional Antônio Carlos Jobim (☎21 3398 5050, ⓦaeroportogaleao.net), is 20km north of the city, serving destinations abroad and throughout Brazil, including most state capitals.

Facilities In the arrivals hall, you'll find tourist information desks (daily 6am–3am; ☎21 3398 4077) supplying information about the city. Changing money is not a problem as there are bank branches and ATMs in the arrivals hall and on the airport's third floor. Departure desks are split into three sections: internal Brazilian flights from Sector A; sectors B and C for international flights.

By bus to the city centre To reach a hotel in Centro, take a/c premium bus #2145 (daily 5.30am–9.30pm; R$14), which runs to Santos Dumont airport via Centro. City buses #324 and #326 also link Centro with the airport, but are not a great idea if you've just arrived with all your worldly wealth and baggage. For the Zona Sul (Copacabana, Ipanema and around), premium bus #2018 (daily 5.30am–11pm; R$16) runs to the Rodoviária Novo Rio and along the coast to Flamengo, Copacabana, Ipanema and Leblon. Alternatively, get a BRT bus two stops to Vicente de Carvalho, where you can change onto the *metrô*, for R$11 altogether, including a rechargeable R$3 Bilhete Único Carioca (see page 91).

By taxi to the city centre During the night, when these buses don't run, a taxi ride is the only option. Buy a ticket at the taxi desks, near the arrivals gate, and give it to the driver at the taxi rank; a ticket to Centro costs R$56 and to Botafogo, Copacabana R$74, Ipanema R$68. Most hotels and hostels can arrange an airport pick-up for a similar price, and may even offer it for free. Above all, don't risk accepting a lift from one of the unofficial drivers hanging about in the airport – robbery at their hands is far from uncommon. The ride takes about 15min into the centre or approximately 30min to Zona Sul, unless you hit rush hour.

SANTOS DUMONT

Santos Dumont airport (☎21 3814 7070, ⓦaeroporto-santosdumont.net) at the north end of the Parque do Flamengo in the city centre mainly handles the shuttle ervices to and from São Paulo. The airport's facilities ıclude a *guarda volumes* (left luggage office).

ɜy tram to the city centre The VLT tram line #1 has a top in front of the airport, from where regular trams serve he city centre, the port area and Rodoviária Novo Rio bus erminal.

ɜy taxi to the city centre Taxis (yellow with a blue tripe) are readily available from outside the terminal, nd fares are posted up at the airport's northernmost exit - R$18 to Centro, R$33 to Copacabana, R$41 to Ipanema, lightly more at night.

ɜy bus to the city centre You can take a premium bus rom the north end of the forecourt (to your right as you xit the arrivals hall) or cross Avenida General Justo on the edestrian walkway at the north end of the forecourt and atch an ordinary bus from the stop on the other side: #483 o Botafogo or #SV474 to Copacabana.

Destinations São Paulo (approximately every 15min, am–10.30pm; 1hr); plus a few flights to destinations in he states of Rio and Minas Gerais.

BY BUS

All major intercity bus services arrive at the Rodoviária Novo Rio (21 3213 1800, novorio.com.br), 3km north of Centro in the São Cristovão *bairro*, close to the city's dockside at the corner of Avenida Rodrigues Alves and Avenida Francisco Bicalho. The tourist office desk (daily 5am–midnight) is located in the arrivals hall – they'll give you a map and advise which buses to catch. There are spotlessly clean showers at the rodoviária (R$8, soap and towel included), and a *guarda volumes* (left luggage office).

Booking tickets Leaving Rio by bus, it's best to book a couple of days in advance for popular in-state destinations such as Búzios or Paraty if travelling at weekends, and for international and popular interstate routes, or for any journeys immediately before or after Carnaval. The bus companies' ticket offices are inside the terminal. You can reach the rodoviária on VLT tram lines #1 and #2 and on bus #331, #349 or #443 from Centro, #442, #443, #445 or #485 from Copacabana, and #404 or #443 from Ipanema.

By bus, tram or taxi to the city centre On arrival either purchase a voucher for a taxi (R$25 to Centro, R$30 to Botafogo, R$43 to Copacabana), or catch premium bus #2017 along the coast towards Copacabana, Ipanema and Leblon (5.50am–9.30pm; R$8). You can also cross the road to the ordinary bus terminal in Praça Hermes, where you can pick up several lines including #443 and #TRO-4 to Centro, Flamengo, Botafogo, Copacabana, Ipanema and beyond. For Centro, you can take the VLT tram, which stops right outside the Rodoviária.

International destinations Asunción (6 weekly; 28hr); Buenos Aires (6 weekly; 40–45hr); Santiago de Chile (1 weekly; 72hr). For Montevideo, change at São Paulo.

Domestic destinations Angra dos Reis (approximately hourly; 3hr); Belém (1 daily; 51hr); Belo Horizonte (17 daily, most overnight; 6hr 30min); Brasília (3 daily; 20hr); Búzios (8 daily; 3hr); Cabo Frio (1–2 hourly; 2hr 45min); Campo Grande (2 daily; 24hr); Florianópolis (1 daily; 18hr); Fortaleza (1 daily; 46hr); Foz do Iguaçu (5 daily; 23hr); Ouro Preto (3 daily; 7hr); Paraty (12 daily; 4hr 30min); Petrópolis (every 40min; 1hr 30min); Porto Seguro (1 daily; 19hr); Recife (6 weekly; 36hr); Salvador (1 daily; 32hr); São Luis (1 daily; 50hr); São Paulo (approximately every 15min; 6hr); Teresópolis (hourly; 1hr 45min); Vitória (10 daily; 8hr).

GETTING AROUND

BY METRÔ

Rio's *metrô* (www.metrorio.com.br), inaugurated in 1979, runs Monday to Saturday 5am–midnight, Sunday and public holidays 7am–11pm, with supposedly three lines (1, 2 and 4), but in practice just two. Linha 1 runs from Uruguai station in the *bairro* of Maracanã through Centro, and Copacabana to Ipanema, where the same train continues on what is called Linha 4 to Jardim Oceanico at the eastern end of Barra de Tiujuca. Linha 2 comes in from Pavuna, north of the city, via the Maracanã stadium, and merges with Linha 1 at Central, continuing with it to Botafogo, except on Sundays when it runs to Estácio instead. The system is very efficient and the trains air-conditioned, which is a relief if you've just descended from the scorching world above. During rush hours (Mon–Fri 6–9am & 5–8pm) one carriage is reserved for women only. Tickets are R$4.30, and various combined *metrô*/bus fares are available. You can buy individual tickets, but if you're going to use public transport a lot, consider getting a rechargeable Bilhete Único Carioca card (see below).

BILHETE ÚNICO CARIOCA

The **Bilhete Único Carioca** is a rechargeable card that can be used on the *metrô* and buses in Rio, and also in Niteroí, and is the only form of payment accepted on the VLT tram system. It can be purchased and charged up with credit in machines (but not in the ticket office) at many (but not all) *metrô* stations, and at all VLT tram stops. The card costs R$3, and is supposed to save you time queuing at *metrô* ticket offices, which it can do, except that often the queue for the machines to charge it up is longer than the queue to buy tickets (VLT stops tend to have shorter queues than *metrô* stations). On buses, at present anyway, you can always pay in cash instead.

BY BUS

Rio's buses (@rioonibus.com) are extremely handy. They run till midnight and you never have to wait more than a few moments for one Numbers and destinations are shown on the front of the bus, and bus stops often have signs to tell you which routes stop there and where they go. Fares are usually R$3.60.

Practicalities You get on at the front, pay the seated conductor (the price is on a card behind his head) or place a rechargeable card on the reader, and then push through the turnstile and find yourself a seat. Buses can get very full at rush hour (around 7–9am & 5–7pm), so if your journey is short, start working your way to the back of the bus as soon as you're through the turnstile; you alight at the back. If the bus reaches the stop before you reach the back, haul on the bell and the driver will wait. In the beach areas of the Zona Sul, especially along the coast, bus stops are not always marked. Stick your arm out to flag the bus down, or look for groups of people by the roadside facing the oncoming traffic, as this indicates a bus stop.

Safety When crowded, buses may attract opportunistic thieves and pickpockets. As a precaution therefore, don't leave wallets or money in easily accessible pockets and don't flash cameras around. Have your fare ready or use a rechargeable card (see page 91) so that you can pass through the turnstile immediately – pickpockets often work the entrance – and make sure that you carry any items in front of you as you pass through the turnstile. Buses known to carry mostly tourists (such as those to Sugar Loaf Mountain) are particularly considered easy targets by thieves.

BRT buses In addition to ordinary buses, there are special (and more expensive) rapid-transit of BRT buses (@brtrio.com), which have specially dedicated corridors to tale them though the traffic in certain parts of town, mostly in the suburbs. There are four main BRT corridors, each with stopping (*parador*) and express services. The most useful BRT route is from Galeão airport to Vicente de Carvalho *metrô* station.

BY TRAM AND LIGHT RAIL

Trams Rio's oldest trams, the *bondes* (pronounced "bonjis") climb from near Largo da Carioca, across the eighteenth century Aqueduto da Carioca (Arcos de Lapa), up to Sant Teresa (see page 72) Mon–Sat 11am–4pm every 20min.

VLT Of more practical use, a new tram (or light rail) service called the VLT (*Veículo Leve sobre Trilhos* or "Light Vehicle on Rails"; ☎0800 000 0858, @vltrio.rio) has two lines: line 1 from Santos Dumont airport and line 2 from Praça XV which both run, by different routes, through Centro to the Rodoviária Novo Rio. There are plans for a third line too. The only way to pay a VLT fare is with a Bilhete Único Carioc (see page 91), which can be bought from and charged a machines at all VLT stops. The VLT runs daily 7am–midnigh and the fare is R$3.80.

BY FERRY AND HYDROFOIL

From Praça XV de Novembro, ferries (@www.grupoccr com.br) transport passengers across Guanabara Bay to Praça Araribóio in central Niterói (daily 6.30am–11.30pm Mon–Fri every 20min, Sat every 30min, Sun hourly 20min; R$5.90) and Paquetá Island (Mon–Fri 5.30am–midnight, Sat, Sun & public holidays 4.30am–midnight approximately every 2hr; last boat back Mon–Fri 11.10pm Sat & Sun 11.30pm; R$5.90). There's also a hydrofoil service to Eastação Charitas near Niterói (Mon–Fri 6.50am–8.10pm; 2–3 hourly; 10min; R$16.50).

BY TAXI

Taxis in Rio come in two varieties: yellow ones with a blue stripe that cruise the streets, and the larger, newer, a/c radio cabs, which are white with a red-and-yellow stripe and are ordered by phone. Both have meters, and unless you've pre-paid at the airport, you should insist that they are activated The flag, or *bandeira*, over the meter denotes the tariff.

Prices Generally speaking, Rio's taxi services are reasonably priced (Centro to Ipanema costs around R$37, Botafogo to Copacabana around R$15) and it is not in the cabbies

RIO'S USEFUL BUS ROUTES

Between Centro and the Zona Sul, most buses run along the coast as far as **Botafogo**; those for **Copacabana** continue around the bay, past the Rio Sul shopping centre, and through the Pasmado Tunnel; those for **Leblon**, via Jóquei (the Jockey Club), turn right at Botafogo and travel along Avenida São Clemente. Useful websites for finding bus routes are @onilinhas.com.br/rio-de-janeiro and @vadeonibus.com.br.

From Rodoviária Novo Rio #361, #332, #443 to Centro; #497 to Lapa and Catete; #404, #441 or #443 to Copacabana; #404 or #443 to Ipanema.

From Avenida Rio Branco #442 to Copacabana and Ipanema, #443 to Copacabana, Ipanema and Leblon.

From Avenida Beira Mar, Lapa (near Praça Deodoro): #TR-10 (via Jardim Botânico and the Jockey Club/Jóquei), #TRO-2 and #TRO-4 (via Praia do Botafogo) to Leblon; #309 and #409 via Botafogo to Jardim Botânico.

From Copacabana #TRO-1, TRO-,3, TRO-4, #415, #442, #455 to Centro; #435, #455, #456, #457 to Maracanã.

nterest to alienate tourists by ripping them off. At night prices are about ten percent higher. Radio cabs are thirty percent more expensive than the regular taxis, but they are reliable: companies include Coopertramo (21 2209 9292, radio-taxi.com.br) and Transcoopass (21 2209 1555, transcoopass.com.br). Rio is also covered by Uber (uber.com/cities/rio-de-janeiro).

BY CAR

Rio's road system is characterized by a confusion of one-way streets, tunnels, access roads and flyovers, and parking is either difficult or impossible. Lane discipline is not much adhered to, overtaking on the right appears to be mandatory and, between 10pm and 6am, to avoid an armed hold-up, you need only slow down at a red traffic light. If you rent a car, it's best to only use it for trips out of town, thus avoiding the worst of Rio driving; consider collecting it on a Sunday morning when traffic is at its lightest.

Car rental Most companies are represented at the international airport and, in Centro, at Santos Dumont airport. In Zona Sul, they have offices in the following locations, all on Avenida Princesa Isabel in Copacabana: Avis, at no. 350 (0800 725 2847); Hertz, no. 500 (0800 701 7300); Localiza, no. 150 (21 3575 5250); Unidas, no. 168 (0800 771 5158 or 21 3873 2521).

BY BICYCLE

Cycling – along with skateboarding and rollerblading – is particularly good on Sundays when the beach roads along Parque de Flamengo are closed to motorized traffic.

City bikes Rio' has a city bike system (BikeRio), with orange bicycles (painted with the logo of Itaú bank) available at ranks citywide. You will need a mobile phone and credit or debit card to liberate them. A daily pass to use them is R$5, a monthly pass (for which you need to register) R$10. There's no further payment for any journey of less than an hour, and it's R$5/hr thereafter. You will find the necessary information at bikerio.tembici.com.br, or you can call 21 4003 6054.

Bike rental Bike in Rio (21 98474 7740, bikeinriotours.com) rents bikes at R$14/hr or R$100/day. In Ipanema you can rent bikes from Bike Tours at Rua Barão da Torre 175, casa 14 (21 96671 6683) for R$15/hr or R$50/day.

INFORMATION

Tourist information There are two official tourist agencies in the city. Information about the city of Rio is from Riotur (rio.rj.gov.br/riotur, visit.rio), which distributes maps and brochures and has information booths at Rodoviária Novo Rio, both airports, Praça XV, Copacabana (21 2298 7890), Ipanema, Lapa and dotted about town. Information about other parts of the state of Rio is put out by TurisRio (www.turisrio.rj.gov.br), based at Rua Uruguaiana 118 in Centro (21 3803 9366).

TOURS

Bike in Rio 21 98474 7740, **bikeinriotours.com.** Bicycle tours of Rio (four different ones) and bicycle rentals.

★ **Favela Tour** 21 3322 2727, **favelatour.com.br.** Marcelo Armstrong's walking tours of the Rocinha and Vila Canoas *favelas* (see page 85).

Helisight 21 2511 2141, **helisight.com.br.** Panoramic helicopter rides from Morro da Urca, including a 4–5min jaunt around Sugar Loaf Mountain and Copacabana for R$230 per person or a full hour for R$1860 per person (minimum three people). Needless to say, the views are absolutely breathtaking.

Jungle Me 21 4105 7533, **jungleme.com.br.** Hikes in Parque Nacional da Tijuca (see page 87) and a Brazilian cooking class.

★ **Rio Hiking** 21 2552 9204, **riohiking.com.br.** Organizes hikes in Parque Nacional da Tijuca (see page 87) and bar-hopping tours of Lapa (see page 102), as well as out-of-town excursions.

ACCOMMODATION

There's usually no shortage of **accommodation** in Rio, but a huge variation in prices, not just from season to season but from day to day depending on demand; even basic hostels vary their prices on a daily basis. In principle, **high season** is from December to February, when advanced reservations are recommended, with the highest prices of all at Christmas and Carnaval. If you arrive at these times without a booking, it's advisable to either make one through a tourist office, or leave your luggage in the *guarda volumes* (baggage offices) at the *rodoviária* or Santos Dumont airport while you look, as lugging heavy bags around Rio in high summer is not recommended. During **Carnaval**, most hotels and hostels only accept bookings for a minimum of four nights' stay. In low season on the other hand, many hotels lower prices by between thirty and fifty percent. The highest concentrations of **budget places** are in Glória, Catete and Flamengo, with numerous good **hostels** in Botafogo, Copacabana and Ipanema. Oasis (oasiscollections.com) offer apartments in Rio from around R$200 a day for a one-bedroom unit (sleeping two). **Prices** quoted below include breakfast, unless stated otherwise.

1

CENTRO, CINELÂNDIA AND LAPA

Belga Hotel Rua Dos Andradas 129, Centro 21 2263 9086, belgahotel.com.br; Urugaiana; map p.62. The rooms are small (standard rooms have double beds only) but they use their space economically at this well-designed, cool and modern city-centre hotel in a 1927 Art Deco building, where the bar and restaurant have a Belgian theme and serve Belgian beer and bar snacks as well as hosting early music evenings (6.30–10pm) most Wednesdays and Fridays. R$207

Hotel Arcos Rio Palace Av Mem de Sá 117, Lapa 21 2242 8116, arcosriopalacehotel.com.br; Cinelândia; map p.62. A busy, well-equipped hotel that's secure, inexpensive and ideally situated for enjoying Lapa's nightlife, which you can look down on from the rooftop pool terrace. The street outside can get quite busy (double glazing keeps most of the noise out), and some of the beds are a bit on the hard side. R$311

Hotel Belas Artes Rua Visconde do Rio Branco 52, Centro 21 2252 6336, hotelbelasartes.com.br; Presidente Vargas; map p.62. This small city-centre hotel in a pretty 1930s building has three types of simply furnished but impeccably clean rooms at slightly varying rates, but all are good value. R$140

Hotel Ibis Rio Santos Dumont Av Marechal Câmara 280, Centro 21 3506 4500, ibis.com; Cinelândia; map p.62. Located just 200m from Santos Dumont airport, and ideal for a late arrival or early departure. Like most Ibis hotels in Brazil, the 330 rooms here are compact yet very comfortable, and offer excellent value, although breakfast is not included. R$268

Hotel Marajó Rua São Joaquim da Silva 99, Lapa 21 2224 4134, hotelmarajorio.com; Cinelândia; map p.62. An excellent budget choice with modern facilities, clean, spacious rooms and friendly service in the heart of vibrant Lapa very near to the Escadaria de Selarón. Rooms at the front can be noisy at night. R$166

Windsor Guanabara Av Presidente Vargas 392, Centro 21 2195 6000, windsorhoteis.com; Urugaiana; map p.62. Expense-account visitors tend to stay at this lone luxury hotel in the city centre. It lacks character but is good value and well run, with spacious guest rooms, a comfortable lounge, a business centre and the added bonus of a pool. Rates are generally cheaper at weekends. R$350

SANTA TERESA

★ **Casa Áurea** Rua Áurea 80, Santa Teresa 21 3081 4652, pousada-casa-aurea-rio.com; map p.62. In a charming house dating from 1871, this lovely *pousada* has twelve simple rooms, some with private bathrooms and a/c. Breakfast is served in the attractive courtyard garden, with the friendly, multilingual staff always on hand for local advice. Dorms R$70, doubles R$220

THREE PLACES TO STAY IN A FAVELA

Favela life is hard (see page 84), but the community spirit can be great. These are poor neighbourhoods, and some are very rough, but others are very welcoming, and give a taste of Rio life beyond the glamorous facade. Here are three places where you can stay in small, friendly *favelas* and see how the other half live.

Babilônia Rio Hostel (Babilônia) See page 95

The Maze (Tavares Bastos) See page 95

Varandas do Vidigal (Vidigal) See page 97

★ **Hotel Santa Teresa** Rua Almirante Alexandrino 660, Santa Teresa 21 3380 0200, santateresahotelrio.com; map p.62. Once a down-at-heel hostel, this imposing 1860s building has been transformed into one of Rio's most beautiful and efficiently run hotels. The guest and communal rooms are decorated in natural colours, using a mix of fibres and woods to convey a modern Brazilian look. Many of the rooms have views of Centro and the bay, as does the infinity pool. Rs942

GLÓRIA, CATETE AND FLAMENGO

Golden Park Hotel Rua do Russel 374, Glória 21 2555 2700, nacionalinn.com.br; Glória; map p.75. This medium-sized hotel has modern facilities including a sauna and a small rooftop pool. Rooms are well kitted-out, but be sure to request one at the front, where you'll get more light and have a park view. R$938

Hotel Inglês Rua Silveira Martins 20, Catete 21 2558 3452, hotelingles.com.br; Catete; map p.75. This small, long-established and pleasantly old-fashioned hotel is one of the best-value places to stay in Catete. The rooms are a little bit sombre, but all have bathrooms, a/c, TV and *frigobar*, and the staff are friendly and helpful. R$230

Hotel Regina Rua Ferreira Viana 29, Flamengo 21 3289 9999, hotelregina.com.br; Catete; map p.75. Rooms are on the small side but they are well looked after and feature all the basics: comfortable beds, minibars and a/c, pleasant public areas and an excellent location one block from the beach. Actual prices are usually substantially lower than this published "rack" rate. R$500

Imperial Hotel Rua do Catete 186, Catete 21 2112 6000, imperialhotel.com.br; Catete; map p.75. Spacious, modern rooms are housed in a distinguished-looking 1880s building well located near the *metrô* and the park. Parking is available and there's also a decent-sized pool, which is unusual for a hotel in this price category. R$186.90

★**The Maze** Rua Tavares Bastos 414, Casa 66, Catete 21 2558 5547, themazerio.com; Catete or Largo do Machado; map p.75. The most interesting place to stay in Rio, and a work of art in itself, designed and run by the BBC's former Rio correspondent, and famous for its jazz nights (see page 105), it has a range of rooms, all en-suite, none exactly rectangular. With stunning panoramic views of Guanabara Bay, it has featured in movies and music videos, and has accommodated numerous celebrities and film stars. The *favela* around it is friendly, with no security issues day or night – indeed, there's a big BOPE (SWAT-style police) station right behind the hotel. Minibuses and motorbike taxis from the junction of Tavares Bastos with Bento Lisboa will take you up there. On Sundays they have a R$69 curry buffet, serving the best and most authentic Indian food in the whole of Brazil. R$140

Windsor Flórida Rua Ferreira Viana 81, Flamengo 21 2195 6800, windsorhoteis.com.br; Catete; map p.75. A sleek, modern hotel, with light-coloured wood and cool cream decor in the rooms, the nicest of which overlook the gardens of the neighbouring Palácio do Catete. Amenities include a rooftop pool, a gym, a good restaurant and a business centre. R$493.35

BOTAFOGO

Enseada Rio Hostel Praia de Botafogo 462, Casa 5 21 2226 0461, enseadariohostel.com.br; Botafogo; map p.76. A quiet little hostel in an old house located on an alleyway with a couple of other hostels. Dorms of various sizes include one for women only. Dorms R$40, doubles R$150

Hotel Mercure Botafogo Mourisco Rua da Passagem 39 21 2131 1212, mercure.com; Botafogo; map p.76. Oriented to business travellers, this 110-room hotel offers large, comfortable rooms (ask for one with a view towards the Corcovado), an outdoor pool and a reasonable restaurant. Rates vary with demand, but tend to be cheaper if booked online. R$464

★**Vila Carioca Hostel** Rua Estácio Coimbra 84 21 2535 3224, vilacarioca.com.br; Botafogo; map p.76. Not as raucous as some hostels but extremely friendly, with an attractive lounge and terrace-garden for relaxing. Located on a quiet, safe street a block from the *metrô*. Dorms R$35, doubles R$130

COPACABANA AND LEME

Copacabana's beach scene won't appeal to everybody, and while the area has certainly seen better days, it still has by far the greatest concentration of places to stay in the city, ranging from hostels to luxury hotels. Leme – really a continuation of Copacabana – is less frenetic thamks to its location at the far end of the stretch of beach in the opposite direction to Ipanema. Edifício Jucati at Rua Tenente Marones de Gusmão 85 (21 2547 5422, edificiojucati.com.br; map p.81) has self-catering studio apartments for R$150 per night for two people.

Apa Hotel Rua República do Peru 305, Copacabana 21 2548 8112, www.apahotel.com.br; Cardeal Arcoverde; map p.81. This is a decent mid-range hotel well located in a central area of Copacabana. The rooms are airy and spacious, all with a/c and balconies, and the ones that sleep four are particularly good value. Online prices are somewhat lower. Doubles R$388.50, quadruples R$441

★**Babilônia Rio Hostel** Ladeira Ari Barroso 50, Babilônia, Leme 21 3873 6826, babiloniariohostel.com.br; Siqueira Campos; map p.76. In a friendly little *favela* just above Leme, this bright and breezy hostel offers ocean views, a cool vibe and clean, airy dorms with three-storey bunks. Three-quarters of their electricity is generated by their own solar panels. It's a slight climb to get to, but there are motorbike taxis on hand at the bottom of the hill in case you're feeling lazy. Breakfast is R$5 per person extra. Dorms R$30, doubles R$100

Bamboo Rio Hostel Rua Lacerda Coutinho 45, Copacabana 21 2236 1117, bamboorio.com; Siqueira Campos; map p.81. Six blocks from the beach in a quiet, leafy suburb, *Bamboo Rio* is a hostel with refreshingly colourful, a/c rooms, a little plunge pool, great atmosphere, and a pleasant garden with wild monkeys. Excellent value – though prices can double or more over holidays. Dorms R$30, doubles R$100

Biarritz Hotel Rua Aires Saldanha 54, Copacabana 21 2287 6086, biarritzhotel@terra.com.br; Cantagalo; map p.81. Basic and unexciting, but clean and friendly place with everything you need (hot water, a/c) located in a quiet side-street one block back from Avenida Atlântica and the beach. R$299

Che Lagarto Hostel Rua Barata Ribeiro 111 21 3209 0348, chelagarto.com; Siqueira Campos; map p.81. Located in central Copacabana, three blocks from the beach, this well-established hostel is one of four *Che Largarto* places in Rio, with four- to six-bed dorms. They have another branch at Rua Santa Clara 304 with private rooms (R$120 weekdays, R$150 weekends), and similar properties in Ipanema. Prices may be less (or more) depending on the day. Dorms R$75

★**Copacabana Palace Hotel** Av Atlântica 1702, Copacabana 21 2548 7070, copacabanapalace.com.br; Cardeal Arcoverde; map p.81. Anyone who's anyone has stayed in this gloriously maintained Art Deco landmark, which, despite Copacabana's general decline, remains a great experience. Although every possible facility is on offer, there's a curious lack of communal areas, apart from the large pool in a central courtyard. All in all, this is a great place to relax, if you can afford it. R$2094

Hotel Acapulco Copacabana Rua Gustavo Sampaio 854, Leme 21 3077 2000, acapulcohotel.com.br;

1

Ⓜ Cardeal Arcoverde; map p.81. This comfortable, highly recommended hotel is in a quiet location near the beach, a couple of minutes' walk from the Cardeal Arcoverde *metrô* station. Rooms are modern, reasonably spacious and well decorated; some of the balconies just about offer a beach view, and the staff are very helpful. R$300

Hotel Atlantis Copacabana Rua Bulhões de Carvalho 61, Copacabana ➊ 21 2521 1142, Ⓦ atlantishotel.com.br; Ⓜ General Osório; map p.81. In a quiet location just one block from Ipanema, this good-value hotel has bright, gleaming rooms done out in white and apricot, and helpful, efficient staff. The small rooftop pool has great views. R$350

Hotel Porto Bay Rio International Av Atlântica 1500, Copacabana ➊ 21 2546 8000, Ⓦ portobay.com; Ⓜ Cardeal Arcoverde; map p.81. A cut above Copacabana's other seafront hotels, partly thanks to the attentive staff, but mainly down to the well thought out design of the place. Protruding windows give lots of light and panoramic views of the beach, and there's a rooftop pool and a good restaurant. Prices do not usually include breakfast. R$580

Hotel Santa Clara Rua Décio Vilares 316, Copacabana ➊ 21 2256 2650, Ⓦ hotelsantaclara.com.br; Ⓜ Siqueira Campos; map p.81. Delightful *pension*-style hotel, excellent value, quiet and very homey, with friendly, helpful staff. The rooms are simple but have everything you need. R$255

Hotel Toledo Rua Domingos Ferreira 71, Copacabana ➊ 21 2257 1990, Ⓦ hoteltoledo.com.br; Ⓜ Siqueira Campos; map p.81. Not the slickest hotel in Copacabana, but a decent mid-range choice, just a block from the beach, with large if slightly chintzy rooms and the air of a friendly seaside guesthouse. R$317

Rio Design Hotel Rua Francisco Sá 17, Copacabana ➊ 21 3222 8800, Ⓦ riodesignhotel.com; Ⓜ Cantagalo; map p.81. One of the few hotels in Rio that dares to be a bit different. Each floor has been conceived by a different Brazilian designer, with some much more successful than others. Decor differs in terms of colour, tone and texture, but all the rooms are well equipped, if on the small side. Located less than a block from the beach. R$518

Rio Othon Palace Hotel Av Atlântica 3264, Copacabana ➊ 21 2106 1500, Ⓦ othon.com.br; Ⓜ Cantagalo; map p.81. With almost 600 guest rooms, this is a favourite of tour groups. The hotel has all the facilities you'd expect of a place this size and price, including several bars and restaurants, a rooftop pool and a business centre. Rooms facing the front have marvellous ocean views. R$575

Windsor Excelsior Av Atlântica 1800, Copacabana ➊ 21 2195 5800, Ⓦ windsorhoteis.com; Ⓜ Cardeal Arcoverde; map p.81. Well-run upper-end choice in the middle of Copacabana's beachfront. Rooms are small but well equipped, with tasteful decor, the staff are supe professional and the rooftop pool has spectacular view: R$451

Windsor Martinique Rua Sá Ferreira 30, Copacaban ➊ 21 2195 5200, Ⓦ windsorhoteis.com; Ⓜ Cantagalc map p.81. Popular hotel located near the quiet, wester end of Copacabana, close to the Forte de Copacabana Modern rooms have large, exceptionally comfortable bed and there's a small rooftop pool. R$341

ARPOADOR, IPANEMA AND LEBLON

Bonita Rua Barão da Torre 107, Ipanema ➊ 21 222 1703, Ⓦ bonitaipanema.com; Ⓜ Nossa Senhora da Paz map p.76. Bright candy pink on the outside, but wit rather more subdued blue and white decor in the rooms this little *pousada* was once the home of jazz and boss nova legend Tom Jobim, who lived here in the early 1960 at the height of his career. History aside, the place is quiet it's pretty, and it even has a pool – all in all, excellent value Dorms R$70, doubles R$199

Caesar Park Hotel Av Vieira Souto 460, Ipanema ➊ 2 2525 2525, Ⓦ sofitel.com; Ⓜ Nossa Senhora da Paz map p.76. One of Rio's finest hotels, the *Caesar Par* features every modern luxury that its celebrity guest would expect. Even the most basic of rooms are vast, wit elegant furniture and huge beds. The rooftop restauran and pool have superb views, and the hotel provide security and lifeguards on the beach fronting the property Rates do not include breakfast. R$788

Hostel New Ipanema Rua Barão da Torre,175, Cas 1, Ipanema ➊ 21 2522 2665; Ⓜ General Osório; ma p.76. This small hostel is a bit pokey, but prices are lov for Ipanema (and even lower out of season), it's decen enough if you're on a tight budget, and there are a coupl more cheap hostels in the same alley. Dorms R$70, double R$120

Hotel Fasano Rua Viera Souto 80, Ipanema ➊ 2 3202 4000, Ⓦ fasano.com.br; Ⓜ General Osório; ma p.76. Ultra stylish – with prices to match (breakfast *no* included) – this Philippe Starck-designed hotel is *the* place to stay for visiting rock stars, supermodels and the like Rooms are on the small side, but their breathtaking ocea views, modern tropical-hardwood furnishings and cutting edge technology make them stand out. The rooftop coffe shop and infinity pool, and the hotel's trendy bar are idea celebrity-spotting hangouts. R$2964

Hotel Ipanema Plaza Rua Farme de Amoedo 34 Ipanema ➊ 21 3687 2000, Ⓦ goldentulipipanemaplaza com; Ⓜ General Osório; map p.76. Rooms and suites a this four-star hotel (part of the Dutch-owned Golden Tuli chain) are tastefully furnished with neutral, earthy tones and there's a small rooftop pool with wonderful beac views. It's popular with gay visitors thanks to its proximity to the beach's gay strip. R$574

★ **Ipanema Inn** Rua Maria Quitéria 27, Ipanema 21 2529 1000, ipanemainn.com.br; Nossa Senhora da Paz; map p.76. This excellent-value and very popular hotel is just a block from the beach and in one of the most fashionable parts of Ipanema. Comfortable rooms, while small, can squeeze in an extra (fold-out) bed. R$476

Lemon Spirit Hostel Rua Cupertino Durão 56, Leblon 21 2294 1853, lemonspirit.com; Antero de Quintal; map p.76. It's difficult to believe that there's this hostel in the heart of Leblon, just one block from the beach and in one of the oldest buildings in this exclusive *bairro*. All rooms are a/c, there's a guest kitchen and a nice patio. Dorms R$70

Mango Tree Hostel Rua Prudente de Moraes 594 21 3083 5031, mangotreehostel.com; Nossa Senhora da Paz; map p.76. A block from *posto* 9 on the beach, this is easily Ipanema's best hostel option. Spacious dorms, grand bathrooms and an overgrown garden with hammocks. Prices for the dorms fall by about half out of season. Dorms R$88, doubles R$208

Margarida's Pousada Rua Barão da Torre 600, Ipanema 21 2239 1840, margaridaspousada.com; Nossa Senhora da Paz; map p.76. Don't expect any frills, but do expect to feel right at home in this small, friendly B&B, where the rooms have a TV, fridge and compact bathroom. Book well ahead, however, as it fills up fast. R$220

Marina All Suites Rua Delfim Moreira 630, Leblon 21 2172 1100, allsuites.hoteismarina.com.br; Antero de Quintal; map p.76. The largest of Leblon's hotels has been revamped as an all-suite deluxe boutique hotel, with designer decor and what it bills as an "exclusive ambience", not to mention a beachside location and two snazzy bar restaurants, although it has to be said that the suites aren't actually as big as you might imagine; then again, neither are the prices. R$259

San Marco Hotel Rua Visconde de Pirajá 524, Ipanema 21 2540 5032, sanmarcohotelipanema.com.br; Nossa Senhora da Paz; map p.76. A good deal for its location, on the main shopping street just a few minutes from the beach. There are three grades of room, differing only in size – the economy rooms are small but still very neat and tidy. R$236.25

★ **South American Hotel Copacabana** Rua Francisco Sá 90, Arpoador 21 2227 9161, reservas@southamericanhotel.com.br; General Osório; map p.76. A few blocks' walk to Copacabana and Ipanema beaches, this excellent-value hotel offers bright, larger than average rooms, IKEA-style modern furnishings, a good buffet breakfast and a small rooftop pool. Typical prices are usually around half this official "rack" rate. R$470

Varandas do Vidigal Rua Madre Ana Coimbra, casa 3 (off Av Goulart), Vidigal 21 3114 3661, varandasdovidigal.com.br; map p.58. Amazing sea views make the climb worthwhile, at this super-friendly hostel in a vibrant community located to the west of Leblon. Buses #177, #521 and #522 and airport bus #2018 will take you to the entrance of the *favela*, from where there is transport up the hill. Dorms R$30, doubles R$125

EATING

Rio is well served by **restaurants** offering a wide variety of cuisines. *Cariocas* generally dine late, and restaurants don't start to fill up until after 9pm. Last orders are usually taken around midnight, but there are places where you can get a meal at 2am. Eating out in Rio can get pretty **expensive**, but there's no shortage of low-priced places to grab a lunchtime meal, or just a snack and a drink. There are numerous hamburger joints around town, but bear in mind that the beef used may well come from the Amazon, where immense ranches are displacing Indians, peasants and trees at a criminal rate; you'll get better and cheaper food at any *galeto* or *lanchonete*, of which there are plenty, though many are closed at night.

CENTRO, CINELÂNDIA AND LAPA

The restaurants in the city centre cater largely for people working in the area, and at lunchtime the service is rushed. There are lots of cheap eating places around Praça Tiradentes.

Ancoramar Praça Marechal Âncora 186, Centro 21 3513 1842, ancoramar.com.br; Uruguiana; map p.62. Housed in the remaining tower of the 1908 municipal market, this cool, green, octagonal building provides a superb view of Guanabara Bay. Waiters in uniform serve the likes of spiced seabass with plantain chutney (R$95) or pan-fried king prawns in rock-lobster sauce (R$278 for two). Mon–Fri 11am–5pm, Sat & Sun 11.30am–6pm.

Bar Ocidental Rua Miguel Couto 124, Centro 21 2253 4042; Uruguiana; map p.62. On a small pedestrianized street that runs alongside Rio Branco all the way up from Sete de Septembro, this is not a posh gaff, nor located in a posh neighbourhood, but you can sit at a table outside and enjoy an early evening *chopp* (R$6) and a plate of fresh sardines (R$2.50 per fish). Mon–Sat 7am–10pm.

Beduino Av Presidente Wilson 123 21 2524 5142, arabebeduino.com.br; Cinelândia; map p.62. Popular and inexpensive Arabic restaurant, where a full meze spread will set you back R$62.90, or you can get just three meze dishes for R$32.76. A great option

TOP 5 SEAFOOD RESTAURANTS

Caranguejo See page 99
Marius See page 99
Rio-Minho See page 98
Shirley See page 99
¡Venga! See page 100

for vegetarians and carnivores alike. Mon–Sat 7am–11.15pm.

Brasserie Rosário Rua do Rosário 34, Centro 21 2518 3033; Uruguiana; map p.62. Light dishes such as quiches and omelettes dominate the menu, but you can also get a steak (R$65) or the fish of the day (R$74). The bakery is especially good, serving delicious cakes and wonderful bread and sandwiches. Mon–Fri 11am–9pm, Sat 11am–6pm.

★ Confeitaria Colombo Rua Gonçalves Dias 32, Centro 21 9967 0081, confeitariacolombo.com.br; Uruguiana or Carioca; map p.62. Founded in 1894, this splendidly decorated Art Nouveau café-patisserie – a true relic of Rio's *belle époque* – is a wonderful place to take tea and cakes, although you may have to queue. There's also a rather plain-looking branch in the Forte de Copacabana. Mon–Fri 9am–7pm, Sat 9am–5pm.

Cosmopolita Travessa do Mosqueira 4, Lapa 21 2224 7820; Cinelândia; map p.62. An excellent Portuguese restaurant established in 1926, with a loyal, rather bohemian, clientele. Fish dishes, and especially those based on saltfish (all of which are R$120), are the firm favourites. Mon–Thurs 8am–10pm, Fri & Sat 8am–11pm.

Dona Vegana Av Marechal Floriano 13, Centro 21 2283 2012; Uruguiana; map p.62. A vegan *por quilo* restaurant, where R$44.90 will net you a kilo of animal-free grub, or you can pop in for a vegan *petisco*, or even some vegan salami. Mon–Fri 8am–6pm.

★ Rio-Minho Rua do Ouvidor 10, Centro 21 2509 2338; Uruguiana; map p.62. The *Rio-Minho* has been going strong since 1884, serving tasty Brazilian food, if a bit on the pricey side. The kitchen concentrates on seafood and the fish of the day (R$145) is always a treat, although they also do a superb *bobó* of *langostinhas* (Dublin bay prawns, which are not really prawns but pygmy lobsters; R$178). Mon–Fri 11am–4pm.

SANTA TERESA

Adega do Pimenta Rua Almirante Alexandrino 296 21 2224 7554, adegadopimenta.com.br; map p.62. Most people go to this moderately priced German spot for the sausages (R$42.90), but the duck (R$62) is also excellent. All dishes are served with an accompaniment of your choice such as sauerkraut or red cabbage, and there's German beer to wash it all down. Mon–Fri noon–10pm, Sat noon–8pm, Sun noon–6pm.

★ Aprazível Rua Aprazível 62 21 2508 9174, aprazivel.com.br; map p.62. Excellent, though expensive, French-influenced Minas Gerais dishes, plus an attractive terrace with wonderful views across Rio. The carnival-style octopus (with potatoes, olives, courgettes and aubergine; R$101) is a wondrous creation, and the goat (R$89) is roasted to perfection. Advance booking advised. Tues–Sat noon–11pm, Sun noon–6pm.

Bar do Arnaudo Rua Almirante Alexandrino 316 21 2210 0817, facebook.com/BarDoArnaudo; map p.62. Just up from the *Adega do Pimenta*, this is an excellent mid-priced place to sample traditional food from Brazil's Northeast such as *carne do sol* (sun-dried meat, served with sweet manioc; R$58) and *caldinho de feijão de corda* (bean soup with pork scratchings; R$6). Daily 11.30am–8pm.

Bar do Mineiro Rua Paschoal Carlos Magno 99 21 2221 9227, bardomineiro.net; map p.62. Inexpensive and authentic country-style food in an old bar that could be in any small town in Minas Gerais. Try the *carne seca abóbora* (dried meat in pumpkin purée; R$92) and there are also good beers and an excellent range of cachaça. Tues–Sun 11am–1am.

Espírito Santa Rua Almirante Alexandrino 264 21 2507 4840, espiritosanta.com.br; map p.62. Offers multi-regional Brazilian cuisine, the focus being on adaptations of flavoursome dishes from the Amazon, Bahia and Minas Gerais (seafood *bobó* R$68), with a fair few vegetarian versions (veg *moqueca* R$40.50). The dining room has a designer-rustic look, or you can eat on the terrace and enjoy wonderful views of the *bairro*. Daily noon–midnight.

GLÓRIA, CATETE AND FLAMENGO

Restaurants, *galetos* and *lanchonetes* are concentrated around the Largo do Machado, with small restaurants serving Brazilian, German, Italian, Japanese or Peruvian food along Rua Barão do Flamengo. On Sundays, *The Maze* (see page 95) offers an excellent curry lunch buffet.

Adega Portugália Largo do Machado 66a, Catete 21 2558 2821, adegaportugalia.com.br; Largo do Machado; map p.75. Don't miss out on the delicious house speciality at this popular bar/restaurant: casserole of tender roast goat (R$64.90), washed down with copious quantities of cold *chopp*. Daily 11am–midnight or later.

Julieta de Serpa Praia do Flamengo 340, Flamengo Flamengo; map p.75. Housed in the prettiest building in Flamengo, a mansion built in 1920, this extremely elegant, formal French restaurant offers top-notch dining (filet mignon R$70, fish of the day R$80) amid wonderful fin-de-siècle decor. There's also a bar and lavishly decorated tearoom, both of which are super-posh. Wed–Sat 7–11.30pm, Sun noon–5pm.

Lamas Rua Marquês de Abrantes, Flamengo 18 21 2556 0799, cafelamas.com.br; Flamengo; map p.75. This ever-popular restaurant has been serving well-prepared Brazilian food since 1874 (the R$95 Oswaldo Aranha steak – pan-fried with lots of garlic – is a staple). Always busy, with a vibrant atmosphere and clientele of artist and journalist types. Mon–Thurs & Sun 9.30am–2.30am, Fri & Sat 9.30am–3am.

Tacacá do Norte Rua Barão do Flamengo 35-R Flamengo 21 2205 7545; Largo do Machado; map p.75. A *lanchonete* (cheap diner) with a difference: here you can try delights from the Amazon like the signature dish, *tacacá* (yellow shrimp and cassava hot pepper soup; R$27), and easily the best *açaí* in Rio, served with tapioca and granola (R$24). Mon–Sat 9am–11pm, Sun 9am–7pm.

BOTAFOGO AND URCA

Bar Urca Rua Cândido Gaffrée 205, Urca ⓣ21 2295 3744, ⓦbarurca.com.br; map p.76. Equally good for a cold beer and *petiscos* or a seafood meal, this traditional neighbourhood gathering point, with a street bar and a restaurant upstairs, serves dishes such as fish surprise (fish fillet on prawn and nut rice; R$110 for one, R$160 for two) or prawn *bobó* (R$138 for one, R$181 for two). Restaurant: Mon–Sat 11.30am–11pm, Sun 11.30am–8pm; bar: Mon–Fri 6am–11pm, Sat 8am–11pm, Sun 8am–8pm.

Cobal Rua Voluntários da Pátria 446, Humaitá; ⓜBotafogo; map p.76. Humaitá's impressive indoor market, where you can take your pick of the moderately priced but excellent *lanchonetes* serving Brazilian Northeastern, Italian and Japanese food; this is a very popular lunch and evening meeting point for local residents. Daily 7am–11pm.

Garota da Urca Av João Luiz Alves 56, Urca ⓣ21 2541 5040; map p.76. *Garota da Urca* boasts one of the best views of any Rio restaurant, looking back towards Botafogo and the Corcovado, and the food – Brazilian with Italian twists – is decent enough, or you can stop by for just a drink. Try the *peixe a garota* – fish pieces with broccoli and rice (R$85). Daily 11am–2am.

★ **Miam Miam** Rua General Góes Monteiro 34, Botafogo ⓣ21 2244 0125, ⓦmiammiam.com.br; ⓜBotafogo; map p.76. Located in a nineteenth-century house typical of Botafogo, with a relaxed dining area decorated in a retro 1960s style, this treasure of a restaurant deserves going slightly out of the way for. Chef Roberta Ciasca comes up with modern Brazilian food at its most delicious – incorporating fresh, local ingredients presented with a European twist (palm heart *tagliarini* with prawns, for example, at R$78.90). They also plan to reintroduce their tasting menu (probably for around R$180). Tues–Fri noon–3.30pm & 7pm–midnight, Sat 1pm–midnight.

Ouioui Rua Conde de Irajá, 85, Botafogo ⓣ21 2527 3539; map p.76. *Miam Miam*'s sister restaurant, specializing in modern international cuisine, where everything is served in the form of mini-dishes at around R$40 a go, with options such as duck risotto, or saltfish with onion, egg and tapenade. Mon–Fri 7pm–midnight, Sat & Sun 8pm–midnight.

COPACABANA AND LEME

Arab Av Atlântica 1936, Copacabana ⓣ21 2235 1884; ⓜSiquiera Campos; map p.81. At this reasonably priced Lebanese and North African restaurant, you can enjoy meze (Lebanese *hors d'oeuvres* such as hummus or tabbouleh) at R$27 a portion, with main courses such as lamb couscous for R$62. Though the menu is rather heavy on meat choices, vegetarians certainly won't go hungry. Mon 5pm–1am, Tues–Sun 9am–1am.

★ **Bar do David** Ladeira Ari Barroso 66, Chapéu Mangueira ⓣ21 2542 4713; ⓜSiquiera Campos; map p.76. Up in a little *favela* just above Leme, chef David has received press accolades for excellent shrimp *bobó*, seafood croquettes, and in particular his signature seafood *feijoada* (R$45). It's also a great place for just a drink, but it does get quite rammed at weekends. Tues–Sun 11.30am–9pm.

★ **Caranguejo** Rua Barata Ribeiro 771, Copacabana ⓣ21 2235 1249, ⓦfacebook.com/ocaranguejocopacabana; ⓜCantagalo; map p.81. Excellent street-corner seafood joint, where you can start with a dozen crab claws for R$39 before you tuck into a succulent prawn stroganoff (R$186). Daily 11am–1am.

Cervantes Av Prado do Júnior 335-B and Rua Barata Ribeiro 7 ⓣ21 2275 6147, ⓦrestaurantecervantes.com.br; ⓜSiquiera Campos; map p.81. Doing a roaring trade day and night, you can try their speciality thick-wedge meat sandwiches (steak with cheese and pineapple R$32) in the stand-up bar on Barata Ribeiro or the sit-down restaurant on Prado do Júnior (they're joined at the back), the latter also serving steak meals (house-style *filet mignon* R$0). Tues–Sun noon–4am.

Deck Av Atlântica 2316, Copacabana ⓣ21 2256 3889, ⓦdeckrestaurante.com.br; ⓜSiquiera Campos; map p.81. This always-busy restaurant offers lunchtime buffets for R$20–26 until 4.30pm, then dishes such as fish steak in caper sauce (R$70) or seafood risotto (R$90) thereafter. Daily noon–midnight.

La Trattoria Rua Fernando Mendes 7, Copacabana ⓣ21 2255 0781 ⓦlatrattoriario.com.br; ⓜCardial Arcoverde; map p.81. Moderately priced premises serving the best Italian food in the *bairro*. Among the excellent range of pasta dishes, the *penne ai quattro formaggi* costs R$46.50, or there are prawn-stuffed cannelloni for R$51.80. Daily 11am–midnight.

Marisqueira Rua Barata Ribeiro 232, Copacabana ⓣ21 2547 2930; ⓜCardial Arcoverde; map p.81. For over fifty years, this restaurant has been serving well-prepared Portuguese-style food, with meat dishes such as roast goat or suckling pig (R$140), or a *mariscada* (seafood casserole) for R$105. Mon–Sat 11.30am–11.30pm, Sun 11.30am–8pm.

Marius Av Atlântica 290, Leme ⓣ21 2275 0632, ⓦmarius.com.br; ⓜCardial Arcoverde; map p.76. Rio's best-known place for oysters, crabs, rock lobster, prawns and other seafood choices, but also good for grilled meats. The menu is fixed at R$150 for a meat or fish platter, not including drinks or afters. Daily noon–11pm.

Shirley Rua Gustavo Sampaio 610a, Copacabana ⓣ21 2275 1398; ⓜCardial Arcoverde; map p.81. Great

1

little Spanish seafood restaurant, where a pukka paella for two will set you back R$135, or you can try the *zarzuela* (saffron-infused fish casserole) for R$55.80, and wash it down with a bottle of Rioja. Service is formal but friendly. Daily noon–midnight.

¡Venga! Av Atlântica 3880, Copacabana ⓣ21 3264 9806 ⓦvenga.com.br; ⓜGeneral Osório; map p.81. The best of three bars in this little chain, specializing in seafood, Spanish-style, especially tapas, made largely with locally caught fish landed right here in Copacabana. *Pulpo a la gallega* (boiled octopus drizzled with olive oil) will set you back R$72, or you can go the whole hog and tuck into a seafood paella at R$118 for two. Mon–Wed & Sun noon–midnight, Thurs–Sat noon–1.30am.

IPANEMA

Bazzar Rua Barão da Torre 538 ⓣ21 3202 2884, ⓦbazzar.com.br; ⓜNossa Senhora da Paz; map p.76. A super-cool, very modern restaurant, with elegantly functional, almost Japanese-style decor. House specialities include palm hearts and plantain in coconut milk (R$59) or rabbit in mustard sauce with mashed sweet potato and oyster mushrooms (R$75). Mon–Sat noon–midnight, Sun noon–7pm.

Bazzar Lado B Livraria da Travessa bookshop, Rua Visconde de Pirajá 572 ⓣ21 2249 4977, ⓦbazzar.com.br; ⓜNossa Senhora da Paz; map p.76. Rio's best bookshop also has a snacky café branch of *Bazzar*, which is super-cool and modern in style – a perfect spot for a break from Ipanema's main shopping area, with coffee and light meals such as spaghetti in tomato sauce for R$44, or *alla carbonara* for R$49. Mon–Sat 10am–11pm, Sun noon–11pm.

Big Nectar Rua Teixeira de Melo 34-A ⓣ21 2522 3949 and Rua dos Jangadeiros 15-B ⓣ21 2247 1459, ⓦbignectar.com.br; ⓜGeneral Osório; map p.76. At opposite ends of Ptaça General Osório, these bright little street-corner diners serve up juices, snacks and cheap combos (R$21–23) round the clock. Nothing special, but handy when you need them. There's another branch in Copacabana (at Av Nossa Senhora de Copacabana 985). Daily 24hr.

Casa da Feijoada Rua Prudente de Morais 10 ⓣ21 2247 2776, ⓦcozinhatipica.com.br; ⓜGeneral Osório; map p.76. Usually served only on Saturdays, *feijoada* is offered seven days a week here (R$93), along with other traditional, moderately priced and extremely filling Brazilian dishes. Daily noon–midnight.

Delírio Tropical Rua Garcia D'Ávila 48, Ipanema ⓣ21 3624 8164, ⓦdelirio.com.br; map p.76. Just a block from the beach and the best value for lunch you'll find anywhere near it, with lots of veggie options such as salads (R$16.50–25 and grilled trout (R$18.90), as well as light fish or meat options. In fact it's part of a chain, with

TOP 5 RESTAURANTS FOR REGIONAL CUISINE

Aprazível (Mineiro) See page 98
Bar do Arnaudo (Northeastern) See page 98
Bar do Mineiro (Minas Gerais) See page 98
Espírito Santa (various regions) See page 98
Tacacá do Norte (Amazon) See page 98

other branches around town. Mon–Sat 11am–9pm; Sun winter 11am–7pm; Sun summer noon–8pm.

Felice Caffé Rua Gomes Carneiro 30, Ipanema ⓣ21 2522 7749, ⓦwww.felice.com.br; ⓜGeneral Osório, map p.76. Excellent café and ice-cream parlour, where a one-scoop cornet will cost you R$11, and two scoops is R$20. Daily noon–midnight.

Fontes Galeria Astor, Rua Visconde de Pirajá 605 ⓣ21 2512 5900, ⓦfontesipanema.com.br; map p.76. *Fontes* does inexpensive dishes made with only natural ingredients, mostly vegetarian. The menu changes daily but typical dishes include aubergine (eggplant) au gratin (R$14.60), and on Saturdays a hearty vegetarian *feijoada* is served (R$17). Mon–Fri 11am–9.20pm, Sat 11am–8pm.

Gula Gula Rua Barão da Torre, 446 ⓣ21 3322 2150 ⓦgulagula.com.br; ⓜJardim de Alah; map p.76. A good choice of reasonably priced and very tasty salads and grilled dishes (such as Angus steak at R$64) makes this an Ipanema favourite – and in fourteen other spots around the city. The set menu is R$39.90. Daily noon–midnight.

Mil Frutas Café Rua Garcia d'Ávila 134-A, Ipanema ⓣ21 2521 1384, ⓦmilfrutas.com.br; map p.76. Ice-cream parlour boasting dozens of flavours – including exotic Brazilian fruit such as *pitanga* and *jaboticaba* – that vary according to the season, at R$14 for one scoop, R$2[illegible] for two. There are other branches around town. Mon–Fri 10am–midnight, Sat & Sun 9.30am–midnight.

New Natural Rua Barão de Torre 173, Ipanema ⓣ21 2287 0301; ⓜNossa Senhora da Paz; map p.76. Really good mainly vegetarian organic *por quilo* lunch place (R$49/kg) that always has a couple of meat choices too. Expect numerous salads, soya dishes and fresh juices. Daily 7am–10pm.

Satyricon Rua Barão de Torre 192 ⓣ21 2521 0627 ⓦsatyricon.com.br; ⓜGeneral Osório; map p.76. Mediterranean seafood dishes are the house speciality (snapper baked in rock salt, for example, at R$125), though there's also a range of interesting pasta choices, too. The ingredients are as fresh as can be and the dishes beautifully presented, but it's just a touch too formal. Daily noon–midnight.

★ Zazá Bistrô Tropical Rua Joana Angélica 40 ⊕21 2247 9101, ⊕zazabistro.com.br; ⊕General Osório; map p.76. Light-hearted, imaginative fusion cuisine, colourful decor and a terrace with a street-life view make this a popular spot with tourists and trendy locals alike. Dishes include chicken curry in coconut milk (R$72) or seared tuna with mash and wasabi (R$79). Mon–Thurs 6.30pm–12.30am, Fri noon–6pm & 7pm–12.30am, Sat 1–6pm & 7pm–1am, Sun 1–6pm & 7pm–midnight.

LEBLON

Antiquarius Rua Aristides Espínola 19 ⊕21 2294 1049; ⊕Antero de Quental; map p.76. This old-school Portuguese restaurant is especially good for seafood, such as prawns in champagne sauce (R$195) or squid cooked Portuguese-style in a *cataplana* open casserole (R$140), but the meat dishes and rich desserts are also good. Very classy and definitely no shorts allowed. Tues–Sat noon–midnight, Sun noon–7pm.

Celeiro Rua Dias Ferreira 199 ⊕21 2274 7843, ⊕celeiroculinaria.com.br; ⊕Antero de Quental; map p.76. Rio's best *por quilo* restaurant, with an extremely varied salad bar, excellent bread and delicious desserts. Well worth the sometimes long wait for a table, and the price (over twice the amount you'd normally expect to pay at a *por quilo* restaurant; R$172.60/kg). Mon–Sat 9.30am–4.30pm.

Confeitaria Kurt Rua General Urquiza 117-B ⊕21 2294 0599, ⊕confeitariakurt.com.br; ⊕Antero de Quental; map p.76. Set up in the 1940s by a refugee fleeing the Nazis, this is *the* place in Rio to indulge in some outrageously delicious Jewish and central European-style cakes and pastries (R$10–16) while sipping a fine espresso coffee and watching the world go by. Mon–Fri 8am–7pm, Sat 9am–6pm.

Mercado Cobal do Leblon Rua Gilberto Cardoso; ⊕Antero de Quental; map p.76. Locals of all ages flock to this excellent fruit and veg market, where the abundant and affordable *lanchonetes* serve everything from pizza and sushi to regional Brazilian dishes. Mon–Sat 8am–6pm.

Nam Thai Rua Rainha Guilhermina 95b ⊕21 2259 2962, ⊕namthai.com.br; ⊕Antero de Quental; map p.76. Rio's top Thai restaurant, where you can start with a spicy, tangy *tom yam kung* (hot-sour prawn soup; R$38) followed by tender aromatic duck breast in a red curry sauce (R$76). Mon 7–11.30pm, Tues–Fri noon–11.30pm, Sat noon–1am, Sun noon–10.30pm.

Sushi Leblon Rua Dias Ferreira 256 ⊕21 2512 7830, ⊕sushileblon.com; ⊕Antero de Quental; map p.76. Superb sushi (R$11–17), along with other Japanese-inspired dishes such as king crab, octopus and green bean tempura (R$122), are offered at this stylish restaurant – a well-known meeting point for actors, models and artists. Mon–Sat noon–1am, Sun noon–midnight.

★ Zuka Rua Dias Ferreira 233 ⊕21 21 3205 7154, ⊕zuka.com.br; ⊕Antero de Quental; map p.76. The unforgettable fusion cuisine at this elegant modern restaurant includes honey-glazed duck with couscous (R$98) or steak with herb ghee with goat's cheese risotto and crunchy leeks (R$103). Mon 7pm–1am, Tues–Fri noon–4pm & 7pm–1am, Sat 1pm–1am, Sun 1pm–midnight.

LAGOA, JARDIM BOTÂNICO AND GÁVEA

Bar Lagoa Av Epitácio Pessoa 1674, Lagoa; map p.76. Tucked into the southern shores of the lake by Ipanema, this is the cheapest and oldest (dating back to 1934) of the waterside restaurants. *Bar Lagoa* is usually full of local families, attended to by white-coated waiters delivering beer, German sausage and enormous smoked pork chops (R$68). Arrive by 9pm to bag a seat on the patio, from where there's a good view of the lake. Daily noon–2pm.

Couve-Flor Rua Pacheco Leão 724, Jardim Botânico ⊕21 2239 2191, ⊕couveflor.com.br; map p.76. The range and quality of the salads and hot meals make *Couve-Flor* one of Rio's most popular *por quilo* restaurants (R$74.90 at weekdays, R$89.90 on weekends). Brazilian dishes predominate but there's much more besides, and don't forget to leave room for dessert: the guava cheesecake is remarkable. Mon–Fri 11.45am–4pm, Sat & Sun 11.45am–6pm.

Guimas Rua José Roberto Macedo Soares 5, Gávea (off Praça Santos Dumont) ⊕21 2259 7996, ⊕restauranteguimas.com.br; map p.76. A small, intimate restaurant near the Jockey Club with a happy atmosphere, catering for an arty and intellectual crowd. The food is delicious, and, unusually, the *couvert* (wholemeal bread and pâté), is worth the price. Try steak in a mustard, cream and wine sauce (R$76) and leave space for the delectable chocolate and cream pudding (R$25). Though this is one of Rio's best restaurants, it's not too expensive. Daily noon–midnight.

★ Olympe Rua Custódio Serrão 62, Jardim Botânico ⊕21 2539 4542, ⊕olympe.com.br; map p.76. Celebrity chef Claude Trosgros makes regular expeditions to the Amazon and other remote regions in search of new ingredients and ideas. Returning to Rio, he reinvents these elements, fusing them with classical and *nouvelle* styles of French cuisine. Try the *menu confiance* (tasting menu) at R$390 with five dishes or R$450 with seven. Somewhere for a special occasion – or to impress. Mon–Fri noon–4pm & 7.30pm–midnight, Sat 7.30pm–midnight.

Pax In the Jockey Club, Rua Jardim Botânico, Gávea ⊕21 2540 9017, ⊕victoriario.com.br; map p.76. Enjoy good, reasonably priced Brazilian and international food, such as the house steak in herb sauce with rösti potatoes (R$68) in this restaurant overlooking the racetrack. Mon–Fri 6pm–midnight, Sat & Sun noon–midnight.

A NIGHT OUT IN LAPA

Clubs and music bars are particularly concentrated in **Lapa** (see page 71), where samba, *choro* and other local rhythms play to an enthusiastic and overwhelmingly local crowd. It's on **Friday and Saturday nights** that Lapa really comes to life, with crowds spilling onto the sidewalks, and food and drink stalls set up under the Arcos de Lapa at the eastern end of Avenida Mem de Sá. Here you'll find cheap snacks and, more to the point, well mixed **caipirinhas** for just R$5 a go. A good place to make for then is **Rua Joaquim da Silva**, where the packed bars pull in a mix of *bairro* residents and college students. West along **Mem de Sá, Rua do Lavradio** attracts a more well-heeled crowd, and **Rua Gomes Freire** is also a good hunting ground for bars and clubs. All of these thoroughfares are safe enough, but it's best not to wander off alone into badly lit side streets, especially when drunk, and obviously you won't want to take valuables with you anyway. Some places in Lapa charge on the door for entry, but often there's just a minimum consumption requirement; particularly in more expensive places, you don't pay at the bar, but get a coupon on entry, which your orders are marked up on, and you pay for them all together before leaving. Truth is though, the bars that are free to enter are as good as, or indeed better, than places which charge, and those R$5 caipirinhas served on the street in plastic cups are just as delicious as the ones you pay four or five times more for in a posh bar (but only buy from stalls where they mix it up fresh each time). For those who feel uncomfortable going alone, or want to be guided round, Rio Hiking (see page 93) regularly take **small groups** bar-hopping in Lapa (R$330 per person, excluding drinks).

DRINKING AND NIGHTLIFE

In most regions of Brazil, beer comes to your table in a bottle, but in Rio draught beer (*chopp*, pronounced "shopee") predominates. For early evening drinks and *petiscos*, office workers flock to the Arco de Teles area, the pedestrian zone centred on Travessa do Comércio and Rua Ouvidor in the many unassuming bars here. Later on, the action shifts to Lapa, one of the most important nightlife spots in Rio (see above). The best way to find out what's on and where in Rio is to consult *Caderno B*, a separate section of the *Jornal do Brasil*, which lists cinema, arts events and concerts; *O Globo*, too, details sporting and cultural goings-on in the city. *Veja*, Brazil's answer to *Newsweek*, includes a weekly Rio supplement with news of local events; the magazine reaches the newsstands on Sunday. Regardless, you should never find yourself stuck for options: there's no end of things to do come nightfall in a city whose name is synonymous with Carnaval (see page 105), samba and jazz. Note that some clubs may ask for ID before allowing entry (a photocopy of your passport should suffice).

BARS

Academia da Cachaça Rua Conde Bernadotte 26, Leblon ⊕21 2529 2680, ⊕academiadacachaca.com.br; Ⓜ Antero de Quental; map p.76. A good place to sample Brazil's national spirit, this small and always crowded bar has over a hundred brands available to sample. Treat the drink with respect at all times, and remember, the top-whack brands are for sipping straight: it's the cheaper ones that are used to make caipirinhas. Daily noon–1am.

Armazem do Chopp Rua Marquês de Abrantes 66, Flamengo ⊕21 2225 1796, ⊕armazemdochopp.com.br; Ⓜ Flamengo; map p.75. Beer hall serving decent-quality food in large quantities. The terrace overlooks the street, and the *bolinhas de bacalhau* (saltfish croquette balls; R$27.20 for five) are an excellent accompaniment to an ice-cold glass of *chopp*. On Fridays in particular it tends to stay open late. Daily 11am–2am (or later).

Armazem São Thiago (Bar do Gomez) Rua Aurea 26, Santa Teresa ⊕21 2232 0822, ⊕armazemsaothiago.com.br; map p.62. Founded in 1919, this grand old bar still looks much the same as it did then. The atmosphere's great, the sandwiches are filling, the beer's ice-cold, and they even do a decent house cachaça (as well as a huge selection of other fine ones). Mon–Sat noon–1am, Sun noon–10pm.

Bar Astor Av Viera Souto 10, Ipanema ⊕21 2523 0085, ⊕barastor.com.br; Ⓜ General Osório; map p.76. The Rio branch of this São Paulo bar (see page 511) is rather different from its SP parent, and the attempts at Art Deco style sit a bit oddly on the beachside at Ipanema, but actually the Rio branch has a style of its own, with a wide shaded terrace out front and an excellent selection of high-grade booze. Mon–Wed 6pm–1am, Thurs 6pm–2am, Fri 1pm–3am, Sat noon–3am, Sun noon–10pm.

Bar Bukowski Rua Álvaro Ramos 270, Botafogo ⊕21 2244 7303, ⊕facebook.com/barbukowskirio; Ⓜ Botafogo; map p.76. Rio's top rock bar, named after American poet and author Charles Bukowski, plays rock music – live or on vinyl – all night long, in a suitably dark space in a lovely old house, decorated with rock posters, and one of Chuck Berry's old guitars, with a beer garden out back (sheesha pipes available), a mock-up of the entrance to CBGB's and great beer. Fri 6.30pm–6am, Sat 9pm–6am.

Bar Luiz Rua Carioca 39, Centro ⊕21 2262 6900, ⊕barluiz.com.br; Ⓜ Carioca; map p.62. Rio's oldest *cervejaria*, serving German food such as kassler smoked sausage (R$55) with ice-cold *chopp*, was called *Bar Adolfo* until World War II. It's long been a popular meeting place for journalists and intellectuals, and although it's a little faded these days, it's still a bustling, enjoyable spot. Mon & Sat 11am–5pm, Tues–Fri 11am–9pm.

Ganjah Coffeeshop Rua do Rezende 76, Lapa ⓣ21 98700 0420; ⓜCinelândia; map p.62. Modelled on an Amsterdam coffee shop, this place has everything such an establishment might have – coffee, tobacco, smokers' prerequisites – with the one rather salient exception, although they do have beer to compensate. It's all very laidback, as you might expect, with a smaller branch at Praia de Botafogo 454 in Botafogo, and a couple more in the Sana and Vidigal neighbourhoods. Mon & Tues 10am–10pm, Wed 10am–midnight, Thurs–Sat 10am–2am.

Garota de Ipanema Rua Vinícius de Morais 49, Ipanema ⓣ21 2522 0340; ⓜGeneral Osório; map p.76. Always busy, this bar entered the folk annals of Rio de Janeiro when the song *The Girl from Ipanema* was written here one night by the composer Tom Jobim. While certainly touristy (with unexceptional food), there are few better places in Ipanema for a beer (R$9.50 for a 350ml *chopp*). Daily 11am–2am.

Lapa Esquina Rua Joaquim Silva 141, Lapa ⓣ21 2242 7980, ⓦlapaesquina.blogspot.com.br; MCinelândia; map p.62. This little corner bar comes alive Sunday, Monday and Tuesday evenings with samba sounds, and in the daytime on weekdays it serves very low-priced lunch dishes such as salmon and mash, or veg with salad, all for R$20–22. Mon, Tues, Thurs & Fri noon–3am, Sat & Sun 9pm–3am.

CLUBS

Although Rio's discos attempt sophistication, the end result is generally bland. Too often they pump out a steady stream of British and American hits, interspersed with records from Brazil's own dreadful pop industry. The fashionable nightclubs that attract both *cariocas* and tourists are all found in the Zona Sul, but for a more authentically local experience you'd be far better off at the music venues in Lapa (see page 102). Cover charges tend to vary on different nights.

LGBT RIO

If you're expecting Rio's **LGBT nightlife** to rival San Francisco's or Sydney's, you may be disappointed. In general, nightlife is pretty integrated, with gay men, lesbians and heterosexuals tending to share the same venues; apart from transvestites who hang out on street corners and are visible during Carnaval, the scene is unexpectedly discreet. The strip of beach between Rua Farme de Amoedo and Rua Teixeira do Melo in Ipanema is the best-known daytime gay meeting point, and Rua Farme de Almoedo is home to several gay- and lesbian-oriented cafés and bars, at their liveliest on Friday and Saturday nights. At Carnaval time there are often **gay carnival balls** (see page 108). Useful **websites** on gay and lesbian Rio include ⓦgayrio4u.com, while ⓦarco-iris.org.br offers more political and campaigning insights but is only in Portuguese.

BARS

Quiosque Rainbow Av Atlântica, beachside, opposite Copacabana Palace hotel, Copacabana ⓣ21 7832 0126; ⓜCardeal Arcoverde; map p.81. This beachside kiosk serving drinks is particularly popular as a meeting place for Rio's transgender community. Daily 9am–3am.

To Nem Ai Rua Farme de Amoedo 57, Ipanema ⓣ21 1224 7840; map p.76. This bar, done out darkly in black with blue lighting, is of course open to all, but Ipanema's gay community tend to meet up here for an afternoon drink, or to get in the mood before heading out clubbing of an evening. Mon–Fri 11.30am–3am, Sat & Sun noon–3am.

CLUBS

Boate 1140 Rua Capitao Menezes 1140, Praça Seca ⓣ21 3017 1792, ⓦboate1140.com; map p.58. Out in the Zona Oeste, this club is especially famous for its spectacular drag shows. It's quite a way out of town, 1.5km from Madureiro station on the suburban train line (which doesn't run late anyway), but can be reached from Centro on buses #363 or #371. Thurs–Sun 11pm–5am.

Galeria Cafe Rua Teixeira de Melo 31-E, Ipanema ⓣ21 2523 8250, ⓦgaleriacafe.com.br; ⓜGeneral Osório; map p.76. A bright little club catering to all branches of the LGBT community, and indeed anyone else who fancies coming along, and on Sundays it becomes a little indoor market with fashion displays. Wed–Sat 11pm–5am, Sun 11am–8pm.

Turma OK Rua dos Inválidos 39, Centro ⓣ21 3177 0181, ⓦturmaok.com.br; ⓜUruguaiana; map p.62. Run by the oldest LGBT group in town, this city-centre venue hosts excellent parties every weekend. Fri 9pm–Sun midnight.

The Week Rua Sacadura Cabral 154, Saúde ⓣ21 2253 1020, ⓦtheweek.com.br; map p.62. The Rio branch of a São Paulo gay nightclub pumping out house music all night long. It's very popular so expect to queue. Sat 11.30pm–5am or later.

1

FROM SAMBA TO SYMPHONIES: RIO'S LIVE MUSIC SCENE

Rio has a tradition of **jazz** music that extends well beyond *The Girl from Ipanema* and is well worth checking out. **Samba** shows where members of Rio's more successful samba schools perform glitzy music and dance routines are usually tourist affairs, but often worth catching. Alternatively, check out the samba school rehearsals (see page 108), held mainly in the Zona Norte from August to February.

For some accordion-driven swing from Brazil's Northeast, look for a **forró** club. The term *forró* (pronounced "fawhaw") originates from the English "for all", a reference to the dances financed by English engineering companies for their manual labour forces, as opposed to the balls organized for the elite. *Forró* can often be found in **gafieiras**: founded as ballrooms for the poorer classes, these became big in the 1920s and remain popular today because they are places where *cariocas* can be assured of traditional dance music.

So far as **classical music** is concerned, Rio is the home of the Orquestra Sinfônica Brasileira, based at the Theatro Municipal (see page 69), which is also home to the city's ballet troupe and opera company.

Casa da Matriz Rua Henrique Novaes 107, Botafogo ⊤21 2266 9691; Ⓜ Botafogo; map p.76. An extremely stylish, aggressively modern club that features more Brazilian music than is typical of discos – though this varies throughout the week. Entrance R$30–50. Wed–Sat 10pm–4am or later.

Castelo das Pedras Estrada de Jacarepaguá 3600, Favela Rio das Pedras, Jacarepaguá ⊤21 3415 2992, Ⓦ facebook.com/castelo.daspedras; map p.58. Rio's premier *funk Carioca* venue, with 3000-strong crowds of sweating, gyrating bodies. Fri–Sun 11pm–4am.

Comuna Rua Sorocaba 585, Botafogo ⊤21 3029 0789, Ⓦ comuna.cc; Ⓜ Botafogo; map p.76. A split personality of electronica parties, art exhibitions, film screenings and even food makes this warehouse-style space a truly communal entertainment centre. Tues, Wed & Sun 6pm–1am, Thurs–Sat 6pm–2am.

Espaço Acústica Praça Tiradentes 2, Centro ⊤21 2232 1299, Ⓦ espacoacustica.com.br; map p.62. Helping along the resurgence of one of Rio's most historic central squares, this is a hip yet unpretentious place to catch some of the best DJ talent in town. Electro/pop/rock/Brazilian mash-up. Fri & Sat from 10pm.

Fosfobox Rua Siquiera Campos 143, Copacabana ⊤21 2548 7498, Ⓦ fosfobox.com.br; Ⓜ Siquiera Campos; map p.81. A basement club that attracts a partly gay crowd on some nights, and is fun and friendly on all nights as hedonistic punters shake the floor nightly to a mix of jolly house sounds. Wed–Sat 11pm–5am.

LIVE MUSIC VENUES

Clubs and music bars are particularly concentrated in Lapa, where samba, *choro* and other local rhythms play to an enthusiastic and overwhelmingly local crowd, but of course there are plenty of venues elsewhere in the city too, notably in Centro and in the Zona Sul beach areas.

LAPA

Café Cultural Sacrilégio Av Mem de Sá 81 ⊤21 3970 1461, Ⓦ sacrilegio.com.br; Ⓜ Cinelândia; map p.62. A small, old town house with a great atmosphere and killer *batidas* (cachaça-based cocktails). The place attracts some great *choro* singers who perform classical works, as well as samba and fusion rock-samba artists. Tues–Thurs 7pm–2am, Fri 7pm–4am Sat 9pm–4am.

Carioca da Gema Av Mem de Sá 79 ⊤21 2221 0043, Ⓦ barcariocadagema.com.br; Ⓜ Cinelândia; map p.62. Stop in for very reliable *choro* and samba: Teresa Cristina, one of Rio's greatest female samba voices, puts in regular appearances. Mon–Fri 7pm–5am, Sat & Sun 8pm–5am.

Circo Voador Rua dos Arcos ⊤21 2533 0354, Ⓦ circovoador.com.br; Ⓜ Cinelândia; map p.62. Whereas other Lapa clubs have a very mixed-age clientele, with its programme of rap, funk and fusion samba-punk-rock, *Circo Voador*, set in a large circus tent, is dominated by young people who come to dance and discover new bands. Fri, Sat and sometimes other days, usually from 10pm.

Democráticos Rua do Riachuaelo 93, Lapa ⊤21 2252 4611, Ⓦ clubedosdemocraticos.com.br; Ⓜ Cinelândia; map p.62. Rio's oldest *gafieira* (people's ballroom), dating from 1867, this large, atmospheric old venue is the best place in town to catch some *forró* (Wed), and good for samba too (Thurs–Sun). Wed 10pm–3am, Thurs–Sat 10pm–4am, Sun 8–11.45pm.

Rio Scenarium Rua do Lavradio 20 ⊤21 3147 9000, Ⓦ rioscenarium.art.br; Ⓜ Cinelândia; map p.62. Located in an old baronial townhouse filled with antiques, this is nonetheless one of the liveliest places in Lapa. More popular for its music than its dancing, the venue has several landings from which visitors can watch the daily shows on the stage below. While specializing in *choro*, samba and local fusions are also performed. Reservations recommended on weekends, when queues are long. Tues & Wed 7pm–1am, Thurs 7pm–2am, Fri 7pm–5am, Sat 8pm–5am.

Teatro Odisséia Av Mem de Sá ⓣ21 2226 9691, ⓦfacebook.com/teatroodisseia; ⓜCinelândia; map p.62. In an old theatre, featuring an eclectic mix of recorded and live Brazilian sounds from rock to samba. Wed–Fri 7.30pm–2am, Sat 7.30pm–6am, Sun 2pm–midnight.

ELSEWHERE

Bip Bip Rua Almirante Gonçalves 50d, Copacabana ⓣ21 2267 9696, ⓦfacebook.com/barbipbip; ⓜCantagalo; map p.81. It's just a tiny *botequim* (little bar), but it has a huge reputation for samba, with customers taking over the surrounding streets. They play samba on Thursday, Friday and Saturday (Mon & Tues are *choro*, Wed is bossa nova), but the big night is Sunday, when famous old-timers often perform. Daily 7–11.45pm.

Blue Note Rio Av Borges de Medeiros 1424, Lagoa ⓣ21 3799 2500, ⓦbluenoterio.com.br; ⓜAntero de Quental; map p.76. A Rio outpost of New York City's famous jazz club, it certainly attracts the big names, but charges outrageous entry fees to see them (R$600 on occasion), although you can usually see local talent here for less than R$100. Wed–Sun 6.30pm–2am.

Estudantina Praça Tiradentes 79, Centro ⓣ21 2232 1149, ⓦfacebook.com/gafieira.estudantina.oficial; ⓜUruguaiana; map p.62. A venerable old *gafieira* whose decor recalls its roots dating back to 1928. Attracting locals and visitors of all ages, the live bands keep up to 1500 dancers moving. Wed–Sun 8pm–2am.

★ Feira Nordestina Campo de São Cristovão, São Cristovão (near Quinta da Boa Vista) ⓣ21 2580 5335, ⓦfeiradesaocristovao.org.br; ⓜSão Cristovão; map p.58. This crafts fair mutates on weekend nights into a huge party – or rather, collection of parties – featuring everything from samba and *forró* to pop and karaoke. You can just wander from one to the other, sampling the music all night as you might sample the food and handicrafts by day. Fri 10am–Sun 9pm.

Gafieira Elite Rua Frei Caneca 4, Centro ⓣ21 2232 3217, ⓦgafieiraelite.xpg.uol.com.br; ⓜCentral; map p.62. Smaller and more traditional in style than most *gafieiras* (with less modern music and dancers wearing formal attire), this one – itself established in 1930 – is hidden away inside a grimy but once quite pretty pink nineteenth-century building. Fri–Sun 10pm–3am or later.

The Maze Rua Tavares Bastos 414, Casa 66, Catete ⓣ21 2558 5547, ⓦthemazerio.com; ⓜCatete; map p.75. If you can, do try to coincide with the jazz evenings held on the first Friday of each month in an unusual venue that also offers bed and breakfast (see page 95), with spectacular views across Rio, run by a British jazz enthusiast and attracting solid local performers. They also sometimes have extra Friday evenings – see the website for details. Fri (when gigs)10pm–4am.

Metropolitan Av Ayrton Senna 3000, Barra da Tijuca ⓣ21 2156 7300, ⓦmetropolitanrio.com.br; map p.58. The largest music venue in Rio (and officially currently named KM de Vantagens Hall) the Metropolitan attracts Brazilian and international stars; programmes and tickets are available at ⓦpremier.ticketsforfun.com.br – expect to pay upwards of R$100.

ENTERTAINMENT

CINEMAS

Most European and American films are quickly released in Brazil and play with their original soundtracks. Cinemas are quite inexpensive (R$15–25), with *Jornal do Brasil* and the Rio supplement of the weekly magazine *Veja* listing what's on and where. Some of Rio's historical cinemas have now been restored and reopened, notably the 1926 Odeon at Praça Floriano 7, one of the original cinemas that gave Cinelândia its name, while the 1909 Cine Theatro Iris at Rua da Carioca 49, Centro – the oldest cinema still in use in the city – has become something now almost equally historical: a grindhouse showing porn flicks (R$20, 3 performances daily).

FESTIVALS (OTHER THAN CARNAVAL)

Film festival Rio hosts one of Latin America's most important international film festivals, the Festival do Rio (ⓣ21 3035 7107, ⓦfestivaldorio.com.br), which takes place over two weeks in late September or early October and screens over four hundred films from dozens of countries in cinemas all over the city.

Rock in Rio The Rock in Rio festival (ⓦrockinrio.com), born in Rio but not exclusive to the city, claims to be the biggest music festival in the world, attracting millions of fans and some of the very top names in rock music. Though it started way back in 1985, it has only been an annual event since 2010. The festival sometimes migrates to Lisbon or Madrid, but Rio was its original home, and is where it is usually held. Its Rio venue, the Cidade do Rock in Barra da Tijuca, was built specifically for the festival.

CARNAVAL

Carnaval is celebrated in every Brazilian city, but Rio's party is the biggest and flashiest of them all. From the Friday before Lent to the following Tuesday (Shrove Tuesday, the last day before Lent, better known by its French name, Mardi Gras), the city shuts up shop and throws itself into the world's most famous manifestation of unbridled hedonism. Carnaval's greatest

1

THE HISTORY OF CARNAVAL

All Roman Catholic countries have a **Carnival** (Carnaval in Portuguese) to let their hair down before the start of Lent – the seven-week fast period leading up to Easter during which parties and celebrations were traditionally banned. In the Azores, Carnaval was particularly wild, and this quickly became a feature in Brazil too, for which the Azores were a staging post. In **Rio**, anarchy reigned in the streets for four days and nights, the festivities often so riotous that in 1843 they were officially banned – but of course the ban was ignored. In the mid-nineteenth century, members of the social elite held **masquerade balls**, and processions of carriages decorated in allegorical themes made their first appearance, beginning the ascendancy of the procession over the general street melée. Rio's masses, denied admission to the balls, had their own music – *jongo* – and they reinforced the tradition of street celebration by organizing in *Zé Pereira* bands, named after the Portuguese tambor that provided the basic musical beat. The organizational structure behind today's **samba schools** (*escolas da samba*) is partly a legacy of those bands sponsored by migrant Bahian port workers in the 1870s – theirs was a more disciplined approach to the Carnaval procession: marching to stringed and wind instruments, using costumes and appointing people to coordinate different aspects of the parade.

Music written specifically for Carnaval emerged in the early twentieth century, by composers such as Chiquinho Gonzaga, who wrote the first recorded samba piece in 1917 (*Pelo Telefone*), and Mauro de Almeida e Donga. In the 1930s, recordings began to spread the music of Rio's Carnaval, and competition between different samba schools became institutionalized: in 1932, the Estação Primeira Mangueira school won the first prize for its performance in the Carnaval parade. The format has remained virtually unchanged since, except for the emergence in the mid-1960s of the **blocos** or **bandas**: street processions by the residents of various *bairros*, who eschew style, discipline and prizes and give themselves up to the most traditional element of Carnaval – street revelry.

quality is that it has never become stale, thanks to its status as the most important celebration on the Brazilian calendar, easily outstripping Christmas and Easter. In a city riven by poverty, Carnaval represents a moment of freedom and release. And at the end of the very intense long weekend, there's a brief collective hangover before attention turns to preparing for the following year's event.

INFORMATION

See ⓦ rio-carnival.net for a complete schedule of events. Carnaval dates obviously depend on the dates for Easter (see page 43).

THE PARADES

Rio's purpose-built parade ground, the **Sambódromo** (Rua Marquês de Sapucaí, Ⓜ Praça Onze), is the scene of all-night parades (*desfiles*) by the samba schools (see page 107) – this is the most formal part of the Carnaval, and is ticketed. The parades start at 9pm, with eight Division 1 schools performing over two nights (Sun & Mon). Unless you have a very tough backside, you will find sitting through a ten-hour show an intolerable test of endurance. Most people don't turn up until 11pm, by which time the show is well under way and hotting up considerably.

Tickets There are a number of different seating options, from grandstands, which are basically concrete steps where you sit where you like, to private chairs, boxes and luxury suites. Bear in mind that the more deluxe and exclusive your seat, the less you will be part of the party, Grandstand tickets start at R$91 for the main parades, with luxury seats going at up to R$1239 a go. Tickets are available from the organizers (ⓦ rio-carnival.net), or from agents such as Rio.com (ⓣ 1 800 800 260 2700 or ⓣ 1 305 420 6900 in the US or Canada, ⓣ 020 3129 3573 in the UK, ⓣ 02 8015 5419 in Australia, ⓦ rio.com) or Bookers International (ⓣ 1 866 930 6020 in the US or Canada, ⓦ carnivalbookers.com), or at premium prices from travel agents in Rio, and should be booked well in advance.

STREET CELEBRATIONS

Of course the real Carnaval carnival is not the formal parade but the street celebrations, which centre on the evening processions that fill Avenida Rio Branco (Ⓜ Largo do Carioca or Ⓜ Cinelândia). Be prepared for the crowds and beware of pickpockets: even though the revellers are generally high-spirited and good-hearted, you should keep any cash you take with you in hard-to-reach places (like your shoes), wear only light clothes and leave your valuables locked up at the hotel. The processions include samba schools (though not the best); Clubes de Frevo, whose loudspeaker-laden floats blast out the frenetic dance music typical of the Recife Carnaval; and the Blocos de Empolgacão, including the Bafo da Onça and Cacique de Ramos clubs, between which exists a tremendous rivalry. After the official parades, the Division 1 samba schools take over the Sambódromo, with Division 2 on Avenida Rio Branco and Division 3 on Avenida 28 de Setembro, near the

Maracanã. There are also *rancho* bands playing a traditional *carioca* carnival music that predates samba.

BLOCOS

In whatever *bairro* you're staying there will probably be a *bloco* or *banda* – a small samba school that doesn't enter an official parade – organized by the local residents; ask about them in your hotel. These schools offer a hint of what Carnaval was like before it became regulated and commercialized. Starting in mid-afternoon, they'll continue well into the small hours, the popular ones accumulating thousands of followers as they wend their way through the neighbourhood. They all have a regular starting point, some have set routes, others wander freely; but they're easy to follow – there's always time to have a beer and catch up later.

Recommended blocos Some of the best *blocos* are: the Banda da Glória, which sets off from near the Glória *metrô*; the Banda da Ipanema (the first to be formed, in 1965), which gathers behind Praça General Osório in Ipanema; the Banda da Vergonha do Posto 6, starting in Rua Francisco Sá in Copacabana; and the Carmelitas de Santa Teresa, which gathers in the *bairro* of the same name. There are dozens of others, including several in each *bairro* of the Zona Sul, each providing a mix of music, movement and none-too-serious cross-dressing – a tradition during Carnaval in which even the most macho men indulge.

THE SAMBA SCHOOLS

The **samba schools**, each representing a different neighbourhood or social club, are divided into three leagues that vie for top ranking following the annual Carnaval parades. Division 1 (the top league) schools play in the Sambódromo, Division 2 on Avenida Rio Branco and Division 3 on Avenida 28 de Setembro, near the Maracanã.

Preparations start in the year preceding Carnaval, as each school mobilizes thousands of supporters to create the various parts of their display. A theme is chosen, music written and costumes created, while the dances are choreographed by the **carnavelesco**, the school's director. By December, rehearsals have begun and, in time for Christmas, the sambas are recorded and released to record stores.

The main procession of Division 1 schools – the **desfile** – takes place on the Sunday and Monday nights of Carnaval week in the purpose-built **Sambódromo**, further along the avenue beyond the train station; the concrete structure is 1.7km long and can accommodate 90,000 spectators. The various samba schools – involving some 50,000 people – take part in a spectacular piece of theatre: no simple parade, but a competition between schools attempting to gain points from their presentation, which is a mix of song, story, dress, dance and rhythm. The schools pass through the Passarela da Samba, the Sambódromo's parade ground, and the judges allocate points according to a number of criteria. Each school must parade for between 85 and 95 minutes, no more and no less.

Regardless of the theme adopted by an individual samba school, all include certain basic elements within their performances. The **bateria**, the percussion section, has to sustain the cadence that drives the school's song and dance; the *samba enredo* is the music, the *enredo* the accompanying story or lyric. The **harmonia** refers to the degree of synchronicity between the *bateria* and the dance by the thousands of **passistas** (samba dancers); the dancers are conducted by the **pastoras**, who lead by example. The **evolução** refers to the quality of the dance, and the choreography is marked on its spontaneity, the skill of the *pastoras* and the excitement that the display generates. The costumes, too, are judged on their originality; their colours are always the traditional ones adopted by each school. The **carros alegóricos** (no more than 10m high and 8m wide) are the gigantic, richly decorated floats, which carry some of the **Figuras de Destaque** ("prominent figures"), among them the **Porta-Bandeira** ("flag bearer") – a woman who carries the school's symbol, a potentially big point-scorer. The **Mestre-Sala** is the dance master, also an important symbolic figure, whose ability to sustain the rhythm of his dancers is of paramount importance. The **Comissão da Frente**, traditionally a school's "board of directors", marches at the head of the procession, a role often filled these days by invited TV stars or sports teams. The bulk of the procession behind is formed by the **alas**, the wings or blocks consisting of hundreds of costumed individuals each linked to a part of the school's theme.

In addition to a parade, every school has an **Ala das Baianas** – a procession of hundreds of women dressed in the flowing white costumes and African-style headdresses typical of Salvador – in remembrance of the debt owed to the Bahian emigrants, who introduced many of the traditions of the Rio Carnaval procession.

1

CARNAVAL BALLS

It's the Carnaval balls (*bailes*) that really signal the start of the celebrations – warm-up sessions in clubs and hotels for rusty revellers, which are quite likely to get out of hand as inhibitions give way to a rampant eroticism. The balls start late, normally after 10pm, and the continual samba beat supplied by live bands drives the festivities into the new day. At most of the balls, *fantasia* (fancy dress or costume) is the order of the day, with elaborate costumes brightening the already hectic proceedings; don't worry if you haven't got one, though – just dress reasonably smartly. You'll often have to pay an awful lot to get into these affairs, as some of the more fashionable ones attract the rich and famous, but the city's *gafeiras*, notably Democráticos (see page 104), often put on more affordable events. There are a number of gay balls, too, which attract an international audience, notably the one at the *Rio Scala*.

Copacabana Palace Hotel ☎ 21 2545 8790. There's none grander than the Baile Mágico held at the *Copacabana Palace Hotel* (see page 95), drawing the elite from across the world. For the privilege of joining in, expect to pay over US$1000 (R$3500), although one or two standing tickets are slightly less – black tie or an extravagant costume is obligatory.

Fundição Progresso Rua dos Arcos 24, Lapa ☎ 21 3212 0800, ⓦ fundicaoprogresso.com.br. Usually arrange appearances by top samba schools at balls in the run-up to Carnaval.

Monte Libano Av Borges de Medeiros 701, Leblon ☎ 21 2512 8833, ⓦ clubemontelibano.com.br. A series of big parties in the run-up to Carnaval, often with a "last days of Rome" flavour, and quite sexually charged, though safe to attend, and reasonable at around R$80 a ticket.

Rio Scala Avenida Treze de Maio 23, Cinelândia ☎ 21 2511 4140, ⓦ scalario.com.br. In recent years, the *Rio Scala* club has become an important centre for balls, with a different line-up each night, including a gay ball.

CARNAVAL REHEARSALS

If you can't make Carnaval, give the shows put on for tourists in the Zona Sul a miss and get a taste of the samba schools at the *ensaios* (rehearsals). They take place at weekends from August to February: phone to confirm times and days. After New Year, Saturday nights are packed solid with tourists and prices triple. Instead, go to one on a midweek evening or, better still, on Sunday afternoon when there's no entrance fee and locals predominate.

Most of the schools are in distant *bairros*, often in, or on the edge of, a *favela*, but there's no need to go accompanied by a guide. It's easy, safe and not too expensive to take a taxi there and back (there are always plenty waiting to take people home). Of the schools, **Mangueira** is certainly the most famous; it has a devoted following, a great atmosphere and includes children and old people among its dancers. The gay-friendly **Salgueiro** has a more white, middle-class fan base.

The **Cidade do Samba** (see page 68), a purpose-built arena and studio complex in Centro, is an even easier way of observing Carnaval preparations. All the Division 1 schools are represented here and their daily musical and dance demonstrations are produced for the public.

SAMBA SCHOOLS

Beija-Flor Rua Pracinha Wallace Paes Leme 1025, Nilopolis ☎ 21 2247 4800, ⓦ beija-flor.com.br. Founded 1948; blue and white.

Grande Rio Rua Wallace Soares 5–6, Centro ☎ 21 2671 3585, ⓦ academicosdogranderio.com.br. Founded 1988; red and green.

Mangueira Rua Visconde de Niterói 1072, Mangueira ☎ 21 2567 3419, ⓦ mangueira.com.br. Founded 1928; green and pink.

Moçidade Av Brasil 31146, Padre Miguel ☎ 21 3332 5823, ⓦ mocidadeindependente.com.br. Founded 1955; green and white.

Portela Rua Clara Nunes 81, Madureira ☎ 21 3256 9411, ⓦ gresportela.org.br. Founded 1923; blue and white.

Salgueiro Rua Silva Telles 104, Tijuca ☎ 21 2238 9226, ⓦ salgueiro.com.br. Founded 1953; red and white.

SHOPPING

It's not hard to find things to buy in Rio, but surprisingly difficult to find much that's distinctively Brazilian. The best shopping area is Ipanema, with a wealth of boutiques lining **Rua Visconde de Pirajá** and its side streets. music (vinyl and CDs) and designer fashions, especially beachwear, make good purchases. Sales assistants in music stores are usually delighted to offer recommendations and you'll be able to listen before you buy.

MARKETS

Babilônia Feira Hype Parque de Figueiras, Av Borges de Medeiros 1426, Lagoa, and three other venues ☎ 21 2267 0066, ⓦ babiloniafeirahype.com.br; Ⓜ Jardim de Alah; map p.76. A good selection of handicrafts as well as clothes and jewellery by young designers hoping to get noticed. Irregular weekends (check website for dates), Sat & Sun 2–10pm.

Feira Nordestina Campo de São Cristovão, São Cristovão (near Quinta da Boa Vista) ☎ 21 2580 5335, ⓦ feiradesaocristovao.org.br; Ⓜ São Cristovão, or any bus marked "São Cristovão" (including #312 from Av Rio

1

Branco); map p.58. Set up in the nineteenth century by the first wave of immigrants from the Northeast, with 700 stalls (many run by people in traditional costume) selling Northeastern handicrafts, caged birds and food and drink, all to the sound of Northeastern music. Best buys are hammocks, leather bags and hats, *literatura de cordel* (illustrated folk-literature pamphlets), herbal medicines and spices. Weekends are best, when migrants enjoying their day off listen to live music here in the evenings; R$5 entry between Fri 6pm & Sun noon (otherwise free). Tues–Thurs 10am–6pm, Fri 10am–Sun 9pm.

Ipanema Hippie Market Praça General Osório, Ipanema; ⓜ General Osório; map p.76. Once it really was for hippies, but nowadays it's just a touristy arts and crafts market, where they sell furnishings, interior design and trendy knick-knacks. Sun 7am–8pm.

CRAFTS AND SOUVENIRS

Lapa e Arte Rua Teotônio Regadas 16, Lapa ⓣ 21 2051 7901, ⓦ lapaearte.com; ⓜ Cinelândia; map p.62. At the better end of the tourist tat market, this is a place to buy souvenirs such as Rio key-rings, Rio shot glasses, Rio purses and Rio handbags, as well as carvings, ceramics, T-shirts and flip-flops. You can undoubtedly buy many of these things more cheaply elsewhere, but it's worth a browse. Mon–Sat 9am–7pm, Sun 10am–7pm.

La Vereda Rua Almirante Alexandrino 428, Largo dos Guimarães, Santa Teresa ⓣ 21 2507 0317, ⓦ lavereda.com.br; map p.62. One of the best handicraft shops in town, with a varied collection from all over Brazil, including work by local artists. Mon–Sat 10am–8pm, Sun 10.30am–8pm.

Loja Artíndia Museu do Índio, Rua das Palmeiras 55, Botafogo; ⓜ Botafogo; map p.76. The best place in the city for Amerindian crafts – an excellent selection of basketry, necklaces, feather items and ceramics, with the tribes and places of origin all clearly identified. The shop, along with the museum, was closed for an upgrade on our last visit, but due to reopen at some point in 2018. Tues–Fri 9am–5.30pm, Sat & Sun 1–5pm.

O Sol Rua Corcovado 213, Jardim Botânico ⓣ 21 2294 6198, ⓦ osolartesanato.org.br; map p.76. A non-profit outlet selling folk art including basketware, ceramics, woodcarvings and table linen. Mon–Fri 9am–6pm, Sat 9am–1pm.

CLOTHES, ACCESSORIES AND COSMETICS

Although not a shopping mall, Ipanema's Rua Visconde de Pirajá has similar stores to those found in the likes of Rio Sul and Shopping Leblon, while on the side roads are some more unusual boutiques. Brazil has some great designer brands (although not cheap), and most of the best ones have outlets in Rio.

Bumbum Rua Visconde de Pirajá 602, Ipanema ⓣ 21 2512 1029, ⓦ bumbum.com.br; ⓜ Nossa Senhora da Paz; map p.76. The world's first ever designer bikini store, and what better name for the place where *fio dental* ("dental floss") thongs were invented? If you do want to don one of their flimsier creations however, remember to get a *depilação de virilha* (bikini wax) first. Mon–Fri 9am–8m, Sat 9am–6pm.

Garota de Ipanema Rua Vinicius de Moraes 53-A, Ipanema ⓣ 21 2521 3168, ⓦ garotadeipanemabrasil.com.br; ⓜ General Osório; map p.76. Founded by Heloisa Paez Pinto, the very girl about whom Tom Jobim wrote his famous song, this little fashion store sells beachwear and swimwear, including T-shirts featuring a facsimile of the words and music as jotted by Jobim. Mon–Sat 10am–7pm.

Gilson Martins Rua Visconde de Pirajá 462, Ipanema ⓣ 21 2227 6178, ⓦ gilsonmartins.com.br; ⓜ Jardim de Alah or ⓜ Nossa Senhora da Paz; map p.76 & p.81. Brightly coloured and interesting designs of bags and other accessories – often featuring silhouettes of Sugar Loaf Mountain and Christ the Redeemer, or the colours of the Brazilian flag – are the hallmark of this Brazilian designer, who also has shops in Copacabana at Av Atlântica 1998 and Rua Figueiredo Magalhães 304 (slightly different hours). Mon–Fri 9am–8pm, Sat 9am–7pm.

H. Stern Rua Garcia d'Ávila 113, Ipanema ⓣ 21 2106 0000, ⓦ hstern.com.br; ⓜ Nossa Senhora da Paz; map p.76. If you're after a seriously posh bit of bling, this, the world headquarters of the internationally renowned jewellery chain, is the place to visit. They even have a museum of sorts, where they show you how gemstones are excavated and cut. Their pieces are absurdly expensive (one ring can easily cost thousands of dollars), but they're often very pretty, especially under showroom lights; don't however go flashing them about while strolling through the *favelas*. Mon–Fri 10m–7pm, Fri 10am–4pm.

Originallis Shopping de Gávea, Rua Marquês de São Vicente 52, shop 158, Gávea ⓣ 21 3529 0793, ⓦ originallisaromas.com.br; map p.76. Brazil's answer to the Body Shop or Lush, the chain sells natural soaps infused with essential oils – the colours and smells are fantastic. Mon–Sat 10am–10pm, Sun noon–10pm.

MUSIC AND BOOKS

Livraria da Travessa Rua Visconde de Pirajá 572, Ipanema ⓣ 21 3205 9002, ⓦ travessa.com.br; ⓜ Nossa Senhora da Paz; map p.76. Their English-language section is small, but they have an excellent stock of Brazilian art and coffee-table books on Brazilian subjects, plus a good selection of CDs and a decent restaurant (see page 100). Mon–Sat 9am–11pm, Sun 10am–11pm.

Musicale Av Nossa Senhora de Copacabana 1103c ⓣ 21 2267 9607, ⓦ musicale.com.br; ⓜ Cantagalo; map p.81. For those in search of that rare Brazilian groove, this is a real enthusiasts' store, where you can browse through thousands of hard-to-find used CDs and LPs featuring all the local genres, with listening stations to check that the disk in your hand really is the one you were after. Mon–Fri 10am–7pm, Sat 10am–4pm.

Saraiva Megastore Rua do Ouvidor 98a, Centro ⓣ 21 2507 9500, ⓦ saraiva.com.br; Ⓜ Uruguaiana; map p.62. The largest bookshop in Centro, although its stock, including its English-language section, is rather limited. Mon–Fri 8.30am–7.30pm, Sat 9am–2pm.

DIRECTORY

Consulates Argentina (ⓣ 21 3850 8150); Australia (ⓣ 21 3824 4624); Canada (ⓣ 21 2543 3004); Peru (ⓣ 21 2551 9596); UK (ⓣ 21 2555 9600); Uruguay (ⓣ 21 2553 6030); US (ⓣ 21 3823 2000); Venezuela (ⓣ 21 2554 5955).

Health If you're unlucky enough to need medical treatment in Rio, forget about the public hospitals as they're extremely crowded and the level of treatment may be poor. You can, however, get excellent medical care privately: hospitals with good reputations include Hospital Samaritano, Rua Bambina 98, Botafogo (ⓣ 21 3444 1000, ⓦ hsamaritano.com.br), and Hospital Copa d'Or, Rua Figueiredo de Magalhães 875, Copacabana (ⓣ 21 2545 3600, ⓦ copador.com.br). Hotels will have lists of English-speaking doctors (ask for a *médico*), and your consulate should have a list of professionals who speak English.

Laundry Most hostels have laundry facilities; hotel laundry services are expensive. Good prices for service washes and dry cleaning are offered by Laundromat Integral, Rua Farme de Amoedo 55, Ipanema (Mon–Sat 8am–6pm), and Lavandería Almirante, Rua Almirante Gonçalves 50, Copacabana (Mon–Fri 7am–7pm, Sat 7am–2pm).

Money and exchange Main bank branches are concentrated in Av Rio Branco in Centro and Av N.S. de Copacabana in Copacabana. Note that although most banks remain open until 4.30pm, you can usually exchange money only until 3pm or 3.30pm. Many travel agents will also change money (often at better rates), and there are ATMs throughout the city, but not all will take foreign cards.

Police The beach areas have police posts located at regular intervals. The Tourist Police (DEAT) are located at Av Afrânio de Melo Franco 159 (opposite the Teatro Casa Grande), Leblon (ⓣ 21 2332 2924); they are helpful, speak English and efficiently process reports of theft or other incidents (open 24hr). Women are otherwise best off going to the Delegacia Especial de Atendimento a Mulher at Rua Visconde do Rio Branco 12, Centro (ⓣ 21 2334 9859).

Post offices Correios are open Mon–Fri 9am–5pm. Locations include: Rua Primeiro do Março (corner of Rosario) in Centro; Av N.S. de Copacabana 540 in Copacabana; Rua Visconde de Pirajá 452, Ipanema; Av Ataúlfo de Paiva 822, Leblon.

Public holidays In addition to the normal Brazilian public holidays (see page 43), most things close in Rio on January 20 (Dia de São Sebastião) and March 1 (Founding of the City).

Visa and tourist-card renewal If you're going to stay in Brazil for over six months and need to extend your visa or tourist card, apply in person at the Polícia Federal's office at Galeão airport (Terminal 1, 3rd floor, Sector A; Mon–Fri 8am–4pm; ⓣ 21 3398 3182) – it's always best to arrive early, well before opening if possible, to avoid a long wait in line, and and make sure you have all the essential documentation ready before you go (see page 27).

Ilha de Paquetá

The one-square-kilometre **ILHA DE PAQUETÁ** in the north of Guanabara Bay makes an easy day-trip so is very popular with *cariocas* at weekends. It was first occupied by the Portuguese in 1565 and later was a favourite resort of Dom João VI, who had the São Roque chapel built here in 1810. Nowadays, the island is almost entirely given over to tourism. About two thousand people live here, but at weekends that number is multiplied several times by visitors here for the tranquillity – the only motor vehicle allowed is an ambulance – and the beaches, which, sadly, are now heavily polluted. Nevertheless, it makes for a pleasant day's excursion – with colonial-style buildings that retain a certain shabby charm – and the trip is an attraction in itself. If possible, time your return to catch sunset over the city as you sail back. Weekdays are best if you want to avoid the crowds, or come in August for the wildly celebrated **Festival de São Roque**.

When you disembark at the ferry terminal, head along the road past the Yacht Club and you'll soon reach the first **beaches**: Praia da Ribeira and Praia dos Frades. Praia da Guarda, a few hundred metres on, has the added attraction of the *Lido* hotel's restaurant and the **Parque Duque de Mattos**, with its exuberant vegetation and panoramic views from the top of the Morro da Cruz, a hill riddled with tunnels dug to extract china clay.

ARRIVAL, GETTING AROUND AND INFORMATION — ILHA DE PAQUETÁ

By ferry Ferries run from near Rio's Praça XV de Novembro in Centro (approximately every 2hr; Mon–Fri 5.30am–midnight, Sat, Sun & holidays 4.30am–midnight; last boat back Mon–Fri 11.10pm, Sat & Sun 11.30pm; R$5.90).

By bicycle The best way to get around Ilha de Paquetá is by bicycle, which are available to rent very cheaply by the ferry terminal.

By horse-drawn cart You can take a ride in a small horse-drawn cart (*charrete*), or rent one by the hour if you want to take your time exploring and stop off along the way – not that there's a great deal to see.

Information The island doesn't have a tourist office as such, but you can often get information from the Casa de Artes cultural centre, Praça de São Roque 31 (daily 10am–5pm; ⓣ 21 3397 2124, ⓦ casadeartespaqueta.org.br).

Niterói and around

Across the strait from Rio, at the mouth of Guanabara Bay, lies **NITERÓI**, founded in 1573, and until 1975 the capital of the old state of Guanabara. Though lacking the splendour of the city of Rio, Niterói, with a population of half a million, has a busy commercial centre, an important museum and lively nightlife. *Cariocas* sometimes sneer that the only good thing about Niterói is its views back across Guanabara Bay to Rio, and it's true that the vistas are gorgeous on a clear day, but Niterói has a lot more to offer, not least for admirers of the work of Brazilian modernist architect **Oscar Niemeyer**.

Teatro Popular

Caminho Niemeyer • Daily 9am–5pm; guided tours (in Portuguese or English) on request from the on-site tourist office • Free • ⓦ teatropopularoscarniemeyer.art.br

Just north of Niterói's ferry terminal, and right by the bus station, a small group of Oscar Niemeyer's buildings includes his 2007 **Teatro Popular**, with jolly tiled murals, and flowing lines that echo the shape of Sugar Loaf Mountain. Close by is Niemeyer's low-domed memorial to the popular state governor **Roberto Silveira**, who died in a helicopter crash in 1961, and the higher dome of the **Fundação Oscar Niemeyer**, which, seen from above (or on Google Maps), takes the form of an eye.

Ilha da Boa Viagem

A couple of kilometres south of central Niterói, the **Ilha da Boa Viagem**, connected to the mainland by a causeway leading from Vermelha and Boa Viagem beaches, is open to the public only on irregular occasions, although there is talk of opening it more regularly, probably on Fridays and weekends. When accessible, it offers excellent views across to Rio, as well as the ruins of a 1663 fort guarding the entrance to the bay and a small seventeenth-century chapel.

Museu de Arte Contemporânea

Av Almirante Benjamin Sodré • Tues–Sun10am–6pm (closing at 7pm on weekends in summer) • R$10, free on Wed • ⓦ culturaniteroi.com.br/macniteroi

Oscar Niemeyer's **Museu de Arte Contemporânea**, more commonly just MAC, opened in 1996 on a promontory south of central Niterói by the Praia da Boa Viagem. The flying-saucer-shaped building offers a 360-degree perspective of Niterói and across the bay to Rio and hosts a worthy, though not very exciting, exhibition of late twentieth-century Brazilian art, as well as temporary exhibitions, which are rarely of much interest. Instead, the real work of art is the building itself, whose curved lines are simply beautiful. The views of the headland, nearby beaches and Guanabara Bay as you walk around inside are breathtaking.

The beaches

Niteroí's beaches, reached from the centre along the beautiful bayside road by bus #33, are every bit as good as those of Rio's Zona Sul. The first you come to after the Museu de Arte Contemporânea is **Icaraí**, followed by **São Francisco**. The bus terminates at **Jurujuba**, but **Piratininga**, beyond that (served by bus #39 and #39A from central Niteroí), is better still.

São Francisco Xavier

Av Quintino Bocalúva, São Francisco • Open by request Mon–Fri 9am–6pm, Sat 9am–noon • Free • T 21 2711 1670

Between Icaraí and Jurujuba beaches, just 600m from the Charitas ferry terminal, is a pretty, seventeenth-century colonial church, **São Francisco Xavier**. In fact it is kept closed up most of the time, but the priest lives next door and will usually open it up on request during official visiting hours.

Fortaleza de Santa Cruz

Jurujuba • Tues–Sun 10am–5pm, guided tours (1hr) every 30min • R$10 • T 21 2710 7840

A hot 2km walk from the last stop on bus #33 (don't forget to take water) is the **Fortaleza de Santa Cruz**, dating from the sixteenth century. One of a slew of forts built at strategic points to guard the entrance to Guanabara Bay, it is still in use as a military establishment, and it's a soldier who guides you round. As the nearest point across the bay from Rio's Sugar Loaf Mountain, the fort offers particularly good views.

Museu de Arqueologia de Itaipu

Praia de Itaipu • Tues–Fri 10am–5pm, Sat & Sun 1–5pm • R$10; Wed free • T 21 3701 2994 • Take bus #537 from Niterói bus station

To the east of Niterói, beyond the bay, the restaurants, bars and hotels fill up with *cariocas* at weekends. Near Itaipu beach, half an hour by bus from Niterói, the **Museu de Arqueologia de Itaipu** (also called the Museu Socioambiental de Itaipu) in the ruined eighteenth-century Santa Teresa convent, is worth a visit for its collection of ceramics and other artefacts excavated from ancient burial mounds.

ARRIVAL AND INFORMATION — NITERÓI

By ferry Passenger ferries (R$5.90) from a station by Praça XV de Novembro (see page 60) serve central Niterói (Estação Praça Arariboia), and hydrofoils (R$18.50) run to the Niemeyer-designed Charitas terminal (Estação Charitas). The passenger ferry is best for views, and the Niterói terminal is handiest for the Museu de Arte Contemporânea; the Charitas terminal is also better for most of the beaches.

By taxi/car/bus You can reach Niterói from Rio by car, taxi or bus across the14km-long Ponte Costa e Silva, the Rio–Niterói bridge.

Tourist offices There are helpful tourist information offices by the Niterói ferry terminal (daily 9am–5pm; T 0800 282 7755) and at the entrance to the Teatro Popular site (daily 9am–6pm; T 21 2611 1462, W niteroiturismo.com.br).

EATING

Da Carmine Rua Mariz e Barros 305, Icaraí T 21 3602 4988, W dacarmine.com.br. Serves the city's best pizzas by far (margherita R$43), and offers cheap "executive lunches" weekdays until 4pm. Mon 6–11.30pm, Tues–Sun noon–4pm & 6–11.30pm.

Mercado de São Pedro Rua Visconde do Rio Branco, Niterói. Niterói's fish market is also the main fish market for Rio. As well as seeing an incredible variety of gleaming fresh seafood downstairs here, you can also eat upstairs, where some forty restaurants of various sizes serve delicious fish creations – expect to pay around R$65–90 per head. Tues–Fri 6am–4pm, Sat & Sun 6am–noon.

Verdanna Grill Av Quintino Bocaiúva 603 (on the coast road, 400m north of Charitas ferry terminal) T 21 2610 5585, W verdanna.com.br. The best place on the Niterói coast to satisfy a meat craving, where a *rodizio* (mixed grill) will set you back R$72.80 (although special offers sometimes reduce this). Mon–Thurs noon–11pm, Fri & Sat noon–11.30pm, Sun noon–10pm.

1

The Costa do Sol

East of Niteroi are three large **lakes**, called Maricá, Saquerema and Araruama, which are also the names of adjoining towns. The brush around them is full of wildlife and the lakes are separated from the ocean by long, narrow stretches of white sand. This forms the **Costa do Sol**, where a string of popular resorts, most importantly Búzios, and some of the state's best beaches, attract visitors from Rio and beyond, particularly at weekends.

Saquarema and around

SAQUAREMA, 100km east of Rio, is a small town in a beautiful natural setting, squeezed between the sea and its 16km-long lagoon, retaining vestiges of its origins as a fishing village. Local anti-pollution legislation means that the environment still sustains much wildlife, including the *microleão* monkey, which you may be able to glimpse on a walk into the nearby forests. Saquarema has a healthy agricultural sector, too, based on fruit cultivation, and orchards surround the town. The main business here nowadays, though, is holidaymaking: you'll find holiday homes, arts and crafts shops and young surfers here in abundance.

Saquarema is widely rated as second only to Florianópolis (see page 572) as Brazil's surfing capital, and the **Praia de Itaúna**, 3km from town, is a favourite with surfers, who gather every year for the National Championship in mid-May. A strong undertow makes its waters potentially dangerous for the casual swimmer, so if you want to swim, head instead for the **Praia da Vila**, where the seventeenth-century church, Nossa Senhora de Nazaré (daily 8am–5pm), stands on the rocky promontory. For fishing, the **Praia de Jaconé** is a popular haunt, stretching 4km west of Saquarema.

ACCOMMODATION AND EATING — SAQUAREMA AND AROUND

Hotel Fazenda Sítio Nosso Paraíso Estrada do Rio Seco 115 (off Rodovia Amaral Peixoto, 16km north of Saqarema) ☎ 22 9969 1969, nosso-paraiso.net. Set amid 25 acres of lush farmland a 20min shuttle-bus ride from the beaches, this hotel has its own bar, swimming pool and sauna. Meals are made using the farm's own produce, and the hotel can be reached on buses from Rio or Niterói travelling to Bacaxá via RJ-106. R$200

Maasai Travessa Itaúna 17, Praia de Itaúna ☎ 22 2651 1092, maasai.com.br. A great-value beachside hotel where the rooms are spacious and the attractive grounds include a pool. They've also got a bar and restaurant, and rent out bicycles to guests. R$360

Cabo Frio and around

During summer, and especially at weekends, **CABO FRIO** is at a pitch of holiday excitement, generated by the out-of-towners who come here to relax in the fresh sea breeze. The town was founded in the late sixteenth century, but it was only really in the twentieth century that it developed, thanks to the salt and tourist industries. Built around sand dunes, Cabo Frio has plenty of **beaches** and is the main transport hub for the eastern end of the Costa do Sol. The **canalside** area to the north of the centre is very lively, particularly in the evenings and at weekends, when its bars and restaurants are full.

The closest beach to town is the **Praia do Forte**, which marks the southern end of the town centre. At its eastern end, the fort of **São Mateus** (irregular hours, but most likely summer Sat & Sun 9am–5pm) was built by the French in 1616 for protection against pirates. The town's other beach, **Praia da Barra**, is larger and more popular. Six kilometres north in the direction of Búzios, near Ogivas, **Praia do Peró** is a good surfing spot, peaceful and deserted on weekdays, and just to its south, the small **Praia das Conchas** has sand dunes and clear, calm, blue waters.

ARRIVAL AND INFORMATION

CABO FRIO AND AROUND

By bus The bus station is on Avenida Júlia Kubitschek, 2km northwest of the centre. Local buses to São Pedro da Aldeia and Arraial do Cabo stop next to it, those for Buzios stop just across Avenida Júlia Kubitschek. Intercity buses from Cabo Frio serve Niterói (20 daily), Rio, São Paulo and Petrópolis, but travelling to Santos or Bahia, your best bet is to take a bus to the sugar-cane-processing town of Campos to pick up a connection.

Tourist office On Av Contorno (daily 8am–6pm; ⊕22 2647 6227). Also see ⊕cabofrioturismo.com.br for local information.

ACCOMMODATION AND EATING

Fun Hostel Rua Jorge Lóssio 1318 ⊕22 2647 3531, ⊕cabofriofunhostel.com.br. The best hostel left in Cabo Frio offers en-suite dorms and private rooms, spacious public areas and big breakfasts. Prices fall somewhat out of the Dec–Feb high season, when it's also a lot quieter. Dorms R$60, doubles R$200

Hotel Malibu Palace Av Hilton Massa 900 (Av do Contorno at Av Nilo Peçanha) ⊕22 2647 8000, ⊕malibupalace.com.br. A good holiday hotel on the beachfront facing Praia do Forte, with large rooms and a good pool, not to mention a sauna, jacuzzi and massage room. Discounts are usually available, especially if you're staying for a few days or more, although rooms with ocean views cost half as much again as a standard room. R$450

Porto Fino Rua Jorge Lóssio 160 ⊕22 2643 6230, ⊕pousadaportofino.com. One of the better-value accommodation choices among several options on a long street that runs east–west through town parallel with Praia Forte. R$330

Pousada Boulevard Rua Marechal Floriano (Boulevard Canal) 237 ⊕22 2643 3095, ⊕pousadaboulevard.com. The location's brilliant if you want to be in the heart of Cabo Frio's canalside bars and restaurants, and it's worth paying a bit extra for a room at the front with a big balcony (although the ones at the back are quieter). This bright and airy posada also has a pool and even a sauna, and service comes with a big smile. R$350

Tia Maluca Rua Av dos Pescadores (Boulevard Canal), at the junction with Travessa Nações Unidas ⊕22 2647 4158, ⊕tiamaluca.com.br. Among the bustling restaurants and bars lining the canalside, which comes alive every evening (but especially Fridays and Saturdays), this decent seafood joint does a neat line in prawn *bobó* for R$45.70. Daily 11.30am–midnight.

São Pedro da Aldeia

Jesuit mission & church: Praça da Matriz • Daily 5–8pm • Free

The small town of **SÃO PEDRO DA ALDEIA**, located north of Cabo Frio at the northeastern end of the Lagoa de Araruama, is built around a Jesuit **church** and mission house, which date back to 1617. Perched on a hill above the shores of the lake, the town provides a marvellous view over the nearby **saltpans**, which look like a patchwork quilt on the edge of the lagoon.

ACCOMMODATION

SÃO PEDRO DA ALDEIA

Aldeia dos Ventos Rua João Martins 160 ⊕22 2621 2919. On a street leading downhill from the church by the pretty, blue-and-white municipal library, this is the cheapest *pousada* in town, with simple rooms, but all with a/c and TV. R$200

Pousada Ponta da Peça Praia do Sudoeste (5km west of town) ⊕22 2621 1181, ⊕pontadapeca.com.br. A *pousada* built in Spanish colonial style offering well-appointed rooms, a pretty garden with a pool, and stunning views across the lagoon and surrounding countryside. R$240

Arraial do Cabo

Six kilometres south of Cabo Frio, **ARRAIAL DO CABO** nestles among sand dunes, surrounded by hills. The **beaches** around Arraial do Cabo are some of the most beautiful in the state and are usually packed in high season. **Praia dos Anjos** is perfectly fine considering the area behind it is so built up, though you'd do much better by walking north (15min) along a path over a steep promontory to the unspoilt **Praia do Forno**. A boat ride is required to reach the stunning Praia do Pontal and the **Ilha de Cabo Frio**, a small, pristine island with powdery white beaches, sand dunes and superb views from its 390m peak (boats leave from Praia dos Anjos and charge around R$55 per person for a four-hour excursion). Another attractive beach is **Prainha**, north of town, which is a lot less developed than Praia dos Anjos, but can still get crowded in season.

ACCOMMODATION

ARRAIAL DO CABO

Capitão n'Areia Rua Santa Cruz 7, off Praia dos Anjos ☎22 2622 2720, 🌐capitaopousada.com.br. Looks like a shopping arcade from the street, but has a pleasantly maritime feel within, and the added attraction of a pool, not to mention a gym and sauna. R$395

Estalagem do Porto Rua Santa Cruz 12 ☎22 2622 2892, 🌐estalagemdoporto.com.br. A small *pousada* just north of Praia dos Anjos with rather poky rooms around a little garden. R$380

Marina Dos Anjos Hostel Rua Bernardo Lens 145 ☎22 2622 4060, 🌐marinadosanjos.com.br. An excellent youth hostel, which is quiet, clean and friendly, with a nice little garden, private rooms and six-bed dorms. Dorms R$73, doubles R$220

Búzios

Armação dos Búzios, or just **BÚZIOS**, is an immensely scenic resort full of high-spending beautiful people, and very popular with Argentines, on a peninsula north of Cabo Frio. Armação, the main settlement, is built in a vaguely colonial style, its streets lined with restaurants, bars and chic boutiques, and has been nicknamed "Brazil's St Tropez". It comes then as little surprise to find that it was "discovered" by none other than Brigitte Bardot, who stumbled upon it while touring the area in 1964. Despite being transformed overnight from humble fishing village to playground of the rich, Búzios didn't change much until some serious property development took hold in the 1980s. Now, during high season, the population swells from 22,000 to well over 150,000, and the fishing boats that once ferried the catch back to shore take pleasure-seekers beach-hopping and scuba diving. Outside of this period, though, it's hard not to be taken in by the peninsula's sheer beauty, with March, April and May the perfect time to visit, as tourists are relatively few, prices low and the weather pretty perfect.

Manguinos, Armação and Ossos

Búzios consists of three main settlements, each with its own distinct character. **Manguinos**, on the isthmus, is the main service centre, with a tourist office, a medical centre, banks and petrol stations. Midway along the peninsula, linked to Manguinos by a road lined with brash hotels, is **Armação**, an attractive village where cars are banned from some of the cobbled roads. Most of Búzio's best restaurants and boutiques are concentrated here, along with some of the resort's nicest *pousadas*, and there's also a helpful tourist office on the main square, **Praça Santos Dumont**. A fifteen-minute walk along the Orla Bardot that follows the coast from Armação, passing the lovely seventeenth-century **Igreja de Nossa Senhora de Sant'Ana** on the way, brings you to **Ossos**, the oldest settlement, comprising a pretty harbour, a quiet beach (though don't swim in the polluted water) and a few bars, restaurants and *pousadas*.

The beaches

Within walking distance of all Búzios' settlements are beautiful white-sand **beaches** – 27 in total – cradled between rocky cliffs and promontories, and lapped by crystal-clear waters. The beaches are varied, with the north-facing ones having the calmest and warmest seas, while those facing the south and east have the most surf. Though the beaches at Búzios' urban centre of Armação look good, the water is polluted and swimming should be avoided; a short distance to the northeast, however, are the very clean waters of the small, rather isolated and extremely picturesque beaches of **Azeda** and **Azedinha**, as well as the rather larger **João Fernandes**, the best place around here for snorkelling. Further east is **Praia Brava**, bordering a fine, horseshoe-shaped bay that's rarely overcrowded. On the north of the peninsula, to the west of Armação, is the **Praia da Tartaruga**, where the water is pristine and, apart from some bars, there are few buildings. South of Armação, the lovely bay of **Praia da Ferradura** is quite built up (and consequently crowded), but further out is the appealing **Praia de Tucuns**, a long stretch of sand that attracts surprisingly few people. On the beaches, you can rent kayaks or *pedalôs*, or indulge in a little windsurfing or snorkelling.

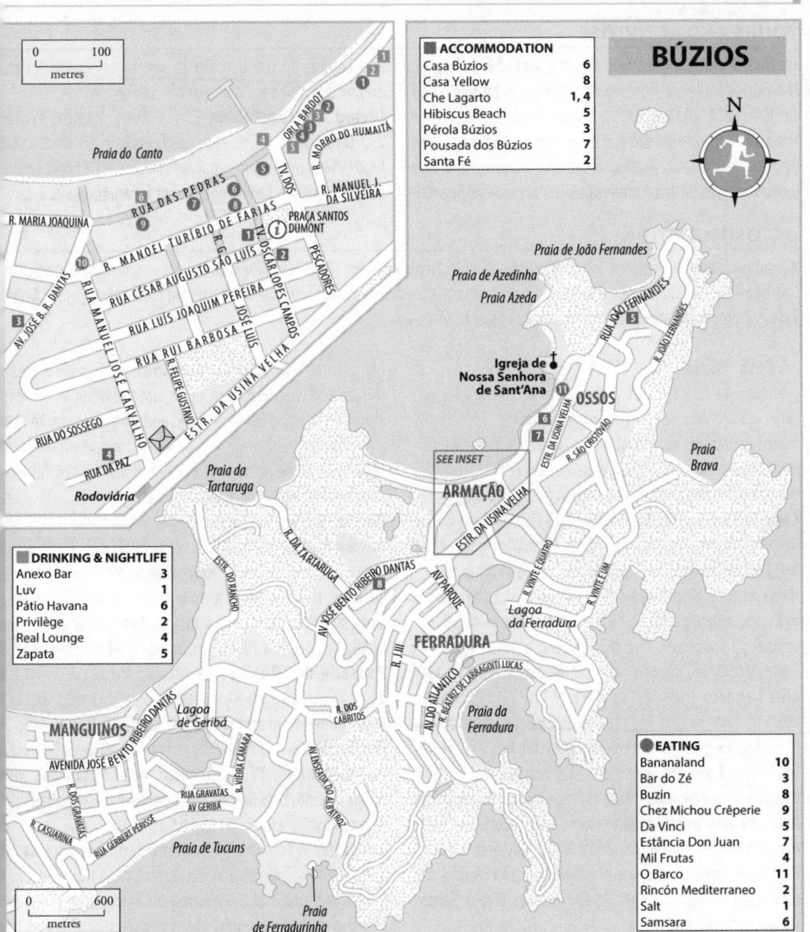

ARRIVAL AND DEPARTURE

BÚZIOS

By bus The rodoviária consists of a couple of shelters on Estrada da Usina, at the junction of Rua Manoel de Carvalho (which leads towards Praia de Armação), with a ticket office across the street. Eight daily buses serve Rio (3hr), with just two weekly (Fri & Sun) to Campos (3hr) for points north and east. Local buses to Cabo Frio (50min) run along Estrada da Usina, terminating on Estrada da Usina Velha, a block off Praia da Armação.

GETTING AROUND AND INFORMATION

By minivan/taxi Minivans (R$3.50) ply the peninsula's main road, but taxis charge rates that are fixed and posted up at their ranks (for example in Praça Santos Dumont; ☎ 22 2623 2160), with most beach-to-beach journeys costing R$20–30.

Information The main tourist office is out at Pórtico de Búzios, the entry into town on the RJ-102 highway, 4km west of central Armação, at the far end of Av José Bento Ribeiro Dantas (daily 9am–10pm; ☎ 22 2623 4254, Ⓦ buzios.rj.gov.br/informacoes_turisticas). A handier, though erratically open, kiosk is on Armação's main square, Praça Santos Dumont (supposedly Mon–Thurs & Sun 8am–9pm, Fri & Sat 8am–10pm, but often closed; ☎ 22 2623 2099). There's a handy listings website at Ⓦ buziosonline.com.br.

1

TOURS AND ACTIVITIES

Búzios Trolley A good way to get oriented is to hop on the Búzios Trolley, a sightseeing vehicle run by Tour Shop Buzios (22 2623 4733, tourshop.com.br). It leaves their office at Orla Bardot 550 every day at 9am, noon and 3pm on a 2hr tour, passing by twelve beaches and two lookout points, with a commentary in Portuguese, Spanish and English on the peninsula's vegetation, microclimate and history; R$60 including drinks and snacks.

Diving and snorkelling Búzios Divers, Rua das Pedras 232 (22 2623 0670, buziosdivers.com.br) lead scuba trips (R$300 per person, equipment included). People on the beaches rent snorkelling equipment for around R$25 a day.

ACCOMMODATION

Accommodation in Búzios is fairly expensive, and in **high season** (Dec–Feb) reservations are essential, although the tourist offices will do their best to help you find a room. If nothing's available in Búzios, you might consider staying in **Cabo Frio**, where rooms are cheaper and usually easier to come by.

★**Casa Búzios** Rua Morro do Humaitá, Casa 1, Armação 22 2623 7002, pousadacasabuzios.com; map p.117. Very friendly home from home, with lovely rooms betraying an attention to detail that makes this more a luxurious B&B than a *pousada*. There's an attractive garden with ocean views and a small pool. R$400

Casa Yellow Rua de Mandrágora 13 (off Av José Bento Ribeiro Dantas, 1km southwest of central Armação) 22 2623 3419, casayellowbuzioshostel.com; map p.117. Here's where you can be a scruffy backpacker and stay cheaply in Búzios, although it's a bit of a walk to the beach. Sill, the company's congenial, and there's even a small pool. Dorms R$50, doubles (available out-of-season only) R$130

Che Lagarto Rua da Paz 7 22 2623 1173, chelagarto.com; map p.117. This little hostel opened by the Che Lagarto chain is extremely handy for bus departures (and indeed arrivals). There are only dorms here, but Che Lagarto have a separate place at Praça Santos Dumont 280 for those who want a private room. Both locales are basic and functional, nothing special, but clean and friendly. Prices are somewhat cheaper off-season and during the week. Dorms (Rua da Paz) R$40, doubles (Praça Santos Dumont) R$250

Hibiscus Beach Rua 1, no. 22, quadra C, Praia de João Fernandes 22 2623 6221, hibiscusbeach.com.br; map p.117. Spacious bungalows, each with a small terrace and wonderful sea views, are the order of the day at this welcoming British-owned and -run *pousada*. There's a good-sized pool, and the area's best snorkelling beach is very close, while Armaçao's nightlife is a 5min taxi ride (or 20min walk) away. R$570

Pérola Búzios Av José Bento Ribeiro Dantas 222, Armação 22 2620 8507, perolahotels.com; map p.117. All the facilities you'd expect of a luxury hotel including stylish modern furniture, a fitness centre and spa and a large, beautiful pool. Although there's no sea view, the hotel is located just 200m from Rua das Pedras. R$828

Pousada dos Búzios Rua Alto do Humaitá 11 22 2623 6060, pousadadosbuzios.com.br; map p.117. A cut above your average Búzios *pousada*, this is quite a plush little place, with a variety of rooms, all nice and fresh, equipped with a TV and frigobar, helpful staff and just 200m up from Orla Bardot. Discounts are usually available (big ones off-season). R$685

Santa Fé Praça Santos Dumont 300, Armação 22 2623 6404, pousadasantafe.com; map p.117. Rooms are simple but well cared-for at this little *pousada*. The the staff are friendly, the decor is attractive and it's right in the centre of Armação, good value and very popular thanks to its proximity to Búzios's nightlife. R$260

EATING

With few exceptions, **restaurants** in Búzios are predictably expensive. The best places to eat are in Armação, especially along Rua das Pedras and Orla Bardot, which were originally part of (and have continuous numbering with) Avenida José Bento Ribeiro Dantas. Less expensive options include some excellent *por quilo* restaurants in the town centre, especially on Rua Manoel Turíbio de Farias, which runs immediately parallel to Rua das Pedres. Cheapest of all, and often excellent, are the beachside *barracas* selling oysters and grilled fish.

Bananaland Rua Manoel Turíbio de Farias 50 22 2623 2666, restaurantebananaland.com.br; map p.117. One of the best *por quilo* restaurants in Búzios (R$89.50/kg). The choice among the buffet of salads and hot dishes is outstanding. Daily 11.30am–11.30pm.

Bar do Zé Orla Bardot 382 22 2263 4986; map p.117. Celebrities from Rio congregate here: it specializes in creative seafood dishes (snapper in passion fruit sauce R$84, octopus in oyster sauce R$96), but the main point of this place to see and be seen. Mon 6pm–midnight, Tues–Sun 1pm–midnight.

Buzin Rua Manoel Turíbio de Farias 273 22 2633 7051; map p.117. The extensive and sophisticated range of dishes at this pleasant and moderately priced *por quilo* restaurant (R$88.90/kg) includes salads, seafood and excellent Argentine beef. Daily noon–12.30am.

Chez Michou Crêperie Rua das Pedras 90 ☎ 22 2623 5137, ⓦ chezmichou.com.br; map p.117. Thanks to its open-air bar, cheap drinks and imaginative crêpes (*doce de leite* crêpe R$18, chicken curry crêpe R$22), this has long been Armação's most popular hangout. Open until dawn, when it serves breakfast to the patrons pouring out of the nearby clubs. Daily 12.30pm–around 6am.

Da Vinci Rua das Pedras 286 ☎ 22 2623 7098, ⓦ info buzios.com; map p.117. The best Italian food in town, with 25 varieties of wood-oven pizzas (small margherita R$24) and other hearty dishes (*lasagne ai quattro formaggi* R$34), perhaps not quite like mamma used to make, but not a bad attempt. Daily noon–1am.

Estância Don Juan Rua das Pedras 178 ☎ 22 2623 2169, ⓦ estanciadonjuan.com.br; map p.117. An airy Argentine restaurant serving first-rate meat to a demanding (mainly Argentine) clientele. If cuts of beef mean little to you, opt for the *bife de chorizo*, the Argentine standard (sirloin strip; R$81). Most days noon–1am, closes one day a week (usually Tues or Wed).

Mil Frutas Orla Bardot 362 ☎ 22 2623 6436, ⓦ mil frutas.com.br; map p.117. The best ice cream in town, offering flavours both familiar and exotic – from *capuaça* to "Romeu e Julieta" (guava and cream). One scoop costs R$14, two scoops R$22. Mon–Thurs & Sun 11am–midnight, Fri & Sat 11am–1am.

★ **O Barco** Av José Bento Ribeiro Dantas 1054, Armação ☎ 22 2629 8307; map p.117. An unpretentious little fish restaurant where you can tuck into some seriously tasty seafood without breaking the bank. There's fried fish for R$30, or garlic prawns for R$38, all served with a smile on a terrace by the seafront. Daily except Tues 10am–11pm.

Rincón Mediterraneo Orla Bardot 422 ☎ 22 2623 4644; map p.117. Spanish food, especially seafood, is the mainstay at this largish restaurant facing Armação beach, where specialities include *bacalao a la vizcaiana* (saltfish stewed Basque-style in tomato sauce; R$78), and of course paella (R$155 for two). They also have good lunchtime set menus. Mon, Tues & Thurs–Sun noon–11pm.

Salt Orla Bardot 468 ☎ 22 2623 6769, ⓦ restaurante salt.com.br; map p.117. Top marks for creativity to this modern restaurant where succulent salmon in creamy ginger sauce will set you back R$69, or you can try the lobster medallions wrapped in Parma ham with walnut, celery and lime qinoa for R$98. Tues–Sun 5pm–midnight.

Samsara Rua Santana Maia 684, just off Rua das Pedras ☎ 22 2623 1080; map p.117. Vegetarian *por quilo* restaurant offering an excellent lunch buffet of hot and cold dishes (R$65.90/kg), featuring interesting pasta offerings that make use of fresh, organic produce. Entry is via the Indian-style bells and joss-sticks shop downstairs. Tues–Sun noon–10pm.

DRINKING AND NIGHTLIFE

Nightlife is concentrated along Rua das Pedras and the Orla Bardot. It's impossible to exaggerate how crowded Armação gets in January and February, but even in the off-season Rua das Pedras is quite lively on weekend nights.

Anexo Bar Orla Bardot 392 ☎ 22 2623 6837, ⓦ anexo barbuzios.com.br; map p.117. Hang out and be chic at Búzios's primo bar, where the food's good, the drinks are well mixed, and the company's elegant. You can of course come here just for a beer or a cocktail, but most customers grab a bite too and make an evening of it. Daily 5pm–3am.

Pátio Havana Rua das Pedras 101 ☎ 22 2623 2169, ⓦ patiohavana.com.br; map p.117. The *Pátio Havana* is a restaurant and bar at the upper end of the price scale that's worth checking out for the first-rate jazz artists from Rio, São Paulo and abroad who play here at weekends. Free entry; live music Sat & Sun from 8pm. Mon & Wed–Fri 6pm–midnight, Sat & Sun 1pm–midnight.

Privilège Orla Bardot 500 ☎ 22 8819 0465, ⓦ privilege net.com.br; map p.117. A poppy, slightly glitzy resort disco favoured by bright young things from Rio, which plays upbeat house sounds. *Luv*, next door, is rather similar. Thurs–Sat 11pm–late, sometimes also other days.

Real Lounge Búzios Rua das Pedras 275 ☎ 22 2623 8387, ⓦ facebook.com/realsushibuzios; map p.117. This sushi restaurant transmogrifies on weekend nights into a club called *La Resistencia*, which is the place to head in Búzios if you care more about the music (house and techno) than you do about being among pretty people and showing off your clothes. Restaurant daily 9am–5pm & 6pm–12.30am; club Thurs–Sat 11pm–6am.

Zapata Orla Bardot 352 ☎ 22 2623 0973; map p.117. Rougher and readier than the more expensive nightclubs, with an often quite raucous atmosphere fuelled by the free beers included in the (after 11pm) entrance fee. Bar Tues–Sun 5–11pm; club Wed–Sat 11pm–5am.

Barra de São João and Rio das Ostras

An hour or so up the coast from the Costa do Sol there are beautiful **beaches** around the pretty colonial villages of **Barra de São João** and **Rio das Ostras**. If you want to stay round here, you'll find *pousadas* in both these places, though there's been much

1

uncontrolled development along this stretch of coast, leading to pretty hideous results. Near Rio das Ostras, the iodized waters of the **Lagoa da Coca-Cola** (yes, really) boast medicinal qualities.

Petrópolis

Sixty-six kilometres directly north of Rio de Janeiro, high in the mountains, stands the imperial city of **PETRÓPOLIS**. In fine weather, the journey from Rio is glorious. On the way up, sit on the left-hand side of the bus for great views along a one-way road, bordered by naked rock on one side and a sheer drop on the other; the return to Rio is made by a slightly different route that also snakes its way through terrifying mountain passes. The landscape is dramatic, climbing among forested slopes that give way suddenly to ravines and gullies, while clouds shroud the surrounding mountains.

In 1720, **Bernardo Soares de Proença** opened a trade route between Rio and Minas Gerais, and in return was conceded the area around the present site of Petrópolis as a royal land grant. Surrounded by stunning scenery, and with a gentle, alpine summer climate, it had by the nineteenth century become a favourite retreat of Rio's elite. The arrival of German immigrants contributed to the development of the town, and has much to do with its curious European Gothic feel. Dom Pedro II took a fancy to Petrópolis and in 1843 designated it the summer seat of his government. He also established a German agricultural colony, which failed because of the unsuitability of the soil, and in 1849 – with an epidemic of yellow fever sweeping through Rio – he and his court took refuge in the town, thus assuring its prosperity.

You can easily visit Petrópolis as a day-trip from Rio, or instead continue to Teresopólis or inland. It's possible to ignore the traffic congestion and fumes of the commercial area, as most sights are in the older, quieter part of town. Although Petrópolis is quite spread out, you can easily stroll around it, taking in plenty of elegant nineteenth-century mansions, particularly along **Avenida Koeller** and **Avenida Ipiranga**.

HISTORIC BUILDINGS IN PETRÓPOLIS

Historic buildings in Petrópolis worth checking out include:

Casa da Ipiranga Av Ipiranga 716. Virtually unchanged since being built in 1884 for a wealthy coffee merchant; set in a park designed by Emperor Dom Pedro II's gardener (interior currently closed pending restoration, but you can see the outside and eat at the *Bordeaux* restaurant in its grounds; see page 123).

Casa Santos Dumont Rua do Encanto 22. An 1918 Alpine chalet, former home of a famous local aviator, containing personal memorabilia; R$8. Tues–Sun 9.30am–5pm.

Casa Stefan Zweig Rua Gonçalves Dias 34 ⓦcasastefanzweig.org. Home of an Austrian writer and refugee who committed suicide here in 1942 with his young wife, Lotte; the house has an exhibition on refugees from Nazism in Brazil; free. Fri–Sun 11am–5pm.

Cervejaria Bohemia Rua Alfredo Pachá 166. Brazil's oldest brewery, set up by German immigrants in 1853, stopped production in 1973 and now houses an exhibition on the history of beer; R$36. Mon–Thurs noon–5pm, Fri–Sun 10am–6pm.

Museu Casa do Colono Rua Cristóvão Colombo 1034. A simple house built in 1847, exhibiting possessions and photos of Petrópolis's nineteenth-century German immigrants; free. Tues–Sun 8.30am–4pm.

Palácio Quitandinha Av Joaquim Rolla 2, Quitandinha, 5km south of town. A grand casino (the biggest in South America), which closed following a gambling ban just five years after its 1941 construction; R$8, with free guided tours available in Portuguese. Tues–Sat 9.30am–7pm.

Palácio Rio Negro Av Koeller 255. Dating from 1896, this elegant primrose-yellow mansion was the summer palace of Brazil's presidents until 1960; free. Tues–Sat 10am–5pm.

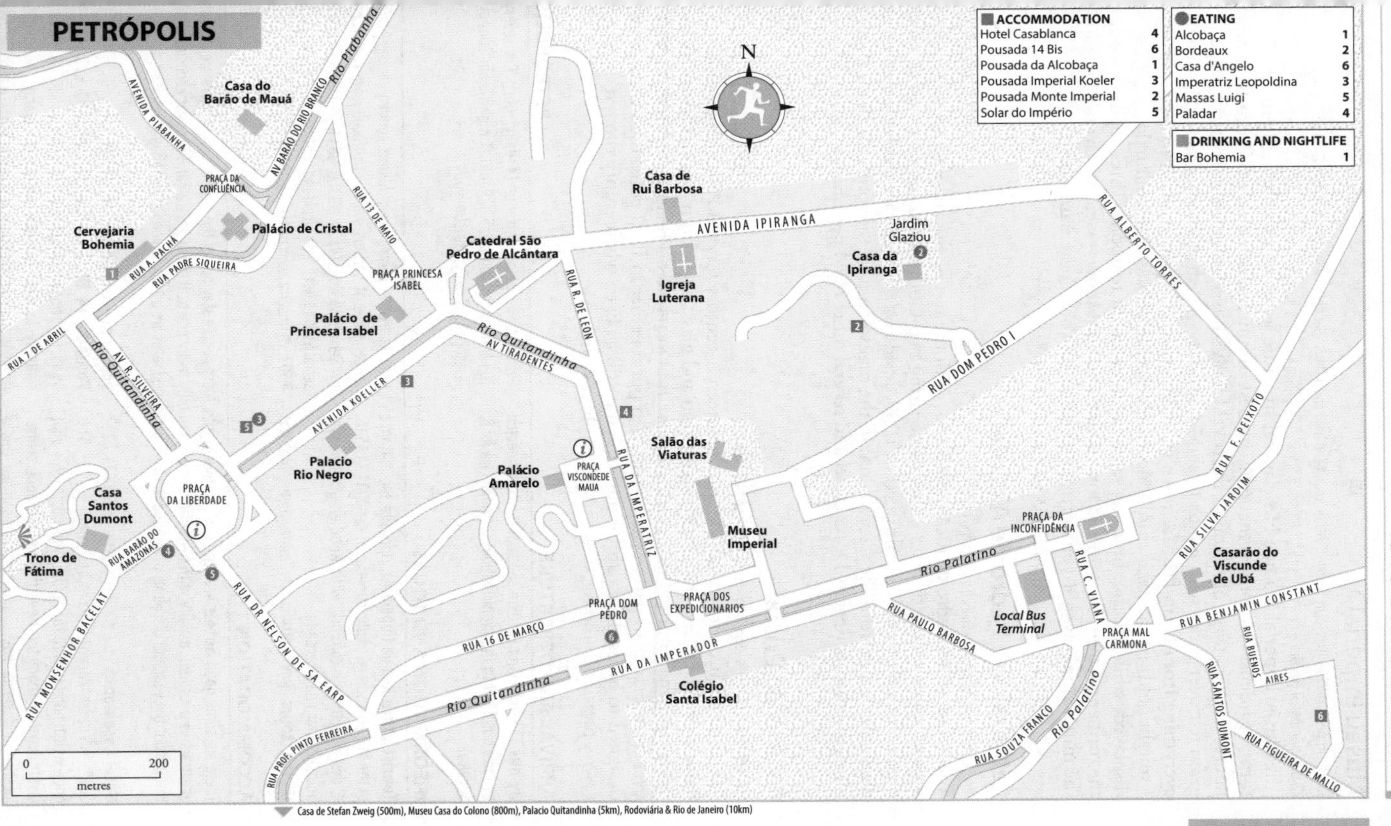
PETRÓPOLIS
ACCOMMODATION
Hotel Casablanca 4
Pousada 14 Bis 6
Pousada da Alcobaça 1
Pousada Imperial Koeler 3
Pousada Monte Imperial 2
Solar do Império 5
EATING
Alcobaça 1
Bordeaux 2
Casa d'Angelo 6
Imperatriz Leopoldina 3
Massas Luigi 5
Paladar 4
DRINKING AND NIGHTLIFE
Bar Bohemia 1
N
Casa do Barão de Mauá
Palácio de Cristal
Cervejaria Bohemia
Palácio de Princesa Isabel
Palacio Rio Negro
Catedral São Pedro de Alcântara
Casa de Rui Barbosa
Igreja Luterana
Casa da Ipiranga
Jardim Glaziou
Salão das Viaturas
Museu Imperial
Palácio Amarelo
Colégio Santa Isabel
Local Bus Terminal
Casarão do Viscunde de Ubá
Casa Santos Dumont
Trono de Fátima
PRAÇA DA LIBERDADE
PRAÇA DA CONFLUÊNCIA
PRAÇA PRINCESA ISABEL
PRAÇA VISCONDEDE MAUA
PRAÇA DOM PEDRO
PRAÇA DOS EXPEDICIONARIOS
PRAÇA DA INCONFIDÊNCIA
PRAÇA MAL CARMONA
AVENIDA PIABANHA
AV BARÃO DO RIO BRANCO
Rio Piabanha
RUA 13 DE MAIO
RUA A. PACHA
RUA PADRE SIQUEIRA
RUA 7 DE ABRIL
AV R. SILVEIRA
Rio Quitandinha
AVENIDA KOELLER
AV TIRADENTES
RUA R. DE LEON
AVENIDA IPIRANGA
RUA DA IMPERATRIZ
RUA DOM PEDRO I
RUA ALBERTO TORRES
RUA F. PEIXOTO
RUA SILVA JARDIM
RUA DA IMPERADOR
RUA 16 DE MARÇO
Rio Palatino
RUA PAULO BARBOSA
RUA C. VIANA
RUA BENJAMIN CONSTANT
RUA BUENOS AIRES
RUA SANTOS DUMONT
RUA FIGUEIRA DE MALLO
RUA SOUZA FRANCO
RUA DR NELSON DE SA EARP
RUA PROF. PINTO FERREIRA
RUA BARÃO DO AMAZONAS
RUA MONSENHOR BACELAT
0 200
metres
Casa de Stefan Zweig (500m), Museu Casa do Colono (800m), Palacio Quitandinha (5km), Rodoviária & Rio de Janeiro (10km)

1

Museu Imperial

Rua da Imperatriz 220 • Tues–Sun 11am–5.30pm; sound and light show Thurs–Sat 8pm • R$10; show R$20 • ⓣ 24 2233 0300, ⓦ museuimperial.gov.br

The **Museu Imperial** is a fine Neoclassical structure set in beautifully maintained formal gardens. Once the remarkably modest summer palace of Dom Pedro II, it now houses a fascinating collection of the royal family's bits and pieces. On entry, you're given felt over-shoes with which to slide around the polished floors, and inside there's everything from Dom Pedro's crown (639 diamonds, 77 pearls, all set in 2kg of finely wrought gold) to the regal commode. In the former stables, the royal railway carriage is displayed, while another building serves as an excellent **tearoom**. Three nights a week the former palace is illuminated for a **sound and light show** – well worth attending for the music alone, even if you don't understand the Portuguese narration.

Catedral São Pedro de Alcântara

Rua São Pedro de Alcântara • Daily 8am–6pm • Free

The **Catedral São Pedro de Alcântara** blends with the rest of the architecture around but is much more recent than its rather overbearing neo-Gothic style suggests – while work began in 1884, it was only finished in 1939. Inside on the walls are ten relief sculptures depicting scenes from the Crucifixion; in the mausoleum lie the tombs of Dom Pedro himself, Princess Regent Dona Isabel and several other royal personages.

Palácio de Cristal

Rua Alfredo Pachá • Tues–Sun 9am–6pm • Free • ⓣ 24 2247 3721

Like a miniature version of London's nineteenth-century Crystal Palace, Petrópolis's **Palácio de Cristal**, likewise made of cast iron and glass, dates from 1884. The town's last slaves were manumitted in a ceremony here four years later. Prefabricated and shipped over from France in parts, which were then put together in Petrópolis, the Palácio was designed to be used for exhibitions, which it still is. Even when empty though, it's the town's prettiest building, and extremely photogenic.

ARRIVAL AND DEPARTURE — PETRÓPOLIS

By bus The rodoviária is 10km south of town, connected by local bus #100 to the municipal bus terminal (via Av R. Silveira).

Destinations Belo Horizonte (4 daily; 6hr); Rio (every 30–40min; 1hr 30min); São Paulo (1 nightly; 6hr 30min); Teresópolis (7 daily; 1hr 30min).

INFORMATION AND TOURS

Tourist office Rua da Imperatriz, opposite the entrance to the Museu Imperial (daily 9am–5pm; ⓣ 0800 024 1516, ⓦ destinopetropolis.com.br), with another office (same hours) in Praça da Liberdade.

Hiking tours Town attractions aside, Petrópolis has easy access to some lovely hiking country – day- and longer hikes at various scales of difficulty are organized by Serra Trekking (ⓣ 24 99266 8811, ⓦ facebook.com/serratrekking.net) and Trekking Petrópolis (ⓣ 24 223 7607, ⓦ rioserra.com.br/trekking).

ACCOMMODATION

There are some good **hotels** near the city's historic sights. Most people stay out of the centre, where there are dozens of attractive *pousadas*, usually with beautiful gardens, but only really practical if you have a car. Prices vary considerably throughout the year, but discounts of about a third off our quoted rates are usually given for weekday stays.

Hotel Casablanca Rua da Imperatriz 286 ⓣ 24 2242 6662, ⓦ casablancahotel.com.br; map p.121. This once-stylish hotel next to the *Palácio Imperial* is somewhat institutional in character. Nevertheless, the pool, central location and clean, well-appointed rooms make this a popular city-centre choice. Wi-Fi R$345

Pousada 14 Bis Rua Buenos Aires 192 ⓣ 24 223 0946, ⓦ pousada14bis.com.br; map p.121. A lovely centrally located *pousada* with jolly orange bedrooms (the superior upstairs ones get more light), a nice garden and a collection of memorabilia related to celebrated local aviator Santos Dumont. R$220

★ **Pousada da Alcobaça** Rua Dr Agostinho Goulão 298, Corrêas (6km northeast of Petrópolis) 24 2221 1240, pousadadaalcobaca.com.br; map p.121. A fairly simple yet extraordinarily comfortable *pousada* located a few kilometres from the entrance of the Parque Nacional da Serra dos Órgãos. The gardens, flowers (inside and out), superb meals (see page 123) and the owners' warm welcome make this the most delightful of Petrópolis's country inns. R$528

Pousada Imperial Koeler Av Koeller 99 24 2243 4330, pousadaimperialkoeler.com.br; map p.121. A relatively modest 1875 mansion on one of Petrópolis's grandest avenues, a short walk from the city's historic sites. Decorated in period style, the rooms are simple yet comfortable, with the most attractive facing the avenue. Midweek, the price drops by nearly half. R$435

★ **Pousada Monte Imperial** Rua José Alencar 27 24 2237 1664, pousadamonteimperial.com.br; map p.121. Located on a hilltop, this *pousada* has the look and air of an Alpine inn and is a stiff walk from the town's attractions. Rooms are quite small but appealing, and there's a nice garden with a pool, too; the English-speaking owner is extremely friendly. R$380

Solar do Império Av Koeller 376 24 2103 3000, solardoimperio.com.br; map p.121. Set among the city's most elegant residences, this Neoclassical mansion is now a luxurious hotel. All the rooms have been restored to their period splendour, while every modern convenience and comfort is also offered. The grounds include a small indoor pool, and there's a fine restaurant (see page 123). R$590

EATING

Alcobaça Rua Dr Agostinho Goulão 298, Corrêas 24 2221 1240, pousadadaalcobaca.com.br; map p.121. This country inn (20min by taxi or bus from the centre) is a delightful setting for a leisurely lunch or dinner. They use fresh ingredients such as local dairy produce, freshwater fish, and vegetables and herbs from the kitchen garden, and the food is both unpretentious and excellent. Be sure to allow time after lunch for a gentle walk in the beautiful gardens. Reservations advisable. Daily 1–5pm & 7–9pm.

Bordeaux Av Ipiranga 716 24 2242 5711, bordeauxvinhos.com.br; map p.121. In the converted stables of one of Petrópolis's most beautiful stately homes (see page 120), the moderately priced Italian- and French-influenced offerings here include salmon carpaccio to start (R$36) with solid meat dishes such as steak au poivre (R$54) to complement the excellent wine list. Mon–Sat noon–midnight.

Casa d'Angelo Rua do Imperador 700 24 2242 0888; map p.121. A *chopperia* (beer bar) and restaurant, slap-bang in the centre of town, which has been filling Petropolitan bellies with solid grub since 1914. Lunchtime *pratos executivos* (weekdays till 4pm) go for R$24.90, or you can tuck into a supper-time stroganoff for R$49, and of course wash it down with an ice-cold glass of *chopp*. Tues–Sun 11am–midnight.

★ **Imperatriz Leopoldina** Solar do Império hotel, Av Koeller 376 24 2103 3000; map p.121. The chef

COFFEE COUNTRY

To many people, Brazil means **coffee** like Assam means tea, and in the nineteenth century it did dominate the coffee trade, but Rio's coffee boom – centred on the **Paraiba Valley**, some 200km west of Petrópolis – was actually short-lived. It only got under way in the 1820s, and collapsed in 1888 with the abolition of slavery, on which the plantation owners were completely dependent. More resourceful farmers migrated to São Paulo to take advantage of Italian and other immigrant labour and the availability of fertile, well-watered land. Back in Rio state, single-crop farming in the hilly terrain had eroded the soil, and felling the forest to plant coffee had altered the climate, causing drought, so the coffee barons had to abandon their *fazendas* (plantations) or look for other uses of their land. Dairy farming was eventually found to work, and today almost all the land is given over to cattle grazing. Evidence of the coffee boom is most clearly apparent in the **fazenda houses** that are left standing in various states of repair.

With a few days and, ideally, a car, a visit to the Paraiba Valley can be fascinating. It can be reached in two hours from Rio, and is a convenient stop-off between Petrópolis and Paraty. A particularly attractive place to make for is **Rio das Flores**, a sleepy little spot dotted with grand *fazenda* house.

INFORMATION AND ACCOMMODATION

The Paraiba Valley towns all have **tourist information offices**, among which the one in Rio das Flores is at Rua Aniceto de Medeiros Corrêa 156 (daily 8am–5pm; 24 2458 1271). They can usually help with visiting old coffee **fazendas**; among these, the slightly run-down look of *Fazenda Campos Eliseos*, established in 1847, contrasts with the beautifully preserved 1820 *Fazenda Santa Justa* where the period decor on the *casa grande* could come straight from the pages of a coffee-table book.

has given a contemporary slant dishes inspired by Empress Leopoldina's supposed love of Brazilian ingredients and flavours. Favourites include trout with almonds (R$59) and steak au poivre vert (R$73). Daily noon–12.20pm.

Massas Luigi Praça da Liberdade 185 ⓣ24 2246 0279, ⓦmassasluigi.com.br; map p.121. Although considered the best Italian restaurant in town, its pasta offerings, including cannelloni or lasagne for R$48.90, may disappoint purists. You won't, on the other hand, leave hungry. Mon–Thurs & Sun 11am–midnight, Fri & Sat 11am–1am.

Paladar Praça da Liberdade 229 ⓣ24 2243 1143 ⓦpaladarpetropolis.com.br; map p.121. A *por quilo* buffet with a varied choice of salads and Brazilian hot dishes (R$65.90/kg). Located within a nineteenth-century mansion, you can either eat indoors or on the shaded terrace overlooking Praça da Liberdade. Tues–Sun 11am–midnight.

DRINKING

Bar Bohemia Rua Alfredo Pachá 166 ⓣ24 2020 9050, ⓦbohemia.com.br; map p.121. The Bohemia brewery's tap-house is a modern, largely outdoor bar where you can sample the range of beers produced by the brewery (mostly R$8.50 for 600ml), along with bar food that supposedly complements specific brews. There's an additional R$10 charge per customer for the musical entertainment. Tues–Fri 5pm–midnight, Sat & Sun 11am–midnight.

Teresópolis

While **TERESÓPOLIS** can be reached directly from Rio by bus, the most scenic route is from Petrópolis – 40km through the **Serra dos Órgãos**, much of which is a national park (see page 125). The state's highest town (872m), Teresópolis owed its initial development to the eighteenth-century opening of a road from Rio to Minas Gerais. Like Petrópolis, it was a favoured summer retreat (for Empress Teresa Cristina, for whom the town was named), and though smaller than Petrópolis it also shares some of its Germanic characteristics, including a benevolent alpine climate. The town itself is dull, centred on a main street that changes its name every couple of blocks, but the surrounding countryside is interesting. There are also magnificent views, especially over the Baixada Fluminense from **Soberbo**, where the Rio highway enters Teresópolis.

ARRIVAL AND INFORMATION — TERESÓPOLIS

By bus The rodoviária is at the southern end of Av Delfim Moreira, very near the centre.

Destinations Petrópolis (7 daily; 1hr 30min); Rio (hourly; 1hr 45min).

Tourist office Praça Olimpica, a square on Av Lúcio Meira (Mon–Sat 8am–6pm; ⓣ21 2742 5561).

ACCOMMODATION

Intercity Teresopolis Rua Rui Barbosa 611, Agriões ⓣ21 2741 4000, ⓦintercityhoteis.com.br. A handy if functional four-star chain hotel located at the southern end of the town centre near the municipal theatre. It won't get any marks for style and panache, but it scores well for cleanliness and efficiency, and it's got everything you need for a good night's sleep. R$350

★ **Rosa dos Ventos** 22km from town, on the road towards Nova Friburgo ⓣ21 2644 8833, ⓦhotelrosadosventos.com.br. The best of the hotels in the picturesque hills around Teresópolis, set in beautiful park-like gardens with several restaurants, swimming pools and an extensive network of trails. R$769

Várzea Palace Hotel Rua Sebastião Teixeira 41 ⓣ21 2742 0878, ⓦvarzea.palace.nafoto.net. A beautiful white building that was once the most elegant place in town to stay. Only faint traces of its former luxury remain, but the place is clean, welcoming and extremely good value, with discounts midweek. R$140

EATING AND DRINKING

Dona Irene Rua Tenente Luís Meireles 1800, Bom Retiro (1km east of the rodoviária) ⓣ21 2742 2901, ⓦdonairene.com.br. A Russian restaurant offering "the food of the Tsars". You start with *borscht*, naturally, moving on to main courses such as *pojarski* (chicken in creamy cheese sauce) or *veranike* (chicken in sour cream). The fixed price for a meal without drinks is R$150. Tues–Sat noon–midnight.

Vagão Av Lúcio Meira 833 ⓣ21 2643 3034, ⓦvagaobeer.com. A lively bar, with a big choice of international beers, with food from burgers (from R$28–42) to steaks (from R$33). There's a kids' play area, and true to its name ("wagon"), you can eat and drink in a genuine old train carriage. Tues–Fri 6pm–midnight, Sat noon–1am, Sun noon–midnight.

Parque Nacional do Itatiaia

Between the borders of São Paulo and Minas Gerais • Plateau area daily 7am–6pm (last entry 2.30pm); lower area daily 8am–5pm • R$32 • ⓣ 24 3352 1292, ⓦ icmbio.gov.br/parnaitatiaia

Nestling in the northwest corner of the state, 165km from Rio, the **Parque Nacional do Itatiaia** is the oldest national park in Brazil, founded in 1937 and covering 120 square kilometres of the Mantigueira mountain range. People come here to climb – favourites are the **Pico das Agulhas Negras** (2787m) and the **Pico de Prateleira** (2540m) – and it is also an important nature reserve. There are two separate entrances to the park: the lower area entrance is accessible by bus from Itatiaia, but the plateau area entrance is not served by public transport, so you will have to make your own arrangements for getting there; buses from Itatiaia to Caxambu will drop you at the state line, a 14km hike from the plateau area entrance.

The park has waterfalls, primary forest, wildlife and orchids. Natural springs and streams here combine to form the Bonito, Preto, Pirapitinga and Palmital rivers, supplying the massive hydrographic basin of the Paraíba plate, and giving much-needed oxygenation to the Paraíba watercourse in one of its most polluted stretches.

Itatiaia

The town of **ITATIAIA**, on the BR-116, is surrounded by beautiful scenery and makes a good base: it has plenty of **hotels**, mainly found along the Estrada do Parque Nacional, the 2km-long road that links the town and park, plied by local buses from the rodoviária.

Penedo

The small town of **PENEDO** is 14km away from Itatiaia, to which it is connected by regular buses, and is also a good base for visiting the Parque Nacional do Itatiaia. Penedo was settled in 1929 by immigrants from Finland, one of numerous Finnish utopian communities established in Latin America at that time. With vegetarianism and agricultural self-sufficiency among their founding tenets, the Finnish community struggled to survive as they discovered that the land they occupied was unsuitable for cultivation. Those who opted to remain turned to tourism and the area gradually

PARQUE NACIONAL DA SERRA DOS ÓRGÃOS

One of Brazil's most beautiful mountain regions, the **Parque Nacional da Serra dos Órgãos** (daily 8am–5pm; lower part R$33, upper part R$53; ⓦ icmbio.gov.br/parnaso) straddles an area of highland Atlantic rainforest between Petrópolis and Teresópolis. The main features of the park are dramatic rock formations that resemble rows of organ pipes (hence the range's name), dominated by the towering **Dedo de Deus** ("God's Finger") peak. There are tremendous **walking** possibilities in the park, with the favourite peaks for those with mountain-goat tendencies being the Agulha do Diablo (2050m) and the Pedra do Sino (2263m); the latter has a path leading to the summit, a relatively easy three-hour trip (take refreshments). There are some campsites but no equipment for rent, so you'll need to come prepared.

There are entrances with **visitors' centres** near Petrópolis (ⓣ 21 2236 0464) and Teresópolis (ⓣ 21 2642 4072). At **Petrópolis** the entrance is near the village of Corrêas (served from Petrópolis by citybus #600). From Corrêas you can take bus #611, which leaves you a kilometre short, or #616, which takes you a bit nearer. At **Teresópolis** it's just south of town and much easier to access, served by hourly local buses (on the hour, destination "Soberbo") heading south along Avenida Lúcio Meira, with more frequent buses (to "Alto") leaving you a fifteen-minute walk away.

became popular with weekenders from São Paulo and Rio, who come for the horse riding and to buy the chocolates, jams, preserves and liquors produced here. Much is made of this Nordic heritage, despite the fact that today only a very small minority of the population are of Finnish origin, but one handy spin-off of the Finnish legacy for visitors is that most of the town's hotels have a sauna.

Clube Finlândia

Museum: Av das Mangueiras 2601 • Sun 9am–5pm • R$10 • 24 3351 1374, clubefinlandiablog.blogspot.com.br

An association dedicated to preserving Penedo's Finnish heritage, the *Clube Finlândia* puts on evenings of **Finnish folk dances** on the first Saturday of every month (9pm–1am). It also runs the **Museu Finlandês da Dona Eva**, which displays documents and photos illustrating the history of Finnish immigration in the region, along with works by local Finnish-Brazilian artists, and costumes, textiles and crafts; it usually only opens on Sundays, although it has been known to open on other days too occasionally.

Visconde de Maua area

The valley of the Rio Preto, stretching eastwards from the upper area of the park along the Rio–Minas Gerais state line towards the town of Visconde de Maua, is a popular beauty spot dotted with picturesque waterfalls, most notably those at Escorrega and Santa Clara. Unfortunately however, these are inaccessible by public transport, so you'll need your own vehicle to reach them.

ARRIVAL AND INFORMATION

By bus Itatiaia is served by buses from Rio (6 daily; 3hr 10min) and São Paulo (12 daily; 4hr). Local buses serve Penedo (roughly hourly; 20min) and the lower park entrance (4 daily; 15min).

PARQUE NACIONAL DO ITATIAIA

Visitors' centre 8.5km north of Itatiaia on the road to the lower park entrance (daily 8am–5pm; 24 3352 1461). Provides information and maps, and has a small Museu Regional da Fauna e da Flora.

ACCOMMODATION AND EATING

ITATIAIA

Hotel do Ypê Estrada Parque Nacional (15km from Itatiaia town) 24 3352 1296, hoteldoype.com.br. A hotel inside the park with rooms and chalets, lawns and a pool, surrounded by forest and wildlife (loads of birds, even toucans on occasion), with lots of hiking trails nearby. Wi-fi (rather eratic) in the reception area only. Prices include full-board. R$400

Vista Linda Estrada do Parque Nacional 50 24 3352 1124, vistalindahotel.com.br. You need to head 3.5km down a dirt track off the Estrada do Parque Nacional to reach this place, where you can stay in well-equipped chalets set in beautiful countryside, with facilities such as a pool and sauna. It's a great place to get away from it all, enjoy the views and appreciate the area's natural beauty. R$350

PENEDO

Koskenkorva Estrada das Três Cachoeiras 3882 24 3351 2532, koskenkorvafinland.wixsite.com/koskenkorva restauran. One of the country's only Finnish restaurants. The Finnish-style trout in dill sauce (R$45) is particularly worth trying. Mon, Tues, Thurs & Fri noon–5pm & 7–10pm, Sat noon–11pm, Sun noon–6pm.

Pequena Suécia Rua Toivo Suni 33 24 3351 1275, pequenasuecia.com.br. An excellent hotel in the middle of Penedo, with a choice of rooms or chalets, a pool and Finnish-style sauna, a Swedish restaurant and even its own jazz club. Includes breakfast. R$250

Rei das Trutas Av das Mangueiras 69 24 3351 1387, reidastrutas.com.br. A great place to sample the local trout, served fresh or smoked, plain or with a choice of sauces and garnishes, one of the best being *truta a belle meunièra* with prawns, capers and mushrooms (R$54.90). Mon–Thurs 11.15am–9.30pm, Fri & Sat 11.15am–10.30pm, Sun 11.15am–6pm.

Rio das Pedras Rua Resende 39 24 99208 9805, fazendariodaspedras.com.br. A quiet place by a river (the "Rio da Pedras" of its name), where you can stay in a room with a veranda or in a pretty little Alpine-style chalet in the grounds. There is a two-day minimum stay at weekends. R$225

The Costa Verde

The mountainous littoral and calm green waters of the aptly named **Costa Verde** ("Green Coast") provide a marked contrast to the sand and surf of the coastline east of Rio. One of Brazil's truly beautiful landscapes, the Costa Verde has been made much more accessible by the **Rio–Santos BR-101 Highway**, which has led to an increase in commercial penetration of the region, and threatens its ecosystem (see page 127). The Costa Verde's biggest attractions for visitors are the offshore island of **Ilha Grande**, with its lovely beaches, and the quaint old colonial town of **Paraty**.

Angra dos Reis

Most boats to Ilha Grande leave from the slightly shabby town of **ANGRA DOS REIS**, 152km west of Rio, which was founded in 1556 and became a port for exporting agricultural produce from São Paulo and Minas Gerais. There isn't much to see or do here, but you may end up staying the night between boat and bus journeys.

ARRIVAL AND INFORMATION — ANGRA DOS REIS

By bus The bus station is 1.5km east of the Estação Santa Luzia boat station, but buses to Paraty (19 daily; 2hr) and Rio (approximately hourly; 3hr), stop in front of the boat station anyway.

Tourist office Av Ayrton Senna, equidistant between the bus station 700m to its east, and the boat station (Estação Santa Luzia) 700m west (daily 8am–5pm; ☎24 3369 7704). There's also a tourist office branch at the boat station (daily 7am–7pm).

ACCOMMODATION AND EATING

Acropolis Marina Av Jair Toscano de Brito 500 (near the bus station) ☎24 3377 2650, hotelacropolisangradosreis.com.br. If you need a place with a pool, this is it. The rooms are decent enough and the breakfasts are good, but the staff aren't exactly on the ball. R$350

THE "GREEN" COAST?

There's no doubt that the **Costa Verde** is one of Brazil's most beautiful stretches of coast, but the fate of this 280km stretch of lush vegetation, rolling hills and tropical beaches hangs in the balance between rational development and ecological destruction, and so far the signs augur badly. Ecologists warn that fish stocks in the Bay of Sepetiba, which covers almost half the length of the Costa Verde, are in constant danger of destruction because of pollution. It's not surprising that so many hotel and holiday-home complexes are appearing on the hillsides and in the picturesque coves. What is incredible, however, is that the coast was *also* chosen as the location of two constructions with the potential to cause the most environmental destruction – an oil terminal and a nuclear power plant.

The Petrobrás **oil terminal** is, at least, out of sight, located 25km east of Angra dos Reis, so you only need contemplate the damage that an oil spill could wreak on this ecologically fragile stretch of coast when you pass the barrack-like housing complexes for the Petrobrás workers on the BR-101.

More worrying are the **nuclear power plants**, Angra-1 and Angra-2, some 40km west of Angra. It's difficult to imagine a more insane place to put a nuclear reactor. Not only would there be enormous difficulties should an emergency evacuation be necessary, as the mountains here plunge directly into the sea, but in addition the plant is in an earthquake fault zone, in a cove that local Indians call *Itaorna*, the Moving Rock.

The safety record of Angra-1 has been under particular scrutiny, and since 1985 it has been shut down for unspecified repairs over twenty times. Officials insist that there have been no radiation leaks beyond the plant, but environmentalists, who say there may be cracks in the reactor's primary container system, want the entire complex closed for good. The future, however, looks certain: it would be humiliating to abandon the project – and there would be huge problems in decommissioning the plant. In any case, the plants supply about half the electrical power used in the state of Rio de Janeiro, a figure that is set to increase greatly when work on a long-delayed third reactor (Angra-3) is completed in 2018.

1

Cherry Rua Pereira Peixoto 64 ⓣ 24 3365 0567. Simple little hotel in the centre of town, not far from the boat station, whose rooms (all with bathroom) are bright, airy and good value, so long as you make sure you get one with an outside window. R$160

Fogão de Minas Rua Júlio Maria 398 ⓣ 21 3365 4877. A decent *por quilo* restaurant offering a good choice of fish, meat and salad dishes (R$55.90/kg), near the quayside west of the boat station. Daily 11am–4pm.

Restaurante Pensãp de Tio Ivan Rua Júlio Maria 102 ⓣ 24 99818 4066. Almost directly opposite the boat station, this no-nonsense diner serves up cheap but good food, with a choice of simple meat of fish dishes with rice and salad an R$17 a go. Mon–Sat 11am–4pm.

Ilha Grande

ILHA GRANDE comprises 193 square kilometres of mountainous jungle, historic ruins and beautiful beaches, excellent for some scenic tropical rambling. The island is a state park and the authorities have been successful at limiting development and maintaining a ban on motor vehicles. The main drawback is the ferocity of the insects, especially during the summer, so come equipped with repellent.

Ilha Grande offers lots of beautiful **walks** along well-maintained and fairly well-signposted trails, but it's sensible to take some basic precautions. Be sure to set out as early as possible and always inform people at your *pousada* where you are going – in writing if possible. Carry plenty of water with you, and remember to apply sunscreen and insect repellent at regular intervals. Darkness comes suddenly, and even on a night with a full moon the trails are likely to be pitch-black due to the canopy formed by the overhanging foliage; it's best to carry a flashlight – most *pousadas* will be happy to lend you one. Whatever you do, avoid straying from the trail: not only could you easily get hopelessly lost, but there are also rumours of booby traps primed to fire bullets, left over from the days when the island hosted a high-security prison.

Carnaval is well celebrated in Ilha Grande and much more relaxed than the Rio experience. Also watch for the **Festival of São João** (Jan 20), and the February **Pirate Regatta**.

Brief history

According to legend, the pirate **Jorge Grego** was heading for the Straits of Magellan when his ship was sunk by a British fleet. He managed to escape with his two daughters to Ilha Grande, where he became a successful farmer and merchant. In a fit of rage, he murdered the lover of one of his daughters, and shortly afterwards, a terrible storm destroyed all his farms and houses. From then on, Jorge Grego passed his time roaming the island, distraught, pausing only long enough to bury his treasure before his final demise. If there is any treasure today, though, it's the island's **wildlife**: parrots, exotic hummingbirds, butterflies and monkeys abound in the thick vegetation.

Vila do Abraão

As you approach the low-lying, whitewashed colonial port of **VILA DO ABRAÃO**, the mountains rise dramatically from the sea, and in the distance there's the curiously shaped summit of Bico do Papagaio ("Parrot's Beak"), which rises to a height of 980m and can be reached in about three hours. There's really very little to see in Abraão itself, but it's a pleasant enough base from which to explore the rest of the island.

Antigo Presídio

The ruins of the **Antigo Presídio** lie a half-hour walk west along the coast from Abraão. Originally built as a hospital, it was converted to a prison for political prisoners in 1910 and was finally dynamited in the early 1960s. Among the ruins, you'll find the *cafofo*, the containment centre where prisoners who had failed in escape attempts were immersed in freezing water.

Antigo Aqueduto and around

Just fifteen minutes inland from Abraão, and overgrown with vegetation, stands the **Antigo Aqueduto** that used to channel the island's water supply. There's a fine view of the aqueduct from the **Pedra Mirante**, a hill near the centre of the island, and, close by, a waterfall provides the opportunity for a cool bathe on a hot day.

The beaches

Boat tours to the beaches depart from Abraão's jetty around 10.30am, with stops for snorkelling (equipment provided) and at a beach, where you'll be picked up later in the day to arrive back in Abraão around 4.30pm • Day-trip R$100/person

For the most part, the island's **beaches** – Aventureiro, Lopes Mendes, Canto, Júlia and Morcegoare to name a few – are still wild and unspoilt. They can be most easily reached by **boat** and beaches can also be reached on **foot** – there are some lovely quiet spots within an hour's walk of Abraão.

Praia da Parnaioca

The hike from Abraão across the island to **Praia da Parnaioca** takes about five hours. By the coconut-fringed *praia* is an old fishing village abandoned by its inhabitants for fear of escaped prisoners from a second prison that was built on the island. It closed in April 1994, but not before earning the island something of a dangerous reputation, as escapes were not infrequent. Today, the only dangers come from *borachudos*, almost invisible but vicious gnats that bite without your hearing them or, until later, feeling them. A tiny fishing community has slowly been established here, and if you need to stay over you should have little trouble finding a room to rent and something to eat. Many of the other beaches have a *barraca* or two selling snacks and cold drinks, but you should bring supplies with you.

ARRIVAL AND INFORMATION — ILHA GRANDE

By ferry CCR Barcas (www.grupoccr.com.br/barcas) run ferries to Ilha Grande's Vila do Abraão from Mangaratiba (daily 8am, also Fri 10pm, returning daily 5.30pm; 80min; R$16.60) and Angra dos Reis (Mon–Fri 3.30pm, Sat & Sun 1.30pm, returning daily 10am; R$16.60); Costa Verde buses from Rio connect with these, but you need to take their 5am bus to connect with the 8am ferry at Mangaratiba.

By private boat Private boats (R$25) also do the crossing to the island from Angra (6 daily; 90min) and Conceição de Jacarei (roughly hourly 8.30am–6pm; 90min). If you have a car, you'll have to leave it on the mainland, but can get advice at the ferry terminals on where to find a secure parking spot.

Services Come with plenty of cash: there are no ATMs, exchange facilities are limited (one travel agency, near the boat station, will sometimes change foreign currency) and most *pousadas* and restaurants do not accept credit cards.

Tourist office At the boat station (daily 7am–7pm), with online information at ilhagrande.org.

ACCOMMODATION

Accommodation is mostly around Vila do Abraão, and when you arrive you may be approached by youths intent on taking you to a room in a **private house** (around R$80 per person) – a good option if you're on a tight budget. **Pousadas** in Abraão are mostly quite simple (though they tend to be more expensive than places of similar quality on the mainland), while those elsewhere on the island tend to be more exclusive and have greater levels of comfort. Reservations in the **high season**, especially at weekends, are absolutely essential; in the off-season prices are halved.

Água Viva Rua da Praia 26, Abraão 21 2688 4716, aguaviva.ilhagrande.com.br. Located near the jetty amid a busy strip of shops and restaurants, the rooms are well equipped and impeccably clean, and the breakfast is good, but the wi-fi can be slow and the atmosphere a bit impersonal. R$400

Holandês Hostel Off Rua da Assembleia 24 3833 7979, holandeshostel.com.br. Popular, friendly and well looked-after youth hostel near the Assembléia de Jesus church. The garden is lovely, and even the dorms have a loving touch about them. It's a little bit of a climb from the beach, but worth it. Dorms R$60, doubles R$250

★ **Lagamar** Praia Grande de Araçatiba 24 3021 2738, pousadalagamar.com.br. The nicest of several charming little *pousadas* in this quiet fishing hamlet, offering generous seafood meals, caipirinhas and a wholesome breakfast served in as beautiful a setting as you could imagine. R$400

Manacá Praia do Abraão 333 ⓣ 24 3361 5404, ⓦ ilhagrandemanaca.com.br. Right on the beach, very quiet (no TVs), upstairs rooms with a sea view cost slightly more than the ones downstairs around the banana tree garden. R$360

★ **Naturália** Abraão, just off the beach ⓣ 24 3361 9583, ⓦ pousadanaturalia.net. Set back slightly uphill from the beach, all the guest rooms have breathtaking sea views from their balconies. Breakfast is always a treat, and the friendly manager is usually on hand to offer advice on hikes or boat trips, but wi-fi is only available in the public areas. R$400

EATING AND DRINKING

Café do Mar Praia do Abraão. A great little bar and beach restaurant serving up the day's catch in various formats, notably with coconut or mango sauce (R$55). For those in need of a wake-up, they do a nice espresso too, but they're best known for their thrice-weekly barbecues (Mon, Wed & Sat 7pm). Daily 10am–11pm; closed Fri in winter.

Lua e Mar Rua Praia do Abraão 329 ⓣ 24 3361 5113. The best beachside restaurant in this stretch. Check out their seafood risotto (R$90) or their seafood *moqueca* (R$93). Mon, Tues & Thurs–Sun 11am–11pm.

Tarituba

About 60km from Angra dos Reis, **TARITUBA**, a charming little fishing village just off the coast road, is still relatively untouched by tourism. Any bus going along the coast will let you off at the side road that leads to the village, and there are buses several times a day from Paraty, 35km further west.

There's not much to the village – a pier along which fishing boats land their catches, a pretty church and a few *barracas* on the beach serving fried fish and cold drinks – and it's simply a place to relax in, away from the often brash commercialism of Angra and Paraty. Bear in mind that here, as right along the coast, the *borachudos* and mosquitoes are murder, so bring plenty of insect repellent and mosquito coils with you.

ACCOMMODATION — TARITUBA

Pousada de Carminha ⓣ 24 3371 6661, ⓦ pousadadacarminha.blogspot.com.br. Simple but very friendly, and right on the beach, offering rustic chalets with either private or shared bathrooms. R$200

Pousada Tarituba ⓣ 24 3371 6614, ⓦ pousadatarituba.com.br. The most comfortable place in town, where large rooms with private verandas and hammocks overlook the pool and beach beyond. R$250

Paraty and around

About 300km from Rio on the BR-101 is the Costa Verde's main attraction, the town of **PARATY**. The town centre's narrow cobbled streets (closed to cars) are bordered by houses with inner courtyards full of brightly coloured flowers and hummingbirds. The cobbles of the streets are arranged in channels to drain off storm water, allowing the sea to enter and wash the streets at high spring tides. Although businesses in the historic centre are overwhelmingly geared to tourists, the wider community has not been totally engulfed by wealthy outsiders. It's a great place to wander around, each corner bringing another picturesque view, small enough that there's no danger of getting lost, and safe at any hour of the day or night.

Brief history

Inhabited since 1650, the centre of Paraty (or, officially, Vila de Nossa Senhora dos Remédios de Paraty) has remained fundamentally unaltered since its heyday as a port for the export of **gold** from Minas Gerais to Portugal. Before Portuguese settlement, the land had been occupied by the **Guaianá Indians**, whose old trails the Portuguese gold routes now followed. But inland raids and pirate attacks at sea forced the Portuguese to switch to a direct route from Minas Gerais to Rio, bypassing Paraty, whose fortunes declined. Apart from a short nineteenth-century boom in coffee shipping and cachaça production, Paraty remained off the beaten track. It therefore remained unchanged, meaning UNESCO now considers Paraty one of the world's most important examples of Portuguese colonial architecture, and the old city has the status of a national monument.

Nossa Senhora dos Remédios

Praça da Matriz • Daily 9am–5pm • Free

Dating back to 1646, **Nossa Senhora dos Remédios** is Paraty's main church and the town's largest building. As in most small colonial towns in Brazil, each of Paraty's churches traditionally served a different sector of the population, and this was built for the local bourgeoisie. It underwent major structural reforms in the late eighteenth century, but the exterior, at least, has since remained unchanged.

Igreja das Dores

Rua Fresca • Sat & Sun 1.30–6pm • Free

The graceful **Igreja das Dores**, with its small cemetery, located by the sea, three blocks from Nossa Senhora dos Remédios, was founded in 1800 for Paraty's aristocracy, who wanted their own church. The aristos were not the only class who had their own church: the town's slaves had the **Igreja do Rosário** on Rua do Comércio, constructed in 1725 and closed for restoration at last check.

Igreja de Santa Rita dos Pardos Libertos and around

Rua Santa Rita • Antiga Cadeia: Mon–Fri 9.15am–noon & 2.15–5pm • Free

At the southern edge of town, **Igreja de Santa Rita dos Pardos Libertos** is the oldest and architecturally most significant of Paraty's churches. Built in 1722 for the freed mulatto population, the structure is notable for its elaborate Portuguese Baroque facade. Next to it, the late eighteenth-century jail, known as the **Antiga Cadeia**, is now the public library.

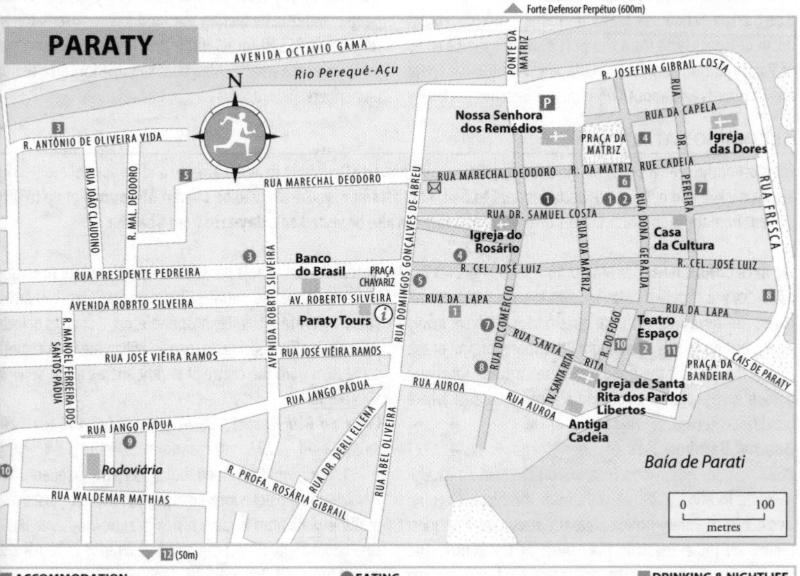

ACCOMMODATION
- Arte Colonial 10
- Bambu Bamboo 1
- Caminho do Ouro 9
- Casa do Rio Hostel 3
- Casa Turquesa 11
- Che Lagarto Hostel 5
- Flor do Mar 8
- Pousada da Marquesa 4
- Pousada do Ouro 7
- Solar dos Gerânios 6
- Tropical 12
- Vivenda 2

EATING
- Banana da Terra 2
- Bartholomeu 1
- Casa do Fogo 4
- Istanbul 9
- Le Gite d'Indaiatiba 6
- Margarida Café 5
- Marlim 10
- Quintal das Letras 8
- Sabor da Terra 3
- Thai Brasil 7

DRINKING & NIGHTLIFE
- Paraty 33 1
- Teatro Espaço 2

SHOPPING
- Emporio da Cachaça 1

1

Casa da Cultura

Corner of Rua Dona Geralda and Rua Samuel Costa • Tues–Sun 10am–10pm • Free • ⓦ casadaculturaparaty.org.br

The beautifully maintained **Casa da Cultura** is worth stopping by for its art and photography exhibitions, and occasional music and dance performances, especially on Thursday evenings (8–10pm), and on Sundays for children.

Forte Defensor Perpétuo

Morro de Vilha Velha (north of the old town, across the Rio Perequé-Açu) • Tues–Sun 9am–noon & 1–4.30pm • Free

The **Forte Defensor Perpétuo** was built in 1703 to defend Paraty from pirates preying on gold ships leaving the port. It underwent restoration in 1822, The twenty-minute walk up from town is rewarded with good views and a collection of old cannons. The fort also has a small **Museu de Artes e Tradições Populares**, with a display of basketware and musical instruments.

ARRIVAL AND INFORMATION PARATY

By bus The rodoviária is about 500m west of the old town on Rua Jango Pádua, two blocks south of Av Roberto Silveira. Destinations Angra dos Reis (19 daily; 2hr); Paraty-Mirim (11 daily; 45min); Rio (12 daily; 5hr); São Paulo (5 daily; 5hr); São Sebastião (2 daily; 3hr); Trindade (roughly hourly; 45min); Ubatuba (13 daily; 1hr 15min).

Tourist office Av Roberto Silveira 1993, Portal de Paraty (2km west of the centre; daily 8am–8pm; ⓣ 24 3371 1897), with a more convenient office at Av Roberto Silveira 1 on Praça Chayariz (daily 9am–9pm; ⓣ 24 3371 1222).

TOURS AND ACTIVITIES

Tours/bicycle rental Excursions to outlying beaches and the surrounding countryside are offered by Paraty Tours, Av Roberto Silveira 11 (ⓣ 24 3371 1327, ⓦ paratytours.com.br), who also rent out mountain bikes for R$60 a day, and have maps showing suggested routes.

Boat trips Schooners leave from the Praia do Pontal north of Paraty, and from the port quay, for the beaches of Paraty-Mirim, Jurumirim, Lula and Picinguaba. There are 65 islands and about two hundred beaches to choose from in the vicinity. Tickets for trips out to the islands typically costing R$50 per person, leave Paraty at 11am stop at three or four islands for swimming opportunities and return at 4pm. These trips can be pretty rowdy affairs with the larger boats capable of carrying several dozen people and usually blaring out loud music. Alternatively for around R$300 (or R$200 in the low season) you can easily charter a small fishing boat suitable for three to five passengers.

ACCOMMODATION

For most of the year, it's easy to find accommodation, but from late December to after Carnaval and for special events, the area is packed and hotel space becomes hard to find. At other times, you're likely to be offered **discounts** of up to fifty percent from the high-season prices given below. Paraty can also be visited on a **day-trip** from Ubatuba.

★ **Arte Colonial** Rua da Matriz 59 (ex-292) ⓣ 24 3371 7347, ⓦ pousadaartecolonial.com.br; map p.131. All rooms are furnished with antiques and most have lovely views, but it's worth spending a little more for one of the two at the front of the building. There's a small courtyard garden with a plunge pool, and a communal area where breakfast is served. R$330

Bambu Bamboo Rua Glauber Rocha 9 ⓣ 24 3371 8629, ⓦ bambubamboo.com; map p.131. In a peaceful riverside location a 20min walk from the historic centre, this is one of Paraty's most pleasant *pousadas*. The guest rooms are more spacious than most in the centre, and there's a large pool in the attractive garden, with spa treatments available. R$300

Caminho do Ouro Estrada Paraty–Cunha Km 4 ⓣ 24 3371 6548, ⓦ pousadacaminhodoouro.com.br; map p.131. Set amid unspoilt forest, by a small river and near waterfalls, this simple *pousada* is a perfect place to escape the crowds that sometimes impinge on Paraty's charms. The owners are extremely hospitable, great sources of local advice and offer delicious Franco-Brazilian meals. Although some 8km from the centre of Paraty, there's a bus service. R$350

Casa do Rio Hostel Rua Antônio Vidal 144 (ex-120) ⓣ 24 3371 2223, ⓦ casadoriohostel.com.br; map p.131. Somewhat cramped, but otherwise excellent, this official youth hostel is located alongside the river, just a few minutes' walk from Paraty's historic centre, and even has a small pool. Helpful staff can organize a range of beach and inland tours. Dorms R$79, doubles R$212

Casa Turquesa Rua Dr Pereira 65 (ex-50) ⓣ 24 3371 1037, ⓦ casaturquesa.com.br; map p.131. A boutique *pousada* that has established itself as *the* place for wealthy *paulistas* to stay in Paraty. The nine suites spring straight

ACADEMY OF COOKING AND OTHER PLEASURES

For an unusual dining experience, drop by the **Academy of Cooking and Other Pleasures** at Rua Dona Geralda 288 (T 24 3371 6025, W chefbrasil.com) to find out about events hosted by Yara Castro Roberts. A professional cook and restaurant consultant, she has done much to encourage interest in Brazilian food through cookery classes, television segments and writing. Several evenings a week, Yara gives demonstrations in her home, alternating between menus drawn from Rio, Bahia, the Amazon and Minas Gerais, her home state. The high point of the evening comes when Yara and her guests sit around her dining-room table to enjoy food and wine and sample some fine cachaças, of which she is a connoisseur. The evening, which lasts 8 to 11pm, costs R$270 per person, with groups limited to eight or so people.

from a design magazine mixing modern furniture and fabrics with the overall rustic-chic look, although the courtyard (with a plunge pool) and lounge with bar are rather compact. R$1810

Che Lagarto Hostel Rua Benina Toledo do Prado 22 T 24 3371 1564, W chelagarto.com; map p.131. One of the better offerings from this popular hostel chain, fun and sociable with spacious communal areas, largely outside in the garden, although it's true that the dorms are rather less spacious. Dorms R$72, doubles R$198

Flor do Mar Rua Fresca 257 T 24 3371 1647, W pousada flordomar.com.br; map p.131. A sweet little *pousada* with just seven rooms facing the mangroves near the marina. It's very homey and quiet with simple but ample rooms, a pretty garden and charming owners. R$350

Pousada da Marquesa Rua Dona Geralda 99 (ex-69) T 24 3371 1263, W pousadamarquesa.com.br; map p.131. Discreet luxury *pousada* offering an attractive pool and wonderful views of the town from the bedrooms. Avoid the rooms in the annexe, as they're on the small side. R$605

Pousada do Ouro Rua Dr Pereira 145 T 24 3371 2033, W pousadaouro.com.br; map p.131. The least expensive luxury *pousada* in Paraty, boasting a range of tastefully furnished rooms – spacious and light in the main building, but rather small and dark in the annexe. There's a lovely walled garden and a good-size pool, too. R$650

Solar dos Gerânios Rua Dona Geralda 4, Praça da Matriz T 24 3371 1550, E s.geranio.s@hotmail.com; map p.131. This beautiful and long-established *pousada* is filled with rustic furniture and curios. The rooms are small and spartan but impeccably kept; most have a balcony and all have a private bathroom. The *pousada* is superb value (prices remain the same all year), but because it's popular, reservations are usually essential – request a room overlooking the *praça*. R$170

Tropical Rua Waldemar Mathias 169 (ex-38) T 24 3371 2020, W paratytropical.com.br; map p.131. Set in a residential area just south of the rodoviária. Rooms are plain, but ask for one on the upper floor, as they're quieter and have better ventilation. R$258

★ **Vivenda** Rua Beija-flor 9 T 24 3371 4272, W vivendaparaty.com; map p.131. A 15min walk from the historic centre, this modern, elegant, yet immensely relaxing B&B has a double room and two spacious bungalows with kitchenettes set around a leafy patio garden and pool. The owner is a perfect host, providing local advice (and caipirinhas) without ever being overbearing. If it's full, the *Maris Paraty* next door is very similar in style. R$528

EATING

★ **Banana da Terra** Rua Dr Samuel Costa 198 T 24 3371 1725, W restaurantebananadaterra.com.br; map p.131. Paraty's most interesting restaurant, emphasizing local ingredients (especially bananas and plantains) and regional cooking. The grilled fish with garlic-herb butter and banana is delicious (R$90), as are the wonderful banana desserts. Mon, Wed & Thurs 6pm–midnight, Fri–Sun noon–4pm & 7pm–midnight.

Bartholomeu Rua Dr Samuel Costa 176 T 24 3371 5032; map p.131. A relatively simple but good and moderately priced menu that gives pride of place to Argentine beef filled with Roquefort (R$200 for two), and seafood *moqueca* (R$74). Mon–Thurs 7–11.30pm, Fri–Sun noon–4pm & 7–11.30pm.

★ **Casa do Fogo** Rua da Ferraria (aka Rua Comendador José Luiz) 404 (ex-390) T 24 3371 3161, W casadofogo.com.br; map p.131. Attractively presented, immensely flavourful vegetable, seafood and meat dishes, all flambéed with local cachaça – R$34 for prawns, or R$30 for the vegetarian flambée with palm hearts. Daily 6–11pm,

Istanbul Rua Manuel Torres, Shopping Colonial T 24 9974 9638; map p.131. Great kebabs (R$22) as well as Turkish-style falafel (R$17) and Turkish coffee at this friendly and great-value snack bar with tables upstairs, just across from the bus station. Tues–Sat noon–10pm.

Le Gite d'Indaiatiba BR-101, Km 562, Graúna (17km from Paraty) T 24 3371 7174 or 99999 9923, W legitedindaiatiba.com.br; map p.131. At this outstanding restaurant, the French chef serves a few classic dishes as well as his own creations based on local

FESTIVALS IN PARATY

May, June and July see frequent **festivals** in Paraty celebrating local holidays, and the town's square comes alive during this time with folk dances – *cerandis*, *congadas* and *xibas* – showcasing the European and African influences on Brazilian culture. While such goings-on certainly demonstrate that local traditions can survive against the onslaught of tourism, they are small in scale compared with newly established events. Taking place since 2002 over the course of a week in July, the **Festa Literária Internacional de Parati** (**FLIP**) immediately established itself as Brazil's single most influential literary gathering, with panels featuring some of the most important writers from across the world. For the FLIP programme, see ⓦflip.org.br.

ingredients. Set inland from Paraty, the mountainside location is stunning, and it's a wonderful place to spend an afternoon – or longer, as it's also a *pousada* (bring a towel and you can use the *cachoeira*). If you don't have your own transport, phone ahead for a possible lift. Advance reservation is obligatory. Daily except Tues 1.30–8.30pm.

Margarida Café Praça Chafariz ⓣ24 3371 2441, ⓦmargaridacafe.com.br; map p.131. A very popular tourist restaurant where a prawn *moqueca* for two goes for R$166, or you can opt for a rack of lamb at R$85. Daily noon–midnight.

Marlim Eua da Floresta 395 ⓣ24 3371 5369; map p.131. Cheap eats every lunchtime at the no-frills diner near the bus station. Fish or squid with beans, rice and a bit of salad are R£22, and fresh fried sardines are even cheaper. Daily 11am–10pm.

Quintal das Letras Rua do Comércio 362 (ex-58) 395 ⓣ24 3371 1568, ⓦpousadaliteraria.com.br; map p.131. There's some top-notch gastronomy going on in this rather refined restaurant where they come up with fine dishes such as beef tournedos with a cake of brie and cassava (R$78) or lamb couscous with cinnamon (R$75), and they do wonderful things with crab and salt-cod. Not cheap, but worth it, Daily 11am–10pm.

Sabor da Terra Av Roberto Silveira 618 (ex-180) ⓣ24 3371 2384, ⓦparaty.com.br/sabordaterra; map p.131. Paraty's best *por quilo* restaurant (R$40.80/kg), offering a wide variety of inexpensive hot and cold dishes that include a choice of grilled meats. Daily 11am–10pm.

Thai Brasil Rua do Comércio 308 ⓣ24 3371 2760, ⓦthaibrasil.com.br; map p.131. Well-presented, moderately priced Thai food served in a bright and attractive setting. The German owner has created remarkably authentic dishes, with the fish being especially good (fish green curry R$52; prawn green curry R$75). Mon–Sat 6pm–midnight.

NIGHTLIFE AND ENTERTAINMENT

Paraty 33 Rua Maria Jácome de Mello 357 ⓣ24 3371 7311, ⓦparaty33.com; map p.131. Head through the bar/restaurant at the front to Paraty's only proper nightclub, which mostly functions at weekends, with dance DJs, rock bands and bossa nova, depending on the evening. The programme is posted on their website. Fri & Sat 11.30pm–4am (sometimes other days too, especially in season).

Teatro Espaço Rua Dona Geralda 327 ⓣ24 3371 1575, ⓦteatroespaco.com.br; map p.131. This small theatre is the home of the puppet troupe Grupo Contadores de Estórias (ⓦecparaty.org.br), whose wordless performances nimbly leap between comedy and tragedy, exploring such adult themes as death, sex and betrayal (you must be 14 years or over to attend). The theatre sometimes hosts other events too. Wed & Sat 9pm.

SHOPPING

Emporio da Cachaça Rua Dr Samuel Costa 270 ⓣ24 3371 6329; map p.131. Shop selling a wide variety of local cachaças. It isn't a bar, but they do dispense free samples, and they also sell a lot of brands in miniature-size bottles, which is handy if you want to try out a few different ones. Mon–Fri & Sun 9.30am–10pm, Sat 9.30am–11pm.

Paraty-Mirim

Seventeen kilometres southwest of Paraty, including 8km along an unpaved road (to be avoided after heavy rains), is **Paraty-Mirim**, an attractive bay with calm water ideal for swimming. Although there are a couple of bars serving food, there's nowhere to stay at the beach itself.

ARRIVAL AND DEPARTURE PARATY-MIRIM

By bus There are eleven buses a day from Paraty (9 on Sun), with a journey time of about 45 minutes.

ACCOMMODATION AND EATING

Vila Volta Off Paraty–Paraty-Mirim road, 8km from beach ⓣ 24 99957 5476, ⓦ vilavolta.com.br. A rustic but comfortable *pousada* run by a Dutch-Brazilian couple; here you'll find a friendly reception, an extremely peaceful setting, excellent Dutch-Indonesian-Brazilian food, trails and natural swimming pools. R$220

Trindade

Some of the best beaches around Paraty are near the village of **Trindade**, 21km southwest of Paraty and reached by a steep, but good, winding road. Sandwiched between the ocean and Serra do Mar, Trindade has reached the physical limits of growth, the dozens of inexpensive *pousadas*, holiday homes, camping sites, bars and restaurants crammed with tourists in the peak summer season. The main beach is nice enough, but you're better off walking away from the village across the rocky outcrops to Praia Brava or Praia do Meio, where the only signs of development on what are some of the most perfect mainland beaches on this stretch of coast are simply a few bars.

ARRIVAL AND DEPARTURE — TRINDADE

By bus 17 buses run daily on the route from Trindade to Paraty (45min), supplemented by minibuses.

ACCOMMODATION

Ponta da Trindade Rua Pastor Enozir 123 ⓣ 24 3371 5113, ⓦ paraty.com.br/trindade/ponta.asp. Located right on the beach, with immaculate rooms, this place also offers camping space. Doubles R$280, camping/person R$60

Pousada Agua do Mar Rua Pastor Enozir 108 ⓣ 24 2122 2212, ⓦ pousadaaguadomartrindade.com.br. Just across the way from the beach, upstairs rooms here have a/c, while the downstairs rooms have ceiling fans, but compensate with a hammock out front. R$250

Pouso Trindade Av Principal de Trindade 1950 ⓣ 24 3371 5121, ⓦ pousotrindadeinn.com.br. A welcoming place on the village's main road, but still only 50m from the beach, offering bright rooms with a/c upstairs or with ceiling fans downstairs. R$200

Trindade Hostel Av Principal de Trindade 2250 ⓣ 24 3379 5324. This is the most economical place to stay in Trindade, and the most sociable too. It's a small place, but very friendly, with a communal kitchen for use of guests, a nice veranda, and each dorm has its own bathroom. Dorms R$75, doubles R$240

Fazenda Bananal

Estrada da Pedra Branca • Daily 9am–6pm • R$20 • ⓣ 24 3371 0039, ⓦ facebook.com/pg/fazendabananalparaty

A well-signposted side road from the Paraty–Cunha road at Km 4 leads 900m to a seventeenth-century farm complex called the **Fazenda Bananal** (also known as Fazenda Murycana). It originally served as an inn for travellers on the Caminho do Ouro and also as a toll post where the royal tax of twenty percent on goods was levied. The most interesting of its restored buildings is the **casa grande**, but the whole estate has been extensively restored and revamped as an educational project promoting sustainable agriculture, which they'll happily explain to you if your Portuguese is up to it. It also has a good restaurant.

Cachoeira das Penha

At Km 6 on the Paraty–Cunha road, signs point to the **Cachoeira das Penha**, a waterfall up in the mountains that offers a chance to bake on the sun-scorched rocks of the river gully and then cool off in the river. From here you can descend from rock to rock for a few hundred metres before scrambling up to a road above you.

Ponte Branca

About 2km along the road from the Cachoeira das Penha, just across a small bridge, you'll enter **PONTE BRANCA**. At the far end of the village, overlooking the river, is the *Villa Verde* restaurant, where you can take a break and enjoy a cold drink. The easy walk here from the waterfall takes you through the hills and valleys, and past tropical-fruit plantations – all very pleasant. If you don't have your own transport, you'll probably manage to get a lift back to Paraty from the restaurant or you can wait by the Cunha road for a bus.

Minas Gerais and Espírito Santo

TIRADENTES

Minas Gerais and Espírito Santo

Brazil's historic hinterland since the seventeenth century, Minas Gerais is blessed with an incredibly rich cache of colonial towns and Baroque art, as well as a mountainous interior laced with waterfalls and unspoiled reserves. The state's political and commercial heart, Belo Horizonte lies in the centre of a booming mining and agricultural zone that has made the state one of the powerhouses of Brazil, running from the coffee estates of western Minas to the mines and cattle pastures of the Rio Doce valley, in the east. The neighbouring state of Espírito Santo is best known for its beaches, though several Italian and German towns add colour to its hilly inland regions.

All *mineiros* would agree that the soul of the state lies in the rural areas, in the colonial-era hill and mountain villages and the towns of its vast **interior**. Explorers flocked to the region following the discovery of gold in 1693, and Minas Gerais' **cidades históricas**, "the historic cities", represent some of the finest examples of Portuguese colonial architecture in the nation. They are repositories of a great flowering of eighteenth-century Baroque **religious art**; *arte sacra mineira* was the finest work of its time in the Americas, and Minas Gerais can lay claim to indisputably the greatest figure in Brazilian cultural history – the mulatto leper sculptor, **Aleijadinho**, whose magnificent work is scattered throughout the state's wonderfully preserved historic cities. The most important of the *cidades históricas* are **Ouro Preto**, **Mariana** and **Sabará**, all within easy striking distance of **Belo Horizonte**, the state's modern capital, and **Congonhas**, **São João del Rei**, **Tiradentes** and **Diamantina**, further afield.

With the exception of its coastal resorts, **Espírito Santo** is almost completely off the tourist map, though the interior of the state has some claim to being one of the most beautiful parts of Brazil. Espírito Santo's capital **Vitória** boasts a fine location (on an island surrounded by hills and granite outcrops) and a smattering of historic sights, while nearby **Vila Velha** is a major beach resort. The best way to view the interior is to make the round of the towns that began as German and Italian colonies, the so-called **Região dos Imigrantes**: **Santa Teresa**, **Santa Leopoldina**, **Santa Maria** and **Domingos Martins** – the last on the road to the remarkable sheer granite face of **Pedra Azul**, one of the least-known but most spectacular sights in the country.

INHOTIM

Highlights

❶ **Museu de Arte da Pampulha** One of several important buildings in Pampulha dreamed up by Oscar Niemeyer, amid Roberto Burle Marx-designed gardens. See page 147

❷ **Inhotim** One of the world's great outdoor art museums, with mind-blowing installations and contemporary galleries set among lush, tropical gardens. See page 151

❸ **Diamantina** The hometown of Juscelino Kubitschek is the most remote, traditional and intriguing of the colonial mining towns. See page 156

❹ **Ouro Preto** Nowhere in the country is there a richer concentration of Baroque art and architecture than here. See page 168

❺ **The Prophets by Aleijadinho, Congonhas** Amazingly, the master sculptor of Brazilian Baroque produced his best work after leprosy deformed his hands. See page 178

❻ **Tiradentes** Perfectly preserved eighteenth-century town, dominated by the magnificent Igreja Matriz de Santo Antônio. See page 183

❼ **Moqueca capixaba** Don't leave Vitória without sampling its renowned seafood stew – a sumptuous blend of shrimp, crab and spices. See page 191

HIGHLIGHTS ARE MARKED ON THE MAP ON PAGE 140

Belo Horizonte and around

One of the biggest cities in Brazil and the capital of Minas Gerais, **BELO HORIZONTE** is a vast, sprawling metropolis of high-rises seemingly sprouting up between the hills like needles. From the centre, the jagged, rust-coloured skyline of the Serra do Espinhaço, which gave the city its name, is always visible on the horizon – it's still being transformed by the mines gnawing away at the "breast of iron". But while it may not be as historic as the rest of the state, it's difficult not to be impressed by the city's scale and energy. Moreover, the centre of Belo Horizonte – increasingly a middle-class enclave with standards of living that compare to parts of Scandinavia, despite the recent economic turndown – is surprisingly safe for such a big city, and is graced by some truly excellent art galleries and museums that seem to specialize in making otherwise dry subjects intriguing.

The **central zone** is contained within the inner ring road, the **Avenida do Contorno**, and laid out in a grid pattern, crossed by diagonal *avenidas*, which makes it easy to find your way around on foot. The spine of the city is the broad **Avenida Afonso Pena**, with the rodoviária at its northern end, in the heart of the downtown area. The only places beyond the Contorno you're likely to visit are the artificial lake and Niemeyer buildings of **Pampulha**, to the north.

Brief history

Despite its size and importance, Belo Horizonte is little more than a century old, founded in 1893 as "Cidade de Minas" on the site of the impoverished village of Curral del Rei – of which nothing remains. Designed by Aarão Reisa and shaped by the novel ideas of "progress" that emerged with the new Republic, it was the first of Brazil's planned cities, inaugurated in 1897 and renamed Belo Horizonte nine years later. As late as 1945 it had only 100,000 inhabitants; now it has twenty times that number (some five million if one includes the city's metropolitan hinterland), an explosive rate of growth even by Latin American standards.

Museu de Artes e Ofícios

Praça Rui Barbosa (Praça da Estação) 600 • Tues 9am–9pm, Wed–Sun 9am–5pm • Free • ⓣ 31 3248 8600, ⓦ mao.org.br

The tone of Belo Horizonte's highly creative museums is set by the **Museu de Artes e Ofícios**, a repository of traditional trades and industries set within the wonderfully enigmatic premises of the renovated **train station** (a tunnel beneath the tracks connects the two sides). Essentially this is a huge display of machinery and tools from the nineteenth and twentieth centuries, but there are some truly intriguing exhibits, including a video of the process of traditional sugar refining, huge, antique sugar boiling vats, leather tanning drums and copper *alambiques* (distilleries). Labels are in Portuguese only, but most displays have moveable laminated cards with English translations. The station, one of the city's most elegant buildings, is part of the attraction here, a Neoclassical confection built in 1922. It's among Brazil's finest examples of "tropical Edwardiana", although these days the station's platforms are used only by commuters riding the city's *metrô* (the museum is completely separate – enter via the main station entrance).

Mercado Central

Av Augusto de Lima 744 • Mon–Sat 7am–6pm, Sun 7am–1pm • ⓣ 31 3274 9434, ⓦ mercadocentral.com.br

Constructed in 1929 in what is now the scrappy commercial heart of Belo Horizonte, the **Mercado Central** is a sprawling indoor market of almost four hundred stalls. An incredible variety of goods is on offer, ranging from the usual fruit, vegetables, cheeses and meats to cachaças, spices, medicinal herbs, kitchen equipment, rustic handicrafts and *umbanda* and candomblé accessories. It's also a great place to eat or drink (see page 154).

Avenida Afonso Pena and around

Running southeast from **Praça Sete**, and the rodoviária, the broad **Avenida Afonso Pena** which bisects Belo Horizonte is home to some of the city's showcase buildings. On Praça Sete itself stands the granite obelisk dubbed "*pirulito*" (the "lollipop"), erected in 1922 to celebrate Brazil's independence centenary. Humming with activity, the square is usually full with office workers (this area is the city's main financial district), street hustlers, bars and *lanchonetes* that stay open until midnight (even later at weekends). South along Afonso Pena, between Rua da Bahia and Avenida Álvares Cabral, the Art Deco–influenced **Prefeitura** (town hall) at no. 1212 was built in the 1930s in a burst of civic pride; just a short distance on are the imposing **Palácio da Justiça** at no. 1420 (completed in 1913), and the **Escola da Música**, each supported by elegant Corinthian columns.

CâmeraSete – Casa da Fotografia de Minas Gerais

Av Afonso Pena 737 • Tues–Sat 9.30am–9pm • Free • ⓣ 31 3236 7400, ⓦ fcs.mg.gov.br

Housed in a Neoclassical gem, the **CâmeraSete – Casa da Fotografia de Minas Gerais** hosts high-quality exhibitions (revolving three months or so) of twentieth-century Brazilian art and photography, enhanced by videos and interactive installations.

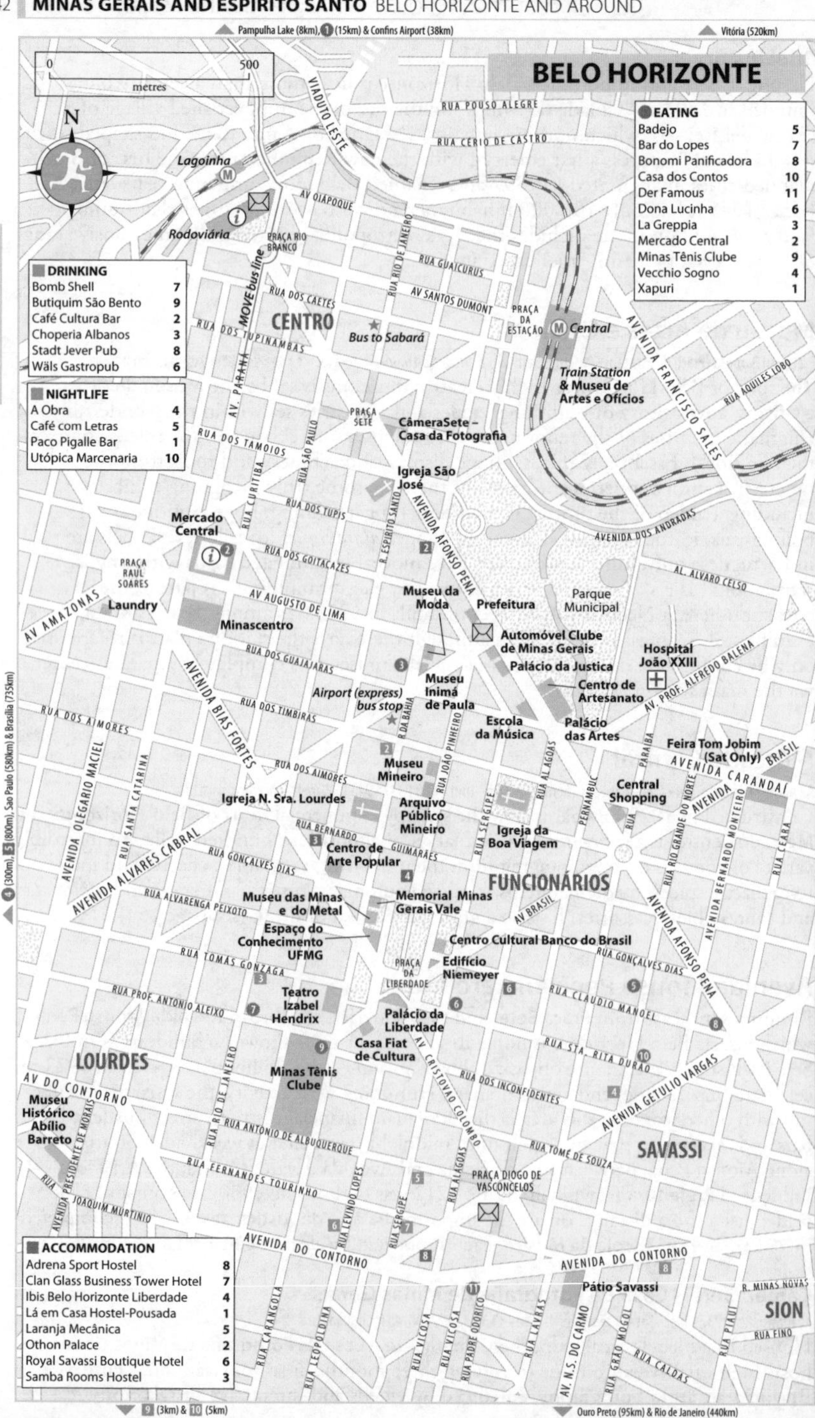
BELO HORIZONTE
Pampulha Lake (8km), 1 (15km) & Confins Airport (38km)
Vitória (520km)
4 (300m), 5 (800m), São Paulo (580km) & Brasília (735km)
9 (3km) & 10 (5km)
Ouro Preto (95km) & Rio de Janeiro (440km)
0 500 metres
N
EATING
Badejo 5
Bar do Lopes 7
Bonomi Panificadora 8
Casa dos Contos 10
Der Famous 11
Dona Lucinha 6
La Greppia 3
Mercado Central 2
Minas Tênis Clube 9
Vecchio Sogno 4
Xapuri 1
DRINKING
Bomb Shell 7
Butiquim São Bento 9
Café Cultura Bar 2
Choperia Albanos 3
Stadt Jever Pub 8
Wäls Gastropub 6
NIGHTLIFE
A Obra 4
Café com Letras 5
Paco Pigalle Bar 1
Utópica Marcenaria 10
ACCOMMODATION
Adrena Sport Hostel 8
Clan Glass Business Tower Hotel 7
Ibis Belo Horizonte Liberdade 4
Lá em Casa Hostel-Pousada 1
Laranja Mecânica 5
Othon Palace 2
Royal Savassi Boutique Hotel 6
Samba Rooms Hostel 3
CENTRO
FUNCIONÁRIOS
LOURDES
SAVASSI
SION
Lagoinha
Rodoviária
Central
Train Station & Museu de Artes e Ofícios
Bus to Sabará
CâmeraSete – Casa da Fotografia
Igreja São José
Mercado Central
Laundry
Minascentro
Museu da Moda
Prefeitura
Parque Municipal
Automóvel Clube de Minas Gerais
Palácio da Justica
Hospital João XXIII
Centro de Artesanato
Palácio das Artes
Museu Inimá de Paula
Airport (express) bus stop
Escola da Música
Feira Tom Jobim (Sat Only)
Museu Mineiro
Central Shopping
Igreja N. Sra. Lourdes
Arquivo Público Mineiro
Igreja da Boa Viagem
Centro de Arte Popular
Museu das Minas e do Metal
Memorial Minas Gerais Vale
Espaço do Conhecimento UFMG
Centro Cultural Banco do Brasil
Edifício Niemeyer
Teatro Izabel Hendrix
Palácio da Liberdade
Casa Fiat de Cultura
Minas Tênis Clube
Museu Histórico Abílio Barreto
Pátio Savassi
PRAÇA RIO BRANCO
PRAÇA DA ESTAÇÃO
PRAÇA SETE
PRAÇA RAUL SOARES
PRAÇA DA LIBERDADE
PRAÇA DIOGO DE VASCONCELOS
VIADUTO LESTE
RUA POUSO ALEGRE
RUA CERIO DE CASTRO
AV OIAPOQUE
MOVE bus line
RUA GUAICURUS
RUA RIO DE JANEIRO
AV SANTOS DUMONT
RUA DOS CAETES
RUA DOS TUPINAMBAS
AV. PARANÁ
AVENIDA FRANCISCO SALES
RUA AQUILES LOBO
RUA DOS TAMOIOS
RUA SÃO PAULO
RUA CURITIBA
RUA DOS TUPIS
R. ESPIRITO SANTO
AVENIDA AFONSO PENA
AVENIDA DOS ANDRADAS
AL. ALVARO CELSO
RUA DOS GOITACAZES
AV AMAZONAS
AV AUGUSTO DE LIMA
RUA DOS GUAJAJARAS
AVENIDA BIAS FORTES
RUA DOS TIMBIRAS
R DA BAHIA
RUA JOÃO PINHEIRO
AV. PROF. ALFREDO BALENA
RUA DOS AIMORES
AVENIDA OLEGARIO MACIEL
RUA SANTA CATARINA
RUA AL AGOAS
RUA PARAIBA
AVENIDA BRASIL
AVENIDA CARANDAÍ
AVENIDA ALVARES CABRAL
RUA BERNARDO GUIMARÃES
RUA SERGIPE
RUA PERNAMBUCO
RUA RIO GRANDE DO NORTE
AVENIDA BERNARDO MONTEIRO
RUA CEARA
RUA GONÇALVES DIAS
RUA ALVARENGA PEIXOTO
AV BRASIL
RUA TOMÁS GONZAGA
RUA PROF. ANTONIO ALEIXO
RUA CLAUDIO MANOEL
RUA STA. RITA DURÃO
AV CRISTOVÃO COLOMBO
RUA DOS INCONFIDENTES
AVENIDA GETULIO VARGAS
AV DO CONTORNO
RUA RIO DE JANEIRO
RUA ANTONIO DE ALBUQUERQUE
AVENIDA PRESIDENTE DE MORAIS
RUA FERNANDES TOURINHO
RUA TOMÉ DE SOUZA
RUA JOAQUIM MURTINIO
RUA LEVINDO LOPES
RUA ALAGOAS
AVENIDA DO CONTORNO
R. MINAS NOVAS
RUA FINO
RUA CARANGOLA
RUA LEOPOLDINA
RUA VIÇOSA
RUA PADRE ODORICO
RUA LAVRAS
AV. N.S. DO CARMO
RUA GRÃO MOGOL
RUA CALDAS
RUA PIAUI

Igreja São José

Rua Tupis 164 at Av Afonso Pena • Mon & Wed–Sun 6.30am–9pm, Tues 6.30am–4pm • Free • ⓣ 31 3273 2988, ⓦ igrejasaojose.org.br

Given its relatively recent origins, Belo Horizonte lacks the historic churches of other Minas Gerais towns, but the **Igreja São José**, which was completed in 1910, almost makes up for this with a spectacular painted interior by the German artist Wilhelm Schumacher. The walls and ceiling are smothered in paintings and murals, and while it's no Sistine Chapel, the overall effect of the faux medieval and Renaissance imagery is certainly awe-inspiring. The building itself was constructed in an eclectic "Neo-Manueline" style (a re-imagining of Portuguese late Gothic architecture), though it was also influenced by the Art Nouveau movement of the period.

2

Museu da Moda

Rua da Bahia 1149 • Mon–Fri 9am–9pm, Sat & Sun 10am–2pm • Free • ⓣ 31 3277 9248

One block west from Avenida Afonso Pena, the **Museu da Moda** or fashion museum occupies an incongruous Manueline-style structure that was built in 1914 for the city council known as the "Castelinho da Bahia". The whimsical interior of the building, with its wood panelling, Art Nouveau stained glass and sweeping staircase, is worth a look alone, while the roster of changing exhibits all have a sartorial angle (though English labelling is rare).

Museu Inimá de Paula

Rua da Bahia 1201 • Tues, Wed, Fri & Sat 10am–6.30pm, Thurs noon–8.30pm, Sun 10am–4.30pm • Free • ⓣ 31 3213 4320, ⓦ museuinimadepaula.org.br

One of Minas Gerais' most famous sons is commemorated at the **Museu Inimá de Paula**, though his work is not always on display – the building primarily hosts high-quality **contemporary art** exhibitions. The museum's permanent collection incorporates some eighty works by de Paula, including some piercing self-portraits, but check ahead to see if they are on show. There is a permanent reconstruction of de Paula's studio on the first floor, enhanced with some personal effects. De Paula, who died in 1999, was a member of the "Movimento Modernista de Fortaleza" in the 1940s – his unique "single stroke" style is considered the greatest Brazilian expression of Fauvist or Modern art. The building itself is an Art Deco beauty, completed for the private Clube Belo Horizonte in 1928.

Palácio das Artes

Av Afonso Pena 1537 • **Galleries** Tues–Sat 9.30am–9pm, Sun 4–9pm • Free • ⓣ 31 3236 7400, ⓦ fcs.mg.gov.br • **Centro de Artesanato Mineiro** Mon–Fri 9am–7.30pm, Sat 9am–1.30pm, Sun 8am–12.30pm • ⓣ 31 3272 9513, ⓦ centrodeartesanatomineiro.com.br

Completed in 1971 to a design by Hélio Pinto Ferreira, the **Palácio das Artes** is one of the finest Modernist buildings in the city. The *palácio* is divided into a number of well-laid-out **galleries**, with changing exhibitions concentrating on modern Brazilian art, a couple of small **theatres** and one big one, the **Grande Teatro**. The *palácio* is also one of the very few places in Belo Horizonte where you'll come across a good display of the state's distinctive arts and crafts, inside the **Centro de Artesanato Mineiro**.

Igreja Nossa Senhora da Boa Viagem

Rua Sergipe 175 • Daily 24hr • Free • ⓣ 31 3222 2361, ⓦ igrejaboaviagem.org.br

The city's most sacred shrine, the **Igreja Nossa Senhora da Boa Viagem**, was inaugurated in 1922 to mark the centenary of Brazilian independence. Though the fairytale Neo-Gothic exterior looks fancy, in contrast to Igreja São José (see above) the all-white interior is very plain. It's best known as the home of the **Santuário de Adoração Perpétua** ("Sanctuary of Perpetual Adoration"), accessible 24hr (there's a special side entrance 9pm–6am, when the rest of the church closes). Devotees come to pray and contemplate the star-like sacred vessel (called a monstrance) at the altar at the end of

MARKETS IN BELO HORIZONTE

It's worth making an effort to be in Belo Horizonte on a Sunday morning for the **Feira de Arte e Artesanato** (Sun 8am–2pm; T 31 3277 4914). One of the best of its kind anywhere in the country, with buyers and sellers coming from all over Brazil, this massive market takes over the Avenida Afonso Pena bordering the Parque Municipal. An excellent place for bargains, the market is split into sections, with related stalls grouped together – jewellery, leather goods, lace, ceramics, cane furniture, clothes, food, paintings and drinks, to name but a few.

On Saturdays you can visit the **Feira Tom Jobim** (8am–5pm) – effectively two connected markets in Santa Efigênia (Av Carandaí between Av Brasil and Rua Ceara) – an antique fair and a massive street food market. Take bus #9501 from Afonso Pena between Tupis and Espírito Santo.

the church, symbolizing the presence of Jesus. Currently it remains the city's cathedral, though it will eventually be usurped by a new building, the **Catedral Cristo Rei**, which is under construction in the northern neighbourhood of Juliana to a design by Oscar Niemeyer (slated for completion in 2021).

Museu Mineiro

Av João Pinheiro 342 • Tues, Wed & Fri 10am–7pm, Thurs noon–9pm, Sat, Sun & holidays noon–7pm • Free • T 31 3269 1109, W circuitoculturalliberdade.com.br

The tiny but beautifully presented art collections in the **Museu Mineiro** are enhanced by the elegant Neoclassical building it occupies, completed in 1897 and one of the first in Belo Horizonte. The building served as the state senate from 1905 to 1930. Today the Sala das Colunas is a gorgeous space housing a variety of religious statuary, while the Sala das Sessões (the old senate room), with its rose-hued walls and painted ceiling intact, displays the work of local painters from the twentieth century (mostly landscapes).

The highlight, however, is the small collection of six vibrant paintings by Minas Gerais Baroque master **Manuel da Costa Ataíde** (1762–1830) in the "Sala do Colecionador"; Ataíde is best known for painting the São Francisco church in Ouro Preto (see page 172). Labels are in Portuguese only.

Centro de Arte Popular

Rua Gonçalves Dias 1608 • Tues, Wed & Fri 10am–7pm, Thurs noon–9pm, Sat & Sun noon–7pm • Free • T 31 3222 3231, W circuitoculturalliberdade.com.br

A lesser-visited treasure trove of high-quality popular or "naïve" art, the **Centro de Arte Popular** contains several permanent galleries of wooden carvings, sculptures and artefacts illustrating the rich folk art traditions of Minas Gerais. Most of the work on display is twentieth century or contemporary (with some English labelling), by masters such as **Geraldo Teles de Oliveira** ("GTO"), but also includes ex-votos and everyday items such as pots and jars. Don't miss the stunning **wall murals** in the garden at the back, by Brazilian graffiti artists.

Praça da Liberdade and around

The park-like **Praça da Liberdade** occupies the highest point in the centre of Belo Horizonte, designed to be the political heart of the new capital in the 1890s. With the construction of the new city government complex in the northern suburbs in 2010, the plaza's stately buildings have been converted to a fine ensemble of **museums**. With its beautiful *ipê* trees and imperial palms, Edwardian bandstand and fountains, the square itself is a wonderful place to sit and relax. The plaza is dominated by the elegant Neoclassical-style **Palácio da Liberdade**, built between 1895 and 1898 as the residence of the president of Minas Gerais (tours have been suspended for some time; check circuitoculturalliberdade.com.br for the latest). Also look out for the **Edifício Niemeyer** apartment building at the southeast corner (at Av Brasil), whose flowing lines were designed by architect Oscar Niemeyer (the building was completed in 1960); it remains one of Belo Horizonte's most prestigious residential city-centre addresses.

Memorial Minas Gerais Vale

Praça da Liberdade at Gonçalves Dias • Tues, Wed, Fri & Sat 10am–5.30pm, Thurs 10am–9.30pm, Sun 10am–3.30pm • Free • 31 3343 7317, memorialvale.com.br

The highly imaginative and entertaining galleries of the **Memorial Minas Gerais Vale** are more like artistic representations of various aspects of Minas Gerais culture and history than a typical museum. Local artist **Lygia Clark** is commemorated with a small shrine-like video gallery, while influential poet **Carlos Drummond de Andrade** gets a room piled with books, suit jackets and a tree – you get the picture. With 31 rooms, there are ones dedicated to the state's ancient cave paintings, a wonderful mini opera house and a collection of scale models of the historic towns of Minas Gerais. The main caveat: nothing is labelled in English. Housed in the former Secretaria de Estado da Fazenda (the state finance department) building, completed in 1897, the grand interior staircase and open areas are almost as impressive as the exhibits.

Museu das Minas e do Metal

Praça da Liberdade 680 • Tues–Sun noon–6pm (Thurs till 10pm); last entry 1hr before closing • Free • 31 3516 7200, mmgerdau.org.br

One of the city's most artfully designed museums, the **Museu das Minas e do Metal** successfully makes the otherwise dry subjects of mining and minerals utterly absorbing, with a series of dimly lit, whimsical galleries combining interactive exhibits, video and moody, New Age background music. You could easily spend a couple of hours here (labels are in English, but video and audio is Portuguese only). The dreamy Mirage Gallery, where images of rare stones behind glass are serenaded by recordings of Brazilian rock singer **Fernanda Takai** reading *Romanceiro da Inconfidência* – Cecilia Meireles' poem celebrating the doomed Minas freedom movement (see page 170) – sets the stage. There are tributes to the "prince of geologists" **Djalma Guimarães**, as well as a fabulous display of his collection of precious gems and rock; the mesmerizing *Sharp Tongue* installation (a huge, expressive, twisting steel sculpture); a room of hanging metal tubes representing the elements of the periodic table; and a fascinating terminal allowing you to compare the current price of commodities such as beans, gold and cotton with past decades. The museum is housed in another Neoclassical confection known as the "pink building", completed in 1897 as the Secretaría do Interior.

Espaço do Conhecimento UFMG

Praça da Liberdade • Tues–Fri & Sun 10am–5pm, Sat 10am–9pm • Free; planetarium R$6 • 31 3409 8350, espacodoconhecimento.org.br

The **Espaço do Conhecimento UFMG** or "palace of knowledge" is primarily targeted at kids, and contains a planetarium plus several galleries focusing on the creation of the universe, life on earth and the environment. The museum is the only one on the Praça da Liberdade to feature flashy, purpose-built premises, though the complex also incorporates the old headquarters of the Dean of the Universidade Federal de Minas Gerais.

Centro Cultural Banco do Brasil

Praça da Liberdade 450 • Daily except Tues 9am–9pm • Free • 31 3431 9400, culturabancodobrasil.com.br/portal/belo-horizonte

The grand sandy-coloured building on the east side of Praça da Liberdade contains the **Centro Cultural Banco do Brasil**, an atmospheric gallery venue with a wide range of temporary art exhibitions sponsored by the central bank. The building opened in 1930 to house the Secretaria de Segurança e Assistência Pública; its original, imposing granite staircase and Art Nouveau stained glass are still intact, and its wonderful airy inner courtyard now topped with a glass roof.

Museu Histórico Abílio Barreto

Av Prudente de Morais 202 • Tues & Fri–Sun 10am–5pm, Wed & Thurs 10am–9pm • Free • ☎ 31 3277 8573 • Bus #8103 (marked "Nova Floresta/Santa Lúcia") from Av Amazonas between Rua Espírito Santo and Rua dos Caetés; if you ask the conductor for the Museu Histórico, you'll be dropped on Av do Contorno, a block away, from where there are signs to the museum

Just outside the city centre, the **Museu Histórico Abílio Barreto** usually hosts interesting temporary exhibits on aspects of city history (everything from football to the history of the original settlement of Curral del Rei), though not much is labelled in English. The leafy garden area outside contains old train engines, carriages and a rare Minas *fazenda* (farmhouse), the **Fazenda do Leitão**, built in 1883 with a lovely wooden veranda and now a sort of monument to the region's old way of life. Exhibits inside highlight how folks used to live in Curral del Rei and Belo in the 1950s and 1990s, through antique furniture, photos and mediocre artwork.

Pampulha

Some 10km north of the city centre, the wealthy district of **Pampulha** is best known for the Mineirão football stadium and the complex of **Oscar Niemeyer** Modernist buildings set around the **Lagoa da Pampulha**, an artificial lake rich in birdlife. Despite a green algae problem and a fair amount of pollution, the lake sustains cormorants, the moorhen-like common gallinule, grebes, ibis, egrets, owls, herons and even large **capybara**, the fat, beaver-like creature you might spy basking on the lakeshore (alligators also live in the lake, but it's rare to see them). The lake was opened in 1938 as a reservoir, but in 1940 then-mayor of Belo Horizonte, **Juscelino Kubitschek**, commissioned Niemeyer and landscape designer **Roberto Burle Marx** to build a complex of buildings around it to create a leisure hub for the rapidly expanding city. Things didn't quite work out: it was years before the church was actually used, the **yacht club** (still there) was defunct after the lake was considered too polluted for watersports, and today the area is a posh residential district – a development which Niemeyer and Burle Marx, with their socialist ideals, would presumably be horrified by.

Casa do Baile

Av Otacílio Negrão de Lima 751 • Tues, Wed & Fri–Sun 9am–5pm, Thurs 9am–9pm • Free • ☎ 31 3277 7443

The curvaceous **Casa do Baile** ("house of dance") was designed by Oscar Niemeyer in 1942 to be a dance hall, but like most of the other buildings around the lake it didn't serve its original purpose for long. Today it displays small temporary exhibits on local art and architectural themes. Nearby is the **tourist office** (see page 152), designed to be a boat terminal in the 1940s, but serving as a bar from 1954 to 2007.

Igreja de São Francisco de Assis

Av Otacílio Negrão de Lima 3000 • Tues–Sat 9am–5pm, Sun 11am–2pm • R$3 • ☎ 31 4101 1174

The construction of the **Igreja de São Francisco de Assis**, with its striking curves, *azulejo* frontage and elegant bell tower, provides a roll call of the greatest names of Brazilian Modernism: Burle Marx laid out its grounds, Niemeyer designed the church, Cândido Portinari did the tiles and murals depicting the fourteen Stations of the Cross and Alfredo Ceschiatti (best known for his gravity-defying angels in Brasília's cathedral) contributed the bronze baptismal font. The church's design was decades ahead of its time and it's astonishing to realize that it dates from 1943. So shocked was the intensely conservative local Catholic hierarchy by the building's daring that he archbishop refused to consecrate it and almost twenty years passed before Mass could be held there. Note that it's a 2km walk around the lake from the Casa do Baile to the church.

Casa Kubitschek

Av Otacílio Negrão de Lima 4188 • Tues 9am–9pm, Wed–Sun 9am–6pm • Free • 31 3277 1586, bhfazcultura.pbh.gov.br

President of Brazil from 1956 to 1961, **Juscelino Kubitschek** (see page 158) is Minas Gerais' favourite son (he's viewed as the father of modern Brazil), starting his rise to power as mayor of Belo Horizonte in 1940. As the driving force behind the Pampulha project, it's fitting that Niemeyer designed JK's summer home along the lakeshore in 1943, now open to the public, complete with most of its Modernist furniture and interiors (the basement/garage presents changing exhibits dedicated to the development of Pampulha or other Modernist Brazilian themes), with English labelling throughout. A sculpture unveiled in 2016 of all four men most associated with Pampulha – JK, Niemeyer, Burle Marx and Portinari – stands on the lakeshore opposite the house, dubbed *Eterna Modernidade*.

Museu de Arte da Pampulha (MAP)

Av Otacílio Negrão de Lima 16585 • Tues–Sun 9am–5pm • Free • 31 3277 7946, bhfazcultura.pbh.gov.br

Set on a small peninsula jutting out into the northern side of the lake, the **Museu de Arte da Pampulha** is a product of two geniuses at the height of their powers. **Niemeyer** – influenced here heavily by Le Corbusier – created a boxy-style building typical of International Modernism, all straight lines and right angles at the front but melting into rippling curves at the back, with a marvellous use of glass; while **Burle Marx** set the whole thing off beautifully, with an exquisite garden framing the building both front and back. It was completed in 1942 as a casino, but the Brazilian government abolished gambling four years later and not until 1957 was the building inaugurated as an art museum. Aficionados of contemporary and Modernist Brazilian art will enjoy the modest temporary exhibitions inside, the galleries and main auditorium linked by ramps, though it's really the building that makes a visit worthwhile (you can sip coffee at the café and enjoy the lake views at the back).

Estádio Mineirão and Museu Brasileiro do Futebol

Av Coronel Oscar Paschoal 932 • Tues 9am–8pm, Wed–Fri 9am–5pm, Sat & Sun 9am–1pm • R$20 • 31 3499 4312, estadiomineirao.com.br/museu-e-visita

In addition to the Oscar Niemeyer connection, Pampulha is known for the **Mineirão** football stadium, the "Giant of Pampulha", and its **Museu Brasileiro do Futebol**. The museum, which has English labelling, chronicles the history of the stadium and its most famous matches (top team **Cruzeiro** play here), while one-hour guided **tours** (hourly, first-come, first-served; not available on public holidays or match days) take in the locker rooms, press room, stands and pitch where Brazil were crushed 7–1 by Germany in the semi-finals of the 2014 World Cup, which was dubbed "The biggest shame in history" by *Lance!*, the major Brazilian sports newspaper.

FOOTBALL IN BH

One of the better teams in Brasileiro Série A, **Cruzeiro** (the "Foxes") play at the Mineirão (they won the league in 2013 and 2014), and they're worth catching if you're in Belo Horizonte during a home game. Local derbies, especially against Atlético Mineiro (known as "Galo", after their mascot, a rooster), also a top Série A team (they won South America's Copa Libertadores in 2013 and the Copa do Brasil in 2014), are torrid and very entertaining affairs (if you attend, prepare to learn a lot of Brazilian swear words). Tickets are around R$15 for the *arquibancada* (stands), rising to R$75 for better seats.

Sabará

Strung out along the valley of the Rio das Velhas a short drive east from the edge of Belo Horizonte's sprawling suburbs, **Sabará** has retained a relaxed, small-town feel that befits its historic past – founded in 1674, it was the first major centre of gold mining in the state. While its cobbled streets, rickety old homes and small plazas are appealing enough, Sabará's gorgeous **churches** are the real draw, austere on the outside but choked with spectacular ornamentation inside. Sabará's proximity to Belo Horizonte (around 20km) and the frequency of the **bus** link makes it an easy day-trip: start early and avoid visiting on Monday when most sights are closed.

Praça Santa Rita

Standing in **Praça Santa Rita**, you're in the centre not just of the oldest part of Sabará, but of the oldest inhabited streets in southern Brazil. Today the cobbled square is a small, humble affair with a bandstand, a couple of cheap restaurants and a bank.

Prefeitura

Rua Dom Pedro II • Mon–Fri 8am–5pm • Free

There are a number of impressive eighteenth-century buildings near Praça Santa Rita, notably the **Prefeitura**. Completed around 1773 as the local priest's residence, it became the town hall in 1871. You can poke your head inside the main entrance hall to see the jacaranda staircase and original ceiling paintings, but the rest of the building is off limits.

Teatro Municipal

Rua Dom Pedro II • Daily 8am–noon & 1–5pm • Free

You can take a peek inside the **Teatro Municipal**, just beyond Praça Santa Rita, to glimpse the Italian Baroque-style interior, bamboo ceiling, three circles of boxes and rattan chairs in the orchestra seats. This incarnation dates back to 1819, though the first opera house was erected here around 1770.

Nossa Senhora do Rosário dos Pretos

Praça Melo Viana • Tues–Sun 8–11am & 1–5pm • R$2

A short walk up Rua Dom Pedro II from Praça Santa Rita lies the much bigger **Praça Melo Viana**, shaded by giant palms and the place to catch local buses. At the top end lies the unfinished church of **Nossa Senhora do Rosário dos Pretos**, looking a bit like a ruined castle. Slaves who worked in the gold mines began paying for it and building it in typical Portuguese-colonial style in 1768, but with the decline of the mines the money ran out with only the chancel and sacristy completed by 1780. Although sporadic restarts were made during the nineteenth century, it was never more than half-built, and when slavery was abolished in 1888 it was left as a memorial. Today the chancel/chapel and sacristy remain the only covered sections within the crumbling walls, housing a mildly interesting collection of religious art.

Nossa Senhora do Carmo

Rua do Carmo • Tues–Sat 9–11.30am & 1–5pm, Sun 1–5pm • R$5

A "third-phase" Baroque church a short walk east along Rua Borba Gato and then Rua do Carmo from Praça Melo Viana, **Nossa Senhora do Carmo** demonstrates the remarkable talents of **Aleijadinho** (see page 166), who oversaw its construction and contributed much of the decoration between 1763 and 1778. The interior manages to be elaborate and uncluttered at the same time, with graceful curves in the gallery, largely plain walls, comparatively little gilding and a beautifully painted ceiling. Aleijadinho left his mark everywhere: the imposing soapstone and painted wood pulpits, the banister in the nave, and above all in the two statues of São João

da Cruz and São Simão Stock (in the two *retábulos* on either side of the nave). You can tell an Aleijadinho from the faces: the remarkably lifelike one of São Simão (facing the altar, he is on the left) is complete with wrinkles and transfixed by religious ecstasy.

Museu do Ouro

Rua da Intendência • Tues–Fri 10am–5pm, Sat & Sun noon–5pm • R$1 • ⓣ 31 36711848

The small but absorbing **Museu do Ouro** ("gold museum") is a short but steep walk behind the Nossa Senhora do Carmo, a memorial to the trade that made the town rich in the eighteenth century. The museum occupies a creaking, slanting wooden colonial building built around 1730 to serve as the royal foundry and mint, as well as the living quarters of the official "Intendência" who oversaw the operation and collection of taxes from the balcony overlooking the inner courtyard – a function it served until 1833.

The lower rooms are full of scales, weights, pans and other mining instruments, and a strongroom containing plaster-cast replicas of eighteenth-century gold bars. There's also the **Sala dos Inglês**, a room dedicated to the mostly British engineers and mining companies who helped revive extraction of the region's mineral wealth in the nineteenth century, using the deep mining techniques established in Cornwall (the British-owned **St John d'el Rey Mining Co** operated the famed Morro Velho mine between 1830 and 1960).

Upstairs you'll find living quarters decorated circa 1750 with a collection of colonial furniture, porcelain and *arte sacra* (including a *Sant'ana Mestra* by Aleijadinho), as well as the **Sala dos Quatros Continentes** and its handsomely painted ceiling representing the four continents known at the time it was built.

Igreja Matriz de Nossa Senhora da Conceição

Praça Getúlio Vargas s/n • Tues–Sun 9am–noon & 2–5pm • Free • ⓣ 31 3671 1724, ⓦ nsconceicao-sabara.blogspot.com.br

Sabará's most spectacular church, **Igreja Matriz de Nossa Senhora da Conceição**, is a 1.5km walk from Praça Santa Rita, its modest red-and-white exterior situated on the work a day Praça Getúlio Vargas at the eastern end of town. The interior, however, is another story: completed between 1710 and 1714, it's a jaw-dropping example of the so-called first and second phases of *barroco mineiro*. Inside the bejewelled cave-like interior is a row of heavily carved and gilded arches on each side of the nave, a beautifully decorated ceiling, and almost every space is smothered with paintings and murals the closer you get to the altar. Check out the doors on either side of the apse (especially on the left facing the altar) – for an added dose of the exotic these feature painted panels with unmistakable red and gold Chinese influences, most likely added by craftsmen from the Portuguese colony of Macau (or at least, someone who had been there).

Igreja de Nossa Senhora de Ó

Largo Nossa Senhora de Ó • Daily 8am–noon & 1.30–5pm • Free (donation suggested) • ⓣ 31 3671 1724

From Praça Getúlio Vargas it's another 1km (well signposted) trek to Sabará's most enigmatic church, the tiny **Igreja de Nossa Senhora de Ó**. Located, incongruously, in a quiet residential area on the other side of the Rio das Velhas, it doesn't look in the least Brazilian: its simple, irregularly shaped exterior is topped off by the kind of tower more usually seen on colonial churches in China, complete with pagoda-like flying eaves at the corners. The cramped, lavishly decorated interior, dominated by a gilded arch over the altar and smothered with gorgeous paintings and murals, also shows some oriental influences; the octagonal painted panels in the arch feature unmistakably Chinese-style boats, birds and pagodas. Constructed between 1717 and 1720 (the "Ó" supposedly comes from the loud "oh" given out by churchgoers during services), the most likely explanation is that, like the Conceição church, Chinese craftsmen from Macau were responsible for the design.

RRIVAL AND DEPARTURE

y plane Belo Horizonte has two airports: Aeroporto nternacional Tancredo Neves (31 3689 2700, www.bh-irport.com.br), usually referred to as Confins, the name of he nearby town, 38km north of Belo Horizonte; depending n traffic, the journey into town can take over an hour. City uses run at 10–30min intervals (24hr) to the main rodoviária n the centre (R$12.25), while posher *executivo* buses (every 0–30min, 6am–12.30am; R$26.75; conexaoaeroporto. om.br) drop you in the centre at Av Alvares Cabral 387, near ua da Bahia. Taxis from Confins cost around R$120–130 on he meter, depending on traffic; from the airport it's usually heaper to fix the price in advance (around R$110, cash or redit card) at the taxi booths at the main terminal exit (this also where the bus ticket booths are). The barely used ampulha (31 3490 2001) is 9km from the centre.

y train The train station (31 3279 4366) is on Praça da stação. Apart from the local *metrô* commuter line, there's only ne passenger service out of Belo Horizonte, the Estrada de erro Vitória a Minas, which is the connection with Vitória (daily .30am; 13hr; R$58; 0800 285 7000), returning at 7am. The rain was given a trendy makeover in 2015 (it's operated by ale, the second-largest mining company in the world). You an buy tickets at the station or online (tremdepassageiros. ale.com; the Vitória station is "Cariacica").

By bus The huge rodoviária (31 3271 3000) is on Praça Rio Branco, an easy walk from the commercial centre of the city (for taxis, head to the dedicated rank at the underground level; street level is just for drop off). A new terminal is being built in the far less convenient northern suburb of São Gabriel (7.5km from the centre), but legal and funding problems have stalled the project for years; if it does finally open in 2018/2019, it will be connected to the metro and local bus system – taxis from here into the centre will be around R$45. For travel within the state, look for the Pássaro Verde (Ouro Preto, Mariana, Diamantina; passaroverde.com.br) and Viação Sandra (Congonhas, São João del Rei; viacaosandra.com.br) desks inside the terminal; you can also catch buses to Confins airport here. There are lockers ($13/30hr) and left luggage ($12–40/ day) on the underground level.

Destinations Brasília (9 daily; 10–11hr); Campo Grande (4 daily; 23–25hr); Congonhas (hourly; 2hr); Cuiabá (2 daily; 25–29hr); Diamantina (8 daily; 5hr); Mariana (14 daily; 2hr–2hr 15min); Ouro Preto (hourly 6am–11pm; 1hr 55min); Rio (18 daily; 6–8hr); Salvador (1 daily; 24hr); São João del Rei (7 daily; 3hr 30min); São Lourenço (3 daily; 5hr 30min–7hr); São Paulo (hourly; 8hr); Vitória (13 daily; 8–9hr).

ART IN THE JUNGLE

It comes as a bit of a shock to find the world's largest open-air art museum in an otherwise suburban backwater an hour's bus journey from Belo Horizonte. But that's exactly what's on offer at **Inhotim Instituto Cultural**, just outside the non-descript town of Brumadinho (Tues–Fri 9.30am–4.30pm, Sat & Sun 9.30am–5.30pm; R$44, Wed free; access to golf cart transport routes around the park R$28 extra; 31 3571 9700, inhotim.org.br), an exhibition of over four hundred pieces of contemporary art across ten galleries, set amid an incredible 106 acres of lush botanical reserve. Opened officially in 2006, the collection includes paintings, sculpture, photos, videos and installations by both Brazilians and international artists – among them outstanding works by Hélio Oiticica, Cildo Meireles, Vik Muniz and Amilcar de Castro – dating from the 1960s to the present. Inhotim's appeal goes beyond art, however, with **gardens** of orchids, palms and rare tropical species landscaped by Burle Marx. The huge estate also boasts one of the best-preserved sections of Atlantic forest in Brazil. The project was conceived and primarily funded by iron-mining tycoon Bernardo Paz, who bought up land around his ranch from the 1980s onwards and started filling the spaces with art.

You'll need a full day at Inhotim – walking the whole site will take some effort (and many of the paths are steep), but unless it's especially hot (bring water) or you are short of time, there's no real need to pay for the golf carts. There are plenty of places to take a rest and the on-site restaurants and cafés, while pricey, are all pretty good and beautifully located.

GETTING THERE

The site lies 60km southwest of Belo Horizonte; Saritur **buses** leave from the rodoviária in the city (Sat, Sun & hols at 8.15am, arriving at 10am, R$36.20; returning at 5.30pm, reaching Belo Horizonte at 7.25pm, R$32.50; 31 3419 1800, saritur.com.br). Shuttle vans also make the trip, departing the Inhotim Savassi store, Antônio de Albuquerque 909, with a minimum four people (Sat & Sun departing 8.15pm; R$60 return; 31 3571 9796). Taxis from central Belo Horizonte will charge around R$200 (one-way).

Saritur also runs three daily buses to Brumadinho (7am, 11am & 3pm; 1hr 35min; R$20.30), from where taxis charge around R$20 to Inhotim (only one bus returns, though, at 8.35am; R$16.55).

GETTING AROUND

BY BUS

The city's bus system (bhtrans.pbh.gov.br) works along the same lines as elsewhere in Brazil (pay as you enter), with the exception of the MOVE bus rapid transit (BRT) system, which works like a subway, with dedicated bus lanes and stations – its main use for visitors is for travelling between the centre and Pampulha (see page 146). You need to buy a BHBUS card or a stored value "Cartão Unitário" to go through the electronic turnstiles (buy them at kiosks outside the station), with single rides R$4.05. Other buses charge R$2.85 or R$4.05 depending on the route (fares are posted on the bus). Virtually all routes include a stretch along Av Afonso Pena, which is usually the most convenient place to catch a bus if you are staying in the centre.

BY METRO

The one-line city *metrô* (daily 5.15am–11pm; R$1.80/ride) was built with commuters rather than tourists in mind and serves only to link the suburbs with the centre.

BY TAXI

With distances being short between most points of interest in the centre, taxi rides (BH Táxi 31 3215 8081, bh.taxi.br; Coopertramo 31 3454 5757, coopertramo.com.br) are not very expensive; the meter starts at R$4.70, so figure on R$10–15 for most rides within the centre (or R$20–25 for Pampulha).

BY CAR

Car rental Numerous options at the airports, plus: Hertz at Av Prof. Magalhães Penido 101, Pampulha (31 3492 1919); Localiza at Av Bernardo Monteiro 1567 (31 3247 7956); and Unidas at Av Bias Fortes 1019, near Praça Raul Soares (31 3586 5000).

PAMPULHA

Getting to and around the Lagoa da Pampulha can be tricky without your own transport; it's pleasant enough to walk along the waterside path, but it's some 19km in all, and unless it's mid-winter, it's often very hot. Buses and taxis are unfortunately hard to come by; one possibility is to get a taxi to the Niemeyer church (see page 146), then walk back to the tourist centre (2km) and get them to call another one. Getting to the Museu de Arte is even trickier – it's another 1hr walk from the tourist centre.

By bus/minibus There a handful of useful local bus and minibus routes around the Lagoa da Pampulha. MOVE buses #50 and #51 run direct to Estação Pampulha (40min), at Av Portugal, on the eastern side of the lake from downtown BH (Av Santos Dumont, between São Paulo and Rio de Janeiro); bus #8550 runs from São Gabriel metro station along the southern side of the lake to the zoo and back, but on Sundays and holidays only (8.30am–4.30pm, every 30min; R$4.05); S51 circular minibus runs 2–3 times an hour (every 30min Sat & Sun; R$4.05) around most of the lake, while bus #512 (R$2.85) runs around the lake between 9am and 6pm daily, but only every 2hr or so (hourly Sat & Sun).

SABARÁ

By bus In central Belo Horizonte catch either bus #4988 or #4987 (every 15min 4am–midnight; R$4.05; 40min) from Rua dos Caetés, at the junction with Rua Rio de Janeiro. Buses terminate at Sabará bus station on Rua Ajuda at the far eastern end of town (opposite the giant ArcelorMittal steel plant). Get off before this: ask the driver to drop you at the best stop for the *centro histórico*, which should be somewhere on Av Prefeito Vitor Fantini (the name of BR-262 as it skirts the old town along the river). From here it's a short walk up Rua Dom Pedro II to Praça Santa Rita. Buses back to Belo Horizonte are best caught on the same stretch of road (there's a bus stop close to the junction of Rua Dom Pedro II and Av Prefeito Vitor Fantini).

By taxi Belo Horizonte taxis should take you to Sabará without any fuss, though they'll use the meter: expect to pay around R$60 one-way from downtown, depending on where you start.

INFORMATION

Tourist offices Mercado Central, Av Augusto de Lima 744 (Mon & Tues 8am–4.20pm, Wed–Sat 8am–5.20pm, Sun & hols 8am–1pm; 31 3277 4691); Tancredo Neves (Confins) airport (Mon–Fri 8am–10pm, Sat & Sun 8am–5pm; 31 3689 2557); rodoviária, Praça Rio Branco (daily 8am–5pm; 31 3277 6907); and the tourist information centre on the lake at Av Otacílio Negrão de Lima 855, Pampulha (Tues–Sun 8am–5pm; 31 3277 9987).

ACCOMMODATION

There are scores of hotels within easy reach of the rodoviária. There are some good options in the pleasant **Savassi** area, an easy taxi or bus ride (or a 20min walk) from the centre, and a few in **Funcionários**, midway between the two. For those on a tight budget, there are a several decent **youth hostels** to choose from.

★ **Adrena Sport Hostel** Av Getúlio Vargas 1635, Savassi 31 3657 9970, adrenasporthostel.com.br; map p.142. Fun, chilled out hostel with an extreme sports theme in buzzing Savassi; the bilingual staff are a mine of information, there's a full kitchen and bar on site and the dorms are clean and cosy (with fans). Also offers comfy "stand up" rooms for four people (one double and two bunks) and private bathroom. Cash only. Dorms R$50, doubles R$140

Clan Glass Business Tower Hotel Rua Gonçalves Dias 30, Funcionários 31 3615 1300, clan.com.br; map p.142. For a little more comfort, try this centrally located business hotel with modern, stylish rooms (with a/c and good cable TV) and wonderful buffet breakfasts. R230

Ibis Belo Horizonte Liberdade Av João Pinheiro 602, Centro 31 2111 1500, accorhotels.com; map p.142. This efficient and ever-popular hotel on the edge of Funcionários is typical of the chain (there are several branches in the city). Located in an attractive renovated old mansion with a modern tower building behind, the no-frills rooms are small, but each has a shower and all are a/c. R$132

Lá em Casa Hostel-Pousada Rua Eurita 30, Santa Tereza 31 3653 9566, laemcasahostel.com; map p.142. An attractive HI-affiliated hostel in BH's bohemian quarter, a short ride from the centre and with numerous traditional *botecos* nearby. Dorms and simple en-suite doubles are available, with an excellent breakfast included. Dorms R$38, doubles R$120

Laranja Mecânica Rua Rodrigues Caldas 714, Santo Agostinho 31 3309 5881, laranjamecanicahostel pousada.com; map p.142. Popular hostel and pousada (named after the cult movie *A Clockwork Orange*), just inside the Contorno, 2km southwest of the centre. Dorms are simple but stylish, while doubles come with or without bathrooms. Splashes of orange and murals inspired by the movie pay homage to the hostel's namesake. Dorms R$40, doubles R$140

Othon Palace Av Afonso Pena 1050, Centro 31 3247 0000, othon.com.br; map p.142. A huge, refurbished 1970s skyscraper with friendly and highly professional staff, well-equipped rooms and a fine rooftop pool. Be sure to request a room on one of the upper floors facing out from the front of the building – the views across the Parque Municipal and onwards to the Serra do Curral are spectacular. R$185

Royal Savassi Boutique Hotel Rua Alagoas 699, Savassi 31 2138 0000, royalhoteis.com.br; map p.142. Overall the best luxury choice in the city, with elegant contemporary rooms, cable TV, gym and a sauna on site. R$240

Samba Rooms Hostel Av Bias Fortes 368 31 3267 0740, sambaroomshostel.com.br; map p.142. Popular hostel in the central Lourdes district, set in a pretty canary-coloured 1930s mansion, offering bright double rooms (with private or shared bathrooms) and dorms with basic breakfast and ceiling fans. Communal kitchen, lounge and guest-use computer available. Laundry R$25 per 15kg/30lb. Dorms R$50, doubles R$110

COMIDA MINEIRA

Though not well-known outside the country, Minas Gerais' tasty **regional cuisine**, *comida mineira*, is one of Brazil's most distinctive – based mainly on pork, the imaginative use of vegetables, *couve* (a green vegetable somewhat like kale), and the famous *tutu*, a thick bean sauce made by grinding uncooked beans with manioc flour and cooking the mixture. Stews often include the excellent Minas sausages, which is smoked and peppery. Many of the dishes originate from the early mule trains and *bandeirante* expeditions of the eighteenth century, when food had to keep for long periods (hence the use of salted pork, now usually replaced by fresh). There are also small stores everywhere serving Minas Gerais' *doces* (cakes and sweetmeats), local cheeses, made both from goats' and cows' milk, and, of course, cachaça. Typical dishes include:

Carne picadinha A straightforward, rich stew of either beef or pork, cooked for hours until tender.

Costelinha Stewed ribs of ham.

Dobradinha Tripe stew cooked with sweet potatoes.

Doce de leite A rich caramel sludge.

Feijão tropeiro ("Mule driver's beans"). A close relative to *tutu a mineira*, with a name that betrays its eighteenth-century origins; it features everything that is in a *tutu* but also has beans fried with *farinha* (manioc flour), egg and onion thrown into the mix.

Frango ao molho pardo Definitely one for hardened carnivores only: essentially chicken cooked in its own blood. It's better than it sounds, but rather bitter in taste.

Frango com quiabo Chicken roasted with okra and served sizzling with a side plate of *anju*, a corn porridge that *mineiros* eat with almost anything.

Tutu a mineira Roasted pork served with lashings of *tutu*, garnished with steamed *couve* and *torresmo* (an excellent salted-pork crackling) – most common of all dishes, found on every menu.

EATING

CENTRAL BELO HORIZONTE

Badejo Rua Rio Grande do Norte 836, Savassi 31 3261 2023, restaurantebadejo.com.br; map p.142. Restaurant specializing in the dishes and fresh seafood of Espírito Santo. If you won't be visiting that state, at least try one of the distinctive *mocquecas* – a tomato-based fish stew, unlike the Bahian dish of the same name which uses coconut milk. Tues–Fri 11.30am–5pm & 6–11.30pm, Sat 11.30am–11.30pm, Sun 11.30am–5pm.

Bar do Lopes Rua Professor Antônio Aleixo 260, Lourdes 31 3337 7995; map p.142. This relaxed open-front bar has been in operation since 1963 – making it historical by BH standards – with all-white tile decor and street seating. Serves delicious *petiscos*, including its famed *porção de lula à dorée* (crispy calamari), French baguette sandwiches and Portuguese sardine sandwiches. Mon & Sun 11am–3pm Tues–Sat 11am–midnight.

Bonomi Panificadora Av Afonso Pena 2600, Funcionários 31 3261 3460, casabonomi.com.br; map p.142. Located in a rustic building with an easy-to-miss sign, this bakery and takeaway serves excellent light meals (salads, pasta, soups and sandwiches from R$30), wonderful cakes and what may be the best bread anywhere in Brazil. Tues–Sat 8am–10.30pm, Sun 8am–8pm.

Casa dos Contos Rua Rio Grande do Norte 1065, Savassi 31 3261 5853, restaurantecasadoscontos.com.br; map p.142. Local favourite since 1975, serving traditional Italian and Brazilian cuisine, but also serving as a popular bar (mains R$21–60). Mon 11.30am–3pm & 6pm–2am, Tues–Thurs 11.30am–2am, Fri & Sat 11.30am–3am, Sun 11.30am–1am.

Der Famous Av do Contorno 6399, Santo Antônio 31 8417 9537; map p.142. Justly lauded gourmet hotdog joint (try the "Karl Marx"; R$23.50), featuring huge, German-style sausages. Tues–Thurs 5–11pm, Fri 6pm–1am, Sat 12.30pm–1am, Sun 12.30–11pm.

★ **Dona Lucinha** Rua Sergipe 811, Funcionários 31 3261 5930, donalucinha.com.br; map p.142. Offers a gut-busting but very authentic *comida mineira* buffet for around R$60 per person – it's not cheap, but top quality, with a vast range of meats, stews and vegetable dishes, and the wonderful pudding-like desserts are all helpfully labelled in English. Dona Lucinha herself (born in Serro) a bit of a legend, even penning a cookbook you can bu here. Tues–Fri noon–3pm & 7–11pm, Sat noon–4pm 7–11pm, Sun noon–4.30pm.

La Greppia Rua da Bahia 1196, Centro 31 327 2055; map p.142. A rare downtown BH restaurant wi some history and great-value tasty Brazilian and Italia meals and snacks, any time day and night. Try the R$2 unlimited lunchtime buffet, or evening pasta *rodizio* wi dessert for R$25. Daily 24hr.

★ **Minas Tênis Clube** Rua da Bahia 2244, Lourde 31 3516 1310, minastenisclube.com.br; ma p.142. The tennis club's excellent-value (R$35/perso plus drink) lunch buffet is one of the city centre's bes kept secrets. Choose a table on the terrace overlooking th tennis courts, gardens and pool and marvel at the club's A Deco splendour. The food's good too – a varied selectio of salads and local dishes, from rich stews and *feijoad* to grilled fish and creamy mashed potatoes. Mon–F 11am–3pm.

★ **Vecchio Sogno** Rua Martim de Carvalho 7 Santo Agostinho 31 3292 5231, vecchiosogn com.br; map p.142. Widely considered to be one of th best restaurants in the city (mains R$72–119), with a imaginative mix of Italian, French and Brazilian dishe Try the duck lasagne with wild mushrooms or the he gnocchi with a prawn sauce, and don't miss the banan *tarte tatine* served with *queijo-de-minas* ice cream. Mon Thurs noon–midnight, Fri noon–1am, Sat 6pm–1am Sun noon–6pm.

PAMPULHA

★ **Xapuri** Rua Mandacaru 260, Pampulha 31 349 6198, restaurantexapuri.com.br; map p.142. Th superb *comida mineira* here includes dishes you're unlike to find elsewhere, such as the *moranga recheada com carn seca* (pumpkin stuffed with dried meat). The atmospher is that of an old country house, the kitchen's wood-fire stoves and ovens clearly visible – and it's a good place t purchase *artesanato* as well as *doces* (sweets) made on th premises. Mains R$34–129. It's easiest to take a taxi here Tues–Sat noon–11pm, Sun noon–6pm.

EATING AT THE MERCADO CENTRAL

The city's Mercado Central (see page 141) is an atmospheric and popular place to grab lunch, a sandwich or a cold beer. There are several stand-up bars around the edges, but *Bar da Tia* (31 3274 9648) and the classy *Botiquin do Antônio*, which opened in 1963 (daily 7am–6pm 31 9267 6593), have the most character.

The most popular sit-down joint is *Casa Cheia* (Mon–Sat 10.30am–6.30pm, Sun 10am–1pm; 31 3274 9585) a small but excellent restaurant – if it's full and you can't wait, the row of buffet canteens behind it down the steps are acceptable standbys (try *Bom Grill*; 31 3273 2333).

SABARÁ

★ **Barroco** Praça Santa Rita 14 ☎31 3671 4696. Friendly local bar and restaurant with a rustic interior of wooden counter and tables (plus giant map of the town), serving cold beers, cheap lunch buffet of *mineira* favourites (R$14) and a menu of hearty steaks, pork chops, roast chicken and tilapia to share (mains R$30–50). Mon–Wed & Sun 8am–11pm, Thurs–Sat 8am–1am.

Santíssimo Bar Praça Melo Viana 34 ☎31 3671 2147. By far the coolest place for a drink in town, on a terrace overlooking Praça Melo Viana, though its main focus is creating innovative pizza toppings. Tues–Sun 6pm–3am.

DRINKING AND NIGHTLIFE

Belo Horizonte's chic nightlife is concentrated in **Savassi**, but you'll find lively pockets of bars and clubs throughout the central area, and there's a flourishing live music scene in the city. Most days of the week, the bottom end of **Rua da Bahia** between Avenida Afonso Pena and Praça da Estação is buzzing; the bars put out tables under the palm trees and the action goes on until the small hours.

BARS

Bomb Shell Rua Sergipe 1395, Savassi ☎31 8930 3640; map p.142. Contemporary *boteco* with DJs spinning anything from funk *carioca* to jazz standards or rock and pop: check the schedule. Nice eats for sharing, too. Mon & Sun 6pm–midnight, Tues–Fri 6pm–1am, Sat 1pm–1am.

Butiquim São Bento Rua Kepler 131, São Bento ☎31 3047 9596; map p.142. A traditional-looking *boteco*, yet this is a young and friendly bar, with live MPB (Música Popular Brasileira) on Fridays and Saturdays. Play pool in the back room, sip cocktails or try one of the 28 kinds of beer. Tues–Thurs 5.30pm–1am, Fri 5.30pm–2am, Sat noon–2am, Sun noon–11pm.

★ **Café Cultura Bar** Rua da Bahia 1416, Lourdes ☎31 3653 5992, Ⓦcafeculturabar.com.br; map p.142. Atmospheric coffee shop and bar set inside a handsome 1904 building, with live rock'n'roll and MPB. Mon–Fri 11am–2pm & 6pm–1am, Sat 6pm–1am.

Choperia Albanos Rua Rio de Janeiro 2076, Lourdes ☎31 3292 6221, Ⓦalbanos.com.br; map p.142. Excellent German-style microbrewery and pub in a 1936 town house (the original branch is at Pium-1 611), with a beer-hall set-up and lots of outdoor tables. Mon–Fri 6pm–1am, Sat & Sun noon–1am.

Stadt Jever Pub Av Cotorno 5771 ☎31 3223 5056, Ⓦstadtjever.com.br; map p.142. German-style pub with great beer from local Cervejaria Wäls, pork knuckle and *sauerkraut*, a popular balcony and all sorts of whimsical touches such as a table dedicated to Elvis and an ox-cart hanging from the ceiling. Mon–Wed 6pm–1am, Thurs 6pm–2am, Fri & Sat 6pm–3am, Sun 6pm–midnight.

★ **Wäls Gastropub** Rua Levindo Lopes 358, Savassi ☎31 3582 5628, Ⓦwalsgastropub.com.br; map p.142. Stylish bar dedicated to serving local Wäls craft beers, with a decent selection on tap from its session IPA to its "Petroleum", a Russian Imperial Stout. Mon–Wed 11.30am–midnight, Thurs 11.30am–1am, Fri 11.30am–2am, Sat noon–2am, Sun noon–11pm.

CLUBS AND LIVE MUSIC

A Obra Rua Rio Grande do Norte 1168, Funcionários ☎31 3215 8077, Ⓦaobra.com.br; map p.142. Live rock venue and club with a roster of decent local bands. Prices are not bad: beers are R$8, caipirinhas R$12, with cover ranging from R$15–30. Wed & Thurs 8pm–midnight, Fri & Sat 10pm–6am.

Café com Letras Rua Antônio de Albuquerque 781, Savassi ☎31 3225 9973, Ⓦcafecomletras.com.br; map p.142. Café, bar, bookshop and cultural space, with a calendar of live music (mostly jazz) and book launches throughout the year. DJs spin most nights. R$3.50–8 cover charge. Mon–Thurs noon–midnight, Fri & Sat noon–1am, Sun 5–11pm.

Paco Pigalle Bar Av do Contorno 2314, Floresta (between Av dos Andradas and Av Assis Chateaubriand) ☎31 3222 4948; map p.142. Plays a mix of hip-hop, reggae, salsa and disco to a high-spending, trendy crowd. Fri & Sat 10pm–5am.

Utópica Marcenaria Av Raja Gabáglia 4700, Santa Lúcia ☎31 3296 2868, Ⓦutopica.com.br; map p.142. Popular live music venue located a few kilometres south of Centro, with a lively, diverse crowd: plays samba on Thursdays, rock/MPB on Friday, funk/soul on Saturday and *forró* on Sunday. Cover R$20–30. Fri & Sat 9pm–3am, Sun 7pm–1am.

DIRECTORY

Consulates Argentina, Rua Ceará 1566, 6th floor, Funcionários (☎31 3047 5490); Canada, Av do Contorno 4520, 8th floor (☎31 3213 1651); US, Edifício Celta, Rua Maranhão 310, Santa Efigênia (☎31 3956 0800); UK, Rua Fernandes Tourinho 669/702 (☎21 2555 9600).

Hospital Pronto Socorro do Hospital João XXIII, Av Alfredo Balena 400, Santa Efigênia (☎31 3239 9200). Ambulance ☎192.

Laundry Lavanderia Just a Sec, at Rua dos Guajajaras 1268, Centro (Mon–Fri 8am–6pm, Sat 8am–1pm).

Money and exchange Banks are concentrated downtown on Av João Pinheiro, between Rua dos Timbiras and Av Afonso Pena. Bank ATMs are common throughout the city.
Police ⓣ 190. For a visa or tourist permit extension, go to the Polícia Federal at Rua Nascimento Gurgel 30, in Guiterrez (ⓣ 31 3291 2359).
Post office Av Afonso Pena 1270 (Mon–Fri 8.30am–6pm, Sat 9am–noon); the Savassi branch is at Rua Pernambuco 1322 (Mon–Fri 9am–6pm, Sat 9am–noon) and there's also a branch at the bus station (Mon–Fri 9am–7pm, Sat 9am–noon).

2

Estrada Real: the Diamond Road

In 1695, gold was discovered in the hills of Minas Gerais, and a north–south road system dubbed the **Estrada Real** or "royal highway", was established soon after, linking **Ouro Preto** (see page 168) with the coastal ports of Rio and Paraty. When diamonds were discovered further north in 1727, the road was extended 302km to **Diamantina** – and this section became known as the **Diamond Road** (Caminho dos Diamantes). Today it's still possible to follow the old route, which cuts into the foothills of the **Serra do Espinhaço**, the highlands that form the spine of the state, though it's much easier to do so with your own transport. Rough and violent mining camps in their early days, the towns here were soon transformed by mineral wealth into treasure houses, not merely of gold, but also of Baroque art and architecture. Well preserved and carefully maintained, along with the towns of the **Old Road** (see page 177), they form one of the most impressive sets of colonial remains in the Americas.

Diamantina

Nestled in the heart of the Serra do Espinhaço, the northern terminus of the Diamond Road, **DIAMANTINA** was the original starting point of the Estrada Real and remains the most isolated of the state's historic towns. Named after the abundant diamond reserves hereabouts, first exploited in the 1720s, the town was designated a UNESCO World Heritage Site in 1999 – the narrow stone-flagged streets, with their overhanging Chinese-style eaves and perfectly preserved colonial houses, are exactly as they have been for generations.

While the streets are either too narrow or too steep even for Brazil's intrepid local bus drivers, the place is small enough for you to get your bearings very quickly. The central square in the old town is **Praça Conselheiro Mata**, which has the cathedral built in the middle of it – everyone calls the cathedral and the square "Sé"; most of the sights and places to stay are within a stone's throw of here. Diamantina justifies a couple of days' wandering around in its own right, but you should also try to take in the scenery and nearby waterfalls and pools.

Museu do Diamante

Rua Direita 14, Praça Conselheiro Mata • Tues–Sat 10am–5pm, Sun 9am–1pm • Free • ⓣ 38 3531 1382, ⓦ museudiamante.blogspot.com

Contrary to the name, the **Museu do Diamante** is not a diamond museum, but does make an effort to give you an idea of daily life in old Diamantina – like all the town's museums, labels are in Portuguese only. The tiny room behind the entrance desk is

THE DIARY OF HELENA MORLEY

Visitors to Diamantina often find inspiration in the *Diary of Helena Morley* by American poet **Elizabeth Bishop**, who came to live in Brazil in 1952. The book is actually an English translation of a real diary of a local girl (aged 12 to 15) growing up in Diamantina during the 1890s – "Helena Morley" was the pseudonym of Alice Dayrell, the daughter of a frustrated diamond miner of English descent. The evocative description of life in rural Brazil at a time when slavery had just been abolished and modernization was beginning to take sway makes for fascinating reading. Bishop spent three years translating the diary and visited Diamantina, which she describes in the introduction as having changed very little between the 1890s and 1950s.

devoted to the town's mining history – in addition to the old tools, scales, maps and prints is an enormous cast-iron English safe, brought by ox cart all the way from Rio in the eighteenth century (it took eighteen months to get here). Inside is a pile of (replica) uncut diamonds and emeralds, plus a selection of very real precious stones, jewellery and minerals (the reason for the armed guards patrolling the museum).

Other rooms are dedicated to religious icons and eighteenth-century oratorios, a bizarre wall of carved legs, arms and hands (remnants of devotional *santos* or religious statues), antique guns and swords, a mouldering sedan chair and an extravagant top hat box. There is also an appalling display of whips, chains and brands used on slaves right up until the late nineteenth century. The atmospheric colonial house itself once belonged to José da Silva e Oliveira Rolim, aka **Padre Rolim** (1747–1835), a major figure in the Inconfidência Mineira (see page 170), but barely remembered here.

Catedral Metropolitana and Praça de Se

Praça da Sé (Praça Conselheiro Mata) • Mon–Sat 8am–6pm; Sun Mass only • Free • ⓣ 38 3531 1094, ⓦ arquidiamantina.org.br

The grand **Catedral Metropolitana de Santo Antônio**, built in the 1930s on the site of a much older colonial church, is spacious but relatively plain inside, but the central square itself, the Praça da Sé, is worth savouring. It's lined with *sobrados* (colonial mansions), many of them with exquisite ornamental bronze and ironwork, often imported from Portugal – look closely and you'll see iron pineapples on the balconies. Most impressive of all are the serried windows of the **Casa da Intendência**, completed in 1735, and the ornate **Banco do Brazil** building next to it, on the north side of the cathedral – possibly unique in Brazil in that it spells the country name the old way, with a "z".

Igreja de Nossa Senhora do Carmo

Rua do Carmo • Tues, Thurs & Fri 2.30–5pm, Sat 9am–noon & 2–5pm, Sun for Mass only • R$3

Diamantina's most enticing church is the **Igreja de Nossa Senhora do Carmo**, built between 1765 and 1784. Legend has it that Diamantina's richest diamond contractor,

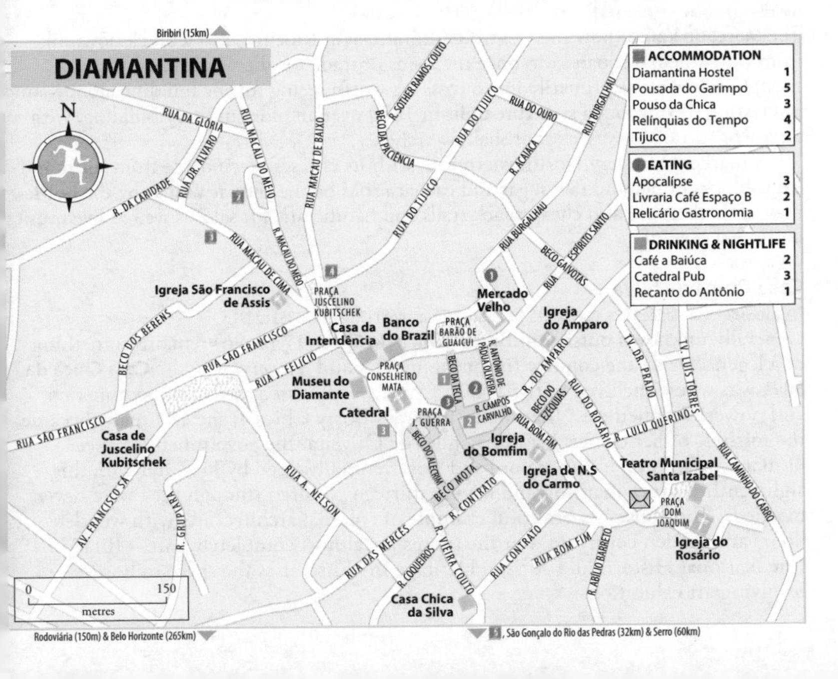

JUSCELINO KUBITSCHEK

Juscelino Kubitschek, one of Brazil's great postwar presidents, was born in Diamantina in 1902 and spent the first seventeen years of his life in the town. His enduring monument is the capital city he built on the Planalto Central, Brasília, which fired Brazil's and the world's imaginations and where his remains are interred (he was killed in a road accident in 1976). The house where he lived between the ages of 5 and 18, **Casa de Juscelino Kubitschek**, is preserved as a shrine to him (Tues–Sat 8am–5pm, Sun 8am–1pm; R$10; ☎ 38 3531 3607), on the steep Rua São Francisco (no. 241, uphill from his statue at the bottom). Juscelino had a meteoric political career, fuelled by his energy, imagination and uncompromising **liberal** instincts. You can understand his lifelong concern with the poor from the small, wattle and daub house where he spent his early life in poverty (Juscelino was from a poor Czech-gypsy family). Restoration has rather flattered the house, which is evident if you look at the photos of how it was when he lived here; with the exception of Lula, no Brazilian president has come from a humbler background. Today the tiny rooms (plus the modern annexe) explore aspects of Kubitschek's life, with old photos and documents, but labels are in Portuguese only. **September 12**, Kubitschek's birthday, is Diamantina's most important *festa*, featuring music of all kinds performed in the town's *praças* late into the night. Many still don't believe his death was a genuine accident. The massive turnout for Juscelino's **funeral** in Brasília in 1976 was one of the first times Brazilians dared to show their detestation of the military regime.

João Fernandes de Oliveira, made sure the tower was built at the back of the church rather than the front, as was usual, so the bells didn't disturb his lover's beauty sleep, the formidable **Chica da Silva** (see below). The interior is atypically florid, its two main features a rich, intricately carved altar screen by Portuguese artist José Soares de Araújo and a rare gold-sheathed organ, built in Diamantina in 1782. Note that, as is typical in Diamantina, the church is often closed.

Mercado Velho

Praça Barão do Guaicuí • Fri 6am–11pm, Sat 6am–3pm, Sun 8am–noon • Free

The **Mercado Velho** (now the Centro Cultural David Ribeiro), just a block downhill from the cathedral square, was once the focus of trade for the whole region, and though it now exists primarily for tourists it's worth seeing for the building alone – an interesting tiled wooden structure built in 1889 over an older military building, with a facade of rustic but very elegant shallow arches.

The market has a very Northeastern feel, with its cheeses, *doces* made from sugar and fruit, blocks of salt and raw sugar and cachaça sold by the shot as well as by the bottle – these days there are also cheap snack stalls and handicrafts for sale, as well as live music on Friday evening.

Casa Chica da Silva

Praça Lobo de Mesquita 266 • Tues–Sat noon–5.30pm, Sun 8.30am–noon • Free • ☎ 38 3531 2491

Generally unknown outside of Brazil, **Chica da Silva** (1732–96) remains something of a legend inside the country (inspiring movies and *telenovelas*) – the **Casa Chica da Silva** was where she lived in the 1760s. Chica was a born a slave, but became rich and powerful nonetheless (her nickname was "Bossy Chica"); she eventually became the mistress of her owner, João Fernandes de Oliveira, the government overseer of diamond mining in the region, and was eventually freed by him, living in this eighteenth-century mansion and having thirteen children (though they were never married). The house is a beautiful example of colonial architecture, with wooden floors and garden courtyard, but the rooms are almost completely bare – IPHAN (the National Historic and Artistic Heritage Institute) uses the space to host revolving art exhibitions.

Casa da Glória

Rua da Glória 298 • Daily 9–5pm • R$1 • ⓣ 38 3531 1394

More worthwhile for the building than its contents, the **Casa da Glória** is one of the city's most iconic structures, two blue and white colonial buildings linked by the **Passadiço da Glória**, Diamantina's own "Bridge of Sighs". Owned by the Institute of Geology (Universidade Federal de Minas Gerais or UFMG), sections of both buildings are open to visitors. The main entrance is in the Casa da Glória itself, constructed between 1770 and 1780 and named after its first owner, one Dona Josefa Maria da Glória. There's a short introductory video (with English subtitles), then several artfully restored exhibit rooms, with polished wood floors, tiny, intricate windows and a modest collection of gemstones and minerals. In the nineteenth century, the house became the residence of the town diamond inspectors, before reverting to the church in 1864 and later becoming a school (there's a room dedicated to the Colégio Nossa Senhora das Dores). You can walk across the bridge (built 1878) to the other building, constructed in 1850 and previously serving as an orphanage (just one large hall here is open to visitors, with geological maps of Brazil).

Igreja de Nossa Senhora do Rosário dos Pretos

Largo do Rosário (Praça Dom Joaquim) • Open sporadically Tues–Sat (not lunchtimes)

The beautiful white church at the bottom of Rua do Rosário (the city's oldest), **Igreja de Nossa Senhora do Rosário dos Pretos**, with its Chinese-influenced, tiled roof tower, and classic pale-blue trim, is best known in Brazil for the large tree growing in front of it (the "Gameleira"). Look closely and you can see a large distorted wooden cross embedded in the trunk and lower branches, the "Arvore da Cruz". The story behind this reads like something from a Gabriel García Márquez novel, but did really happen. The year the old Sé church was knocked down, in 1932, the padre of Rosário planted a wooden cross outside his church to commemorate the chapel old Diamantina had originally been built around. A fig tree sprouted up around it so that at first the cross seemed to flower – there's a photo of it at this stage in the Museu do Diamante – and eventually, rather than knocking it down, the tree grew up around the cross and ended up absorbing it (other stories claim this is where a wrongly executed slave was buried). The church was built between 1728 and 1732 to serve Diamantina's slave population and features a marvellous Baroque altar and a simple, yet stunning, painted ceiling by José Soares de Araújo.

ARRIVAL AND DEPARTURE — DIAMANTINA

By car The fastest route to Diamantina from Belo Horizonte (or Confins airport) is to stick to the main roads (BR-40 via Sete Lagoas, then MG-231 and MG-259; 4hr). Heading south you join the "Diamond Road" proper, with the route to São Gonçalo (40km) relatively easy to follow once you've left the warren of roads in the centre (the road to São Gonçalo should be paved all the way by the end of 2018).

By bus Although the rodoviária is not far from the centre of town, it's on a steep hill, and the only way back to it once in the centre is by taxi (around R$12), unless you have the legs and lungs of a mountain goat.

Destinations Belo Horizonte (6–7 daily; 5hr); São Paulo (1 daily; 13–14hr); Serro (2 daily; 2hr; 30min).

INFORMATION

Tourist information Praça Antônio Eulálio 53 (Mon–Sat 9am–6pm, Sun 9am–2pm; ⓣ 38 3531 9532, ⓦ diamantina.mg.gov.br). You're unlikely to find anyone who speaks English, but the staff can point you towards hotels and offer advice on excursions.

ACCOMMODATION

Diamantina Hostel Rua do Bicame 988 ⓣ 38 3531 5021, ⓦ diamantinahostel.com.br; map p.157. This HI hostel is spotless and has a great view, yet the rooms are a little dark and not especially inviting. It's a 15min (uphill) walk from town and 10min from the rodoviária; R$5 cheaper for HI members. Wi-Fi. Dorms R$59

Pousada do Garimpo Av da Saudade 265 ⓣ 38 3531 1044, ⓦ pousadadogarimpo.com.br; map p.157. A 10min walk from the centre on the western continuation of Rua Direita, this is the largest and most comfortable place

TOP TRIPS FROM DIAMANTINA

The region **surrounding Diamantina** is rich in history and scenery as well as opportunities for off-the-beaten-track adventure.

PARQUE ESTADUAL DO BIRIBIRI

With your own transport you can drive 12km along a bone-jarring dirt road (passable with a normal car if dry) through the arid **Parque Estadual do Biribiri** (daily 9am–6pm; free; entrance signposted on Av Geraldo Édson Nascimento, off BR-367; ⓣ 38 3531 3919), just north of town. At around 7km from the entrance, the road passes the **Cachoeira da Sentinela**, a series of gentle cascades and enticing swimming holes on the Ribeirão das Pedras. The abandoned textile mill town of **Biribiri** itself (officially daily 7am–6pm), at the end of the road, existed from 1876 to 1972, with the romantic mill ruin now off limits, though you can still wander the small collection of handsome white and blue colonial-style buildings (including the restored chapel), a hotel (*Pousada Vila do Biribiri*; ⓦ pousadaviladobiribiri.com.br) and two simple restaurants around a small green.

GRUTA DO SALITRE

The **Gruta do Salitre** is an enchanting cave with a small waterfall outside, on a dirt track signposted south of Diamantina on the road to the village of Extração (aka Curralinho) – allow 2hr for the hike, one-way, from town. Though nominally open every day, official guides are only around at certain times (usually Sat 2–5pm, Sun 9am–noon; free; parking R$10). Visits must be otherwise arranged in advance with Instituto Biotrópicos in Diamantina (Mon–Fri 9am–noon & 2–5pm; Praça JK 25, ⓣ 38 3531 2197, ⓦ biotropicos.org.br), which organize local guides and secure parking at the site. They can also help with rides to the cave (there's no public transport).

to stay in town; it's friendly, well equipped and has a pool. R$293

Pouso da Chica Rua Macau de Cima 115 ⓣ 38 3531 6190, ⓦ pousodachica.com.br; map p.157. A beautifully restored eighteenth-century property with simple guest rooms in both the historic main house and in newer outbuildings decorated with locally made rustic furniture and textiles. R$298

★ **Relínquias do Tempo** Rua Macau de Baixo 104 ⓣ 38 3531 1627, ⓦ pousadareliquiasdotempo.com.br; map p.157. Located in a wonderfully converted nineteenth-century home just up from the cathedral, this simple bu[t] delightful *pousada* is filled with rustic period furnishing[s] and decorated with handicrafts from the Jequitinhonh[a] valley. R$315

★ **Tijuco** Rua Macau do Meio 211 ⓣ 38 3531 1022 ⓦ hoteltijuco.com.br; map p.157. This 1951 Osca[r] Niemeyer creation has fairly spartan but perfectl[y] adequate rooms. It's worth paying for one of the slightl[y] more expensive "*luxo*" rooms, which are larger and brighte[r] and have balconies offering wonderful views acros[s] Diamantina. R$220

EATING

Apocalípse Praça Barão do Guaicuí 78 ⓣ 38 3531 3242; map p.157. A popular and classy *por quilo* (around R$54/kg) restaurant in a grand building across from the old market: the menu includes Italian dishes and *comida mineira*, plus sublime desserts. Daily 11am–3.30pm, Thurs–Sat also 7–11pm.

★ **Livraria Café Espaço B** Beco da Tecla 31 ⓣ 38 3531 6005; map p.157. Just off the cathedral square, this is the place for good coffee (R$4.75) and cakes (R$9–10) late into the evening, in a dimly-lit bookshop. Also does conventional main dishes (R$16–40), and offers free wi-fi Mon–Sat 9am–midnight, Sun 10am–1pm.

Relicário Gastronomia Rua Joaquim Gomes d[a] Costa 59 ⓣ 38 3531 3242; map p.157. One of the bes[t] resaturants in town, next to the Mercado Velho, adorne[d] with antiques and works of art, and specializing i[n] contemporary Brazilian and *mineira* cuisine. Tues–Thur[s] 6pm–midnight, Fri 6pm–1am, Sat noon–1am, Su[n] noon–3pm.

DRINKING

At weekends Diamantina comes alive, when locals and Brazilian tourists mingle, snack and booze at the outdoor tables i[n] tiny **Praça Correa Robelo** and narrow **Beco da Tecla**, both just off the main square. Nearby **Praça Barão do Guaicu[í]** is also often the centre of all-day and late-night revels over Friday and Saturday. Look out for the tasty craft beers from loca[l] brewer **Cerveja Diamantina** (ⓦ cervejadiamantina.com.br).

Café a Baiúca Rua Quitanda 13 ⓣ38 3531 3181; map p.157. This is usually *the* place to snack and drink on Fridays and Saturdays, at the apex of Praça Correa Robelo, with a decent spread of booze and bar snacks (the locals favour chips/fries, *batatas fritas*). Grab a table outside, but be prepared to wait at weekends. Mon–Wed 8am–midnight, Thurs–Sat 8am–3am.

★ **Catedral Pub** Rua Direita 68 ⓣ38 3531 3627, ⓦcatedral.pub; map p.157. Stylish bar in an old house on the main plaza, with narrow interior, exposed wattle and daub walls, and huge menu of craft beers (mostly local), ordered via tablet (R$16–25), including Cerveja Diamantina, Krug and Cerveja Wäls (from Belo Horizonte). Food served at the back (burgers R$28–36). Daily 10am–1am.

Recanto do Antônio Beco da Tecla 39 (an alleyway off the Praça Barão do Guaicuí) ⓣ38 3531 1147; map p.157. Chilled-out spot with the appearance of a country tavern, serving beer, wine, sausage and *carne do sol*. Tues–Sun 11am–3pm & 6pm–midnight.

São Gonçalo do Rio das Pedras

The charming colonial village of **SÃO GONÇALO DO RIO DAS PEDRAS**, 40km south of Diamantina, lies in rolling hills above the Rio das Pedras. In the centre, at the top of grassy Largo Felix Antônio, stands a pretty church, **Igreja Matriz de São Gonçalo**, dating from the 1780s and containing wonderfully vivid ceiling paintings featuring the popular medieval Portuguese priest and village namesake St Gonçalo de Amarante (though it's often closed). There are a few handicraft shops here (and shops selling home-made sweets), convenience stores and restaurants, usually open from noon onwards. The southern end of the village is anchored by another simple colonial church, **Igreja de Nossa Senhora Rosário**. The area around the village is known chiefly for its six attractive (and easily accessible) waterfalls, including the **Cachoeira da Rapadura**.

ARRIVAL AND DEPARTURE — SÃO GONÇALO DO RIO DAS PEDRAS

By car The reasonably well signposted 40km road between Diamantina and São Gonçalo is gradually being paved and should be complete by the end of 2018 (it will be rough in parts, but passable in a normal car, until then). The short section between São Gonçalo and Milho Verde should be paved by the end of 2019.

Milho Verde

Just 5km south of São Gonçalo, the village of **MILHO VERDE** is another result of the eighteenth-century mining boom. The countryside around is laced with hiking trails and waterfalls, notably the 30m-high **Cachoeira do Piolho,** 3km from the centre. Milho Verde was also the birthplace of Chica da Silva (see page 158), who was baptized in the simple crimson and white **Igreja de Nossa Senhora dos Prazeres**, thought to be one of the oldest churches in the region. The **Capela de Rosário** at the southern end of town is perhaps the most captivating in all Minas, a tiny colonial chapel with a small tiled tower on a large grassy plaza overlooking the mountains. You'll find several basic restaurants and *pousadas* around here.

ARRIVAL AND DEPARTURE — MILHO VERDE

By car The road south to Serro is paved and in excellent condition.

Serro

Established in 1702 as a gold mine camp, and set amid scintillating hill country 27km south from Milho Verde, **SERRO** remains blissfully undeveloped, its steep slopes crammed with gorgeous colonial architecture little changed from the eighteenth century. Rarely visited by tourists, it's the best place to appreciate the leisurely pace of life in small-town Minas. There are six handsome colonial churches, their interiors easily a match for anything in Diamantina in terms of artistic splendour (though opening times can be erratic), and Serro is also the centre for some of the best artisanal **cheese** made in Minas Gerais ("Queijo do Serro").

Igreja de Santa Rita and around

Praça Modesto J Oliveira • Mon & Thurs 1–4.50pm, Wed, Fri & Sat 8–11.50am (closed Tues; open Sun for services only) • Free • ☎ 38 3541 1221

Serro is dominated by the pilgrimage chapel of **Igreja de Santa Rita**, high above the centre – there are fine **views** across the town and towards the surrounding countryside from here. Completed around 1745, the chapel is something of a town symbol, with most eagle-eyed residents claiming they can tell the time from the French-made tower clock, even from the base of the hill. The humble wood-plank interior is painted to look like veined green and pink marble, while the venerated statue of St Rita stands below Mary on the altar. The most pleasant (if exhausting) way to reach the chapel is via the 57 stone steps cut into the slope from central **Praça João Pinheiro**, home of the larger **Igreja Nossa Senhora do Carmo** (nominally Mon–Fri 9am–noon, Sat 10am–noon), inaugurated in 1781.

Igreja da Matriz de Nossa Senhora da Conceição

Praça Matriz (Rua Nelsom de Sena 8) • Mon, Tues & Sun 8–11.50am, Wed & Fri 1–4.50pm • Free

A short walk east along Rua Alferes Luís Pinto from Praça João Pinheiro brings you to the twin Chinese-influenced towers of the **Igreja da Matriz de Nossa Senhora da Conceição**. Dating from the 1770s, the church is one of the biggest and most beautiful Baroque churches in the state; the ornate ceiling painting of a Madonna surrounded by clouds, angels and baubles was painted by Manuel Antônio Fonseca in 1888.

Chácara do Barão do Serro

Rua Maria José de Morais 84 • Tues–Sat 8–11.50am & 1–4.50pm, Sun 8–11.50am • Free • ☎ 38 3541 2005

Easily recognizable from a clump of palms just across the river (a five-minute walk from the Conceição church) is the **Chácara do Barão do Serro**, which now houses the town's Centro Cultural. The old farmhouse is a fascinating example of a nineteenth-century *casa grande*, and you are free to wander through the main building and the former slaves' quarters outside.

Museu Regional Casa dos Ottoni

Praça Cristiano Otoni 72 • Tues–Sat 10am–6pm, Sun 8am–noon • R$2 • ☎ 38 3541 1440

Serro's **Museu Regional Casa dos Otoni**, housed in an eighteenth-century mansion on the other side of the valley from Conceição church, contains a reasonable collection of period drawings and paintings, kitchen equipment and furniture belonging to the once influential Ottoni family.

ARRIVAL AND INFORMATION — SERRO

By bus The rodoviária (☎ 38 3541 1366) is almost in the centre at Praça Ângelo Miranda, so you can ignore the attentions of the taxi drivers and walk uphill for some 30m to the heart of town. Construction of new bus station on the edge of town was still delayed at the time of research, but it could be complete by 2019. Buses run to Conceição do Mato Dentro (1 daily; 2hr 30min); Diamantina (3 daily; 2hr 30min; @passaroverde.com.br) and Belo Horizonte (5 daily; 5hr 35min–6hr 45min). Viação Transfácil (☎ 38 3541 4091) usually runs two buses a day to Milho Verde (1hr) and São Gonçalo (1hr 30min).

By car The road between Serro and Milho Verde is excellent and paved; you can also drive direct to Serro from Diamantina (90km) on the paved BR-367 and BR-259 in around 1h 30min. The road to Conceição do Mato Dentro (64km) is paved only half of the way, but is usually in good condition.

Information The helpful tourist office (Mon–Sat 8am–5pm, Sun 8am–noon; @serro.mg.gov.br) is in the centre at Rua Nagib Bahmed 3, though it's rare to find English speakers.

ACCOMMODATION AND EATING

Dodoia e Júnior Rua Fernando Vasconcelos 240 ☎ 38 3541 1322. There are few places to eat in Serro, but this simple canteen in an old house above the centre offers a tasty buffet of regional dishes (salads, potatoes, pumpkin, beef and pork stews, rice, beans) for just R$13. Daily 11.30am–3pm & 6pm–midnight.

Pousada Do Queijo Rua Nagib Bahmed 75 ☎ 38 354 2622. Rooms are small and simple (with basic satellite TV and fan), but the views are fantastic, there's a decent buffet breakfast and it's in the centre of town. R$145

Conceição do Mato Dentro and around

Some 65km south of Serro, **CONCEIÇÃO DO MATO DENTRO** is at the heart of another enticing region of hills and waterfalls, notably the **Cachoeira do Tabuleiro.** In town, the historic centre runs north–south from the small **Coreto do Rosário** to the twin-towered **Igreja Matriz de Nossa Senhora da Conceição** (closed for renovation until 2019), which dates from the early eighteenth century, and the bustling Praça Ubaldina Ferreira, where you'll find basic tourist information, several decent bakeries and simple canteens. From here you can walk up to the **Capela de Santana** for fine views across town. East of the centre, the massive hilltop **Santuário Bom Jesus do Matozinhos** contains rare Baroque carved figures, produced between 1805 and 1811 (though the church was almost completely rebuilt in an incongruous Neogothic style 1930s).

2

Cachoeira do Tabuleiro

Parque Natural Municipal do Tabuleiro • Daily 8am–5pm (hikes to the upper falls permitted to begin until 11am; to the lower falls until 2pm) • R$10

Some 18km from Conceição do Mato Dentro via dirt roads (passable in normal car when dry), just beyond the village of Tabuleiro, the spectacular **Cachoeira do Tabuleiro** is the third-tallest waterfall in Brazil (273m), a thin ribbon of water plunging off a sheer granite cliff face. The falls lie within the **Parque Natural Municipal do Tabuleiro** – you can park your car at the park entrance (where there's toilets and usually some park rangers); from here there are two hiking trails to the falls themselves. The rugged, very tough 8km (one-way) path to the top of the falls (signposted "Alto de Cachoeira"; allow 2–3hr each way) usually requires a guide, while the steep track to the base (signposted "Cachoeira"; 2.5km one-way; 1–2hr), where there are a series of icy cold swimming holes in the Ribeirão do Campo, can be tackled solo. There's an observation deck ("Mirante") around 800m from the entrance station, but it's a long way from the falls.

ARRIVAL AND DEPARTURE — CONCEIÇÃO DO MATO DENTRO

By bus Buses link Conceição do Mato Dentro with Belo Horizonte (8 daily; 3hr 20min–4hr) and Serro (5 daily; 1hr 30min–2hr 45min). The bus station lies just beyond the northern edge of town. From Mato Dentro there are also buses to Tabuleiro, which pass its hostel (Mon, Wed & Fri at 3pm, Sat at 2pm; R$5); otherwise taxis charge around R$80.

By car The MG-10 between Serro and Conceição is in good condition, but the central section is dirt road. Heading south to Serra do Cipó the road is paved.

ACCOMMODATION

Tabuleiro Eco Hostel Rua Joaquim Costinha 01B, Tabuleiro, Conceição do Mato Dentro ⓣ 31 3654 3288, ⓦ tabuleiro-eco-hostel8.webnode.com. The ideal place to stay for the Cachoeira do Tabuleiro, and can help with transportation; offers double rooms (with private or shared bathrooms), comfy mixed dorms and spots for camping. No internet, but buffet breakfast included. Cash only. Camping **R$40**, dorms **R$65**, doubles **R$150**

Parque Nacional da Serra do Cipó

Rua do Eugenho, Serra do Cipó (MG-10) • Daily 8am–6pm (last admission 3pm) • Free • ⓣ 31 3718 7151

Southwest of Conceição do Mato Dentro, MG-10 winds its way for some 65km across the upland landscapes of the **Parque Nacional da Serra do Cipó**, offering stupendous vistas in all directions. This park encompasses limestone hills, rugged valleys and grasslands, Atlantic forest and numerous pools and waterfalls – enticing you to trek, bike, rock-climb, kayak and swim. Rare bird species such as the Cipó canastero and hyacinth visorbearer attract serious birders, while other fauna out includes wolves, jaguars, monkeys and the sapo de pyjama (pyjama frog). Entry to the park itself is free, and though at weekends the principal trails draw day-trippers in numbers, during the week it's often near-deserted. Access to the park is from the small village of **SERRA DO CIPÓ** (aka Cardeal Mota) at the edge of the reserve, spread out for several kilometres along MG-10, with plenty of cheap bars, restaurants and *pousadas*.

The main park area offers two trails up gradually rising river valleys to various waterfalls and canyons. The longer (up to 28km round-trip) follows the Mascates valley to the **Cachoeira do Farofa** (after about 8.5km); the path continues for another 6km to cross the Rio Mascates then into the narrow Bandeirinhas canyon. The other main trail leads up the Vale do Bocaina to two waterfalls, the **Cachoeira do Gavião** and **Cachoeira das Andorinhas** (8km or 2hr one-way).

Cachoeira Grande

Serra do Cipó (MG-10) • Daily 8am–6pm • R$30 • T 31 3718 7044

The impressive **Cachoeira Grande** is contained within a privately managed reserve south of Serra do Cipó village on the Rio Cipó (around 1km walk from the centre; the entrance is on MG-10). Beyond the entrance gate, a 1km trail passes several minor cascades and swimming holes along the river, culminating at a 60m-wide waterfall plunging 10m over a rocky ledge.

Cachoeira Véu da Noiva

Serra do Cipó (MG-10) • Daily 8am–4pm • R$11/1hr, R$30/day • T 31 3718 7096, W acmmg.com.br/veu-da-noiva

On the northern edge of Serra do Cipó village, a YMCA-affiliated holiday camp contains the **Cachoeira Véu da Noiva** ("Bride's Veil"), a ribbon of water plunging 70m down a sheer cliff into an enticing cold-water pool (there's another natural swimming pool on the short walk up to the falls). Chalets here start at R$174 for two people, with camping from R$40 per person.

ARRIVAL, INFORMATION AND TOURS — SERRA DO CIPÓ

By car The park is clearly signposted from paved MG-10, in Serra do Cipó (Cardeal Mota); the main park office and entrance for the Mascates valley is 3km from the main road (the turning is around 2km south from the centre of the village, just beyond the Cachoeira Grande); for the Vale do Bocaina look for Rua do Engenho in the centre of Serra do Cipó.

By bus Buses (11–12 daily; 2hr 10min–2hr 35min; R$27–35; W saritur.com.br and W serro.com.br) ply the route from Belo Horizonte to Serra do Cipó; you can also travel from Serro (4–5 daily; 3hr 25min–4hr 15min; R$42–44).

Information Visit W serradocipo.com and W serradocipo.com.br for more information and details on accommodation (camping is not permitted in the park).

Tour operators Bela Geraes Turismo (T 31 3718 7394, W belageraes.com.br); Cipó Aventuras (T 31 9974 0878, W cipoaventuras.blogspot.com).

ACCOMMODATION AND EATING

Hotel Cipó Veraneio MG-10 Km 95 T 31 3718 7000, W cipoveraneiohotel.com.br. Very comfortable option, right at the turn-off to the park, with a pool overlooking the Rio Cipó and compact, modern rooms that have LCD TVs and ceiling fans. R$230

Pousada Adega Cipó Alameda das Bromélias 68 (MG-10 Km 97) T 31 3718 7296, W pousadaadegacipo.com.br. Attractive and comfortable chalets and en-suite double rooms, with a swimming pool, sauna and breakfast located on a dirt road parallel to the main road. R$130

Mariana

Around 215km south of Serra do Cipó, the Estrada Real reaches lovely **MARIANA**, founded in 1696 and named after King Dom João V's wife Maria Ana de Austria. In the first half of the eighteenth century the town was far grander than its younger rival Ouro Preto, just 12km to the west, and acted as the administrative centre of the gold mines of central Minas until the 1750s. The town can be visited as a day-trip from Ouro Preto (30min by bus away), but it's also a great place to stay should you wish to escape the tourists. The main commercial drag, **Avenida Salvador Furtado**, cuts through the centre of town, with the colonial district just to the south and the train station to the north.

THE PARQUE NATURAL DO CARAÇA AND THE RED WOLVES

The surprisingly isolated **Parque Natural do Caraça** lies just 20km south of the Estrada Real (at Barão de Cocais, halfway between Serra do Cipó and Mariana), on winding roads. The park forms a protected section of the rugged Sierra do Espinhaço best known for the **Santuário do Caraça** (daily 8am–5pm; R$10) at its heart, a former Catholic seminary and school. The school was founded on the site of a 1774 hermitage in the 1820s, and for 150 years educated the upper classes of Minas Gerais, including generations of Brazilian politicians. In 1968 a fire destroyed much of the building, and today what remains serves as a spartan church-run **pousada** (see below).

The Neogothic church of **Nossa Senhora Mãe dos Homens**, added in 1883, was also spared by the fire, and has beautiful French stained-glass windows, marble and soapstone carvings and a seven-hundred-pipe organ built in the seminary itself. A small **museum** is attached to the church and displays items rescued from the fire, including English and Chinese porcelain and furniture.

The major attraction here, however, is the **maned wolves** (*lobo-guará*) that live in the surrounding woods (they look like large foxes with reddish fur) – there's a long-standing (though extremely dubious from an ecological point of view) tradition of monks leaving food for them near the church at night (guests are permitted to watch, but if the crowd is big they'll stay away). There are also plenty of **signed walks** of varying difficulty on the tracks through the mountains – information is available from the hotel. The nearby lake, **Banho do Belchior**, provides a good opportunity for swimming from its small beaches and there are also several natural pools by the waterfalls within the park.

The park lies at the end of a well-surfaced and signposted road 20km south of the MG-129 between Barão de Cocais and Catas Altas; without a car you'll have to take a 2hr journey by bus from Belo Horizonte to Barão de Cocais (every 2hr, 6am–8.30pm; R$33.35; Ⓦ passaroverde.com.br), and then take a taxi the rest of the way (at least R$110; call Ⓣ 31 3837 1812). There's only bus daily from Catas Altas to Barão (7.30am; 55min; R$8.70), returning at 7.20pm.

ACCOMMODATION

Pousada do Caraça Complexo Santuário do Caraça, Serra do Caraça Ⓣ 31 3837 2698, Ⓦ santuariodocaraca.com.br. The old *colegio* offers a wide range of clean but basic accommodation in various buildings (no a/c, TV or wi-fi) with lunch provided for R$25. The cheapest is the dorm-like Casa da Porte, but doubles with bathrooms are much more expensive. Reservations essential. Dorms **R$84**, doubles **R$173**

Catedral de Nossa Senhora da Assunção

Praça Cláudio Manoel • Tues–Sun 7am–5pm; organ recitals Fri 11.30am, Sun 12.15pm • R$4; organ recitals R$30 • Ⓦ arqmariana.com.br

Dominating Praça Cláudio Manoel, the oldest church in Mariana is the **Catedral de Nossa Senhora da Assunção** (Catedral da Sé), begun in 1713 and choked with gilded Rococo detail. This is very much an Aleijadinho family venture: his father, Manoel Francisco Lisboa, designed and built it, while Aleijadinho contributed the carvings in the sacristy and a font. The interior is dominated by a massive German Schnitger **organ** dating from 1701 and donated by the king of Portugal in 1753. Look closely and you can see Chinese-style decorations carved by slaves, who also worked the bellows. You can hear the organ in action, in twice-weekly recitals. The cathedral was closed in 2016 for a major restoration, which should be complete by the end of 2018.

Museu Arquidiocesano de Arte Sacra

Rua Frei Durão 49 • Tues–Fri 8.30am–noon & 1.30–5pm, Sat & Sun 9am–3pm • R$5 • Ⓣ 31 3557 2581

Although it has been overshadowed by Ouro Preto for over two centuries, you can still get a good idea of Mariana's early flourishing at the **Museu Arquidiocesano de Arte Sacra** inside the old bishop's palace, the Casa Capitular. The Rococo building is magnificent, with parts dating from the first decade of the eighteenth century, when it began life, bizarrely, as a prison for erring churchmen, some of whom were notorious for being the worst cut-throats of the *paulista* expeditions. Between 1720 and 1756 the

ALEIJADINHO

Although little is known of his life, we do know roughly what the renowned sculptor **Aleijadinho** looked like. In the Museu do Aleijadinho in Ouro Preto (see page 172), a crude but vivid portrait shows an intense, aquiline man who is clearly what Brazilians call *pardo* – of mixed race. His hands are under his jacket, which seems a trivial detail unless you know what makes his achievements truly astonishing: the great sculptor of the *barroco mineiro* was presumed to be a leper, and produced much of his best work after he had lost the use of his hands.

Antônio Francisco Lisboa was born in **Ouro Preto** in 1738, the son of a Portuguese craftsman; his mother was probably a slave. For the first half of his exceptionally long life he was perfectly healthy, a womanizer and *bon viveur* despite his exclusively religious output. His prodigious talent – equally on display in wood or stone, human figures or abstract decoration – allowed him to set up a workshop with apprentices while still young, and he was much in demand. Although always based in Ouro Preto, he spent long periods in all the major historic towns (except Diamantina) working on commissions, but never travelled beyond the state. Self-taught, he was an obsessive reader of the Bible and medical textbooks (the only two obvious influences in his work), one supplying its imagery, the other underlying the anatomical detail of his human figures.

In the late 1770s, Aleijadinho's life changed utterly. He began to suffer from a progressively debilitating disease, thought to have been **leprosy**. As it got worse he became a recluse, only venturing outdoors in the dark, and became increasingly obsessed with his work. His physical disabilities were terrible: he lost his fingers, toes and the use of his lower legs. Sometimes the pain was so bad his apprentices had to stop him hacking away at the offending part of his body with a chisel.

Yet despite all this, Aleijadinho actually increased his output, working with hammer and chisel strapped to his wrists by his apprentices, who moved him about on a wooden trolley. Under these conditions he sculpted his masterpiece, the twelve massive figures of the prophets and the 64 life-size Passion figures for the basílica of the **Santuário do Bom Jesus de Matosinhos** (see page 178) in Congonhas, between 1796 and 1805. The figures were his swansong; failing eyesight finally forced him to stop work and he ended his life as a hermit in a hovel on the outskirts of Ouro Preto. The death he longed for finally came on November 18, 1814; he is buried in a simple grave in the church he attended all his life, Nossa Senhora da Conceição in Ouro Preto.

building was extended and became the bishop's palace; the door and window frames are massive, built in beautifully worked local soapstone.

Inside, the **collection** of *arte sacra* and colonial furniture is distinguished by its quality and age. The stairwell is dominated by a powerful painting of *Christ's Passion* by Mariana native **Manuel da Costa Ataíde** – his best-known work. The stairs lead up to a number of graceful colonial rooms, including the luxurious private quarters of the bishops, which contain the largest number of **Aleijadinho** figures anywhere outside a church.

Praça Gomes Freire

By far the prettiest part of Mariana, languid **Praça Gomes Freire** contains a bandstand, trees and pond, lined on all sides by colonial *sobrados* (two-storey mansions). In the northwest corner (on the Travessa São Francisco) lies the **Chafariz São Francisco**, an ornamental fountain dating from 1801.

Praça Minas Gerais

The two churches on Praça Minas Gerais (São Francisco de Assis and the less interesting Nossa Senhora do Carmo) around the corner from Praça Gomes Freire, with their ornate facades and comparatively restrained interiors, are typical of the third phase of *barroco mineiro*. However, the combination of the two churches with the equally graceful eighteenth-century **Casa da Câmara e Cadeia** makes the bare grass square here an extremely photogenic spot. Note the *pelourinho* in the centre, a 1970s ornamental version of what surely would have been a far more grimy whipping-post (to which slaves and miscreants were tied and beaten) – the original was destroyed in 1871.

Igreja de São Francisco de Assis

Praça Minas Gerais • Tues–Sun 8am–noon & 1–5pm • R$4 (guided tours from R$20)

The **Igreja de São Francisco de Assis**, finished in 1794, has the finest paintings of any Mariana church, as befits **Manuel da Costa Ataíde**'s burial place. The numbers on the church floor are where members of the lay Franciscan brotherhood are buried; Ataíde is number 94. Inside you'll see a fine sacristy as well as an altar and pews by Aleijadinho, who, in addition, put his signature on the church in his usual way, by sculpting the sumptuous soapstone "medal" over the door.

Basílica de São Pedro dos Clérigos

Largo de São Pedro (Rua Dom Silvério) • Tues–Sat 9am–noon & 2–5pm, Sun 9.30am–noon • R$4

From Praça Minas Gerais it's a short uphill walk via the unspoilt Rua Dom Silvério to the mid-eighteenth-century **Basílica de São Pedro dos Clérigos** that overlooks the town, framed by groves of towering palm trees. The sumptuous facade was started in 1752, but the church was never formally completed. The object is not so much to check out the Basílica interior (though you might want to climb the tower), but to enjoy the view of the town stretched out before you; if you follow the path along the edge the views are even better.

Igreja Nossa Senhora do Rosário dos Pretos

Rua Monsenhor Horta 226 • Daily 9am–noon & 1.30–5pm • R$2

Built on a hill just west of the centre between 1752 and 1758 by Mariana's free and enslaved black population, the **Igreja Nossa Senhora do Rosário dos Pretos** reopened in 2017 after an incredible restoration, resuming its place as one of Mariana's most beautiful Baroque churches. Inside there are artfully carved altars by Portuguese-born Francisco Vieira Servas, plus ornate ceiling work by local genius Manuel da Costa Ataíde. The church will eventually contain the Museu Vieira Servas, dedicated to the former artist.

Mina da Passagem

Rua Eugenio Eduardo Rapallo • Mon & Tues 9am–5pm, Wed–Sun 9am–5.30pm; tours last 1hr • R$70 • T 31 3557 5000, W minasdapassagem.com.br • Take the Ouro Preto–Mariana bus (R$4.35) and ask to get off at the stop opposite the mine; taxis from Ouro Preto charge R$40 one-way, and R$20/hr to wait for you

Four kilometres from Mariana (on the road to Ouro Preto), the historic gold mine of **Mina da Passagem** is one of the area's more unusual sights. Gold was first extracted here in 1719, making it one of the oldest deep-shaft gold mines in the country. Long since closed, the site exists today as a tourist attraction. Once you've purchased tickets, walk to the mine head via the tiny museum (full of rusting equipment) and craft store.

At the mine head you line up to board what for many tourists is the main attraction: a rickety open-seat railcar that trundles 315m down a steep slope into the main tunnel (be careful of bumping your head). The railcar is driven by a drum cable powered by a vintage 1825 **British steam engine**, now adapted to run on compressed air. At the bottom, guides lead you around the dripping, muddy but fairly spacious main tunnel, with smaller galleries branching off into the gloom in all directions. Tours end at a small, crystalline floodlit **lake**, 120m underground, and round off with a demonstration of gold panning back on the surface, complete with real gold. Note that you are supposed to stay with your guide underground, though they rarely speak English – you'll be very bored if you don't understand Portuguese (ask at the ticket office if there are any English-speakers available).

ARRIVAL AND INFORMATION — MARIANA

By train The "Trem da Vale" tourist train links Mariana with Ouro Preto, 12km to the west. Timetables can change, but trains usually depart Ouro Preto on Fri & Sat at 10am and 2.30pm, returning from Mariana at 1pm and 4pm; on Sun trains depart Ouro Preto at 10am and 4pm, and from Mariana only at 2.30pm. Tickets are R$46 one-way or R$66 return (the "panoramic wagon" is R$70/R$90); in the January and July peak seasons (and holidays) rates rise to R$50 one-way or R$70 return (R$76/R$100 for panoramic seats). The train station is located near the centre at Praça Juscelino Kubitschek (open Wed–Sun 8.30am–5pm; T 31 3557 3844).

By bus Transcotta buses from Ouro Preto (daily 5.30am–11.30pm; every 30min; R$4.35) stop right in the centre of town at Praça Tancredo Neves (Av Salvador Furtado) – Rua Padre Lopes leads one block south to Praça Cláudio Manoel from here. If you're coming from Belo Horizonte (at least 14 daily 5.30am–midnight; 2hr–2hr 35min) or São Paulo (3 daily; around 11hr), you'll arrive at the rodoviária (T 31 3557 1122), on the main road a couple of kilometres from the centre; if you don't wish to walk into the centre, catch one of the buses from Ouro Preto, which pass through the rodoviária every 30min or so.

Information Praça Tancredo Neves, opposite the bus stop (Tues–Sun 8am–noon & 1.30–5pm; T 31 3557 1158, W mariana.org.br). There's also a smaller office at Rua Direita 91, a short walk into the old town, which can also supply maps (Mon–Fri 8am–5pm; T 31 3558 2314).

ACCOMMODATION AND EATING

Chantilly Confeitaria Rua Frei Durão 32 T 31 3557 3195. The best café on Praça Gomes Freire, in a building dating back to 1925, offering mouthwatering cakes, chocolates, coffee, quiche and *empadas*. Daily 10am–9pm.

★ **Pousada do Chafariz** Rua Cônego Rego 149 T 31 3557 1492, W pousadadochafariz.com.br. Excellent, centrally located accommodation, with simple but adequate en-suite rooms (with fan) in a lovely old house and generous buffet breakfast (included). Small outdoor pool, pool table and limited parking (free). R$230

Rancho Praça Gomes Freire 108 T 31 3558 1060, W ranchorestaurante.com.br. Tasty local cuisine is kept warm on a wood-fire stove here, as well as a selection of pizzas (from R$30). Also does a lunchtime *mineira* buffet (R$26). Tues–Sun 11am–3pm & 6pm–midnight.

Scotch & Art Bar Praça Minas Gerais 57. Great location for an evening tipple, with a terrace overlooking the churches on the plaza and a menu of tasty bar snacks. Tues–Sun 6.30pm–2am.

Ouro Preto and around

The most enchanting of all the colonial towns in Minas Gerais, **OURO PRETO** lies 100km southeast of Belo Horizonte at the central hub of the **Estrada Real**, its narrow, cobbled streets straddling impossibly steep hills topped with Baroque churches and lined with an assortment of candy-coloured eighteenth-century homes and mansions. Unsurprisingly, the town is also the most visited in the region, but it's far from becoming a giant museum; touristy shops and restaurants dominate the centre, but this remains a working town with a population of over 70,000 – get up early on a weekday and you'll see locals drinking coffee on the way to work, smell smoke from wood fires and hear church bells ringing for the faithful. Other than just soaking up the historic ambience, art and architecture are the main attractions here (it was capital of the state until 1897), though Ouro Preto is also a tempting place to load up on the precious stones – notably **tourmaline** and **imperial topaz** – and jewellery Minas Gerais is known for.

It was in these cities that the **Inconfidência Mineira**, Brazil's first bungling attempt to throw off the Portuguese yoke, was played out in 1789. And here the great sculptor

FESTIVE OURO PRETO

Ouro Preto has an extremely popular street **Carnaval** (Jan/Feb) that attracts visitors from far afield, so be sure to reserve accommodation far in advance. Likewise, at **Easter** (Semana Santa) the town becomes the focus of a spectacular series of plays and processions lasting for about a month before Easter Sunday itself; the last days of the life of Christ are played out in open-air theatres throughout town.

2

Antônio Francisco Lisboa – **Aleijadinho** or the "little cripple" – spent all his life (see page 166), leaving behind him a collection unmatched by any other figure working in the contemporary Baroque tradition.

Brief history

Less than a decade after gold was struck at Sabará, a *paulista* adventurer called **Antônio Dias** found "black gold"– alluvial gold mixed with iron ore – here and named his camp after it (*ouro preto*). It attracted a flood of people as it became clear that the deposits were the richest yet found in Minas, and so many came that they outstripped the food supply.

The early years were hard, made worse by conflict between the Portuguese and *paulista bandeirantes* in 1707, who resisted the Crown's attempts to take over the area. The **Guerra das Emboabas** lasted for two years and was brutal, with ambushes and massacres the preferred tactics of both sides. Ouro Preto was the Portuguese base, and troops from here drove the *paulistas* from their headquarters at Sabará and finally annihilated them near São João del Rei. From then on, Ouro Preto was the effective **capital** of Minas, although it wasn't officially named as such until 1823. Indeed, compared to places like nearby Mariana, Ouro Preto was a late developer; all but two of its churches date from the second half of the eighteenth century.

THE INCONFIDÊNCIA MINEIRA

Ouro Preto is most famous in Brazil as the birthplace of the **Inconfidência Mineira** (the "Minas Conspiracy"), the first attempt to free Brazil from the Portuguese. Inspired by the French Revolution, and heartily sick of the heavy taxes levied by a bankrupt Portugal, a group of twelve prominent town citizens – known as the Inconfidentes – led by **Joaquim José da Silva Xavier** began in 1789 to discuss organizing a rebellion. Xavier was a dentist, known to everyone as Tiradentes ("teeth-puller"). Another of the conspirators was **Tomás Gonzaga**, whose hopeless love poems to the beautiful **Marília Dirceu**, promised by her family to another, made the couple into the Brazilian equivalent of Romeo and Juliet: "When you appear at dawn, all rumpled/like a badly wrapped parcel, no ribbons or flowers/how Nature shines, how much lovelier you seem".

The conspiracy proved a fiasco and all were betrayed and arrested before any uprising was organized. The leaders were condemned to hang, but the Portuguese, realizing they could ill afford to offend the inhabitants of a state whose taxes kept them afloat, arranged a **royal reprieve**, commuting the sentence to exile in Angola and Mozambique. Unfortunately the messenger arrived two days too late to save Tiradentes, marked as the first to die. He was hanged where the column now stands in the square that bears his name, his head stuck on a post and his limbs dispatched to the other mining towns to serve as a warning.

The gold gave out about the time Brazil finally became independent in 1822, but for decades the town survived as an administrative centre and university town; a **school of mining** – now a federal university – was founded in 1876. After the capital moved to Belo Horizonte, steady decline set in, though the populist government of Getúlio Vargas brought back the bodies of the Inconfidêntes (see page 170) to a proper shrine, and sensitively restored the crumbling monuments. Since the 1980s, **tourism** and **aluminium** production have been the city's main sources of income, the latter attracting job-hungry migrants, many of whom end up living in hillside *favelas*.

Museu de Ciência e Técnica

Praça Tiradentes 20 • Tues–Sun noon–5pm • R$10 • ⓣ 31 3559 3118

At the heart of Ouro Preto lies its main square, **Praça Tiradentes**, dominated by the **Escola de Minas**, which is housed in the old governor's palace. Established in 1876, it's still the best mining school in the country and now affiliated with the Universidade Federal de Ouro Preto. The main building doubles as the absorbing **Museu de Ciência e Técnica**, its galleries scattered around the central courtyard in between ramshackle lecture rooms. The museum primarily explores the history of mining, minerals and metals in Minas Gerais through models and old machinery (there's also a fossil section), though the main draw is the **Mineralogy** gallery where gold, huge amethyst and quartz crystals, silver, diamonds and other precious stones are beautifully displayed. Labels in the museum are in Portuguese only, but there are English translations on cards in most rooms. The building itself, with a fine marble entrance, dates from the 1740s, but the inside was gutted during the nineteenth century and not improved by it.

Museu da Inconfidência

Praça Tiradentes 139 • Tues–Sun 10am–6pm • R$10 • ⓣ 31 3551 1121, ⓦ museudainconfidencia.gov.br/en

The illuminating **Museu da Inconfidência** is housed in the former **Casa de Câmara e Cadeira**, the old city hall and prison, a glorious eighteenth-century palace that provides a perfect example of the classical grace of Minas colonial architecture with its beautifully restored interior, though many of the huge, dimly lit rooms, so well suited to the display of *arte sacra*, were once dungeons. The museum is primarily a shrine to the doomed Inconfidência (see page 170), with the ground floor charting the early history of Ouro Preto leading up to the 1789 plot through relics of eighteenth-century daily life, from sedan chairs, saddles and kitchen utensils (including the seal the bishop used to stamp his coat of arms on his cakes), to horrendous instruments used to punish slaves.

The spiritual heart of the museum is an antechamber holding original documents – including the execution order and birth and death registrations of **Tiradentes** – leading into a solemn room containing his remains and those of his fellow conspirators, marked with simple, flat tombstones. Most of the conspirators died in Africa, some in Portugal; all but Tiradentes were exiled for the rest of their lives and never returned to Brazil. There's another small section dedicated to the Imperial period, while upstairs the focus switches to religious art and antique furniture, though the highlight is the room dedicated to **Aleijadinho** containing original letters, several statues and even a chair designed by the master. The museum has English labelling throughout.

Igreja Nossa Senhora do Carmo

Rua Brigadeiro Musqueira • Tues–Sat 8.30–11.10am & 1–5.10pm, Sun 10am–3pm • R$4 • ⓣ 31 3551 2601 • No photos permitted

Just off Praça Tiradentes, the **Igreja de Nossa Senhora do Carmo** is one of the finest churches in Ouro Preto. It was designed by Manoel Francisco Lisboa, Aleijadinho's father, and construction began just before his death in 1766. Aleijadinho himself then took over the building of the church and finished it six years later. He contributed the carving of the exterior and worked on the ornate, gilt interior, on and off, for four decades. Two of the Rococo side chapels in the main church (São João and Nossa Senhora da Piedade) were among the last commissions he was able to complete, in 1809; the accounts book for the time has Aleijadinho complaining he was paid with "false gold". The 1776 baptismal font in the **sacristy** at the back is a masterpiece; this room also features a wonderful painted ceiling.

Museu do Oratório

Adro de Igreja do Carmo 28 • Daily except Tues 9.30am–5.30pm • R$5 • ⓣ 31 3551 5369, ⓦ museudooratorio.org.br

Just behind the Igreja de Nossa Senhora do Carmo is the **Museu do Oratório**, housed in the artfully restored Casa do Noviciado (1753–66), which was once the meeting house for the lay society attached to Nossa Senhora do Carmo – Aleijadinho is said to have lived here while working on the church. On display is a high-quality collection of eighteenth- and nineteenth-century oratorios (small Catholic altars or shrines) from throughout Brazil, including a fine example by **Manuel da Costa Ataíde.**

Although there are some glittering shrines featuring gold and silver (and even sea shells) on the top floor, the most touching examples are the portable and "bullet" oratorios in the basement, carried by muleteers and other travellers to protect themselves from danger. Don't miss the amazing "**trunk altar**" with its painted interior, and the fascinating Afro-Brazilian oratorios on the ground floor, where African gods are depicted to look like Catholic saints. An English-language guide is available.

Igreja de Nossa Senhora do Pilar

Praça Mons. Castilho Barbosa • Tues–Sun 9–10.45am & noon–4.45pm • R$10 • ⓦ ouropretoparoquiadopilar.com.br

Ouro Preto's oldest and most spectacular church is **Igreja de Nossa Senhora do Pilar**, with an ornate exterior even by Baroque standards. It was begun in 1711 and the interior is a wild explosion of glinting Rococo, liberally plastered with gold. The best carving was done by Francisco Xavier de Brito, who worked in Minas from 1741 until his early death ten years later – and about whom nothing is known except that he was Portuguese and influenced Aleijadinho. He was responsible for the astonishing **arch** over the wedding-cake altar, where the angels supporting the Rococo pillars seem to swarm out of the wall on either side. Look out for the paintings symbolizing the four seasons in the apse. The small **sacristy** at the back (which contains an oratorio by Aleijadinho) and the old crypt below the church form the **Museu de Art Sacra** (same hours), which contains all sorts of religious bits and pieces – huge crosses, episcopal staffs, vestments and the like.

Casa dos Contos

Rua São José 12 • Tues–Sat 10am–5pm, Sun 10am–3pm • Free • T 31 3551 1444

The perfectly proportioned **Casa dos Contos**, a grand old Baroque mansion built in the 1780s by João Rodrigues de Macedo, now serves as an art gallery and museum. Macedo was one of the town's wealthiest men, but he was also part of the Inconfidência movement (see page 170); the house was appropriated as a prison in 1789, where conspirator Manuel da Costa died in his cell. In 1803 the property was seized to pay Macedo's debts and it served as the **Fazenda Real**, a foundry where the Crown extracted its fifth of the gold and assembled armed convoys to escort it down to Rio for shipment to Portugal.

The collection is no more than moderately interesting and is labelled in Portuguese only. It includes the **Casa do Moeda** exhibit in the 1821 annexe (used as the mint) charting the tortured history of Brazil's currency, a collection of dusty old books and documents and several temporary art exhibitions on the ground floor. The building itself is half the attraction – an imposing four-storey staircase dominates the entrance hall, while the mansion is constructed around a beautiful courtyard large enough for a dozen cavalry troopers. The most interesting places radiate off this courtyard: the tiny **cell** (behind the stairs) where da Costa died in 1789, the **slave quarters** or *senzala*, which now contain a display of old tools, manacles and chains, and the old **slave kitchen** with its giant scales.

Igreja de São Francisco de Assis

Largo do Coimbra • Tues–Sun 8.30am–noon & 1.30–5pm • R$10 • No photos permitted

The most beautiful church in Ouro Preto, the **Igreja de São Francisco de Assis**, was begun in 1765, and no other contains more works by Aleijadinho. The magnificent exterior soapstone panels are his, as is virtually all the virtuoso carving, in both wood and stone, inside; Aleijadinho also designed the church and supervised its construction. In 1801 the church commissioners contracted the best painter of the *barroco mineiro*, **Manuel da Costa Ataíde**, to decorate the **ceilings**. It took him nine years, using natural dyes made from plant juices and powdered iron ore, and his work has stood the test of time far better than other church paintings of the period. The squirming mass of cherubs and saints is framed within a cunning trompe l'oeil effect, which extends the real Baroque pillars on the sides of the nave into painted ones on the ceiling, making it seem like an open-air canopy through which you can glimpse clouds. There are also painted *azulejos* in the apse that look remarkably like the real thing.

Museu do Aleijadinho

Until the Conceição church reopens (see page 174), items from the **Museu do Aleijadinho** (W museualeijadinho.com.br) have been temporarily located inside São

CONCEIÇÃO NEARS COMPLETION

One of Ouro Preto's grand colonial churches, the **Nossa Senhora da Conceição** (aka Matriz de Antônio Dias) has been closed for extensive renovations for several years; it's not expected to reopen fully until at least late 2018 or 2019, though its bright white and yellow-trim facade was completed in 2017 and the interior is partially accessible for Mass while work continues (though you may not see much, other than the workers). It's primarily famous for being the church Aleijadinho belonged to and where he is buried (along with his father, Manuel Francisco Lisboa). Check the latest situation at the tourist office (see page 175).

Francisco (same hours). You'll find the collection in the side rooms and sacristy at the back, including the four magnificent rosewood lions that once served as supports for the plinth on which coffins were laid. Aleijadinho, never having seen a lion, drew from imagination and produced medieval monsters with the faces of monkeys. There's also a sensual crucifix and a baptismal font from 1779, as well as a small collection of paintings by various contemporaries, including a replica of a portrait of Aleijadinho by Euclásio Pena Ventura.

Igreja de Santa Efigênia

Rua Santa Efigênia • Tues–Sun 8.30am–4.30pm • R$5 • ☎ 31 3551 5047 • From Praça Tiradentes walk along Rua Cláudio Manoel down to the river, cross over and climb up Rua Santa Efigênia

Slightly out from the town centre is the fascinating **Igreja de Santa Efigênia**, the church for slaves, constructed between 1733 and 1785 on a hill 1km from Praça Tiradentes. Although plain in comparison to what you'll see in Ouro Preto's other churches, the artwork here is well worth the steep climb and the **views** towards town are outstanding. The altar was carved by Javier do Briton, the mentor of Aleijadinho; the interior panels are by Manoel Rabelo de Souza; and the exterior image of Nossa Senhora do Rosário is by Aleijadinho himself. Slaves contributed to its construction by smuggling gold in their teeth cavities and under their fingernails.

Mina do Chico Rei

Rua Dom Silvério 108 • Guided tours daily 8am–5.30pm • R$25 • ☎ 31 3552 2866

If you don't have time to get to the Mina da Passagem **gold mine** near Mariana (see page 167), it's worth visiting the cheaper **Mina do Chico Rei**, right in the centre of Ouro Preto. Founded in 1702, barely seven years after gold was first struck in Sabará, the mine operated until 1888. Though visually not as striking as the Mina da Passagem, it nonetheless boasts some impressive statistics, which give an idea of just how rich Ouro Preto must once have been: the mine, constructed on five levels, contains an astonishing eighty square kilometres of tunnels and vaults (only 300m of damp, narrow passages are open to the public). The mine was worked by slaves; there's also a small exhibit of the horrendous objects used to shackle and punish them. You'll also learn about the mine's namesake, a semi-legendary Congolese slave dubbed "Chico Rei", said to have hid enough gold from the mines to later free himself and his son.

ARRIVAL AND INFORMATION — OURO PRETO

By train The "Trem da Vale" tourist train links Ouro Preto with Mariana (see page 164), 12km to the east, which makes for a very pleasant day-trip. The train station – built in 1889 – is located south of the city centre at Praça Cesário Alvim (Wed–Sun 8.30am–5pm; ☎ 31 3551 7310).

By bus All long-distance buses arrive at the rodoviária (☎ 31 3559 3252), an easy 10min walk westwards from Praça Tiradentes at Rua Padre Rolim 661, though you'll want to grab a taxi if you have accommodation anywhere else in town – the hills are very steep. There is a local bus to Mariana operated by Transcotta (daily 5.30am–11.30pm; R$4.35)

PRECIOUS STONES OF OURO PRETO

Ouro Preto is littered with jewellery stores selling the region's **precious stones**, notably tourmaline, topaz and imperial topaz (the latter is only found here). The quality is usually very good, and despite the touristy focus, prices are much cheaper here than in the US or Europe and the trade is well regulated; try *Brasil Gemas* at Praça Tiradentes 74 (T 031 3551 4448).

from Praça Tiradentes (no need to go to the rodoviária) – you pay as you board. Heading to destinations in northern or southern Minas Gerais, it's usually a lot faster to travel via Belo Horizonte, assuming you start early enough.

Destinations Barão de Cocais (2 daily; 1hr); Belo Horizonte (hourly 6am–8pm; 2hr); Brasília (1 daily; 13hr 30min); Mariana (every 30min; 30min); Rio (2 daily; 6hr 40min); São João del Rei (2 daily; 4–5hr); São Paulo (1 daily; 11hr 30min).

By taxi Taxis in Praça Tiradentes charge around R$250 to drive to central Belo Horizonte, but it depends exactly where you want to go – the airports will be more like R$320. Taxis to Mariana charge around R$60 one-way. Try private operators such as Edson Loredo (T 31 8893 7563, E edslor@gmail.com).

Tourist office On the east side of Praça Tiradentes at no. 41 (daily 8am–5pm; T 31 3559 3269, W ouropreto.org.br).

2

ACCOMMODATION

Ouro Preto gets very crowded at **weekends** and **holidays**, so it's a good idea to reserve a room in advance, while during Carnaval or at Easter you'd be wise to book several months ahead.

Grande Hotel de Ouro Preto Rua Senador Rocha Lagoa 164 T 31 3551 1488, W grandehotelouropreto.com.br; map p.169. Opened in 1940, this building is one of architect Oscar Niemeyer's earliest creations – though not one of his best. The "standard" rooms at this three-star hotel are on the small side and overlook the garden, but the suites have tremendous views. Offers good service and there's a nice pool in the Burle Marx–designed gardens. R$255

Hostel Goiabada com Queijo Rua do Pilar 44 T 31 3552 3816, E goiabadacomqueijohostel@gmail.com; map p.169. No frills hostel accommodation with super-helpful owners, clean bunk-bed dorms with parquet floors, communal kitchen and TV room. Smaller and more intimate than other hostels in town (14 people maximum). Cash only. Dorms R$45

★ **Hotel Pousada do Arcanjo** Rua São Miguel Arcânjo 270 T 31 3551 4121, W arcanjohotel.com; map p.169. This grand and luxurious mid-eighteenth-century building features rooms decorated with period furniture and artwork (plus a/c and satellite TV). Rich buffet breakfast and afternoon tea (daily 5–7pm) included. Free rides to Praça Tiradentes, and free parking. R$291

Pousada Laços de Minas Rua dos Paulistas 43 T 31 3552 2597, W pousadaemouropreto.com.br; map p.169. Enticing historical digs, with a blend of old and new decor in common areas giving it a boutique feel. Rooms are rustic and simple but comfy enough, with satellite TV and smart, modern bathrooms (no a/c or fan, though, and no mosquito nets on the windows). Also does decent breakfast (included) and free afternoon coffee and cakes daily 5–7pm. Note that it's a steep walk up to the main square. R$269

★ **Pousada dos Meninos** Rua do Aleijadinho 89 T 31 3552 6212, W pousadadosmeninos.com.br; map p.169. Comfortable, cosy and stylish option run by friendly hosts Fabricio and Romulo, with wood floors, tasty breakfast, free wine and cheese every afternoon and rooms that come with ceiling fan, satellite TV, fridge and portable heaters. R$220

Pousada Nello Nuno Rua Camilo de Brito 59 T 31 3551 3375, W pousadanellonuno.com.br; map p.169. A very pretty, small *pousada* built around a courtyard. The rooms are attractively furnished in natural woods and the artwork is mostly by the proprietor who works in her printing atelier in the same building. R$170

Pouso do Chico Rei Rua Brigador Mosqueira 90 T 31 3551 1274, W pousodochicorei.com.br; map p.169. A small eighteenth-century house converted into a pleasant *pensão* (formerly graced by pre-eminent Brazilian singers Vinicius de Moraes and Dorival Caymmi), filled with a collection of rustic antiques that would do credit to a museum. There's a wonderful view from the reading room on the first floor, plus excellent breakfasts are served. Complimentary tea and cake are available at any time. There are only six rooms, so book in advance. Cash only. Limited parking. R$175

Rock in Hostel Rua Brigadeiro Musqueira 14 T 31 3551 3165, W rockinhostelouropreto.com.br; map p.169. This spotless hostel in a beautiful nineteenth-century mansion right in the centre (chiming bells can be an issue) features a rock'n'roll theme (with its three dorms and two doubles dedicated to stars such as Elvis Presley, Jimi Hendrix, The Beatles and Jim Morrison). Decent breakfast included, with shared kitchen and TV room. Towels cost R$5 extra. Can be cold in winter. Dorms R$55, doubles R$130

★ **Trilhas de Minas Hostel** Praça Antonio Dias 21 ⓣ31 3551 6367, ⓦtrilhasdeminashostel.com; map p.169. Popular hostel on the edge of the historic centre (at the bottom of a steep slope), with compact but cosy dorms and doubles, all with wooden beds and parquet floors plus fine views of the city and pleasant outdoor deck. Decent breakfast included. Incredibly helpful staff, though English-speakers are rare. Can be cold in winter. Cash only. Dorms R$55, doubles R$150

Viva Chico Rei Hostel Praça Antônio Dias 14 ⓣ31 3552 3328, ⓦvivachicoreihostel.com; map p.169. Wonderfully located hostel with heaps of charm, dorms (mixed and female only) with stylish bunks and spacious doubles (with fans), thoughtful owners and delicious buffet breakfast in the communal kitchen. Cash only. Dorms R$60, doubles R$170

EATING

★ **Bené da Flauta** Rua São Francisco de Assis 32 ⓣ31 3551 1036, ⓦbenedaflauta.com.br; map p.169. Fine dining in a lovely colonial building, this restaurant specializes in French and Italian dishes but also has some tasty local specials; a *mineira* buffet is served at lunch. Located right alongside the Igreja Francisco de Assis, near Praça Tiradentes, the views across town from the first-floor dining room are quite spectacular. Mains R$40–69. Daily noon–11.45pm.

Café Geraes Rua Conde de Bobadela (Rua Direita) 122 ⓣ31 3551 5097; map p.169. Restaurant with fairly priced sandwiches and soups, delicious cakes and wine, as well as more extensive dinners, all served inside the gorgeous interior of an old town house (dinner mains R$40–59), with live jazz piano (Thurs–Sat eve). The hip *Escadabaixo Bar* is downstairs too. Daily except Tues noon–midnight.

Casa do Ouvidor Rua Conde de Bobadela (Rua Direita) 42 ⓣ31 3551 2141, ⓦcasadoouvidor.com.br; map p.169. A particularly appealing choice for *mineira* cuisine is this rather elegant restaurant, in a beautifully converted colonial townhouse. Mains range R$43–81, pasta R$29; try the exquisite stewed chicken (*frango com quiabo*; R$63 for two people). Daily 11am–3pm & 7–10pm.

★ **Chafariz** Rua São José 167 ⓣ31 3551 2828; map p.169. Established by the Tropia family in 1958, this restaurant has become something of a local institution (the house is the birthplace of poet Alphonsus de Guimaraens), with pleasantly rustic decor and smooth service. Their *mineira* buffet is R$55 and also usually includes *feijoada*. Tues–Sun 11am–6pm.

Chocolates Ouro Preto Praça Tiradentes 111 ⓣ31 3551 3213, ⓦchocolatesouropreto.com.br; map p.169. Ouro Preto's most popular chocolatier offers excellent espresso (R$3.50) as well as hot chocolate (R$6–8), rich, tempting brownies and even local microbrews from Cervejaria Ouropretana in its casual café. Also has free wi-fi. Mon–Thurs & Sun 9am–7pm, Fri & Sat 9am–10pm.

O Passo Pizza Jazz Rua São José 56 ⓣ31 3552 5089, ⓦopassopizzajazz.com; map p.169. If you've had your fill of *mineira* cooking, one of the few alternatives is the pizza (and wine) served at this stylish place with a terrace (often with live jazz, and delightful views onto a small park and the river. You can expect to pay about R$36–41 for a medium pizza or R$39–44 for a plate of pasta. Daily noon–midnight.

Ópera Café Rua Conde de Bobadela 75 (inside the Pousada Solar da Ópera) ⓣ31 3551 6844; map p.169. Stylish café serving superb local coffee, croissants, cakes (guava cheesecake) and pastries, but also more extensive menus of steaks and fish (mains R$25–75). Mon 1–8pm, Tues–Sun 10am–8pm.

Quinto do Ouro Rua Conde de Bobadela (Rua Direita) 76 ⓣ31 3552 2633; map p.169. Thankfully, for those on a tight budget, there are several cheap places to eat in town, including this attractive *lanchonete*, with an excellent buffet (R$30). Tues–Sun 11am–3pm.

DRINKING AND NIGHTLIFE

During term time, and at the weekend, steep **Rua Conde de Bobadela** (aka Rua Direita), leading up to Praça Tiradentes, is packed with students spilling out of bars and cafés. Beer drinkers should try one of the excellent local microbrews from **Cervejaria Ouropretana** (ⓦouropretana.com.br), available all over town.

★ **Bar Barroco** Rua Conde de Bobadela (Rua Direita) 106 ⓣ31 3551 3032; map p.169. Hip student dive bar with wooden benches and graffiti-smothered walls. Has plenty of live music (mostly MPB and jazz) and tasty *coxhimba* (fried chicken or cheese-filled *pasteles*). Mon–Sat noon–2am.

Chopp Real Rua Barão de Camargos 8 ⓣ31 3551 1584; map p.169. A few psychedelic paintings decorate this popular joint, with tables on the cobbled street in front the perfect spot for a *chopp* on a warm evening. There's live bossa nova or MPB most nights from 8pm, though the food isn't that great. Daily noon–2am.

O Sótão Rua São José 201 ⓣ31 3552 3804; map p.169. Fun, colourful paintings decorate this student-friendly place with straw lightshades casting shadows on the walls. Does cheap buffets at lunch and excellent *rodízio* (Tues–Sun from 5pm; R$27), as well as cachaças and light bites such as filled pancakes. From 8pm live and relaxing samba, MPB and bossa nova set the mood. Tues–Sun noon–2am.

ON THE TRAIL OF THE WOOLLY SPIDER MONKEY

Ouro Preto is one of the launching points for trips to the relatively isolated **Reserva Particular do Patrimônio Natural Feliciano Miguel Abdala** (preservemuriqui.org.br), best known as a refuge for the endangered **northern muriqui woolly spider monkey**, as well as rare **buffy-headed marmosets** and thriving colonies of brown howler and tufted capuchin monkeys. Most of the pristine reserve (which covers around ten square kilometres), a private venture established by the late Feliciano Abdala, is smothered in dense forest (Mata Atlântica) and contains the Estação Biológica de Caratinga research station. The reserve is open daily 8am–5pm, but all visitors must be accompanied by a guide (see website); rates range R$150–300 per person depending on the size of your group and amount of time spent here – the chance of a spider monkey sighting is very high. Pássaro Verde runs one daily bus (5.30am; 5hr 30min) between Ouro Preto and **Caratinga** (returning at 4pm), where you can switch to a local bus heading to Rio Doce (2hr; ask to be let off at the reserve; the entrance is 2km from where the bus stops). Pássaro Verde also runs two daily buses from Belo Horizonte to Ipanema (9am & 8.30pm; 8hr 20min), from where it's just 1hr by local bus from the reserve. The nearest accommodation is at Santo Antonio do Manhuaçu on the edge of the reserve (see website). Note that the dry season is from April to September with the rainy season from October to March, but it can be very hot year-round.

DIRECTORY

Hospital Santa Casa de Misericórdia, Rua José Moringa 20, Bairro Bauxita (24hr; 31 3551 1133).

Laundry Ask at your hotel/hostel as there are no self-service laundries downtown. Nacente Lavanderia, at Rua dos Inconfidentes 5 (Mon–Fri 8am–5pm, Sat 8am–noon), picks up and drops off washing.

Money and exchange All the major banks with ATMs and exchange facilities are located along Rua São José; HSBC (31 3551 2048) is at Rua São José 201, while Banco do Brasil is at Rua São José 189.

Post office Rua Conde de Bobadela (Rua Direita) 180 (Mon–Fri 9am–5pm; 31 3551 1855); also at Rua Getúlio Vargas 233 near Rosário church (Mon–Fri 9am–5pm, Sat 9am–noon).

Around Ouro Preto: Lavras Novas

An easy day-trip from Ouro Preto, **LAVRAS NOVAS** is another small colonial town rapidly being developed as a tourist attraction, with its quaint cobbled streets, enticing boutique hotels and smattering of waterfalls and historic sights. Chief among the latter is the main church, the pretty **Igreja Nossa Senhora dos Prazeres** on central Praça Pedro Fernandes Marins, dating from around 1727.

ARRIVAL AND ACTIVIVITIES — LAVRAS NOVAS

By bus Transcotta operates buses (Mon–Fri 3 daily; Sat & Sun 1 daily; 45min) between Ouro Preto and Lavras Novas, usually from the train station at Praça Cesário Alvim (check with the tourist office).

Tours and activities For local tours and activities, from rappelling and rafting to ATV rental and kayaking, contact Nefelibatas Aventuras & Expedições, Rua Nossa Senhora dos Prazeres 887 (98701 4495, nefelibatas.com).

Estrada Real: the Old Road

From Ouro Preto, the **Estrada Real** splits into two, with the **Old Road** (Caminho Velho) running south all the way to the coast at Paraty, via Tiradentes, while the less enticing "New Road" runs down to Rio. All the historic cities on the Old Road have centres barely touched by modern developers; a few, like **Tiradentes**, look very much as they did two centuries ago. All have ravishing Portuguese churches, steep cobbled streets, ornate mansions and drip with colonial history. Further south, the hills rising into mountains near the state border harbour a cluster of **spa towns** – the **Circuito das Águas**, or "Circuit of the Waters", as the spa resorts of **São Lourenço** and **Caxambu** are collectively known.

Congonhas

Though it has roots in a mining community founded in 1734, **CONGONHAS** is an otherwise unexceptional modern town but for a single, showstopping sight: Aleijadinho's **The Prophets**. It's a long way to travel just to see one thing, but this is no ordinary work of art; if one place represents the flowering of *barroco mineiro*, this is it – the spiritual heart of Minas Gerais.

Santuário do Bom Jesus de Matosinhos

Praça da Basílica, Rua de Aleijadinho (off Rua Feliciano Mendes) • Tues–Sun 7am–6pm • Free • ⓣ 31 3731 1591

Built on a hill overlooking the southern side of town, with a panoramic view of the hills around it, the **Santuário do Bom Jesus de Matosinhos** comprises a central basilica and a magnificent sloping plaza (Jardim dos Passos) studded with palms and what look like six tiny mosques with oriental-like domes. These are, in fact, small **chapels** commemorating episodes of the Passion ("Janelas dos Passos"); each is filled with life-size cedarwood statues dramatizing the scene in a tableau (66 figures in total), the slope symbolizing the ascent towards the Cross.

Looking down on them from the parapets of the terrace leading up to the basilica itself are twelve towering soapstone **statues** of Old Testament prophets, remarkably dramatic, larger than life-size, full of movement and expression. Everything, the figures and the statues, was sculpted by **Aleijadinho** (see page 166). His presumed leprosy was already advanced, and he could only work with chisels strapped to his wrists. The results are astonishing, a masterpiece made all the more moving by the fact that it seems likely it was a conscious swan-song on Aleijadinho's part – there is no other explanation for the way a seriously ill man pushed so hard to finish such a massive undertaking whose theme was immediately relevant to his own suffering.

The Rococo-style **basilica** at the heart of the complex is modelled on the shrine of Bom Jesus in Braga, in northern Portugal. The basilica was completed in 1772; Aleijadinho and his disciples worked on the chapels from 1796 to 1800, and then focused on the prophets until 1805. **Manuel da Costa Ataíde** is thought to have added the bright paints to the statues in the chapels around 1808. Don't miss the small **Salão dos Ex-Votos** ("Hall of Miracles"), off to the side of the church itself, a hall plastered with the ex-votos of the faithful.

Museu Congonhas

Alameda Cidade de Matosinhos de Portugal 77 • Tues & Thurs– Sun 9am–5pm, Wed 1–5pm • R$10 (free Wed) • ⓣ 31 3731 1591, ⓦ museudecongonhas.org.br

Just off the main church plaza, the **Museu Congonhas** is a modern addition to the hilltop, its collection primarily focussed on religious art, ex-votos and carved *santos* (there's also a decent café here).

Museu da Imagem e Memória

Rua Bom Jesus 250 • Tues–Sun 9am–5pm • Free • ⓣ 31 3731 6110

To learn more about the history and personalities of Congonhas (including infamous faith healer Zé Arigó), walk down the precipitous Ladeira Caminho da Historia (aka "steep street") from the main church to the small but informative **Museu da Imagem e Memória** (near another historic church, the **Igreja de São José Operário**).

ARRIVAL AND GETTING AROUND — CONGONHAS

By bus Getting to Congonhas is easy by bus from Belo Horizonte (hourly 6am–9pm; 1hr 10min–2hr) and São João del Rei (6–7 daily on the Belo-bound bus; 1hr 50min); check schedules at ⓦ viacaosandra.com.br. It's possible to start out from either place, visit Bom Jesus in Congonhas and still get to São João del Rei or Belo Horizonte by the evening, but only if you begin your trip early.

To Bom Jesus de Matosinhos From Congonhas's main rodoviária, a couple of kilometres out of town (Av Mauá at Av Júlia Kubitscheck) catch the local bus (every 30min–1hr; R$3.60; 15min) marked "Basílica", which takes you all the way up the hill to the church; it's impossible to miss. The bus to take you back to the rodoviária leaves from the parking bay behind the church. Taxis charge R$15–20.

ACCOMMODATION AND EATING

Hotel Colonial Praça da Basílica 76 ⓣ31 3731 1834, ⓦhotelcolonialcongonhas.com.br. Most people visit Congonhas on a day-trip, but if you decide to spend the night this is the most comfortable option, right alongside the basilica, with its own small pool. The hotel's restaurant, *Cova do Daniel*, is also the best place to eat, with a menu of authentic *comida mineira* (*tutu à mineira* and *feijão tropeiro* are specialities). Mon 9am–6pm, Tues–Sun 11am–11pm. R$150

2

São João del Rei

Dating back to a simple mining camp established in 1704 on the São João River, **SÃO JOÃO DEL REI** has all the usual trappings of the Estrada Real – gilded Baroque churches, well-stocked museums and colonial mansions – but uniquely it's also a thriving modern town, easily the largest of the state's historic cities, with a population of just over 89,000 and a major student presence thanks to UFSJ (Universidade Federal de São João del Rei).

São João is divided into two main districts, each with a colonial area, separated by a narrow stream – the Córrego do Lenheiro – which runs between the broad **Avenida Tancredo Neves**, on the north side, and **Avenida Hermílio Alves**, which turns into **Avenida Eduardo Magalhães**, to the south. Relatively small and easy to find your way around, these districts are linked by a number of small bridges, including two eighteenth-century stone ones (Ponte da Cadeia and Ponte do Rosário), and a narrow, late nineteenth-century footbridge made of cast iron.

Igreja de São Francisco de Assis and around

Praça Frei Orlando • Mon 8am–4pm, Tues–Sat 8am–5pm, Sun after Mass 9.15am–2.30pm • R$4 • ⓣ32 3372 3110, ⓦvotdesaofranciscodeassis.org.br

The most impressive of the town's colonial churches and a wonderful example of *barroco mineiro*, the **Igreja de São Francisco de Assis** overlooks the towering

palms of Praça Frei Orlando (on the southern side of the old town). The church, started in 1774, is exceptionally large, with an ornately carved facade by a pupil of **Aleijadinho**. The master himself contributed the intricate decorations of the side chapels, which can be seen in all their glory now the original paint and gilding have been stripped off. Also here is the **grave of Tancredo Neves** (see page 647), in the cemetery behind the church.

Across from São Francisco church at Praça Frei Orlando 90, the tourism office shares space with the **Museu Tomé Portes del Rei** (daily 8am–5pm; free), the charming, rickety old townhouse once the home of poet Bárbara Heliodora (whose husband, Alvarenga Peixoto, was one of the Inconfidêntes). It's full of all sorts of bric-a-brac, junk, old photos and antiques, including huge scales from 1735.

Memorial Tancredo Neves

Rua Padre José Maria Xavier 7 • Thurs–Sat 9am–5.30pm, Sun & holidays 9am–3.30pm • R$2 • T 31 3371 7836, W memorialtancredoneves.com.br

The **Memorial Tancredo Neves** displays a collection of personal artefacts, awards, photographs, videos and documents relating to the former president's life – those intrigued by Brazil's political history will love this, but you have to read Portuguese to get the most out of it (there's nothing in English). Neves never lived in this nineteenth-century townhouse – the family home was, and continues to be, **Solar dos Neves** (see below). Exhibits here cover his early days in São João (Neves was born in the city in 1910), through his political career to the euphoric campaign of 1984–85, when he shepherded Brazil out of military rule and was elected president (see page 647). Tragically, he died before he took office – the final galleries are appropriately sombre, dealing with his funeral and ending with a shrine-like room containing a portrait and death-mask of the beloved leader. Neves is buried in a relatively humble black marble tomb with his wife in the cemetery behind São Francisco (see above).

Igreja da Nossa Senhora do Rosário

Praça Embaixador Gastão da Cunha (Rua Getúlio Vargas) • Tues–Sun 8–11am • Free

One block north from Avenida Tancredo Neves lies the colonial area around **Rua Getúlio Vargas**. The western end is home to the small **Igreja da Nossa Senhora do Rosário** (note the limited opening hours), built for the town's slave population in around 1719, which looks onto a cobbled square dominated by two handsome colonial mansions; the one nearest the church is the **Solar dos Neves** (closed to the public), the house where Tancredo lived between 1957 and 1985, and still owned by his family.

Museu de Arte Sacra

Praça Embaixador Gastão da Cunha 8, Rua Getúlio Vargas • Mon–Fri noon–5pm, Sat 9am–1pm • R$7 • T 32 3371 7005, W museudeartesacra.com.br

Contained within another sensitively restored building (a former jail), the **Museu de Arte Sacra** boasts a small but enchanting collection of religious art; chalices, silver halos, carvings of saints, painted oratorios, crucifixes, huge silver processional crosses and so on (the lack of English labelling doesn't take anything away from the experience). Highlights include a finely painted, full-size wooden statue of St George by Mestre do Cajuru, and a head of Christ attributed to Aleijadinho (now attached to a larger sculpture of Jesus roped to a whipping post, the *Cristo Flagelado*).

Catedral Basílica de Nossa Senhora do Pilar

Rua Monsenhor Gustavo 61 at Rua Getúlio Vargas • Mon 6–10.30am, Tues–Sun 6–10.30am & 1–8pm • R$5 • T 32 3371 2568

Almost next door to the Museu de Arte Sacra is a magnificent early Baroque church, now the **Catedral de Nossa Senhora do Pilar**, started in 1721. Beyond the rather plain exterior, you'll discover an interior that is gorgeously decorated – only Pilar in Ouro

Preto and Santo Antônio in Tiradentes are as liberally plastered with gold. The gilding is seen to best effect over the altar, a riot of Rococo pillars, angels and curlicues. The ceiling painting is all done with vegetable dyes, and there's a beautiful tiled floor in the porch area.

Igreja de Nossa Senhora das Mercês

Praça Dom Pedro II (Largo das Mercês) • Mon–Fri 8am–noon & 1.30–5pm, Sat & Sun 8am–noon • Free

The **Igreja de Nossa Senhora das Mercês**, behind the cathedral at the end of sleepy Praça Dom Pedro II, dates from 1751 (but was largely rebuilt in the 1800s) and is notable for the variety and artistry of the graffiti – some of it dating back to the nineteenth century – etched into its stone steps.

Museu Regional de São João del-Rei

Rua Marechal Deodoro 12 • Tues–Fri 9.30am–5.30pm, Sat & Sun 9am–1pm • Free • 32 3371 7663

Housed in a magnificently restored mansion dubbed the Casarão do Comendador (built for prominent businessman João Antônio da Silva Mourão in around 1859), the **Museu Regional** contains a curious collection of historic artefacts (labelled in Portuguese only), from antique furniture and wonderfully decorated oratorios, to an ornate, painted sedan chair and a small pipe organ, smothered in murals. Perhaps the most fascinating pieces here are the eighteenth-century *ex votos* on the first floor, vivid folk paintings detailing the trials both masters and slaves experienced: José Alves de Carvalho was stabbed in the chest while crossing a bridge on the way home in 1765; a slave called Antônio had his leg broken and was half-buried for hours in a mine cave-in. Also on the first floor, look out for the several figures of saints – crafted with a simplicity and directness that makes them stand out – made by ordinary people in the eighteenth century.

Igreja de Nossa Senhora do Carmo

Largo do Carmo, Av Getúlio Vargas • Mon–Sat 7am–noon & 2–5pm, Sun 7am–noon & 5.30–7pm • R$2

The elegant facade of **Igreja de Nossa Senhora do Carmo** dominates a beautiful triangular *praça* at the eastern end of Avenida Getúlio Vargas. It's another church designed by Aleijadinho in the eighteenth century – note his exquisite sculptures around the entrance.

Museu Ferroviário

Av Hermílo Alves 366 • Wed–Sat 9–11am & 1–4pm, Sun 9am-12.30pm • Free • 32 3371 8485 • Enter through the main train station

Rail aficioandos should make for the nineteenth-century train station, where the **Museu Ferroviário** charts the history of rail transport, from James Watt and George Stephenson et al, through to the genesis of Brazilian railways and the **Maria Fumaça** or "**Smoking Mary**" (see page 182) in the 1870s (primarily through information boards and paintings labelled in Portuguese only). It also houses the first engine to run on the track here, an old "Baldwin" steam locomotive like you see in Westerns, made in Philadelphia in 1880.

ARRIVAL AND INFORMATION — SÃO JOÃO DEL REI

By train The tourist steam train service, the *Maria Fumaça*, leaves São João station (Av Hermílo Alves 366; ticket office Thurs & Fri 9–11am & 1–4pm, Sat 9am–1pm & 2–4pm, Sun 9am–1pm; 32 3371 8485, vli-logistica.com/pt-br/trem-turistico) for the 12km ride to Tiradentes on Fri & Sat at 10am and 3pm, returning at 1pm and 5pm, and on Sun at 10am and 1pm, returning 11am & 2pm (R$50 one-way, R$60 return; 35min).

By bus The rodoviária (Rua Ver. Eli Araújo 142; 32 3373 4700) is 1.5km northeast of the centre; take a local *Presidente* bus (R$3) into the centre. Taxis (32 3371 2028) charge R$15–20.

Destinations Belo Horizonte (7–8 daily; 3hr 30min); Caxambu (4 weekly; 3hr); Congonhas (6 daily; 1hr 50min); Ouro Preto (2 daily; 4hr); Rio (3 daily; 5hr 30min); São Paulo (8 daily; 6hr–8hr 30min); Tiradentes (every 40min; 30min).

Information Praça Frei Orlando 90 (daily 8am–5pm; 32 3372 7338).

ACCOMMODATION

Finding somewhere to stay is rarely a problem as accommodation in São João is plentiful and good value, though hotel and *pousadas* here are not nearly as attractive as those in neighbouring **Tiradentes** (see page 183). Bear in mind however, that the town is a popular spot for **Carnaval**, and **Easter** celebrations also attract huge numbers of visitors; at these times advance reservations are essential.

★ **AZ Hostel** Rua Marechal Bitencourt 73 ⓣ 32 98854 2842, ⓦ azhostel.com.br; map p.179. Bright, spotless hostel with female- and male-only dorms, tiled floors, colourful artwork, simple but comfy en-suite doubles and extra helpful owner (Flávia Frota). Sheets, towels and soaps included, plus free use of bikes. Breakfast is provided through vouchers for local cafés, including the highly rated *Taberna d'Omar* (see below). No parking. Cash only. Dorms R$65, doubles R$150

Pousada Beco do Bispo Rua Beco do Bispo 93 ⓣ 32 3373 0992, ⓦ becodobispo.com.br; map p.179. The poshest digs in town can be found at this stylish central option, with beautifully decorated rooms (a/c and satellite TV), great breakfast, fabulous outdoor pool and a friendly English-speaking host, Nitza. Free parking. R$225

Pousada Rotunda Rua Conselheiro Belisário Leite de Andrade Neto 100 ⓣ 32 3372 2699, ⓦ pousadarotunda.com.br; map p.179. Next to the train station, this enchanting, whimsical choice features rustic rooms set around a quiet courtyard, rooftop pool, cable TV and a pool table. R$240

Pousada Villa Magnólia Rua Ribeiro Bastos 2 ⓣ 32 3373 5065, ⓦ pousadavillamagnolia.com.br; map p.179. Just outside of the historic centre, this romantic candle-lit inn is top of the range, excellent value and has a gorgeous outdoor pool. The rooms are decked out in period style, and come with flat-screen TVs. Free parking. R$186

EATING

Biscoiteria Tradição Mineira Travessa Lopes Bahia 18 ⓣ 32 3371 2020; map p.179. Seek out this small store in the commercial heart of town to load up on traditional *mineira* sweets and biscuits. Mon–Sat 9am–5pm.

Churrascaria Ramon Praça Severiano de Rezende 52 ⓣ 32 3371 3540; map p.179. Long-standing, excellent and good-value *churrasco* and *mineiro* food, with all the usual barbecued meats (and zesty home-made mayonnaise) in a lively, family-friendly atmosphere. Set lunch from R$20. Steaks R$59–88. Daily 11.30am–6pm.

Restaurante Rex Av Hermílio Alves 146 ⓣ 32 3371 1449; map p.179. Perfectly adequate and reasonably priced *por quilo* restaurant (R$32–40/kg) in a charming old building (next to the Teatro Municipal), with a huge selection of traditional items in a spacious, clean dining room. Try and get a table on the balcony. Daily 11am–3.30pm.

★ **Taberna d'Omar** Rua Getúlio Vargas 242 ⓣ 32 99123 7856; map p.179. Small but superb coffee shop and artisanal bakery, selling all manner of breads, cookies and *pão de queijo* (cheese bread; from R$2), hot chocolate (R$4.50), plus more substantial dishes (such as quinoa crusted sole; R$40). Mon & Tues 7am–7pm, Wed–Sat 7am–midnight, Sun 7am–4pm.

★ **Villeiros** Rua Padré Maria Xavier 132 ⓣ 32 3372 1034; map p.179. Justly popular traditional restaurant in nineteenth-century mansion (the daughter of Tancredo Neves still takes lunch here), with superb *comida mineira* – the *por quilo* buffet lunch is always busy (around R$36/kg), so try and arrive early. Daily 11.30am–4pm (buffet served till 3pm).

SMOKING MARY

If you're in São João between Friday and Sunday, don't miss the half-hour **train ride** (see page 184) to the colonial village of **Tiradentes**, 12km away. There are frequent buses too, but they don't compare to the trip on a nineteenth-century steam train, with immaculately maintained rolling stock from the 1930s. You may think yourself immune to the romance of steam and be bored by the collection of old steam engines and rail equipment in São João's railway museum (see page 181), but by the time you've bought your ticket you'll be hooked: the booking hall is right out of a 1930s movie, the train hisses and spits out cinders, and as you sit down in carriages filled with excited children, it's all you can do not to run up and down the aisle with them.

Completed in 1881, as the textile industry took off in São João, this was one of the earliest rail lines in Brazil, and the trains were immediately christened **Maria Fumaça** (**"Smoking Mary"**). The half-hour ride is very scenic, following a winding valley of the Serra de São José, which by the time it gets to Tiradentes has reared up into a series of rocky bluffs. Sit on the left leaving São João for the best views, and as far from the engine as you can: steam trains bring tears to your eyes in more ways than one.

'iradentes

Vith its quaint historic houses converted into posh boutiques, galleries, restaurants nd wine shops, **TIRADENTES** is a complete contrast to São João, just 11km away. hough it gets mobbed by Brazilian tourists (especially *cariocas*) at the weekends, nd costs here are the most expensive in Minas, it's popular for good reason. During he week the romantic architecture, chirping parrots, high-quality arts and crafts, lossoms and sublime food are hard to resist. Although it was founded as early as 1702, y the 1730s Tiradentes (originally Vila de São José do Rio das Mortes) had already een overshadowed by São João and is now little more than a sleepy village with a opulation of just under 8000 (it was re-named after the Brazilian revolutionary hero n 1889). The core is much as it was in the eighteenth century, straggling down the side f a hill crowned by the twin towers of the **Igreja Matriz de Santo Antônio**. The main quare, the attractive **Largo das Forras**, was landscaped by Roberto Burle Marx, today inged by shops, cafés and the small but picturesque **Capela do Bom Jesus da Pobreza** Sat & Sun 9am–4pm; free).

greja Matriz de Santo Antônio

ua da Câmara at Padre Toledo • Daily 9am–5pm; concerts Fri 8.30pm • R$5; organ concerts R$40 • ⓣ 32 3355 1238

Begun in 1710 and completed around 1750, the **Igreja Matriz de Santo Antônio** is one f the earliest and largest of the Minas Baroque churches; in 1732 it began to acquire he gilding for which it is famous, becoming in the process one of the richest churches n any of the mining towns. The church was decorated with the special extravagance of he newly rich, using more gold, the locals say, than any other church in Brazil, save the Capela Dourada in Recife. Whether this is true – and Pilar in Ouro Preto is probably s rich as either – the glinting of the gold around the lavish altar is certainly jaw-dropping, and the entire wooden ceiling is smothered in murals. The beautifully carved oapstone panels on the facade (1810) are now not thought to be by Aleijadinho, as ome still believe, but by his pupil, Cláudio Pereira Viana, who worked with the master n his last projects. Linger on the steps of the church to enjoy the view of the old town, ramed by the crests of the hills – if you had to take one photograph to represent Minas Gerais, this would be it. Popular **organ concerts** (40min) take place in the church very Friday at 8.30pm – the beautifully painted organ is one of the most eye-catching bjects in the church.

Museu da Liturgia

ua Jogo de Bola 15 • Mon & Thurs–Sat 10am–5pm, Sun 10am–1.30pm • R$10 • ⓣ 32 3355 1552, ⓦ museudaliturgia.com.br

The **Museu da Liturgia**, a relatively new, stylish religious art museum, inside the shell f the old Casa Paroquial next to Santo Antônio, is a little more creative than your verage *museu de arte sacra*. Its galleries use interactive exhibits, touchscreens and neditative background music, in addition to the rare collections of massive silver andleholders, multicoloured altar palms and stunning silver halos and crowns, to shed ight on aspects of Catholic tradition, ceremonies and theology. Each gallery contains a aminated guide in English.

Museu Padre Toledo

ua Padre Toledo 190 • Tues–Sun 10am–5pm • R$10 • ⓣ 32 3351 1549

The **Museu Padre Toledo** is named after one of the Inconfidêntes and is located in his eighteenth-century mansion (this is where the conspirators first met in 1788). Toledo, who was pastor at Santo Antônio church between 1777 and 1789, obviously didn't et being a priest stand in the way of enjoying the pleasures of life; the two-storey *obrado* must have been very comfortable, and even though the lavish **ceiling paintings** (artist unknown) are dressed up as classical allegories, they're not the sort of thing you would expect a priest to commission, featuring, as they do, so much naked flesh. The rooms are mostly empty save for a handful of religious carvings, statues and paintings

HIKING TIRADENTES

Tiradentes is surrounded by some ravishing countryside and the hilly terrain of the Serra de São José, and **hiking** has become a major attraction for visitors. As the trails are poorly marked, you're best off going with a guide. Caminhos e Trilhas (Rua Custódio Gomes 13; T 32 3355 1811) lead small groups on fairly easy hikes, stopping at spots where there are natural pools and picnic areas and views of Tiradentes. The closest target is the **Mãe d'Água**, a natural spring just a ten-minute walk from the centre, while the **Trilha Carteiro** takes around three hours and leads up to the nearest ridge. Uai Trip, Rua Henrique Diniz 119 (T 32 3355 1161, W uaitrip.com.br), provides guides for R$95, as well as arranging horse-riding, rafting and biking.

(plus a painting of Dom Pedro I receiving tribute from an indigenous chief), but are enlivened by some contemporary extras such as touch-screen terminals highlighting the building's history (Portuguese only; English leaflets available), and mirrors to allow easier examination of the ceiling.

Igreja da Nossa Senhora do Rosário dos Pretos

Praça Padre Lourival (Rua Direita) • Tues–Sun 9am–noon & 2–5pm • R$3

There is no more eloquent reminder of the harsh divisions between masters and slaves than the small **Igreja da Nossa Senhora do Rosário dos Pretos**, a chapel built by slaves from around 1708 for their own worship. There is a small gilded altar here – some colonial miners were freed slaves working on their own account – and two fine figures of the black St Benedict stand out, but overall the church is moving precisely because it is so simple and dignified.

Museu de Sant'Ana

Rua Direita 93 (entrance on Rua da Cadeia) • Daily except Tues 10am–7pm • R$5 • T 32 3355 2798, W museudesantana.org.br

Housed in the old public jail (Cadeia Pública), the **Museu de Sant'Ana** is a fascinating museum of religious art, focusing specifically on images of **St Anne**, the Catholic patron saint of home and family, and the mother of Mary (and grandmother of Jesus), though as the museum points out, this is really a much older folk tradition – akin to the "Earth Mother" or Goddess tradition – adopted by the Catholic church later. The four beautifully presented galleries display around three hundred images of St Anne, mostly carved icons collected in Brazil by museum founder Angela Gutierrez (whose father established Construtora Andrade Gutierrez, one of Brazil's biggest construction companies). Everything is labelled in English (the free audioguides simply read these out).

ARRIVAL AND INFORMATION — TIRADENTES

By train The tourist steam train service, the *Maria Fumaça* (see page 182), leaves Tiradentes station (Praça Estação; ticket office Thurs 9–11am & 1–4pm, Fri 9am–1pm & 2–5pm, Sat 9am–noon & 1–5pm, Sun 9am–noon & 1–2pm; T 32 3371 8485, W vli-logistica.com/pt-br/trem-turistico) for the 12km ride to for São João del Rei on Fri & Sat at 1pm & 5pm and on Sun at 11am & 2pm (R$50 one-way, R$60 return; 35min).

By car Tirandentes is served by good, paved roads from Belo Horizonte (190km; 3hr) via Congonhas (117km; 2hr), and São João del Rei (11km; 25min). Parking (free) is fairly easy along the streets during the week.

By bus The rodoviária is in the centre of town off Rua Gabriel Passos. Buses leave regularly for São João del Rei (Mon–Fri 5.50am–7pm, every 40min, Sat & Sun 7am–7pm, every 1hr 30min–2hr; 30min; R$3.65), from where you can connect to other destinations. Taxis charge R$50 (one-way) for the trip.

Tourist information Rua Resende Costa 71, in the town hall on Largo das Forres (Mon–Thurs & Sun 9am–6pm, Fri & Sat 9am–8pm; T 32 3355 1212).

ACCOMMODATION

Finding a place to stay in Tiradentes is rarely a problem, as a good proportion of the town's population have turned their homes into **pousadas** (there are well over fifty), many of which are exceptionally comfortable. During **Carnaval**, over **Easter** and in **July**, advanced reservations are essential, and most *pousadas* will only accept bookings of at least four nights

dara Hostel Rua Custódio Gomes 286 ☎32 3355 579, ⓦodarahosteltiradentes.com.br. Excellent udget option, a short walk from the centre, with clean iixed, male- and female-only dorms (all with just three unks) with fans, plus two en-suite family rooms with itchenettes for up to five people. Friendly, English-peaking staff. Dorms R$40, doubles R$130

'ousada Marília de Dirceu Rua Agostino José Cabral 95 ☎32 3355 1962, ⓦpousadamariliadedirceu.com.r. Charming hotel loaded with character, its simple but osy rooms featuring parquet floors, flat-screen TVs with able, fans, modern bathrooms with beautiful tiling, and alconies; typical *mineira* breakfast and afternoon tea ncluded. Free parking. R$162

★ **Pousada Toque Mineiro** Rua Fernão Dias Paes 381 ☎32 3355 1917, ⓦtoquemineiro.com.br. Quite possibly ne of the best *pousadas* in the state, located south of the entre and ideal for those touring by car. The beautifully furnished rooms overlook a lush garden courtyard (there's also outdoor and indoor pools) as part of a posh but rustic condo development, with plenty of free parking and the best buffet breakfast (included) anywhere. Free snacks available daily 2–10pm. R$250

Pouso Lar Doce Lar Rua Martim Paolucci 160 ☎32 8854 9442, ⓦpousolardocelar.com/pt-br. Great central location just off the Largo das Forras, with comfy, period-style rooms (with space for three people) with parquet floors, flat-screen cable TV and free parking nearby. Cash only. R150

Torre Hostel Rua Herculano José dos Santos 92 ☎32 9993 20804, ⓦtorrehostel.com.br. One of the cheapest and friendliest places to stay, 1km from centre, with clean, simple rooms and newish dorms, shared kitchen and TV room, plus bike rentals. Free parking (reservation needed). Dorms R$40, doubles R$125

EATING AND DRINKING

Angatu Rua da Cadeia 38 ☎32 9990 35734, ⓦangatutiradentes.com. Beautiful little restaurant serving stylish, ontemporary Brazilian food. Menu changes seasonally, ut might include roast pumpkin, perfectly seared cuts of eef and tender pork chop with smoked aubergine puree. Mains R$59–72. Wed–Fri 7.30–11.30pm, Sat & Sun 12.30–3pm & 7.30–11.30pm.

Chico Doceiro Rua Francisco de Morais 74 ☎32 3355 1900. Lauded local sweetshop, with all the traditional *mineira* treats handmade by octogenarian Chico "the candyman" since 1965, and now by his son; try the exquisite *doce de leite* or *doce de banana* (each piece R$1). The open-front store has just one table inside. Daily 9am–6pm.

★ **Pau de Angu** Estrada para Bichinho, Km 3 ☎32 9948 1692. Four kilometres from the centre along the Estrada Tiradentes–Bichinho, amid beautiful countryside, this is a wonderful rustic restaurant serving *mineiro* food at its best. Most dishes are huge servings of meat and stews, meant for sharing, and range R$75–150. Cash only. Daily except Tues noon–5pm.

Tragaluz Rua Direita 52 ☎32 9968 4837, ⓦtragaluztiradentes.com.br. Modern *comida mineira* with a fun and creative menu like *galinha d'angola* ("Angolan hen") and a justly famed guava and cashew-nut cream cheese dessert (R$25). Most mains R$52–82. Wed–Mon 7pm–midnight.

★ **Virada's do Largo** Rua do Moinho 11 ☎32 3355 1111. Beth Beltrão's restaurant is considered the best in town for *comida mineira*, with home-made *linguiça* sausage (smoke-cured pork), *tutu* (mashed cooked beans) and local cachaça (R$8.50; caipirinha R$18) especially outstanding. Choose single plates (mains R$38–48) or huge sets of pork, chicken, sausage and steaks for three people (R$97). Daily except Tues noon–10pm.

Espírito Santo

A compact blend of mountains and sub-tropical coastline, **Espírito Santo** is one of the smallest states in Brazil (with a population of only 2.6 million), but as Minas Gerais' main outlet to the sea it is strategically very important. To a *mineiro*, Espírito Santo means only one thing: **beaches**. During weekends and holiday seasons, thousands flock to the coast, tending to concentrate on the stretch immediately south of the historic capital **Vitória** – especially the large resort town of **Guarapari**. The best beaches, however, lie on the strip of coastline another 50km south of Guarapari, and in the north of the state, heading towards Bahia. The hinterland of the state, which is far less visited, is exceptionally beautiful – an enticing mix of lush forest, river valleys, mountains and granite hills. Since the latter part of the nineteenth century the area has been colonized by successive waves of Italians, Poles and Germans, their descendants living in small, charming country towns such as **Santa Teresa** and **Domingos Martins**, which combine a European look and feel with a thoroughly tropical landscape. All

2

CIRCUITO DAS ÁGUAS – THE SPA TOWNS

The **spa towns** in the southern portion of Minas Gerais provide soothing relief on the journey to Rio or São Paolo, with a variety of treatments, massages and spring pool bathing on offer. **Caxambu** was a favourite haunt of the Brazilian royal family in the nineteenth century, and the Das Águas Minerais de Caxambu bottling company was established in 1886, along with the basis of the **Parque das Águas de Caxambu** in the centre of town today (daily 7am–6pm; park entry R$5; T 35 3341 3266). It's dotted with eleven oriental-style pavilions sheltering the actual mineral water springs and houses an ornate Turkish-style Balneário de Hidroterapia (bathhouse) completed in 1912 that is very reasonably priced.

If Caxambu is the last word in Edwardian elegance, **São Lourenço**, 30km to the southwest, rivals it with its displays of Art Deco brilliance. Its **Parque das Águas** (daily 7am–8pm; R$5; T 35 3332 3066) is studded with striking 1940s pavilions and has a stunning bathhouse that looks more like a film set for a Hollywood high-society comedy. Since 2002 corporate giant Nestlé has been bottling the water here (and managing the park), under the brand Água Mineral São Lourenço. The park is larger and more modern than the one in Caxambu, with its nine brilliant white fountain pavilions (all housing free mineral water springs), forested hillside and clouds of butterflies and birds. The 1935 Centro Hidroterápico-Balneário, at the park entrance, offers baths (*duchas*), saunas and posh spa treatments (R$42–133). Frequent **buses** link São Lourenço and Caxambu several times daily, as well as with Belo Horizonte, Rio and São Paulo.

ACCOMMODATION

Hotel Brasil Alameda João Lage 87, São Lourenço T 35 3339 2550, W hotelbrasil.com.br. This grand but fairly atmospheric behemoth dominates the Praça Duque de Caixas and offers the works, including four pools and water slides. Parking R$18/day. R$250

Hotel Caxambu Rua Major Penha 145, Caxambu T 35 3341 9300, W hotelcaxambu.com.br. For faded, late nineteenth-century elegance it's hard to beat this old stalwart (open since 1884), 400m from Caxambu's spa, but with its own gym, pools and saunas. Free parking. R$200

Palace Hotel Rua Dr Viotti 567, Caxambu T 35 3341 3341, W palacehotel.com.br. Grand colonial option that opened in 1892, close to the park and with another slew of pools, sauna and massage parlour. Huge buffet breakfast included. R$170

are easy to get to from Vitória, not more than a couple of hours over good roads and linked by frequent buses.

Vitória

Founded in 1551 as the capital of Espírito Santo on an island formed by the Rio Santa Maria delta, **VITÓRIA** is an affluent and well-run seaside city vaguely reminiscent of Rio, with a combination of high-rises, beaches, granite outcrops and irregularly shaped mountains on the horizon. Like Rio, it has an old centre several kilometres from the more fashionable beach districts, which are home to the best nightlife and restaurants – at the beaches you can sample **moqueca capixaba**, the local seafood stew, as well as especially good crab.

Though its beaches attract plenty of Brazilians in the summer and Vitória is renowned for blue marlin and sailfish **fishing**, the economy is not driven by tourism; the city is a base for offshore oil, home to the giant Arcelor-Mittal Tubarão steel plant, Vale iron-ore railway operations and two major ports. Today Vitória is spread out over a vast area: the **centro histórico** contains most of the sights, while the modern financial district lies several kilometres along the Baía de Vitória in **Enseada do Sua**. The name of the street that hugs the shore between the two areas changes as you go eastwards from the rodoviária; initially it's called Avenida Elias Miguel, then Avenida Getúlio Vargas, Avenida Marechal Mascarenhas de Moraes, and finally **Avenida Beira Mar** (the whole stretch is generally referred to by locals as the latter). The main beaches run north from here, beginning with **Praia do Curva da Jurema**.

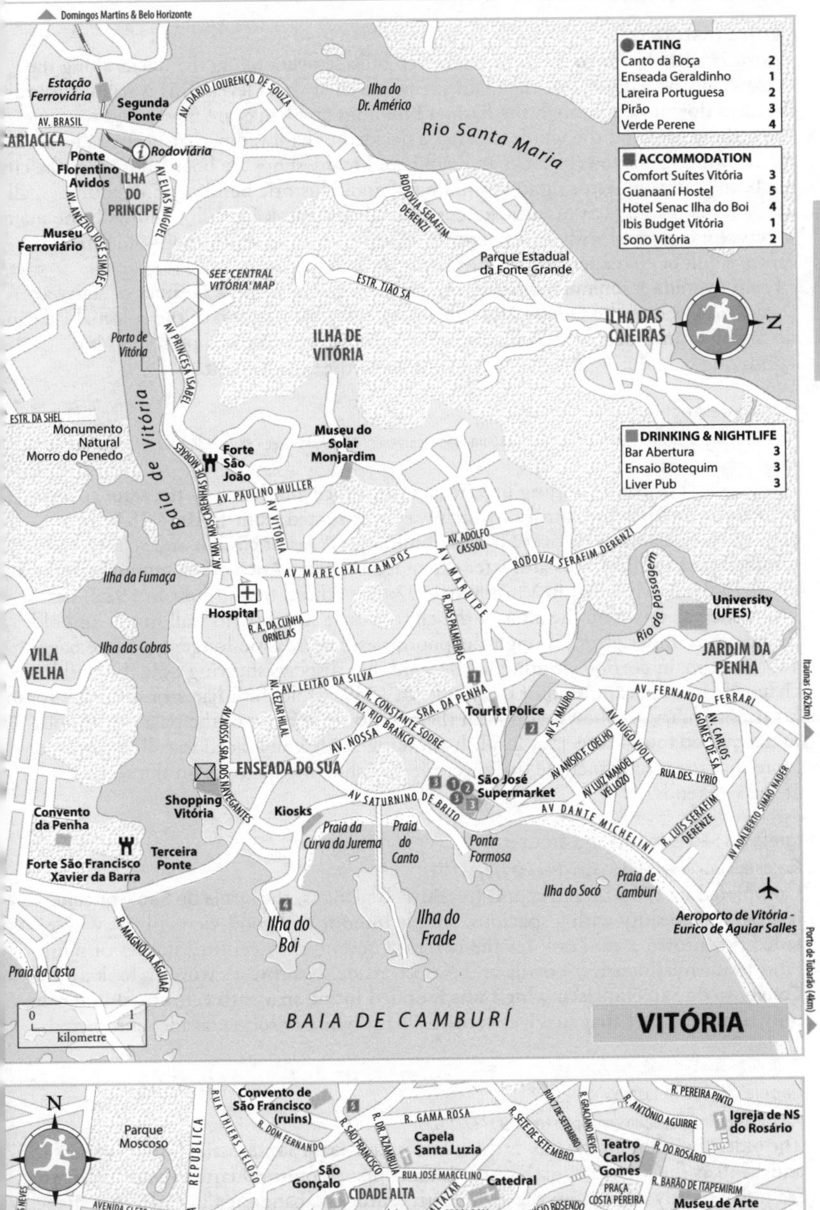
VITÓRIA
EATING
Canto da Roça 2
Enseada Geraldinho 1
Lareira Portuguesa 2
Pirão 3
Verde Perene 4
ACCOMMODATION
Comfort Suítes Vitória 3
Guanaaní Hostel 5
Hotel Senac Ilha do Boi 4
Ibis Budget Vitória 1
Sono Vitória 2
DRINKING & NIGHTLIFE
Bar Abertura 3
Ensaio Botequim 3
Liver Pub 3
Domingos Martins & Belo Horizonte
Estação Ferroviária
Segunda Ponte
AV. BRASIL
CARIACICA
Rodoviária
Ponte Florentino Avidos
ILHA DO PRINCIPE
Museu Ferroviário
Ilha do Dr. Américo
Rio Santa Maria
Parque Estadual da Fonte Grande
SEE 'CENTRAL VITÓRIA' MAP
Porto de Vitória
ILHA DE VITÓRIA
ILHA DAS CAIEIRAS
ESTR. DA SHEL
Monumento Natural Morro do Penedo
Baia de Vitória
Forte São João
Museu do Solar Monjardim
Ilha da Fumaça
Hospital
Ilha das Cobras
VILA VELHA
University (UFES)
JARDIM DA PENHA
Rio da Passagem
Tourist Police
ENSEADA DO SUA
São José Supermarket
Shopping Vitória
Kiosks
Convento da Penha
Forte São Francisco Xavier da Barra
Terceira Ponte
Praia da Curva da Jurema
Praia do Canto
Ponta Formosa
Praia de Camburí
Ilha do Socó
Ilha do Boi
Ilha do Frade
Aeroporto de Vitória - Eurico de Aguiar Salles
Itaúnas (262km)
Porto de Tubarão (4km)
Praia da Costa
BAIA DE CAMBURÍ
0 1 kilometre

CENTRAL VITÓRIA
Parque Moscoso
Convento de São Francisco (ruins)
Capela Santa Luzia
São Gonçalo
CIDADE ALTA
Catedral
PRAÇA DOM LUIZ SCORTEGAGNA
Teatro Carlos Gomes
PRAÇA COSTA PEREIRA
Igreja de NS do Rosário
Museu de Arte do Espírito Santo
MUCANE - Museu Capixaba do Negro
Colegio Maria Ortiz
Palácio de Anchieta
PRAÇA JOÃO CLIMACO
PRAÇA 8 DE SETEMBRO
PRAÇA PIO XII
Banco do Brasil
AVENIDA JERÔNIMO MONTEIRO
AVENIDA PRINCESA ISABEL
AVENIDA MASCARENHAS DE MORAES
AVENIDA FLORENTINO AVIDOS
Port
0 100 metres

2

Centro histórico

Vitória's **centro histórico** is built into a steep hillside overlooking the docks along the narrow Baía de Vitória, but the main streets are all at shore level. This is still technically the city's downtown, though the flashier buildings and banks are now based way out along Beira Mar and the whole area has a decidedly shabby, down-at-heel air about it – many of the 1960s tower blocks are empty and many shops are boarded up. Yet the city has been gradually restoring its sprinkling of grand historic buildings and churches, all of them manned by enthusiastic guides (though few speak English), and with the main streets still crammed with locals perusing cheap stores and snack shops the historic centre is full of character and an intriguing place to explore.

From **Avenida Jerônimo Monteiro**, the main shopping street, a number of stairways (*escadarias*) lead to the **Cidade Alta** (the upper city), the location of the colonial Palácio de Anchieta and most of the churches. With so many people and police around, wandering here during the day is safe, but avoid the area at night.

Palácio de Anchieta

Praça João Clímaco • Tues–Fri 9am–5pm, Sat & Sun 9am–4pm; tours every 20–30min • Free • ⓣ 27 3636 1032, ⓦ es.gov.br/governo/palacio-anchieta

The grandest historic building in Vitória is the office and home of the state governor, the **Palácio de Anchieta**, most of which was constructed from 1910 to 1912 in an elegant Neoclassical style over far older buildings. A Jesuit church and school was founded here in the 1570s and later expanded by **Padre Anchieta**, a seminal religious figure in Brazil who died in Vitória in 1597. His official **tomb** (built in 1922) lies inside the palace where the altar of the church once stood (with wall mural and old foundations under glass), though the poor priest's body is no longer here (see page 189). The main corridor leading to the tomb has displays showing how the building changed after the expulsion of the Jesuits in 1759, while the adjacent exhibition room hosts temporary art shows with local themes. To see the rest of the palace you must join a **guided tour** – to get an English-speaking guide you'll need to call in advance. Note that tours only include the governor's lavish living quarters on the second floor at the weekends.

Igreja de São Gonçalo and around

Rua São Gonçalo • Tues–Sun 9am–5pm • Free • ⓣ 27 3233 2856

Completed in 1766 by slaves and free Afro-Brazilians, the **Igreja de São Gonçalo** is a Baroque beauty with a spacious, simple interior and good views of the whole, faded downtown area. Look for the two rare, seventeenth-century statues of saints (and Jesuit missionaries) Loyola and Xavier inside. Nearby, it's worth a look at the **Convento de São Francisco** which was founded in the sixteenth century, though the only historical part that survives is the brilliant white Baroque facade, completed 1744–84.

Capela de Santa Luzia

Rua José Marcelino • Tues–Sun 9am–5pm • Free • ⓣ 27 3222 3219

The oldest building in the city is the humble **Capela de Santa Luzia**, built between 1537 and 1540 as the private church of the island's first colonist, Duarte Lemos. What you see today mostly dates from the eighteenth century – abandoned in 1928, the chapel was a ruin until restoration work in the 1940s. The simple whitewashed chapel with its rustic, wooden Baroque altar would not be out of place in a Portuguese village, a vivid reminder that the coast of Espírito Santo was one of the first parts of Brazil Europeans settled. Opposite lies the old **Masonic Lodge**, completed in 1913 and a wedge of Neoclassical blue between the concrete.

atedral Metropolitana

raça Dom Luiz Scortegagna • Daily 7am–7pm • Free • 27 3223 0590

)ominating the largely dull, modern concrete buildings on Praça Dom Luiz cortegagna, the vast Neogothic **Catedral Metropolitana** was modelled in part on Cologne Cathedral, though there are also Art Nouveau influences in its lattice-work owers. Work on the cathedral began in 1920 on the site of the city's first church 1550), and was only completed in 1970. Inside, the main attraction is the stained lass, a wonderfully luminous series of works completed from 1933 to 1943 (the image f St Cecilia over the entrance is most famous), and touched off with a more modern lisplay over the altar (installed in 2013).

2

'raça Costa Pereira

The *centro histórico*'s most pleasant square is shaded **Praça Costa Pereira**, a busy edestrian intersection. There are a number of distinguished-looking buildings urrounding the *praça*, the most notable being the **Teatro Carlos Gomes**, a replica of La Scala in Milan, built between 1925 and 1927 when the rebuilding of Vitória was at its eight – the plaza itself was only opened in 1912 and enlarged in 1924.

greja de Nossa Senhora do Rosário

ua do Rosário (off Rua Pereira Pinto) • Tues–Sun 9am–5pm • Free

To reach the whitewashed **Igreja de Nossa Senhora do Rosário** you need to walk up a once-elegant flight of steps, now sprayed with graffiti, up a steep hillside off Rua do Rosário. The church dates back to 1765 when it was built by slaves and free Afro-Brazilians in just two years (Nossa Senhora do Rosário was the apparition of Mary thought to protect slaves), but the elegant facade you see today was mostly constructed in the nineteenth century. Its plain interior houses an impressive Baroque altar, while original ossuaries line the side corridor.

Museu de Arte do Espírito Santo

Av Jerônimo Monteiro 631 • Tues–Fri 9am–6pm, Sat & Sun 10am–5pm • Free • 27 3132 8393

Vitória's **Museu de Arte do Espírito Santo** is housed in another historic gem on the edge of the *centro histórico*, this time the government urban planning office completed in 1925. Exhibits rotate, usually with a contemporary theme – note that the museum can be closed in between installations.

Museu Ferroviário

Estrada de Ferro Vitória a Minas (Rua Vila Isabel), Argolas • Jan Tues–Sun 10am–6pm; Feb–Dec Tues–Fri 8am–5pm, Sat & Sun 10am–6pm • Free • 27 3333 2484, museuvale.com • Buses #516, #559, #572, #573, #574 and #597 all run here

Directly across the *baía* from downtown Vitória is the fascinating **Museu Ferroviário**, housed in a former train station built in 1927. Focusing on the history of the **Vitória-to-**

FIRST FATHER: PADRE ANCHIETA

Padre Anchieta, the first of a series of legendary Jesuit missionaries from Spain and Portugal to Brazil, is most famous for being one of the two founders of São Paulo, building the rough chapel the town formed around in the sixteenth century and giving his name to one of the city's main avenues, the Via Anchieta. He was a stout defender of the rights of indigenous peoples, doing all he could to protect them from the ravages of the Portuguese and pleading their case several times to the Portuguese Crown; he was also the first to compile a grammar and dictionary of the Tupi language. Driven out of São Paulo by enraged Portuguese settlers, he retired to Vitória, died in 1597 and was finally canonized. His body, however, only remained here for some fifteen years; in a story that would confuse Tolstoy with its complexity, Anchieta's bones were broken up and sent to various Brazilian cities to act as holy relics (a fragment is supposed to remain here, and also in the city of Anchieta).

Minas railway, constructed in the early twentieth century to carry iron ore to the coast from the interior, the exhibits include a steam engine and carriages, a model railway and maps, documents, photographs and company memorabilia relating to the 664km line.

The beaches

Come evening and at weekends, old Vitória is pretty well deserted and the action shifts to the middle-class **beach districts**, where all of the best shops, hotels and restaurants are located. All the main city beaches are attractive, with palm trees and promenades in the best Brazilian tradition. At the northern end of the strip in the Jardim da Penha neighbourhood, **Praia de Camburi** is a gorgeous, wide stretch of sand with beach volleyball courts and bars located strategically along the promenade à la Copacabana. It's not good for swimming, however: the beach is overlooked by the port of Tubarão in the distance, where iron ore and bauxite are either smelted or loaded onto supertankers.

Praia da Curva da Jurema and around

At the southern end of the beach strip lies the appealing **Praia da Curva da Jurema** in the Enseada do Sua district, popular for kayaking and sailing but not recommended for swimming because of nearby shipping – backed by posh condos, this is where the rich flaunt themselves on the sands, though the **kioskos** at the end provide relatively cheap snacks and booze. Curva da Jurema is hemmed in by two islands, both elite enclaves of large, modern houses: **Ilha do Frade**, linked by bridge to the mainland with two tiny but attractive beaches (Praia Ilha do Frade and Praia das Castanheiras); and **Ilha do Boi**, now attached to the mainland and also boasting two small strips of sand that are popular with families and good for snorkelling (Praia Grande and Praia da Direita). Just to the north of Frade is **Praia do Canto** in the district of the same name, a pretty beach but facing the local marina. If you want to take a dip, you're better off crossing the bay to Vila Velha (see page 192) or travelling further along the coast.

ARRIVAL AND DEPARTURE — VITÓRIA

By plane Vitória airport (Aeroporto Eurico de Aguiar Salles; ⓣ 27 3235 6300) is situated a couple of kilometres from Camburi beach on Av Fernando Ferrari, some 11km north of the *centro histórico*. Bus #212 (Mon–Sat R$3.20; Sun R$2.80) runs from the airport via Camburi beach and the old centre to the rodoviária (around 1hr). Taxis operate on a well-managed fixed-rate system; line up and tell the despatcher where you want to go; you'll get a receipt telling you how much the fare will be (pay the driver): R$21 to Camburi, R$27 to Praia do Canto and R$37 to the *centro histórico*.

By train Over in the mainland district of Cariacica, the daily train from Belo Horizonte pulls into the Estação Ferroviária Pedro Nolasco (ⓣ 27 3226 4169), 1km west of the rodoviária; it's connected to the city and rodoviária by yellow buses marked "Terminal Itacibá" and by most of the city's orange buses, including those marked "Jardim América" and "Campo Grande". You can buy tickets at the station or online (ⓦ tremdepassageiros.vale.com).

Destinations Belo Horizonte (daily at 6am; 13hr; from R$73 one-way; calling at all stations, including Governador Valadares and Itabira). Trains make the return journey to Vitória at 6.30am.

By bus The city's enormous, modern rodoviária (ⓣ 27 3222 3366) is only 1km from the centre (Av Alexandre Buaiz 350), and all local buses from the stop across the road run into the city; returning from the centre, most buses from Av Jerônimo Monteiro pass the rodoviária and will have it marked as a destination on their route cards. If you're heading straight for the beaches on arrival, any bus that says "Aeroporto", "UFES", "Eurico Sales" or "Via Camburi" will take you to Camburi; for the southern beaches you need "P. da Costa", "Vila Velha" or "Itapoan" – all can be caught at the stops outside the rodoviária or in the centre. Like the airport, taxis at the bus station tend to charge according to a fixed-rate system: it's R$17 into the *centro histórico*.

Destinations Belo Horizonte (6 daily; 8hr); Domingos Martins (13 daily; 1hr); Guarapari (every 30min; 1hr); Linhares (4 daily; 3hr); Rio (hourly; 7hr 30min); Salvador (2 daily; 17hr); Santa Teresa (10 daily; 2hr–2hr 30min); São Paulo (5 daily; 14hr); Venda Nova (hourly; 3hr).

INFORMATION

Tourist information There are tourist information booths ("CAT", for Centro de Atendimento ao Turista) at the rodoviária (Mon–Fri 8am–9pm, Sat 9am–4pm; ⓣ 27 3203 3666); at the airport (daily 7am–8.30pm; ⓣ 27 3235 6350); and kiosk 6 on Camburi beach (daily 9am–5pm); all of which have lists of hotels, brochures and city maps (see also ⓦ vitoria.es.gov.br)

ETTING AROUND

tória is **not pedestrian-friendly**; beyond the *centro histórico* and beach promenades, few people walk anywhere, with rs, taxis and buses the main forms of transportation.

y bus From the *centro histórico* it's easy to catch buses to e beach districts; bus #500 goes over the massive Terceira onte ("third bridge") to Vila Velha. Bus #509 and #508 run l the way down the beaches and across into Vila Velha; om the rodoviária take bus #503. Most buses charge $3.20 Mon–Sat, and R$2.80 on Sun (express or "*seletivo*" uses are R$5.40–6.25).

By taxi Taxi meters start at R$4.44, with most fares across the city or over the bridge to Vila Velha no more than R$28; it's around R$35–45 from the old centre to the airport.

Car rental At the airport: Avis (T 27 3327 2348); Localiza (T 0800 99 2000); Unidas (T 27 3327 0180).

2

ACCOMMODATION

he choice for accommodation is generally between the modern establishments in the **beach suburbs** and the less xpensive, older hotels in the **centre** (which becomes desolate at night). For really cheap places, there's a row of rather rim hotels facing the main entrance of the rodoviária.

★ **Comfort Suítes Vitória** Av Saturnino de Brito 1327, raia do Canto T 27 3183 2500, W atlanticahotels. om.br; map p.187. This ex-Novotel remains extremely vell maintained, with an extensive range of business and eisure facilities (including an excellent pool). The spacious nd comfortable a/c rooms come with cable LCD TV and are ompetitively priced online; reservations highly advised. A free shuttle runs hourly (Mon–Fri 6–11pm) to Shopping Vitória and the bars in the Triângulo das Bermudas district. Popular with small conferences and parties, it tends to be either totally full or nearly empty. R$250

Guanaaní Hostel Rua Coronel Monjardim 49, Centro listórico T 27 3233 4455, W guanaanihostel.com; map .186. Excellent hostel accommodation in a lovely 1920s nansion right on the edge of the historic centre; simple ut clean dorms (including female only; R$45), decent reakfast (shared kitchen) and cheap double rooms with an and cable TV. Dorms R$35, doubles R$100

Hotel Senac Ilha do Boi Rua Bráulio Macedo 417, Ilha do Boi T 27 3345 0111, W hotelilhadoboi.com.br; map p.187. Set amid the secluded, high-end *Ilha do Boi*, the very comfortable and tastefully decorated rooms here offer beautiful sea views. The facilities include a large pool and a good restaurant serving both local and international dishes.

Ibis Budget Vitória Av Nossa Senhora da Penha 1993 T 27 3205 6155, W accorhotels.com; map p.187. The a/c rooms are small but comfortable at this excellent budget hotel, and the service is efficient. It's 500m from Praia do Canto, 3km from the airport and extremely popular; reservations are advised. R$115

★ **Sono Vitória** Rua Alberto Bella Rosa 95, Jardim da Penha T 27 99511 5479, W sonovitoria.com; map p.187. Vitória has slowly developed a hostel scene, and this is the best so far, a short walk from Camburi beach (north of the centre). The a/c dorms (female or mixed) feature stylish cubicle-like "pods" with individual light and power outlets, and there are simple en-suite doubles with cable TV. There are seven spotless modern, shared bathrooms, a swimming pool, free bikes and an on-site Portuguese language school. Dorms R$40, doubles R$120

EATING

Local cuisine, which is pretty good, is based around seafood, and **crab** is a key ingredient for many dishes. No stay in Vitória is complete without trying the *moqueca capixaba*, a distinctive local seafood stew in which the sauce is less spicy and uses more tomatoes than the better-known Bahian variety. Northwest of the *centro histórico*, the **Ilha das Caieiras**, situated near the mangrove forests, is where you'll find the most traditional *moqueca capixaba* restaurants.

Canto da Roça Rua João da Cruz 280, Praia do Canto T 27 3227 8747; map p.187. Offers a typical *mineiro* lunch buffet (R$43–53) in an attractively rustic, open-air setting in the city's "Bermuda Triangle" bar district. Mon–Sat 11am–3pm & 6pm–midnight, Sun 11am–4pm.

Enseada Geraldinho Rua Aleixo Netto 1603, Praia do Canto T 27 3324 6360; map p.187. Geraldo Alves opened his first seafood restaurant in the 1980s, with this branch opening in 2011. His specialities – *moqueca capixaba* (R$45–75), fish stews and fresh sea bass – remain top-notch. Mon–Sat 11am–11pm, Sun 11am–5pm.

★ **Lareira Portuguesa** Av Saturnino de Brito 260 T 27 3345 0329, W lareiraportuguesa.com.br; map p.187. Serves authentic Portuguese dishes (mostly seafood) in a very romantic setting, replete with Portuguese tiling and lush garden. Mains (for two sharing) R$120–180. Mon–Sat 11.30am–3pm & 6.30pm–midnight, Sun 11.30am–4.30pm.

★ **Pirão** Rua Joaquim Lírio 753, Praia do Canto t 27 3227 1165, w piraovitoria.com.br; map p.187. One of the best places for crab and *moqueca capixaba* (R$130–175 for two), the walls are smothered with photos of fans, regulars and Brazilian celebrities (whom you probably won't recognize). Mon–Fri 11am–4pm & 6–11pm, Sat & Sun 11am–5pm.

Verde Perene Escadaria Maria Ortiz 29, Centro t 2 3019 6069; map p.187. Excellent Chinese vegetaria restaurant in the old town, serving wholesome dish such as spinach lasagne, spring rolls, noodles and sus and a popular buffet (around R$42/kg). Mon–Fri 11am 2.30pm, Sat 11.30am–3pm.

DRINKING AND NIGHTLIFE

Vitória's nightlife is concentrated in a couple of areas. The **Triángulo das Bermudas** (Bermuda Triangle) in Praia d Canto (the streets around Rua Joaquim Lírio and Rua João da Cruz) has loads of bars and the area attracts people from a backgrounds. On a stretch of Ave Anísio Fernandes Coelho just west of Camburi beach, near the Universidade Federal d Espírito Santo (UFES), there´s another string of bars (popularly called **"Rua da Lama"** or Mud Street).

Bar Abertura Rua Joaquim Lírio 811, Praia do Canto t 27 3376 1478, w barabertura.com.br; map p.187. Huge bar (part of a mini-chain), with a decent menu of local food and snacks, live music and the usual choice of cold beers and cocktails. Mon & Tues 4pm–1am, Wed 4pm–2am, Thurs 4pm–3am, Fri & Sat 2pm–5am, Sun 2pm–midnight.

Ensaio Botequim Rua Joaquim Lírio 778, Praia do Canto t 27 99904 5360, w ensaiobotequim.com.br; map p.187. Stylish open-front lounge bar and restaurant, which offers a decent *feijoada* on Sundays (1–4pm; R$34.90) and live samba Thurday to Saturday evenings. Cover R$10–15 from 10pm on show nights. Tues–Thu 6pm–12.30am, Fri 6pm–2.30am, Sat 5pm–2.30am Sun 4pm–midnight.

Liver Pub Rua Joaquim Lírio 820, Praia do Canto t 2 99944 1204, w liverpub.com.br; map p.187. Englis rock'n'roll and Beatles-themed pub with a sort of pseud English-style red-brick interior, but lots of fun all th same. It has a menu of international and Brazilian dishe (including fish and chips), live rock bands and DJs. We 8pm–1am, Thurs 9pm–3am, Fri & Sat 10pm–4am, Su 3–10pm.

DIRECTORY

Banks and money HSBC has a branch at Rua Abiail do Amaral Carneiro 41 in Enseada do Sua, but there are Brazilian banks all over the city.

Hospital 24hr healthcare is available at Pronto Socorro do Coração, Av Leitão da Silva 2351, Santa Lúcia (t 27 3327 4833).

Police The tourist police station (open 24hr) is at Rua Joã Carlos de Souza 730, Barro Vermelho.

Post offices Av Jerônimo Monteiro and Av República i the centre, Rua Sampaio 204 at Praia do Canto and in th Shopping Vitória.

Vila Velha

The massive **Terceira Ponte** ("Third Bridge"; cars R$1; no pedestrians) connects Vitória with **VILA VELHA** on the other side of the Baía de Vitória, the state's largest city, with roots that actually go back further than those of its neighbour (1535). Though governed separately, the two cities effectively form a single metropolitan area, with people commuting in both directions, and it's an easy day-trip, with buses running over the bridge from Vitória's beach districts to Vila Velha. Whereas Vitória is the state's administrative centre, Vila Velha is primarily a popular beach resort, with the usual wall of high-rise condos lining attractive **Praia da Costa**, a safe place for swimming. Otherwise the main reason to visit is the spectacularly located **Convento da Penha**, soaring high above both cities.

Convento da Penha

Rua Vasco Coutinho, Prainha • Mon–Sat 5.15am–4.45pm, Sun 4.15am–4.45pm; Sala das Milagres daily 8am–4.45pm • Free • t 27 3329 0420, w conventodapenha.org.br • A taxi from Praia da Curva Jurema in Vitória should be around R$25; otherwise get a bus; #509/#508 runs all the way down the beaches and across into Vila Velha (R$3.20) or from the rodoviária take bus #500; then from downtown Vila Velha walk or get a taxi to the convent

The most memorable sight in the whole Vitória area, the **Convento da Penha** traces its foundation to a simple hermitage founded way back in 1558 by one Father Pedro

Palacios (though the current complex dates to 1650). Perched on a granite outcrop towering over the city, the site is worth visiting not so much for the convent itself – interesting though it is – as for the gasp-inducing panoramic views. It is a major pilgrimage centre and in the week after Easter thousands come to pay homage to the **Virgem da Penha** (a venerated image of Mary originating around 1569 in Portugal), the most devout making the climb up to the convent on their knees.

You can drive or take a taxi to the car park at the top (from where there is another short, steep climb to the chapel), or take one of the two walks up from the lower entrance. The steepest and most direct is the fork off the main road to the left, shortly after the entrance gate, where a cobbled (and extremely uneven) path leads up to the convent. Less direct, but considerably easier and with better views, is the winding Rua Luísa Grinalda – a very pleasant thirty-minute walk. Once at the top, the city is stretched out below you, Vitória to the north framed by the silhouettes of the mountains inland and, to the south, by the golden arcs of Vila Velha's beaches. The chapel's builders thoughtfully included a **viewing platform**, which you reach through a door to the left of the main **sanctuary**, itself a relatively simple space remodelled in 1910, with a marble, wood and gilt altar framing the famous Mary statue (the side corridor displays paintings representing the foundation of the chapel). There's also a *Pietà* by Carlo Crepaz (1961) in the main entrance. On the way up from the car park be sure to visit the **Sala das Milagres**, which houses a collection of photos, *ex votos*, artificial limbs and artefacts from grateful pilgrims. By the car park itself is a small café and a 1950s replica of the first chapel, the **Capela São Francisco.**

Guarapari

The most enticing beaches south of Vitória are around the town of **GUARAPARI**, 54km to the south of the state capital. There are dozens of hotels here – mostly white skyscrapers catering for visitors from Minas Gerais. If you fancy raucous nightlife and holiday-making Brazilian-style, then Guarapari is the place; the beaches around here are among the finest in southern Espírito Santo, with a pleasant backdrop of hills covered in tropical vegetation, and they're extremely popular in the summer. If you need to escape to somewhere more tranquil, a mere 7km to the south of central Guarapari, accessible by a short trail from the fishing village Meaípe, is tiny **Praia dos Padres**, a protected area lapped by a wonderfully green sea. **Meaípe** itself has some excellent restaurants, a long sandy beach, and is also a good place to stay overnight.

ARRIVAL AND DEPARTURE — GUARAPARI

By bus Buses run hourly between Vitória and Guarapari (daily 7.30am–9.30pm; 1hr 15min). Guarapari's bus station is at João Gomes de Jesus 50 in the centre of town, a short walk from the main beach. Buses also run every 30min–1hr from here to points south including Anchieta (40min).

ACCOMMODATION AND EATING

★ **Cantinho do Curuca** Av Santana 96, Meaípe ⓣ 27 3272 2000. The most popular restaurant in the area is especially recommended for its *bolinhos de aipim* and *moqueca capixaba* (from R$100) though everything is good. Mon–Sat 11am–10pm, Sun 11am–9pm.

Pousada Enseada Verde Rua Duarte Matos 27, Meaípe ⓣ 27 3272 1376, ⓦ enseadaverde.com.br. Close to the beach, set on a hillside with views along the coast, this cheap hotel offers basic but comfy rooms and has a pool. Free parking. **R$140**

★ **Violeta Meaípe Hotel** Rua da Enseada 96, Meaípe ⓣ 27 3272 2000, ⓦ hotelvioleta.com. Conveniently attached to the *Curuca* restaurant, this cosy option is a short walk from the beach and popular with families. The rooms feature a clean, contemporary style, with breakfast included. **R$175**

Anchieta

Twenty kilometres south of Guarapari, the town of **ANCHIETA** is one of the oldest settlements in the state. Built on the site of a Tupi village converted by the Jesuits in the 1560s, it was granted town status in 1759 as "Benevente". An important fishing port, Anchieta is one of the few places along this stretch of coast where life isn't focused on tourism, and, as such, the hotels here are mainly grim – visit for the day.

Santuário Nacional Padre Anchieta

Praça da Matriz • Daily 8am–7.30pm; museum daily 8am–5pm • R$5 (church free) • ⓣ 28 3536 2335, ⓦ santuariodeanchieta.com

Of particular interest in Anchieta is the imposing **Santuário Nacional Padre Anchieta**, which dominates the town from a hilltop position on the Praça da Matriz. Built sometime around the late sixteenth century as a Jesuit mission, the complex includes a church, the Igreja Nossa Senhora da Assunção, and the small but well-kept Museu Nacional São José de Anchieta, commemorating the evangelical work among indigenous peoples of the sixteenth-century Jesuit priest **José de Anchieta**, who spent his last days here (see page 189). His cell, where he died in 1597, is preserved, as is, rather gruesomely, a piece of his actual tibia bone.

ARRIVAL AND DEPARTURE — ANCHIETA

By bus Buses run between Guarapari and Anchieta every 30min–1hr (daily 7.30am–9.30pm; 40min), and also to Vitória (2hr 10min). Heading south, the town has 3 daily services to Rio (9.30am, 10pm & 10.30pm; 6–7hr).

Regência

Some 115km north of Vitória via ES-10 lies the village of **REGÊNCIA**, a fishing community at the mouth of the Rio Doce of barely two thousand inhabitants, noted for its **surf** breaks. In summer, the village comes alive with young sun-seekers and surfers from Belo Horizonte and Vitória. In Brazil the village is best known as the home of **Caboclo Bernardo**, the humble fisherman who saved 128 navy sailors from the wrecked naval cruiser *Imperial Marinheiro* in 1887 – a festival celebrates the local hero every June. Outside the rainy season (Oct–Dec) the unpaved roads leading to Regência are always passable, but it's often slow going, with buses stopping frequently.

Centro Ecológico de Regência (Projeto Tamar)

Rua Principal (in the centre of the village) • Tues–Sun 8am–noon & 1–5pm • Free • ⓣ 27 3274 1905, ⓦ projetotamar.org.br

Projeto Tamar's **Centro Ecológico de Regência** monitors a 35km stretch of coast near here where, between October and January, sea turtles of all kinds come to lay their eggs. Tamar's work is charted inside the centre, which also contains a giant humpback whale skeleton and an aquarium of marine life. At the **Reserva Biológica de Comboios** (same hours; free), another Tamar base 7km south of Regência, interns guide you through exhibits explaining the turtles' life cycle and to tanks where you can view mature turtles.

Museu Histórico de Regência

Rua Principal, in front of the football stadium • Mon–Fri 8–11.30am & 1–5pm, Sat & Sun 8.30–11.30am & 1–5pm • Free • ⓣ 27 3377 0011

The village of Regência itself holds little of interest, apart from the small **Museu Histórico de Regência**, which charts local history through old photographs and artefacts. Outside in the grounds is the village landmark, the preserved top section of the **Farol do Rio Doce**, a nineteenth-century lighthouse.

ARRIVAL AND ACCOMMODATION — REGÊNCIA

By bus It's easiest to visit by car; by bus you'll have to travel to Linhares on the main BR-101 highway, and take a slow bus to Regência (3 daily; 1hr 30min).

Pousada Careba Rua da Praia ⓣ 27 9720 6744, ⓔ pousadacareba@gmail.com. There are several simple *pousadas* right on the beach, including this simple option with a couple of restaurants serving simple fish-based meals nearby. R$85

Itaúnas

The alluring village of **ITAÚNAS**, 270km north of Vitória near the Bahia border, lies on the edge of the **Parque Estadual Itaúnas**, best known for its 30m-high sand dunes. Beneath these dunes lies the original town that was engulfed and evacuated in the 1970s after the vegetation surrounding it had been cleared for farmland. It is said that occasionally the **dunes** shift in the wind to uncover the spire of the old church. The beaches are long and – with only low-lying vegetation – exposed, but at the height of the summer are extremely popular with students, drawn by the place's party atmosphere, where *axê* music pounds from the bars until the small hours of the morning. Very different in atmosphere to coastal settlements further south, Itaúnas is said to be where northeastern Brazil begins.

Keep your ears open for **forró** music – which may owe its popularity in Rio and São Paulo to tourists returning from Itaúnas; dances here typically get going around midnight and continue until 10am. The craziest time is July, when the **Festival Nacional de Forró** attracts revellers from all over Brazil. Bring cash with you – there are no banks or ATMs in Itaúnas.

2

Parque Estadual de Itaúnas

Daily 8am–5pm • Free • ☎ 27 3762 5196

Other than simply soaking up the magnificent views from the giant sand dunes, the best way to appreciate the **Parque Estadual de Itaúnas** is to explore some of its well-maintained trails. The easiest is the **Trilha do Tamandaré**, which runs for around 700m from the bridge and park office to the ruins of the Casa do Tamandaré, then another 400m to the beach, while the **Trilha das Dunas** runs across the top of the dunes (beginning at the end of the dirt road beyond the Rio Itaúnas bridge). Hikes are also possible along the beach, 8km north to **Riacho Doce**, a small, isolated creek and a usually deserted beach right on the Bahia state border – there are some simple kiosks serving food on both sides of the border (which are often closed), plus the more dependable *Pousada e Restaurante do Celsao*. Note that at the time of research the creek had been dry for some time, thanks to ongoing drought in the area.

ARRIVAL AND DEPARTURE ITAÚNAS

By bus Buses stop at the main plaza in town, around 1km from the beach, which lies across the Rio Itaúnas bridge. To get here you'll first have to take a bus to Conceição de Barra (27km from Itaúnas), which has three daily connections from Vitória via Viação Águia Branca (6.40am, 11.40am & 4pm; 5hr 10min–5hr 50min; ⓦ aguiabranca.com.br). For Bahia and points north, you'll have to take a frequent bus from Conceição to São Mateus (45min), 56km from Itaúnas, and change there. From Conceição, Viação Mar Aberto buses trundle along the dirt road to Itaúnas three times daily (usually 7am, 12.30pm & 3.30pm; returning 8am, 1.30pm & 4.30pm; 40min), with extra buses in the peak summer periods.

By taxi Taxis charge around R$80 one-way from Conceição, and around R$180 from São Mateus.

ACCOMMODATION

Arte Vida Hospedagem Rua Demerval Leite da Silva 450 ☎ 27 99892 6330. Basic but bargain hostel a short walk from the beach, with shared kitchen, bar and clean, mixed dorms. Until its own website is up and running, reserve a bunk on ⓦ booking.com. Dorms **R$30**

Hospedaria Cosanostra Rua Demerval Leite da Silva (Praça da Igreja) ☎ 27 99627 1138, ⓦ mapadavilaitaunas.com.br/pousada-cosanostra.htm. Popular hotel with excellent value en-suite doubles, with balconies, fans and patio access, plus larger family-size rooms for up to four people (R$160). **R$100**

Pousada Casa da Praia Rua Dercilio F. da Fonseca ☎ 27 3762 5028, ⓦ pousadacasadapraiaitaunas.com.br. No-frills but friendly, and blending in with the environment, this charming inn offers sea views, a/c rooms, TV lounge and a wholesome breakfast (featuring home-made breads and cakes). **R$160**

Pousada dos Corais Rua Maria Ortiz Barcelos 154 ☎ 27 3762 5200, ⓦ pousadadoscorais.com.br. Central option with clean, simple a/c rooms (with flat-screen TVs and solar-heated shower), a tiny outdoor pool, a balcony with hammocks and a hearty breakfast. **R$250**

EATING AND DRINKING

A Casa di Berê Rua Lionório Lisboa Vasconcelos ☎27 99986 1228. Popular Italian bistro, best known for its home-made pasta dishes and the speciality dessert, *sorvete de queijo com goiabada*, Brazilian white-cheese ice cream with guava sauce perfected by owner Berê herself. Daily noon–10pm.

★ **Bar Forró** Rua Ítalo Vasconcelos 98 ☎27 3762 5087, forrodeitaunas.com. Legendary bar with a huge dance floor that is the focus for all *forró*-related merriment during the festival, and usually year-round – otherwise check out *Buraco do Tatu*, down the street at Rua Ítalo Vasconcelos 49. Fri & Sat 10pm–6am (daily during festivals).

Crepe Samba Kone Av Bento Daher ☎27 99952 1195. Part café, part live music venue, with a simple menu of various crêpes (R$21–24) accompanied by an energetic programme of live bossa nova and "sambarock". Cover charge after 10pm. Daily 8pm–4am.

2

Região dos Imigrantes

The coffee-smothered hills and forests of **inland Espírito Santo** offer an easily accessible slice of rural Brazilian life, with the most interesting section dubbed **REGIÃO DOS IMIGRANTES** ("region of immigrants"), for good reason. In the nineteenth century, this largely undeveloped wilderness was colonized by boatloads of hopeful German and Italian peasants who, miraculously, managed to clear sections of forest and create a viable agricultural economy in just a few years. Though the towns they created are typically Brazilian today, subtle signs of their European roots remain – Lutheran churches and vineyards, incongruously squashed between the coffee plantations, for example – and the **scenery** is magnificent. To the far west lies **Pedra Azul**, a grey granite outcrop almost 1000m high that's one of the unsung natural wonders of Brazil.

GETTING AROUND REGIÃO DOS IMIGRANTES

By car You can travel the region fairly easily by bus, though renting a car in Vitória will give you more flexibility – the northern loop, taking in Santa Teresa, Santa Maria and Santa Leopoldina, can be completed in a day, as can the trip out to Pedra Azul, though you'll get more out of it by staying the night in one of the local *pousadas*.

Santa Teresa

Some 90km northwest from central Vitória, **SANTA TERESA** might seem like a typical, bustling Brazilian country town studded by coffee bushes, palms and mango trees, but intriguing remnants of its Italian origins make it a good place to start a tour of inland Espírito Santo. The first Italian colonists arrived here in 1875, and the last shipload of Italian immigrants docked in Vitória in 1925. Today the town is quite large, sprawling along the Rio Timbuí valley for several kilometres, though the compact, historical centre lies at the western end between the rodoviária and pretty **Praça Augusto Ruschi**, full of flowers, trees and fluttering hummingbirds. Walking from the bus station to the square you'll pass the small tourist centre and **Galeria Artesanto** (with cheap bottles of local wine, cachaça and even grappa).

Igreja Matriz

Rua Coronel Bonfim • Mon–Fri & Sun 8am–5pm, Sat 8am–noon • Free • ☎27 3259 1662

The town's Italian-influenced, blue-striped **Igreja Matriz** was completed with roundels and cupola in 1906. The pale blue interior is quite plain, but the names of the first colonists are engraved on a plaque on its outside wall. The street adjacent to the church is lined with old houses built in the 1920s, local bars and decent Italian restaurants.

Casa de Virgílio Lambert

Rua São Lourenço • Wed–Sun 9–11am & 12.30–5pm • R$2 • ☎27 3259 1611

A short walk up Rua São Lourenço from the Igreja Matriz you'll see the surviving two-storey wattle-and-daub houses put up by the first Italian immigrants; oldest of all is the **Casa de Virgílio Lambert**, a farmhouse built around 1876 and now a simple museum.

Museu de Biologia Professor Mello Leitão

Av José Ruschi 4 • Tues–Sun 8am–5pm • Free • ① 27 3259 1182

Santa Teresa is full of flowers, and of hummingbirds feeding off them, and in the early twentieth century they aroused the interest of one of the first generation of Italians to be born here, **Augusto Ruschi**. He turned a childhood fascination into a lifetime of study, becoming a pioneering natural scientist and ecologist decades before it was fashionable, and ultimately founded the **Museu de Biologia Professor Mello Leitão** (named in tribute to a former teacher) in 1949 around his home, now the museum administrative centre (Ruschi lived here from 1937 till his death). Ruschi died in 1986, at the age of 71, after being poisoned by the secretions of a tree frog he collected on one of his many expeditions into the forest.

You won't learn much about Ruschi's remarkable life at the museum, which does display a few old photos in one of its exhibition halls (Portuguese labels only), but which is essentially a small **botanical garden**, replete with rather sad-looking cages of parrots, marmosets, an aviary, a snake house and even a hall of Ruschi's dusty stuffed-bird and animal collection. What makes a trip really worthwhile, however, is the **observação de beija-flores**, a mesmerizing deck of bird feeders swarming with **hummingbirds**, oblivious to the humans watching them. Ruschi specialized in the study of hummingbirds, becoming the world's leading expert in the field and, in the later years of his life, was almost single-handedly responsible for galvanizing the state government into action to protect the exceptional beauty of the interior of Espírito Santo; that so much forest remains is due in no small measure to him.

Cachaça da Mata

Rodovia Santa Teresa, Itarana, Km 5 (Vale de São Lourenço) • Tues–Sun 9am–5pm; call ahead to check • ① 27 3225 1739, ⓦ damata.com.br

Some 5km west of town on the road towards Santa Maria, **Cachaça da Mata** is the producer of the best **cachaça** in Espírito Santo and a fascinating place to visit, its traditional buildings and furnaces redolent of the region's early years. The best time to come here is during the September-to-December harvest, during which you can see every stage of the distilling process, but visitors are welcome to tastings throughout the year.

ARRIVAL AND INFORMATION — SANTA TERESA

By bus The rodoviária (① 27 3259 1300) lies at the western end of town on Rua Ricardo Pasolini, an easy walk from most of the sights; Lírio dos Valles (ⓦ viacaoliriodosvales.com.br) runs the most useful buses.

Destinations Santa Leopoldina (7am, 10.40am, 2.20pm; 1hr 20min); Santa Maria (11am & 6pm; 1hr); Vitória (10–11 daily; 2hr–2hr 30min).

Information For tourist information visit the Prefeitura at Av Jerônimo Verloet 145 (Mon–Fri 8am–6pm; ① 27 3259 2268; ⓦ santateresa.es.gov.br).

Money and exchange A branch of the Banco do Brasil with an ATM is opposite the Prefeitura.

ACCOMMODATION AND EATING

Booking ahead is essential during the **Festa do Imigrante Italiano de Santa Teresa**, an annual celebration of Italian culture and traditions that takes place over a four-day period, coinciding with the last weekend of June. **Italian food** rules in Santa Teresa, and is probably the most obvious sign of its roots. Don't expect Tuscan levels of perfection, obviously, but it's all pretty good.

★ **Bar Elite** Rua Coronel Bonfim Júnior 104 ① 27 9736 8488. This café/bar founded in 1920 opposite the church is hard to beat for ambience, retaining a classic Italian feel with the bar on top of an antique vitrine, ageing photos lining the walls, locals reading the paper and dusty bottles of wines in cabinets. Stick with beer, wine and cachaça – the coffee is served sweet from a flask. Hours tend to be irregular in practice. Daily 9am–8pm.

Café Haus Av José Ruschi 287 ① 27 3259 1329, ⓦ restaurantecafehaus.com.br. Charming little café specializing in gourmet Brazilian coffee and delicious cakes and sweets (you can also buy local products in the shop).

It also offers more substantial German and Italian dishes; think creamy lasagne and amazing flambéed bananas. Thurs & Sun 11am–4pm, Fri & Sat 11am–11pm.

Claid's Biscoitos Av José Ruschi 241 ⊕27 3259 1368, claids.com.br. This local institution produces classic Italian-style *biscotti* worth sampling and taking away – flavours include coconut, chocolate, cashew, almond, pepper, bacon and even champagne. Mon–Sat 9am–6pm.

Hotel Pierazzo Av Getúlio Vargas 115 ⊕27 3259 1233, hotelpierazzo.com.br. This is your only option in town. It's a no-frills ageing hotel with basic but adequate, clean en-suite rooms (with ceiling fan and local TV) and a decent breakfast included. R$130

Piaceri Alla Tavola Rua Colonel Bomfim Júnior 70 ⊕27 3259 2999. The pasta, pizza and other typical Italian dishes here are excellent quality, most produce is sourced locally and mains cost around R$30. The restaurant is housed in an attractive nineteenth-century home. Tues–Sun 11am–3pm & 7–11pm.

Pousada Vita Verde Estrada de Aparecidinha ⊕27 3259 3332, pousadavitaverde.com. This is the most comfortable place to stay, 2km from the town centre, with a converted farmhouse that has two chalets and seven cosy suites set amid beautiful countryside. Fifty percent deposit required in advance. R$240

Santa Maria de Jetibá

The road between Santa Teresa and **SANTA MARIA DE JETIBÁ** (the ES-261) passes through hilly terrain, densely cultivated with coffee bushes, interspersed with pine plantations and, on the steepest of hillsides, patches of Mata Atlântica. Santa Maria is another thriving country town, but this time with Pomeranian (German) roots. Virtually the entire population is descended from mid-nineteenth-century immigrants from Pomerania (now part of Poland) and today remains bound together by a common heritage based on the continued use of the *Pommersch Platt* dialect and membership in the Lutheran Church.

The main commercial centre lies at the southern end of town, along **Avenida Frederico Grulke**, a busy thoroughfare lined with shops, and tiny **Praça Saudável**, with its German-themed kiosks. Nearby, the **Prefuitura** or "Radhaus" is a giant, Hanseatic-looking structure, with the fairly ineffectual tourist office (really a small craft shop) nearby.

Museu da Imigração Pomerana

Rua Dalmácio Espíndula • Tues–Sun 9am–5.30pm • Free

The history of the area's settlement is commemorated by the small **Museu da Imigração Pomerana** near the town hall at the end of Rua Dalmácio Espíndula. Inside is a handful of artefacts chronicling life in the town, with labels in English (and German).

ARRIVAL AND DEPARTURE — SANTA MARIA DE JETIBÁ

By bus Buses run between here and Santa Teresa at 5.10am, 1pm and 3pm (1hr) from along Av Frederico Grulke.

ACCOMMODATION AND EATING

Food is very definitely Brazilian in Santa Maria, though one odd German legacy remains: at the handful of buffet/*churrasco* canteens along Av Frederico Grulke, surprisingly good **sauerkraut** is served (with the usual, bland, local sausages).

Hotel PommerHaus Av Frederico Grulke 455 (above the Banco do Brasil) ⊕27 3263 1718, hotelpomerhaus@limainfo.com.br. This excellent-value hotel is right in the centre, with fairly basic rooms and an easy-to-spot "German" facade. No lift, so be prepared for stairs. R$105

Santa Leopoldina

From Santa Maria it's an incredibly winding 33km to **SANTA LEOPOLDINA** (commonly known as just Leopoldina), through thickly forested hills and gorges (you can also drive straight from Santa Teresa, skipping Santa Maria, but only on a dirt road). Leopoldina is lower down, more tropical and subsequently hotter than its neighbours, and the town is smaller and more sleepy, laid out along one street and the Rio Santa Maria. The *centro histórico* is a small but oddly compelling strip, with a Lutheran church high above and a smattering of 1920s buildings. While the town's German character has faded almost entirely, the outlying parts of the *município* are still mainly inhabited by descendants of Germans, many of whom have retained the language or dialect of earlier generations.

Museu do Colono

Av Presidente Vargas 1501 • Wed–Sun 9am–5pm, holidays 1–5pm (sometimes closes noon–1.30pm) • Free • ⓣ 27 3266 1250

The interesting **Museu do Colono** is housed in a mansion built in 1877 for the Holzmeisters, who were once the leading German family in town. Today the museum spotlights the early decades of German settlement with photographs – including some fascinating ones of the construction of the road to Santa Teresa in 1919 – along with relics and documents.

ARRIVAL AND INFORMATION — SANTA LEOPOLDINA

By bus The bus drops you at one end of the main street, Rua do Comércio (aka Av Presidente Vargas); Lírio dos Valles (ⓦ viacaoliriodosvales.com.br) runs the most useful buses.

Destinations Santa Teresa (6.50am, noon & 3.30pm; 1hr 20min); Vitória (8.20am, noon & 3.30pm; 1hr 10min).

Domingos Martins and around

The oldest and the most German of the inland towns is **DOMINGOS MARTINS**, 42km west of Vitória on the north side of the Belo Horizonte highway (BR-202) – as soon as you turn off the main road you are greeted by the obligatory "Wilkommen" sign. The town's name was changed from Santa Isabel in 1921 in honour of Brazilian freedom fighter Domingos José Martins. Though it's a modern, typical Brazil country town these days, its Pomeranian roots are very much in evidence, through a sprinkling of triangular wooden houses modelled after alpine chalets, well-maintained German *Strasse* name tiles on every street and the odd bit of German kitsch along the main drag, **Avenida Presidente Vargas**. Halfway along lies **Praça Arthur Gerhardt**, the immaculately manicured main square with a **colonists' monument**, and ringed by faux Bavarian *Hofs* (even the public toilets) and the genuinely Hanseatic tower of the **Igreja Luterana**, dating from 1887 and said to have been the first tower permitted on a Protestant place of worship in Brazil (the church dates from 1866). Running parallel to Vargas, pedestrianized **Rua João Baptista Wernersbach** is lined with small shops and restaurants.

Almost completely surrounded by steep hills, Domingos Martins is high enough to be bracingly fresh by day (542m) and distinctly cold at night – if you stay the night, your *pousada* will fill you in on all the **hiking trails** and **waterfalls** in the area.

Casa da Cultura (Museu de Historia)

Av Presidente Vargas 531 • Tues–Fri 8–11.30am & 1–5pm, Sat & Sun 10am–4pm • R$1 • ⓣ 27 3268 2550

The most impressive historic building in Domingos Martins is the **Casa da Cultura**, housed in the 1915 courthouse on the otherwise humdrum main street. Upstairs the tiny **Museu da Historia** acts as the local community museum, a storehouse of old German documents, obsolete Austro-Hungarian *kronen* and assorted bric-a-brac from old shoes and pipes to antique cameras and a German clock from 1870, though the most fascinating items are the black-and-white photos of the old town and its original settlers. You can watch a ten-minute video on the town (in English) downstairs.

ARRIVAL AND INFORMATION — DOMINGOS MARTINS AND AROUND

By bus Get off the bus at the first stop in the town, rather than continuing to the rodoviária on Rua Bernadino Monteiro. Buses shuttle between here and Vitória 8–10 times daily (1hr). For Belo Horizonte you'll have to get to the main highway and flag a bus down.

Information The Casa da Cultura doubles as an information centre (ⓦ www.domingosmartins.es.gov.br).

ACCOMMODATION AND EATING

★**Caminho do Imigrante** Rua João Baptista Wernersbach 155 (also known as Rua de Lazer) ⓣ27 3268 1137. One of the nicer, sit-down restaurants on this popular strip, with live music on Saturday nights and Sunday lunch (usually accordion players), and traditional home-made *mineira* (and Italian) food cooked over a wood stove. Mains R$19–50. Mon–Fri 10.30am–2.30pm, Sat 10.30am–4.30pm & 7pm–midnight, Sun 10.30am–4pm.

Fritz Frida Av Presidente Vargas 782 ⓣ27 3268 1808. Restaurant and bar with a wonderfully kitsch alpine facade, right opposite the main plaza, and a menu of all the usual German favourites, fondues and pizzas washed down with jugs of Brahma *chopp* (craft beers R$8–15). Mains R$60–120. Mon & Wed–Sat 10am–11pm, Sun 11am–11pm.

Hotel Pousada Solar da Serra Rua Pedro Gerhardt 191 ⓣ27 3268 2080, ⓔpousadasolardaserra@hotmail.com. By far the best option in the centre of town (though if you have a car, you can opt for one of the many *fazendas* in the countryside nearby). The small but comfy rooms here come with TV, breakfast buffet and either a/c or fan. Wi-fi (free) tends to work near reception only. R$120

Pousada e Restaurante Delícias da Tilápia Estrada do Chapeu ⓣ27 9983 3006, ⓦdeliciasdatilapia.com.br. Rustic restaurant and hotel on the Huver family farm (third-generation Germans), 5km northwest of town. The restaurant serves *tilapia* (farmed on site, from R$42) all sorts of ways and the chalets offer cosy accommodation (which includes breakfast and broth in the evening). Mon–Thurs 8am–4pm, Fri & Sat 8am–9pm, Sun 8am–5pm. R$275

Pedra Azul

Parque Estadual da Pedra Azul: Rota do Lagrato (Rodovia Angelo Girardi) Km 2 • Trails open Dec–Feb daily 8am–3.30pm; March–Nov usually open Tues–Sun, call ahead to confirm (tours can be scheduled from 9am to 1.30pm only) • Entry free, tours with guide R$10 • Call ⓣ27 3248 1156 (Mon–Fri 8am–5pm), ⓦpedraazul.com.br

Some 45km west of Domingos Martins the Belo Horizonte Highway (BR-262) passes the most remarkable sight in Espírito Santo, a towering, bare granite mountain shaped like a thumb (with a lizard shape, on its side), and almost 1000m high – the **PEDRA AZUL**, or "blue stone". Its peak is actually 1822m above sea level, the other eight hundred accounted for by the hill country from which it sprouts. It's like an enormous version of the Sugar Loaf in Rio, except no vegetation grows on its bare surface, which rears up from thick forest and looks so smooth that from a distance it appears more like glass than stone. During the day sunlight does strange things to it – it really does look blue in shadow – but the time to see it is at either dawn or sunset, when it turns all kinds of colours in a spectacular natural show.

Pedra Azul forms the centrepiece of a state park, the **Parque Estadual da Pedra Azul**; the park is clearly signposted on BR-262 at Km 88, where a narrow road ("Rota do Lagarto", aka ES-10) starts at *Pousada Peterle* (see page 201) and snakes into the hills for around 2.5km to the actual park entrance. Here you'll find a small shop where you can leave your car; a path leads from here for 800m to a small **visitors' centre** (at 1250m) with exhibits on local fauna and flora. Officially you are supposed to hike the trails from here with a **guide**, and these must be **pre-booked** at least 24 hours in advance (usually in Portuguese only); check ahead, as trails close after heavy rain (in the summer).

The two most popular trails are the easy **Trilha da Pedra Azul** (1.9km round-trip) to the base and viewpoints along the way, and the harder **Trilha das Piscinas Naturais** (2.5km round-trip), which takes you up to a series of nine, crystal-clear freshwater pools, 97m up the slopes via rope walk (scaling the peak itself is strictly forbidden). You can swim in the pools, but it's icy cold.

ARRIVAL AND DEPARTURE — PEDRA AZUL

By bus Travelling here by bus is a hassle but possible; you can take frequent Aguia Branca buses (17 daily; 2hr; ⓦaguiabranca.com.br) from Vitória to Belo Horizonte and ask to get off at *Pousada Peterle* (BR-262 Km 88); you'll have to walk the 2.5km from here. All buses to Belo Horizonte will pass here, but express services may not want to stop – check in advance.

ACCOMMODATION AND EATING

★**Casa da Bica** BR-262 Km 69.5, Alto Santa Maria ⓣ27 3288 4064, ⓦcasadabica.com. Great restaurant on the main highway, 20km east of the park, with an exceptional buffet ($50/kg) of local and mountain specialities (beef, sausages, mash, pumpkin, beans, hash) served in a rustic setting opposite a waterfall and old-fashioned water wheel. There's also a huge dessert selection. Daily 7am–6pm.

Pousada Aargau ES-164 Km 7, São Paulo do Aracê ⓣ27 3248 2175, ⓦpousadaaargau.com.br. On the continuation of the park access road, ES-164, some 6km beyond Pedra Azul, this simple, clean and friendly option is located in some of the most beautiful countryside in the area. Owned and run by the son of Swiss immigrants, the *pousada* also offers an enormous *café colonial*, available every day. R$180

Pousada Peterle BR-262 Km 88 ⓣ27 3248 1243, ⓦpousadapeterle.com.br. Near the access road for the park (ES-164), this rustic-looking hotel consists of several modern chalets, all with superb views, and an Italian buffet-style restaurant. Daily 11am–3.30pm. R$240

Bahia

WATERFALL IN THE BAHIAN SERTÃO

Bahia

With over 1000km of coconut-fringed beaches and the most agreeable climate in the region – hot and sunny, but not as blistering as elsewhere –Bahia ("bai-ee-a") has long been one of the country's most popular destinations for foreign visitors. Constituting over a third of Northeast Brazil, it sits to the south of the region's other states but stands apart, primarily because of the strength of its Afro-Brazilian culture. This is especially true in the capital Salvador, where the legacy of slavery has influenced everything from music and capoeira to dialect, festivals, candomblé and the local cuisine.

At the state's heart are the **Chapada Diamantina Mountains**, offering breathtaking trekking and climbing opportunities, while a string of inland colonial towns, including **Cachoeira**, lies within striking distance of Salvador. Further south lies **Ilhéus**, hometown of writer Jorge Amado, and the thriving beach resort of **Porto Seguro**, whose early settlement pre-dates even Salvador's. All along the coast are tiny, off-the-beaten-path villages and towns with spectacular beaches and a languid, laidback lifestyle. Beyond the coastline, the Bahian *sertão* is massive, a desert-like land that supports some fascinating towns such as the ex-mining base of **Lençóis**.

Exploring the state is easy enough by **bus**, though you'll have a lot more freedom renting a **car**, especially when it comes to exploring the coast. Enclaves such as Sítio do Conde and Mangue Seco north of Salvador, and Barra Grande and Caraíva to the south offer the prospect of tranquil swathes of sand and simple village life.

Salvador

High above the enormous bay of Todos os Santos (All Saints), **SALVADOR** has an electric feel from the moment you arrive. This is the great cultural and historical centre of Brazil, where Afro-Brazilian heritage is strongest and where capoeira, candomblé and *samba de roda* were created. The *centro histórico* is a magical place, a melange of narrow cobbled streets, peeling purple walls, grand Baroque churches, kids kicking footballs, rastas, locals sipping bottled beer on plastic chairs, the wafting aroma of herbs and the almost constant beating of drums, especially as the sun sets. Beyond the old town Salvador is a vast, sprawling city, with a vibrant beach life, modern skyscrapers and plenty of *favelas*. The divide between the rich and poor is as big here as anywhere else in Brazil, but security has improved a lot in recent years.

The **centro histórico** is the traditional heart of Salvador, but in the last century the city also expanded into the still elegant areas of **Vitória**, **Garcia**, **Graça**, **Barris** and **Canela**, to

MORRO DE SÃO PAULO

Highlights

❶ **Capoeira** Watch nimble displays of this Afro-Brazilian martial art at an organized capoeira school. See page 213

❷ **Pelourinho** The vibrant backstreets of the Pelourinho offer Salvador's best live music and the most beautiful architecture in Brazil. See page 213

❸ **Candomblé celebrations** The dance rituals of this religious cult can be memorable if you're lucky enough to catch one. See pages 216 and 230

❹ **Cachoeira** One of the most beautiful colonial towns in Bahia lies in the lush Recôncavo plantation zone. See page 228

❺ **Morro de São Paulo** Bahia's party centre is also home to some jaw-dropping stretches of sand. See page 235

❻ **Ilha de Boipeba** Soak up the quiet on the stunning beach at Bahia's best – and least commercialized – offshore island, where there are just a few *pousadas* and absolutely no road traffic. See page 238

❼ **Parque Nacional da Chapada Diamantina** There's plenty of diverse terrain to keep hikers happy in this huge national park. See page 246

HIGHLIGHTS ARE MARKED ON THE MAP ON PAGE 206

the south, and down to the suburb of **Barra**, the headland at the mouth of the bay. From Barra, a broken coastline of coves and beaches, large and small, is linked by the twisting **Avenida Oceânica**, which runs along the shore for 22km through the other main beach areas, **Ondina**, **Rio Vermelho**, **Pituba** and **Itapuã** (near the airport). Inland, the district of **Caminho das Árvores**, a forest of contemporary skyscrapers clustered around the vast **Salvador Shopping** mall, is fast becoming the new business centre. This "new downtown" area is a long way from anything of interest, though all the best business hotels are there.

Brief history

Salvador was officially founded in 1549 by Portuguese conquistador **Tomé de Sousa**, who chose the city for its inaccessible perch 70m above sea level. It was the scene of a great battle in 1624, when the Dutch destroyed the Portuguese fleet in the bay and stormed and captured the town, only to be forced out again within a year by a joint Spanish and Portuguese force. For the first 300 years of its existence, Salvador was the most important port and city in the South Atlantic – Rio only replaced it as capital in 1763.

Salvador was also Brazil's main slave port, and the survivors of the brutal journey from the Portuguese Gold Coast and Angola were immediately packed off to city

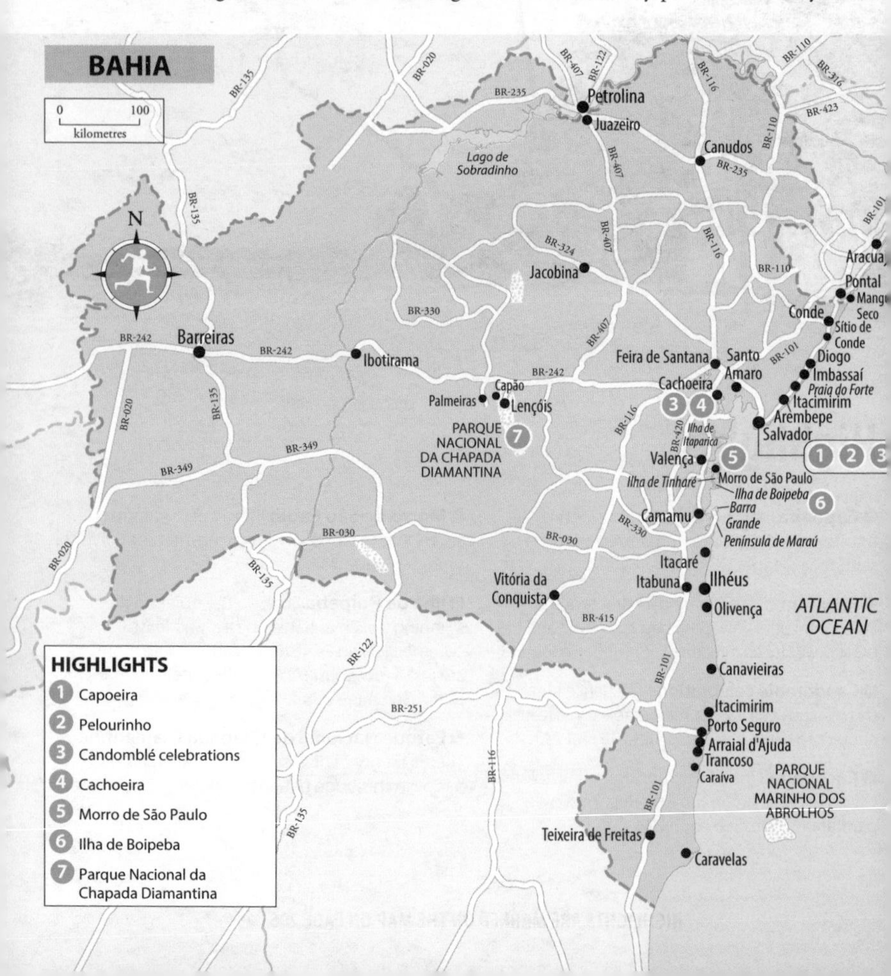

PERSONAL SAFETY IN SALVADOR

Salvador (especially the *centro histórico*) has more reported **robberies** and **muggings** of tourists than anywhere else in Bahia, and possibly Brazil, and the main safety advice for travelling in Brazil should be adhered to (see page 46). However, trouble is much easier to avoid than the statistics suggest. The vast majority of tourists who get mugged go exploring along pretty, but deserted, narrow streets. However enticing this might seem, never wander off the main drags or down ill-lit side streets in the day or at night, and don't use the **Elevador Lacerda** (see page 208) after early evening. Again, though it seems tempting (because it's so close), never walk up and down the winding roads that connect the Cidade Alta and the Cidade Baixa. Be careful using **city buses**, especially on Sundays when there are few people around, and avoid wandering the backstreets of Barra at night.

If you stick to these rules you should have no problems: the main tourist area around the **Pelourinho** is heavily policed and busy until quite late at night, and is therefore relatively safe. Needless to say, leave expensive jewellery, watches and electronics in the hotel while touring the old city, and if you are mugged, do not resist.

construction gangs or the plantations of the **Recôncavo**; today, their descendants make up the bulk of the population. Much of the plantation wealth of the Recôncavo was used to adorn the city with imposing public buildings, ornate squares and, above all, churches. In the 1800s the region survived the decline of the sugar trade by diversifying into tobacco and spices – especially peppers and cloves. Though the city has effectively been in elegant decline since the nineteenth century – largely bypassed by industrialization – today it's Brazil's fourth-largest city, a major port and oil-refining centre with a population close to four million and a booming tourist industry.

Cidade Alta

Salvador's **centro histórico** is built around the craggy, 70m-high bluff that dominates the eastern side of the bay, and is split into upper and lower sections. **Cidade Alta** (or simply "Centro") is strung along its top, linked to the less interesting **Cidade Baixa** (the old commercial centre, aka "Comércio") by precipitous streets and the towering Art Deco lift-shaft of the **Elevador Lacerda**. Cidade Alta is the cultural centre of the city,

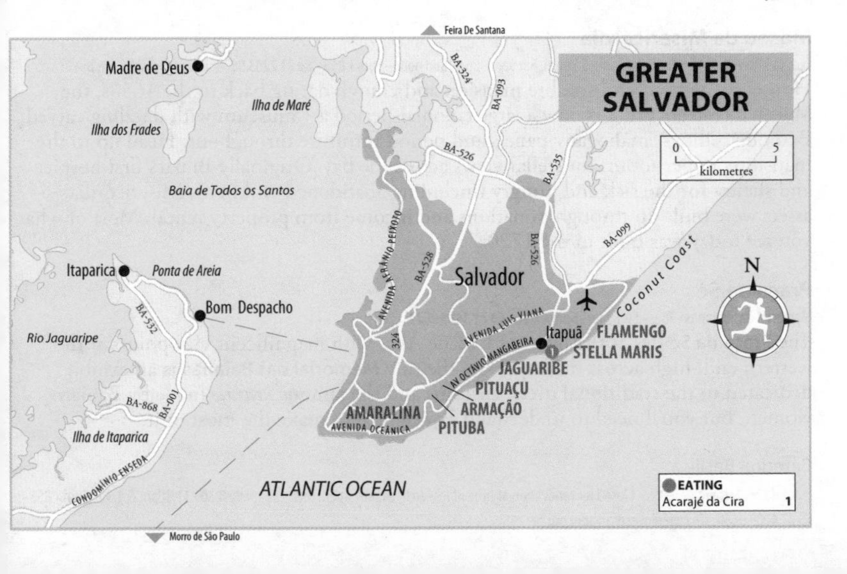

GOING UP AND DOWN FROM THE OLD TOWN

The best way to zip between the Cidade Alta and the Cidade Baixa (for boat tours and the Mercado) is via the 73.5m-tall **Elevador Lacerda** (24hr; R$0.15) on the **Praça Municipal**, though it is best avoided late at night. Simply pay at the turnstiles and line up for the next car (every few minutes). The elevator was designed by its namesake Antônio Francisco de Lacerda and dates back to 1873, though it was given its current Art Deco makeover in 1930 and the equipment has been replaced several times.

Further along the cliff, the **Plano Inclinado Gonçalves** (daily 6am–10pm; R$0.15), a funicular railway dating back to 1874, links Praça Ramos de Queiroz (off Praça da Sé) with Rua Francisco Gonçalves in Cidade Baixa.

and the section known as the **Pelourinho** is the groovy old district with colourful and hilly winding streets, its most vibrant and beguiling neighbourhood.

Palácio do Rio Branco

Praça Municipal • Mon–Fri 9am–5pm, Sat & Sun 9am–1pm • Free • T 71 3316 6814

The best spot to begin a walking tour of the city is at the **Praça Municipal**, the square dominated by the impressive **Palácio do Rio Branco**, the old governor's palace which was in use until 1979. Burnt down and rebuilt during the Dutch wars, the building features regal plaster eagles added by nineteenth-century restorers, who turned a plain colonial mansion into an imposing palace in 1919. The fine interior is a blend of Rococo plasterwork, polished wooden floors and painted walls and ceilings. The exhibit inside, the **Memorial dos Governadores**, houses pieces from the colonial era and portraits of former governors.

Memorial da Câmara de Municipal

Praça Municipal 3 • Mon–Fri 8am–noon & 2–6pm • Free • T 71 3320 0308

On the east side of Praça Municipal lies the **Memorial da Câmara Municipal**, the old seventeenth-century city hall (the current, characterless, 1980s Prefeitura Municipal is just opposite on the plaza), graced by a series of elegant yet solid arches and now home to a small, well-presented museum. Exhibits chronicle the history of the city from its founding by Tomé de Sousa (whose statue stands in the plaza outside), including the state legislature, and the history of the building, which dates back to 1660.

Museu da Misericórdia

Rua da Misericórdia 6 • Tues–Fri 8am–5.30pm, Sat 9am–5pm, Sun noon–5pm • R$6 • T 71 2203 9835, W santacasaba.org.br

Housed in a grand and sombre mansion and church dating back to the 1650s, the **Museu da Misericórdia** is now a large colonial-period art museum with dazzling carved Baroque ceilings, mahogany panels and period furniture throughout. Head up to the mansion's upper rooms for stellar views across the bay. Originally Brazil's first hospice and shelter for the sick and hungry (including abandoned children), Misericórdia's assets were built up through donations and income from property rental. Most of what you see today was built in the 1720s.

Praça da Sé

Memorial das Baianas • Tues–Sun 9am–6pm • Free • T 71 3488 0622

The **Praça da Sé** lies at the heart of Cidade Alta, with magnificent viewpoints at the western end, high across the bay. Here the tiny **Memorial das Baianas** is an exhibit dedicated to the traditional dress, customs and the famous *acarajé* made by Bahian women, but you'll need to understand Portuguese to make the most of it.

Catedral Basílica

Praça da Sé, Terreiro de Jesus • Closed for renovation at time of research, usually open: Mon–Sat daily 8.30–11.30am & 1.30–5pm • R$3 • T 71 4009 6666, W arquidiocesesalvador.org.br

At the end of the Praça da Sé, facing the adjoining square known as the **Terreiro de Jesus**, is the **Catedral Basílica.** The core of the structure was completed in 1672 and it was once the chapel of the largest Jesuit seminary outside Rome. Its Mannerist interior is one of the most beautiful in the city – particularly the Portuguese tiling and stunning panelled ceiling of carved and gilded wood, which gives the church a light, airy feel that's an effective antidote to the overwrought Rococo altar and side chapels.

To the left of the altar is the tomb of **Mem de Sá**, third viceroy of Brazil from 1556 to 1570, and the most energetic and effective of all Brazil's colonial governors. It was he who supervised the first phase of building in Salvador, in the process destroying the Caeté people.

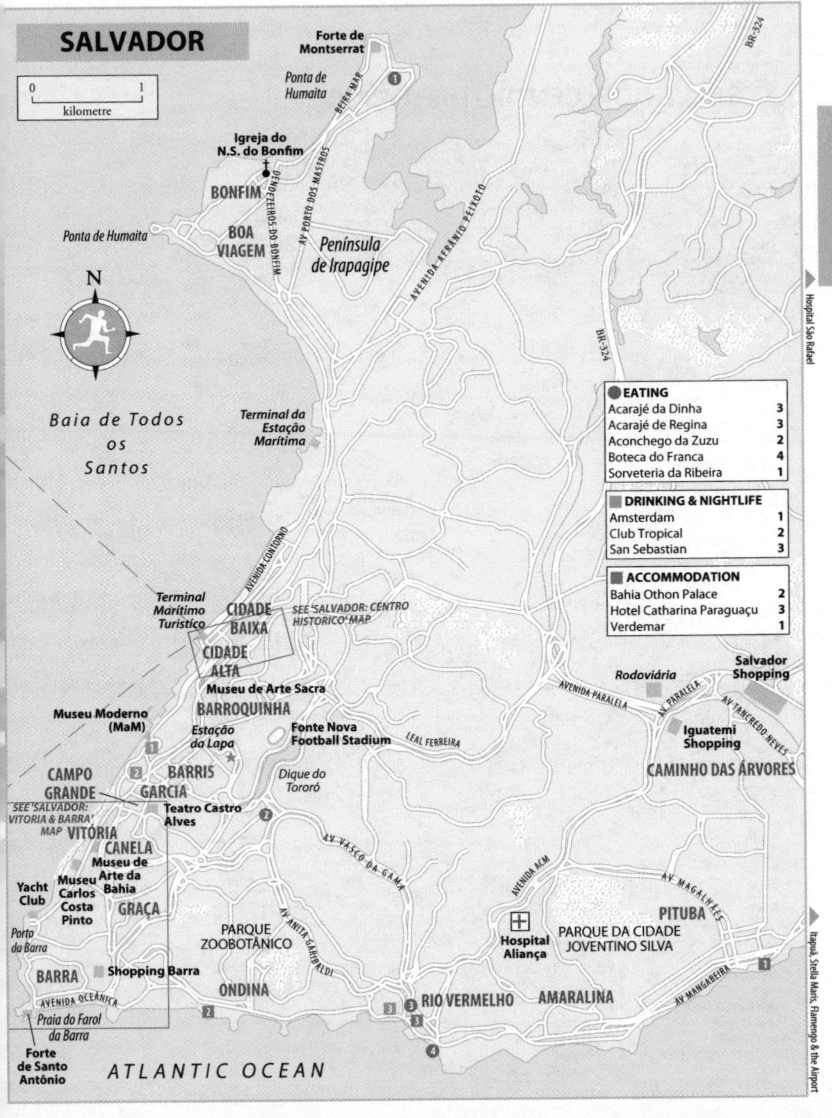

Museu Afro-Brasileiro

Terreiro de Jesus • Mon–Fri 9am–5pm • R$6 • ☎ 71 3283 5540, ⓦ mafro.ceao.ufba.br

Next to the cathedral stands one of the best museums in the city, the **Museu Afro-Brasileiro**, contained within a large nineteenth-century building that used to be the university's medical faculty (and is still part of the Universidade Federal da Bahia). The main building houses three collections, one on each storey. Most labelling is Portuguese only, so grab a written English guide at the entrance.

The ground floor

The museum's largest and best collection is on the **ground floor**, recording and celebrating the African contribution to Brazilian culture. Four rooms are dedicated

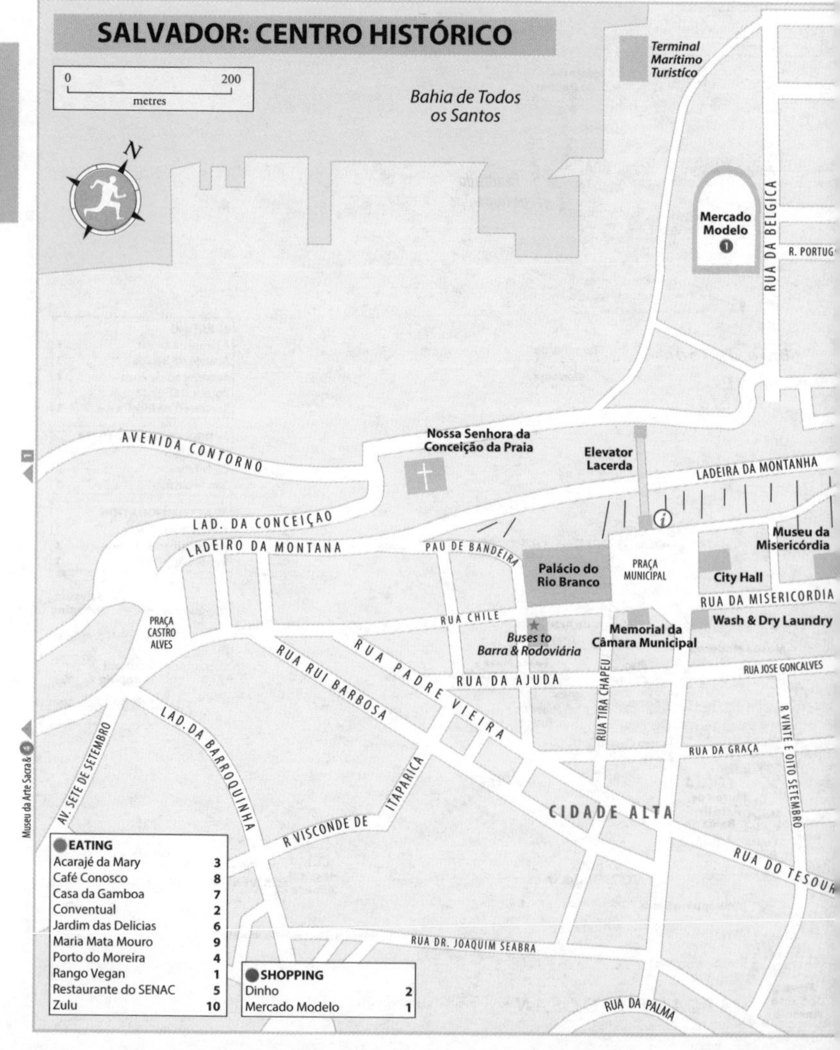

to different aspects of black culture – popular religion, capoeira, weaving, music and carnaval – and everything, for once, is very well laid out. The section on capoeira, the balletic martial art the city's slaves developed (see page 213), is fascinating, supported by photos and old newspaper clippings.

There are other highlights, too: the gallery of large photographs of candomblé leaders (some dating from the nineteenth century), most in full regalia and exuding pride and authority, and a special room dedicated to the famous **carved wood panels** by Carybé, Bahia's most famous artist, in the exhibition room past the photo gallery. Argentine by birth, Carybé came to Salvador in 1950 to find inspiration in the city and its culture. The carved panels in the museum, imaginatively decorated with scrap metal, represent the gods and goddesses of candomblé.

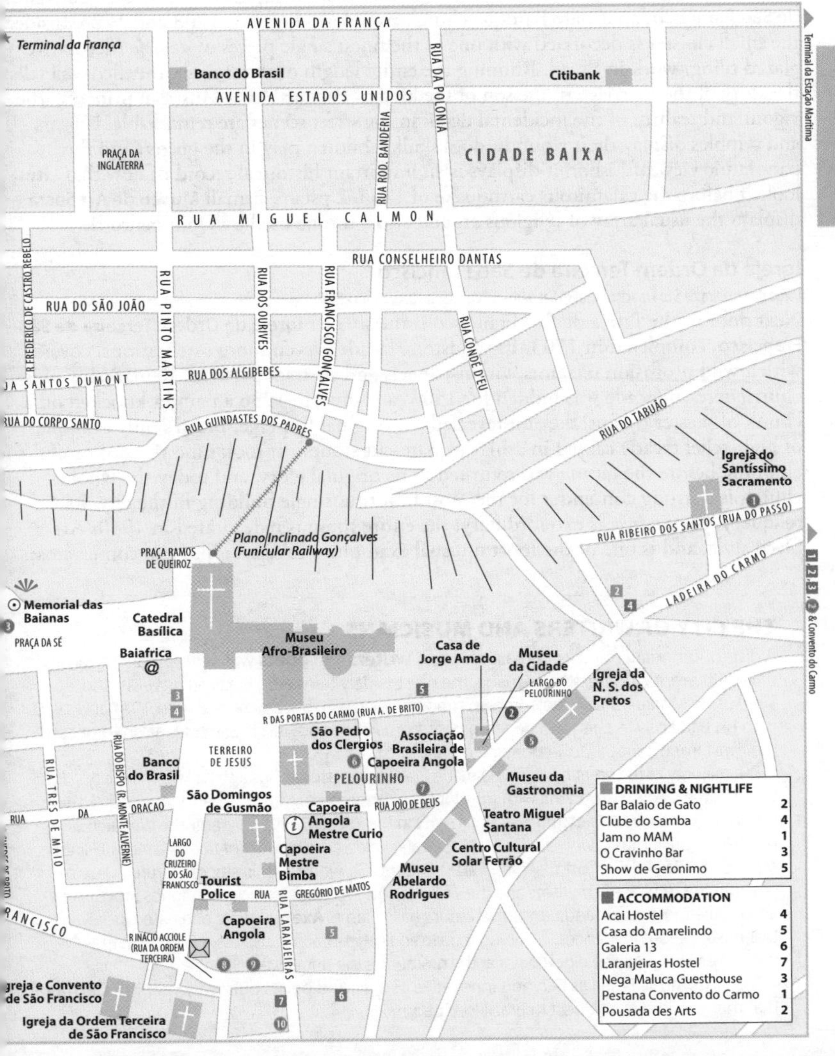

Museu Arqueológico e Etnológico

The first floor houses a rather dull exhibition on the university's faculty of medicine, dominated by busts and dusty bookcases. Better is the **basement**, a section known as the **Museu Arqueológico e Etnológico**. Largely given over to fossils and artefacts from ancient burial sites, it also incorporates tribal costume, basketry and rock art, as well as the only surviving part of the original Jesuit college, a section of the cellars in the arched brickwork at the far end. A diagram at the entrance to the museum shows how enormous the college was, extending all the way from what is now the Praça da Sé to Largo do Pelourinho.

Igreja e Convento de São Francisco

Largo do Cruzeiro de São Francisco • Daily 9am–6.30pm • R$5 • ⓣ 71 3322 6430

Dominating the eastern end of tranquil Largo do Cruzeiro de São Francisco (an extension of Terreiro de Jesus) is the superb, carved stone facade of the **Igreja e Convento de São Francisco**, an ornate Baroque church completed between 1708 and 1723. Inside, the small cloister is decorated with one of the finest single pieces of *azulejo* (decorative glazed tiling) work in Brazil. Running the entire length of the cloister, the tiled **wall** tells the story of the marriage of the son of the king of Portugal to an Austrian princess. The vigour and realism of the incidental detail in the street scenes are remarkable: beggars and cripples display their wounds, dogs skulk, children play in the gutter; and the panoramic view of Lisbon it displays is an important historical record of how that city looked before the calamitous earthquake of 1755. Upstairs a small **Museu de Art Sacra** displays the usual array of religious art and also a throne used by Dom Pedro II.

3

Igreja da Ordem Terceira de São Francisco

Largo do Cruzeiro de São Francisco • Tues–Sat 9am–6.30pm, Sun 10am–5pm • R$5

Next door to the Igreja de São Francisco is the smaller **Igreja da Ordem Terceira de São Francisco**, completed in 1703. Its sandstone facade is even more ostentatious, covered with a wild profusion of saints, virgins, angels and abstract patterns. Remarkably, this churrigueresco facade was hidden for 150 years, until in 1936 a painter knocked off a chunk of plaster by mistake and revealed the original frontage, Brazil's only example of high-relief facade carved in ashlar (square-cut stones). It took nine years of careful chipping before the facade was returned to its original glory, and today the whole church is a strong contender for the most beautiful single building in the city. Its **reliquary**, or *ossuário*, is extraordinary; the entire room is redecorated in 1940s Art Deco style, and is one of the most unusual examples you're ever likely to come across.

THE CITY OF WRITERS AND MUSICIANS

A disproportionate number of Brazil's leading **writers** and **poets** were either born in Salvador or lived there, including Jorge Amado, the most widely translated Brazilian novelist, and Vinícius de Morães, Brazil's best-known modern poet, who lived here between 1974 and 1980 with his Bahian wife. Gregório de Matos was born in Salvador in 1636 and went on to become the most important Baroque poet in colonial Brazil.

The majority of the great names who made Brazilian **music** famous also hail from the city – João Gilberto, the leading exponent, with Tom Jobim, of bossa nova; Astrud Gilberto, whose quavering version of *The Girl from Ipanema* was a global hit in the 1960s; Dorival Caymmi, the patriarch of Brazilian popular music, who died in 2008; Caetano Veloso, the founder of *tropicalismo*; the singers Maria Bethânia and Gal Costa; and MPB artist Gilberto Gil, who was Minister of Culture in Lula's government. Timbalada rhythms and the world-renowned black musician Carlinhos Brown are among the most recent additions to Salvador's hall of fame. **Axé** is a genre originated in Salvador that mixes various influences, including reggae and calypso, and is also associated with the Candomblé religion. The biggest star at the moment is the singer Ivete Sangalo.

The city's music is still as rich and innovative as ever, and bursts out every year in a **Carnaval** that many regard as the best in Brazil (see page 226).

CAPOEIRA

Capoeira began in Angola as a ritual fight to gain the nuptial rights of women when they reached puberty; since then it has evolved into a graceful semi-balletic art form somewhere between fighting and dancing. It did so because African slaves were denied the right to practise their ritual fighting, and so disguised or changed it into the singing and dancing form seen today. Displays of capoeira – often accompanied by the characteristic rhythmic twang of the **berimbau** – usually take the form of a pair of dancers/fighters leaping and whirling in stylized "combat".

The *capoeiristas* normally create a **roda**, a circle of spectators including drummers, *berimbaus*, singing and clapping. The basic method of moving around the *roda* is the *ginga*, a standing, stepping motion that includes the *role* (rolling) and *au* (cartwheeling) movements, respectively. The players then attack each other and defend themselves using these basic methods, along with a range of kicks such as the spinning *armada*. To avoid the kicks, players fall into various stances like the *queda de tres*, a crouching position with one arm raised to defend the head. Only the feet, hands and head of the players should touch the floor during the game.

There are regular displays – largely for the benefit of tourists but interesting nevertheless – on Terreiro de Jesus and near the entrances to the Mercado Modelo in Cidade Baixa, where contributions from onlookers are expected. You'll find the best capoeira, however, in the **academias de capoeira**, organized schools with classes that anyone can watch, free of charge (though donations are suggested). The oldest and most famous school, the Associação de Capoeira Mestre Bimba, named after the man who popularized capoeira in Salvador in the 1920s, is still the best. Saturday afternoon is the best time to visit a school.

CAPOEIRA SCHOOLS

Associação Brasileira de Capoeira Angola Rua Gregório de Matos 38 ☎71 9266 7881, Ⓦabca.portalcapoeira.com. Runs biweekly classes (call to confirm times).

Associação de Capoeira Mestre Bimba Rua das Laranjeiras 1 (also known as Rua Francisco Muniz Barreto), Pelourinho ☎71 3322 0639, Ⓦcapoeiramestrebimba.com.br. Named after legendary pioneer of "Capoeira Regional", Mestre Bimba (1899–1974). Visitors welcome Mon–Fri 10am–noon & 4–9pm, Sat 10am–noon; classes Tues–Fri 7.15pm & 8.15pm.

Capoeira Angola Irmões Gêmeos e Mestre Curió Rua Gregório de Matos 9 (upstairs), Pelourinho ☎71 3321 0081, Ⓔmestrecurio@yahoo.com.br. Established by the great Mestre Curió in 1982; Curió was a student of legendary Mestre Pastinha (1889–1981), spiritual godfather of "Capoeira Angola". Call for times.

Pelourinho

If you head down the narrow Rua Alfredo de Brito leading from **Terreiro de Jesus** and emerge onto the steep, cobbled **Largo do Pelourinho** you'll see one of the most romantic sights in Brazil, much as it was during the eighteenth century. The area of Cidade Alta around the square is known simply as the **Pelourinho**, or just Pelô (named after the whipping post that once stood in the plaza), famed for its gorgeous architecture, shops, music, dining and nightlife.

Igreja de Nossa Senhora do Rosário dos Pretos

Largo do Pelourinho • Mon–Sat 8am–noon & 1–5pm, Sun 9.30am mass only • R$3 • ☎71 3241 5781

Lined with solid colonial mansions, the Largo do Pelourinho is dominated by the oriental-looking towers of the **Igreja de Nossa Senhora do Rosário dos Pretos**, built by and for slaves over many decades in the 1700s and still with a largely black congregation.

Casa de Jorge Amado

Largo do Pelourinho • Mon–Fri 10am–6pm, Sat 10am–4pm • R$5 (free on Wed) • ☎71 3321 0070, Ⓦjorgeamado.org.br

At the top of the Largo do Pelourinho, the **Casa de Jorge Amado** is a museum dedicated to the life and work of the hugely popular Brazilian novelist, though there are also travelling displays with a literary theme. Amado was born in Itabuna in the south of Bahia, but he attended high school in Salvador and spent much of his later life here, dying in the city in 2001. Among the permanent exhibits are panels representing his books, a biographical timeline and personal effects, with some captions in English.

3

Museu da Cidade

Largo do Pelourinho 3 • Mon–Fri 10am–5pm; closed for renovation at time of research • R$2; free on Thurs • T 71 3321 1967

Housed in an attractive Pelourinho mansion next to the Casa de Jorge Amado, the **Museu da Cidade** offers similarly jaw-dropping views over the old town. Displays include paintings and sculpture by young city artists – some startlingly good and some pretty dire – while luxuriously dressed dummies show off Carnaval costumes from years gone by. There are models of candomblé deities and an exhibit featuring the personal belongings of the greatest Bahian poet, **Castro Alves**, with some fascinating photographs from the beginning of the twentieth century.

Centro Cultural Solar Ferrão

Rua Gregório de Matos 45 • Tues–Sat 1–5pm • R$1 • T 71 3116 6743, W www.ipac.ba.gov.br

Housed in a beguiling seventeenth-century mansion, the **Centro Cultural Solar Ferrão** comprises four exceptional art collections. The **Museu Abelardo Rodrigues** – named after its Pernambuco-based founder – houses a fascinating ensemble of Catholic art from the sixteenth century onwards, while other galleries are dedicated to African art (**Coleção Claudio Masella de Arte Africana**), the folk art and masks of Bahia and the Northeast (**Coleção de Arte Popular**) and Brazilian musical instruments (**Musicais Tradicionais Emília Biancardi**).

Ladeira do Carmo

From Largo do Pelourinho, a steep climb north up Ladeira do Carmo rewards you with two more exceptional examples of colonial architecture: on the left is the **Convento da Ordem Primeira do Carmo**, now the *Pestana Convento do Carmo* hotel (see page 222), open to non-guests, and on the right the **Igreja da Ordem Terceira de Nossa Senhora do Carmo**, which dates from 1828 – both are built around large and beautiful cloisters, with a fine view across the old city at the back.

Museu da Arte Sacra

Rua do Sodré 276 • Mon–Fri 11.30am–5.30pm • R$10 • T 71 3283 5600, W mas.ufba.br

Despite the concentration of riches in Cidade Alta, you'll have to leave the old city proper to find the **Museu da Arte Sacra**, one of the finest museums of Catholic art in Brazil. It's housed in the former Convento de Santa Teresa d'Ávila, a magnificent building built between 1667 and 1676 with much of its original furniture and fittings still intact, and with galleries on three floors surrounding a cloister. The chapel on the ground floor is lavishly decorated with elaborate, gilded carvings, and it leads into a maze of small rooms stuffed with a remarkably rich collection of colonial art, primarily dating from the sixteenth to eighteenth centuries. The collection of Baroque work by **José Teófilo de Jesus** and **José Joaquim da Rocha**, founders of the Bahian school of painting, is especially good.

Museu de Arte Moderno (MaM)

Av do Contorno s/n • Tues–Sun 1–6pm • Free • T 71 3117 6139, W jamnomam.com.br/mam • Walk from the bottom of the Lacerda elevator or bus #1051 south from here (though doesn't stop very near)

Located in the whitewashed Solar do Unhão, a beautiful sixteenth-century building just north of the marina is the city's contemporary art museum, **Museu de Art Moderno (MaM)**. There are four galleries in total showing exhibits that change every month or two, largely focusing on local artists but occasionally featuring national and international works. Be sure to stay to see the gorgeous sunset over Bahia Todos Santos, and even take a dip in the water at the adjacent beach. On Saturday evenings, the museum hosts jazz performances (7–9.30pm; R$8).

CANDOMBLÉ

Candomblé, a popular Afro-Brazilian blend of Christian and African religious belief, permeates Salvador. Its followers often dress in white and worship together in ecstatic dance rituals accompanied by lots of drumming and singing, or otherwise communicate with and make offerings to the Orixás spirits – personal protectors, guides and go-betweens for people and their creator-god Olorum.

A candomblé cult house, or *terreiro*, is headed by a *mãe do santo* (literally "holy mother") or *pai do santo* ("holy father"'), who directs the operations of dozens of novices and initiates. The usual objective is to persuade the **spirits** to descend into the bodies of worshippers, which is achieved by **sacrifices** (animals are killed outside public view and usually during the day), offerings of food and drink, and above all by drumming, dancing and the invocations of the *mãe* or *pai do santo*. In a central dance area, devotees dance for hours to induce the trance that allows the spirits to enter them. Each deity has its own songs, animals, colours, qualities, powers and holy day; there are different types of candomblé, as well as other related Afro-Brazilian religions like *umbanda*.

If you go to a *terreiro*, there are certain **rules** you must observe. A *terreiro* should be respected and treated like the church it is. Clothes should be smart and modest: long trousers and a clean shirt for men, a non-revealing blouse and trousers or long skirt for women. The dancing area is a sacred space and no matter how infectious you find the rhythms you should do no more than stand or sit around its edges. Don't take photographs without asking permission from the *mãe* or *pai do santo* first, or you will give offence. You may find people coming round offering **drinks** from jars, or items of **food**: it's impolite to refuse, but watch what everyone else does first – sometimes food is not for eating but for throwing over dancers, and the story of the gringos who ate the popcorn intended as a sacred offering is guaranteed to bring a smile to any Brazilian face.

To make contact with candomblé practitioners and attend a session, either book through a tour operator or approach a *terreiro* directly. It's important to call and check times, dates and terms of access or ask the tourist information office in the Pelourinho (see page 221) for help in booking. Below is a list of *terreiros* (none is especially close to the *centro histórico*, so take a taxi and arrange for it to wait):

Axé Opo Afonja Rua Direita de São Goncalo do Retiro 557 ☎ 71 3384 5229, 🌐 bit.ly/AxeOpoAfonja.

Terreiro do Oxum Rua Helio Machado 108, Bairro Bocado Rio ☎ 71 3232 1460.

Terreiro de Oxossi Rua 6 de Janeiro 29 (white house, by entrance to Escolinha Rosa Vermelho), Bairro Sete de Abril ☎ 71 3393 1168.

Cidade Baixa

Cidade Baixa, the part of the city at the foot of the bluff in the *centro histórico*, takes in the docks, the old harbour – dominated by the circular sixteenth-century **Forte de São Marcelo** (sadly off limits) offshore – **the ferry terminals** and the main city **market**. Once the commercial heart of the city, "Comércio", as the neighbourhood is also known, is now the most neglected part of the city. Restoration of some of the older buildings has begun, but most of the neighbourhood is shabby, uninteresting and best avoided.

Mercado Modelo

Praça Visconde de Cayrú 250 • Mon–Sat 9am–7pm, Sun 9am–2pm • Free • ☎ 71 4102 9414

There is one essential stop in Cidade Baixa: the **Mercado Modelo**. This is a huge, covered arts and crafts market, always crowded with Bahians as well as tourists and with the best selection of *artesanato* in the city. Not everything is cheap, so it helps to have the confidence to haggle. Some of the nicest souvenirs are the painted statues of candomblé deities – look for signs saying *artigos religiosos*. The Neoclassical building itself is a joy, a spacious nineteenth-century cathedral to commerce; constructed around 1861 as the city customs house, the building became the market in 1971, after the original burnt down. There is always something going on here, with displays of capoeira common (and donations expected). There is an **information office** sometimes staffed to the left of the front entrance, while upstairs you will find a couple of good **restaurants** and at the back several cheap **bars**.

Igreja do Nosso Senhor do Bonfim

Largo do Bonfim, Bonfim • Mon 9am–5pm, Tues–Thurs 7am–5pm, Fri 6am–6.30pm, Sat 7am–5pm; Masses throughout the day • Free • ⊕ 71 3316 2196 • Take the buses marked "Bonfim" or "Ribeira" from the Estação da Lapa or from the bottom of the Lacerda elevator

The Igreja do Bonfim, as everyone calls the **Igreja do Nosso Senhor do Bonfim**, sits on a hill on the Itapagipe Peninsula, overlooking the bay 9km north of the *centro histórico*. The church looks relatively ordinary, but it attracts thousands of devotees from all over Brazil. Though the tradition came from Portugal, Nosso Senhor do Bonfim ("Our Lord of the Good End", represented by the crucified Jesus in the moment of his death) is also associated with Oxalá, father of the Orishas in the **candomblé** religion (see page 216), explaining its special status in Bahia.

The church – completed in 1754 – is not, by any means, the oldest or most beautiful in the city but it's easily the most interesting. The force of popular devotion is obvious from the moment you arrive. The large square in front of the church is lined with stalls catering to the hundreds of pilgrims who visit every day, and you'll be besieged by small children selling **fitas** (multicoloured ribbons to tie around your wrist for luck and to hang in the church when you make your requests) – it's ungracious to enter without a few. It's always at least half-full of all kinds of people worshipping with almost hypnotic fervour – from middle-class matrons to uniformed military officers to peasants from the *sertão* and women from the *favelas*. Inside, note the Neoclassical *retábulo* (altarpiece) and the painted wooden ceiling, completed around 1820 – there are also paintings by José Teófilo de Jesus in the sacristy and side rooms.

Museu dos Ex-Votos do Senhor do Bonfim

Igreja do Nosso Senhor do Bonfim • Tues–Sat 9am–noon & 2–5pm • Free

For a clearer idea of what Bonfim church means to the people of Bahia, go to the right of the nave where steps lead up to the **Museu dos Ex-Votos do Senhor do Bonfim**. The incredibly crowded antechamber where you buy your ticket gives you an idea of what to expect: it's lined to the roof with thousands of small photographs of supplicants, with notes pinned to the wall requesting intervention or giving thanks for benefits received. Every spare centimetre is covered with a forest of ribbons, one for each request, some almost rotted away with age. Hanging from the roof are dozens of body parts – limbs, heads, even organs such as hearts and lungs – made of wood or plastic (from anxious patients asking for protection before an operation), or silver (from

BONFIM FESTIVALS

Salvador's two main popular festivals of the year, besides Carnaval (see page 226), take place either in or near the Igreja do Nosso Senhor do Bonfim (see page 217). On New Year's Day the **Procissão no Mar**, the "Sea Procession", sees statues of the seafarers' protectors, Nosso Senhor dos Navegantes and Nossa Senhora da Conceição, carried in a decorated nineteenth-century boat across the bay from the old harbour to the church of Boa Viagem where thousands wait to greet them. Nossa Senhora da Conçeicão is then taken back by land in another procession to her church near the foot of the Lacerda elevator. The celebrations around both churches go on for hours, with thousands drinking and dancing the night away.

On the second Thursday of January comes the **Lavagem do Bonfim**, "the washing of Bonfim", second only to Carnaval in scale. Hundreds of *baianas*, women in the traditional all-white costume of turban, lace blouse and a billowing long skirt, gather in front of the Igreja de Nossa Senhora da Conceição, and a procession follows them along the 12km seafront to the Igreja do Bonfim, with tens of thousands more lining the route. At the church, everyone sets to scrubbing the square spotless, cleaning the church and decorating the exterior with flowers and strings of coloured lights. That evening, and every evening until Sunday, raucous celebrations go on into the wee hours, and the square is crowded with people. The focus switches on the Monday to **Ribeira**, the headland beyond Bonfim, for a completely secular preview of Carnaval.

ICE CREAM BREAK

★ **Sorveteria da Ribeira** Praça General Osório 87 in Ribeira ☎ 71 3316 5451, Ⓦ sorveteriadaribeira.com.br; map p.209. Salvador's most famous ice-cream shop lies on the waterfront a short taxi ride from Igreja da Bonfim. Founded by Italian immigrant Mario Tosta, the *Sorveteria da Ribeira* has been knocking out sweet icy treats since 1931, with flavours ranging from coconut and chocolate to tapioca and exotic Brazilian fruits such as *açai* and *biribiri* (scoops from R$7). Daily 9am–10pm.

relieved patients giving thanks after successful surgery). Some people blessed by a particularly spectacular escape pay tribute by leaving a pictorial record of the miracle: photos of smashed cars the driver walked away from, or crude but vivid paintings of fires, boat sinkings and electrocutions.

Upstairs in the museum proper is the oldest material and recent offerings judged worthy of special display. The more valuable *ex votos* are displayed here in ranks of cases, classified according to the part of the body: silver heads and limbs you might expect, even silver hearts, lungs, ears, eyes and noses, but the serried ranks of silver kidneys, spleens, livers and intestines are striking. There are also football shirts (the city's two big teams always make a visit at the start of the season).

Vitória and Barra

Some 4km south of the *centro histórico*, Avenida 7 de Setembro runs along the bay through the leafy, middle-class suburb of **Vitória**, home to several intriguing museums and where the coast is blocked off by posh condos with their own lifts down to the water. The road ends at **Barra**, a lively neighbourhood of mid-range hotels, restaurants and bars popular with Brazilian tourists, and a couple of beaches: the **Praia Porto da Barra**, always heaving with sunbathers and swimmers, and the quieter **Praia do Farol da Barra**, popular with surfers. Barra also boasts three Portuguese-era forts, though only one, **Forte de Santo Antônio**, is open to the public.

Museu de Arte da Bahia

Av 7 de Setembro 2340, Vitória • Tues–Fri 1–7pm, Sat & Sun 2–7pm • Free • ☎ 71 3117 6902 • Local buses and the *executivo* service to Barra via Vitória leave from the Praça da Sé

The **Museu de Art da Bahia** is housed in a gorgeous Neoclassical confection, the Palácio da Vitória, built in 1925 for the state education and health department, but incorporating many features from older buildings. The small galleries here contain a focused collection of Bahian landscapes and decorative arts from the eighteenth and nineteenth centuries, including furniture, beds, Chinese porcelain, glassware and Baroque paintings from the Bahian School, including some of the best works by **José Teófilo de Jesus**.

Museu Carlos Costa Pinto

Av 7 de Setembro 2490, Vitória • Mon & Wed–Sat 2.30–7pm • R$10 • ☎ 71 3336 6081, Ⓦ museucostapinto.com.br/capa.asp • Local buses and the executive bus to Vitória leave from the Praca da Sé

Set in a modern "US-colonial style" mansion completed in 1958, amid tranquil gardens, the **Museu Carlos Costa Pinto** contains a precious and eclectic collection of fine and decorative arts. The collection was put together by businessman Carlos de Aguiar Costa Pinto (1885–1946) and donated to the city by his wife – the building was to have been the family home, but it was never lived in. The museum features rooms dedicated to antique crystal from the Baccarat glassworks in France, ornate tortoiseshell fans, Japanese lacquerware, ivory carvings from Goa, dazzling silverware and the spectacular gold jewellery and silver amulets traditionally worn by creole women. There's also an intriguing modern painting exhibit to counter all that religious art elsewhere, with the vaguely Impressionistic work of local boy Prisciliano Silva, and the naturalistic art of Alberto Valença.

Museu Náutico da Bahia

Largo do Farol da Barra, Av Oceânica, Barra • Tues–Sun 9am–6pm; daily Jan & July 9am–6pm • R$15 • 71 3264 3296, museunauticodabahia.org.br • Local buses and the *executivo* service to Barra leave from the Praça da Sé

The **Museu Náutico da Bahia** sits within the picturesque **Forte de Santo Antônio** on the windy Barra point, where the Atlantic Ocean becomes the bay of Todos os Santos. It houses a collection of seafaring instruments, maps, model boats, art and a small amount of written historical information (all labelled in English). Founded in 1534 as a wattle-and-daub construction, this was the first European fort on the Brazilian coast, meant to defend the newly founded settlement and access to the bay (the current fortifications date from 1696 to 1702). Most people come for the views from the terrace above the museum; it's a popular place to have a cocktail as the sun sets. The 1890, 22m lighthouse (**Torre do Farol**) that sprouts above the fort is usually off limits, though there are sometimes tours.

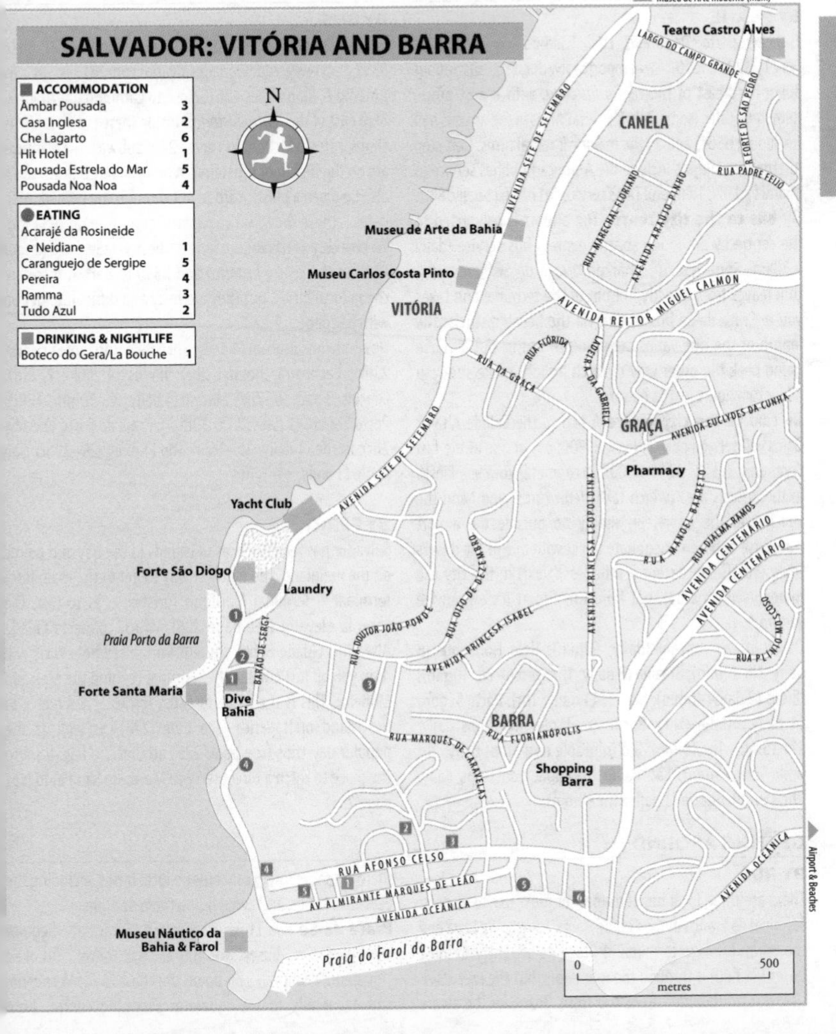

The beaches

East of Barra there are several kilometres of much cleaner, less crowded **beaches** all the way to the **Coconut Coast** (see page 231). The initial few bays in Ondina and Rio Vermelho contain fairly small, unappealing strips of sand, and the first place worth stopping is the boardwalk at **Amaralina** (though packed at weekends), 7km from Barra, and the long, wide stretch of beach backed by restaurants and condos 4km further on at **Armação** (though the water is not clean enough to swim here). The beaches at **Pituaçu** (Corsario) and **Patamares** are a little wilder and emptier, while **Jaguaribe** (18km from Barra) is another popular strip. **Itapuã**, 21km east of Barra, is the last of the main city beaches, but is past its best, and you should keep going another 3–5km to the most enticing sands at **Stella Maris** and **Flamengo** (45min by taxi from the *centro histórico*), both featuring hotels, kiosks selling booze and hordes of beautiful people in high season.

ARRIVAL AND DEPARTURE — SALVADOR

BY PLANE

The Aeroporto Deputado Luis Eduardo do Magalhães (☎71 3204 1010, Ⓦaeroportosalvador.net) sits about 30km northeast of the *centro histórico*, with a post office, numerous cafés (some 24hr), several ATMs in the arrivals hall (including HSBC) and all the major car rental firms. Non-stop international flights include the American Airlines service to Miami (1 daily; 10hr) and TAP's service to Lisbon (1 daily; 8hr).

By bus to the city centre The airport is connected to the centre by an hourly shuttle express bus service (daily 7.30am–8pm; R$6.50), marked "Praça da Sé/Aeroporto", that leaves from directly in front of the terminal and takes you to Praça da Sé bus station via the beach districts. The length of the ride varies according to traffic, but if you're going back the other way to catch a flight make sure you allow two hours just to be safe.

By taxi to the city centre A taxi to the Cidade Alta or Barra will set you back at least R$100; pay at one of the Taxi Coometas (☎71 3244 4500, Ⓦcoometas.com.br) kiosks in the arrivals area (which take credit cards) and hand the voucher to the driver; or, simply go outside the airport concourse doors and negotiate direct with one of the drivers (they will usually accept a little less). Taxis in the city use meters (see page 33), but from the airport it's a fixed fee system.

Destinations Aracaju (daily; 50min); Belo Horizonte (6 daily; 1hr 40min); Brasília (7 daily; 1hr 50min–2hr 10min); Ilhéus (3 daily; 40min); Maceió (1 daily; 1hr); Porto Seguro (4 daily; 50min–1hr); Recife (multiple non-stops daily; 1hr 15min–1hr 30min); Rio (multiple non-stops daily; 2hr 5min–2hr 35min); São Paulo (multiple non-stops daily; 2hr 35min); Vitória (3 daily; 1hr 40min).

BY BUS

Salvador's well-organized, large rodoviária (☎71 3616 8357, Ⓦwww.rodoviariadesalvador.com.br) is at Av. Antônio C. Magalhães 4362, close to Caminho das Árvores 8km east of the *centro histórico*. Inside there is a post office, shops, cafés, a McDonald's and a 24hr Subway. Ticket offices are on the first floor (upstairs). When you buy a ticket you'll also be given a plastic card to get through the embarkation gates – these show you've paid the departure tax (R$1.40).

To the city centre From here it's best to take a taxi (about R$40 to the *centro histórico* and R$50 to Barra); there are cheap local buses, but they are busy and difficult to get on with baggage.

Destinations Aracaju (4 daily; 5hr); Belo Horizonte (1 daily; 23hr); Cachoeira (hourly; 2hr); Ilhéus (4 daily; 8–9hr); Lençóis (3 daily; 6–7hr); Maceió (4 daily; 9hr 30min–12hr); Porto Seguro (1 daily; 11hr 30min); Praia do Forte (2 daily; 2hr); Recife (1 daily; 12–16hr); Rio (1 daily; 28–30hr); São Paulo (1 daily; 33–35hr)

BY FERRY

Salvador has ferry services to islands in the bay and points on the mainland. The quickest way to get to the main ferry terminal – Terminal Maritimo Turístico – is to take the Lacerda elevator (see page 208), which connects Cidade Alta with Cidade Baixa, though from elsewhere taxis will drop you off just outside the terminal (behind the Mercado Modelo). This is the place to catch ferries – *lanchas* – to the island of Itaparica (see page 228), as well as the popular day-trips (see page 229) around the bay. It's also the place to catch a direct ferry to Morro de São Paulo (see page 235).

GETTING AROUND

BY BUS

There are three local bus terminals of most use to visitors: Terminal da França in the Cidade Baixa, Estação da Lapa and the *centro histórico* terminal at Praça da Sé. Entry to most buses (R$3.60) is through the rear doors, but the *executivos* (R$5.30) are boarded from the front. However, be aware there are some safety concerns on local buses, including the executive buses, and avoid riding them at night.

Praça da Sé Rua Chile (near Praça Municipal). Regular and *executivo* buses to Barra; the latter (marked "Iguatemi") continues on down the coast to Rio Vermelho, and eventually to the Iguatemi shopping centre, from

THE SALVADOR BUS

An easy (and safe) way to tour the city is to take the **Salvador Bus** (☎ 71 3356 6425, 🌐 salvadorbus.com.br), an open-topped double-decker tourist service that makes a loop four times a day (Mon–Sat) around the main attractions: tickets start at R$60 for one day (one loop is 4hr, but you can hop-on, hop-off). Buses run from Rio Vermelho along the coast, past Barra up to the Praça Municipal and Mercado Modelo before taking in the Bonfim church and eventually ending up at the Salvador Shopping mall. Check the website for the latest times.

where you can easily walk back across to the *rodoviária*; this is the fastest way to reach the *rodoviária* by public transport, though still count on at least 45min in transit. The "Aeroporto" service, meanwhile, follows the same route until Rio Vermelho, before continuing along past Pituba to Itapuã, and on to the airport – cutting journey times to any of the beach areas to at least half that of a regular city bus.

Estação da Lapa Av Vale do Tororó, Barris. Well laid-out, with destinations clearly labelled. To reach the centre, any bus with "Sé", "C. Grande" or "Lapa" on the route card will do.

Terminal da França Avenida da França (next to the ferry terminal). Services include #12–14 to Lapa, #342 to the rodoviária plus numerous to Bonfim.

BY TAXI

Taxis are plentiful, although all the beach areas except Barra are a long ride from the centre. Meters start at R$4.80 and will quickly top R$50 for rides across the city.

Taxi companies Radio Taxi Comtas (☎ 71 3377 6311); Chame Táxi (☎ 71 3241 2266, 🌐 chametaxisalvador.com.br); Teletáxi (☎ 71 3341 9988, 🌐 teletaxisalvador.com.br).

INFORMATION AND ACTIVITIES

Tourist information The tourist office at the Lacerda Elevator on Praça Municipal (Mon 9am–6pm, Sat 9am–2pm; ☎ 71 3321 3127, 🌐 bahia.com.br) has helpful staff (some speak English). There are also information desks at the airport (daily 7.30am–11pm; ☎ 71 3204 1244), in the Pelourinho at Rua das Laranjeiras 2 (daily 8.30am–6pm; ☎ 71 3321 2133) and at the rodoviária (daily 8.30am–6pm; ☎ 71 3450 3871). An additional source of information is the tourist hotline, "Disque Bahia Turismo (24hr; ☎ 71 3103 3103).

Diving and scuba Dive Bahia Porta da Barra, Av Sete de Setembro 3809, on the seafront (☎ 71 3264 3820, 🌐 divebahia.com.br), offers dive trips (including the Sacramento shipwreck) in the bay (R$340, includes full equipment and guide), and Discovery Scuba trips for beginners (R$200–370).

Travel and tour companies Privé Tur, Rua Manuel Andrade 55, Sala 3, Pituba (☎ 71 3205 1400, 🌐 privetur.com.br), organizes city tours, beach trips and schooner cruises. Tours Bahia, Rua das Laranjeiras 05 sala 1, Pelourinho (☎ 71 3320 3280, 🌐 toursbahia.com.br), offers a range of good-quality services, covering city tours, airline tickets, transfers and money exchange.

ACCOMMODATION

Salvador is the second most popular tourist destination in Brazil and correspondingly full of hotels. Unless you want be near the beaches, the best area to head for is **Cidade Alta**, not least because of the spectacular view across the island-studded bay. The wealthy suburb of **Barra** has by far the closest of the beaches to the centre, and plenty of cafés and nightspots, though the best resorts lie strung out along 25km of coast east of here.

CENTRO HISTÓRICO

★ **Acai Hostel** Rua do Passo 7, San Antonio ☎ 71 3241 1039, 🌐 acaihostel.com; map p.210. Located just down from the Pelourinho and leading up into the San Antonio neighbourhood, this fun hostel offers pod beds, which are a nice change from standard dorm bunks. They offer a daily caipirinha or shot, but no breakfast. There's also a lively bar next door. Dorms R$30

Casa do Amarelindo Rua das Portas do Carmo 6, Pelourinho ☎ 71 3266 8550, 🌐 casadoamarelindo.com; map p.210. Step into a little oasis in the heart of the Pelourinho, with terracotta floors, tropical plants and sculptures of *orixas* (gods) dotted around the tranquil reception area. It's worth the splurge for the lovely rooms, which have comfy beds and flat-screen TVs, as well as DVD and CD players. There's a small rooftop pool, and a panoramic terrace from which you can soak up the views of the Baía de Todos os Santos. R$640

Galeria 13 Rua da Ordem Terceira (aka Rua Inácio Accioli) 23, Pelourinho ☎ 71 3266 5609, 🌐 hostelgaleria13.com; map p.210. An interesting backpacker pad where English is spoken. Great breakfast buffet served until midday, plus luggage store. Have an afternoon dip in the pool or unwind in the dimly lit Moroccan chill-out room. Free amazing happy hour caipirinhas. Dormitories and en-suite doubles have a/c. Guests get a ten percent discount at *Galeria 13*'s restaurant, *Zulu*, which serves traditional cuisine with vegetarian options. Dorms R$50, doubles R$160

★ **Laranjeiras Hostel** Rua da Ordem Terceira (aka Rua Inácio Accioli) 13 ☎ 71 3321 1366, 🌐 laranjeirashostel.

com.br; map p.210. This lively hostel in the heart of the historic centre has good security, relaxing hammocks, and long thin dorms with high top bunks. The crêperie in the lobby and mezzanine chill-out area are great for mingling. Dorms R$55, doubles R$140

Nega Maluca Guesthouse Rua dos Marchantes 15 71 3242 9249, negamaluca.com; map p.210. This Israeli-owned hostel has windy, narrow corridors and dorms with deposit boxes for valuables, as well as sockets and lamps above each bed. There's a rooftop terrace with hammocks overlooking the upper part of Salvador, as well as a chill-out area at the back. Dorms R$45, doubles R$110

Pestana Convento do Carmo Rua do Carmo 1, Pelourinho 71 3327 8400, pestana.com; map p.210. The place to splurge in the old town, inside the grandest of convents, this hotel is very exclusive and centrally located. The rooms are very comfortable with all modern conveniences, but the highlights are probably the pool, bar and romantic restaurant in the courtyard and cloisters (open to non-guests). R$400

3

Pousada des Arts Rua Direita de Santo Antônio 90 71 3012 5964, pousadadesarts.com.br; map p.210. Set in a stunning four-storey colonial mansion dating from 1740, this smart *pousada* has palatial rooms, some with excellent views of the Santo Antônio Church. *Berimbaus* (percussion instruments) decorate the walls on the ground floor while upstairs local wooden furniture gives the place a warm, cosy touch. Good discounts in low season. R$210

BARRA

★ **Âmbar Pousada** Rua Afonso Celso 485 71 3264 6956, ambarpousada.com.br; map p.219. Friendly *pousada* with simple but neat, cosy rooms on two storeys, with or without bathrooms, set around an attractive courtyard. Good breakfast included, though the dining room has slightly dreary tablecloths and an old-fashioned feel. Staff are helpful and Barra beach is just a 10min walk away. Dorms R$40, doubles R$120

Casa Inglesa Rua Eng. Milton Olvieira 71 3022 0564, casainglesasalvador.com; map p.219. Small guesthouse on a quiet residential street with seven bedrooms, each with a/c and minibars. Services include private Bahian cuisine cooking classes and capoeira lessons. R$350

Che Lagarto Av Oceánica 84 71 3235 2404, chelagarto.com; map p.219. Part of the ubiquitous chain of party hostels throughout South America. Th Salvador branch has a prime location on the waterfron an upstairs terrace bar (happy hour 6–8pm), and a pizzeri downstairs. They can arrange tours and excursions. Dorms R$50, doubles R$165

Hit Hotel Av Sete de Setembro 3691 71 3264 7433 hithotel.com.br; map p.219. A modern hotel with cool, spacious lobby overlooking the beach, pretty goo service, a restaurant and bright, contemporary style room with LCD TVs, fridge and sea views. R$189

Pousada Estrela do Mar Rua Afonso Celso 119 7 3022 4882, estreladomarsalvador.com; map p.219 A pleasant *pousada*, less than two blocks from the seafron near the lighthouse, with a small courtyard, nice breakfas room and English-speaking owners. The suite has a terrac and there are larger rooms suitable for families; cable T and a/c are standard. R$190

Pousada Noa Noa Av Sete de Setembro 4295 71 326 1148, pousadanoanoa.com; map p.219. One of th more popular *pousadas* in Barra, right on the seafront, offerin a variety of simple, bright and private a/c rooms, a hammoc area, terrace, garden and friendly service. R$170

ONDINA

Bahia Othon Palace Av Oceânica 2294, Praia d Ondina 71 2103 7100, othon.com.br; map p.209 The grande dame of Salvador beach resorts is a little pas its prime, but still occupies a stunning location betwee two narrow beaches, with a huge pool, mountainou breakfast buffet and ageing but comfortable rooms, al with dramatic sea views. R$208

RIO VERMELHO

★ **Hotel Catharina Paraguaçu** Rua João Gomes 128 71 3334 0089, hotelcatharinaparaguacu.com.br; map p.209. One of Bahia's most elegant hotels, in a beautifully restored nineteenth-century residence full o character. Rooms are comfy with a/c and cable. For some reason, taxi drivers have difficulty finding it even though it's on a main road. R$187

PITUBA

Verdemar Av Otávio Mangabeira 513 71 3797 4333, verdemar.com.br; map p.209. Comfortable hotel set in one of the cheapest of all the beach areas, Pituba, and handily close to the airport, although a little far from the centre. Plain but comfy rooms have a/c and cable TV. R$169

EATING

Eating out is one of the major pleasures of Salvador, and the local cuisine, **comida baiana**, is deservedly famous. There's a huge range of restaurants and, although Cidade Alta has an increasing number of stylish, expensive places, it's still quite possible to eat well for less than R$30, though easier to spend R$50 plus, including drinks. Especially at **Barra** and **Rio Vermelho**, the seafront promenade is lined with bars, cafés and restaurants.

FILHOS DE GANDHI, CARNAVAL, SALVADOR

DIRETOR

CENTRO HISTÓRICO

Café Conosco Rua da Ordem Terceira do São Francisco 4, Pelourinho ☎71 8415 2332, facebook.com/Cafeconosco; map p.210. Attractive café set in an early eighteenth-century house; good coffee, quiche and cakes (R$4–5) handmade by owner Nilza Ribeiro, free wi-fi and a tranquil escape from the hubbub of the streets. Mon–Fri 10am–7pm, Sat 10am–4pm.

Casa da Gamboa Rua João de Deus 32, Pelourinho ☎71 3321 3393, bit.ly/CasadaGamboa; map p.210. One of the district's top restaurants, and worth a splurge, it serves mainly Bahian dishes; expect to pay about R$90 per head. The interior is decorated with local paintings. Mon–Sat noon–4pm & 6–11pm.

Conventual Rua do Carmo 1, Santo Antonio ☎71 3329 3316, terezapaim.com.br; map p.210. Based in the cloisters of the exclusive *Convento do Carmo*, just a short stroll from the heart and heat of the Pelourinho, this is probably the city's most expensive restaurant. It has a mainly Portuguese menu, full of excellently prepared and presented dishes, plus there's a large and fancy bar. The best reason to eat here, however, is to enjoy the ambience of the leafy and crafted stone courtyard and cloisters. Daily 7am–11pm.

★ **Jardim das Delicias** Rua Maciel de Cima 12, Pelourinho ☎71 3321 1449; map p.210. Fantastic Bahian and international cuisine is served here – the shrimp in cassava cream and *moquecas* are especially good. Cover charge (R$5) for gentle live music most weekend evenings, and there's indoor and outdoor seating, in a lovely garden. Mains cost R$40–60. Mon & Wed 4–11pm, Tues & Thurs–Sat noon–11pm.

Maria Mata Mouro Rua da Ordem Terceira (aka Rua Inácio Accioli) 08, Pelourinho ☎71 3321 3929 mariamatamouro.com.br; map p.210. One of th finest Bahian restaurants in the district, with prices to matc whatever you choose will be divine and lovingly presente Very busy at weekends, so it's best to book a table in advanc Mains cost R$45–75 per person. Daily noon–11pm.

★ **Porto do Moreira** Largo do Mocambinho 488 ☎7 3322 4112, bit.ly/PortodoMoreira; map p.210 Unassuming local lunch spot with creative Bahian dishe and a long history – it was founded in 1938 by Portugues immigrant José Moreira da Silva and is now managed b his two sons (the restaurant and the plaza featured in Jorg Amado's novel *Dona Flor and Her Two Husbands*). Dishe from R$25–40. Daily 11am–3pm.

Rango Vegan Rua do Passo (Rua Ribeiro dos Santos 62, San Antonio ☎71 3488 2756; map p.210 Herbivores will want to head straight to San Antonio an *Rango Vegan*, a quaint vegan spot on the hillside. Men items include burgers made from lentils, curries, rice dishe and tofu "fish" fillets and fried corn nuggets with chic peas. Menu changes daily, with dishes for R$20–40. Tues-Fri noon–8pm, Sat noon–11pm.

★ **Restaurante do SENAC** Largo do Pelourinho ☎7 3321 5502, www.ba.senac.br; map p.210. Municipa restaurant-school in a finely restored colonial mansion (onc a legendary capoeira school). It looks very expensive from th outside, but it's good value for what you get. You pay a se charge for the lunch *buffet típico* upstairs – about R$56 – an take as much as you want from a choice of around forty dishe (and twelve desserts), all helpfully labelled so you know wha you're eating. On street level is a simpler "*buffet por quilo*" optior (pay by weight; Mon–Fri only). Daily 11.30am–3.30pm.

ACARAJÉ: FIVE OF THE BEST

Salvador's signature street food is **acarajé**, the delicious deep-fried black-eyed pea dough stuffed with seafood (shrimps), peanuts and spicy sauces (*vatapá*). Vendors who serve *acarajé* are generally women ("*baianas*"), dressed in traditional all-white cotton dresses and headscarves (city statutes mean they have to wear this costume). *Acarajé* is usually R$7–8 per serving. Rivalry is fierce between stalls, with local competitions to name the best each year:

★ **Acarajé da Cira** Rua Aristídes Milton, Posto 12, Itapuã ☎71 3249 4170; map p.207. It's a long taxi ride from town but this is the locals' pick for the best *acarajé* in the city year after year. There is a second branch at Largo da Mariquita, Rio Vermelho. Daily 10am–midnight.

Acarajé da Dinha Rua João Gomes 25, Largo de Santana, Rio Vermelho ☎71 3334 4350; map p.209. Famous stall in Rio Vermelho's main plaza that is packed each night – it has long queues and is not quite up to the hype, but a fun, buzzy place to snack with a cold beer all the same. Tues–Fri 6–11.30pm, Sat noon–3pm & 6–11.30 pm, Sun noon–3pm.

Acarajé da Mary Praça de Se; map p.210. The stall most tourists are likely to visit, but it's actually not bad and often very spicy; wash your *acarajé* down with some fresh *agua de coco*. Daily 11am–6pm.

Acarajé de Regina Largo de Santana/Rua Guedes Cabral, Rio Vermelho ☎71 3232 7542; map p.209. Friendly competition to *Dinha* is provided by this similarly fêted stall. Tues–Fri 3–10.30pm, Sat & Sun 10am–9pm.

Acarajé da Rosineide e Neidiane Azevedo Fernandes (in front of Instituto Mauá), Barra ☎71 3347 3899; map p.219. Best of many vendors along Barra beach. Mon–Fri 10am–8pm, Sat & Sun 10am–6pm.

COMIDA BAIANA

The secret of Bahian cooking is twofold: a rich seafood base and the abundance of traditional West African **ingredients** like palm oil, nuts, coconut and ferociously strong peppers. *Vatapá*, a bright yellow porridge of palm oil, coconut, shrimp and garlic, looks vaguely unappetizing but is delicious. Other dishes to look out for are *moqueca* (seafood cooked in the inevitable palm-oil-based sauce); *caruru* (with many of the same ingredients as *vatapá* but with the vital addition of loads of okra); and *acarajé* (deep-fried bean cake stuffed with *vatapá*, salad and optional hot pepper). Bahian cuisine also has good **desserts**: *quindim* is a delicious small cake of coconut flavoured with vanilla, which often comes with a prune in the middle.

Zulu Rua de Laranjeiras 15, Pelourinho ⓣ71 98784 3172; map p.210. The owners of the hostel *Galeria 13* also run this travellers' favourite. The menu includes Bahian-inspired burgers, great *moqueca* (fish stew, which you can learn how to make at the cooking class offered by the hostel), homemade bread and a large selection of craft beers. Mains R$30–90. Daily noon–11pm.

BARRA

Caranguejo de Sergipe Av Oceânica s/n ⓣ71 2132 0798, ⓦfacebook.com/caranguejodesergipe; map p.219. Best spot on the waterfront for seafood, with a vast array of options from fresh octopus and lobster to oysters and freshly caught fish, though the house speciality is crab. They offer a good set lunch special for R$15; mains cost around R$80. Mon 4pm–midnight, Tues–Sun 11am–midnight.

★ **Pereira** Av Sete de Setembro 3959 ⓣ71 3264 6464, ⓦfacebook.com/pereirarestaurante; map p.219. Stylish spot with a cool interior and pleasant terrace overlooking the road and beach. The meals – especially the seafood and salad – and drinks are great but expensive (mains around R$60). Tues–Sun 11.30am–4pm & 5pm–midnight, Sat till 1am.

Ramma Rua Lord Cochrane 76 ⓣ71 3264 0044, ⓦrammacozinhanatural.com.br; map p.219. This classic wholefood café provides an excellent range of tasty and healthy *comida por quilo* at lunchtimes. Get there well before 1pm to avoid the crowds. Figure on R$20–35. Daily 11.30am–3.30pm.

Tudo Azul Av Sete de Setembro 3701 ⓣ71 9104 8011, ⓦfacebook.com/restaurantetudoazul; map p.219. This modest Swiss/Brazilian fusion place is great for a relatively cheap meal and cold beer – think "Swiss" potatoes, *moqueca* and fresh shrimp. Staff hand out salted popcorn while you wait for a table, and the names of customers are scribbled on the walls. Mains R$30–55. Mon–Fri 10am–10pm, Sat & Sun 9am–10pm.

RIO VERMELHO

Boteca do Franca Rua Borges dos Réis 24 ⓣ71 3334 2734, ⓦfacebook.com/BotecoDoFranca; map p.209. Local favourite with chequered tablecloths, where the menu features regional specialities as well as giant plates of rice dishes, like *arroz de polvo* (octopus) and *camarão* (shrimp). Mains R$60. Daily noon until the last customer leaves.

GARCIA

★ **Aconchego da Zuzu** Rua Quintana Bocaiuva 18, Garcia ⓣ71 3331 5074; map p.209. Enjoyably different and highly Bahian, this small family-run restaurant sits in a courtyard on a backstreet of the Garcia suburb. Choose from a wide range of local cuisine – try the *peixa au molho de camarão* (fish in shrimp sauce). Superb, traditional percussion music is sometimes performed. Tues–Fri 11.30am–4pm, Sat & Sun 11.30am–5pm.

DRINKING AND NIGHTLIFE

You'll find Salvador's most distinctive bars and nightlife in the **Pelourinho**, though **Barra** also attracts the party crowd and other venues are scattered all over the city (Amaralina and Pituba are probably the liveliest areas to head for, and Friday and Saturday nights are best). Other than the weekend, Tuesday is a big night out, a tradition known as **Terça da Benção** ("blessed Tuesday"). Bars aside, undoubtedly the biggest attraction of the area is the chance to hear **live music**: Salvador has spawned several musical genres, and in recent years has overtaken Rio to become the most creative centre of Brazilian music. Some of the best music in the city comes from organized cultural groups who have public rehearsals around their own clubhouses in the weeks leading up to Carnaval (see page 226). For the rest of the year, the **clubhouses** are used as bars and meeting places, often with music at weekends. Check out ⓦsalvadorcentral.com and ⓦagendacultural.ba.gov.br for up-to-the-minute listings of cultural events and live music.

BARS

Bar Balaio de Gato Rua do Passo 10; map p.210. Dive bar located adjacent to the *Acai Hostel* just down from the Pelourinho. There's a big Tuesday party featuring live traditional samba music, which draws a fun crowd of locals and travellers. Free entry. Daily 10pm–2am.

O Cravinho Bar Largo Terreiro de Jesus 3 ⊕71 9314 6022, ⓦocravinho.com.br; map p.210. Traditional place to start the evening, preferably with a glass of *infusões* (specially flavoured cachaça), the most popular – *cravinho* – made from essence of clove or ginger. This place gets busy Tues evenings (the busiest weekday night in Pelourinho) and at weekends. Daily 11am–around 11pm.

LIVE MUSIC VENUES

Clube do Samba Largo do Terreiro de Jesus 5 ⊕71 9361 1508, ⓦclubedosamba.com.br; map p.210. Often hosts live samba acts on Saturdays and Sundays, and various local groups during the week. Cover R$10. Tues, Fri & Sat 5pm–midnight, Sun 4–10pm.

Jam no MAM Av Contorno (Cidade Baixa) ⊕71 3241 2983, ⓦjamnomam.com.br; map p.210. Live jazz, samba, blues and bossa nova every Sat evening at the Museu de Arte Moderna da Bahia, which also hosts temporary exhibitions, in the old Solar do Unhão. Take a taxi to get here. Cover R$8. Sat 7–9:30pm.

Show de Gerônimo Praca Pedro Arcanjo, Pelourinho; map p.210. Don't miss this weekly live performance by Gerônimo (a veteran *Salvadorian* songwriter) supported by his band Mont'Serrat, renowned for its classy horn section – though sadly, this only occurs during high seasons of Holy Week and December. Tues 7–10pm.

ENTERTAINMENT

3

★ Teatro Miguel Santana Rua Gregório de Matos 49, Pelourinho ⊕71 3322 1962, ⓦbalefolcloricodabahia.com.br. During the week (except Tues), the Balé Folclórico da Bahia perform athletic Afro-Brazilian dance (R$50) at this old theatre; it's best to buy tickets in advance from the box office (open from 2pm). Mon–Sat 8–9.15pm.

SHOPPING

Dinho Praca José Alencar 16, Pelourinho ⊕71 3213 0416, ⓦdinhoartes.com.br; map p.210. A shop of high-quality, handmade, traditional percussion instruments. Mon–Sat 9am–6pm.

Mercado Modelo Praça Visconde de Cayrú 250; map p.210. The best arts and crafts market in Salvador, located in Cidade Baixa (see page 216). Mon–Sat 9am–7pm, Sun 9am–2pm.

DIRECTORY

Consulates US, Av Tancredo Neves 1632, Room 1401, Salvador Trade Center, Torre Sul, Caminho das Árvores (⊕71 3113 2090).

Hospitals Hospital Aliança, Av Juracy Magalhães Jr. 2096, Rio Vermelho (⊕71 2108 5600, ⓦhospitalalianca.com.br); Hospital São Rafael, Av São Rafael 2152, São Marcos (⊕71 3409 8000).

Internet Try Baiafrica Internet Café on the Praça da Sé (R$8/hr) or Lan House de Tega, Rua Alfonso Célso, 70, in Barra.

Laundry O Casal at Av Sete de Setembro 3564, Barra (⊕71 3203 8000); Lavanderia Maria, Ladeira do Carmo 30, Pelourinho (⊕71 4102 6405; R$50 per load).

CARNAVAL

Having steadfastly resisted commercialization, **Carnaval** (February/March) in Salvador has remained a street event of mass participation. The main hubs of activity are **Cidade Alta**, especially the area around Praça Castro Alves – which turns into a seething mass of people that, once joined, is almost impossible to get out of – and, in recent years, **Porto da Barra** (see page 218), equally crowded and just as enjoyable. This is an expensive and a hectic time to stay in Salvador; all accommodation more than doubles in price, and with added costs like paying to join a *bloco* or participate in a *camarote* (a venue with good views over the Carnaval route and an organized party thrown in for the duration), you are likely to be spending in excess of R$600–700 a day.

From December onwards Carnaval groups hold **public rehearsals** and dances all over the city. The most famous are **Grupo Cultural Olodum**, whose students rehearse on Saturday afternoons (2–5pm) in front of their school at Rua das Laranjeiras 30 (⊕71 332 8069). Another group **Ara Ketu** organize public rehearsals in the Pelorinho, often during the month of January (ⓦfacebook.com/oficialaraketu). These rehearsals get very crowded, so be careful with your belongings. One of the oldest and best loved of the *afoxés* (candomblé-inspired musical groups) is **Filhos de Gandhi** ("Sons of Gandhi"), founded in the 1940s, who have a clubhouse in Rua Gregório de Matos, near Largo do Pelourinho, easily recognized by the large papier-mâché white elephant in the hall.

Information about Carnaval is published in special supplements in the local papers on Thursday and Saturday. Tourist offices also have schedules, route maps, and sometimes sell tickets for the Campo Grande grandstands.

LGBT SALVADOR

Salvador has a small but dynamic **gay scene**, with its own gay pride parade every September (part of the "Semana da Diversidade"). Visit www.ggb.org.br for insights into the Bahian LGBT community (Portuguese only).

CIDADE ALTA AND AROUND

Amsterdam Ladeira dos Aflitos 71 98114 9433, facebook.com/AmsterdamSalvador; map p.209. This new club, located just down from the Museu de Arte Moderno, features house music and DJs on Fridays and pop music on Saturdays. Popular with young bohemians and students. R$30 (occasionally have an open bar for R$50). Fri & Sat from 11.45pm–6am.

Club Tropical Rua Gamboa de Cima, Campo Grande 24 71 3336 8915, boatetropical.com.br; map p.209. The oldest LGBT club in Salvador, it attracts a local crowd and has drag shows at 3am. R$25. Fri & Sat 11pm–5am.

RIO VERMELHO

San Sebastian Rua Praia da Paciência 71 3561 0411, sansebastianoficial.com.br; map p.209. Upmarket club heavy on EDM that attracts a trendy crowd. R$35. Fri & Sat 11pm–5am.

BARRA

Boteco do Gera Rua Dias d'Avila 71 3264 0420; & **La Bouche** 71 9887 0531, bit.ly/LaBoucheBar; map p.219. These two outdoor bars located on the small pedestrian walkway of Rua Dias d'Avila, which is a predominantly gay area. It gets going around 10pm. High season (Dec & Carnaval) daily from 7pm; low season Thurs–Sun.

Money and exchange There are several places where you can change money in the Pelourinho area, while Banco do Brasil has several branches, all with Visa ATMs, including one on the Terreiro de Jesus. Citibank has a branch at Av Estados Unidos 558, Cidade Baixa.

Pharmacies Farmácia Sant'ana, Praça Azevedo Fernandes, Barra (71 3267 8970); Drogaleve, Praça da Sé 6, Pelourinho (71 3322 6921).

Police The tourist police (Delegacia de Proteção ao Turista) are at Praça Anchieta 14, Cruzeiro do São Francisco, Pelourinho (71 3322 1188).

Post office Praca da Inglaterra s/n (Mon–Fri 9am–5pm; correios.com.br).

Day-trips from Salvador

Many of Bahia's gems lie just outside the city of Salvador: sparsely populated islands dotted with sleepy fishing villages, which you can visit by ferry or on day cruises; while inland you'll find the idyllic colonial town of **Cachoeira**. Cradled amid lush green hills and set around a tranquil lake, it's well worth a day-trip.

Baía de Todos os Santos

To get a closer look at the enticing islands scattered across the **Baía de Todos os Santos** – 31 of them, mainly uninhabited or home to a few simple fishing villages – most visitors join **day-long cruises** on private schooners from Salvador; the kiosks in the city's Terminal Turístico in Cidade Baixa are the easiest places to buy tickets (see page 229). It's less busy during the week, but these boats have their advantages; if you manage to get on one full of Brazilian tourists you're likely to have a very lively time.

Ilha dos Frades

A favourite target of Salvador day-trip boats, 6km-long **Ilha dos Frades** is best known for its gorgeous beaches and unspoiled interior of Mata Atlântica (a protected reserve), though there are also three small villages on the island with a permanent population of around 1100. Boats tend to stop at the **Praia da Ponta de Nossa Senhora** at the southern tip (R$0.80 for entry via the pier; not included in tours), the best and calmest beach, where several bars and restaurants cater to the daily tide of sun-worshippers. Other than lounging on the sands and swimming, you can make the short hike up the hill to

FUTEBOL SALVADOR

Long overshadowed by its big brothers in the south, Salvador now has two teams that regularly compete in Série A, and was a host city for the World Cup in 2014. **Esporte Clube Bahia** (esporteclubebahia.com.br) play at the Arena Fonte Nova (Ladeira da Fonte das Pedras, Nazaré); it's easy to get to, 5km west of the city's main bus station. Bahia's main rival is **Esporte Clube Vitória** (ecvitoria.com.br) aka "Leão da Barra", who play at the Estádio Manoel Barradas, also known as the Barradão, a much smaller stadium 18km northeast of the old centre. The two teams meet in heated games known simply as the "Ba–Vi". It's usually possible to buy tickets (from R$25–140) at the stadium just before a game, but as always your hotel should be able to help.

the eighteenth-century **Igreja de Nossa Senhora de Guadalupe** (restored in 2012), for sensational views across the bay.

Ilha de Itaparica

3

A narrow, 36km-long island, the **Ilha de Itaparica** was taken over by the Jesuits in 1560, making it one of the earliest places to be settled by the Portuguese. It's now very much seen as an appendage of Salvador, whose inhabitants flock to its beaches at weekends, and have built villas by the score along the strip known as **Ponta de Areia**. It's quiet enough during the week, though, and big enough to find calmer spots even at the busiest times. Itaparica is also famous for its fruit trees, especially its mangoes, which are prized throughout Bahia.

The main town, also called **ITAPARICA**, was briefly the capital of Bahia, though little evidence remains of those times: its most famous sight is the **Fonte da Bica** (Rua Antônio Calmon and Travessa 25 de Outubro), a natural spring of mineral water still framed by its 1842 tiled facade and a favourite spot for Brazilian tourists and locals to fill up their water bottles – the three taps are said to represent love, health and money (the water is safe to drink and supposedly rich in health benefits). At the other end of the *centro histórico*, the **Fortaleza São Lourenço**, which dates back to 1711, makes a nice photo-op along the shore, but is otherwise a military base and off limits.

ARRIVAL AND GETTING AROUND — ILHA DE ITAPARICA

By ferry Passenger ferries (daily 6am–2.30pm, every 30min; R$5–6; 40min) leave from Salvador's Terminal Marítimo Turístico for the terminal at Mar Grande south of Itaparica town near the beaches; try to avoid taking the ferry at the weekend when hundreds of locals line up to make the crossing.

By bus For getting around once you're there, use the *kombis* (minibuses) and buses that ply the coastline, or rent bicycles (rental places are easily spotted by the bikes piled up on the pavement).

ACCOMMODATION AND EATING

Club Med Itaparica Estrada Praia da Conceição 71 3681 8800, clubmed.com.br. Yes, Itaparica has a full-on Club Med resort with all the amenities, luxuries and hedonistic temptations you'd expect, set directly on 300m of its own beachfront. Meals and booze are all-inclusive. Weekly rate R$3304

Portal das Águas Av 25 de Outubro, Marina de Itaparica, Centro, Itaparica 71 3631 3239. Modern, stylish restaurant overlooking the marina, with a menu of pastas, pizzas, fresh seafood and traditional Bahian food. Wed–Sun noon–9pm.

Posada Claro de Luar Av Beira Mar 200, Ponta de Areia 71 3631 1163. Spacious a/c rooms (with TV) are offered at this friendly B&B near the beach that is run by an Argentine couple. Breakfast is excellent, and there are plenty of beach buffet restaurants nearby. R$138

Cachoeira and around

The most rewarding day-trip inland from Salvador takes in the elegant colonial town of **CACHOEIRA** in the heart of the **Recôncavo**, the Portuguese plantation zone named after the concave shape of the Bahia Todos Santos. The Recôncavo arcs out from Salvador along 150km of shoreline, before petering out in the mangrove swamps around the town of Valença. It's one of the most lush and tropical regions in Brazil, with palm-covered hills and colonial towns breaking up the green and fertile coastal plains; you'll still see some of the sugar cane that made the area so rich, though these days there are plenty of empty, overgrown fields overtaken by jungle. The twin towns of Cachoeira and **São Félix** are only a few kilometres apart across the Rio Paraguaçu, spanned by a single-track **iron box-girder bridge** (built by British engineers in 1885 and opened by Emperor Dom Pedro himself). Cachoeira is easily the more impressive, its vibrant Afro-Brazilian culture, wide, shady plazas and profusion of gorgeous Baroque buildings evidence of the sugar boom in the eighteenth century.

In a sign of the times, buses now pull in at a tiny rodoviária, overlooked by the grand, derelict train station worthy of *belle époque* Europe. Freight trains still pass over the bridge (stopping traffic), and run through the station, but the whole structure is an abandoned shell. Much of the old town is similarly crumbling away, though restoration has picked up in recent years as the town develops its tourist potential. Cachoeira was the birthplace of **Ana Néri**, known as "Mother of the Brazilians", who organized nursing services during the Paraguayan War (1865–70). Note that street signs are hard to make out in Cachoeira, and even shops and restaurants are poorly marked.

Casa da Câmara e Cadeia

Praça da Aclamação • Mon–Fri 8am–1pm & 2–5pm • Free

The finest and most spacious square in the town is **Praça da Aclamação**, lined with eighteenth-century civil buildings from the golden age of Cachoeira, including the Prefeitura and the **Casa da Câmara e Cadeia**. Built between 1698 and 1712, this relatively simple building served as town hall and jail (it was also briefly the seat of provincial government in 1822). Today it still holds city council meetings. Inside is a small museum about the history of the building and slavery in the region.

Conjunto do Carmo

Praça da Aclamação s/n • Tues–Sat 8am–noon & 2–5pm, Sun 9am–noon • R$4

The south side of Praça da Aclamação is dominated by the huge bulk of the eighteenth-century **Conjunto do Carmo**, beautifully restored in 2006: the complex includes the main church or **Ordem Primeira do Carmo** (now a convention centre), a Carmelite convent (**Convento do Carmo**) converted into a *pousada* (see page 231), and the **Igreja da Ordem Terceira do Carmo** on the left, open to visitors and built mostly between 1702 and 1724. Inside is a small **Museu do Arte Sacra** that includes Chinese-influenced carvings and statues from Macau and a venerated image of the Senhor dos Passos.

Museu Regional da Cachoeira

Praça da Aclamação 4 • Mon–Fri 8am–noon & 2–5pm, Sat & Sun 8am–noon • Free • ⓣ 75 752 1123

On the west side of Praça da Aclamação, housed in the former townhouse of a plantation owner dating from 1723, the **Museu Regional da Cachoeira** contains a collection of period furniture from Rio de Janeiro, most belonging to one Baron de Cabo Frio.

BAÍA DE TODOS OS SANTOS BOAT TOURS

All day-trips around the bay depart from the **Terminal Turístico** ferry terminal in the Cidade Baixa, with several kiosks selling tickets. Most follow similar routes; departing at around 9am daily, they usually make stops at the beach on Frades (2hr 30min) and then Ponta de Areia on Itaparica (2hr). Snacks such as fruit are included, but otherwise food is not. You'll be back at the Salvador terminal by 5.30pm. During the boat ride you'll be offered fruits (free) cold beers (extra) and be entertained by local samba musicians – standards are usually high. Tours are usually R$50 per person; see ⓦ passeiosasilhas.com.br or call ⓣ 71 8771 5949.

Igreja Matriz de Nossa Senhora do Rosário

Rua Ana Néri and Praça 13 de Maio

The impressive **Igreja Matriz de Nossa Senhora do Rosário** was constructed between 1674 and 1754. As with most churches in Cachoeira, this one has been robbed all too frequently and is usually shut, but if you can get in you'll see two huge, jaw-dropping 5m-high *azulejo* panels dating from the 1750s. Upstairs the **Museu das Alfaias** preserves art works from the now ruined Convento São Francisco.

Museu Hansen Bahia

Rua 13 de Maio 13 • Tues–Fri 9am–5pm, Sat 9am–1pm • Free • T 75 3425 1453, W hansenbahia.com.br

Housed in a renovated 1830 residence, the small **Museu Hansen Bahia** is dedicated to the work of German engraver Karl Heinz Hansen (1915–78), who was born in Hamburg, emigrated to Brazil in 1950 and settled in Salvador five years later. After a spell back in Germany, he returned to Salvador for good in 1966, naturalized and adopted the artistic name "Hansen Bahia". From 1970 onwards he spent the last years of his life in São Felix and donated his work to this museum, including the startling *Via Crucis* series. You can also visit the **Museu-Casa**, in São Félix, the former home of the artist (free – ask at the museum for current exhibits).

Capela de Nossa Senhora da Ajuda

Largo da Ajuda • Often closed • Free

Climb up the narrow, cobbled Rua da Ajuda, and you'll come to a peaceful little square that contains the **Capela de Nossa Senhora da Ajuda**, the city's oldest church. Begun in 1595 and completed eleven years later, it just about qualifies as sixteenth century, which makes it a rarity. Sadly, the simple but well-proportioned interior is usually closed to visitors for fear of thieves, but if you knock on the door there might be someone around to let you in.

Santa Casa da Misericórdia

Praça Doutor Milton • Mon–Fri 2–5pm • Free

A couple of blocks along Rua Lauro de Freitas past the market you'll come to the fine Praça Doutor Milton, with its Baroque public fountain and the early eighteenth-century bulk of the **Santa Casa da Misericórdia**, a colonial hospital from 1734, which has a beautiful chapel and small garden attached.

CANDOMBLÉ IN CACHOEIRA

Cachoeira is known all over Brazil for the intensity of its **candomblé** traditions, with some *terreiros* still conducting rituals in African dialects nobody otherwise speaks, recognizable as variants of West African and Angolan languages. One of the best-known candomblé events is Cachoeira's fiesta of **Nossa Senhora da Boa Morte**, which always begins on the first Friday before August 15. It's staged by a sisterhood, the Irmandade da Boa Morte, founded by freed women slaves in the mid-nineteenth century, partly as a religious group and partly to work for the emancipation of slaves by acting as an early cooperative bank to buy people their liberty. All the local candomblé groups turn out with drummers and singers, and although the name of the fiesta is Catholic it's a celebration of candomblé, with centre stage held by the dignified matriarchs of the sisterhood. The other great day in the candomblé year is the **Festa de Santa Barbara**, on December 4 in São Félix, dedicated to the goddess Iansã. There are several other fiestas worth catching, like the **São João** celebrations from June 22 to 24, while five saints' days are crammed into the last three months of the year; check with the tourist office (see page 231) for exact dates.

Dedicated to the all-female Boa Morte religious society, the **Centro Cultural da Irmandade da Nossa Senhora da Boa Morte**, Rua 13 de Maio (daily 9am–noon; by donation), features costumes worn in the Fiesta Nossa Senhora da Boa Morte, as well as other Candomblé art exhibits and a photo gallery.

WOODCARVERS OF CACHOEIRA

There's a lively tradition of **woodcarving** in Cachoeira and several sculptors have studios open to the public. One of the best is **Louco Filho** (nephew of legendary Louco, who died in 1992), who displays his wonderful elongated carvings in his studio at Rua 13 de Maio 18, which tends to open Mon–Fri 9am–4pm. **Doidão** (aka José Cardoso de Araújo, another nephew of the original Louco) was another popular sculptor from Cachoeira, but alas he died in 2017.

Central Cultural Dannemann

Av Salvador Pinto 29, São Félix • Mon–Fri 8am–noon & 1–5pm • Free • T 75 3438 2500, W terradannemann.com

The main reason for going over the bridge to **São Félix** is the great view back across the Rio Paraguaçu, with the colonial facades of Cachoeira reflected in the water. The only real sight over here is the **Central Cultural Dannemann**, named after the founder of the eponymous **cigar company** (W dannemann.com), Geraldo Dannemann, who came to Brazil from Germany in 1872. Today Dannemann's original cigar factory operates as an art and cultural centre for temporary exhibitions, though cigars are still hand-rolled in the traditional way at the back (you can buy them here).

ARRIVAL AND INFORMATION

By bus Cachoeira's tiny rodoviária is in Praça Manuel Vitorino, opposite the old train station and the bridge over the Rio Paraguaçu. Salvador buses (operated by Santana) tend to end or begin their routes across the bridge in São Félix, stopping at Cachoeira, and run hourly (R$25/2hr).

Tourist information There's a small tourist office in the yellow municipal building a block up from the Casa da Câmara e Cadeia on Rua Benjamin Constant (daily 8am–noon & 2–4pm), but the staff don't speak English or Spanish, and no maps are given.

Services On central Praça Dr Milton there's a branch of Bradesco bank and a post office.

ACCOMMODATION AND EATING

Baiana's Point Rua Virgilio Reis T 75 3425 4967. Enticing Brazilian restaurant set on a short pier into the Rio Paraguaçu, just off the main promenade; a great spot for drinks or dinner. Daily 9am–10pm.

O Pouso da Palavra Praça da Aclamação 8 T 75 3425 2528, W bit.ly/BaianaPoint. Eighteenth-century town house on the main plaza, which is now a cosy café, art gallery and bookshop, founded by poet and photographer Damário Dacruz (who died in 2010). It also has free wi-fi and is open late on Fridays for live concerts. Daily 11am–10pm, Fri until midnight.

Pousada do Convento Praça da Aclamação T 75 3425 1716, W pousadadoconvento.com.br. Gorgeous premises that was once part of the seventeenth-century convent and Conjunto do Carmo; it has a pool, attractive patio and a bar, though some of the rooms could do with a renovation – check inside before you move in. Also has a decent restaurant known for its huge portions (daily 11am–10pm). R$90

Pousada do Guerreiro Rua 13 de Maio 14 T 75 3215 1104, W facebook.com/pg/pousadaguerreiro. Solid no-frills option in the centre of town, with spacious, wood-floor rooms that have fans; you can often find half-price rates online. R$100

Pousada Pai Thomas Rua 25 de Junho 12 T 75 3425 3182, W pousadapaithomaz.com.br. In a great location near the waterfront, this *pousada* and restaurant is housed in a colonial building that was refurbished in 2016. It features basic, clean rooms with big beds, while the downstairs restaurant has a nice ambiance and features a solid menu of regional and international dishes. R$90

The Coconut Coast

The coastline immediately north of Salvador, known as the **COCONUT COAST**, is essentially a long palm-fringed sandy beach all the way to Aracaju (see page 252). Access to the best bathing spots and seaside facilities is limited to a few settlements, each with its own distinctive flavour. **Arembepe** has long been seen as an alternative type of place, stuffed as it is with hippy beach shops. Further north, **Praia do Forte** is a popular resort town and famous across Brazil for the Tamar Project, which works with sea turtles. Near here are the truly laidback villages of **Imbassai**, **Diogo** and **Mangue Seco**, all superbly peaceful and yet with plenty of bars and cafés to enjoy in the balmy evenings.

Arembepe

Some 50km north of Salvador (30km north of Itapuã and the airport), **AREMBEPE** is a now-gentrified former hippy hangout, though still peaceful and pretty, with a pleasant little beach sheltered by a coral reef popular with turtles. The town lies on a well-beaten tourist track, but don't be put off by this – it's a beautiful coastline and the beaches are long enough to swallow the crowds. Most people stop off on the way to Praia do Forte for just a few hours, but there are plenty of places to spend the night.

A fifteen-minute walk from the centre of town brings you to the **Aldeia Hippie**, the "Hippie Village" made famous in the 1960s and 1970s when Mick Jagger, Janis Joplin and other stars enjoyed its pleasures. It has vestiges of its hippy past, but is now known more as a fine place to cool off in the Capivara River in the late afternoons.

Projecto Tamar

Estrada Geral do Projeto Tamar • Daily 9am–5pm • R$6 • T 71 98127 0038, W tamar.org.br

Projecto Tamar runs a small Centro de Visitantes with displays on the group's conservation work with turtles, as well as cute but injured turtles saved from the wild – it's not as big as the centre at Praia do Forte (see page 233), but a good introduction all the same.

ARRIVAL AND DEPARTURE — AREMBEPE

By bus Regular buses from Salvador's Estação da Lapa, Terminal da França and rodoviária run northeast along the coastal road (Estrada do Coco aka BA-099) to Arembepe (R$6; 1hr).

ACCOMMODATION AND EATING

★ **Mar Aberto** Largo de São Francisco 43 T 71 3624 1257, W marabertorestaurante.com.br. *Mar Aberto* is known for its memorable fresh fish dishes – especially the legendary fish balls (*bolinho de peixe*) – and dazzling views across the beach. Try the *bacalhau ao molho de ervas* (cod in herb sauce) or traditional *moquecas*. Mains cost R$35–65. Mon–Thurs 11.30am–9pm, Fri & Sat 11.30am–11pm, Sun noon–6pm.

Pousada A Capela Praia do Piruí (south of town), Rua do Pirui 50 T 71 3624 2708, W pousadaacapela.com.br. Located on a gorgeous, clean and tranquil strip of Piruí beach (where coral pools form at low tide), this lodge contains ten modern, comfy rooms overlooking the sea. R$180

Itacimirim

Fifteen kilometres northeast of Arembepe lies the barrier island beach of **ITACIMIRIM**. It is not as developed as many resorts, though there are a few hotels and lots of upmarket weekend residences. Out of high season and during the week, you can have this palm-fringed paradise with several natural pools to swim in more or less to yourself; high-tide swells make this a good place to surf too (you can usually rent boards from shacks on the beach).

ARRIVAL AND DEPARTURE — ITACIMIRIM

By bus Itacimirim is a short drive (5km) south of Praia do Forte (see page 233); buses between Salvador and Forte will drop you on the highway (BA-099) from where its 2km to the beach.

ACCOMMODATION

Hotel Pousada Praia das Ondas Rua Principal de Itacimirim 60 T 71 9630 9030, W praiadasondas.com.br. Boasts luxurious a/c rooms (with a balcony or a patio with a hammock), amid leafy gardens with two outdoor pools and a hot tub. Also has excellent restaurant. R$375

Pousada Dourada Ilha do Meio 182 T 71 9271 0122, W facebook.com/PousadaDouradaItacimirim. Simple, clean and modern accommodation in a small house, with poo and a/c, though it's not on the beach. One English-speaking owner (Vincent). R$160

Praia do Forte

The hip little resort of **PRAIA DO FORTE**, some 83km north of Salvador, has a small but dazzling palm-lined beach and an array of arty craft shops, restaurants and bars along the main pedestrianized street, Alameda do Sol. There's also a pretty church right on the waterfront, the **Igreja São Francisco de Assis do Litoral**, completed in 1900.

Castelo Garcia D'Avila

Alameda Farol • Daily 8am–5pm • R$10 • ⓣ 71 3676 1133, ⓦ fgd.org.br

The **Castelo Garcia D'Avila** is a ruined fortress some 5km inland from town. The fort was one of the first major structures built by the Portuguese in Brazil (it has its origins way

THE LITORAL VERDE: ON THE ROAD TO RECIFE

Renting a car one-way is becoming a popular option for travelling **between Salvador and Recife**, affording a lot more flexibility, especially when it comes to exploring the coast of Bahia (which is a lot more enticing than the interior). North of Praia do Forte the coast is generally known as the **Litoral Verde**, with a bridge across the Rio Jacaré making driving to Acaraju in Sergipe (see page 252) easier than ever before on BA-099 and SE-100. Travelling by bus is a hassle but possible, though the Linha Verde (ⓣ 71 3460 2050) buses from Salvador tend to stick to the main road (BA-099); just tell the driver where you want to get off then walk or rent a *moto-taxi*.

IMBASSAÍ

There are beautiful palm-fringed beaches just 16km further north of Praia do Forte, around **Imbassaí**; they tend to be less busy, making it easier to find cheaper accommodation. The town is separated from the beach by the Rio Barroso and a giant sand dune (there's a footbridge across), 2km from the highway. *Pousadas* are available on both sides, with the beach side obviously more appealing.

DIOGO

For a peaceful place to stay, head to the village of **Diogo**, 5km north of Imbassaí; look for the right turn at Km 69 on BA-099 (signposted). The road turns into track by the time it reaches the village, 1km further along; from the village, a footpath crosses the river and leads through some attractive dunes before reaching a massive, usually empty, beach, with a few *barracas* and rustic eating spots.

SÍTIO DO CONDE

Some 85km north of Diogo on BA-099 lies the small town of **Conde**, with the beach resort of **Sítio do Conde** another 10km east on BA-233. It's a good base for another dazzling section of coast, from Barra do Itariri, 12km south, to Seribinha, 13km north.

MANGUE SECO

Around 50km north of Conde on a sandy spit that juts out between the Rio Real (the Sergipe border) and the ocean, Mangue Seco is blissfully remote, only accessible by boat or 4WD along bumpy tracks (the village is thought to have inspired Jorge Amado's novel *Tieta*). Surrounded by vast white-sand dunes and empty swathes of beach, the village is connected to Pontal (Sergipe) by boat (15min; R$60), another village connected to the town of Estância (Sergipe) by bus just twice a day (taxis from R$60). From Estância there are regular onward services to Aracaju (see page 252), in the Northeast, with Coopertalse (R$11.50; ⓦ coopertalse.com.br).

ACCOMMODATION

Cosy Pousada O Forte Praia da Costa, Mangue Seco ⓣ 79 9952 0813, ⓦ pousadaoforte.com. This luxurious option has twelve eco-friendly bungalows with a/c, TV and DVD player. Also offers private transfers from Salvador for R$450 for up to four people. **R$230**

Pousada Luar Praia Praia de Imbassaí ⓣ 71 3677 1030, ⓦ luardapraia.com.br. Good choice, right on the beach, with simple but comfy a/c rooms and buffet breakfast. Pick-up service from Salvador R$220. **R$180**

Pousada Talismã Sítio do Conde (on the beach) ⓣ 75 9991 3138, ⓦ facebook.com/pousadatalisma. Excellent beachfront option, with just five cosy rooms, all with TV and fridge. **R$100**

Pousada Too Cool na Bahia Diogo ⓣ 71 9952 2190, ⓦ toocoolnabahia.com.br. Popular option in the village of Diogo, with stylish and comfortable a/c chalets with views of the sea and Rio Imbassaí. **R$260**

back in 1551, but most of what you see today dates from the eighteenth century). The ruins are still an impressive sight and there's a restored chapel and small visitor centre.

Projeto Tamar

Av Farol Garcia D'Ávila • Daily 8.30am–5.30pm• R$24 • 71 3676 0321, projetotamar.org.br

One of the highlights of Praia do Forte is a visit to the local headquarters of **Projeto Tamar**, the conservation organization working to save and protect Brazil's threatened turtle population. Four species of turtle nest off the coast of Bahia, with their favoured spots at the end of the main drag here, beyond all the craft shops and stalls. Inside the Tamar reserve, you can see many turtles in large aquariums, most of them injured and unlikely to survive in the wild. The nesting season is from September to March.

ARRIVAL AND INFORMATION — PRAIA DO FORTE

By bus Buses leave regularly from the top of the main street (Alameda do Sol) for Salvador with Linha Verde (daily 9am–6pm; 3 daily; around R$10) and for further north up the coast to Imbassaí. Day-trips by boat from Salvador generally cost R$90/person (passeiosasilhas.com.br).

Information For general tourist information check out praiadoforte.org.br (there is no tourist office).

ACCOMMODATION AND EATING

Bar do Souza Alameda do Sol 71 3676 1386. Located at the entrance to the town, this lauded seafood restaurant and bar is known for its *bolinho de peixe* (fish balls) and *moqueca* (fish stew). It also features live music. Daily 10am–1am.

Pousada Ogum Marinho Alameda do Sol 71 3676 1165, ogumarinho.com.br. Close to the beach at the end of the main street, this posher option has cosy a/c rooms, a nice hammock veranda and a pool. R$360

Pousada Tia Helena Alameda das Estrelas 286 71 3676 1198, tiahelenapraiadoforte.com.br. This simple but clean choice is the closest you'll get to budget accommodation in high season, just 200m from the beach. Rooms come with ceiling fan, TV and private shower. (lobby only) R$180

Praia do Forte Hostel Rua da Aurora 155 71 3676 1094, albergue.com.br. Simple HI accommodation a 5min walk from the beach, with self-catering kitchen and a games room with a TV. Dorms and private rooms have a choice of a/c or fan. Prices for HI members are ten percent cheaper. Dorms R$80, doubles R$280

Terra Brasil Av ACM s/n 71 3676 1705. It's a local chain, but this modern Brazilian/Italian restaurant offers the best value on a now highly overpriced strip, with draught beer, decent seafood, good *moqueca* and excellent risottos. Mains are R$26–65. Daily noon–midnight.

The southern coast of Bahia

The BR-101 highway is the main route to the **southern coast of Bahia**, a region immortalized in the much translated and filmed novels of **Jorge Amado**, born in Itabuna. From the bus window you'll see the familiar fields of sugar replaced by huge plantations of *cacau* (cocoa). Southern Bahia produces two-thirds of Brazil's cocoa, almost all of which goes for export, making this part of Bahia the richest agricultural area of the state. The *zona de cacau* seems quiet and respectable enough today, with its pleasant towns and prosperous countryside, but in the last decades of the nineteenth century and the first decades of the twentieth, it was one of the most turbulent parts of Brazil. Entrepreneurs and adventurers from all over the country carved out estates here, often violently – a process chronicled by Amado in his novel *The Violent Land* (see page 671).

Valença

South of Salvador, the coast becomes swampy and by the time you get to **VALENÇA** you're in mangrove country. The city lies on the banks of the Rio Una, about 10km from the sea, at the point where the river widens into a delta made up of dozens of small islands, most of which support at least a couple of fishing villages. Today, it's also an increasingly popular destination for tourists from Salvador – mainly as a stop-off point for the nearby island resort of **Morro de São Paulo** and the pristine beaches of **Ilha de Boipeba**.

There are a couple of colonial churches – the **Igreja do Sagrado Coração de Jesus** (1801) and the more interesting **Igreja de Nossa Senhora do Amparo**, built in 1757 on a hill affording beautiful views over the city and accessed from near the market. The local beach, the **Praia de Guaibim**, is 18km north of town.

The boatyards

By far the most absorbing thing Valença has to offer is its **boatyards**, the *estaleiros navais*, along the river 500m downstream from the central Praça Admar Braga Guimarães. A whole series of wooden boats is produced here, largely by hand, ranging from small fishing smacks to large schooners, and local boat-builders are renowned throughout the state for their skill. Provided you don't get in the way – try going around midday, when work stops for a couple of hours – and ask permission, people are pleased to let you take a closer look and often take pride in showing off their work.

ARRIVAL AND DEPARTURE — VALENÇA

By bus Valença's rodoviária (☎75 3641 4894) is close to the centre of town, which is just a few blocks' walk away along the riverside towards the market. From Valença you can travel to Salvador via Bom Despacho and Itaparica by local van, and then the ferry across to Salvador, thereby reducing the journey by 150km. As of this writing there weren't direct bus services to Salvador from Valenca. Águia Branca (🌐aguiabranca.com.br) also runs 1 daily service to Porto Seguro (8hr 40min) for R$90–101; 2 daily to Ilhéus (4hr 45min; R$39–52); 3–4 daily to Camamu (2hr 25min; R$15); and 2 daily to Itacaré (3hr 20min; R$25). Viação São Geraldo (🌐saogeraldo.com.br) runs a daily service direct to Rio de Janeiro (9.30am; R$280; 25hr).

By ferry There are daily departures to Boipeba (see page 238) and Morro de São Paulo (see below) from the wharf along the river.

ACCOMMODATION AND EATING

Da Mara Travessa Pelicano Praia de Guaibim ☎75 3643 1393, 🌐bit.ly/RestaurantedaMara. You'll have to visit Guaibim beach for the best food in the area; this sleek, modern beach restaurant is well known throughout Brazil thanks to flattering media coverage over the years, and it still knocks out classic Bahian seafood, especially the fish and shrimp *moquecas*. It also has live music. Daily 10am–11pm.

Guaibim Hotel Praça da Independência 74 ☎75 3641 4114, 🌐guaibimhotel.com.br. Welcoming and good-value modern hotel in the centre of town, with small but cosy rooms. The restaurant serves *feijoada* every Saturday. 📶 R$80

Portal Rio Una Rua Maestro Barrinha ☎75 3641 5050, 🌐portalhoteis.tur.br. Ageing but comfy option surrounded by tropical gardens and pool, with TVs in a/c rooms, balconies and free wired internet. Also convenient for the ferries. Breakfast is R$41 extra. 📶 (lobby only) R$260

Morro de São Paulo

Covering the tip of the island of **Tinharé**, some 60km south of Salvador by sea (and 10km from Valença), the beach resort of **MORRO DE SÃO PAULO** ("mor-who de san paolo") is quite unlike anything else in Bahia. Safe, friendly, and with no cars and a string of gorgeous beaches lined with palm trees, reggae bars, hip *pousadas* and great seafood restaurants, it boasts a tropical, laidback beach scene reminiscent of Thailand or the Philippines – the main beaches are backed by jungle-clad mountains and you're as likely to hear Daft Punk as Sergio Mendes in the bars. Note, however, this is no longer a backpacker haven – far from it. Brazil's middle class – not to mention hordes of weekenders from Salvador – have been coming here for a while now, and though cheap hostels remain, posher *pousadas*, lounge bars and restaurants are far more prevalent. Between November and March (especially at weekends, which are best avoided altogether), Morro is utterly swamped with visitors, though at other times it can still seem relatively peaceful and undeveloped. If you want quiet, untouched beaches, head to Boipeba (see page 238); if you want to party with Brazilians, come to Morro.

Fortaleza do Tapirandú

Caminho do Fortaleza • Daily 24hr • Free

Once you've disembarked at the Morro ferry dock, walked through the historic **Portaló** (sea gate) paths take you up a short hill to the centre of the town, or left along the coast to the **Fortaleza do Tapirandú**. The coastal path follows the line of old walls to what's left of the Portuguese fortress, now nothing more than a ruined shell with a few rusty cannons amid the palms. The walls along the way have been restored, however, and the rest of the fort may receive the same treatment in the future – it dates back to the 1630s, though what you see today was mostly constructed in the 1750s. Just beyond the fort are the natural saltwater pools of the **Praia da Pedra do Facho**, a great place to swim at high tide and rarely busy.

Praça Nossa Senhora da Luz and around

Tiroleza do Morro: daily 9am–5pm • R$50 • T 75 8183 9874, W tiroleza.com.br

At the top of the hill from the ferry dock is tiny **Praça Nossa Senhora da Luz**, where you can carry on to the centre of town or turn left for the **Farol do Morro de São Paulo** (lighthouse). The plaza itself is dominated by the Neoclassical **Igreja Nossa Senhora da Luz**, built around 1845 over an earlier structure, with a simple but pretty interior of gold gilt and a Chinese-style roof. The path up to the lighthouse is a short but steep climb through the jungle, and the main reason for the hike is the viewpoint behind the 89m-high tower (built in 1855 on the site of another old fort, but still in use and off limits). From here, the whole of the beach strip is visible, though it is often obscured by the mobs of eager zipliners lining up for the 70m-high **Tiroleza do Morro** that shoots 340m down to the beach.

Praça Aureliano Lima and Fonte Grande

The heart of Morro is pretty **Praça Aureliano Lima**, lined with restaurants and the seventeenth-century **Casarão** ("big house"), once the home of the Portuguese captain of the guard and where Dom Pedro II spent the night in 1859 – it's now the *Pousada O Casarão* (see page 237). A **craft market** is held in the plaza every night (6pm–midnight). Turn left for Rua Caminho da Praia, the main road to the beaches, which is also crammed with shops and restaurants, or right for the **Fonte Grande**, the town's old water source in a much quieter part of the town. The current Baroque fountain and its domed cistern date from 1746.

The beaches

Five main beaches line the coast southeast of Praça Aureliano Lima and the town centre. The **Primeira Praia** (aka Prainha), at the lower end of Rua Caminho da Praia, has a few beach bars and cheapish accommodation, but isn't the nicest of the beaches and it's worth heading five minutes further south to **Segunda Praia** (or Praia da Poca), popular with the in-crowd from all over Brazil and boasting the island's best beach bars, swimming and snorkelling. The boardwalk finally peters out at **Terceira Praia** (Praia da Caeira), much narrower but pleasant and more laidback than Segunda Praia, with the ocean lapping the edge of wooden beach bars when the tide is in. The long (and quite glorious) **Quarta Praia** – divided into several sections around the headland from Terceira Praia – is the least developed stretch of sand. **Praia do Encanto** is little more than an extension of Quarta Praia, but has deeper natural pools. In the other direction, southwest of the centre, lies a series of less busy beaches leading up to the village of **Gamboa** – you can walk here via the Fonte Grande or take a ferry from the main dock.

ARRIVAL AND DEPARTURE — MORRO DE SÃO PAULO

All ferries to Morro arrive at the main dock, just below the town centre. Just inside the grand eighteenth-century Portaló (sea gate) lies a ticket office; as of 2017, there is no longer an arrival tax. When you leave by ferry, you must pass through the Cais do Porto on the pier itself to pay the R$10 "**Taxa de Embarque**" but you can tack this fee onto your ferry ticket upon purchase.

BY PLANE

It's possible to fly between Salvador airport and Morro, but by chartered air taxi only; try Aerostar (71 3612 8600, aerostar.com.br) or Addey (71 3377 1993, addey.com.br).

BY BOAT

From Valença Passenger ferries (call 75 3641 3011 for information) chug between Valença and Morro every hour (usually on the half hour, until 6.20pm) via Gamboa (R$4), costing R$25 and taking about 90min to get there. There's also a faster *lancha rapida*, which takes 30–40min but costs about R$25 (these go when full, which can be every few minutes during summer weekends). Heading back, for both services just turn up at the main dock in Morro and then you pay on board.

From Salvador Several boats run back and forth between the Terminal Turístico in Salvador (see box, page 229) and the ferry dock in Morro every day, beginning at 8am and usually running every hour or so till 2.30pm – boats back usually start at 5am with the last one at 3.30pm. Fares start at around R$95 for a one-way trip on a fast boat (*lancha*) or larger catamaran (usually a bit cheaper coming back); trips take about 3hr, but be warned, the sea can be rough, even on a fine day. See Bio Tur (biotur.com.br) or Passeios às Ilhas (passeiosasilhas.com.br) for more information.

INFORMATION AND TOURS

Information For information see morrodesaopaulo.com.br. There is no public tourist information point on Morro, but most hostels and *pousadas* can provide a wealth of info about the island and tours.

Services Cash is king in Morro, so make sure you bring enough. There are ATMs at aBanco do Brasil on the main plaza, and Bradesco on the main street but these often run out. Cyber Fonte internet café on Rua Fonte is open daily 8am–10pm (R$6/hr).

Boipeba and boat tours The cluster of kiosks along the path from the dock to the plaza (and along the beaches) all sell ferry tickets and the standard day-trip around Ilha de Boipeba (see page 238) which costs R$100; they take in the natural pools at Garapuá (along the southern coast of Tinharé), Boca da Barra beach on Boipeba, with another beach stop, plus a final stop on Ilha de Cairu as the boat makes a complete circumnavigation of Tinharé. If you intend to stay on Boipeba it's best to book a boat in Valença (see lanchaspuroprazer.com.br). You can also take a 4WD drive followed by a short boat ride to Boipeba from Segunda Praia (see page 239).

ACCOMMODATION

Accommodation on the island is all **expensive** relative to Salvador, particularly at holiday times. Most of the larger places are self-contained *pousadas*, with their own restaurant and bar. Nearly all places are within a stone's throw of the beaches.

MORRO DE SÃO PAULO

Che Lagarto Hostel Rua da Fonte Grande 11 75 3652 1018, chelagarto.com. Basic rooms and dorms, all with a/c, and a shared TV room, bar, table tennis and barbecue area – drinks are cheap and the owners lay on free popcorn to munch. Dorms R$45, doubles R$320

Morro Hostel Travessa Prudente de Moraes 11 2302 3163, thehostelmorro.com.br. The rooms are a little pricey at this newer, well-regarded hostel, but the place is clean and rooms are spacious and towels are provided. There is a simple buffet breakfast included and, like the other hostels, Morro offers communal dinner nights. Dorms R$58, doubles R$165

Porto de Cima Rua Porto de Cima 53 75 3652 1562. Excellent value, this is a simple inn set in lush gardens with pretty, rustic rooms, handmade furniture and hammocks, all 250m from the wharf. R$260

Pousada O Casarão Praça Aureliano Lima 190 75 3652 1022, ocasarao.net. Attractive early seventeenth-century mansion, this place offers both spacious a/c apartments and chalets with private balconies and hammocks, plus a little pool. R$230

★ **Pousada Natureza** Praça da Amendoeira (on the path to the lighthouse) 75 3652 1044, hotelnatureza.com. This spot has lovely rooms with hammock verandas, some apartments with jacuzzis, a patio bar set in attractive gardens and a pool. R$260

THE BEACHES

Hostel Rosa dos Ventos Rua Chalon, Terceira Praia 75 3652 1529, hostelrosadosventos.com.br. Solid, clean budget choice 5min from Segundo Praia, with a communal kitchen (till 11pm) and a sociable bar where you can swap stories with other travellers. There are a/c doubles and larger rooms with two bunks that can function as dorms. Adequate breakfast included. Dorms R$90, doubles R$240

Le Terrace Beach Hotel Segunda Praia 75 3652 1308, leterrace.com.br. Right on the sands in the heart of the action, this is the most enticing boutique hotel on the strip, with simple but stylish rooms that have LCD TVs and a/c (some with kitchenette too). R$300

Pousada Farol do Morro Rua Domingos Olindino Ramos 160, Primeira Praia 75 3652 1036, faroldomorro.com.br. Framed by a faux lighthouse, this affable place offers small but adequate a/c rooms with hammocks on balconies, scenic views and a small pool. R$210

Praia do Encanto Praia do Encanto (Quarta Praia) 75 3652 2000, praiadoencanto.com.br. This elegant *pousada* has some very comfortable apartments and some less expensive (but still comfortable) chalets, plus a good bar, restaurant and three pools in a tranquil stretch of the strip. Doubles R200

Villa das Pedras Segunda Praia 75 3652 1075, villadaspedras.com.br. Luxurious option, with its own beachside pool enclosed in lovely green gardens; all rooms have a/c, minibar and cable TV, and come with a fabulous breakfast buffet. R$450

EATING AND DRINKING

There are several good restaurants around the **Praça Aureliano Lima** and **Caminho da Praia** in town, with cheaper menus in the smaller, no-frills places towards the Fonte Grande. Most restaurants on the beaches double as bars, and drinks prices are usually standardized – R$8 for a beer, R$10 for caipirinhas – but look out for happy-hour deals. **Segunda Praia** can be smothered in tables on summer weekends, and you'll need to arrive early to snag one; further along the scene is more laidback.

MORRO DE SÃO PAULO

Bianco e Nero Rua Caminho da Praia 75 3652 1097. Top spot for pizza and other Italian classics (the name is a tribute to Juventus), steaks and seafood (mains R$25–45; pizzas R$50), on an enticing terrace overlooking the main drag. Mon 5.30–11.45pm, Tues–Sun noon–11.30pm.

Café des Artes Praça Aureliano Lima 157 75 99162 3668. Elegant place on the main plaza with a great afternoon coffee service (4–7pm) food and coffee combinations from R$9, including the petit gateau Baiana, a decadent coconut/chocolate/ice cream dish, and seafood dishes (R$40–100) like coconut shrimp with banana puree. It's all about the old-fashioned ambience and location. Daily 3–11pm.

Morena Bela Rua da Fonte Grande. This cheap joint knocks out stews, chicken, seafood and especially tasty *moquecas* for about R$25 per plate, with seating on plastic chairs and tables in a sleepy street. No sea views, but this is a real bargain. Daily 11.30am–midnight.

Papoula Rua da Lagoa 6 75 9867 3601, facebook.com/papoulaculinaria.artesanal. Popular local spot with a hippy vibe, *Papoula* has many à la carte items, including pizzas, sandwiches and salads. Good, cheap lunch specials are on offer and there are many vegetarian options. Get there right at noon, because the place fills up quick. Mon–Sat noon–11pm.

THE BEACHES

Chez Max Between Segunda and Terceira Praia 75 3652 1103, pousadachezmax.com. The Italian chefs here knock up better thin-crust pizza for your *reais* and pasta dishes, with, relaxed vibe and good music. Expect to pay R$35–65 per person. Daily 6pm–11pm.

Marilyn Café Segunda Praia 75 3652 1625. The place to be seen on the beachfront, with prime people-watching, quality cocktails and a surprisingly good menu for such a pretentious spot; try the *moqueca* (R$75 for two people), or fried fish ($80 for two people). Daily 9am–late.

★ **Pedra Sobre Pedra** Segunda Praia. Right at the north end of the beach, where the path comes down the hill, this bar is perched on a wooden deck with magnificent views, cold beers, snacks and decent caipirinhas. Open 24hr.

NIGHTLIFE

Pulsar Disco Club Caminho do Fortaleza 1 (the path to the Fortaleza do Tapirandú) 75 8104 3372, pulsardisco.com.br. Morro's party central is an Ibiza-style club that really gets going in the summer, with decent guest DJs from all over Brazil. Cover charge R$10–50. Sat midnight–8am.

Toca do Morcego Rua Caminho do Farol 11 (on the path up to the lighthouse) 75 3652 1355, tocadomorcego.com. Morro's second major club is located in the jungle, with a fine roster of DJ talent, scintillating views and more of a lounge-bar vibe. Cover R$80, but you can pick up flyers in advance for reductions. Sunset sessions Tues–Sun 4.30–10pm; club only Fri (but five nights a week in summer) midnight–6am.

Ilha de Boipeba

The beaches on the **Ilha de Boipeba**, separated from the Ilha de Tinharé by the Rio do Inferno, are even more beautiful than those at Morro de São Paulo, but much less developed, still possessing the tranquillity that Morro hasn't seen for over twenty years. The settlement here is small and scattered across the island, with a few facilities, including a decent number of restaurants and several *pousadas*. The beaches are simply gorgeous, and there's good snorkelling at the coral reefs near the Ponta da Castelhauos at the southernmost point of the island.

ARRIVAL AND ACTIVITIES — ILHA DE BOIPEBA

By plane There is a six-seater single-prop aircraft shuttle between Salvador airport and Boipeba (3 daily; 30min; R$610 one-way, plus R$30 boarding fee paid in Boipeba). Contact Bahia Terra for bookings (T 75 3653 6017, W boipebatur.com.br).

By car/boat From Morro's Segunda Praia you can take a 4WD drive (3 daily last at 5pm; 1hr; R$105) followed by a short boat ride to Boipeba (W boipebatur.com.br), or join a tour to the island (see page 237). Speedboats also run to Boipeba direct from Valença (50min; R$44). See W boipebatur.com.br to book tickets.

Activities It's possible to arrange outdoor activities through your *pousada*, including canoeing in the mangrove swamps, spotting wildlife in the coastal woodlands and horse riding on the beach, as well as surfing and diving.

ACCOMMODATION AND EATING

Casa Bobô Vila Monte Alegre, Moreré T 75 9930 5757, W pousadacasabobo.com. Managed by the indefatigable (English-speaking) Myriam and Nilton, this is a justly popular choice so book ahead; everything is spotless, beautifully crafted and maintained, with three cosy rustic-chic bungalows and healthy breakfasts, on a hill just a short walk or tractor ride from the pier. Wi-Fi R$300

Pousada Lua das Águas Rua da Praia, Praia Boca da Barra T 75 3653 6015, W luardasaguas.com.br. Very attractive bungalows with hammock verandas and a palm-thatched circular beach restaurant that serves some of the best seafood south of Fortaleza. Wi-Fi Daily noon–8pm (9pm in December). R$230

Pousada Santa Clara Travessa Da Praia 5 (Praia Boca da Barra) T 75 3653 6085, W santaclaraboipeba.com. Just a short walk from town, this hotel offers luxurious, spacious rooms but is best known for its good Bahian cooking (Tues–Sun 4–9pm). Wi-Fi (public areas). R$300

Barra Grande

Isolated out on the tip of the Península de Maraú, **BARRA GRANDE** is a blissfully untouched village at the heart of vast tracts of sandy beaches and the pristine waters of the Baía de Camamu. Things are changing, but for now the village retains a rustic appeal hard to beat – there's little to do but lounge on the sands or hike along the beaches. Most *pousadas* are located in Barra Grande village itself (where the ferries come in), while **Taipús de Fora** is a 7km strip of palm-fringed beach (20min drive south of Barra), facing an incredibly rich reef on the Atlantic side of the peninsula, with pools forming at low tide (you can also stay here).

ARRIVAL AND GETTING AROUND — BARRA GRANDE

By bus and boat Most people come by boat from Camamu; slow ferries depart from the pier hourly (6am–5pm; 1hr 40min; R$10), while faster speedboats (R$120) can be hired to make the trip in 40min. Camamu lies on BA-001, 325km south of Salvador and linked to it with regular buses (5hr); buses also depart from here to Itacaré (multiple daily; 55min; R$11), Ilhéus (4 daily; 2hr 20min; R$28) and Valença (3 daily; 2hr 25min; R$13).

By car Getting here with your own wheels (preferably 4WD) is possible in dry weather, but the drive entails a 50km ride of very poor, grinding dirt and sand tracks (BR-030).

By 4WD Local 4WD transports shuttle between the beaches when full (R$10).

ACCOMMODATION AND EATING

★ **Pousada Arte Latina** Praia de Taipús de Fora T 73 99903 768, W pousadaartelatina.com.br. Excellent choice on the Atlantic side of the peninsula, this rustic-chic inn is run by friendly owners Priscila and Pablo and has beautifully decorated rooms. They also do great drinks and food. Wi-Fi Daily 8–10am & 6–10pm. R$250

Pousada Ponta da Mutá Rua do Anjo, Barra Grande T 73 3258 6028, W pousadapontadomuta.com.br. Wonderfully located near the beach, with a choice of ocean or garden view apartments, all with a/c, TV/DVD, ceiling fans and hammock on the balcony or terrace. Wi-Fi R$300

Itacaré

Some 55km south of Camamu, **ITACARÉ** is a small fishing port off the main highway, BA-001, but much better known as a backpacker destination and haven for **surfing** and all manner of water-based adventure sports, including rafting and canoeing. The main town and port lies on the mouth of the Rio de Contas, with most of the *pousadas* and restaurants on Rua Pedro Longo, east of the centre; a short walk to the north lies **Praia da Concha**, lined with *barracas* and good for swimming, while the surf beaches lie to the east and south – you'll need a car to reach most of them, theough the idyllic **Praia do Resende** is located 200m south of town off the main road and is signposted.

ARRIVAL AND DEPARTURE — ITACARÉ

By bus The rodoviária lies just off the main road into town, Av Boa Vista (BA-654), a 15min walk from Rua Pedro Longo. Buses run frequently to Ilhéus (7am–7.40pm; 1hr 40min; R$17) but much less regularly to and from Camamu (multiple daily, last at 3pm; 55min) and Valença (multiple daily; 3hr). From Salvador it's best to take the ferry across to Bom Despacho on Ilha Itaparica and take the Águia Branca bus (aguiabranca.com.br) to Ilhéus, which should stop at Itacaré (check before you get on) – it takes around 4hr.

INFORMATION AND TOURS

Services There are currently three ATMs in town (including a Banco do Brasil three blocks away from the bus terminal) and most cafés and restaurants have wi-fi.

Tours and surfing Try Brazil Trip Tour (73 9996 3331, facebook.com/braziltriptour) on Rua Pedro Longo for a full range of activities, including trips along the Península de Maraú. For surfing instruction, contact the well-respected EasyDrop school (73 3251 3065, easydrop.com) at Rua João Coutinho 140. November to April is the best time for beginners, with rates ranging R$150–270 per day.

ACCOMMODATION AND EATING

Cantina d'Italia Rua Pedro Longo 282 73 3251 2677, facebook.com/cantinaitacare. Locals recommend this as the best Italian in town. Best is the *rodizio* (all-you-can-eat for R$29.90) pizza, pasta and lasagne on offer every night. Daily noon–11pm.

Casarão Verde Hostel Av Castro Alves, Praia da Coroa 73 3251 2037, casaraoverdehostel.com.br. Fun hostel in a gorgeous pea-green mansion built in 1913. The elegant dorms are spacious and clean (with fans), and there are basic doubles with shared bathroom and fan. You can opt to have breakfast included or not (R$7–10 more). Dorms R$37, doubles R$105

Itacaré Hostel Praca Santos Dumont #2 73 3251 2402, facebook.com/itacare.hostel. This solid hostel offers cheap dorms and rooms just off the main drag (though not quite as atmospheric as *Casarão Verde*), with a choice of, a/c dorms and fan-cooled or a/c doubles and fully equipped kitchen. Friendly owner Junior speaks some English and can help organize tours and transfers. Dorms R$45, doubles R$80

Manga Rosa Rua Pedro Longo 249 073 3251 3095, restaurantemangarosa.com.br. Relatively expensive restaurant in the heart of town, popular with tourists but still a good bet for decent Brazilian dishes, pasta and seafood, though you are paying for the location (and really good free wi-fi). Mains cost R$35–45. Mon–Sat noon–11pm, Sun 5–11pm.

★ **Pousada Casa Tiki** Rua C 30, Praia da Concha 73 99804 8901, pousadacasatiki.com.br. Gorgeous hotel with four simple but immaculate, colourful rooms, all with a/c, and lush gardens and breakfast included. R$240

Ilhéus

In literary terms **ILHÉUS**, 70km south of Itacaré at the mouth of the Rio Cachoeira, is the best-known town in Brazil, as the setting for **Jorge Amado**'s most famous novel, *Gabriela, Cravo e Canela*, translated into English as "Gabriela, Clove and Cinnamon". If you haven't heard of it before visiting Ilhéus, you soon will; it seems like every other bar, hotel and restaurant is either named after the novel or one of its characters. Traditionally Ilhéus has also been popular for its lively city beaches, though given the options now available to the south and north, these need not detain you long.

Catedral de São Sebastião

Praça Don Eduardo • Daily 8am–noon & 2–5pm • Free

The city's landmark **Catedral de São Sebastião** on Praça Don Eduardo looks like a Romanesque wedding cake, with a 48m-high dome, but was actually started in 1931 and only dedicated in 1967. It replaced an older chapel deemed too small for the city and demolished.

Igreja Matriz de São Jorge

Praça Rui Barbosa • Tues–Sun 10am–6pm • Free; R$10 for museum

Dating back to a structure completed in the 1570s, the **Igreja Matriz de São Jorge** (closed for renovation at time of research) is the oldest church in the city (though most of what you see today is seventeenth century), containing an old and venerated image of Saint George (São Jorge). The sacristy serves as a small **Museu de Arte Sacra**, with the usual church silverware, various religious sculptures and antique furniture on display.

Museu Casa de Cultura Jorge Amado

Rua Jorge Amado 21 • Mon–Fri 9am–12.30pm & 2–6pm, Sat 9am–1pm • R$5 (R$2.50 for students) • 73 3634 8986

Housed in an ornate mansion commissioned by Amado's father in 1926, the **Museu Casa de Cultura Jorge Amado** was once the home of the city's most famous son and now contains exhibits on the region's chocolate industry and Amado himself. Born in Itabuna in 1912, Amado moved to Ilhéus when he was a baby, and spent much of his life here and in Salvador.

3

The beaches

Apart from the centre, you'll find the main concentration of bars in Ilhéus along the fine beach promenade of the Avenida Soares Lopes, east of the centre – the beach itself called simply **Avenida** – though much of it is polluted and not recommended for bathing. There are other beaches to the south: **Do Cristo** is on the river with a statue of Christ the Redeemer, and tiny **Da Concha** and **Do Sul** are south of the Rio Cachoeira. Some 6km south of the centre lies the area's best beach, **Praia dos Milionários**, lined with coconut palms. Some 8km south lies **Cururupe**, where there are a series of bars, some holiday homes and groves of palm trees. **Backdoor**, the famous right **surf break**, is at Km 14, while the beaches of the suburban community of **Olivença** begin at Km 17 – **Batuba** (batubabeach.com.br) and then Praia de Olivença itself. Other than the sands, the main attraction in Olivença is the tranquil **Balneário Tororomba**, a public swimming bath built around mineral water from the Rio Tororomba.

ARRIVAL AND DEPARTURE — ILHÉUS

By plane Aeroporto Jorge Amado is 3km from the centre on Rua Brig. Eduardo Gomes, on the south side of the river (73 3234 4000); taxis should be around R$30. Localiza (73 3231 8158) has a car rental desk in the terminal and there are several ATMs. Most regional carriers operate flights here, notably from Belo Horizonte, Rio, Salvador and even Porto Seguro.

By bus The rodoviária (73 3634 4121) is on Praça Cairu, 3.5km west of the centre of Ilhéus, but buses outside marked "Centro" or "Olivença" will take you into town; from the centre take the "Teotônio Vilela" or "Salobrinho" buses (15min; R$3.10). Destinations Itacaré (every hour; 1hr 40min); Porto Seguro (4 daily; 6hr); Rio (1 daily; 17hr); Salvador (3 daily; 8); São Paulo (1 daily; 28hr); Vitória (2 daily; 15hr).

ACCOMMODATION AND EATING

★ **Bar Vesúvio** Praça Dom Eduardo 73 3634 2164, barvesuvio.com. Yes, it's a tourist trap, but this is one of the most famous bars in Brazil thanks to Amado's *Gabriela, Cravo e Canela*. It has a genuine history that goes back to the 1910s and really was frequented by indolent cocoa farmers. Dishes named after "Nacib"– the Middle Eastern owner in the novel – are still served, with cold draught beer (R$6) and *pastel árabe* (a sweet cake, a bit like baklava; R$5.50). Mon–Fri 3–11pm, Sat & Sun 11.30am–11pm.

Bataclan Av 2 de Julho 77 73 3633 4701, bataclan.com.br. Fashionable restaurant, gift shop and arts centre associated with the famed Amado novel (it was a brothel until the 1940s), with a room dedicated to the former owner and Amado character "Maria Machadão". Mains R$50–60. Mon–Sat 10am–11pm.

Ilhéus Hotel Rua Eustáquio Bastos 144 73 3084 4733, ilheushotel.com.br. This grand old canary-coloured building is loaded with character, a faded 1930s highrise by the water in the centre of town. Rooms are simple but adequate (some with sea views), and come with fan or a/c and TV. **R$100**

Pousada Pier do Pontal Lomanto Júnior 1650 73 3221 4000, pierdopontal.com.br. Solid mid-range choice on the south side of the river, near the airport, with modern but rustic-chic style rooms, all with cable TV and a/c. Also has sushi restaurant. **R$310**

Porto Seguro

The most popular destination in southern Bahia is the resort area around **PORTO SEGURO**, where Cabral supposedly "discovered" Brazil in 1500. Founded in 1526, the port has some claim to being the oldest town in Brazil, and buildings still survive from that period, but the modern city is a no-nonsense beach resort in the mould of Spain's Costa del Sol – it can be a fun place to party, but if you value character keep on going to Arraial (see page 243).

Cidade Alta

The colonial area, **Cidade Alta**, is built on a bluff overlooking the town, with fine views out to sea and across the Rio Buranhém. The **Igreja da Misericórdia**, begun in 1526, is one of the two oldest churches in Brazil. The **Igreja de Nossa Senhora da Pena**, nearby, dates from 1773 but is said to contain the oldest religious icon in Brazil, a St Francis of Assisi, brought over in the first serious expedition to Brazil, in 1503. There are the ruins of a Jesuit church and chapel (dating from the 1540s) and a small, early fort; the squat and thick-walled style of the churches shows their early function as fortified strongpoints in the days when attacks by indigenous tribes were common. Near the ruins of the Jesuit college on Praça Pero Campos de Tourinho, and encased in glass, the **Marca do Descobrimento** is a 2m-high column sunk to mark Portuguese sovereignty in 1503; nearby is the **Museu do Descobrimento** (daily 9am–3pm; R$3), a small museum which adds context with displays on the early history of the region.

The beaches

North of town is a string of superb beaches along the Beira Mar coast road. The nearest, **Praia Curuípe**, is 3km away and has some natural pools and reefs, as well as beachside restaurants. More popular, and just 1km further away, is **Praia Itacimirim**. These beaches, and others further north (notably Mundaí, 6km, and Taperapuá, 7km – both good for scuba diving), are connected to Porto Seguro by regular seafront buses ($R4).

ARRIVAL AND INFORMATION — PORTO SEGURO

By plane Porto Seguro Airport is 2km from the centre, with flights from Belo Horizonte, Ilhéus, Rio, Salvador and Vitória. Taxis to the centre or beaches are around R$20–30.

By bus The rodoviária is 1.5km out of town, but taxis are cheap and plentiful (R$25–35 for the centre or beaches).

Destinations Belo Horizonte (2 daily; 17hr); Ilhéus (3 daily; 4hr); Rio (1 daily; 18hr 30min); Salvador (1 daily; 11hr 30min); São Paulo (1 daily; 17hr); Vitória, Espírito Santo (2 daily; 10hr 15min).

Tourist information There are several tourist information offices: at the rodoviária, the airport (although operating hours can be erratic), and in the centre of town at the Secretaria de Turismo, Av Portugal 350 (Mon–Fri 8am–5pm; 73 7811 3450, portosegurotur.com).

ACCOMMODATION AND EATING

Hotel prices in Porto Seguro vary astonishingly between **high and low season**: a budget hotel in November can triple in price by Christmas (remember this when considering the high-season prices quoted). **Cidade Baixa**, below the colonial area, is where the nightlife action is; the riverside Av 22 de Abril and its continuation, Av Portugal, are a mass of bars, restaurants and hotels known at night as Passarela do Álcool, or "Alcohol Street".

Best Western Shalimar Praia Av Beira Mar 1, Praia do Cruzeiro 73 3288 7000, shalimar.com.br. Standard, spacious chain a/c rooms, but with pool, gym, sauna, jacuzzi and free wi-fi. R$270

Hotel Estalagem Rua Marechal Deodoro 66 73 3288 2095, hotelestalagem.com.br. Excellent-value hotel located in a colonial building from 1810 close to the Passarela do Álcool, which has been carefully and tastefully renovated. Rooms are small, but have a/c and cable TV and there's a swimming pool; it's a 10min walk from the centre. R$135

Rabanete Rua Saldanha Marinho 83 73 3288 2743, facebook.com/RabanetePortoSeguro. Justly popular local restaurant – à la carte dishes are on offer but the buffet *por quilo* (R$42) is the best way to go. Leave room for the amazing desserts and avoid lunch between 1pm and 2pm when it tends to be mobbed. Daily noon–10pm.

Arraial d'Ajuda

Just south of Porto Seguro across the Rio Buranhém, **ARRAIAL D'AJUDA** is a lively beach resort that can become very crowded, though the further you get from the bars and the restaurants on **Praia Mucugê**, the easier it is to find a peaceful spot. Compared to Seguro, however, it retains a lot more charm, with narrow lanes and chilled-out *pousadas*.

ARRIVAL AND DEPARTURE — ARRAIAL D'AJUDA

By ferry/bus Catch the ferry from the centre of Porto Seguro for the 10min journey across the Rio Buranhém (24hr; every hour after midnight; R$3). From the other side, buses (R$3.10) climb the hill and drop you in the centre of town. Don't stay on the bus after this or you'll find yourself making a very boring round-trip.

ACCOMMODATION AND EATING

Arraial d'Ajuda Hostel Rua do Campo 94 73 3575 1192, arraialdajudahostel.com.br. The local hostel offers clean dorms and doubles with a/c 10pm–7am only (24hr in privates). Dorms R$55, doubles R$160

Pousada Marambaia Alameda dos Flamboyants 116 73 3575 1275, hotelmarambaia.com.br. Clean, chalet-style rooms around a peaceful, lush courtyard, complete with swimming pool and gently jangling cowbells. R$195

Pousada Pé-na-Estrada Rua Jequitibá 60 73 3575 3878, penaestradapousada.com.br. Excellent mid-range option close to the Praia Mucugê with spotless rooms and flat-screen TVs. A big breakfast is included. R$205

3

ON THE ROAD TO ESPÍRITO SANTO

Heading south between Salvador and Vitória (see page 186) and Rio (see page 57), if you have your own car you can be more flexible to explore the numerous beaches and villages along **the southern coast** of Bahia.

CARAÍVA

If you want to get away from civilization in this part of Bahia you have to go south to **Caraíva** on the banks of the Rio Caraíva, not accessible by road (cars are parked on the other side of the river, which is crossed by canoe). Two buses (2hr) a day leave from Arraial and Trancoso, but it's a bumpy ride on 32km of dirt road. Once there, you'll find superb beaches, a few rustic places to stay, some good food and plenty of peace and quiet.

CARAVELAS

On the banks of the Rio Caravelas, in the extreme south of Bahia, lies **Caravelas**, an attractive colonial port town, and nearby **Praia do Grauçá**. Both are – despite the growth of tourism – very relaxing places. Caravelas is also the jumping-off point for the Parque Nacional Marinho dos Abrolhos.

PARQUE NACIONAL MARINHO DOS ABROLHOS

The main reason people visit the southern region of Bahia is to see the extraordinary profusion of marine and bird life in the **Parque Nacional Marinho dos Abrolhos**, an archipelago of five islands lying 72km from Caravelas (landing is only allowed on one island, Siriba). Among the clear waters and coral reefs here live all kinds of rare fish, sea turtles and birds, and between July and early November the waters are home to humpback whales taking refuge from the Antarctic winter. Various agents in Caravelas can arrange day-trips for around R$330 (3hr one-way), leaving at 7am and returning at 5pm (includes lunch and a snack); try Horizonte Aberto at Av das Palmeiras 313 (73 3297 1474, horizonteaberto.com.br).

ACCOMMODATION

Memoan Hostel Caraíva 61 3297 2415, memoanhostel.com.br. This hostel has clean dorms and doubles and communal kitchen. Dorms R$60, doubles R$110

Pousada Liberdade Av Ministro Adalício Nogueria 1551, Caraíva 73 3297 2415, pousadaliberdade.com.br. Spacious, well-equipped (a/c, fridge, TV) modern chalets as well as more basic doubles, just a few minutes by car from town. R$120

EATING AND NIGHTLIFE

RESTAURANTS

Restaurante Do Paulo Pescador Praça São Braz 116 ⊕73 3575 1242, ⊕paulopescador.com.br. Justly popular Italian-Brazilian emporium serving a fusion of spaghetti with *moqueca*, lots of fresh seafood and roast meats. Wed–Sun noon–10pm.

Rosa dos Ventos Alameda dos Flamboyants 24 ⊕73 3575 1271. Lauded open-air restaurant with fresh seafood, excellent goulash and amazing *apfelstrudel* (seriously). Count on R$50/person. Daily 4pm–midnight.

CLUB

Morocha Praia Mucugê ⊕morochaclub.com. Mucugê is the place to come for a night out, especially this club, which has live rock music daily (6pm–4am) except Sundays.

Trancoso and around

TRANCOSO is a more relaxed, chilled-out backpacker resort than Arrail d'Ajuda. On foot it's a beautiful walk – 12km down the beach from Arraial – but you have to ford a couple of rivers so be prepared to get wet. Some 25km south of Trancoso, **Praia do Espelho** is another jaw-dropping strip of sand and offshore reef.

3

ARRIVAL AND DEPARTURE — TRANCOSO AND AROUND

By bus Buses run hourly (8am–6pm; 1hr; R$10) from Arraial d'Ajuda to Trancoso.

ACCOMMODATION

Mata N'ativa Pousada Estrada do Arraial ⊕73 3668 1830, ⊕matanativapousada.com.br. Offers lovely accommodation in tropical gardens by a river; English, Italian and French are spoken, and there are four rooms with a/c and private bathrooms. R$390

Pousada Enseada do Espelho Praia do Espelho ⊕73 99985 4608, ⊕enseadadoespelho.com.br. Luxury accommodation, with drape-lined beds and elegant furnishings, cable TV and a/c. R$560

The Bahian sertão

The **Bahian sertão** is immense: an area considerably larger than any European country and constituting most of the land area of Bahia state. Much of it is semi-desert, with endless expanses of rock and cactus broiling in the sun. But it can be spectacular, with ranges of hills to the north and broken highlands to the west, rearing up into the tableland of the great **Planalto Central**, the plateau extending over most of the state of Goiás and parts of Minas Gerais. No part of the Bahian *sertão* is densely populated, and most of it is positively hostile to human habitation; in some places, no rain falls for years at a stretch. By far the most popular route into the region is westwards along the BR-242, which eventually hits the Belém–Brasília highway in Goiás: en route you'll pass the old mining town of **Lençóis**, gateway to the staggering natural wonders of the **Chapada Diamantina** – one of Brazil's best and most accessible trekking areas.

Lençóis

Some 425km west of Salvador, **LENÇÓIS** is an ex-mining town and the main tourist centre in the Chapada Diamantina region. The name of the town, meaning "sheets", derives from the camp that grew up around a diamond strike in 1844. The miners, too poor to afford tents, made do with sheets draped over branches. Lençóis is a pretty little town, set in the midst of the spectacular Parque Nacional da Chapada Diamantina (see page 246). Most of its fine old buildings date back to the second half of the nineteenth century, when the town was a prosperous mining community, attracting diamond buyers from as far afield as Europe.

The centre of the town, between two lovely squares, Praça Otaviano Alves and Praça Horácio de Matos, is made up of cobbled streets, lined with well-proportioned two-storey nineteenth-century houses with high, arched windows. On Praça Horácio, the **Subconsulado Francês**, once the French consulate, was built with the money of the European diamond-buyers, who wanted an office to take care of export certificates.

Mercado Cultural

Praça Aureliano Sá • Mon–Sat 6pm–11pm • Free

The **Mercado Cultural**, next to the bridge over the Rio Lençóis that runs through the centre, is where most of the diamonds were sold and now houses craft stalls – it has Italian- and French-style trimmings tacked on to make the buyers feel at home.

Salão das Areias

Local **artesanato** is very good, particularly the bottles filled with coloured sand arranged into intricate patterns; get a guide to take you to the **Salão das Areias** on the outskirts of town, where you can see the sand being gathered and put into bottles by local artisans.

ARRIVAL AND INFORMATION — LENÇÓIS

By plane Azul operates one daily flight (1hr) between Salvador and the tiny airport outside Coronel Octaviano Alves (20km from Lençóis), where taxis will take you into town (R$100; agencies run transfers for R$25) or to destinations inside the Parque Nacional da Chapada Diamantina.

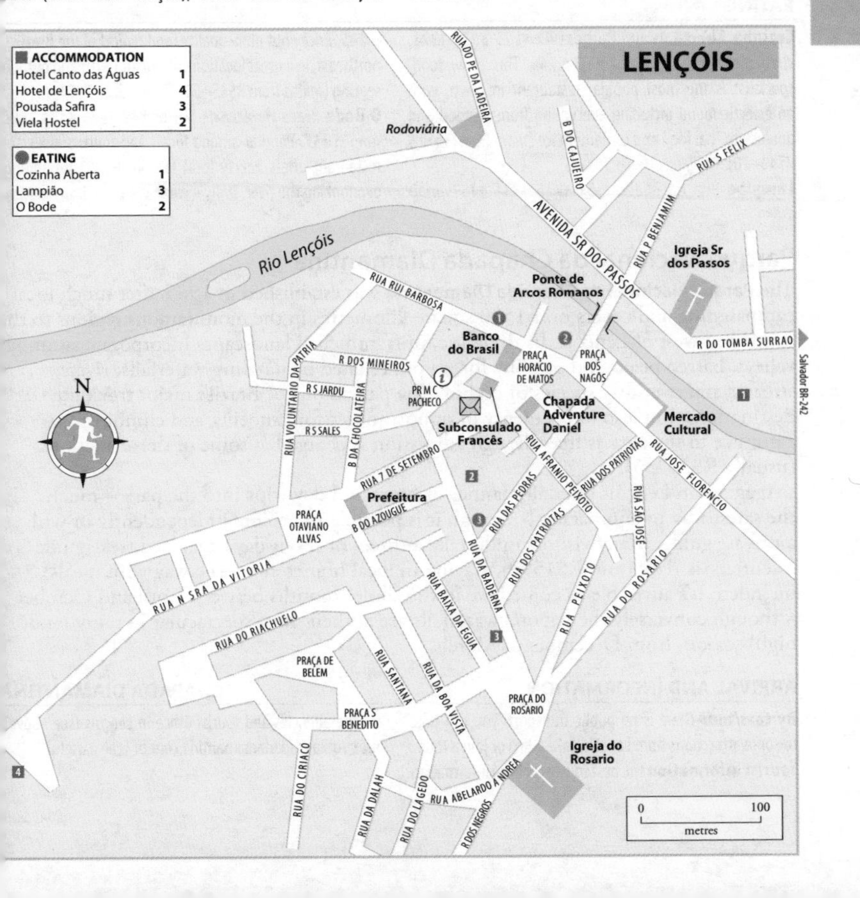

By bus Three Real Expresso (T 0800 883 8830, W realexpresso.com.br) buses a day make the 6hr journey from Salvador to Lençóis, all arriving at the main rodoviária in town; departures at the time of research were 7am, 1pm, & 11pm (R$80). Buses return to Salvador at 7.30am, 1.15pm, and 11.35pm.

Tourist information Information is available from the Associação dos Conductores de Visitantes at Rua 10 de Novembro 22 (daily 8am–noon & 2–8pm; T 75 3334 1425).

Services Banco do Brasil has a branch at Praça Horácio de Matos 56.

ACCOMMODATION

★ **Hotel Canto das Águas** Av Senhor dos Passos 1 T 75 3334 1154, W lencois.com.br; map p.245. Expensive but excellent option, with luxurious rooms, well- kept gardens, a meditation and massage area and a beautiful riverside location; hearty breakfasts and a pool included. R$344

Hotel de Lençóis Rua Altina Alves 747 T 75 3334 1102, W hoteldelencois.com; map p.245. Located mainly in a small mansion with spacious, modern rooms, this attractive place is set in the heart of sweet-smelling gardens with its own lauded restaurant. R$320

Pousada Safira Rua Miguel Calmon 124 T 75 3334 1443; map p.245. This is one of the friendliest budget options but with just a few small rooms, all with their own bathroom. It's a little hard to find in the backstreets at the heart of town. Breakfast is included. (public areas) R$100

Viela Hostel Travessa do Tamandaré s/n T 75 3334 1271, W facebook.com/vielahostel; map p.245. Located in the centre, this is a very popular and economical place to stay. *Viela* has two kitchens and two TV rooms (one with Netflix), and a pool table. Breakfast is not served. Dorms R$50, doubles R$150

EATING

Cozinha Aberta Av Rui Barbosa 42 T 75 3334 1321, W cozinhaaberta.com.br; map p.245. This "slow food" specialist is the most popular restaurant in town, with an eclectic menu including everything from seafood and goulash to Thai food and cardamom ice cream (most mains R$40–70). Daily noon–10.30pm.

Lampião Rua da Baderna 51 T 75 3334 1157; map p.245. Pricey but high-quality food typical of the Brazilian northeast, in a great location with rustic decor and outdoor seating (mains from R$35–50). Tues– Sun 5–11pm.

O Bode Praca Horácio de Matos 849 T 75 3334 1600; map p.245. Popular among locals and tourists alike, this restaurant offers hearty local fare in rustic surroundings overlooking the river. Daily except Wed lunch until 4pm.

Parque Nacional da Chapada Diamantina

The **Parque Nacional da Chapada Diamantina** was established in 1985 after much local campaigning and covers over 1500 square kilometres in the mountainous regions to the south and west of Lençóis. Its dramatic, untrammelled landscapes incorporate swampy valleys, barren peaks and scrubby forest, punctuated by dazzling waterfalls, rivers, streams and over fifty species of orchid. The park is one of Brazil's major **trekking** destinations, but also offers plenty of opportunities for canoeing and climbing. Entrance to the park is free, though admission is charged at some of the attractions (usually R$25–35).

Agencies in Lençóis offer all manner of **tours** and **day-trips** into the park – much the safest way to approach it – though it is possible to explore independently or with a private guide. Many visitors undertake a three- or seven-day organized trek (guide essential; six days from R$1590), staying in local houses along the way with meals included. It's advisable to come here in the cooler months between April and October – though conversely the region's waterfalls are at their most spectacular in rainy (and high) season, from December to March.

ARRIVAL AND INFORMATION — CHAPADA DIAMANTINA

By taxi/tour There is no public transport; you can hike to some attractions from Lençóis, take a taxi or join a tour.

Tourist information The best sources of local information are the agencies and tourist office in Lençóis (see above) but W guiachapadadiamantina.com.br is also useful.

THE TRAGIC HISTORY OF CANUDOS

Today just a typical small town in the *sertão*, 400km north of Salvador, **Canudos** provided the backdrop for one of the most remarkable and tragic events in Brazilian history. Canudos was founded in 1893 by messianic religious leader **Antônio Conselheiro**, an itinerant preacher who gathered thousands of followers (including landless farmers, former slaves and indigenous people) disenchanted with the central Brazilian government in Rio. Within a few years this autonomous community numbered 30,000 people.

They were dubbed "rebels" by the central government, and attempts were made to bring Canudos to heel in 1896 and 1897, but the first three expeditions were resoundingly defeated; in the worst shock the young republic had suffered to that point, the third force, led by Paraguayan war hero **Colonel Moreira César**, was completely annihilated. A fourth expedition was sent late in 1897, just after Conselheiro had died of fever; this time Canudos fell, almost all of its defenders massacred and raped, and the 150 survivors sent to prisons or brothels.

The brutality of the final assault was not fully appreciated at the time, though the events were immortalized by **Euclides da Cunha** in *Os Sertões* (1902), translated into English as "Rebellion in the Backlands". Cunha didn't see the fighting himself, only the aftermath, and essentially regarded the Brazilian interior (and Canudos) as highly primitive. Conselheiro's town remained a wasteland for many years, and the old church ruins were drowned in the 1970s by dam construction. Velho Canudos – "new" Canudos – now lies a few kilometres down the road. On what remains of the old site lies a statue of Antônio Conselheiro and the tiny, single-room **Museu Histórico de Canudos** (Mon–Fri 8am–noon, 2–5pm; free) containing trinkets salvaged from the site (pistols, buttons, needles and the like). When the reservoir is low, you can still spy some of the ruins poking out of the water.

3

TOURS

To make the most of the park you'll need a proper guide, as the countryside can be difficult to negotiate. Standard rates for independent guides are between R$150 and R$200 per day for a group of five or six people, though it can be tough to find someone who speaks good English. Ask at the tourist office in Lençóis (see page 246) or at the agencies below.

Chapada Adventure Daniel Praça Horácio de Matos 114, Lençóis ⊕75 3334 1933, ⊕chapadaadventure.com.

Extreme Eco Adventure Av 7 de Setembro 15, Lençóis ⊕75 3341 1727, ⊕extremeecoadventure.com.br.

H20 Travel Adventures Rua do Pires, Lençóis ⊕75 3334 1229, ⊕h2otraveladventures.com.

ACCOMMODATION

Most visitors to the park base themselves in Lençóis (see page 244), but there several other towns and villages in the region that offer accommodation, notably the bohemian community of **Capão**, 70km from Lençóis (hikeable in two or three days) and 20km from **Palmeiras** (via good dirt road), on the other side of the park; *coletivos* shuttle between Palmeiras and Capão for around R$20 (30min); a taxi will be R$60–70.

Pousada do Capão Vale do Capão ⊕75 3334 1034, ⊕pousadadocapao.com.br. Elegant rooms with rustic but artsy decor, lovely balconies and big breakfast included. R$200

Pousada Pé no Mato Ladeira da Vila 2, Caeté-Açú (Vale do Capão) ⊕75 3344 1105, ⊕penomato.com.br. Offers simple but adequate rooms with fans, dorms and more comfortable suites and chalets with verandas, TVs and fans. Dorms R$60, doubles R$120, suites and chalets (minimum three nights) R$190

Pousada Sincorá Av Paraguaçu 120, Andaraí ⊕75 3335 2210, ⊕sincora.com.br. Colonial-style house with cosy, clean a/c rooms with TVs and fridge; whopping breakfast included. Doubles R$95, camping R$12

The Northeast

PORTO DE GALINHAS

The Northeast

Long regarded as one of Brazil's poorest areas, the Northeast is now a region with a modern economy and a continously growing tourism business. Despite having the most dazzling coastline in South America, a buzzing beach scene and an exuberant culture that blends samba, reggae and African influences, the area, divided politically into eight separate states, has not been spoilt by tourism. There are major cities along the coast: some, such as Recife, Olinda, São Luís and Fortaleza, have deep colonial heritage; others, such as Maceió and Natal, have developed mostly in recent decades. All of these cities have their own city beaches plus more idyllic and deserted resorts hidden up and down the coast. The Ilha de Fernando de Noronha, hundreds of kilometres offshore, is one of the finest oceanic wildlife reserves in the world – expensive, but perfect for ecotourism.

While most travellers stick to **the coast**, it's the semi-arid region inland, the **sertão**, where the stereotypes, traditions and legends of the Northeast have most endured. There is still much poverty here and the land still suffers periods of intense drought; yet in the wet season it is transformed for a few glorious months to a verdant green, and there are some intriguing destinations to uncover, from ancient petroglyphs to poignant reminders of folk hero **Lampião**.

Alagoas and Sergipe

The smallest Brazilian states and long ignored by travellers, **Alagoas** and **Sergipe** have developed rapidly in recent years, shedding their reputation as the poorest parts of the nation and boasting their own dizzying stretches of pristine white sands. Though lacking the romance of Rio and Salvador, the two state capitals of **Maceió** and **Aracaju** offer fine beaches and a smattering of history, while some genuinely well-preserved colonial towns are a short bus ride away. This part of Brazil is also noted for its quality **crabs**, while its **festivals** are some the biggest; Aracaju's **Forró Caju** music festival attracts over one million revellers every June.

Along with Bahia, this region was at the heart of Brazil's sugar boom in the nineteenth century, though most of the population remained grindingly poor through to the 1980s (sugar is still a major crop). Thanks in part to a minor offshore oil boom,

SPINNER DOLPHIN, FERNANDO DO NORONHA

Highlights

❶ **Capela Dourada, Recife** This fabulous eighteenth-century church is a riot of gold gilt and lavish oil paintings. See page 270

❷ **Olinda** Best visited during Carnaval, when colourful parades snake through beautifully preserved colonial streets. See page 278

❸ **Porto de Galinhas** One of Brazil's most beautiful beaches, this place really comes to life during high season, when sound systems and DJs from Recife's trendiest clubs move out here. See page 284

❹ **The sertão** Take a road-trip into the dusty heartlands of old Brazil, home to mysterious prehistoric petroglyphs, dinosaurs, *vaqueiros* and the bandit Lampião. See page 286

❺ **Fernando de Noronha** A gorgeous archipelago visited by thousands of dolphins early each morning. See page 287

❻ **Jericoacoara** With some of the finest beaches and best surf and wind in Brazil, Jericoacoara lies deep within the giant dunes of the Ceará coast. See page 309

❼ **São Luís** Tropical, torpid city of faded colonial elegance, beaches, Bumba-meu-boi and reggae bands. See page 316

HIGHLIGHTS ARE MARKED ON THE MAP ON PAGE 252

a degree of affluence has been brought to parts of the coast, though travel inland through the tropical scrub forest (*caatinga*), and potholed roads, rickety buses and ramshackle villages are still in evidence. This is despite Alagoas in particular wielding an inordinate amount of influence on the national stage over the years: ex-presidents **Floriano Peixoto** (1839–95) and **Deodoro da Fonseca** (1827–92) both hailed from the state, while **Fernando Collor de Mello** (b. 1949), the ex-president impeached for corruption in the 1990s, remains leader of a powerful political dynasty based in Maceió (he's currently the federal senator for Alagoas).

Aracaju

Some 325km north from Salvador, **ARACAJU**, the capital of **Sergipe**, comes as a surprise. Gone is the dominant Afro-Brazilian culture of Bahia (though still a major influence in festivals), replaced with a more typical multi-racial Brazilian mix, while the city itself is the kind of affluent, ordered place more associated with the southeast, with a thicket of condos expanding the city ever outwards. Much of its wealth comes from the exploitation of the Sergipe Basin oilfields since the 1960s (just offshore), though the city is relatively new, founded in 1855 as one of the nation's first purpose-built state capitals. Today, Aracaju has multiple centres: the *centro histórico* on the Rio Sergipe is its traditional heart and retains much of its commerce and civic buildings, though the best nightlife, restaurants and recreation have moved south to the **beaches** especially **Atalaia**. Other than a couple of good museums, there are no real major sights in the city, but you can base yourself here to visit the two colonial gems of **São Cristóvão** and **Laranjeiras**.

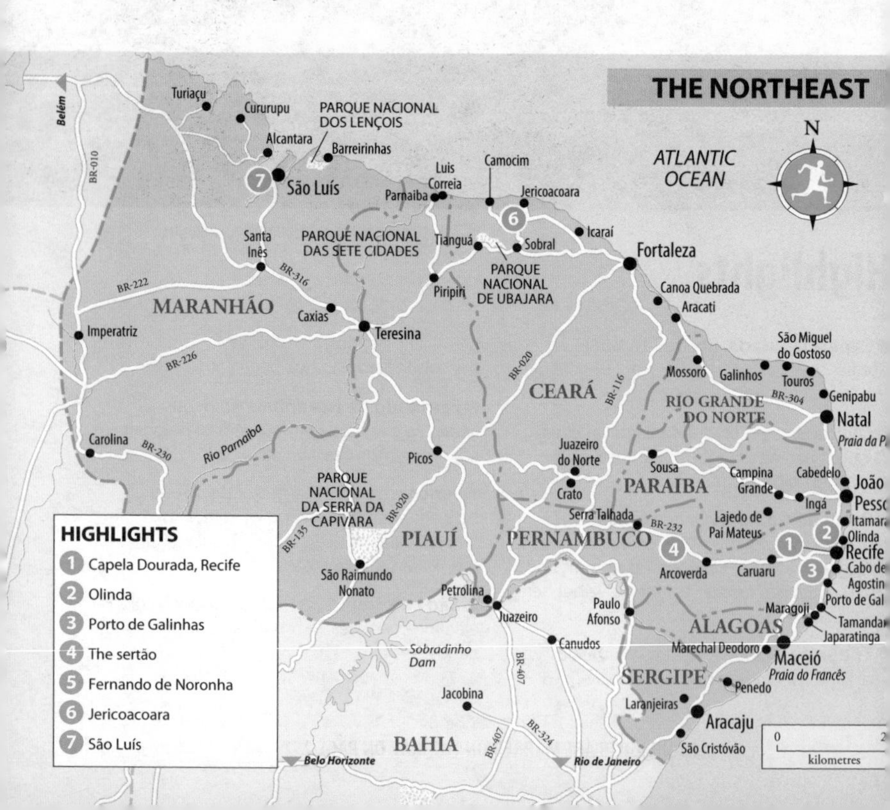

Praça Olímpio Campos and around

The heart of Aracaju's *centro histórico* is the wide, lush space of **Praça Olímpio Campos**, dominated by the lavish French Gothic-style **Catedral Metropolitana** (daily 8am–8pm; free; ⊕79 3214 3418), built in 1862 and dedicated to the Nossa Senhora da Conceição. Check out the unusual decorative interior – smothered in trompe-l'œil paintwork. The small **market** in front sells examples of the state's "*renda Irlandesa*" (Irish lace), and local snacks. On the north side, the **Centro de Turismo** (see page 254) is located in the faded French-Empire-style Escola Normal (1911). Behind it in the same building is the **Rua do Turista**, a pleasant courtyard lined with craft stores (Tues–Sat 8am–7pm, Sun 9am–6pm), and a modern arcade with cheap cafés, Cinema Vitória and a stage. A small **Museu do Artesanato** (same as store hours) displays a selection of arts and crafts from around the state.

Palacio Museu Olímpio Campos

Praça Fausto Cardoso • Tues–Fri 10am–5pm, Sat 9–1pm • Free • ⊕79 3198 1461 • ⊕palacioolimpiocampos.se.gov.br

Built between 1859 and 1863, Aracaju's original Palacio do Goberno (Governor's mansion) is preserved as the **Palacio Museu Olímpio Campos**, a grand, Neoclassical showcase of nineteenth-century art and architecture. Guides show you around various ornate rooms (generally Portuguese only), from the old bedrooms to lavish dining and reception rooms and the grand staircase decorated with vaguely Art Nouveau murals – there's also a scale model of the city in 1920–40. Outside in the plaza, overlooking the Rio Sergipe, is a statue of local hero **Fausto Cardoso**, leader of a failed 1906 revolt.

Museu da Gente Sergipe

Av Ivo do Prado 398 • Tues–Fri 10am–4pm, Sat & Sun 10am–3pm • Free • ⊕79 3218 1551, ⊕www.museudagentesergipana.com.br

Opened in 2011, the **Museu da Gente Sergipe** is the pride and joy of Aracaju, a hip interactive museum that introduces the people and culture of the state. Visits begin with a ten-minute film highlighting the sights and festivals of Sergipe, while temporary art exhibits and a decent café (see page 254) take up the ground floor. Upstairs the permanent exhibits tackle everything from flora and fauna to famous people of Sergipe with innovative displays (including a video tunnel and holographic characters) and games testing everything from ingredients in local dishes to your ability to sing local *repente* songs. The building itself is a grand Neoclassical pile completed in 1926 as the Colegio Atheneu Pedro II (high school). Though everything is in Portuguese, English-speaking students are often on hand to act as guides (free).

Teleférico Aracaju

Rua Fortaleza • Tues 9.30am–4pm, Wed–Fri 9.30am–5pm, Sat & Sun 8.30am–5.30pm • R$20 • ⊕79 3205 1305, ⊕bit.ly/telefericoaracaju

Aracaju's cable car, the **Teleférico Aracaju**, soars over the green expanse of the Parque da Cidade on the northern edge of the city, a patch of Mata Atlântica that includes the local zoo. The ride ends on top of the Morro do Urubu with an image of Nossa Senhora da Conceição and stellar views across the city.

Atalaia and the beaches

Aracaju's city **beaches** are not great, especially considering what lies ahead, but they do boast some excellent restaurants known for their crab dishes (see page 254), and a couple of attractions. The two main ones are Atalaia Velha and Atalaia Nova. Four-kilometre-long **Atalaia Velha** lies about 5km south from the city centre and is the more developed of the two. It's easy to get there by bus, but the whole area is rather soulless and uninspiring. The major landmark is the chequered **Farol de Atalaia** (lighthouse). **Atalaia Nova** lies on Santa Luzia across the Rio Sergipe, accessible via the 1.8km-long Ponte João Alves or by boat ("*tototo*") from the *hidroviária* in the city centre (every 10min; R$2); you can then get a bus to Atalaia Nova from the ferry terminal. Although the beach itself isn't great, the island is a pleasant place to stay – hotels are expensive, but there are plenty of rooms for rent.

4

Oceanário de Aracaju

Av Santos Dumont 1010, Atalaia • Daily 9am–9pm • R$20 • 79 3214 3243, tamar.org.br

Brazil's Tamar Project runs the **Oceanário de Aracaju**, comprising aquariums crammed with local marine life and many of the turtles Tamar saves each year. There is also a focus on the ecosystems of the Rio São Francisco, as well as lectures, video screenings and classes.

ARRIVAL AND DEPARTURE — ARACAJU

By plane The modern airport (79 3212 8500) is 12km south of the old centre, but quite close to the beaches; buses marked "Centro/Aeroporto" will get you into the *centro histórico* (R$3.50). For taxis, pay in advance for Comtaju Taxi (R$40 to *centro histórico*, R$30 to Atalaia).

By bus The new rodoviária (79 3238 3900) is 4km west of the old centre, connected by frequent local buses to the centre (R$3.50); taxis will cost around R$40 to Atalaia and R$25 to the *centro histórico*. The old rodoviária Velha (Terminal do Centro), which serves mainly local destinations, is five blocks north of Praça Olímpia Campos. The latter is a more chaotic place, though useful TV screens list departures and you can pay on board – this is where to catch minibuses for São Cristóvão (see page 256) and Laranjeiras (see page 255).

Destinations Maceió (14 daily; 4hr); Penedo (1 daily; 3hr 15min); Recife (3 daily; 8hr); Salvador (9 daily; 5hr).

INFORMATION AND GETTING AROUND

Tourist information The most convenient information desk (daily 8am–8pm; 79 3214 8848), lies inside the Centro de Turismo though there's not much here and rarely English-speakers.

By taxi Taxis are reliable in Aracaju, with meters starting at R$5.50, and most trips around town less than $30.

By bus Local buses charge R$3.50, with numerous services shuttling between Atalaia and the *centro histórico*.

ACCOMMODATION

Aju Hostel e Pousada Rua François Hoald 276, Atalaia 79 3223 4332, ajuhostel.com. Solid budget option 3km from the airport, with clean, modern premises, en-suite a/c doubles and spacious a/c dorms, all including breakfast. Dorms R$50, doubles R$150

Hotel Jangadeiro Rua Santa Luzia 269 79 3211 1350, jangadeirose.com.br. Options in the *centro histórico* are generally poor, but this is the best of the bunch, an ageing, grim-looking business hotel with adequate rooms and service, free wi-fi that's a bit hit-and-miss and reasonable breakfast. If you stay down here, remember virtually everything shuts after 7pm and all weekend. R$160

Pousada Dos Caminhos Rua Dr Bráulio Costa 89, Atalaia 79 3243 4315, pousadadoscaminhos.com.br. Justly popular B&B near the Passarela do Caranguejo, with cosy rooms, cable TV, good internet and hearty breakfasts. R$130

Radisson Hotel Aracaju Rua Dr Bezerra De Menezes 40, Atalaia 79 3711 3300, radisson.com. This luxury chain hotel is the poshest place to stay in town, with all the amenities you'd expect (pool, jacuzzi, gym, LCD TVs, cable TV), right on the beach. R$360

EATING AND DRINKING

★ **Café da Gente** Av Ivo do Prado 398 79 3246 3186. This stylish café and bar (at the Museu da Gente) offers a tranquil escape from the city, with a pleasant patio, excellent espresso, snacks and light meals. Tues–Sun 10am–8pm.

Calles Bar da Tapas Av Santos Dumont 188 79 3025 2725, facebook.com/callesbardetapas. Good choice if you are longing for a wide selection of beer from various Brazilian microbreweries (around R$30 for 500ml bottles) and Spanish-style tapas, including *batatas bravas* (R$20) and squid with *aioli* (R$29). Mains $R42–49. Mon–Thurs & Sun 6pm–midnight, Fri & Sat 6pm–2am.

★ **Cariri** Av Santos Dumont, Atalaia 79 3243 1379, facebook.com/caririsergipe. The most famous restaurant along the "Passarela do Caranguejo" ("crab passage"), a sort of homage to the *sertão* known not just for their Northeastern cuisine but also boisterous *forró* shows, live music and dancing that takes place at the back in the *Casa de Forró* (Thurs, Fri & Sun from 10pm). Daily 10am–5am.

Churrascaria Sal e Brasa Av Santos Dumont, Atalaia 79 3255 1644, salebrasa.com.br. This steakhouse chain offers excellent value, with weekday dinner buffets just R$39. Includes salads, hot dishes and sushi, in addition to the usual mounds of roast meat. Sometimes a pianist entertains customers (R$8 cover will be added to your bill). Mon–Thurs 11.30am–4pm & 6–11.30pm, Fri & Sat 11.30am–11.30pm, Sun 11.30am–10pm.

Cumbuca Rua Pacatuba 113 79 3211 9122. Clean, compact and modern choice for a hearty buffet lunch downtown, with rates from around R$39/kg. Mon–Fri 11.30am–3.30pm.

República dos Camarões Av Santos Dumont 79 3255 3361. Seafood specialist with a focus on shrimps

TRIPS ALONG THE CÂNION DO XINGÓ

Some 200km northwest of Aracaju, the stunning **Cânion do Xingó** – on the Rio São Francisco – is a popular day-trip (around R$160 inclusive), though the van ride there is three to four hours one-way – staying the night in nearby **Piranhas** (where the bandit Lampião was killed and his head displayed in 1938) is much less rushed (regular buses run from Aracaju to Canindé de São Francisco, an entry point for visits to the dam, river and canyon, or Piranhas for around R$25). Catamarans (8am, 9am, 10.30am, 11.30am, 12.30am, 2pm & 3pm; R$90, cash only) depart the dock at *Karranca's* restaurant (T 79 9 9869 6428, W facebook.com/Karrancas), 10km from Canindé de São Francisco on the banks of Lago São Pedro (just upriver from Xingó dam); the three-hour trips traverse the lake, stopping at the end of the canyon for a swim or to take a canoe ride into the narrowest section and a cave, the Gruta do Talhado (R$10 extra). Lunch buffet at the restaurant is R$40 extra. Nozes Tur (Av Santos Dumont 340 T 79 3243 7177, W www.nozestur.com.br) arranges trips from Aracaju.

served in a range of tempting combos; try the *camarão a quatro queijos* (shrimp with four cheeses). Reckon on R$50/head. Mon–Fri 11.30am–4pm & 6–11pm, Sat 11.30am–11pm & Sun 11.30am–9pm.

DIRECTORY

Internet Try Centernet at Rua João Pessoa 64 (Mon–Fri 8am–6pm, Sat 9am–2pm).

Money and exchange Bradesco and Santander have branches on Praça Olímpio Campos.

Post office Rua Laranjeiras 229 (Tues–Fri 9am–5pm).

4

Laranjeiras

Dominated by hills crowned with old *engenho* (mill) chapels, the pleasantly decrepit town of **LARANJEIRAS** is a languid colonial relic on the Rio Cotinguiba, a reminder of the time when sugar made the *sergipano* coast one of the most strategically valuable parts of Brazil. Today it's little more than a sleepy backwater some 20km north of Aracaju, littered with half-ruined mansions and churches, though restoration is gearing up as tourism develops and it boasts a couple of small but enticing museums. With little in the way of accommodation, and eating generally restricted to snack stalls, make this a day-trip from the capital.

Praça Matriz

Museu de Arte Sacra: Praça Matriz 39 • Tues–Sun 8am–5pm • Free • T 79 3281 2486

The heart of town is **Praça Matriz** (also called Praça Dr Heráclito Diniz Gonçalves), an elegantly faded square ringed by low-rise official buildings. The grand Baroque **Igreja Matriz Sagrado Coração de Jesus** dates from 1791 (though most of what you see today was completed around 1905). Housed in a mansion built for the Sobral Franco family in the 1890s, the **Museu de Arte Sacra** contains a small collection of religious art, statues and paintings culled from churches in the area.

Museu Afro-Brasileiro and around

Rua José do Prado Franco 19 • Tues–Fri 10am–5pm, Sat & Sun 1–5pm • R$5 • T 79 3281 2418

The illuminating **Museu Afro-Brasileiro** chronicles slave life on the sugar plantations in the region up to emancipation in 1888, as well as highlighting aspects of candomblé religion. The Neoclassical building itself was completed in the nineteenth century for the Brandão family, and is known as the Casa Aquiles Ribeiro. Walk here from Praça Matriz along Rua José do Prado Franco and you'll pass the ornate **Igreja Presbiteriana**, completed in 1899. The Protestant congregation was founded here, controversially, in 1884 by American pastor and missionary Alexander Latimer Blackford (1829–90).

Praça Josino Meneses

At the western end of the old town, **Praça Josino Meneses** is a once richly adorned plaza now virtually abandoned to the elements. Romantic ruins of an old hospital, theatre and police station line the fringes, while the centre is dominated by the elegant but crumbling tiled façade of the **Nossa Senhora da Conceição dos Pardos**. Built between 1834 and 1860, the church is finally being restored. Don't miss the **Ponte Nova**, the footbridge over the Rio Cotinguiba here; despite its name, the cobblestone beauty was completed in the first half of the nineteenth century.

Casa do Artesanato and around

Av Rotary • Mon–Fri 8am–10pm, Sat 8am–1pm, Sun 2–5pm • Free

The **Casa do Artesanato** opened in this new building in 2011 opposite the bus station, given over to *artesanato* and relics of plantation life, though the quality is not especially good. The large grey building next door is the **Trapiche**, a nineteenth-century warehouse, now a performance space (Centro do Tradição). Further along is the nineteenth-century **Mercado Municipal**, which tends to run only on Saturdays.

ARRIVAL AND INFORMATION — LARANJEIRAS

By bus Coopertalse (coopertalse.com.br) and São Pedro run minibuses to Laranjeiras (every 20–30min; 30min; R$2.30) from Aracaju's Terminal Velha (see page 254). These terminate at the tiny bus station in the old town, one block from the main plaza (you should be able to see the church spires).

Tourist information Keep walking down the main road (Av Rotary) from the bus station and you'll see the Bureau de Informações Turísticas (Mon–Sat 9am–5pm; 79 3281 1805) a couple of blocks down on the right, housed in the old Padaria Barroso (bakery); no one is likely to speak English but you can grab a useful map here. Inside is also the small Galeria de Artes Horácio Hora, showcasing local artists.

4

São Cristóvão

Founded in 1590 and Sergipe's state capital until 1855, **SÃO CRISTÓVÃO** has a wonderfully preserved *centro histórico*, perched high above the modern, commercial part of town some 23km southwest of Aracaju, on the estuary of the Rio Vaza-Barris. Packed into the small area around **Praça São Francisco** is the full panoply of a colonial administrative centre, including an old governor's palace, a parliament building and half a dozen period churches.

Museu de Arte Sacra

Praça São Francisco • Tues–Sat 10am–4pm, Sun 10am–1pm • R$5 • 79 3261 1580

Dominating the beautifully maintained but rather bare Praça São Francisco is the seventeenth-century Igreja e Convento de São Francisco, now home to the **Museu de Arte Sacra**. Around five hundred pieces of religious art are displayed inside; don't miss the beautiful interior of the church itself, decorated with paintings.

Santa Casa de Misericórdia da São Cristóvão

Praça São Francisco • Daily 10am–12.30pm & 2–5pm • Free

This historic hospital foundation dates back to the early seventeenth century and is operated by the Ordem Imaculada Conceição (a Catholic order) as a home for old nuns. You can view its humble, timber-roofed chapel or "Antiga Igreja" (with a canvas panel by José Teófilo de Jesus behind the altar), the sacristy with ornate, carved stone font (*lavabo*) and small garden grotto.

Museu Histórico de Sergipe

Praça São Francisco • Tues–Sun 10am–4pm • R$5 guide included • 79 3261 1435

The Antigo Palácio Provincial – the old provincial governor's house – now serves as the regional history museum, **Museu Histórico de Sergipe**. The building remained in use from 1855 to 1960, and today contains period furniture, art exhibits, displays on the *cangaço* (rural bandits) such as Lampião, and the locally renowned painting by Romantic artist Horácio Hora of Ceci e Peri, characters in José de Alencar's still popular novel *O Guarani* (1857).

Praça Getúlio Vargas

A short walk along Rua Cel. Erondino Prado from Praça São Francisco lies its overgrown, elegant sibling, **Praça Getúlio Vargas**, ringed by some pristine examples of colonial townhouses with *balcão corrido* (balcony). The main church here – and the primary church in town – is **Igreja Matriz Nossa Senhora do Vitória** (Tues–Sat 10am–4pm, Sun 9am–1pm), with roots in the early seventeenth century, but destroyed by the Dutch in the 1640s and rebuilt in the eighteenth century.

Igreja e Convento de Nossa Senhora do Carmo

Praça Senhor Dos Passos • Tues–Sun 10am–4pm, Sun 9am–1pm • Free

The small, usually deserted Praça Senhor Dos Passos contains the impressive bulk of **Igreja e Convento de Nossa Senhora do Carmo**, completed between 1745 and 1766, as well as the smaller **Igreja da Ordem Terceira** to the left (the buildings are connected by a cloister). The latter church is better known as the Igreja de Nosso Senhor dos Passos, and is actually more enticing architecturally, with ornate chapels, altars and the small **Museu dos Ex-Votos** inside, festooned with the photos and objects (mostly wooden arms and legs) left by devotees. The "**Blessed Irmã Dulce**", the Salvador-born nun dubbed the "good angel of Bahia", lived in the convent between 1933 and 1934 – a small exhibit honours her memory (beatified in 2011, she is on track to become the first Catholic saint born in Brazil).

Igreja Nossa Senhora do Amparo

Largo do Amparo at Rua Messias Prado • Tues–Sat 10am–4pm, Sun 9am–1pm • Free

Completing the line-up of major colonial relics in São Cristóvão is the mouldering Baroque tower of **Igreja Nossa Senhora do Amparo**, completed in the eighteenth century and one of the tallest structures in the town. The interior is spacious but adorned in a relatively simple Baroque style.

ARRIVAL AND INFORMATION — SÃO CRISTÓVÃO

By bus Minibuses run to São Cristóvão (hourly; 40min; R$2.35) from Aracaju's Terminal Velha (see page 254); these usually drop you off on the hill just below Praça São Francisco. Walk back down the hill (across the old train tracks) to the tiny bus station to catch one back.

Tourist information The small information centre on Praça São Francisco (Mon–Fri 10am–4pm, Sat & Sun 10am–1pm) is staffed by enthusiastic volunteers, but English is rarely spoken – at the time of writing the town had no maps either, but this should change. Next door (same hours) is the Casa do Folclore, a gallery dedicated to local festivals and various town characters, big puppets and some drawings by Nivaldo Oliveira (Portuguese labels only).

EATING

Eating in São Cristóvão usually means perusing the snack stalls and cheap *lanchonetes* near the bus station in the commercial part of town. The town is noted for its cakes: *queijada* (a bit like cheesecake, made with coconut); and *bricelets* (loosely based on the thin Swiss waffle cookie, with a mild orange flavour), usually sold in Santa Casa de Misericórdia (see page 256).

Petisku's Bar e Restaurante Praça Getulio Vargas ⓣ 79 3261 2763. Friendly little diner and bar on the main plaza, knocking out home-cooked regional dishes and serving cold beers. Mon–Sat 10.30am–3pm.

Penedo

A couple of hours, and some 120km, northeast of Aracaju is the sparkling colonial town of **PENEDO**, across the border in Alagoas. Originally developed to control the illegal export of lumber by French merchant ships in the sixteenth century, it was occupied by the Dutch between 1637 and 1645, who built the original fort here. Penedo is strategically placed at the mouth of the mighty **Rio São Francisco**, and it's still a busy little place, much of whose life revolves around the river and the waterfront – the only way to cross the river here is by ferry. Indeed, while the town is worth exploring on foot, the main attractions along the São Francisco are best accessed on a boat tour (see below).

Igreja de Nossa Senhora da Corrente

Praça 12 de Abril • Tues–Fri 8am–5pm, Sat & Sun 8am–4pm • Free

There are several colonial churches in Penedo, the most attractive of which is the early eighteenth-century *azulejo*-decorated **Igreja de Nossa Senhora da Corrente**, started around 1764 with a stunning gold-leaf Rococo *retábulo* (altarpiece) inside. According to local tradition, escaped slaves took refuge inside the church via a "secret passage" to the right of the high altar.

Convento de São Francisco e Igreja Nossa Senhora dos Anjos

Rua 7 de Setembro 218 (Praça Rui Barbosa) • Tues–Fri 8am–5pm, Sat & Sun 8am–4pm • R$2 • ⓣ 82 3551 2279

This combined convent and church was completed around 1759, with a small museum of antique furniture and religious art inside. The Baroque church itself is richly adorned with a fine trompe l'oeil ceiling by Pernambucan artist Libório Lázaro Lial (1784) and a gilded gold altar.

Casa de Penedo

Rua João Pessoa 126 • Mon–Sat 9am–noon & 2–4pm • R$3 • ⓣ 82 3551 4198, ⓦ casadopenedo.com.br

Largely displaying the cache of historic photos, books and documents collected by local doctor Francisco A. Sales, the tiny **Casa de Penedo** acts as small museum and cultural centre. Among the exhibits are rooms dedicated to Francisco Inácio de Carvalho Moreira, the one-time Barão do Penedo, writer Elysio de Carvalho and the visits of invading Dutch prince John Maurice of Nassau (1637) and Dom Pedro II (1859) to Penedo.

Museu do Paço Imperial

Praça 12 de Abril 21 • Tues–Sat 11am–5pm, Sun 8am–noon • R$4

The **Museu do Paço Imperial** is housed inside an elegant eighteenth-century *sobrado* (mansion), with displays of period furniture and religious art, though it also makes a lot of the fact that Dom Pedro II stayed here in 1859. There's a memorial to former town mayor Raimundo Marinho too.

ARRIVAL AND DEPARTURE — PENEDO

By bus Penedo is linked to Maceió by one daily bus (4hr 15min; R$30.50; ⓦ realalagoas.com.br) arriving and departing the Terminal Rodoviário, Av Duque de Caxias (ⓣ 82 3551 2602), near the centre. Aguiabranca runs one daily bus to Salvador (6am; 11hr; R$95; ⓦ aguiabranca.com.br) via Aracaju (3h 20min; R$18), though local vans (*topiques*) on the waterfront also ply to and from the Sergipe capital. From Aracaju, Aguiabranca (3h 20min; R$18) run buses to Penedo departing at 2.50pm.

TRIPS TO THE FOZ DO SÃO FRANCISCO

There are some dazzling golden sand beaches at the mouth of the Rio São Francisco, an area known as **Foz do São Francisco**. Many tourists visit on day-trips from Aracaju (R$160), but you can also negotiate trips with local boats in Penedo or **Piaçabuçu**, 28km down river; from here boats take around 45min (R$120 for four people) to reach the beaches. Piaçabuçu itself is a sleepy and little-visited fishing village, accessible by local vans/*topiques* (40min; every 30min; R$2) or taxi from Penedo.

TOURS

★ **Farol da Foz Ecoturismo** Av Ulisses Guedes 228, Bairro Brasília, Piaçabuçu ⓣ 82 9975 1975, ⓦ faroldafozecoturismo.com. Excellent guided tours to Foz do São Francisco by dune buggy (R$280 for up to four people) or by boat (R$70/person) from Piaçabuçu.

ACCOMMODATION AND EATING

Forte da Rocheira Rua da Rocheira 2 82 3551 3273. One of the town's better restaurants lies right on the waterfront with fabulous river views. They specialize in fish (especially the local tilapia), but also more exotic dishes such as *moqueca de jacaré* (alligator stew). Daily 11am–4pm.

Hotel São Francisco Av Floriano Peixoto 237 82 3551 2273, hotelsaofrancisco.tur.br. The most comfortable place to stay in the heart of town, with a nice pool and a/c rooms featuring, *frigobar* and HD TVs. R$250

Pousada Colonial Praça 12 de Abril 21 82 3551 2355. This historic gem overlooks the river, offering simple but adequate a/c rooms, an alright restaurant, excellent views and cable TV, though it's not as comfy as the newer hotels in town – you're paying for location and ambience. R$140

Maceió

Like Aracaju 280km to the south, **MACEIÓ**, the state capital of Alagoas, is a nineteenth-century creation, but there the comparisons end. Maceió is twice as big and a burgeoning beach resort, its attractive beaches and clear, turquoise waters attracting plane-loads from all over Brazil. It's also smack in the middle of a far longer strip of some of the best beaches in the country, all easily accessible on day-trips. Most visitors congregate in the affluent and lively resort area that starts at **Pajuçara**, a few kilometres to the east of downtown, built along a spectacular beach. The somewhat down-at-heel **city centre** itself, just inland from a more polluted (and generally deserted) stretch of sand and the grubby port district, remains the commercial, administrative and uninspiring heart of the city, with a few *belle époque* buildings and enticing museums.

Praça dos Martírios

The best place to get some sense of the old Maceió is **Praça dos Martírios** (aka Praça Floriano Pexioto, after the statue of the first Republican president in the centre), once the finest square in the city, but nowadays most of its elegance has faded away. Other than the church, the plaza's main buildings include the old **Intendência da Capital**, completed on the south side in 1909, the **Palácio do Governo** and **Museu de Arte da Fundação Pierre Chalita** (see below). Don't miss the public phone booth in the shape of a mussel shell on the south side.

The elegant **Igreja Bom Jesus dos Martírios** (Mon–Sat 8am–12.30pm & 2–5pm, Sun 7am–1pm) was completed between 1877 and 1881, with its two towers and facade smothered in blue-and-white *azulejo* tiling. Inside there are some fine tile murals in the apse, and a revered shrine to Nossa Senhora da Cabeça.

4

Museu Palácio Floriano Pexioto

Praça dos Martírios 517 • Mon–Fri 8am–4pm • Free • 82 3315 7874

Completed in 1902, Maceió's old Palácio do Governo is now the **Museu Palácio Floriano Pexioto**, its stately upper-floor rooms decorated with period furniture, art (including work by **Rosalvo Ribeiro**) and silverware. Also inside are excellent exhibitions on local poet **Lêdo Ivo** and **Aurélio Buarque de Holanda** (creator of Brazil's first dictionary). You must be accompanied by a guide (ask at the desk in the lobby), but English-speakers are rare and there are no English labels.

Museu de Arte da Fundação Pierre Chalita

Praça dos Martírios 44 • Mon–Fri 8am–noon & 2–6pm • Free • 82 3223 4298, cultura.al.gov.br/politicas-e-acoes/museus/cadastro-de-museus-alagoanos/5-metropolitana/maceio/museu-de-arte-pierre-chalita

The faded, pink confection at the northern end of Praça dos Martírios is the **Museu de Arte da Fundação Pierre Chalita**, an intriguing wood-floor art gallery housing the private collection of painter **Pierre Chalita** (1930–2010). The main floor contains eighteenth-century paintings and religious art (Baroque altars, calvaries and statues), including two works attributed to the workshop of **Caravaggio**, while Chalita's own Expressionist, often unsettling, work is featured upstairs. The basement is mostly filled with modern and contemporary work of Alagoas artists including Chalita's wife, Solange.

Museu do Instituto Histórico e Geográfico

Rua João Pessoa 382 • Mon–Fri 8am–noon • R$4 • 82 3223 7797, bit.ly/MuseuHistoricoGeografico

The small **Museu do Instituto Histórico e Geográfico** is chiefly worth visiting for its Afro-Brazilian artefacts (some relating to the Quebra do Xangô massacre of 1912), and various relics and photographs of the bandit leader **Lampião** (see page 261), including the famous "team photo" of his severed head along with those of his wife and leading gang members. The building is the handsome nineteenth-century home of Américo Passos Guimarães, acquired by the Institute in 1909.

Praça Dom Pedro II

Praça Dom Pedro II (marked by a bust commemorating the emperor's visit here in 1859) is dominated by the mid-nineteenth-century **Catedral Metropolitana** (1859), a vast but fairly unexceptional space dedicated to city patron saint **Nossa Senhora dos Prazeres.** The other main building complex here is the **Provincial Assembly**, housed in the old Palácio Tavares Bastos (1850), with the Ministério da Fazenda (Ministry of Finance) on the opposite side of the plaza (1902). From here you can walk west into the commercial heart of the city, pedestrianized **Rua do Livramento** and **Avenida Moreira Lima**, with the usual smattering of shops and cheap cafés.

Museu Théo Brandão

Av da Paz 1490 • Tues–Fri 9am–5pm (sometimes closed for lunch) • R$2 • 82 3214 1711, ufal.edu.br

The UFAL (Universidade Federal de Alagoas) runs the **Museu Théo Brandão**, housed in the grand *belle époque* mansion known as Palacete dos Machados, incongruously marooned along the desolate seafront near the port. Inside, the folk art collection of teacher and folklorist Theotônio Vilela Brandão is arranged in a series of artfully presented galleries: hanging displays of ex-votos, rooms of ceramic pots, lace and huge festival puppets and headgear. Students are on hand to guide you, but rarely in English, and labels are Portuguese only.

4

THE LEGEND OF LAMPIÃO: BRAZIL'S ROBIN HOOD

Lampião was born **Virgulino Ferreira da Silva** in 1897 in the Northeastern state of Pernambuco. As Virgulino grew up, he and his family got involved in local feuding and they ended up on the wrong side of the law. Virgulino's father was killed in a police raid on his home, turning Virgulino, only 25 years old, into a bandit gang leader – one of the region's "cangaceiros" – and a deadly threat to the local establishment for the next fifteen years. The **Robin Hood of Brazil** image he cultivated belies the reality of a complex, vain and brutal man. It is perhaps his boldness that made him stand out, often fighting battles when his gang was outnumbered more than three to one (though his elaborate handmade costume must have helped).

The law finally caught up with Lampião in 1938. The police detachment that shot him, his wife, Maria Bonita, and his closest lieutenants preserved their heads in alcohol so that they could be shown in market towns in the interior, the only way to convince people he really had been killed – even today, the Brazilian media occasionally publish pictures of an old man who died in 1996 and bears a striking resemblance to Lampião.

Jaraguá

Once the booming commercial heart of the city, the port district of **Jaraguá**, halfway between the centre and Pajuçara, fell on hard times after World War II and has now been regenerated, its old warehouses converted into stores and a clutch of museums, mostly along **Rua Sá e Albuquerque.**

Museu do Comércio de Alagoas

Rua Sá e Albuquerque 467 • Mon–Fri 9am–noon & 1–5pm • R$2 • T 82 3597 8550

The **Museu do Comércio de Alagoas**, housed in the stately Associação Comercial building (1928), has a mildly interesting collection of old maps, documents and ledgers laying out the trade history of the state, and a much less enticing exhibit on global technology since 1900 (though the "old" 1970 mainframe computer is fun).

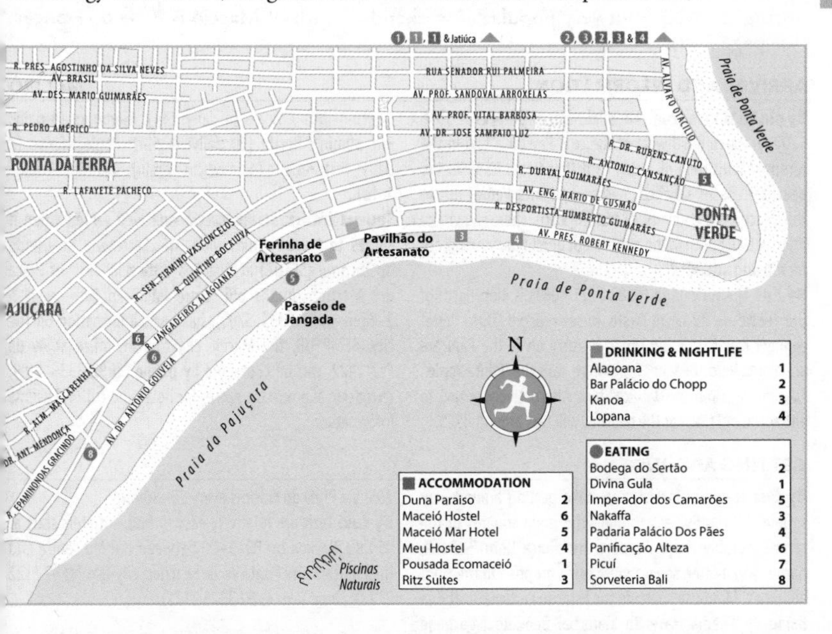

Casa da Patrimônio and Fundação Pierre Chalita

Casa da Patrimônio Rua Sá e Albuquerque 157 • Tues–Sun 11am–5pm • Free • ☎ 82 3551 5295 **Fundação Pierre Chalita** Praça Manoel Duarte 77 • Mon–Fri 8am–11am & 2–5pm, Sat 8am–11am • Free

The **Casa da Patrimônio** is an old sugar warehouse at the end of Rua Sá e Albuquerque, artfully converted to display eight hundred pieces of the eclectic Tânia de Maya Pedrosa collection of folk art, carvings, puppets, masks and ex-votos. The nearby **Fundação Pierre Chalita** has also taken over two huge warehouses to display the larger, vibrant canvases of patron Pierre Chalita (see page 259).

Pajuçara and Ponta Verde beaches

The main Maceió resort area begins at **Pajuçara**, whose curving road and wide mosaic promenade are studded with palm trees. Though there are always plenty of umbrellas and chairs for rent, cold beers and tasty snacks on offer, the water is not always the cleanest here – to swim, head out to the main reef offshore (see page 263). The only attraction as such is the craft market, the **Ferinha de Artesanato**, and its twin across the road, the two floors of **Pavilhão do Artesanato** at Avenida Silvio Carlos Viana 1447. Pajuçara curves into the **Ponta Verde**, which continues around the headland and north to Jatiúca, where things get slightly less crowded.

Litoral Norte

Ponta Verde and the neighbouring beach of Jatiúca are the beginning of the **Litoral Norte**, a series of fine sands to the north of Maceió. The best way to get to them is to take buses marked "Mirante" or "Fátima" from the centre, which take you along the coast as far as **Pratagi** (also called Mirante da Sereia), 13km north, where there are coral pools in the reef at low tide. You can get off the bus anywhere that takes your fancy; the main beaches, in order of appearance, are **Cruz das Almas** (surf beach), **Jacarecica** (surf beach), **Guaxuma** (swimming beach), **Garça Torta** (swimming beach) and **Riacho Doce** (surf beach, but also famed for its locally made sweet coconut treats). All these beaches are less crowded than the city beaches during the week, but very popular at weekends. South of Maceió is **Praia do Francês** (see page 264).

ARRIVAL AND INFORMATION — MACEIÓ

By plane Maceió's Zumbi dos Palmares airport (☎ 82 3036 5200) is 22km northwest of the city. Pay for a taxi in the terminal with cash or credit card (fixed-rate R$65 to the beaches). Buses labelled "Aeroporto-Ponta Verde" run to the beach districts every 45min (R$3.50). There is a visitor information booth in the airport, but don't hold your breath for it being attended.

By bus The rodoviária (☎ 82 3221 4081) is 4km north of the centre on Av Leste Oeste. Buses marked "Ouro Preto" connect it with the old town; to carry on to the Pajuçara and Ponta Verde beaches from there, take the "Ponta Verde", "Jardim Vaticano" or "Jatiúca" bus. Alternatively, a taxi to either the old town or the beaches will cost around R$20.

Destinations Aracaju (4 daily; 5hr); Maragogi (4 daily; 3hr 30min); Recife (10 daily; 4–5hr); Paulo Afonso (2 daily; 4hr); Penedo (4 daily; 2hr 30min); Salvador (4 daily; 11hr).

Tourist information Maceió isn't well served when it comes to tourist information. The Secretaria de Estado do Turismo (SETUR) at Rua Boa Vista 453, just off Praça dos Martírios in the old centre (Mon–Fri 8am–noon & 2–6pm; ☎ 82 3315 5700), has basic information on the city. SEMPTUR, the Maceió city tourism office at Av da Paz 1422, can be contacted by phone (☎ 82 3336 4409, 🌐 maceio.al.gov.br/semptur) for hotel and cultural events information.

GETTING AROUND

By bus Frequent local buses make getting around very simple. All routes pass through the main squares in the centre, notably Praça Deodoro and Praça Dom Pedro II, names you'll often see on route cards propped in the front windows. Minibuses outside the Estação Ferroviária at Rua Barão de Anádia travel to Marechal Deodoro (see page 265) via Praia do Francês every 20–30min.

By taxi Taxis are relatively easy to find – meters start at R$4.85. Reckon on R$15–20 between the old centre and the Pajuçara and Ponta Verde beaches. City Taxi (☎ 82 2122 2727); Ligue Taxi (☎ 82 3326 2121).

PAJUÇARA'S REEF POOLS

The real highlight of Pajuçara beach lies offshore, where the "**piscinas naturais**" (natural pools) form along the nearby reef at low tide. Though it can get busy on holidays and weekends, there are usually plenty of tropical fish around and the water is spectacular. Local **sailboats** known as *jangadas* (R$35/person) depart from the Passeio de Jangada at Pajuçara beach during low tide (during the day), roughly opposite the Radisson hotel.

ACCOMMODATION

★ **Duna Paraiso** Rua São Pedro 427, Garça Torta ⓣ 82 3355 1646, ⓦ dunaparaiso.com; map p.260. Just six rustic-chic bungalows on Praia da Garça Torta, north of the city, a tranquil getaway that doesn't accept kids under 12. Superb breakfasts and friendly Italian owners, Ivan and Graziella. Book in advance. **R$420**

Maceió Hostel e Pousada Rua Jangadeiros Alagoanos 1528, Pajuçara ⓣ 82 3231 7762, ⓦ maceiohostel.com.br; map 260. Maceió has a few very modern and comfortable hostels and this is one of them. It's 100m from the beach and staff are usually helpful and friendly. Breakfast is decent, and all rooms have a/c. Dorms **R$80**, doubles **R$220**

★ **Maceió Mar Hotel** Av Álavaro Octacílio 2991, Ponta Verde ⓣ 82 3142 0001, ⓦ maceiomarhotel.com.br; map p.260. Quality hotel with very spacious and comfortable rooms, plus a bar and sauna; located close to the southern end of Praia de Ponta Verde. Offers fine views over the ocean, and is a great spot to take in December's Carnaval. **R$587**

★ **Meu Hostel** Rua Senador Ezechias Jerônimo da Rocha 134, Cruz das Almas ⓣ 82 3185 4410, ⓦ meu-hostel.com; map p.260. This gem of a new hostel has superb facilities and excellent staff. Beautifully decorated with turquoise accent colours and bright paintings, it's as pleasing to the eye as it is comfortable. Dorms come with towels and lockers – pay a little extra for a bed in the four-bed dorm and you get your own pod, Japanese style, but more spacious. There's a pool and a great table upstairs with board games for socializing. Dorms **R$65**, doubles **R$200**

★ **Pousada Ecomaceió** Av Desembargador Valente de Lima 204, Jatiuca ⓣ 82 3317 8551, ⓦ pousadaecomaceio.com.br; map p.260. Stylish hotel with cool contemporary a/c rooms, LCD cable TVs and furniture made with eco-friendly materials such as coconut fibre and bamboo. English-speaking staff. **R$270**

Ritz Suites Rua Elias Ramos de Araujo 140 Cruz das Almas ⓣ 82 3312 2000, ⓦ ritzsuites.com.br; map p.260. Situated just across the road from the beach, this four-star hotel offers modern and stylish rooms, as well as an inviting pool with sea view. Facilities include a bar, restaurant, gym and steam room. Free parking. **R$567**

EATING

THE BEACHES

★ **Bodega do Sertão** Av Júlio Marquês Luz 62, Jatiúca ⓣ 82 3327 4446, ⓦ bodegadosertao.com.br; map p.260. This Northeastern (*sertão*), rustic-themed restaurant is a big tourist favourite but fun nonetheless, that serves food *por quillo* (R$7/100g) with typical dishes such as *carneiro guisado* (mutton stew) and *carne de sol*. Decent choice of cachaças *alagoanos* also. Mon–Sat 11.30am–10pm, Sun 7am–10pm.

Divina Gula Rua Eng. Paulo Brandão Nogueira 85, Jatiúca ⓣ 82 3235 1016, ⓦ facebook.com/divina.gula.oficial; map p.260. Justly popular restaurant for authentic *mineira* (Minas Gerais) food such as *picanha na chapa* and *tropeiro mineiro (R$75)*, as well as quality *mineira* cachaça. Tues–Thurs & Sun noon–midnight, Fri & Sat noon– 2am.

Imperador dos Camarões Av Dr António Gouveia 607, Pajuçara ⓣ 82 3231 4134, ⓦ imperadordoscamaroes.com.br; map p.260. This place wins kudos for novelty value only; the primary reason for a visit is to try their now infamous "invention", *chiclete de camarãos* (R$54.90; literally "shrimp bubblegum"), basically shrimps smothered in strings of melted cheese. You will love it or hate it. Though their roasted shrimp (*espeto de camarão*) is good, most of the seafood here is just so-so. Mains R$55–70. Daily 11.30am–11.30pm.

Nakaffa Rua Dep José Lages 395, Ponta Verde ⓣ 82 3027 3747, ⓦ facebook.com/nakaffa; map p.260. Stylish coffee shop two blocks from the beach with excellent espresso (R$4.90), sandwiches and salads (around R$20–30): an a/c-cooled sanctuary from Skol and caipirinhas. Daily noon–10pm.

Panificação Alteza Rua Jangadeiros Alagoanos 732, Pajuçara ⓣ 82 3231 0447; map p.260. This venerable bakery has been open since 1967, knocking out mouth-watering cakes, savoury pastries and gourmet coffee. Mon–Sat 6am–8pm.

★ **Picuí** Av da Paz 1140, Jaraguá ⓣ 82 3223 8080, ⓦ picui.com.br; map p.260. Fêted restaurant from celebrity chef Wanderson Medeiros, with a menu of Brazilian cuisine like *prato da boa esperança* (sun-dried beef, mashed cassava and rice; R$72.50) in an artsy space.

4

Daily 11.30am–5pm.

Sorveteria Bali Av Dr Antônio Gouveia 451, Pajuçara 82 3231 8833, sorvetesbali.com.br; map p.260. The place for Brazilian ice cream, from traditional flavours (chocolate, vanilla) to those exotic local tastes (*jaca, mangaba, acerola*). Mon–Thurs & Sun 10am–midnight, Fri & Sat 10am–1am.

CENTRO

Padaria Palácio Dos Pães Rua do Comércio 672 82 3326 3114; map p.260. Most of the options in the centre are simple lunch counters and *lanchonetes*, and this is the classic example, a no-frills place serving locals since 1970, with bar stools, cakes, sandwiches and the cheese "X-burgers". Daily 6am–8pm.

DRINKING AND NIGHTLIFE

For **nightlife**, the area around Rua Sá de Albuquerque (in the Jaraguá district) is a fashionable part of the city that's especially lively from Thursday to Saturday, when the main street is closed off to traffic and the bars and restaurants put their tables outside. Otherwise stick to the beach bars (*barracas*) in Pajuçara and Ponta Verde, or the strip further north in Jatiúca.

Alagoana Rua Deputado Luiz Gonzaga Coutinho 125, Jatiúca 82 9 9122 9338, facebook.com/casadechoppalagoana; map p.260. Good place to start the evening on the Jatiúca strip, with an open beer tent/beer garden format, selling Brahma (R$4.99; half price 4–7pm Tues & Wed), decent seafood and featuring live MPB, pop rock and *sertanejo* bands. Mon–Fri 4pm–1am, Sat & Sun 11am–midnight.

Bar Palácio do Chopp Rua Boa Vista 15 82 3223 5488; map p.260. No-nonsense beer hall, something of a local institution in the heart of the pedestrianized shopping area in the centre (look for the Chinese-style roof), selling beer and tasty bar food. Note, however, this is a day-time only joint. Mon–Sat 9am–7pm.

★ **Kanoa** Av Silvio Carlos Viana, barraca 25, Ponta Verde 82 3235 3943, facebook.com/kanoabeach; map p.260. This is the best bar on the beach, always packed with the in-crowd and featuring great DJs and live bands (MPB, *sertanejo*). Cover charged most evenings (R$10). Daily 9am–midnight.

Lopana Av Silvio Carlos Viana, barraca 27, Ponta Verde 82 3231 7484, lopana.com.br; map p.260. Cool beach bar with tables on the sand, live music, cold beers and great snacks (fried prawns, *carne de sol*), plus their own *jangada* (sailboat; up to 7 people) you'll see offshore. Cover charged most evenings (R$10). Mon–Fri 10am–midnight, Sat & Sun 9am–1am.

4

DIRECTORY

Emergencies 190; Federal Police 82 3216 6700.

Internet Toy Entretenimento e Accesso Digital, Rua São Francisco de Assis 385, Jatiúca (daily 10am–10pm).

Money and exchange Banco do Brasil is on the first block of Rua do Livramento, close to the corner with Rua Boa Vista, in the centre of the city.

Post office The post office is at Rua João Pessoa 57 in the centre near the Asamblea building, with a branch in Shopping Centro de Artesanato Jaraguá, Rua Sá da Albuquerque 417.

Praia do Francês

Twenty-four kilometres south of Maceió, the coast road (AL-101) loops around **Praia do Francês**, which even by Alagoan standards is something special. An enormous expanse of white sand, surf and thick palm forest, it even boasts several *pousadas* and a burgeoning restaurant scene. Most folks end up at the northern end, a protected lagoon formed by a large reef offshore; surfers take in the pounding waves at the less busy and unsheltered end. Beach bars line the northern section, while Avenida Dos Corais and Rua da Algas run parallel to the sand and are lined with shops and restaurants. Given its proximity to Maceió, it's no surprise Francês has effectively become a city beach – don't expect peace and quiet.

ARRIVAL AND DEPARTURE — PRAIA DO FRANCÊS

By minibus Real Alagoas (realalagoas.com.br) run daily buses (R$5) departing the Estação Ferroviária in Maceió for Marechal Deodoro via Praia do Francês.

By car Parking just behind the beach in Praia do Francês is R$10 (daily 8am–5.30pm).

ALAGOAS: BEST OF THE BEACHES

If your time in Alagoas is short, you can go to one of the agencies in Maceió, which offer a plethora of easy day-trips to the best beaches in the state, many of which are hard to reach without your own transport.

LITORAL SUL

(listed in km south of Maceió)

- **Barra de São Miguel** (38km) and **Praia do Gunga** (42km). São Miguel is the gateway to the incredible white-sand headland of Gunga – you have to take a boat across the Rio São Miguel (R$35). Day-trips are usually R$45.
- **Dunas do Marapé** (Jequiá da Praia; 77km). Gorgeous beach where the Jequiá River meets the sea, surrounded by mangroves. Day-trips around R$120.

LITORAL NORTE

(listed in km north of Maceió)

- **Angra de Ipioca** (16km). Long stretch of golden sands, backed by coconut palms. Day-trips from R$45.
- **Barra de Santo Antônio** (46km). Tranquil fishing village near a fine beach on a narrow neck of land jutting out from the coast a short canoe ride away (Praia Tabuba), and good, fresh seafood is served in the cluster of small beachside hotels. There are twenty daily buses between Maceió and Santo Antônio.
- **Japaratinga** (117km). An even more laidback fishing village and resort of coral reefs and shallow, warm waters, just 11km south of Maragogi (see page 266) and easily reached by van from there (R$3).

TOUR AGENCIES (MACEIÓ)

Jaragua Turismo Rua Dr Messeias de Gusmão 188 ⓣ 82 3337 2780, ⓦ jaraguaturismo.com.

Maceió Turismo Rua Firmino de Vasconcelos 685, Pajuçara ⓣ 82 3327 7711, ⓦ maceioturismo.com.br.

Transamérica Turismo Av Dr Antônio Gouveia 487 ⓣ 82 2121 7373, ⓦ www.transamericatur.com.br.

4

ACCOMMODATION AND EATING

Dona Madalena Av dos Corais 1 ⓣ 82 3260 1369. One of the best restaurants in the area, with specials such as the house lobster (*lagosta da Madalena*), shrimp risotto and pumpkin shrimp (*camarão na abobora*). Around R$25/head. Thurs–Sun noon–10pm.

Hotel Ponte Verde Rua da Algas 300 ⓣ 82 3263 6100, ⓦ praiadofrances.hotelpontaverde.com.br. Purists may not like the biggest, most luxurious hotel on the beach, but all things considered it hasn't made much difference to the already booming beach scene, with compact but cosy a/c rooms, exceptional service and excellent food; considerably cheaper during low season (R$330). **R$770**

Padrino Av dos Corais 7 ⓣ 82 3260 1143. Fabulous Italian food from *carioca* Alexandre Nigro (mains R$20–43), tasty pastas with various sauces (crab, prawn and meat) and fresh salads. Mon–Sat noon–11pm, Sun noon–10pm.

Pousada Cachoeira do Sol Rua Recanto dos Coqueirais ⓣ 82 3260 1298. Comfy B&B with simple, but comfortable rooms and an inviting garden with hammocks. Communal kitchen and 24hr reception. **R$150**

Marechal Deodoro

The beautifully preserved colonial town of **MARECHAL DEODORO** ("mar-ay-shao deodoro") lies just 24km south of Maceió via AL-101 and AL-215. Once the booming capital of the Captaincy of Alagoas (Maceió replaced it in 1839), today it's no more than a small market town, built on rising ground on the banks of the Lagoa Manguaba, with streets that are either dirt or cobbled – its low-strung adobe homes seem almost Central American, with not a single building that looks as if it were constructed this century. Nor is it simply preserved for tourists to gawp at: the locals spit in the streets, gossip and hang about in bars as they would anywhere else, and there's a real air of small-town tranquillity.

Museu de Arte Sagrada

Praça Pedro Paulinho (Rua São Francisco at Rua Dr Melo Moraes) • Mon & Wed–Sat 9am–5pm • Free • ☎ 82 221 2651

Tiny **Praça Pedro Paulinho** is dominated by the imposing facade of the 1790s **Igreja de Santa Maria Magdalena**, with the older **Convento de São Francisco**, finished in 1684, attached. The church itself is bare save for the incredibly lavish Rococo altar, ceiling paintings and a similarly elaborate side chapel. The convent is built around a cloister, with the main galleries of the excellent **Museu de Arte Sagrada** on the first storey. Everything on display is high Catholic religious art, with little concession made to the tropical setting save for the large number of portrayals of São Benedito, the black patron saint of the slaves who manned the *engenhos* (sugar mills) all around and built most of Marechal Deodoro itself. The highlight of the collection, extracted from churches all over the state, is the group of seventeenth- to nineteenth-century statues of saints and the Virgin Mary. Most are no more than 30cm high, made of wood or plaster, and intricately painted. There's also a gallery of life-size (and frighteningly lifelike) carved wooden bodies of the Passion of Christ, replete with gruesome wounds.

Casa Museu Marechal Deodoro

Rua Marechal Deodoro • Mon–Sat 8am–5pm • Free • ☎ 82 9998 3520

Down the road curving to the right past the Convento de São Francisco is the modest house that was the birthplace of **Marechal Deodoro** in 1827 (he lived here for sixteen years), proclaimer and first president of the Republic in 1889; it's now preserved as the **Casa Museu Marechal Deodoro**. Deodoro, the son of an army officer, was the first Brazilian to mount a military coup, unceremoniously de-throning the harmless old emperor Dom Pedro II, but he proved an arrogant and inept president, the first in a depressingly long line of incompetent military authoritarians. Dissolving Congress and declaring a state of siege in 1891, he did everyone a favour by resigning when he couldn't make it stick. There's no hint, of course, of his disastrous political career in the museum, which is basically a mildly interesting collection of personal effects and period furniture.

Igreja Matriz de Nossa Senhora da Conceição

Rua Capitão Bernardino Souto • Mon–Sat 8am–5pm • Free

Completed in 1783, the **Igreja Matriz de Nossa Senhora da Conceição** is the town's pretty white and yellow main church, with a simple interior featuring a gorgeous hand-carved wood altarpiece. The church lies at the end of the long plaza-like swathe of Rua Capitão Bernardino Souto, lined with more colonial relics and accessed via Rua Dr Ladislau Neto from the main part of town.

ARRIVAL AND DEPARTURE — MARECHAL DEODORO

By bus and minibus Buses and minibuses from Maceió run to Marechal frequently (30–40min), generally via Praia do Francês. Minibuses (R$3) depart from outside the Estação Ferroviária on Rua Barão de Anádia. On arrival in Marechal buses and minibuses take a snaking route through the town; get off in or close to Praça Pedro Paulinho (from where you can jump onto any bus heading back).

By colectivo *Colectivo* taxis are easy to find (near the lagoon at the end of Rua Barão de Alagoas), charging R$3 for the run to Praia do Francês (assuming the car is full).

Maragogi

Some 130km north of Maceió, just 15km before the border with Pernambuco state, the beautiful beachside settlement of **MARAGOGI**, also known as Caribbean Brazil, is a soothing place to break the journey north, with a wide swathe of golden sand and a smattering of appealing *pousadas* and simple restaurants. Other than lazing around, the main draw is the **Área de Preservação Ambiental Costa dos Corais** marine reserve, a pristine combination of reef and sand bar rich in marine life – at low tide pools of crystal-clear water form between the coral. Three areas are open to visitors: **Galés**, 6km offshore (30min by boat), and **Taocas** and **Barra Grande** further north. Local agencies offer day-trips to Galés from R$80 (plus R$15 for snorkelling and R$130 for diving).

ARRIVAL AND TOURS — MARAGOGI

By bus Real Alagoas (realalagoas.com.br) runs 2 buses daily between Maceió and Maragogi (departing 4am & 11am; returning 6.30am & 1.30am; R$30); they also run 2 buses to Recife.

Tours Most tour agencies in Maceió can arrange day-trips to Maragogi from R$75.

ACCOMMODATION AND EATING

Pousada Barra Velha AL-101 Norte, Sítio Barra Velha, Praia de Peroba (14km north of Maragogi) 82 3296 8105, pousadabarravelha.com.br. Clean and comfortable standard suites with colourful local artworks, as well as bigger, circular chalets. R$336

Pousada Camurim Grande AL-101 Norte Km 124 82 3296 2044, camurimgrande.com.br. Enticing luxury accommodation right on the beach at the southern end of town, with a huge pool ringed by palms, cosy wood chalets and bungalows all equipped with LCD TVs and hammocks. Breakfast and dinner included. (public areas) R$1790

Restaurante Maragaço Av Senador Rui Palmeira 1001 82 3296 2041. One of several high-quality seafood restaurants along the beach in town, a small no-frills place with some outdoor seating but where the focus is on the food. Mains around R$50–60. Mon, Tues & Thurs–Sun 11am–11pm.

Pernambuco

Though the state of **Pernambuco** cuts deep into the interior of Brazil, once again it's the coast that provides the greatest allure, with a series of stunning beaches and beach resorts and two intriguing but contrasting cities: the modern behemoth of **Recife**, the state capital, and the beautiful colonial town of **Olinda**, the second-oldest city in Brazil. Both host raucous **Carnavals** that attract revellers from all over Brazil. Historically the region is known for being occupied by the Dutch between 1630 and 1654; the state's most famous son is one Luiz Inácio da Silva (**Lula**), who was born dirt-poor in 1945 in Caetés, 250km from Recife – he went on to become one of the nation's most successful presidents (2003–10), but was in 2017 sentenced to nearly ten years in prison for corruption.

Recife

The Northeast's largest metropolitan area, **RECIFE** ("her-see-fey") is a dynamic, sprawling city of over four million with a booming economy and two major ports. The city centre – the three islands of Santo Antônio, Boa Vista and Bairro do Recife – remains a chaotic, and sometimes shabby place, where scrappy street vendors, markets, polluted drains and heavy traffic contrast with crumbling Art Nouveau buildings and a profusion of colonial churches. It's actually a compelling mix, once you get used to it (a bit like Rio's old downtown), is completely safe (during the day at least), and the regenerated **Bairro do Recife** area in particular is a real gem, more akin to *belle époque* Europe than to the rest of Brazil. Most of the money – and the middle class – lives in the beachside district of **Boa Viagem**, a forest of high-rise condos and beach hotels to the south, though it's not as much of a resort area as Maceió – shopping malls and businesses have moved out here, but it remains a residential area at heart.

Though Recife officially dates its foundation to 1537, it was the Dutch that really developed the city following their conquest of Olinda in 1630 (see page 635). They made Recife the capital of their Brazilian colony, as it had a fine natural harbour that Olinda lacked. The Dutch drained and reclaimed the low-lying swampy land, and the main evidence of their presence today is not so much their few surviving churches and forts dotted up and down the coast (the Portuguese destroyed virtually everything when they recaptured the area in 1654), as the very land on which the core of Recife is built.

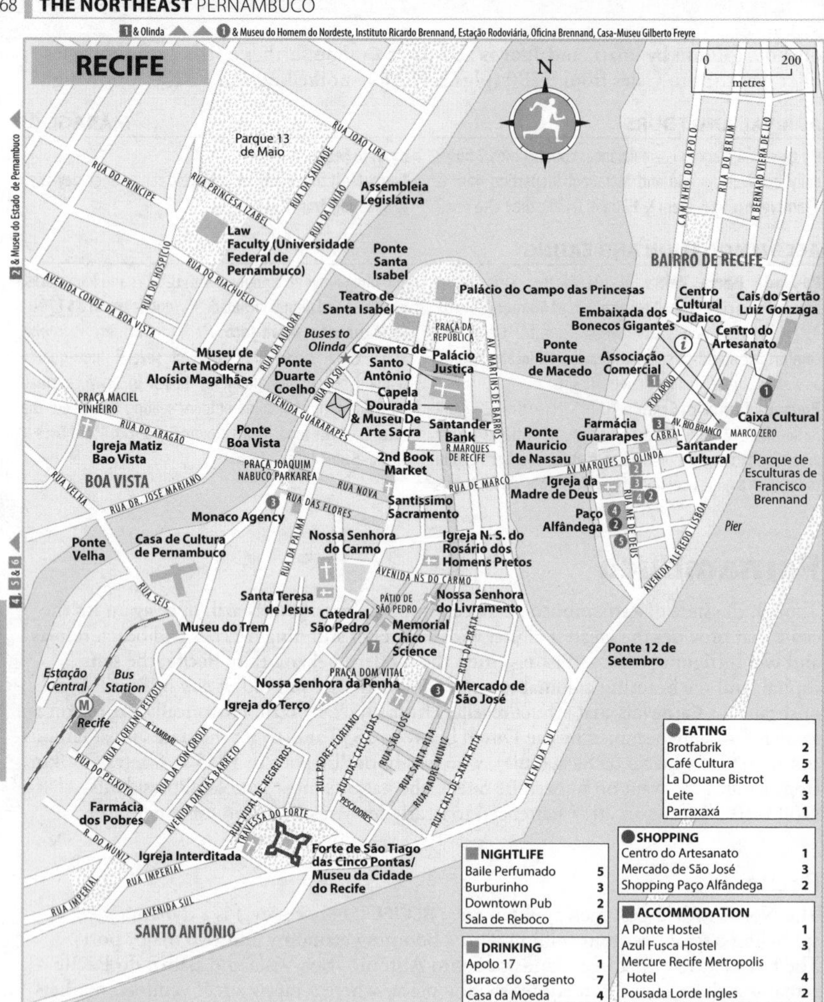

Avenida Dantas Barreto and the Praça da República

The broad **Avenida Dantas Barreto** forms the spine of the central island of **Santo Antônio**, lined with street markets almost its entire length, and criss-crossed with a web of crowded, narrow lanes lined with stalls and shops. It ends in the much quieter **Praça da República**, filled with majestic palms and surrounded by Recife's grandest public buildings – the **Palácio do Campo das Princesas**, the **Teatro Santa Isabel** (opened in 1850 and still in use) and the **Palácio da Justiça**, a grand French Empire-style pile completed in 1930 (closed to visitors).

Basílica de Nossa Senhora do Carmo

Av Dantas Barreto, at Rua Tobias Barreto • Daily 7am–8pm • Free • ⓣ 81 3224 3174, ⓦ basilicadocarmorecife.org.br

Recife's grandest church was completed in around 1767 next to the Convento do Carmo, and dedicated to the city's patron saint (Virgem do Carmo). The spacious,

CAPELA DOURADA, RECIFE

Rococo interior features an array of gilt gold *retábulos*, not quite as lavish as the Capela Dourada (see below), but impressive nonetheless.

Capela Dourada

Rua do Imperador s/n • **Chapel and museum** Mon–Fri 8–11.30am & 2–5pm, Sat 8–11.30am • R$5 • ☎ 81 3224 0530, Ⓦ capeladourada.com.br **Igreja do Convento de Santo Antônio** Mon–Fri 8–11.30am & 2–4.30pm, Sat 9–11.30am • Free

The most enticing attraction in central Recife is the **Capela Dourada** (Golden Chapel), housed inside the Franciscan complex **Convento do Santo Antônio**. Established in 1606, the convent was incorporated into the Dutch fortress here in the 1630s, and it was largely rebuilt between 1702 and 1777. You enter via the **Museu Franciscano de Arte Sacra**, a small but precious collection of religious carvings and statuary (all with good English labelling), before walking through a quiet cloister to the chapel itself. Finished in 1724, the Baroque interior is smothered in lavish wall-to-ceiling ornamentation, everything covered with gold leaf – in between are panels of oil paintings, mostly the work of José Ribeiro de Vasconcelos (between 1759 and 1761), including one of the "Twenty-six Martyrs of Japan", crucified in Nagasaki in 1597 (and not especially Japanese-looking). What really gilded the chapel, of course, was sugar cane: the sugar trade was at its peak when it was built, and the sugar elite were building monuments to their wealth all over the city. From the chapel you can peer into (but not enter) the main convent church, the **Igreja do Convento de Santo Antônio**, remodelled in the Rococo style 1753 to 1770. The church entrance is back on the street, next door to the museum entrance – ask someone in the office to let you into the main cloister. Though simpler than the Capela Dourada, the cloister and the church feature gorgeous **azulejos** (painted tiles), representing scenes from the Bible and the life of St Anthony.

Pátio de São Pedro

Tiny **Pátio de São Pedro** lies just off Avenida Dantas Barreto, a tranquil, pedestrianized plaza ringed with some lovely old bars and restaurants, and dominated by the **Igreja São Pedro dos Clerigios** (closed for major renovation at the time of writing).

Memorial Chico Science

Pátio de São Pedro 21 • Mon–Fri 9am–5pm • Free • ☎ 81 3355 3158, Ⓦ www.recife.pe.gov.br/chicoscience

The small but poignant **Memorial Chico Science** celebrates the life of the creator of **mangue beat** (a fusion of rock, funk and hip-hop with the traditional music of Brazil's Northeast), who died in a car accident here in 1997. Chico was born Francisco de Assis França in Olinda in 1966, and founded mangue beat in 1991 with fellow local musician Fred 04.

Casa da Cultura de Pernambuco

Rua Floriano Peixoto s/n • Mon–Fri 9am–7pm, Sat 9am–6pm, Sun 9am–2pm • Free • ☎ 81 3224 2850, Ⓦ casadaculturape.com.br

Opposite Recife's old train station, the forbidding **Casa da Cultura de Pernambuco** was the city's prison from 1855 to 1973, but is now an arts and crafts centre, the cells converted into little boutiques and one or two places for refreshment. The prison was cunningly designed, with four wings radiating out from a central point, so that a single warder could keep an eye on all corridors (**Cell 106** has been preserved as it was). The quality of the goods on offer here is high, but the multi-level interior, cells and metal walkways are worth seeing, regardless of whether you want to shop.

Museu da Cidade

Forte das Cinco Pontas s/n • Tues–Sun 9am–5pm • Free • ☎ 81 3355 9540, Ⓦ museudacidadedorecife.org

Recife's **Museu da Cidade** occupies the star-shaped Forte das Cinco Pontas, built in 1630 by the Dutch but remodelled many times since then. Notable chiefly as the last place where the Dutch surrendered in 1654, the structure is usually more interesting than the temporary exhibits inside (often with an architectural theme, in Portuguese only), with a neat central Plaza da Armas and wide battlements on all sides.

Museu de Arte Moderna Aloísio Magalhães

Rua da Aurora 256, Boa Vista • Tues–Fri noon–6pm, Sat & Sun 1–5pm • Free • ⓣ 81 3355 6870, ⓦ blogmamam.wordpress.com

Housed in a wonderfully restored nineteenth-century mansion in Boa Vista, just over the Rio Capibaribe from Santo Antônio, the **Museu de Arte Moderna Aloísio Magalhães** features prestigious travelling exhibitions of mainly Brazilian contemporary artists, many among Pernambuco's best. Don't miss the painted tile mural by Ricardo Brennand (see page 272) in the courtyard out the back, completed in 1965 and dubbed "O Grande Sol".

Bairro de Recife (Recife Antigo)

Until only a few years ago, the **Bairro do Recife** (also known as **Recife Antigo**) was a dangerous, run-down area inhabited mainly by drunks and prostitutes, but the investment of millions by the local authorities and private businesses has brought about something of a transformation in both the look and feel of the area. The grand, brightly painted *belle époque* buildings here are quite spectacular, and it's a pleasant place to wander during the day. In addition, the streets and *praças* are stocked with bars and cafés (see page 275), which are very busy at weekends and lunchtimes.

Centro Cultural Judaico

Rua do Bom Jesus 197 • Tues–Fri 9am–5.30pm, Sun 2–5.30pm • R$10 • ⓣ 81 3224 2128

The **Sinagoga Kahal Zur Israel** or simply the **Centro Cultural Judaico** was the site of the first synagogue built in the whole of the Americas; it dates back to 1639 when Jews started coming to Dutch-controlled Brazil (the Dutch were remarkably tolerant of Jews, considering the period). Sadly, once the Portuguese retook the city in 1654 the Jews were booted out, and the synagogue was destroyed – today all that remains is the foundation, the excavated Mikvah (ritual bath) and some original brick walls. Upstairs there's a re-creation of what it might have looked like in its heyday (with Torah), plus exhibits on the seventeenth-century community (Sephardic) and the Azkenazi Jews who returned here in the nineteenth century. Some exhibits are labelled in English, and there are usually English-speaking guides on hand.

Embaixada dos Bonecos Gigantes

Rua do Bom Jesus 183 • Daily 8am–6pm • R$20 • ⓣ 81 3441 5102, ⓦ bonecosgigantesdeolinda.com.br

The **Embaixada dos Bonecos Gigantes** is a small, quirky museum displaying some of the giant **puppets** used in the Olinda Carnaval, many of them celebrities, from Lampião to a scary-looking Michael Jackson. Informative guides add context, but rarely speak English.

Marco Zero (Praça Barão Rio Branco)

Santander Cultural Av Rio Branco 23 • Only open during Carnaval (check with the tourism office beforehand) • Free **Caixa Cultural** Av Alfredo Lisboa 505 • Tues–Sat 10am–8pm, Sun 10am–5pm • Free • ⓣ 81 3425 1915, ⓦ caixacultural.com.br **Cais do Sertão Luis Gonzaga** Av Alfredo Lisboa S/N • R$10 • Tues–Fri 9am–5pm (last entry 4.30pm), Sat & Sun 1–5pm (last entry 4.30pm) • ⓣ 81 4042 0484, ⓦ caisdosertao.org.br

Lying at the heart of the Bairro do Recife's regeneration is Praça Barão Rio Branco, known simply as "**Marco Zero**" for the "Km 0" marker in the centre. Surrounding the plaza are venues for high-quality travelling art shows, the **Santander Cultural** and **Caixa Cultural**. Both occupy gorgeously renovated buildings (the British-dominated old River Plate Bank and the 1912 Banco de Londres respectively). On the other side of the plaza lies the **Centro do Artesanato** (see page 277), with views across the river to the totem-like 32m-high Torre de Cristal in the **Parque de Esculturas Francisco Brennand** (boats charge R$5 to go across, daily 8am–5pm). Beyond the Centro do Artesanato lies the beautifully and very Informative **Cais do Sertão Luiz Gonzaga**, showcasing exhibits on the traditions, life, music and culture of the *sertão*. On the other side of the island lies the **Paço Alfândega**, a 1732 convent that became a customs house in 1826 and is now a posh shopping mall (see page 277). Next door stands the elegant **Igreja da Madre de Deus**, dating back to 1679.

Museu do Homem do Nordeste

Av 17 de Agosto 2187, Casa Forte • Tues–Fri 8.30am–5pm, Sat & Sun 2–6pm • R$6 • T 81 3073 6363, W www.fundaj.gov.br • Take the "Dois Irmãos" bus from outside the post office or from Parque 13 de Maio in Boa Vista

Founded by Gilberto Freyre (see pages 668 and 669), the **Museu do Homem do Nordeste** is an introduction to the history and culture of the Northeast. It's split into several galleries, each devoted to one of the great themes of Northeastern economy and society: sugar, cattle, fishing, popular religion, festivals, ceramics and so on. The museum's strongest point is its unrivalled collection of **popular art** – there are displays not just of handicrafts, but also of cigarette packets, tobacco pouches and, best of all, a superb collection of postwar bottles of cachaça.

Museu do Estado de Pernambuco

Av Rui Barbosa 960, Graças • Tues–Fri 9am–5pm, Sat & Sun 2–5pm • R$6 • T 81 3184 3174, W museudoestadope.com.br • Take the "Dois Irmãos" bus from outside the post office or from Parque 13 de Maio

The Pernambuco state history museum, the **Museu do Estado de Pernambuco**, occupies an elegant nineteenth-century mansion in Graças that once belonged to the son of the Barão de Beberibe. Here you'll find prehistoric and indigenous artefacts, antique furniture, Chinese porcelain, some fine engravings of Recife as it was in the early part of the last century, all of them by English artists, and upstairs there are good paintings by Telles Júnior, which give you an idea of what tropical Turners might have looked like.

Casa Museu Gilberto Freyre

Rua Dois Irmãos 320, Apipucos • Mon–Fri 9am–4.30pm • R$10 • T 81 3441 1733, W facebook.com/fundacao.gilbertofreyre • Take an Uber (R$30 from Boa Viagem) or taxi (around R$50)

Fans of the lauded Brazilian author of *The Masters and the Slaves* Palácio da Justiça should make the pilgrimage to his nineteenth-century house, the **Casa Museu Gilberto Freyre**, now a museum commemorating his life (1900–87) with books, personal effects and the creaky old rooms frozen in time. The enthusiastic guides speak very little English.

Instituto Ricardo Brennand

Alameda Antônio Brennand, Várzea • Tues–Sun 1–5pm • R$30 • T 81 2121 0352, W institutoricardobrennand.org.br • Taxis will charge at least R$150 round-trip from Boa Viagem; or take bus #40 on Av Domingos Ferreira (in Boa Viagem) or Av Agamenon Magalhães (bordering Boa Vista) and take it to the end of the line; walk to the end of the road, and turn right onto Rua Isaac Buril; the institute is at the end of this road on the left

Though quite a trek from the city centre, the **Instituto Ricardo Brennand** and nearby Oficina Brennand (see below) are the most beguiling attractions in the region, the former a museum in the northern suburbs housed in a faux Tudor castle, the "Castelo São João" (complete with working drawbridge). Inside is the Museu de Armas, with over three thousand medieval Asian and European weapons, suits of armour and the like, but also tapestries, stained glass and antique European furnishings – all rather jarring considering the palm trees outside. In the adjacent Pinacoteca building there's changing art exhibitions, a gallery of nineteenth-century Brazilian landscape paintings and a fascinating space dedicated to the **Dutch occupation of Brazil** (including the world's largest collection of paintings by Frans Post).

Oficina Brennand

Propriedade Santos Cosme e Damião (off Rua Gastão Vidigal), Várzea • Mon–Thurs 8am–5pm, Fri 8am–4pm • R$20 • T 81 3271 2466, W brennand.com.br • For transport, see Instituto Ricardo Brennand above; the oficina is a short walk south of the Instituto

Beyond the Instituto Ricardo Brennand, past rows of workers' cottages and a brickworks, you come to **Oficina Brennand**, where **Francisco Brennand** (the cousin of entrepreneur Ricardo), born in Recife in 1927, displays thousands of his own whimsical sculptures, decorated tiles, paintings and drawings. The main building is actually an old tile factory, but now part of a vast open-air sculpture park surrounded by pristine Mata Atlântica forest.

Boa Viagem

Regular buses make it easy to get from the city centre to **Boa Viagem** and the beach, an enormous skyscraper-lined arc of sand that constitutes the longest stretch of urbanized seafront in Brazil (over 7km), protected by the slim *arrecife* (reef) just offshore. Though most of the good hotels and restaurants are here, swimming is not really a good idea; over fifty **shark attacks** have been reported here since 1992, more than twenty of which were fatal (though in reality sharks rarely come beyond the reef, and surfers are most at risk). Nevertheless, the beach itself is sandy, attractive and relatively relaxed on weekdays, and it's generally a lot quieter than other resorts, partly because of sheer size, and also because so much seafront is dominated by residential condos, not hotels.

ARRIVAL AND DEPARTURE RECIFE

By plane Recife's large, modern Aeroporto Internacional dos Guararapes-Gilberto Freyre (☎81 3322 4188, ⓦaeroportorecife.net) is only 11km from the city centre, at the southern end of Boa Viagem. You can pay for fixed-rate taxis at the arrivals halls (COOPSETA ☎81 3462 1584), which will cost around R$30 to Boa Viagem, R$45 to Santo Antônio (city centre) and R$80 to Olinda, or opt for a pay-by-meter *taxi comum*, which are about the same, assuming it's not rush hour. Prices are higher if you arrive between 10pm and 6am. Alternatively, for Boa Viagem take either the a/c bus #042 from outside the airport (every 20min, 5am–11.55pm; R$3.20), or bus #040 (every 20min, 5am–11.55pm; R$3.20) from nearby Praça Ministro Salgado Filho. For Boa Vista (city centre), take bus #163 (every 20min, 5am–11pm; R$3.20) from the same *praça*. The *metrô* (see page 274) also runs from just south of the airport (connected by walkway) to Estaçâo Central terminal (not the beach).

Destinations Fortaleza (8–12 daily; 1hr 15min–1hr 25min); Lisbon (1 daily; 7hr 35min); Miami (1 daily; 8hr 20min); Panama City (1 daily; 7hr 20min); Rio (26–32 daily; 5hr 20min–7hr 50min); Salvador (7–10 daily; 1hr 10min–1hr 20min); São Paulo (11–15 daily; 3hr–3hr 30min).

By bus The rodoviária is about 14km west of the centre at BR-232 Km 15, Coqueiral (☎81 3452 1103), though this is not really a problem since the *metrô* (see page 274) whisks you very cheaply (R$1.60) and efficiently into the centre, gliding through various *favelas*. It will deposit you at the old train station, called Estação Central (or simply "Recife"). To get to your hotel from there, you're best off taking a taxi. Taxis from the bus station to Boa Viagem or the city centre should be about R$45–55 on the meter.

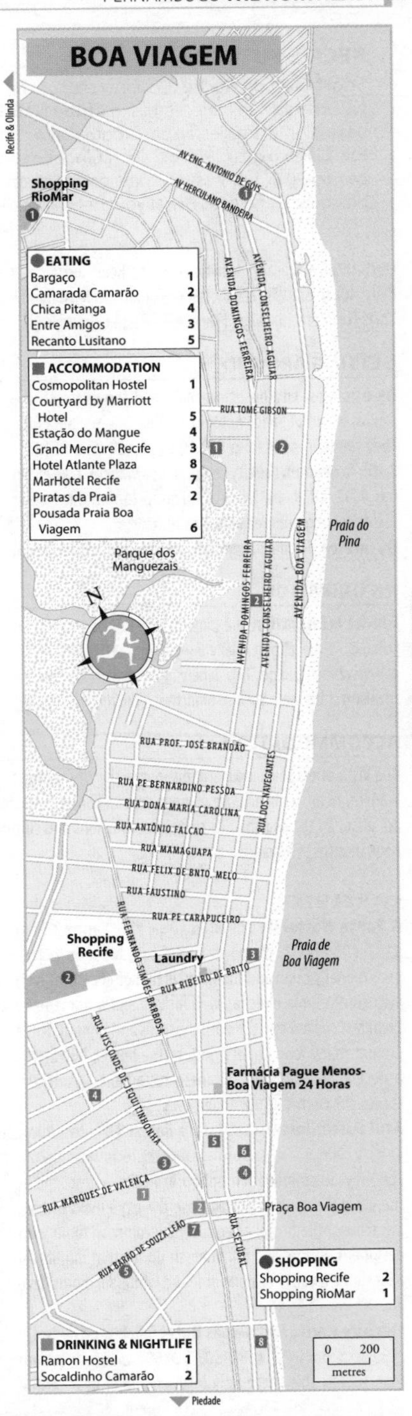

RECIFE FUTEBOL

Sport Club do Recife (sportrecife.com.br) is fanatically supported in the city, with a historic rivalry with Recife-based **Clube Náutico Capibaribe** (nautico-pe.com.br), which has a slightly smaller fan base (both play in Série A). Games between the two are known as the "Clássico dos Clássicos". Sport Clube's new Arena da Copa should have been completed by mid-2015, but was still under construction at the time of writing with a continuously postponed end date. Ask at your hotel about buying tickets.

Destinations Aracaju (4 daily; 7–11hr); Belo Horizonte (1 daily; 40hr); Brasília (2 daily; 48hr); Caruaru (at least hourly; 2hr); Fortaleza (5 daily; 13hr); João Pessoa (hourly; 2hr); Maceió (8 daily; 4hr 30min); Natal (9 daily; 5hr); Porto de Galinhas (every 30min; 1hr); Rio (2 daily; 38–41hr); Salvador (2 daily; 12–16hr); São Paulo (1–3 daily; 45–50hr).

GETTING AROUND

By bus Most city buses originate and terminate on the central island of Santo Antônio, on Rua Cais de Santa Rita. They range in price from R$2.10 to R$3.20 (Sun R$1.60–2.20). To get from the city centre to Boa Viagem, take either bus #042, #039, #032 or #071. For up-to-date timetables see www.granderecife.pe.gov.br.

By metrô Recife's light rail system runs 5am–11pm (R$1.60; metrorec.com.br), but is only really useful for travellers as a way of getting to the city centre (Estação Central or just "Recife") from the airport or bus station.

By taxi Taxis use meters that start at R$4.85; reckon on R$25–30 between Boa Viagem and the city centre, and R$45–50 between Boa Viagem and Olinda.

4

INFORMATION

Tourist information The most helpful tourist information point is at the airport (daily 8am–6pm; 81 3182 8299, www2.recife.pe.gov.br), where you may find English-speaking staff. There are also branches at the rodoviária (daily 7am–7pm; 81 3182 8298), Praça de Boa Viagem (daily 8am–8pm; 81 3182 8297. Alternatively, there's the tourist hotline, the Apoio ao Turista (24hr; 81 3182 8299), on which you should be able to find someone who speaks English.

ACCOMMODATION

Boa Vista offers some excellent options in the city centre, though most of the city's hotels and hostels are located in Boa Viagem, near the beach. An obvious area to consider staying in is nearby Olinda (see page 278), where the high prices are offset by the charm of its colonial conversions and culture. As ever, if you want to visit during Carnaval, you'll need to book months in advance.

CITY CENTRE

A Ponte Hostel Rua Capitao Lima 410, Santo Amaro 81 3034 6603, apontehostel.com.br; map p.268. Exceptionally clean and small hostel that offers dorms with very comfortable beds, as well lockers and a homemade breakfast cooked to order with couscous and tapioca. There are not many food outlets close to the hostel, but there's a decent and affordable Chinese restaurant around the corner. Dorms R$50, doubles R$150

Azul Fusca Hostel Rua Mariz e Barros 328 (2nd floor) 81 97906 6338, azulfuscahostel.com; map p.268. The only accommodation option in Recife Antigo, this is the place if you want to stay close the city's main historic attractions. The hostel offers a stylish common room with designer furniture and minimalistic dorms that might feel a bit sterile if you're not into grey and white. All rooms have a/c. Dorms R$45

Mercure Recife Metropolis Hotel Rua Estado de Israel 203, Ilha do leite 81 3087 3700, mercure.com; map p.268. This is the only luxurious hotel near central Recife; it offers a pool, gym and a restaurant, though most apartments also have their own kitchen. R$250

★ **Pousada Lorde Ingles** Rua Padre Inglês 90, Boa Vista 81 3048 0034, pousadalordeingles.com.br; map p.268. Set in a beautiful yellow villa, this excellent *pousada* with kind and helpful staff offers comfortable, bright and modern rooms with *frigobar*, LCD TV and a/c, as well as a decent breakfast buffet. Extra plus for location – just outside the hotel you'll find street vendors selling drinks and food, making it easy to grab a cheap and delicious snack. R$200

BOA VIAGEM

Cosmopolitan Hostel Rua Paulo Setúbal 53 81 3204 0321, cosmopolitanhostel.com; map p.273. Decent budget option, with basic en-suite doubles and spotless dorms, TV lounge (cable TV and DVDs), shared kitchen and breakfast included. Dorms R$39, doubles R$109

Courtyard by Marriott Hotel Av Eng Domingos Ferreira 4661 81 3256 7700, marriott.com; map

RECIFE CARNAVAL

Carnaval in Recife is overshadowed by the one in Olinda, but the city affair is still worth sampling. The best place for **Carnaval information** is the tourist office, which publishes a free broadsheet with timetables and route details of all the Carnaval groups (*blocos*). The most famous is the Galo da Madrugada; the most common are the *frevo* groups (trucks called *freviocas*, with an electric *frevo* band aboard, circulate around the centre, whipping up already frantic crowds); but most visually arresting are *caboclinhos*, who wear modern Brazilian interpretations of a traditional Amazon Indian costume – feathers, animal-tooth necklaces – and carry bows and arrows, which they use to beat out the rhythm as they dance. It's also worth trying to see a *maracatu* group, unique to Pernambuco: they're mainly Afro-Brazilian, and wear bright costumes, the music an interesting (and danceable) hybrid of African percussion and Latin brass.

In Recife, the **main events** are concentrated in Santo Antônio and Boa Vista. Carnaval officially begins with a trumpet fanfare welcoming Rei Momo, the Carnaval king and queen, on Avenida Guararapes at midnight on Friday, the cue for wild celebrations. At night, activities centre on the grandstands on Avenida Dantas Barreto, where the *blocos* parade under the critical eyes of the judges; the other central area to head for is the Pátio de São Pedro. During the day, the *blocos* follow a **route** of sorts: beginning in Praça Manuel Pinheiro, and then via Rua do Hospício, Avenida Conde de Boa Vista, Avenida Guararapes, Praça da República and Avenida Dantas Barreto, to Pátio de São Pedro. Good places to hang around are near churches, especially Rosário dos Pretos, on Largo do Rosário, a special target for *maracatu* groups. Daylight hours is the best time to see the *blocos* – when the crowds are smaller and there are far more children around. At night, it's far more intense and the usual safety warnings apply.

p.273. Standard four-star hotel with English speaking staff, comfortable and stylish rooms, very good breakfast buffet and a pleasant roof top pool. All rooms have a/c, ironing board, LCD TV and work desk. R$329

Estação do Mangue Rua Raimundo Gomes Gondim 26 ⊕81 3049 2626, ⊕estacaodomangue.com.br; map p.273. Justly popular hostel, a short walk from the beach, with communal TV room and kitchen, simple dorms and private rooms. Buffet breakfast included. Dorms R$50, doubles R$150

Grand Mercure Recife Av Boa Viagem 4070 ⊕81 3201 8200, ⊕accorhotels.com; map p.273. Standard luxury high-rise, with superb beach views, plush lobby and rooms with all comforts and facilities, including gym and pool. R$300

Hotel Atlante Plaza Av Boa Viagem 5426 ⊕81 3302 4446, ⊕ponteshoteis.com.br; map p.273. Large and well located in the centre of the beach and nightlife, this luxurious hotel boasts elevators with panoramic views, plus a bar, restaurant, swimming pool, fitness suite and sauna. R$279

MarHotel Recife Rua Barão de Souza Leão 451 ⊕81 3302 4446, ⊕ponteshoteis.com.br; map p.273. One of the best mid-range options on the beach, with good service and rooms with balcony, a/c, LCD TV and cable TV. R$242

Piratas da Praia Av Cons Aguiar 2034 (3rd floor), at Rua Prof. Osias Ribeiro ⊕81 3326 1281, ⊕piratasdapraia.com; map p.273. Neat pastel dorms with primary-coloured portraiture and some private rooms; all have fans and a/c. Co-working space for digital nomads (R$5/hr) and lockers available. Breakfast included. Dorms R$46, doubles R$106

Pousada Praia Boa Viagem Rua Petrolina 81 ⊕81 3039 5880, ⊕pousadapraiaboaviagem.com; map p.273. A decent and more intimate option to the usual high-rise hotels in Boa Viagem, this *pousada* offers clean rooms with a/c, LCD TV and *frigobar* and 24hr reception. Just two blocks from the beach. (public areas) R$180

EATING

Recifense cuisine revolves around **fish** and **shellfish** – try *carangueijo mole*, crabs cooked in a spicy sauce until shells and legs are soft and edible, which solves the problem of digging out the meat; small crabs called *guaiamum*; and *agulhas fritas* (fried needle-fish), as well as the local dessert *cartola* (grilled banana with cheese, cinnamon and granulated sugar). In Bairro do Recife, Rua da Bom Jesus is transformed into an open-air food and arts market, Feira do Bom Jesus (Sun 10am–6pm).

CITY CENTRE

★ **Brotfabrik** Rua da Moeda 87, Recife Antigo ⊕81 3424 2250, ⊕brotfabrik.com.br; map p.268. Bakery that almost pulls off the Dutch theme in a spacious old warehouse with espresso (from R$4.10), pastries, rye bread, *salgados*, sandwiches (R$9.70–12.90) and bite-sized pizzas (*brotinho*; R$10.90), as the constant queue attests. Mon–Fri 7am–7pm.

Café Cultura Av Paulista 2073, Bairro do Recife; map p.268. Located on the second floor of the beautiful bookshop Livraria Cultura, this café offers excellent coffee and hot chocolate. Perfect If you want to escape the sun and have a light snack and cake. Mon–Sat 10am–10pm, Sun noon–9pm.

La Douane Bistrot Paço de Alfândega 35, Bairro do Recife ☎81 3224 5799, ⓦladouane.com.br; map p.268. Located in the wonderfully converted Alfândega shopping mall, this plush restaurant is favoured by local politicians and businessmen. Waiting staff are immaculately turned out and the food is Mediterranean in flavour with a Brazilian bent – splash out on the *bacalhau da restauração* with stuffed potato (R$78). The three-course set menu is very good value for money (R$50). Mon–Sat 9am–9pm, Sun noon–8pm.

Leite Praça Joaquim Nabuco 147, Santo Antônio ☎81 3224 7977; map p.268. This classy place in a very stylish nineteenth-century interior serves tasty local and Portuguese dishes (lots of cod dishes, beef tongue in madeira sauce and the like). The restaurant was founded in 1882, but this building dates from around 1905. Mon–Fri & Sun 11.30am–4pm (closed Sat).

Parraxaxá Rua Igarassu 40, Casa Forte ☎81 3268 4169, ⓦparraxaxa.com.br; map p.268. A little piece of the *sertão* transplanted to the city, this celebrated *por quilo* place is themed around the talismanic bandit Lampião, with *cantina*-style tables and chairs, and a daily buffet bulging under the weight of backcountry specialities such as sun-dried beef and all manner of deliciously stodgy puddings (around R$63.90/kg). A perfect lunchstop after the nearby Museu do Homem do Nordeste (see page 272). Note that the branch in Boa Viagem isn't as good. Daily 7am–10pm.

BOA VIAGEM

★ **Bargaço** Av Antônio de Góes 62, Pina ☎81 3465 1847, ⓦrestaurantebargaco.com.br; map p.273. Sophisticated seafront restaurant serving regional and Bahian seafood dishes and especially tasty shrimp and lobster *moqueca* (most dishes are designed for two). Potent caipirinhas. Mon–Thurs & Sun noon–midnight, Fri & Sat noon–1am.

★ **Camarada Camarão** Rua Baltazar Pereira 130 ☎81 3325 1786, ⓦocamarada.com.br; map p.273. Heaven for seafood lovers, this popular and airy restaurant serves prawns in all shapes and forms. Food is fresh and tasty – try the *praia do paraíso* (lightly battered prawns with garlic and onion R$45). Most dishes are for two people sharing and there are two more branches in Recife. Tues & Wed 5–11pm, Thurs–Sat 11.30am–midnight & Sun 11.30am–8pm.

★ **Chica Pitanga** Rua Petrolina 19 ☎81 3465 2224, ⓦchicapitanga.com.br; map p.273. Long one of the most sought-after *por quilo* places in Recife, with a bright stylish interior and tables that you'll likely have to wait patiently to snag a table (go early). At R$75/kg at lunch (R$82 at weekends) and R$64/kg at dinner, it isn't cheap but you get what you pay for, with a dazzling buffet heavy on seafood, with a great selection of salads and always in flux. Mon–Fri 11.30am–3.30pm & 5.30–10pm, Sat & Sun 11.30am–4pm & 6–10pm.

Entre Amigos Rua Marquês de Valença 50 ☎81 3312 1000, ⓦwww.entreamigosobode.com.br; map p.273. Famed for its braised goat, hence the nickname "O Bode" (the goat) – the main event is served a bewildering number of ways, from goat paella to goat in wine sauce with sweet potato (mains to share R$70–95). Daily 11.30am–3am.

Recanto Lusitano Rua Antônio Vicente 284 ☎81 3462 2161, ⓦrecantolusitano.com.br; map p.273. Serving traditional Portuguese food since 1980; dishes range R$80–110 but are good for two people to share. Tues–Sat 11.45am–3pm, 6.45pm–1.30am; Sun 11.45am–4pm.

DRINKING

Most of the city-centre **bars** are in the Bairro do Recife (Recife Antigo) with the scene at its noisiest in and around Praça do Arsenal. The liveliest area in Boa Viagem is around Praça de Boa Viagem (quite a long way down the beach from the city centre, near the junction of Av Boa Viagem and Rua Bavão de Souza Leão).

CITY CENTRE

Apolo 17 Rua do Apolo 170, Bairro do Recife ☎81 9579 1655, ⓦfacebook.com/apolo17galeriacafe; map p.268. Bar serving a wide selection of beers, pizzas (R$18–28) and snacks (R$12–27) in the heart of Recife Antigo. The focus here is on the live music (pop, rock, Indie), so expect few tables and people standing up during the gigs. Wed–Sat 6pm–midnight.

Buraco do Sargento Pátio de São Pedro 33, Santo Antônio ☎81 3224 7522, ⓦfacebook.com/buracodosargento; map p.268. This classic old-school bar and café has stood on this plaza since 1955, housed in the headquarters of the Batutas de São José (one of Recife's *blocos de carnaval*). Stand around the granite counter-top or sit on a table outside, sipping Brahma or cachaça and snacking on *galinha cozido* (chicken gizzards; R$20). Mon–Fri 9am–5pm.

Casa da Moeda Rua da Moeda 150, Bairro do Recife ☎81 3224 7095, ⓦfacebook.com/Casa-da-Moeda-Comes-Bebes-153714391322446; map p.268. For a taster of Recife's bohemian side visit the bar run by local photographer and artist Sergio Altenkirch and decorated with his work. Join the alternative crowd to drink cachaça nd snack, and to enjoy live music (from jazz and blues to ock). Mon–Wed & Sun 5pm–1am, Thurs 5pm–2am, Fri pm–3am, Sat 6pm–3am.

BOA VIAGEM

Ramon Hostel Rua Olávo Bilac 20B 81 ⓣ3036 6930, ⓦfacebook.com/ramonhostelbar; map p.273. Part of hostel, *Ramon Hostel*, this bar is a great budget option, as Spanish-speaking staff, serves ice-cold beers, as well as pizza Argentina style (with loads of cheese). The atmosphere is friendly and relaxed and the place is usually packed. Tues–Sun 6pm–late.

Socaldinho Camarão Av Visconde de Jequitinhonha 106 ⓣ81 3462 9500; map p.273. If you fancy some football action, head here and join the locals for a beer over a gripping game of Brazilian *futebol* as you munch on some *peixe a móda* (R$50 for three people). Mon–Fri 11.30am–midnight, Sat 11am–2am, Sun 11am–midnight.

NIGHTLIFE

Recife lives and breathes **live music**. While the city Carnaval throbs its own frenetic sounds, the *frevo*, *afoxê* and *maracatu*, they've long been hybridized into the city's most famous musical export, *manguebeat*, a style that exerts a huge influence on acts you can either see for free, in the Pátio de São Pedro (see page 270) and at Marco Zero (see page 271) or, for a modest fee, in the bars and clubs of Bairro do Recife (Recife Antigo), where tables spill onto the street into the small hours. Look out, especially, for performances by Orquestra Contemporânea de Olinda (ⓦorquestraolinda.com.br), perhaps the most promising of the area's manguebeat inheritors.

Baile Perfumado Rua Carlos Gomes 390, Prado ⓣ81 3033 4747; map p.268. With a capacity of 5000, this live music venue puts on rock/pop gigs including national acts like singer and guitarist Humberto Gessinger. Tickets are usually in the region of R$80. Located well out in the suburbs (5km west of the centre) in Prado, so take a taxi. Opens according to show times.

Burburinho Rua Tomazina 106, Bairro do Recife ⓣ81 3224 5854, ⓦbarburburinho.com.br; map p.268. Long the venue in Recife to hear local music in a sweaty nightclub setting, much of it in a tribute vein, this place puts on everything from the new generation of local artists influenced by the 1990s mangue-beat explosion, to homages as diverse as The Cure and Creedence Clearwater Revival. Cover usually R$10–30. Tuesdays free. Hours vary; currently runs sessions with unsigned acts Tues and tribute nights Sat.

Downtown Pub Rua Vigário Tenório 105, Bairro do Recife ⓣ81 3424 5731, ⓦdowntownpub.com.br; map p.268. This place, which is more of a club than a pub with its lighting system and polished interior, lays it on thick with the Anglophone rock and tribute nights, but you can sometimes land lucky with decent live reggae. Cover R$40. Fri & Sat 10pm–5am.

Sala de Reboco Rua Gregório Júnior 264, Cordeiro ⓣ81 3228 7052, ⓦsaladereboco.com.br; map p.268. If you're really keen to pick up some authentic *forró pé-de-serra nordestino* (Northeastern Brazilian folk dance) skills, then it's worth your while heading out to the suburbs (bus #040 if you're not taking a taxi; ask the driver where to get off) to one of the country's best *casas de forró*, drawing a loyal and passionate crowd as well as some of Brazil's best *forrozeiros*. Cover normally R$20. Thurs–Sat 10pm–late.

4

SHOPPING

Centro do Artesanato Av Alfredo Lisboa (Marco Zero), Armazém 11, Bairro do Recife ⓣ81 3181 3451, ⓦwww.portaldoartesanato.pe.gov.br; map p.268. Former warehouse on the waterfront that acts as a showcase for folk art and the traditional crafts of Pernambuco. Mon–Sat 8am–7pm & Sun 8am–4pm.

Mercado de São José Rua São José, Santo Antônio; map p.268. Opened in 1875, this is the oldest public market in Brazil. Stock up on some local crafts, or simply peruse the stacks of curious herbal medicines and everyday items as locals go about their daily shopping. Mon–Sat 6am–6pm, Sun 6am–noon.

Shopping Paço Alfândega Rua da Alfândega 35, Bairro do Recife ⓣ81 3194 2100, ⓦpacoalfandega.com.br; map p.268. Chic, refurbished 1732 convent that became a customs house in 1826 and now houses the typical range of Brazilian chain stores and fast-food outlets as well as the swanky *La Douane Bistrot* (see page 276). Mon–Sat 9am–9pm, Sun 11am–8pm.

Shopping Recife Rua Pe. Carapuceiro 777, Boa Viagem ⓣ81 3464 6000, ⓦwww.shoppingrecife.com.br; map p.273. Suburban shopping mall, one of Brazil's largest. Mon–Sat 9am–10pm, Sun noon–9pm.

Shopping RioMar Av República do Líbano 251, Pina ⓣ81 3878 0000, ⓦ riomarrecife.com.br; map p.273. Big and flashy shopping centre with over 350 stores including high fashion and international brands, a spacious food court, cinema and even a bowling alley.

DIRECTORY

Consulates UK, Av Agamenon Magalhães 4775, 8th floor (ⓣ81 2127 0200); US, Rua Gonçalves Maia 163, Boa Vista (ⓣ81 3416 3050).

Hospital Real Hospital Português de Beneficência, Av

Agamenon Magalhâes 4760, Boa Vista (T 81 3416 1122).
Internet LAN Games Rua Waldemar Nery Carneiro Monteiro 104 (T 81 3031 5104).
Laundry Prima Clean Rua Carlos Pereira Falcão 112, Boa Viagem (T 81 3037 1249). A bit pricey (R$45/load; same day delivery).
Money and exchange Most banks have ATMs. The Banco do Brasil has branches at the airport (Mon–Fri 10am–4pm), Av Dantas Barreto 541 and Av Rio Branco 240. Shopping centres all have ATMs, banks and mone changing facilities (Mon–Sat until 9pm). The Brades bank on Conde de Boa Vista has an ATM that accepts mo Visa cards.
Pharmacy Farmácia Pague Menos, Av Cons Aguiar 463 Boa Viagem, 24hr (T 81 3301 4220).
Post office Correio building at Av Guararapes 250 in Sant Antônio (Mon–Fri 9am–5pm); and a branch in the Bair do Recife, Av Marquês de Olinda 262.

Olinda

OLINDA is, quite simply, one of the largest and most beautiful complexes of **colonial architecture** in Brazil: a maze of cobbled streets, hills crowned with brilliant white churches, pastel-coloured houses, Baroque fountains and graceful plazas. It's quite different to Salvador's gorgeous but in-your-face Pelourinho (see page 213), with a laidback, small-town feel, calm, languid streets laced with palm and mango trees and just single- or two-storey buildings – wandering around even at night is pretty safe. Founded in 1535, the old city is spread across several small hills looking back towards Recife, but it belongs to a different world; it's here that many of the larger city's artists, musicians and liberal professionals live, and there's a significant gay community. Olind is most renowned, though, for its **Carnaval**, famous throughout Brazil.

Though a city in its own right, Olinda is effectively a suburb of Recife these days: a high proportion of the population commutes into the city, which means that **transport links** are good, with buses leaving every few minutes. Olinda's old colonial centre is built slightly back from the sea, but arching along the seafront and spreading inland behind the old town is a modern Brazilian city of nearly 400,000 people – known as **Novo Olinda**, it's the usual bland collection of suburbs and chaotic commercial streets, with little of interest.

Alto da Sé

A good spot to have a drink and plan your day is the **Alto da Sé** (the highest square in town), not least because of the stunning view of Recife's skyscrapers shimmering in the distance, framed in the foreground by the church towers, gardens and palm trees of Olinda. There's always an arts and crafts **market** going on here during the day, peaking in the late afternoon, as well as the permanent **Mercado Artesanato da Sé**.

Igreja de São Salvador

Alto da Sé • Daily 9am–5pm • Free • T 81 3271 4270

The main attraction on the Alto da Sé is the **Igreja de São Salvador** or just Igreja da Sé, reconstructed between 1656 and 1676 after the Dutch had destroyed the original. Inexplicably, the facade was given a bland Mannerist makeover in the 1970s, and the interior is now more of a museum than a living church, its former chapels used to display desultory religious art (including a Cristo Redentor statue). At the back of the church is a patio from where you'll have the best views of the surrounding area and Recife.

Museu de Arte Sacra de Pernambuco

Rua Bispo Coutinho 726, Alto da Sé • Tues–Sun 10am–5pm • R$10 • T 81 3184 3154

Halfway along Praca da Sé lies the **Museu de Arte Sacra de Pernambuco**, holding a moderately interesting sample of religious art saved from the region, in a seventeenth-century bishop's palace.

Convento de São Francisco

Rua São Francisco 280 • Daily 9am–noon & 2–5.30pm • R$2 • T 81 3429 0517

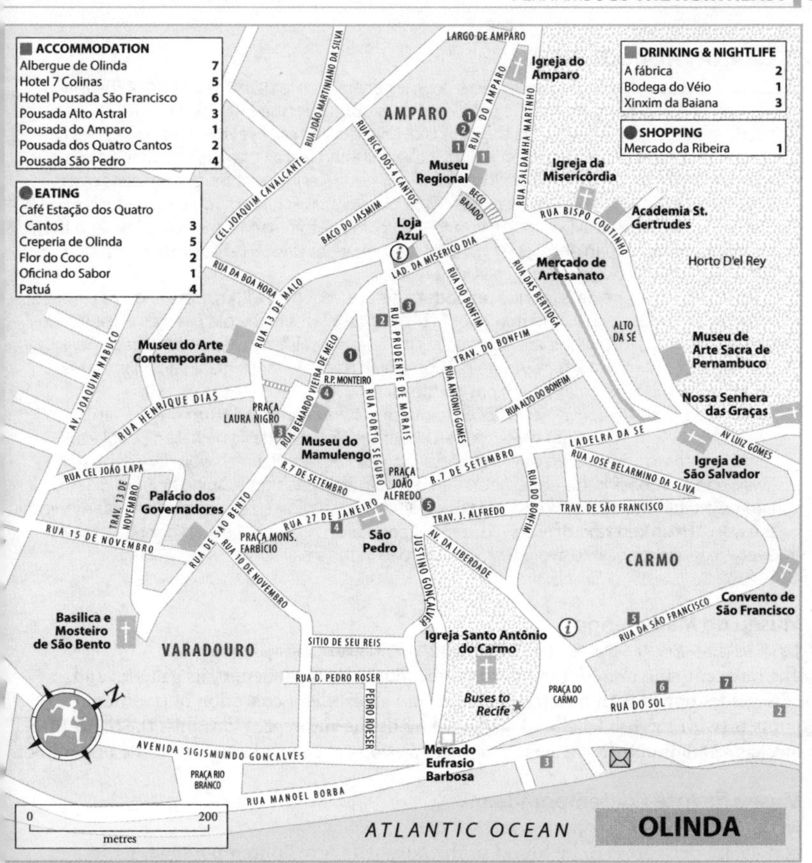

If you have time to see only one church in Olinda, make it the **Convento de São Francisco**. Established in 1577 as the first Franciscan church in Brazil, most of what you see today was rebuilt in the eighteenth century, and though the interior is well maintained there is enough peeling wall and crumbling plaster to give a sense of great antiquity. You enter through the **Capela da Senhora Sant' Ana**, which leads into a cloister adorned with sixteen tiled *azulejo* panels depicting the life of St Francis of Assisi, created 1734–35 (all have good English labels). To the left is the main church, **Nossa Senhora das Neves**, with the highlight the attached **Capela de São Roque** with its gilded altarpiece and painted ceiling. The **sacristy** at the back contains a gorgeous Baroque cabinet carved from jacaranda wood, while behind the convent there's a grand patio with the original seventeenth-century well and views of the ocean.

Museu Regional de Olinda

Rua do Amparo 128 • Tues–Fri 9am–5pm • R$2 • ☎ 81 3184 3159

The eighteenth-century former residence of the Bishop of Olinda now houses the **Museu Regional de Olinda**, a collection of miscellaneous historical objects, from antique furniture, paintings and panels to religious art, including an altar that once stood in the Igreja da Sé.

CARNAVAL IN OLINDA

Olinda's **Carnaval**, with a massive 560 *blocos*, is generally considered to be one of the three greatest in Brazil, along with those of Rio and Salvador. It overshadows the celebrations in neighbouring Recife and attracts thousands of revellers from all over the Northeast. Like the other two great Brazilian Carnavals, Olinda has a style and feel all its own: not quite as large and potentially intimidating as in either Rio or Salvador, the fact that much of it takes place in the winding streets and small squares of the old city makes it seem more manageable. The music, with the local beats of *frevo* and *maracatu* predominating, the costumes, and the enormous *bonecos* (papier-mâché figures of folk heroes, or savage caricatures of local and national personalities), make this celebration unique.

The tourist office has lists of the hundreds of groups, together with **routes** and approximate times, but there is always something going on in most places in the old city. The most famous *blocos*, with mass followings, are Pitombeira and Elefantes; also try catching the daytime performances of *travestis*, transvestite groups, which have the most imaginative costumes – ask the tourist office to mark them out on the list for you.

Inevitably, with so many visitors flocking into the city, **accommodation** during Carnaval can be a problem. You might as well forget about hotels in Olinda if you haven't booked a room months in advance. It's easier to find a room in Recife, but, unless you dance the night away, transport back in the small hours can be difficult; buses start running at around 5am, and before then you have to rely on taxis, which means paying an exorbitant fare and running the risk of **drunken taxi drivers** – dozens of people are killed on the road during Carnaval every year, and it's best to avoid travelling by road in the small hours.

Museu do Mamulengo

Rua São Bento 344 • Mon–Fri 9.30am–5pm • R$2 • T 81 3493 2753, W museudomamulengo.blogspot.com.br

The most enticing museum in Olinda is the **Museu do Mamulengo**, its galleries and passages festooned with flowery wallpaper and an excellent collection of traditional puppets (with English labelling), arranged by theme and type. Don't miss the hand-turned mechanical diorama downstairs, and the depictions of bandit Lampião on the upper floor.

Museu de Arte Contemporânea

Rua 13 de Maio 149 • Tues–Fri 9am–1pm • Free • T 81 3184 3153

Serious modern art is to be found in the **Museu de Arte Contemporânea**, set in a handsome building dating from 1756 and once used as a jail by the Inquisition. Exhibits tend to change, but the permanent collection includes work from Brazilian artists Portinari, Cícero Dias, Telles Junior, Wellington Virgolino, Burle Max and Francisco Brennand.

Basilica e Mosteiro de São Bento

Rua de São Bento s/n • Daily 9am–11.45am & 2–5pm • Free (donation requested during Mass) • T 81 3429 3288

The grand **Basilica e Mosteiro de São Bento** bookends Rua de São Bento, with palm trees swaying in the courtyard, and brown-robed monks still attending daily prayers. It's another institution destroyed by the Dutch, then slowly rebuilt between 1654 and 1759. The Benedictine monastery section is off limits but the church interior is open, its lavish *retábulo* (main altarpiece) seemingly solid gold, the apse further enhanced by ornate ceiling paintings.

Igreja Santo Antônio do Carmo

Praça do Carmo (enter at the back, on the left-hand side) • Tues–Sat 9–11am & 2–5pm • R$2 donation • T 81 3494 7573

Majestically sited on a small hill overlooking Praça do Carmo, **Igreja Santo Antônio do Carmo** dates from 1720 but was given a pristine makeover in 2012, though it remains quite subdued in terms of ornamentation and the exterior quickly suffered from the humidity of the sea. The main exception is the lavish gold *retábulo* inside, a flamboyant Rococo-Baroque hybrid.

ARRIVAL AND INFORMATION

OLINDA

By bus From Recife, take bus #1983 or #1992 from Rua do Sol in central Recife; from Boa Viagem, take bus #910 (R$3.35). Buses follow the seafront road (PE-001 aka Av Sigismundo Gonçalves); get off in Praça do Carmo, just by Olinda's main post office, from where it's a 2min walk up into the old city.

By taxi A taxi from Boa Viagem should be around R$45–50 (on the meter), and around R$30 from the city centre. From Recife bus station reckon on at least R$60, and R$80 from the airport.

Tourist information Information and maps are available from Casa do Turista on Rua de São Bento 742 (daily 8am–7pm; ☎81 3305 1060, ⓦolinda.pe.gov.br).

ACCOMMODATION

In Olinda prices vary enormously throughout the year (March, June & Aug–Nov is cheapest). During Carnaval (Feb/March), it's virtually impossible to get a room unless you've booked months in advance.

Albergue de Olinda Rua do Sol 233 ☎81 3429 1592, ⓦalberguedeolinda.com.br; map p.279. Located on a busy main road by the seafront, this bright and tasteful HI hostel has a bucolic little garden with hammocks and a pool, ideal for mingling with other travellers. Dorms are a bit on the plain side with just the bare necessities, but they're clean enough and the place itself has a friendly vibe. Breakfast included. Wi-Fi Dorms R$60

★ **Hotel 7 Colinas** Ladeira de São Francisco 307 ☎81 3493 7766, ⓦhotel7colinas.com.br; map p.279. This fabulous hotel right in the centre of Olinda is set in beautiful gardens with modern sculpture and a fine swimming pool. There's a range of rooms, suites and luxury apartments, and a good restaurant, too. Breakfast included. Wi-Fi R$352

Hotel Pousada São Francisco Rua do Sol 127 ☎81 3429 2109, ⓦpousadasaofrancisco.com.br; map p.279. Located on the main road but quite close to the seafront, this place has a good-sized pool, a games room and 45 bright, comfortable rooms, with antique wooden or tile floors and Afro-Brazilian art decorating the walls. All have a/c, fridge and cable TV. Breakfast included. Wi-Fi R$220

Pousada Alto Astral Rua 13 de Maio 305 ☎81 3439 3453, ⓦpousadaaltoastral.com; map p.279. This *pousada* is decorated with naïve art and with a handsome wrought-iron staircase, plus there's a pool. The rooms are warm, wildly painted and superb value – ask for any of the ones at the back, or, if there are four of you, go for room no.8, which is spacious and with leafy views over the city. The staff here are incredibly friendly and the breakfast area (lavish spread included in price) is perfect for socializing Wi-Fi R$150

Pousada do Amparo Rua do Amparo 199 ☎81 3429 6889, ⓦpousadadoamparo.com.br; map p.279. Not cheap, but a quality place set in a colonial mansion. Beautifully decorated rooms, blending original wood and antique pieces with contemporary amenities and art, a restaurant, simple but very atmospheric spa and a pool. Wi-Fi R$350

★ **Pousada dos Quatro Cantos** Rua Prudente de Morais 441 ☎81 3429 0220, ⓦwww.pousada4cantos.com.br; map p.279. Beautiful, small nineteenth-century mansion with a leafy courtyard, right in the heart of the old city. A range of rooms and suites available; all with a/c. Wi-Fi R$293

Pousada São Pedro Rua 27 de Janeiro 95 ☎81 3439 9546, ⓦpousadapedro.com; map p.279. A spiral staircase leads up to the more expensive rooms in the main house of this charming *pousada*, while the cheaper rooms are around the pool area at the back. All have a/c. Breakfast included. Wi-Fi R$190

EATING

The best place to go for cheap eating and drinking is the Alto da Sé. The tasty street food here, cooked on charcoal fires, can't be recommended too highly; try the Bahian *acarajé* (around R$10), which you get from women sitting next to sizzling wok-like pots – bean-curd cake, fried in palm oil, cut open and filled with green salad, dried shrimps and *vatapá*, a yellow paste made with shrimps, coconut milk and fresh coriander.

Café Estação dos Quatro Cantos Rua Prudente de Moraes 440 ☎81 3429 7575, ⓦfacebook.com/e4cantos; map p.279. Laidback café set in the backyard of an art gallery, handicrafts store and cultural space, with decent espresso, huge salads ($24–30), simple dishes like pasta bolognese (R$20) and snacks. Tues–Thurs & Sun 2–9pm, Fri & Sat 2–10pm.

Creperia de Olinda Praça João Alfredo 168 ☎81 3429 2935; map p.279. This agreeable crêperie is decorated with knick-knacks, local art and exposed brickwork, and has an open-air patio. The scrumptious crêpes come in both sweet and savoury varieties (from R$9–41) and they even do a curried version with chicken (R$32). Daily 11am–11pm.

Flor do Coco Rua do Amparo 199 ☎81 3429 6889, ⓦpousadadoamparo.com.br; map p.279. *Pousada* restaurant boasting excellent regional cuisine, including both local fish dishes, duck (R$62) and great pastas. Mains between R$54 and R$69. Mon–Fri 6–11.30pm, Sat & Sun noon–5pm & 6–11.30pm.

★ **Oficina do Sabor** Rua do Amparo 335 ☎81 3429 3331, ⓦoficinadosabor.com; map p.279. After two

THE TORNEIO DOS REPENTISTAS

There are plenty of festivals other than Carnaval (see page 280) in Olinda. Definitely worth catching if you happen to be visiting in late January is the **Torneio dos Repentistas**, which is centred on and around the Praça da Preguiça and lasts for three days. A *repentista* is a Northeastern singer-poet who improvises strictly metered verses accompanied only by a guitar. Olinda's *torneio* is one of the most famous events of its kind in the region, bringing in *repentistas* from all over the Northeast who pair off and embark on singing duels while surrounded by audiences; the audiences break into spontaneous applause at particularly good rhymes or well-turned stanzas.

decades of supplying Recife and Olinda's chattering classes with exquisitely prepared Pernambucan cuisine, the reputation of this place precedes it. And with an interior that's hardly ostentatious, the emphasis is squarely on the food; splashing out on dishes such as their pumpkin stuffed with fish and shrimp in a passion fruit and coconut sauce serving two (R$144) is all worth it. Tues–Thurs 11.30am–4pm & 6pm–midnight, Fri & Sat 11.30am–1am, Sun 11.30am–5pm.

Patuá Rua Bernardo Vieira de Melo 79 ⓣ 81 3055 083[illegible] ⓦ restaurantepatua.com.br; map p.279. Olinda's fête seafood specialist always delivers, paired with magnifice[illegible] views of the city. Try their sumptuous *auê-oyá* (seafoo[illegible] with coconut milk; R$56.90), or Peixe Delícia de Olinda, bizarre (but delicious) combination of fish fillets, chee[illegible] and banana (R$42.90). Tues & Wed 11am–3pm, Thurs [illegible] Fri 11am–3pm & 6–10pm, Sat 11am–4pm & 6–11pm Sun 11am–4pm.

DRINKING AND NIGHTLIFE

4

Olinda's relaxed atmosphere draws many *recifenses* at night, when tables and chairs are set on squares and pavements, an[illegible] bars that are tucked away in courtyards amid spectacular tropical foliage make for the perfect escape. There's always plen[illegible] of music around, and, at weekends, a lot of young Brazilians out for a good time.

A fábrica Praça do Fortim do Queijo ⓣ 81 9 8727 3030, ⓦ facebook.com/afabricabar; map p.279. This is Olinda's hippest bar and club, semi-alfresco with a great location close to several hostels on Rua do Sol and a busy schedule that includes live samba (Wed) and pop rock (Sat). Cover R$6. Wed–Sun 5pm–late.

★ **Bodega do Véio** Rua do Amparo 212 ⓣ 81 3429 0185, ⓦ facebook.com/BodegaDoVeio; map p.279. A ridiculously convivial general store-cum neighbourhood bar of the kind you still find in rural Brazil, with brooms propped up against the walls and shelves stacked to the ceiling with everything from soap powder to beans an[illegible] of course, booze. From mid-afternoon onwards, peop[illegible] are crammed up against the counter and spilling onto th[illegible] cobbled streets, and there's usually some kind of live mus[illegible] at weekends. Mon–Sat 9am–11pm, Sun 9am–8pm.

Xinxim da Baiana Av Sigismundo Gonçalves 74[illegible] ⓣ 81 3439 8447; map p.279. Bahían-themed bar an[illegible] restaurant where local *forró de rabeca* stars, Quartet[illegible] Olinda, made their name. Still a good place for mus[illegible] new and old, as well as other myriad cultural happening[illegible] Tues–Thurs & Sun 7pm–2am, Fri & Sat 7pm–4am.

SHOPPING

Mercado da Ribeira Rua Bernardo Vieira de Melo 160; map p.279. Built in the sixteenth century, Olinda's oldest market offers a few shops selling craft goods; large festiva[illegible] puppets are displayed in the hall at the end. Daily 8am–6pm.

DIRECTORY

Money and exchange There are no ATMs in Olinda's historical centre, but there's a Banco24horas ATM at the petrol (gas) station on Av Pres. Kennedy on the right-hand side coming from Recife.

Pharmacies Farmácia Bicentenária, Rua S Miguel 27[illegible] Novo Olinda (ⓣ 81 3429 2148).

Post office Praça João Pessoa s/n (Mon–Fri 9am–5pm ⓣ 81 3439 2203).

North from Recife

Beyond Recife, highway BR-101 runs inland for some 120km north to João Pessoa (see page 289). Though there's little to see en route, there is one place where it's worth heading back to the coast: from the pleasantly run-down colonial town of **Igarassu** to the island of **Itamaracá**.

garassu

he second-oldest city in Brazil, 32km north of Recife, **IGARASSU** was founded by the ortuguese in 1537 on a ridge rising out of a sea of palm trees: the name means "great anoe" in the language of the Tupi Indians, the cry that went up when they first saw he Portuguese galleons. Though it's nothing like Olinda, a few relics of its past remain n the historic centre (Sítio Histórico de Igarassu); the modest **Igreja dos Santos Cosme Damião**, the oldest church in Brazil, is still there on the ridge (the first church was ounded in 1535, but this one dates to the 1590s).

Auseu Pinacoteca de Igarassu

ua Barbosa Lima at Rua Dantas Barreto • Mon–Fri 8–11.30am & 1.30–4.30pm • R$2 • ⓣ 81 3543 0258

ust down the hill from the Igreja dos Santos Cosme e Damião, the **Convento de Santo Antônio** was founded in 1588 and is now home to the **Museu Pinacoteca de Igarassu**, museum of religious art stuffed with paintings and panels that date back to the eventeenth century.

raia da Gavôa

ome 14km east of Igarassu, there are a couple of upmarket places to stay at the leasant **Praia da Gavôa**, popular with Brazilian tourists for watersports and its shallow, alm waters. It's hard to get here without your own transport, however.

ARRIVAL AND DEPARTURE IGARASSU

Hourly buses to Igarassu, with easy connections to Itamaracá, leave from Avenida Martins de Barros on Santo Antônio in Recife, opposite the *Grande Hotel*.

4

tamaracá

ome 16km northeast of Igarassu, **ITAMARACÁ** is connected to the mainland by a auseway. Local legend has it that the island was once the site of the Garden of Eden, and the short drive across the causeway from Itapissuma promises much, passing among housands of palm trees lapped by fields of sugar cane. While the **beaches** around the sland are very good – **Praia do Sossego** is especially wide and lined with palms – the own of **Itamaracá** itself is something of a disappointment, and you are better off making for the southern end of the island, an area known as **Vila Velha** around **Forte Orange.**

Forte Orange

Estrada do Forte • Tues–Sun 9am–5pm • Free • ⓣ 81 3544 1080

Constructed by the Dutch in 1631 and rebuilt by the Portuguese in 1654, **Forte Orange** is one of the best-preserved colonial forts in Brazil. Displays inside shed light on the Dutch presence in the region, as well as the excavations completed on site. The enthusiastic guides are excellent, though few speak English – everything is labelled in English, however.

Ilhota da Coroa do Avião

Boats from Forte Orange • R$10/person return (5min); fix a time for pick-up

Visiting the ravishing **Ilhota da Coroa do Avião** at low tide is a real treat, even though it can get mobbed in high season (when the jet-skis arrive). The island is really just a large sand bar in the middle of the Rio Jaguaribe, which can only be reached by boat from Itamaracá. There are a few stalls and *barracas* on the island but not much else, and no toilets.

Centro de Mamíferos Aquáticos

Estrada do Forte • Daily: Jan–March 9am–5pm, April–Dec 9am–4pm • R$10 • ⓣ 81 3544 1056, ⓦ icmbio.gov.br/cma

To learn more about the local marine life, visit the **Centro de Mamíferos Aquáticos**, dedicated to the preservation of the endangered **manatee**, with displays, videos and giant tanks that harbour the gentle "sea cows" as well as other rescued sea creatures.

ACCOMMODATION **ITAMARACÁ**

Orange Praia Hotel Estrada do Forte 81 3544 1170, hotelorange.com.br. Pricey but convenient place to stay right in the heart of the action near all the main sights with spacious comfy rooms with LCD TVs. R$320

South from Recife

The coast south of Recife has the best **beaches** in the state, beginning with the **Cabo de Santo Agostinho** area but especially **Porto de Galinhas**, a once scrappy fishing port that has been transformed into one of Brazil's most well-known Further south lies the enticing village of **Tamandaré**, which – for now at least – remains a much sleepier place.

Cabo de Agostinho and around

Some 35km south of Recife, **CABO DE AGOSTINHO** is a small town near an especially rich section of coast, beginning with **Praia do Paiva** just south of the Rio Jaboatao. From here the beachside development continues more or less without a break for 13km to **Gaibú**, a sizeable resort town with palm trees, bars and surf – it's a good base for beach-hopping.

Just south of Gaibú lies the cape of **São Agostinho** itself, a pleasant walk uphill through palms and mango trees. Some 3km from central Gaibú a signposted dirt road to the left leads out onto a promontory where the forest suddenly disappears and leaves you with a stunning view of the idyllic, and usually deserted, beach of **Calhetas**, the waters offshore especially popular for scuba diving and underwater fishing. A little further south on the main road is another left turn to **Vila Nazaré**. During the Dutch occupation, there was vicious fighting here, and most of the village remains in ruins. Beyond the seventeenth-century **Igreja de Nazare** and adjacent ruins of the Convento Carmelita, there are the pulverized remains of a fort and burnt-out shells of Dutch buildings. There's also a plaque commemorating the Spanish conquistador Yanez Piñon, blown south by storms on his way to the Caribbean in 1500. He is thought to have put in here for shelter a couple of months before Cabral "discovered" Brazil. The cape is crisscrossed with several walking trails; keep going beyond the Igreja de Nazare and you'll come to tiny **Praia do Paraíso** on the south side of the cape, overlooking Praia Suape and the port complex beyond.

ARRIVAL AND DEPARTURE **CABO DE AGOSTINHO**

By bus Bus #195 runs between Recife's Terminal de Passageiros Santa Rita and Cabo de Agostinho every 30min (R$3.50); from here there are frequent local buses to Gaibú and the beaches.

By car From Recife, avoid the BR-101 highway and take PE-009 along the coast instead.

ACCOMMODATION AND EATING

★ **Namoa** Av Beira Mar 87, Praia de Gaibú 81 3512 0035, namoa.com. Comfortable boutique option close to the beach (and 1km from Calhetas), with fifteen stylish, contemporary rooms and cosy restaurant (daily 11am–10pm) overlooking the waves. R$330

Pousada Touit Rua Joaquim Leão Neto 179, Praia de Gaibú 81 3522 6020. Laidback inn 80m from the beach, with lush gardens, bright and airy a/c rooms and a bar. R$220

Porto de Galinhas

The days of **PORTO DE GALINHAS**, 65km south of Recife, being a sleepy fishing port are long gone, and it's now a popular beach resort, with pedestrianized streets, shops selling beachwear and souvenirs, gorgeous palm-fringed strips of sand and several luxurious hotels and *pousadas*. The town itself lies in the centre of the main strip around a central square, Pracinha, with Praia do Cupe and Praia Muro Alto to the north, and Maracaípe (4km) and Serrambi (10km) beaches to the south. From the main Porto beach **jangadas** (R$25/person, plus R$15 for snorkel) will take you out o the small, natural coral pools just off the coast, and there is some excellent **surfing** t Maracaípe. Staying in Maracaipé is a good choice if you want to get away from the rowds, although keep in mind that the sea is a bit rougher here.

The name, which means "Chicken Port", derives from a history of slave running; fter the British forcibly halted the slave trade with Africa in the 1850s, tax-dodging, ife-dealing smugglers would arrive here proclaiming they had a shipment of 'Angolan chickens".

RRIVAL, INFORMATION AND TOURS — PORTO DE GALINHAS

By bus Bus #195 (hourly 5.30am–8.30pm; R$10.90) links ecife with the inland village of Nossa Senhora do Ó (often onfused with Galinhas) via the airport, departing Terminal le Passageiros Santa Rita in Recife.

Tourist information Rua Beijupirá (daily 9am–8pm; 81 3552 1728). The small office is opposite the Banco Santander ATM.

Buggy tours Lines of dune buggies (R$50–70 for 2–3hr) wait at the sea end of Rua da Esperança, which connects the beach with the Pracinha. They'll act as taxis, running up and down the beaches for R$15–20/trip.

ACCOMMODATION AND EATING

BarCaxiera Rua da Esperança 458 81 3552 1913, barcaxeira.com.br. A pleasantly decorated restaurant with colourful chairs, tiled walls and friendly service that serves decent seafood (R$42.90–52.90) and *macaxeiras gratinadas* (various types of gratins with everything from shitake mushroom to cod topped with plenty of melted cheese; R$32.90–43.90). Try the fried prawns with broccoli rice and a divine pineapple dressing (R$52.90). Live music every evening, cover charge R$4. Daily noon–11pm.

Beijupirá Rua Beijupirá s/n 81 3552 2354, beijupiraporto.com.br. Visit this seafood restaurant (part of a small chain) for unbelievably tasty shrimp, lobster and local *sobremesas* (desserts). Mains around R$60. Mon–Sat noon–midnight, Sun noon–5pm.

Beach Hostel Praça Dez s/n 81 3552 1227. A short stroll from the beach, in a quiet part of town, this Argentine-owned hostel with multilingual staff offers female/male dorms and doubles with a/c, as well as a small pool and a very chilled atmosphere. Buffet breakfast (although a bit mediocre) is included in the room rate. Dorms **R$40**, doubles **R$140**

Hostel Brisas do Mar Rua Beira Mar 100, Praia de Maracaípe 81 3552 3417, maracabana.com.br. A laidback and small hostel, beautifully located right on the beach. Offers a bar and restaurant serving simple dishes, a six-bed dorm and private rooms with fan. The dorm is a bit crammed when full, but the location is hard to beat. Breakfast not included (R$15). Dorms **R$80**, doubles **R$250**

Pousada Maracabana Rua Beira Mar 254, Praia de Maracaípe 81 3552 3417, maracabana.com.br. Excellent option right on Maracaípe beach, with a/c rooms with balcony and partial sea views and restaurant serving reasonably priced local and vegan dishes. **R$240**

Pousada Porto Verde Loteamento Recanto Praça 1 Lote J 81 3552 1410, pousadaportoverde.com.br. With an enticing garden and colourful rooms, this is the most beautiful B&B in town. Most rooms have a terrace with a hammock, as well as TV, *frigobar* and a/c. There's an inviting pool, a library and a café on site. Breakfast included. **R$230**

Pousada São Jorge Rua da Carauna 234, Praça 04 81 3552 1681, pousadasaojorge.net/porto-de-galinhas.html. Clean and comfy mid-range option near the main beach, with its own small pool and bright rooms with TV and wooden floors. **R$229**

Tapioca da Praia Rua da Esperança 340 81 8773 6197. The place to grab a cheap local snack after a hard day on the beach; the "tapioca" (cassava) rolls stuffed come in all sorts of combos, though it's hard to beat the *frango com queijo* (chicken and cheese). Daily 2–10.30pm.

Village Porto de Galinhas PE-09 Km 5.5 81 3552 4200, villageportodegalinhas.com.br. Standard luxury resort on the beach, with spacious, modern rooms, four swimming pools, beach bar and dance club. **R$672**

4

Tamandaré

Some 57km south of Porto de Galinhas (by road), fishing still dominates the village of **TAMANDARÉ** – for now, at least – with *jangadas* drawn up on the beaches and men repairing nets, though even here weekend houses for city slickers are becoming common. Around 8km to the north lies **Praia dos Carneiros**, a spectacular and deservedly popular beach, with a selection of attractive *pousadas* and restaurants and the picture-perfect **Capela de São Benedito** framed by coconut palms.

ARRIVAL AND DEPARTURE

TAMANDARÉ

By bus Buses depart from Av Dantas Barreto in Recife (Mon–Sat 5.20am & 2.20pm, Sun 4pm; 3hr). From Porto de Galinhas you'll have to go to Ipojuca first, then to Rio Famoso and from there look for another bus to Tamandaré.

By van For points south you'll need to take a regular van from Tamandaré to Barreiros (40min; R$3.35), and change there.

By moto-taxi The easiest way to zip between Tamandaré and Praia dos Carneiros is by *moto-taxi* (R$7–R$10), which can be flagged down anywhere in the centre.

ACCOMMODATION AND EATING

Beijupirá Praia Dos Carneiros ⓣ81 9 8653 9409, ⓦbeijupiracarneiros.com.br. One of the loveliest and most excluisve restaurants in Praia Dos Carneiros, serving fresh seafood including whisky flambéed lobster served in a pineapple (R$122) and prawn curry with coconut milk, mango and banana (R$71). Make sure to grab a table by the beach bar and enjoy the superb views. Bring your swimsuit. Daily 9am–4pm.

Bora Bora Praia Dos Carneiros ⓣ81 3676 1482, ⓦbbcarneiros.com.br. This always crowded beach bar and restaurant is a local institution, with shady *palapas* in between the palms, fresh if pricey seafood (R$40–95) and free wi-fi. Parking $R30/day. Can sometimes be mobbed by tour groups in high season. Daily 9am–5pm.

Hostel 81 Rua São José 61 ⓣ81 3676 2472, ⓦhostel81.com.br. Conviniently located just across the street from the beach, this hostel offers basic dorms, a small pool and an oddly located shared kitchen separate from the main building. The facilities could do with a bit more love from the owners, but the location for the price is hard to beat. Dorms R$50, doubles R$160

Pousada Beira Mar Av Almirante Tamandaré 140 ⓣ81 3676 1567, ⓦpousadabeiramartamandare.com. Decent mid-range option right on the beach, with eight cosy a/c rooms, flat-screen TVs and sea views. R$240

★ **Tapera do Sabor** Rua Sergipe s/n ⓣ81 3676 1509, ⓦtaperadosabor.com.br. Airy, yet intimate restaurant with a lush and enticing garden that serves excellent

4

INTO THE SERTÃO

In contrast to the gentle scenery of the coastal routes out of Recife, heading **inland** brings you abruptly into a completely different landscape, the spectacular and forbidding **sertao**. The *sertanejo* people, too, has a distinct look; they tend to be short, have high cheekbones and they speak Portugues with a distinctive accent.

If you rent a car you can make a fascinating **loop through interior Pernambuco and Paraíba** between Recife and João Pessoa – and although you can also take buses, it will take you much longer. Before heading off make sure you are equipped with an updated road map or a GPS (some parts of the interior have poor network coverage – relying on online navigation apps is not your best option). For any questions about the destinations you can ask at the usually very helpful tourism offices in Recife and Fortaleza (although English is not always spoken), but don't expect them to have too much information as the interior is far off the beaten track. However, there should be no problems finding accommodation en route. These are the highlights.

PERNAMBUCO

- **Bezerros** (105km west of Recife). Home of renowned *cordel* artist and printer, **Jota Borges**, who has a small museum and showroom, Memorial J. Borges & Museu da Xilogravura on BR-232 Km 106 (Mon–Fri 8am–5.30pm & Sat 8am–noon; free; ⓣ81 9214 0410).
- **Caruaru** (30km west of Bezerros). Home of the largest market in the Northeast (Feira de Caruaru; daily 6am–5pm), the largest *forró* festival (Festa de São João, held in June), and the Museu do Barro e do Forró (Tues–Sat 8am–5pm, Sun 9am–1pm; R$2), a homage to local ceramic arts and Luiz Gonzaga, the godfather of *forró*.
  - **Alto do Moura** (7km from Caruaru). Every other house on the only street, Rua Mestre Vitalino, is a potter's workshop, with kilns resembling large beehives in the yards behind. The home of the master of the craft, Mestre Vitalino (1909–63), is now the Museu Casa do Mestre Vitalino (Mon–Sat 9am–5pm, Sun 9am–noon; free), housing tools, personal effects and some of his works (his son Severino looks after the place). Bode Assado do Luciano at Rua Mestre Vitalino 511 (Mon–Fri 11am–4pm, Sat & Sun 11am–6pm) is the best place to try the regional specialities, roasted goat and *buchada*, goat casserole.
- **Nova Jerusalém** (at Brejo da Madre de Deus, 90km northwest of Caruaru). Truly bizarre: a granite replica of the old city of Jerusalem (a third of the size), built in the 1960s by a local entrepreneur to

eafood by friendly staff. Most dishes serve two (R$84–10), but there's a handful of options for one person (around $55). There's an extensive list of starters – don't miss the prawns with onion (R$58) and ask for the homemade spicy sauce. Tues–Thurs noon–4pm & 6–9pm, Fri & Sat noon–10pm, Sun noon–9pm.

ernando de Noronha

he staggeringly beautiful and environmentally protected archipelago of **FERNANDO DE NORONHA** lies in the equatorial Atlantic some 545km from Pernambuco and 350km rom Natal. Boasting sixteen stunning **beaches**, it's also hard to beat for **snorkelling** nd **scuba diving** – its clear water stretches down to a depth of 40m in places, with a vhite sandy sea bottom, plenty of coral, crustaceans, turtles, dolphins and a wide range of fish species and shoal types. There's just one a small catch – visiting Noronha is xtremely expensive.

European explorers first came here in 1503, and after a struggle between various powers, vith the Dutch running the show from 1700 to 1736, the islands ended up under the ontrol of the Portuguese in 1737 (the archipelago got its name from the Portuguese nerchant Fernão de Loronha). Lisbon considered the islands strategically important nough to build the **Forte dos Remédios**, of which only some remains can now be seen.

In recent years, the archipelago has become well known as an ecotourist destination. Most of it is protected within the **Parque Nacional Marinho de Fernando de Noronha** (@parnanoronha.com.br), created in 1988 in order to maintain the ecological wonders

4

host an annual Passion of Christ performance. Thousands come to watch five hundred costumed actors re-create the Passion on nine stages, each representing a Station of the Cross. The play is performed daily from the Tuesday before Easter to Easter Sunday.

- **Parque Nacional do Catimbau** (170km west of Nova Jerusalém). Exotic sandstone formations including the Sítio de Alcobaça, hundreds of 2000-year-old cave paintings, and the wild landscapes of the *caatinga*. Arco Verde is the nearest town.
- **Serra Talhada** (163km northwest of Catimbau): Visit the town where Lampião, the king of *cangaço* (bandits), was born in 1897, taking in the Museu do Cangaço in the old train station (Mon–Fri 8.30am–noon & 2–5.30pm, Sat 8am–noon; free).

CEARÁ

- **Juazeiro da Norte** (200km northwest of Serra Talhada). The main centre of the deep *sertão*, famed for being the home of a young priest, Padre Cícero Romão Batista, who is said to have performed miracles in the 1890s and came to be seen as a living saint: thousands come on a massive pilgrimage on July 20 each year to his tomb in Nossa Senhora do Perpétuo Socorro, his statue on the hill that looks down on the town (topped with a chapel and a museum of ex votos), and his house, signposted from the church where he is buried.

PARAÍBA

- **Sousa** (190km northeast of Juazeiro). Home to one of the Northeast's more unusual sights, the Vale dos Dinossauros. "Dinosaur Valley" was formed by the sedimentary basin of the Rio Peixe where various prehistoric reptiles left their footprints, preserved in stone, at 32 sites in the area around the town.
- **Lajedo da Pai Mateus** (300km southeast of Sousa). Area with some of the most enigmatic rock formations anywhere, including the "*feijao da caatinga*", giant granite boulders, but also the pyramid-like slabs of Sacas de Lá.
- **Campina Grande** (70m east of Pai Mateus). Best known for its market, held every Wednesday and Saturday, the Museu de Arte Assis Chateaubriand (Tues–Fri 9am–6pm, Sat & Sun 2–6pm; free), crammed with Brazilian modern art, and its festivals (the Fest São João in June and its out-of-season Carnaval, the Micarande, held in late April).
- **Pedra do Ingá** (Ingá, 40km east of Campina and 110km west of João Pessoa). Huge rock (15m by 3m) smothered in beautiful petroglyphs, a mind-bending 6000 years old.

NORONHA TAXES AND FEES

All visitors to Fernando de Noronha are expected to pay the **Taxa de Preservação Ambiental** (R$70.66/day for first four days, then increasing by varying amounts for each extra day), which goes toward protecting the environment. You pay by credit card or with cash on arrival at the airport. At the time of writing (and fees do go up every year), a four-day stay cost R$282.66; seven days R$449.43. This is in addition to accommodation and the **Parque Nacional Marinho de Fernando de Noronha admission fee**, hard to avoid if you want to visit the best beaches. This is R$178 for up to ten days, paid at the park visitor centre in Vila Boldró (daily 8am–10pm).

that have been preserved by the islands' isolation from the rest of Brazil. The vegetatio is fairly typical Northeastern *agreste*, but the wildlife is magnificent: birdwatchers will be amazed by the variety of **exotic birds**, including several types of pelican, and you'll be moved by the remarkable sight of thousands of **dolphins** entering the bay every day between 5am and 6am, viewed from the harbour.

The largest and only inhabited island (there are 21 altogether), **Ilha de Fernando de Noronha** is just 10km long and much of it also falls within the park boundaries. The main settlement is **Vila dos Remédios**, surrounded by a few smaller villages, linked by one main road. The most famous beaches – all pristine tropical paradises with turquoise waters – lie inside the park (daily 8am–6.30pm): **Baía dos Porcos**, **Praia do Leão** and **Praia do Sancho.**

4

ARRIVAL AND GETTING AROUND — FERNANDO DE NORONH

By plane To reach the islands, you must fly from either Recife (1hr 15min) with Azul or Gol, or Natal (1hr 10min) with Azul. As with other domestic routes, prices vary considerably according to demand and time of year, though expect to pay a lot more than an equivalent flight on the mainland (one-way fares rarely dip below R$500). Aeroporto Governador Carlos Wilson (T 81 3619 1633) lies in the centre of the main island – taxis charge around R$30 into town.

Getting around On the main island, buggies (R$28C day), 4WD jeeps (R$1000/day) and motorbikes (R$15C day) can be rented from several operators, includin Locbuggy in Vila do Trinta (T 81 3619 1490, W locbugg com.br) and Morro do Farol Locadora (T 81 3619 0127 Many hotels and *pousadas* rent out their own buggie which can work out to be less expensive.

INFORMATION

Tourist information You'll find the information kiosks at the airport and at the port (daily 8am–6pm; W www.noronha.pe.gov.br), while the Parque Nacional Marinho Centro de Visitantes (daily 8am–10.30pm; T 81 3619 1171) lies 10km to the south near the airport.

Money Bradesco has 24hr ATMs at the airport that shoul accept all cards; in Vila dos Remédios there is a branch c Banco Santander (Mon–Fri 8am–1pm) and several ATMs.

ACCOMMODATION

Pousada Golfinho Rua São Miguel 144, Vila dos Remédios T 81 3619 1837. This cosy B&B passes for budget accommodation on Noronha, 400m from Praia do Meio. Small but comfy rooms come with satellite TV. **R$180**

Pousada Maravilha Vila do Vai Quem Sabe (BR-363), Baía do Sueste T 81 3619 0028, W pousadamaravilha.com.br. Luxurious option with gorgeous views over the ocean, a posh spa, tempting infinity pool and wood framed bungalows and apartments. **R$1480**

Pousada do Vale Rua Pescador Sérgio Lino 18 T 8 3619 1293, W pousadadovale.com. Expensive guesthous made almost entirely out of wood, set in the lush hills of th island and just 250m from the beach. Rooms have woode floors, spacious beds and a/c. **R$1400**

EATING AND NIGHTLIFE

Bar de Cachorro Vila dos Remédios (Praia do Cachorro). When it comes to nightlife, your choices essentially come down to sitting on the beach with a beer or enjoying the ramshackle ambience at open-air "Dog Bar", where locals often join the tourists for bouts of frenzied *forró* and samba. Daily noon–midnight.

Mergulhão Praia do Porto T 81 3619 0215 W mergulhaonoronha.com.br. Innovative fusion cuisin blending Brazilian and Mediterranean flavours (lot of seafood, pastas) with rustic chic interior, handsom views over the port and delicious cocktails. Mon–Sa noon–11pm.

FERNANDO DE NORONHA ACTIVITIES

Other than just lounging on the (usually) half-empty beaches, there are plenty of activities on Noronha. **Hiking trails** through the park area allow good **birdwatching** and usually end up at remote beaches, but require a guide (from R$80–100/person, minimum of two people) – it's rare to find one who speaks English, though. Your *pousada* will be able to recommend someone. Various companies also offer **boat trips** around the archipelago, departing from the port at the northeastern tip of the main island (from R$130–180/person including transport to the harbour; T 81 3619 1307). Several companies specialize in PADI courses (from R$2200) and **scuba-diving** trips (around R$400 for two-tank dives, including equipment).

TOUR OPERATORS

Águas Claras Alameda do Boldró T 81 3619 1225, W aguasclaras-fn.com.br.

Atlantis Divers T 81 3619 1371, W atlantisdivers.com.br.

Noronha Divers Terminal Turístico do Cachorro T 81 36191 1128, W facebook.com/noronhadivers.

Paraíba

Like most of the Northeast, the state of **Paraíba** was developed by the Portuguese as a major sugar producer, though also like its neighbours, the big draw today is its sun-drenched coastline, the most easterly in all the Americas. **João Pessoa**, capital of the state, is the most attractive of the smaller Northeastern cities, with some of the finest urban beaches in the area, a beautiful setting on the mouth of the Rio Sanhauá and colonial remnants, including one of Brazil's finest churches. Out of the city, Paraíba is blessed with many wonderful **beaches** north and south along its 140km coastline. Unlike some other parts of the Northeast, however, many of its beaches are, for the time being, largely undeveloped and many require somewhat difficult journeys by bus and then on foot or by taxi to reach them. The inland *sertão* also contains some intriguing destinations, notably the mesmerizing **Pedra do Ingá** (see page 287).

4

João Pessoa

Founded in 1585, **JOÃO PESSOA** is one of the oldest cities in Brazil, with a spruced-up *centro histórico* complementing a relatively low-key but popular 20km strip of resort development along the city's two main beaches, **Cabo Branco** and **Tambaú**. Despite a growing number of hotels, the bone-white sands remain stunningly beautiful and, out of season, tourists are still few and far between.

The centre of João Pessoa is dotted with **colonial churches**, **monasteries** and **convents**, just west of a small lake known simply as the **Lagoa**. At the city's core is **Praça João Pessoa**, which contains the state governor's palace and the local parliament; most of the central hotels are clustered around here. The oldest part of the city is just to the north of Praça João Pessoa, where Rua Duque de Caxias ends in the Baroque splendour of the **Igreja de São Francisco**. The steep Ladeira de São Francisco, leading down from here to the lower city and the bus and train stations, offers a marvellous tree-framed view of the rest of the city spread out on the banks of the **Rio Sanhauá**.

To the east of Lagoa, Avenida Getúlio Vargas leads out of town towards the skyscrapers and beachside *bairros* of Cabo Branco and Tambaú, separated by the futuristic, luxury *Tambaú Hotel* (see page 292). This area is also where you'll find the highest concentration of bars and clubs. The southern boundary of the city is the lighthouse on **Ponta de Seixas**, the cape at the far end of Cabo Branco, the most easterly point of Brazil.

Centro Cultural de São Francisco

Rua Duque de Caxias (Praça de São Francisco) • Mon 2–5pm, Tues–Sun 9am–noon & 2–5pm • R$4 • T 83 3218 4505

João Pessoa's most spectacular church is the **Igreja de São Francisco**, which sits in splendid isolation atop the hill that bears its name, and now forms part of the **Centro**

Cultural de São Francisco. The exterior alone is impressive enough. A huge courtyard is flanked by high walls beautifully decorated with *azulejo* tiling, with pastoral scenes in a series of alcoves. These walls funnel you towards a large early eighteenth-century church that would do credit to Lisbon or Coimbra: its most remarkable feature is the tower topped with an oriental dome, a form that the Portuguese encountered in Goa and appropriated for their own purposes. Beyond the church are the chapels and cloister of the **Convento de Santo Antônio**, notably the gold-smothered altars of **Capela da Ordem Terceira de São Francisco**, while upstairs there's the excellent **Museu Sacro e de Arte Popular** (museum of popular and sacred art).

Catedral Basílica de Nossa Senhora das Neves

Praça Dom Ulrico • Mon–Fri 1.30–5.30pm; Sat Mass 6pm, Sun Mass 6am, 9am & 6pm • Free • ⓣ 83 3221 2503

The mother church of João Pessoa, the **Catedral Basílica de Nossa Senhora das Neves** is a brilliant white wedding cake of a structure, with a well-proportioned interior that, for once, forgoes the Rococo excesses of many colonial churches (this incarnation of the church was inaugurated in 1894). Its large, rather plain facade fronts a small square with majestic views north to the wooded river valley and, to the west, green suburbs.

Mosteiro de São Bento

Av General Osório 36 • Tues–Sat 2–5pm • Free • ⓣ 83 3214 2923

The seventeenth-century **Mosteiro de São Bento** has a simple, beautifully restored Baroque interior with a lovely curved wooden ceiling. Today the monastery acts as display space for temporary art exhibitions and venue for classical concerts.

Hotel Globo

Pátio de São Frei Pedro Gonçalves 7 • Mon–Fri 9am–5pm, Sat 9am–4pm • Free • ⓣ 83 3221 4635

The most visited site in the *centro histórico* is the compact **Hotel Globo**, an Art Deco gem built in 1928 by hotelier Henriques Siqueira. Its heyday – when it hosted some of the biggest celebrities in the country – only lasted until the late 1930s, and has served as a cultural centre and small museum of decorative arts. The hotel building has been closed since 2013 when it was severely damaged during a storm and was, at the time of writing, still closed for refurbishment.

Igreja de Nossa Senhora do Carmo

Rua Visconde de Pelotas (Praça Dom Adauto) • Mon–Fri 9.30–11am • Free • ⓣ 83 3221 9400

The eighteenth-century **Igreja de Nossa Senhora do Carmo** is well worth a look, both for its ornate Baroque exterior and the gold-leaf-covered altar inside. The old Carmelite convent next door was converted into the Palácio Episcopal in 1906.

City beaches

The beach areas of Tambaú (7km east of the centre) and Cabo Branco just to its south are linked to the centre by frequent buses from the Anel Viário and the local bus station. The **Cabo Branco** seafront is especially stylish, with a mosaic pavement and thousands of well-tended palm trees to complement the sweep of the bay. **Tambaú** is a lot livelier, dominated by its eponymous hotel, which forms one end of a small square, Praça Vicente Trevas. To the north of Tambaú lies **Praia de Manaíra**, a far less enticing, narrow wedge of beach bordered by Avenida João Maurício and a promenade.

Mercado de Artesanato Paraibano

Av Senador Rui Carneiro 241, at Av Nossa Senhora dos Navegantes • Mon–Sat 9am–7pm, Sun 9am–5pm • ⓣ 83 3247 3135

Lying midway between the two beach districts, the **Mercado de Artesanato Paraibano** showcases Paraíba's distinctive *artesanato*: painted plates and bowls, and striking figurines made out of sacking and wood.

BOLERO DE RAVEL

One of the most popular rites of passage for Brazilian tourists to the Northeast is spending a Saturday evening nursing cocktails along the Rio Jacaré in **Cabedelo** (10km north of João Pessoa), being serenaded by a rendition of Ravel's **Boléro** (the music famously used by British Olympic gold medal skaters Torvill and Dean) by saxophonist **Jurandy**, who plays in a canoe on the river – all very Kenny G. circa 1980s. Concerts begin at 6pm, with violinist Isabelle Soares also getting in on the action later on. To be fair, it can be lots of fun, with plenty of music and dancing before and after the main performance. Local tour operators can arrange trips for around R$40 per person; if you have a group, a taxi might be cheaper (around R$40 each way).

Estação Cabo Branco

Av João Cirillo da Silva • Tues–Fri 9am–6pm, Sat & Sun 10am–7pm • Free • T 83 3214 8303, W joaopessoa.pb.gov.br/estacaocb • Bus #507

Some 6km south of Tambaú, the **Estação Cabo Branco** is a typically futuristic glass and concrete cultural centre designed by Oscar Niemeyer and opened in 2008. The changing exhibitions here, mostly on local contemporary art and film, are a bit hit-and-miss, and it's the three main buildings that draws most attention (the newest section, the **Estação das Artes**, opened in 2012 and was designed by Amaro Muniz). The **Museu de Ciência** and Planetarium in the main building, the Torre Mirante, has permanent exhibits on robotics, astronomy and the general concepts of physics and chemistry – all very educational but with little labelled in English.

Ponta de Seixas

Overlooking the ocean next to the Estação Cabo Branco, a plaque and the **Farol do Cabo Branco** (lighthouse) at **Ponta de Seixas** mark Brazil's easternmost point. From here, it's only 2200km to Senegal in Africa, less than half the distance to Rio Grande do Sul in the south of Brazil or the state of Roraima in the north. At the odd-looking lighthouse you'll find a park and a couple of tacky souvenir shops, but the main draw here is the **view**, which is glorious – Cabo Branco beach stretches out before you in an enormous arc, 6km long.

ARRIVAL AND INFORMATION — JOÃO PESSOA

By plane The Aeroporto Internacional Presidente Castro Pinto (T 83 3041 4200) lies just 12km west of the city centre and is connected to the rodoviária by regular buses; taxis into the *centro histórico* cost around R$40 (R$60 to the beaches).

By bus The rodoviária (T 83 3221 9611) is conveniently near the city centre. Any bus (R$2.30) from the Terminal de Integração (local bus station), opposite the rodoviária's entrance, takes you to the city's one unmistakeable, central landmark: the Lagoa. Taxis from the rodoviária to the beaches should be around R$30, and just R$12 to the *centro histórico*.

Destinations Campina Grande (hourly; 1hr 45min); Fortaleza (2 daily; 9hr); Juazeiro do Norte (7 daily; 10–11hr); Natal (8 daily; 3hr); Recife (13 daily; 2hr); Salvador (1 daily; 22hr).

Tourist information Official information is available from the state tourist board, PB-Tur (W destinoparaiba.pb.gov.br), at the rodoviária (daily 8am–6pm; T 83 3222 3537), the airport (daily 9am–4pm) and in the Centro de Turismo in Tambaú, opposite the *Tropical Tambaú Center Hotel* at Av Almirante Tamandaré 100 (daily 8am–7pm; T 83 3247 0505). See also W joaopessoa.pb.gov.br.

GETTING AROUND

By bus All bus routes converge on the circular Anel Viário skirting the lake, some en route to the beach districts (#510, #511 and #513), others heading further afield, including to the northern beaches, the neighbouring town of Cabedelo and the village of Penha (#507A) to the south of the city.

ACCOMMODATION

Lagoa Park Hotel Parque Sólon de Lucena 19 T 83 3015 1414, W lagoaparkhotel.com.br. There's not a lot of choice in the city centre, but this is the best option, with adequate rooms, some with great views over the Lagoa, friendly staff, decent breakfast and great location. R$260

Manaíra Hostel Av Major Ciraulo 380 T 83 3247 1962, W himanairahostel.com.br. The only HI-affiliate in town, this is a well-kept house with small pool and garden just 300m from the beach at Praia de Manaíra; offering dorms (with a/c or fan), doubles and family rooms. The bathrooms are shared and sex-segregated. Prices for members are R$10–15 less. Dorms R$60, doubles R$135

★ **Slow Hostel** Av Cajazeiras 108 83 3021 7218, slowhostel.net. Excellent hostel 50m from Praia de Manaíra with memorable home-cooked breakfast and clean dorms with a/c. Dorms R$45

Tambaú Hotel Av Almirante Tamandaré 229 83 2107 1900, tambauhotel.com.br. Built in the 1970s and one of the city's landmark Modernist buildings (it looks a bit like a flying saucer but, amazingly, was designed not by Niemeyer but by Sérgio Bernardes), this luxury beachside hotel offers a sauna, pool, games room, fitness suite and classy restaurant – though it's a little faded and you're paying for the location (and the novelty). R$330

★ **Verdegreen Hotel** Av João Maurício 255 83 3044 0000, verdegreen.com.br. Eco-friendly (though pricey) solar-powered option, with decor made from natural materials, huge breakfast buffet, spacious a/c rooms, free bikes and complimentary coconut water on arrival. R$460

EATING

★ **Mangai** Av Edson Ramalho 696 83 3226 1615, mangai.com.br. A smart place (part of a mini-chain) boasting a wide range of Northeastern and *sertão* dishes, with much of the produce coming fresh from the restaurant's own ranch; this is regional cooking at its best (buffet-style; R$59.90/kg). Daily 11am–10pm.

★ **NAU Frutos do Mar** Rua Lupércio Branco 130, Manaíra 83 3021 8003, site.naufrutosdomar.com.br. Hordes of Brazilian tourists pile into this stylish seafood joint at the weekends, eager to sample its lauded "*camarão nau*" and *moquecas*, but the hype is almost justified – the shrimp and fish here are some of the freshest and tastiest in the Northeast. Reckon on at least R$70/head. Mon–Wed noon–3.30pm & 6–10pm, Thurs–Sat noon–3.30pm & 6–11pm, Sun 11.30am–3.30pm & 6–10pm.

Olho de Lula Av Cabo Branco 2300 83 3247 3249. Popular, if slightly exclusive, seafood restaurant overlooking the beach (opposite the beach bar of the same name) with a menu featuring freshly grilled *garoupa* (R$68) and *moquecas* (R$80) for sharing. Indoor and outdoor seating. Daily 10am–1am.

Recanto do Picuí Rua Mírian Barreto Rabelo 120 83 3246 7789. Serves some of the best *sertão* food in the city; the *carne de sol* here is excellent, best accompanied by green beans and *batata doce assado* (roast sweet potatoes). Mon–Sat 11am–10pm, Sun 11am–4pm.

Tábua de Carne Av Rui Carneiro 648, Tambaú 83 3247 5970. Located on one of the roads running away from the beach, this rustic-themed place is a good choice for meat, *carne de sol* and tasty *sertão* food (mains R$40–65). Daily 11.30am–11.30pm.

4

DRINKING AND NIGHTLIFE

João Pessoa has a surprisingly rich but fluctuating **music scene** for a city of its size, concentrated in some of the character-laden bars and venues in the *centro histórico* where Rua Braz Florentino remains the unofficial *beco cultural* ("culture alley") despite police crackdowns. At the Tambaú seafront the beach kiosks are the most fun, but the square in front of the *Tambaú Hotel* is also a relaxed place for a drink and some live music.

Cachaçaria Philipéia Rua Duque de Caixas 83 8718 8080. Cool cachaça bar that gets especially busy on Saturdays after the "Sabadinho Bom" *chorinho* party (*choro* is the Brazilian instrumental music genre) in nearby Praça Rio Branco ends around 4pm. Try the house speciality, Cachimbinho, cachaça with honey and lemon for just R$3/shot. Mon–Thurs 2–6pm, Fri & Sat noon–6pm & 10pm–3.30am.

Centro Cultural Espaço Mundo Praça Antenor Navarro 53 83 3021 5233, facebook.com/espacomundo. Housed in an historic mansion in the old centre, this cultural space and bar hosts live music and art exhibitions, and sells CDs (there's also a lunch buffet Mon–Fri 11am–3pm for just R$20/kg). Mon–Wed 11am–2pm, Thurs 11am–2pm & 8pm–1am, Fri 11am–2pm & 8pm–3am, Sat 8pm–3am.

Giramundo Av Almirante Tamandaré 634, Tambaú 83 3023 1660. Seafood kiosk on the beach best viewed as a fun bar, with an excellent range of microbrews, German-style sausages and buzzing atmosphere – no live music, though. Mon–Thurs 6pm–1am, Fri & Sat 6pm–2am.

Vila Do Porto Praça de São Frei Pedro Gonçalves 8 83 3222 6900. This restaurant bar hosts some of the best dance parties in the city. Cover is usually R$15. Mon 7pm–12.30am, Fri 4pm–5am, Sat 10pm–5am.

Jacumã and around

Some 30km to the south of João Pessoa lies the small seaside town of **Jacumã**, jumping-off point for the gorgeous **Praia Coqueirinho** (2km further south), lined with *barracas* and popular at the weekends. Another 4km south is **Praia de Tambaba,** the first officially recognized nudist beach (men can only enter accompanied by a woman) in the Northeast (though there is a non-nudist section).

ARRIVAL AND DEPARTURE **JACUMÃ**

Getting to Jacumã by bus from João Pessoa is easy (every 40min), but from here you'll be reliant on taxis or *moto-taxis* for the beaches (R$15–20).

Rio Grande do Norte

Until the late 1980s, the small state of **Rio Grande do Norte** and its capital, **Natal**, were sleepy, conservative backwaters rarely visited by tourists. But two things have transformed the state into one of the Northeast's biggest tourist centres: **beaches** and **buggies**. North of Natal, the *sertão* rolls down practically to the coast, and the idyllic palm-fringed beaches give way to massive sand dunes. From Genipabu j you can drive in a beach buggy for 250km of uninterrupted dunes as far as Areia Branca, near the border with Ceará. And if you haven't yet tried Brazilian **caju** (cashews), you will here – locals are genuinely proud of the local crop and the dubious honour of having the **world's largest cashew tree**, though the local **mangoes** are just as good.

Natal

Founded by the Portuguese in 1599 on the banks of the Rio Potengi, **NATAL** is now a laidback seaside city of over one million. Though its languid old town contains a few sights, Natal is essentially a major beach resort, with all the action on the Atlantic side of the city. From here the giant dunes and dazzling beaches of the state are easily accessible on day-trips (often via those infamous beach buggies). As befits a popular resort, Natal is also a party town; **forró** originated in this part of the Northeast, and at places such as Rastapé you can watch and learn how to dance with the help of locals.

Downtown Natal is the usual scrappy, bustling affair, centred on the **Avenida Rio Branco**, which runs past the oldest (and far more sleepy) part of the city, **Cidade Alta**, and terminates just to the right of a scruffy square, Praça Augusto Severo, site of the useful central bus station.

Forte dos Reis Magos

Av Presidente Café Filho • Daily 8am–4.30pm • R$3 • ⓣ 84 3202 2006 • Take a taxi (R$30 one-way from Cidade Alta) and ask it to wait

Natal's premier historical site is the distinctive, whitewashed **Forte dos Reis Magos**, which dominates the mouth of the Rio Potengi and dates back to 1598. The name commemorates the date that construction began on January 6, the Christian feast of the Epiphany that honours the biblical "Three Kings" of the "natal". Inside the fort, the old stone courtyard and low walls give the impression of great antiquity, with a small Moorish-like chapel in the middle housing images of the Three Kings (you'll see their images all over the city). Small exhibits on the history of the fort occupy the old, dank rooms, and the views back towards the city, the river and the new **Ponte Newton Navarro** suspension bridge from the battlements are spectacular.

Praça Sete de Setembro

Espaço Cultural Palácio Potengi • Tues–Sat 8am–6pm • Free • ⓣ 84 3211 4620

The oldest part of Natal is formed by the closely packed streets and small squares of **Cidade Alta**, clustered around the administrative heart of the city, **Praça Sete de Setembro**. The plaza is dominated by the **Palacio Potengi**, built in tropical Neoclassical style in 1873 as the Provincial Assembly and now the **Espaço Cultural Palácio Potengi**, with changing art displays by mainly local artists in the austere, simply furnished

4

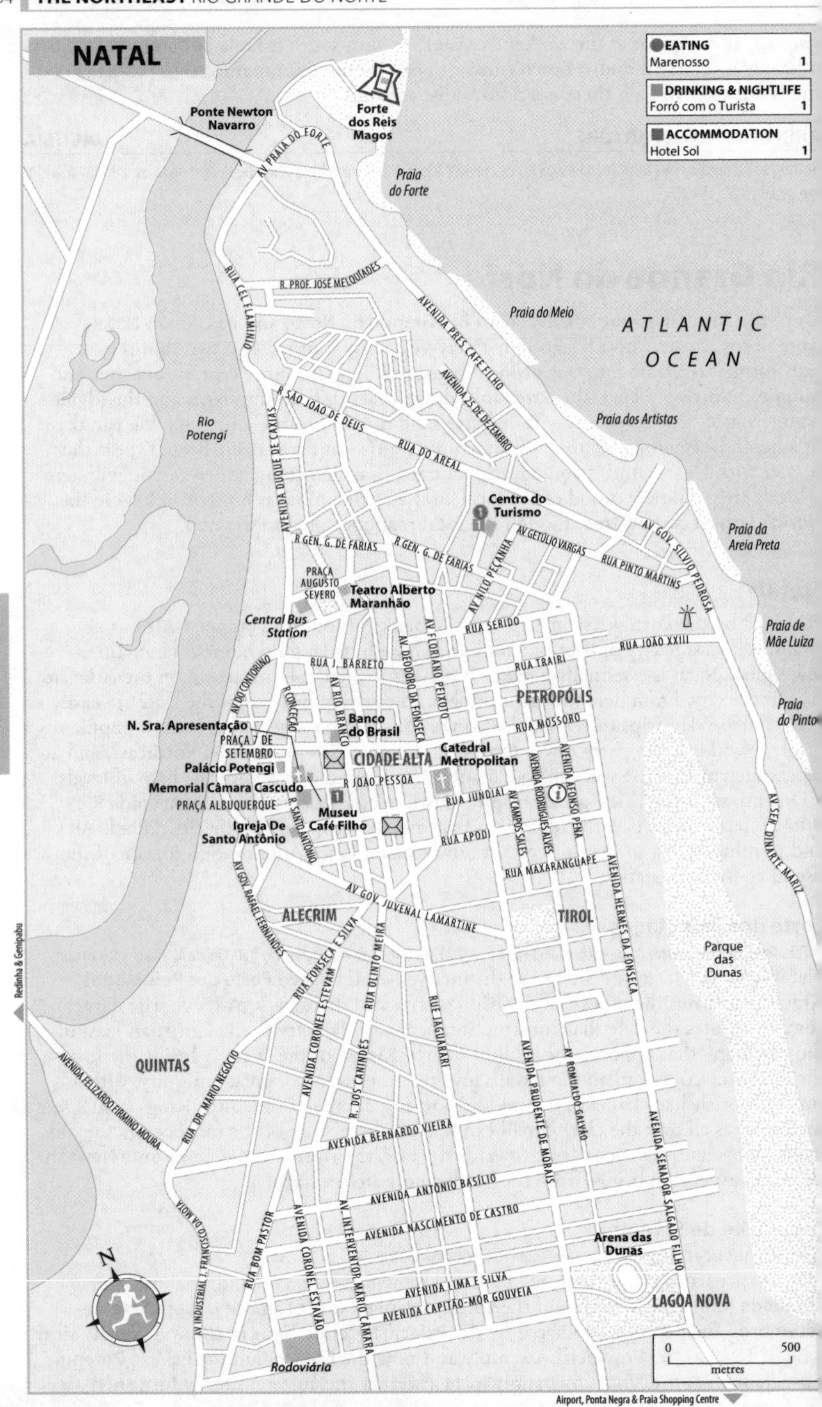
NATAL
EATING
Marenosso 1
DRINKING & NIGHTLIFE
Forró com o Turista 1
ACCOMMODATION
Hotel Sol 1
Ponte Newton Navarro
Forte dos Reis Magos
AV PRAIA DO FORTE
Praia do Forte
RUA CEL ELAMINO
R. PROF. JOSÉ MELQUIADES
AVENIDA PRES CAFE FILHO
Praia do Meio
ATLANTIC OCEAN
AVENIDA 25 DE DEZEMBRO
R SÃO JOÃO DE DEUS
RUA DO AREAL
Rio Potengi
AVENIDA DUQUE DE CAXIAS
Praia dos Artistas
Centro do Turismo
AV GETÚLIO VARGAS
AV GOV. SILVIO PEDROSA
Praia da Areia Preta
RUA PINTO MARTINS
R GEN. G. DE FARIAS
PRAÇA AUGUSTO SEVERO
Teatro Alberto Maranhão
AV NILO PEÇANHA
Central Bus Station
RUA SERIDO
RUA JOÃO XXIII
Praia de Mãe Luiza
RUA J. BARRETO
RUA TRAIRI
AV DO CONTORINO
R CONCEÇÃO
AV RIO BRANCO
AV. DEODORO DA FONSECA
AV FLORIANO PEIXOTO
PETROPÓLIS
Praia do Pinto
Banco do Brasil
RUA MOSSORO
N. Sra. Apresentação
PRAÇA 7 DE SETEMBRO
CIDADE ALTA
Catedral Metropolitan
Palácio Potengi
AVENIDA RODRIGUES ALVES
AVENIDA AFONSO PENA
Memorial Câmara Cascudo
R JOÃO PESSOA
RUA JUNDIAÍ
AV CAMPOS SALES
PRAÇA ALBUQUERQUE
R. SANTO ANTÔNIO
Museu Café Filho
Igreja De Santo Antônio
RUA APODI
RUA MAXARANGUAPE
AV SEN. DINARTE MARIZ
AV GOV. RAFAEL FERNANDES
AV GOV. JUVENAL LAMARTINE
ALECRIM
TIROL
AVENIDA HERMES DA FONSECA
RUA FONSECA E SILVA
RUA OLINTO MEIRA
Parque das Dunas
Redinha & Genipabu
AVENIDA CORONEL ESTEVAM
RUE JAGUARARI
QUINTAS
R. DOS CANINDÉS
AVENIDA PRUDENTE DE MORAIS
AV ROMUALDO GALVÃO
AVENIDA FELIZARDO FIRMINO MOURA
RUA DR. MARIO NEGÓCIO
AVENIDA BERNARDO VIEIRA
AVENIDA SENADOR SALGADO FILHO
AVENIDA ANTÔNIO BASÍLIO
AV INDUSTRIAL J. FRANCISCO DA MOTA
RUA BOM PASTOR
AVENIDA CORONEL ESTAVÃO
AV. INTERVENTOR MÁRIO CÂMARA
AVENIDA NASCIMENTO DE CASTRO
Arena das Dunas
N
AVENIDA LIMA E SILVA
AVENIDA CAPITÃO-MOR GOUVEIA
LAGOA NOVA
0
500
metres
Rodoviária
Airport, Ponta Negra & Praia Shopping Centre

period rooms. Opposite lies the striking blue **Prefeitura Municipal** (aka Palácio Felipe Camarão), completed in 1922, and the grimly Modernist **Assembleia Legislativa do Rio Grande do Norte**.

Teatro Alberto Maranhão

Praça Augusto Severo • ⓣ 84 3222 3669

The restored **Teatro Alberto Maranhão**, a Neoclassical gem built between 1898 and 1904, is arguably the most elegant building in the city, and still hosts concerts and shows.

Praça Albuquerque

Igreja Nossa Senhora da Apresentação Daily 4.30–6pm • Free **Memorial Câmara Cascudo** Tues–Sat 9am–4.30pm • Free • ⓣ 84 3222 3293

In languid, almost half-forgotten Praça Albuquerque, you'll find the **Igreja Nossa Senhora da Apresentação**, once Natal's cathedral and built in 1862, with a fairly unexceptional interior (the bewilderingly ugly hulk of a modern cathedral opened at the end of Rua João Pessoa in 1988). At the southern end of the plaza the **Memorial Câmara Cascudo** celebrates the life and work of **Luís da Câmara Cascudo**, the beloved *natalense* folk writer, housed in a Neoclassical mansion built in 1875 with a statue of the great man outside.

Igreja de Santo Antônio

Rua Santo Antônio 683 • Mon–Fri 8–11.30am & 2–5.30pm, Sat 8–11.30am • Free **Museu de Arte Sacra** Tues–Sat 8am–5pm • Free • ⓣ 84 3211 4236

The most historical and photogenic church in Cidade Alta is the **Igreja de Santo Antônio**, a Baroque gem in white and blue also known as the Igreja do Galo, after the eighteenth-century bronze cock crowing on top of its Moorish tower.

Completed between 1766 and 1799, it features a relatively humble interior with a wood-carved *retábulo*. Next door is the **Museu de Art Sacra**, a fairly small collection of religious art work, oratorios and statuary, with much of the upstairs dedicated to **Padre João Maria** (1848–1905), who was beatified in 2002.

4

BEACHES BY BUGGY: TRIPS FROM NATAL

Going to Natal without riding a **beach buggy** is a bit like going to Ireland and not drinking Guinness – you may or may not enjoy it, but you might as well try it seeing as you're there. After a period of explosive, unregulated growth, the scene today is much more subdued and controlled – you won't see buggies on any of the city beaches, and you'll have to arrange a trip with agents or hotels. Whichever operator you choose, make sure they are licensed by SETUR (they should have official ID cards and beach buggies marked with their SETUR number).

There are two basic kinds of buggy experience: a day- or half-day trip, which involves riding either north or south down the coast, mainly along the beaches (the *bugeiro* will perform a few stunts along the way, surfing the sand dunes, but it's mainly an opportunity to explore the beautiful coastline around Natal); or pay by the ride or by the hour for fairground-type stuff on specific beaches, especially at **Genipabu**, 10km to the north of Natal. Here the *bugeiros* make full use of the spectacular sand dunes to push your heart through your mouth. Trips cost R$90–100, plus a R$10 fee to enter the dunes area. Some operators include Genipabu on longer tours along the coast: these cost around R$440 per buggy (or R$110 per person) and include visits to Lagoa de Jacumã and Praia Muriú. It's possible to travel all the way from **Natal to Fortaleza** and even **Jericoacoara** – the mother of all buggy trips takes three to four days and costs R$1800 and up (six days to Jericoacoara).

BUGGY TOUR OPERATORS

Marazul Passeios de Buggy Rua Vereador Manoel Sátiro 75, Ponta Negra ⓣ 84 3204 7910, ⓦ marazulreceptivo.com.br.

Top Buggy Av Moema Tinoco 1559, Genipabu ⓣ 84 4141 6262, ⓦ topbuggy.com.br.

Museu Café Filho

Rua da Conceição 601 • Tues–Sat 9am–5pm, Sun 11am–5pm • R$1 • ⓣ 84 221 2938

Just off Praça Sete de Setembro is the **Museu Café Filho**, dedicated to the only *rio grandense* to become president of Brazil, local boy **João Café Filho**, who became Vargas' vice-president in 1950 (he became president in 1954 after Vargas' suicide, but only lasted two years) – a corrupt and incompetent paternalist, despite the attempts by the museum to present him as a statesman. But he had the good taste to live in a fine two-storey mansion (completed in 1820), which is worth seeing – more than can be said for the yellowing papers and heavy furniture of the long-dead president.

Centro de Turismo

Rua Aderbal de Figueiredo 980 • Mon–Sat 8am–7pm, Sun 8am–6pm • ⓣ 84 3211 6149 • **Casa de Milagros** • Tues–Sat 10am–5pm • Free • ⓣ 84 9984 8530

Located in the old city prison, perched on top of a hill in Petrópolis (surrounded by *favelas*), the **Centro de Turismo** boats a lovely café, *Marenosso* (see page 298), as well as scores of quality arts and crafts stalls, with an emphasis on cotton products. The complex dates back to the late nineteenth century, becoming a poorhouse in 1911 and a prison between 1945 and 1969. Part of the same complex but with a separate entrance, the **Casa de Milagros** is a small but fascinating collection of ex-votos and religious statuary from all over Rio Grande do Norte housed in an old chapel; no English labels, but the walls of wooden legs, arms, breasts, animals and actual photos of gruesome injuries more than compensate. This is currently the venue for the Thursday-night **Forró com o Turista** (see page 298).

City beaches

Parque das Dunas Av Alexandrino de Alencar • Tues–Sun 8am–6pm • R$1 (R$2 with trails) • ⓣ 84 3201 3985, ⓦ parquedasdunas.rn.gov.br

Natal's beaches are the main tourist draw, though the primary city beaches have waned in popularity in recent years. Beginning at the Forte dos Reis Magos, arcs of sand sweep along the bay between land and an offshore reef, with a small collection of stalls at **Praia do Forte**. The main strip is the **Praia dos Artistas** further down, lined with *quiosques* serving the usual array of cold drinks and food, and numerous hotels and bars are strung along the inland side of the seafront, which gets lively on weekend evenings. Beyond the headland is the **Praia da Areia Preta**, though the reasonable beach here is lined with condo high-rises and there's little action. From here the **Via Costeira** takes you to **Ponta Negra**, 10km away on the ocean side of the **Parque das Dunas**, a range of huge dunes that you can climb.

Ponta Negra

Following close on the heels of Bahia's Morro de São Paulo, **Ponta Negra** is one of the finest resort beaches in the Northeast. Running along a sweeping bay under steep sandy cliffs some 14km from downtown Natal, it is magnificent, sheltered from the biggest Atlantic rollers, though still good for **surfing**. The resort town – a southern suburb of Natal – crowds around the beach, and has expanded rapidly in recent years, jam-packed with places to stay and often quite crowded; bars and restaurants range from trendy beach shacks to serious seafood restaurants, and there's a constant party atmosphere. A pleasant pedestrian promenade runs just above the beach; above this lies a zone of smaller hotels and apartments, while a short but fairly steep climb further up the hill brings you to Avenida Engenheiro Roberto Freire (RN-063), the main highway. The promenade ends at the vast sand dune known as the **Morro do Careca** (you can walk to the foot of the 120m-high dune, but you can't climb on it).

ARRIVAL AND INFORMATION

NATAL

By plane Natal's airport, the Aeroporto Internacional Augusto Severo, is about 15km south of the centre on the BR-101 highway; a taxi to the centre will cost you a fixed rate of about R$25, or you can catch the bus marked "Parnamirim–Natal" (R$2.60) – you'll have to switch to another bus for Ponte Negra. Taxis from the airport to Ponta Negra cost a fixed rate of R$43.

By bus The rodoviária (T 84 3232 7312) is a long way out from the centre, at Av Capitão Mor-Gouveia 1237, in the suburb of Cidade de Esperança, but you can get a local bus (R$2.20) into town at the bus stop on the other side of the road, opposite the rodoviária entrance. Most of these buses from across the road pass through the centre: those marked "Av Rio Branco", "Cidade Alta" and "Ribeira" are the most common. Taxis from the rodoviária into the centre are also plentiful and should cost around R$25, or R$40 to Ponte Negra.

Destinations Fortaleza (6–8 daily; 8hr); João Pessoa (8 daily; 3hr); Recife (9 daily; 4hr 15min); Salvador (2 daily; 21–22hr).

Tourist information Natal's main tourist office is at Rua Jundiaí 644 (Mon–Fri 9am–5pm; T 84 3232 9065, W turismo.natal.rn.gov.br), but your best bet is to ask your accommodation for recommendations and maps.

GETTING AROUND

By bus Natal's bus system is easy to master, and in a hot city with hills and scattered beaches it's worth spending a little time getting used to it – taking taxis can be very expensive. At the central bus station on Praça Augusto Severo, and from Av Rio Branco, you can catch local buses (R$3.50) to most of the places you might want to go to: all the buses to the southern beaches, like Areia Preta and Ponta Negra, can be caught from here or the seafront; buses marked "Via Costeira" head along the southern coastal road out to Ponta Negra. Several bus routes run from the centre to the rodoviária, taking at least half an hour and often longer because of their circuitous routes; buses marked "Cidade de Esperança" are the most direct.

By taxi Meters start at R$4.85, and with things so spread out, expect high fares. A trip between Ponta Negra and the city centre will cost R$40–45, while trips between the latter and the Forte dos Reis Magos are likely to run up another R$20. If sightseeing by taxi, ask the driver to wait, since other than at the main beaches and in the centre it can be hard to hail them on the street. Most Brazilian tourists take city tours or drive their own cars.

ACCOMMODATION

THE CITY CENTRE

Hotel Sol Rua Heitor Carrilho 107 T 84 3201 2208; map p.294. Good-value hotel right in the heart of the old city, with its own restaurant and smallish but pleasant rooms with private baths, a/c, minibar and cable TV. **R$120**

PONTA NEGRA

★ **Albergue da Costa** Av Praia de Ponta Negra 8932 T 84 3219 0095, W facebook.com/alberguedacostahostel. Noted for the exceptionally friendly staff and good-value dorms, with hammocks, hearty breakfast, TV room with DVDs, and a tiny swimming pool. Wi-Fi Dorms **R$55**, doubles **R$150**

★ **Manary Praia Hotel** Rua Francisco Gurgel 9067 T 84 3204 2900, W manary.com.br. On a relatively quiet part of the beach, just a few hundred metres from the main action, this charming, LGBT-friendly hotel is set in mellow garden terraces. They also operate minibus trips into the *sertão* to visit local communities, archeological sites and cave paintings. It has some rooms with hammock balconies looking over the ocean and a large beach terrace. Wi-Fi **R$480**

Pousada América do Sol Rua Erivan França 35 T 84 3219 2245, W pousadaamericadosol.com.br. Newish hotel near the beach with very comfortable rooms overlooking the ocean and great service for the price. It runs a reliable travel agency, too, organizing buggy rides,

THE BIGGEST CASHEW TREE IN THE WORLD

Some 25km south of Natal (and easily reached by bus from the rodoviária), the village of **Pirangi do Norte** is famed throughout the Northeast for having the biggest **caju tree** in the world (aka the **Cajueiro de Pirangi**), over 100 years old and with branches that have spread and put down new roots. Although Brazilians know *caju* as a fruit, its seeds, once roasted, become the familiar cashew nut. It's difficult to believe this enormous (over 8500 square metres) expanse of green leaves and boughs could be a single tree; it looks more like a forest. It still bears over 2.5 tonnes of fruit annually, so it's not surprising that Pirangi is known for its *caju*-flavoured rum. Legend has it that the cashew tree was planted in 1888 by a fisherman named Luiz Inácio de Oliveira, who died at the age of 93 under the shadows of his tree. To wander beneath the branches and climb the viewing platform (daily 7am–6pm) it's R$8 (which includes a shot of cashew juice). Vendors selling cashew nuts and local crafts surround the entrance.

boat trips and excursions as far afield as Fernando de Noronha. R$215

Republika Hostel Rua Porto das Oficinas 123 84 3236 2782, republikahostel.com.br. Stylish hostel in a quiet area a short walk high above the beach, with an all-white-and-blue Mediterranean-like colour scheme and cosy common areas. Small, spotless dorms and doubles. Dorms R$40, doubles R$100

Vila Bonita Pousada Boutique Rua Pedro Fonseca Filho 999 84 2030 9071, pousadavilabonita.com.br. Intimate and lovely *pousada* with only six rooms, each with a minibar, comfortable beds and wooden floors. Spend a bit extra and opt for the two rooms on the upper floor with sea view and private terrace. There's also a rooftop pool and the delicious breakfas. R$400

★ **Visual Praia Hotel** Rua Francisco Gurgel 9184 84 3646 4646, visualpraiahotel.com.br. Large, very comfortable resort-like option located right on the beach, with several pools, a big terrace and a children's play area. R$419

EATING

CITY CENTRE

★ **Marenosso** Rua Aderbal Figueiredo 980, Centro de Turismo, Petrópolis 84 3211 6218, facebook.com/Marenosso; map p.294. Atmospheric restaurant in the Centro de Turismo, high above the city, serving traditional tapiocas (R$7–9), cold beers (R$5), *carne de sol* (R$32–36) and other local dishes (R$37–46). Mon–Wed, Fri & Sat 9am–6pm, Thurs 9am–9pm, Sun 9am–5pm.

PONTA NEGRA

★ **Camarões** Av Engenheiro Roberto Freire 2610 84 3209 2424, camaroes.com.br. Long-standing tourist favourite (its offshoot, Camarões Potiguar, nearby, is equally popular) with delicious specials such as shrimp with quinoa, the signature *camarões potiguar* (shrimp in a coconut milk sauce), and grilled fresh fish. Expect to wait a bit for a table. Mains R$65–95. Mon–Sat 11.30am–3.30pm & 6.30pm–midnight, Sun 11.30am–4pm, 6.30–11pm.

Casa da Taipa Av Praia de Ponta Negra 8868 84 3219 5798, casadetaipatapiocaria.com.br. Rustic, open-air place specializing in regional dishes such as couscous with shrimp but primarily known for its tapioca stuffed with a variety of fillings, from *carne de sol* to cheese and chocolate (R$28) – and their caipirinhas are superb. Mon, Tues & Thurs–Sun 5–11pm.

Cuore di Panna Av Engenheiro Roberto Freire 9028 84 2226 7191, facebook.com/Cuoredipanna Gelateria. Best ice cream in the city (authentic Italian gelato) in a variety of flavours from traditional to tropical fruits, also serving tasty crêpes, good coffee and cakes (R$12). Daily 11am–11pm.

Mar de Sabores Rua Altemar Dutra 47 84 3345 4937, facebook.com/mardesaboresbistro. Straightforward restaurant just a few blocks from the beach with a wide range of dishes on the menu, including, fish, meat, tapioca, snacks and salads. The starters are for sharing or works as a main for one, try the fried fish with fries (R$27.90). Mains between R$22.90 and R$62.90. Tues–Sun noon–9pm (but sometimes close after lunch if not busy).

DRINKING AND NIGHTLIFE

CITY CENTRE

★ **Forró com o Turista** Centro de Turismo, Rua Aderbal de Figueiredo 980, Petrópolis 84 3211 6218, forrocomturista.com.br; map p.294. Every Thursday night the Centro de Turismo hosts this fun evening of live music and dance, for locals as much as tourists. The emphasis here is on participation, so don't expect to sit quietly in a corner (professionals mingle with the crowd to add encouragement). Arrive around 7pm if you want to eat at *Marenosso* first (see above). Entry R$35. Thurs 10pm–1am.

PONTE NEGRA

★ **Botequim Tá Na Hora** Rua Francisco Gurgel 47 84 2010 0034. Best place to drink and listen to music (*forró*, pop rock, *axé* and *sertanejo*) in Ponta Negra, a smart Rio-style place that also serves decent steaks and seafood. Tues–Thurs 6pm–1am, Fri 6pm–2am, Sat 12.30pm–2am, Sun 4pm–midnight.

Decky Bar Av Engenheiro Roberto Freire 9100 84 3219 2471. Always packed bar and club venue, with live bands every night (rock, MPB) but so-so food. Cover mostly R$5–10, R$20 on Saturdays. Wed–Sat 5pm–late.

Hemingway Bar Rua Francisco Gurgel 9125 82 3219 0113. Small, chilled-out modern spot overlooking the ocean on the middle of the promenade, perfect for caipirinhas and cold beers. Daily 9am–9pm.

Rastapé Rua Aristides Porpino Filho 2198 84 3219 0181, rastapecasadeforro.com.br. This "*casa de forró*" features live regional *forró* bands every Wed, Fri and Sat in a rustic, barn-like space. Wed, Fri & Sat 10pm–4am.

Taverna Pub Rua Manoel Augusto Bezerra de Araújo 500 84 3236 3696, tavernapub.com.br. Travellers' favourite for a few beers (it's below the *Lua Cheia Youth Hostal*), in a faux medieval castle with theme nights and live bands. Mon–Sat 10am–4pm.

DIRECTORY

Internet In the Vilarte mall in Ponta Negra (Av Engenheiro Roberto Freire 2107) there's the small phone.com internet café (daily 10am–9pm).

Money and exchange Banco do Brasil at Av Rio Branco 510, Cidade Alta, has ATMs; note that all banks have security checks in Natal and can be jam-packed depending on the time of day and week. Banco24Horas ATMs are the best bet for international credit cards.

Post office Main city centre branches at Rua Princesa Isabel 711 and Av Rio Branco 538.

Praia da Pipa and around

A popular target for independent travellers, **PRAIA DA PIPA** ("Kite Beach") is set in truly idyllic surroundings some 80km south of Ponta Negra, with crystal-clear lagoons, pristine beaches, dolphins regularly swimming near the shore and a wealth of appealing *pousadas* and bars. The main action takes place on 1.5km-long Praia da Pipa itself, with smaller **Praia do Amor** around the headland to the east best for surfing (rental boards are R$80/day). A short walk to the west lies cliff-lined **Baía dos Golfinhos** – where the dolphins come in most mornings – and beyond that **Praia Madeiro**, a popular spot for beginner surfers.

Santuário Ecológico de Pipa

Praia da Pipa–Tibau do Sul Hwy (2km from town) • Daily 8am–5pm • R$10 • ⓣ 84 3201 2007

The **Santuário Ecológico de Pipa** is a small section of preserved coastline – the Chácara do Madeira – above the Baía dos Golfinhos and Praia Madeiro, laced with sixteen fairly easy and short trails that afford a chance to spot local wildlife (birds, snakes, saguis monkeys and the smelly white-eared opossum, or *timbu*). For the best views of the ocean, make for the Passeio do Peroba (300m), which follows the cliffs above the beaches, while the Caminho do Jacú (200m) snakes up to the reserve's highest point, 80m above sea level.

Southern beaches

Some 11km south of Praia da Pipa, and an hour from Natal by bus, the **Barra da Cunhaú** beach is breathtakingly beautiful, with many kilometres of white sands bordered by red sandstone cliffs, natural pools at low tide and usually almost completely deserted – it's becoming popular as a **kite-surfing** destination, however. A further 10km south from here, through sugar-cane plantations and really only accessible by buggy, you'll find the **Lagoa da Coca-Cola**; this black lake, made acidic by the specific plantlife here, is part of a nature reserve where there are cashew trees as well as fragrant bark trees which are used to make some perfumes.

To get away from people, you have to travel further south to **Praia Sagi**, which lies almost on the border with Paraíba state, some 120km from Natal. This is particularly inaccessible and can only be approached by 4WD vehicles or on foot, but as a result is virtually untouched.

ARRIVAL AND INFORMATION **PRAIA DA PIPA**

By bus and minibus Oceano (ⓣ 84 3311 3333, ⓦ expresso-oceano.com.br) runs buses between Natal and Pipa (6am–6.10pm; Mon–Sat 12 daily, Sun 6 daily; 2hr), terminating on Av Baía dos Golfinhos. Coming from João Pessoa you'll have to change in Goianinha and take one of the local vans that zip over to Pipa every few minutes (5am–midnight; 50min). Local minibuses run along the coast between the main beaches (R$3).

By taxi Taxis charge R$150 from Natal airport, but it's best to arrange one in advance: try Taxi Pipa (ⓣ 84 9996 6687).

Tourist information There is no formal information office in Pipa, but ⓦ pipa.com.br is useful.

SANDBOARDING AND SKIBUNDA

Sandboarding down the mountainous dunes near Pipa on surfboards is big business and lots of fun (the sport originated in Brazil). Most of the action takes place at Praia Cacimbinhas, beyond Praia do Madeiro. If the prospect of wiping out puts you off, Brazilians have developed **skibunda** (literally "bottom-skiing"), where you sit on the board (like a sledge) and zip down the slope in a controlled manner. For sandboarding, real surfing and kite-surfing, contact Trieb Club (ⓦ triebclub.com.br).

4

ACCOMMODATION

Media Veronica Hostel Rua Albacora 267 ⓣ84 9997 7606, ⓦmediaveronicahostel.com. Popular and chilled out hostel 250m from the beach, with clean dorms and doubles, surfboard rental, large balcony with hammocks, shared TV room and kitchen. Breakfast not included. Dorms R$40, doubles R$120

Pousada Berro do Jeguy Rua das Pedrinhas 240 ⓣ84 3246 2395, ⓦberrodojeguy.com.br. Brightly decorated, comfy a/c chalets (with cable TV and terraces with hammocks) set around a relaxing pool, 500m from Praia do Amora. R$231

★ **Pousada Terra dos Goitis** Rua das Acácias s/n ⓣ84 3246 2261, ⓦterradosgoitis.com. Luxurious chalets set within lush, tropical gardens, each one featuring a blend of rustic and contemporary design with canopy-style king beds, kitchen and dining area, and a terrace with sunbeds and hammocks, pluss a small pool. R$475

★ **Sugar Cane Hostel** Rua da Mata 233 ⓣ84 3246 2723, ⓦsugarcanehostel.com.br. Justly popular budget option with spotless dorms and private rooms, kitchen, TV room and breakfast included. They can arrange surf lessons, board rentals and Portuguese lessons. Dorms R$40, doubles R$100

EATING AND DRINKING

★ **Cruzeiro do Pescador** Rua dos Concrizes 1, Chapadão (near Praia do Amora) ⓣ84 3246 2026, ⓦcruzeirodopescador.com.br. Superb, no-nonsense seafood, blending local, Brazilian and Portuguese flavours and using rustic cooking methods (clay pots) to cook paellas, shrimp, fresh fish, cod and also steaks. Mains R$80–110 (for two). Daily 1–4pm & 7–10.30pm.

★ **Golde's** Av Baia dos Golfinhos 748 ⓣ84 9920 2447. This buzzy place was built from scratch on the beach and opened in 2013 by Mattias and Tom, twin brothers from Germany, and they've been knocking out exquisite fusion cuisine ever since, with Thai, French, German and Italian influences. Mains R$45–58. Daily except Tues 6pm–1am.

Macoco Rua do Ceu 90 ⓣ84 9 9159 4602, ⓦfacebook.com/MacocoArtesanal. Bright, colourful, Argentine-run place for soups, pastas (around R$35), empanadas (onion with mozzarella, chicken and tomato pesto; R$7) and perfectly roasted lamb (R$55). Wed–Sun 6–11pm.

Tapas Rua dos Bem Te Vis s/n ⓣ84 9414 4675. Excellent Spanish-inspired restaurant serving not just traditional small plates but Asian-influenced dishes such as curried fish and sesame-encrusted tuna. Mains around R$50. Tues–Sat 6.30–11.30pm.

DIRECTORY

Internet For the internet, Cook.com Cyber Café is at Av Baía dos Golfinhos 888 (R$3/hr).

Money and exchange Banco do Brasil at Av Baía dos Golfinhos 369 is the only bank with an international ATM (daily 8am–10pm).

4

Ceará

The state of **Ceará**, covering a vast area but with fewer than nine million inhabitants, is primarily known for its mind-blowing beaches – it has a coastline of around 600km, a constant ribbon of mostly unspoiled and deserted sands. The area has strong and predictable winds which, combined with good surf, means it's a windsurfer's paradise, and many small fishing villages depend on tourism. The state's capital, **Fortaleza**, is the largest, most modern and cosmopolitan city in the Northeast after Recife and Salvador. In stark contrast are the fun beach towns of **Canoa Quebrada** and **Jericoacoara**, which are among some of the most compelling destinations in the country, where massive dunes and rustling coconut palms line the coast to the horizon. Inland Ceará contains more surprises: the flat and rather dull plains of Rio Grande do Norte gradually give way to ranges of hills, culminating in the extreme west of the state in the highlands and lush cloud forest of the **Serra da Ibiapaba**, the only place in Brazil where you can stand in jungle and look down on desert.

Fortaleza

The languid state capital of Ceará, **FORTALEZA** is a sprawling conurbation of over 2.5 million inhabitants. The city itself contains an odd smattering of sights, though there's nothing special to see, and it's the beaches, bar scene and shopping opportunities

NORTH OF NATAL: THE LITORAL NORTE

North of Natal the **Litoral Norte** runs for some 400km to the Ceará border, lined with massive dunes and beaches almost the whole way – indeed, it's possible to travel all the way to Fortaleza by beach buggy (see page 295). Many of the best beaches – such as Genipabu (see page 295) – can be visited on day-trips from Natal, though travelling independently is also possible. The main bus operator up here is Expresso Cabral (ⓦ expressocabral.com.br). These are the highlights (listed in km north of central Natal):

- **Jacumã** (30km). Small village surrounded by giant dunes, with a small lagoon where visitors can indulge in "Aerobunda" (basically a zipline into the water; R$13) or try the "Kamikaze" (sliding down head first on a short body board: R$13).
- **Maracajaú Reefs** (52km). These spectacular coral formations lie 7km off the coast (accessed by boat from the small village of Maracajaú). Expresso Cabral runs buses to the village from Natal (Mon–Sat 10.15am & 1.15pm), and on to Zumbi.
- **Touros** (85km). The closest South American city to Africa (2,865km) is a working fishing port, best known for Brazil's largest lighthouse, the Farol do Calcanhar (62m). Cabral runs buses ten times daily (five on Sun) from Natal.
- **São Miguel do Gostoso** (100km). Friendly town amidst gorgeous, generally empty white-sand beaches with plenty of seafood restaurants, cheap *pousadas* and world-class kitesurf and windsurfing school Clube Kauli Seadi (ⓦ clubekauliseadi.com). Cabral runs buses from Natal and Touros five times daily (four on Sun).
- **Galinhos** (160km). Remote village stranded dramatically on a sandbar, with long swathes of empty beach on all sides. Access is from the tiny port of Pratagil, where boats regularly shuttle across the lagoon ($4; 10min). Pratagil is connected to Natal by Cabral bus (2 daily; 3hr).

that make it an obvious pit stop on the road north – there's plenty of good *artesanato* to seek out, notably lace and leather, and Fortaleza is the largest centre for the manufacture and sale of hammocks in Brazil. The city initiated a spate of new projects designed to increase its tourist appeal, including the beautification of the beachfront **Avenida Beira Mar** and the redevelopment of chic shopping street **Rua Monsenhor Tabosa**, completed in 2014. However, other plans, such as a new cruise ship terminal and the giant aquarium, **Acquário**, have ground to a halt. Not everyone was happy with the money being spent: the city's World Cup 2014 stadium, the shimmering **Arena Castelão**, inflamed protests about poor public services in 2013 and the aquarium garnered a similar reaction.

Centro forms the gritty commercial, administrative and religious heart of the city, though it's little more than a heaving, budget shopping district. Most of the action lies to the east, around the main city beaches and the chic middle-class *bairros* of **Praia de Iracema** and **Meireles**. These give way to the *favelas* and docks of the port area, **Mucuripe**, the gateway to the eastern beaches, notably **Praia do Futuro**, beyond which the city peters out – this is where people actually swim (the other city beaches are really for lounging and drinking). Fortaleza's year-round heat is mitigated somewhat by the constant sea breezes sweeping in from the Atlantic, making the beach districts even more enticing.

Centro de Turismo

Rua Senador Pompeu 350 • Mon–Fri 8am–6pm, Sat 8am–4pm, Sun 8am–noon • Free • ⓣ 85 3212 5880

Housed in the city's old prison, completed in 1866 and in use to the 1970s, the **Centro de Turismo** is not a tourist office but a shopping mall of arts and craft stalls, everything from local lace and tasty cashew nuts to hand-crafted dolls, toys and more standard souvenirs. Quality is generally good and prices reasonable, and the main building is surrounded by the one-time exercise yard, shaded by mango trees – a good place to grab a fresh juice from the kiosk here (R$5). Upstairs is the **Museu de Arte e Cultura Populares**, with an excellent collection of *cearense artesanato* of all kinds, though the museum has been closed for several years and was still closed at the time of writing.

FORTALEZA
0 500 metres
EATING
50 Sabores 2
Balu Doces 1
Neide do Camarão 5
Ponto do Guaraná 3
Rei dos Mares 2 4
DRINKING & NIGHTLIFE
Café Pagliuca 1
Mucuripe Club 2
ACCOMMODATION
Albergaria Hostel 1
Fortaleza Mar Hotel 6
Hotel Luzeiros 2
Hotel La Maison 5
Hotel Marina Praia 3
Pousada Arara 4
Ponte dos Ingleses
Breakwater
Praia de Iracema
Ideal Clube
Feira de Artesanato
Praia do Mucuripe
Estação Ferroviaria & local Bus Station
CENTRO
MEIRELES
VARJOTA
ALDEOTA
FATIMA
Bradesco
Barracas
Praia do Meireles
Jardim Japones
Pão de Açúcar Supermarket
Monte Klinikum Hospital
Droga Nunes
Shopping Del Paseo
5à Sec
Buses to Aquiraz
Estação Rodoviária
Shopping Iguatemi
Río Cocó
SEE MAP BELOW FOR DETAIL
Airport

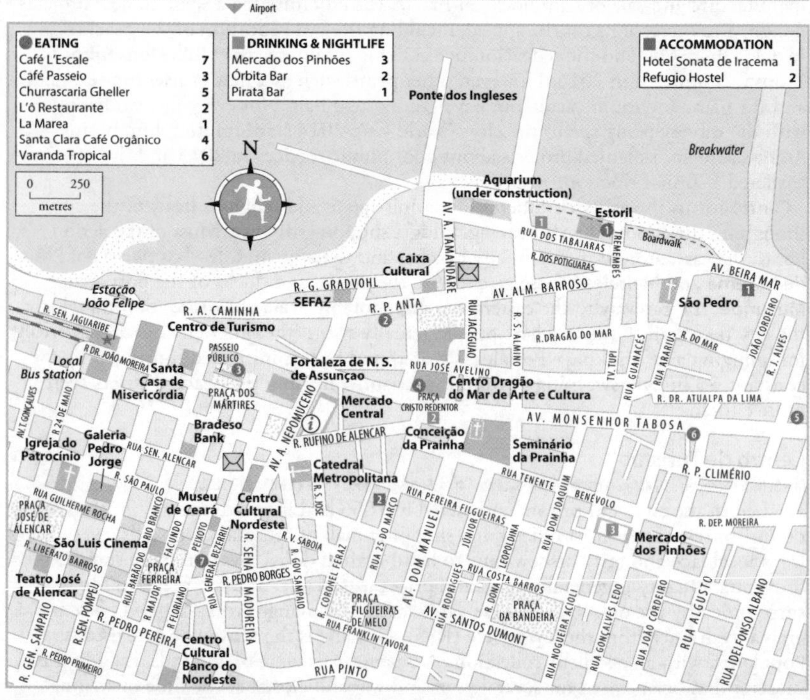
EATING
Café L'Escale 7
Café Passeio 3
Churrascaria Gheller 5
L'ô Restaurante 2
La Marea 1
Santa Clara Café Orgânico 4
Varanda Tropical 6
DRINKING & NIGHTLIFE
Mercado dos Pinhões 3
Órbita Bar 2
Pirata Bar 1
ACCOMMODATION
Hotel Sonata de Iracema 1
Refugio Hostel 2
0 250 metres
Ponte dos Ingleses
Breakwater
Aquarium (under construction)
Estoril
Boardwalk
Caixa Cultural
SEFAZ
São Pedro
Estação João Felipe
Centro de Turismo
Local Bus Station
Santa Casa de Misericórdia
Passeio Público
Fortaleza de N. S. de Assunçao
Centro Dragão do Mar de Arte e Cultura
Mercado Central
Bradeso Bank
Conceição da Prainha
Seminário da Prainha
Igreja do Patrocínio
Galeria Pedro Jorge
Catedral Metropolitana
Museu de Ceará
Centro Cultural Nordeste
Mercado dos Pinhões
São Luis Cinema
Teatro José de Alencar
Centro Cultural Banco do Nordeste

Passeio Público and Praça dos Mártires

One of the few survivors of nineteenth-century Fortaleza, the **Passeio Público** is a short pedestrian promenade designed in the 1860s. It cuts through the pleasantly shady **Praça dos Mártires**, a lush tropical park framed by the elegant **Santa Casa de Misericórdia de Fortaleza**, the first city hospital, completed in 1861. The Passeio looks out across the warehouses to the distant waterfront, and stallholders set up chairs and tables under the trees, from where they sell cold drinks and simple food. It's also a good place for a sit-down lunch.

Mercado Central and Feira José Avelino

Rua Alberto Nepomuceno 199 • Mon–Fri 7am–6pm, Sat 7am–4pm, Sun 7am–2pm • T 85 3454 8586, W mercadocentraldefortaleza.com.br

Fortaleza's once modern but now a bit rundown **Mercado Central** is a wonderful place to explore, a huge complex holding hundreds of small stores, most selling *artesanato* for which the city is famed. The market, along with the nearby stores along **Rua José Avelino**, is the best place to buy a hammock in the city: if you're going to use one on your travels, purchase it with care (see page 375). The informal **Feira José Avelino** (along the street of the same name) is effectively a **night market** that runs from Wednesday at 7pm to 8am on Thursday, and from 7pm on Saturday to noon on Sunday – you'll see thousands of buyers and sellers from all over the Northeast loading up buses around Centro on Thursdays and Sundays.

Catedral Metropolitana

Rua Sobral • Daily 7am–6pm • Free • T 85 3226 1129

Looming over Centro like a grimy Victorian throwback, Fortaleza's **Catedral Metropolitana** is a huge Neogothic oddity completed in 1978, though its interior is a surprisingly bright, open space enhanced by dazzling stained-glass windows. Designed by French architect George Maunier, with 75m-high towers, the new cathedral replaced the earlier nineteenth-century incarnation, demolished in 1938.

Museu do Ceará

Rua São Paulo 51 • Tues–Sat 9am–4pm • Free • T 85 3101 2611

Located smack in the middle of Centro's frenetic commercial district, the curious **Museu do Ceará** fits right in with the scruffy, elegant decay of the area, despite occupying the Palacete Senador Alencar, the grand Neoclassical palace completed in 1871 to house the provincial assembly. Ostensibly a museum of the history of the state (there is a small collection of pre-Columbian artefacts), it's best on the nineteenth century, displaying a number of curios sure to delight aficionados. Highlights include odd mementoes of the 1832 Insurreição do Crato (earth in a jar from where leader Joaquim Pinto Madeira was executed, and his blunderbuss); shiny daggers belonging to bandit Lampião (see page 261); the flag of the "Pandaria Spritual" literary group of the 1890s; and a stuffed goat dubbed "Yoyo" that became a virtual city mascot one hundred years ago. There's also a small but poignant gallery dedicated to **Frei Tito**, born here in 1945, who committed suicide in 1974 after being tortured by the military regime.

From the museum you can wander across to the **Praça do Ferreira**, the former heart of the city and still ringed by relatively grand nineteenth-century buildings.

Praça José de Alencar

The city's largest square is **Praça José de Alencar**, a parched, fairly bare space, anchored by a statue of writer and politician José de Alencar, which comes alive in the late afternoon and early evening, when the crowds attract capoeira groups, street sellers of all kinds and *repentistas*. Fortaleza seems to specialize in these street poets, who with great skill and wit gather an audience by improvising a verse or two about those standing around watching, passing round a hat for you to show your appreciation.

Teatro José de Alencar

Rua 24 de Maio 600 (Praça José de Alencar) • Courtyard Mon–Fri 8am–5pm, Sat 8am–noon • Free tours Tues–Fri 9am–5pm hourly; Sat & Sun 2pm, 3pm, 4pm & 5pm • R$4 • ☎ 85 3101 2567

The most elegant building in Fortaleza lies on the south side of Praça José de Alencar, where the beautiful **Teatro José de Alencar** is named after the great nineteenth-century novelist and poet who was a native of the city. Completed in 1910, the theatre's fine tropical-Edwardian exterior is in fact only a facade, which leads into an open courtyard and the main body of the theatre. It is built in ornate and beautifully worked cast-iron sections, which were brought over complete from Scotland and reassembled here. It remains a key space for theatrical performances and concerts. The surrounding gardens were designed by Burle Marx in the 1970s.

Centro Dragão do Mar

Rua Dragão do Mar 81 • Daily 8am–11pm • Free **Museums** Tues–Thurs 9am–7pm, Fri–Sun 10am–8pm • Free • ☎ 85 3488 8625 • **Planetarium** was closed at the time of research with no known opening date

The vast **Centro Dragão do Mar** complex makes a striking contrast to the rest of the city, containing a couple of small museums well worth a peek. Architecturally it's very modern, but its steel and glass curves blend sensitively with the attractive old terraced buildings over and around which it is built. The **Museu de Arte Contemporanea do Ceará** is a bright, well-curated gallery showing primarily local and Brazilian artists in a variety of media, while the **Memorial da Cultura Cearense** hosts various changing exhibits on aspects of Ceará history, art and culture, but also houses a permanent exhibit on the lower levels dedicated to the **Vaqueiros**, the hardy cowboys of the state. This is an enlightening exhibit on Brazil's "leather civilization" touching all aspects of life in the *sertão* (with some English labelling) enhanced with real saddles, stirrups, branding irons and the like. To a certain extent this presents a romantic view of the past, but one that widely conforms to the modern *cearanese* idea of themselves as rugged individuals, albeit paired with their *ocio criativo*, "creative laziness".

There's also a small, shiny-domed **planetarium** (closed at the time of writing), cinemas, an auditorium and a good coffee-shop, the *Torre do Café*, located in the tower that supports the covered walkway between the two main sections of the complex. On the ground level, the **Central de Artesanato do Ceará** sells quality regional arts and crafts. At weekends the bars and restaurants below the complex become a hive of eating, drinking and musical activities.

Praça Cristo Redentor and around

The southern entrance to Centro Dragão do Mar opens onto the **Praça Cristo Redentor**, an otherwise bare space notable for the 35m column of the **Monumento de Cristo Redentor**, raised in 1922 to commemorate the centenary of Brazilian independence. At the western end lies the once elegant but long-abandoned Teatro São José, while the eastern side is dominated by the **Seminário do Prainha**, completed in 1864 around the older Igreja do Prainha (1841). From here it's a pleasant if hot stroll to the beaches along **Avenida Monsenhor Tabosa**, a shopping street given a smart facelift in 2014.

City beaches

The main city beaches are **Praia de Iracema** and the adjacent **Praia do Meireles**, both focal points for Fortaleza's nightlife and broken up by a series of piers (*espigões*), though the boundary between the two beaches is blurry in practice. As beaches go, the Praia do Meireles wins thanks to its greater expanse of sand, though the water is not as clean as the beaches out of town and Iracema is gradually receiving a long-overdue makeover (this is where the new **aquarium** is supposed to open, but don't count on it). The pier here, known as **Ponte dos Ingleses**, is very popular with couples and families in the early evenings and a lovely place to have a beer or simply watch the sunset.

The seafront boulevard is well laid out, punctuated by clumps of palm trees, and there is no shortage of watering holes. By day there are surfers on the waves and beach parties at the *barracas*, and in the early evening it seems everyone in the city turns out to stroll, jog or rollerblade down the **Avenida Beira Mar**, which has replaced the city's squares as the favoured meeting place.

If you're a beach devotee, cleaner water, higher rollers and better seafood are to be had further out past Mucuripe at 7km-long **Praia do Futuro**: take buses marked "Caça e Pesca" (#49) from Rua Castro e Silva in the centre or along Avendia Beira Mar. The beach *barracas* here are very good, and it's the only beach where locals will actually swim.

Porto das Dunas and Beach Park

Beach Park Rua Porto das Dunas 2734 • Daily 11am–5pm (closed Wed & Thurs March–June & Aug–Nov) • R$170 (children up to 12 R$160) • T 85 4012 3000, W beachpark.com.br • Viação São Benedito runs regular buses to Prainha from the rodoviária, but for the Beach Park it's easier to take a tour: Sim 7 Turismo (see page 306) runs daily buses (with hotel pick-up) for R$38 return

Most Brazilian tourists use Fortaleza as a base from which to visit the surrounding beaches, either renting a car, or more typically taking tours (see below). The nearest targets are the surf beaches at **Porto das Dunas** (31km east of the centre via CE-25/CE-40) and **Prainha** (36km east), with a combined length of 11km. Porto das Dunas is best known in Brazil for having an aquatic theme-park called **Beach Park**, the largest of its kind in Latin America and home to the world's tallest water slide (at 41m high, the aptly named **Insano**).

ARRIVAL AND INFORMATION — FORTALEZA

By plane Aeroporto Internacional Pinto Martins is just 6km south of Centro at Av Carlos Jereissati 3000 (T 85 3392 1200). A fixed-rate taxi costs R$45 to Meireles, Iracema and Centro (R$35 to the rodoviária; R$100 to Porto das Dunas). Pay first at the Coopaero (T 85 3392 1500, W coopaero.com.br) desk in the terminal (higher rates apply Mon–Fri 8pm–6am, after 1pm Sat and all day Sun). You can also take a by-the-meter "Taxi Comum" that are nominally a little cheaper, but only if traffic is light. Buses with the route card Aeroporto/Benfica/Rodoviária (#404; R$3.50) run regularly to Praça José de Alencar in the centre via the rodoviária (daily 5.10am–10pm).

Destinations Belém (5 daily; 1hr 50min–3hr 40min); Recife (10 daily; 1hr 15min–1hr 35min); Rio (12–24 daily; 5hr 40min–8hr 15min); Salvador (7–9 daily; 1hr 40min–4hr 20min).

By bus The Rodoviária Engenheiro João Thomé (T 85 3230 1111) is 3km from Centro at Av Borges de Melo 1630, in the southern suburb of Fátima, but getting into town is relatively easy by bus (R$3.50). A taxi costs around R$30 from the rodoviária to most places in the city.

Destinations Belém (3 daily; 24–26hr); Jijoca de Jericoacoara (16 daily; 5–6hr); Natal (7 daily; 8hr); Parnaíba (5 daily; 8hr); Recife (6 daily; 12–13hr); Salvador (2 daily; 22hr); São Luís (3 daily; 18hr 30min); Teresina (7 daily; 11–12hr).

Tourist information There's a good range of tourist information outlets including a kiosk in the airport (daily 8am–8pm), offices in the Mercado Central (Mon–Sat 9am–5pm; T 85 3105 1475) and on Av Beira Mar (daily 9am–5pm; T 85 3105 2670).

GETTING AROUND

By bus Fortaleza has plenty of local buses (R$3.50). Useful routes that take you to the main beaches and back to the city centre are marked "Grande Circular I" and "Caça e Pesca/Centro/Beira Mar" or #49. The local bus station in Centro is known as Praça da Estação, a large square by the old railway station.

By taxi Taxi meters start at R$4.85 – it's around R$25 between Meireles and Centro. Cooperativa Rádio Táxi de Fortaleza (T 85 3254 5744, W radiotaxifortaleza.com.br) are 24hr.

Car rental All the major companies have desks at the airport, including Avis (6am–11pm; T 85 3392 1369), Localiza/Hertz (24hr; T 85 3308 8350), Movida (24hr; T 0800 606 8686) and Unidas (24hr; T 85 3392 1400).

TOURS

Ernahitur Av Senador Vigilio Tavora 205, 2/F, Room A T 85 3533 5333, W ernanitur.com.br. Arranges packages to Jericoacoara (R$55) and day-trips to Canoa Quebrada (R$55) and Lagoinha (R$45), in addition to all the other major beaches.

Girafatur Rua Tenente Benévolo 13, at Rua Vila Bachá, Meireles T 85 3219 3255, W girafatur.com.br. Tends to specialize in transport and packages to Jericoacoara beaches; punters for the bus are often recruited on the seafront between Iracema and Meireles beaches.

Sim 7 Turismo 85 8750 2500, sim7turismo.com.br. Offers multi-beach packages (6 beaches in 4 days from R$228) as well as the usual day-trips. They also run daily minibuses (7–8am) to Jericoacoara (with hotel pick-up and drop-off) for R$120 return.

ACCOMMODATION

The budget hotels, as ever, tend to be downtown, which hums busily during the day but empties at night – it's best to stay elsewhere. Close by is Praia de Iracema, with a decent enough range of accommodation, while Praia Meireles further south is home to more upmarket hotels.

CENTRO

Refugio Hostel Fortaleza Rua Deputado João Lopes 31 85 3393 4349, refugiohostelfortaleza.com; map p.302. A German-owned and extremely well-run hostel with an environmental conscience, clean dorms and excellent service. The young staff are all English speaking and the shared bathrooms are plenty, spacious and even have hair dryers. Dorms R$30, doubles R$120

PRAIA DE IRACEMA

Albergaria Hostel Rua Antônio Augusto 111, Praia de Iracema 85 3032 9005, albergariahostel.com.br; map p.302. Cheerful hostel close to the beach and nightlife, with small clean dorms and doubles with tiled floors and a/c. Basic breakfast included, and there's a pool table and cold beers (for sale) at the bar. Dorms R$45, doubles R$120

Hotel Sonata de Iracema Av Beira Mar 848 85 4006 1600, sonatadeiracema.com.br; map p.302. Gorgeous renovated mansion and tower on the seafront, with bright, clean a/c rooms with tiled floors, rooftop pool, cocktail bar, stunning ocean views and a modern gym. R$330

PRAIA DO MEIRELES

Fortaleza Mar Hotel Rua Antônio Lima 126 85 3248 8000; map p.302. Excellent deal, close to the beach, with a small but lovely pool, simply furnished a/c rooms with TV and hearty breakfast included. R$205

Hotel Luzeiros Av Beira Mar 2600 85 4006 8585, luzeirosfortaleza.com.br; map p.302. Stylish ocean-front hotel overlooking the beach, with fabulous rooftop pool and rooms featuring a cool contemporary design with purple, beige or red interiors and white tile floors, balconies with sea views, a/c and cable TV. R$215

★ **Hotel La Maison** Av Desembarador Moreira 201 85 3048 4200, hotellamaison.com.br; map p.302. This thirteen-room *pousada* is in a tastefully converted house just a few blocks from the beach; the rooms are pleasant and have TVs, telephones and a/c. French and English are spoken and parking is available. R$159

Hotel Marina Praia Rua Paula Barros 44 85 3242 7734, hotelmarinapraia.com.br; map p.302. A small, spick-and-span hotel, little bigger than a house and less than a block from the beach in the Nautico section of Praia Meireles. It somehow fits 25 apartments into its comfortable and colourful interior, and there's also a little patio out front. R$341

Pousada Arara Av Aboliçao 3806, Mucuripe 85 3263 2277, hotelarara.com.br; map p.302. A friendly hotel in a safe setting, although it's on a main road so not too quiet. Rooms are clean and comfortable although the owners have a penchant for adorning their walls with tropical sunset prints. There's a nice enough pool at the back, as well as a little barbecue area. Breakfast included. R$140

EATING

Downtown, Praça do Ferreira offers a few *por quilo lanchonetes* (self-service cafeterias), and Iracema has a few good restaurants, while the Centro Dragão do Mar has pavement cafés overflowing with people having fun in the evenings. The beaches all have a smattering of good restaurants as well as beach *barracas* offering some of the best deals on seafood. In two or three small streets around Rua dos Tabajaras on Praia de Iracema you'll find a score of brightly coloured bars and restaurants.

CENTRO

Café L'Escale Rua Floriano Peixoto 587 85 3253 1976, lescale.com.br; map p.302. Excellent local pit stop right on Praça do Ferreira (in an Art Nouveau building dating from 1914), with the usual selection of *salgados*, drinks and self-service buffet options. Mon–Thurs 8am–9pm, Sat 8am–4pm.

★ **Café Passeio** Rua Dr João Moreira, Praça do Passeios Público 84 3063 8782; map p.302. Elegant restaurant occupying the old-fashioned kiosks in the park with outdoor seating. It's a self-service Brazilian buffet during the week (R$51.90/kg), with *feijoada* on Saturday and a bigger buffet on Sunday (R$61.90/kg on the weekends). Daily 9am–5pm.

L'ô Restaurante Av Pessoa Anta 217 85 3265 2288, lorestaurante.com.br; map p.302. Cool, slick modern restaurant combining Art Deco and contemporary design with a menu of highly creative nouvelle Brazilian cuisine – think smoked haddock risotto and "aphrodisiac prawns" in cognac (R$89). Mon–Thurs 7pm–midnight, Fri noon–3pm & 7pm–1am, Sat 7pm–1am.

Santa Clara Café Orgânico Rua Dragão do Mar 81 (Centro Dragão do Mar) 85 3219 6900, cafesantaclara.com.br; map p.302. Try the popular espresso (R$3.90) or sip on a chocolate-fringed cappuccino (R$10) at Fortaleza's best coffee joint. Tues–Sun 3–10pm.

PRAIA DE IRACEMA

La Marea Rua dos Tremembés 100 85 3219 2284; map p.302. Lovely two-tier wooden chalet-like place in the heart of the action, nominally a Spanish restaurant but serving primarily Brazilian seafood classics such as *moqueca* (R$29.90), filet mignon (R$25.90) and lobster specials (R$54.90). Daily 6pm–1.30am.

Varanda Tropical Av Monsenhor Tabosa 714 85 3219 5195; map p.302. Open-fronted restaurant on the main road serving a solid range of meat, fish and seafood options, many of which will fill two bellies; if you're alone, try the shrimps in garlic (R$9.90). The buffet is R$27/kg. Mon–Sat 11am–midnight, Sun 11am–5pm.

PRAIA DO MEIRELES

★ **50 Sabores** Av Beira Mar 3958 85 3077 9400, 50sabores.com.br; map p.302. This decades-old Fortaleza institution offers almost double the titular fifty flavours of ice cream, all of which change with the seasons, even if it feels like the weather never does. Try the plum, caipirinha or *maracujá* (R$12 for one huge scoop). One of six branches spread around town. Mon–Sat 10am–10pm, Sun 2–8pm.

Balu Doces Av Monsenhor Tabosa 1717 85 3248 2200, baludoces.com.br; map p.302. Long-standing bakery and café specializing in cakes and irresistible desserts: creamy tarts, crunchy biscotti and fluffy mousse. Mon–Sat 9am–9pm, Sun 10am–9pm.

Churrascaria Gheller Av Monsenhor Tabosa 825 85 3219 3599; map p.302. No-nonsense steakhouse where the buffet is R$37.90 on weekdays (with salads, sushi, pasta and vegetables), though the *rodizio* is so-so. Drinks and desserts are extra. Daily 11am–11pm.

Neide do Camarão Av da Abolição 4772 85 9 8892 8231; map p.302. You buy your shrimp at the door (R$39/kg), choose how you want it prepared, hand it to the waiter, then eat it, preferably washed down with ice-cold beer. Local, authentic and awesome. Daily 5pm–midnight.

Rei dos Mares 2 Rua Visconde de Maua 200 85 3036 2215; map p.302. Great seafood restaurant keeping it old school with white table cloths and handwritten menus. (R$89.90–149.90). Try the *camarão ceara*, grilled prawns with butter and capers (R$89.90) or the lobster (R$115). Daily 11am–11pm.

★ **Ponto do Guaraná** Av Beira Mar 3127-A, at Rua Júlio Ibiapina 85 3086 5650; map p.302. *Guaraná* addicts should head here – there's plenty of flavours to choose from, including lemon, *acerola* and *açaí* (drinks R$7–10). Sandwiches are also available (from R$10). Daily 6am–10pm.

PRAIA DO FUTURO

Croco Beach Av Zezé Diogo 3125 85 3521 9600, crocobeach.com.br. Futuro's most popular beach restaurant, serving huge sharing platters of seafood and a buffet for R$69.90/kg, as well as salads (from R$26.90) and plenty of meat dishes (most mains for two R$62.90–88.90). Also lays on live local bands and MPB Tuesdays and Thursdays (R$25 cover) and DJs/live music at weekends (R$8 cover). Mon–Wed & Sun 8am–6pm, Thurs 8am–2am, Fri & Sat 8am–9pm.

4

DRINKING AND NIGHTLIFE

Fortaleza is justly famous for its **forró**. Nowhere is it so popular, and there is no better way to see what *cearenses* do when they want to enjoy themselves than to spend a night in a *dancetaria* here. One of the busiest nightlife areas is the streets behind the Ponte dos Ingleses.

Café Pagliuca Rua Barbosa de Freitas 1035 85 3324 1903, facebook.com/cafepagliuca; map p.302. An arty, rustic bohemian vibe makes this one of the mellowest spots in town for a quiet drink and some live jazz, bossa and MPB (Tues–Sat 9.30pm–midnight). There's Chilean red from R$50 a bottle and the food includes a range of authentic Italian risotto (try the house recipe, R$40). R$20 cover. Tues–Thurs 5.30pm–midnight, Fri noon–midnight, Sat noon–1am.

Mercado dos Pinhões Praça Visconde 41 85 3251 1299; map p.302. Perhaps the best place to get a sense of how locals take their *forró* and *chorinho* seriously, this old 1890s *mercado* is an arts and craft market by day (Mon–Fri 9am–noon & 2–5pm), but morphs into an authentic *forró* dance hall on Thursday, Friday and Sunday evenings. Thurs, Fri & Sun 5pm–midnight.

Mucuripe Club Travessa Maranguape 108 85 3254 3020; map p.302. Veteran superclub hosting some of the country's biggest DJs, singers and bands in several themed areas including a film-set-like, colonial-style street, a huge "arena" for live shows and a hi-tech clubbing area, with a music policy covering everything from rock, funk and electronica to samba, *axé* and *forró*. No flip-flops or shorts. Cover varies according to event (usually R$30–60). Fri & Sat 9.30pm–5am.

Órbita Bar Rua Dragão do Mar 207 85 3453 1421, orbitabar.com.br; map p.302. A Fortaleza institution, with live Brazilian and international indie/alternative, blues, electronica and even – for those who like their twang – a night (Thurs) dedicated to the delights of surf-rock. Check out their radio station, orbitaradio.com.br. Cover R$10–30. Thurs–Sun 9pm–5am.

Pirata Bar Rua dos Tabajaras 325, Praia de Iracema ☎85 4011 6161, @pirata.com.br; map p.302. The most famous place in Fortaleza and Brazil to get your fix of *forró*. By cannily cornering the club-less wilds of *segunda-feira*, this unashamed tourist trap has generated more than its fair share of publicity – the *New York Times* famousl called it "the craziest place on earth on a Monday night and a Brazilian magazine rated it as one of the 1001 place to see in the country before you die. Get ready to dance ti you drop. Cover R$40. Mon 8pm–5am.

DIRECTORY

Consulates UK, British Honorary Consulate, Rua Leonardo Mota 501, Meireles (☎85 242 0888); US, Torre Santos Dumont, Av Santos Dumont 2828, Suite 708, Aldeota (☎85 3021 5200).

Hospital Monte Klinikum Hospital, Rua República do Libano 747 (☎85 4012 0012, @monteklinikum.com.br).

Internet Cyber Café, Av da Abolição 2659, Meireles (Mon–Sat 8.30am–10pm).

Laundry Lavanderia São Luíz at Av da Abolição 2679 (Mon–Fri 8–11.30am & 12.30–6.30pm, Sat 8am–1pm) for drop-off service; the branch of Lav & Lev (@lavelev.com.br) next door at Av da Abolição 2685 has self-service coin-operated machines (powder available).

Money and exchange Bradesco have an ATM in the cit centre on Rua Senador Alencar 144. Banco24horas als have ATMs at Av Beira Mar 2982 and Av da Abolição 2900.

Pharmacy Farmácia Santa Branca, Av da Universidad 3089, Benfica (☎85 3223 0000).

Police The tourist police are open 24/7 and can be foun at Av Almirante Barroso 805, Praia da Iracema (☎85 310 2488).

Post office The central post office is at Rua Senador Alenca 38 (Mon–Fri 8am–5pm); in Miereles there is a branch at A Monsenhor Tabosa 1561 (Mon–Fri 9am–5pm).

Canoa Quebrada

4

Ceará's best-known and most fashionable beach, **CANOA QUEBRADA** lies 148km southeast of Fortaleza, its deep emerald waters, enticing sands and massive, cathedral-like dunes making it a big hit with foreigners and young Brazilians alike. The atmosphere is relaxed by day, and lively at night. Certainly, if you want company and *movimento* (action) it's the beach to head for, and there's fun **buggy-riding** to be had in the sand dunes of the surrounding coast (R$160–260), with trips easily organized at your *pousada*.

ARRIVAL AND DEPARTURE

CANOA QUEBRADA

By bus São Benedito (@gruposaobenedito.com.br) runs four buses daily from Fortaleza's rodoviária direct to Canoa (6am, 11am, 1.30pm & 5.30pm; 3hr 15min). Alternatively, most tour operators in Fortaleza run door-to-door minibus services (see page 305). Coming from Natal and the south you'll have to take a bus to Aracat (13km southwest of Canoa), and catch the São Benedit bus there; alternatively, for the Canoa leg, minibuses ru every 30min and charge around R$3, while taxis will as for R$25–30.

ACCOMMODATION

★ **Il Nuraghe** Rua Decida Da Praia ☎88 3421 7418, @nuraghe-canoa.com. Justly popular solar-powered hotel, a rustic-looking property with a long, tranquil pool area and simple but stylish contemporary a/c rooms (with kitchenette and LCD TVs), a short walk from the beach. R$215

Pousada Aruanã Rua dos Bugueiros ☎88 3421 7154, @pousadaaruana.com.br. Great-value, two-storey place overlooking the beach and arranged around a relaxing pool area, with simple but stylish modern a/c rooms and satellite TV. R$145

Pousada Azul Marinho Rua Leandro Bezerra ☎88 3421 7003, @azul-marinho.com. Set high above the beach, the best feature here is the stunning, panoramic sea view, though the rooms are comfy enough (with a/c and TVs) and there's an outdoor pool. R$155

★ **Pousada Fortaleza** Rua Descida da Praia 76 ☎88 3421 7019, @pousadafortaleza.com. Just 200m from the beach, this was one of the early pioneering *pousadas* here and has developed comfortable a/c apartments equipped with *frigobars*, TVs and hammocks. There's also a pool and sound information on kite-boarding, one of the more popular beach activities. R$90

EATING AND DRINKING

Most of the evening action in Canoa takes places along the eastern end of the main drag, Rua Dragão do Mar, known here as "Broadway Street". There are also several *barracas* along the beach itself, where reggae parties usually kick off after midnight at the weekends.

PRAIA DAS FONTES AND MORRO BRANCO

Some 90km southeast of Fortaleza lies the spectacular **Labirinto do Morro Branco**, where the coastline crumbles into a series of jagged crimson, gold and chalky sand-dune cliffs, overlooked by a lighthouse. Nearby, the **Praia das Fontes** is a pleasant spot to lounge on the sands. Both places are around 5km from the small town of **Beberibe**, accessible by bus from Fortaleza – São Benedito's service to Canoa stops here (see page 308) – though most travellers visit on day-trips from the city (see page 305).

Barraca Antônio Coco (on the beach) 88 3421 7000, antoniococo.com.br. Superb seafood (fresh fish, prawns, lobster) and regional dishes served in one of the best *barracas* on the beach, equally appealing for a laidback beer or caipirinha, with tables on the beach and on the shady balcony. Free showers and buggy rides back to your hotel. Daily 9am–10pm.

Costa Brava Rua Dragão do Mar 2022 88 3421 7088. Spanish restaurant cooking up great pans of delicious paella crammed with fresh seafood, grilled prawns and (mains R$40–70). Daily 5pm–midnight.

Jericoacoara

Ceará's most enticing beach, and arguably one of the world's finest, **JERICOACOARA** lies 300km northwest of Fortaleza with huge dunes of fine white sand and turquoise *lagoas*. It is quite probably Brazil's best location for wind and surf activities, and most tour agents in Fortaleza offer packages here (see page 305). It's no longer off the beaten track or a budget destination, but development has so far not spoiled the languid atmosphere of the place, and there are plenty of spots to stay as well as several outfits renting out surfboards and windsurfing equipment. **Kite-surfing** is also very popular here, particularly at Praia do Prea, a small fishing village some 10km down the beach (43km by road).

The village lies within a small but protected national park (Parque Nacional de Jericoacoara), with vehicle access highly restricted (for now at least) and the main "streets" little more than sandy trails. The main drag is Rua Principal, with Rua do Forró (where buses arrive) to the north and Rua São Francisco and Rua das Dunas to the south near the dunes. Watching the mesmerizing sunsets atop the **Pôr do Sol** dune is one of the highlights of Brazil.

Tatajuba

A small village in the dunes 25km west of Jericoacoara, **Tatajuba** is a popular excursion by buggy or 4WD (around R$250 for four). The primary draw is the idyllic freshwater lagoon here, where you can take *jangada* rides, laze in waterside *barracas* or loll in hammocks that actually dip into the cooling water.

ARRIVAL AND INFORMATION — JERICOACOARA

By plane Aeroporto de Jericoacoara is 30km from the beach area. Azul run direct flights from Belo Horizonte (3 weekly Tues, Fri & Sun; 2hr 55min), São Paulo (1 weekly Sat; 3hr 30min) and Recife (3 weekly Wed, Fri & Sat; 1hr 30min). Gol runs flights to São Paulo (2 weekly Wed & Sat; 3hr 30min).

By bus "Jeri" remains accessible only via a bumpy unpaved trail through the dunes, with most buses going only as far as Jijoca, 20km south of the beach. Fretcar runs two daily buses from Fortaleza to Jeri, with a change to 4WD transport in Jijoca (7.45am; & 3.30pm; 5hr 15min; R$83; fretcar.com.br), with an additional 4.30am service Fri–Mon. Buses make the return journey at 6.15am and 2.55pm, with an additional 4.55pm service Fri–Mon.

To and from Icaraí From Icaraí (see page 310) you'll have to take the 5.50am Fretcar bus to Amontada (1hr), where four Fretcar buses a day zip up to Jijoca (2hr 25min); simply reverse the route heading in the other direction (buses depart Amontada for Icaraí at 5.50pm). From Icaraí there is a daily bus (5.30am) to Fortaleza.

To Lençóis and São Luís Moving on further west to Parque Nacional dos Lençóis and São Luís, Fretcar buses connect Jijoca with Camocim (2 daily; R$15; 1hr 30min), from where there are buses to Parnaíba (3 daily; R$25; 2hr 45min). From Parnaiba you take the bus to São Luis.

By truck or buggy From Jijoca, *camionetes* (small 4WD trucks/jeeps) run back and forth to Jeri for around R$10–20, though they tend only to run frequently between 6am and 10am – otherwise beach buggies will make the trip for around R$80.

Tours Tour operators also offer direct door-to-door transfers between Fortaleza and Jeri for around R$75–100

4

THE LITORAL OESTE

Northwest of Fortaleza the **Litoral Oeste** is lined with massive dunes and beaches almost the whole way to Jericoacoara – indeed, it's possible to travel around by beach buggy (see page 295). Travelling by bus is time-consuming but possible (most places are connected to Fortaleza); the main operator is Fretcar (ⓦfretcar.com.br). In addition to just lazing on vast wedges of sand, **kite-surfing** and **windsurfing** are major pursuits in these parts, with Cumbuco and Paracuru fun places to learn. For a quieter, more laidback experience, aim for the village of Icaraí. These are the east-coast highlights (listed in km north of central Fortaleza):

- **Cumbuco** (30km). Best known as the kite-surfing centre of the Northeast, best June to January. Beginner courses (10hr) start at around R$800. See ⓦcumbuco.com.
- **Paracuru** (88km). Party town that gets crowded during weekends, but is less frenetic during the week when surfing and kite-surfing on the beaches are popular. See ⓦparacuru.tur.br. Hourly buses from Fortaleza (2hr; R$8.70), and one daily to Paraipaba (5pm; 1hr; R$3).
- **Lagoinha** (105km). Gorgeous strip of sand, with as yet minimal development (though day-trips from the city are popular). The closest bus is Paraipaba, from where taxis run to Lagoinha. Hourly buses from Fortaleza (2hr; R$9.20).
- **Trairi** (125km). Several idyllic, untrammelled beaches are accessible from this small town: **Mundaú** (17km) protected by a 100m reef, and **Fleicheiras** (11km) more deserted still. Fretcar buses go direct to both places via Paraipaba: Fleicheiras (6 daily; 3hr 20min; R$13.85); Mundaú (3 daily; 3hr 45min; R$14.15).
- **Icaraí** (196km). End-of-the-road-type fishing village, barely touched by tourism, with a lovely beach and a handful of places to stay. Fretcar runs one bus daily from Fortaleza (2.30pm; 4hr 20min; R$21.20). Moving on, you'll have to get a bus to Amontada (5.50am; 1hr; R$5), and change there for buses to Jijoca for Jericoacoara (4 daily; 2hr 25min).

4

(see page 305). Officially, Fretcar is the only company allowed to run transfers to and from Jericoacoara. Transfers arranged by tour operators therefore always include an excursion to a tourist sight (although they don't necessarily make a stop for this on the day of travel) to get around this. In Jeri you can also get direct transfers via 4WD to Lençóis, jumping-off point Barreirinhas, for around R$1500 (for up to four people) – expensive but a huge time-saver (1 day of travel). Excellent Global Connection (ⓣ88 9 9900 2109, ⓦglobalconnection.tur.br), with English-speaking staff, can help you book flights, bus tickets and transfers.

Tourist information For information on the village visit ⓦjericoacoara.com. Please note that you need to pay a fee (sustainable tourism tax) of R$5 per day to stay in Jericoacoara. It's paid at the Tourism office in Jijoca or can be paid in advance online at ⓦspeedgov.com.br/satjij/servlet/formtaxaing. You'll be asked to show your payment receipt at the entrance of Jericoacoara.

Money and exchange There are no banks or ATMs in Jeri, so make sure you bring enough cash. The closest ATM is in Jijoca.

ACTIVITIES

Capoeira The Brazilian dance/martial art (see page 213) is popular here, with lessons around R$30/hr. Most agents and *pousadas* can book these for you.

Dune buggy tours Can be arranged through your *pousada* or the kiosk on the main plaza, with rates (per vehicle) ranging R$120 for a couple of hours in the nearby dunes, to R$250 for 5hr excursions to Tatajuba and beyond. For longer expeditions as far as São Luís or Fortaleza see Jeri Off Road (ⓦjeri.tur.br).

Kite-surfing The region is a major kite-surfing centre. Contact Rancho do Kite (ⓦranchodokite.com.br) or Downwind Brazil (ⓦdownwindbrasil.com) for lessons and excursions. ClubVentos also offer kite-surfing (see below).

Sand boarding Is no longer allowed to protect the sand dunes from deteriorating.

Surfing The best spot for beginners is in the bay in front of town; Praia Malhada is best for more experienced surfers (Dec–April sees the biggest waves). ClubVentos Surf School (ⓣ88 3669 2288, ⓦclubventos.com) offers wind surfing lessons (R$198–504) and board rental for from R$112/day.

Windsurfing Tikowind Jeri, Rua das Dunas 30 (ⓣ88 9662 9291, ⓦticowindjeri.com) or ClubVentos are your best bets for lessons and board rentals (boards from R$80/day; lessons from R$100/hr). The wind is strongest July–Dec.

ACCOMMODATION

Casa Fufi Rua do Ibama ⓣ88 9773 0303, ⓦcasafufi.com.br. Fabulous hillside property boasting luxurious bungalows and apartments (with stylish decor, flat-screen TVs and kitchen), set in lush gardens around a pool. Minibar items included in the rate. R$280

Onda Blue Brasil Rua Principal 2 ⊕88 9680 6880, ⊕ondabluebrasil.com.br. Handsome boutique property a short walk from the beach, with bright, hip a/c rooms (finished in red and white), pool, and excellent views. R$175

Pousada da Renata Rua da Escola ⊕88 3669 2109, ⊕pousadadarenata.com. Homely accommodation 500m from the beach, with pleasantly decorated, simple a/c doubles with either a balcony or a patio. R$150

Pousada do Tadeu Rua Principal ⊕88 9918 6915. This is what passes for "budget" in Jeri these days, with barebones but clean en-suite doubles and family rooms, simple shared kitchen and balcony with hammocks. Basic breakfast included. R$90

Pousada Windjeri Rua do Forró 33 ⊕88 3669 2090, ⊕windjeri.it. Popular Italian-run inn, with attractively rustic chalets and rooms just 50m from the beach, all with TVs, *frigobars*, a/c and hot showers. Fortaleza airport pick-up for R$450. R$155

EATING AND DRINKING

Espaço Aberto Rua Principal 104 ⊕88 3669 2063. Good bet for superb fish (try the *peixe-verde* or *peixe tropical* with banana) and seafood, run by an affable *carioca* Beto (for around R$20 per head). Daily noon–11pm.

Kaze Sushi Bar Rua do Forro s/n ⊕88 99961 5791, ⊕kazesushibar.com. Cosy and nicely decorated restaurant serving tasty and beautifully presented sushi. The staff is friendly and there's a decent selection of sake on bottle (Japanese rice wine; R$69–212), fish and meat carpaccio (R$33–43) and a great selection of temaki (sushi rolls; R$13–39) and big platters to share with up to 74 pieces of sushi (R$59–321). Daily 6–11.30pm.

★ **Naturalmente** Rua da Praia s/n. This excellent and chilled-out restaurant right on the beach serves delicious savoury crêpes (R$16–39) with wholesome salads or stuffed with everything from *calabresa* (Brazilian styled Italian sausage) to chicken breast. There's also a good range of sweet pancakes (R$18–24). Daily noon–11pm.

Pizzaria Nômade Rua da Farmácia ⊕88 3669 2134. Great spot with rustic, Northeastern decor, best known for tasty pizza (try the prawn and cream cheese), but it also cooks up decent pasta and has a reasonable wine list. Daily 6pm–midnight.

Tortuga Jeri Rua São Francisco ⊕88 9725 2500. Healthy and wholesome sandwiches, wraps, soups and light meals with plenty of vegetarian and vegan options. Reverts to chilled-out bar in the evenings. Dishes R$15–45. Mon–Sat 5–11pm.

4

Parque Nacional de Ubajara

Rodovia da Confiança (off CE-187), 5km northeast of the town of Ubajara (325km west of Fortaleza) • **Visitors' centre** Tues–Sun 9am–4pm • ⊕88 3634 1388 **Cave tour** Tues–Sun 8am–4pm (last entry 2pm) • R$5 (R$10 via the trail) **Cable car** Tues–Sun 9am–2.30pm • R$4 one-way (closed at the time of research) **Guides' cooperative** ⊕88 3634 2365 • Services start at around R$55/day

Few travellers stray far from the dazzling beaches along the coast of Ceará, and in truth there is little to detain you in much of the dusty *sertão*-blown interior of the state. There is one exception, however: the caves of the **Parque Nacional de Ubajara** in the **Serra da Ibiapaba**, the beautiful hills and cloud-forest highlands that run down the border between Ceará and Piauí. Everything here is green and fertile; the temperature, warm but fresh with cool breezes, is an immense relief, and the contrast with the conditions only half an hour's drive away below couldn't be more marked. The park itself is very small (at less than six square kilometres it is in fact Brazil's smallest national park), but has a **visitors' centre**. A cooperative of local guides can show you round the park's eco-trails, large caves and impressive waterfalls (you can't walk around without a guide); they are also a good source of up-to-the-minute local information.

Gruta de Ubajara

From the park *mirante* (viewpoint) beyond the entrance gate, a three-minute **cable car** (*teleférico*) swoops down 550m to the cave complex of the **Gruta de Ubajara**, huge caverns with fantastical formations of stalactites and stalagmites that extend 450m into the mountain (with a 35m elevation loss). For hikes along the 7km trail down to the cave mouth, guides prefer to start in the morning (8am, 9am & 10am), so you do the bulk of the walk before the heat gets up; take liquids, and wear decent walking shoes. Going down takes a couple of hours, returning twice that, but there are streams and a small waterfall to cool off in along the way.

ARRIVAL AND DEPARTURE

PARQUE NACIONAL DE UBAJARA

The park entrance lies a 20min walk along the road from the town of Ubajara, or you can take a taxi for R$25.

By bus From Jericoacoara you'll have to take the Fretcar (fretcar.com.br) bus from Jijoca to Camocim (2pm; R$12; 1hr), then take the 2.30pm (the connection is very tight) Guanabara bus to Sobral (3hr; R$13.55; expressoguanabara.com.br), then take the 6.50pm Guanabara bus to Ubajara (2hr; R$16.60).

Destinations Brasília (daily at 10.30am; 15hr); Fortaleza (5 daily; 7hr; R$35–45; expressoguanabara.com.br); Teresina (daily at 10am; 5hr).

ACCOMMODATION

Ubajara is a pleasant place to stay, a small, friendly town nestling in picturesque hills, with a couple of simple but perfectly adequate hotels near the church and quiet square, together with one or two bars and restaurants. The best options, however, lie just outside town.

Neblina Park Estrada do Teleférico 88 3634 1270, neblinaparkhotel.com.br. Standing in splendid isolation at the foot of a hill covered with palm forest, this comfy option has a restaurant and swimming pool, and is remarkable value; you can also camp here. Camping R$30, doubles R$110

Sítio do Alemâo 88 9961 4645, sitio-do-alemao.20fr.com. Spotless German-run hotel (they also speak English) 1.5km from the park entrance, with five cosy chalets set in lush, tropical gardens and banana palms. Taxis should charge around R$20 from Ubajara. Breakfast included. R$70

4

Piauí

Oddly shaped **Piauí**, with a narrow neck of coastline 66km long broadening out inland, is the most typically "Northeastern" state in the region. It has just over three million inhabitants, by far the lowest population density in the Northeast, and remains one of the poorest states in Brazil. There are really only three places worth making for: the pleasant coastal town of **Parnaíba**, which has excellent beaches; the **Parque Nacional de Sete Cidades**, good walking country with weird and striking rock formations; and the **Parque Nacional da Serra da Capivara**, the oldest inhabited prehistoric site found in Brazil with over four hundred archeological sites and the largest concentration of rock paintings in the world. Few travellers spend much time in the capital, **Teresina**, strategically placed for breaking the long bus journey between Fortaleza and São Luís.

Teresina

Brazil's hottest state capital, **TERESINA** sits far inland on the east bank of the Rio Parnaíba, where it bakes year-round in an average temperature of 40°C (which means it regularly gets hotter than that). Founded in 1852, its main claim to fame is being Brazil's first planned city. The rains, meant to arrive in February and last for three or four months, are not to be relied upon – though twice in the last twenty years they have actually flooded the city. Thankfully, given the heat, most of the things worth seeing and doing are reasonably close to each other.

Central de Artesanato Mestre Dezinho

Praça Pedro II (Rua Paissandu 1276) • Mon–Fri 9am–6pm, Sat 9am–3pm • Free • 86 3222 5772

The former headquarters of the military police is now the **Central de Artesanato Mestre Dezinho**, an arts and crafts market showcasing locally made products, especially those made from leather and *buriti* palm.

BUMBA-MEU-BOI

Museu do Piauí

Praça Marechal Deodoro da Fonseca • Tues–Fri 8am–6pm, Sat & Sun 8am–noon • R$2 • ☎ 86 3221 6027

Overlooking the central plaza, the **Museu do Piauí** is housed in the old palace of the state governors, built in 1859. The *palacio* has been beautifully restored, with the exhibits well displayed in simple, elegant rooms, many with high arched windows and balconies perched just above the crowded market stalls. The collection is the usual eclectic mix, and pride of place goes to a collection of early radios, televisions and stereograms, a must for lovers of 1950s and 60s kitsch. There are also fossils as well as fine examples of the two things that distinguish *artesanato* in Piauí: sculpture in *buriti* palm and beautifully tooled leather.

ARRIVAL AND INFORMATION — TERESINA

By plane Teresina airport (☎ 86 3133 6270) lies 3.5km north of the centre via Av Centenário. The terminal contains Banco do Brasil and Bradesco ATMs, a post office and all the major car rental companies. Taxis (Cooperativa Cootaero ☎ 86 3225 2530) charge around R$15 into town.

By bus The rodoviária (☎ 86 3218 1514) is 6km southeast of the city centre. Frequent buses run into the centre (R$2.50), while taxis will cost around R$25 (on the meter).

Destinations Belém (7 daily; 14–15hr); Brasília (3 daily; 25hr); Fortaleza (6 daily; 10hr); Parnaíba (10 daily; 5hr 30min–7hr); Piripiri (20 daily; 3hr 20min); São Luís (10 daily; 6hr 30min–8hr).

Tourist information There's a tourist information post at the rodoviária (Mon–Fri 8am–noon & 2–6pm, Sat 8am–noon; ☎ 86 3216 5510).

ACCOMMODATION AND EATING

Favorito Grill Rua Prof. Mário Batista 69 ☎ 86 3233 3333, ⓦ favoritorestaurante.com.br. *Piauienses* excel at meat (try *paçoca*, prepared with shredded jerky and manioc meal), the best of which can be found at this lively local hangout, which also serves the city's best *feijoada Teresina* every Sat with live samba. Budget for R$50–75/head. Tues–Sun noon–11pm.

Hotel Teresinha Av Getúlio Vargas 2885 ☎ 86 3211 0919. Top budget option in the centre, with no-frills but adequate rooms, with breakfast and satellite TV included, though the white tiling everywhere gives it a bit of an institutional feel. R$100

Luxor Piauí Praça Mal. Deodoro 310 ☎ 86 3131 3000, ⓦ www.luxorpiaui.com.br. Plush business hotel in the city centre overlooking the river, with a restaurant, modern rooms (with cable TV) and a pool. R$210

Restaurante São João Av Nossa Senhora de Fátima 2575. Top local restaurant, best for its high-quality, mouthwatering *carne de sol* served by weight (300g, 500g or 1kg). Daily 5–10pm.

Parnaíba and around

PARNAÍBA, with its attractive natural anchorage on the Rio Igaraçu, was founded in 1761, almost a century before Teresina. For the Portuguese, it was the obvious harbour from which to ship out the dried meat and *carnaúba* (a wax derived from *carnaúba* palm) of the interior and, in the nineteenth century, it was a thriving little settlement;

PREHISTORIC PARK

The prehistoric wonders of the **Parque Nacional da Serra da Capivara** (daily 6am–6pm; ☎ 89 3582 2085) are well off the beaten track, and you really need your own transport to make a trip worthwhile. The park covers an area of over 1000 square kilometres in the southern section of Piauí (530km from Teresina), and contains a mind-boggling ensemble of rare prehistoric cave paintings and petroglyphs (some 657 sites, of which 173 can be visited), with traces of human occupation going back thousands of years. The highlight is the **Boqueirão da Pedra Furada**, a giant hole in the rock, where evidence of humans goes back 48,000 years. Park entry is R$28, plus a fee for guides (mandatory; R$75/day for up to six people). **São Raimundo Nonato** (20km from the park) is the main service town for the region and home to the **Museu do Homem Americano** (Tues–Sun 9am–5pm; R$15; ⓦ fumdham.org.br), an essential first stop. Without a car you'll have to pay a taxi R$150 round-trip to get to the park from here (includes waiting time). Buses link Teresina with São Raimundo four times daily (9–10hr).

you can still see the chimneys of the cotton factories put up by British entrepreneurs a century ago. When the river silted up, the port moved to Luiz Correia at the mouth of the river, and the town slipped into decline. Today, Parnaíba has a lazy feel, but is still the second-largest city in the state, with around 145,000 inhabitants. Located anywhere else, it would be a thriving resort town; the **beaches** nearby are excellent. There's some beach accommodation here, but it's often fully booked at busy times of year. One of the best beaches is close to **Luiz Correia**, a fishing village 8km north of Parnaíba, with a small modern port attached. From here you can either walk or get the bus to the huge and popular **Praia de Atalaia**. At weekends practically the city's entire population decamps here and the crowded bars reverberate to *forró* trios. A less crowded beach, **Coqueiro**, is 12km from here, but there are only a couple of buses there a day.

ARRIVAL AND DEPARTURE — PARNAÍBA

By bus The rodoviária (T 86 3323 7300) is on Av Pinheiro Machado (5km from the centre), with connections to Fortaleza (5 daily; 8–10hr), Teresina (7 daily; 5–7hr) and São Luís (3 daily; 8–9hr). Frequent buses run from here into the centre (R$2.20), while taxis will cost around R$25 (on the meter).

ACCOMMODATION

Casa de Santo Antônio Hotel de Charme Praça Santo Antônio 988 T 86 3322 1900, W mvchoteisdecharme.com.br. This boutique is the best place to stay in town (with prices to match), with luxurious a/c rooms featuring a cool contemporary take on eighteenth-century styles, LED TVs, and cable TV. Wi-Fi **R$347**

Pousada Chalé Suiço Av Pe. Vieira 448, Bairro de Fátima T 86 3321 3026. Decent budget options are thin on the ground in Parnaíba, but this is the best choice, with very small but clean and cosy rooms (a/c but cold showers), pool, breakfast included and helpful owners. Wi-Fi (public areas only) **R$80**

Parque Nacional das Sete Cidades

24km northeast of the town of Piripiri or 190km northeast of Teresina • BR-222 Km 64 • Daily 8am–5pm • Free; guided tours from R$80 on foot (5hr) and R$60 by car (3hr) • T 86 3343 1342

The **Parque Nacional das Sete Cidades** comprises 63 square kilometres of nature reserve that could hardly be more different from the forest reserve of Ubajara, a couple of hundred kilometres east. Here it's the spiky, semi-arid vegetation of the high *sertão* that is preserved – cacti and stubby trees. The really special feature of the park is its eroded **rock formations**, many streaked with prehistoric carvings up to five thousand years old. From the air they look like the ruins of seven towns, hence the name of the area, and their striking shapes have given rise to all sorts of crackpot theories about the area having been a Phoenician outpost in the New World. In fact the rock sculpting is the entirely natural result of erosion by wind and rain.

Despite its good facilities and its position near the main Teresina–Fortaleza highway, not as many people visit the park as you might expect. Consequently, it's the ideal place to get off the beaten track without actually venturing far from civilization.

Exploring the park

Walking in Sete Cidades is not particularly difficult in physical terms, but guides – which you pick up at the visitors' centre 5km beyond the entrance – are mandatory. Prices differ based on time/how many of the seven formations you visit and form of transport (ranging from tours on foot and bike to tours in a 4WD). If biking or walking, bear in mind that the park does get extremely hot; plenty of water is essential. The **rock formations** themselves make very good landmarks and their different shapes have lent them their names: the "Map of Brazil", the "Tortoise", the "Roman Soldier", the "Three Kings", the "Elephant" and so on.

4

ARRIVAL AND INFORMATION

By bus or taxi From Piripiri's main plaza a staff bus leaves at 7am to the park, which visitors can sometimes hitch a lift on. Otherwise you'll have to take a taxi (R$60). From the park entrance it's 5km via unpaved road to the visitors' centre.

Destinations from Piripiri Fortaleza (5 daily; 7–9hr); Parnaíba (6 daily; 3–5hr); Teresina (20 daily; 3hr 20min).

PARQUE NACIONAL DAS SETE CIDADES

ACCOMMODATION

Califórxnia Hotel Rua Dr Antenor de Araújo Freitas 546, Piripiri 86 3276 1645. With the park accommodation currently abandoned, staying in Piripiri is your only option, with this modern hotel one of only a handful of decent places. It's fairly characterless but comfy, with a/c rooms and breakfast included. R$100

Maranhão

Maranhão is where the Northeast and Amazônia collide. Although classed as a Northeastern state by Brazilians, its climate, landscape, history, and capital of **São Luís** are all *amazônico* rather than *nordestino*. Drought is not a problem here; the **climate** is equatorial – humid, hot and very wet indeed. The rainy season peaks from January to April, but most months it rains at least a little, and usually a lot – although only in concentrated, refreshing bouts for most of the year. The **coast** also changes character: the enormous beaches of the Northeast give way, from São Luís westwards, to a bewildering jumble of creeks, river estuaries, mangrove swamps and small islands, interspersed with some of the most remote beaches in Brazil – almost 500km of largely roadless coastline with towns and villages accessible only from the sea. For most travellers there are two primary targets: the dozy, historic and immensely appealing colonial city of **São Luís**, home to the **Bumba-meu-boi** in June, and the wondrous dunes of the **Parque Nacional dos Lençóis**.

4

São Luís

The steamy, tropical capital of Maranhão, **SÃO LUÍS** has the potential to be one of the most compelling destinations in all Brazil, with a gorgeous, albeit half-decayed, colonial heart and an enticing Afro-Brazilian cultural heritage that has spawned the nation's biggest **reggae** scene and the **Bumba-meu-boi** (see page 321). São Luís is far larger than it seems from the compact, crumbling **centro histórico**; built on **Ilha de São Luís** within the larger delta formed by the **Pindaré** and **Itapicuru** rivers, over a million people live here, most of them in sprawling *favelas*. The middle classes tend to live in the high-rises in the beach areas of Ponta da Areia, São Francisco and Olho d'Agua, linked to the rest of the city by a ring road and the bridge across the Rio Anil. The commercial heart of the city lies just to the east of the *centro histórico*, with pedestrianized **Rua Grande** the main drag, running east from elegantly faded Praça João Lisboa – wander up here during the day to get a taste of the city's chaotic, bustling shopping zone.

Yet it's really the *centro histórico* that makes São Luís so special, with its cobbled streets, **azulejos** (see page 316), smattering of museums and the ubiquitous black vultures lurking on tile roofs. Though parts might appear intimidating, exploring is safe enough

THE AZULEJOS OF SÃO LUÍS

On narrow, steep streets leading down to the river you'll see the lovely, glazed-tile frontages, the **azulejos**, which are the signature of São Luís. Salvador has finer individual examples of *azulejo*, but taken as a whole the *azulejos* of colonial São Luís are unmatched for the scale of their use and their abstract beauty – you'll see them plastered all over the old town, in various stages of restoration and decay. Most are early nineteenth century; some, with characteristic mustard-coloured shapes in the glazing, date back to the 1750s. Remarkably, many of the oldest tiles arrived in São Luís by accident, as ballast in cargo ships.

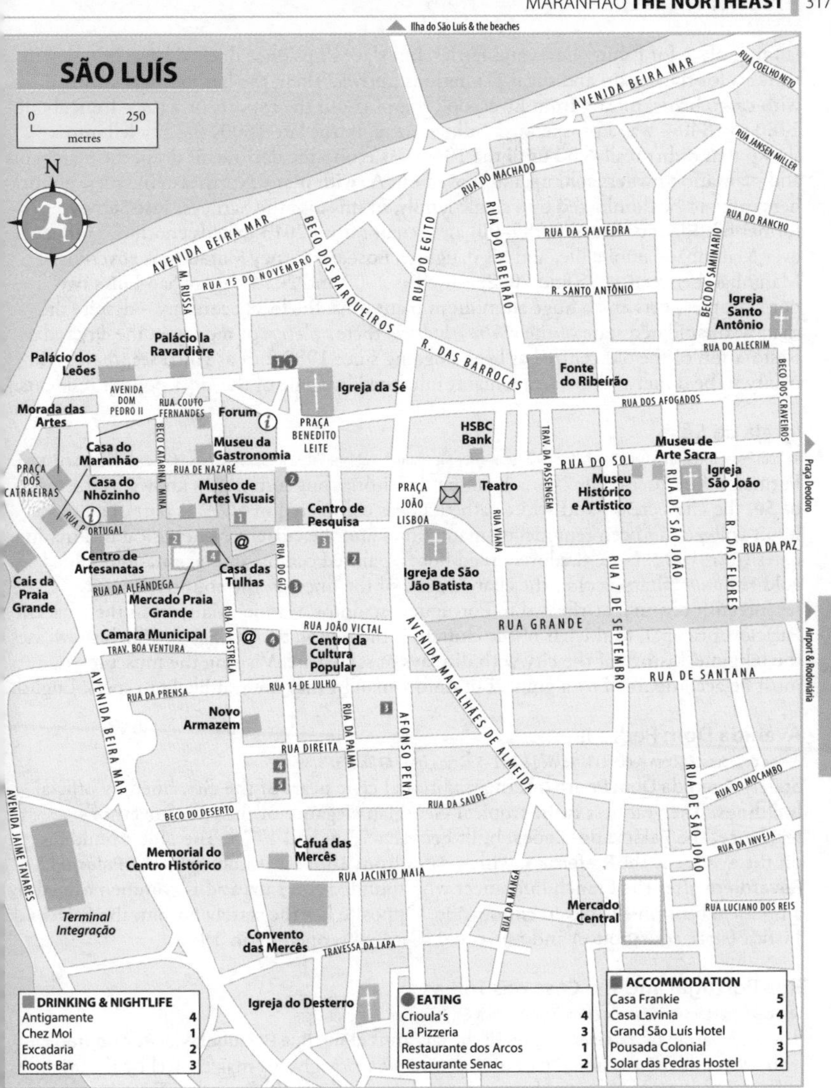

4

during the day, and the similarly intriguing old town of **Alcântara** across the river adds to the appeal. You should also bear in mind that many streets have two names – Rua do Trapiche, for example, is also known as Rua Portugal – and signage is quite poor.

Brief history

São Luís was actually founded by the French in 1612, who managed to hold on to "France Équinoxiale" (little more than a fort) for three years before being kicked out by the Portuguese. The Dutch sacked the city and held the area for three years from 1641, building the small fort that now lies in ruins on a headland between Calhau and Ponta da Areia. Over the next hundred years, the original shacks were replaced by some of the finest colonial buildings in northern Brazil. Now the waterfront is no more than a landing place for fishing boats and ferries, but slave ships once docked here, bringing in workers for the cotton and sugar plantations upriver. Then, the harbour was crowded with cargo boats, mostly from Liverpool, shipping out the exports of what – from about 1780 to 1840 – was a prosperous trading centre. In the late 1800s the city fell into a slump that didn't really end until the 1960s. As economic decline bit deep, the merchant and plantation owners sold up and moved on. As with many Northeastern cities, politics here came to be dominated by a single family, in this case the Sarneys; **José Sarney**, former president of Brazil (1985–90) and senator until 2013, wields enormous influence over Maranhão's public life, and his daughter, **Roseana Sarney Murad**, was governor of Maranhão between 1995 and 2002, as well as 2009 and 2014. Today São Luís's two ports, iron exports and a huge aluminium plant drive the local economy – despite the shabby, dilapidated state of the *centro histórico*, there's plenty of money in the city today. Restoration of the old centre has been ongoing since 1989, but as you'll see, there's still plenty to be done, and the area remains inhabited by some of the city's poorest residents.

Igreja da Sé

Av Dom Pedro II • **Church** Daily 8–11.30am & 2–6pm • Free **Museum** Daily Mon–Sat 9am–5pm • R$2 (guide included and mandatory)

Formally the Catedral de Nossa Senhora da Vitória, but commonly known as the **Igreja da Sé**, the city's cream-and-white cathedral was completed in 1699 as part of an older Jesuit college. It's been remodelled many times and the current Neoclassical incarnation dates from 1922. Note the lovely tiled floors, painted ceiling and ostentatious gilded gold *retábulo* (altarpiece) in the chancel, one of the finest in the country from the seventeenth century, attributed to Portuguese sculptor Manuel Manços. In the adjacent Palácio Episcopal, to the left of the church, is the **Museu de Arte Sacra**, which showcases the religious history of the city with displays of sacred art. Visiting the museum you must be accompanied by a guide, but unfortunately, they are not likely to speak English

Avenida Dom Pedro II

Palácio dos Leões: Av Dom Pedro II • Mon, Wed & Fri 2–5.30pm • Free • ☎ 98 3232 9789

Stately **Avenida Dom Pedro II** is the traditional civic heart of the city, lined by official buildings. The grandest is the tropical Georgian elegance of the state governor's residence, the **Palácio dos Leões**, built between 1766 and 1776. The oldest building on the avenue is the **Prefeitura**, which dates from 1689: it is known as the **Palácio La Ravardière** after the French buccaneer who founded São Luís and is commemorated by a piratical bust on the pavement outside. Opposite lies the stately **Fórum**, the Palácio da Justiça (state courthouse) and not as old as it looks, opening in 1948.

Rua Portugal and the Casa das Tulhas

Casa das Tulhas Largo do Comercio • Mon–Fri 6am–8pm, Sat 6am–6pm, Sun 6am–1pm

The finest array of *azulejos* facades in the city runs along **Rua Portugal** (aka **Rua do Trapiche**). This area is the best-restored part of the *centro histórico*, given a magical feel by the brightly coloured tiles, and has several bars and restaurants and a lively street life. The main focus is the hodgepodge of buildings in the centre of Lago do Comercio that make up **Mercado da Praia Grande**, also known as **Casa das Tulhas** ("Granary House"). This nineteenth-century market (completed in 1861) is now ringed with stalls selling *artesanato*, locally produced foods (such as cachaça, *camarão seco* or dried shrimp, and *tiquira*, the local brandy), quality cotton clothing, hammocks and tablecloths, with a few snack stalls in the centre.

More handicrafts await at the western end of Rua Portugal, near the water, where the **Centro de Artesanatos** (no. 152) occupies the old premises of merchant Adelino Silva, who served as Portuguese consul from 1968 to 1983. Local painters sell their work in the old warehouses nearby, dubbed **Morada das Artes** (Mon–Sat 9am–5pm; free). Opposite is the **Casa do Maranhão**, the vast customs house completed in 1873 and currently closed indefinitely for renovation.

Museu de Artes Visuais

Rua Portugal 273 • Tues–Fri 9am–5pm, Sat & Sun 9am–4pm • R$2.50 • ☎ 98 3218 9938

The city's main art museum, the **Museu de Artes Visuais** begins with a comprehensive survey of Portuguese **azulejos** – panels of all types and patterns from the eighteenth to the twentieth century – and includes a special display on **Catulo da Paixão Cearense**, the poet and musician, who was born in the city in 1863. Two floors of galleries upstairs are dedicated to a mixed bag of paintings and sculpture by local artists, organized by theme – women, landscapes and so on – which make it a lot more digestible. Local painter **Ambrósio Amorim** (1922–2003) features heavily, as does the naïve cityscapes of José Erasmo Campello, and there are portraits of local poet Gonçalves Dias and writer João Francisco Lisboa.

Casa do Nhôzinho

Rua Portugal 185 • Tues–Sun 9am–6pm • Free • ☎ 98 3218 9951

The **Casa do Nhôzinho**, an annexe of the Casa de Cultura Popular (see below), is a large, cellar-like space with wood-beam ceilings and stone floors, housing a collection of model boats and an exhibit on *buriti* palm crafts that segues into a store selling products made by a local cooperative. The centre is named after folksy *buriti* palm sculptor Antônio Bruno Pinto Nogueira (aka Nhôzinho), who died in the city in 1974.

Centro de Pesquisa de História Natural e Arqueologia

Rua do Giz 59 • Mon–Fri 8–11am & 2–4pm • Free • ☎ 98 3218 9906

One of the quirkiest museums in the old centre, the **Centro de Pesquisa de História Natural e Arqueologia** is worth a quick peek, with a slightly tatty dinosaur exhibit downstairs (scale models and fossil finds in Maranhão), and a more interesting, and better maintained, gallery upstairs highlighting pre-Columbian Tupi-Guarani artefacts found in the state. There's also a small room dedicated to the present-day **Ka'apor** and **Canela** indigenous cultures of Maranhão, though English labelling is minimal.

Centro de Cultura Popular (Casa da Festa)

Rua do Giz 221 • Tues–Sun 9am–6pm • Free • ☎ 98 3218 9924

Housed in another atmospheric old mansion, the **Centro de Cultura Popular Domingos Vieira Filho** (aka Casa da Festa) is primarily dedicated to the city's African-influenced religious festivals and rituals, with three levels of displays of costumes, folk art and instruments used for Bumba-meu-boi, candomblé rituals and the like.

Memorial do Centro Histórico

Rua da Estrela 562 • Mon–Fri 9am–6pm • Free • ☎ 98 3231 9075

Housed in the nineteenth-century Solar dos Vasconcelos, the **Memorial do Centro Histórico** boasts a couple of small but interesting exhibits (assuming you can read Portuguese). The first room is dedicated to the restoration of the *centro histórico*, with scale models of the main projects, while the second gallery contains models and information boards about the region's iconic sailing boats – you'll see the real thing in the bay.

Cafuá das Mercês

Rua Jacinto Maia 54 • Mon–Fri 9am–5pm • R$2

Down at the southern end of the *centro histórico*, in one of the scruffier parts of town, lies the tiny **Cafuá das Mercês**, an eighteenth-century "slave house". Slaves who survived the journey across from West Africa were marched up here from the harbour and kept in the holding cells until they could be auctioned off in the small square outside – note the narrow slit windows. Today it contains two small exhibit rooms dedicated to Afro-Brazilian culture with just a handful of displays – the old *pelourinho* (whipping post) in the courtyard outside is a stark reminder of the original purpose of the building.

Convento das Mercês

Rua da Palma 502 • Mon–Fri 8am–7pm, Sat 8am–noon • Free • T 98 3221 3724, W www.fmrb.ma.gov.br

Thanks to the omniscient largesse of the Sarney clan (see page 318), the seventeenth-century **Convento das Mercês**, long abandoned, opened as a lavish art space and museum in 1990, part of the "Fundação José Sarney". In 2009 the complex was handed back to the state, but after a series of ongoing (and confusing) court cases, allegations of corruption and re-launches, the **Fundação da Memória Republicana Brasileira** is running the space, with a permanent multimedia exhibit ("Memória da República Brasileira") on the political history of Brazil, a gallery dedicated to ex-president **José Sarney** (of course) and the official gifts he received during his tenure.

Igreja do Desterro

Largo do Desterro • Mon–Fri 9am–6pm • Free

Many **churches** in the city have exteriors dating from the seventeenth century, though none of the interiors has survived successive restorations. The most beautiful of these is the **Igreja do Desterro**, with its Byzantine onion domes, at the southern end of the *centro histórico*. The first church on this site was built in 1618, but was thoroughly looted by the Dutch. After the whole thing collapsed in 1832, the local Afro-Brazilian community rallied around activist José Lé and rebuilt it.

Museu Histórico e Artistico do Maranhão

Rua do Sol 302 • Tues–Sun 9am–5pm • R$5 • T 98 3218 9920

This intriguing museum (another José Sarney initiative) comprises two parts, the first section offering a glimpse of what life was like during the golden age of São Luís. Housed in the **Solar Gomes do Souza**, a high-ceilinged mansion completed around 1836, the upstairs has been beautifully renovated with period furniture and decorative arts once common here – Chinese porcelain, jade, a ninteenth-century *chocolateira* and plenty of crystal. Look out also for an actual Picasso, *Tauromaquia*, one of his bullfighting series.

Next door, but part of the same complex and entrance fee, the **Museu de Arte Sacra** occupies the Sobrado do Barão de Grajaú, named after owner and politician Carlos Fernandes Ribeiro who was made "baron" in 1884. Inside are some moderately interesting religious artworks from the seventeenth, eighteenth and nineteenth centuries (some of the collection may transfer to the new cathedral museum). As with most museums in town, you'll be chaperoned by enthusiastic guides (Portuguese only).

Ilha do São Luís: the beaches

The north coast of São Luís island is blessed with a chain of excellent **beaches**, most of which can be reached by bus (R$2.10; Sun R$1.05) from the **Terminal de Integração** in the centre of town (you pay as you enter the terminal; bus platforms are clearly labelled with destinations). Though all of them look enticing, there are a few catches: the water around here is not the cleanest, so swimming is not a great idea; the tides can be a real pain – during low tide the water can recede for kilometres; the surf can be dangerous and people drown every month; and swimming after sunset is not a good idea, as there are occasional attacks by sharks attracted by the kitchen waste dumped by ships offshore. Assuming this little list doesn't put you off, all the main beaches can be tranquil places to while away the afternoon on the (usually clean) sands, or to enjoy a cold beer in the ubiquitous beach bars.

Ponta da Areia is the closest beach to the city centre, located by the ruins of the Forte São Marcos, though the water here is polluted. Some 8km out of town, the dune beach of **Calhau** is larger and more scenic (though it tends to be windy and a hangout for kitesurfers); when the tide is out there is a lovely walk along the sands from Ponta da Areia, two hours' leisurely stroll west. After Calhau comes **Olho d'Agua**, 12km out and equally fine, close to the dunes but also windy and well developed with condos and beach kiosks. **Araçagi**, 19km from town, is the loveliest beach of all, an expansive stretch of sand that's also studded with bars and restaurants. It's served by hourly buses, but if you want to make

BUMBA-MEU-BOI

Bumba-meu-boi, which dominates every June in São Luís (generally starting on Santo Antônio's day, **June 13**), is worth making some effort to catch: there's no more atmospheric popular festival in Brazil. A dance with distinctive music, performed by a costumed troupe of characters backed by drummers and brass instruments, it blends the Portuguese, African and Indian influences of both the state and Brazil. It originated on the plantations, and the troupes the *maranhenses* rate highest still come from the old plantation towns of the interior – Axixá, Pinheiro and Pindaré. To mark the day of São João on **June 24**, the interior towns send their bands to São Luís, where at night they sing and dance outside churches and in squares in the centre. Seeing the spectacular dances and costumes, and hearing the spellbindingly powerful music echoing down the colonial streets, is a magical experience. Everything revolves around the **Igreja de São João Batista**, on Rua da Paz, and the **Igreja de Santo Antônio**, four blocks north. Many choose to follow the *bois*, as the troupes are called, through the streets: if you feel less energetic, the best place to see everything is Praça de Santo Antônio, the square in front of the church where all the *bois* converge, in which you can sit and drink between troupes.

Bumba-meu-boi has a stock of characters and re-enacts the story of a plantation owner leaving a bull in the care of a slave, which dies and then magically revives. The bull, black velvet decorated with sequins and a cascade of ribbons, with someone inside whirling it around, is at the centre of a circle of musicians. The songs are belted out, with lyrics declaimed first by a lead caller, backed up only by a mandolin, and then joyously roared out by everyone when the drums and brass come in. *Bumba* drums are unique: hollow, and played by strumming a metal spring inside, they give out a deep, hypnotically powerful backbeat.

Bumba-meu-boi starts late, the troupes not hitting the centre until 11pm at the earliest, but people start congregating, either at the waterfront or in the square, soon after dark. *Bois* don't appear every night, except during the last few days before the 24th: ask at the place where you're staying, as everyone knows when a good *boi* is on. The best day of all is **June 29** (St Peter's Day), when all the *bois* congregate at the Igreja de São Pedro from 10pm until dawn.

it back the same day, you'll need to rent a car. **Raposa**, a simple village on a beach, 30km and an hour away by bus from Praça Deodoro or Rua da Paz, is the end of the line.

São José do Ribamar

The Ilha do São Luís isn't just beaches – the island also supports several thriving fishing ports, the most appealing of which is the relaxed, friendly town of **SÃO JOSÉ DO RIBAMAR**, which you can reach on the bus marked "Ribamar" from Praça Deodoro.

It's 32km to São José, about an hour's drive, a lovely route through thick palm forest and small hills. The bus deposits you in the small town centre, where straggling houses on a headland have sweeping views of a fine bay. São José is an important fishing town, as well as being a centre of skilled boat-building by traditional methods – you can see the yards, with the half-finished ribs of surprisingly large boats, behind the houses running inland from the small landing quay and large beach.

ARRIVAL AND DEPARTURE — SÃO LUÍS

By plane A taxi from the Aeroporto Internacional Marechal Cunha Machado (T 98 3217 6101), to *centro histórico* (14km), is a fixed-rate R$53 (check the current price with the dispatchers outside the terminal). Alternatively, you can catch the bus outside marked "São Cristóvão". All the major car rental companies have desks in the terminal and there are several ATMs (Santander and Banco do Brasil among them).

By bus From the rodoviária, a taxi to the *centro histórico* costs about R$30. Alternatively, local buses (R$2.10) run between the rodoviária and the Terminal de Integração Praia Grande, the bus station by the waterfront in the centre.

Destinations Belém (1–2 daily; 13hr); Brasília (1 daily; 36hr); Fortaleza (3 daily; 18–20hr); Imperatriz (3 daily; 11hr 30min); Parnaíba (3 daily; 8–9hr); Teresina (8 daily; 7hr 30min).

By ferry Passenger ferries to Alcântara (see page 323) depart the Cais da Praia Grande terminal in the centre and cost R$12–14 one-way. Departure times vary according to the tides (which can vary considerably, but there is usually an early departure 6.30–7am and an afternoon ferry

3–4pm – check the day before). Boats usually return to São Luís at 4pm. Four companies share the route, including late Imperador (☎ 98 9105 9301). The crossing is rarely rough but the ferries are little more than ageing fishing boats.

INFORMATION AND GETTING AROUND

Tourist information The availability of the tourist information office at Praça Benedito Leite can be unreliable (usually daily 10am–5pm; ☎ 98 3212 6211). There's also the Secretaria de Turismo at Rua Portugal 165 is (Mon–Sat 8am–7pm & Sun 9am–3pm). Both offices supply similar maps and basic information, but rarely have English-speakers. The kiosk at the airport (☎ 98 3244 4500) is open 24hr (though not always manned).

On foot You shouldn't need to use public transport very much in the old centre: the area of interest is small and most things are within walking distance.

By taxi Radio taxis are available from Coopertaxi (☎ 98 3245 4404) and it won't be more than R$10 around town.

Car rental Localiza (☎ 98 2109 3900).

ACCOMMODATION

Most of the city's luxury hotels lie well outside the centre, near the beaches, but to get a flavour of the city's atmosphere there's no substitute for staying in the *centro histórico*. You should be aware, however, that there are extremely loud reggae nights (normally Wed, Thurs & Fri) here that may keep you awake well into the early hours.

Casa Frankie Rua 28 de Julho 394 (Rua do Giz) ☎ 98 3222 8198, casafrankie.com; map p.317. A beautifully restored colonial mansion in the heart of the old centre, this affordable and well cared for *pousada* offers spacious rooms with desks, wardrobes and dark wooden floors, as well as a tranquil pool area. All rooms come with fan and shared bathrrom. Make sure to chat with owner Frankie and if you're lucky he might take you to Sao Luis coolest and most authentic cachaça shop/bar. Breakfast not included. R$80

Casa Lavinia Rua 28 de Julho 380 (Rua do Giz) ☎ 98 8103 1842, casalavinia.com; map p.317. Gorgeous mid-nineteenth-century colonial mansion with just four romantic suites decked out in period style with four-poster beds, mosquito nets and polished wood floors. R$200

Grand São Luís Hotel Praça Dom Pedro II 299 ☎ 98 2109 3500, grandsaoluis.com.br; map p.317. Comfortable but not as luxurious as it once was, this ageing concrete 1970s throwback is well located in the historic centre but generally cocooned from the noisy party nights. Great views across the river, nice circular pool, cable TV, and strong a/c. Decent restaurant and big buffet breakfast included. R$225

Pousada Colonial Rua Afonso Pena 112 ☎ 98 3232 2834, facebook.com/hpcolonial; map p.317. Finely maintained mansion offering basic rooms (old beds, TV but no cable, slow wi-fi) but good service in pleasant surroundings, close to the historic centre. R$135

Solar das Pedras Hostel Rua da Palma 127 ☎ 98 3232 6694, ajsolardaspedras.com.br; map p.317. Barebones but cheerful youth hostel right in the heart of the action in Praia Grande (in a nineteenth-century home) with tidy dorms and double rooms. Prices for members are R$5–10 lower. Dorms R$40, doubles R$90

EATING

At weekends virtually the entire city moves to the beaches, which are large enough to swallow up the masses without getting too crowded. You will quickly discover one of the delights of this coast: the seafood. The beach stalls do fried fish, the prawns are the size of large fingers, and whatever they don't cook you can buy fresh from a stream of vendors. One thing you won't find outside Maranhão is *cuxá* – a delicious dish made of crushed dried shrimp, garlic and the stewed leaves of two native plants. Another local culinary icon is Guaraná Jesus, a bright pink soft drink produced here since 192[illegible] and now owned by the Coca-Cola Company. Note, however, that the restaurants most fêted by locals tend to be a long way from the centre and hard to reach unless you have a car.

Crioula's Rua do Giz at Rua João Vital ☎ 98 3221 0985; map p.317. Traditional, spacious dinner hall for buffet *por quilo* lunches, with an old-time *maranhense* flavour (as well as *doce de espécie*, the coconut dessert typical of Alcântara). Mon–Sat 11am–3pm & 6–10pm.

La Pizzeria Rua do Giz 129 ☎ 98 3182 8794; map p.317. Brazilian traveller and foreign backpacker fave for dinner, with a friendly vibe, decent thin-crust pizzas and cold beers (mains R$12–30). Daily 6.30pm–midnight.

Restaurante dos Arcos Grand São Luís Hotel, Praça Dom Pedro II 299 ☎ 98 3167 3200, grandsaoluis.com.br; map p.317. Movers and shakers pile in to this hotel restaurant for the excellent lunch buffet (Mon–Fri noon–3pm; R$30); they also serve dinner buffets (Mon–Thurs R$55, Fri R$65) with themes that differ through the week. Daily noon–3pm & 7–10pm.

★ **Restaurante Senac** Rua de Nazaré 242 ☎ 98 319[illegible] 1100, www.ma.senac.br/unidades/restaurante-escola; map p.317. Excellent restaurant that's a training ground for serious apprentice chefs and waiting staff (SENAC is a culinary college). Lunches are buffet-style (you can also opt for à la carte, but it's less value for money), with a vast selection of salads, seafood (including the famous *cuxá* rice), meat and desserts, all for R$42 (all you can eat). It's a bit 1980s, with a live pianist, but great value. Get there early. Dinner is à la carte (mains R$40–116). Mon–Thurs & Sat noon–3pm, Fri noon–3pm & 7–11pm.

DRINKING AND NIGHTLIFE

The largest concentration of clubs and bars is just over the bridge, in the São Francisco suburb – but these are mostly on the tacky side. In the centre, Rua da Estrela is a good bet for music and a drink, and the city's street-bars and cafés burst into life at festival times and on Wednesday to Friday nights, when reggae can blast out till dawn. The most famous reggae bars are out along the beaches.

Antigamente Rua da Estrela 220 ⊕98 232 3964; map p.317. Traditional restaurant and bar with French-influenced menu, an antique-looking interior and chairs outside – a great place to drink and check out the scene. Live *chorinho* (Tues–Sat), as well as MPB, with jazz also on Tuesdays. Mon–Sat 10am–late.

Chez Moi Rua da Estrela 143 ⊕98 3221 5877; map p.317. Big club venue on Fridays, with DJs spinning on the first floor and live Brazilian bands upstairs. Sundays are all about live Brazilian rock. Cover R$15–30. Fri 10pm–4am, Sun 7pm–2am.

Excadaria Rua Portugal 39 ⊕98 8409 5383; map p.317. Weekend party hub, with live samba and *sertanejo*, a cosy bar, potent caipirinhas and well-heeled locals. Fri & Sat 10pm–4am.

Roots Bar Rua da Palma 85 ⊕98 3221 7580; map p.317. One of the predominant, hubs for reggae in the centre, with huge DJ parties every Friday. Wed & Thurs 6pm–2am, Fri 9pm–5am.

DIRECTORY

Internet Try Cyber Café Praia Grande at 48 Rua João Victal (R$2.50/hr, minimum R$1.25); the Poeme-Se bookshop also has a few terminals (R$1/15min; R$4/hr), and there's a basic internet café at Rua de Nazaré 328.

Money and exchange There's an ATM at the HSBC bank on Rua do Sol 105 (ATM daily 6am–10pm). Several branches of Banco do Brasil are located in the centre – Av Dom Pedro II, for example (Mon–Fri 10am–4pm).

Post office The central Correios is at Largo do Carmo (Mon–Fri 8am–5pm).

4

Alcântara

Set in a rich tropical landscape on the other side of the bay from São Luís, **ALCÂNTARA** is now no more than a poor village built around the ruins of what was once the richest town in northern Brazil. Settled briefly in 1613 by the French, the Portuguese formally established Alcântara in 1648, but São Luís had already eclipsed the town by the end of the eighteenth century – for the last two hundred years it has been left to moulder quietly away, and as a result makes an enticing target for a day-trip. Highlights include the walk through overgrown cobbled streets to the central **Praça da Matriz** (aka Praça Gomes de Castro), where you can see the ruins of the Igreja São Matias, the eighteenth-century **Câmara Municipal** (City Hall) and the old *pelourinho* (whipping post). **Rua da Amargura**, one block east of the main plaza, is perhaps the most poignant thoroughfare, once lined with the richest mansions in Brazil, now all ruins. Among the remains are the **Palácio Negro** – the former slave market – as well as the palaces of the imperial barons (Barões) of Pindaré, São Bento, Mearim and Grajaú.

In recent years Alcântara has become famous for being the location of the **Brazilian Space Agency** (Agência Espacial Brasileira; ⊕aeb.gov.br) launch site – Brazil launched its first rocket into space in 2004 and has launched many more since then (mostly for satellites). The site is strictly off limits.

Igreja de Nossa Senhora do Desterro

Rua Barões de São Bento, off Rua das Mercês • Bell shelter open 24hr • Free

From the main pier, narrow **Ladeira do Jacaré** leads up into the town centre towards Rua das Mercês and Praça da Matriz, passing tiny **Igreja das Mercês** (usually closed) and the **Igreja de Nossa Senhora do Desterro** on the way. There's not much to the simple, white Desterro church itself (which dates back to the 1650s), and the real highlight here is the stunning view back across the bay and over to Ilha do Livramento. Look for the small shelter containing two **bells** at the overlook – local tradition claims that if you ring one of the bells three times, your wish will come true.

Igreja São Matias

Praça Matriz

Dominating the languid main plaza, the **Igreja São Matias** is essentially just a ruined facade, standing in the middle of the square like a ghostly outline of a church. Construction began in the mid-1700s, but though it was used for services it was never completed and the church was abandoned in 1884.

Museu Casa Histórica de Alcântara

Praça Matriz 7 • Tues–Fri 9am–3pm, Sat & Sun 9am–1pm • R$3 • ☎ 98 3337 1515

On the main plaza opposite Igreja São Matias, the **Museu Casa Histórica de Alcântara** evokes the life of the rich colonial planters with exhibits and period rooms containing original furnishings (and slave quarters). Portuguese businessman José Maria Correia de Souza built the house itself in the early nineteenth century, a gift for his daughter Mariana and her husband, the noted politician Barão (baron) de São Bento. The views from the second floor are spectacular.

Casa do Divino

Rua Grande 88 • Tues–Sun 9am–3pm • R$1

Rua Grande leads north from Praça Matriz, passing the **Casa do Divino**, a colonial townhouse attractively adorned with *azulejos* (painted tiles). The exhibit inside is dedicated to Alcântara's biggest festival, the **Festa do Divino Espírito Santo**, with displays of objects, altars and instruments used during the celebrations. The festival takes place in the weeks running up to the seventh Sunday after Easter (Pentecost Sunday, usually in May), with exuberant parades that blend Portuguese Catholic and African traditions – local sweets (*doces*) and liquors (*licores*) are dolled out for free at this time. During the celebrations, the Casa do Divino serves as festival headquarters.

Igreja de Nossa Senhora do Carmo

Praça do Carmo (Rua Grande) • Daily 9am–1pm • R$2

At the end of Rua Grande lies the most beautiful church in Alcântara, the simple, twin-towered **Igreja de Nossa Senhora do Carmo**, an all-white Baroque structure built by the Carmelite Order around 1665. The church is one of the few in town to be comprehensively restored and is still an active centre of worship, with a grand altar of gilded carvings, Portuguese tiles, sculptures and side altars. The ruins surrounding the church are all that remain of the **Carmelite convent** established here in the 1640s, and abandoned in 1890.

Casa de Cultura Aeroespacial

Praça Nossa Senhora do Rosário 98 (off Rua Silva Maia) • Tues–Fri 9am–3pm, Sat & Sun 9am–1pm • R$3 • ☎ 98 3216 9263

This small and rather unorganized exhibit, for the moment at least, is the closest you can get to Brazil's space programme, with models of all the rockets launched into space from the nearby Brazilian Space Agency, including some full-size replicas in the gardens outside.

ARRIVAL AND DEPARTURE — ALCÂNTARA

By ferry The only way to reach Alcântara is by passenger ferry from the Cais da Praia Grande terminal in São Luís (see page 321). Day-trips are possible, with boats usually departing 7–8am and returning 3–4pm depending on the tides.

Parque Nacional dos Lençóis

São Luís is the nearest major city to what is arguably one of the most beautiful natural phenomena in Brazil, the wilderness of the **Parque Nacional dos Lençóis**, a desert some 370km to the east covering around 300 square kilometres. What makes it so special is that it is composed of hundreds of massive sand dunes that reach towering heights but are subject to prolonged rainfall. The result is that the dunes are sprinkled with literally hundreds of crystal-clear freshwater lagoons during the rainy season (Feb–May), with two of the largest, Lagoa Azul and Lagoa Bonita, big enough for swimming. The best time to go is between May and August when the water levels are at its highest.

ARRIVAL AND TOURS — PARQUE NACIONAL DOS LENÇÓIS

By bus and boat The main gateway to the park is the small, attractive town of Barreirinhas on the Rio Preguiças, 255km east of São Luís. From São Luís, Cisne Branco (W cisnebrancoturismo.com.br) runs 4 daily buses (6am, 8.45am, 2pm & 7.30pm; 4hr 30min; R$51) to Barreirinhas. From Barreirinhas, it's a 3hr journey down the Rio Preguiças to the dunes themselves, usually on a day-trip to the small village of Atins (R$60); if you hire a boat, expect to pay at least R$300 (1hr 30min).

By 4WD From Barreirinhas you can also hitch a ride on 4WD trucks that usually depart in the mornings (R$25; 2hr). From Barreirinhas it's possible to arrange 4WD transport to Parnaíba (R$650 for up to six people) and 7-day expeditions to Jericoacoara (R$1750/person, minimum two people).

Tours São Paulo Ecoturismo, Av Brasília 108, Barreirinhas (T 98 3349 0079, W saopauloecoturismo.com.br), runs minibus transfers between São Luís and Barreirinhas (daily 7am; 4–5hr; R$50), as well the full array of tours into the park (R$60–100). They can also arrange longer trips to Jericoacoara. Tropical Adventure, Av 31 de Março 15, Barreirinhas (T 98 3349 1987, W tropicaladventure.com.br), offers a similar line-up of services.

ACCOMMODATION

Gran Lençóis Flat Residence Estrada de São Domingos, Barreirinhas T 98 3349 6000, W facebook.com/granlencoisflat. The place to stay for extra comfort near the park, with compact, modern a/c rooms with balcony, a huge pool, sauna and a decent restaurant. (in rooms) R$315

Pousada do Rio Rua Cazuza Ramos 700, Barreirinhas T 98 3349 1255, W pousadadorioma.com.br. Simple but cosy a/c rooms in two blocks with a cool location; the hotel is right on the Rio Preguiça, with hammocks and its own private beach where you can swim. Decent breakfast included. R$270

Pousada Sossego Do Cantinho Rua Principal 2, Barreirinhas T 98 3349 0753, W sossegodocantinho.com.br. Just four stylish chalets with rustic stone floors and wooden furnishings, set in pleasant gardens near the river. LCD satellite TV and breakfast buffet included. Barreirinhas centre is a 5min boat ride from the hotel. R$310

The Amazon

ALTER DO CHÃO

The Amazon

The Amazon is a vast forest – the largest on the planet – and a giant river system. It covers over half of Brazil and a large portion of South America. This forest extends into Brazil's neighbouring countries (Venezuela, Colombia, Peru and Bolivia), where the river itself begins life among thousands of different headwaters. In Brazil only the stretch between Manaus and Belém is actually known as the Rio Amazonas: above Manaus the river is called the Rio Solimões up to the border with Peru, where it once again becomes the Amazonas. It forms by far the biggest river system in the world; eight of the world's twenty longest rivers are in the Amazon basin, along with a fifth of the planet's fresh water.

In its upper reaches, the Rio Solimões from Peru to Manaus is a muddy light brown, but at Manaus it meets the darker flow of the Rio Negro and the two mingle together at the famous "meeting of the waters" to form the Rio Amazonas. There are something like 80,000 square kilometres of **navigable river** in the Amazon system, and the Amazon itself can take ocean-going vessels virtually clean across South America, from the Atlantic coast to Iquitos in Peru.

The Amazon is far more than just a river system. The **rainforest** it sustains is a vitally important cog in the planet's biosphere and covers an area of over six million square kilometres. The rainforest is an enormous carbon sink, and if it burns the implications for global warming – as well as biodiversity – hardly bear thinking about.

Politically divided between the states of Pará and Amapá, the eastern Amazon is essentially a vast area of forest and savannah plains centred on the final 1100km or so of the giant river's course. **Belém**, an Atlantic port near the mouth of the estuary, which has undergone something of an urban renaissance in recent years, is the elegant capital of Pará and a worthwhile place to spend some time. The city overlooks the river and the vast **Ilha do Marajó**, the world's largest maritime-fluvial island, given over mainly to cattle farming, but with some lovely freshwater beaches.

Amapá, a small state on the northern bank of the Amazon opposite Belém, is a poor and little-visited area, although it offers the opportunity of an adventurous overland route to French Guiana and on into Suriname, Guyana and Venezuela. Apart from Belém and the area around it, the most interesting section of the eastern Amazon is the western part

VER-O-PESO MARKET, BELÉM

Highlights

❶ **Jungle river trips** Take in the lush forest scenery, fascinating river settlements and the beautiful sight of the river itself. See page 333

❷ **Ver-o-Peso Market** Belém's traditional market is a great place to watch the local trade, with vendors displaying all manner of goods, including fish, meats, crafts, wicker products and Amazonian herbal remedies. See page 336

❸ **Ilha do Marajó** The world's largest fluvial-maritime island lies at the mouth of the Amazon River and is the only place in the world where police ride buffalo. See page 348

❹ **Alter do Chão** Close to Santarém, this beautiful bay boasts a Caribbean combination of white sand and turquoise water that flows from the river Tapajós. See page 358

❺ **Teatro Amazonas** Built at the height of the rubber boom, this spectacular European opera house is in one of the least likely locations. See page 367

❻ **Amazon wildlife** Make sure to spend at least a few days in the jungle if you want to spot magnificent toucans, alligators and much more. See page 376

❼ **Acre's geoglyphs** Float over the Amazon rainforest in a hot-air balloon and take in the lush vegetation and mysterious geoglyphs from high above. See page 395

HIGHLIGHTS ARE MARKED ON THE MAP ON PAGE 330

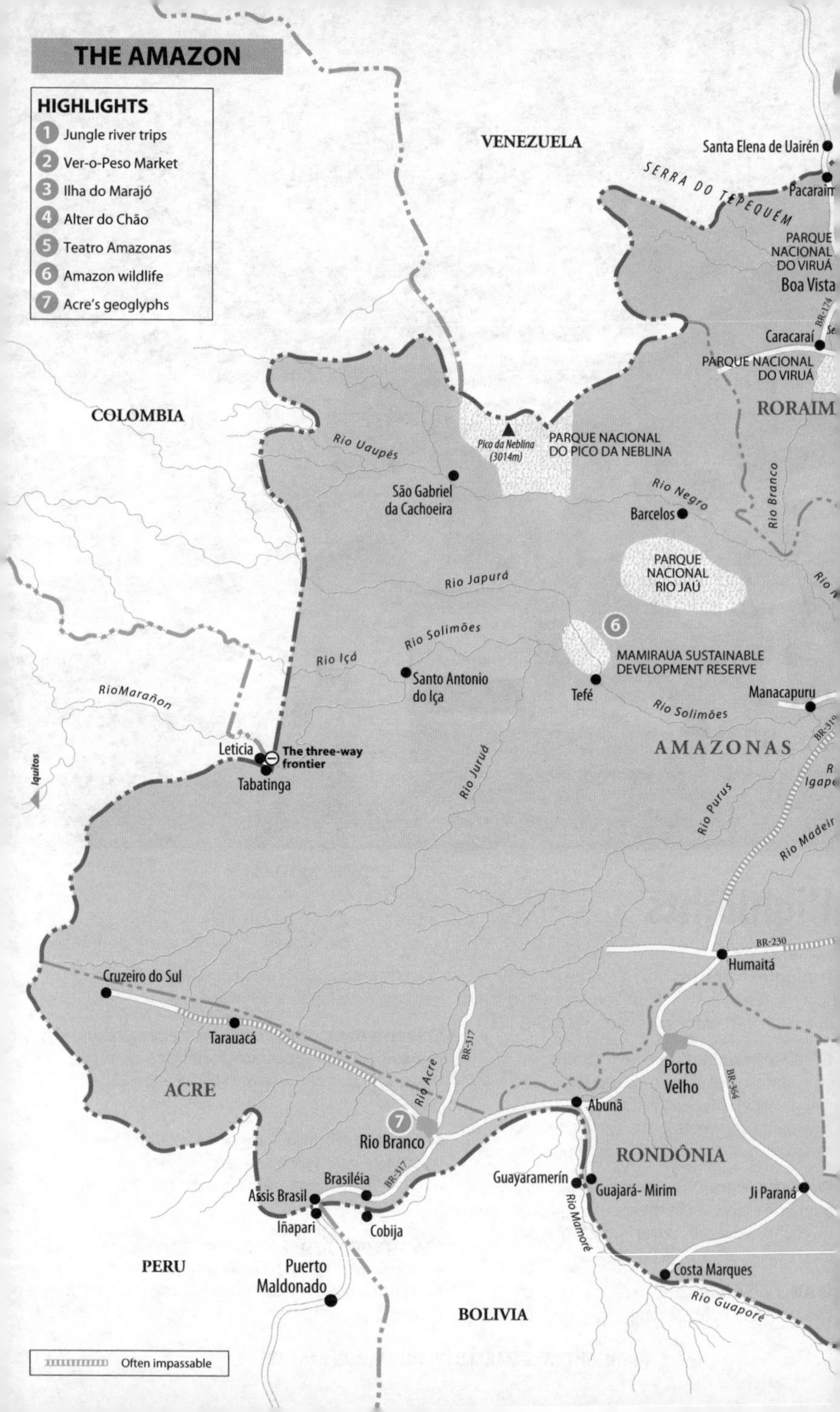

THE AMAZON
HIGHLIGHTS
1 Jungle river trips
2 Ver-o-Peso Market
3 Ilha do Marajó
4 Alter do Chão
5 Teatro Amazonas
6 Amazon wildlife
7 Acre's geoglyphs
VENEZUELA
Santa Elena de Uairén
SERRA DO TEPEQUÉM
Pacaraim
PARQUE NACIONAL DO VIRUÁ
Boa Vista
Caracaraí
PARQUE NACIONAL DO VIRUÁ
RORAIM
COLOMBIA
Pico da Neblina (3014m)
PARQUE NACIONAL DO PICO DA NEBLINA
Rio Uaupés
São Gabriel da Cachoeira
Rio Negro
Barcelos
Rio Branco
PARQUE NACIONAL RIO JAÚ
Rio Japurá
Rio Solimões
MAMIRAUA SUSTAINABLE DEVELOPMENT RESERVE
Rio Içá
Santo Antonio do Iça
Tefé
Manacapuru
RioMarañon
Rio Solimões
AMAZONAS
Leticia
The three-way frontier
Tabatinga
Iquitos
Rio Juruá
Rio Purus
Rio Madeir
BR-230
Humaitá
Cruzeiro do Sul
Tarauacá
BR-317
Rio Acre
Porto Velho
BR-364
ACRE
Abunã
Rio Branco
RONDÔNIA
Brasiléia
BR-317
Guayaramerín
Guajará- Mirim
Ji Paraná
Assis Brasil
Iñapari
Cobija
Rio Mamoré
PERU
Puerto Maldonado
Costa Marques
Rio Guaporé
BOLIVIA
Often impassable

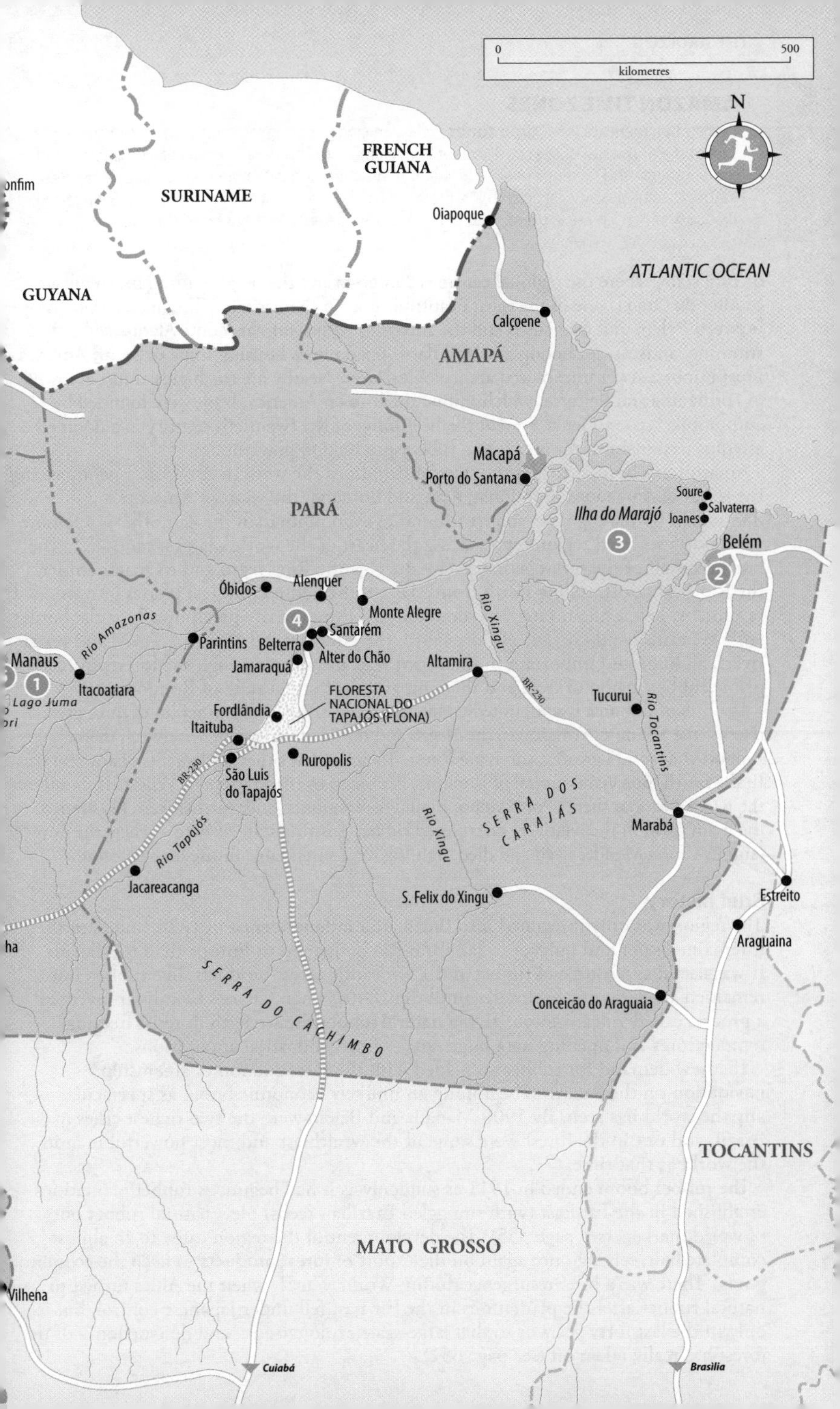

0
500
kilometres
N
FRENCH GUIANA
SURINAME
GUYANA
onfim
Oiapoque
ATLANTIC OCEAN
Calçoene
AMAPÁ
Macapá
Porto do Santana
PARÁ
Soure
Salvaterra
Joanes
Ilha do Marajó
3
Belém
2
Óbidos
Alenquer
Monte Alegre
Rio Xingu
Rio Amazonas
4
Santarém
Parintins
Belterra
Alter do Chão
Manaus
Itacoatiara
1
Lago Juma
Jamaraquá
Altamira
BR-230
Tucurui
Rio Tocantins
FLORESTA NACIONAL DO TAPAJÓS (FLONA)
Fordlândia
Itaituba
Ruropolis
São Luis do Tapajós
BR-230
SERRA DOS CARAJÁS
Rio Xingu
Marabá
Rio Tapajós
Jacareacanga
S. Felix do Xingu
Estreito
Araguaina
SERRA DO CACHIMBO
Conceicão do Araguaia
TOCANTINS
MATO GROSSO
Vilhena
Cuiabá
Brasilia

AMAZON TIME ZONES

Remember, there are three **time zones** in the Amazon region. Belém and eastern Pará are on the same time as the rest of the coast, except from October to February when Bahia and the states of the Southeast and the South switch to "summer time", leaving Belém an hour behind. At the Rio Xingu, about halfway west across Pará, the clocks go back an hour to Manaus time. Tabatinga, Rio Branco and Acre, in the extreme west of the Amazon, are another hour behind again.

of Pará state, where the regional centre is **Santarém** and the neighbouring beach village of **Alter do Chão** is one of the most beautiful spots in the Amazon. The main throughway between Belém and Manaus is still the Amazon, with a stop at **Monte Alegre**, set amid a stunning landscape of floodplains and flat-topped mesas housing some of South America's most important yet unexplored archeological sites. Nearby are the highly unusual towns of **Fordlândia** and **Belterra**, which mimic small-town America; both were founded by automobile tycoon Henry Ford at the beginning of the twentieth century in a doomed attempt to transform the area into a rubber production powerhouse.

An arbitrary border divides the state of Pará from the western Amazon. Encompassing the states of **Amazonas**, **Rondônia**, **Acre** and **Roraima**, the western Amazon is dominated by the big river and its tributaries even more than the east. This is a remote and poorly serviced region representing the heart of the world's largest rainforest. The northern half of the forest is drained by the gigantic Rio Negro and its major affluent, the Rio Branco. Travelling north from Manaus the dense rainforest phases into wooded savannahs, before the mysterious mountains of Roraima rise precipitously at the border with Venezuela and Guyana. To the south, the rarely visited Madeira, Purús and Juruá rivers, all huge and important in their own way, meander through the forests from the prime rubber region of Acre and the rampantly colonized state of Rondônia.

The hub of this area is undoubtedly **Manaus**, more or less at the junction of three great rivers – the Solimões/Amazonas, the Negro and the Madeira – which, between them, support the world's greatest surviving forest. There are few other settlements of any real size. In the north, **Boa Vista**, capital of Roraima, lies on an overland route to Venezuela. South of the Rio Amazonas there's **Porto Velho**, capital of Rondônia, and, further west, **Rio Branco**, the main town in the relatively unexplored rubber-growing state of Acre – where the now famous Chico Mendes lived and died, fighting for a sustainable future for the forest.

Brief history

The region was only integrated into Brazil after **independence** in 1822, and even then it remained safer and quicker to sail from Rio de Janeiro to Europe than to Manaus. It was useful as a source of timber and a few exotic forest products, like rubber, but remained an economic backwater until the 1840s, when Charles Goodyear invented a process called vulcanization, giving **natural rubber** the strength to resist freezing temperatures and opening up a huge range of new industrial applications.

The new demand for rubber coincided with the introduction of **steamship navigation** on the Amazon, beginning an unlikely economic boom as spectacular as any the world has seen. By 1900 Manaus and Belém were the two richest cities in Brazil, and out in the forest were some of the wealthiest and most powerful men in the world at that time.

The rubber boom ended in 1911 as suddenly as it had begun, as rubber plantations established in the Far East (with smuggled Brazilian seeds) blew natural rubber out of world markets (see page 355). The development of the region came to an almost complete halt, relying once again on the export of **forest products** to keep the economy going. There was a brief resurgence during World War II, when the Allies turned to natural rubber after the plantations in the Far East fell under Japanese control, but it is only in the last forty years or so that large-scale exploitation – and destruction – of the forest has really taken off (see page 652).

RIVER JOURNEYS

Any journey up the Rio Amazonas is a serious affair. The river is big and powerful and the boats, in general, are relatively small, top-heavy-looking vessels on two or three levels. As far as **spotting wildlife** goes, there's very little chance of seeing much more than a small range of tropical forest birds – mostly vultures around the refuse tips of the ports en route – and the occasional river dolphin, although your chances increase the smaller the craft you're travelling on, as going upriver the smaller boats tend to hug the riverbanks, bringing the spectacle much closer. Going downstream, however, large and small boats alike tend to cruise with the mid-stream currents, taking advantage of the added power they provide. Whichever boat you travel with, the river is nevertheless a beautiful sight and many of the settlements you pass or moor at are fascinating.

WHAT TO PACK

It's important to **prepare** properly for an Amazon river trip if you want to ensure your comfort and health. The most essential item is a **hammock**, which can be bought cheaply (from about R$40 in the stores and markets of Manaus, Santarém or Belém, plus two lengths of rope (*armador de rede*) to hang it from – hooks may not always be the right interval apart for your size of hammock. All hammock shops sell the ropes and you need to get them at the same time as you buy your hammock. Loose **clothing** is fine during daylight hours but at night you'll need some warmer garments and long sleeves against the chill and the insects. A **blanket** and some **insect repellent** are also recommended. Enough to **drink** (large bottles of mineral water are the best option) and extra **food** – cookies, fruit and the odd tin – to keep you happy for the duration of the voyage may also be a good idea. Virtually all boats now provide mineral water, and the food, often included in the price, has improved on most vessels, but a lot of people still get literally sick of the rice, meat and beans served on board, which is, of course, usually cooked in river water. However, the breakfasts are often delicious, heavy on delicious Brazilian fruits, ham, cheese and coffee. Most of the larger boats also have canteens, which sell snacks, noodles and beer. If all else fails, you can always buy extra provisions in the small ports the boats visit. There are toilets on all boats, though even on the best they can get filthy within a few hours of leaving port. Again, there are exceptions, but it's advisable to take your own roll of **toilet paper** just in case.

BOAT TYPES

There are a few things to bear in mind when choosing **which boat** to travel with, the most important being the size and degree of comfort. The size affects the length of the journey: most small wooden boats take up to seven days to cover Belém to Manaus, and the larger vessels generally make the same journey in five to six days (four to five days downriver).

Better value, and usually more interesting in the degree of contact it affords among tourists, the crew and locals, is the option of taking a **wooden riverboat** carrying both cargo and passengers. There are plenty of these along the waterfront in all the main ports, and it's simply a matter of going down there and establishing which ones are getting ready to go to wherever you are heading, or else enquiring at the ticket offices; these vessels are essentially water-borne buses and stop at most towns along the way. You'll share a deck with scores of other travellers, mostly locals or other Brazilians, which will almost certainly ensure the journey never becomes too monotonous. The most organized of the wooden riverboats are the larger **three-deck vessels**. All of these wooden vessels tend to let passengers stay aboard a night or two before departure and after arrival, which saves on hotel costs, and is handy for travellers on a low budget.

ACCOMMODATION

There's room for debate about whether hammock space is a better bet than a **cabin** (*camarote*), of which there are usually only a few. Though the cabins can be unbearably hot and stuffy during the day, they do offer security for your baggage, as well as some privacy (the cabins are shared, however, with either two or four bunks in each) and, in most cases, your own toilet (which can be a blessing, especially if you're not very well). The hammock areas get extremely crowded, so arrive early and establish your position: the best spots are near the front or the sides for the cooling breezes (it doesn't really matter which side, as the boat will alternate quite freely from one bank of the river to the other), though the bow of the boat can get rather chilly if the weather conditions turn a bit stormy.

GETTING AROUND

BY BOAT

The rivers are the traditional and still dominant means of travel. In the east, further along from Santarém, are the small ports of Parintins and Itacoatiara. The former is home to the internationally known Boi Bumbá festival (see page 357) and the latter has bus connections with Manaus, though the roads are often very hard-going in the rainy season (Dec–April). From Itacoatiara it's a matter of hours till Manaus appears near the confluence of the Negro and Solimões rivers. It takes another five to eight days by slow boat to reach the Peruvian frontier, and even here the river is several kilometres wide and still big enough for ocean-going ships.

BY CAR

For a long time river travel was virtually the only means of getting around the Amazon region, but in the 1960s the **Transamazônica** – Highway BR-230 – was constructed, cutting right across the south of Amazônia and linking the Atlantic coast (via the Belém–Brasília highway) with the Peruvian border. Inaugurated in 1972, it remains an extraordinary piece of engineering, but is now increasingly bedraggled. Lack of money to pay for the stupendous amount of maintenance the network needed has now made much of it impassable. West of Altamira it has practically ceased to exist, apart from the Porto Velho–Rio Branco run and odd stretches where local communities find the road useful and maintain it. The same fate has met other highways like the Santarém–Cuiabá and the Porto Velho–Manaus. With the exception of the Belém–Brasília, Cuiabá–Rio Branco and the Manaus–Boa Vista highway corridors, transport in the Amazon has sensibly reverted to the rivers.

From Manaus Travel is never easy or particularly comfortable in the western Amazon. From Manaus it's possible to go by bus to Venezuela or Boa Vista, which is just twelve hours or so on the tarmacked BR-174 through the stunning tropical forest zone of the Waimiris tribe, with over fifty rickety wooden bridges en route. You can also head east to the Amazon river settlement of Itacoatiara. The BR-319 road from the south bank close to Manaus down to Porto requires 4WD vehicles, having been repossessed by the rains and vegetation for most of its length.

From Porto Velho The Transamazônica continues into Acre from Porto Velho to the quirky town of Rio Branco, from where the BR-317 has been paved all the way to Puerto Maldonado in the Peruvian Amazon, with road links on to Cusco and the Pacific coast beyond. Access is easy from here into Bolivia, too; and, from Porto Velho, the paved BR-364 offers fast roads south to Cuiabá, Mato Grosso, Brasília and the rest of Brazil.

Belém

Although less well known than Manaus, **BELÉM**, the only city in the Amazon that is truly old, has much more to offer: an unspoilt colonial centre, one of Brazil's most distinctive cuisines, a stunning collection of architectural survivals from the rubber boom and, to cap it all, an **urban revitalization** over the last couple of decades that has seen new parks, imaginatively restored historic buildings and leisure complexes transform its centre and riverfront into easily the most attractive city for tourism in the Amazon.

Belém remains the economic centre of the North and the Amazon's main port. The wealth generated by the rubber boom is most evident in the downtown area, where elegant central avenues converge on two luxuriant squares: **Praça da República** and **Praça Batista Campos.** These border the old heart of the city, the harbour and colonial centre – the focus of intensive revitalization efforts in recent years, which have transformed the riverfront into the Amazon's most attractive and interesting urban space.

The first thing visitors will notice, however, is the always hot – and often wet – **climate**, which takes some getting used to by day (at night, however, it's always pleasant). The rain is torrential and the **rainy season** runs from January to May. Fortunately it falls as showers rather than persistent rain, and typically the skies clear after an hour or so of even the most intense downpour. The central zone of the city is lined by **mango trees**, over a century old and proportionately massive, which provide shade and protection from the broiling sun. When strolling around, be sure to do so slowly, and remember mangoes ripen in October – keep half an eye and ear out for falling fruit or you're in for a lump on your head and some intensive shampooing.

Brief history

Founded just a couple of decades later than the colonial cities of the Northeast coast, Belém at its heart looks very much like them, with the obligatory Portuguese fort,

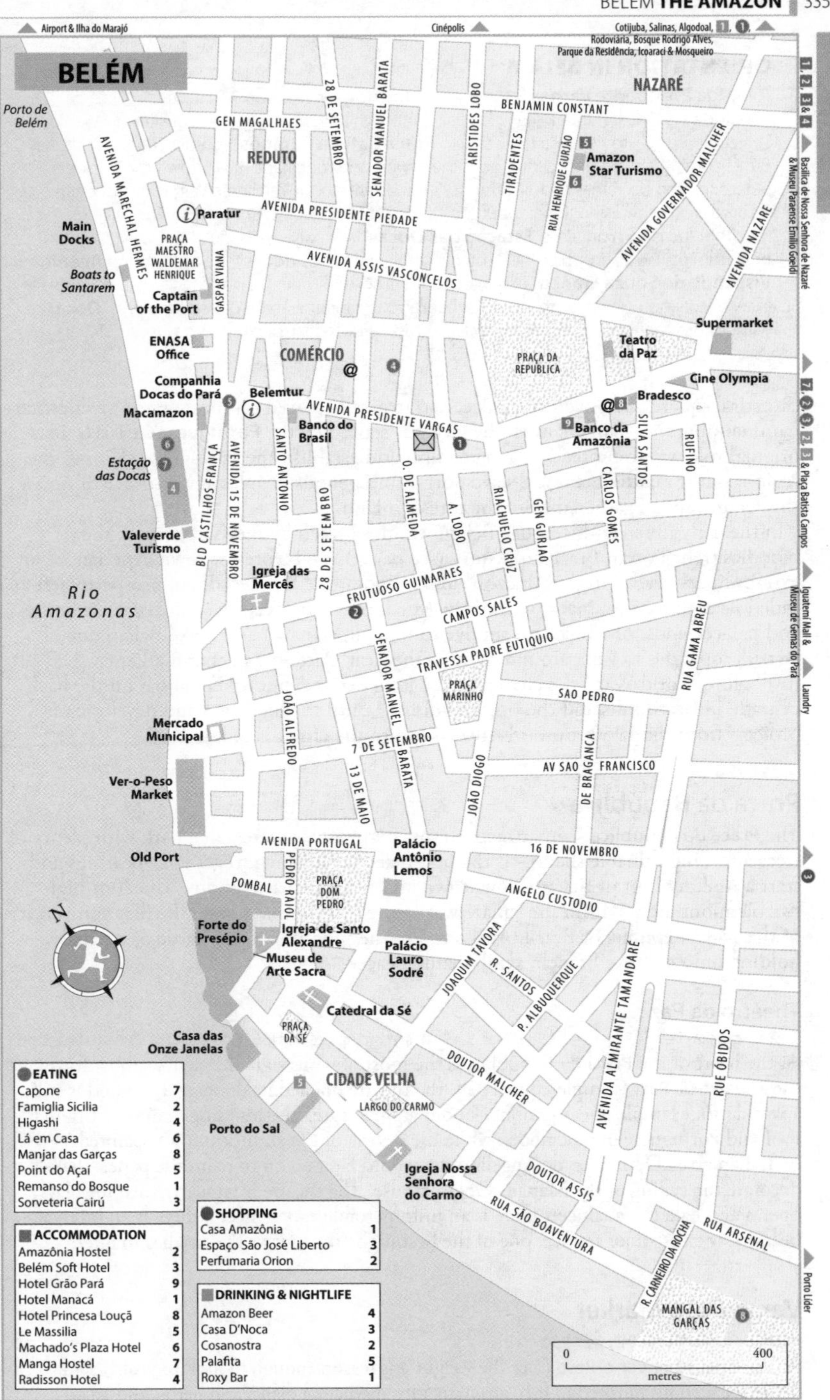
BELÉM
Airport & Ilha do Marajó
Cinépolis
Cotijuba, Salinas, Algodoal, 1, 1, Rodoviária, Bosque Rodrigo Alves, Parque da Residência, Icoaraci & Mosqueiro
NAZARÉ
REDUTO
COMÉRCIO
CIDADE VELHA
Porto de Belém
Main Docks
Boats to Santarem
Captain of the Port
ENASA Office
Companhia Docas do Pará
Macamazon
Estação das Docas
Valeverde Turismo
Rio Amazonas
Paratur
Belemtur
Banco do Brasil
Amazon Star Turismo
Teatro da Paz
Supermarket
Cine Olympia
Bradesco
Banco da Amazônia
PRAÇA DA REPUBLICA
Igreja das Mercês
PRAÇA MARINHO
Mercado Municipal
Ver-o-Peso Market
Old Port
Palácio Antônio Lemos
PRAÇA DOM PEDRO
Forte do Presépio
Igreja de Santo Alexandre
Museu de Arte Sacra
Palácio Lauro Sodré
Catedral da Sé
PRAÇA DA SÉ
Casa das Onze Janelas
Porto do Sal
LARGO DO CARMO
Igreja Nossa Senhora do Carmo
MANGAL DAS GARÇAS
Basílica de Nossa Senhora de Nazaré & Museu Paraense Emílio Goeldi
& Placa Batista Campos
Iguatemi Mall & Museu de Gemas do Pará
Laundry
Porto Líder
PRAÇA MAESTRO WALDEMAR HENRIQUE
GEN MAGALHAES
BENJAMIN CONSTANT
28 DE SETEMBRO
SENADOR MANUEL BARATA
ARISTIDES LOBO
TIRADENTES
RUA HENRIQUE GURJÃO
AVENIDA GOVERNADOR MALCHER
AVENIDA NAZARE
AVENIDA MARECHAL HERMES
AVENIDA PRESIDENTE PIEDADE
AVENIDA ASSIS VASCONCELOS
GASPAR VIANA
AVENIDA PRESIDENTE VARGAS
BLD CASTILHOS FRANÇA
AVENIDA 15 DE NOVEMBRO
SANTO ANTONIO
O. DE ALMEIDA
A. LOBO
RIACHUELO CRUZ
GEN GURJAO
CARLOS GOMES
SILVA SANTOS
RUFINO
FRUTUOSO GUIMARAES
CAMPOS SALES
TRAVESSA PADRE EUTIQUIO
RUA GAMA ABREU
SAO PEDRO
JOÃO ALFREDO
SENADOR MANUEL BARATA
7 DE SETEMBRO
13 DE MAIO
JOÃO DIOGO
DE BRAGANCA
AV SAO FRANCISCO
AVENIDA PORTUGAL
PEDRO RAIOL
POMBAL
16 DE NOVEMBRO
ANGELO CUSTODIO
JOAQUIM TAVORA
R. SANTOS
P. ALBUQUERQUE
AVENIDA ALMIRANTE TAMANDARÉ
RUE ÓBIDOS
DOUTOR MALCHER
DOUTOR ASSIS
RUA SÃO BOAVENTURA
R. CARNEIRO DA ROCHA
RUA ARSENAL
0 400 metres
EATING
Capone 7
Famiglia Sicilia 2
Higashi 4
Lá em Casa 6
Manjar das Garças 8
Point do Açaí 5
Remanso do Bosque 1
Sorveteria Cairú 3
ACCOMMODATION
Amazônia Hostel 2
Belém Soft Hotel 3
Hotel Grão Pará 9
Hotel Manacá 1
Hotel Princesa Louça 8
Le Massilia 5
Machado's Plaza Hotel 6
Manga Hostel 7
Radisson Hotel 4
SHOPPING
Casa Amazônia 1
Espaço São José Liberto 3
Perfumaria Orion 2
DRINKING & NIGHTLIFE
Amazon Beer 4
Casa D'Noca 3
Cosanostra 2
Palafita 5
Roxy Bar 1

5

ORIENTATION IN BELÉM

Avenida Presidente Vargas is the modern town's main axis, running from the Praça da República and the landmark Teatro da Paz right to the riverfront. A short walk down Avenida Serzedelo Correa, to the east, takes you to **Praça Batista Campos**, another central landmark. Buses coming into Belém's centre from the airport and rodoviária travel down the dock road before turning up Vargas. Most of the city's hotels are along Presidente Vargas, or just off it.

There is one confusing thing about the city that's important to understand. The main riverfront focus for nightlife is "**Estação das Docas**" (see page 337). You might want to get a boat from the docks, in which case you need to head for "**as docas**". The area around **Avenida Visconde de Souza Franco**, a couple of streets north of Travessa Benjamin Constant, is also a likely destination, however, thanks to its bars and restaurants. This region is known as "**Docas**", without the definite article, which creates immense potential for confusion with taxi drivers.

cathedral square and governor's palace. Strategically placed on the Amazon river estuary commanding the main channel, the city was settled by the **Portuguese** in 1616. Its original role was to protect the river mouth and establish the Portuguese claim to the region, but it rapidly became a slave port of indigenous peoples and a source of *cacao*, timber and spices gathered from the forests inland.

In the early nineteenth century Belém was devastated by the Cabanagem, the bloodiest rebellion in Brazilian history (see page 339), before the town experienced an extraordinary revival in the Amazon **rubber boom**; the few decades of prosperity left an indelible architectural mark on the city. Much of the proceeds were invested in houses and palaces, most of which still survive (unlike in Manaus) and make Belém one of Brazil's top cities to walk around, despite the heat. After the rubber market crashed just before World War I the city entered a long decline, but it kept afloat on the back of trade in Brazil nuts and the timber industry until the highways and development projects from the 1960s onwards turned it into the city it is today.

Praça da República

The **Praça da República** – an attractive cross between a square and a park with plenty of trees affording valuable shade – is the best place from which to get your bearings and start a walking tour of Belém's downtown and riverfront attractions. The 20m-high marble monument within the square was erected to commemorate the first anniversary of the 1889 Republic of Brazil. At the top of the monument is a statue of a female holding onto an olive branch, symbolizing peace.

Theatro da Paz

Praça da República • Tues–Fri 9am–6pm, Sat 9am–noon, Sun 9–11am • Hourly guided tours R$6 • ☎ 91 4009 8750, Ⓦ theatrodapaz.com.br

At the heart of the Praça da República is the most obvious sign of Belém's rubber fortunes: the **Theatro da Paz**. Completed in 1874, the theatre opened its doors in 1878 and is still a wonderful example of early rubber-boom architecture. The building retains its original roof and Portuguese mosaic floors, while the ceiling of the auditorium was painted by Italian artist Domenico de Angelis, who would later go on to paint the panels that decorate the ceiling of the Manaus Opera House. The theatre is regularly used for plays, operas and ballets – a concert there is an unforgettable experience; if there is an interval, head for the first-floor terrace, one of the best night-time views the city has to offer.

Ver-o-Peso Market

Boulevard Castilhos França • Daily 6am–9:30pm • Free

An essential stop, **Ver-o-Peso** ("see the weight") is reason enough in itself to visit Belém. There are sections devoted to fish, aromatic oils, medicinal plants and herbs, and an expanding sector selling locally produced craft goods. The market is at its most interesting from around 4am, when the boats from the interior start coming in with the two Pará products the city needs above all else: fish and *açaí*, a palm fruit from which one brews a purple mush that is a staple of Amazonian cuisine, and which no self-respecting *paraense* can get through the day without drinking straight, eating mixed with a variety of ingredients or freezing and consuming as ice cream. The fish is either sold right on the dockside or hauled into the cast-iron market overlooking the harbour. (Scots reminded of home are quite right, as the sections were made in Scotland in the 1890s and then assembled here.) The *açaí* comes bundled up in baskets woven from the palm leaves, and is immediately pounced on by traders and customers in a hubbub of shouting and early-morning bustle.

Getting there at a more realistic hour, around 8am, there is still plenty of fish to see in the old market, and stretching beyond it are, in order, an equally fascinating medicinal herbs and spices market, all grown in backyards or fresh from the forest; the colonial customs house, now restored; and a more orthodox market under modern awnings which is a good place to buy hammocks, mosquito nets, football shirts and other necessities.

Mercado Municipal

Boulevard Castilhos França • Mon–Fri 7am–4pm, Sat 8am–1pm • Free

The faded but still impressive wrought-iron entrance to the **Mercado Municipal** is another rubber-boom survival that today displays meats. The iron bars above were added to keep the vultures away from the meat and fish the market sold when it was built.

Estação das Docas

Av Boulevard Castilho s/n • Mon–Sat 10am–late, Sun 9am–late • ⓣ 91 3212 5525, ⓦ estacaodasdocas.com.br

Along the riverfront is the **Estação das Docas**, a row of old warehouses that has been converted into a complex of restaurants, bars, stalls, exhibition spaces, shops and a cinema/theatre, where you can choose between strolling inside in the air conditioning or outside along the river (a great option at night). The designers sensibly kept everything intact and reconditioned it, rather than building anew, so you can still see the old loading cranes, now painted bright yellow. A wonderful touch is the hydraulic loading trolley, which runs beneath the warehouse roof: it has been turned into a moving stage where live music serenades the crowds every night.

Estação das Docas is great at any time of day but comes into its own at night. You can take your pick of a row of restaurants, the music is good, the atmosphere is lively and the river traffic is a constantly fascinating backdrop.

Cidade Velha

Across from Ver-o-Peso in the opposite direction to Estação das Docas is the colonial heart of Belém, **Cidade Velha**. The small Neoclassical building on the water's edge is the

THE SUNDOWNER RIVER CRUISE

It's worth going on the **sundowner river cruise**, which leaves from the Estação das Docas at 5.30pm (Tues–Sun; 1hr 30min; R$50); tickets can be bought from the Valeverde Turismo office (see page 343). It may look like a cheesy tourist thing to be doing – a suspicion not exactly laid to rest by the colossally vulgar boat sporting a large, fibreglass figurehead – but it's wonderful. The city is best seen from the river, the guides are friendly, the tourists are mainly Brazilian and, best surprise of all, the live "regional music and dancing" is in fact genuinely regional and excellent. The boat returns to its starting point ninety minutes later, invariably with most of its passengers dancing. Drinks and light refreshments are served at reasonable prices, with *tacacá* soup (see page 345) the highlight.

old *necrotério*, where dead bodies from villages in the interior without a priest would be landed so they could be given proper burial in the city.

Forte do Presépio

Praça Dom Frei Caetano Brandão • Tues–Fri 10am–6pm, Sat & Sun 10am–2pm • R$2 • ⓣ 91 4009 8828

The bulk of the old Portuguese fort, the **Forte do Presépio**, is mostly mid-eighteenth century, though its earliest parts date from the 1620s. There is a small, very interesting (and air-conditioned) **Museu do Encontro** inside displaying archeological fragments from the pre-colonial period, along with beautiful indigenous ceramics and urns. The most enjoyable thing to do, however, is walk the battlements, with views down to the harbour and across the river.

Praça da Sé

The cathedral square outside the city fort, the **Praça da Sé**, looks very much as it did in the late eighteenth century; it is a wonderful place to sit at night and admire the views before moving on to the many options for eating and drinking in the neighbourhood.

Catedral da Sé

Praça da Sé • Mon 2–9pm, Tues–Fri 7am–8pm, Sat 7–10am & 4–10pm, Sun 6am–noon & 4–8.30pm • Free • ⓣ 91 2121 3722

The mid-eighteenth-century cathedral known universally as the **Catedral da Sé** is the starting point of the Círio procession (see page 341). Its interior is largely Neoclassical, while its Baroque exterior is classically Portuguese (although in fact built by an Italian, Antônio Landí). The nave is lit up by eighteen iron chandeliers and decorated with beautiful nineteenth-century frescoes. With a height of 8m, the cathedral's organ is the largest in Latin America.

Museu de Arte Sacra

Praça Dom Frei Caetano Brandão • Tues–Fri 10am–5pm, Sat & Sun 9am–1pm • R$6 • ⓣ 91 4009 8802

The **Museu de Arte Sacra** is worth visiting for the wonderful **Igreja de Santo Alexandre**, to which it is attached. Belém's first church, it was founded by Jesuits in the seventeenth century and executed with local labour. Over the centuries the church fell into disrepair – the original ceiling has been entirely replaced – with parts of the red cedar interior eaten away by termites. Today, the church has been wonderfully restored and is still hired out for weddings. The museum itself displays religious objects; note the controversial icon of the Virgin Mary breastfeeding baby Jesus.

Casa das Onze Janelas

Praça Dom Frei Caetano Brandão • Art galleries: Tues–Fri 10am–5pm, Sat & Sun 9am–1pm • R$4 • ⓣ 091 4009 8825

Dating from the early eighteenth century, the **Casa das Onze Janelas** was originally the town jail and then an arsenal; today it is a cultural centre, with a couple of contemporary art galleries. There's a marvellous view of the river from a terrace behind the building, a great place to arrive in the late afternoon and watch the sunset over the river.

Palácio Antônio Lemos

Praça Dom Pedro II • Mon–Fri 10am–6pm, Sat & Sun 9am–1pm • Free • ⓣ 91 3114 1026

The **Palácio Antônio Lemos**, finished in the 1890s at the height of the rubber boom, has an elegant blue-and-white Neoclassical colonnaded exterior and a series of airy, arched courtyards that are occasionally used as galleries for travelling exhibitions. Upstairs is the **Salão Nobre**, a huge suite of reception rooms running the entire length of the frontage, featuring crystal chandeliers, beautiful inlaid wooden floors and Art Nouveau furniture. A separate section of the palace houses the **Museu de Arte do Belém**, with a selection of paintings dating back to the eighteenth and nineteenth centuries.

THE CABANAGEM REBELLION

The **Cabanagem Rebellion** ravaged the region around Belém for sixteen months between January 1835 and May 1836, in the uncertain years following Independence and the abdication of Pedro I. What started as a power struggle among Brazil's new rulers rapidly became a revolt of the poor against racial injustice: the *cabanos* were mostly black and indigenous or mixed-race settlers who lived in relative poverty in *cabaña* huts on the flood plains and riverbanks around Belém and on the lower Amazon riverbanks. Following years of unrest, the pent-up hatred of generations burst in August 1835. After days of bloody fighting, the survivors of the Belém authorities fled, leaving the *cabanos* in control. Many of the area's sugar mills and *fazendas* were destroyed, and their white owners put to death. Bands of rebels roamed throughout the region, and in most settlements their arrival was greeted by the non-white populations spontaneously joining their ranks, looting and killing.

The rebellion was doomed almost from the start, however. Although the leaders attempted to form a revolutionary government, they never had any real programme, nor did they succeed in controlling their own followers. A **British ship** became embroiled in the rebellion in October 1835, when it arrived unwittingly with a cargo of arms the authorities had ordered before their hasty departure a couple of months previously. The crew were killed and their cargo confiscated. Five months later, a British naval force arrived demanding compensation from the rebels. The leader of the *cabanos*, Eduardo Angelim, met the British captain and refused any sort of compromise; British trade was now threatened, and the squadron bombarded and blockaded Belém. In May 1836 a force of 2500 Brazilian soldiers under the command of **Francisco d'Andrea** drove the rebels from Belém. Mopping-up operations continued for years, and by the time all isolated pockets of armed resistance had been eradicated, some 30,000 people are estimated to have died – almost a third of the region's population at that time.

Palácio Lauro Sodré

Praça Dom Pedro II • Tues–Fri 10am–6pm, Sat & Sun 10am–2pm • R$2; Tues free • ☎ 91 4009 9831

The dazzling white **Palácio Lauro Sodré** was built in the 1770s by Antônio Landí, a talented émigré Italian who, as an artist, sketched the first scientifically accurate drawings of Amazonian fauna. It was here that the joint Portuguese–Spanish border commissions set out to agree the frontiers of Brazil in colonial times. Pará's independence from Portugal in 1822 and adhesion to the Republic in 1888 were declared from here, and it was on the main staircase that President Lobo de Souza was shot down on January 7, 1835, in the early hours of the Cabanagem Rebellion (see above). The palace later became the centre of days-long street fighting at the rebellion's height, which left hundreds dead.

Today it houses the **Museu do Estado do Pará**, showcasing historical pieces and a small collection of stunning Art Nouveau furniture. It is the building itself, however, that is the real highlight. The reception rooms overlooking the square were rebuilt at the turn of the twentieth century with no expense spared and, perhaps even more than the Manaus opera house, give an idea of what an extraordinary period the rubber boom was.

Largo do Carmo

It's worth taking a stroll around the gorgeous, perfectly preserved **Largo do Carmo**, an eighteenth-century square dominated by the church of the same name, built by Antônio Landí. During the *belle époque* the Largo do Carmo was beautified with pretty mango trees and new paving in an effort to encourage the use of open spaces and emulate a European way of life, where public gardens were a place of distraction and relaxation.

Mangal das Garças

Passagem Carneiro da Rocha • Tues–Sun 9am–6pm • Tickets needed for the aviary, Museum of Navigation, *borboletário* and observation tower, and available from a kiosk at the bottom of the observation tower; combination ticket R$15; individual tickets R$5 • ☎ 91 3242 5052, Ⓦ mangaldasgarcas.com.br • Free parking

Set on the banks of the Guamá River, the park of **Mangal das Garças** is a pleasant spot for a stroll. It is dominated by an **observation tower** with wonderful river and city views from the top. Within its grounds, the **Museum of Navigation** includes miniature models of Amazon boats and displays on boatbuilding. A wooden walkway leads out to a platform over the mudflats, where the combination of shade, river traffic and birdlife is hypnotic. Here there is an **aviary**, home to numerous species of birds, including the spectacular scarlet ibis and pretty tanagers. Nearby the **Borboletário Márcio Ayres** butterfly sanctuary was named after a pioneering Amazonian conservationist who died tragically young of cancer. The air here is cool and comes from pipes high above spraying water droplets to create the humidity and moisture the butterflies need.

São José Liberto

Praça Amazonas • Tues–Sat 9am–6:30pm, Sun 10am–6pm • Free entry to complex; Gemology Museum of Pará R$6 (free on Tuesday) • ⓣ 91 3344 3500, ⓦ saojoseliberto.com.br

Once a church and then the city prison, **São José Liberto**'s often grim history has vanished without trace in an imaginative restoration and conversion: it is now a cultural complex housing an exhibition space, the fascinating **Museu de Gemas do Pará**, and a number of workshops where you can see gem cutters at work and purchase their output directly.

The entrance hall is a modern annexe built onto the colonial core, and has a café. The highlight (apart from the air conditioning) is the stalls selling the best of local handicrafts (see page 345) – most notably the very distinctive tribal-influenced ceramics produced at Icoaraci (see page 346). Buying here will save you a long bus ride, and it's exactly the same stuff (although rather more expensive). The space is also often used for shows and live music performances in the late afternoon and evening, especially at weekends; it's always worth asking if anything is scheduled.

The **gemology museum** and **jewellery workshops** are in the colonial part of the building; the workers ply their trade behind glass walls, for all the world like fish in an aquarium, with a number of bijou shops displaying the finished products nearby. The gemology museum offers a fascinating display of over 4000 precious and semiprecious stones (cut and uncut) in a strongroom; among the highlights is the fossilized trunk of a psaronius tree that dates back approximately 250 million years.

Basílica de Nossa Senhora de Nazaré

Praça Justo Chermont • Mon–Sat Masses 7am–6pm (Sat till 5pm), Sun 6.30am–8pm • Free • ⓣ 91 4009 8400, ⓦ facebook.com/basilicadenazareoficial/

Created in 1908, and supposedly modelled on St Peter's in Rome, the **Basílica de Nossa Senhora de Nazaré** rates – internally at least – as one of the most beautiful churches in South America. It somehow manages to be ornate and simple at the same time, its cruciform structure bearing a fine wooden ceiling and attractive Moorish designs that decorate the sixteen main arches. Most importantly, however, this is home to one of the most revered images in Brazil, the small **Nossa Senhora de Nazaré** statue. There is the usual cluster of legends about the image's miraculous properties, and for *Paraenses* it is something like a combination of patron saint, first port of spiritual help when trouble strikes and symbol of the city. Wherever they are, someone from Belém will do whatever they can to be back in the city in October for Brazil's most spectacular religious festival, the **Círio de Nazaré** (see page 341), when the image is paraded around in front of enormous crowds.

Museu Paraense Emílio Goeldi

Av Governador Magalhães Barata 376 • Wed–Sun 9am–5pm • R$3 • ⓣ 91 3182 3200, ⓦ museu-goeldi.ru

Opened in 1895, the institute for scientific research, or **Museu Paraense Emílio Goeldi**, is more of a botanical garden and a zoo than a museum. The gardens are attractive as

CÍRIO DE NAZARÉ

Círio de Nazaré climaxes on the second Sunday of October, but for weeks beforehand the city is preparing itself for what in Belém is by far the most important time of year. The centre is swept and cleaned, houses and buildings on the image's route (much of the centre of town) are decorated and festooned with bunting and posters in the saint's yellow and white colours, and hotels fill up while anticipation builds. On the **Friday night** before the climax hundreds of thousands of people accompany a cortege with the small Nossa Senhora de Nazaré statue (see page 340) is borne aloft on a flower-covered *palanque* down Avenida Nazaré from the Basílica, through Praça da República to a chapel where it spends the night. It is quite a spectacle; hundreds of thousands of people quietly and in perfect order walking along with the image, residents of buildings applauding and throwing flowers as it passes, with choirs stationed at improvised stages en route serenading it with hymns.

Saturday morning is, in some ways, the visual highlight. The image is put onto a decorated boat for the *procissão fluvial* and sailed around the riverfront, accompanied by dozens of boats full of devotees, so the sailors and riverboats so central to the life of the city get a chance to show their devotion too. This is best seen from the battlements of the fort or the walkway next to it, but get there no later than 10am or the places will be taken. The next part of the festivities is secular; around 1pm a riotous procession dominated by young people, with bands and drummers, wends its way through the Praça da Sé, down Rua Siqueira Mendes, and ends up at the Largo do Carmo, where groups set up on stage and entertain the multitude with excellent regional music until the evening.

Sunday morning is the climax, when the decorated *palanque* makes its way back through the centre of town and up Avenida Nazaré to the Basílica. The crowd tops a million, but is unintimidating: the atmosphere is saturated with devotion and everyone is very orderly – at least away from the cortege. The self-flagellating side of Catholicism is much in evidence: the image is protected on its travels by a thick anchor rope snaking around the cortege, and those with sins to pay for or favours to ask help carry the rope, where the squeeze of bodies is intense – at the end of the day the rope is stained red with blood from the hands of devotees. The especially devout follow the cortege on their hands and knees, with equally bloodstained results after several kilometres of crawling on asphalt. The image is usually back at the Basílica by noon, when families unite for the *Paraense* equivalent of a Thanksgiving or Christmas dinner, with turkey being substituted with *pato no tucupí*, duck in *tucupí* sauce, and *maniçoba*, a fatty, smoky-tasting stew of pork and manioc leaves, which takes days to prepare. All in all, the largest and most spectacular religious festival in Brazil is worth going to some trouble to catch – but be sure to book your hotel well in advance.

well as educational, and any money you spend here also supports a wide programme of research in everything from anthropology to zoology. This is one of only two Brazilian research institutes in the Amazon, and it plays a vital role in developing local expertise.

A small **zoo** is set in the compact, but beautifully laid out, botanical gardens. Tapirs, manatees, big cats, huge alligators, terrapins, electric eels and an incredible selection of birds make this place an important site for anyone interested in the forest, and by Brazilian standards the animals are reasonably kept, too. The aquarium here has 25 species of fish and six species of reptiles, including the *matamata* turtle.

Parque da Residência

The grounds of the leafy **Parque da Residência**, formally the official residence of the governor, have been converted into a small park and cultural centre. This very pleasant spot houses a theatre, where the old governor's limo is displayed in the foyer.

Bosque Rodrigo Alves

Av Almirante Barroso 2453, Bairro do Marco • Tues–Sun 8am–5pm • R$2 • Take the bus from the centre marked "Almirante Barroso" (R$3.10; 30min)

Inspired by Paris's Bois de Boulogne, the **Bosque Rodrigo Alves** is an entire city block of trees as tall as a five-storey building. Though not as domesticated as the botanical

SAFETY IN BELÉM

Belém is not especially dangerous, but the usual cautions apply regarding **security**. Be careful about walking the narrow streets off **Presidente Vargas** around **Praça da República** at night, as it's been a red-light district for centuries. The *Bar do Parque* on the Praça next to the Theatro da Paz is one of the loveliest places to sit and drink a beer in the city, but it's unfortunately infested by pimps, prostitutes and various low-lifes drawn like a magnet by the hope of snaring a rich tourist from the *Hilton* across the road. The whole area around **Ver-o-Peso** market is an essential sight, but keep a sharp eye on your pockets and be careful about cameras and bags. The riverfront street leading down from the **fort** to the harbour is picturesque but to be avoided at night and treated with caution even in daylight. Though bustling during the week, the whole central area empties at **weekends**, when you should not stray off the main streets.

garden, it's well kept and gives you a sample of the jungle around the city. Here you'll be able to stroll along pretty tree-shaded paths flanked by the occasional animal enclosure; you'll find hundreds of turtles, and a café by the side of an artificial lake.

The highlight, however, is without doubt the **Amazon manatee**, the *peixe-boi* (literally, fish-cow, and up close you see why – it's big). These mammals are increasingly rare in the wild. As this is the only chance you will have to see one in the Amazon, the opportunity is not to be missed: they are astonishing creatures, combining breathtaking ugliness with sheer grace as they move through the water. The enclosure at the Bosque includes a bridge built over the water – where manatees graze on aquatic grasses – allowing you within a few metres.

ARRIVAL AND DEPARTURE — BELÉM

By plane Belém international airport is 15km out of town. Regular buses (every 15min; 40min; R$3.10) connect the airport to the city centre. A taxi from the airport costs R$45 (30min).

Destinations Brasília (2 non-stop flights daily; 2hr 30min); Macapá (5 daily; 1hr); Manaus (5 daily; 2hr); Santarém (5 daily; 1hr 30min) and at least once daily to all other major Brazilian cities. TAP has weekly flights from Lisbon to Belém (8hr).

By boat Larger riverboats dock at the Porto de Belém near the town centre, from where you can walk or take a local bus up Av Presidente Vargas (not recommended if you have luggage or if it's late at night), or catch a taxi (R$15). Macamazon, with offices at Boulevard Castilho França 716 (T 91 3222 5604), serves Macapá (Mon 11am, Wed & Thurs noon & Sat 2pm; 24hr; hammock R$60, double cabin R$225); Santarém (Tues–Fri 7pm; 3 days; hammock R$200, double cabin R$800) and Manaus (Tues–Fri 6pm; 5 days; hammock R$250, double cabin R$1050). Tuesday departures to Santarém and Manaus leave from Porto Líder at Bernardo Sayão s/n (best to take a taxi here for R$10; alternatively bus #328 from either the airport or Av Almirante Tamandare), while Wednesday to Friday departures leave from the Porto de Belém (taxi R$5 from centre).

By bus Belém's rodoviária (T 91 3266 2625, W www.rodoviariadebelem.com.br) is in the district of São Bras, about 3km from the centre. There are plenty of bus companies with services to major destinations, including Itapemirim (T 91 3226 3382) with daily buses to Belo Horizonte (41hr; R$391) and São Paulo (49hr; R$449), and Salvador (daily 3pm; 34hr; R$387). Itapemirim and Guanabara (T 91 3323 1992) have daily services to Fortaleza (daily at 7.30am, noon & 1pm; 24hr; R$200). Any bus from the stops opposite the entrance to the rodoviária will take you downtown (R$3.10; 20min). A taxi into town costs roughly R$25.

By car For car rental try Localiza, Av Governador José Malcher 1365 (T 91 3201 1251), also with a kiosk at the airport; or Dallas Rent a Car, Tv Quintino Bocaiuva 1273 (T 91 3182 2237).

INFORMATION AND GETTING AROUND

Tourist offices The friendly state tourism agency Paratur is at Praça Waldemar Henrique (Mon–Fri 8am–5pm T 091 3110 8700); there is also a Paratur window at the airport (daily 8am–6pm; T 91 3210 6330). The municipal Belemtur is on the 13th floor at Av Presidente Vargas 158 (Mon–Fri 8am–4pm; T 091 3230 3926); there are no signs indicating the offices of Belemtur – just walk into the building and take the lift to the 13th floor.

Buses The centre is easily walkable. The Port of Belem, for example, is no more than a 15–20min walk from most points in the centre. Those staying near the bus terminal can take any of the city buses towards Boulevard Shopping (#976, #930, #548, #439), and they will let you out in the city centre's main artery, Av Visc. de Souza Franco.

Taxis A taxi from outside central Belem to the centre should cost no more than R$10. Cooperdoca Rádio Táxi T 91 3241 3555; Águia Rádio Táxi T 91 2764 4000.

TOUR COMPANIES

Amazon Star Turismo Rua Henrique Gurjão 210 ⊙91 3212 6244 or 24hr ⊙9982 7911, ⊕amazonstar.com.br. An excellent French-run agency specializing in ecotourism. Their half-day tour (Mon, Wed, Fri, R$170, min. two people) through the streams of the Rio Guamá includes a short jungle trek and is a great introduction to the Amazon's flora and fauna. Multi-lingual guides are available.

Valeverde Turismo Estação das Docas (⊙91 3218 7333) and at the airport ⊙91 3210 6333, ⊕valeverdeturismo.com.br. A reliable tour company offering city tours and packages to the surrounding area. Both offices offer excursions to Ilha dos Papagaios, an island near Belém where tens of thousands of parrots zoom out of the trees at dawn, an unforgettable sight at R$180 a head, including pick-up from your hotel at 4.30am – it's worth the bleary eyes. Guides speak good German and French, as well as English.

ACCOMMODATION

Amazônia Hostel Av Governador José Malcher 592 ⊕amazoniahostel.com.br; map p.335. Belém's first hostel features beautiful wooden floors and lovely high ceilings. Rooms are set on two floors, with separate male and female dorms with a/c; they're a bit small, but are comfortable, with sturdy bunks and personal lockers. There's a communal chill-out area with TV. Ten percent discounts for HI members. Friendly, helpful staff; but don't expect anyone to respond to emails, and standards have slipped in recent years. Dorms **R$40**, doubles **R$80**

Belém Soft Hotel Av Braz de Aguiar 612 ⊙91 3323 3400, ⊕belemsofthotel.com.br; map p.335. The corridors of this hotel are a bit sterile although the tiled double rooms decked out in a mellow layer of green paint are very clean, with king-sized beds. Accommodation is set on thirteen floors and each a/c room is equipped with fridge, safe and cable TV. **R$165**

Hotel Grão Pará Av Presidente Vargas 718 ⊙91 3321 2121, ⊕hotelgraopara.com.br; map p.335. This excellent-value hotel offers spacious a/c rooms set on fifteen floors with cable TV and fridges. The hotel interior is a bit dull and staff are a little absent-minded but the price doesn't get much better than this. **R$130**

★ **Hotel Manacá** Travessa Quintino Bocaiuva 1645 ⊙91 3222 9224, ⊕manacahotel.com.br; map p.335. A lovely mid-range option in a smart area of town featuring nineteen cosy rooms with wooden decor, which are kept spotless. Breakfast is served by the little pool area, which has a pretty hedged privacy screen and wooden loungers. **R$175**

Hotel Princesa Louçã Av Presidente Vargas 882 ⊙91 4006 7000, ⊕facebook.com/hotelprincesabelem; map p.335. Formerly the *Belém Hilton*, this hotel dominates the Praça da República. It was built in the 1980s, and neither Hilton nor the current owners have updated it much; it still very much retains a feel from bygone days but there's a well-equipped gym and small outdoor pool. **R$250**

Le Massilia Rua Henrique Gurjão 236 ⊙91 3222 2834, ⊕facebook.com/hotellemassilia; map p.335. A little oasis of calm in the middle of the hustle and bustle of Belém, this French owned place is an excellent mid-range choice. Rooms are set around a leafy patio with hammocks, loungers and a pool – perfect for a refreshing dip in Belém's stifling heat. Most of the spacious a/c rooms feature an open brick wall, with larger duplex rooms sleeping three and four set on the first floor. **R$160**

Machado's Plaza Hotel Rua Henrique Gurjão 200 ⊙91 3347 9800, ⊕machadosplazahotel.com.br; map p.335. This functional hotel just off Praça da República is mainly aimed at business travellers. The stairways are brightened up with local Paraense crafts and the a/c rooms are welcoming, with wooden furniture, fridges and TVs. There's a teensy rooftop pool – more of a jacuzzi really. **R$134**

Manga Hostel Av Ceará 290 ⊙91 3347 2800, ⊕mangahostelbelem.com.br; map p.335. New hostel founded in a multi-storey home near the bus station. The facilities are stunning, with modern amenities and features like flat-screen TVs, a/c, an expansive kitchen with bar, outdoor patio and best of all, a swimming pool (the only hostel in Belem that can claim one), perfect to beat Belem's often scorching heat. It's an oasis of calm in an otherwise hectic neighbourhood. Also near to Lider supermarket and ATMs. Dorms **R$55**, doubles **R$125**

★ **Radisson Hotel** Av Comandante Brás de Aguiar 321 ⊙91 3205 1399, ⊕atlanticahotels.com.br; map p.335. The city's best option: the a/c rooms here are spacious and comfortable with modern amenities, and all feature a partitioned work space with desk. There's an inviting rooftop pool with views over the city, along with a gym and large sauna. **R$410**

EATING

Belém is a great place to eat out and get acquainted with the distinctive dishes of the Amazon region (see page 345). **Estação das Docas** and the **Docas** area around Avenida Visconde Souza Franco are good places to start, and they are two of the city's main focuses for nightlife as well. **Street food** is also good, even for those not on a budget: fantastic roast leg of pork sandwiches (*pernil*) can be had from the stall on the corner by the Cine Olimpia, on Praça da República, and for the more adventurous palate, *tacacá* and *açaí* are safe and delicious from the stalls of Dona Miloca, in front of the Goeldi museum, and Maria do Carmo (as well as a few other stalls) in front of the Colégio Nazaré on Avenida Nazaré, just before the Basílica. Other cheap eating options are off **Presidente Vargas** but cater mainly for the lunchtime office crowd.

Capone Estação das Docas, Av Castilhos França ☎91 3212 5566 facebook.com/CaponeRistorante; map p.335. The lunchtime buffet (R$61) at this popular restaurant in the Estação das Docas features local specialities as well as a selection of pastas; you can choose your own pasta sauce, sizzled in front of your very eyes. The evening à la carte menu includes risotto (R$49.90), pizza (R$52) and pasta (R$42). Mon 9am–midnight, Tues 9am–7pm, Wed & Thurs 9am–midnight, Fri & Sat noon–1am, Sun 9am–midnight.

Famiglia Sicilia Av Conselheiro Furtado 1420 ☎91 4008 0001, famigliasicilia.com; map p.335. This popular Italian restaurant features a mezzanine floor that looks over the main dining area, decorated with world clocks and a rather unusual choice of flowery and stripey chairs. The menu includes tasty home-made pastas (RS$54), risottos (RS$88) and meats (R$74). Mon–Sat 6.30pm–midnight.

Higashi Rua Ó de Almeida 509 ☎91 3230 5552; map p.335. This informal restaurant offers a good *por quilo* buffet that includes salmon, shrimp and crab; on the first floor there's an eat-all-you-can buffet (daily except Sat; R$23.49) – there's not as much on offer but it's a bargain for those who arrive with an empty belly. Daily 11am–3pm.

Lá em Casa Estaçao das Docas, Av Castilhos França ☎91 3212 5588, laemcasa.com; map p.335. One of the most popular restaurants in town, offering a lunchtime buffet (S$64; noon–3pm) featuring all manner of regional dishes. In the evenings it's à la carte; try the "*menu Paraense*" (R$35/person or R$69/two) – a perfect introduction to Pará's cuisine – or the *corridinho de peixe* (R$69.90), featuring the very best fish from the Amazon. Mon–Thurs & Sun noon–midnight, Fri & Sat noon–3am.

★ **Manjar das Garças** Mangal das Garças park, Praça Carneiro da Rocha ☎91 3242 1056, manjardasgarcas.com.br; map p.335. This large a/c restaurant with a rustic thatched roof serves excellent regional cuisine and is especially popular over the weekends when families head here for lunch and an afternoon stroll in the park. There's a popular all-you-can-eat lunchtime buffet (R$76) and mellow live music daily. Tues–Sat noon–4pm, 8pm–2am, Sun noon–4pm.

Point do Açaí Boulevard Castilho França 744 ☎91 3212 2168, pointdoacai.net; map p.335. Top up your vitamin count here with *açaí*, the crushed berries of the *açaí* palm tree that are the Amazon's "superfood", rich in all manner of vitamins and antioxidants. Mains are served with a jug of *açaí* – try the *chapa mista paraense* (serves three; R$135), a platter of local fish, meats and vegetables. The *açaí* experience doesn't finish with your meal – you will be presented with a toothbrush with your bill to brush away the berry's deep shade of purple that stains your lips and teeth. Mon & Sun 11am–4pm, Tues–Sat 11am–10.30pm.

Remanso do Bosque Av Rômulo Maiorana 2350 ☎91 3347 2829, restauranteremanso.com.br; map p.335. One of the city's best restaurants offering excellent fish dishes that come grilled, baked or cooked in a wood-fire oven (R$68–132). Meat lovers can go for the pork belly (R$26), and to round off your meal make sure to try the *bolinho de tapioca assado*, a warm tapioca pudding served with ice cream (R$22). Tues–Thurs 11.30am–3pm & 7–10.30pm, Fri & Sat 11.30am–3.30pm & 7.30–11.30pm, Sun 11.30am–3pm.

Sorveteria Cairú Travessa 14 de Março at Gov José Malcher 1570 ☎91 3246 9129; map p.335. This hugely popular ice-cream place offers over many exotic flavours (R$5 per scoop) of regional fruits like *graviola* (soursop), *cupuaçu*, *manga* and the much sought-after *açaí*. Plenty of branches across town, including at the Estação das Docas. Daily 8am–11.45pm.

DRINKING AND NIGHTLIFE

Belém's real **nightlife** rarely begins much before 10 or 11pm, with Estação das Docas and the Docas area around Visconde de Souza Franco being the main focus in the centre.

Amazon Beer Estação das Docas, Av Castilhos França ☎91 3039 1456, amazonbeer.com.br; map p.335. This microbrewery at the Estação das Docas offers seven types of locally brewed beer (starting at R$6.60) to be enjoyed with the place's famed pork banger (*linguiça de metro*; R$36), which is one metre long. Mon–Thurs 5pm–midnight, Fri 5pm–2am, Sat noon–2am, Sun noon–midnight.

Casa D'Noca Travessa 9 de Janeiro 1677 ☎91 3229 1792, facebook.com/casadnoca; map p.335. A great spot for some Brazilian live music – mainly samba. Bands take centre stage daily and crowds spill onto the dance floor; there's also an outdoor area to enjoy a drink or two. Wed & Thurs 6pm–midnight, Fri 6pm–2am, Sat noon–2am, Sun noon–midnight.

Cosanostra Travessa Benjamin Constant 1499 ☎91 3241 1068; map p.335. With a bit of an English pub feel to it, this dimly lit drinking hole attracts Belém's bohemians who meet here over beers (R$6.50) and gin and tonics (R$12) until the wee hours. Grub is ordered at the bar. Mon–Sat noon–3am.

Palafita Rua Siqueira Mendes 264 ☎91 3212 6302; map p.335. Located on the riverfront, this rustic bar on stilts is a good spot for a late afternoon caipirinha (R$6) as you watch the sun set; it's also worth heading here for the

AMAZON CUISINE

As you might expect from the richest freshwater ecosystem in the world, **fish** takes pride of place in **Amazonian cooking**, and you'll come across dozens of species. There are many kinds of huge, almost boneless fish, including *pirarucu*, *tambaqui* and *filhote*, which come in dense slabs sometimes more like meat, and are delicious grilled over charcoal. Smaller, bonier fish, such as *surubim*, *curimatã*, *jaraqui*, *acari* and *tucunaré*, can be just as succulent, the latter similar to a large tasty mullet. Fish in the Amazon is commonly just barbecued or fried; its freshness and flavour need little help. It's also served *no escabeche* (in a tomato sauce), *a leite de coco* (cooked in coconut milk) or stewed in *tucupí*.

The other staple food in Amazônia is **manioc**. *Farinha*, a manioc flour consumed throughout Brazil, is supplied at the table in granulated form – in texture akin to gravel – for mixing with the meat or fish juices with most meals, and is even added to coffee. Less bland and more filling, manioc is also eaten throughout Amazônia on its own or as a side dish, either boiled or fried (known as *macaxeira* in Manaus and western Amazônia, or *mandioca* elsewhere). A more exciting form of manioc, **tucupí**, is produced from its fermented juices. This delicious sauce can be used to stew fish in or to make *pato no tucupí* (duck stewed in *tucupí*). Manioc juice is also used to make *beiju* (pancakes) and *doce de tapioca*, a tasty cinnamon-flavoured tapioca pudding. A gloopy, translucent manioc sauce also forms the basis of one of Amazônia's most distinctive dishes, *tacacá*, a shrimp soup gulped from a gourd bowl and sold everywhere from chichi restaurants to street corners. Other typical regional dishes include *maniçoba*, pieces of meat and sausage stewed with manioc leaves, and *vatapá*, a North Brazil version of the Bahian shrimp dish.

Finally, no stay in the Amazon would be complete without sampling the remarkable variety of **tropical fruits** the region has to offer, which form the basis for a mouthwatering array of *sucos* and ice creams. Most have no English or even Portuguese translations. Palm fruits are among the most common; you are bound to come across *açaí*, a deep purple pulp mixed with water and drunk straight, with added sugar, with tapioca or thickened with *farinha* and eaten. Other palm fruits include *taperebá*, which makes a delicious *suco*, *bacuri* and *buriti*. Also good, especially as *sucos* or ice cream, is *acerola* (originally it came over with the first Japanese settlers in the 1920s, although Amazonians swear it is regional), *peroba*, *graviola*, *ata* (also called *fruta de conde*) and, most exotic of all, *cupuaçú*, which looks like an elongated brown coconut and floods your palate with the tropical taste to end all tropical tastes.

good regional food (mains R$35) that on weekends can be enjoyed to the sound of live *carimbó*, *forró* and pop-rock bands. Tues–Sun noon–midnight.

★ **Roxy Bar** Av Senador Lemos 231 ⓣ 91 3224 4514, ⓦ roxybar.com.br; map p.335. Attracting well-heeled Belenenses, the queue at this hugely popular joint forms way before the doors even open and you'll always see eager customers outside waiting to be seated. The trendy interior features bare brick walls, funky paintings and a fun menu with dishes named after famous movie stars. Mains R$45. Also has a location at Shopping Bosque Grão-Pará near the airport. Daily 7pm–12.30am (Fri & Sat until 3am).

CINEMAS

Cine Olympia Av Presidente Vargas 918 ⓣ 91 3230 5380, ⓦ facebook.com/cineolympiabelem. Run by the local government, Belém's oldest cinema screens art-house movies and foreign films. Entry is free. Screenings usually at 6pm.

Cinépolis Boulevard Shopping Av Visconde de Souza Franco 776 ⓣ 91 3241 4045, ⓦ cinepolis.com.br. Within the Boulevard Shopping Centre, this cinema shows the latest blockbuster movies.

SHOPPING

Belém is one of the best places in the world to buy **hammocks** (essential if you are about to go upriver) – look in the street markets between Av Presidente Vargas and Ver-o-Peso, starting in Rua Santo Antônio.

Casa Amazônia Av Presidente Vargas 512 ⓣ 91 9144 7317; map p.335. This small shop has a decent selection of local crafts on offer. Mon–Fri 8am–5pm, Sat 8am–noon.

Espaço São José Liberto Praça Amazonas ⓣ 91 3344 3500, ⓦ saojoseliberto.com.br; map p.335. Within the complex of São José Liberto (see page 340) there are stalls displaying all manner of arts and crafts from all over Pará, including ceramics, traditional handicrafts, adornments, woven objects, aromatic herbs and regional liqueurs. Tues–Sat 9am–6.30pm, Sun 10am–6pm.

Perfumaria Orion Tv Frutuoso Guimarães 270 ⓣ 91 3241 3726 ⓦ perfumariaorion.com.br; map p.335. This tiny place produces and sells a wide range of rainforest oils, scents and cosmetic products. Mon–Fri 8am–6pm, Sat 8am–noon.

5

DIRECTORY

Hospital Hospital Guadalupe, Rua Arciprestes Manoel Teodoro 734 (☎ 91 4005 9877).

Internet Servicos E Solucões, Av Presidente Vargas 144 (Mon–Sat 8am–6pm; R$5/hr; ☎ 91 3222 0350);

Laundry Lav & Lev Travessa Dr Moraes 576 (Mon–Sat 8am–6pm; wash R$15, dry R$15; ☎ 91 3223 7247).

Money and exchange Banco da Amazônia, Av Presidente Vargas 800; Bradesco, Av Presidente Varga 988; Banco do Brasil, 2nd floor, Av Presidente Vargas 248 There are also a number of ATMs in the Estação das Docas Many of the larger shops, travel agents and hotels wi change dollars.

Post office The central post office (Mon–Fri 9am–5pm) i at Av Presidente Vargas 498.

Around Belém

There are interesting places around Belém, although you should mostly resist the temptation to swim at the river beaches anywhere close to the city. The locals, indifferent to high faecal counts, regularly do, but it plays havoc with the unaccustomed. The best bet for a day at the beach, if a day is all you have, is **Mosqueiro**. If you have longer, head for the altogether more enticing destinations of **Algodoal** and **Marajó** – further afield but worth the effort.

Icoaraci

The easiest of the beaches to reach from Belém is **ICOARACI**, with local buses from anywhere downtown taking about an hour. Walk towards the river from the bus terminus and you'll hit the two things that make the trip worthwhile. One is the **ceramic workshops** on the paved and reconditioned riverfront, which sell distinctive pottery based on the ancient designs of the local indigenous tribes. The skill involved in shaping, engraving, painting and firing these pots is remarkable. Some of the ceramics are very large and, except to the expert eye, barely distinguishable from the relics in the Goeldi museum. They are cheap and the shops are used to crating things up for travellers; for a little extra they will deliver to your hotel the following day.

ARRIVAL AND DEPARTURE — ICOARACI

By bus Regular buses connect Belém's city centre to Icoaraci (every 15min; 1hr; R$13.50).

EATING

★ **Na Telha** Rua Siqueira Mendes 263 ☎ 91 3227 0853. It's worth heading to Icoaraci to sample the mouthwatering fresh and seafood dishes served in *telhas* (casseroles) at this long-standing favourite. The menu includes a selection of *os mais pedidos*, the most popular dishes (around R$85) – you won't go wrong with any of these. Dishes are big enough for two, and try if you can to get there during the week, since it's packed at the weekend. Mon–Fri 11am–4pm & 6–11pm, Sat until 11am–3pm, 7.30–10pm, Sun 11am–3pm.

Mosqueiro

MOSQUEIRO, some 70km east of Belém, is actually an island but well connected to Belém by a good road and bridge; the ride is pleasant, and a fine opportunity to see the country beyond the city. Unfortunately, the beaches close to the town are picturesque but too dirty to swim at, and you need to take a local bus from the main square to the best option, **Praia do Paraíso**, about half an hour away. Stay on the bus until the end of the line and you'll find yourself at a gorgeous headland, with a hotel behind you and a clean, swimmable beach in front.

ARRIVAL AND DEPARTURE — MOSQUEIRO

By bus Regular buses from Belém's rodoviária make the journey to Mosqueiro (every 30min; 2hr; R$12).

5

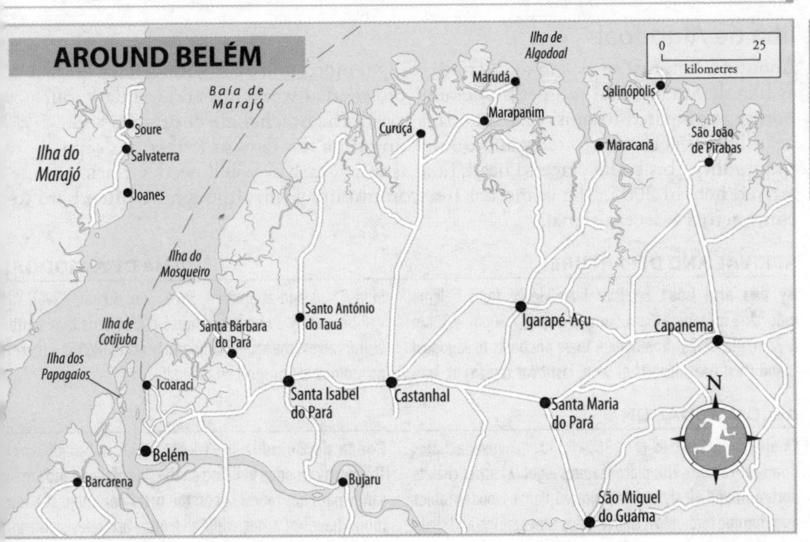

ACCOMMODATION AND EATING

Hotel Fazenda Paraíso Praia do Paraíso ⊕91 3618 2022, ⊕hotelfazendaparaiso.com.br. Located on Praia do Paraiso, this hotel restaurant with tables spilling onto a sunny stretch of beach also offers seating in a shaded area that is complemented by a refreshing sea breeze. The speciality here is pan-fried fish – try the *pescador na telha (*R$85), large enough for three to four people. Accommodation is either in neat and tidy small doubles or in 22 clean and colourful chalets sleeping three, four and eight, with some giving onto the pool area. Mon–Thurs 8am–7pm, Fri 8am–10.30pm, Sat & Sun 8am–11.30pm. **R$230**

Ilha de Cotijuba

Just 18km northeast of Belém, the haven of **Ilha de Cotijuba** is replete with beautiful beaches, rainforest and access to *igarapé* creeks. It's the perfect place for birdwatching and nature walks. In 1990 the island was made an Environmental Protection Area, encouraging conservation efforts and prohibiting motorized vehicles. The island's communities subsist on fishing, agriculture and tourism.

ARRIVAL AND DEPARTURE — COTIJUBA

By boat There are regular boats from the port of Icoaraci to Cotijuba (hourly; 45min; R$5).

Salinas

Located 240km east of Belém, **SALINAS** is one of Pará's most visited beach resorts. There are two beaches here: Praia Masarico and Praia Atalaia. The former is rather built up, while the latter is considered to be one of the state's nicest stretches of coast. The beaches here have fine white sand and green-grey waters because of the sediment carried by the Amazon River.

ARRIVAL AND DEPARTURE — SALINAS

By bus There are regular bus services running to Salinas that leave from outside Belém's rodoviária (daily 6.30am, 9am, 1pm, 4.15pm & 6pm; 4hr; R$25).

5

Ilha de Algodoal

About 160km east of Belém and wonderfully remote, **Ilha de Algodoal** (also known as Ilha de Maiandeua) can get moderately crowded at weekends and holidays, but nothing compared to most places on this coast. The beaches are enormous and beautiful. If you want to relax and do nothing for a few days or longer in sleepy tranquillity, this is the place to head.Take as much cash as you'll need; electricity only arrived here in 2005. The island has free community wi-fi, although it's often hard to come across a decent signal.

ARRIVAL AND DEPARTURE — ILHA DE ALGODOAL

By bus and boat Excelsior buses leave from Belém's rodoviária to Marudá (6am, 9am, 12.30pm, 2.30pm, 4.30pm & 7pm; 4hr; R$25) from where there are boats to Algodoal island (first boat departs at 9am, last boat returns at 3pm Mon–Thurs and at 5pm Fri, Sat & Sun; 40min; R$10). You will be met by a number of horse-pulled carts that shuttle visitors across the sandy paths and beaches (R$15) – there is no motorized transport on the island.

ACCOMMODATION

Chalês do Atlântico 91 3854 1130, pousadachalesdoatlantico.com. This place features eight colourful chalets dotted around a leafy area with potted plants, wooden tables and chirping birds. Most chalets have a mezzanine and sleep up to four; some are nicer than others so take a look at a few before settling in. There are also four welcoming doubles and a small restaurant serving local dishes. **R$150**

Ponta do Boiador 91 9811 5622, boiador.com. This pretty wooden building on the side of the island's main sandy path has rooms set on the first floor; more spacious rooms have hot water, while all feature a/c, television and a small balcony with hammock and sea views. There's a large breezy area with deckchairs looking directly onto a lovely stretch of beach. **R$240**

Ilha do Marajó

The **Ilha do Marajó** is a vast, 40,000-square-kilometre island of largely uninhabited mangrove swamps and beaches in the Amazon river delta opposite Belém. Roughly the size of Switzerland, it is by some way the largest river island in the world. Created by the accretion of silt and sand over millions of years, it's a wet and marshy area. The western half is covered in thick jungle, the east is flat savannah; it's swampy in the wet season (Jan–June) and brown and firm in the dry season (June–Dec). Originally inhabited by the Marajoara, famed for their ceramics, these days the savannah is dominated by *fazendas* where water buffalo are ranched; over 500,000 of them roam the island, and supplying meat and hides to Belém is Marajó's main trade. Among the most spectacular sights are the flocks of scarlet ibis (*guará*), which can vary in colour from flamingo pink to blood red. Common on Marajó but an endangered species in the rest of Brazil, they are born white – it is the red crabs they eat that turn their feathers red over time. Marajó has beautiful sandy **beaches**, and it's become a popular option for Brazilian sunseekers and ecotourists alike. On all beaches, be mindful of **stingrays** – they are particularly common on Marajó. Stick to places with waves and moving water, and avoid wading in rivers and streams.

Brief history

Although it was settled by Jesuits in the seventeenth century, Marajó's earliest inhabitants left behind thousand-year-old burial mounds, in which many examples of distinctive Marajó pottery were found. The most spectacular are large funeral urns, decorated with geometric engravings and painted designs – the best examples are in the Museu Goeldi in Belém (see page 340). When the Jesuits established their cattle ranches, the island was inhabited by the Aurá, who lasted no more than a few decades; later its vast expanses offered haven to runaway slaves and to refugee indigenous peoples who wanted to trade with Belém without too much direct interference from white settlers. Water buffalo, ideally suited to the marshy local conditions, were imported from India during the rubber boom – or, if you believe local legend, were part of a French cargo bound for Guiana and escaped when the ship sank. River navigation around Marajó is still tricky, the course of the channels constantly altered by the ebb and flow of the ocean tides.

Salvaterra

The first town you come across upon alighting the ferry to Ilha do Marajó is **SALVATERRA**. The town itself doesn't offer much to visitors, although just outside town is Praia Grande, the island's longest stretch of freshwater beach. Buffalo roam the surrounding countryside, characterized by large tracts of boggy fields. Salvaterra is a major fruit-growing region – its pineapples are said to be among the sweetest in the country.

Joanes

The sleepy town of **JOANES** is the perfect spot to head to if you want to get away from it all – there's a wonderful 2km stretch of beach just by the town's only hotel. In the seventeenth century Jesuits settled in Joanes to evangelize the island's indigenous peoples – you can still see the ruins of a seventeenth-century Jesuit church here.

Soure

The largest town on the island is **SOURE**, where most visitors head for at first. It is home to pleasant beaches where you can relax under the shade of ancient mango trees. The town is linked to Salvaterra and Joanes, on the other side of the estuary, by a regular ferry service. One of the best beaches on the island is Praia do Pesqueiro, about 8km from Soure – a lovely wild stretch of coast with a handful of restaurants that make for a perfect lunch spot.

ARRIVAL AND GETTING AROUND — ILHA DO MARAJÓ

By boat From Belém's Terminal Hidroviário on Av Marechal Hermes there are daily fast boats (1hr 30min) and slow boats (3hr) to Ponto de Camará on Ilha do Marajó (slow boat 6.30am, 2.30pm, fast boat 2pm; slow boat returning 6.30am & 3pm, fast boat at 7am; R$25–35). Additional departures are occasionally added on holidays and at weekends. At Ponto de Camará buses to Salvaterra (30min; RS$8), Joanes (20min; R$10) and Soure (40min; R$12) meet the boats, although your best bet is to contact Edgar Augusto who can organize pick-up in a comfortable a/c van and will drop you off at your hotel (T 91 3741 1441, E edgar-transporte@hotmail.com).

By car If you're travelling by car you'll need to catch a ferry boat (T 91 3246 7472, W henvil.com.br) from Porto de Icoaraci, 13km from Belém. Ferries leave daily from Porto de Icoariaci for Ponto de Camará on Ilha do Marajó (check timetable in advance, generally: Tues, Fri & Sat 7am on, returning at 4pm; Mon, Tues, Wed, Thurs, Sat, Sun ferries leave at 8am (R$153/medium-sized car; 3hr). Ferries also leave from the Terminal Hidroviario in Belem, with Empresa Master Motors, for Soure (daily at 8.15am returning at 5.30am).

INFORMATION

Tourist information The Soure municipal tourist office is at 1 Rua between Travessa 13 & 14 close to the Trapiche Municipal, near to the river crossing (Mon–Fri 7.30am–6pm, although opening hours are erratic; T 91 8298 8087, E secretaria-turismo-soure@hotmail.com).

Services There are four banks in Soure with ATMs including Bradesco, Rua 2 541 at Travessa 16, and Banco do Brasil, Rua 3 1560, between Travessa 17 & 18. For internet, try Cyber Gigabyte at 2 Rua Travessa 15 524 (Mon–Sat 8.30am–12.30pm & 3.30–8.30pm; R$5/hr; T 91 3741 1826).

TOURS

Tour agencies Mururé Turismo (T 91 4005 5656, W mururetturismo.com.br) and Rumo Norte (T 91 3225 5915, W rumonorte.tur.br) are reliable agencies that organize tours to the interior of Marajó as well as day-trips to *fazendas* (ranches).

Fazenda tours *Fazendas* usually offer buffalo rides, canoeing through mangroves, alligator spotting and treks (a combination of these starts from approximately R$100; about 2hr). You can also visit *fazendas* independently, although it's wise to book ahead, especially in high season. Among the most established in Soure are Fazenda Araruna (T 91 3741 1474), Fazenda Bom Jesus (T 91 3741 1243) and Fazenda São Jerônimo (T 91 99365 4375, E fazenda.saojeronimo@hotmail.com).

5

ACCOMMODATION

SOURE

Casarão da Amazônia 4 Rua 626 corner Travessa 9 ⓣ 91 3741 1988, ⓦ facebook.com/hotelcasaraoamazonia. An Italian architect was flown in to restore this beautiful colonial building, which now houses five comfortable rooms (some smaller than others). An additional five rooms are set in a separate building facing the yard; beds are sturdy and comfortable with amenities including TV, a/c and fridge. The restaurant looks onto the pool area, which makes a refreshing addition in Marajó's heat. R$200

Hostel Tucupi Rua Prolongamento 7, between streets 34 and 35 ⓣ 91 98105 5264. This charming house sits on an expansive bit of property, and represents the island's only hostel. Rooms are shared with individual beds. Owners can help organize transfers through Edgar Transport. Dorms R$60

Hotel Ilha do Marajó Travessa 2 between Rua 7 & 8 ⓣ 91 3741 1315, ⓦ iaraturismo.com.br. This large hotel looking right onto the beach has a series of adequate rooms that could do with a splash of paint. The upside is that there are plenty of facilities, including a volleyball court, tennis court and a very decent-sized pool. R$250

Paracauary Eco Pousada 3km outside Soure ⓣ 91 3225 5915, ⓦ paracauary.com.br. Three kilometres outside Soure, this eco-resort is set amid a beautiful tract of forested land. The simply furnished yet welcoming rooms have forest views, and there's a pool to cool off too. Staff can organize tours on the island. R$250

Pousada O Canto do Francês 6 Rua corner Travessa 8 ⓣ 91 3741 1298, ⓦ bit.ly/OCantoDoFrances. Some of the a/c rooms at this French-owned *pousada* open onto a wide airy corridor with large modern paintings, while others look onto the spacious garden at the back. All feature dark chocolate-coloured furniture and are decorated with artisanal paintings from Pará. Cards are accepted, and there's ten percent discount if you pay cash. (some rooms) R$180

SALVATERRA

Pousada dos Guarás Praia Grande de Salvaterra ⓣ 91 4005 5656, ⓦ pousadadosguaras.com.br. This lovely resort looks right onto a wonderful stretch of freshwater beach; accommodation is dotted around a verdant garden shaded by palm trees, and facilities include a pool, beach volleyball, massage area, and horse and buffalo riding. R$234

JOANES

★ **Ventania do Rio-mar** ⓣ 91 3646 2067, ⓦ pousadaventania.com. This excellent Belgian-run *pousada* is set on a windy headland with exceptional views over the beach. Accommodation is in nine rustic, colourful rooms with mosquito nets; there are also four more spacious rooms sleeping three and four. Bathrooms have cold water only. R$130

EATING

Delícias da Nalva 4 Rua 1051 between Travessa 20 and 21, Soure ⓣ 91 8301 0110. This friendly family-run place is Soure's best restaurant – the food is lovingly prepared by Nalva who has been rustling up excellent local dishes for three decades. At R$90 the recommended *banquete marajoara*, an excellent introduction to the island's cuisine, is not cheap, although it's worth the splurge. Along with buffalo meat dishes (R$50), the menu also embraces chicken (R$50) and fish (R$50), along with home-made desserts (R$10). Don't forget to try the delicious home-made liqueur made with seasonal fruits. Daily 10am–10pm.

Solar do Bola Oitava Rua, Travessa 9, Soure ⓣ 91 3741 2196, ⓦ solardobola.com.br. Regarded by locals as the best restaurant in town, Solar do Bola offers local favourites. There's the *peixe al molho de camarão* (fish in shrimp sauce), and the *filé a solar* (buffalo steak). It's a decent budget option because the mains are easily big enough to serve two. Mains start at around R$45. Daily 11.30am–2.30pm & 6.30pm–midnight.

SHOPPING

Ilha do Marajó is renowned for its beautiful **ceramics** and **buffalo leather** products. It's worth taking the time to have a look at one of the places below – you can see craftsmen at work at all three, who are usually delighted to tell customers more about their trade and give a live demo where possible.

Arte Marajó Travessa 23 1069, between Rua 12 & 13 ⓣ 91 3741 1396, ⓔ artemarajo@hotmail.com. This pleasant little shop with a leafy work area at the back sells pretty ceramic bowls and pots as well as wooden crafts. Daily 8am–5pm.

Curtume Marajó 2 Rua Travessa 4, Bairro Novo ⓣ 91 8078 4215. Displays a selection of ceramics, buffalo saddles and buffalo leather products such as sandals and purses. The attached shop has a larger selection of leather products; make sure you take a look at the work area behind the shop where workers dye leather at the tanneries. Daily 8am–7pm.

Mbarayo Cerámica Travessa 20 between Rua 3 & 4 ⓣ 91 98465 9714, ⓦ facebook.com/Mbarayó-Cerâmica-Marajoara-136976656469887/. This itty-bitty shop displays a small selection of tribal ceramics including masks and pots, as well as necklaces. The owner will happily demonstrate how the ceramics are made – a fascinating process that involves using wild pig and anaconda teeth, a fish spine and a stingray barb. Daily 8am–6pm.

Macapá

On the north bank of the Amazon and right on the equator, **MACAPÁ** is the gateway to the state of Amapá and home to three-quarters of its population. This is one of Brazil's poorest and least populated regions. Traditionally it was dependent on rubber exports, but manganese was discovered in the 1950s and this, together with timber and other minerals, is now the main source of income. Amapá doesn't have much going for it, other than as a transit route to **French Guiana** (see page 352), and it suffers the most marked dry season in the Amazon, running from June to December, when it can get extremely hot. Macapá fights it out with Palmas in Tocantins for the title of dullest state capital in Brazil, but at least it's cheap, and a couple of sights that will keep you entertained for a few hours.

Casa do Artesão

Av Azarias Neto s/n • Tues–Sun 8am–5.30pm • Free • ⓣ 96 3223 5444

This handicraft centre promotes and supports artisans in the city and surrounding areas, and as such it's a great spot to buy souvenirs, such as crafts, paintings, earrings and woodwork, at very reasonable prices.

Fortaleza de São José de Macapá

Rua Cândido Mendes s/n • Tues–Sun 8am–6pm, • Free

The one highlight of Macapá is the **Fortaleza de São José de Macapá**, one of the largest colonial forts in Brazil, built in 1782 from material brought over as ballast in Portuguese ships, in response to worries that the French had designs on the north bank of the Amazon.

Marco Zero do Equador

Rodovia JK, Km 2, Bairro do Zerão • Daily 8am–8pm • Free

Located right at the borderline between the northern and southern hemispheres, **Marco Zero** is Macapá's pride. Here visitors can take a snapshot with one foot to the north and the other to the south of the equator. The nearby stadium is allegedly the only place in the world where two teams in one game play in different hemispheres.

Museu Histórico Joaquim Caetano da Silva

Av Mário Cruz 0376 • Tues–Sun 9am–6pm • Free • ⓣ 96 3223 5441

The small **Museu Histórico Joaquim Caetano da Silva** traces the history of the state of Amapá and its people from colonial times until the twentieth century. There's a handful of objects on display including beautiful wooden boats, musical instruments and a few archeological finds, although the majority of the museum consists of informative panels – sadly, though, none is translated into English.

Museu Sacaca

Av Feliciano Coelho 1509 • Tues–Sun 9am–5pm • Free • ⓣ 96 3212 5362, ⓦ facebook.com/museusacaca/

The beautiful open-air **Museu Sacaca** collaborates closely with Amapá's institute of scientific and technological research. The museum reproduces the habitat of the people of the forest, with replicas including a demonstration of nut-gathering and processing and riverside dwellings and a floating market used to trade medicines, weapons, salt, fabrics and other native products to isolated communities. Visitors take in the exhibits strolling along wooden walkways within the pretty grounds; the entire complex is a lovely verdant spot that feels a world apart from Macapá's monotonous centre.

CROSSING INTO FRENCH GUIANA

One reason to come to Macapá is to travel on to **French Guiana** (or Guyane). The key road in the state connects Macapá with the town of **OIAPOQUE**, on the river of the same name that delineates the frontier. The road isn't asphalted all the way, but even where it's dirt it's usually good going in the dry season; in the wet season, however, it can easily double travel time.

From Macapá's rodoviária catch a **bus** to Oiapoque (daily 5pm & 7pm; 10hr, though can take up 24hr or longer in the rainy season; R$92); there are also 4WD services that shuttle passengers (7hr, can take longer in the rainy season; R$150). Once in Oiapoque, you can catch a boat (every 5min; 10min; €10) across to Saint-Georges. (Alternatively walk over the bridge; there's no bus that runs across.) Brazilian **exit stamps** can be obtained from the border police *(Police des Frontiéres)* at the southern road entrance into Oiapoque; on the other side you have to check in with the *gendarmes* in Saint-Georges. From here you can hop on a bus to **Cayenne** (3hr; €35).

CROSSING THE BORDER

If you are not a citizen of an EU country, the US or Canada, you will need a **visa** to enter French Guiana, which it's best to try to arrange before you leave home. If you're going to travel overland, buy **euros** in Belém or Macapá. You can get them in Oiapoque but the rates are worse, and you can't depend on changing either Brazilian currency or US dollars for euros in the border settlement of Saint-Georges in Guyane.

ARRIVAL AND INFORMATION — MACAPÁ

By plane The airport is 4km from town on Rua Hildemar Maia (☎96 3223 2323). LATAM, Gol and Azul serve Belém (6 daily; 40min), from where there are connections to numerous national and international destinations. A taxi to the centre from here is about R$15.

By boat The port is 25km southwest at Porto do Santana, connected to Rua Tiradentes in the city centre by bus (40min; R$3.10).

Destinations Belém (Mon–Wed & Fri–Sun daily 10am, Thurs noon; 24hr; hammock R$60, cabin for two R$225); Santarém (daily 10am; 24hr; hammock R$120).

By bus The rodoviária (☎96 3251 3435) is at Jardim Felicidade, about 4km outside town on the BR-156; from there, local buses run to Rua Tiradentes in the centre (every 15min; 20min; R$3.10).

Information There's a small tourist office at the Eliezer Levy Pier on Av Beira Mar (daily 8am–1pm & 3–7pm).

ACCOMMODATION

Hotel Do Forte Av Beira Rio 248 ☎96 3223 2855, ⓦhoteldoforte.com. One of the city's most comfortable options offering clean and tidy rooms, along with a pool which, despite being small, offers a much welcome respite from the city's stifling heat. Pricier *executivo* rooms have river views, although they're not really worth the extra expense. There's an open-air gym as well as a lovely rooftop terrace with little gazebos and river views – the perfect spot to catch a little evening breeze. R$225

Hotel Ibis Rua Tiradentes 303 ☎96 2101 9050, ⓦibis.com. An excellent budget option offering clean practical rooms with private bathrooms, a/c units and cable TV. There's a small pool table in the lobby area, along with a restaurant serving very reasonably priced food. R$180

★ **Hotel Pousada Ekinox** Jovino Dinoa 1693 ☎96 3223 0086, ⓦekinoxmacapa.com. This lovely *pousada*, has comfortable spacious rooms set around a pretty verdant patio. All rooms are equipped with a/c and cable TV and the restaurant serves up very good nosh too. They don't accept walk-ins – make sure to ring or email ahead to make a reservation. R$180

EATING

Cantinho Baiano Av Acelino de Leão ☎96 3223 4153, ⓦcantinhobaianoap.com.br. On the river front, this a/c restaurant specializes in fish and shrimp dishes – try the *peixe região dos lagos* (fish served with *jambú* risotto; R$79). Dishes are big enough to share, although if you're travelling alone they will make single portions at sixty percent of the dish price. Mon–Sat 11am–3pm & 6–11.30pm, Sun 11am–3.30pm.

Churrascaria Santa Rita Av Mendonça Furtado 2084 ☎96 3223 0670. Macapá's best *por quilo* restaurant offers a wide range of salads, fish and excellent *churrasco* for meat lovers. Prices are reasonable, the service is good and the food certainly makes it worth visiting. Tues–Sun 11am–3pm.

Restaurante Estaleiro Av 1 de Maio 52 ☎96 3222 8375. Set in a pretty wooden building resembling a ship with anchors lying outside, the real draw here is the excellent seafood, served by friendly waiters dressed in sailors' outfits. Tues–Fri 7.30pm–midnight, Sat 7.30pm–midnight & noon–3pm, Sun noon–3pm.

BOAT ON THE RIO NEGRO

5

Santarém

Around 700km west of Belém – but closer to 800km as the river flows – **SANTARÉM** is the first significant stop on the journey up the Amazon, a small city of over 200,000 people, which still makes it the fifth largest in the Brazilian Amazon. Santarém is located at the junction of the **Tapajós River** and the Amazon; the waters mix in front of the city and the contrast between the muddy Amazon and the deep blue and turquoise of the Tapajós is as spectacular as the much better-known merging of the Rio Negro and the Amazon in front of Manaus. During the dry season (June–Nov) the Tapajós drops several metres, fringing the entire river system with stunning white-sand beaches. Santarém is a rather unattractive town of concrete blocks; base yourself instead in nearby Alter do Chão (see page 358), a laidback beach resort and the perfect base for exploring some of the most beautiful river scenery the Amazon basin has to offer.

The area around Santarém (see page 358) has been transformed by a soy-growing boom, and the docks are now dominated by a Cargill grain terminal. But don't be deceived: there are plenty of things to do in the surrounding region, which is still largely (and inexplicably) unvisited by tourists.

The waterfront

By far the most interesting place in Santarém, at any hour of the day or night, is the **waterfront**. There are always dozens of boats tied up here, with the accompanying bustle of people and cargoes being loaded and unloaded, and constant activity in the shops and outfitters by the water. You will probably have to wander along the

THE RISE AND FALL OF AMAZONIAN RUBBER

In 1874 an Englishman named **Henry Wickham** settled at Santarém with his wife and went on to be almost single-handedly responsible for the collapse of the Amazon rubber boom, smuggling quantities of valuable rubber seed from the heart of the Amazon (at a price of £10 for every 1000 seeds) to the Royal Botanical Gardens in London and from there to British-owned plantations in Asia that were already prepared and waiting. It took over twenty years for the first crop to mature to anywhere near peak production, but when it did the bottom fell out of the Brazilian rubber market.

British plantations in Asia produced four tons of rubber in 1900, but 71,000 tons by 1914. This was not only more than Brazil was producing, but also a great deal cheaper, since the plantations were far more efficient than the labour-intensive wild-rubber-tree tapping practised in the Amazon. Rubber was to feature again in local history through the development of the towns of **Belterra** (see page 360) and **Fordlândia** (see page 361), both accessible from Santarém, set up by automobile tycoon Henry Ford with the intent of establishing the world's largest rubber production centre.

waterfront anyway to find boats to points elsewhere, but a sunset stroll is reason enough to venture down this way.

Centro Cultural João Fona

Praça Santarém • Mon–Fri 8am–5pm • By donation

The **Centro Cultural João Fona** is located in a fine building inaugurated in 1868 and standing in splendid isolation on Praça Santarém. The highlight of the collection is some stunning tribal pottery, small but elaborately decorated and around 2000 years old. The building itself is also very pleasant and the shady internal courtyard is a good spot to hide from the sun on a hot day.

Museu Dica Frazão

Rua Floriano Peixote 281 • Daily 8am–6pm • By donation • ☎ 93 3522 1026

The unique **Museu Dica Frazão** was founded by its eponymous owner, who personally gave enthusiastic tours of her museum until her death in 2017, aged 96. On display are stylist and artist Dica's handmade clothes, all made exclusively using natural fibres such as roots, palm and bark. The pieces on display are replicas of clothing sold to individuals all over the world – according to a story once told by Dica, one of her tablecloths is in the Vatican with the pope. There's a pretty outfit from the 1960s, a wedding dress and other inventive garb on display; there's also a little shop where you can purchase handmade accessories.

ARRIVAL AND DEPARTURE — SANTARÉM

By plane Santarém airport (☎ 93 3522 4328) is at Praça Eduardo Gomes s/n about 15km from the centre with a bus connection to Av Rui Barbosa (every 30min; 20min; R$3.50). A taxi to the centre is R$75 and to Alter do Chão R$100. Travelling from the town centre, take the "Aeroporto" bus, not to be confused with "Aeroporto Velho", which goes nowhere near the airport. LATAM, Azul and Gol have connections to Belém (4 daily; 1hr) and Manaus (3 daily; 1hr).

By boat Boats to Manaus and Belém dock at the Estação das Docas on Av Cuiabá to the west of the city centre. Buses run from the port to the city centre (every 45min; 15min; R$3.50). Boats to Porto da Santana near Macapá leave by Praça Tiradentes to the west of town. Note that there's an additional fee if you pay by card.

Destinations Belém (Mon, Fri & Sat at noon; hammock R$200, cabin for two R$800); Manaus (Mon–Sat 11am; 42–50hr; hammock R$180, cabin for two R$600); Porto da Santana (for Macapá; daily at 6pm; 24hr; hammock R$120).

By bus The rodoviária, 3km from the centre, is connected to the city by local buses (every 20min; 10min; R$3.25).

Destinations Campo Grande, Mato Grosso do Sur (daily 6.30am & 4pm; 48hr; R$576); Cuiabá, Mato Grosso (daily, 6.30am, 3pm, 4pm & 9.30pm; 36hr; R$383).

INFORMATION AND TOURS

Tourist information The tourist office is at the Terminal Fluvial Turístico at Av Tapajós s/n (Mon–Fri 8am–8pm, Sat 2–8pm; 93 3523 2434).

Tours The most reliable company in town is Santarém Tur at Rua Adriano Pimentel 44 (93 3522 4847, santaremtur.com.br) who organize city tours, FLONA trips and tours of nearby Alter do Chão.

ACCOMMODATION

The accommodation in Santarém is largely uninspiring. It's much better to base yourself in nearby **Alter do Chão**, which offers a number of pleasant *pousadas* in beautiful surrounding. If you're just here for a night to catch another boat, there are plenty of centrally located options not too far from the boat docks.

Barrudada Tropical Hotel Av Mendonça Furtado 4120 93 99146 4996, barrudadatropicalhotel.com.br; map p.354. There's nothing too tropical about this place – it's a massive concrete structure with over two hundred rooms on the outskirts of town. It is, however, the city's best hotel and features an appealing round pool that is a real treat in Santarém's hot and sticky weather. The mellow coloured rooms are clean and comfortable – try and secure one on the third floor from where there are views of the city and beyond. **R$150**

Brisa Hotel Rua Senador Lameira Bittencourt 5 93 3522 1018, brisahotel@hotmail.com; map p.354. This is probably Santarém's most atmospheric hotel, featuring a little touch of greenery, wooden furniture and yellow hues. The a/c rooms are clean and have private bathrooms, although there is only one room with a window (facing the back of the building). **R$80**

Central Hotel Av Tapajós 258 93 3522 4920; map p.354. Run by the same management as *Mistura Brasileira*, this hotel has equally claustrophobic narrow corridors painted in bright blue; the rooms are on the small side here too, with just a tiny window flap giving onto the interior. There is a handful of more spacious (and slightly more expensive) rooms upstairs with windows, so you're better off going for one of those. (reception only) **R$50**

Mistura Brasileira Av Tapajós 23 93 3522 4819; map p.354. Right by the *por quilo* restaurant of the same name, this centrally located hotel has clean but small and stuffy a/c rooms with cold water; most are dark with no windows as they face onto the bright blue interior corridor; try and ask for one of the four rooms with window. **R$100**

Tapajós Center Hotel Av Tapajós 1827 93 3522 5353, tapajoscenterhotel.com.br; map p.354. On the southern end of Av Tapajós, this new addition to Santarém offers decent rooms in a concrete block; all have a/c, private bathroom and cable TV. Some rooms look onto the river but can get a bit noisy at night as they also face the town's main artery. **R$170**

EATING

Mistura Brasileira Av Tapajós 23 93 3522 4819; map p.354. This laidback place is a good spot for a *por quilo* lunch (R$31.90), with a very decent selection of fish, meat and vegetable dishes. It's among the best buffet restaurants in town. Daily 11am–3pm.

Nossa Casa Rua São Cristovão 54 93 9197 6354; map p.354. This warm and welcoming family-run restaurant features bare brick walls and little colourful knick-knacks decorating scattered shelves. The menu features new additions every six months or so, giving the owner and chef some time to come up with original creations taking in clients' suggestions. Try the bestselling mega *tapajós* (fresh *pirarucu* fish with cheese, oregano, *jambu* risotto and *farofa* with plantain; R$79 for two people). Mon–Sat 7pm–midnight.

★ **Peixaria Rayana** Av Rui Barbosa 3596 93 3523 0349, peixariarayana.com.br; map p.354. This local institution has been going strong for years and is by far the city's best restaurant. The place itself is very laidback, with plastic chairs and simple decor, but the food is truly exceptional – and wonderfully cheap. The speciality is fish that comes grilled, fried or boiled. The popular *pirarucu na manteiga* (*pirarucu* in butter sauce; R$57) is big enough for two. Mon–Sat 11am–4pm & 6pm–midnight, Sun 11am–4pm.

Piracema Av Mendoca Furtado 73 93 3522 7461, restaurantepiracema.com.br; map p.354. This is one of Santarém's best and most popular restaurants. Guests dine in cosy surroundings with intimate lighting. Mon–Sat 11am–3pm, 7–11.30pm, Sun 11am–4pm.

Sorveteria Nido Av Doutor Mendonca Furtado 2590 93 3522 7130; map p.354. This *sorveteria* offers a selection of about fifteen exotic flavours including Brazil nut, *açaí* and all manner of local fruits – scoop away at the self-service *por quilo* ice-cream stand (R$45) and sprinkle with your toppings of choice. Daily 11am–11pm.

DRINKING AND NIGHTLIFE

Boteco do Sorriso Rua do Imperador 622 93 99147 3003, facebook.com/BotecodoSorriso; map p.354. One of the city's best spots for some live music, this friendly bar buzzes late at night when pop-rock and MPB bands play until the early hours (10.30pm–2am). There are over twenty types of wine, cocktails and 3.5l beer towers (R$45), along with fish and meat dishes (small snacks start at R$11; plates serving two are R$51) to refuel. Tues–Sat 7pm–2:30am.

Mascotinho Praça Manoel de Jesus Moraes s/n ⓣ93 99216 8546; map p.354. This relaxed bar on the riverfront promenade attracts plenty of locals who head here to watch the sun set with a beer (R$5); the pleasant river breeze is an added bonus. Daily 5–11.45pm.

SHOPPING

Muiraquitã Rua Senador Lameira Bittencourt 131 ⓣ93 3522 7164; map p.354. The city's largest souvenir shop sells all manner of wooden crafts, jewellery, tablemats and more. Daily 10.30am–6.30pm.

DIRECTORY

Hospital Hospital Municipal de Santarém, Av Presidente Vargas 1539, Santa Clara ⓣ93 3523 2155.

Internet Cyber Sonic, Travessa dos Mártires 12 (Mon–Fri 8am–10pm, Sat 8am–9pm; R$5/hr; ⓣ93 3522 1540).

Money and exchange All major banks are along Av Rui Barbosa; Bradesco is at no. 756, Banco do Brasil at no. 794 and HSBC at no. 493.

Post office Praca da Bandeira 81 (Mon–Fri 9am–5pm).

BOI BUMBÁ IN PARINTINS

Parintins, an otherwise unremarkable, small river-town with a population of around 100,000 lying roughly halfway between Santarém and Manaus, has become the unlikely centre of one of the largest mass events in Brazil – the **Boi Bumbá** celebrations, which take place in the last weekend of June every year. The official name is the **Festival Folclórico de Parintins**, but it is often called Boi Bumbá after the name for a funny and dramatized dance concerning the death and rebirth of an ox traditionally performed at the festival. The festival's roots go back at least a hundred years, when the Cid brothers from Maranhão arrived in the area bringing with them the Bumba-meu-boi musical influence from the culture-rich ex-slave plantations.

Tens of thousands of visitors arrive annually at the Bumbódromo stadium, built to look like a massive stylized bull, which hosts a wild, energetic **parade** by something resembling an Amazonian version of Rio samba schools – and the resemblance is not coincidental, the organizers having consciously modelled themselves on Rio's Carnaval. The event revolves around two schools, **Caprichoso** and **Garantido**, which compete, parading through the Bumbódromo, where supporters of one school watch the opposing parade in complete silence. You thus have the strange spectacle of thousands of people going wild while the other half of the stadium is as quiet as a funeral, with roles reversed a few hours later. Boi Bumbá has its high point with the enactment of the death of a **bull**, part of the legend of the slave Ma Catirina who, during her pregnancy, developed a craving for ox tongue. To satisfy her craving, her husband, Pa Francisco, slaughtered his master's bull, but the master found out and decided to arrest Pa Francisco. Legend, however, says a priest and a witch doctor managed to resuscitate the animal, thus saving Pa Francisco; with the bull alive once more, the party begins again at fever pitch, with a frenetic rhythm that pounds away well into the hot and smoke-filled night.

PRACTICAL INFORMATION

The parade is undeniably spectacular, and the music infectious. But if you're going to participate, remember joining in with the Caprichoso group means you mustn't wear red clothing; if you're dancing with the Garantido school, you need to avoid blue clothes. During the festival, forget about **accommodation** in any of the town's few hotels: they are booked up months in advance. Your best chance is simply to stay on a **boat**; in all the towns and cities of the region – notably Manaus and Santarém – you will find boats and travel agencies offering all-inclusive packages for the event, with accommodation in hammocks on the boats. Most of the riverboat companies offer three- or four-day **packages**, costing between R$200 and R$700. The trips (26hr from Manaus, 20hr from Santarém) are often booked well in advance, and are advertised from March onwards on banners tied to the boats. There is a lot of petty thieving and pickpocketing, so take extra care of anything you bring with you.

Around Santarém

The area around Santarém is richly rewarding, with a variety of day-trips possible out to **Alter do Chão** and **Belterra**, as well as boat journeys further afield. Due north, on the opposite bank of the Amazon, is the town of **Alenquer**, the jumping-off point for the lovely waterfall of **Vale do Paraíso** and the mysterious rock formations at **Cidade dos Deuses**.

Travelling south along the Tapajós River will take you to **Fordlândia**, set up in the late 1920s by Henry Ford to help create an Amazonian rubber plantation, while east from Santarém is **Monte Alegre**, the jumping-off point for the Monte Alegre rock paintings that date back over 13,000 years. To head into less disturbed forest and consequently have better access to wildlife, your best bet is one of the tour operators in Alter do Chão; an excellent option is a visit to the **Floresta Nacional do Tapajós**, a national park some 64km out of town down the Santarém–Cuiabá highway.

Alter do Chão

The lovely beach resort of **ALTER DO CHÃO** is a beautiful bay in the Rio Tapajós overlooked by two easily climbable hills, one the shape of a church altar, giving the place its name. In recent years Alter do Chão has become something of a cult destination on the alternative travel circuit.

From July to November the bay is fringed by **white-sand beaches**, which combine with the deep blue of the Tapajós to give it a Mediterranean look. During the week you'll almost have the place to yourself, while weekends see the tranquillity shattered, as *santarenhos* head out en masse for the beach – be careful if you're heading back to Santarém on a weekend afternoon as many drivers on the road will be drunk.

Ilha do Amor

The stunning **Ilha do Amor** is a white-sand beach just across from Alter do Chão. In the dry season the sandbank is accessible either by wading or by rowing boat (5min; R$5/person), and laidback shaded restaurants provide the fried fish and chilled beer essential to the full enjoyment of the scene. It's well worth taking the time to climb up to the **Morro de Cruzeiro** viewpoint, from where there are breathtaking views of the Tapajós River, Lago Verde and the Amazon rainforest.

Lago Verde

Alter do Chão sits at the shores of the beautiful **Lago Verde**, surrounded by verdant forest rich in fauna including monkeys, macaws, agoutis and armadillos. The lake has some lovely secluded spots perfect for a swim. The best way to explore the area is

PIRANHAS AND STINGRAYS

One thing definitely worth bearing in mind if you are swimming anywhere in the Amazon is that piranhas and stingrays (*raia*) are common. **Piranhas** are actually much less of a problem than you would expect. Forget any films you have seen; they don't attack in shoals, prefer still water to currents and no death or serious injury from piranha attack is on record. Nevertheless, they can give you a nasty bite and are indeed attracted to blood. They frequent particular spots, which locals all know about and avoid, so ask for advice.

Stingrays are more of a problem. They love warm, shallow water and are so well camouflaged that they are practically invisible. If you tread on one, it will whip its sting into your ankle, causing a deep gash and agonizing pain for at least 24 hours. However, stingrays really hate noise, crowds, waves and strong currents, and so are rarely found on regularly used beaches, such as Alter do Chão, near Santarém, but off the beaten track, they are an ever-present threat. You can minimize the danger by wearing canvas boots or trainers and by splashing and throwing sand and stones into shallow water if you intend to swim there.

through a guided tour with one of the agencies in Alter do Chão; alternatively, you can explore the lake with one of the boatmen along the waterfront.

ARRIVAL AND DEPARTURE — ALTER DO CHÃO

By bus From Santarém's Praça Tiradentes you can catch a bus to Alter do Chão (hourly; 45min; R$3.60).

TOURS

Many **tour operators** organize reasonably priced forest treks, fishing expeditions, boat trips and other excursions in the area. Prices start from R$60–100 depending on the type of boat (slow or fast) for a 2hr boat trip on the **Lago Verde**. A fun way to explore town is to rent a **tandem bike** (R$20/hr); Santos Locacões at Copa Cabana 150 (daily 8am–11pm) has a range of tandem bikes as well as a six-seater cycle (R$60).

Gil Serique Av Copacabana ⊕93 9115 8111, ⊕gilserique.com. This one-man outfit is run by friendly Gil, whose love for the rainforest and all things nature avidly comes across in all of his fun tours. He has plenty of experience, having worked as a naturalist and lecturer, as well as on a number of TV documentaries. He mainly organizes trips to FLONA and to the less explored flood plains east of Santarém by the Rio Maicá.

Mae Natureza Praça 7 de Setembro s/n ⊕93 3527 1264, ⊕facebook.com/maenaturezaecoturismo. This well-established Argentine-run agency specializes in eco-tourism trips; they organize tours to FLONA, the Parque Nacional da Amazônia and Canal do Jarí, among others.

Vento em Popa Rua Francisco Branco 15 ⊕93 9154 2120, ⊕receptivo.ventoempopa@gmail.com. This agency organizes airport transfers, hotel bookings, boat rides and full-board trips overnighting in the Amazon jungle.

Ynca Turismo Av Pedro Teixeira 500 ⊕93 9145 9560, ⊕yncaamazontoursbrazil.fr.gd. Located in the *Beloalter* hotel, this friendly operator organizes tours to Lago Verde in Alter do Chão, kayaking trips, FLONA trips, Santarém city tours and visits to the meeting of the waters. Also arranges trips to the Monte Alegre rock paintings.

ACCOMMODATION

Tour operators can help you to **rent a house** in Alter do Chão, which is the most economic form of accommodation if you fancy staying a week or two – which many people do, once they see the place. Prices can jump significantly in December.

Agualinda Hotel Rua Dr Macedo Costa s/n ⊕93 3527 1314, ⊕agualindahotel.com.br. Accommodation here is within a peach-coloured building with clay-coloured doors a couple of blocks back from the river front; the 32 a/c rooms are kept in shipshape condition, and all have private bathroom and TV. R$130

★ **Albergue da Floresta** Tv Antônio de Sousa Pedroso s/n ⊕93 99209 5656, ⊕alberguedafloresta@hotmail.com. This laidback place offers rustic accommodation integrated within the jungle's natural environment; timber walkways lead to cosy rooms set in colourfully painted wooden houses. There's a breezy kitchen for guests' use and overall a very chilled-out vibe. Bed sheets are an extra R$10. Hammock R$25, dorms R$50, doubles R$150

Beloalter Hotel Rua Pedro Teixeira 500 ⊕93 3527 1230, ⊕beloalter.com.br. Alter do Chão's most high-end hotel offers comfortable if a bit tired a/c rooms with hot showers. The draw here is the swimming pool along with the pretty stretch of beach at the back of the property. (reception only) R$280

Coracão Verde Pousada Rua Dom Macedo Costa 837 ⊕93 3527 1262, ⊕pousadaclaudia.com.br. This *pousada* features three-bed dorms (male and female) and doubles facing one another. The decor is slightly kitsch (in some rooms more than others), with chintzy sheets, plastic flowers and other curious trimmings. Dorms R$25, doubles R$100

Pousada Encantos da Amazônia Tv Prof. Juvêncio Navarro 38 ⊕93 9123 9115, ⊕pousadaencantosdaamazonia.com. A pleasant choice offering ten spacious a/c rooms which open onto a courtyard, some of which are in better nick than others. The bamboo and wooden chalets are the best of the lot, with warm and welcoming interiors featuring natural materials. There's a kitchen for guests' use and a little patch of land where the owners grow herbs and vegetables. Prices halve in low season. R$250

Pousada Mingote Tv Agostinho A. Lobato s/n ⊕93 3527 1158, ⊕pousadadomingote.com.br. In the centre of town just off the main square, this *pousada* is dotted with a few curios and potted plants. The rooms, mostly decorated with paintings of local wildlife, are neat and tidy – try and secure one of the three rooms with pretty views over the square and riverfront. R$240

Pousada Sombra do Cajueiro Rua Pedro Teixeira 200 ⊕93 3527 1370, ⊕pousadasombradocajueiro.com.br. This small *pousada* features six a/c rooms set around a leafy courtyard with hammocks shaded by *cajueiros* (cashew trees), while breakfast is served next to a large mango tree. There are pleasant touches like wicker lamps and hammocks, and all rooms have TVs and fridges. R$150

Pousada do Tapajós Hostel Rua Lauro Sodré 100 ☎93 9210 2166, pousadadotapajos.com.br. This hostel offers clean tiled dorms with wooden bunks, personal lockers and private bathrooms. There's a pleasant garden with hammocks and barbecue area, along with a kitchen for guests' use. Call ahead to organize airport pick-up (R$70). Dorms R$50, doubles R$180

EATING

★**Farol da Ilha** Rua Ladro Sodré s/n ☎93 99236 6704. This breezy restaurant on the riverfront features wooden tables and colourful paintings made by an Italian artist who used to live next door. There are some tasty dishes on the menu, such as *peixe ilha dos macacos* (R$82), which goes down a treat – stuffed fish with shrimps, banana and *farofa* cooked and served wrapped in a banana leaf. Thurs–Sun 10am–10pm.

Restaurante Tribal Tv Antônio Lobato s/n ☎93 99211 9549. Set on two floors, this open-fronted restaurant decked out in natural materials is a pleasant spot for a meal; seating is either within the main building or in the shaded sandy area with wooden benches and hammocks. Dishes are for two, with mains starting from R$50. Daily 11am–4pm & 7pm–last customer leaves.

DRINKING AND NIGHTLIFE

★**Espaço Alter do Chão** Rua Lauro Sodré 74 ☎93 98401 6144, espacoalter.com.br. Known locally as *Borô*, after the owner's name, this laidback cultural centre gets packed over the weekends when *carimbó* and reggae bands take centre stage; virtually all the square flocks here once the other bars have closed down, and the sandy dancefloor remains packed until closing. Daily 11am–midnight.

Mae Natureza Praça 7 de Setembro s/n ☎93 3527 1264, maenaturezaecoturismo.com.br. This travel agency morphs into a happening bar at night, in particular on Thursday and Saturday evenings (and sometimes Tues) when live bands play *carimbó*, MPB and other Brazilian musical flavours, livening up the entire square. Tables spill onto the street, with drinking and dancing until closure. Tues–Sun 6pm–2am.

SHOPPING

★**Arariba** Rua Dom Macedo Costa ☎93 3527 1251, araribah.com.br. This excellent shop encourages tribal arts and crafts production, with beautiful pieces of indigenous art from ninety ethnic tribes available for purchase. It's the perfect spot to buy wonderful Amazonian souvenirs, including ceramics, hammocks, masks, musical instruments and books. Highly recommended. Mon–Thurs & Sun 9am–noon & 3–8pm, Fri & Sat 9am–noon, 3–9pm.

The Floresta Nacional do Tapajós (FLONA)

An essential day-trip is to the **Floresta Nacional do Tapajós (FLONA)**, the most easily accessible national park from Alter do Chão and Santarém. Some 5450 square kilometres of preserved upland forest riddled with trails, it includes around 50km of Tapajós river frontage, where there are a number of small communities living within the reserve's boundaries. The forest is magnificent, with primary rainforest towering over the secondary scrubland, which the area around has been reduced to by waves of colonization over the last fifty years (soy growers being merely the latest of a succession of new arrivals).

ARRIVAL AND TOURS — FLORESTA NACIONAL DO TAPAJÓS (FLONA)

Tours The easiest way of visiting the Floresta is as part of a package organized by a tour operator in Santarém (see page 356) or Alter do Chão (see page 359).

By bus You can catch a bus to Jamaraquá from where you can hire a local guide to take you around the park (R$100/day up to five people) – contact the head of the community Conceição who can help organize this (☎93 9124 5750). Buses run from Santarém's Av Rui Barbosa by the Banco do Brasil (daily at 11am; 2hr 30min; R$10). The return bus leaves at 4am so you'll have to spend the night at the town's basic *pousada* (dorms R$30, doubles R$60).

Belterra

The unusual town of **BELTERRA** is a quiet little place that looks bizarrely like an American country village on the wrong continent. It mimics small-town America exactly, with whitewashed wooden houses, immaculate gardens, fire hydrants, churches and spacious tree-lined streets. The only jarring note is the potholed roads. The town

PREHISTORIC FINDS

Thirty kilometres east of Santarém, and more easily accessible by river than by road, is a nineteenth-century sugar plantation called **Taperinha**. During an excavation there in 1991, American archeologist Anna Roosevelt unearthed **decorated pottery** almost 10,000 years old. This suggested that the Amazon basin was settled before the Andes, and that the Americas had been settled much earlier than previously thought. Later excavations in **Monte Alegre** confirmed that the middle Amazon played an important role in the prehistory of the Americas, with cave and rock paintings dotting the surrounding hills also being dated at around 10,000 years old.

About two thousand years ago, tribal culture in the region entered a particularly dynamic phase, producing some superbly decorated ceramics comparable in their sophistication with Andean pottery; there are beautiful pieces in the Centro Cultural João Fona in Santarém (see page 355) and even more in the Museu Goeldi in Belém (see page 340).

was set up in the 1930s by automobile tycoon Henry Ford when his rubber plantation in Fordlândia (see below) was struck with blight. Today, Belterra is better preserved than its sister settlement Fordlândia; there's not much to do within the town itself, except stroll around and take in its highly unusual buildings.

ARRIVAL AND ACCOMMODATION — BELTERRA

By bus There are regular buses to Belterra from Santarém's Av Rui Barbosa by the Banco do Brasil (every 30min; 1hr; R$5).

Pousada Cajutuba Rua Cajutuba 3, Aramanai ☎ 93 99183 1200. This *pousada* is in a charming house with a wraparound terrace fronted by a rolling-green lawn, with lovely views of the Rio Tapajos. It also has a restaurant that serves various fish dishes and even ox meat (R$60–$100). Doubles R$120

Fordlândia

The town of **FORDLÂNDIA**, 233km south of Belterra, was set up by automobile tycoon Henry Ford in the 1920s as part of a doomed attempt to transform the area into the world's largest rubber plantation. Here, Ford cleared vast tracts of forest to plant thousands of rubber trees. Rubber tappers and their families were housed in the centre, while American dignitaries lived in larger residences on the outskirts. Virtually all of the materials used to build the town were brought over from the United States, including the large riverside warehouse, the rubber factory and all its heavy machinery. The rubber trees were eventually struck with a fungus that stumped their growth, leading Ford to abandon the land and establish the town of Belterra. Today, this sleepy town is still functional, and walking around is extremely atmospheric, with trees growing through the roof of the rubber processing factory and machinery still lying around, including 1920s bulldozers and trucks.

ARRIVAL AND ACCOMMODATION — FORDLÂNDIA

By boat Slow boats leave Santarém for Fordlândia daily at 4pm returning at 8pm (10–12hr; R$50); fast boats take much less time and cost just a fraction more (daily 10am & noon; 4hr 30min; R$73), returning from Fordlândia at noon and 2pm (daily) when the boat from Itaituba stops by. Note that sometimes the boat fills up in Itaituba and won't stop in Fordlândia if there are no seats available.

Pousada Americana Av Boa Vista 31 ☎ 93 3505 3073, facebook.com/pousadaamericana. A surprisingly good accommodation choice in remote Fordlândia, this welcoming family-run guesthouse offers clean and spacious a/c rooms. Owner Rita rustles up some tasty meals at reasonable prices (R$25) and Guilherme gives impromptu tours. R$120

Alenquer and around

About 111km north of Santarém, through a maze of islands and lakes on the north bank of the Amazon, is **ALENQUER**, a typical small Amazon river town rarely visited by tourists. The town is rather dull and won't on its own detain you for more than an hour or so. The streets are pleasant, the waterfront occasionally bustles and has a good view of the river, and there are a couple of atmospheric public buildings from the days of the rubber boom. However, the surrounding countryside is strikingly beautiful with lakes, an abundance of wildlife and the rustic tourist complex of **Vale do Paraíso**, centred around the gorgeous **Cachoeira Paraíso**, a lovely waterfall that is accessible by road. Another reason to visit the area is to see **Cidade dos Deuses**, a unique complex of rock formations hidden within the jungle.

ARRIVAL AND DEPARTURE — ALENQUER AND AROUND

By boat Slow boats leave Santarém for Alenquer (Mon–Fri & Sun 8am, Sat noon; 6hr; R$35); fast boats leave from the Hidroviária de Santarém on Av Tapajós (daily 9am & 6.30pm, returning to Santarém 6.30am & 4pm; 2hr 30min; R$48; ⓣ93 4523 0788, ⓦtapajosexpresso.com.br). From Alenquer there are also boats to Manaus (Fri & Sat 10am; 2 days; R$120 including meals). Manaus to Alenquer boats leave Tues & Wed at 11am (36hr).

ACCOMMODATION AND EATING

Hotel Detinha Av Getúlio Vargas 563 ⓣ93 3526 1005. Alenquer's most comfortable hotel offers a/c rooms with private bathroom (cold water only). (erratic) R$80

Panificadora Fima Tv Doctor Arnaldo Morais 87 ⓣ93 3526 2921. Passengers arriving at the port flock to this little bakery the second the boats dock for their morning *cafezinho*, which comes with bread and butter for just R$5; if you're feeling more peckish you can have a *cafezinho* with bread, cheese and ham for R$15. There's also a selection of tasty pastries and even Middle Eastern *kibbeh* (R$5). Mon–Sat 6am–8.30pm, Sun 6am–noon.

Pepita Hotel Rua Coaraci Nunes 713 ⓣ93 9137 8469. Set in a tiled black-and-yellow building with a touch of greenery out the front, this *pousada* offers decent accommodation and a friendly atmosphere; the rooms are a bit run-down and the tattered sofas in the communal area could do with a make-over, but the pretty building makes up for it. Ask for a "new" room, in better shape than their predecessors. R$60

Vale do Paraíso

The best reason for visiting Alenquer is the stunning **Vale do Paraíso**, a forested valley dotted with a series of beautiful waterfalls hidden deep within the jungle about 60km from Alenquer. There are three main falls here: the first one you come across is the gorgeous **Paraíso**, with water gently cascading down a series of stone steps into a glade in the forest with a beautiful chestnut-coloured pool of cool water perfect for a dip. Below the falls you can wade with care through shallow rapids, but watch your step on the sharp-edged rocks.

About 800m further along a forest path is **Véu de Noiva** with a fall of 20m; the deep chocolate-coloured pool here is a fun spot to dive and jump in from the rocks, shaded by dense jungle. Make sure you go with a guide (*Pousada Vale do Paraíso* can arrange for someone to take you) who will be able to tell you where the water is deepest. The last is **Preciosa**, measuring 35m and the tallest of all. Its pool is not as appealing for a swim as the other two, although it makes for a good spot to abseil (you can arrange this through *Pousada Vale do Paraíso*).

If you're up for something even more wild, get a guide to take you to **Chuva de Prata**, an 85m-high fall hidden deep within the jungle. It's a trek of about four hours, and if you're feeling adventurous you can sling hammocks between two trees and sleep in the depths of the forest (do not even dream of doing this without a guide). There are networks of trails through the forest, and on weekdays you're likely to have the place to yourself. It's the perfect spot to unwind in tranquillity for a few days.

ARRIVAL AND DEPARTURE — VALE DO PARAÍSO

By bus There are regular bus services from Alenquer (Mon–Sat 9am, Sun 7am; 1hr 30min; R$10). From the highway it's a 13km walk to Vale do Paraíso – call ahead to *Pousada Vale do Paraíso* who can pick you up from the junction (R$25 by motorbike; R$50 by car), or even fetch you directly from Alenquer (R$200).

ACCOMMODATION

Pousada Vale do Paraíso Vale do Paraíso, PA254, Ramal da Cachoeira 93 3526 1284, valedoparaiso.tur.br. This pretty rustic *pousada* offers accommodation in colourful A-framed and square huts set around the lovely Paraíso waterfall; you can roll out of bed and head straight for a refreshing dip in the coffee-coloured pool. The homemade food is excellent and there's a laidback open-fronted communal area with owner Zé Alfredo's eclectic collection of knick-knacks along with hammocks to swing in. The *pousada* organizes activities including abseiling, trekking and nocturnal walks with night-vision monocles to spot wildlife. If you're looking for somewhere properly Amazonian to hang out for a few days, it's perfect. **R$80**

Cidade dos Deuses

Taxi from Alenquer R$200 return including waiting time; *Pousada Vale do Paraíso* can help organize this – you can visit the area by taxi on the way to Vale do Paraíso

A spectacular spot near Alenquer not to be missed is **Cidade dos Deuses**, literally City of the Gods, an awe-inspiring complex of rock formations lying deep in the jungle. You can explore the area on foot – keep your eyes peeled for ancient rock paintings. Not much is known about the formations nor the paintings, but it's widely believed the area was used as a religious temple to worship the gods and possibly even for ritual purposes.

Monte Alegre and around

Most of the town of **MONTE ALEGRE**, 111km east of Santarém, is built along the brow of a steep hill with spectacular views out across marshes and freshwater lakes, with the Amazon to the south and jagged hills to the north and west the only pieces of high ground between Belém and Manaus. With its obvious strategic advantages, this was one of the first places on the Amazon to be colonized by Europeans; a small group of English and Irish adventurers settled here in the 1570s, almost fifty years before Belém was founded. The Portuguese soon expelled them, and Monte Alegre was a ranching and farming settlement, then a centre of the rubber trade.

However, there is a much longer history of human settlement in the region. At various points the hills behind the town are covered in spectacular **indigenous rock paintings** that range from abstract geometric patterns through to stylized representations of animals and human stick figures and the most compelling images of all: palm prints of the ancient painters themselves.

Monte Alegre Rock Paintings

Guides: Nelsi Sadeck, Rua do Jaquara 320 (93 3533 1430, 93 9653 4785, nnsadeck@yahoo.com.br), is the most knowledgeable (R$450, up to six people)

The rock paintings have been dated at 13,150 years old, making Monte Alegre one of the most important archeological sites in South America. Some of the paintings are on rockfaces large enough to be seen from the road, but others are hidden away, requiring a steep climb to see them, so wear good shoes. Also, whatever time of year you go, it is likely to get very hot during the day: take plenty of water, a hat, mosquito repellent and sunscreen. There are six main sites where you can view the paintings – most with incredible views over the surrounding area. You will only be able to visit by **4WD** and you will need a **guide.**

ARRIVAL AND DEPARTURE — MONTE ALEGRE AND AROUND

By boat Slow boats leave Santarém daily at 2pm (8hr; R$30) returning daily at 8pm; fast boats leave from the Hidroviária de Santarém on Av Tapajós daily at 4pm (2hr 30min; R$43), returning to Santarém daily at 5.45am. From Monte Alegre there are departures to Manaus (Tues & Thurs 8pm, Fri & Sun eve, times vary; 3 days; R$130), Macapá (daily at midnight; 24hr; R$120) and Belém (Fri & Sun, with one added service on Mon every 15 days – times vary; 2 days; R$130).

ACCOMMODATION AND EATING

Dona Marita Av Aviador Pinto Martins 607 93 9139 3355. This welcoming restaurant with dangling lampshades and seating set around a small leafy courtyard offers plenty of local specialities, including *filé de pirarucú*

5

BIRDWATCHING AROUND MONTE ALEGRE

The water world **around Monte Alegre** is one of the richest birding sites in Amazônia. All along the banks of the Amazon, huge freshwater lakes are separated from the river by narrow strips of land. Depending on the time of year, the lakes either flood over the surrounding land, become marshland or even, in places, sandy cattle pasture. The whole area is thick with **birdlife**: huge herons, waders of all kinds and a sprinkling of hawks and fish eagles. At sunset, thousands of birds fly in to roost in the trees at the foot of the town. The stunning waterscapes set against the dramatic backdrop of hills make a boat trip really worth doing, even if you can't tell an egret from your elbow. Take everything with you for the time you'll be out – trips on nearby Lago Taxipá are usually a couple of hours long.

stuffed with cheese and fried banana (R$45). On Sundays there's an all-you-can-eat lunch buffet (R$30). Tues–Sat 11.30am–3pm & 4–11.30pm, Sun lunch only.

Hotel Shalon Tv Joaquim José Correa 467 93 3533 1700. This drab hotel midway between the Cidade Alta and the Cidade Baixa offers a selection of simple tired rooms with paper-thin doors. Staff at reception seem to be away more often than not, but if you hang around for a bit someone is bound to come and greet you. R$70

Hotel Shekinah 93 3533 1489, facebook.com/hotelshekinahPR. This hotel is probably the best Monte Alegre has to offer; the a/c rooms feature wooden furniture and are brightened up with a splash of yellow or green paint. (some rooms) R$100

Tonica Rua Enarnes Chaves 147 93 3533 1976. This friendly family-run restaurant is worth visiting for the tasty homemade cooking (R$30/kg). It couldn't get any more local than this, with seating in the backyard virtually shaded by rows of washing. Mon–Sat 11am–3pm.

Manaus

MANAUS is the capital of Amazonas, a tropical forest state covering around one and a half million square kilometres. The city is also the commercial hub of the Amazon region. Most visitors are surprised to learn Manaus isn't actually on the Amazon at all, but on the Rio Negro, 6km from the point where that river meets the Solimões to form (as far as Brazilians are concerned) the Rio Amazonas. Just a few hundred metres away from the tranquil life on the rivers, the centre of Manaus perpetually buzzes with energy. Escaping from the frenzy is not easy, but there is the occasional quiet corner, and the Opera House square and some of the city's museums make up for the hectic pace downtown. In the port and market areas, pigs, chickens and people selling hammocks line the streets, and despite the sprucing up the town underwent for the 2014 World Cup, there's an atmosphere that seems unchanged in centuries.

For the Amazon hinterland, Manaus has long symbolized "civilization". Traditionally, this meant simply that it was the **trading centre**, where the hardships of life in the forest could be escaped temporarily and where manufactured commodities to make that life easier – metal pots, steel knives, machetes and the like – could be purchased. Virgin jungle seems further from the city these days, but there are still waterways and channels within a short river journey of Manaus where you can find dolphins, alligators, kingfishers and the impression, at least, that humans have barely penetrated. Most visitors to Manaus rightly regard a multi-day **river trip** as an essential part of their stay, and there are also a number of nearby sites that make worthwhile day-excursions, most notably the **meeting of the waters** of the yellow Rio Solimões and the black Rio Negro, and the lily-strewn **Parque Ecológico do Janauary**.

Brief history

Established as a town in 1856, the name Manaus was given for the Manaós tribe, which was encountered in this region by São Luís do Maranhão while he was exploring the area in 1616. Missionaries arrived in 1657 and a small trading settlement, originally known as São José da Barra, evolved. The city you see today is primarily a product of the **rubber boom** and in particular the child of visionary state governor **Eduardo Ribeiro**, who from 1892 transformed Manaus into a major city. Under Ribeiro the Opera House was completed, and whole streets were wiped out in the process of laying down broad Parisian-style avenues, interspersed with Italian piazzas centred on splendid fountains. In 1899 Manaus was the first Brazilian city to have trolley buses and the second to have electric street lights.

At the start of the twentieth century Manaus was an opulent metropolis run by elegant people, who, despite the tropical heat, dressed and housed themselves as fashionably as their counterparts in any large European city. This heyday lasted barely thirty years; Ribeiro committed suicide in 1900 and by 1914 the rubber market was collapsing fast. There was a second brief boost for Brazilian rubber during World War II, but today's prosperity is largely due to the creation of a **Free Trade Zone**, the Zona Franca, in 1966. Over the following ten years the population doubled, from 250,000 to half a million, and many new industries moved in, especially electronics companies. An impressive international airport was opened in 1976 and the floating port was modernized to accommodate the new business.

Today, with just over two million inhabitants, Manaus is an aggressive **commercial and industrial centre** for an enormous region. It boasts one of the world's largest motorcycle assembly plants and over half of Brazil's televisions are made here. Landless and jobless Brazilians also flock here looking for work, particularly as there are more prospects in Manaus than in many parts of the Northeast.

The docks and around

The **port** is an unforgettable spectacle, with a constant throng of activity stretching along the riverfront, while the ships moored at the docks bob serenely up and down. Boats are getting ready to leave or, having just arrived, are busy unloading. People cook fish at stalls to sell to the hungry sailors and their passengers, or to the workers once they've finished their shift of carrying cargo from the boats to the distribution market. During the day there's no problem wandering around (although watch your personal belongings), and it's easy enough to find out which boats are going where just by asking. At night, however, this can be a dangerous area and is best avoided, as many of the river men carry guns.

The **Porto Flutuante**, or floating docks, here were built by a British company at the beginning of the twentieth century. To cope with the Rio Negro rising over a 14m range, the concrete pier is supported on pontoons that rise and fall to allow even the largest ships to dock here year-round (the highest recorded level of the river was in 1953, when it rose some 30m above sea level).

Alfândega

From the Praça Adalberto Valle, the impressive **Alfândega** or Customs House, on Avenida Floriano Peixoto, stands between you and the floating docks. Erected in 1906, the building was shipped over from England in prefabricated blocks and the tower once acted as a lighthouse guiding vessels in at night.

Mercado Municipal

Rua dos Barés • Mon–Sat 6am–6pm, Sun 6am–noon • Free

Along the riverfront is the covered **Mercado Municipal**, whose elegant Art Nouveau roof was designed by Eiffel during the rubber boom and is a copy of the former Les Halles

THE WESTERN AMAZON CLIMATE

The western Amazon normally receives a lot of **rain** – up to 375cm a year in the extreme west and about 175cm around Manaus. In ordinary circumstances, the area's heaviest rains fall in January and February, with a relatively dry season from June to October. The humidity rarely falls much below eighty percent, and the temperature in the month of December can reach well above 40°C. This takes a few days to get used to; until you do it's like being stuck in a sauna with only air conditioning, shady trees, a breeze or cool drinks to help you escape.

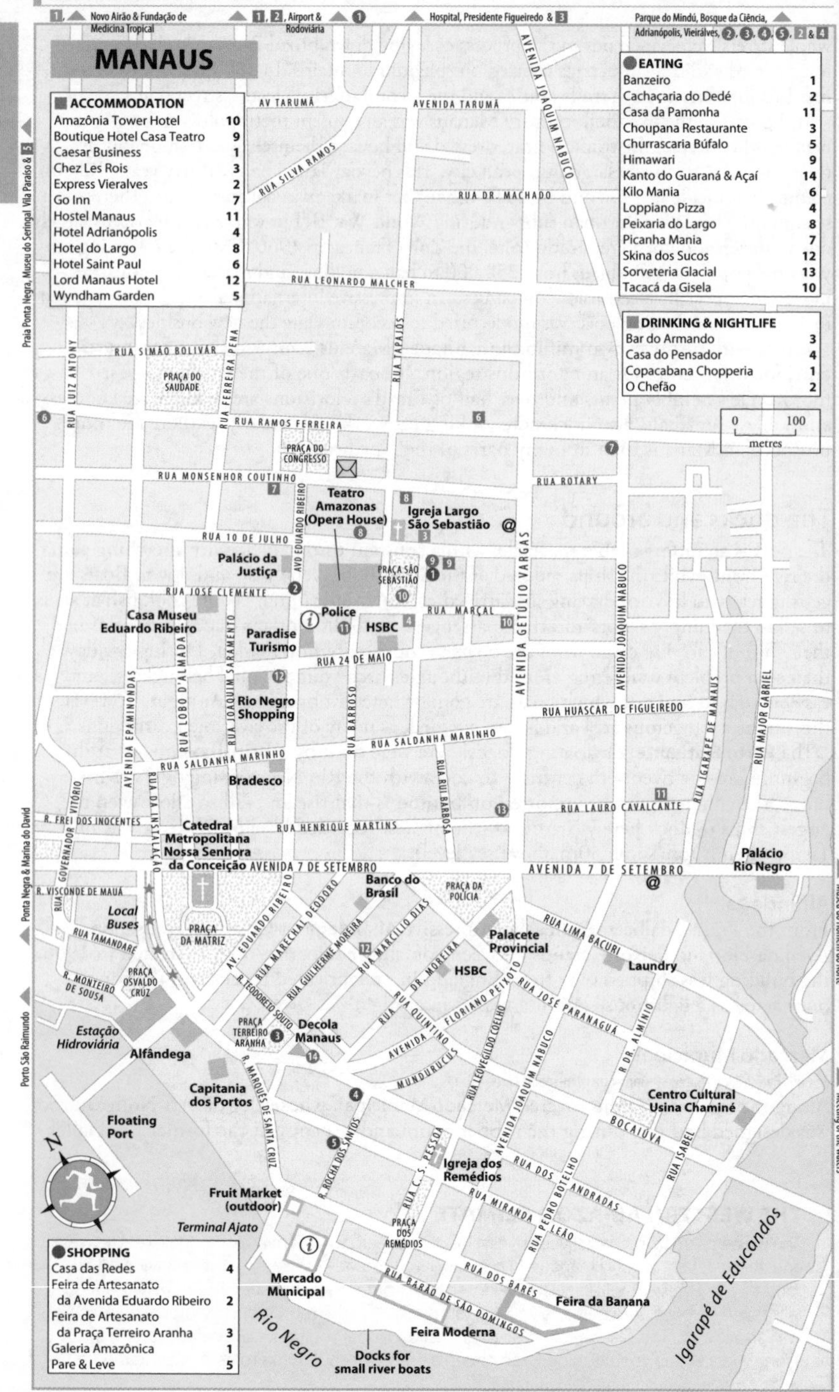

MANAUS
ACCOMMODATION
Amazônia Tower Hotel 10
Boutique Hotel Casa Teatro 9
Caesar Business 1
Chez Les Rois 3
Express Vieralves 2
Go Inn 7
Hostel Manaus 11
Hotel Adrianópolis 4
Hotel do Largo 8
Hotel Saint Paul 6
Lord Manaus Hotel 12
Wyndham Garden 5
EATING
Banzeiro 1
Cachaçaria do Dedé 2
Casa da Pamonha 11
Choupana Restaurante 3
Churrascaria Búfalo 5
Himawari 9
Kanto do Guaraná & Açaí 14
Kilo Mania 6
Loppiano Pizza 4
Peixaria do Largo 8
Picanha Mania 7
Skina dos Sucos 12
Sorveteria Glacial 13
Tacacá da Gisela 10
DRINKING & NIGHTLIFE
Bar do Armando 3
Casa do Pensador 4
Copacabana Chopperia 1
O Chefão 2
SHOPPING
Casa das Redes 4
Feira de Artesanato da Avenida Eduardo Ribeiro 2
Feira de Artesanato da Praça Terreiro Aranha 3
Galeria Amazônica 1
Pare & Leve 5
0 100 metres
Novo Airão & Fundação de Medicina Tropical
Airport & Rodoviária
Hospital, Presidente Figueiredo
Parque do Mindú, Bosque da Ciência, Adrianópolis, Vieirálves
Praia Ponta Negra, Museu do Seringal Vila Paraíso
Ponta Negra & Marina do David
Porto São Raimundo
Museu do Homem do Norte
Meeting of the Waters
Parque Ecológico do Janauary
Teatro Amazonas (Opera House)
Igreja Largo São Sebastião
Palácio da Justiça
Casa Museu Eduardo Ribeiro
Paradise Turismo
Police
HSBC
Rio Negro Shopping
Bradesco
Catedral Metropolitana Nossa Senhora da Conceição
Banco do Brasil
Palacete Provincial
Palácio Rio Negro
Laundry
Local Buses
Estação Hidroviária
Alfândega
Decola Manaus
Capitania dos Portos
Floating Port
Centro Cultural Usina Chaminé
Igreja dos Remédios
Fruit Market (outdoor)
Terminal Ajato
Mercado Municipal
Feira da Banana
Feira Moderna
Docks for small river boats
Rio Negro
Igarapé de Educandos
Praça do Saudade
Praça do Congresso
Praça São Sebastião
Praça da Polícia
Praça da Matriz
Praça Osvaldo Cruz
Praça Terreiro Aranha
Praça dos Remédios
Av Tarumã
Avenida Tarumã
Avenida Joaquim Nabuco
Rua Silva Ramos
Rua Dr. Machado
Rua Leonardo Malcher
Rua Simão Bolívar
Rua Luiz Antony
Rua Ferreira Pena
Rua Tapajós
Rua Ramos Ferreira
Rua Monsenhor Coutinho
Rua Rotary
Rua 10 de Julho
Avd Eduardo Ribeiro
Rua José Clemente
Rua Marçal
Avenida Getúlio Vargas
Rua 24 de Maio
Rua Huascar de Figueiredo
Rua Igarapé de Manaus
Rua Major Gabriel
Avenida Epaminondas
Rua Lobo d'Almada
Rua Joaquim Sarmento
Rua Barroso
Rua Saldanha Marinho
Rua Rui Barbosa
Rua da Instalação
Governador Vitório
R. Frei dos Inocentes
Rua Henrique Martins
Rua Lauro Cavalcante
Avenida 7 de Setembro
R. Visconde de Mauá
Rua Tamandaré
R. Monteiro de Sousa
Av. Eduardo Ribeiro
Rua Marechal Deodoro
Rua Guilherme Moreira
Rua Marcílio Dias
R. Teodoreto Souto
Rua Dr. Moreira
Rua Lima Bacuri
Rua Quintino
Avenida Floriano Peixoto
Rua José Paranaguá
R. Dr. Almínio
Avenida Mundurucus
Rua Leovegildo Coelho
Avenida Joaquim Nabuco
Bocaiúva
Rua Isabel
R. Marquês de Santa Cruz
R. Rocha dos Santos
Rua C. S. Pessoa
Rua dos Andradas
Rua Miranda Leão
Rua Pedro Botelho
Rua dos Barés
Rua Barão de São Domingos

market in Paris. Inaugurated in 1882 and restored in 2009, the market traditionally features an assortment of tropical fruit and vegetables, jungle herbs, scores of different fresh fish and indigenous craft goods jumbled together. Just to the east of this market is the **Feira Moderna**, selling food, clothes and other goods, while further along is the colourful **Feira da Banana**, or banana market, displaying mountains of bananas and plantains, along with other exotic fruits.

Catedral Metropolitana Nossa Senhora da Conceição

Praça Osvaldo Cruz s/n • Open for worship and Mass • Free

The **Catedral de Nossa Senhora da Conceição**, more commonly known as Igreja Matriz, is a relatively plain building, surprisingly untouched by the orgy of adornment that struck the rest of the city – though judging by the number of people who use it, it plays a more active role in the life of the city than many showier buildings. The original cathedral, built mainly of wood and completed in 1695 by the Carmelite missionaries, was destroyed by fire in 1850, and the present building dates from 1878, with most of its materials brought from Europe (mainly Portugal). Around the cathedral are the **Praça Osvaldo Cruz** and the **Praça da Matriz**, shady parks popular with local courting couples, hustlers and sleeping drunks.

Casa Museu Eduardo Ribeiro

Rua José Clemente 322 • Tues–Fri 9am–2pm, Sun 9am-2pm• Free • ⓣ 92 3631 2938

The **Casa Museu Eduardo Ribeiro** was the former residence of journalist and politician Eduardo Ribeiro, who transformed Manaus into one of the world's finest capitals during the golden years of the rubber boom. The interior is laid out like a wealthy town house typical of its time, with lovely pieces of furniture and other artefacts; the beautiful rocking chair is original. Within the same building are also the headquarters of the Amazon Academy of Medicine.

Teatro Amazonas

Praça Largo de São Sebastião • Tues–Sat 9am–5pm, visits via 20min guided tours only, leaving every 30min • R$20 • ⓣ 92 3232 1768

Several blocks north away from the river lies the city's most famous symbol, the **Teatro Amazonas** or Opera House, which seems even more extraordinary lying in the midst of all the rampant commercialism hereabouts. The whole incongruous, magnificent creation, designed in a pastiche of Italian Renaissance style by a Lisbon architectural firm, cost over R$6 million. After twelve years of building, with virtually all the materials – apart from the regional wood – brought from Europe, the Opera House was finally completed in 1896. Its main feature, the fantastic cupola, was created from 36,000 tiles imported from Alsace in France. The theatre's main curtain, painted in Paris by Brazilian artist Crispim do Amaral, represents the meeting of the waters and the local water-goddess Iara. The four painted pillars on the ceiling depict the Eiffel Tower in Paris, giving visitors the impression, as they look upwards, that they are actually underneath the tower itself. The chandeliers are of Italian crystal and French bronze, and the theatre's seven hundred seats, its main columns and the balconies are all made of English cast iron. If you include the dome, into which the original curtain is pulled up in its entirety, the stage is 75m high.

Major restorations have taken place in 1929, 1960, 1974 and in 1990, when the outside was returned from blue to its original pink. Looking over the upstairs balcony down onto the road in front of the Opera House, you can see the black driveway made from a special blend of rubber, clay and sand, originally to dampen the noise of horses and carriages as they arrived. Regular performances continue to be held at the theatre.

5

Praça São Sebastião

In front of the Teatro, the wavy black-and-white mosaic designs of the **Praça São Sebastião** represent the meeting of the waters, and are home to the Monument to the Opening of the Ports, a marble-and-granite creation with four ships that represent four continents – America, Europe, Africa and Asia/Australasia – and children who symbolize the people of those continents. The Praça São Sebastião is getting trendier by the year, with a growing number of interesting shops, bars and arty cafés.

Igreja Largo São Sebastião

Rua 10 de Julho • Daily 6am–10pm

Also on the Praça São Sebastião is the beautiful little **Igreja Largo São Sebastião**, built in 1888, and, like many other churches in Brazil, with only one tower due to the nineteenth-century tax levied on those with two towers.

Palácio da Justiça

Avenida Eduardo Ribeiro 833 • Tues–Fri 9am–2pm, Sun 9am–1pm • Free • ⓣ 92 3248 1844

The beautifully preserved **Palácio da Justiça** was inaugurated in April 1900 and until April 2006 served as the main state court. The building was inspired by French Imperial architecture and English Neoclassicism, and today serves as a cultural centre and museum. Its sumptuous interior features polished wooden floors and wonderfully high ceilings, while above the central portico is a statue of the Greek goddess Themis, personifying justice and eternal law; contrary to traditional representation, the goddess here is not blindfolded.

Centro Cultural Usina Chaminé

Av Lourenço da Silva Braga s/n • Tues–Fri 9am–2pm, Sat 9am–1pm • Free • ⓣ 92 3633 3026

This interactive museum located in a lovely mansion displays all manner of artefacts, oils, herbs and spices of indigenous life that are aimed at stimulating the five senses. There are temporary exhibitions, plus theatrical and musical performances.

Palacete Provincial

Praça da Polícia • Tues–Sat 9am–2pm • ⓣ 92 3631 6047

The **Palacete Provincial** is a cultural complex housing four museums and the Pinacoteca do Estado Amazonas, a permanent art exposition featuring the works of local, national and international artists. The **Museu da Imagem e do Som do Amazonas** (or Image and Sound museum) houses audiovisual and multimedia displays of Amazonian culture, while the **Sala de Arqueologia** (or Archeological Room) showcases archeological finds unearthed in the Amazon region, including tools, utensils and ancient burial jars. The **Museu Tiradentes** displays military memorabilia, while the **Museu de Numismática** houses a collection of Ancient Greek and Roman coins as well as old Brazilian currency.

Palácio Rio Negro

Av Sete de Setembro s/n • Tues–Fri 9am–2pm, Sat 9am–1pm • Free • ⓣ 92 3232 4450

The **Centro Cultural Palácio Rio Negro** is a gorgeous colonial-period mansion built in the early twentieth century by the wealthy German rubber merchant Waldemar Scholz. Scholz's dream in the Amazon was short-lived; with the collapse of the rubber boom, he was forced into remortgaging his home. The State acquired the mansion in 1918 for a paltry sum and it became the seat of the government of Governor Pedro d'Alcantara. Today, the building functions as a cultural centre and museum with lovely varnished *acapú* and *pau amarelo* floors and displays of beautiful period furniture.

Museu do Homem do Norte

Centro Cultural dos Povos da Amazônia, Praça Francisco Pereira da Silva s/n, Bairro Crespo • Mon–Fri 9am–2pm • Free • 92 2125 5323 • Bus #611, #705, #706, #712, #713 or #715 from Praça da Matriz

With a collection of over 2000 objects, the fascinating **Museu do Homem do Norte** (Museum of Northern Man) offers an insight into the life and traditions of the Amazon's diverse tribes. It provides an excellent introduction to the region, with informative displays on pre-colonial societies, tribal rituals and medicinal herbs, along with exhibitions on *guaraná* and rubber production.

Meeting of the waters

The most popular and widely touted day-trip around Manaus is to the **meeting of the waters**, some 10km downstream, where the Rio Negro and the Rio Solimões meet to form the Rio Amazonas. The alkaline Solimões absorbs the much more acid Rio Negro over several kilometres. For this distance the waters of the two rivers continue to flow separately, the muddy yellow of the former contrasting sharply with the black of the latter. Interestingly, the Rio Negro is always warmer than the Solimões. The lighter colour of the Solimões is mainly due to the high levels of soil suspended in the water, which has mostly come here as runoff from the Andes. The Rio Negro is particularly dark because most of its source streams have emerged in low-lying forests where rotting vegetation rather than heavier soil is absorbed into the river drainage system. It creates a strange sight, and one well worth experiencing.

Parque Ecológico do Janauary

The beautiful **Parque Ecológico do Janauary** is an ecological park of 90 square kilometres some 7km from Manaus on one of the main local tributaries of the Rio Negro. Tours to the meeting of the waters usually also include a visit here; you'll be transferred to smaller motorized canoes to explore its creeks (*igarapés*), flooded forest lands (*igapós*) and abundant vegetation. In the rainy season you have to explore the creeks and floodlands by boat; during the dry season – between September and January – it's possible to walk around.

Praia Ponta Negra

Bus #120 from Praça da Matriz (40min; R$3.10)

The river beach at **Praia Ponta Negra**, about 13km northwest of Manaus near the *Hotel Tropical*, is a very popular local excursion, and at weekends is packed with locals. Once the home of the Manaós, today the beach is an enjoyable spot for a swim, with plenty of bars and restaurants serving freshly cooked river fish. The beach is at its best between September and March, when the river is low and exposes a wide expanse of sand, but even when the rains bring higher waters and the beach almost entirely disappears, plenty of people come to eat and drink.

VICTORIA AMAZONICA

One of the highlights of the Manaus area is the abundance of **Victoria amazonica** (previously *Victoria regia*), the extraordinary giant floating lily for which Manaus is famous. Found mostly in shallow lakes, it flourishes in the rainy months. The plant, named after Queen Victoria by an English naturalist in the nineteenth century, has huge leaves – some over 1m across – with a covering of thorns on their underside as protection from the teeth of plant-eating fish. The flowers are white on the first day of their life, rose-coloured on the second, and on the third they begin to wilt: at night the blooms close, imprisoning any insects that have wandered in, and releasing them again as they open with the morning sun.

5

Parque do Mindú

Rua Perimental s/n • Tues–Sun 8am–4pm • Free • Bus #422 from Praça da Matriz (1hr; R$3.10)

The **Parque do Mindú**, out in the direction of the airport in the Parque Dez district, about 6km from the centre, is the city's largest expanse of public greenery, incorporating educational trails where visitors can walk along suspended walkways. The park is home to a number of species of flora and fauna, including agoutis and the endangered primate tamarin. The park is a pleasant spot for a stroll; it gets busy on weekends when locals head over from Manaus.

Bosque da Ciência

Av Otávio Cabral s/n, Aleixo • Tues–Fri 9am–noon & 2–4pm, Sat & Sun 9am–4pm • R$5 • T 92 3643 3192, W bosque.inpa.gov.br • Bus #125, #215, #515 or #517 from Praça da Matriz (1hr; R$3.10)

The **Bosque da Ciência** is an ecological park of about 130,000 square metres located to the west of Manaus. It was created by the Instituto Nacional de Pesquisas de Amazônia (National Institute for Amazon Research; INPA), and is home to otters, manatees, monkeys, snakes and birds. The museum within the grounds displays the giant leaf of the coccoloba plant, the largest ever found in the Amazon measuring 250cm by 144cm.

Museu do Seringal Vila Paraíso

Igarapé São João, Tarumã Mirim • Daily 8am–4pm • R$5 • T 92 3631 3632 • Catch a boat from the Marina do David in Ponta Negra (hourly; 40min; R$12)

The **Museu do Seringal Vila Paraíso** re-creates the living and working conditions of rubber barons and tappers from the beginning of the twentieth century. The rubber baron's mansion displays lovely pieces of furniture and memorabilia, including a gramophone, a 1911 piano, an Italian sewing machine and other objects imported from the Far East. Within the grounds are also a chapel, the modest housing quarters of a rubber tapper and a rubber-smoking hut where liquid latex was solidified into rubber bales.

ARRIVAL AND DEPARTURE — MANAUS

BY PLANE

Manaus serves all major Brazilian destinations. The Aeroporto Internacional Eduardo Gomes (T 92 3652 1212) is at Av Santos Dumont 1350, Tarumã, 17km from the town centre. Be warned that petty crime is an issue on city buses, so a taxi, Uber or transfer service are advised. A taxi to/from town is about R$75. Many tour operators offer airport pick-up if you're booked with them; Antônio Gomes of Amazon Antonio Jungle Tours (see page 376) offers airport pick-up for R$80 (up to four people), while Geraldo Mesquita of Amazon Gero Tours (see page 377) can organize a van pick-up for up to twelve people (R$120). The airport is served by bus #059, #306 and #813; if travelling from the centre, catch a bus from Praça Matriz. There is also an express bus from the airport (daily 3am–11pm; R$20).

Destinations Belém (2 non-stop flights daily; 2hr); Boa Vista (1 daily; 1hr 20min); Brasília (5 daily; 3hr); Porto Velho (4 daily; 1hr 30min); Rio Branco (multiple connecting flights daily; 2hr 40min); Rio de Janeiro (2 daily; 4hr); São Paulo (3 daily; 4hr).

BY BOAT

Slow boats Slow boats dock at the Estação Hidroviária where you also need to go to buy boat tickets to most destinations.

Destinations (via slow boat) Belém (Wed & Fri noon; 4 days; hammock R$200, double cabin R$1050); Porto Velho (Tues & Fri 6pm; 4 days; hammock R$200/250, double cabin R$600); Santarém (daily except Sun 11am; 30hr; hammock R$100, double cabin R$400); Tabatinga (Wed & Fri 11.30am; 6 days; hammock R$350, double cabin R$1000).

Speedboats Speedboats depart from the Terminal Ajato (T 92 3622 6047) on the riverfront by the Estação Hidroviária.

Destinations (via speedboat) Tefé, for the Mamirauá Sustainable Development Reserve (Mon & Wed–Sun 6am, Tues 7am; 14hr; R$230, Tues R$260); Tabatinga (Wed & Fri 7am; 9hr 30min; R$520).

River cruises Amazon Clipper (W amazonclipper.com.br), Think Jungle (W thinkjungle.com) and TourTheTropics, W tourthetropics.com) run excellent river cruises; standard cruises start from R$2150 for 3 days/2 nights, while the smarter premium cruises start from R$3000 for 3 days/2 nights.

BY BUS

The rodoviária (T 92 3642 5808) is at Rua Mário Ipiranga 2348, Florês, some 6km north of the centre; buses #201,

202, #203, #222, #214, #223, #227 and #228 connect the tation to the city centre (40min; R$3.10).

estinations Boa Vista (multiple daily; 12hr; R$157); Porto a Cruz, Venezuela (with a change of bus in Boa Vista; Tues, hurs & Sat at 7pm; 36hr; R$310); Puerto Ordaz, Venezuela with a change of bus in Boa Vista; Tues, Thurs & Sat at 7pm; 0hr; R$300).

BY CAR

ar rental Amore Rent a Car, Av Emilio Moreira 1405 at Av Barcelos 2028, Praça 14 de Janeiro (92 3233 0900, amorerentacar.com.br); Avis, Av Raimundo Parente 38 (92 2127 2847, avis.com) and at the airport (800 725 2847); Localiza, Rua Major Gabriel 1558, Praça 14 de Janeiro (92 3233 4141, localiza.com) and at the airport; Hertz, at the airport (800 701 7300, hertz.com).

BY TAXI

Tucuxi Radio Taxi (92 2123 9090); Manaus Rádio Táxi (92 3236 4220); Tocantins (92 3321 6300).

NFORMATION AND TOURS

ourist information Amazonastur is at Rua Tapajós 74 (Mon–Fri 8am–2pm, Sat & Sun 8am–noon; 92 123 3800, www.visitamazonas.am.gov.br) and an nformation desk at the airport (daily 7am–10pm; 92 652 1656).

ravel agents Decola Manaus, Av Djalma Batista, 735 (92 3088 6222, 92 9152 0320, decolamanaus.com.br), is a reliable and efficiently run agency that can book national and international flights, hotels, car rental, boat trips and more; Paradise Turismo, Av Eduardo Ribeiro 654 (92 3633 8301, paradisetur.com.br), has plenty of offices around town and offers similar services to Decola Manaus. There are also a number of jungle tour operators (see page 376).

ACCOMMODATION

There are a number of hotels in the centre, although most of the best accommodation lies outside in the neighbourhoods of **Punta Negra**, **Vieiralves** and **Adrianópolis**. A number of areas are unsafe at night, in particular in the city centre – make sure you check with your hotel before venturing out into the streets. The area close to the **Teatro Amazonas**, particularly along Rua 10 de Julho, is increasingly popular as a place to stay.

Amazônia Tower Hotel Av Getúlio Vargas 227 92 3028 3891, amazoniatowerhotel.com.br; map p.366. This hotel right in the city centre is a good option, featuring spotless a/c rooms with modern amenities, gym and pool. The hotel doesn't have masses of character, but it's without a doubt among the best in this part of town; staff are welcoming and helpful. R$140

★ **Boutique Hotel Casa Teatro** Rua 10 de Julho 632 92 3633 8381, casateatro.com.br; map p.366. A stone's throw away from the Opera House, *Casa Teatro* is more of a doll's house than a hotel, with itsy-bitsy rooms and hallways decorated with the owner's little knick-knacks, all for sale, from teapots to old phones. The nine suites have private bathrooms, while the twins – all a serious squeeze – feature bunks and shared bathrooms. There's a lounge area that's chock-a-block with curios, and a chill-out rooftop gazebo from where there are unobstructed views of the Opera House. R$310

Caesar Business Av Darcy Vargas 654, Bairro da Chapada 92 3306 4700, caesar-business-manaus.h-rez.com; map p.366. This business hotel is among the city's best, offering comfortable a/c rooms with modern amenities, and a business centre. There's a rooftop gym and terrace, along with a helipad, with great views over the city and the Rio Negro, a sauna and an inviting pool on the mezzanine level. R$270

Chez Les Rois Travessa dos Cristais 1, Conj. Manauense, Nossa Senhora das Graças 92 3015 5638, chezlesrois.com.br; map p.366. About 4.5km north of the centre, this peaceful *pousada* offers ten a/c rooms in a pretty colonial building; scattered bookshelves and little knick-knacks add to the cosy ambience. Breakfast is served by the pool. Inquire about discounts. R$110

Express Vieiralves Av Rio Branco 95 92 3303 9933, expressvieiralves.tur.br; map p.366. This budget hotel located in the Vieiralves district, about 3.5km north of the centre, is a superb option, with spotless rooms, modern amenities, a welcoming restaurant and excellent service. The hotel is perfectly located for Rua Rio Branco, one of the city's most buzzing spots, and home to plenty of bars and restaurants; it makes for a great alternative to staying in the city centre. R$130

Go Inn Rua Monsenhor Coutinho 560 92 3306 2600, atlanticahotels.com.br; map p.366. This is an excellent downtown option featuring welcoming rooms with modern amenities set on five floors, each with safe, fridge and a/c units. Staff are friendly and it's just a short walk to the city's major sights. R$140

Hostel Manaus Rua Lauro Cavalcante 231 92 3233 4545, hostelmanaus.com; map p.366. This HI-affiliated backpacker favourite located in a pair of lovingly restored mansion-style houses offers shared a/c or fan dorms with sturdy bunks and lockers. There's a large communal lounge area, a small patio garden, a rooftop terrace for breakfast with great views towards the Palácio Rio Negro, and kitchen and laundry facilities. HI members get a ten percent discount. Dorms R$40, doubles R$95

Hotel Adrianópolis Rua Salvador 195 ☎ 92 2101 2000, hoteladrianopolis.tur.br; map p.366. Perfect for self-caterers, this recently refurbished hotel features sixty large rooms, each with living area, veranda and kitchenette with hobs. There's also a twentieth-floor pool with great views over the city, a gym and sauna. R$200

Hotel do Largo Rua Monsenhor Coutinho 790 ☎ 92 3304 4751, hoteldolargomanaus.com.br; map p.366. This budget hotel just one block away from the Opera House features great-value rooms with private bathrooms. The hallways are a bit sterile, with tacky carpeting, and the breakfast is nothing to write home about, but the price cannot be beaten. R$160

Hotel Saint Paul Rua Ramos Ferreira 1115 ☎ 92 2101 3800, hotelsaintpaul.tur.br; map p.366. At just 500m from the Opera House, this is one of the best options in the centre. The a/c rooms are comfortable with modern amenities, TV, minibar and safe. There's also a little pool, fitness centre and restaurant. R$180

Lord Manaus Hotel Rua Marcílio Dias 217 ☎ 9 3622 2844, lordmanaus.com.br; map p.366. Th reception has a bit of a retro feel to it, with a 1980s-sty bar decked out in dark leather, but the 100-plus room are comfortable; the *executivos* curiously have sinks in th bedroom itself, while the pricier suites are much large with grander bathrooms. There are also a few standar rooms reserved for smokers – they're not the best th hotel offers, with carpeted floors and a bit of a musty fee to them. Substantial discounts available (up to fifty percen off) – simply ask. R$160

Wyndham Garden Av Coronel Teixeira 1320A, Pont Negra ☎ 92 4009 8200, wyndham.com; map p.36 This sleek lodging option is located in the happening Pont Negra district, 15km west of the city centre, is one of th city's best hotels, offering spacious, well-appointed room set on sixteen floors. There's a sauna, gym and infinity poo looking right onto the river; it's a great spot for a sundowne soaking up the much welcome river breeze. R$200

EATING

Most of the city's best restaurants are outside the centre in **Punta Negra**, **Vieiralves** and **Adrianópolis**, a taxi rid away. One traditional dish you should definitely try is **tacacá** – a soup that consists essentially of yellow manioc-root juic in a hot spicy dried-shrimp sauce. It's often mixed and served in traditional gourd bowls (*cuias*) and is usually sold in th late afternoons by *tacacazeiras* (street-food vendors).

★ **Banzeiro** Rua Libertador 102, Adrianópolis ☎ 92 3234 1621, restaurantebanzeiro.com.br; map p.366. The Amazonian cuisine at this renowned restaurant attracting well-heeled *Manauenses* is superb, embracing African and European creations using exotic local ingredients. The interior features minimalist yet sophisticated decor recalling life in the jungle, including a wooden canoe and oars. Try the *tambaqui con crosta de castanha e banana assada* (*tambaqui fish* with Brazilian nuts; R$131). Mon–Thurs 11.30am–3pm & 6.30–11pm, Fri & Sat 11.30am–4pm & 6.30–11pm, Sun 11.30am–4pm & 7–10pm.

Cachaçaria do Dedé Manauara Shopping, Av Mario Ypiranga 1300, Adrianópolis ☎ 92 3236 6642, cachacariadodede.com.br; map p.366. This cosy bar and restaurant is jam-packed with foodstuffs stacked on shelves, along with floor-to-ceiling bottles of alcohol, with over 150 types of cachaça on offer (there are allegedly over 800 stacked away). The food's great too – fish lovers should try the oven-cooked cod (*bacalhau manauara*; R$69.90), while meat lovers can go for the *carne do sol de filé do dedé* (R$92.90). Mon–Thurs 10am–11pm, Fri & Sat 10am–midnight, Sun noon–10pm.

Casa da Pamonha Rua Barroso 375, Centro ☎ 92 3234 7086 casadapamonha.com; map p.366. This vegetarian restaurant offers a *por quilo* self-service (R$42.90) of regional dishes, including *tapioca* with Brazilian nuts and *tucumã* (palm), and offers vegan and sugar-free options along with a handful of gluten-fre products. The bread is home-made (try the delicious *pã de milho*, or cornbread) and the freshly squeezed juice (R$6–10) are well worth trying. Mon–Fri 7am–7pm, Sa 7am–2pm.

Choupana Restaurante Rua Recife 790, Adrianopóli ☎ 92 3635 3878, choupanarestaurante.com.b map p.366. Some of the city's best regional cuisine i on offer at this pleasant airy restaurant, reminiscent of a indigenous building with natural materials and woode furniture. The *tucupí* duck baked in manioc juice an *jambu* leaves (R$118) is excellent, and the barmen rustl up creative cocktails using fresh local fruits. Mon–Sa 11.30am–11pm, Sun 11am–4pm.

★ **Churrascaria Búfalo** Rua Pará 490 ☎ 92 363 3773, churrascariabufalo.com.br; map p.366. Wit multiple locations around town, this is an absolute mus for any foodie, and in particular meat lovers. This branch in Vieiralves, offers a *por quilo* lunch buffet (R$89.90) and features 25 types of succulent meat served by waiter dressed in typical *gaúcho* clothing; the buffet feature paella, cod, salmon and a vast selection of salads. Fo dessert, try the ice cream/cake dish *petit gateau* (R$25 Mon–Thurs 11.30am–3pm & 6.30–11pm, Fri & Sa 11.30am–3.30pm & 7–11pm, Sun 11.30am–4pm.

Himawari Rua 10 de Julho 618, Centro ☎ 92 3233 2208, facebook.com/RestauranteHimawariManaus; ma p.366. This Japanese restaurant offers plenty of sashim and sushi dishes (R$70) of salmon, shrimp, octopus and tuna, along with a good selection of udon noodles (R$40), although the real draw here is the Peruvian *ceviche* (R$30). Mon–Wed 6–11pm, Fri & Sat 6–11pm, Sun 6–10pm.

Kanto do Guaraná & Açaí Av Floriano Peixoto, loja 15, Centro ⓣ92 3233 1693; map p.366. This no-frills hole in the wall is just the place to grab an energizing *guaraná*-based drink or a cup of *açaí* (R$5) as you explore town; there's plenty to choose from. For a real boost try the "Popeye" drink, rustled up with spinach, guarana, ginseng, granola, banana, *açaí*, Amazonian herbs and even quail eggs (R$6). Mon–Sat 7am–6pm.

Kilo Mania Rua Ramos Ferreira 390 ⓣ92 3633 2236, ⓦkilomaniamanaus.com.br; map p.366. Set on two floors, this *por quilo* restaurant with orange decor is a popular lunch choice for those working in and around the centre. The *por quilo* buffet (R$48.90) features plenty of dishes, including a very decent selection of meats and local fish. Daily 11am–3pm.

Loppiano Pizza Rua Major Gabriel 1080 ⓣ92 3642 1234, ⓦloppiano.com.br; map p.366. This open-fronted pizzeria with chequered tablecloths is among the city's best; you can watch the *pizzaiolo* at work preparing all manner of pizzas, including an Amazonian-style *pizza tacacá* with *jambú*, shrimps and olives (R$76.70). And save a space for their dessert pizzas, which include everything from fried banana pizzas to chocolate, pineapple, dulce de leche and M&M toppings. Mon–Thurs & Sun 5–11.30pm, Fri & Sat 5pm–12.30am.

Peixaria do Largo Rua 10 de Julho 491 ⓣ92 3234 8462; map p.366. Once housing the employees of the Manaus Opera House just opposite and thereafter a ballet academy, this building has been fully refurbished to re-create the city's atmosphere at the height of the rubber boom; the smartly dressed waiters sport bow ties, but the atmosphere is laidback and the menu features excellent fish options, including *tambaqui*, *tucunaré*, *pirarucu* and *dourado* – all big enough to share. Mains roughly R$75. Mon–Sat 11am–2pm.

★ **Picanha Mania** Rua Ramos Ferreira 1684 ⓣ92 3234 8054, ⓦpicanhamania.com.br; map p.366. Specializing in *picanha* (fillet steak), this large restaurant with impeccable speedy service also offers beef ribs (R$8.90/100g), pork ribs (R$21) and spring chicken (R$21), with individual sides starting at R$5 and up to R$25 for combos; the broccoli rice is particularly tasty. Mon–Thurs & Sun 11.30am–3pm & 6.30–11pm, Fri & Sat 11.30am–3pm & 6.30pm–midnight.

Skina dos Sucos Av Eduardo Ribeiro 629 ⓣ92 3233 1970; map p.366. This superb little café packed with fruits specializes almost exclusively in tropical juices (R$10) with all manner of exotic names, half of which you will probably have never heard of. For a further vitamin boost, try the *açaí*, crushed berries highly rich in anti-oxidants. Mon–Sat 7am–7pm.

Sorveteria Glacial Rua Getulio Vargas 585, Centro ⓣ92 8826 0041, ⓦglacial.com.br; map p.366. This hugely popular chain serves 24 flavours of exotic ice cream – just grab a cup and scoop away at the self-service, sprinkle with toppings and pay at the counter (R$5/100g). Mon–Thurs 10am–11pm, Fri & Sat 10am–midnight.

Tacacá da Gisela Largo São Sebastião s/n ⓣ92 8801 4901, ⓦfacebook.com/tacaca.gisela; map p.366. This friendly stall right by the Opera House only serves *tacacá* (R$18), a speciality of the Brazilian Amazon traditionally enjoyed in the late afternoon and a must-try; it's made of *tucupi* (boiled manioc), *jambu* (anaesthetic leaves that will leave your tongue numb for quite some time), tapioca starch, dried shrimps and hot pepper, served in a calabash tree bowl. Daily 4–10pm.

DRINKING AND NIGHTLIFE

The best bars and clubs are outside the centre in **Ponta Negra**, **Vieiralves** and **Adrianópolis**, along with Avenida do Turismo in **Tarumã**, 18km north of the city centre (taxi R$80), which is lined with restaurants and bars. In the centre, the bars by the **Praça do Teatro** are frequented by tourists and locals alike – can be the rest of the area dodgy and unsafe.

★ **Bar do Armando** Rua 10 de Julho, Centro 593 ⓣ95 3232 1195, ⓦfacebook.com/BarDoArmando; map p.366. This local institution has been going strong for years – you'll be hard pushed to find a table, especially at weekends. Locals flock here for the delicious *bolinhos de bacalhau* (*bacalhau* fritters; R$25), washed down with ice-cold beer (Skol R$8). The *pernil* (ham) sandwich (R$15) is also a real winner. Mon & Tues 10am–1am, Wed–Sat 10am–2am, Sun 5pm–midnight.

Casa do Pensador Rua José Clemente 632, Centro ⓣ92 9981 9556, ⓦfacebook.com/casadopensador; map p.366. Formerly a school (it translates as "The House of the Thinker"), this bar and restaurant with tables spilling onto the square is a great spot for a sundowner as you soak in the views of the Opera House. Try the tasty *peixe à delícia* (R$30), grilled fish served with rice and potatoes. Daily 4–11pm.

Copacabana Chopperia Av do Turismo s/n ⓣ92 3584 4569, ⓦcopacabanachopperia.com; map p.366. This large breezy bar is a popular spot along Av do Turismo and gets packed over the weekends. Local bands play on Fridays, and on Sundays it's *pagode* and samba. Beers (R$6), cocktails (R$10). Thurs–Sat 8pm–3am, Sun 2.30pm–2am.

O Chefão Av Mário Ypiranga, 1300 Manauara Shopping ⓣ92 3236 2605; map p.366. This longstanding Irish-style pub has been redone with a Godfather theme (not

5

clear why) and is set in the Manaura Shopping Mall. Decor features chequered wooden floors, a handful of comfy armchairs and plenty of curios dotted about. There are plenty of local and imported beers (R$8), and bar snacks starting at R$18 and burgers (R$20). There's live rock music on Fridays. Daily 10am–10pm.

SHOPPING

Casa das Redes Santana Rua dos Andradas 106 ⓣ 95 3232 7660; map p.366. One of the best places to buy hammocks, with a huge variety of all colours and sizes; prices for singles start at R$50, for doubles R$70. Mon–Fri 8am–5pm, Sat 8am–4pm.

Feira de Artesanato da Avenida Eduardo Ribeiro Av Eduardo Ribeiro; map p.366. This lively Sunday-morning street market which appears out of nowhere in the broad Avenida Eduardo Ribeira, behind the Teatro Amazonas, displays crafts, herbal remedies, cosmetics made with local products, and food stalls. Sun 7am–1pm.

Feira de Artesanato da Praça Terreiro Aranha Praça Terreiro Aranha; map p.366. By the riverfront, this market is one of the best spots to buy crafts, and at reasonable prices, too. Mon–Sat 8am–6pm.

★ **Galeria Amazônica** Rua Costa Azevedo 272, Largo do Teatro, Centro ⓣ 92 3233 4521, ⓦ galeriamazonica.org.br; map p.366. This lovely shop displays traditional and contemporary products of the Amazon, such as pottery, sculptures, paintings and mats. Prices are high but so is the quality. Mon–Sat 10am–8pm.

Pare & Leve Rua Rocha dos Santos 95 ⓣ 92 3233 1733; map p.366. An excellent health-food shop selling all manner of natural and wholewheat products along with a range of juices, ideal for self-caterers; the walls are lined with foodstuffs from dried fruits to wild mushrooms. Mon–Sat 7.30am–6pm.

DIRECTORY

Consulates Colombia, Vereador Manoel Marçal, 651-A Parque 10 de Novembro (ⓣ 92 3234 6777); Peru, Av Constelação 16 (ⓣ 92 3236 0585); UK, Rua Poraquê 240, Distrito Industrial (ⓣ 92 3613 1819); Venezuela, Rua Rio Jurai 10 (ⓣ 92 3584 3922).

Health The Fundação de Medicina Tropical, Av Pedro Teixeira 25 (ⓣ 92 2127 3555, ⓦ www.fmt.am.gov.br), also known as the Hospital de Doenças Tropicais, specializes in tropical illnesses; Hospital Santa Júlia, Av Ayrão 507 (ⓣ 92 2121 9000, ⓦ hospitalsantajulia.com.br).

Internet *Palace Cyber Café*, Av 7 de Setembro 1428 (daily 8am–11pm; R$5/hr); *Top Cyber*, Av Getúlio Vargas 821 (Mon–Sat 9am–10pm; R$5/hr; ⓣ 92 9154 5815).

Laundry Lavanderia Brilhante, Rua Lima Bacuri 126 (Mon–Sat 7:30am–5pm, ⓣ 92 3232 1214).

Money and exchange Bradesco, Av Eduardo Ribeiro 475; HSBC, Rua Dr Moreira 226 and Rua 24 de Maio 439; Banco do Brasil, Guilherme Moreira 315.

Police The tourist police are in the same building as the tourist office on Av Eduardo Ribeiro (ⓣ 92 98842 1769).

Post office Praça do Congresso 90 (Mon–Fri 8am–4pm, Sat 8am–noon).

Around Manaus

The area around Manaus is the obvious place in the Brazilian Amazon for **jungle** river trips. However, you have to be prepared to travel for at least a few days out of Manaus if you are serious about spotting a wide range of wildlife. The city offers many **organized tours** (see page 376) bringing visitors into close contact with the world's largest tropical rainforest. Unfortunately, though, the forest in the immediate vicinity is far from virgin. Over the last millennia it has been explored by indigenous peoples, missionaries, rubber gatherers, colonizing extractors, settlers, urban folk from Manaus and, more recently, a steady flow of eco-minded tourists.

The amount and kind of **wildlife** you get to see on a standard jungle tour depends mainly on how far away from Manaus you go and how long you can devote to the trip. **Birds** including macaws, hummingbirds, jacanas, cormorants, herons, kingfishers, hawks, chacalacas and toucans can generally be spotted – but you need luck to see hoatzins, trogons, cock-of-the-rock or blue macaws. You might see alligators, snakes, sloths, river dolphins and a few species of monkey on a three-day trip – though you can see many of these anyway at INPA or the Parque Ecológico do Janauary (see page 369). Sightings for **large mammals** and **cats**, however, are very rare, though chances are increased on expedition-type tours of six days or more to deep-forest places like the Rio Juma. On any trip, make sure to get some time in the smaller channels in a canoe, as the sound of a motor is a sure way of scaring every living thing out of sight.

BUYING A HAMMOCK

Cloth hammocks are the most comfortable and attractive, but they're also heavier, bulkier and take longer to dry out if they get wet. Less comfortable, but more convenient, much lighter and more durable are **nylon hammocks**. You should be able to get a perfectly adequate cloth hammock, which will stand up to a few weeks' travelling, from around R$30 for a single and R$60 for a double; for a nylon hammock, add R$10 to the price; you'll pay more for elaborate handwoven ones. Easing the path to slinging hammocks once you get home are metal *armadores*, which many hammock and most hardware shops sell; these are hooks mounted on hinges and a plate with bolts for sinking into walls. When buying a hammock, make sure it takes your body lying horizontally across it: sleeping along the curve is bad for your back. A good hammock shop in Manaus is Casa des Redes (see page 374) on Rua dos Andradas.

If you want to sleep in the forest, either in a lodge, riverboat or, for the more adventurous (and perhaps those on a low budget), swinging in a hammock outside in a small jungle clearing, it really is worth taking as many days as you can to get as far away from Manaus as possible.

Presidente Figueiredo

Located 107km north of Manaus, **PRESIDENTE FIGUEIREDO** sits at the heart of waterfall country. It is also home to numerous caves and verdant jungle rich in fauna, with paths snaking through beautiful scenery. It's the ideal spot for ecotourists; there are plenty of places to stay, although it's also possible to visit as part of a day-trip from Manaus with Amazon Eco Adventures (see page 376).

ARRIVAL AND INFORMATION — PRESIDENTE FIGUEIREDO

By bus There are buses from Manaus's rodoviária (daily 6am, 10am, 12.30pm, 5pm & 9.20pm, returning to Manaus 6am, 10am, 12.30pm, 5pm & 9pm; 2hr; R$29).

Tourist information The friendly CAT tourist office is just by the rodoviária along the BR-174 at the Praça da Cultura, Km 107 (daily 8am–5pm; ❶92 3324 1308, ⓦpresidentefigueiredo.am.gov.br). This is where you can hire registered guides for the day.

ACCOMMODATION AND EATING

Café Regional Priscila Estrada Cachoeira 23 ❶92 9171 3776. This hugely popular café is an obligatory pit stop for anyone passing through Presidente Figueiredo along the BR-174; breakfast is their big thing, with excellent home-made tapioca with cheese, nuts and *tucumã* (native palm; R$18) and delicious *farofa de carne sol* (R$10). Daily 5am–7.30pm.

Hotel Iracema Falls BR174, Km 115 ❶92 9250 4370, ⓦhoteliracemafalls.com.br. This large complex at the entrance to the Iracema Falls features accommodation in yellow bungalows dotted around a large plot of verdant land. Rooms are simply decorated with wooden furniture and the occasional painting, and there's a large breezy restaurant as well as a pool, two kiddie pools and a volleyball court. R$150

Novo Airão

NOVO AÍRÃO, a small jungle town on the west bank of the Rio Negro, is 115km northwest of Manaus. Its main attraction is the chance to feed **pink dolphins** from the floating restaurant run by Doña Marilda, north of the town's small port (daily 8am–noon & 2–5pm on the hour; R$15, kids half price; ❶92 9235 9155) – a practice that is frowned upon by some. Since the Archipelago Anavilhanas on the other side of the river was made a national park in 2008, it is no longer possible to swim with the dolphins.

ARRIVAL AND INFORMATION — NOVO AÍRÃO

By boat Slow boats from Manaus leave Tues & Fri at 8pm, returning to Manaus Mon, Thurs & Sun at 8pm (8–9hr; R$45).

By bus From Manaus's rodoviária, Aruanã has daily bus services from Manaus to Novo Airão with Emtram and

Master at 6.15am & 10.45am and 3.15pm, returning to Manaus at 6am, 1.30pm & 3.45pm (4hr; R$43).

By taxi A taxi from Manaus to Novo Airão is R$55 per person per car (up to 4 people), which makes it worth it if there's a group of you. Driver Nilson can arrange pick-up (92 9221 5147).

Information There is an information centre at Av Ajuricaba s/n, Bairro Nova Esperança (daily 8am–5pm).

ACCOMMODATION

Mirante do Avião Rua São Domingos 3 92 3365 1644, mirantedogaviao.com.br. This quirky, eco-friendly hotel is downright idyllic, with solar panels, a veggie garden and recycling facilities is shaped like an overturned boat; rooms are entirely made of local wood and decorated with artisanal furniture. Multi-day packages including transfers, food, guides and tours start at R$2451. Suites R$850

Pousada Bela Vista Av Presidente Getulio Vargas 47 92 3365 1023, pousada-belavista.com. This pleasant *pousada* features small but comfortable a/c rooms decorated with fun, colourful paintings of Amazonian wildlife and tribes; there are views of the Rio Negro from the breakfast table, while the beautiful Anavilhanas archipelago lies just across the river. There are hammocks to sit back in and the *pousada* organizes tours (starting at R$160 for 1hr tour) in the area of Anavilhanas National Park. R$200

JUNGLE TOUR OPERATORS AND LODGES IN MANAUS

Jungle lodges offer travellers the opportunity to experience the rainforest while maintaining high levels of comfort, even elegance; there are scores of lodges, most operated by tour companies. There are plenty of phony agencies and touts at the airport and in the city centre ready to rip off naïve tourists, so be careful. Make sure you personally visit a tour agency (never hand over money to anyone on the street or at the airport, even if they claim they work for a given agency). You can also check with Amazonastur (visitamazonas.am.gov.br) for reports on complaints against particular tour operators. It's much better to book in advance on the internet, although make sure the company actually exists – touts have even set up fake websites and scammed tourists online.

The most dependable and comfortable way to visit the rainforest is to take a **package tour** that involves a number of nights in a jungle lodge. The lodges invariably offer hotel-standard accommodation, full board and a range of activities including alligator spotting, piranha fishing, trips by canoe and transport to and from Manaus. Some lodge-based tours integrate the opportunity to spend a night or two camping out in the forest. The least expensive options offer hammock-space accommodation, perhaps combined with a night in the forest; the most expensive include at least four-star comfort.

TOUR OPERATORS

Amazon Antonio Jungle Tours Rua Iauro Cavalcante 231, Centro 92 3234 1294, 92 9961 8314, www.antonio-jungletours.com. Run by native tour guide Antônio Gomes, this experienced operator organizes jungle tours from two to ten days with stays at his pleasant ecolodge powered by solar panels 200km from Manaus along the Rio Urubu. Accommodation is in native-style chalets, bungalows and dorms; there's a canopy tower with wonderful views over the river and rainforest, and a floating sundeck with loungers. Plenty of exciting activities are offered, including alligator spotting, piranha fishing, paddle canoeing and camping in the jungle. Price per day at the lodge starting from $R250. He also runs the *Cumaru Pousada*, a smaller lodging option 240km downstream from Manaus along the Rio Urubu. Guests stay in jungle bungalows and dorms, each with river views. Activities include birding, canoe trips and alligator spotting. Price per day starting at R$300.

Amazon Eco Adventures Rua 10 de Julho 509 92 883 1011, amazonecoadventures.com. This one-man outfi is run by experienced Pedro Neto. He only works with sma groups (maximum 7 people), which means that you'll b zooming along the river in his very own speedboat to see th meeting of the waters, as opposed to sitting in a large boa with dozens of other tourists. As a result, his tours are slightl more expensive, but well worth it. Pedro also organize panoramic flights and day-trips to Presidente Figueiredo (see page 375), plus he runs a beautiful floating lodge. He's th only operator doing the Maruaga trail and cave.

Amazon Explorers Av Sete de Setembro, 827, Líde Hotel, Centro 92 3232 3052, amazonexplorers tur.br. This reputable operator runs a reservation service for smart jungle lodges and luxury boat rental and organizes jungle tours with boat accommodatio (promotional packages start around R$180/person pe day with transfers) and a 6hr trip to the meeting of th waters and Parque Janauary. As a travel agency, it offers ticketing service for day-trips as well as air and boat trave

Pousada Tarântula Rua Nova Esperança, Bairro Sto. Elias 44 ☎92 9110 9185, ✉tarantula@amazonia expeditions.com.br. This tranquil *pousada* outside of town has pretty leafy grounds with a pleasant pool area; rooms are tiled and nicely decorated with paintings of Amazonian wildlife. There's a barbecue area and a kitchen that guests are welcome to use. It's a nice spot to sit back and have some peace and quiet. R$190

EATING

★ **Flor do Luar** South of town ☎92 9418 0865. This floating restaurant just south of town serves exceptional food; the talented chef from São Paulo has years of experience working in some of the country's top restaurants. She rustles up creative dishes exclusively using seasonal products with an emphasis on bringing out the genuine flavours of the Amazon (mains start at around R$80). It's only open on weekends for lunch, but if you're in town another day just call ahead and the chef will come in especially for you. Fri–Sun 10am–5pm.

Sabor do Sul Av Tiradentes 5 ☎92 9231 8273. This popular restaurant is one of the best in town, serving simple home-made dishes that will really hit the spot. It's a laidback place, but if you're after authentic Amazonian cooking this is where it's at. The menu includes plenty of fresh fish dishes (R$55) along with meats (R$59). Daily 11am–3pm.

Amazon Gero Tour Dez de Julho 679, Centro ☎92 9983 6273, ⓦamazongerotours.com. One of the most reliable and experienced operators, the owner Geraldo (Gero) Mesquita organizes tours mainly to the Mamori and Juma areas. Great rainforest accommodation is available in Gero's own *Ararinha Jungle Lodge*, located on the scenic and peaceful Lago Arara (see page 378) just off the Parana do Mamori. It offers a range of prices and levels of comfort from family suites and standard rooms to hammock space in the round viewing platform above the circular restaurant. Tours include boat and canoe trips, jungle hiking and visits to native people, with accommodation in hammocks, overnight in the bush, visiting or staying at local family houses, or in luxury lodge accommodation.

Amazona Tours Av Djalma Batista, Casa Center, No. 735 ☎92 3088 6222, ⓦamazonatours.com. This agency specializes in river cruises, with accommodation in hammocks or cabins, and tours in the Amazon region. They also offer short trips to the meeting of the waters, fishing and alligator spotting, as well as transfer services, city tours, hotel bookings and flight reservations for the whole of Brazil. They also have their own jungle lodge.

Iguana Rua Dez de Julho 663, Centro ☎92 3633 6507, ☎92 9105 5660, ⓦamazonbrasil.com.br. Based next to the *Hotel Dez de Julho*, this company, which operates regularly in the Juma and Mamori areas, is able to organize most kinds of trips, from overnights in the forest to longer lodge- or camp-based trips. They have an attractive lodge in the Juma area that offers private wooden cabins with own shower room or shared dorms.

Maia Expeditions Rua Badajós 62 ☎92 3613 4683, ⓦmaiaexpeditions.com. This highly experienced operator offers private boat expeditions in cabins and hammock accommodation, along with high-end yacht trips. The company runs the lovely *Amazon Turtle Lodge*, a sustainable lodge with eighteen suites 100km southeast of Manaus in the beautiful Mamorí region. The lodge aims to develop and improve living standards by providing English lessons, educating residents about tourism, organic food production and preserving the environment, with the underlying aim of self-sustainability.

LODGES

Anavilhanas Lodge ☎92 3622 8996, ⓦanavilhanas lodge.com. This boutique lodge is located just across the river from the Parque Nacional do Anavilhanas, one of the world's largest freshwater archipelagos with over four hundred islands. Accommodation is in well-appointed bungalows or cottages, there's a welcoming bar and lounge area, and an open-fronted restaurant with superb home cooking. Excursions are fun and educational, and include trips into the beautiful Anavilhanas archipelago, a UNESCO World Heritage Site. All-inclusive packages/person for 3 days/2 nights from R$2800

Dolphin Lodge ☎92 3663 0392, ⓦdolphinlodge.tur.br. Located along the peaceful banks of the Rio Mamori, 78km southeast of Manaus, this welcoming lodge offers accommodation in rustic wooden rooms with private bathrooms. There is plenty to see and do in the immediate vicinity; the area here is rich in macaws, dolphins, birds and alligators, to name a few. All-inclusive packages for minimum three people for 2 days/1 night per person from R$638

Juma Lodge ☎92 3232 2707, ⓦjumalodge.com. This smart lodge offers accommodation in twenty well-appointed forest- and lake-view bungalows sitting on stilts perching among the treetops. Four of the bungalows have solar-heated water, and the welcoming restaurant with rustic furniture has wonderful views over the lake. All-inclusive packages/person for 2 days/1 night from R$2308

Mamirauá Sustainable Development Reserve

Located about 600km west of Manaus, the **Mamirauá Sustainable Development Reserve** is a spectacular area of relatively untouched, seasonally flooded *várzea*-type vegetation offering close contact with the flora and fauna, including pink dolphins. It was Brazil's first sustainable development reserve, aimed at nature conservation and sustainable practices, while providing employment to local communities.

ARRIVAL AND ACCOMMODATION — MAMIRAUÁ RESERVE

By boat There are boats from Manaus to Tefé (see page 370); or you can arrange transport here via the lodge.

Uakari Floating Lodge 97 3343 4160, pousadauacari.com.br. This rustic lodge makes it possible to explore the unspoilt surroundings from a comfortable and welcoming base within the reserve. Three-night minimum stay R$2210

The upper Rio Negro

The **UPPER RIO NEGRO** flows into Manaus from northwestern Amazonas, one of the least explored regions of South America. The area remains is a wonderful place to venture if you're looking to get off the beaten track. The main towns along the Rio Negro are **Barcelos**, the jumping-off point to Brazil's highest waterfall, and **São Gabriel da Cachoeira**, providing access to Brazil's highest peak, the Pico da Neblina.

Barcelos and around

The pleasant little town of **BARCELOS** is one of the stopping-off points for boats heading further upstream. The town attracts plenty of fishermen – its waters are highly rich

THE RIOS NEGRO AND SOLIMÕES

The **Rio Negro** region has a very distinctive beauty influenced by the geology of the Guiana Shield where the main river sources are, and the consequent soil types and topography. The dark (nearly black) waters are very acidic and home to far fewer mosquitoes than you find in other regions. The Negro also tends to have less abundant wildlife than some of the lakes and channels around the Rio Solimões. You can still see much the same species in both regions, but the densities are lower on the Rio Negro and many of its tributaries. Plenty of tours combine both the Solimões and Negro rivers in their itineraries.

Unlike the Rio Negro, the waters of the **Rio Solimões** are a murky brown, as they carry a large quantity of sediment from the Andes mountains. On the river is the beautiful **Lago Mamori**, which offers reasonably well-preserved forest conditions in which you'll see plenty of birds, alligators and dolphins and have the chance to do some piranha fishing. Slightly further into the forest, the **Parana do Mamori** is a quieter river-like arm from Lago Mamori and a zone where numerous birds, sloths, pink dolphins, caiman and monkeys are easily spotted. **Lago Arara**, accessed from the Parana do Mamori, is a beautiful and relatively well-preserved corner in this area. As well as wildlife, the Parana do Mamori allows close contact with the local riverine communities of *caboclo* people (the settlers who have been here for generations and who dedicate their time to fishing, farinha making, cattle ranching and tapping rubber). The Parana do Mamori is connected to the quieter **Lago Juma**; from here the **Rio Juma** region is accessible. It's remote and malarial, but excellent for wildlife.

Much further south of Manaus, the **Rio Igapó Açu** area is one of the best sites for wildlife and, despite its remoteness, it can also be easily reached from Manaus (by boat and road) in a five- or six-day trip; there are no lodges here, but it is possible to stay with locals and ideally your guide will have good contacts. West of Manaus, on the north bank of the Solimões, **Manacapuru**, also accessible by road and boat, is closer to large population centres and therefore offers more in the way of a visit to lakes and plant-familiarization walks, including access to Brazil-nut tree trails. It's also an area where visitors can make interesting excursions up smaller tributaries in search of birdlife, alligators and spectacular flora, such as the gigantic **samaúma tree** with its buttress base (one of the tallest trees in the Amazon).

JUNGLE TERMS

There are a few Brazilian **jungle terms** every visitor should be familiar with: a *regatão* is a travelling-boat-cum-general-store, which can provide a fascinating introduction to the interior if you can strike up an agreeable arrangement with one of their captains; an *igarapé* is a narrow river or creek flowing from the forest into one of the larger rivers (though by "narrow" around Manaus they mean less than 1km wide); an *igapó* is a patch of forest that is seasonally flooded; a *furo* is a channel joining two rivers and therefore a short cut for canoes; a *paraná*, on the other hand, is a branch of the river that leaves the main channel and returns further downstream, creating a river island. The typical deep-red earth of the Western Amazon is known as *tabatinga*, like the city on the frontier with Peru and Colombia; and regenerated forest, like secondary growth, is called *capoeira*.

in fish, in particular peacock bass – and it's possible to arrange fishing trips for one or more days. Barcelos is also the jumping-off point to **Mariuá**, Brazil's largest freshwater archipelago, and the **Cachoeira do El Dorado**, the country's highest waterfall at 353m.

ARRIVAL AND DEPARTURE — BARCELOS AND AROUND

By plane Trip has flights to Barcelos from Manaus (Tues & Fri 12.30pm; 1hr), returning to Manaus same day at 5.30pm.

By slow boat Slow boats leave Manaus Tues, Wed & Fri at 6pm, returning to Manaus on Mon at 6pm, Wed at 11am, Fri at 6pm & Sat at noon & 6pm (R$120 hammock space; R$300 cabin for two including meals).

By fast boat Fast boats from Porto São Raimundo in Manaus leave Tues & Fri at 3pm (R$180/person including meals; 12hr), returning to Manaus Tues & Fri at 7pm.

Tours There are no official tour operators in Barcelos. To book tours to the Cachoeira do El Dorado, contact manausbooking.com, or arrange a tour at the *Hostel Barcelos* (the owner, Gerry, can organize tours upon request). The tourist office also keeps a list of local guides with boats who can be hired per day.

ACCOMMODATION

Hostel Barcelos Rua Anauali 46, Bairro São Francisco 97 99157 5271, hostelbarcelos.com. Run by an expat from Luxembourg, this welcoming hostel offers fan-cooled private rooms and dorms. There's a swimming pool, barbecue area and breezy verandas where travellers can while away a few hours swinging in their hammocks. The hostel has its own large motorized canoe that can be hired, with guide, for trips and expeditions ranging from half a day to several weeks (R$150 per day), as well as an inflatable kayak that can be used for free. Guests can also rent tents and pick their own jungle beach to camp on. They also lend bikes to guests. Open from September to March only. Book ahead. (though slow) Doubles **R$30**, hammock dorms **R$15**

Parque Nacional do Jaú

Located on the west bank of the Rio Negro, just below the confluence with the Rio Branco, is Brazil's largest national park – the 23,000-square-kilometre **Parque Nacional do Jaú**, which cannot be entered alone or without official permission; it is always best to do this through a local tour operator (see page 376) who has the necessary contacts with IBAMA and the national-park offices. It takes time and money to visit the park, but this is exceptionally remote forest and well conserved.

São Gabriel da Cachoeira and around

The town of **SÃO GABRIEL DA CACHOEIRA** has the largest indigenous population of the country, and is a beautiful place where the jungle is punctuated by volcanic cones, one with a Christ figure standing high on its flank. It's a laidback town, with a surprisingly good choice of accommodation and dining options, mainly because of its strong military presence (near the Colombian and Venezuelan borders). The area surrounding São Gabriel is entirely home to indigenous peoples, and while this means it's a hassle for tourists to acquire necessary permits to enter these territories (permits can be

YANOMAMI TOURS: A WARNING

Some tourists are offered trips to the **Yanomami** or other **indigenous reserves**. These are difficult to obtain these days following outbreaks of violence between miners and the Yanomami. Such a trip is only possible with valid permission from IBAMA (Rua Ministro João Gonçalves de Souza, Km 1, BR-319, Distrito Industrial; T 92 3878 7100, W ibama.gov.br) and FUNAI (offices in Brasília; W funai.gov.br), which you have to obtain yourself. If a company says they already have permission, they're probably lying, as each visit needs a new permit. In any case, permission is generally impossible to get, so that the trips offered may actually be illegal and could land you in serious trouble. Of course, the ethics of such visits are in any case clear: isolated indigenous groups have no immunity to imported diseases, and even the common cold can kill them with devastating ease.

obtained usually in a few days through FOIRN, Federação das Organizações Indigenas do Rio Negro, in town; Av Alvaro Maia 79; T 97 3471 1632, T 97 3471 1001, W foirn.org.br), it makes this one of the Amazon's most pristine regions to visit.

Pico da Neblina

São Gabriel is the jumping-off point for **Pico da Neblina**, which, at 3014m, is Brazil's highest peak. However, the National Park Pico da Neblina has been closed since 2003, as a result of tour companies exploiting the local Yanomami Indians as guides yet paying them paltry wages. In the intervening years the Yanomami have organized and now control access. They have agreed to reopen the park by the end of 2018, at which point hundreds of Yanomami will oversee tourism in the area.

Bela Adormecida

The 1000m-high mountain of **Bela Adormecida** is easily reachable from São Gabriel. Getting there involves navigating one of the area's most scenic rivers, the Rio Curicuriari. It's also possible to camp at the summit – ask at *Pousada Pico da Neblina*.

ARRIVAL AND DEPARTURE — SÃO GABRIEL DA CACHOEIRA AND AROUND

By boat Boats arrive at Porto Camanaus, about 25km from São Gabriel. Shared taxis meet incoming boats (R$20/person; 25min). A private taxi to the town is R$60. Buses also connect the town to the port; buses meet the boats, while if you're heading to the port from town catch a bus from Av Sete de Setembro along the beach (Mon–Sat at 6am, 7am, noon & 3pm, Sun 7am & 3pm; 40min; R$6).

Slow boats Slow services leave Porto São Raimundo in Manaus on Fri at 3pm and 6pm returning to Manaus on Fri at 8am and noon (3 days; R$390).

Fast boats Boats depart Manaus on Fri and Sat at 10am (24hr; R$480), returning to Manaus on Mon and Tues at 7am. It's a good idea to take your own mattress – you can stretch out on the floor and get a decent night's sleep.

ACCOMMODATION

Pousada Pico da Neblina Rua Capitão Euclides 322 T 97 9168 0047, W pousadapicodaneblina.com. This large yellow house sitting on a hill has lovely views over the beach. Accommodation is in private rooms with bathrooms, dorms, hammocks or tents. The friendly Australian owner, who is also the owner of the long-established *Hostel Manaus* in Manaus, can provide plenty of information on the area, as well as organize tours. Dorms R$25, doubles R$45

The three-way frontier

The point where Brazil meets Peru and Colombia is known as the **three-way frontier**, and it's somewhere you may end up staying for a few days sorting out red tape or waiting for a boat. The best place to stay is in **Leticia** in Colombia, from where you can also head out on jungle trips. A fleet of *moto-taxis*, *lanchas* and Colombian *moto carros* connect the three countries at very reasonable prices. For many centuries the three-way frontier has been home to the

Tikuna, once large in number, but today down to a population of around 10,000. Their excellent handicrafts – mainly string bags and hammocks – can be bought in Leticia.

Tabatinga

TABATINGA is not the most exciting of towns, and is pretty dodgy, especially at night. Travellers who usually end up here waiting for a boat or plane to Manaus or Iquitos prefer to hop over the border to Leticia for the duration of their stay, even if they don't plan on going any further into Colombia. Tabatinga is the place to complete Brazilian exit (or entry) formalities with the Polícia Federal (see page 382).

ARRIVAL AND DEPARTURE — TABATINGA

By plane Azul has one daily flight to Manaus (1hr 40min). A taxi from the airport to the city centre is R$20 (10min), to the centre of Leticia R$30 (20min). Moto taxis can't pass beyond the border.

By slow boat There's a slow boat to Manaus on Wed & Sat and every other week on Tues leaving from Tabatinga's Porto do Voyagem at noon (3 days; R$330). Plenty of small boats make the journey from Tabatinga and Leticia to Santa Rosa (10min; R$5).

By fast boat Fast boats to Manaus leave from Portobras at Rua Duarte Coelho 10 (Sat & Sun 11am; 30hr; R$500).

ACCOMMODATION

The accommodation options in Tabatinga are poor – a good reason to head over to **Leticia** – though there are a couple of hotels that will do the trick for the night.

Hotel Solimões Tv Doze 1-261 ☎ 97 9186 2793. This option is located in the centre of town, a couple blocks from the water. It's a simple affair with long, bright corridors and clean rooms. Solid breakfast of fruits and breads. R$120

Takana Hotel Rua Osvaldo Cruz 970 ☎ 97 3412 3557. Make your way down a corridor lined with colourful wooden statuettes of Amazonian wildlife and exotic masks to reach a series of comfortable darkish rooms set around a green courtyard; the suites are substantially better than the standards, with king-sized beds and wooden furniture. Tabatinga's best hotel. R$140

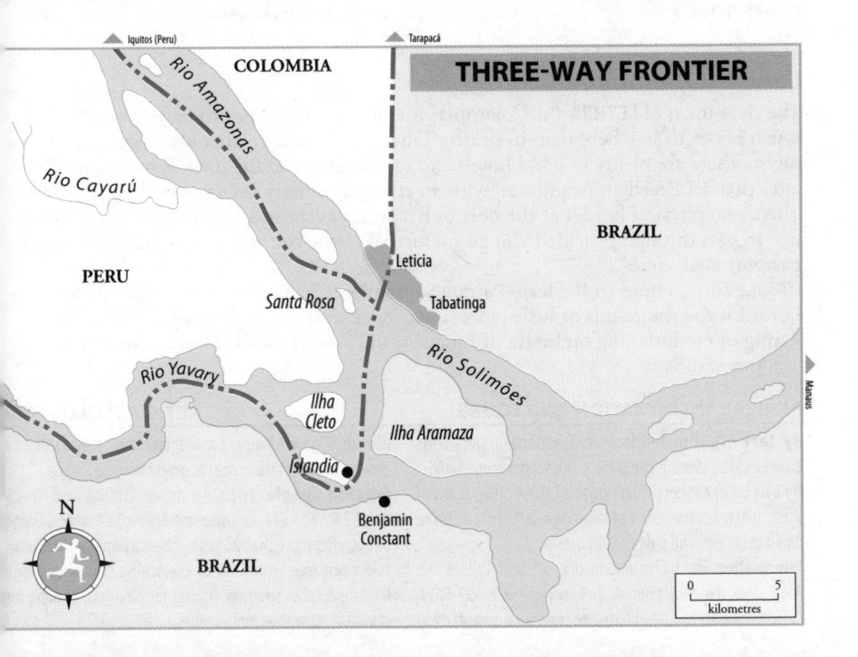

5

CROSSING TO COLOMBIA AND PERU

If you're arriving from **Colombia**, or heading into Colombia from Brazil, you'll need to go to the Polícia Federal at Av da Amizade 26 (daily 8am–noon & 2–6pm; 97 3412 2047) for your passport entry or exit stamp and visitor card; you'll then need to go to Leticia airport to get a Colombian entry stamp.

Heading into **Peru**, many boats leave from Tabatinga (Tues–Sun 5am; 12hr; R$200), although Peruvian authorities and passport control are in Santa Rosa (10min; R$5), a military post over the river, where all Peru-bound boats have to stop for passport and customs control; you'll need to get your exit stamp in Tabatinga the day before. Arriving from Peru, you'll need to go to the Polícia Federal in Tabatinga for your Brazilian passport entry stamp and visitor card.

CONSULATES

Brazilian Vice-consulate Carrera 9a #13-84, Leticia (Mon–Fri 8am–2pm; +57 592 7530).

Colombian Consulate Rua General Sampaio 623, Tabatinga (Mon–Fri 7am–1pm; 97 3412 2104, tabatinga.consulado.gov.co).

Peruvian Consulate Calle 11 5-32, Leticia (Mon–Fri 8am–noon & 2–4pm; +57 8 592 7755).

EATING

Bella Epoca Rua Pedro Teixeira 589 97 3412 3496. This popular self-service restaurant offers thirty options of home-made dishes at lunchtime (R$38/kg), including beans, meats, salads, plantains, *farofa* and mash. In the evenings, it's pizza only, rustled up using home-made dough. Daily 11am–4pm & 6pm–midnight.

Restaurante Três Fronteiras Do Amazonas Ru Barbosa s/n 97 9151 7060. This welcoming airy restauran lined with verdant plants and built in natural material specializes in Amazonian fish dishes (starting at R$34) including *tambaqui* and *tucunaré*. It's one of Tabatinga's mos atmospheric restaurants. Daily 10am–11pm.

DIRECTORY

Internet Star Tech Tecnologia, Rua Santo Dumont 325, Dom Pedro I (daily 8.30am–12.30pm & 2–9.30pm; R$5/hr; 97 9171 5238).

Money and exchange There are no money-changers ir Tabatinga – not legal ones anyway; you will need to head over to Leticia to change currency.

Leticia (Colombia)

The river town of **LETICIA** (in Colombia) is a pleasant little spot to base yourself – it's much better to stay here than in nearby Tabatinga, even if you're only about for one night. There are plenty of good hotels and restaurants, and the town is overall much safer than its Brazilian neighbour, with an efficient military presence and police force. There's no physical border at the port or between Leticia and Tabatinga; though you're free to pass through provided you go no further in the country, you should carry your passport at all times.

Make sure to head to the leafy **Parque Santander**, locally nicknamed Plaza de los Loros for the thousands of little parrots that flock to its trees, dancing in the air and letting out a deafening orchestra of squawks; the parrots can be found here around 4.30pm and 5am.

ARRIVAL, INFORMATION AND TOURS

LETICIA (COLOMBIA)

By taxi A taxi to Leticia from Tabatinga airport costs around R$30 (15min). There are also cheaper *moto-taxis*.

By bus Buses connect Tabatinga and Leticia (R$2); many of them only reach the centre of Tabatinga, but some do come down the main road past the airport.

Information The tourist information office at Calle 8, no. 9–75 (Mon–Fri 7am–noon & 2–5pm; +57 8 592 5810, facebook.com/amazonasmidestino) give out a map of Leticia and Tabatinga, are happy to answer questions; they also have a desk at the airport (open daily to meet incoming flights).

Amazon Jungle Trips Av Internacional No. 6–25 +57 8 592 7377, amazonjungletrips.com.co. Going strong after more than 25 years, offers a popular three-day two-night tour with a bit of everything (swimming in a lagoon, dolphin spotting, fishing for piranhas, looking fo caimans), as well as longer tours.

ACCOMMODATION

★ Amazon B&B Calle 12 No. 9–30 ⊙ +57 8 592 4981, ⊙ amazonbb.com. In the style of an upmarket safari lodge, with a choice of spacious rooms and even more spacious bungalows. They don't have a/c or a pool, but there are ceiling fans and a jacuzzi, crisp white sheets and a peaceful garden space, as well as a variety of local tours. COP$225,000

La Jangada Carrera 10 No. 6–37 ⊙ +57 312 451 0758, ⊙ lajangadamazonas.com. Top marks for friendliness and helpfulness to this long-running travellers' hostel. The fan-cooled rooms and dorms are clean and airy, you can book jungle adventures. The kitchen whips up a simple breakfast, which is included. They also have a forest lodge at Km15, where you stay in the woods, check the local birdlife, and swim in a natural pool. Dorms COP$27,000, doubles COP$55,000

Waira Suites Carrera 10 No. 7–36 ⊙ +57 8 592 4428, ⊙ wairahotel.com.co. There are two pools and two restaurants at this rather chic little establishment, all done out in white, with splashes of colour in the rooms. They have a/c and hot water too. The best rooms are upstairs at the front with big balconies. COP$296,000

EATING

El Cielo Av Internacional No. 6–11 ⊙ +57 8 592 3723. A pioneering restaurant serving what they call "fusión amazónica" – essentially, experimental modern cuisine using traditional local ingredients. You can start with *canoas* (plantain stuffed with prawns; COP$15,000) or, if you want to be more adventurous, *canajois* (*mojojoy* jungle grubs stuffed with meat; COP$14,000), before moving on to the house speciality, *casabes*, consisting of a cassava-bread base, served pizza-style, with a choice of locally inspired meat, fish or vegetable toppings (COP$15,000). Mon–Sat 5.30–10.30pm.

★ Tierras Amazónicas Calle 8 No. 7–50 ⊙ +57 8 592 4748. Cool, open-fronted restaurant serving large portions of perfectly cooked fish, with a choice of local species and preparations. The *pescado a la pupeca* (fish fillet steamed in a banana leaf) is particularly succulent at COP$30,500, and you can wash it down with juices such as *borojó*, *copoazú* or *kamu-kamu* (COP$4500) Tues–Sat 10.30am–10.30pm, Sun 10.30am–9pm.

Tierras Antioqueñas Calle 8 No. 9-03 ⊙ +57 314 224 4056. This relaxed restaurant with wooden tables lining the street is a good spot for a quick bite to eat; the menu features *bandeja paisa* (a big plate of meat, rice, beans and plantain) for COP$20,000, or do you a fish cooked in coconut milk for the same price. It's also a top spot to have a typical Colombian breakfast of *caldo* (beef rib broth) with plantain, rice and cornbread on the side (COP$6000). Daily 7am–9pm.

DIRECTORY

Internet Internet connectivity in Leticia is dire, though a new network should be installed in 2018. Internet cafés include: Tentel.net, Calle 9 No. 9–09 (Mon–Sat 8.30am–12.30pm & 2.30–8.30pm, Sun 9am–2pm & 4–9pm; COP$2000/hr); Servientrega, Calle 8 No. 9–50 (Mon–Fri 7am–1pm & 2–9pm, Sat 8am–1pm & 2–9pm, Sun 9am–1pm; COP$2400/hr).

Money and exchange There are banks with ATMs dotted around town; Bancolombia is at Cra 11 No. 9–52. Moneychangers are concentrated on C8 by the port, and on any given day will offer varying rates for Colombian pesos, reais, soles, dollars and euros, so shop around before you choose one.

Roraima

In the far north of Brazil, the state of **RORAIMA**, abutting Guyana and Venezuela, is notable mainly for the mountains and rock formations with high table-top plateaux to the north of the region. These mountains continue into Venezuela and Guyana where they were made famous by Sir Arthur Conan Doyle's book *The Lost World*. Most of Roraima state, however, is relatively flat grassland.

Brief history

When discovered in the mid-eighteenth century, Roraima's grasslands were considered ideal cattle country. The current national borders weren't settled until the early part of the twentieth century. During the early 1990s, a massive gold rush generated an influx of 50,000 *garimpeiros*, mainly in the northwest, against the Venezuelan border in the territory of the **Yanomami**, Amazonian tribal peoples living on both sides of the border.

In 1989 the plight of the Yanomami, whose lands were being invaded by prospectors, brought about an international outcry that forced the Brazilian government to announce that they would evacuate all settlers from Yanomami lands. But the project was abandoned almost as soon as it began; protection of the region's valuable **mineral reserves** was deemed to necessitate the strengthening of the country's borders and the settlement of the area. Following the successful demarcation of Yanomami lands in 1992, and the territory's official recognition by the Federal State, things have improved and there are now fewer *garimpeiros* prospecting in Yanomami forests.

Boa Vista

BOA VISTA is a fast-growing city of 313,000 people, an unrelentingly hot, modern and concrete monument to its Brazilian planners who laid it out on a grand but charmless scale; traffic islands divide broad, tree-lined boulevards and a vast Praça do Centro Cívico, swirling with traffic, from which streets radiate unevenly. Clearly this is meant to be a fitting capital for the development of Roraima – and there are large stores full of ranching and mining equipment that reflect that growth. Busy as it is, though, Boa Vista has far to go to fulfil its ambitious designs.

The huge streets often seem half empty, reflecting the waning of the gold boom after the initial rush in the late 1980s and early 1990s, and many of the old hotels and gold-trading posts have closed down, or have turned into travel agencies, small-time banks and restaurants. The new layout obliterated many of the town's older buildings, which means there's little of interest to see in the city itself. Most visitors to Boa Vista are on business or travellers passing through on the overland route from Venezuela to Manaus.

Praça do Centro Cívico

The Praça do Centro Cívico lies at the heart of the city and is home to the **Monumento ao Garimpeiro**, or Monument to the Miners, which portrays a miner sifting gold, thereby paying tribute to the former backbone of the economy. On the south side of the square is the **Catedral Cristo Redentor**, built in the 1960s with an interesting curvaceous and airy design. Its stain-glassed windows are shaped like fish, while the ceiling is reminiscent of the hull of a huge wooden boat, giving visitors the impression of being underwater. Also note the long windows that from a distance take on the shape of a harp.

The waterfront

Down in the old waterfront district, connected to the *praça* by the main shopping street, Avenida Jaime Brasil, you'll find a cluster of sights, including the imposing concrete **Monumento Aos Pioneiros,** or Monument to the Pioneers, which symbolizes the arrival of the first families to the city and the alleged integration of the indigenous population with the Portuguese colonialists. Note the shape of the monument, which is reminiscent of nearby Mount Roraima.

Nearby is the pretty, bright yellow **Igreja Nossa Senhora do Carmo**, with its original 1920s Germanic-style features. A short walk away is the beautifully preserved Neoclassical **Prelazia**; originally erected in 1924 and intended as a hospital, it became the official residence of priests and the bishop. In 1950 the building became the seat of the government, while also continuing to serve as the episcopal residence.

Casa do Artesanato

Rua Floriano Peixoto 423 • Mon–Fri 9am–6pm • Free

The **Casa do Artesanato** opposite the Igreja Nossa Senhora do Carmo on the riverbank is worth a visit; its selection of handicrafts is not wide but there's some interesting stuff and it's all very cheap. Nearby there are plenty of small shops selling similar artefacts. It's a good spot to buy souvenirs.

EMPEROR TAMARI

5

Praia Grande

Boat from Boa Vista's Porto do Babazinho (10min; R$6)

Opposite Boa Vista on the other side of the Rio Branco is **Praia Grande**, a large sand bar that is a pleasant spot to visit when the water is low between December and April. Given that the beach emerges only at certain times of the year, there is no infrastructure so make sure to bring water and food.

ARRIVAL AND DEPARTURE — BOA VISTA

By plane The airport (95 3198 0119) is about 4km northwest of the centre. Buses marked Caracã and Aeroporto connect the airport to the centre (hourly; 15min; R$3.75), although they run irregularly. It's safest to take a taxi (5min; R$45).

By bus The rodoviária is 5km south of the city on Av das Guianas. Regular buses (every 20min; 10min; R$3.75) and shared taxis (5min; R$4) connect the station to Praça do Centro Cívico in the city centre; a taxi is R$30.

Destinations Bonfim (for Guyana; daily 7am, 10am, 2pm & 4.30pm; 1hr 30min; R$20); Manaus (daily 9am, 7pm, 8pm & 9pm; 11–12hr; R$157); Pacaraima (for Venezuela; daily 7:30am; 3hr; R$30); Puerto La Cruz, Venezuela (Tues, Thurs & Sat 7am; 24hr; R$160); Puerto Ordaz, Venezuela (Tues, Thurs & Sat 7am; 18hr; R$140).

By shared taxi Shared taxis use the Terminal de Integração João Firmino Neto, commonly known as Terminal do

Caimbé, on Av dos Imigrantes to the west of the centre. They leave when all six seats are full; there are normally more passengers in the mornings and therefore less of a wait.
Destinations Bonfim (1hr 30min; R$40); Pacaraima (2hr 30min; R$50); Santa Elena de Uairén (3hr; R$50).
By car Car rental: Localiza, Av Glaycon de Paiva 1630 (☎ 95 3224 7045, @ localiza.com), and at the airport (☎ 95 3224 1876); Hertz have a booth at the airport (☎ 95 3198 0165).

INFORMATION, ACTIVITIES AND TOURS

Information The DETUR tourist office is at Rua Coronel Pinto 267 (Mon–Fri 8am–noon; ☎ 95 3623 2365); there's also an information office on the riverfront just opposite the Igreja Nossa Senhora do Carmo on Rua Floriano Peixoto (Mon–Fri 8am–noon & 2–6pm; ☎ 95 3621 3975).

Makunaima Expedições Rua Floriano Peixoto 136 ☎ 95 3624 6004, @ makunaima.com. This friendly agency specializes in birdwatching tours in the Parque Nacional do Viruá; other activities including trekking, city tours, bike tours and kayaking. They also rent bikes for R$40/day.

Porto do Babazinho Av Major Williams 1, São Pedro ☎ 95 9111 3511. Rents out kayaks (R$8/hr), windsurfing boards (R$25/hr) and stand-up boards (R$30/hr). They also offer windsurfing lessons (R$200 for five sessions), kite-surfing lessons (R$600 for six sessions) and stand-up board lessons (R$60/session).

Roraima Adventures Rua Cel Pinto 86, sala 106 ☎ 95 3624 9611, @ roraima-brasil.com.br. This agency specializes in trips to Mount Roraima; trips are for 7, 8 or 9 days (prices from R$2507/person). They also organize trips to Angel Falls in Venezuela (3 days; starting from R$1920).

ACCOMMODATION

Aipana Plaza Hotel Praça Centro Cívico 974 ☎ 95 3212 0800, @ aipanaplaza.com.br; map p.386. Boa Vista's best hotel is located right on the main square; the spacious a/c rooms feature wooden furniture and flat-screen TVs. There's a pleasant pool area with loungers and a café-bar, along with an indoor restaurant serving great food. **R$270**

Boa Vista Eco Hotel Av Glaycon de Paiva 1240 ☎ 95 3623 0746, @ boavistaecohotel.com; map p.386. One of the city's newest hotels, this option offers nearly one hundred comfortable a/c rooms with modern amenities, all fully equipped with fridge, TV and safe – albeit in somewhat soulless surroundings. There are plans to build a pool on the 9th floor, and there are nice views over the surrounding area from the rooftop terrace. **R$250.50**

Cristal Hotel Av Nossa Senhora da Consolata 3447 ☎ 95 3621 1410, @ cristalhotel.tur.br; map p.386. Located a few minutes' walk from the bus station, this newer place has safely become the area's best accommodation option. Rooms are comfortable if slightly tattered around the edges and there's a pool in the back yard. This is the best option if you've got an early bus trip. **R$190**

Hotel Barrudada Rua Araújo Filho 228 ☎ 95 2121 1700, @ hotelbarrudada.tur.br; map p.386. Just one block from the main square, the a/c rooms here give onto a series of long narrow corridors; they're nothing to write home about but are perfectly comfortable, and there's a pool too – a welcome addition in Boa Vista's heat. Up to fifty percent discount if paying cash. **R$100**

Hotel Ideal Rua Araújo Filho 481 ☎ 95 3224 1010, @ hotel-ideal88@hotmail.com; map p.386. A decent budget option offering neat and plain tiled rooms with wooden furniture and private bathrooms; cheaper accommodation is fan only, while slightly pricier rooms have additional comforts such as a/c, fridge and TV. **R$80**

Uiramutam Palace Hotel Av Cap. Ene Garcêz 427 ☎ 95 3198 0000, @ uiramutam.com.br; map p.386. A reliable mid-range option featuring standard and deluxe rooms – the former substantially better and well worth the extra reais, with freshly painted walls and refurbished bathrooms. The pool is a pleasant spot for an afternoon dip. **R$120**

EATING

Meu Cantinho Av Ene Garces s/n ☎ 95 3224 0667; map p.386. Looking over the Praça das Aguas, this local institution is without a doubt the best place to dig into all manner of freshly grilled meats; the roasted rump steak (R$55) served with rice is superb. Also worth trying is the shrimp risotto (*risotto de camarão*) Tues-Sun 8pm–midnight.

Mr Quilo Rua Inácio Magalhães 328 ☎ 95 3623 9185; map p.386. With a very decent selection of grub on offer, this is one of the best places in the city centre for a *por quilo* lunch (R$53). There's plenty to choose from, including fish, meats and veggie dishes, along with a wide selection of desserts. Mon–Sat 11.30am–2.30pm.

Peixada Tropical Rua Ajuricaba 1525 ☎ 95 3224 6040, @ facebook.com/peixadatropical; map p.386. This local favourite with outdoor roadside seating and a laidback atmosphere specializes in fish dishes; the bestseller here is the *à delícia*, fried fish with white sauce and cheese served with fried banana (R$45 for two). There's live music on Saturday and Sunday afternoons between 1pm and 5pm. Daily 11am–midnight.

Tulipa Av Major Williams 1373 ☎ 95 3224 2150; map p.386. One of the best places in Boa Vista for a *por quilo* lunch (R$40), with a huge selection of dishes including salads, vegetables and fish, along with an entire section solely dedicated to freshly grilled meats. Daily 11.30am–3pm.

5

DRINKING

Pit Stop Av Cap. Ene Garces, 95 3624 5884; map p.386. An old, local institution in the heart of Centro, *Pit Stop* is a big open-air bar that gets rowdy at weekends. Come for the beer and bar snacks. Daily 24hr.

Territorio Bar Orla Taumanan, on the waterfront 95 98122 6966, facebook.com/territoriobarbv; map p.386. This fun bar on Boa Vista's waterfront promenade has a nice vibe with a spacious patio – it's a great place to sip a cocktail (caipirinhas R$9; beers R$6) and listen to live music (Thus–Sun from 9pm). Tues–Sun 5pm–midnight.

DIRECTORY

Consulates Guyana, Av Benjamin Constant 388, Centro (95 224 0799); Venezuela, Av Benjamin Constant 968, São Pedro (95 3623 9285).

Hospital Hospital Geral de Roraima, Av Brigadeiro Eduardo Gomes 1364 (95 2121 0600).

Money and exchange Banco do Brasil is at the corner of Av Glaycon de Paiva and Av Amazonas on the Praça Cívico; Bradesco is at the corner of Av Getúlio Vargas and Av Jaime Brasil.

Post office Praça Centro Cívico 176 (Mon–Fri 8am–5pm, Sat 8am–noon).

Around Boa Vista

Situated as it is on the northern edge of the Amazon forest, where it meets the savannah of Roraima, the region around Boa Vista boasts three different forms of ecosystem: tropical rainforest, grassland savannah plains and the "Lost World"-style tepius mountains, flat plateau-like rock rising out of the savannah. Still fairly undeveloped in terms of its tourism infrastructure and so best visited on tours, the area is exceptionally beautiful, with a wealth of river beaches, and has a very pleasant climate (hot with cooling breezes).

Serra Grande

About 50km from Boa Vista is the beautiful **Serra Grande**, which, at a height of 850m, offers plenty of trekking opportunities. The area is home to pretty cascading waterfalls, natural pools and lush vegetation, and there are wonderful views from high up of the Rio Branco, Boa Vista and beyond.

Serra do Tepequém

Located 210km from the city, the **Serra do Tepequém** is one of Roraima's highlights. The area was a mining settlement for over eight decades, reaching its heyday in the 1930s and 1940s. The remnants of the area's diamond mining history are visible today, as the soil rapidly erodes amid lush greenery; it is nonetheless spectacularly rich in flora and fauna, and it's not uncommon to spot anteaters, turtles, herons, macaws and hawks.

Parque Nacional do Viruá

The **Parque Nacional do Viruá** protects an area of 2270 square kilometres of dense forest and savannah in the south of Roraima state. The park possesses some of the richest fauna among Brazil's protected areas, with over 110 mammals, 420 fish species and over 1150 vertebrates. The area is also home to over 520 species of birds, making the park a true paradise for birdwatchers and one of the country's prime destinations for ecotourism. The best time to visit is during the dry season (Sept–April), with large open tracts of vegetation facilitating animal spotting.

Santa Elena de Uairén (Venezuela)

The journey from Boa Vista to **Venezuela**, across a vast flat savannah that is dusty in the dry season and boggy in the wet, offers very little in the way of scenery, but there is a great deal of wildlife: white egrets, storks and all sorts of waders in the rainy season, flycatchers, hawks and the occasional large animal, such as the giant anteater. As the border approaches, the land begins to rise slightly; to the northeast, at the point where Brazil, Guyana and Venezuela meet, lies **Monte Roraima**, the fourth-highest peak in Brazil at 2875m.

The small town of **SANTA ELENA DE UAIRÉN** has the real feel of a border town in its low, corrugated-roof houses and dusty streets, and serves as a base to explore Mount Roraima. You can see the whole place in an hour's walk, but there's a handful of agencies who run tours to local waterfalls and native communities. Various traders will accept cash US dollars or Brazilian currency – ask around at one of the hotels.

ARRIVAL AND DEPARTURE — SANTA ELENA DE UAIRÉN (VENEZUELA)

TO VENEZUELA

By bus From Boa Vista's rodoviária there are buses to Pacaraima at the Venezuelan border (daily 7.30am; 3hr; R$30), from where you can catch a taxi to Santa Elena (R$5; 30min/person). Shared taxis from Boa Vista's Terminal de Integração João Firmino Neto, known as Terminal do Caimbé, also ply the route (2hr 30min; R$45/person), although you might as well take a shared taxi directly (3hr; R$50). There are onward buses into Venezuela from Santa Elena to Ciudad Bolívar (daily at 7pm; 12hr; R$15), stopping off at Puerto Ordaz (11hr; R$15).

TO BRAZIL

By bus If you're heading into Brazil, you'll have to make your way to the border and then catch a bus (3hr; R$27) or shared taxi (2hr 30min; R$50/person) from Pacaraima, just across the border in Brazil, to Boa Vista. Alternatively, you can organize a shared taxi all the way from Santa Elena to Boa Vista (3hr; R$65). There are no direct buses travelling from Santa Elena into Brazil.

TOURS

Backpacker Tours Calle Urdaneta ⊕+58 289 995 1430, ⊕+58 414 886 7227, ⊕backpacker-tours.com. This reliable German-run agency with high-quality equipment (tents, bikes and trucks) offers multi-day treks to Mount Roraima, Chirikayen and Auyan Tepui, as well as plenty of tours around Venezuela including to Angel Falls, Los Llanos and the Orinoco Delta. Also offers multi-day bike trips.

ACCOMMODATION AND EATING

Backpacker Tours & Pousada Los Pinos Los Pinos 98, Urbanizacion Akurima, ⊕+58 289 995 1430, ⊕backpacker-tours.com. This German-owned *pousada* largely catering to backpackers offers ten spacious, colourful rooms right in the centre of town. The jacuzzi and pool (with waterslide) will knock your socks off. There's a reliable affiliated travel agency and the attached restaurant, *Caney*, with outdoor patio, is a great spot for a meal and an evening beer or cocktail. Sat & Sun 6–10pm, plus Sun lunch. **R$45**

Hotel Anaconda Calle Ikabaru ⊕+58 289 995 1011. This is Santa Elena's most comfortable hotel, featuring a/c rooms with minibar, a welcoming lounge area and an inviting swimming pool with deckchairs (erratic) **US$15**

Bonfim

The small town of **Bonfim** 125km northeast of Boa Vista is the nearest access point for travelling onwards to Guyana. It's nothing more than a dull border town, although it does attract a fair few Brazilians who head over to Guyana to shop, as their Brazilian reais are worth much more there. A bridge crosses over the river into Guyana, with customs and immigration on both sides.

Rondônia

A large, partially deforested region in the southwest corner of the Brazilian Amazon, the state of **RONDÔNIA** (named after the famous explorer Marechal Cândido Rondon, Brazilian military officer and a lifelong supporter of indigenous populations) has a reputation for unbridled colonization and very rapid "development". The state was only created in 1981, having evolved from an unknown and almost entirely unsettled zone (then the Territory of Guaporé) over the previous thirty years. The first phase of its environmental destruction began in the 1980s when roads and tracks, radiating like fine bones from the spinal highway **BR-364**, backbone of modern Rondônia that links the state more or less from north to south, began to dissect almost the entire state, bringing in their wake hundreds of thousands of settlers and many large companies who have moved in to gobble up the rainforest. Poor landless groups are a common sight – some the surviving representatives of once-proud tribes – living under plastic sheets at the side of the road.

The state is not exactly one of Brazil's major tourist attractions, but it is an interesting area in its own right, and offers a few stopping-off places between more obvious destinations. Its main city, **Porto Velho**, is an important rainforest market town and pit stop between Cuiabá in Mato Grosso and the frontier state of Acre. Rondônia also offers **border crossings** to Peru and Bolivia and **river trips** to Manaus.

Porto Velho

The capital of Rondônia state, **PORTO VELHO** overlooks the Amazon's longest tributary, the mighty Rio Madeira. In the 1980s, settlers arrived in enormous numbers in search of land, jobs and, more specifically, the mineral wealth of the area: gold and casserite (a form of tin). As in most regions, the gold boom has bottomed out and the empty gold-buying stores are signs of the rapid decline. Seen from a distance across the river, Porto Velho looks rather more impressive than it does at close quarters, its newest buildings are reaching for the sky and the younger generation ensures that its weekend partying helps bring a modern Brazilian vibe to the city through music. The town mainly serves as a jumping-off point to lodges in the area; there's really nothing much to do in the town itself.

Museu da Estrada de Ferro Madeira–Mamoré

Av Sete de Setembro at Av Farqhuar • Mon–Sat 9am–3pm • Free • ⓣ 69 3901 3196

The **Museu da Estrada de Ferro Madeira–Mamoré**, once jam-packed with fascinating period railway-themed exhibits – including an entire and quite spectacular locomotive, built in Philadelphia in 1878 – has unfortunately been left in a profound state of disrepair, all but abandoned by the municipality. Sadly, there is little to recommend it anymore. For railway buffs, there's equipment and other locomotives to see around the old railway terminal adjacent to the museum.

The Madeira–Mamoré (or Mad Maria) Railway was planned to provide a route for Bolivian rubber to the Atlantic, but after a series of setbacks during its forty-year construction it was only completed in 1912 – just in time to see the price of rubber plummet and the market dry up. The line was closed in 1960, and in 1972 many of the tracks were ripped up to help build a road along the same difficult route.

Mercado Cultural

Rua José de Alencar s/n, Praça Getúlio Vargas • Mon–Sat 8am–midnight • Free

By day the **Mercado Cultural** is a cultural centre featuring no more than a handful of paintings and a couple of stalls, but in the evenings it turns into a popular meeting point, with tables spilling onto the street. There's an eclectic range of live music from Monday to Saturday – rock, *forró*, *seresta*, samba and MPB, and it's free for all to watch. Grab a beer and enjoy.

ARRIVAL AND DEPARTURE — PORTO VELHO

By plane Porto Velho's airport (ⓣ 69 3219 7453) is 7km north of town. Local buses run to Av Sete de Setembro (hourly; 30min; R$3.80); a taxi is R$40 (20min). Azul, Gol and LATAM fly to Manaus (2 non-stop daily; 1hr 30min), Rio Branco (1 daily; 50min), Cuiabá (2 daily; 1hr 55min) and Brasília (4 daily; 2hr 55min).

By boat Boats leave from the port to the south of town, including services to Manaus (Wed & Sat at noon; 4 days; hammock R$250, double cabin R$900).

By bus The rodoviária (ⓣ 69 3222 2233) is 2km east of the centre. Regular buses connect the station to Av Sete de Setembro in the city centre (every 15min; 20min; R$3.80). **Destinations** Brasília (1 daily; 46hr; R$436); Cuiabá (daily; 24hr; R$273); Guajará-Mirim (2 daily; 4hr 30min; R$74); Rio Branco (3 daily; 8hr; R$103); São Paulo (1 daily; 60hr; R$473).

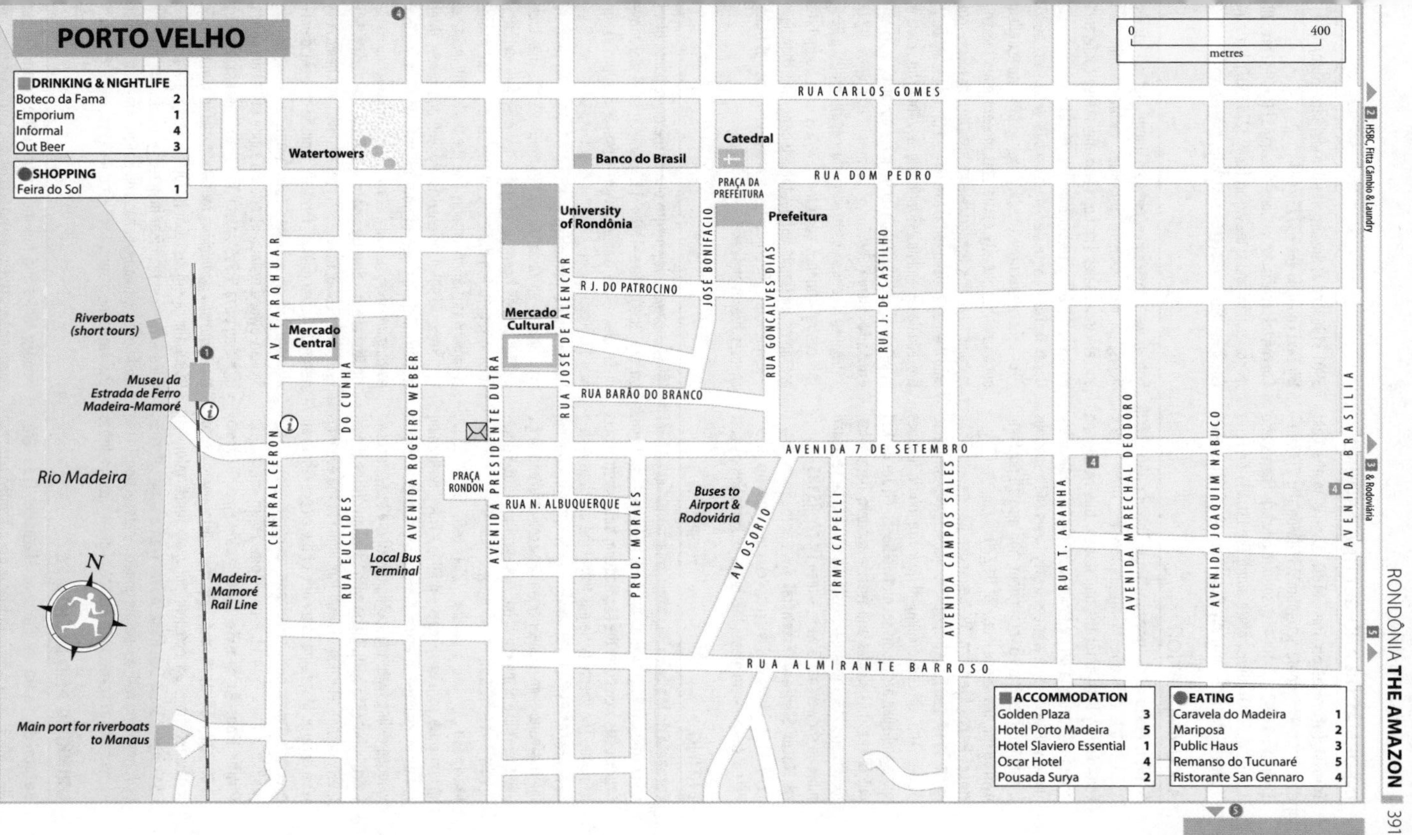
PORTO VELHO
DRINKING & NIGHTLIFE
Boteco da Fama 2
Emporium 1
Informal 4
Out Beer 3
SHOPPING
Feira do Sol 1
0
400
metres
RUA CARLOS GOMES
2, HSBC, Fitta Câmbio & Laundry
Watertowers
Banco do Brasil
Catedral
RUA DOM PEDRO
PRAÇA DA PREFEITURA
Prefeitura
University of Rondônia
AV FARQUHAR
RUA JOSÉ DE ALENCAR
R J. DO PATROCINO
JOSÉ BONIFACIO
RUA GONÇALVES DIAS
RUA J. DE CASTILHO
Riverboats (short tours)
Mercado Central
Mercado Cultural
Museu da Estrada de Ferro Madeira-Mamoré
DO CUNHA
AVENIDA ROGEIRO WEBER
AVENIDA PRESIDENTE DUTRA
RUA BARÃO DO BRANCO
AVENIDA MARECHAL DEODORO
AVENIDA JOAQUIM NABUCO
AVENIDA BRASILIA
CENTRAL CERON
AVENIDA 7 DE SETEMBRO
3 & Rodoviária
Rio Madeira
PRAÇA RONDON
RUA N. ALBUQUERQUE
Buses to Airport & Rodoviária
AV OSORIO
PRUD. MORÁES
IRMA CAPELLI
AVENIDA CAMPOS SALES
RUA T. ARANHA
N
RUA EUCLIDES
Local Bus Terminal
Madeira-Mamoré Rail Line
5
RUA ALMIRANTE BARROSO
Main port for riverboats to Manaus
ACCOMMODATION
Golden Plaza 3
Hotel Porto Madeira 5
Hotel Slaviero Essential 1
Oscar Hotel 4
Pousada Surya 2
EATING
Caravela do Madeira 1
Mariposa 2
Public Haus 3
Remanso do Tucunaré 5
Ristorante San Gennaro 4

INFORMATION AND GETTING AROUND

Tourist information The SETUR office is in the Casa do Turista, Av Sete de Setembro 237 (Mon–Fri 7.30am–1.30pm; ☎ 69 3216 1044, ⓦ setur.ro.gov.br). There's also a CAT municipal tourist office along the Estrada de Ferro Madeira–Mamoré s/n (daily 8am–noon & 2–6pm; ☎ 69 3901 3196) and at the airport (Mon–Fri 8am–5pm).

By taxi Cooptaxi ☎ 69 3225 1414.

Car rental Localiza, Av Gov. Jorge Teixeira 151 (☎ 69 3224 6530, ⓦ localiza.com) and at the airport (☎ 69 3225 7307); Hertz, Av Gov. Jorge Teixeira 786 (☎ 69 3211 0575, ⓦ hertz.com).

ACCOMMODATION

Golden Plaza Av Governador Jorge Teixera 810 ☎ 69 3225 9000, ⓦ hotelgoldenplaza.com.br; map p.391. Conveniently located for the bus station, this welcoming hotel has clean and bright rooms with modern amenities. The airy suites feature white and grey tones and a spacious bathroom. There's wi-fi throughout, and a small pool and gym on the mezzanine level. R$270

Hotel Porto Madeira Av Alexandre Guimarães 3310 ☎ 69 3219 2002, ⓦ hotelportomadeira.com.br; map p.391. This chocolate-coloured low-rise block features spick-and-span a/c rooms set on two floors. All are decked out in chestnut shades and feature modern bathrooms, fridges and TVs. The larger master suite has a large jacuzzi tub, two showers and a wide-screen TV. R$185

★ **Hotel Slaviero Essential** Av Lauro Sodré 2441 ☎ 69 3301 3390, ⓦ slavierohoteis.com.br; map p.391. Part of the Slaviero group, this is one of Porto Velho's best hotels, with tastefully decorated rooms set on eleven floors, all with modern amenities, including mini-bars and electronic safes. The hotel also offers three conference rooms and a 24hr fitness centre. R$200

Oscar Hotel Av Sete de Setembro 934 ☎ 69 2182 0600, ⓦ oscarhotelexecutive.com.br; map p.391. An excellent option right in the city centre, this modern glass building features clean and comfortable rooms; cheaper rooms look onto the interior patio and as a result are a little dark, although the additional amenities, including a 24hr gym, rooftop infinity pool and convention centre, make up for it. R$250

Pousada Surya Av Carlos Gomes 2289 ☎ 69 3223 2407, ⓦ facebook.com/pousadasurya; map p.391. This central option is good for travellers on a budget. Its a/c rooms are simple but get the job done, and they have a formidable buffet breakfast featuring all kinds of fruits, cheeses, breads and cakes. R$170

EATING

Caravela do Madeira Rua José Camacho 104 ☎ 69 3221 6641; map p.391. One of the best restaurants in town, *Caravela* has views over the Rio Madeira, from where it gets its name. The speciality here is fish – the delicious *costela de tambaqui* (R$95) is big enough for two. The welcoming interior features an open-brick wall and colourful paintings, and there's live piano music on Sundays. Tues–Sat 11am–3pm & 6–11pm, Sun 11am–4pm.

Mariposa Av Lauro Sodré 2211 ☎ 69 3223 3312, ⓦ mariposa.com.br; map p.391. This welcoming restaurant painted in warm hues of red and blue with a wooden ceiling featuring spotlights offers a tasty *por quilo* lunch buffet (R$52.90). Along with Brazilian dishes, there's a very decent selection of sushi too, while in the evenings it's à la carte. Make sure to try one of the crêpes (there are over fifty types, both sweet and savoury). Mon 6pm–midnight, Tues–Sun 11.30am–3pm & 6pm–midnight.

Public Haus Av Brasília 1656, Bairro São Cristóvão ☎ 69 3223 6001; map p.391. This microbrewery-cum-restaurant offers an excellent *por quilo* lunch (Mon–Fri R$49.90/kg, Sat & Sun R$54.90/kg) with a large selection of dishes along with a separate grilled meats section. In the evenings it's à la carte, with a range of great *picanha* dishes (R$77), to wash down with one of the great house beers on tap (R$3). Mon–Thurs 11.30am–3pm & 5.30pm–midnight, Fri & Sat 11.30am–3pm & 5.30pm–1am, Sun 11.30am–3pm.

Remanso do Tucunaré Av Brasília 1506, B.N. Senhora das Graças ☎ 92 3301 6271; map p.391. This local institution has been going strong for over four decades, serving superb fish dishes to all and sundry – the names of famous customers proudly line the walls. The *moqueca* (fish stew; R$90) does particularly well and serves three to four; if there's two of you, try the *filé de dourado à parmegiana* (R$80). Daily 11am–3pm & 6–11pm.

★ **Ristorante San Gennaro** Rua Duque de Caxias 568 ☎ 69 3223 2000; map p.391. Located within a beautifully restored building that formerly housed the Madeira-Mamoré railway workers, this warm and welcoming Sicilian-owned restaurant offers a range of Italian dishes including pizza (R$35), pasta (R$70) and meat mains – try the *filetto alla parmigiana* for two (battered filet of steak R$80). The cavernous cellar features bare stone walls and is lined with more than four hundred types of wine from the world over, with an emphasis on Italian, Brazilian, Chilean and Argentine grapes. Tues–Sun 6–11pm.

DRINKING AND NIGHTLIFE

Boteco da Fama Av Pinheiro Machado 1356 ☎ 69 3043 3001; map p.391. This large open-fronted bar with wooden tables and fun murals hosts live country music bands on Tuesdays, while on Fridays and Saturdays there are

LODGES AROUND PORTO VELHO

Pousada Rancho Grande, BR 364, RO140, Linha C20, Lote 23, Cacaulândia 69 98108 0523, ranchogrande.com.br. This German-run lodge in the middle of rainforest and plantations 260km south of Porto Velho offers accommodation in fan-cooled eco-rooms with shared bath and a/c standards with fridge and private bathroom. There's a swimming pool and plenty of activities on offer including football, volleyball and table tennis, as well as birdwatching, jungle walks and fishing trips. Eco-rooms R$158, a/c doubles R$250

Salsalito Jungle Park BR364, Km 43 towards Cuiabá 69 3224 5300, salsalito.com.br. This lovely place has several nice detached bungalows for rent and a floating restaurant in a beautiful part of the river; activities include horse-riding, boat safaris, fishing trips, dolphin spotting and hikes along short forest- and river-edge trails. R$140

Três Capelas Eco Resort BR364, Km 673, Candelas do Jamari 69 3259 1010, trescapelas.com.br. This large eco-resort offers bungalow accommodation, a restaurant, a bar and plenty of facilities including a swimming pool, football field and beach volleyball in a pleasant setting. R$370

rock sessions at 10pm. Sunday afternoons see crowds here at 6pm for some popular *pagode* music. Footie matches are screened here too, and there's an attached club open (Fri & Sat). Beers R$6, cocktails R$16. Tues–Sun 5pm–2am.

Emporium Av Presidente Dutra 3366, Caiari 69 3221 2665, facebook.com/emporiumrestauranteechoperia; map p.391. This pretty bright blue building has tables lining the street, lit up by little electric lanterns. It's a popular spot for food and drinks and there are daily live MPB music sessions at 8pm. Mains R$65, beer R$6. Mon–Sat 6pm–1am.

Informal Av Brasília 1962 69 3221 1912, facebook.com/informalpubpvh; map p.391. This cavernous pub with bare brick walls is packed with retro curios, from old film posters to black-and-white photos of famous rock bands. It's a hugely popular place and can get pretty crowded, especially when the live music kicks off at 11.30pm. Wed–Sat 7pm–4am.

Out Beer João Goulart 3002, corner Av Calama 69 3229 0761, facebook.com/OutBeerSpecial; map p.391. "Drink less and drink well" is the slogan of this bar, and with two hundred beer labels there certainly is plenty of choice; prices range from R$4.50 to a whopping R$280. There are plenty of imported beers too, which customers can enjoy at the little tables within or on the open-air patio. Tues–Thurs 6pm–midnight, Fri, 6pm–2am, Sat 4pm–2.45am, Sun 5pm–midnight.

SHOPPING

Feira do Sol Estrada do Ferro; map p.391. This little market just by the Madeira–Mamoré Museu Ferroviário has a selection of local crafts and other trinkets. Mon–Fri 8am–6pm, Sat & Sun 8am–8pm.

DIRECTORY

Laundry 5 à Sec, Rua Carlos Gomes 2701, São Cristóvão (Mon–Fri 7.30am–6.30pm, Sat 8am–1pm; 69 3229 2215).

Money and exchange HSBC is at Av Jorge Teixeira 1350; Banco do Brasil is at the corner of José de Alencar and Dom Pedro II; Fitta Câmbio at Av Carlos Gomes 1879 (Mon–Sat 8.30am–5.30pm; 69 3223 2104, fittacambio.com) changes US, Canadian and Australian dollars, pound sterling, euros and Swiss francs.

Post office Av Presidente Dutra 2701, corner Av Sete de Setembro (Mon–Fri 8.30am–5pm).

West from Porto Velho: the Bolivian border

Travelling west from Porto Velho soon begins to feel like real pioneering. The further you go, the smaller and wilder the roads, rivers and towns become. The main attractions are **Rio Branco** and the border crossings into Peru, in the state of Acre, and **Guajará-Mirim**, where you can cross into Bolivia (see page 394). The BR-364 is asphalted, although heavy rains still have a habit of washing great sections of it away. Water birds like the *garça real* (an amazing white royal heron) can frequently be spotted from the bus, fishing in the roadside streams and ditches, but the general picture is one of an alarming rate of destruction.

Guajará-Mirim

About 300km from Porto Velho lies **GUAJARÁ-MIRIM**, a little town on the Rio Mamoré originally built as the terminus of the Madeira-Mamoré railway. There's not much to

5

CROSSING INTO BOLIVIA

The town of **Guayaramerín** in **Bolivia** is something of a contrast to its Brazilian counterpart just opposite the river, with dusty roads and not much going for it. However, from here you can travel by road to La Paz, or catch a flight. If you plan on travelling into Bolivia, get your passport stamped in Guajará-Mirim first at the Bolivian consulate, Av Beira Rio 505 (T 69 3541 8622), and visit the Polícia Federal, Av Presidente Dutra 70 (T 69 3541 2437), for an exit stamp before crossing the river.

Scores of **motorboats** connect Guajará-Mirim to Guayaramerín (5min; R$5). The town's access road is unpassable for all of the rainy season (Nov–April), and often during the months outside that too, causing huge delays. In the dry season there are **buses** to La Paz, although flying is a much more reliable option.

ACCOMMODATION

Hotel Balneario San Carlos Calle 6 de Agosto 347 T 591 3 855 3555. This is the town's snazziest option featuring comfortable a/c rooms, swimming pool, billiards table and restaurant. R$260

do in town – the main reason travellers find themselves here is to head over to **Bolivia** or to head up the Mamoré and Guaporé rivers on a trip to the Forte Príncipe da Beira.

ARRIVAL AND DEPARTURE — GUAJARÁ-MIRIM

By bus There are regular buses from Porto Velho to Guajará-Mirim (2 daily; 4hr 30min; R$74).

ACCOMMODATION AND EATING

Eco Tur Pousada Av Francisco Firmo de Matos 755 T 69 3541 3896, W ecoturpousada.com. Located in the centre of Guajará-Mirim, this is one of the town's most decent choices, offering comfortable and spacious rooms with flatscreen TV, along with a reliable buffet breakfast. Staff are friendly, too. R$115

Oasis Av 15 de Novembro 460 T 69 3541 1621. This large breezy restaurant offers a range of tasty lunch dishes (R$40/kg); it's one of the best options in town. Wed–Mon 11am–3pm.

Pakaas Palafita Lodge Estrada da Palheta, Km 16, Rio Pacaas T 69 9978 6050, W pakaas.tur.br. This rustic lodge offers accommodation in 28 comfortable a/c *cabanas* on stilts with private terraces along the Rio Pacaas. The *cabanas* are well spread out, giving off a 2km walkway, and come in different categories, from standards to luxo superior with kingsize bed, TV and fridge. There's an infinity pool and great views over the meeting of the waters. R$250

Rio Branco and around

Crossing from Rondônia into the state of **Acre**, territory annexed from Bolivia during the rubber-boom days in the first years of the twentieth century, there's nowhere to stop before you reach the capital at **RIO BRANCO**. The state is a vast frontier forest zone, so it comes as a real surprise to find Rio Branco is one of Brazil's hippest cities. It's a small and lively place with a surprising number of things to see and do; it's perhaps best known as the home of the famous environmentalist and rubber-tree-tapper Chico Mendes (see page 397).

The riverfront by the **Mercado Velho** (old market) is replete with bars and cafés where music is played and locals hang out in the evenings. Over the weekends, the town comes even more alive when jet-skis zoom up and down the river, as spectators watch and cheer.

Much of the reason for the liveliness is that Rio Branco is a federal **university town**. On top of this, Rio Branco is also a thriving and very busy market town, pivotally situated on the new road and with an active, if tiny, river port.

If you happen to be in Rio Branco during the third week of November, don't miss the **Feira de Produtos da Floresta do Acre** (Acre's Rainforest Products Fair), usually housed in the splendid SEBRAE building on Avenida Ceará (take the Conjunto Esperança bus from the central terminal and follow the signs), and accompanied by local bands.

A FLIGHT OVER ACRE'S GEOGLYPHS

One of the main attractions in the eastern part of Acre state is the area's mysterious **geoglyphs**, discovered in 1977. Since then, a number of other structures have been found, with more and more being unearthed over the years; there are now just under three hundred that have been recorded. While little is generally known about these geometric designs, it is believed that they predate the arrival of European colonialists and may possibly have had religious purposes.

The geometric shapes have an internal area of 10,000 to 30,000 square metres and a depth of up to 5m, and as a result are only really visible from the air. Maanaim Turismo (R$550 per person for three people; ⓣ68 9917 3232, ⓣ68 9214 7131, ⓦmaanaimturismo.com) offer **hot-air balloon rides** over the geoglyphs. As hot-air balloons travel with the direction of the wind and the pilot therefore has no control over where you're heading, flying over the geoglyphs by plane will mean you will be able to spot many more shapes. However, floating over the Amazon rainforest in a hot-air balloon is a truly unforgettable experience; the trip with Eme Amazônia even includes a delicious breakfast in the field you land in.

Gameleira

Lying on the southern bank of the river, the **Gameleira** is the city's historical core. The riverbank is lined with pretty colourful buildings erected during the rubber boom at the end of the nineteenth and beginning of the twentieth century. The lovely Cine Teatro Recreio was built to house cultural and artistic shows. Along the riverbank flutters Acre's large flag, at full mast all year round, reaffirming the people's pride and patriotism in their nascent state.

Parque Urbano Capitão Ciríaco

Av Dr Pereira Pasos s/n • Mon–Sat 4am–6pm • Free

The lovely **Parque Urbano Capitão Ciríaco** is home to native Amazonian flora including approximately four hundred rubber trees, and is a pleasant spot for a stroll. Make sure you head to the rubber-tapper's hut; the friendly tapper Antônio will be happy to tell you more about how latex is extracted from the trees, before being smoked onto bales (leave him a donation; he's usually around Mon–Sat in the mornings).

Mercado Velho

Rua Epaminondas Jacome 2755 • Daily 6am–6pm • Free

Built at the end of the 1920s, the beautiful **Mercado Velho** was one of the city's first brickwork constructions. Today, along with meat, fish and vegetable stalls, it houses a number of craft shops; it's a good spot to buy souvenirs (see page 399). The market also hosts cultural shows, from live music bands to dance performances.

Palácio Rio Branco

Av Getúlio Vargas, Praça Povos da Floresta • Tues–Fri 8am–6pm, Sat 4–9pm • Free • ⓣ68 3223 9240

Inaugurated in 1930, the beautiful **Palácio Rio Branco** is the seat of the government of Acre. The building features Doric and Ionic columns on the main facade and a well-preserved wooden ceiling within. It houses a lovely museum on Acre's history and peoples, with a section on the region's turbulent past, which touches upon the rubber boom, the state's brief independence in the twentieth century and its subsequent annexation to Brazil. Displays include the headwear of Acre's indigenous tribes, decorated with beautiful colourful plumes, and large urns dating back to three thousand years ago that were found near the geoglyphs, thereby providing valuable clues on the area's mysterious shapes.

Quixadá

Estrada do Quixadá, Km 20 • Wed–Sun 9am–5pm • Free • 68 9204 4638 • Local buses from Rio Branco leave daily at 5am, 9am, 11am, 3pm & 7pm, returning daily at 10am, noon, 4pm & 8pm (1hr; R$10 return)

About 20km northeast of Rio Branco on the site of a former *siringal*, or rubber production centre, Quixadá was reconstructed for a Brazilian TV series that focused on the rubber boom and Acre's turbulent history during the twentieth century. The property is now a museum housing clothes, objects and furniture that were used for the TV show, providing an insight into life at the time of Acre's rubber boom. The museum is run by the local community, and is in a peaceful riverside location; it's worth making an afternoon of it, and having lunch at the restaurant on the property. There's also a *pousada* here (see page 398).

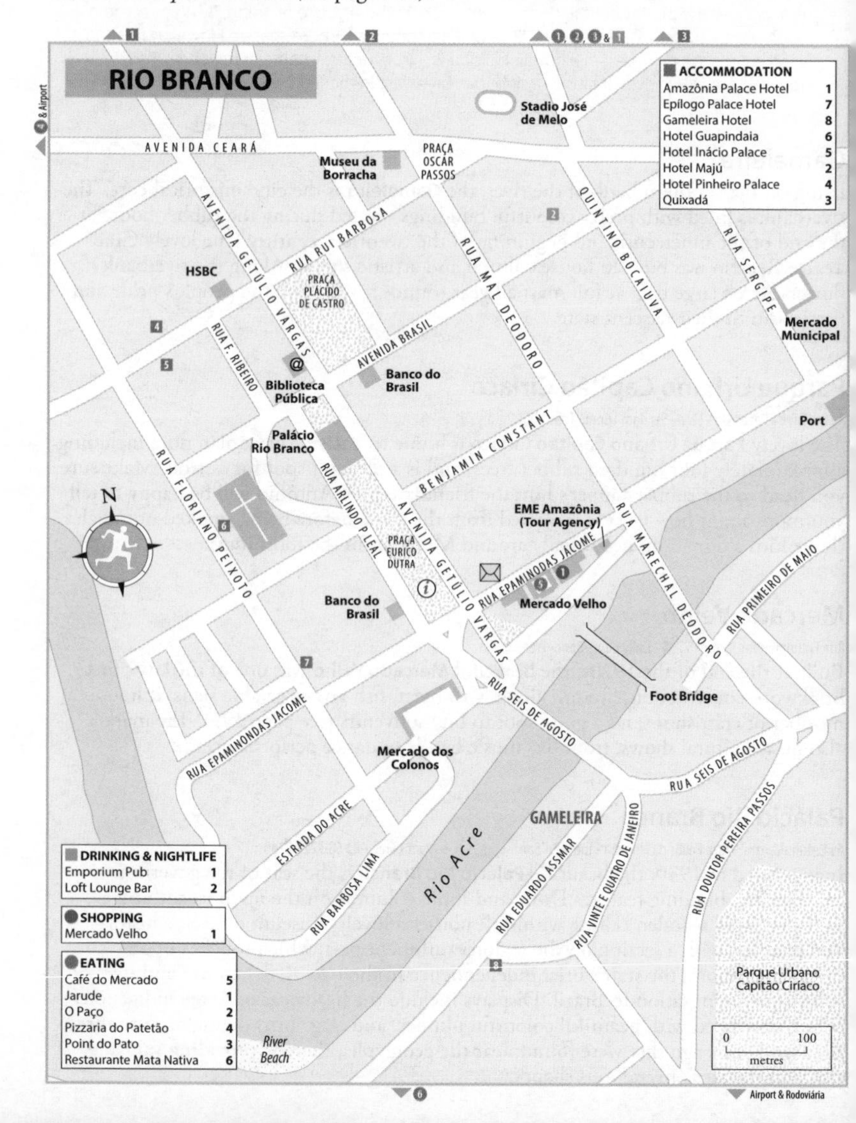

ACRE AND THE RUBBER CONFLICT

The relaxed air of Rio Branco masks many **tensions**, above all to do with population movement – people are still arriving here from the east – and the conflicting claims of small rubber-tappers and multinational companies on the jungle. The tappers, who have lived here for a long time and who know how to manage the forests in a sustainable way, see the multinationals as newcomers who aim to turn the trees into pasture for beef cattle and short-term profit, destroying not only the forest but also many local livelihoods. When hired gunmen working for the cattle ranchers shot dead **Chico Mendes**, the leader of the rubber-tappers' union, in 1988, the plight of the forest peoples of Acre came to the world's attention. Today, the political situation in Acre remains uneasy, with the second- and third-generation tappers and gatherers joining forces with the native population in resisting the enormous economic and armed might of the advancing cattle-based companies.

ARRIVAL AND DEPARTURE

By plane The airport (☎68 3211 1000) is 25km northwest of town, with LATAM, and Gol serving Brasília (4 daily; 3hr) and Porto Velho (one direct daily with Gol; 55min). Buses connect the airport to the city centre, although they are not very regular (every 2hr; 1hr; R$5); a taxi is R$83 (20min).

By bus The rodoviária (☎68 3221 3693, ⓦfacebook.com/RodoviariaInternacionalRB) is at BR-364, Via Verde, Km 125, 8km southwest of town. Regular buses connect the rodoviária to the city centre (every 10min; 15min; R$5); a taxi is R$30 (10min). Eucatur serves plenty of national destinations, including Cuiabá (daily 9pm; 36hr; R$339) and Porto Velho (3 daily; 7hr; R$104). For Brasília it's best to change in Porto Velho (1 daily at 2pm with Andorinha).

By car Car rental from Yes Rent a Car, Rua Isaura Parente 747, Sala 2, Bosque (☎68 3226 4811, ⓦyesrentacar.com.br); iNova, Rua Primavera 275, Conjunto Universitário (☎68 3229 3101, ⓦinovalocadora.com.br).

INFORMATION AND TOURS

Tourist office The regional CAT tourist office, a kiosk below the Palácio Rio Branco on Av Getúlio Vargas (Mon–Sat 8am–6pm, Sun 2–6pm; ☎68 3901 3029), can supply maps of the town and information on hotels and travel in the region. There's an information point at the rodoviária (Mon–Sat 8am–noon & 2–7pm, Sun 8am–noon) and at the airport, which meets incoming flights.

Eme Amazônia Tv da Capitania 40 by the Mercado Velho (☎68 3222 8838, ⓦemeamazonia.com.br) is a reputable operator offering magical hot-air balloon rides (R$790; min 2 people) over the rainforest and geoglyphs, along with boat trips, city tours and bike tours.

Maanaim Turismo The long-established Maanaim Turismo (Av Central 10, Sala 07; ☎68 9971 3232, ⓦmaanaimturismo.com) organizes a wide range of exciting trips to local sites, rubber-tapper and indigenous communities, along with city and river tours. The friendly owner also organizes treks and overnight stays with local communities, week-long trips to Peru, and thrilling flights in four-seater planes over the area's geoglyphs.

ACCOMMODATION

Amazônia Palace Hotel Rua Isaura Parente 259, Bosque ☎68 3223 4525, ⓦamazoniapalacehotel.com.br; map p.396. Located about 2km north of the centre in the Bairro Bosque, this is a great option offering spacious and comfortable a/c rooms with sturdy beds and decked out with new furniture. Staff are friendly. (wi-fi) **R$190**

Epílogo Palace Hotel Rua Floriano Peixoto 470 ☎68 3223 2440, ⓦepilogopalacehotel.com.br; map p.396. The a/c rooms here are brightened up with a splash of green paint; they're a bit run-down, with humming rusty fridges, although given the price they're not too bad at all. (wi-fi) (but poor) **R$150**

Gameleira Hotel Rua 24 de Janeiro 283 ☎68 3222 8861, ⓦgameleirahotel.com.br; map p.396. This oddly shaped building painted in olive green offers surprisingly good-value doubles and triples. There's not much difference between the newer and older rooms, except the former have flat-screen TVs as opposed to larger outdated sets; rooms are a bit small, but the place is kept clean – overall, it's a real steal. (wi-fi) **R$100**

Hotel Guapindaia Rua Floriano Peixoto 550 ☎68 3223 2399, ⓦhoteisguapindaia.com.br; map p.396. With a couple of other locations in town, this place offers compact beige rooms, some of which are in better shape than others – take a look at a couple before settling in. Location is great, just a stone's throw away from Praça Placido de Castro. (wi-fi) **R$170**

Hotel Inácio Palace Rua Rui Barbosa 450 ☎68 3214 7100, ⓦirmaospinheiro.com.br; map p.396. With over one hundred rooms on a series of long narrow corridors the atmosphere here is rather impersonal. The newer, more expensive "gran" *luxo* rooms are not so different from the "old" rooms built over forty years ago; all feature a/c units and television, and guests can use the pool of *Inácio Palace*'s sister hotel *Pinheiro Palace* just across the street. R$126

Hotel Majú Av Nações Unidas 302, Bosque 68 3223 0812, bit.ly/HotelMaju; map p.396. This friendly hotel north of the stadium is the town's best budget option with spotless a/c rooms with TV and fridge, and new modern fittings. There's a living area with sofas and TV on the ground floor, and a garage in a safe setting. R$120

Hotel Pinheiro Palace Rua Rui Barbosa 450 68 3214 7100, irmaospinheiro.com.br; map p.396. With better amenities than its sister hotel *Inácio Palace*, the tiled rooms here are neat and tidy with flat-screen TVs. There are two suites, substantially bigger than the standards, featuring a large jacuzzi tub and shower. There's a decent-sized pool, too. R$180

★ **Quixadá** Estrada do Quixadá, Km 20 68 9204 4638; map p.396. Run by the local community, accommodation at this museum re-creates life during the rubber era in a couple of simply decorated but welcoming rooms sleeping three; there's also a breezy restaurant serving delicious home-made cooking. It's a great place to spend a few days if you want to immerse yourself in community life; locals are friendly and will be happy to tell you more about how they live as well as show you around the area. R$150

EATING

Café do Mercado Rua Epaminondas Jacomé, in the Mercado Velho 68 3223 4567; map p.396. This bustling café with tables spilling onto the riverfront is a great spot to watch life go by as you sip on a cup of coffee and enjoy freshly baked pastries, pancakes or tapioca (R$5–10). The café is just inside the market. Mon–Sat 8am–10pm, Sun 4–10pm.

★ **Jarude Rua** Martiniano Prado 188 68 3224 0266, jaruderestaurante.com; map p.396. The friendly owner here is of Lebanese origin, and her family have been lovingly preparing delicious Arab food for decades. The menu includes home-made hummus (R$29.90), tabbouleh (R$18.90), baba ghanoush (R$27.90) and superb beef and lamb koftas (R$14.90). There's also lamb with Moroccan couscous (R$59.75), served at tables lit by dim red lights. The interior features bare-brick walls, glittering lanterns and a few Middle Eastern knick-knacks. Daily 5–10.45pm (until 11pm on weekends); closed last Sun of the month.

O Paço Parque da Maternidade s/n, Lote 1 68 3028 0001, facebook.com/opacorestaurante; map p.396. This open-fronted restaurant offers a selection of international dishes, including burgers (R$20) and Arab dishes – the *misto árabe* platter (R$55) includes kofta, kibbeh, baba ghanoush, hummus and stuffed vine leaves. There's a daily lunch and dinner buffet (R$70/kg) that also includes a selection of Lebanese dishes. Daily 11am–1am.

Pizzaria do Patetão Av Ceará 2767 68 3226 4242; map p.396. This lively spot buzzes on Sundays, when loud *samba de roda* bands fuel drinking and dancing until the late hours. It's a great little spot to watch life go by, especially over the weekends when the river hums with spinning jet-skis and speedboats. Pizzas from R$28. Tues–Sun 6pm–midnight.

★ **Point do Pato** Rua das Palmeiras 613, Bairro São Francisco 68 3224 8009; map p.396. This simple family-run place in a residential neighbourhood by a skate park has been a catalyst for inventive Amazonian cuisine in Rio Branco. The owner uses simple everyday ingredients and creates creative dishes that are to die for. The *filé de pirarucu* served in chestnut milk is just outstanding (R$60). Tues–Sat 7pm–midnight.

Restaurante Mata Nativa Via Verde Km 2 68 3221 3004, facebook.com/restaurantematanativaac; map p.396. This breezy restaurant with a straw roof attracts plenty of local families for its appetizing regional dishes including *galinha caipira* (R$98 for four people) and *carne do sol* (R$75 for four people), all at extremely reasonable prices. The restaurant features a children's playground. Daily 11am–3pm.

DRINKING AND NIGHTLIFE

Rio Branco is a lively city with plenty of fun bars, many of which **host live music** bands. A great place to meet people in the evening is by **Mercado Velho**, with a range of pleasant bars and cafés.

Emporium Pub Rua Beira do Canal 50, Parque da Maternidade 68 9213 0555; map p.396. This popular bar gets crammed on the weekends, when crowds spill in to sway to reggae, pop, rock and MPB bands. There's a mezzanine level from where you can look down onto the stage and little dancefloor. Drinks R$8, snacks from R$15. Thurs–Sat 6pm–4am.

Loft Lounge Bar Av Brasil 276 facebook.com/loftbar.acre; map p.396. This moody bar in the heart of centro does creative cocktails (R$13), bar food starting at R$18, and live rock music on Friday nights. Popular with locals. Fri 9pm–3am; plus some Sat.

SHOPPING

Mercado Velho Rua Epaminondas Jacome 2755; map p.396. There are a number of shops within the Mercado Velho, selling all manner of goods, including Brazil nuts, herbal remedies and local crafts. Mon–Sat 6pm–noon, some shops open Sun.

DIRECTORY

Consulates Peru, Rua Pernambuco 1040, Bosque (68 3224 2727); Bolivia, Rua Italo Meireles 236 (68 3546 5760).

Internet The Biblioteca Pública, Av Getúlio Vargas 389 (Mon–Sat 8am–9pm; 68 3223 1210) offers free internet.

Money and exchange Banco do Brasil, Rua Arlindo Porto Leal 85.

Post office Rua Epaminondas Jacome 2858 (Mon–Fri 8am–5pm), by the corner with Av Getúlio Vargas.

Brasília and the Planalto Central

OSCAR NIEMEYER'S CATEDRAL METROPOLITANA

Brasília and the Planalto Central

The geographical heart of Brazil is the central highlands (Planalto Central), shared by the states of Goiás, Tocantins and parts of Mato Grosso. This rapidly developing and prosperous agricultural region was, as recently as seventy years ago, still largely inhabited by indigenous peoples, with a few colonial towns precariously linked by oxcart trails to the rest of the country. The founding of Brasília in the late 1950s ended that, shifting Brazil's centre of political gravity from the coast to the interior and opening up an entire region of the country to settlement and development.

Brasília remains the region's main attraction, with its extraordinary **architecture**, a 1950s vision of the future. In recent years, the city has become the base for a mostly Brazilian **ecotourism** boom. People come for the emptiness and beauty of the landscape a few hours north of Brasília, as well as great **hiking** and more specialized outdoor pursuits like caving and rock climbing. The main centre, **Parque Nacional Chapada dos Veadeiros**, is an easy excursion from Brasília. There is also a national park, the **Parque Nacional de Brasília**, on the city's periphery. Within easy reach of Brasília are two colonial towns worth visiting: **Pirenópolis**, and the old capital of Goiás state, **Goiás Velho**, a little-visited jewel that's as beautiful as any of the better-known *cidades históricas* of Minas Gerais.

Brasília

Love it or loathe it, Brazil's capital **BRASÍLIA** is like nowhere else on earth: the world's largest, most successful, and in its own weird way most beautiful planned city. The city has a startlingly space-age feel and look, with a decidedly retro twist. Originally intended for a population of half a million by the year 2000, Brasília and the area around it today has close to five million people and is the only one of Brazil's major metropolitan areas still growing quickly. Brasília also has its own little state, the **Distrito Federal** (Federal District), which includes its *cidades satélites* – poorer satellite cities that house Brasília's low-income workers, who commute into town to serve the needs of the government-employed elite.

Some visitors find Brasília alienating, with its jumble of skyscrapers, malls and massive empty spaces – the absence of planned gardens and parks is the centre's major design flaw. At night the centre is deserted. But beyond the central area, no other Brazilian city has as many trees and parks, and the older residential sections are very pleasant to walk in, with the trees so dense it often seems the housing blocks have been built in the middle of a wood. Most places in Asa Norte and Asa Sul are safe enough to walk around in, but W3 and the deserted central area should be treated with caution at night.

MEMORIAL JK

Highlights

❶ **Catedral Metropolitana** Contemplate the soaring statues of St Peter and the angels from the sunken floor of this landmark cathedral. See page 408

❷ **Memorial JK** Learn about Juscelino Kubitschek, the ambitious president who commissioned the capital, at this intriguing museum devoted to his life. See page 410

❸ **Memorial dos Povos Indígenas** Superb indigenous art is on view inside this elegant museum, itself a dazzling Niemeyer creation. See page 410

❹ **Salto de Itiquira** Best known for its vast waterfall, this delightful park near Formosa makes a worthwhile day-trip from Brasília. See page 418

❺ **Pirenópolis** A charming little mountain town with fresh air, colonial churches and a slew of arty jewellery shops. See page 424

❻ **Goiás Velho** A picturesque colonial town, well preserved and relatively untouched by commercialism, with fine excursions nearby. See page 426

❼ **Parque Nacional Chapada dos Veadeiros** The varied terrain in this national park makes it an ideal spot for hiking. See page 431

HIGHLIGHTS ARE MARKED ON THE MAPS ON PAGES 404 AND 406

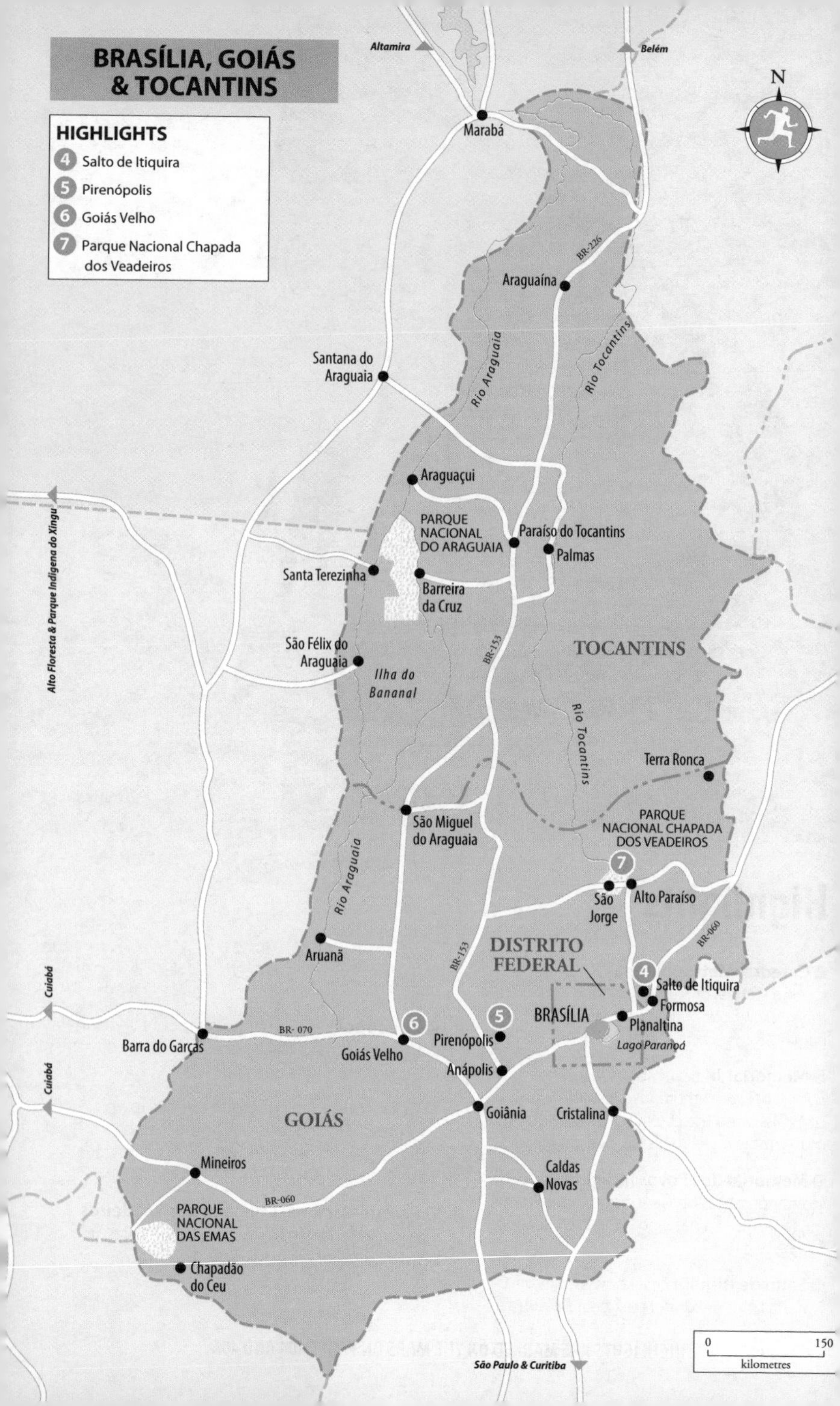

BRASÍLIA, GOIÁS & TOCANTINS
HIGHLIGHTS
4 Salto de Itiquira
5 Pirenópolis
6 Goiás Velho
7 Parque Nacional Chapada dos Veadeiros
N
Altamira
Belém
Marabá
BR-226
Araguaína
Rio Araguaia
Rio Tocantins
Santana do Araguaia
Araguaçui
PARQUE NACIONAL DO ARAGUAIA
Paraíso do Tocantins
Palmas
Santa Terezinha
Barreira da Cruz
Alto Floresta & Parque Indígena do Xingu
São Félix do Araguaia
Ilha do Bananal
BR-153
TOCANTINS
Rio Tocantins
Terra Ronca
São Miguel do Araguaia
PARQUE NACIONAL CHAPADA DOS VEADEIROS
Rio Araguaia
São Jorge
Alto Paraíso
BR-060
Aruanã
BR-153
DISTRITO FEDERAL
Salto de Itiquira
Formosa
Cuiabá
BRASÍLIA
Planaltina
Lago Paranoá
BR- 070
Barra do Garças
Goiás Velho
Pirenópolis
Anápolis
Cuiabá
Goiânia
Cristalina
GOIÁS
Mineiros
Caldas Novas
BR-060
PARQUE NACIONAL DAS EMAS
Chapadão do Ceu
0
150
kilometres
São Paulo & Curitiba

Brief history

The idea of a **Brazilian inland capital** goes back to colonial times but fulfilment of the idea had to wait until 1956 when **Juscelino Kubitschek** became president, on the promise he would build the city if he won the election. He had to get it finished by the end of his term of office, so work soon began in earnest.

The site was quickly selected by aerial surveys but the city then had to be planned, financed and built at a site 125km from the nearest rail line, 190km from the nearest airport, over 600km from the nearest paved road. Still, in **Oscar Niemeyer**, the city's architect, Brasília had South America's most able student of Le Corbusier, who was contracted to design the buildings, and alongside him, **Lúcio Costa** was hired for the awesome task of Brasília's urban planning. His **city plan** is described variously as being in the shape of a bow and arrow, a bird in flight or an aeroplane. The main public buildings, government ministries, palace of justice and presidential palace are in the "fuselage", an 8km-long grass mall known as the **Eixo Monumental** (Monumental Axis).

Exactly three years, one month and five days after the master plan was unveiled, 150,000 people arrived in Brasília for the official **inauguration**, in April 1960 (the event is celebrated today as the Festa da Cidade on April 21 each year). There were still years of work ahead, but in time, the city slowly grew.

Financial and environmental costs

Brasília quickly paid for itself. The rapid **development of the planalto** that followed transformed the region into one of the most developed agricultural areas in the country, and the taxes, jobs and production that were generated swiftly made the decision to build Brasília seem inspired. The costs have proved to be more environmental than financial, with the rapid conversion of much of the *planalto* to farmland and the destruction of forest along the Belém–Brasília highway corridor. As ever, those with most cause to complain were the **indigenous peoples** of the *planalto*, notably the **Xavante**, who did what they could to halt the tide, but by the 1970s they were all confined to reservations a fraction of the size of their previous territories.

The Praça dos Três Poderes

The focus of the Brazilian government complex, at the southern end of the **Esplanada dos Ministérios** (a wide, open space between the two Via Um central roadways, flanked by ministries), is the **Praça dos Três Poderes**, which means Square of Three Powers, those being the legislature (Congress), executive (president) and judiciary (law courts). Niemeyer designed them all, and they're rightly regarded as among the best modernist buildings in the world. The combination of white marble, water pools, reflecting glass and the airy flying buttresses on the presidential palace and supreme court make these buildings remarkably elegant. The ugly flagpole at the centre of the square was installed by Brazil's military regime over Niemeyer's protests. At night floodlighting and internal lights make the square even more impressive; a slow walk or bus ride around the Esplanada in the early evening, when people are still working and the buildings glow like Chinese lanterns, is a must.

BRASÍLIA'S CLIMATE

Brasília's **rainy season** (Oct–March) can be torrential. The best time to come is immediately afterwards, from April to June, when the trees are in bloom and the climate is pleasant and mild. July to September is the **dry season**, when the sun beats down hard, everything dries out and hot winds blow fine red dust over everything. This time of year is extraordinarily dry – humidity levels are comparable with the Sahara. If you do come during this time, drink as much water as you can and don't skimp on the sunscreen. Fortunately, night always comes as a relief as temperatures drop and freshness returns.

Congresso Nacional

Praça dos Três Poderes • Tues & Thurs–Sun 9am–5pm (Wed by online advance reservation); tours (1hr) every 30min; tours in English must be booked in advance online • Free but photo ID required • No sandals or sleeveless T-shirts, or shorts during the week or during parliamentary recess • 61 3216 1771, www2.congressonacional.leg.br/visite & facebook.com/pg/visitacaocongresso

The **Congresso Nacional**, with its tall twin towers, is the most recognizable landmark in Brasília. The two large "bowls" on either side of the towers house the Senate Chamber (the smaller, inverted one) and the House of Representatives, and were designed so that the public could climb and play on them, though the only people allowed there now are the patrolling soldiers of the Polícia Militar. Visitors can attend debates when in session, however – something you might want to enquire about at the front entrance desk. The chambers themselves are a hoot – they come over today as retro 1960s, but haven't aged as well as that phrase implies.

Palácio Itamaraty

Praça dos Três Poderes • Tours Mon–Fri 9am, 10am, 11am, 2pm, 3pm, 4pm & 5pm, Sat & Sun 9am, 11am, 2pm, 3pm & 5pm • Tours must be booked in advance by phone or by email (visita@itamaraty.gov.br) • Free but photo ID required • No sandals, shorts or sleeveless T-shirts • 61 2030 8051, itamaraty.gov.br

The **Palácio Itamaraty**, which houses the Foreign Office, combines modern and classical styles. It's built around elegant courtyards, sculptures and gardens, and inside its airiness and sense of space are breathtaking, well set off by a carefully chosen selection of modern art and wall hangings. Outside, the marble *Meteor* sculpture by Bruno Giorgi is a stunning piece of work, its five parts representing five continents.

Palácio do Planalto

Praça dos Três Poderes • Sun 9.30am–2pm; flag ceremony Mon–Thurs, Sat & Sun 8am & 6pm, Fri 8am & 5pm • Free but photo ID required • No sandals, shorts or sleeveless T-shirts • 61 3411 2317

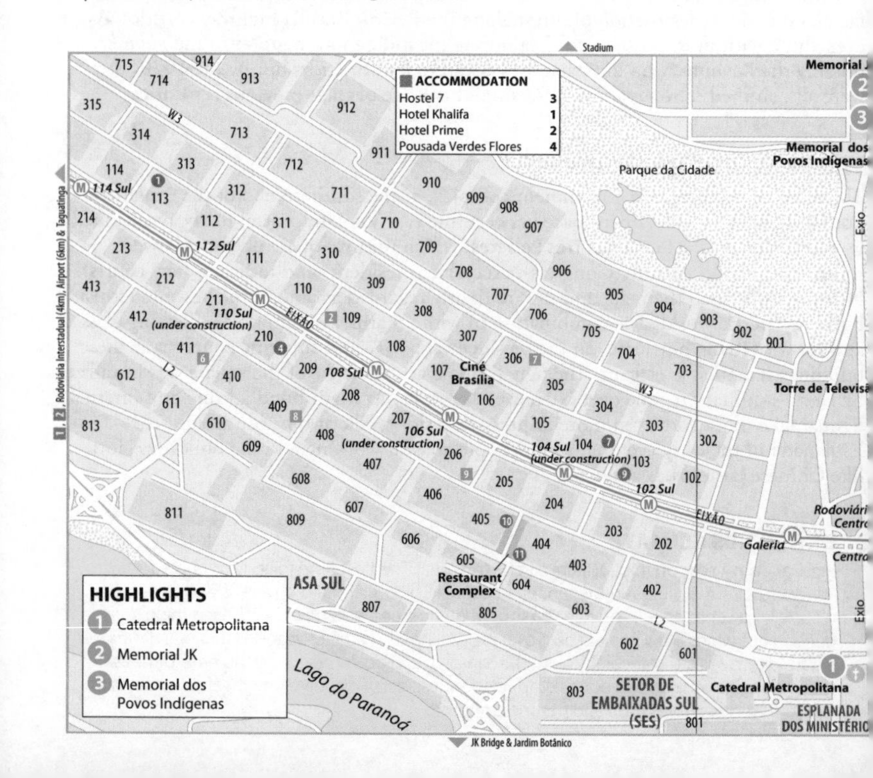

North of the Congresso Nacional, the **Palácio do Planalto** houses the president's office, which can be visited by guided tour. This is the most spectacular Niemeyer building; the interior is dominated by sleek columns and a glorious, curving ramp. They raise and lower the flag out the front twice daily, with a full ceremony, accompanied on Friday evenings by a band.

Museu da Cidade

Praça dos Três Poderes • Tues–Sun 9am–6pm • Free • ☎ 61 3223 3728

In the middle of Praça dos Três Poderes, an oblong marble structure balanced on a plinth with a bust of Juscelino Kubitschek is the **Museu da Cidade** (**or Museu Histórico de Brasília**). This curious building was intended to house a small exhibition on the history of Brasília, but in fact it is almost entirely empty, with just inscriptions on its walls of quotes about the new city from Kubitschek, Niemeyer and the then Pope Pius XII.

Panteão da Pátria Tancredo Neves

Praça dos Três Poderes • Tues–Sun 9am–6pm • Free • ☎ 61 3325 6244

Although it wasn't built until 1985, the **Panteão da Pátria Tancredo Neves** was conceived in 1954 following the unexpected death of president-elect Tancredo Neves (see page 647). Designed by Oscar Niemeyer in the form of a dove, it isn't a tomb, but a monument to honour a raft of national heroes – fourteen so far, starting with Tiradentes – whose names are inscribed in a *Livro de Aço* ("Book of Steel"), displayed within. There's also a small exhibition about Tancredo Neves, and on the top floor a stained-glass window by Marianne Peretti, who designed the windows in the Catedral Metropolitana.

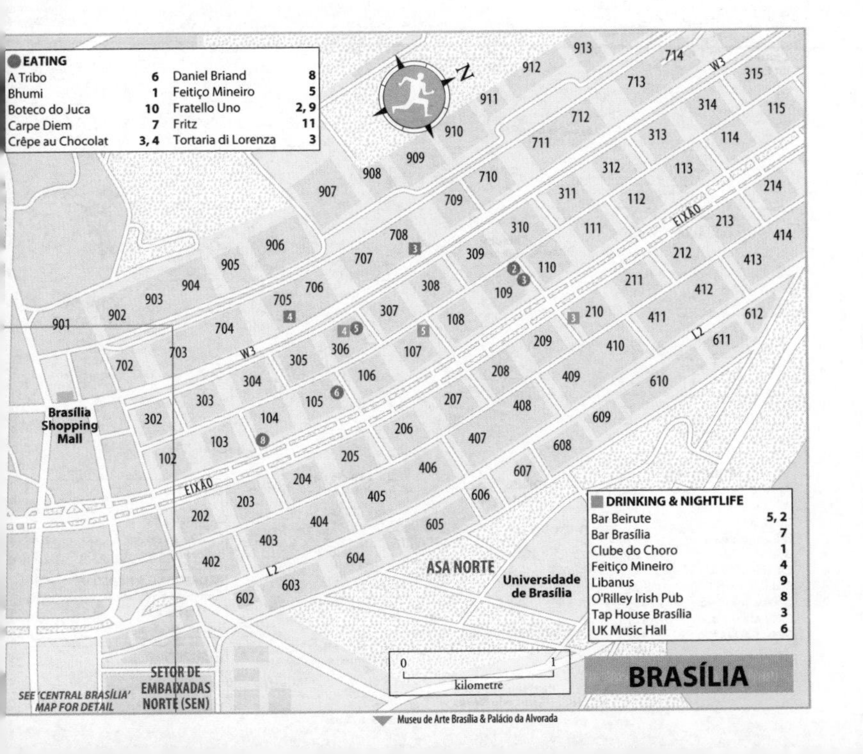

Catedral Metropolitana

Sector Cultural Sul • Mon, Wed, Thurs, Sat & Sun 8am–5pm, Tues & Fri & Sun 10.30am–5pm, but no entry during Mass, and no shorts allowed • Free

Between the ministries and the downtown rodoviária, and within walking distance of either, the **Catedral Metropolitana** is one of Brasília's most striking edifices. Marking the spot where the city of Brasília was inaugurated in 1960, it is built in the form of

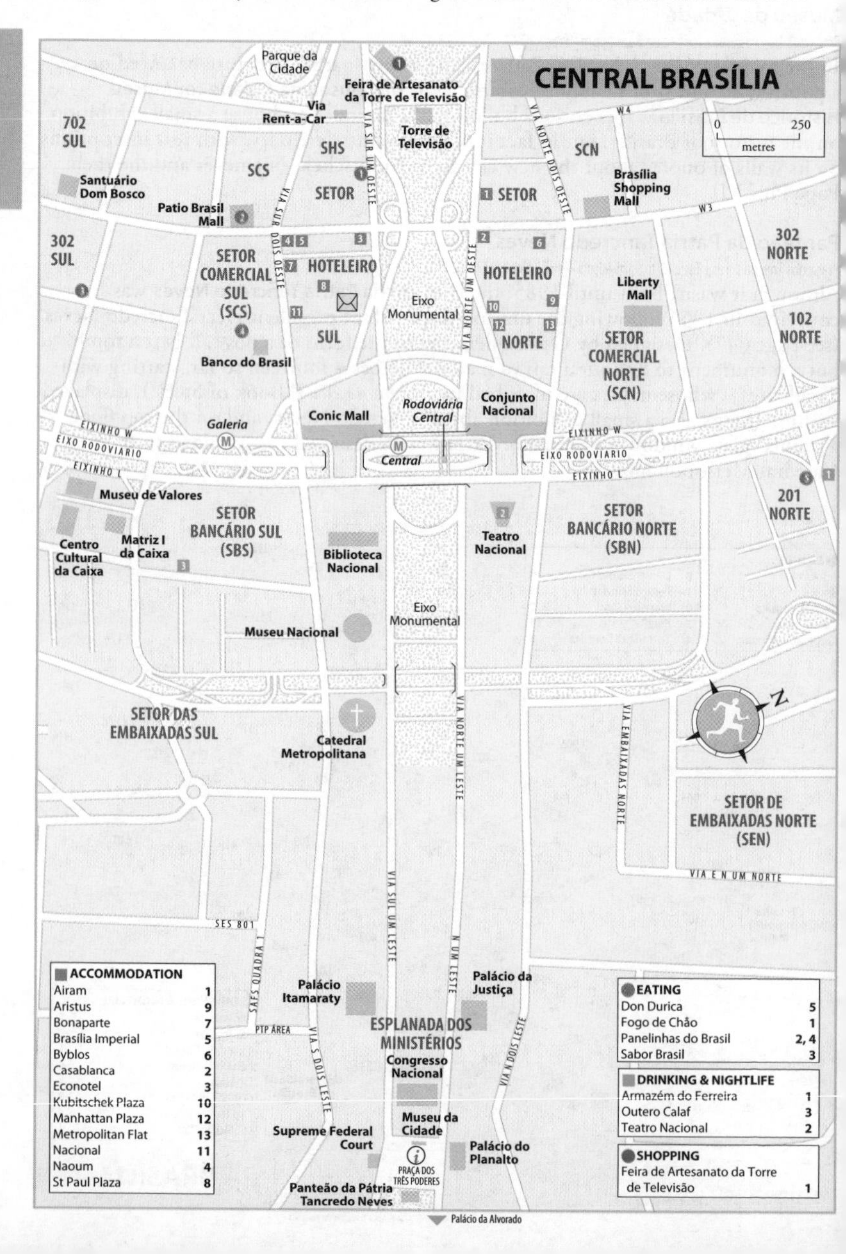

ACCOMMODATION

Airam	1
Aristus	9
Bonaparte	7
Brasília Imperial	5
Byblos	6
Casablanca	2
Econotel	3
Kubitschek Plaza	10
Manhattan Plaza	12
Metropolitan Flat	13
Nacional	11
Naoum	4
St Paul Plaza	8

EATING

Don Durica	5
Fogo de Chão	1
Panelinhas do Brasil	2, 4
Sabor Brasil	3

DRINKING & NIGHTLIFE

Armazém do Ferreira	1
Outero Calaf	3
Teatro Nacional	2

SHOPPING

Feira de Artesanato da Torre de Televisão	1

an inverted chalice and crown of thorns; its sunken nave puts most of the interior floor below ground level. Some of the glass roof panels in the interior reflect rippling water from outside, adding to the sense of airiness, while the statues of St Peter and the angels suspended from the ceiling (the inspired gravity-defying creations of Brazilian sculptor Bruno Ceschiatti) help to highlight the feeling of elevation.

Museu Nacional and around

Sector Cultural Sul • Tues–Sun 9am–6.30pm • Free • 61 3325 6410, www.cultura.df.gov.br/nossa-cultura/museus/museu-nacional.html

One of Niemeyer's last Brasília buildings, finished only in 2006, the **Museu Nacional** is a white dome with protruding walkways, just northwest of the cathedral, which bears a striking resemblance to Michael Rennie's spaceship in *The Day the Earth Stood Still*. Despite its name, it doesn't actually have any permanent exhibits, but houses within its cool inner space temporary exhibitions of modern art.

Very close by is another of Niemeyer's last Brasília buildings, the rather more terrestrial-looking **Biblioteca Nacional** (National Library), which opened in 2007.

Teatro Nacional

Sector Cultural Norte • Mon–Sat 8am–noon & 2–6pm • Free • 61 3325 6239, www.cultura.df.gov.br/nossa-cultura/teatro-nacional.html

On the north side of the Eixo Monumental, the **Teatro Nacional** is a marvellous, largely glass-covered pyramid built in the form of an Aztec temple. It's set at an angle to let light into the lobby, which often hosts good art exhibitions with futuristic and environmental themes. Inside the theatre are three halls: the Martins Pena, the Villa-Lobos (the largest, seating 1200) and the much smaller Alberto Nepomuceno. The theatre also hosts concerts (see page 417) and is the main city venue for **ballet and dance**, sustained by an appreciative audience among Brasília's government and diplomatic corps.

Palácio da Alvorada

Peninsula de Alvorada • Wed 2.30–4.50pm • Free • 61 3411 2317, www2.planalto.gov.br/presidencia/palacios-e-residencias-oficiais/palacio_alvorada • Bus #0.104 or #104.2 from platform A16 at the Rodoviária Central; if you go by taxi, ask the driver to wait for you in the car park to the right, as taxis rarely pass by here

To complete your tour of Niemeyer gems, it's worth taking the short bus or taxi ride to the president's official residence, the **Palácio da Alvorada**, considered by many the most beautiful of the architect's buildings. The residence is nestled behind an emerald-green lawn and beautifully manicured gardens, which perfectly set off the brilliant white of its exterior, with Niemeyer's signature slender buttresses and its blue-tinted glass. Somehow the fact that you're usually only allowed to see it from fifty metres away adds to its delicateness and elegance.

It is now possible to visit the **interior**, on Wednesdays only, but reserve on line in advance or turn up at least an hour early to get a ticket as numbers are limited and demand is high. Inside, it all looks a bit too modern for a presidential residence: the most striking feature is the gold-tiled wall in the entrance hall, inscribed with one of Juscelino Kubitschek's platitudes about the city. The tour is guided, but in Portuguese only.

Museu de Valores

SBS Q.3, Bloco B, Lote 1 • Tues–Fri 10am–6pm (last entry 5.30pm), plus 1st Sat of month 2–6pm • Free, but photo ID required • 61 3414 2093, www.bcb.gov.br/?museu

The most interesting place to visit within easy walking distance of the rodoviária can be found in the unlikely setting of the **Central Bank building**, the unmistakeable concrete-and-black-glass skyscraper in Setor Bancário Sul, visible from anywhere in the centre. Tucked away by the building's rear entrance is the **Museu de Valores** or

Museu da Moeda (Money Museum), where you'll find a quirky but fascinating display of Brazilian currency from colonial times. It's very interesting as social history, but overshadowed by the second part of the display, an extraordinary exhibition behind armoured glass of the largest gold nuggets ever found in Brazil – most dating from the 1980s, when the Central Bank was buying nuggets from the Amazon gold rush.

Torre de Televisão

Eixo Monumental Oeste • Daily 8am–8pm • Free • ⓣ 61 3412 2712

The 218m-high **Torre de Televisão** (TV Tower), built in 1967, is an obvious city landmark, and its viewing platform is a great place from which to put Brasília into perspective. Indeed, there's no better place in town for watching the sun set – though frustratingly there is no bar to watch it from. At weekends the tower is also popular for the **craft market** held just to its west (see page 417).

Parque da Cidade

Asa Sul (most central entrance on Eixo Monumental Oeste) • Daily 5am–midnight • Free • ⓣ 61 3329 0400

A short walk from Setor Hoteleiro Sul, the enormous **Parque da Cidade** (City Park) – also called **Parque Sara Kubitschek** after JK's wife – is a massive mosaic of playgrounds, jogging tracks, bars and restaurants, picnic grounds, artificial lakes, parklands and woods. If you want to walk or jog in Brasília, this is the place to do it. The southern entrance, a block away from the hotel sector, is where many of the attractions are concentrated, including an enjoyably tacky **funfair**. The best time to visit is Sunday morning, when the locals turn out en masse to jog, work out, sunbathe or read the paper, while dozens of kiosks and street-sellers tout everything from chilled green coconuts to shiatsu massage.

Memorial JK

Eixo Monumental Oeste • Daily 9am–6pm • Free • ⓣ 61 3226 7860, ⓦ memorialjk.com.br • Best reached by one of the many buses heading up the Eixo

The **Memorial JK (Juscelino Kubitschek)** is topped by a rather Soviet-looking statue of Brasília's founder standing inside an enormous question mark and pointing down the Eixo towards the heart of government. The museum below reverently reproduces JK's library and study, while the man himself lies upstairs in state in a black marble sarcophagus, backlit by an extraordinary combination of purple, violet and orange lights. There's a fascinating display of mementoes of JK and the city, including photos and video clips of his funeral and the dedication of the Memorial – in turning out in their hundreds of thousands in his honour, the population of the Distrito Federal made the first important anti-military demonstration.

Memorial dos Povos Indígenas

Eixo Monumental Oeste • Tues–Fri 9am–5pm, Sat & Sun 10am–5pm • Free • ⓣ 61 3344 1154, ⓦ www.cultura.df.gov.br/nossa-cultura/museus/memorial-dos-povos-indigenas.html

Southeast of the JK Memorial is another Niemeyer building, the white and curving **Memorial dos Povos Indígenas**, which houses one of the best collections of **indigenous art** in Brazil, much of it from the *planalto* itself, produced by the indigenous groups who inhabit the headwaters of the Xingú River. Highlights are the extraordinary ceramic pots of the Warao, the Xingú's ceramic specialists, beautifully adorned with figures of birds and animals, and vivid, delicate featherwork. The rotating exhibits and regular travelling shows are always fascinating, but the building alone is worth the visit; the gallery is set in a long, downward curve around a circular courtyard, the smoked glass set against Niemeyer's trademark brilliant white exterior.

Santuário Dom Bosco

702 Sul, Bloco B (on Via W3 Sul) • Daily 8am–6pm • Free • ⓣ 61 3223 6542, ⓦ santuariodombosco.org.br

Built to honour Brasília's patron saint, **Giovanni (John) Bosco**, a nineteenth-century Italian priest who prophesied the rise of utopian city at this latitude in South America, the **Santuário Dom Bosco** is a nice enough piece of modern architecture on the outside. From within, however, it is completely bathed in a heavenly blue light from the brilliant floor-to-ceiling stained glass that surrounds it on all sides. The glass, square panes in twelve shades of blue to represent the brilliance of Brasília's sky, is arranged in 16m-high panels, twenty on each side of the church, making a total of 2200 square metres of window. Nor does the glasswork end there, as the interior of the church is embellished with a huge chandelier made from 7400 pieces of Ventian Murano crystal.

Asa Sul

The **residential areas** of Brasília are rarely thought of as a destination for visitors, but the older areas are by far the best place for a stroll during the day. The oldest *superquadras* are all in **Asa Sul**; 108 Sul was the first to be completed in the whole city. The adjacent blocks from 107 down to 104 were all built shortly after and make for a great **urban walk** – take a bus or walk up W3 Sul, get off at the 508 block, walk two blocks down, and then start strolling towards the centre.

Jardim Botânico

Setor de Mansões Dom Bosco, Lago Sul • Tues–Sun 9am–5pm • R$5 • Bus #147.3 or #197.3 from platforms A8–9 at the Rodoviária Central; a taxi costs around R$60 from the centre • ⓣ 61 3366 5597, ⓦ www.jardimbotanico.df.gov.br

Brasília's **Jardim Botânico** is a calm and well-organized retreat where you can experience the flora and fauna of the *cerrado* at first hand. There's an information centre, a large display of medicinal plants of the region, a herb garden, and over forty square kilometres of nature reserve with an extensive network of trails. It's good hiking, but make sure you bring a hat and water.

OSCAR NIEMEYER

Oscar Niemeyer (1907–2012) was the greatest architect Latin America has produced. He's best known for his unique contribution to Brasília, but during his long and highly productive life he left his mark on most of Brazil's major cities, especially Rio and Belo Horizonte. Widely regarded as the most influential modernist architect of the twentieth century after Le Corbusier, he also designed important buildings abroad, including the Serpentine Gallery in London and the Le Havre Cultural Centre in France.

Born in Rio in 1907, he was influenced as a student by Le Corbusier's geometric ideas on urban planning and design; his first major commission, the building of the Ministry of Education in Rio in 1937, now known as the Palácio Gustavo Capanema, shows this influence clearly. By the 1940s Niemeyer began to show his independence and originality with a series of buildings in the Belo Horizonte suburb of Pampulha, which gave a recognizably Brazilian twist to Le Corbusier, adding curves, ramps and buttresses to buildings decades ahead of their time. Niemeyer's designs were **controversial**: the São Francisco church in Pampulha (see page 146) was completed in 1943 but not consecrated until 1959, so reluctant was the Catholic Church to endorse such a radical departure. But the germs of Brasília were clearly evident in his work in Pampulha, a decade before the new capital was begun.

After Brasília, Niemeyer became an **international star** and beyond criticism in his own country, which had its advantages: he was the only militant Communist never to be troubled by the military dictatorship. He built a number of other unforgettable buildings, the most spectacular being the Museum of Modern Art in Niterói (see page 112), across the bay from Rio, perched like a modernist flying saucer over the sea.

Parque Nacional de Brasília

SMAN, Zona Industrial,,Asa Norte • Daily 8am–5pm (last entry 4pm) • R$26 • ☎ 61 3233 6897 • Bus #128.1 or #128.3 from platform A at the Rodoviária Central, or a taxi costs around R$45 from the centre

For a taste of the *cerrado* before heading deeper into the *planalto*, head across the Lago Paranoá's striking **JK Bridge** to the **Parque Nacional de Brasília**, the city's very own national park. Located at the far end of Asa Norte, it's the only area of native vegetation large enough around Brasília to support proper wildlife populations. During the week, you will have the place largely to yourself, and while the park itself is enormous, visitors are restricted to its southern corner, where the main attractions are two very large **swimming holes**, Piscina Velha and Piscina Nova, both a short, well-signposted walk from either of the two entrances, and built around a stream, preserving the natural flow of the water. When there is nobody there, this is a lovely spot – especially for a picnic. You may spot capuchin monkeys leaping acrobatically through the trees, but they have become used to scavenging picnic remains so take care not to leave food lying around, and be sure to pack plastic bags away as the monkeys regularly choke on them.

Although the swimming holes get very crowded at weekends, virtually everyone sticks to the water, so if you want space and some solitude, head up the slope to a small fenced trail through a section of gallery forest and continue up the hill until you come up onto open *cerrado* savannah. Here you'll find another much longer trail, a 7km circuit called the **Água Cristal** (crystal water trail), which lives up to its name, taking you through a number of clearwater streams before dumping you back more or less where you started.

ARRIVAL AND DEPARTURE — BRASÍLIA

By plane The airport (☎ 61 3364 9000) is 12km south of the centre, served by bus #0.102 and #102.1 from platform A17 at the Rodoviária Central. There's also a pricier "executive bus" that does a loop from the airport up and down both sides of the Eixo Monumental and round the hotel zones. A taxi from the airport to the hotel sectors is around R$50. Brasília is second only to Rio and São Paulo for number and frequency of flights, although they are exclusively domestic, serving most state capitals.

Destinations Belém (2–6 daily; 1hr 35min); Belo Horizonte (8–12 daily; 1hr 15min); Campo Grande (2–5 daily; 1hr 45min); Manaus (3–5 daily; 2hr 55min); Recife (5–7 daily; 2hr 30min); Rio (14–24 daily; 1hr 45min); Salvador (5–8 daily; 1hr 55min); São Paulo (1–4 hourly 5am–9.30pm; 1hr 45min).

By bus Inter-city buses use the Rodoviária Interstadual at the far end of the Asa Sul (☎ 61 3234 2185). It's most easily reached by *metrô* (Ⓜ Shopping), but is also served by bus #108.8 from platform A4 at the Rodoviária Central, or you can take a cab (around R$45 from the hotel zone).

Destinations Alto Paraíso (3 daily; 4hr); Belém (1 daily; 36hr); Belo Horizonte (6 daily; 11hr); Cristalina (5 daily; 2hr 15min); Cuiabá (5 daily; 20hr); Formosa (roughly hourly; 2hr); Fortaleza (1 daily; 45hr); Goiânia (roughly hourly; 2hr 30min); Pirenópolis (4 daily; 3hr); Recife (2 daily; 36hr); Rio (3 daily; 20hr); Salvador (3 daily; 26hr); São Paulo (12 daily, mostly overnight; 14hr).

GETTING AROUND

By taxi The city has a good taxi service. Flag a taxi down when you want one, or pick one up at the many ranks throughout the city; every *superquadra* has at least one. A cab from the Rodoviária Central to the Congresso Nacional should cost around R$20. Brasília is also covered by Uber.

On foot Brasília is built for cars, and isn't really made for walking. You can see its central sights on foot if you don't mind a bit of a hike, but particularly in the hot season, negotiating the city's wide-open spaces can be quite exhausting. At the very least, slap on some sunscreen and carry water with you.

By bus City bus routes radiate out from the Rodoviária Central, which marks the dead centre of town. It's on three levels, with shops, toilets and snack bars, and computer terminals near the platforms to tell you what bus you need and which platform to find it at, although they are in Portuguese only. Pickpockets work the bus queues, especially during the rush hour, so make sure your valuables are not somewhere vulnerable. Bus fares are mostly R$3.50–5.

By metrô Brasília's *metrô* (🌐 www.metro.df.gov.br) starts at the Rodoviária Central and heads up the Asa Sul to the satellite towns of Taguatinga, Samambaia and Ceilândia, but it doesn't serve the Asa Norte at all. It's fast but not frequent and some stations on it are not yet operational. Tickets are R$5 and the system is open 6am–11.30pm Monday to Saturday, but only 7am–7pm on Sundays.

By car Car rental costs start at R$130 for a day with unlimited mileage and insurance. A warning, though:

Brasília, uniquely among Brazilian cities, is blanketed by speed cameras. If you're caught jumping a light or speeding in a rented car, the fine will be taken off your credit card. Rental firms with offices along the airport road include Avis (61 3364 9905), Hertz (61 3221 4400), Movida (0800 606 8686) and Unidas (61 3365 2955). Avoid paying a hefty surcharge at the airport by heading into town by taxi and renting from there; highly recommended is Via Rent-A-Car (SHS Q6 Cj. A, Bloco F, Loja 50, next to the *Hotel Melia*; 61 3322 3181, viadfrentacar.com.br).

INFORMATION

Tourist information The city's tourist office is in Praça dos Três Poderes (daily 8am–6pm; 61 3214 2764, turismo.df.gov.br), with a desk at the airport, give out a free map with information about all the main sights.

Listings The city's main newspaper, the *Correio Brasiliense*, publishes a daily listings supplement, the *Guia*, with comprehensive information on films, exhibitions, live music and opening hours.

ADDRESSES IN BRASÍLIA

Although initially quite confusing, Brasília is laid out with geometric precision. It is neatly divided into **sectors**: residential (each with its own shopping and other facilities), hotel, embassy, banking and commercial. The residential wings are divided into *superquadras* with numbers like 205 Norte or 706 Sul. "Norte" and "Sul" refer to the two *asas* ("wings") of the city, which spread out from a central backbone called the **Eixo Monumental**, where all the important buildings are located. Running up the middle of each wing is the city's other main axis, the Eixo Rodoviário, universally known as the **Eixão** (the roads parallel to it are called Eixinhos, or "little *eixos*" – the main one is W3). The Eixão meets the Eixo Monumental at the Rodoviária Central (central terminal for city buses), which marks the very centre of town.

The number of each *superquadra* tells you exactly where it is. Heading south along the Eixão, for example, the blocks to its west are numbered 101 Sul, then 102 Sul, 103 Sul and so on, while those directly to its east are numbered 201 Sul, then 202 Sul, 203 Sul and so on. Heading westwards from 103 Sul, the blocks start with an odd number: 303 Sul, then 503 Sul, then 703 Sul. Heading eastward, they start with an even number: 203 Sul, then 403 Sul, then 603 Sul. Our map (see map p.406) shows how this works. This system is exactly mirrored in the northern wing.

Addresses in Brasília are like grid references. They look like mathematical gobbledygook, but there is a perfect logic to them which is easy once you get used to it. For example, the address 504 Norte, Bloco I, Casa 20 is in the northern wing (Asa Norte). From the fact that it is 504 rather than 501, 502 or 503, we know that it is four blocks north of the centre. As it begins with an odd number (504 rather than 604), we know that it is west rather than east of the Eixão, and 504, rather than 104 or 304, tells us that it is three blocks away from the Eixão. "Bloco I" is the actual block within the *superquadra*. "Casa 20" means it is house no. 20 – it might otherwise be "Loja 20" (shop no. 20) or "Lote 20" (lot no. 20). Shops are found in commercial zones between the residential blocks. Closer to the centre there are special zones like the SHN and SHS (Setor Hoteleiro Norte and Sul), where all the hotels are located.

The terminology you are most likely to come across includes:

Asa Norte/Asa Sul General terms for the two "wings" (*asas*) of the city, comprising the avenues Eixo Rodoviário Norte and Eixo Rodoviário Sul, and the roads running off and parallel to them (the latter lettered "W" to the west, and "L" to the east, eg W-3 Norte, L-4 Sul).

CLN/CLS or **SCLN/SCLS** (Setor) Comércio Local Norte/Sul. The shopping areas between the residential *superquadras*.

Eixinho The smaller roads running parallel to the Eixão.

EQN/EQS Entrequadras Norte/Sul (literally "between *quadras*"). Small blocks in the commercial areas between *superquadras*.

SBN/SBS Setor Bancário Norte/Sul. The two banking sectors either side of the Eixo Monumental.

SCN/SCS Setor Comercial Norte/Sul. The two commercial office block areas, set back from the Conjuntos de Diversões shopping centres. Often confused with CLN/CLS.

SDN/SDS Setor de Diversões Norte/Sul. The two shopping centres (*conjuntos*) either side of Eixo Monumental.

SEN/SES Setor de Embaixadas Norte/Sul. The embassy sectors, east of the bank sectors.

SHIN/SHIS Setor de Habitações Individuais Norte/Sul. The two peninsulas that jut into Lago Paranoá.

SHN/SHS Setor Hoteleiro Norte/Sul. The hotel sectors either side of the Eixo Monumental, west of the rodoviária.

SQN/SQS or **SHCN/SHCS** Superquadras Norte/Sul. The individual *superquadras* in the main residential wings, Asa Norte and Asa Sul.

Websites aboutBrasília.com has hotel and restaurant listings and city satellite maps. vemviverBrasília.df.gov.br, put up by the Distrito Federal's government, lists various useful facilities including car rental firms and money changers. souBrasília.com reviews restaurants, bars and other facilities, but only in Portuguese. vejabrasil.abril.com.br/Brasília is Veja magazine's online selection of the city's best restaurants and bars (in Portuguese).

ACCOMMODATION

Most hotels are concentrated in the **central hotel sectors**, with official ("rack rate") prices way above their equivalents elsewhere. Actual budget places are few and far between, and are either *pousadas* – unlicensed, and below the standards of the worst hotels – or else are located out in satellite towns. In fact, an out-of-town location can be an advantage, as it will have shops, cheap *lanchonetes* and so on nearby, and *metrô* connections to the centre are reasonably fast. Even in the centre, hotels may not be anything like as pricey as they appear, since most offer considerable **discounts** – often well over 50 percent – especially at weekends and in December and January, and many never actually charge the official rate at all (the rates we quote here are the official rates for weekday reservations and include breakfast). Private B&B rentals such as those on airbnb.com are often the best value. Staying in the campsites north of town is not recommended: besides being unsafe, it costs much the same as accommodation in Brasília.

CENTRAL HOTEL SECTORS

Airam SHN Q.5, Bloco A 61 2195 4000, www.airamhotel.com.br; map p.408. A good-value mid-range hotel midweek, with fine views from the upper floors, but no weekend discounts. It's seen better days, but it isn't bad value for the price. R$269

Aristus SHN Q.2, Bloco O 61 3328 8675, aristushotel.com.br; map p.408. One of the cheaper options, especially at weekends when they offer discounts of around 50 percent. The rooms are good, with a/c and a fridge, the ones on the bottom floors costing less than those at the top. R$343

Bonaparte SHS Q.2, Bloco J 0800 701 9990 or 61 2104 6600, bonapartehotel.com.br; map p.408. A good and well-equipped top-notch hotel, with a gym and big pool. The rooms are actually suites, with a sitting room and kitchenette, and although the official rate is high, it rarely applies: generally speaking you can expect to pay just over half in the week, and substantially less than that at weekends. R$1123

Brasília Imperial SHS Q.3, Bloco H 61 3425.0000, Brasíliaimperialhotel.com.br; map p.408. Cool white rooms, a gym but no pool, and an official rate that's never actually charged – in reality you'll probably pay less than half, especially at weekends. R$650

Byblos SHN Q.3, Bloco E 61 3326 1570, byblos hotelexpress.webnode.com; map p.408. A low-rise hotel, clean but a bit spartan – the rooms are big but quite plainly furnished, with a choice of fan or (for R$220) a/c. R$180

Casablanca SHN Q.3, Bloco A 61 3328 8586, casablancaBrasília.com.br; map p.408. Close to the Eixo Monumental and within sight of the TV Tower, a small and friendly three-star hotel with cool cream and beige decor in the rooms. Discounts almost always apply, especially if you book online. R$280

Econotel SHS Q.3, Bloco B 61 3204 7337; map p.408. Generally the cheapest of the city-centre hotels, depending on who's offering what discounts. It's housed in a squat grey building that doesn't look too prepossessing, but it's actually fine inside: the rooms are cool and quite spacious, and all have TV, a/c and a fridge. R$239

Kubitschek Plaza SHN Q.2, Bloco E 61 3329 3333, kubitschek.com.br; map p.408. Tall five-star whose lobby and corridors are decorated with photos from the life of Juscelino Kubitschek, with cream, beige and grey decor in the rooms. For good views, it's worth asking for an upper-floor room facing the Esplanada dos Ministerios. Substantial discounts almost always apply (even during the week in high season, you'll pay somewhat less than half the official rate), in which case it can be quite a bargain. R$897

Manhattan Plaza SHN Q.2, Bloco A 61 3319 3060, manhattan.com.br; map p.408. Less extravagant than its stable-mate the *Kubitschek Plaza*, but really just as good: the rooms are bigger, all with balconies, and with the room numbers illuminated on the floor of the corridor. It's particularly good value at weekends, when the price falls substantially. R$682

Metropolitan Flat SHN Q.2, Bloco H 61 3533 8888, atlanticahotels.com.br; map p.408. Not top-of-the-range but fine for a four-star, and the rooms are indeed "flats" with a kitchenette for those who want to self-cater. The pool on the roof is small, but who cares – it's a rooftop pool. Views are good if you get a room high up facing the Esplanada dos Ministerios, and good discounts are usually on offer (half to two-thirds at weekends). R$335

★ **Nacional** SHS Q.1, Bloco A 61 3321 7575, hotelnacional.com.br; map p.408. The oldest of the big hotels, opened in 1960 and a real period piece – certainly the hotel that best embodies Brasília's retro vibe. The cavernous lobby is particularly vintage, and mirrors make the corridors seem endless. Queen Elizabeth and Prince Philip stayed here in 1968. Big discounts usually apply – over 50 percent at weekends. R$826

Naoum SHS Q.3, Bloco J ☎61 3212 4545, @naoumhoteis.com.br; map p.408. A modern little hotel aimed at the business market but very reasonably priced and in a great central location, with rooms set around a snazzy little atrium. R$318

St Paul Plaza SHS Q.2, Bloco H ☎61 2102 8400, @hotelstpaul.com.br; map p.408. Good-value, business-like hotel with smallish but well-equipped rooms, balconies with great views – especially if you ask for a high room on the side facing the Esplanada dos Ministérios – and a rooftop pool. Discounts of over 60 percent make this place particularly good value at weekends. R$544

ELSEWHERE

Hostel 7 708 Norte, Bloco I, Loja 20 ☎61 3033 7707, @hostel7.com.br; map p.406. A clean and modern hostel, with mixed and female-only dorms, in a residential area near some handy shops. Dorms R$55.90, doubles R$140

Hotel Khalifa QS5, Lote 30, Taguatinga ☎61 3356 5011, @hotelkhalifa.com.br; map p.406. Way out of town but only 400m from Taguatinga Sul *metrô* station, this is how far you have to come to find a budget hotel. It isn't luxurious, but it's clean enough, the rooms have TV and a fridge, although not all have outside windows, and – what you won't get in central Brasília – there's a cheap bar-cum-lancheonete next door and a small supermarket round the corner. R$80

Hotel Prime QS5 Rua 800, Lote 60, Taguatinga ☎61 3967 6006, @hotelprime.com.br; map p.406. A good-value budget hotel in Taguatinga (300m from Taguatinga Sul *metrô* station). Rooms are surprisingly large, many with balconies, some with a/c. It's on a busy road, however, so you may prefer a room at the back. R$110

Pousada Verdes Flores 705 Norte, Bloco A, Casa 40 ☎61 3447 8694, ⓔpousadaverdesflores@hotmail.com; map p.406. Not great value considering that discounts often bring the prices of city-centre hotels down to much the same level, but it has the advantage of being in a residential neighbourhood, and the rooms aren't at all bad, with a/c and bathroom, although not all have outside windows. R$149

EATING

A Tribo 105 Norte, Bloco B, Lojas 52–9 ☎61 3039 6430; map p.406. Semi-vegetarian (they serve fish and chicken but no red meat) self-service offering what they call "natural food", and it's certainly good, very flavoursome, with enough proper options for vegetarians too (buffet prices R$65.90 Tues–Fri, R$68.90 Sat & Sun). Tues–Sat 11.30am–3pm, Sun noon–4pm.

★ **Bhumi** 113 Sul, Bloco C, Loja 34 ☎61 3345 0046, @facebook.com/BhumiOrganico; map p.406. This is really an organic wholefood shop with café and restaurant attached, but the restaurant rather overshadows the grocery store. The vegetarian lunchtime self-service is wonderful (R$52.90/kg), although the soups they serve in the evenings are pretty hearty too. Daily: shop 8am–10pm, restaurant noon–3pm (self-service) & 6–10pm (soups).

Boteco do Juca 405 Sul, Bloco A, Loja 4 ☎61 3242 9415 @botecodojuca.com.br; map p.406. A great-value *a vontage* (that is, eat as much as you want) lunchtime buffet (noon–3pm) for just R$15.90; come the evening (from 6.30pm), there's a low-priced pizza/pasta buffet instead (R$21.90 weekdays, R$23.90 weekends). Daily noon–midnight.

★ **Carpe Diem** 104 Sul, Bloco D, Loja 1 ☎61 3325 5301, @carpediem.com.br; map p.406. Deservedly the best-known bar/restaurant in town: great atmosphere, renowned politico hangout and reasonably priced. Famous among locals for the best lunch buffet (R$59.90) in the city, and for the Saturday *feijoada a vontage* (R$59.90). Mon–Sat noon–2am, Sun noon–11pm.

Crêpe au Chocolat 109 Norte, Bloco C, Loja 5 ☎61 3340 7009, @facebook.com/crepeauchocolat; map p.406. Sweet crêpes of course, but savoury ones too – a carpaccio in mustard sauce crêpe for example (R$28.70), with an "Afrodite" (passion fruit and white chocolate crêpe; R$22.80) for afters. Yum. There's a second branch at 210 Sul, Bloco B, Loja 24 (☎61 3443 2050). Daily 11am–midnight.

Daniel Briand 104 Norte, Bloco A, Loja 26 ☎61 3326 1135, @cafedanielbriand.com; map p.406. This upmarket French-owned patisserie and coffee-house is highly recommended (especially for a late R$41–50 breakfast) and serves the best quiche and cakes in town (quiche lorraine R$65/kg). There's nowhere better for a cup of coffee while you read. Tues–Fri 9am–10pm, Sat & Sun 8.30am–10pm.

Don Durica 201 Norte, Bloco A ☎61 3326 1045, @dondurica.com.br; map p.408. Serves an excellent lunch buffet of traditional, quite heavy Brazilian food, such as stewed rabbit and various dishes of lamb, pork and suckling pig (R$71/kg). Mon 11am–7pm, Tues–Sun 11am–11pm.

Feitiço Mineiro 306 Norte, Bloco B, Lojas 45–51 ☎61 3272 3032, @feiticomineiro.com.br; map p.406. Even without the live music in the evenings (see page 416), this spot is worth patronizing for the food alone: a buffet of *comida mineira* (Minas Gerais food; lunch Mon–Thurs R$38.50/kg, Fri–Sun R$44.50/kg, supper R$82/kg), heavy on the pork, bean sauce and sausages, prepared the traditional way on a wood-fired stove. Mon–Sat noon–midnight, Sun noon–5pm.

Fogo de Chão SHS Q.5, Bloco E ☎61 3322 4666, @fogodechao.com.br; map p.408. The best option if you're staying in one of the nearby hotels and don't feel like going far – good, varied and unlimited *churrascaria* of excellent char-grilled meats (R$138), infinitely preferable to any of the hotel restaurants. Daily noon–midnight.

Fratello Uno 103 Sul, Bloco A, Loja 36 ⓣ 61 3225 0031, ⓦ fratellounopizzaria.com.br; map p.406. Best pizza in town: wood-fired kiln and original ingredients. Try the eponymous Fratello (R$68), topped with sweet pickled aubergine. There's another branch at 109 Norte, Bloco D, Loja 19 (ⓣ 61 3447 8989). Mon–Thurs & Sun 6.30pm–midnight, Fri & Sat 6.30pm–12.30am.

Fritz 404 Sul, Bloco D, Loja 35 ⓣ 61 3226 8033; map p.406. This spot is known for its German food, with plenty of schnitzels and wurst (*knackwurst* with fries R$42.90), and best of all, real German beer. Mon–Sat noon–11pm, Sun noon–4pm.

Panelinhas do Brasil Pátio Brasil Shopping mall, Loja 03P ⓣ 61 3037 2322, ⓦ panelinhasdobrasil.com.br; map p.408. A Brasília-based Brazilian-style fast food chain (and that's fast food, not junk food), serving as its name suggests, *panelhinas* (little hot pots) of tasty Brazilian grub, mostly at R$18.30. There's another branch in the SCS at Quadra 3, Bloco A, Loja 10, and more around town. Mon–Sat 10am–10pm, Sun 2–8pm.

Sabor Brasil 302 Sul, Bloco A, Lojas 1–5 ⓣ 61 3226 5942; map p.408. Good value near the city centre: a big varied lunchtime buffet with lots of salads, fish, meat and good vegetarian options for R$54.90/kg Monday to Friday, R$69.90/kg at weekends. Mon–Fri 11.30am–2.30pm & 6pm–1am, Sat 11.30am–3pm & 6pm–1am, Sun 11.30am–3pm.

Tortaria di Lorenza 109 Norte, Bloco C, Loja 19 ⓣ 61 3347 0474; map p.406. Gooey pastries (custard-filled éclair R$8) and espresso coffee (R$5) make this an ideal spot for some Continental-style elevenses or a sugar-and-caffeine pick-me-up. Daily 8am–10pm.

DRINKING AND NIGHTLIFE

Every June, Brasília hosts the **Brasília International Film Festival** (BIFF; ⓦ biffestival.com), showcasing new South American and international movies, mostly at the Cine Cultura in Liberty Mall (SCN Q.2 Bloco D; ⓣ 61 3326.1399, ⓦ cinecultura.com.br).

BARS

Armazém do Ferreira 202 Norte, Bloco A, Loja 57 ⓣ 61 3327 8342, ⓦ armazemdoferreira.com.br; map p.408. Popular with politicians, this place is best towards midnight, when it gets very crowded. The tables outside are very pleasant, huddled under trees. Tues–Thurs 4pm–1am, Fri & Sat noon–1am, Sun noon–4pm.

★ **Bar Beirute** 107 Norte, Bloco D, Lojas 19 & 29 ⓣ 61 3272 0123, ⓦ barbeirute.com.br; map p.406. What you don't get to check out too often in the Arab world is what works so well here: the excellent way meze and cold beer complement each other. A selection of hot meze goes for R$45, a selection of cold ones for R$42. This is a second branch; the original one at 109 Sul, Bloco A, Lojas 2–4 (ⓣ 61 3244 1717) being rather less spacious. Daily 11am–1am.

Bar Brasília 506 Sul, Bloco A, Loja 18 ⓣ 61 3443 4323, ⓦ barBrasília.com.br; map p.406. A remarkably successful re-creation of an old-style Rio bar, with what most Brasília drinking holes completely lack: a bit of atmosphere. If it wasn't for the name, you'd almost think you were somewhere else entirely. Mon–Sat 11.30am–midnight, Sun 11.30am–5pm.

Libanus 206 Sul, Bloco C, Loja 36 ⓣ 61 3244 9795, ⓦ libanus.com.br; map p.406. Perennially crowded spot serving up excellent-value Lebanese food (three meze with Middle Eastern bread R$45.90); swings and slides at the back make it a good place for families in the afternoons, when really it's just a restaurant, but it turns into a bar with a young and humming scene at night. Mon–Thurs & Sun 11am–1am, Fri & Sat 11am–2am.

Tap House Brasília 210 Norte, Bloco B, Lojas 53–75 ⓣ 61 3033 6909, ⓦ ilovebeertaphouse.com.br; map p.406. With thirty craft beers on tap and loads more by the bottle, this is a place to come to if you care about your beer (although the bar snacks aren't bad either). Tues–Sun noon–midnight.

LIVE MUSIC VENUES

Clube do Choro Sector de Divulgação Cultural, Bloco G, Eixo Monumental ⓣ 61 3224 0599, ⓦ clubedochoro.com.br; map p.406. In a concrete Niemeyer Building west of the Torre de Televisão, this is as good a club venue as you'll find anywhere in the country. It's especially lively on Thursdays and Fridays, when it specializes in *choro*, the oldest – and arguably most beautiful – Brazilian musical genre, played here by masters young and old to an appreciative, knowledgeable audience. It turns into a *gafieira* (dance hall) on Saturday night, with its own house band and older, intimidatingly good dancers. Mon–Sat 9–11pm.

Feitiço Mineiro 306 Norte, Bloco B, Lojas 45–51 ⓣ 61 3272 3032, ⓦ feiticomineiro.com.br; map p.406. A *mineiro* restaurant (see page 415) where you can see first-class live traditional Brazilian music while you dine or drink. Tues–Sat, usually from 10pm.

O'Rilley Irish Pub 409 Sul, Bloco C, Loja 36 ⓣ 61 3244 2424, ⓦ orilley.com.br; map p.406. Yes, rilley: an Irish-style pub in Brasília, and you can really get a Guinness here too (or German lager, or British ale). The music is rock, and the bands are live. All in all, a decent craic. Wed–Sat 8pm–2am.

Outero Calaf Edifício João Carlos Saad, SBS Quadra 2, Lojas 4–6 ⓣ61 3322 9581, ⓦcalaf.com.br; map p.408. Busy after work until late, this is the place in Brasília on Mondays for samba-rock, or samba on Tuesdays and Saturdays. Lunch Mon–Fri 11.30am–3pm; music Mon–Thurs & Sun 10pm–3am, Fri & Sat 6.30pm–3am.

Teatro Nacional Sector Cultural Norte ⓣ61 3325 6239, ⓦwww.cultura.df.gov.br/nossa-cultura/teatro-nacional.html; map p.408. All three halls in this amazing building (see page 409) host classical and popular concerts, and this is where visiting megastars, Brazilian and otherwise, are most likely to play.

UK Music Hall 411 Sul, Bloco B, Loja 28 ⓣ61 3257 1993, ⓦukmusichall.com; map p.406. Known locally as the "UK-Brasil Pub", this smallish music venue spins a Brit-rock-leaning music selection with some reggae, blues and soul thrown in for good measure. Thurs–Sat 9pm–2am.

6

SHOPPING

Brasília's city centre is dominated by malls, with no independent shops bar a few at the Rodoviária Central, and the city doesn't really have many outlets for crafts.

Feira de Artesanato da Torre de Televisão Eixo Monumental Oeste, just west of the Torre de Televisão ⓦfeiradatorredf.com.br; map p.408. The market at the base of the TV Tower sells clothes, accessories and handicrafts, from hammocks to meticulously pin-pricked dried leaves and items made from Tocantins's beautiful "golden grass" (*capim dourado*), as well as places to stop for a drink or a snack. Since the federal agency for Indigenous peoples, FUNAI, closed its crafts stores, this is the best place in town to find Indigenous handicrafts. Fri–Sun 7am–6pm.

DIRECTORY

Embassies The Setor de Embaixadas Sul (SES, covering blocks 801 Sul–815 Sul) is southwest of the cathedral along Av das Nações. The Setor de Habitações Individuais Sul (SHIS) is out near the airport in Lago Sul. Argentina, SES Q.803, Lote 12 (ⓣ61 3212 7600); Australia, SES Q.801, conj. K, Lote 7 (ⓣ61 3226 3111); Bolivia, SES, Q.809, Lote 34, (ⓣ61 3366 2238); Canada, SES Q.803, Lote 16 (ⓣ61 3424 5400); Colombia, SES Q.803, Lote 10 (ⓣ61 3214 8900); Ecuador, SHIS Q.10, conj. 8, Casa 1 (ⓣ61 3248 5560); Guyana, SHIS Q.5, conj. 19, Casa 24 (ⓣ61 3248 0874); Ireland SHIS Q12, conj 5, Casa 9 (ⓣ61 3248 8800); New Zealand, SES Q.809, conj 16, Casa 1 (ⓣ61 3248 9900); Paraguay, SES Q.811, Lote 42 (ⓣ61 3242 3968); Peru, SES Q.811, Lote 43 (ⓣ61 3242 9933); South Africa, SES Q.801, Lote 6 (ⓣ61 3312 9500); Suriname, SHIS Q.9, conj. 8, Casa 24 (ⓣ61 3248 3595); UK, SES Q.801, conj. K, Lote 8 (ⓣ61 3329 2300); Uruguay, SES Q.803, Lote 14 (ⓣ61 3322 1200); US, SES Q.801, Lote 3 (ⓣ61 3312 7000); Venezuela, SES Q.803, Lote 13 (ⓣ61 2101 1010).

Money and exchange Confidence Cambio (ⓦconfidence cambio.com.br) at Patio Brasil mall (unit 2, by the north entrance; Mon–Fri 10am–9pm, Sat 10am–6pm), Brasília Shopping mall (unit 204; Mon–Fri 10am–10pm, Sat 10am–6pm) and in the arcade in front of the *Hotel Nacional* (Mon–Fri 8am–5pm); indeed, they may give you better rates in the hotel itself – ask at reception.

Post office The main post office (Mon–Fri 9am–5pm) is a small, white building in the open grassy space behind the *Hotel Nacional*, with branch offices around town including 408 Sul and EQN 405/406.

Goiás state

Beyond the Distríto Federal, the hill-studded, surprisingly green *cerrado* of **Goiás state** extends towards another relatively modern planned city, **Goiânia**, and the historic old towns of **Pirenópolis** and **Goiás Velho**. Although gold mining started in a small way during the seventeenth century, the first genuine settlement didn't appear until 1725. These days agriculture is the main activity: ranching is important, but it is soybean production that is booming, driving the conversion of the dwindling remnants of *cerrado* into enormous farms. The small rural towns are all increasingly prosperous as a result, and the state road system is excellent by Brazilian standards.

In the north of Goiás is the heart of the *planalto*, a jumble of cliffs, spectacular valleys and mountain ranges in and around the national park of **Chapada dos Veadeiros**, excellent for hiking and a thoroughly worthwhile excursion from Brasília, although you'll need a few days to do it justice. Over on the western border with Mato Grosso, the **Parque Nacional das Emas** has less spectacular landscapes but is wilder, a little more inaccessible (although still easily reached from Brasília), and a better place to see wildlife.

Formosa and the Itiquira waterfall

Parque Municipal do Itiquira, highway GO-524 • Daily 9am–5pm; last entry for the salto trail at 1pm • R$10 • ⓣ 61 3981 1234, ⓦ parquemunicipaldoitiquira.blogspot.com.br

If you only have time for one day-trip from Brasília, your best bet is to take the two-hour bus ride to the town of **FORMOSA**, not so much for the place itself, pleasant though it is, as for the stunning waterfall and park of **Salto de Itiquira**. The park is about 40km away, but it's worth the trip: the drive is beautiful, with the spectacular 90m waterfall visible from far away as a white line against the towering cliffs of the Serra Formosa. Surrounding the waterfall is a municipal park, well laid out with a series of swimholes that make it a great place to spend the day. The most spectacular of all is at the very top of the salto trail, where the waterfall comes plunging down. The park is at its best during the week, when it's less crowded.

ARRIVAL AND DEPARTURE — FORMOSA AND THE ITIQUIRA WATERFALL

By bus and taxi Buses from Brasília depart approximately hourly for the 2hr journey to Formosa, but buses from town to the waterfall and park are infrequent; haggling with a local taxi driver at the bus station should get you a return trip for around R$140.

By car The park is well signposted and easy to find if you are in a rented car.

EATING

Dom Fernando GO-116, Km 6 ⓣ 61 99968 2983, ⓦ domfernando.com.br. Although there is a snack bar at the Salto de Itiquira car park, by far the best place to eat is the *Dom Fernando* restaurant, with an excellent buffet of local food, and freshly grilled meats to order (R$44, including dessert). It's located in splendid isolation on the road to the waterfall, but is only open weekends and holidays. Sat, Sun & public holidays 11.30am–4pm.

Cristalina

From Brasília, an easy day-trip involves taking a two-hour bus ride to **CRISTALINA** on the Goiás plateau. Indeed, the journey itself is one of the main reasons to go, as you'll pass through the distinctive rolling hills of the *planalto* along the BR-040 towards Belo Horizonte. Prospectors who came here looking for gold in the early eighteenth century came across a large quantity of rock crystal; the European market opened up over a century later, and today Cristalina is an attractive, rustic town, based around the mining, cutting, polishing and marketing of semi-precious stones. Quartz crystal and Brazilian amethyst can also be bought here at very reasonable prices, mostly from enormous warehouses on the edge of town that pull in passing motorists.

ARRIVAL AND DEPARTURE — CRISTALINA

By bus There are four daily buses from Brasília to Cristalina (2hr).

ACCOMMODATION AND EATING

Churrascaria Rodeio Rua 7 de Setembro 1237 ⓣ 61 3612 1980. An excellent *churrasco* restaurant, particularly worthwhile on Sundays when the R$55 *rodizio* includes roasted game. Daily 11am–4pm & 6–11pm.

Cristal Park Hotel Rua Otaviano de Paiva 900 ⓣ 61 3612 5517, ⓦ cristalparkhotel.com.br. A modern hotel in a slightly odd-looking building, with bright but smallish rooms, reasonable standards of comfort, usual mod cons (a/c, TV, fridge) and handy for Cristalina's main concentration of bars and restaurants. R$160

Hotel Attie Praça José Adamian 34 ⓣ 61 3612 6671. A friendly, good-value little hotel, nothing fancy but centrally located and perfectly adequate. The rooms, though not large, have everything you need in the way of a/c, TV and a fridge. R$120

THE PLANALTO

The topography and ecology of the **planalto** are unique, known in Brazil as the *cerrado*, only partly translated by the word "savannah". Much of it looks startlingly African: red earth, scrubby vegetation, dusty in the dry season, missing only the giraffes and zebras. What makes it spectacular is the topography, which begins to break up the high plains into a series of hill ranges, cliffs, mesas, plateaus and moorland almost as soon as you start heading north from Brasília. This irregular landscape is situated between two enormous watersheds, the Paraná to the south and the Amazon to the north, both of which have the headwaters of major tributaries in the *planalto*. The hills and mountains are riddled with thousands of **rivers and streams**, forming spectacular waterfalls and swimholes.

As ecotourism grows, so too do the **threats**. Development here is far more intense than in the Amazon. The ranchers who spearheaded the early wave of settlement of the *planalto* are still there, but giving way to large-scale commercial agriculture, especially soybeans. This has underlain the development of the two largest cities in Goiás, **Goiânia**, the state capital, and **Anápolis**, and as it becomes one of the world's breadbaskets much of the *planalto* now looks like the US Midwest, with endless geometric fields and irrigation canals stretching to the horizon. Over sixty percent of the native vegetation has been converted to farmland or pasture, compared to fifteen percent of the Amazon, and the unique flora and fauna of the *cerrado* – the giant anteater and armadillo, the maned wolf, the glorious wildflowers that speckle the area with colour in the rainy season – are all increasingly endangered. If things continue at the present rate, within a generation the only islands of true *cerrado* left will be the national parks.

Goiânia

GOIÂNIA was founded in 1933 (giving it a trove of **Art Deco architecture**), and became the state capital four years later. With over a million inhabitants, and both cheaper and more alive than Brasília, with good transport connections, Goiânia earns its living as a market centre for the surrounding agricultural region, which specializes in beef and soybeans.

One of the first things visitors note when they arrive in Goiânia is the size of the place. The main node of the city's concentric city plan is the **Centro Cívico**, at the head of Avenida Goiás, whose broad and leafy pavement extends all the way down its middle. The two most obvious tourist sights – the **Centro Cultural Oscar Niemeyer** and the **Museu Memorial do Cerrado** – are both some way out from the city centre.

Bosque dos Buritis

Daily 7am–8pm • Museum Rua 1, no. 605, Setor Oeste • Tues–Fri 9am–noon & 1–5pm, Sat & Sun 10am–4pm • Free • T 62 3524 1196

Just two blocks west of the Centro Cívico, the woods of the **Bosque dos Buritis** spread over 125,000 square metres and contain a huge water-jet fountain as well as the free but small and not very exciting **Museu de Arte de Goiânia (MAG)**, which displays paintings of the city and stone sculptures.

Museu Zoroastro Artiaga

Praça Dr Pedro Ludovico 17, Setor Central • Tues–Fri 9am–5pm, Sat & Sun 9am–3pm • Free • T 62 3201 4676

Just next to the Centro Cívico, the **Museu Zoroastro Artiaga** exhibits mainly artefacts, crafts and art from the region, but also houses roaming exhibitions, sometimes of ethnographic interest.

Praça Universitária

Museu Antropológico: Av Universitária 1166, Setor Leste Universal • Tues–Fri 9am–5pm • Free • T 62 3209 6010, W museu.ufg.br
Buses including #019, #027, #164 or #257 from Centro Cívico

A fifteen-minute walk or short bus ride from the Centro Cívico, the **Praça Universitária** is a tree-shaded open space among the faculties of the Universidade Federal de Goiás. The Praça's paved areas are much favoured by the city's skateboarders, while the grassy areas double as an **open-air sculpture gallery** featuring interesting modern works such as Julio Valente's *Venus 2000* and Leía Leal's *Gestante*.

Among the faculty buildings on the southern side of Praça Universitária, the University's **Museu Antropológico** is home to a surprisingly wide range of traditional indigenous handicrafts and hosts regular temporary exhibitions too.

Jardim Zoológico

Parque Lago das Rosas, Av Anhanguera, Setor Oeste • Tues–Sun 8.30am–5pm • R$5 • ☎ 62 3524 2390

One of the town's main outdoor features, the **Jardim Zoológico**, located some nine long blocks west of Avenida Goiás along Avenida Anhanguera, is a pleasant and well-managed public park. At its northern end around the muddy Lago das Rosas, the park is home to a number of semi-tame monkeys, while the southern corner houses a large and well-stocked **zoo**, which is a must for anyone interested in wildlife. You'll see *emas* (rheas), *tuiuiús* (red-throated storks) and *jacarés* (alligators) closer here than you will in the wild.

Museu de Ornitológia

Av Pará 395, Setor Campinas • No fixed hours: call ahead to arrange a visit • R$3 • ☎ 62 3233 5773

Easily the most interesting museum in town, even for non-birdwatchers, is the **Museu de Ornitológia**, out in the Campinas sector, which displays around six thousand stuffed

GOIÂNIA'S ART DECO HERITAGE

Founded in 1933, Goiânia still boasts a fair few buildings in the **Art Deco** style of that era. Top of the list is the **former train station**, located at the northern end of Avenida Goiás. At the avenue's opposite end, a 1942 **clocktower** is one of several tasty Art Deco constructions that embellish the Centro Civico, including the **Museu Zoroastro Artiaga** (see page 419), and the green 1937 **Palácio das Esmeraldas**, which is the state governor's residence. Arguably the most impressive Art Deco building in town is the **Teatro Goiânia** on Avenida Anhanguera, but keep your eyes peeled, and you'll see Art Deco styling on the city's older buildings all over the place.

birds, mostly with an eye to distinguishing different species for the benefit of those studying them in the wild. The museum also features mammals and reptiles.

Centro Cultural Oscar Niemeyer

Av Dep. Jamel Cecílio, Quadra Gleba, lote 1, no. 4490, Setor Fazenda Gameleira (4km southeast of the centre; bus #193 from the Centro Civico will take you to the Flamboyant shopping mall, about 500m from the site) • Museu de Arte Contemporânea: Tues–Fri 9am–5pm, Sat, Sun & public holidays 1am–5pm • Free • T 62 3201 4932, W facebook.com/mac.gomuseu

Brazil's great modern architect, Oscar Niemeyer, didn't design the **Centro Cultural Oscar Niemeyer** which bears his name, but he certainly inspired it. It's a plaza of four structures, designed to honour several Brazilian architects, artists and intellectuals. There's a large library, a red, triangular monument to human rights, and a very Niemeyeresque UFO-shaped music hall, but of most interest to visitors is the cylindrical **Museu de Arte Contemporânea (MAC)**, which houses a small collection of Brazilian and international painting, including works by Goiás's own native sons, D.J. Oliveira and Cléber Gouvêa.

Museu Memorial do Cerrado

Av Enger, Jardim Mariliza • Tues–Sun 8am–noon & 1–5pm • R$12 • T 62 3946 1723 • Bus #002 from Centro Cívico, or around R$40 by cab

The **Museu Memorial do Cerrado** is a large and well laid-out museum, model village and eco-centre developed on the site of an old estate some 10km southeast of the city centre, with displays on geology, indigenous cultures and the wildlife and flora of the *cerrado*. There are also botanical gardens, a plant nursery with both common and endangered *cerrado* plant species and a fascinating model of a nineteenth-century *cerrado* village, including everything from the village shop and church to the bordello.

ARRIVAL AND TOURS — GOIÂNIA

By plane Santa Genoveva airport (T 62 3265 1500) is 8km northeast of the centre, served by bus #225, #262 and #280.
Destinations Belo Horizonte (1–3 daily; 1hr 15min); Brasília (2–5 daily; 40min); Rio (1–3 daily; 1hr 45min); São Paulo (roughly hourly; 1hr 45min).

By bus The rodoviária (T 62 3240 0000) is 2km north of the centre, or around 15min on foot from Setor Central along Avenida Goiás. A taxi to the centre will cost around R$25. Leaving by the south entrance, you'll find motorbike taxis, and also shared taxis to Brasília, which leave when full and are slightly faster than buses.
Destinations Alto Paraíso (2 daily; 6hr); Brasília (roughly hourly; 2hr 30min); Caldas Novas (4 daily; 3hr); Goiás Velho (10 daily; 3hr); Palmas (3 daily; 14hr); Rio (1 daily, 22hr); São Paulo (8 daily; 15hr).

By car There are several places to rent a car in town: Achei, Av T-6 no. 338, Setor Bueno (T 62 3215 8060); Localiza, Av T-23 no. 955, Setor Bueno (T 62 2765 6450); and Unidas, Praça Capitão Frazão, Santa Genoveva (T 62 3207 1757).

ACCOMMODATION

Araguaia Av Araguaia 664, Centro T 62 3212 9800, W araguaiahotel.com.br; map p.420. Overlooking the little Praça Antônio Lisita, this hotel has small rooms, not all of which have outside windows, but it's good value none the less, and very centrally located. **R$140**

Augustus (Plaza Inn) Av Araguaia 702, Centro T 62 3216 6600, W plazainn.com.br; map p.420. Located on the Praça Antônio Lisita, this is an efficient business hotel with good rooms, a pool and sauna. The staff are attentive, if a little formal, and they do a good breakfast. **R$206**

6

Castro's Park Av República do Líbano 1520, Setor Oeste 62 3096 2000, castrospark.com.br; map p.420. Luxurious hotel with immaculate service, as well as swimming pools and a superb restaurant. Outside of holiday times it's a good place to try for discounts, which can be as much as two-thirds off the official rate. R$705

Itajubá Rua 4 no. 93, Centro 62 3212 4440, hotel itajuba.com.br; map p.420. Unassuming little family hotel, friendly and well located, with plain but clean rooms and low prices. R$90

Joman Av Goiás 1710, Centro 62 3212 0608, hotel joman@hotmail.com; map p.420. Between the centre and the bus station, this is a simple but good-value hotel. The rooms, set rooms around a lawn, are plain and functional with metal doors, but they're clean and comfortable, and they've all got a/c. R$120

Oft Place Av Anhanguera 4999, Centro 62 3224 9666, oftplacehotel.com.br; map p.420. Sparkly pictures of the Brooklyn Bridge by a local artist welcome you into the lobby of this refurbished hotel with large, airy rooms, and discounts if you book and pay in advance. $139

Papillon Av República do Líbano 1825, Setor Oeste 62 3508 1500, papillonhotel.com.br; map p.420. A luxury modern hotel with rooftop pool, sauna and bar, as well as exceptionally comfortable rooms and great breakfasts, and usually discounts. R$478

EATING

In Goiânia and Goiás Velho, locals are justly proud of their cooking. Delicacies range from pasties (*empadões*) to roast pork with fried banana (*leitão assada com banana frita*) and rice with *pequí* fruit (which needs to be eaten with great care if you don't want a mouthful of hard-to-remove spines – whatever you do, don't bite into the pip).

Árabe Av 83 no. 205, Setor Sul 62 3218 6296, restaurantearabe.com.br; map p.420. Goiânia has a large population of Lebanese descent and this is the best Arabic food in town, with a bakery and takeaways too. Roast lamb with three side dishes will set you back R$49.90. Mon–Sat 8am–11pm, Sun 8am–6pm.

Cerrado Alimentos Orgânicos Rua 10 no. 342 (at Rua 93), Setor Sul 62 3213 4388; map p.420. This is really an organic food store, and you can certainly pop in to buy fruit and veg, or just a juice, but they run an organic restaurant too. A lunchtime buffet of organic foods (not necessarily vegetarian, although most options are) will set you back R$42.90 on weekdays, or just two reais more on Saturdays. Mon–Sat 11.30am–2pm.

★ **Chão Nativo I** Av República do Líbano 1809, Setor Oeste 62 3223 5396, chaonativo1.com.br; map p.420. The city's best self-service lunch spread, with salads, vegetable dishes, meats and stews, many of which are traditional *goiâno* cooking made on a wood-burning stove. The best deal is all-you-can-eat (including coffee and afters) for R$44.20 weekdays, R$48.90 weekends (slightly lower if paying cash). Mon–Sat 11am–3pm, Sun 11am–4pm.

Kabanas Av T-3 no. 2693, Setor Bueno 62 3093 3393, kabanas.com.br; map p.420. 2km southwest of the centre, in the heart of Setor Bueno's upmarket drinking zone, this is a very pleasant combined bar-restaurant next to a park, excellent for either eating or drinking, with dishes such as seafood risotto for R$85. Very good *petiscos* (bar snacks – the Brazilian equivalent of tapas). Tues–Fri 5pm–midnight, Sat & Sun 10am–midnight.

Piquiras Bougainville shopping mall (Rua 9 no. 1855), Setor Marista 62 3945 9900, piquiras.com; map p.420. One of the city's better all-round restaurants, with reliably good-quality food (steak in mushroom sauce R$59), and a posh grocery store attached. You can find it inside the mall, or via its own entrance at the corner of Rua 38 with Rua 32. Mon–Sat 11am–11pm, Sun 11am–8pm.

Restaurante Popular Dona Lourdes Rua 72 no. 524 62 3224 6450; map p.420. Home-style Brazilian food, lots of it, and cheap (R$25 unlimited buffet). There are several meat options, vegetables, salads, rice and beans; you serve yourself straight out of the pot, find a place at one of the tables, and tuck in. Unfortunately, it's open lunchtime only. Mon–Sat 11am–2.30pm.

DRINKING AND NIGHTLIFE

Praça Tamandaré is a good place to start the evening, with a number of bars and cafés and, later on, nightclubs on or near the square. Another important area for **bars** is Setor Bueno, 2km southwest of the centre, in the vicinity of the *Kabanas* restaurant (see above), where you'll find a number of upmarket drinking establishments.

Celsin & Cia Rua 22 no. 475 (at Rua 15), Setor Oeste 62 3215 3043, celsinecia.com.br; map p.420. A buzzing bar-restaurant, where people stop by for supper, weekend lunch, or just a few beers or caipirinhas. The best seats are outside under the awning. Mon–Fri 5pm–2am, Sat 11am–2am, Sun 11am–5pm.

Kombinado Rua 10 no. 304 (at Rua 93), Setor Sul 62 98201 6693; map p.420. A large local bar with a pool table where they play rock and MFB (Brazilian pop), sometimes with live music at weekends. Tues–Sun 7pm–3am.

WATERFALL, PARQUE NACIONAL CHAPADA DOS VEADEIROS

GOIÂNIA'S MARKETS

The **Feira Hippie** is a fascinating street market open every Sunday from early in the morning until mid-afternoon, dominating the stretch of Avenida Goiás from Rua 4 up to the Praça do Trabalhador. Originally a market for local crafts people, it has evolved to incorporate a wide range of more general alternative handicrafts, plus a global variety of socks, underwear, watches, electrical goods and all kinds of imported plastics. The same locale hosts a clothes market on Saturdays. If you're around on a Saturday between 5 and 10pm, head for the **Feira da Lua**, which sells mainly *artesanato* in the tree-studded and lively Praça Tamandaré, a few blocks west of the Centro Cívico. The smaller **Feira do Sol**, on the Praça do Sol in the Setor Oeste, has around two hundred stalls selling crafts, antiques, foods, pets and fine arts every Sunday between 4 and 9pm. During the week, the **Mercado Aberto** on Avenida Paranaiba flanking Avenida Goiás sells cheap clothes, its western side transforming itself in the evenings into a hangout for local bikers.

Yes Bar Rua 2 no. 159 (at Rua 8), Centro ⓣ 62 3645 2612; map p.420. A handy spot in the centre for a beer, which turns into a rather campy (but fun) dancehall on Fridays and Saturdays, with eclectic sounds and nice, cold beer, but it doesn't really get going until late. Mon–Thurs 5.30pm–1am, Fri & Sat 5.30pm–5am.

Pirenópolis

PIRENÓPOLIS, a picturesque market town of about 16,000 people, straddles the Rio das Almas, 112km north of Goiânia in the scrubby mountains of the Serra dos Pireneus. Founded by *bandeirantes* in 1727 as a gold-mining settlement, it's a popular weekend retreat for residents of Brasília and often very busy during main Brazilian holidays, but well supplied with accommodation to suit all budgets.

There's a vibrant **alternative scene** here, reflected in a handful of interesting bars, organic cafés and New Age stores, but Pirenópolis is most famous in Brazil for its **silverwork**, mostly inset with semiprecious stones. The craft was introduced here by hippies in the 1980s, and today the jewellery of over two hundred artisans, much of it Asian-influenced, is sold in dozens of shops around town.

Igreja Matriz de Nossa Senhora do Rosário and around

Praça de Matriz • Wed–Sun 9am–noon & 2–5pm • Free

Right in the centre of town, the **Igreja Matriz de Nossa Senhora do Rosário** was previously an attractive colonial edifice and the oldest church in Goiás. Tragically, it was almost completely destroyed by fire in 2002, and although it has been rebuilt, only parts of the walls are actually original.

The buildings surrounding the church are also very pretty. Across the street to its east, the 1899 **Teatro de Pirenópolis** often has shows that cater to tourists, while the former cinema, **Cine Pireneus** two doors down on Rua Direita, no longer shows films but still has its 1936 Art Deco facade.

Igreja Nosso Senhor do Bonfim

Rua Bonfim da Serra dos Pireneus • Fri–Sun 1–6pm • R$2

The town centre's only remaining colonial church is east along the very attractive Rua Bonfim da Serra dos Pireneus. **Igreja Nosso Senhor do Bonfim**, built in the 1750s, is famous for its image of Nosso Senhor do Bonfim, the very impressive white statue of Christ that was originally carried here by two hundred slaves.

Museu das Cavalhadas

Rua Direita 39 • Fri–Sun 10am–5pm • R$2

Between the remains of Rosário and the rodoviária, you'll find the small **Museu das Cavalhadas**, located in a family's front room. The museum contains displays of incredible carnival costumes from the **Festo do Divino Espírito Santo**, a lively and largely horse-mounted religious festival that takes place in the town exactly six weeks after Easter Sunday. The festival combines dances with mock battles from the Crusades, and the costumes include ornate metal armour, demonic masks and animal heads.

Museu de Arte Sacra

Rua do Caremo • Wed–Sat 2–6pm, Sun 10am–5pm • R$2

Swimming and sunbathing spots line the river by the **Ponte de Madeira** – the old wooden bridge linking the town centre with the Carmo *bairro* on the north bank. Just over the bridge, on the north side of the river, the **Museu de Arte Sacra** is housed in the **Igreja de Nossa Senhora do Carmo**, a church built by slave labour in the 1750s. Pride of place among the religious images displayed within goes to an eighteenth-century statue of the town's patroness, the eponymous Nossa Senhora do Carmo, by local Baroque sculptor José Joaquim Veiga Valle.

Santuário Vagafogo

Daily 9am–4pm • R$20 • Take a motorbike taxi from next to the rodoviária or from the junction of Avenida Sizenando Jayme with Rua Joaquim Alves in the centre of town (motorbike taxis 20min; around R$40 round trip; ☎ 62 3331 1948)

One very worthwhile excursion into the surrounding countryside is to the **Santuário Vagafogo**, a beautifully preserved patch of gallery forest with streams, swimholes, trails with walkways over the muddy patches and stairs up the steep sections, and a hammock-strung gazebo to relax in after your walk. Look hard and you can see the remains of colonial gold-mining beneath the undergrowth – part of the main trail is an eighteenth-century sluice bed. At weekends, you can eat first in the small restaurant at the reserve entrance (see page 426) and walk it off down the trails. Access is a problem, since it is not well signposted and lies some 6km out of town; your best bet is to take a motorbike taxi. It is a bumpy but enjoyable ride down a dirt track, with pleasant scenery. Once there, hiking back is easy, or arrange to be picked up again.

ARRIVAL AND INFORMATION — PIRENÓPOLIS

By bus The rodoviária (☎ 62 3331 1080) is on the eastern edge of town on Av Neco Mendonça, a 10min walk from the centre. There are four daily buses to Brasília (3hr) but only one direct to Goiânia (2hr), although there are five to Anápolis (1hr 10min), where there are frequent onward connections; coming the other way, check the times of buses from Anápolis to Pirenópolis in advance (currently 8am, 11am, 2pm, 3.30pm & 6.15pm), and get a bus from Goiânia a good 90min earlier to make the connection.

Tourist information Information is available from the Centro de Atendimento ao Turista, Rua Bonfim da Serra dos Pireneus (Mon–Sat 9am–6pm, Sun 9am–4pm; ☎ 62 3331 2633). Beware of tour operators falsely claiming to be tourist information offices.

ACCOMMODATION

A popular local resort, Pirenópolis has dozens of **hotels** and **pousadas** to choose from, many of them merely private homes with a few rooms for rent. The quality is generally well above average, and discounts are usually available out of season. The prices we quote here are for midweek occupancy: many hotels charge more at weekends.

Hostel and Camping Pirenopolis Rua Matutina 4 ☎ 62 98153 2571, ⓦ jardimsecretohostel.com.br. This small hostel, with an even smaller camping area, is so laidback it's almost asleep, and it doesn't serve breakfast, although there's a kitchen to make your own, and a coffee bar is under construction. Wi-fi is stronger in some areas than in others. Dorms R$50; camping/person R$30.

Hotel Rex Praça Emmanoel Lopes 15 ☎ 62 3331 1121. Located on a small square behind the church, this family-operated hotel in former slaves' quarters has simple rooms, some rather small, along the edge of a traditional courtyard, and usually offers the best deals in town for a single room (R$100). R$170

Pousada Cavalhadas Praça da Matriz ☎ 62 3331 1261, ⓦ pousadacavalhadas.com.br. This is the most central hotel in town, just opposite the Igreja Nossa Senhora do Rosário. The rooms are small, but have a homely, rustic feel. R$180

Pousada Lara Rua Direita 11 ☎ 62 3331 1294, ⓦ pousadalara.com.br. Clean and neat: the rooms (all with a/c and a fridge) are around a yard at the back, with a small pool. R$200

Pousada dos Pireneus ⓣ62 3331 7300, reservations ⓣ61 2101 7818, ⓦpousadadospireneus.com.br. This is the main upmarket place in town, with its own rambling gardens, a pool, a small water-park with slides that kids will love, and horse-riding facilities – including amusing 20min jaunts by carriage through town for just R$20 per person. Weekend prices are considerably higher at R$620. R$445

Pousada Walkeriana Rua do Rosário 37 (on Praça do Rosário) ⓣ62 3331 1260, ⓦpousadawalkeriana.com.br. One of the grander places in town, with rooms set around a large and pleasant courtyard with a swimming pool. Prices are nearly double at weekends at R$460. R$R$240

★ **Pouso do Sô Vigário** Rua Nova 25 ⓣ62 3331 1206, ⓦfacebook.com/pousodosovigario. One of the town's nicest hotels, in a former priest's residence, it has been embellished with a/c, a pool and a sauna, but still retains a real old-fashioned charm. At weekends (Fri & Sat), you have to take a R$486 two-night package. R$225

EATING

Aravinda Bar and Restaurant Rua do Rosário 25 ⓣ62 3331 2409, ⓦfacebook.com/aravinda.pirenopolis. A solid Brazilian restaurant, specializing in fish, in a street of good eating places, where you can dine inside, or out on the pavement. Try the fish *moqueca* (R$62), or *peixa na telha* (fish baked in an earthenware dish; R$45). Daily 11am–1am.

As Flôr Av Sizenando Jaime 16 ⓣ62 3331 1276. Just R$26 here buys you a whole spread of salads, meats, rice, beans and fried manioc that you'll never get through (but if you do, they'll bring you more), and they throw in coffee and dessert too. A real bargain. Tues–Sat 11am–3pm.

Dill Rua do Rosário 17 ⓣ62 3331 2046. In the most bustling part of town come evening time, with tables spread out in the street, this popular cachaçaria has hundreds of different brands of cachaça on offer, some to be sipped straight, others to make caipirinhas, and for those who don't like cachaça there's also a big selection of beers and other drinks on the menu. Daily 10.30am–1am.

Santuario Vagafogo Rua do Carmo, Km 6 ⓣ62 3335 8515. At weekends and on holidays, the small restaurant at the reserve entrance serves quite superb, very reasonably priced brunches (R$68), using home-grown ingredients: the jams and pickles using *cerrado* fruits are deliciously unusual. Sat, Sun & public holidays 11am–2pm.

Tempero do Rosário Praça de Matriz 27 ⓣ62 3331 2706. In the main square, just across the street from the church, this popular lunchtime buffet restaurant offers a big choice of salads, meats and pasta dishes (mostly lasagnes) for just R$23.90 per person. Mon–Fri 11am–4pm, Sat & Sun 11am–5pm.

Vitória Rua Direita 13 ⓣ62 3331 2772. A great-value unlimited lunchtime buffet for just R$15. The price doesn't include afters, but for R$2 you can round off your meal with an excellent home-made passion-fruit mousse. Mon & Wed–Fri 11am–3pm, Sat & Sun 11am–4pm.

Goiás Velho

Renowned for its religious architecture and historic feel, **GOIÁS VELHO** – originally known as Vila Boa, and now often just called Goiás – is the state's main settlement west of Goiânia. Strung along and up a steep valley cut by the Rio Vermelho, it is one of the most beautiful colonial towns in Brazil. At its heart is the pretty little **Praça Dr Tasso de Camargo**, commonly known as the Praça do Coreto after its rather charming 1923 Art Nouveau bandstand (*coreto*), which now houses an ice-cream shop. The calm elegance of its cobbled streets and squares, and its lack of commercialism, largely thanks to a remote location well to the north of the country's other eighteenth-century mining zones, has made it the best-preserved colonial town in the country. It is simply

TOURS FROM PIRENÓPOLIS

A number of guides and agencies offer ecological **tours** of the surrounding region, taking in sites within the **Parque Estadual da Serra dos Pirineus** and the **Reserva Ecológica Vargem Grande**. The region boasts many great trails and a host of impressive waterfalls, including the Abade, Inferno and Corumbá.

Morro Alto Turismo Rua das Margaridas Rua Direita 27, ⓣ62 3331 3348, ⓦmorroalto.tur.br. Runs excursions to the Parque da Serra dos Pirineus and various local waterfalls.

Savanah Ecotrilhas ⓣ62 9624 1207, ⓦsavanah.tur.br. Runs tours to several destinations, including the Parque da Serra dos Pirineus and the Cachoeiras dos Dragões (where there are eight waterfalls).

gorgeous, fully deserving its status as a UNESCO World Heritage Site. Unfortunately, however, all of the town's **churches** have had their interiors ruined by a combination of fires and misguided "improvements" – the worst example being the slave church of Rosário dos Pretos just north of the river, which was levelled on its bicentenary in 1934 and replaced by an incongruous Gothic structure that rather mars the town.

Founded in 1726 as a gold-mining settlement by the *bandeirantes*, Goiás Velho was the state capital until 1937. Nowhere else in Brazil is there a stronger sense of the colonial past, palpable in the cobbled streets and the many well-preserved eighteenth- and nineteenth-century buildings. Its timeless atmosphere is enhanced every year during the colourful, torchlit Easter **Fogaréu** procession, and apart from the town itself, the surrounding countryside offers good **hiking** amid the trails, waterfalls and swimholes characteristic of the *cerrado*.

Palácio Conde dos Arcos

Praça Dr Tasso de Camargo • Tues–Sat 8am–5pm, Sun 8am–1pm • R$4 • ☎ 62 3371 0266

The **Palácio Conde dos Arcos**, built in 1755, was the old governor's palace and has the usual clunky period furniture. Its best feature is an attractive Portuguese-style garden. The most interesting exhibits inside the building are actually relatively modern, such as a nineteenth-century photo of the great-grandfather of two-term Brazilian president Fernando Henrique Cardoso, proudly pointed out by the museum guide who accompanies you, and the original application documents for their UNESCO World Heritage listing, reverently displayed in a velvet case.

Museu de Arte Sacra da Boa Morte

Entrance in side of Igreja da Boa Morte on Rua Luiz do Couto, just off Praça Dr Tasso de Camargo • Tues–Sat 9am–5pm, Sun 9am–1pm (but often closed, especially at lunchtime, in which case ask at the Palácio Conde dos Arcos across the street) • R$4 • ☎ 62 3371 1087

The town's **Museu de Arte Sacra da Boa Morte**, in the 1779 Igreja da Boa Morte, contains a small collection of religious paintings and statues mainly dating from the eighteenth and nineteenth centuries. Unfortunately the interior of the church it's housed in is of no interest, having been "improved" to death by misguided modernizers.

Museu das Bandeiras

Praça Brasil Ramos Caiado • Tues–Sat 9am–noon & 1–6pm, Sun 9am–1pm • Free • ☎ 62 3372 1133

The **Museu das Bandeiras**, situated up the hill on the Praça Brasil Ramos Caiado, recounts the story of the gold rush through artefacts including slave shackles and chains. A unique feature is the building itself, which has a combined governor's office and council chamber upstairs and jail downstairs – an arrangement typical of early eighteenth-century Brazilian towns. The room to the right of the entrance desk was once part of the jail and has changed very little since it was built.

Casa de Cora Coralina

Rua Dom Cândido 22 • Tues–Sat 9am–4.45pm, Sun 9am–1pm • R$8 • ☎ 62 3371 1990

The **Casa de Cora Coralina** was the home of a local poet who never left the town in all of her 96 years of life but used it as raw material and became nationally famous. Located on the corner of a colonial street overlooking the Rio Vermelho, the museum is a hotchpotch of old furniture, photos and manuscripts, giving a glimpse into small-town life.

ARRIVAL AND INFORMATION — GOIÁS VELHO

By bus The rodoviária (☎ 62 3371 1510) is 1km south of town, served by ten daily buses to Goiânia (3hr), where you'll generally need to change for points beyond.

By motorbike taxi The best way to get around, other than your own two feet, is with the local motorbike taxis; you'll see a stand of them in most squares, and there is one opposite the rodoviária; agree the price before you go.

Tourist information The Centro de Atendimento ao Turista is in the centre of town at Rua Moretti Foggia 20 (Mon–Fri 8am–6pm, Sat 8am–12.30pm & 2–6pm, Sun 9am–noon; ☎ 62 3371 7713).

6

EXPLORING THE COUNTRYSIDE AROUND GOIÁS VELHO

If you need to cool off in the afternoon after walking the old city streets, take a trip out to the natural swimming pool out by the **Cachoeira Grande waterfalls** on the Rio Vermelho, just 7km east of town – the best (and cheapest) way to get there is on the back of one of the local motorbike taxis. The pool is pleasant when quiet, but it can get crowded at weekends. The most beautiful sight in the area is the **Cachoeira das Andorinhas** (Swallow Waterfall), 8km out of town, which makes for a wonderful day-trip. On the only road out of town, cross the Rio Vermelho, passing by the pretty church of **Igreja de Santa Bárbara**, perched on a small hill overlooking the municipal cemetery. Take the dirt road to the left of the church (signposted *Hotel Fazenda Manduzanzan*). The waterfall is another kilometre from here – when in doubt, always bear left. The last few hundred metres rise steeply through a forested gorge before ending at a glorious, tree-choked swimhole with a waterfall and – true to its name – swallows darting around. A highlight is a natural rock chamber that channels part of the waterfall into a cavern.

Remember Goiás is hot year-round – and baking hot in the dry season – so the usual precautions of carrying water, sunscreen and a hat apply. To save yourself some effort, consider having a motorbike taxi drop you off at the trail entrance (around R$20), thereby halving the distance you need to walk, or arrange a time for a motorbike taxi to pick you up if you don't feel like walking at all. Also consider heading out early for the trek, stopping afterwards at the *Hotel Fazenda Manduzanzan* for lunch.

ACCOMMODATION

Araguaia Av Dr Deusdeth Ferreira de Moura 8 ⓣ62 3371 1462, ⓦbit.ly/HotelAraguaia. A friendly, inexpensive, family-run hotel located southeast of town on the way up to the university. Perks include a fridge in the room and free chilled drinking water at the reception. The best rooms are at the back, with views over the wooded hillside behind; some come with a/c (R$120). R$90

★ **Casa da Ponte** Rua Moretti Foggia ⓣ62 3371 4467, ⓔcasadapontehotel_@hotmail.com. Slap-bang in the middle of town, right by the wooden bridge (hence the name: "House of the Bridge") linking the two banks of the river, this place offers a bit of old-fashioned charm and, if you get in there quick when making your reservation, views over the river too. Excellent value, although you pay a bit more for a/c (R$300). R$220

Pousada do Ipê Rua Luiz Guedes de Amorim 22 ⓣ62 3371 2065, ⓦpousadadoipe.com. An upmarket *pousada* in a lovely old house north of the river, with essentials such as a/c and a pool, a garden full of fruit trees (cashew, mango, guava, even jackfruit), and a choice of good rooms in the main building or larger chalets (R$245) out back by the river. R$215

Serrano Av Dr Deusdeth Ferreira de Moura (almost at the top, 1km southeast of town) ⓣ62 3371 1825, ⓔhotel_serrano@hotmail.com. The pictures in the lobby are a bit kitsch, but the rooms are pretty spacious and a very good deal for the price, especially for single occupancy, which is half the price of a double. R$100

Vila Boa Morro Chapéu do Padre (1km southeast of town, off Av Dr Deusdeth Ferreira de Moura) ⓣ62 3371 1000, ⓦhotelvilaboa.com.br. A good-value upmarket choice, on a wooded hillside with lots of wildlife-spotting opportunities, not to mention cosy rooms, a good restaurant and a large pool. R$267

EATING

Casa Do Doce Cristalizado Rua Maximiliano Mendes 1 ⓣ62 9651 5759. Crystallized fruit is the local sweet speciality around here, and this is the place to get it, at R$30/kg for any mix you like. There's fig, orange, strawberry, orange peel and ginger or, for the more adventurous, sweet potato. Just don't tell your dentist. Daily 9am–5pm.

Flor do Ipê Rua Boa Vista 32 ⓣ62 3372 1133. Situated across the square from *Pousada Ipê*, there's beautiful outdoor dining area here, where they serve a typical regional buffet (R$35) that includes salads, pork, stewed chicken, okra and regional vegetables like *pequí* – of which, beware (see page 422). Tues–Sun noon–3pm.

Restaurante Braseiro Praça Brasil Ramos Caiado ⓣ62 3371 2892. Real local food cooked on a proper wood stove, with a different selection of dishes daily, and for R$22 you can eat as much as you want. Daily 11am–2pm.

Restaurante Dalí Sabor e Arte Rua 13 de Maio 26 ⓣ62 3372 1640. Not as arty as its name suggests, and pretty traditional food-wise, despite the modern decor, this is a great place to check out the local speciality, *empadão* – meat pie with palm hearts, served in a special bowl to keep it hot (R$10, or R$19 with rice and veg). Tues–Sun noon–4pm & 7pm–midnight.

Rio Araguaia

The huge **Rio Araguaia**, one of the Amazon's main southern tributaries, is what attracts most Brazilians to Goiás. Even though most of the river now falls within the state of Tocantins, the Goiás section has hundreds of fine **sandy beaches** suitable for camping, and some well-established resorts, very popular with the residents of Goiânia and other towns in Goiás. Rich in fish, the Araguaia is particularly busy during the dry season from May to September when the water level drops, and serious anglers come from São Paulo and Goiânia to compete.

6

Aruanã

The gateway to the river is **ARUANÃ**, a small town served by only a few hotels, just over 380km northwest of Goiânia. You can arrange boat trips to go fishing or rent your own boat in Aruanã. The busiest month is July, when it can be difficult to get a room.

ARRIVAL AND DEPARTURE — ARUANÃ

By bus Buses from Aruanã serve Goiás Velho (2 daily; 3hr) and Goiânia (2 daily; 6hr).

ACCOMMODATION

Hotel Araguaia Praça Couto Magalhães 53 ⓣ62 3376 1251. A very green facade greets you at this small hotel, simple enough but the rooms all have TV, a/c and a fridge, and there's even a pool. Discounts are usually available. R$130

Pousada Acauá Rua José Eufrasio de Lima 14 ⓣ62 3376 1294, ⓦacauahotelpousada.com. The best place in Aruanã to stay, and as comfortable as hotels come in this town, with a pool, bar and reasonable restaurant. It offers fishing trips too. R$255

Sesi Aruanã Av Altamiro Caio Pacheco ⓣ62 3376 1221, ⓦwww.sesiaruana.com.br. Large but good-value family-oriented riverside hotel with a big pool (with a slide) to splash about in, plus lots of activities, including bicycles and even banana boats to rent. R$218

Parque Nacional das Emas

Portão do Bandeira entrance on unsurfaced road, 30km northwest of Chapadão do Céu; Portão do Jacuba entrance on BR-359/GO-341, 88km southwest of Mineiros • Daily 8am–6pm (until 10pm during the period of termite luminescence) • R$13 • ⓣ64 3929 6000

Down in the southwestern corner of Goiás state, the **Parque Nacional das Emas** is a *cerrado* reserve in the central Brazilian highlands near the Mato Grosso do Sul border. The park consists of some 1300 square kilometres of fairly pristine *cerrado*, mostly open grasslands pocked by thousands of termite hills, but with occasional clumps of savannah forest. While it lacks the scenic grandeur of Chapada dos Veadeiros, thanks to its relative isolation, it is one of the last places where you can find *cerrado* wildlife in some abundance, supporting an enormous population of **emas** (South American rheas) and also large herds of **veado-campeiro** deer, often shadowed by the solitary **lobo guará** (the maned wolf); all are more easily spotted here than anywhere else in Brazil. The Emas park is also famous for its wide range of variously coloured and extremely large **termite mounds**, which are used by *coruja-do-campo* owls as lookout posts dotted across the flat plain, and are a good source of food for *bandeira* anteaters. Activity from the larvae living inside them makes some of the anthills glow phosphorescently green and blue; this happens mainly around October, when the rains start (a hot day with showers provides the best conditions for it), and is an amazing sight, especially at the beginning of a dark night around the new moon.

Within the park you're restricted to set trails – although here they traverse most of the park. Beware of *mucuim*, irritating tiny ticks that jump onto legs and leave clumps of fantastically itchy reddish bites; wearing long trousers is your best defence. It's possible to rent bicycles and ride the trails, and there's a safari truck with sloped seating so that everybody gets a good view – it takes up to twenty people, costs R$200 between them for a circuit, and can be booked at the Centro de Atendimento ao Turista in Mineiros.

HIRING A GUIDE IN THE PARQUE NACIONAL DAS EMAS

You must hire a local **guide** to explore the park. Together with the transport they arrange, this will set you back between R$200 and R$250 a day depending how many people are in your group. Both Mineiros and Chapadão do Céu have a highly organized association of local guides, who should be your first port of call; they will quote you a price and take care of the formalities with IBAMA, the national parks authority, such as registering entry and exit and paying the R$13 **entrance fee** (you also have to pay your guide's entrance fee).

You will rarely be able to set out until the following day, as cars and drivers have to be found. Given the time it will take to reach the park itself, your best bet is to complete the formalities the day before and set off at dawn the next day.

Mineiros Guides can be located through the Centro de Atendimento ao Turista (CAT) at Av Alessandro Marchió 169 (T 64 3661 0006, E cat.mineiros@gmail.com). The guides' association, Filhos de Cerrado Chapadão, is at Av Alessandro Marchió 169 (T 64 3663 1134, E afc.mineiros.go@gmail.com).

Chapadão do Céu The guides' association (SETA) is on Av Netuno (T 64 3634 1119).

ARRIVAL AND DEPARTURE

By bus It's easy to get to the area by bus from Brasília and Goiânia: the access town of Mineiros is connected by bus to Brasília (4 daily; 10hr 30min) and Goiânia (8 daily; 8hr), and there are also buses from Goiânia to Chapadão do Céu (1 daily; 9hr 30min). However, it's a bit of a logistical challenge from these towns without a car once you're here: distances are long, local buses are almost nonexistent, and you'll have to rely on a guide's contacts to get around (see above).

ACCOMMODATION AND EATING

There is no accommodation in the park itself, apart from a camping area 6km inside the Portão do Bandeira. Otherwise, you'll have to base yourself in the small towns of **Mineiros** or **Chapadão do Céu**, both some distance from the park: Mineiros, with a population of just over 50,000 and more geared more to visitors, is 88km away; Chapadão do Céu, 30km from the park, is more rustic, and much smaller with around 6000 inhabitants. Although there aren't many accommodation options, all are adequate and cheap. As for **dining**, you'll be limited to a couple of *churrascarias* in each town, plus the hotel restaurants – not *haute cuisine*, but satisfying after a day's hiking.

MINEIROS

Dallas Av Alessandro Marchio 223 T 64 3661 1534, W dallashotel.com.br. A range of rooms, all equipped with a/c, TV and a fridge, with more deluxe rooms going all the way up to a presidential suite. R$120

Líder Rua Elias Machado 18 T 64 3661 1149. Centrally located, family-run hotel, and not as basic as you might expect – no a/c, but everything else you need, and with a smile. R$80

Pilões Palace Praça Assis T 64 3661 1547, W piloeshotel.com.br. The best hotel in town, right in the centre, and a decent enough three-star. The rooms are a bit retro, but fine for the price, and they may offer discounts in periods when demand is low. R$195

Pinheiros Rua 8 no. 90 T 64 3661 1942. Great value for the price: the rooms are small but homely, all with bathrooms, some with a/c, and there's parking space too. R$70

CHAPADÃO DO CÉU

Pousada das Emas Rua Ipê Oeste, Q.17, Lote 1 T 64 3634 1986. Although it calls itself a *pousada*, this is really more like a restaurant that rents out a few rooms, but it's actually a pretty good-value if small and modest place to stay, quiet and very welcoming, and all very neat and tidy; a/c rooms for R$80. R$70

Vitor Rua Rua Ipê Leste 213 T 64 3634 1722, W bit.ly/VitorHotel. A smallish hotel in a modern building, homey, comfortable and friendly, with great breakfasts and coffee on tap. R$155

Caldas Novas

More easily accessible than many of Goiás's attractions, the **thermal resorts** of **Caldas Novas**, around 185km south of Goiânia, are incredibly popular with Brazilians from beyond the state. It claims to be one of the world's largest hot-spring aquifers, a massive and very hot natural subterranean reservoir. The healing reputation and the sheer joy of relaxing in these natural spa resorts lure plenty of people from the urban sprawl of the

São Paulo region. While some people do come for long, expensive courses of treatment, most visitors are simply here on holiday, relaxing, sunbathing and taking the waters for a few days or a week.

It gets crowded in the dry season from May to September, but there are thousands of hotel beds within this relatively small town of only around 40,000 people.

ARRIVAL AND INFORMATION — CALDAS NOVAS

By bus The rodoviária is in the centre of town at Av Coronel Bento de Godoy 2095 (64 3454 3530).

Destinations Goiânia (9 daily; 3hr); São Paulo (3 daily; 14hr). For Brasília change at Goiânia.

Tourist information The Centro de Atendimento ao Turista is at Praça Mestre Orlando 462 (daily 8am–5pm; 64 3454 3524).

ACCOMMODATION AND EATING

Dody's Rua Antônio Praça Mestre Orlando 64 3454 5127, facebook.com/dodysrestauranteoficial. Brazilian and particularly local dishes, with the accent on fish as well as regional vegetables such as *pequí* (see page 422). Try the salmon in passion fruit sauce (R$80) or chicken in lemon and herb sauce (R$49). Mon & Tues 6.30–11.45pm, Wed–Sun 11.30am–3.30pm & 6.30–11.45pm.

Hotel Taiyo Thermas Rua Presidente Castelo Branco 115 0800 707 5555 or 64 3455 5555, hoteltaiyo.com.br. A resort hotel with a big water-park and lots of sports facilities and entertainment for adults and children. At weekends, depending on the season, they may require a two-day minimum stay. R$380

Thermas di Roma Rua São Cristóvão 1110, Solar de Caldas 0800 648 9800 or 64 3455 9393, diroma.com.br. A huge thermal spa hotel in a beautiful out-of-town location with panoramic views, over two hundred rooms, nine thermal pools and a sauna. R$590

Parque Nacional Chapada dos Veadeiros

GO-239, Km 36 • Tues–Sun 8am–6pm (last entry at noon) • Free • 62 3455 1114, icmbio.gov.br/parnachapadadosveadeiros

The **Parque Nacional Chapada dos Veadeiros** in the north of Goiás is the heart of the *planalto*, its stunning natural scenery among the most beautiful and distinctive in Brazil. The hundreds of square kilometres of wild and sparse vegetation, extraordinary geological formations, cave systems, waterfalls and hiking trails make this one of the best destinations for **ecotourism** in the country. A few hours north from Brasília and easily accessible by bus, the park has good local support for tourism, and apart from the occasional holidaying diplomat up from the capital, it is still remarkably unknown as a destination to foreign tourists.

HIKING IN PARQUE NACIONAL CHAPADA DOS VEADEIROS

Visitors to the park can hike on four **trails**. The two most popular, each 11–12km long, give you a day's worth of exploring in the most spectacular area of the park, an unforgettable blend of hills and cliff-faces (mostly in the middle distance; fortunately you don't have to climb them), plunging waterfalls, swimholes and forests. You encounter the full range of *cerrado* vegetation as well: *veredas* (open moorlands lined by *burití* palms), *floresta de galeria* (full-sized deciduous forest along watercourses) and *campo sujo* (the classic, shrubby savannah characteristic of Africa).

Of the two trails, one includes the park's main highlight – the marvellous **Salto do Rio Preto**, where two separate waterfalls plunge almost 130m into a pool 440m across. The trail's other notable sight is the **Pedreiras**, a series of natural rock pools. On the other trail, the highlight is **Salto Cariocas**, a series of falls with a sand beach at the top, and you will also pass **Canion 1 e 2**, two canyons cut by the Rio Preto and lined with granite cliffs.

Guides are easily engaged in Alto Paraiso or São Jorge, where hotels and the CAT tourist offices can help you find one. Your guide's first stop will be the IBAMA office to register entry. Take plenty of water and enough food for a day (agree beforehand whether you will be providing your guide's food as well), and stick to the trails, taking your rubbish home with you, and, most importantly, in the dry season **do not smoke**. Fires are the worst problem the park has, often deliberately started, and the vegetation is tinder-dry between July and October. Bringing a change of clothes and swimwear is a good idea as you'll be cooling off in swimholes between treks.

Alto Paraíso de Goiás

The main point of arrival for visitors to the park is **ALTO PARAÍSO DE GOIÁS**, an extremely friendly and relaxing little town on the GO-118 highway, although, if you really want to explore the Chapada, a better base is the village of São Jorge (see page 433), which is much closer to the national park and the best hiking. Alto Paraíso's main drag, **Avenida Ary Valadão Filho**, leads down from the highway through the centre of town, and most of the facilities you'll need are on or near it.

If you want to **hike from Alto Paraíso**, your best bet is to walk 4km up the GO-118 road north of the town, and then take the signposted dirt road right another 3km to the **Cristal waterfall**. The Cristal is at the head of a beautiful valley, where a series of swimholes and small waterfalls has been created by a cool mountain stream as it plunges into the valley.

ARRIVAL AND INFORMATION — ALTO PARAÍSO DE GOIÁS

By bus The rodoviária is off Av Ary Valadão Filho at its top end, near the GO-118 highway.

Destinations Brasília (3 daily, plus one to Taguatinga; 4hr); Goiânia (2 nightly, plus 3 day services weekly; 6hr 30min); São Jorge (1 daily; 30min).

By shared taxi For just slightly more than the bus, there's a shared taxi service to Brasília (T 62 3446 2129 or T 62 99867 8140) leaving Alto Paraíso around 7am, returning around midday, and they'll pick up and drop off at a location of your choice at both ends.

Tourist information The Centro de Atendimento ao Turista (Mon–Fri 8am–6pm, Sat & Sun 8am–8pm; T 62 3446 1159) is on Av Ary Valadão Filho near the rodoviária.

Tourist operators Alternativas, Av Ary Valadão Filho at Praça do Bambú (T 62 3446 1000, W alternativas.tur.br); EcoRotas, Rua das Nascentes 129 T 62 3446 1820, W ecorotas.com.br; Travessia, Av Ary R. Valadão Filho 979 (T 62 3446 1595, W travessia.tur.br). All offer tours in the Parque Nacional Chapada dos Veadeiros from Brasília as well as starting locally.

ACCOMMODATION

There's a distinct **new-age feel** to many of Alto Paraíso's lodgings, be they hippy encampments or upscale **pousadas** offering yoga and meditation for ecotourists and weekend trippers up from Brasília. Places to stay include a plethora of *pousadas*, an out-of-town forest retreat, and two rather quirky places on the main highway.

Camelot Inn GO-118, Km 168 (about 200m north of the junction with Av Ary Valadão Filho) T 62 3446 1581, W pousadacamelot.com.br. Outrageously kitsch but great value: a Monty Pythonesque fake medieval castle, with a pool, bar, sauna, Excalibur stone, Merlin suite and very comfortable Arthurian bungalow-style rooms. R$348

Jardim da Nova Era Rua Joaquim de Almeida 131 T 62 3446 2115, W jardimdanovaera.com.br. A friendly little hostel right in the middle of town, with a kitchen and a small camping space. If it's full, try the *Reges*, directly opposite (less new-age, more football), which has similar prices. Breakfast not included. Dorms R$40, doubles R$100, camping R$30

★ **Mariri Jungle Lodge** 13km east of town T 62 99913 1153, W maririjunglelodge.com. Tree houses and chalets on a hundred-acre plot out in the forest, with great views, backed by a dramatic escarpment, for those who want to be at one with nature, or just do a bit of birdwatching. It's super-ecofriendly, built on permaculture principles, fed with natural springwater and home to three types of monkeys and at least 46 species of birds. They'll pick you up from town if you contact them in advance, and they also have accommodation in town (R$150) at *Eco Nois* on Rua Coleto Paulino, Q.19, Lote 11 (behind Café da Drica). Breakfast not included. Dorms R$100, doubles R$380

Pousada Alfa Omega Rua Joaquim de Almeida 15 T 62 3446 1225, W veadeiros.com.br. Quite an upmarket *pousada* whose rooms are bungalows set in a lovely garden, each with a little veranda. Facilities include a pool, sauna and meditation space. R$270

Pousada dos Guias Rua Zorozimo Barbosa 278 T 62 3446 1231, W pousadadosguias.com.br. Small, friendly and low-priced *pousada* located just a couple of blocks off Av Ary Valadão Filho; rooms with a/c are R$235. R$185

Pousada Maya Rua das Curicadas Q.11, Lotes 4–5 T 62 3446 2062, W pousadamaya.com.br. A supremely relaxing deluxe *pousada* in a woodland setting on the edge of town (follow the signs from the junction of Av Ary Valadão Filho with Rua dos Buritis). Facilities include a pool, yoga, massage and meditation space, and naturally the *pousada* conforms to feng shui specifications. R$480

Road House (Hotel Europa) GO-118 (Rua 1, Q.7), opposite the junction with Av Ary Valadão Filho T 62 3446 1558, W roadhouserotago118.com.br. Alto Paraíso's oldest hotel, now revamped as a biker-style roadhouse, complete with Confederate flags (no racial or political connotations here) and biker motifs, friendly and welcoming to all, with a bar and live music at weekends. Midweek, it's half the price. R$200

Tapindaré Av Ary Valadão Filho 610 62 3446 1778, hoteltapindare.com. A good, modern hotel where the bright, comfortable rooms have just a very slight (and actually rather charming) touch of chintz about them, and there's a small pool, plus a children's pool, spa facilities and a good restaurant. R$250

EATING

Cravo e Canela Av Ary Valadão Filho 1363 (100m from the junction with GO-118) 62 3446 1376, bit.ly/CravoeCanelaBr. Well-presented vegetarian and vegan food, including veggie burgers (R$19), salads (salad of the day R$20), juices, sandwiches and various combos. Mon & Thurs–Sun noon–9pm.

Massas da Mamma Rua São Jose Operario 305 62 3446 1362, bit.ly/MassasdaMamma. Good pasta (spaghetti *alla carbonara* or *alla puttanesca* R$31.90) and other Italian dishes (medallions of beef with mushroom risotto R$57.90) served in a homey little place with pretty tablecloths, near the rodoviária. Daily noon–11pm.

Taj Mahal Av Ary Valadão Filho 638 62 8182 0594. Not a curry house, but a small restaurant purveying reliably good Brazilian and Italian(-ish) food, most notably a very tasty steak parmigiana (R$60). Thurs & Fri 6–11pm, Sat & Sun 11.30am–11pm.

6

São Jorge

To really get to grips with Chapada dos Veadeiros you need to head 37km up a good-quality dirt road to the small village of **SÃO JORGE**, next to the national park's only entrance. You can either hike into the national park from São Jorge or explore the spectacular countryside around the village, which is dotted with waterfalls, strange geological formations and natural swimholes; best are the otherworldly rock formations of the **Vale da Lua**, and the swimholes and waterfalls of **Raizama** and **Morada do Sol**, both a short drive or a two-hour hike away.

As for **finding a guide**, in the unlikely event locals don't come touting for business where you're staying, let the owner know you're interested and someone should be there within a few minutes. Guides charge a daily rate of around R$150 (R$200 if you need one who speaks English). If you want to go on a long hike outside the park, it's still a good idea to hire a guide to make sure you don't get lost.

HIKES AROUND SÃO JORGE

Hiking options around São Jorge are less strenuous than in the national park, but still spectacular. You could easily spend a week doing a series of rewarding day-hikes without even entering the national park, and for those travelling with children, for whom the long hikes in the park are not realistic, these shorter hikes are a great family outing. All destinations are reached by heading along the road that passes the village, either west or east – that is, towards or away from Alto Paraíso.

The most striking hike around São Jorge leads to **Vale da Lua**, a forested valley where the river São Miguel has carved a narrow canyon through an extraordinary series of sculptured granite curves. To get there from the village, head to the main road and continue 4km east – in the direction of Alto Paraíso. On your right you come to a signposted trail into the Vale da Lua. You can either follow the trail directly to a swimhole, or else peel left, along a different route towards the swimhole, by walking down the valley, the best route to see its extraordinary geology. Flash floods can be a problem here in the rainy season, given the narrowness of the gorge, so exercise caution.

Back at São Jorge, heading in the opposite direction, away from Alto Paraíso, will take you, in quick succession, to **Raizama**, a beautiful gorge with a series of swimholes and waterfalls, and **Morada do Sol**, which has less spectacular waterfalls, but more spectacular views up and down the valley. Another 5km up the main road will bring you to a **Águas Termais do Morro Vermelho**, where the owner has channelled a natural warm spring – tepid rather than hot – into a trio of large pools, making this a wonderful place to soak and recover from the walk.

All of the above destinations charge a R$20 **entrance fee**.

ARRIVAL AND INFORMATION

By bus There is only one daily bus to Alto Paraíso (30min; currently leaves São Jorge 6am, returning at 6.30pm).

By taxi A taxi from Alto Paraíso normally costs around R$100, but Táxis do Rick (62 9642 1910) promise a discount to Rough Guide readers, and in São Jorge you may be able to find people at the junction with the main road to share a cab with. Hitchhiking between Alto Paraíso and São Jorge is the other option.

Tourist information The Centro de Atendimento ao Turista (daily 8am–6pm; 62 3446 1090) is in a modern pavilion on Rua Guariroba (São Jorge's main street) at Rua Marmelada.

ACCOMMODATION

Despite its small size, São Jorge has no shortage of **accommodation**, all within five minutes of the village centre. There are also quite a few campsites. At all times of the year, if you're planning to stay in one of the **pousadas**, it's a good idea to call ahead and make a reservation. At **holiday periods**, especially Carnaval and the New Year, São Jorge fills up and can be noisy. A warning: at the height of the dry season (Sept), the village has been known to run out of **water**.

Pousada Casa das Flores Rua Araça 62 3455 1055, pousadacasadasflores.com.br. São Jorge's most upmarket option, where the rooms all have a sitting and a sleeping area. There's a pool, and a fire in the garden every evening, and all sorts of health and beauty treatments are available. A great place for a romantic weekend. Wi-fi in communal areas only. R$257

Pousada Refugio Rua 2 (Rua Pequi), Q.2, Lote 3 61 99177 7669, pousadarefugio.com. You pay just a little bit more if you want an upstairs room with a veranda and view at this good-value, jolly little *pousada* with a pool. R$200

Trilha Violeta Rua 12, Q.7, Lote 5 62 3455 1088, trilhavioleta.com.br. Rooms done out in violet are set around a pretty but narrow little garden. It's very tranquil and friendly, and even the decor isn't as violent as it sounds. R$200

EATING

Buritis Rua 12, Q.7, Lote 10, 62 3455 1044 restauranteburitis.com.br. It's just R$20 for get a choice of pastas and a big choice of sauces at the pasta buffet here. Mon, Tues & Thurs–Sun 1pm–10pm.

Papalua Rua 12, Q.7, Lote 8 62 3455 1085. The best food in town, with a varied menu of Brazilian and international dishes, but open half the week and evenings only. Thurs–Sun (and sometimes Wed) 6pm–midnight.

Pousada Casa das Flores Rua Araça 62 3455 1055, pousadacasadasflores.com.br. The fine restaurant here is open to all, and offers a weekend set lunch (Sat R$45, Sun R$39), and a range of international dishes, including cheese fondue (R$73). Mon–Fri 3–11pm, Sat & Sun 1–11pm.

Tocantins state

Created in 1989, the **state of Tocantins** is not an obvious geographical or cultural unit, merely a political and bureaucratic invention. Most visitors pass through the region rather than spend time around the state's hot and not very exciting towns. The Rio Araguaia, with its many beautiful sandy beaches, forms the state's western frontier, and its huge river island, **Ilha do Bananal**, containing the **Parque Nacional do Araguaia**, is the state's only real attraction, but it is underdeveloped and can be an expensive, tiring headache of a place to get to unless you're taking a guided tour. Otherwise, you may end up changing buses in either **Palmas** or at **Araguaína** – a flyblown settlement in the middle of a largely converted savannah – on your way overland through the state to the Amazon or the Northeast.

Palmas

The state capital of **PALMAS** is a newer example of a Brazilian planned city than Brasília, started in the late 1980s and inaugurated in 1990. Home to around a quarter of a million people, it lies just under 1000km north of Brasília and just over 1200km south of Belém. With long, wide avenues, it has a spacious feel, and a pleasant average temperature of around 27°C. On the banks of the Rio Tocantins, it is set back some

15km from the main Brasília–Belém highway BR-153, and most long-distance transport skirts it.

Praça dos Girassóis

Memorial Coluna Prestes: Mon–Fri 8am–6pm • Free • 63 3218 3312, bit.ly/MemorialPrestes

At Palmas's heart is the vast **Praça dos Girassóis** ("Sunflower Square") which, at 571,000 square metres, is the largest public square in Latin America, and fourth largest in the world. In the middle of it, the **Palácio Araguaia** is the seat of the state government, and not far from that, an impressive giant **sundial** marks the time of day.

The square has a scattering of monuments, most notably, in its southwestern quadrant, Oscar Niemeyer's **Memorial Coluna Prestes**, dedicated to a column of leftists who fought a rather ineffectual insurgency against the First Republic in the 1920s; their leader, Luís Carlos Prestes, later became the general secretary of Brazil's Communist Party. The memorial houses a small exhibition on the history of the column, with a typically Niemeyer-esque curved ramp outside leading up to a statue of Prestes, the floor of the ramp being red to symbolize the column's spilt blood. Continuing the theme, in the same quadrant of the square, the **Monumento aos Dezoito do Forte** honours seventeen soldiers and a civilian who held out in Rio de Janeiro's Forte de Copacabana (see page 82) in a failed 1922 uprising.

ARRIVAL AND TOURS — PALMAS

By bus Buses serve Araguaína (3 daily; 6hr), Goiânia (3 daily; 14hr) and Paraíso do Tocantins (5 daily; 1hr 15min). Change at Goiânia for Brasília and points south. or get yourself to Paraíso do Tocantins, 15km west of town on the BR-153 highway (around R$150 by taxi), where there are departures for Belém (5 daily; 22hr), Brasília (3 daily; 15hr 30), Goiânia (13 daily; 13hr) and São Paulo (1 daily; 28hr).

Tour companies Jalapão Extremo, 1106 Sul Alameda 29, Lote 12 (63 3322 7990, jalapaoextremo.com.br), run one- to seven-day tours in the little-visited Parque Estadual de Jalapão, 120km east of Palmas.

ACCOMMODATION

Casa Grande Av Joaquim Teotônio Segurado 201 Sul, Conjunto 1, Lote 01 63 3216 8000, hotelcg.com.br. Bright, modern, family-friendly hotel with well-equipped rooms and a pool – all-round, a good-value option. R$170

Rio do Sono Av Joaquim Teotônio Segurado 101 Sul, Conjunto 1, Lote 10 63 3213 6800, hotelriodosono.com.br. Palmas's best hotel, where the rooms are a good size. There's an in-house restaurant, bar, sauna and swimming pool, and various excursions on offer, including visits to Araguaia river beaches. R$270

Mato Grosso and Mato Grosso do Sul

SANDSTONE CLIFFS, CHAPADA DOS GUIMARÃES

Mato Grosso and Mato Grosso do Sul

Very Brazilian, in both its vastness and its frontier culture, the Mato Grosso region is essentially an enormous plain, home to the sprawling Pantanal swamp – the best place in Brazil for seeing wildlife, and one of the world's largest wetlands – and rippled by a handful of small mountain ranges. Equally Brazilian, there's a political boundary – a line on a map – across the heart of the swamp, demarcating two mammoth states: Mato Grosso and Mato Grosso do Sul. The latter is slightly less populous, largely comprised of either seasonal flood plain or open scrubland. To the west of Mato Grosso do Sul are Bolivian swamps and forest; the mighty rivers Araguaia and Paraná (one flowing north, the other south) form a natural rim to the east, while the Rio Paraguai and the country named after it complete the picture to the south. The name Mato Grosso, which means "thick wood", is more appropriate to this northernmost state, where thorny scrubland passes into tropical rainforest and the land begins its incline towards the Amazon, interrupted only by the beautiful uplifted plateau of the Chapada dos Guimarães. The simple road network makes getting around fairly hard work, but the variety of landscapes – from swamps and forests to cattle ranches, riverine villages and indigenous reservations – makes the trip a unique one and, for the adventurous traveller, well worth the effort.

Mato Grosso do Sul has a distinct cowboy flavour: close to the border with Paraguay and just a bit further from Argentine *gaúcho* territory, it's not uncommon to end up drinking *tereré* sitting on a horse under the shade of a tree by day or dancing Spanish polkas through the night in some of the region's bars. It's a place where you can forget about the industrialized world and wonder at nature's riches. The downside is that the Brazilian Ministry of Health recommends **yellow fever inoculations** for this area; during the rainy season there are, especially in December, outbreaks of dengue fever.

The state capital, **Campo Grande**, is a useful base from which to start delving deeper into Mato Grosso do Sul or to explore one of the largest and most beautiful wetlands in the world: there's a road connection to **Corumbá**, a frontier settlement on the edge of both **the Pantanal** and Bolivia, and one or two good tour companies operate from Campo Grande itself, so reaching the depths of the swamp is fairly easy. The wetlands, however, are vast, so while you can also get a feel for what it's like from a variety of road-linked places– like **Coxim**, north of the city, or **Aquidauana**, to the west – the flora and fauna is best experienced off-road.

SPECTACLED CAIMAN, THE PANTANAL

Highlights

❶ **Piranha fishing** Reel in your supper with a simple line and hook; the peaceful town of Coxim is a good place to arrange fishing trips, though piranha can be caught easily in pools and lakes throughout the Pantanal. See page 447

❷ **Rio da Prata** A spectacular river with clear water near Bonito, offering excellent snorkelling among a wide range of tropical fish. This region is also great for other adventure and eco pursuits, including whitewater rafting, caving, trekking and horse riding. See page 452

❸ **The Pantanal** The largest concentration of wildlife in the whole of the Americas – a terrific place to spend a few days on eco-safari to see jungle mammals, exotic birds and hundreds of caiman. See page 459

❹ **Ecolodges** Stay a few nights in a Pantanal ecolodge and learn about sustainable tourism while enjoying the local flora and fauna, and tucking into the best regional home-cooked food. See pages 463 and 465

❺ **Chapada dos Guimarães** A breathtaking plateau with a small, pleasant town and lots of trails, this is also the geodesic centre of South America. See page 474

HIGHLIGHTS ARE MARKED ON THE MAP ON PAGE 440

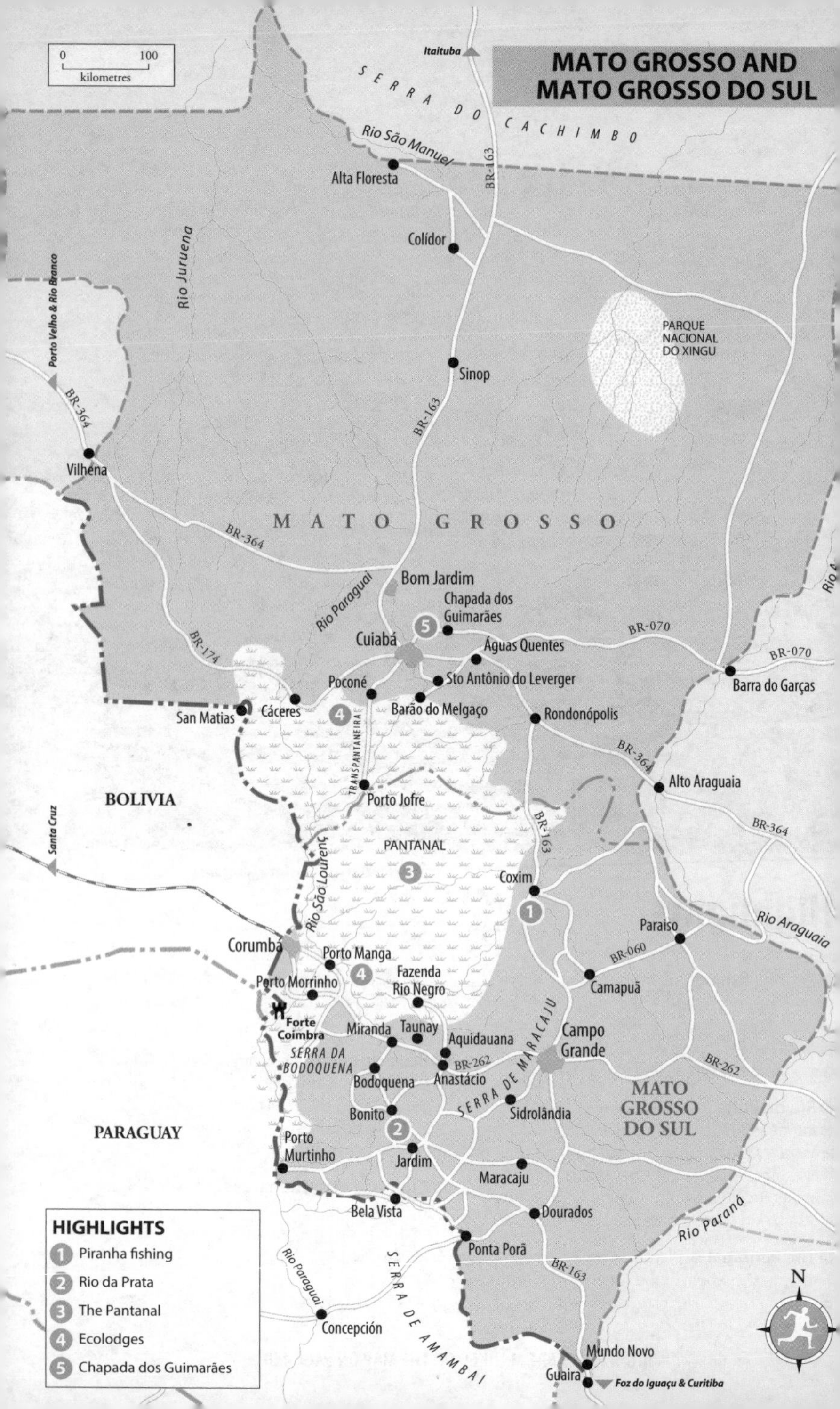

MATO GROSSO AND
MATO GROSSO DO SUL
0
100
kilometres
Itaituba
SERRA DO CACHIMBO
Rio São Manuel
BR-163
Alta Floresta
Colídor
Rio Juruena
Porto Velho & Rio Branco
BR-364
PARQUE
NACIONAL
DO XINGU
Sinop
Vilhena
MATO GROSSO
Bom Jardim
Chapada dos
Guimarães
Rio Paraguai
BR-174
Cuiabá
BR-070
Águas Quentes
Barra do Garças
Sto Antônio do Leverger
Poconé
Barão do Melgaço
Cáceres
San Matias
Rondonópolis
TRANSPANTANEIRA
Porto Jofre
Alto Araguaia
BOLIVIA
PANTANAL
Rio São Lourenço
Santa Cruz
Coxim
Rio Araguaia
Paraiso
BR-060
Corumbá
Porto Manga
Fazenda
Rio Negro
Porto Morrinho
Camapuã
Forte
Coimbra
Miranda
Taunay
Aquidauana
Campo
Grande
SERRA DA
BODOQUENA
BR-262
Anastácio
SERRA DE MARACAJU
Bodoquena
Sidrolândia
MATO
GROSSO
DO SUL
Bonito
PARAGUAY
Porto
Murtinho
Jardim
Maracaju
Bela Vista
Dourados
Ponta Porã
Rio Paraná
Rio Paraguai
SERRA DE AMAMBAI
Concepción
Mundo Novo
Guaira
Foz do Iguaçu & Curitiba
N
HIGHLIGHTS
1 Piranha fishing
2 Rio da Prata
3 The Pantanal
4 Ecolodges
5 Chapada dos Guimarães

TIME ZONES

Mato Grosso and Mato Grosso do Sul are officially **one hour behind** the standard time of Brasília and the coast.

The south of the state is home to the beautiful hills of the Serra da Bodoquena and Serra de Maracaju and, deep in the Bodoquena hills, you can visit the spectacular cave systems, forests and rivers of the **Bonito** area. Further south, 316km from Campo Grande, **Ponta Porã** sits square on the Paraguayan border, from where there's an eight-hour overland route to Asunción.

The region is dominated by the **Pantanal**, one of the world's largest wetland or swamp, which is renowned for its wildlife. In the past, between two million and five million caiman alligators were "culled" annually from the Pantanal, and today it retains possibly the densest population of alligators in the world. This spectacular region is, however, better known for its array of **birdlife**, with around 600 identified species, and its seemingly endless supply of fish, with 240 species – including a great many piranha, which are used in an excellent local soup. Travelling anywhere around here is slow.

Matto Grosso's largest city is **Cuiabá**, with a population of over half a million people. Roads radiate from this commercial and administrative centre like tentacles, extending over the plains in every direction. Cuiabá is a good a springboard for a trip into the north of **Pantanal**, especially if you're on a quest to spot jaguars in **Porto Jofre** (see page 465). Apart from the Pantanal, other nearby tourist destinations include the mysterious and stunning **Chapada dos Guimarães**, and **Bom Jardim** – a natural aquatic attraction north of Cuiabá.

7

GETTING AROUND **MATO GROSSO AND MATO GROSSO DO SUL**

There are three main routes through the two states. Coming from the east and south, two roads fan out around the main Pantanal swamplands in a tweezer-like form: one is the most heavily used road, the **BR-364** through Cuiabá, and the other is the **BR-262**, which runs through Campo Grande to Corumbá. The third road, the **BR-163**, runs from south to north, connecting Campo Grande with Cuiabá and overland routes north to Alta Floresta and beyond, through much of the central Amazon and to Santarém (although many times impassable by buses during rainy season), and south to Paraguay and Asunción.

By plane Given the distances involved, anyone in possession of a Brazilian air pass, or simply limited by time, might well consider the occasional plane hop.

By bus Except on the Campo Grande–Corumbá route, which is monopolized by Andorinha, there are scores of different bus companies competing for the same routes as well as opening up new ones. Each company advertises destinations and departure times at its ticket office windows, making it relatively easy to choose a route and buy a ticket.

Campo Grande and around

Nicknamed the "brunette city" because of its chestnut-coloured earth, **CAMPO GRANDE** has in the last forty years been transformed from an insignificant settlement into a buzzing metropolis with a population of around 800,000. Founded in 1889, the city was only made the capital of the new state of Mato Grosso do Sul in the late 1970s, since when it has almost doubled in size. Its downtown area manages to combine sky-scraping banks and apartment buildings with ranchers' general stores and poky little shops selling strange forest herbs and Catholic *ex votos*. Reminiscent in parts of quiet southern US cities, it's a relatively salubrious **market centre** for an enormous cattle-ranching region, as well as being an important centre of trade routes from Paraguay, Bolivia, Argentina and the south of Brazil. A pioneering place, many of the early twentieth-century settlers here were Arabs, some of whom have since started businesses such as restaurants and hotels. There is also a large Japanese section of the immigrant population, which has left its mark on the local culinary trade. The city also has a number of splendidly planned *praças* and parks with large, leafy trees, bringing wild birds into the modern centre.

An obvious place to break a long journey between Cuiabá or Corumbá and the coast, Campo Grande tries hard to shake off the feeling that it's a city stuck in the middle of nowhere. Apart from the *gaúcho* influence, the town centre is much like that of any other medium-sized city: the generally warm evenings inspire the locals to turn out on the streets in force. People chat over a meal or sip ice-cold beers at one of the restaurants or bars around Avenida Afonso Pena and the Praça Ari Coelho and guitars, maracas and congas are often brought out for **impromptu music sessions**.

The surprisingly modern heart of Campo Grande is based around the **Praça Ari Coelho**, five blocks east of the old rodoviária. Tourism is fairly low-key in the city, but there's enough to keep you interested for a couple of days.

Museu Dom Bosco

7

Av Alfonso Pena 7000, Parque das Nações Indígenas • Tues–Sun 8.30am–4.30pm • R$10 • 67 3326 9788, mcdb.org.br

One of the city's best-known attractions is the **Museu Dom Bosco**, in the university building facing the Praça da República. A fascinating place, it's crammed full of exhibits,

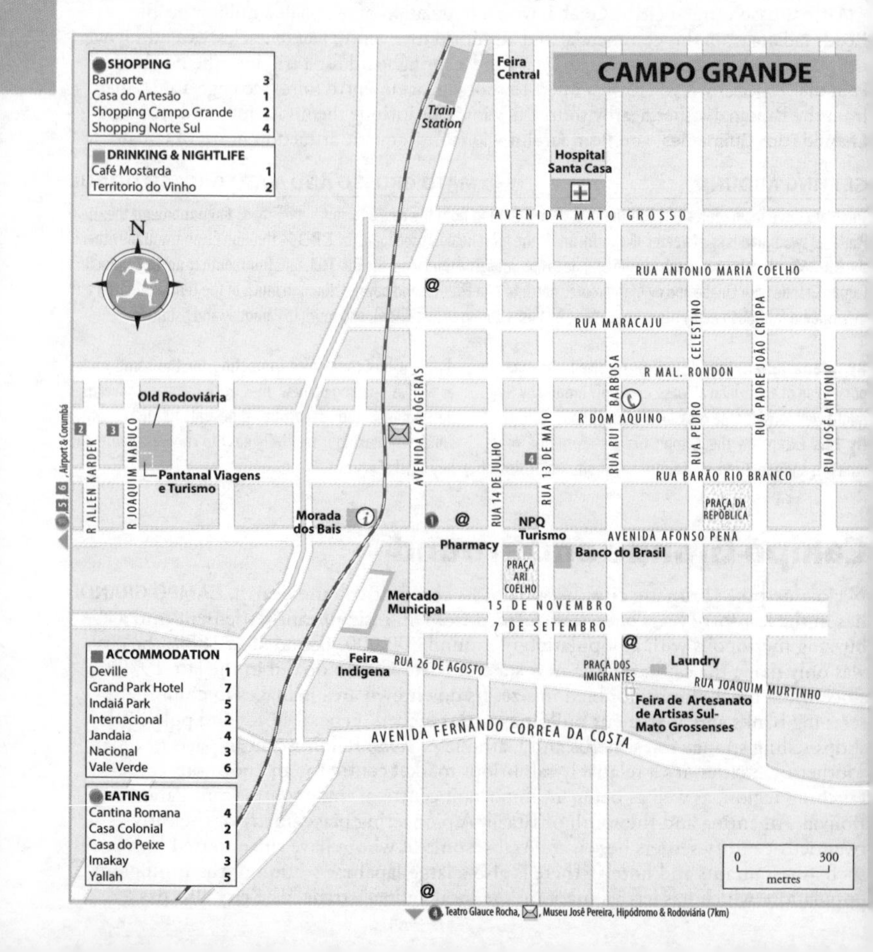

ranging from superb indigenous forest artefacts to over ten thousand terrifying dead insects and some astonishingly beautiful butterflies. Most impressive of all is the vast collection of stuffed birds and animals, including giant rheas (the South American version of an ostrich), anacondas and examples of Brazilian marsupials, the gamba and the quica.

Morada dos Bais

Av Afonso Pena 1661 • Tues–Sat 1–3pm & 4–8pm (live music Wed–Sat 8–11pm) • Free • 67 3311 4458, facebook.com/sescmoradadosbais

This 1918 building houses the Centro de Informações Turisticas e Culturais (Tourist and Cultural Information Office) as well as a small historical museum with period furniture and photos of early Campo Grande, plus a couple of art galleries with changing temporary exhibitions. They also have live music some evenings.

The markets

Mercado Municipal Rua 7 de Setembro 65 • Mon–Sat 6.30am–6.30pm & Sun 6.30am–noon • Free • **Feira Indigena** Rua 26 de Agosto s/n • Mon–Sat 8am–6pm • **Feira Central** Rua 14 de Julho, 3335 • Wed–Fri 3pm–midnight, Sat 3pm–late & Sun noon–late • Free • **Feira de Artesanato de Artistas Sul Mato Grossenses** Praça dos Imigrantes • Mon–Fri 9am–6pm & Sat 8am–noon • Free

The **Mercado Municipal**, built in 1933, sells a good range of inexpensive souvenirs, including cow-horn trumpets, horn goblets and drinking gourds. You can also find leather cowboy boots here. The **Feira Indigena**, just outside the Mercado Municipal, devotes itself to market-garden produce, including lovely honey. Also, the popular **Feira Central**, on Avenida Calogeras at the corner with 14 de Julho, takes place Wednesday to Sunday, attracting indigenous tribesmen selling beads and leatherwork, as well as a few Paraguayans selling toys. But most people come on the weekends to eat Japanese *yaki soba* at one of the many stalls. Thanks to the eclectic mix of local residents, there are other cuisines on offer such as shawarma, *churrasquinho* and pizza. (Many food stalls are closed during the general opening hours and follow their own time table.

Good-quality *artesanato* – mainly leatherwork, embroidery and handicrafts made out of wood – is on sale at the **Feira de Artesanato de Artistas Sul Mato Grossenses**, where there's also a small outdoor café.

Parque dos Poderes and Parque das Nações Indígenas

Av Mato Grosso • **Parque dos Poderes** Mon–Sat 7am–7pm, Sun 8am–6pm • **Parque das Nações Indígenas** daily 6am–10pm • Free • Buses for the Parque dos Poderes can be caught on Av Afonso Pena (travelling east from the centre)

Just beyond the town centre, at the eastern end of Avenida Mato Grosso (and just beside Parque das Nações Indígenas), is the **Parque dos Poderes**. This calm ecological reserve is home to a variety of native plants and a small selection of the region's wild animals as well as numerous government buildings; there are a few short walking trails and the habitat is scrubby woodland. In the huge **Parque das Nações Indígenas**, there's a large lake with an island in the middle, a pier, several bridges and plenty of capybaras that are particularly active at dusk. It's a popular place to practise sports, with a skate park, cycle lanes, and 4km walking trail. While its cultural highlights are, for now, the **Monumento ao Índio** and the **Museu de Arte Contemporânea**, these should, eventually be joined by the **Aquário do Pantanal.** Housed in a futuristic, bullet-shaped building within the park, this is set to be the largest freshwater aquarium in the world, but its opening has been delayed by several years at the time of writing.

Museu de Arte Contemporânea de Mato Grosso do Sul (MARCO)

Av Maria Coelho 6000 • Tues–Fri 7.30am–5.30pm, Sat & Sun 2–6pm • R$10

The small, but usually colourful, **Museu de Arte Contemporânea de Mato Grosso do Sul** (or **MARCO**) is a modern art museum with five rooms and around 1500 works, comprising art exhibitions on local artists as well as temporary exhibits from out-of-state artists. Well-known regional artists represented in the museum include Genésio Fernandes, Lídia Baís and Vânia Pereira.

Memorial da Cultura Indígena

Rua Terena • Tues–Sun 8am–6pm; groups by appointment only • R$2 • ⓣ 67 3314 3544

About fifteen blocks south of the Parque das Nações Indígenas (or east from the centre along Av Joaquim Murtinho), you'll find the **Memorial da Cultura Indígena**, in the Aldeia Indígena Urbana (Urban Indigenous Village), Bairro Tiradentes, where there is a craft workshop, visitor reception and many genuine tribal craft goods for sale, including hand-painted ceramics. Inhabited by people of the Terena tribe, the surrounding brick urban settlement is a planned municipal project. The memorial building itself is an imposing traditional-looking hut with a palm-frond roof standing some 8m tall, which incorporates innovative construction techniques, such as the use of bent bamboo.

ARRIVAL AND DEPARTURE

By plane The airport, Aeroporto Internacional Antônio João (ⓣ 67 3368 6050), is 7km out of town on the road towards Aquidauana. Taxis to the centre cost around R$25. There are several daily flights (Gol, Azul, Avianca and LATAM) to Brazil's main cities and to Cuiabá.

By bus The new rodoviária (ⓣ 67 3026 6789) is situated 7km south of the city centre at Av Gury Marques 1215. There are also several daily bus services from Campo Grande via Dourados and Mundo Novo to Guaira and the amazing Foz do Iguaçu (see page 562), in the neighbouring state of Paraná.

Destinations Alta Floresta (2 daily; 26hr); Anastácio (4–6 daily; 2hr 30min); Aquidauana (1–2 daily; 2h 15min) Belo Horizonte (4–5 daily; 26hr); Bonito (4 daily; 4–6hr); Brasília (1 daily; 25hr); Corumbá (8–9 daily; 7hr); Coxim (7–8 daily; 4hr); Cuiabá (15–17 daily; 11hr 30min); Dourados (18 daily; 4hr); Foz do Iguaçu (1 daily, change at Cascavel; 15hr); Miranda (6 daily; 3hr); Ponta Porã (11 daily; 5–6hr); Rio de Janeiro (4 daily; 24hr); São Paulo (13 daily; 15hr).

Car rental Alamo, Av Duque De Caixas 4355 at the airport (ⓣ 67 3368 6036); Localiza, Av Afonso Pena 318 (ⓣ 67 3348 5500).

INFORMATION

Tourist information Information is readily available at the airport (in theory daily 6am–midnight; ⓣ 67 3363 3116) or in town at either the very helpful Morada dos Bais tourist office on Ave Noroeste 5140 (Tues–Sat 8am–6pm & Sun 9am–noon; ⓣ 67 3314 9968), or during office hours in the Shopping Campo Grande mall (ⓣ 67 3314 3142). As well as information on attractions and accommodation, you'll find a noticeboard with details on cinema, theatre and exhibition listings in Morado dos Bais.

GETTING AROUND

By bus To travel by bus you'll need a reusable bus pass called Assetur *passe de ônibus*, which you can get free from the airport or at kiosks in the city; all fares are set at R$3.70.

By taxi Phone Rádio Táxi on ⓣ 67 3387 1414; Uber is also available in the city and very affordable.

ACCOMMODATION

The area by the old, now abandoned rodoviária on **Rua Joaquim Nabuco 200** is fine during the day but a little rough by night, yet there are reasonable budget and mid-range choices one street west of it, around the junction of **Rua Dom Aquino** and **Rua Allan Kardek**. The more central hotels within a few blocks of the **Praça Ari Coelho** are closer to the modern city's heart. The district south of **Avenida Afonso Pena** also has a dodgy reputation. If in doubt, take a **taxi**.

Deville Av Mato Grosso 4250 ⓣ 67 2106 4600, ⓦ deville.com.br/hotel/deville-prime-campo-grande; map p.442. The city's only five-star hotel is a bit far from the action, but offers spacious and immaculate rooms, an on-site restaurant serving Western food and a terrace with a small pool. Everything is brand new, most of the staff speak excellent English and the breakfast has everything from waffles to eggs, bacon and fresh fruit. R$410

Grand Park Hotel Av Alfonso Pena 5282 ⓣ 67 3044 4444, ⓦ grandparkhotel.com.br; map p.442. Located

TRAVEL AND TOUR COMPANIES IN CAMPO GRANDE

NPQ Turismo Av Afonso Pena 2081, Praça Ari Coelho ⊕67 3325 6162. Good for flights and some bus tickets.

Pantanal Discovery Av Afonso Pena 602 ⊕67 9163 3518, ⊛gilspantanaldiscovery.com.br. One of the main tour operators in Campo Grande, offering low-cost trips into the Pantanal. Enthusiastic owner Gil is quite the salesman, but is clearly passionate about his work and the area, and does go out of his way to make sure you're well looked after in Campo Grande and the Pantanal.

Pantanal Viagens e Turismo Rua Barão do Rio Branco s/n ⊕67 3321 3143, ⊛pantanalviagens.com.br. Family-owned operator offering personalized trips to the Pantanal and Bonito. They work with several lodges, hotels and boats in the area, so you'll have a choice of where to stay.

n front of Campo Grande Shopping, this is one of the city's anciest hotel. Big glass windows throughout the hotel let plenty of light in, and there's a sauna, gym, outdoor pool and decent restaurant. R$480

ndaiá Park Av Afonso Pena 354 ⊕67 2106 1000, ⊛indaiahotel.com.br; map p.442. In a somewhat asteless manner, an animal-skin decorates the lobby loor at this large and modern three-star hotel. There's a pool and decked terrace on the ground floor as well as a restaurant (open Mon–Fri) and piano bar. Offers airport transfers. R$270

Internacional Rua Allan Kardek 223 ⊕67 3384 4677, ⊛hotelinternacionalms.com.br; map p.442. This s the largest and flashiest of the hotels around the old rodoviária, and it's surprisingly well appointed, with TVs and phones in all rooms and even a small pool. Well worth the extra few *reais*. R$145

Jandaia Rua Barão do Rio Branco 1271, on the corner with Rua 13 de Maio ⊕67 3316 7700, ⊛jandaia.com.br; map p.442. This central and slightly outdated luxury hotel with friendly staff has a small oval-shaped terrace pool, gymnasium and a fine restaurant serving some delicious local dishes. The decor is made up of chandeliers, marble floors, leather sofas and a touch of zebra print dotted around. R$210

Nacional Rua Dom Aquino 610 ⊕67 3383 2461, ⊜reservas@hotelnacionalms.com.br; map p.442. Probably the best value of the budget places around the old rodoviária, with a stupendous breakfast featuring tropical fruit and freshly baked breads and cakes. Rooms come with TV, private or shared bathroom and a choice of fan or a/c. It's owned by the people behind the Pantanal Discovery tour operator (see above), so trips to the Pantanal are easily arranged from here. R$85

Vale Verde Av Alfonso Pena 106 ⊕67 3041 3355, ⊛hotelvaleverde.com.br; map p.442. This refurbished hotel has a pool and garden on the ground floor, and friendly staff. It is particularly convenient for late-night arrivals and early-morning departures as it's 5min from the airport by taxi. R$262

EATING

Eating out is an important part of the local lifestyle and this is reflected in the diversity of Campo Grande's restaurants. There are scores of **lanchonetes**, east along Rua Dom Aquino, and, during hot afternoons, the city's many **juice bars** do brisk business: you'll find them on most street corners. This is a cattle-ranching market centre and if you're mad for **beef** you're in for a treat. However, there are also vegetarian options and several good oriental restaurants. For Japanese *yaki soba*, head to the **Feira Central** (see page 443).

★ **Cantina Romana** Rua da Paz 237, ⊕67 3324 9777, ⊛cantinaromana.com.br; map p.442. Easily Campo Grande's top Italian restaurant and pizzeria, the popular *Cantina Romana* serves up large portions of Italian food, including a tasty lasagne. There's a good atmosphere and fine wines, all at very fair prices. Mon–Fri 11am–2pm & 6.30–11pm, Sat & Sun 11am–2.30pm & 6.30–11.30pm.

Casa Colonial Av Afonso Pena 3997, Jardim dos Estados ⊕67 3383 3207, ⊛casacolonial.com.br; map p.442. Primarily a *churrascaria*, this classy place serves excellent Brazilian *rodizio (R$72)*, where you can eat meat till you drop. Expensive, but the decor is refined and there's an impressive wine cellar. Mon 6.30pm–midnight, Tues–Sat 11am–2.30pm & 6.30pm–midnight, Sun 11am–2.30pm.

Casa do Peixe Rua Dr João Pires 1030 ⊕67 3382 7121, ⊛casadopeixe.com.br; map p.442. This long-running, down-to-earth fish restaurant with a sterling reputation has been known to attract Brazilian celebrities passing through Campo Grande. Choose from the all-you-can-eat *rodizio* (R$82) of local fish or order à la carte. Note that most dishes serve two. Mon–Fri 11am–2pm & 6–11pm, Sat 11am–3pm & 6–11pm, Sun 11am–3pm.

★ **Imakaya Oriental y Peruano** Avenida Afonso Pena 4909 ⊕67 3326 5317, ⊛facebook.com/restauranteimakay; map p.442. Upscale Peruvian/Japanese fusion restaurant in Shopping Campo Grande serving a delicious ceviche (R$41) and a mind-blowing tuna sashimi with *foie gras* (R$26). The interior is dark and sleek and there are various pisco based cocktails to choose from. Portions are on the small side, but quality top notch. Mon–Thurs 11.30am–2.30pm & 7–11pm, Fri 11.30am–2.30pm & 7pm–1am, Sat noon–4pm & 7pm–1am, Sun noon–4pm & 7–11pm.

Yallah Rua da paz 95 ⓣ67 3305 1755; map p.442. Small Syrian run restaurant with an English-speaking owner. The menu is extensive and the restaurant serve everything from falafel with pita bread (R$34) an *tabbouleh* to *kibbe* (fried bulgur and minced meat) an Moroccan rice with chicken and cashew nuts (R$27). Th beef kofta (R$37) is good value for money, but avoid th overpriced starter *trio da pastas* (R$30) that is basicall some hummus, yoghurt and baba ghanoush with bread Tues–Thurs 11am–10pm, Fri & Sat 11am–11pm, Su 10.30am–5pm.

DRINKING AND NIGHTLIFE

Most of Campo Grande's action happens at weekends, when the **churrascarias** and other large restaurants generally serve their food to the energetic sounds of Paraguayan polkas and *serrtanejo* folk music. **Nightclubs** come and go at ar alarming speed, but **live music bars** are extremely popular among both young and old.

Café Mostarda Av Afonso Pena 3952 ⓣ67 3301 9990, ⓦbit.ly/CafeMostarda; map p.442. The most popular of Campo Grande's live music bars, *Café Mostarda* lures in the crowds with its buzzing atmosphere, pleasant decor and outdoor seating. The menu is simple and on the pricey side, but the likes of Caesar salad and bite-sized battered fish are perfect accompaniments to ice-cold beers and fruity caipirinhas. Mon, Wed & Thurs 6pm–1am, Fri & Sat 6pm–3am, Sun 5pm–1am.

Territorio do Vinho Rua Euclides da Cunha 48 ⓣ67 3029 8464, ⓦterritoriodovinho.com.br; ma p.442. This classy wine bar attracts well-heeled local with its dimly lit interior, jazz tunes and Italian-Braziliar fusion cuisine. With more than 400 labels on the iPa menu, this is the place to get acquainted with Braziliar wine. Ask about wine tastings and book ahead. Mon–Fri 7pm–1am, Sat 11am–2.30pm & 7pm–late, Sur 11am–2.30pm.

ENTERTAINMENT

Teatro Glauce Rocha 15min out of town in Cidade Universitária ⓣ67 3345 7261. Often hosts interesting Brazilian works. Call for details, or check the local pape *Correio do Estado*.

SHOPPING

The busiest shopping streets in Campo Grande's town centre are mostly congregated in the square formed by Av Calógeras Av Afonso Pena, Rua Cândido Mariano Rondon and Rua Pedro Celestino. A **street market** selling plastic goods anc electronics sets up daily along Rua Barão do Rio Branco between the old rodoviária and Av Calógeras.

Barroarte Av Afonso Pena 4329, Jardim dos Estados; map p.442. Located in a colonial-style house, Barroarte has a wide range of good local ceramics, sculptures and paintings; it's some distance from the centre, but en route to Shopping Campo Grande. Mon–Sat 10am–6pm.

Casa do Artesão Av Calógeras & Av Afonso Pena; map p.442. Located near the Morada dos Bais tourist board, the Casa do Artesão sells crafts that reflect the region's numerous indigenous cultures, including the Terena, the Kadiwéu – whose ancestors were called the Mbaya-Guaicuru – and the Guato peoples. The local works include seed jewellery and painted wood carvings, often depicting mythical symbols like fish-women and totemic figures; all are relatively inexpensive. Mon–Fri 8am–6pm, Sat 8am–noon.

Shopping Campo Grande Av Afonso Pena 4909 ⓣ67 3389 8008, ⓦshoppingcampogrande.com.br; map p.442. A large and flashy shopping centre towards the eastern end of Av Afonso Pena, replete with multiplex cinema and over 170 shops. Mon–Sat 10am–10pm, Sun noon–8pm.

Shopping Norte Sul Plaza Av Ernesto Geisel 2300 ⓣ67 3044 3900, ⓦnortesulplaza.com.br; map p.442. Campo Grande's newest shopping mall is located 2km from the centre in the northern part of the city, and has over 150 shops, several cinemas (including a 3D screen) and the largest food hall in the state. Mon–Sat 10am–10pm & Sun noon–8pm.

DIRECTORY

Consulates If you're heading into either Paraguay or Bolivia from Campo Grande, you should check on border procedures and visa requirements. The Paraguayan consul is at Rua 26 de Agosto 384 (call before to check opening hours; ⓣ67 3384 6610), and the Bolivian consul at Rua Spipe Calarge 99 (Mon–Fri 8am–1pm & 2pm–5pm; ⓣ67 3342 6933).

Hospital The public Santa Casa hospital is at Rua Eduardo Santos Pereira 88 (67 3322 4000). Or if you'd rather go private, there's the 24hr Unimed on Avenida Mato Grosso 1566 near the MARCO (67 3318 6666).

Internet Matrix Cyber Café, Av Calogeras 2069 (67 3029 1206), has efficient a/c, and *Cyber 7*, Rua Sete de Setembro 158 (67 3305 1425).

Laundry Planet Clean, Rua Joaquim Murtinho 135, close to the Praça dos Imigrantes.

Money and exchange There are ATMs by most banks, at the airport and at strategic points in the city, such as the corner of Rua 13 de Maio with Afonso Pena, opposite the main Praça Ari Coelho; you can also change money here (Mon–Fri 10am–5pm); at Shopping Campo Grande on Av Afonso Pena 4909; or at the airport bank.

Pharmacy Drogasil, Av Afonso Pena 2940 (24hr).

Post offices Av Calógeras 2309, on the corner with Rua Dom Aquino (Mon–Fri 8.30am–5pm); Rua Rui Barbosa (Mon–Fri 8am–5pm & Sat 8am–noon).

Coxim

Today, **COXIM** is a quiet town of some 33,000 people, situated on the eastern edges of the Pantanal, and easily reached by bus from Campo Grande. The scrub forest area to the east, north of Campo Grande, was formerly the territory of the **Caiapó** nation, who ambushed miners along the routes to Goiás and Cuiabá from São Paulo, posing a serious threat to Portuguese expansion and development in the mid-eighteenth century.

The centre of the action takes place on the riverfront and around Avenida Virginia Ferreira, where the shops, restaurants and bars are, but the main reason for coming to Coxim is to throw a line during the fishing season between August and October (see below).

ARRIVAL AND INFORMATION — COXIM

By bus The bus takes around 4–5hr from Campo Grande (6–7hr from Cuiabá). There are around 10 daily buses from Campo Grande and 15 daily buses from Cuiabá.

Tourist information The tourist information office (67 3291 2297) in the centre has very unpredictable opening hours.

ACCOMMODATION

The town offers plenty of accommodation possibilities including hotels, *fazendas* and *pousadas*, mostly aimed at **fishing** holiday-makers. There are also several accommodation options 5km away in the neighbouring village of **Silviolândia**.

Hotel Coxim Rodovia Br-163 Km 726 67 3291 1480, facebook.com/hotelcoxim1. This pleasant hotel is probably the fanciest in town, although that's not saying much. It has a decent pool and restaurant, and the clean rooms with large bathrooms have all the regular mod cons. R$200

Hotel Santa Ana Rua Miranda Reis 931 67 3291 1602. Central-ish hotel on the riverfront with basic but clean rooms and friendly service. The generous breakfast is a highlight, as is the pool and sauna. It might be slightly bland, but it does represent good value for money. R$140

FISHING AND SWIMMING AROUND COXIM

Coxim is a fantastic **fishing** centre: the fisherman Pirambero runs excellent trips into the swamp, down the Rio Taquari, to catch piranhas (ask for him at the port). If you're really serious about angling, contact IBAMA, at Rua Floriano Peixoto 151 (67 3291 2310), or the Banco do Brasil for a **temporary fishing permit** (R$30) and, for more detailed local information, try the local fishing club, the late Clube Rio Verde, at Rua Ferreira, Bairro Piracema (67 3291 1246).

Besides fishing, **swimming** in the Rio Taquari around Campo Falls is another popular pastime, in spite of the razor-toothed fish, and, nearby on the Rio Coxim, the **Palmeiras Falls** are a good place for a picnic or to set up camp. From November through to January, the two falls are the best places to witness an incredible spectacle – thousands of fish, leaping clear of the river, on their way upstream to the river's source to lay their eggs. Note that it is strictly forbidden to fish during the **breeding season**, known as *piracema*, which lasts from October to March.

CROSSING THE BORDER TO PARAGUAY

Crossing the border at Ponta Porã is a relatively simple procedure for most non-Brazilians. An **exit stamp** must be obtained from the Polícia Federal at the airport on Rua Batista de Azevedo 770 (Mon–Fri 8am–6pm, Sat & Sun 10am–1pm & 3–6pm; 67 3437 0512) on the Brazilian side, then it's a matter of getting to Av Internacional 4642 to the **Paraguayan consulate** (Mon–Fri 7am–10pm, Sat & Sun 8am–10pm; 67 3431 6312) where you can also get a visa for Paraguay if you need one. If you're pushed for time, catch a cab from the airport; the fare is about R$20.

Once in Paraguay, there's a reasonably good road direct to Concepción, a major source of imports and contraband for Brazilians; daily **buses** make the five- or six-hour trip in good weather. It's another five hours from there to Asunción; there's also a direct service (8hr) from the bus station in Pedro Juan Caballero.

There's no problem **changing money** at decent rates on Av Internacional.

Ponta Porã

7

PONTA PORÃ is an attractive little settlement, right on the Paraguayan border up in the Maracaju hills. The **Avenida Internacional** divides the settlement in two – on one side of the street you're in Brazil, on the other in the Paraguayan town of **Pedro Juan Caballero**. On the Paraguayan side you can polka the night away, gamble your money till dawn or, like most people there, just buy a load of imported goods at the duty-free shops, while the Brazilian side is a little more staid. There's a strange blend of language and character, and a unique *mestizo* cuisine, making it an interesting place to spend a day. Ponta Porã also has a tradition as a distribution centre for *yerba maté* – a herb brewed to make a tea-like drink.

ARRIVAL AND DEPARTURE — PONTA PORÃ

By bus Frequent buses to Campo Grande (9–10 daily; 5hr 30min) and Corumbá (1 daily; 12hr) leave from the main bus station 4km out of town (67 3431 4145).

ACCOMMODATION

Internacional Av Internacional 2604 67 3431 1243. One of the cheapest hotels in town, the popular *Internacional* has simple rooms and friendly service. Rooms overlooking the garden are a little quieter than the others. R$120

Pousada do Bosque Av Presidente Vargas 1151 67 3437 7200, hotelpousadadobosque.com.br. For plush stay it's hard to beat *Pousada do Bosque*, just outside Ponta Porã and surrounded by lush greenery. The old colonial-style building is charming and has a swimming pool as well as a football pitch. R$247

Bonito

Nestling in the Bodoquena hills, around two hours by bus from Miranda, and four from Campo Grande, **BONITO** is a small town, with tourism as the main business. The town comes to life during the main holiday seasons when it's invaded by hordes of young people from southern Brazilian cities, and is always swarming with people looking to visit the excellent **natural attractions** nearby (see page 451) – especially over Christmas and Easter, and in July and August – although the mood, out of season, is surprisingly relaxed and not at all pushy. Situated at the southern edge of the Pantanal, a visit to Bonito can happily be combined with a trip exploring the swamp; indeed, between the two locations it's possible to see a fantastic range of wildlife and several ecological centres.

Culturally Bonito doesn't offer a lot, but in July the four-day **Festival de Inverno** showcases street theatre, art and music.

ARRIVAL AND INFORMATION — BONITO

By bus The rodoviária (67 3255 1606) is located on Rua Aniceto Coehlo, four blocks from the main street Rua Cel. Pilad Rebuá, where many of the town's hotels and most of its tour operators are located. Daily Cruzeiro do Sul buses connect

Bonito with Campo Grande, Corumbá, Dourados and Ponta Porã. You'll need to stay two nights if you want to include even one trip to the caves or rivers (organized tours generally leave around 7.30am), though there are so many possible day- and half-day trips in the area that most people stay longer.

Destinations Campo Grande (3–4 daily; 4–6hr); Corumbá 1 daily Mon–Sat; 5–6hr); Dourados (2 daily; 6hr); Miranda (1 daily; 2hr); Ponta Porã (Mon–Sat 1 daily; 7hr). There are also minibuses operated by Vanzella (T 67 3255 3005, W vanzellatransportes.com.br) to Campo Grande, Dourados, Ponta Porã, and Foz do Iguaçu.

Tourist information The SECTUR tourist information office us at 1780 Rua Coronel Pilad Rebuá (Mon–Sat 9am–5pm; T 67 3255 1449, W turismo.bonito.ms.gov.br and W portalbonito.com.br). Perhaps a better bet are the very helpful staff at the CAT tourist information office at Rodovia Bonito/Guia Lopes Km 0 (Mon–Sat 7am–5pm; T 67 3255 4670).

GETTING AROUND

Taxis Taxis are an easy way of getting about Bonito and its outlying areas, and there are several taxi points in town; Ponto Taxi, Rua Monte Castelo 826 (T 67 3255 1760), charges R$25 a ride in and around town. A cheaper alternative, particularly if you're travelling alone, is taking a *moto-taxi*, or motorbike taxi (R$7 a ride in town, more for trips to sites out of town).

ACCOMMODATION

Finding a place to stay in Bonito should be easy even in **high season**. There is a good number of decent hostels dotted around town and plenty of *pousadas*, which often double up as **tour agencies**. Alternatively, **out-of-town accommodation** is available.

HOTELS AND HOSTELS

Bonito HI Hostel Rua Dr Pires 850 T 67 3255 1022, T 67 3255 1446, W bonitohostel.com.br. Located ten blocks west of the rodoviária and a 20min walk from the town centre, this hostel has a pool, cable TV and hammocks. Dorms and kitchen are kept clean, and the reception staff are very good at helping with trips and transport organization to Bonito's attractions. There are bikes to rent too. Dorms R$60, doubles R$120

Hotel Pousada Águas de Bonito Rua 29 de Maio 1679 T 67 3255 2330, W aguasdebonito.com.br. Romantic *pousada* in town with an eco-conscience. Hammocks in the garden invite relaxation, and there's a sauna, as well as a gym to work off meals from the on-site restaurant, *Encontro das Águas*. The *pousada*'s own travel agency can arrange trips to local attractions. R$420

★ **Muito Bonito Hotel** Rua Coronel Pilad Rebuá 1444 T 67 3255 3077, W pousadamuitobonito.com.br. This *pousada* is on the main road, 500m from the bus station. The staff are very friendly and speak several languages, including English. Rooms are spotless, all with private bathrooms, and there is a pleasant terrace for breakfast. It also has its own tour agency. Minimum stay of two nights in January. R$280

Papaya Hostel Rua Vicente Jacques 1868 T 67 3255 4690, W papayahostelbonito.com. Situated just two blocks from the bus station this hostel has a small pool, English-speaking owners, an outdoor kitchen and hammocks. It offers clean dorms with en-suite bathrooms, as well as private rooms. Great buffet breakfast with homemade cake, fresh juice and cheese and ham. Owners are happy to help book tours both in Bonito and Pantanal. Cash only. Dorms R$60, doubles R$185

Paraíso das Águas Rua Coronel Pilad Rebuá 1884 T 67 3255 1296, W paguas.com.br. You can't get more central than this tidy, welcoming and attractive *pousada* opposite the popular Taboa Bar. There's a pool and modern rooms come with a/c, TV and *frigobar*. Most have views onto the main strip below, but noise levels don't tend to be too much of a problem. R$300

★ **Pousada Olho d'Agua** Rod Bonito Tres Morros Km 1 T 67 3255 1430, W pousadaolhodagua.com.br. Set 3km from the centre on the northwestern end of town, this is no less luxurious than the *Zagaia Eco-Resort*, but arguably more personal and affordable. Offers delightful bungalow accommodation in intimate wooded surroundings, with excellent service and food, and its own tour agency. R$302

Pousada Remanso Av Cel Pilad Rebuá T 3255 1137, W pousadaremanso.com.br. Set on the main strip with quiet rooms facing the back rather than the street this clean *pousada* offers a small swimming pool, hammocks and a buffet breakfast. Staff do not speak English, but are friendly. There's also an affiliated travel agency. R$220

Zagaia Eco-Resort 2km from the centre by the airfield T 67 3255 5500, W zagaia.com.br. Top of the range, ultra-modern complex with three swimming pools, various playing fields, sports fishing, numerous restaurants and even a cabaret – popular with holiday-makers from Rio. R$747

CAMPING

There is a good range of campsites around the Bonito area; you can get their details from the travel agents in town or, in advance, from one of the tourist information offices in Campo Grande (see page 444).

7

Camping do Peralta 67 3255 1901. On the outskirts of town. Per person R$30

Camping Nomadas 67 3255 1729. Near the bus station. Camping/person R$30, chalets/person R$50

EATING AND DRINKING

Cantinho do Peixe Rua Coronel Pilad Rebuá 1437 67 3255 3381. A popular spot with locals, this fish restaurant set in a modern building on the main road serves huge portions of *jacare* (alligator), *pintado* (catfish) and *pacú* (local river fish). Service is good and some of the waiters speak English. Mon–Sat 11.30am–3pm & 6–11pm.

★**Casa do João** Rua Nelson Felicio dos Santos 664 casadojoao.com.br. Wonderful, down-to-earth family-run restaurant specializing in Pantanal cuisine. Try the *traira* (a carnivorous river fish) as a starter (R$38) or the baked *pintado* (river fish) with cheese (R$69). Meat dishes include the filet mignon with rice and chips (R$57). The restaurant was once the owners' family home, and all of the furniture is recycled. Daily except Tues 11am–3pm & 6.30–11pm.

★**Juanita** Rua Nossa Senhora da Penha 854 67 3255 1924, facebook.com/juanitarestaurante. This very popular restaurant set in a yellow house with an inviting veranda specializes in *pacu na brasa*, grilled fresh-water fish (R$89; most portions serve two). Be prepared to wait for a table during high season. Daily except Tues 11am–2.30pm & 6.30–10.30pm.

Pousada Olho d'Agua Estrada Baia das Garças 67 3255 1430. Located 3km from the centre on the northwestern end of town, the restaurant at this pretty *pousada* serves high-quality meals at lunchtime and in the evenings, including pasta, fish and meat dishes; it's best to call to reserve a table in high season. Mains are R$27.20–58.30. Daily noon–3pm & 6.30–11.30pm.

Pastel do Zé Praça da Liberdade on Rua 15 de Novembro. This no-fills place with plastic chairs is where the locals hang out to munch on homemade and very affordable *pastels* (deep-fried *empanadas*) and drink ice-cold beer looking out over the main plaza. The stuffed *empanadas* come straight from the deep fryer – try the one with *carne de sol* and cheese (R$13). Mon–Sat 6–10pm.

Taboa Bar Rua Coronel Pilad Rebuá 1834 67 3255 3598. Graffitied walls, live music and an extensive menu ranging from grilled chicken with rice and buttered vegetables, to soups and salads, make this bar a popular hangout for a twenty- and thirty-something crowd. As the night progresses, you're likely to see Brazilians get up and dance – especially on weekends. Daily 6pm–2am.

Vicio da Gula Rua Coronel Pilad Rebuá 1852 67 3255 2041, facebook.com/viciodagulacafe. Popular and inexpensive corner café in the centre with outside seating, serving exotic fruit juices and milkshakes, burgers (including alligator), sandwiches, and myriad delicious cakes. Daily except Tues 3–11.30pm.

DIRECTORY

Hospital Hospital Municipal (67 3255 3455).

Money and exchange Bradesco, Rua Coronel Pilad Rebuá 1942; Banco do Brasil, Rua Luis da Costa Leite 2279, by the central square.

Pharmacy Farmácia Drogacruz, Rua Coronel Pilad Rebuá 1629.

Post office On the main street Rua Coronel Pilad Rebua 1759 (Mon–Fri 8am–noon and 1–4.30pm).

Around Bonito

The dirt tracks that make up most of the roads around Bonito conceal the fact that ever since the area starred as an "undiscovered" ecological paradise on TV Globo in 1993, it has become one of Brazil's major **ecotourism** destinations. The region is teeming with nature reserves, and boasts crystal-clear rivers and waterfalls for swimming and river snorkelling, interesting caves and excellent opportunities for walking.

Gruta do Lago Azul

20km from Bonito • Daily 7am–2pm • Entrance fee including guide: low season R$50, high season R$65; no children under 5

The **Gruta do Lago Azul** is a large, deep, cathedral-like cave, out beyond the town's tiny municipal airstrip. It's set in forested hills rich in limestone, granite and marble, and full of minerals, as well as a growing number of mercury, uranium and phosphorus mines. Even before the mines, though, these hills, which reach up to about 800m above sea level, were full of massive caves, most of them inaccessible and on private *fazenda* land.

TRIPS FROM BONITO

Bonito's tour companies are unusually well tuned in to the requirements of overseas visitors, and all offer identical trips at identical prices to all the places described here, plus a wide range of other options. The municipality limits the number of visitors to Bonito's natural wonders and systematically enforces a whole array of regulations intended to protect this ecologically "pure" region. Many of the sites charge for entry, and for some, such as the famous Gruta do Lago Azul and Rio da Prata, a guided visit is required. Such **permits** and guides are arranged by the tour companies or hotels themselves. Alternatively, some sites have their own guides. Several hotels, like *Pousada Olho d'Agua* and *Muito Bonito*, have their own tour agencies or can help you arrange a trip with one of the tour companies. Note that very few guides speak English, so if you need an **English-speaking guide** you must request this when you book with an agency or at the hotel. With advance warning, an interpreter or bilingual guide can be organized for an extra fee; the local tour guides association is AGTB (T 67 3255 1837).

Tour companies include: Ygarapé Tours, Rua Coronel Pilad Rebuá 1853 (T 67 3255 1733, W agenciaygarape.com.br), who also offer scuba diving for beginners; Bonitour, Rua Coronel Pilad Rebuá 1957 (T 67 3255 1628, W bonitour.com.br).

INDEPENDENT TRAVEL

Almost all the sites require transport, which makes it virtually impossible to visit them independently. Some hotels, like *Pousada Muito Bonito*, can arrange daily **car rental** for around R$150, and along Rua Coronel Pilad Rebuá you can **rent a bicycle** for the day for around R$30. Another cheap option if you're on your own is to go by **moto-taxi** – there's a firm on almost every corner or you can ask your hotel to order you one. There are a few **minivan** companies that go to the main sights every day at a certain time too – find out their schedules from any of the tour agencies in town.

7

Rediscovered in 1924 by the local Terena people, the entrance to the cave is quite spectacular. Surrounded by some 61 acres of ecological reserve woodland, it has the appearance of a monstrous mouth inviting you into the heart of the earth. At first you climb down a narrow path through vegetation, then deeper down into dripping stalactite territory some 100m below, to the mists hovering above the cave's lake. The Pre-Cambrian rocks of the cave walls are striated like the skin of an old elephant and there are weird rock formations such as the easily recognized natural Buddha. Light streams in from the semicircular cave opening, but only penetrates right to the lake level in the bottom of the cave for 45 minutes on 30 days each year.

Since 1989 a number of expeditions have attempted to fathom the depths of the lake, but with no success (80m is the deepest exploration to date). One of these, a joint French-Brazilian expedition, discovered the bones of prehistoric animals (including a sabre-toothed tiger) and even human remains. The blue waters of the lake extend into the mountain for at least another 300m and are exceptionally clear, with only shrimps and other crustacea able to survive in the calcified water.

Bring closed footwear such as trainers or hiking boots to visit the caves, which can be slippery; visitors wearing flip-flops or sandals will be denied entry.

The Aquário Natural

6km from Bonito • Daily 8am–7pm • Half-day price R$231 (including guide, permit and access to snorkelling equipment and boats) • W aquarionatural.com.br

The **Aquário Natural** complex is justifiably Bonito's next most popular attraction. Located at the source of the Baia Bonita, the Aquário is an incredibly clear spring that is full of fish. Visitors are encouraged to put on a floating jacket, mask and snorkel, and get into the water with the 35 or so species of fish – mainly *dourado* and 35cm *piripitanga* fishes – a ticklish experience with no danger from piranhas, which never swim this far upriver. The sanctuary is accessible by a path from the reception through a swamp and zoo of Pantanal animals – the Trilha dos Animais – home to white-collared peccaries, deer and the majestic *caramugeiro* snail hawk. From the Aquário, the **Bahia Bonita**, a kilometre-long stretch of river, runs down to meet the Rio Formoso, where there's a death-slide (a pulley and rope system for exciting splashdowns into the river).

Tour companies also offer snorkelling trips to the **Nascente Rio Sucuri** (R$202 full day) and the **Rio da Prata** (R$210 full day).

Ecopark Porto da Ilha

13km from Bonito • Daily 9am–5.30pm • Full-day whitewater rafting and stand-up paddle-boarding R$219 • T 67 3255 3021

Around 13km from Bonito down the Rio Formoso, there's an interesting island that has been turned into a public nature reserve, known as the **Ecopark Porto da Ilha**. The Ilha do Padre is surrounded by waterfalls and covers almost twelve acres. Whitewater rafting down to the island (sometimes done by moonlight) is one of the more exciting options available from tour agents in Bonito. Other options include "Bóia Cross" – floating down the river on a rubber tyre, and stand-up paddle-boarding – standing on a surfboard and steering down the river using an oar.

The Formoso is an active whitewater-rafting river (although the rafting itself is very tranquil), though there are also delightful natural swimming spots, lots of exotic birdlife and lush vegetation. It's not quite as beautiful as the Aquário Natural at the river's source, but still very pleasant. Come prepared for biting flies and mosquitoes, and note that the island is annoyingly busy at peak holiday times (such as Easter).

Nascente Azul

Rodovia Bonito, Bodoquena Km 22 • Daily 8am–5pm • Half-day R$200 • T 67 3255 2297, W nascenteazul.com.br

Named "blue spring" because of its turquoise colour, the **Nascente Azul**, 29km from Bonito's centre, offers forty-minute river-snorkelling trips that begin with a 1.8km trail through a forest, passing waterfalls on the way. The spring is 8m deep and full of river fish. There's also a restaurant serving local dishes.

Abismo Anhumas

23km from Bonito • Call for times • R$1270 (rappel and scuba diving) • T 67 3255 3313, W abismoanhumas.com.br

Those seeking a unique adventure will love the **Abismo Anhumas**, 23km from Bonito. This otherworldly abyss has a depth of 72m and is accessed by rappelling down (you need to attend a training session at General Osório 681 in town the day before). Once down, you can admire the majestic stalactite formations before snorkelling or diving (for the latter you need to be certified) in the water, where stalagmites are clearly visible. There's a limit of twenty visitors per day, so be sure to book ahead.

Balneario Municipal

Km 7 on road towards Jardim • Daily 9am–6pm • R$36

Just outside Bonito is the **Balneario Municipal**, a cheap and easy half-day out. It may not be as impressive as the Aquārio Natural, but nevertheless the water is clean and teeming with fish. Snorkelling equipment is available but not necessary as the river is shallow and clear. Swimming in the balneario is hugely refreshing during the hot summer months, but try to get there early as it gets busy during high season. This spot is particularly popular with families and teenagers.

Aquidauana and around

AQUIDAUANA, 140km from Campo Grande, is a lazy-looking place and very hot, sitting under the beating sun of the Piraputanga uplands. Since the demise of passenger trains to Corumbá, it sweats somewhat uncomfortably some distance from the main BR-262 highway, and, though it still serves as one of several gateways into the Pantanal, it's better known for fishing and walking, with some superb views across the swamp. These days, most visitors see little more than the signpost at the crossroads where the highway bypasses the town; if you stop by here, it'll most likely be to use the highway café or toilet facilities at the junction. If you do go into town or stay over here, it's worth enquiring about two nearby but seldom visited sites: the ruins of the **Cidade de Xaraés**, founded by the Spanish in 1580 on the banks of the Rio Aquidauana; and the **Morro do Desenho**, a series of prehistoric inscriptions on the riverbank and in the nearby hills.

The river running through the town boasts some pleasant sandy **beaches**, quite clean and safe for swimming between May and October, and **fishing** championships are an integral part of the annual São João in June festival here.

The neighbouring town (and transport hub) **ANASTÁCIO** – half an hour's walk on the other side of the river – has some nice beaches of its own, but it is best known for the large *jaú* fish (often weighing over 75kg) that live in its river.

7

ARRIVAL AND DEPARTURE — AQUIDAUANA AND AROUND

By bus Several daily buses connect Campo Grande with Aquidauana and Anastácio (2hr), and onwards to Corumbá (7hr). Anastácio is the transport hub of the region, with daily bus services to Bela Vista, Bonito, Miranda and Ponta Porã. Many of the lodges in the Southern Pantanal (see page 463) can be accessed from here via private transfer.

ACCOMMODATION AND EATING

Cabana do Pescador 50km south of Aquidauana just off the BR-419 road towards Bonito ☎67 3255 4981, cabanadopescador.com.br. Luxury fishing lodge on the Rio Miranda, which is a possible base from which to go fishing, horse-riding or take a tour to the Bonito caves (see page 450). The fish-shaped pool is lit up at night. R$360

O Casarão Rua Manoel Antônio Paes de Barros 533 ☎67 3241 2219, facebook.com/ocasaraoaquidauana. One of several decent restaurants in town is the cosy *O Casarão*. This is an expensive spot that serves delicious, though not exclusively Brazilian, dishes and specializes in local fish. The self-service option is good value for money (R$29). Mon–Sat noon–2.30pm & 6.30–11pm, Sun 1–3pm.

Portal Pantaneiro Rua Pandiá Calógeras 1067 ☎67 3241 4329, portalpantaneiro.com.br. Kitted out with local art, this light and airy hotel has a lovely swimming pool and very comfortable rooms with a/c, *frigobar* and TV. The pretty garden is lined with palm trees. R$160

Pousada Pequi Rodovia Br 262 Km 48 ☎67 3245 0949, pousadapequi.com.br. A comfortable lodge by the river with rustic decor, a swimming pool and a restaurant serving hearty Brazilian food. Horse, vehicle and boat expeditions are also available and activities from here include fishing for piranhas. Full board R$900

Miranda

Seventy kilometres northwest of Anastácio, the small town of **MIRANDA** sits straddling the BR-262 at the foot of the Serra da Bodoquena by the Rio Miranda. Once the scene of historic battles, Miranda has been somewhat ignored by visitors since the demise of the old Campo Grande to Corumbá rail service, but it's a pleasant town that is known for excellent fishing and for producing Terena and Kadiwéu artefacts. It's also a good base for visiting Bonito (130km) or the Southern Pantanal swamp (see page 463).

ARRIVAL AND DEPARTURE — MIRANDA

By bus There are six daily buses from Campo Grande to Miranda (3hr 30min).

ACCOMMODATION AND EATING

Hotel Chalé Rua Barão do Rio Branco 685 ☎67 3242 1216, hotelchalems.com.br. A cheap option just up the road from the BR-262. Clean rooms, some newer than others, all with a/c. Family rooms are also available and

THE TERENA

The **Serra de Maracaju** near Campo Grande provided sanctuary for local **Terena** during a period of Paraguayan military occupation in the 1860s. Under their highly ambitious dictator, Solano López, the Paraguayans invaded the southern Mato Grosso in 1864, a colonial adventure that resulted in the death of over half the invasion force, mostly composed of native (Paraguayan) Guaraní. This was one period in Brazilian history when whites and indigenous tribes fought for the same cause, and it was in the magnificent Serra de Maracaju hills that most of the guerrilla-style resistance took place.

The late nineteenth century saw an influx of Brazilian colonists into the Aquidauana and Miranda valleys as the authorities attempted to "populate" the regions between Campo Grande and Paraguay – the war with Paraguay had only made them aware of how fertile these valleys were. Pushed off the best of the land and forced, in the main, to work for new, white landowners, the Terena tribe remained vulnerable until the appearance of **Lieutenant Rondon** (after whom the Amazonian state of Rondônia was named). Essentially an engineer, he came across the Terena in 1903 after constructing a telegraph connection – poles, lines and all – through virtually impassable swamps and jungle between Cuiabá and Corumbá. With his help, the Terena managed to establish a legal claim to some of their traditional land. Considered by FUNAI (the federal agency for indigenous affairs) to be one of the most successfully "integrated" tribal groups in modern Brazil, the Terena have earned a reputation for possessing the necessary drive and ability to compete successfully in the market system –a double-edged compliment in that it could be used by the authorities to undermine their rights to land as a tribal group. They live mostly between Aquidauana and Miranda, the actual focus of their territory being the town and train station of **Taunay** – an interesting settlement with mule-drawn taxi wagons and a peaceful atmosphere. You'll find Terena handicrafts on sale in Campo Grande too.

7

there's a pool, unfortunately located next to the car park. R$145

Pantanal Hotel Av Barão do Rio Branco 609 67 3242 1068, pantanalhotel.com.br. The owner of this very welcoming hotel speaks English and can arrange Pantanal tours. The pool is surrounded by trees and you'll likely be swimming and sunbathing under the watchful eye of resident parrots. It also has a pleasant barbecue area and a good restaurant serving beef jerky (R$30) and various fish mains (R$35–R$45). R$245

Pousada Águas do Pantanal Av Afonso Pena 367 67 3242 1242, aguasdopantanal.com.br. This well-known hotel is full of local character and plants, both indoors and outdoors. A lovely pool, excellent service and a huge breakfast help set it apart from nearby competitors. The on-site tour operator offers personalized trips into the Pantanal and Bonito. R$240

Corumbá and around

Far removed from mainstream Brazil, hard by the Bolivian border and about 400km west of Campo Grande, the city of **CORUMBÁ** provides a welcome stop after the long ride from either Santa Cruz (in Bolivia) or Campo Grande. As an entrance to the Southern Pantanal, Corumbá has the edge over Cuiabá in that it is already there, stuck in the middle of a gigantic swamp, only 116m above sea level, but only really makes a good spring board to Pantanal if you are coming from Bolivia. Commanding a fine view over the Rio Paraguai and across the swamp, the city is small (around 100,000 inhabitants), and is one of Brazil's most laidback places south of the Amazon, basking in intense heat and overwhelming humidity. Even at the port nothing seems to disturb the slow-moving pool games taking place in the bars. There's a very open-plan feel to the city, and the people of Corumbá seem to be equally at home sitting at tables by bars and restaurants, or eating their dinners outside in front of their houses. It's not unusual to be invited into someone's house for food, drinks or – at weekends – a party.

For the party of all parties, time your visit to coincide with Corumbá's **Carnaval** in mid-February, said to be one of the best in Brazil.

Brief history

Corumbá's name, in Tupi, means the "place of stones" and, not surprisingly, Corumbá and the Pantanal didn't start out as a great source of attraction to travellers. As early as 1543, the swamp proved an inhospitable place to an expedition of 120 large canoes on a punitive campaign against the Guaicuru tribe. Sent by the Spanish governor of Paraguay, it encountered vampire bats, stingrays, biting ants and plagues of mosquitoes. And while it doesn't seem quite so bad today, it's easy to understand why air conditioning is such big business here. It was Corumbá's unique location on the old rail link between the Andes and the Atlantic that originally brought most travellers to the town, but, ironically, the same swamp that deterred European invaders for so long has rapidly become an attraction, at the same time that the Brazilian part of the rail link has been closed down.

Praça da Independência and around

Corumbá's life revolves around its **port**, while its transport connections are at the other end of town around the rodoviária and airport; if you're intending to stay more than one night, the port end is your best bet. Within a few blocks of the riverfront you'll find the **Praça da Independência**, a large, shaded park with ponds, a children's playground and a few unusual installations dotted around: a steamroller, imported from England around 1921, whose first job was flattening Avenida General Rondon, and an antique water wheel, also English, which served in a sugar factory until 1932. Early in the day, the *praça* is alive with tropical birds, and by evening it's crowded with couples, family groups and gangs of children relaxing as the temperature begins to drop. The large but otherwise unimpressive church on this square is useful as a prominent landmark to help you get your bearings in this very flat, grid-patterned city.

A block away from the Praça da Independência is the smaller **Praça da República.** On this square stands the stark late nineteenth-century Igreja Matriz Nossa Senhora da Candelária.

Museu de Corumbá

Instituto Luiz de Albuquerque, Rua Delamare 939 • Mon–Fri 7.30–11.30am & 1.30–5.30pm • Free

Facing the local bus terminal is the fascinating **Museu de Corumbá**, which encompasses a collection of indigenous and local artwork, artefacts from the colonial era and an archive of photos that depict Corumbá's colourful history. The museum was closed for restoration at the time of research.

Museu de História do Pantanal (MUHPAN)

Manoel Cassava 275 • Tues–Sat 1–5.30pm • Free • 67 3232 0303, museumuhpan.blogspot.com.br

Corumbá's star attraction is the **Museu de História do Pantanal**, better known as **MUHPAN**. This attractive museum housed in a nineteenth-century building by the port features permanent and temporary exhibitions that focus on the Pantanal's identity. Through informative displays (although only in Spanish and Portuguese), it explores the Pantanal's archeology and the history of human occupation in the region, and the relationship between the two.

ARRIVAL AND GETTING AROUND — CORUMBÁ AND AROUND

By plane The airport (67 3232 3023) is a R$35 taxi ride west of the city centre.

Destinations 4 flights a week (Azul) to São Paulo.

By bus The rodoviária is close to the old train station on Rua Porto Carreiro (67 3231 2033) and is served by daily buses from Campo Grande, Bonito and Ponta Porã. From the rodoviária, it's a 15min walk into town, or there are buses and taxis (R$25) plying the route.

Destinations Anastácio (5 daily; 4hr 25min), Bonito (1 daily; 5hr) Campo Grande via Aquidauana and Miranda (12 daily; 7hr; change in Campo Grande for most onward destinations).

By boat There are plenty of boats waiting on the riverfront off Rua Manoel Cavassa that will take you into the Pantanal swamp or to Bolivia. Ask around at the offices on the waterfront or arrange your boat trip in advance with one of the travel agencies in town.

By car Car rental: Localiza/Hertz is at the airport (Mon–Fri 1–3pm, Sun 12.30–2pm; ⓣ 67 3232 6000, ⓦ localizahertz.com) as well as the centre, Rua Edu Rocha 969 (Mon–Fri 8am–6pm, Sat 8am–6pm; ⓣ 67 3232 6000).

Taxis Ponto Taxi (ⓣ 67 3231 4043; taxi rank at southeast corner of Praça da Independência); Mototaxis (ⓣ 67 3231 7166).

INFORMATION AND TOURS

Corumbá does not have an official tourism office, so your best bet is to ask the staff at your lodging. Budget Pantanal tours are run by the cheap hotels around Rua Delamare, whose touts will probably find you as soon as you get off the bus. Make

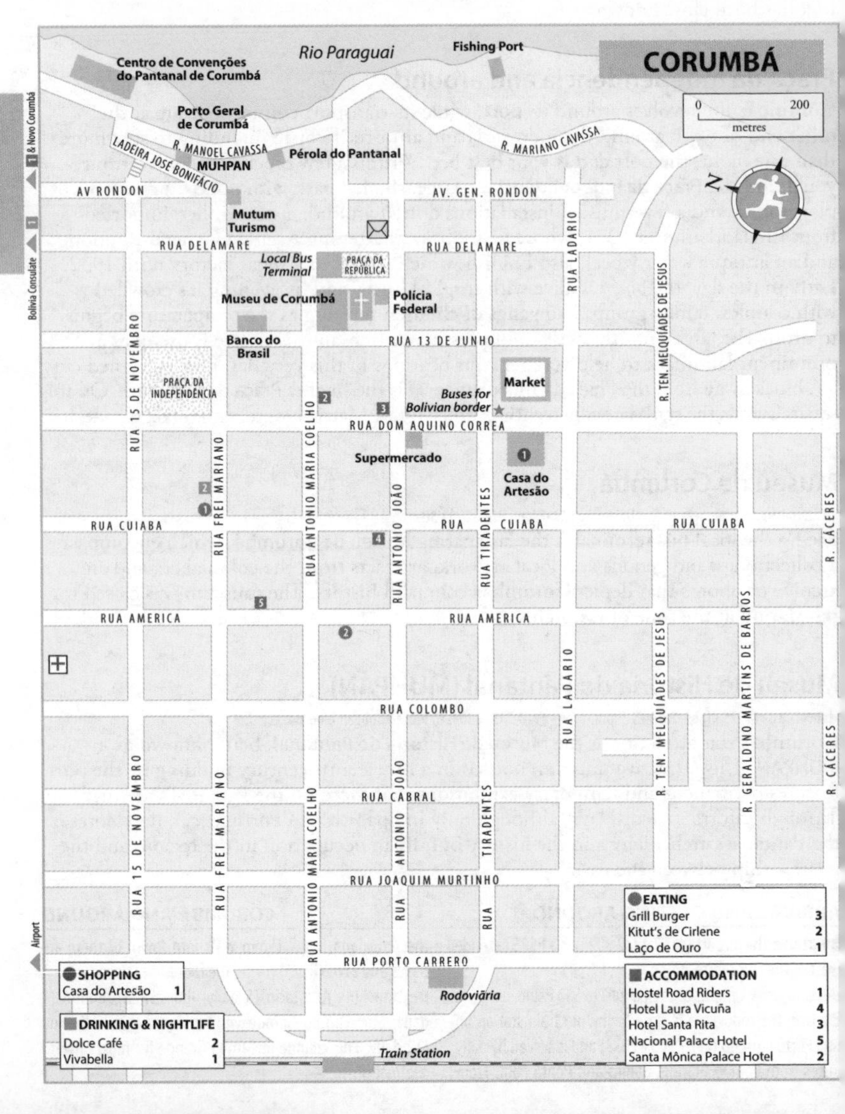

CROSSING THE BORDER TO BOLIVIA FROM CORUMBÁ

To get to the border crossing you take the **bus** from the Praça Independência on Rua Dom Aquino Corréa or a taxi (around R$40). Leaving Brazil, you should get an **exit stamp** from the Polícia Federal at the border (Mon–Fri 8–11am & 2–5pm, Sat & Sun 9am–1pm), before checking through Bolivian immigration and receiving your passport entry stamp. Most countries don't need a **visa** to enter Bolivia, but if you are from the US you should get one from abroad or pick up your Bolivian visa from the consulate at Rua Sete de Setembro 47 in Corumbá (T 67 3231 5605), before you make your way to the border crossing. Entering Brazil from Bolivia is essentially the same procedure in reverse, although US, Australian and Canadian citizens should remember to apply online for their visas at least 72 hours in advance (see page 27).

For **onward travel** in Bolivia, train tickets for Santa Cruz should be bought at La Brasilena train station in Puerto Quijarro, 15min by bus from the Bolivian immigration office at the border. The regular Tren Regional is the cheapest train and departs once a day from Monday to Saturday (19.30hr); the Expreso Oriental leaves on Tuesday, Thursday and Sunday and takes 16 hours; Ferrobus is the fanciest and most expensive of the three, leaving on Tuesday, Thursday and Saturday, taking 14 hours. If travelling on the regular service, bring food, as well as insect repellent, as the lights of the carriages can attract insects at night. Drinking water and a torch are also useful. As timetables vary considerably, check at the station in Corumbá or Quijarro at least a couple of days in advance. It's worth going to Quijarro the day before departure to actually make your booking.

Money can be changed at decent rates at the border.

7

sure you get authorized receipts for any money or valuables you deposit with a tour company or hotel; there have been reports of problems with this kind of practice in Corumbá.

Mutum Turismo Rua Frei Mariano 17 T 67 3231 1818, W mutumturismo.com.br. Deals with flights and ticketing.

Pérola do Pantanal Rua Manoel Cavassa 275 T 67 3231 1460, W peroladopantanal.com.br. Agents for high-end cruises to the Pantanal from Corumbá.

ACCOMMODATION

Hotels in Corumbá vary considerably but their sheer quantity means you should have no trouble finding a room, even from August to October. Out of season, especially January to Easter, there are heavy **discounts**, and prices can be bargained even lower. The most centrally located for shops and the port, and so noisiest at night, is the clutch of cheap (and a bit run down) lodgings around **Rua Delamare**, west of Praça da República. It's worth staying elsewhere.

Hostel Road Riders Rua Firmo de Matos 1 T 67 3232 8143, W hostelroadriders.com.br; map p.456. Set In beautiful villa in a quiet part of town this hostel offers spacious dorms with a veranda looking out over the river. Most staff speak very little English, but owner, Diego, is a true traveller, knows all the best spots in the city and gladly chats with his guests when he is around. Dorms R$50

Hotel Laura Vicuña Rua Cuiabá 775 T 67 3231 5874, W hotellauravicuna.com.br; map p.456. A peaceful place within walking distance of the shops and restaurants. Rooms are very neat and tidy in a traditional fashion, although bathrooms are rather basic. All rooms have phone, TV and a/c. R$150

Hotel Santa Rita Rua Dom Aquino Corréa 860 T 67 3231 5453; map p.456. Rooms are clean and airy at this good-value hotel and the more expensive ones come with a/c and TV. There's also a reasonable on-site restaurant. R$180

Nacional Palace Hotel Rua América 936 T 67 3234 6000, W hnacional.com.br; map p.456. Pretty much top of the range in Corumbá. It's convenient and has a pool complete with water slide (non-residents can use it for R$25) as well as gym equipment, a barbecue area and a snooker table. A whole new building with rooms was also under construction at the time of research. R$315

Santa Mônica Palace Hotel Rua Antônio Maria Coelho 345 T 67 3234 3000, W hsantamonica.com.br; map p.456. Corumbá's largest hotel and best mid-range option in an excellent location. Offers good value for money: the rooms are neat and come with all mod cons including a/c and fridges, and the added luxuries of a pool (non-residents can use it for R$30) and sauna. Ask for a room that doesn't look out onto the street, as these can be noisy. R$262

EATING

There are some decent restaurants in Corumbá and plenty of cheap snack bars throughout town, especially on **Rua Delamare** west of the Praça da República, serving good set meals for around R$20. Being a swamp city, fish is the main local delicacy, with *pacu* and *pintado* among the favoured species.

Grill Burger Rua Eugênio Cunha 11, Maria Leite 67 3232 9974, facebook.com/Grillburgerr; map p.456. A no-frills burger joint a R$20 taxi ride from the centre, this place is well worth the transport cost, and is where the locals come to munch on savoury burgers with plenty of trimmings. The combo deals (R$14–24) with a burger, fries and a drink are very good value. Daily 6.30pm–midnight.

Kitut's de Cirlene Rua America 797 67 3231 8083; map p.456. This family-run restaurant is simply decorated and specializes in local river fish. Try the *pintado à urucum* (R$58) – a lasagne-like dish with fish that comes with plenty of cheese and all the usual trimmings like boiled manioc and *farofa* with banana. Daily 7.30pm–midnight.

Laço de Ouro Rua Frei Mariano 534 67 3232 5555; map p.456. A favourite among locals, this *churrascaria* offers the classic meat *rodizio* as well as à la carte options that include good fish dishes. Also has pleasant outdoor seating and occasional live music. Daily 11am–11pm.

7

DRINKING AND NIGHTLIFE

You'll find bars all over town, though with few exceptions they're spit-and-sawdust joints, rough-looking and a little intimidating at first. The town is not safe at night, so you do need to take care and try to avoid walking the streets after 10pm. The more relaxed bars are those down on the **riverfront** – where you can usually get a game of pool with your drink.

Dolce Café Rua Frei Mariano 572 67 3232 7333, facebook.com/dolcecafecorumba; map p.456. This very popular and spacious restaurant has plenty of outside seating and serves both a good value lunch and dinner buffet (starting from R$45) as well as fish and meat dishes. It's also great for grabbing a beer or sharing a bottle of wine in the evening. There is live music on some evenings. Daily 11am–1am.

Vivabella Arthur Mangabeira 1 67 3232 3396; map p.456. Restaurant-bar with wonderful views of the river, serving ice-cold beer and caipirinhas to locals who mainly come for the quality live music. Get there early on weekends as it gets pretty busy. Tues–Sat 6pm–late.

SHOPPING

Casa do Artesão Rua Dom Aquino Corréa 405 67 3231 2715; map p.456. Housed in Corumbá's most historic edifice – the old prison, dating from 1900 – the Casa do Artesão is a great place to track down some local craft work (especially made of wood and leather), as well as local liquors and *farinha da bocaiúva*, a flour made from palm-tree nuts and reputed to be an aphrodisiac. Mon–Fri 8–11am & 2–5pm, Sat 8–11am.

DIRECTORY

Consulates Bolivia, Rua Sete de Setembro 47 (67 3231 5605); Paraguay, Av Rio Branco 182 B (67 3232 5203).

Hospital Clinica Samec, Rua Colombo 1249 (67 3231 3004).

Laundry Lavanderia Quality, Rua América 311.

Money and exchange For changing money to Bolivian pesos the exchange rate is better at the border than in town. Otherwise, there's a host of banks (some with ATMs) including the Banco do Brasil, Rua 13 de Junho 914 (10am–5pm).

Post office Rua Delamare 708, opposite the church on Praça da República (Mon–Fri 9am–5pm, Sat 8–11.30am).

Forte de Coimbra

80km south of Corumbá • Daily 8.30–11am & 1.30–4pm • Free • 67 3231 2701

Apart from the Pantanal, the most interesting place to visit around Corumbá is the ruin of the eighteenth-century **Forte de Coimbra**, 80km to the south. Theoretically, the fort can only be visited with previous permission from the Exercito Brasileiro in Corumbá, although visitors unaware of this fact are sometimes allowed in: call for authorization.

The Forte de Coimbra was built in 1775, three years before Corumbá's foundation, to defend this western corner of Brazilian territory and, more specifically, to protect the border against invasion from Paraguay. In 1864 it was attacked by the invading

Paraguayan army, which had slipped upriver into the southern Mato Grosso. Coimbra provided the first resistance to the invaders, but it didn't last for long as the Brazilian soldiers escaped from the fort under cover of darkness, leaving the fort to the aggressors. Nearly three thousand Paraguayans continued upstream in a huge convoy of ships and, forging its way north beyond Corumbá, the armada crossed the swamps almost as far as the city of Cuiabá, which was saved only by the shallowness of its river. Nowadays the fort is a pretty dull ruin (except perhaps for military enthusiasts), and it's the boat journey there that's the real draw.

ARRIVAL AND DEPARTURE — FORTE DE COIMBRA

By car and boat The fort is only accessible by water, and is most easily reached via Porto Morrinho, just over an hour's drive from Corumbá's airport. The journey there is an interesting one along the edge of the swamp, and once there you should have little difficulty renting a boat, or finding a guide, to take you a couple more hours downriver to the fort (it will cost at least R$80, however).

By boat from Corumbá It's also possible to approach the fort in traditional fashion, by following the Rio Paraguai all the way from Corumbá in a boat (from around R$300 per tour, depending on the size of your group), but this takes around 7hr one-way and involves going through a tour agency in town. One bonus of going by this route, however, is that you'll pass two little-visited natural caves, Gruta do Inferno and Buraco Soturno, sculpted with huge finger-like stalactites and stalagmites.

The Pantanal

Increasingly known worldwide as the best place for wildlife spotting in South America, the **Pantanal** is fed by rivers and inhabited by rainforest bird and animal species from the Andes to the west and the Brazilian central plateau to the north. Essentially an open swampland larger than France that extends deep into the states of Mato Grosso and Mato Grosso do Sul, it is massive, running 600km north to south. Although the area has only thirty percent natural forest cover, over 4.5 percent of the trees (some 6260 square kilometres) have already been destroyed by human activity – mainly cattle ranching. The region is a stunning blend of swamp water with gallery forest, savannah and lakeside scrub forest, and it is dissected by around 175 rivers into roughly seventeen segments, each with its own distinctive landscape and micro-ecosystem. It was designated a **UNESCO World Heritage Site** in 2000 and is also a Biosphere Reserve; the protected areas of the Pantanal have expanded almost threefold since the late 1990s. This is one of those few destinations in Brazil where you're more likely to find wildlife than nightlife. Capybaras, wild boar, monkeys and yellow anacondas (*sucuri amarela* in Portuguese or *Eunectes notaeus*) all live here, and it's probably the best place to see wild mammals and exotic birds in the whole of the Americas.

You'll find a wide array of wild mammals, reptiles and amphibians in these swamps, plus over 600 bird species. It's quite an experience spending the afternoon on the edge of a remote lagoon in the swamp, surrounded by seemingly endless streams of flying and wading **birds** – toucans, parrots, red and hyacinth macaws, blue herons and the *tuiuiú* (giant red-necked stork). The birdsong and density of wildlife here frequently live up to the exotic soundtrack of Hollywood jungle movies, and in the middle of the swamp it's possible to forget that there are other people in the world – though it's difficult to forget the mosquitoes (although locals say that yellow fever is no longer a big problem in the Pantanal, it is advisable to check with your doctor before departure). The swamp has been a fabulous **fishing spot** for thousands of years and new species of fish and vascular plants are still regularly discovered here. In addition to all this wildlife, it's only fair to mention that you'll still see more cattle and *yacare* caiman (South American alligators) than any other creature, with the exception of **Porto Jofre** (see page 465) where it's common to see up to four or five jaguar sightings in a day, which draws in visitors who run up and down the rivers in speed boats during the dry season.

The southern and northern ends of the Pantanal have the same flora as they are both swampland. In terms of wildlife, they offer similar experiences but each has its own advantage. The animals you see are generally the same, but the **Southern Pantanal** is supposed to offer more chances to spot anteaters and armadillos, and it has more budget options for backpackers. The **Northern Pantanal** is better for those interested in seeing giant otters and jaguars, and the higher prices of tours generally reflects a higher-quality service, though it is possible to find a range of prices in both areas.

When to visit

Although you can visit the Pantanal any time of year, the **dry season**, from April to October, with its peak normally around September, is when you'll see the biggest congregation of wildlife. This is the time when much of the fauna is attracted to the lakes and riverbanks in search of food and water: the swamp's infamous piranha and caiman (South American alligator) populations crowd into relatively small pools and streams, while the astonishing array of aquatic birds follows suit, forming very dense colonies known here as *viveiros*. Treeless bush savannah alternates with wet swamp, while along the banks of the major rivers belts of rainforest grow, populated with troops of monkeys (including capuchin and howler monkeys). Perhaps most importantly, the dry season is when you're almost guaranteed to spot jaguars in the Northern Pantanal as they come to the riverbank for water and to hunt – they retreat deeper into the swamp during rainy season.

During the **rainy season**, from November to March, river levels rise by up to 3m, producing a vast flooded plain with islands of scrubby forest amid oceans of floating vegetation. Deeper into the swamp, transport is necessarily dominated by the rivers, natural water channels and hundreds of well-hidden lagoons, though most of the *fazendas* are still reachable by road. The islands of vegetation created during the rains crawl with wild animals – jaguars, monkeys, tapirs, capybaras (the world's largest rodents) and wild boar, living side by side with domesticated cattle. Many birds are harder to spot, nesting deeper in the forests for the breeding season; nevertheless, there are still plenty of birds and other creatures to see year-round, including hawks and kingfishers.

Note, however, that the previously metronomic regularity of the seasons has become more unpredictable, with the onset of **climate change**, and the "rainy season" isn't actually that rainy: when it does rain, it's usually a tropical downpour that tends to last no more than a couple of hours, and you can still expect glorious sunshine during most days. At other times of the year, much of the Pantanal is still very boggy, though interspersed with open grassy savannah that is studded with small wooded islands of taller vegetation (mainly palm trees).

ARRIVAL AND TOURS — THE PANTANAL

There are three main entry points to the Pantanal: **Corumbá** and **Campo Grande** in Mato Grosso do Sul, or **Cuiabá** in Mato Grosso. You can either rent a car and book a *fazenda* lodge independently, or go through one of the many tour operators in each of these three cities.

TOURS

Most people go on organized tours, entering the swamp in jeeps or trucks and following one of the few rough roads that now connect Corumbá, Aquidauana, Coxim and Cuiabá (via Poconé or Cáceres) with some of the larger *fazenda* settlements of the interior. However, it can be hard to know which freelance operators are reliable, as lists of licensed guides no longer available and there has been reports of scams in Cuiabá, so ask around.

Boat trips It is possible to take small boat trips (around R$300/day/person), from Corumbá or Cáceres – there are no agencies for this sort of trip, so just ask around. Note that if you're in Campo Grande, the trips you might be offered will invariably be luxury cruises.

PANTANAL ESSENTIALS: WHAT TO PACK

- Light-coloured long-sleeved cotton shirts
- Light-coloured trousers
- T-shirts
- Light-coloured cotton field socks
- Trainers or walking shoes
- Waterproof sandals or flip-flops
- Windbreaker
- Fleece jacket
- Sweaters
- Reusable one-litre water bottle
- Camera with a good zoom lens
- Day-pack for camera
- Binoculars
- Long rain poncho
- Sunscreen
- Mosquito repellent
- Sunglasses
- Sunhat
- Small flashlight
- Swimsuit

THE HISTORY OF THE PANTANAL

The **Pantanal** is known to have been inhabited for at least five thousand years. Ceramics were being produced here by 1500 BC and strange mounds were created, possibly ritual sites, around the same era. These were occupied until 1000 AD, then re-utilized by various of the Pantanal's tribal groups: Paiaguá, Gutao, Terna and Mbaya-Guaicuru. At the time of early Portuguese explorations, and the first unsuccessful attempts at populating the region by the Spanish in the sixteenth century, the region was dominated by three main tribes. The horse-riding **Guaicuru**, who lived to the south, adopted stray or stolen horses and cattle from the advancing white settlers, making them an elite group among indigenous tribes. Wearing only jaguar skins as they rode into battle, they were feared by the neighbouring **Terena** (Guana) tribe, who lived much of their lives as servants to Guaicuru families. In many ways, the nature and degree of their economic and social interaction suggests that the two might once have been different castes within the same tribe. Another powerful people lived to the north –the **Paiaguá**, masters of the main rivers, lagoons and canals of the central Pantanal. Much to the chagrin of both Spanish and Portuguese expeditions into the swamps, the Paiaguá were superbly skilled with both their canoes and the bow and arrow.

In 1540, the Spaniard Alvar Nuñez Cabeza de Vaca explored some of the Pantanal. Having previously visited what is now Texas and the southeast US, he was particularly impressed with the extraordinary fishing and healthy constitutions of the people here. Other Spanish adventurers also arrived here in the late sixteenth century, bringing with them the first cattle. They were soon evicted by Brazilian *bandeirantes*, but left their cattle behind to go feral. It wasn't until the **discovery of gold** in the northern Pantanal and around Cuiabá during the early eighteenth century that any genuine settlement schemes were undertaken. A rapid influx of colonists, miners and soldiers led to several bloody battles. In June 1730 hundreds of Paiaguá warriors in 83 canoes ambushed the annual flotilla, which was carrying some 900kg of gold south through the Pantanal from Cuiabá. They spared only some of the women and a few of the stronger black rowers from the flotilla. Much of the gold eventually found its way out of Brazil and into Spanish Paraguay where Cautiguacu, the Paiaguá chief, lived a life of luxury in Asunción until his death 55 years later. The decline of the gold mines during the nineteenth century brought development in the Pantanal to a standstill and the population began to fall.

The twentieth century saw the establishment of unrestricted **cattle-grazing** ranches – *fazendas* – and today over twenty million cattle roam the swamp. Party time here is during the bull castration period, when the local delicacy becomes readily available.

The wildlife trade and ranching were at their peak here between the late nineteenth century and the end of World War II, when the demand for beef in particular dropped off. The Pantanal, however, is still **under threat** from the illegal exploitation of animal skins, fish and rare birds, and even gold panning. The chemical fertilizers and pesticides used on the enormous *fazendas* to produce cash crops such as soya beans are also beginning to take their toll. **Ecotourism** has been heralded as a potential saviour for the swamp, but this will only work if sufficient money is ploughed back into conservation. The Pantanal has its own Polícia Florestal who try to enforce the environmentally friendly regulations that are now being strictly applied: no disposal of non-biodegradable rubbish, no noise pollution, no fishing without a licence (it costs R$250) or between November and January during the breeding season, no fishing with nets or explosives and no removal of rocks, wildlife or plant life.

FAZENDAS

Fazendas Swamping it in comfort is possible at one of numerous of *fazenda*-lodges in the Pantanal, well away from towns and main roads. Most of the *fazenda*-lodges are located east and northeast of Corumbá, and also on either side of the Rio Cuiabá in the north, accessible for the most part via the aborted Transpantaneira road between Poconé and Porto Jofre. With few exceptions *fazenda*-lodges cost upwards of R$350 a night per person, and over R$1000 is not uncommon for some of the most luxurious ones. However, these prices invariably include several activities, including trips by boat or jeep, horse-riding, guided walks or fishing expeditions, as well as meals.

All-inclusive packages Also including nights in *fazenda*-lodges are all-inclusive package tours, though their prices vary wildly, sometimes undercutting the official lodge price, at other times almost doubling it – it's worth shopping around and bargaining. As a general rule, you'll pay less if you deal direct with a *fazenda*-lodge owner in Porto Jofre, Cáceres, Aquidauana and even Corumbá, rather than through their agents. However, some hotels and *fazendas* can only be booked through tour agencies (especially in Porto Jofre) where jaguar tourism has boomed.

INDEPENDENT TRAVEL

The Pantanal is a very difficult place to travel, and setting out independently it is not recommended. Public transportation is at its best poor, there's plenty of wildlife around (jaguars and wild boars) and both a local guide or boatman and driver are required if you want to make it worthwhile. Guides working independently are hard to come across and they tend not to be as tuned into environmental concerns as the guides working for the best tour operators – for example, driving boats with old and noisy motors that disturb the wildlife and getting too close to the animals. If you do go independently, it's important to take all the equipment you need with you, including food, camping gear, a first-aid kit and lots of mosquito repellent.

The Southern Pantanal

Though a little far from the action, **Campo Grande** has good hotels and communications with the rest of Brazil, making it the most obvious entry point into the Southern Pantanal for most visitors. If arriving from Bolivia, however, **Corumbá** is an obvious option from where you can travel into the Pantanal by bus or jeep. The capital of Pantanal, it once had plenty of guides and agencies, as well as boats for rent, but nowadays the tourism mainly evolves around big groups of Brazilians on fishing trips. Some of the most popular *fazenda*-lodges in the region are those in **Nhecolândia**, roughly speaking the area between the *rios* Negro and Taquari east of Corumbá. Many of these benefit from a well-established dirt access road, the MS-184/MS-228 (the old Campo Grande road) also called **Estrada Parque**, which loops off from the main BR-262 highway 300km from Campo Grande near Passo do Lontra (it's well signposted), and crosses through a large section of the swamp before rejoining the same road some 10km before Corumbá.

ACCOMMODATION **THE SOUTHERN PANTANAL**

The following *fazenda*-lodges are accessible from **Corumbá**, **Miranda** or **Aquidauana**; they offer full-board accommodation and swamp trips, and can be booked through the addresses given below or through tour operators. If you book directly through the lodges, transfer costs are usually charged separately.

Hotel Recanto Barra Mansa Rio Negro ⓣ67 3325 6807, ⓦhotelbarramansa.com.br; map p.460. On the north shore of the Rio Negro, 130km from Aquidauana, this small luxury lodge owned by Guilherme Rondon accommodates up to seventeen guests and specializes in game tours and fly-fishing. Daily buses run here from Corumbá, or a helicopter can be arranged if there's been flooding during rainy season. R$1432

Passo do Lontra Park Hotel Rodovia Estrada Parque km 10 off the BR-262 between Campo Grande and Corumbá ⓣ67 3231 6569, ⓦpassodolontra.com.br; map p.460. One of the region's rare, relatively inexpensive options (with substantial reductions in low season), although a minimum number of guests may be required. The lodge specializes in fishing and nature treks. R$400

★ **Refúgio Ecológico Caiman** Rio Aquidauana ⓣ67 3242 1450, ⓦcaiman.com.br; reservation centre in São Paulo where bookings are taken ⓣ11 3706 1800; map p.460. Offering a luxurious Pantanal jungle lodge experience, the *Refúgio* is located some 240km west of Campo Grande and 36km north of Miranda, and covers over 530 square kilometres. There are a handful of lodges and private villas, all with good facilities and a distinctive style to match the surroundings. The ranch works with Projeto Onçafari, a jaguar conservation project, which runs excellent jaguar safaris on the ranch. The main activities include nocturnal safaris, hikes and boat trips. The ranch is still much a working cattle ranch (around seventy percent of the reserve's income is still derived from cattle). The *Refúgio* has its own airstrip and offers transfer services leaving from Campo Grande four times a week. Full board, all activities and bilingual guide services are included in the daily rate. R$3045

The Northern Pantanal

Trips to the Northern Panantal are mainly concentrated around the aborted **Transpantaneira** route. Several lodges, ranging from simple to rustic to luxury, line the road. Tour operators in **Cuiabá** can arrange everything from the four-hour transfer, accommodation at one of the lodges and bilingual guides – and it often works out

LUXURY PANTANAL FISHING TOURS

Luxury fishing boats – essentially floating hotels designed with the Brazilian passion for angling in mind – are an ideal way to encounter the swamp's wildlife on the end of a line, and ultimately on your plate. A stay on one of these for a week starts at around R$1000 a head per day, though the price is full board and usually includes ample drink, food and unlimited use of their small motorboat tenders for exploring further afield. Note that for families with **small children**, any river trip is inadvisable as none of the boats have guard-rails safe enough to keep a toddler from falling in.

Most of the boats are based in Corumbá, with some others in Cáceres, Barão do Melgaço and Cuiabá, and can be booked through tour agents. In high season, they tend to run pre-scheduled trips, departing and returning on Sundays; routes are mentioned where they remain fixed from year to year. Out of season, they're up for rent, with a minimum number of passengers and days invariably demanded, though bargaining is possible. You can find the vessels tied up at their home ports.

FROM CÁCERES

Cobra Grande 65 3223 4203, cobragrande.com.br. A small boat with five cabins and an adequate dining room; book well in advance. Per person/day R$400

Pantanal Vip 65 99941 4181, pantanalvip.com.br. Available for luxury fishing trips. Per person/day R$500

FROM CORUMBÁ

Kalypso Book direct on 67 3231 1460, naviokalypso.com.br or through agents Mutum Turismo (see page 457). Brazil's answer to Nile cruisers, the *Kalypso* is a spacious three-tier affair with berths for 120 passengers and looks like a pile of portacabins on a barge (which is what it once was). The interior is wood-panelled, the restaurant self-service, and there's a pool on top in which to escape the mosquitoes and the heat. Originally designed as a base for fishing trips, it has a number of small motorboats and a giant fridge in which you can keep your catch. There is a minimum stay of six nights. Prices depend on group size; whole boat minimum is R$3000/day.

Millenium 67 3231 3372, opantaneirotur.com.br. This luxury vessel has ten cabins and can only be booked for six days at a time. Prices depend on group size, but expect a minimum of R$2000/day.

cheaper than booking directly. You'll need to stay at the very least to have a full day in the Pantanal – make it three or four nights if you can.

Barão do Melgaço

One of the simplest ways into the northern part of the swamp is to take a four-hour bus from Cuiabá (see page 469) south to **BARÃO DO MELGAÇO**, a small, quiet village on the banks of the Rio Cuiabá. Although not quite in the true swamp, and therefore with less in the way of wildlife, Barão is perfect if you're short on time and just want a taste of the Pantanal. Although Barão is no longer served by regular boats from Corumbá, it might still be worth asking around in case a shallow-draught vessel is covering the journey – an unforgettable experience, right through the centre of the swamp.

ACCOMMODATION — BARÃO DO MELGAÇO

Pousada do Rio Mutum 130km from Cuiaba near the Rio Mutum 65 3052 7022, pousadamutum.com.br; map p.460. In a stunning location on the Baía de Siá Mariana near the Rio Mutum, this *pousada* has chalet style apartments and a lovely pool. Apart from jeep safaris, horse-riding and boat trips, you can visit a riverside community nearby to learn about Pantaneiro customs and traditions. Rates are full board. R$760

Poconé and the Transpantaneira

The most exploited option from Cuiabá is to follow the route south to **POCONÉ**. Like Barão do Melgaço, Poconé is not real Pantanal country, but it's a start and there are a few **hotels** around. The swamp proper begins south of Poconé, along the aborted **Transpantaneira** road. In fact, it's just a bumpy dirt track, often impassable during the rains, but you'll see plenty of wildlife from it, as well as signs marking the entrances to a number of *fazenda*-lodges and *pousadas* set back from the road around various tributaries of the Rio Cuiabá, notably the Pixaim and Rio Claro; although pricey, they all have restaurants and facilities for taking wildlife day-trips into the swamp by boat, on horseback or on foot.

Porto Jofre

The Transpantaneira, a rough track from Poconé to Porto Jofre (4WD is recommended when it's raining and the road gets very muddy), trails off southeast from Porto Cercado to the banks of the Rio Cuiabá itself, and provides access to several *pousadas*. After 145km, having crossed around a hundred wooden bridges in varying stages of dilapidation, the track eventually arrives at **PORTO JOFRE**, a small fishing hamlet and literally the end of the road. This is as far as the Transpantaneira route has got, or ever looks like getting, thanks to technical problems and the sound advice of ecological pressure groups.

ARRIVAL AND DEPARTURE — POCONÉ AND THE TRANSPANTANEIRA

By bus There are daily bus services from Cuiabá's rodoviária (see page 469) as far as Poconé along a paved and smooth 100km stretch of road.

ACCOMMODATION

POCONÉ

Hotel Skala Praça Rondon 64 ⓣ 65 3721 1407; map p.460. This simple little hotel on the main square offers basic but clean rooms at a fair price as well as very friendly service. **R$130**

ALONG THE TRANSPANTANEIRA

All of the following *fazendas* and *pousadas* can be booked through the addresses given below or through tour or travel agents in Cuiabá; some lodges insist on advance reservations. All the lodges offer full-board accommodation, with swamp trips included in the price.

Hotel Pantanal Norte Porto Jofre; office Av São Sebastião 357, Cuiabá ⓣ 65 3637 1593, ⓦ portojofre.com.br; map p.460. This high-end, atmospheric hotel has a monopoly in the area and its own grassy airstrip for wealthy fishermen from São Paulo. There is a lovely pool and games area for when you're not venturing out into the swamp to fish or spot jaguars along the riverbank. March–Oct. **R$700**

Pantanal Jaguar Camp Rodovia Transpantaneira Km 145 ⓣ 65 9 9925 2265, ⓦ pantanaljaguarcamp.com.br; map p.460. Owned by the wonderful Pantanal Nature tour operators, this eco-friendly lodge (complete with septic tanks and solar panels) in the middle of the jungle is perfect for those with a particular interest in jaguars. Their success rate in spotting the elusive creatures is very high, thanks to the owner's passion and expertise. Accommodation is in luxury tents. All guides speak English. **R$670**

★ **Pousada Araras Eco Lodge** Office at Av Ponce de Arruda 670, Várzea Grande ⓣ 65 3682 2800, ⓦ araraslodge.com.br; map p.460. At Km 29 of the Transpantaneira, this long-established *pousada* has an atmospheric brick ranch building with a pool, as well as boats and horses. You'll see animals up close and personal: caimans lurk nearby, howler monkeys swing from the *pousada*'s watch tower and the odd capybara waddles right up to the pool area. Owner André and his wife are pioneers in Brazilian ecotourism and huge efforts go into keeping things sustainable, from the waste system and solar panels, to providing drinking water free of charge to all guests (the only lodge that does this). The home-cooked food is wonderful too. Their nineteen rooms are likely to be full in high season so book as far ahead as possible. If you're into birds, ask about their hyacinth macaw rehabilitation programme. **R$2482**

Pousada Piuval Rodovia Transpantaneira, Km 10 ⓣ 65 3345 1338, ⓦ pousadapiuval.com.br; map p.460. A comfortable spread 119km from Cuiabá with a fine pool and small but pleasant rooms. Well-equipped with horses, open truck and boats for exploring deeper into the swamp. It's also possible to come here just for the day. **R$620**

Pousada Rio Clarinho ⓣ 9998 8888, ⓦ pousadarioclarinho.com.br; map p.460. Authentic and charming, this is a great little rustic lodging based in an old family-run *fazenda* with a good restaurant, viewing tower, horse riding and rowing boats available. The large forested area by the *pousada* makes for fantastic walking trails. **R$625**

Pousada Rio Claro Rodovia Transpantaneira, Km 42 ⓣ 65 3345 2449, ⓦ pousadarioclaro.com.br; map p.460. *Pousada Rio Claro* has direct access to the river of the same name, making canoe trips at dawn that much easier. Comfortable rooms, a pool and good food mean this one's a good choice. **R$695**

Cáceres

Although less frequented than the Porto Jofre route, **CÁCERES** is another good target from Cuiabá, lying 220km west of the city. It's a very pleasant, laidback place, and, given the prices of accommodation along the Transpantaneira, deserves consideration as a base for visiting the Pantanal. On the upper reaches of the Rio Paraguai, which is still quite broad even this far upstream, Cáceres is a relatively new town, made up largely of wooden shacks, bars and pool rooms.

ARRIVAL AND DEPARTURE — CÁCERES

By bus It's a 3-4hr journey by bus to Cáceres from Cuiabá's rodoviária, several of which leave daily.

By plane to Bolivia The only road to go further into the Pantanal than Cáceres is the track that leads on to the Bolivian border settlement of San Matias; from here you can fly to Santa Cruz (best to sort out exit stamp and entry visas first with the Brazilian Federal Police in Cáceres or Cuiabá and the Bolivian Consul in Cuiabá).

ACCOMMODATION

7

Boats There are several reasonably priced boats that operate from here, including the *Babilonia* (65 9989 1896, barcobabilonia.com.br), which has six cabins and usually goes out for seven days at a time. The price depends on the size of the group. Per day from R$852

Hotel Baiazinha Estrada do Barranco Km 60 65 3291 1036, hotelbaiazinha.com.br; map p.460. A lovely little hotel on the Rio Paraguai in the middle of the wilderness, which mainly focuses on fishing. The rooms are clean and there's tasty home-cooked food, a pool and barbecue area. Popular with groups of Brazilian fishermen, so can get a little noisy. R$500

Cuiabá

The southern gateway into the Amazon, **CUIABÁ** has always been firmly on the edge of Brazil's wilderness. In the town itself, modern skyscrapers long ago won the battle for attention, with the ornate facades of crumbling, pastel-shaded colonial villas, churches and shops now hidden. There is a handful of museums, but the real attractions in the city are the lively bars and restaurants: *Cuiabanos* love to drink, eat and dance. The good facilities offered in Cuiabá – in terms of hotels, restaurants and tour companies – mean that ecotourism in the nearby Northern Pantanal is developing rapidly and is being increasingly seen by younger *fazenda* owners as the way forward.

Much to the delight of the *Cuiabanos* (and the disappointment of rivalling Campo Grande), it was Cuiabá that was chosen to represent the region as one of the host cities for the 2014 **World Cup**. With this came a rush to develop the city's infrastructure, including a new light rail system running from the airport to the centre (designed to shuttle fans to and from the stadium), although at the time of research there was no sign of it ever being completed. The Arena Pantanal has a capacity of almost 43,000 people and uses as many sustainable materials as possible. Around the end of June, beginning of July the **Festa de São Benedito** takes place, a local party where the city saint is celebrated with traditional dances, processions and plenty of local food like *bolos de queijo* (cheese balls) and *bolos de arroz* (rice cakes).

Brief history

Following the discovery of a gold field here in 1719 (one version of the town's name means the "river of stars"), the town mushroomed as an administrative and service centre in the middle of **indigenous territory**, thousands of very slow, overland kilometres from any other Portuguese settlement. To the south lay the Pantanal and the dreaded Paiaguá people who frequently ambushed convoys of boats transporting Cuiabá gold by river to São Paulo. The fierce Bororo tribe, who dominated Mato Grosso east of Cuiabá, also regularly attacked many of the mining settlements. Northwest along a high hilly ridge – the Chapada dos Parecis, which now carries the BR-364 to Porto Velho – lived the Parecis people, farmers in the watershed between the Amazon and the Pantanal.

By the 1780s, however, most of these indigenous groups had been either eliminated or transformed into allies: the Parecis were needed as slave labour for the mines; the Bororo either retreated into the forest or joined the Portuguese as mercenaries and hunters; while the Paiaguá fared worst of all, almost completely wiped out by cannon and musket during a succession of punitive expeditions from Cuiabá.

The city's most important development came during the 1890s, when a young Brazilian army officer, Lieutenant **Cândido Rondon**, built a telegraph system from Goiás to Cuiabá through treacherous Bororo territory – assisted no doubt by the fact that he had some Bororo blood in his veins. By 1903 he had extended the telegraph from Cuiabá south to Corumbá, and in 1907 he began work to reach the Rio Madeira, to the northwest in the Amazon basin. Since then, Cuiabá has been pushing forward the frontier of development and the city is still a stepping stone and crossroads for pioneers. Every year, thousands of hopeful settlers stream through Cuiabá on their way to a new life in the western Amazon.

The established farmlands around the city produce abundant crops – maize, fruit, rice and soya – but the city itself thrives on the much larger surrounding **cattle-ranching region**, which contains almost a quarter of a million inhabitants. A large lead-ore deposit is being worked close to the town, and oil has been discovered at neighbouring Várzea Grande (the town where the airport is located); in the longer term, however, it is sustainable industries, like rubber, palm nuts and, of course, ecotourism, that may provide income.

Praça da República and around

The central **Praça da República** is a hive of activity from daybreak onwards. It's the city's main meeting spot, and the cathedral, post office, Palacio da Instrução and the Museu

Histórico all face onto the square, while under the shade of its large trees, hippies from the Brazilian coast sell crafted jewellery and leather work. Just to the northeast of Praça da República, a few narrow central lanes – Pedro Celestino, Galdino Pimentel, Ricardo Franco and Rua 7 de Setembro – form a crowded pedestrian shopping area. Nearby, on Praça do Rosário, you'll find the city's oldest church, the simple but run-down **Igreja Nossa Senhora do Rosário e Capela de São Benedicto**, completed in 1722. Although worth visiting by day, this area is best avoided at night.

Palácio da Instrução

Praça da República 151 • Mon–Fri 1.30pm–7pm • Free

The most interesting old mansion in town is the **Palácio da Instrução**. It houses the city's library on the ground floor, with books spanning children's literature to regional history (in Portuguese). There's a delightful inner courtyard too. Upstairs is the **Pavilhão das Artes**, which holds interesting temporary art exhibitions as well as cultural events and art courses.

Museu Historico de Mato Grosso

Praça da República 131 • Mon–Fri 2–6pm • Free • ⓣ 65 3613 9234

The **Museu Historico de Mato Grosso** depicts Cuiabá's history from eighteenth-century colonial times up until the postwar twentieth century. Artefacts include cannons from the Paraguayan War and nineteenth-century furniture from the former Casa dos Governadores (Governors' House). The museum was closed at the time of research; contact the tourism office for the latest update (see page 470).

Catedral do Bom Jesus

Praça da República s/n • Mass: Mon 6.30pm, Tues–Sat 6.30am & 6.30pm, Sun 7am, 9am, 5pm, 7pm • Free

The **Catedral do Bom Jesus** was built in the 1960s to replace the old cathedral, a beautiful Baroque affair that was then thought old-fashioned. Constructed from pinkish concrete with a square, vaguely Moorish facade, the new cathedral has a predictably vast, rectangular interior; its main altar is overshadowed by a mural reaching from floor to ceiling that depicts a sparkling Christ floating in the air above the city of Cuiabá and the cathedral.

Igreja de Nossa Senhora do Bom Despacho

Praça do Seminario, s/n • Mass: Mon 7am & 6.30pm, Tues–Fri 7am & 4pm, Sat 7am, Sun 8am, 11am & 5pm • Free • ⓣ 65 9973 0516

Sitting on a hill to the south of the city, across the Avenida Tenente Coronel Duarte from the cathedral side of town, the early twentieth-century **Igreja de Nossa Senhora do Bom Despacho** used to dominate the cityscape before office buildings and towering hotels sprang up to dwarf it in the latter half of the twentieth century. It's worth visiting for its splendid religious art collection.

Centro Geodésico da America do Sul

Praça Moreira Cabral, along Rua Barão do Melgaço

The **Centro Geodésico da America do Sul**, by the state assembly buildings, makes a dubious claim: a small post enclosed by a tall, thin pyramid marks what was considered to be, until the advent of satellite topography, the geographical centre of the South American continent. The actual place, for what it's worth, is 67km away in the Chapada dos Guimarães.

Museo da Imagen e do Som

Rua Voluntarios da Patria 118 • Mon–Fri 1–7pm • Free • ⓣ 65 3613 9300

Opposite the tourist office, there's the pleasant if bizarre **Museo da Imagen e do Som** (Museum of Image and Sound), located in an airy colonial mansion that offers a welcome respite from the city's unrelenting heat in its shady inner courtyard. The building houses two permanent exhibitions, mainly featuring historic photos and vintage vinyl record players, cameras and radios, plus changing exhibitions relating to Cuiabá's theatrical past, some of which is more colourful than intelligible to the non-local eye.

Museu do Índio Marechal Rondon

Av Fernando Corréa da Costa, Cidade Universitária • **Museum** Mon–Fri 7.30–11.30am & 1.30–5.30pm, Sat & Sun 7.30–11am • Free • **Zoological garden** Tues–Sun 7.30–11.30am & 1.30–5.20pm • Free • ☎ 65 3615 8007 • Buses #133, #505, #513, #514 and others from Av Tenente Coronel Duarte will take you to the Cidade Universitária

The university-run **Museu do Índio Marechal Rondon** focuses on local tribal culture and features feather, fibre, ceramic and wooden objects representing the material culture of several local tribes, including the Bororo and Nambikwara. The museum is beside the university pool, 5km east of town off BR-364, in the sector known as Cidade Universitária.

Also in the Cidade Universitária is a small **zoological garden** where you'll find swamp creatures including caimans, tapirs and capybaras – a small consolation if you don't have time for a Pantanal tour.

Museu do Morro da Caixa d'Agua Velha

Rua Comandante Costa, s/n • Tues–Fri 9am–noon & 2–6pm, Sat 10am–noon & 1–5pm • R$2 • ☎ 65 3617 1274

This former Roman-style water tank served the city from 1882 to the 1950s and pumped 1.2 million litres of water to the 25 million inhabitants of Cuiabá. Now it houses a **museum** displaying water-related curios, but unless you're particularly into water pipes, it's the building itself that's most impressive. The museum often hosts interesting temporary art exhibitions too.

ARRIVAL AND DEPARTURE — CUIABÁ

Note that going north from Cuiabá, buses only go as far as **Alta Floresta**. Manaus, Itaituba, Santarém and Belém are all advertised by the bus companies, but are reachable only by enormous detours taking several days via Goiânia. The reality for most travellers will be a flight or an intrepid journey by bus (and perhaps river) to some other distant city. The furthest north you can drive is **the Serra do Cachimbo** on the fringes of Pará state. The fastest road is **Highway BR-364** (known as the BR-070 in Mato Grosso) through Cuiabá, which ultimately links São Paulo with Rio Branco and Cruzeiro do Sul.

BY PLANE

The airport (☎ 65 3614 2500), 8km south in Várzea Grande, is connected to the centre by Metropolitano buses (R$2.95) and taxis (from about R$40). From here take the bus marked "Shopping Pantanal", but remember to get off at Av Getúlio Vargas, for the city centre. The construction of the new light rail system from the airport had been stopped at the time of writing and doesn't look like it will ever be completed.

Airlines TAM, Av Isaac Póvoas 586 (☎ 65 3682 1702); Gol (☎ 65 3682 1666).

BY BUS

Both the BR-163 and the BR-364 run to Cuiabá. Whether you're coming from São Paulo, Rio, Brasília or the Northeast, you'll want to take the BR-364 for travelling onwards overland into the western Amazon. The rodoviária (☎ 65 3621 3629) on Avenida Marechal Rondon is a large concrete complex 3km north of the city centre. From here it's a 15min ride into Cuiabá on buses #202, #304 or #309, or 10min by taxi (from R$20).

Bus companies All buses run from the rodoviária; the most useful companies are probably Expresso Rubi and Rapido Chapadense (Chapada dos Guimarães; ☎ 65 3621 1764); TUT (Poconé; ☎ 65 3056 6002, Ⓦ tut.com.br), and Eucatur (for Porto Velho and most major destinations to the south and east; ☎ 65 3901 2140, Ⓦ eucatur.com.br).

Destinations Alta Floresta (2–5 daily; 14hr); Barão do Melgaço (2 daily; 3hr); Brasília (4–8 daily; 20hr); Cáceres (1 daily; 3hr); Campo Grande (16–25 daily; 11hr); Chapada dos Guimarães (Mon–Sat 9 daily, Sun 8 daily; 1hr); Coxim (20 daily; 7hr); Goiânia (12 daily; 15–17hr); Poconé (5 daily; 3hr); Porto Velho (9–13 daily; 23hr); Rio Branco (1–2 daily; 33hr); Rio de Janeiro (2 daily; 31hr); Rondonópolis (12–13 daily; 4hr); São Paulo (2 daily; 24hr-plus).

BY CAR

Car rental Localiza Hertz, Av Dom Bosco 965 (Mon–Fri 8am–6pm & Sat 8am–noon; ☎ 65 3624 7979); Unidas, Av João Ponce de Arruda 920 (daily 24hr; ☎ 65 3682 4052).

TOUR OPERATORS AND GUIDES IN CUIABÁ

All of Cuiabá's **travel agents** offer trips into the Pantanal or to the closer sites, like Chapada dos Guimarães and Nobres (Bom Jardim), although their primary occupation is selling flights within Brazil. For more personal service, however, you'd do better to contact one of the local **tour operators**, which tend to be smaller and offer specialist local knowledge. Tours within the region tend to cost upwards of R$400/day/person including transport, accommodation in *pousadas*, good food, horse riding and photo-safari outings. In **low season** it may be worth bargaining, particularly if there are four or more of you travelling together: you may also have to wait a day or two for enough tourists to make up your group, unless you're happy paying more. If you choose to go with an independent guide make sure to check their guide licence/certificate which should have a Cadastur registration number, as there has been reports of scams. You can cross check the certificate and registration number on ⓦcadastur.turismo.gov.br/cadastur/Certificados.mtur if you ask the guide for his/her CPF number (the Brazilian insurance number). All tour agencies listed below are reputable tour agencies with long experience of taking tourist to Pantanal.

★ **Ecoverde Tours** At Pousada Ecoverde (see page 471) on Rua Pedro Celestino 391 ⓣ65 3624 1386, ⓣ65 9638 1614, ⓦecoverdetours.com.br. Highly recommended company run by the wildlife ecologist Joel Souza, a very reliable operator who speaks excellent English and German, among other languages. Joel works with a number of very good guides.

Pantanal Explorer Av Governador Ponce de Arruda 670, Várzea Grande ⓣ65 3682 2800, ⓦpantanalexplorer.com.br. Run by the inspiring conservationist André Von Thuronyi, Pantanal Explorer offers well-organized trips into the Pantanal and the Amazon. A stay at the wonderful *Pousada Araras Eco Lodge* (see page 465) on the Transpantaneira is likely to be included, where you'll see plenty of local wildlife while staying in comfortable surroundings.

★ **Pantanal Nature** Rua Campo Grande 487 ⓣ65 9994 2265, ⓦpantanalnature.com.br. This fantastic and highly professional tour operator does trips into the Pantanal – offering a choice of different accommodation options – which can be combined with trips to nearby Chapada das Guimarães, Nobres and/or the Amazon in a customized package. They also own the *Pantanal Jaguar Camp* in Porto Jofre (see page 465), which specializes in jaguar-spotting. Owner Ailton Lara is a wonderful guide – both passionate and extremely knowledgeable about the region and its flora and fauna. Highly recommended.

INFORMATION

Tourist information You'll be able to get some limited information from the tourist office in the centre of town on Rua Voluntarios da Patria close to *Pousada Ecoverde* (see page 471), on the corner with Rua Ricardo Franco (in theory daily 9am–6pm; ⓣ65 3613 9300).

ACCOMMODATION

With the rodoviária relatively close by, most people prefer to stay in or near the busy **city centre**, where there's a good range of accommodation options. There are also numerous two- and three-star hotels around the **airport** and on the way into town.

Amazon Plaza Av Getúlio Vargas 600 ⓣ65 2121 2000, ⓦhotelamazon.com.br; map p.467. This is one of the smartest and most comfortable downtown options. Rooms are large with TV and a/c, and there's a small pool and garden patio-bar. Breakfasts are fantastic and the service is good. R$315

★ **Deville** Av Isaac Póvoas 1000 ⓣ65 3319 3000, ⓦdeville.com.br; map p.467. A five-star hotel, at the top of its range, with 174 rooms, an elegant high-ceilinged lobby, Arctic-strength a/c, pool, gym, and a decent restaurant serving Brazilian buffet food as well as à la carte. R$340

Hits Pantanal Av Arthur Bernades 251, Várzea Grande ⓣ65 3363 9977, ⓦhitspantanal.com.br; map p.467. Just by the airport this is a very convenient, albeit pricey, option if you are just passing through town. There is a big pool, rooms are very spacious and have tile flooring, a/c and TVs. For late-night snacks there's a bar serving drinks and simple dishes. It offers free transport to and from the airport and it's worth asking for room discounts. R$390

Hostel Pantanal Backpacker Av Mal Deodoro 2301 ⓣ65 3359 5420, ⓦpantanalbackpacker.com; map p.467. Linked to Youth Hostelling International, this place has all the usual facilities, plus a pool with a waterfall that needs a bit more love and a communal kitchen. Rooms are mostly dorms, though some private doubles are available. The hostel also organizes trips to the Pantanal. Dorms R$50, doubles R$140

Mato Grosso Palace Rua Joaquim Murtinho 170 ⓣ65 3614 7500, ⓦfacebook.com/matogrossopalacehotel; map p.467. This modern hotel is situated in a grand building behind the Palácio Instrução. It has excellent service and pleasant enough rooms, some with good views. Unfortunately there's no pool, but there is a fully equipped gym. R$170

★ **Pousada Ecoverde** Rua Pedro Celestino 391 ⓣ65 3624 1386, ⓦecoverdetours.com.br; map p.467. This lovely *pousada* is based in a safe, self-contained colonial house with patio and rear gardens, right at the heart of the old city centre. It has five rooms, all with fans. Bathrooms are shared, but there are four of them and they're kept clean. There's also a good reference library, a rest area with shade and hammocks, and laundry, as well as links to one of the best Pantanal tour operators (see page 470). Breakfasts are stupendous and very fresh. R$80

EATING

Cuiabá has a surprising range of cuisine and some excellent restaurants. For cheaper eating and *lanches* there are plenty of places in the area around **Praça Alencastro**, at the north end of Travessa João Dias near Rua Comandante Costa, and in the shopping zone between **Rua Pedro Celestino** and **Rua Galdino Pimentel**.

★ **Choppão** Praça 8 de Abril, Goiabeiras ⓣ65 3623 9101, ⓦchoppao.com.br; map p.467. Probably the best and most traditional restaurant-bar in the city centre, *Choppão* is very lively in the evening, with lots of tables in a big corner space and some outside where there is occasionally street entertainment. They serve traditional *escaldo* (egg- and fish-based soup) along with beer and have some fascinating historical photos on the walls. Mains are around R$100 and easily serve three people. Mon, Wed, Thurs & Sun 11am–2am, Tues 5.30pm–2am, Fri & Sat 11am–5am.

★ **Fundo de Quintal** Rua Estevão de Mendonça 1139 ⓣ65 99974 7742; map p.467. This outdoor restaurant is beautifully set in a backyard and decorated with various memorabilia. You'll find traditional local cuisine on the menu that is served in pots giving your meal a very home-away-from-home feeling. Try the *revirado de carne picadinha*, rice with beef and fried plantain (R$41). Mon–Sat 6pm–midnight.

Getúlio Grill Av Getúlio Vargas 1147 ⓣ65 3624 9992, ⓦgetuliogrill.com.br; map p.467. A bar, restaurant and club in one, *Gétulio Grill* is popular with twenty- and thirty-something locals. Typical meat and fish dishes at the restaurant come in big portions, and the bar has outdoor seating where you can watch the cream of Cuiabá cruise by in their dream wagons. Mon–Thurs & Sun 11am–3pm & 5.30pm–midnight, Fri & Sat 11am–3pm & 5.30pm–1am.

Mahalo Presidente Castelo Branco 359, Quilombo ⓣ65 3028 7700, ⓦmahalocozinhacriativa.com.br; map p.467. This fancy restaurant caters to the city's elite with its wine cellar and French-inspired tasting menu (R$194). If you don't feel like going all, pick something from the extensive á la carte menu, such as lamb fillet with goat's cheese (R$89) or orange-flavoured salmon with sweet potatoes (R$76). Mon–Sat 11.30am–2.30pm & 7.30pm–midnight.

O Regionalíssimo Av Manoel José de Arruda 1410, Museu do Rio ⓣ65 3623 6881, ⓦfacebook.com/regionalissimo; map p.467. Excellent, moderately priced *rodízio* with regional dishes in one of Cuiabá's oldest restaurant near the port. In the evening they offer drinks and a buffet of different nibbles (R$30) including fried fish and there's sometimes live music at weekends. Mon 6–9.30pm, Tues–Sat 11am–2pm & 5.30–10pm, Sun 11am–2pm.

Panfrigo Rua Villa Maria 13 ⓣ65 3321 9073 ⓦbit.ly/Panfrigo; map p.467. Just a few blocks from the tourist office and *Pousada Ecoverde*, this very busy bakery is open for great breakfasts and coffee; although you wouldn't expect so, it attracts local celebrities, particularly on weekend mornings. Daily 6am–8pm.

DRINKING AND NIGHTLIFE

Although beer is twice as expensive here as it is on the coast, you'll find that nightlife in Cuiabá revolves mainly around the bars and restaurants in the town centre, especially along **Av Getulio Vargas**. The main nightlife spot, however, is **Praça Eurico Gaspar Dutra**, better known as Praça Popular, lined with good-value restaurants and bars – it's particularly lively on the weekends. Another smaller square popular with locals who eat, drink and make merry to the beats of live Brazilian music on Saturdays and Sundays is the **Praça da Mandioca** in the old town, just down the road from *Pousada Ecoverde*.

Confrade Av Mato Grosso 1000 ⓣ65 3027 2000, ⓦconfrade.com.br; map p.467. Five blocks northeast from Avenida Getúlio Vargas, this enormous microbrewery is one of Cuiabá's trendiest restaurant-bars and the evening focus for young *Cuiabanos*. A good but pricey menu features Brazilian and international dishes – everything from steak (R$62) to baked cod (R$98), as well as very potent cocktails – and of course, a wide range of ice-cold beers. Mon–Sat 11am–3pm & 5pm–2am & Sun 11am–3pm.

Flör Negra Av São Sebastião 2873 ⓣ65 3027 6201,

flornegra.com.br; map p.467. Trendy and sleek wine bar with designer furniture and an inviting cellar with bottles from both the new and the old world. The food is European inspired and beautifully presented, as well as a bit pricey. Four course tasting menu (R$195). Tues–Sat 7.30pm–late.

Hookerz Av Filinto Müller 1398 65 3052 5387; map p.467. This popular bar has its own microbrewery, a sophisticated number of black-and-white photographs hanging on the brick walls and invites a well-dressed crowd, despite its extremely distasteful name. There are burgers to accompany the ice-cold beer and the colourful cocktails. Tues–Sat 5.30pm–2am.

DIRECTORY

Internet LAN Phoenix, Av Tenente Coronel Duarte 07, close to the centre.

Money and exchange Banco do Brasil, Rua Barao de Melgaco 915 (Mon–Sat 10am–4pm) has money exchange and ATM. US dollars can be exchanged in some of the larger hotels.

Post office At Praça da República (Mon–Fri 9am–6pm, Sat 9am–noon).

7

Around Cuiabá

While Cuiabá can't exactly claim to be a resort town, there are some beautiful natural sites to be visited within one to three hours by car from the city, including the clear lakes of **Bom Jardim** and the mountainous scenery of the **Chapada dos Guimarães**.

Bom Jardim

North of Cuiabá, **BOM JARDIM** is famous for offering similar river and cave experiences to Bonito in Mato Grosso do Sul (see page 450), but less crowded. Confusingly, it is often referred to by locals as "Nobres" after the municipality, yet the attractions are in Bom Jardim itself. Located 190km from Cuiabá, it's possible to go just for the day; however, there is a handful of *pousadas*, should you wish to stay the night.

Tourists come to snorkel in crystal-clear rivers teeming with fish, bathe by waterfalls, observe birdlife and visit limestone caves. You can easily book a tour from Cuiabá – all of the operators offer visits and can organize transport and guides (you need a guide to access the main attractions) – or you can book your tour once you arrive in Bom Jardim. Accommodation is also best booked through these tour operators, and it can be cheaper booking a package if you're staying the night.

TOURS **BOM JARDIM**

Anaconda Turismo MT-241, Km 145 65 99998 9944, facebook.com/anacondaturismo. Offers fairly priced trips to all the main attractions in the area and is affiliated with Pousada Lagoa Azul. Packages including trips and accommodation are available.

Rota das Aguas Rodovia MT 241, Km 65 65 3102 2019, rotadasaguas.tur.br. This local tour agency offers multi-day packages and works with private accommodation in chalets as well as *pousadas*. Affiliated with *Pousada Róta das Aguas*.

Águas Quentes

Hotel Aguas Quentes, BR 364, Km 77 Serra de São Vicente • Daily 9am–5pm • R$90 for day pass, including lunch; entry also included in full-board room rates • 65 3614 7500, hotelmt.com.br • Daily buses to the town (1–2hr) from the rodoviária in Cuiabá

The hot baths of **ÁGUAS QUENTES**, 86km east of Cuiabá in the Serra de São Vicente, just off the BR-364 towards Rondonópolis, function as a weekend and honeymoon resort for locals. The baths are within the rather expensive *Hotel Aguas Quentes* and this is the only accommodation option in the area with access. The water, said to be mildly radioactive, comes in four different pools, the hottest at around 42°C, and is regarded as a cure for rheumatism, liver complaints and even conjunctivitis.

SCARLET MACAW

Chapada dos Guimarães and around

A paved road winds its way up to the scenic and increasingly popular mountain village of **CHAPADA DOS GUIMARÃES**, set on the plateau of the same name just 64km from Cuiabá. Located bang on one of the oldest tectonic plates on the planet, it is here on this plateau that the true geodesic centre of South America was pinpointed by satellite, much to the chagrin of the Cuiabanos who stick resolutely to their old 1909 mark; the actual spot, the **Mirante da Geodésia**, is located on the southern continuation of Rua Clariano Curvo from Praça Dom Wunibaldo, 8km away.

Parochial disputes aside, Chapada is an interesting settlement in its own right, containing Mato Grosso's oldest church, the **Igreja de Nossa Senhora de Santana do Sacramento**, a fairly plain colonial temple built in 1779, which dominates the top end of the town's leafy Praça Dom Wunibaldo. These days, with a population nearing eighteen thousand, the village has something of a reputation as a centre for the Brazilian "New Age" movement, with crystal shops, health-food stores and hippy communities.

If you're here in July, you're in for a treat, with the staging of the **Festival de Inverno** – a mix of drama, exhibitions and music, the latter ranging from traditional, sacred and tribal music to funk and rap.

Parque Nacional da Chapada dos Guimarães

Over three hundred square kilometres of the stunning countryside around the village of Chapada dos Guimarães is protected as the **Parque Nacional da Chapada dos Guimarães**. Consisting of a grassy plateau (at 800m the highest land in Mato Grosso), it is scattered with low trees and makes a marvellous backdrop for photographing the local flora and birdlife. Within walking distance, there are waterfalls, fantastic rock formations and precipitous canyons, as well as some interesting, partially excavated archeological sites.

The most spectacular of all the sights in the Parque Nacional da Chapada dos Guimarães is the **Véu de Noiva waterfall**, which drops over a sheer rock face for over 60m, pounding into the forested basin below. Other highlights in the park include – about 25km to the north of the village – the impressive and weird rock formations of **Cidade da Pedra**, some of them up to 300m tall, the spectacular waterfalls of **Cachoeira da Martinha**, 30km further north, and a couple of interesting cave systems – the **Casa de Pedra**, not far from Véu de Noiva and, further afield, the **Caverna Aroe Jari** (the latter with cave paintings). Good views of the Cidade da Pedra can be had from **Porto do Inferno**, a viewing point some 16km from the village on the road into the Chapada from Cuiabá.

All visits must be accompanied by a guide – all of the operators based in Cuiabá can arrange your trip (from around R$100/day/person, depending on how big the group is).

ARRIVAL AND INFORMATION — CHAPADA DOS GUIMARÃES AND AROUND

By bus Nine daily buses (eight on Sundays) run by Expreso Rubi and Chapadense make the 90min journey from Cuiabá's rodoviária to Chapada dos Guimarães.

Tourist information Centro de Apoio Ao Turismo, on the corner of Rua Dr P. Gomez with Rua 7 Perimetral, just a few blocks from Praça Dom Wunibaldo (Mon–Sat 9am–6pm; ⓣ 65 3301 2045, ⓣ 65 3301 1690), is a helpful office that can assist with details of bus times, information on campsites, contact lists for local guides and maps of the Chapada. Information can also be obtained from the national park office (daily 9am–5pm; ⓣ 65 3301 1133), while the website ⓦ chapadadosguimaraes.com.br offers hotel information and so on, though all in Portuguese.

TOURS

Ecoverde Tours (see page 470) can arrange a guide and/or transport for a day-trip or longer excursion here. Pantanal Nature (see page 470) also run tours to the Chapada – you can combine a trip to the Pantanal with the Chapada by opting for their five-day/four-night package tour. There are also a couple of specialist tour agencies that run trips to the Pantanal from Chapada dos Guimarães (see page 475).

PANTANAL TOURS FROM CHAPADA DOS GUIMARÃES

Biodiverse Brazil Tours Rua Perimetral 585 ⓣ65 3301 1961, ⓦbiodiversebraziltours.com. Biologist, bird expert and living encyclopedia, Fabiano Oliveira runs well organized trips to the Pantanal with a clear environmental conscious and guides that speak excellent English. Based in Chapada dos Guimares, but they can arrange pick-ups to the Pantanal from Cuiaba airport. Make sure to book well ahead. It's a bit of a splurge, but you will get what you pay for – clients include film crews and hardcore bird enthusiasts.

Pantanal Jaguar Safaris Estrada Rural Vale do Jamacá ⓣ65 9 9975 4406, ⓦpantanaljaguarsafaris.com. Run by amicable biologist André, this Chapada-based agency runs excellent jaguar safaris in the north of Pantanal on the Paraguay and Cuiabá rivers, as well as to the remote Taiamã Reserve southeast of Cáceres. Make sure to book well in advance.

Eco Turismo Cultural Rua Cipriano Curvo 655A ⓣ65 9 9678 4606, ⓦfacebook.com/ecoturismocultural. Organizes good-value and reliable tours of the region and has an English-speaking guide; their prices depend on numbers but range from around R$100/person a day, upwards.

7

ACCOMMODATION

IN THE VILLAGE

Hotel Turismo Rua Fernando Corréa da Costa 1065 ⓣ65 3301 1176, ⓦhotelturismo.com.br. This pleasant hotel is conveniently located just half a block from the bus station and has comfortable beds and good showers. Breakfast, is however, on the stingy side (for Brazilian standards). There's a small pool and lovely views. R$310

Pousada Bom Jardim Praça Dom Wunibaldo 641 ⓣ65 3301 2668, ⓦpousadabomjardim.com.br. Located right on the central square, this clean and very friendly hotel is good value for money and serves decent breakfasts; some rooms have a/c and are nicer than others. R185

★ **Pousada Cambará** Rua Projetada Florada da Serra ⓣ65 3301 13667. This *pousada* a few minutes' drive from the centre has a lovely garden, and even a football pitch, and is run by a very kind older couple. The helpful owners offer free transfer to town for lunch and dinner, if you don't have your own vehicle. Amazing breakfast with homemade cakes and rooms are all spotless and modern. R$350

Pousada Villa Guimaraes Rua Neco Siqueira 41 ⓣ65 3301 1366, ⓦpousadavillaguimaraes.com.br. This lovely *pousada* housed in a bright yellow building has large comfortable rooms with all the usual mod cons, as well as a pool and living areas to relax in and helpful staff. R$295

SURROUNDING AREA

Pousada do Parque (Park Eco Lodge) Km 52 of the MT-251 towards Campo Verde ⓣ65 9671 6876 or ⓣ65 3682 2800, ⓦpousadadoparque.com.br. This eco-friendly *pousada* is set next to the national park, offers fantastic views of the Chapada and sometimes yoga workshops and is perfect for nature-lovers and birdwatchers. Rooms are on the small side, but you're unlikely to be spending much time in them as the focus here is on the surrounding nature – the treks here are wonderful. R$435

★ **Pousada Cantos da Mata** Estrada Vale do Jamacá s/n ⓣ65 9801 9517, ⓦcantosdamata.com. Beautifully set in the middle of the forest, this small *pousada* with only four rooms Is a secluded treat. Looking out over the trees with no houses in sight make you feel like you're in the middle of the jungle, but actually you're just a 5min drive from town. R$350

EATING

Bistro da Mata Km 2 of the MT-251 towards Campo Verde ⓣ65 3301 3483 or ⓣ 65 98421 8810, ⓦbistrodamata.com.br. It's worth venturing out of the town centre for this romantic restaurant with wonderful views of Cuiabá down below. Get there before sunset and stay for a candlelit dinner. You need to book in advance. Tues, Wed & Sun 10am–3pm, Thurs–Sat 10am–1am.

Dom Kebab Rua Cipriano Curvo 464 ⓣ65 3301 2998, ⓦfacebook.com/domkebabmt. Facing the main square this small restaurant is conveniently located for a quick (and late) snack. The kebabs (around R$16) are fresh, affordable and tasty. Wed–Fri 3pm–midnight, Sat 1–midnight, Sun 1–11pm.

Estilo Av do Penhasco, s/n, Bom Clima, ⓣ65 3301 3430. Doing one thing, but doing it well, Portuguese restaurant *Estilo* is the place to come for *bacalhão* (salted cod) in many different guises. Start off with the delicious *bacalhão* fritters. Fri 7–11pm, Sat 11am–3pm & 7–11pm, Sun 11am–3pm.

Popular Rua Cipriano Curvo 683 ⓣ65 3301 1793. One of the village's most popular restaurants with *comida por quilo* and all you can eat buffet (R$16) at lunchtime and dinner just off the main square. Offers good value for money. Daily 11am–2pm & 6–11pm.

Barra do Garças

Over 500km from Cuiabá, on the frontier between Mato Grosso and Goiás states, **BARRA DO GARÇAS** is a useful and interesting point at which to break a long bus journey. This small and isolated, but still fast-growing town of some 60,000 people sits astride the Rio das Garças, one of the main headwaters of the Araguaia, underneath low-lying wooded hills. It's a surprisingly good base for a variety of nature-based hikes or relaxing hot-water springs, and the nearest river beach, the **Praia de Aragarças**, is barely 1km away. In the mountainous terrain that stretches from Barra do Garças up to the Serra do Cachimbo, the most impressive feature is the highly eroded red-rock cliff of the 700m **Serra do Roncador**, 150km due north of the town. Waterfalls and caves abound in the region; close to the limits of the town there are fourteen waterfalls in the Serra Azul alone, a range that rises to over 800m.

Parque Balneário das Águas Quentes

6km northeast of Barra do Garças • Daily 6am–9.30pm • Small charge • ☎ 66 3405 1313

Just 6km northeast of town, there are more river beaches and the popular natural hot baths of the **Parque Balneário das Águas Quentes**. Besides curing all the usual complaints, the waters are proudly proclaimed by the town's tourist office to have the capacity to augment one's *vitalidade sexual* – you have been warned.

ARRIVAL AND INFORMATION — BARRA DO GARÇAS

By bus Bus connections from the rodoviária on Rua Bororós (☎ 66 3401 1217) along the BR-070 between Cuiabá and Brasília are good, and there is also an airport, Julio Campos, 15km out of town (☎ 66 3401 2218), which is served by Azul who operates three flights a week to Cuiaba and Goiânia.

Car rental Localiza (☎ 66 3861 2140).

Tourist office There is a municipal tourist office, FUNDATUR, on Praça Tiradentes (Mon–Sat 9am–6pm; ☎ 66 3861 2227 or ☎ 66 3861 2344).

TOURS AND ACTIVITIES

Ecotours There are three environmental organizations in town that may be able to help with information on the region and ecotours, as well as possibilities for rock climbing, potholing and canyoning: CELVA, Centro Etno-Ecológico do Vale do Araguaia, Av Araguaia 146 (☎ 66 3861 2018); União Eco-Cultura do Vale do Araguaia, Av Min. João Alberto 100; and the Fundação Cultura Ambiental do Centro Oeste, Caixa Postal 246. Barra do Garças also serves as a possible starting point for visits to the world's largest river island, the Ilha do Bananal, in Tocantins state (see page 434).

Xavante and Bororo reserves For information and to find out about written authorization to enter one of the indigenous reserves, contact FUNAI, Rua Muniz Mariano 3, Setor Dermat (☎ 66 3861 2020).

COLONEL P.H. FAWCETT

Colonel P.H. Fawcett, the famous British explorer, vanished somewhere in this region in 1925, on what turned out to be his last attempt to locate a lost jungle city and civilization. He'd been searching for it on and off for twenty years, as entertainingly told in his edited diaries and letters, *Exploration Fawcett* (see page 669). This last expedition was made in the company of his eldest son, Jack, and a school friend of Jack's, and following their disappearance various theories were put forward as to their fate, including being kept as prisoners of a remote tribe or, more fancifully, adopted chiefs. Possibly, they were murdered out in the wilds, as were dozens of other explorers, although Fawcett had travelled for years among indigenous tribes without coming to any harm. More likely, they merely succumbed to one of the dozens of **tropical diseases** that were by far the biggest killer at the time. But the fate of the colonel still remains a mystery: in 1985, the same team who had identified the body of the Nazi Josef Mengele announced that they had identified bones found in a shallow grave as those of the colonel; but in 1996 another expedition, Expedição Autan, dissatisfied with the Mengele team's evidence, set off to try to make a DNA match, but found no trace of either the colonel or his companions.

ACCOMMODATION AND EATING

Restaurante Vitória Régia Rua Mato Grosso 551 ⓣ 66 3401 1940, ⓦ restaurantevitoriaregia.com.br. This popular lunchtime *por quilo* restaurant serves a good variety of salads and hot dishes, including quality meats straight from the *churrascaria*. Football fans will appreciate the games shown on the TV in the background. Daily 11am–2pm.

Serra Azul Plaza Praça Tiradentes 572 ⓣ 66 3401 6663, ⓦ serraazulplazahotel.com.br. The swishest place to stay in town, although that's not saying much, this hotel is comfortable, if a little soulless. If this one's full, try the sister hotel *Tawfiq's Palace Hotel* on the same square. **R$150**

DIRECTORY

Money and exchange You can change money at the Banco do Brasil on Praça Tiradentes.

Post office The central post office is at Rua 1 de Maio 19.

Alta Floresta

West off the BR-163 some 150km before the Serra do Cachimbo, a dirt road leads to **ALTA FLORESTA**, a rapidly growing frontier town of around 43,000 people, which is increasingly tourist-friendly. Located almost 800km north of Cuiabá, it's a remote but thriving agricultural settlement with regular bus and plane connections to Cuiabá. The town is of little immediate interest, but has in recent years opened its doors to ecotourism in the form of a four-star hotel, the *Floresta Amazonica,* as well as the fantastic luxury lodge *Cristalino Jungle Lodge*. The real reason for visiting this area lies close to the lodge, deeper in the forest on a tributary of the Rio Teles Pires, which ultimately flows into the Amazon. The forest around here is particularly rich in **birdlife**, and there are several set birding trails where you can also see alligators and capuchin, spider and howler monkeys.

ARRIVAL AND DEPARTURE — ALTA FLORESTA

By plane The airport, 2km northwest of Alta Floresta on Av Ariosto da Riva (ⓣ 66 3521 3360; R$30 by taxi), has one daily flight to Cuiabá operated by Azul.

By bus Buses leave from Cuiabá to Alta Floresta six times a day (14hr).

ACCOMMODATION

Cristalino Jungle Lodge 39km north of Alta Floresta ⓣ 11 3071 0104, ⓦ cristalinolodge.com.br. Set in the midst of the forest, this fantastic ecolodge is geared towards serious nature-lovers who want to learn about the surrounding environment, without roughing it. Accommodation is made up of luxury bungalows, but it's environmental sustainability that's the focus here. Guides are extremely knowledgeable about the region and will take you on wonderful trails and to the lodge's two observation towers. Room price includes full board, airport transfer and excursions. **R$1580**

Floresta Amazonica Av Perimetral Oeste 2001 ⓣ 66 3512 7100, ⓦ fah.com.br. A tastefully developed place with over 100 acres of expansive jungle grounds that serves as a base for the associated *Cristalino Jungle Lodge*. There is a great restaurant, lovely rooms with verandas, as well as a pool, sauna and football pitch. **R$245**

Lisboa Palace Hotel Av Jaime V. Campos 251 ⓣ 66 3521 2876, ⓦ www.hotellisboa.com.br. Decent hotel in the town with big, bright clean rooms but no pool. Centrally located and easily accessible from the airport for those just passing by. **R$210**

CICLISTA
SÓ ATRAVESSE NO VERDE

São Paulo

AVENIDA PAULISTA, SÃO PAULO

São Paulo

São Paulo, Brazil's most populous state and home to its biggest city, is Brazil's economic powerhouse. As well as being responsible for nearly half the country's industrial output, it also has an agricultural sector that produces, among other things, more orange juice than any single nation worldwide. Its eponymous city boasts a dizzying variety of cultural centres and art galleries, and the noise from its vibrant fashion and music scenes is heard around the globe. Although most people come here only to visit its capital on business, the state also has excellent sandy beaches that rival Rio's best. Inland, the state is dominated by fields of cattle pasture, sugar cane, orange trees and soya, but some impressive *fazenda* houses still remain as legacies of the days when the local economy was dominated by coffee. To escape scorching summer temperatures, or for the novelty in tropical Brazil of a winter chill, you can also head to Campos do Jordão, one of the country's highest settlements.

São Paulo state's economic pre-eminence is a relatively recent phenomenon. In 1507 São Vicente, the second-oldest Portuguese settlement in Brazil, was founded on the coast near present-day **Santos**, but for over three hundred years the area comprising today's São Paulo state remained a backwater. The inhabitants were a hardy people, of mixed Portuguese and indigenous origin, from whom, in the seventeenth and eighteenth centuries, emerged the **bandeirantes** – frontiersmen who roamed far into the South American interior to secure the borders of the Portuguese Empire against Spanish encroachment, capturing natives as slaves and seeking out precious metals and gems as they went.

It wasn't until the mid-nineteenth century that São Paulo became rich. Cotton production received a boost with the arrival in the late 1860s of Confederate refugees from the American South, who settled around **Santa Bárbara d'Oeste**, about 140km from the then small town of **São Paulo** itself. But after disappointing results with cotton, most of these plantation owners switched their attention to coffee and, by the end of the century, the state had become firmly established as the world's foremost producer of the crop. During the same period, Brazil abolished slavery and the plantation owners recruited European and Japanese immigrants to expand production. Riding the wave of the coffee boom, foreign companies took the opportunity to invest in port facilities, rail lines and power and water supplies, while textile and other new industries emerged, too. Within a few decades, the town of São Paulo became one of Latin America's greatest commercial and cultural centres, growing from a small town into a vast metropolitan sprawl. Although the coffee bubble eventually burst, the state had the resources in place to diversify into other produce and São Paulo's prominence in Brazil's economy was assured.

PRAIA DO BONETE, ILHABELA

Highlights

❶ **Mercado Municipal** Look out for the lovely stained-glass windows at this market, depicting scenes of Brazilian agricultural production. See page 489

❷ **Museu da Imigração do Estado de São Paulo** Explore this fascinating museum, which was once a hostel that tens of thousands of immigrants passed through upon arriving in Brazil. See page 489

❸ **Avenida Paulista** A showcase for modern São Paulo, this avenue also features a few lavish mansions from bygone eras. See page 495

❹ **Paranapiacaba** This remarkable, late nineteenth-century British railway village is a popular base for hikes in the surrounding Mata Atlântica. See page 516

❺ **Casa do Pinhal** An intriguing relic of the state's nineteenth-century coffee boom, this is one of the oldest surviving and best-preserved rural estates in the state of São Paulo. See page 520

❻ **Ilhabela** Protected as a state park, this island – the most beautiful spot on São Paulo's coast – remains unravaged by tourism. See page 528

HIGHLIGHTS ARE MARKED ON THE MAPS ON PAGES 482 AND 484

São Paulo city

Rio is a beauty. But São Paulo – São Paulo is a city. Marlene Dietrich

Nicknamed "Sampa" – the title of a well-known Caetano Veloso song about the city, in which he admits that, "When I arrived here I didn't understand the hard concrete poetry of your streets and the discreet casual beauty of your girls" – the city of **SÃO PAULO** does not have an immediately appealing aesthetic. It's a place most people come to for business; residents of the city, *paulistanos*, boast frequently of their work ethic, supposedly superior to what dominates the rest of Brazil, and speak contemptuously of the idleness of *cariocas* (in reply, *cariocas* joke sourly that *paulistanos* are simply incapable of enjoying anything – sex in particular). Increasingly, though, visitors are also coming to São Paulo to play. Often described, not inaccurately, as "the New York of the tropics", the city lays claim to having surpassed Rio as Brazil's **cultural** centre, with a lively and varied programme of exhibitions and shows. There are several sights associated with the vast influx of immigrants to the city (see page 494), especially in the individual *bairros* where the immigrants and their descendants have established strong local communities.

São Paulo's traditional **Centro** is the area around **Praça da Sé** and **Praça da República**. North of the centre is the red-light district of **Luz**, and just south of the commercial district are São Paulo's "Little Italy", **Bela Vista** (usually referred to as "**Bixiga**"), the traditionally Japanese neighbourhood of **Liberdade** and the smart streets of **Higienópolis**. To the southwest, **Avenida Paulista**, the city's main boulevard, lined by modern high-rise office buildings, divides the centre from **Jardins**, one of the most prestigious of São Paulo's middle- and upper-class suburbs. Yet more plush suburbs, such as **Itaim Bibi**, with its upmarket restaurants and clubs, extend south and west from Jardins towards a business district that stretches along **Avenida Brigadeiro Faria Lima**.

São Paulo lacks the natural beauty of Rio, but it's a place that grows on you as you get to know it. Efficient and business-like, it's also Brazil's most cosmopolitan city, with

AVOIDING TROUBLE IN SÃO PAULO

Assaults and **robberies** are favourite topics of conversation among *paulistanos*, with the city's crime statistics consistently higher than those of Rio. Nevertheless, by using a little common sense you're unlikely to encounter problems. With such a mixture of people in São Paulo, you're far less likely to be assumed to be a foreigner than in most parts of Brazil, and therefore won't make such an obvious target for **pickpockets** and other petty thieves.

At night, pay particular attention around the central red-light district of **Luz**, location of the city's main train stations, and – though not as bad – around **Praça da República**. Also take care late at night in **Bixiga** (also known as Bela Vista), or if you venture into **Praça Roosevelt**. Always carry at least some money in an immediately accessible place so that, if you are accosted by a **mugger**, you can quickly hand something over before they start getting angry or panicky. If in any doubt at all about visiting an area you don't know, don't hesitate to take a **taxi**.

neighbourhoods whose local flavour is much influenced by the cultures of **immigrant communities** who have settled in them – Japanese in Liberdade, Italian in Bixiga, Jewish and more lately Korean in Bom Retiro, to name just a few – and this is of course often reflected in their cuisine. At any rate, in a city with so many museums, theatres, cinemas and parks to its name – not forgetting the hundreds if not thousands of varied bars and restaurants – you certainly have no excuse for being bored.

Brief history

8

In 1554, the Jesuit priests José de Anchieta and Manuel da Nóbrega established a mission station on the banks of the Rio Tietê in an attempt to bring Christianity to the Tupi-Guarani Indians. São Paulo dos Campos de Piratininga, as the site was called, was situated 70km inland and 730m up, in the sheer, forest-covered inclines of the Serra do Mar, above the port of São Vicente. The gently undulating plateau and the proximity to the Paraná and Plata rivers facilitated traffic into the interior and, with São Paulo as their base, roaming gangs of *bandeirantes* set out in search of loot. Around the mission school, a few adobe huts were erected and the settlement soon developed into a trading post and a centre from which to secure mineral wealth. In 1681, São Paulo became a seat of regional government and, in 1711, it was made a municipality by the king of Portugal, the cool, healthy climate helping to attract settlers from the coast.

The coffee boom and urban expansion

With the expansion of **coffee** plantations westwards from Rio de Janeiro, along the Paraibá Valley, in the mid-nineteenth century São Paulo's fortunes improved. The region's rich red soil – *terra roxa* – was ideally suited to coffee cultivation, and from about 1870 plantation owners took up residence in the city, which was undergoing a rapid transformation into a bustling regional centre. In the 1890s, enterprising coffee barons began to place some of their profits into local industry, hedging their bets against a possible fall in the price of coffee, with textile factories being a favourite area for investment.

As the local population could not meet the ever-increasing demands of plantation owners, factories looked to **immigrants** for their workforce (see page 494). As a result, São Paulo's **population** soared, almost tripling to 69,000 by 1890, and to 239,000 by the end of the next decade. By 1950, when it had reached 2.2 million, São Paulo had clearly established its dominant role in Brazil's urbanization. Today, with a population of over eleven million – and over twenty million if you include its sprawling suburbs –São Paulo is the seventh-largest city in the world, and the biggest south of the equator.

In the nineteenth century, most of colonial São Paulo was levelled and replaced by a disorganized patchwork of wide avenues and large buildings, so that today the city's colonial architectural heritage has all but vanished. Some grand **public buildings** were built in the late nineteenth and early twentieth centuries, however, and a few still remain. Even now, conservation is seen as not being profitable, and São Paulo is more concerned with rising population, rising production and rising consumption – factors that today are paralleled by rising levels of homelessness, pollution and crime.

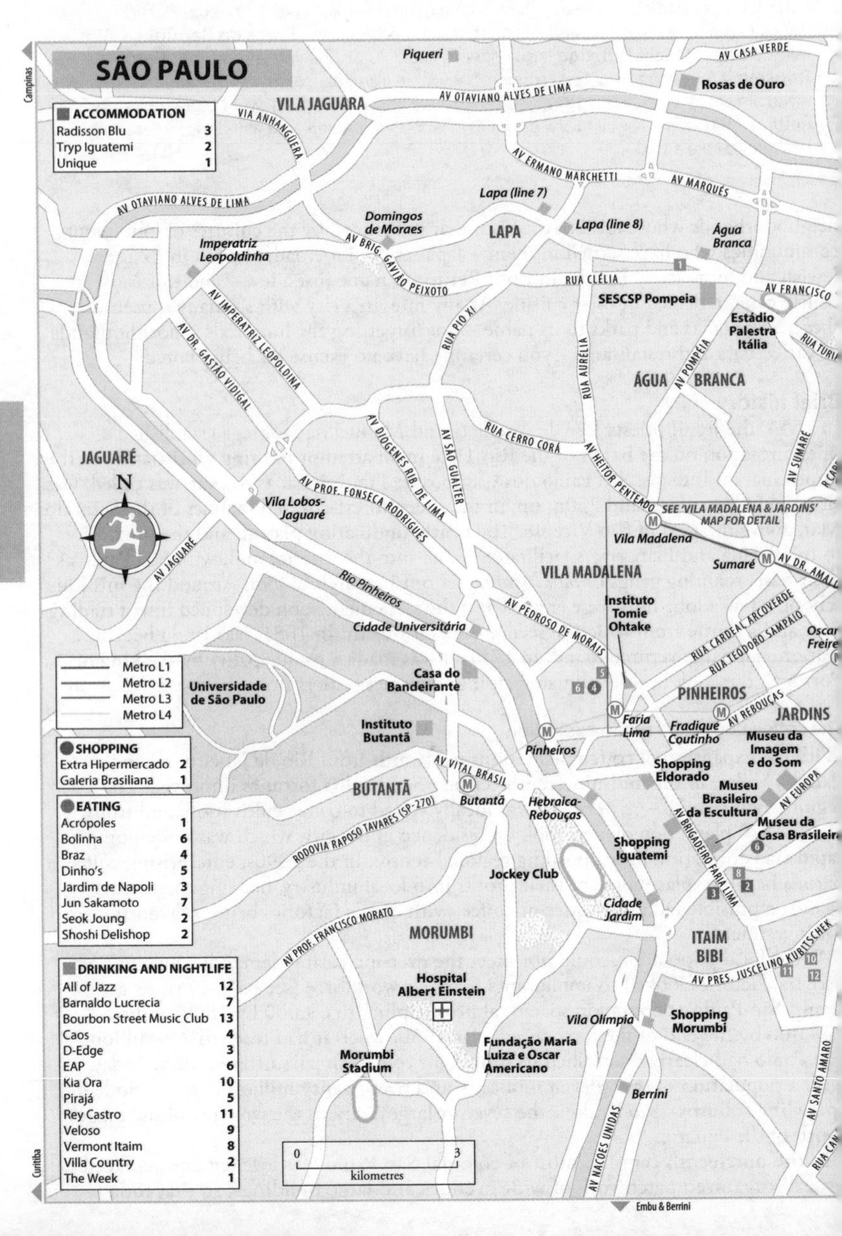

Centro

São Paulo's **Centro** (downtown area) hangs between two main squares, **Praça da Sé** on its eastern side, and **Praça da República** to its west. Its northern edge is marked by the station at Luz, and to its south it borders the strongly Japanese neighbourhood of Liberdade and the traditionally Italian neighbourhood of Bixiga.

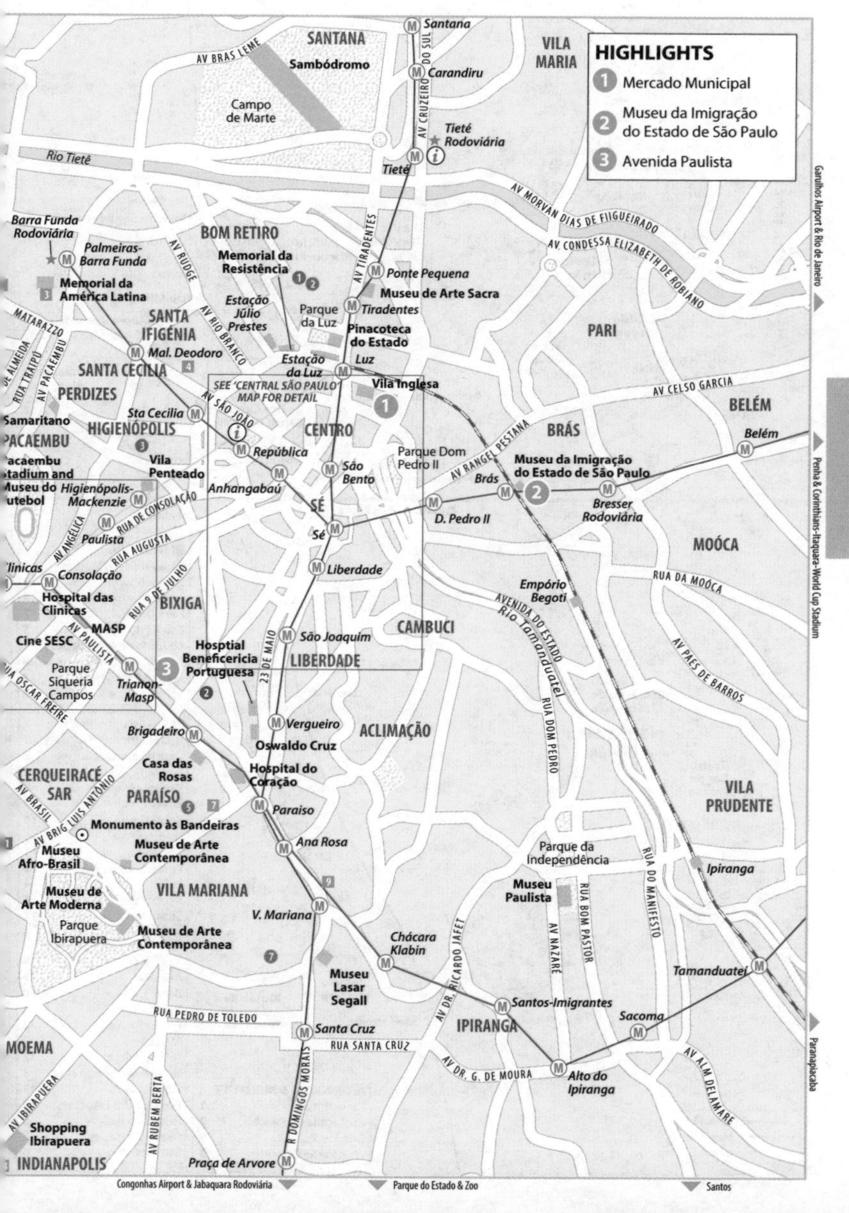

8

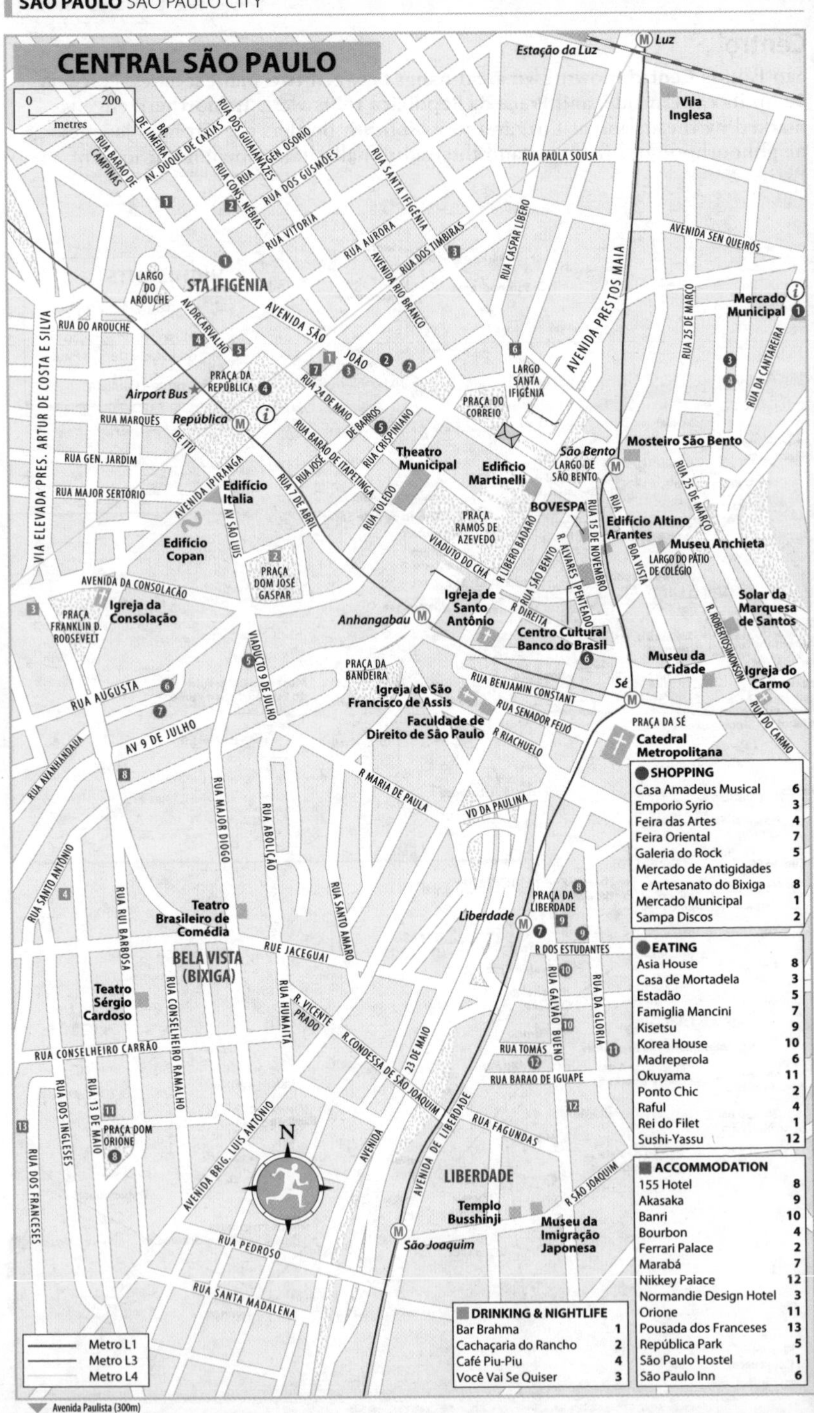
CENTRAL SÃO PAULO
0 200 metres
Estação da Luz
Luz
Vila Inglesa
Rua Paula Sousa
Avenida Sen Queirós
Avenida Prestos Maia
Rua Caspar Libero
Rua Santa Ifigênia
Rua dos Timbiras
Avenida Rio Branco
Rua Aurora
Rua Vitória
Rua dos Gusmões
Rua Gen. Osório
Rua Cons. Nébias
Rua dos Guaianazes
Av. Duque de Caxias
Br. de Limeira
Rua Barão de Campinas
Largo do Arouche
Sta Ifigênia
Avenida São João
Rua do Arouche
Av. Dr Carvalho
Praça da República
Airport Bus
República
Rua Marquês de Itú
Rua Gen. Jardim
Rua Major Sertório
Via Elevada Pres. Artur de Costa e Silva
Avenida Ipiranga
Edifício Italia
Edifício Copan
Av São Luís
Rua 24 de Maio
De Barros
Rua Barão de Itapetinga
Rua José
Rua Crispiniano
Rua 7 de Abril
Rua Toledo
Theatro Municipal
Edifício Martinelli
Praça do Correio
Largo Santa Ifigênia
Mercado Municipal
Rua 25 de Março
Rua da Cantareira
Mosteiro São Bento
São Bento
Largo de São Bento
BOVESPA
Praça Ramos de Azevedo
Viaduto do Cha
R Libero Badaró
R. São Bento
R. Alvares Penteado
Rua 15 de Novembro
Rua Boa Vista
Edifício Altino Arantes
Museu Anchieta
Largo do Pátio de Colégio
Solar da Marquesa de Santos
R. Roberto Simonson
Museu da Cidade
Igreja do Carmo
Rua do Carmo
Avenida da Consolação
Praça Dom José Gaspar
Igreja da Consolação
Praça Franklin D. Roosevelt
Igreja de Santo Antônio
Anhangabau
R Direita
Centro Cultural Banco do Brasil
Sé
Praça da Sé
Catedral Metropolitana
Viaducto 9 de Julho
Praça da Bandeira
Igreja de São Francisco de Assis
Faculdade de Direito de São Paulo
Rua Benjamin Constant
Rua Senador Feijó
R Riachuelo
Rua Augusta
Av 9 de Julho
Rua Avanhandaua
R Maria de Paula
Vd da Paulina
Rua Major Diogo
Rua Abolição
Rua Santo Antônio
Rua Santo Amaro
Rua Rui Barbosa
Teatro Brasileiro de Comédia
Bela Vista (Bixiga)
Rue Jaceguai
Praça da Liberdade
Liberdade
R dos Estudantes
Rua Galvão Bueno
Rua da Glória
Teatro Sérgio Cardoso
Rua Conselheiro Ramalho
Rua Humaitá
R. Vicente Prado
R. Condessa de São Joaquim
23 de Maio
Rua Conselheiro Carrão
Rua Tomás
Rua Barao de Iguape
Rua Fagundas
Rua dos Ingleses
Rua 13 de Maio
Praça Dom Orione
Rua dos Franceses
Avenida Brig. Luis Antônio
Avenida
N
Avenida de Liberdade
Liberdade
R São Joaquim
Templo Busshinji
Museu da Imigração Japonesa
São Joaquim
Rua Pedroso
Rua Santa Madalena
Metro L1
Metro L3
Metro L4
Avenida Paulista (300m)
SHOPPING
Casa Amadeus Musical 6
Emporio Syrio 3
Feira das Artes 4
Feira Oriental 7
Galeria do Rock 5
Mercado de Antigidades e Artesanato do Bixiga 8
Mercado Municipal 1
Sampa Discos 2
EATING
Asia House 8
Casa de Mortadela 3
Estadão 5
Famiglia Mancini 7
Kisetsu 9
Korea House 10
Madreperola 6
Okuyama 11
Ponto Chic 2
Raful 4
Rei do Filet 1
Sushi-Yassu 12
ACCOMMODATION
155 Hotel 8
Akasaka 9
Banri 10
Bourbon 4
Ferrari Palace 2
Marabá 7
Nikkey Palace 12
Normandie Design Hotel 3
Orione 11
Pousada dos Franceses 13
República Park 5
São Paulo Hostel 1
São Paulo Inn 6
DRINKING & NIGHTLIFE
Bar Brahma 1
Cachaçaria do Rancho 2
Café Piu-Piu 4
Você Vai Se Quiser 3

Praça da Sé and around

Praça da Sé, the most convenient starting point of a hunt for what remains of **colonial São Paulo**, is a large expanse of concrete and fountains. During the day the square outside bustles with activity, always crowded with hawkers and people heading towards the commercial district on its western fringes. The **sundial** just outside the cathedral is considered the exact centre of the city from which all road distances to São Paulo are measured, and its inscription indicates the direction of other Brazilian states. At night the square is transformed into a campsite for homeless children, who survive as best they can by shining shoes, selling chewing gum or begging.

Catedral Metropolitana

Praça da Sé • Mon–Fri 7.30am–7pm, Sat 7.30am–5pm, Sun 7.30am–6pm • Free • Ⓜ Sé

Praça da Sé is dominated by the **Catedral Metropolitana**, a huge Neogothic structure with capacity for 8000. Completed in 1954, it replaced São Paulo's eighteenth-century cathedral. Although the building is largely unremarkable, its doorway is interesting for having distinctly tropical details such as coffee beans and crocodiles alongside the more usual apostles and saints.

Pátio do Colégio

Rua Boa Vista • Chapel Tues–Sun 9am–4.30pm; Museu Anchieta Tues–Fri 9am–4.45pm, Sat & Sun 9am–4.30pm • R$8 • Ⓦ pateocollegio.com.br • Ⓜ Sé

Just north of Praça da Sé you'll find the site of the city's origins. The whitewashed Portuguese Baroque **Pátio do Colégio** is a replica of the college and chapel that formed the centre of the Jesuit mission founded here by the priests José de Anchieta and Manoel da Nóbrega on January 25, 1554 (the anniversary celebrated as a citywide holiday). Although built in 1896 (the other buildings forming the Pátio were constructed in the twentieth century), the chapel is an accurate reproduction, but it's in the **Museu Anchieta**, part of the Pátio, that the most interesting sixteenth- and early seventeenth-century relics – mostly old documents, maps and watercolours – are held.

Museu da Cidade

Rua Roberto Simonsen 136 • Tues–Sun 9am–5pm • Free • Ⓣ 11 3241 1081, Ⓦ www.museudacidade.sp.gov.br • Ⓜ Sé

Just off Praça da Sé and around the corner from the Pátio do Colégio is the **Museu da Cidade**. More interesting than the museum's small collection chronicling the development of São Paulo is the building that it's housed in, the **Solar da Marquesa de Santos** – an eighteenth-century manor house that represents the sole remaining residential building in the city from this period.

Igreja do Carmo

Av Rangel Pestana 230 • Mon–Fri 8am–5pm, Sat & Sun 8am–noon • Free • Ⓣ 11 3119 1168 • Ⓜ Sé

Just east of Praça da Sé, the well-preserved **Igreja do Carmo** (or, to give its full title, Igreja da Ordem Terceira do Carmo) was built in 1632 and still retains many of its seventeenth-century features, as well as a fine Baroque high altar that dates from the century after that.

Igreja de São Francisco de Assis

Largo de São Francisco 133 • Daily 7.30am–7pm • Free • Ⓜ Anhangabaú

West of the Praça da Sé (a 2min walk down Rua Senador Feijó), the **Igreja de São Francisco de Assis** is one of the best-preserved colonial buildings in the city. Built between 1647 and 1790, it is a typical Portuguese Baroque church of the period, featuring intricately carved ornaments and an elaborate high altar. While here, step inside the adjoining courtyard of the **Faculdade de Direito de São Paulo** – the country's best and most exclusive law school, and one of its first higher-education institutions, founded in 1824 – and take a look at the huge 1930s stained-glass window depicting the Largo de São Francisco in the early nineteenth century.

Igreja de Santo Antônio

Praça do Patriarca 49 • Mon–Fri 6am–6.30pm, Sat 7–9.30am & 5–6.30pm, Sun 8–9.30am & 5–6.30pm • Free • T 11 3242 2414 • M Anhangabaú

Very near to the **Viaduto do Chá** (a pedestrian bridge linking the two parts of the commercial centre), it's worth visiting the **Igreja de Santo Antônio**, which dates from 1717, although the present-day yellow-and-white facade (squeezed incongruously in between modern shops and office blocks) only dates from the early twentieth century. The interior has been stripped of many of its eighteenth-century accoutrements, but its Baroque altar has been restored, and the simple painted wooden ceiling deserves a look.

The Triângulo

Edifício Altino Arantes: Rua João Brícola 24 • Tues–Sat 9am–7pm, Sun 9am–5pm • R$20 • W farolsantander.com.br • Edifício Martinelli Avenida São João 35 • Roof terrace Mon–Fri 9.30–11am & 2.30–4pm • Free but photo ID required • T 11 3104-2477 • W prediomartinelli.com.br • M São Bento

The **Triângulo**, the traditional banking district and a zone of concentrated vertical growth, lies northwest of the Praça da Sé. The city's first skyscraper, the 35-storey **Edifício Martinelli**, stands at the northern edge of the district, at Avenida São João 35; it was inaugurated in 1929 and remains an important downtown landmark. Two blocks east, at Rua João Brícola 24, the similar-sized **Edifício Altino Arantes** opened in 1947. Modelled on the Empire State Building, it was home to the Banespa bank, and is often referred to as the Banespa building, although it has now been rebranded as Farol Santander. You can take the elevators up to a lookout tower at the top for great views of São Paulo's intense cityscape.

The BOVESPA building

8

Rua 15 de Novembro 275 • Mon–Fri 9am–5pm • Free • T 11 2565 5024, E visite@b3.com.br, W educacional.bmfbovespa.com.br/visitas • M São Bento

São Paulo's stock exchange, located in the **BOVESPA** building, is, after Wall Street, the most active in the Americas. Free two-hour tours are offered to groups of 20–60 people (apply by phone or email), and individuals can tag along with a group if there's one visiting, but the truth is that most of the activity happens behind computer screens these days.

Centro Cultural Banco do Brasil

Rua Álvares Penteado 112 • 9am–9pm; closed Tues • Free • T 11 3113 3651, W culturabancodobrasil.com.br • M São Bento or Sé

The arts are hardly a driving force within the Triângulo, but a distinctive Beaux Arts–style former bank building has been developed as the **Centro Cultural Banco do Brasil** and is a refreshing contrast to the surrounding mammon. The temporary exhibitions on display, which are taken from the bank's own important collections of Brazilian art or those of prominent private collectors, are always worth at least a brief look. Inside, the café is a convenient place for lunch.

Mosteiro São Bento and around

Largo de São Bento • Mon–Fri 6am–6.40pm, Sat & Sun 6am–noon & 4–6.40pm • Free • T 11 3328-8799, W mosteiro.org.br • M São Bento

Incongruously situated just a block away from the high-rise financial district, the **Mosteiro São Bento** provides a different kind of uplifting experience. The monastery's church originally dates from 1598, but has been given a facelift five times (the last one took place in 1912). The interior is more impressive than you might expect given the rather severe exterior; look out for fine detail such as zodiac symbols above the archway just inside the entrance. The rest of the complex is closed to the public, however, as it still provides living quarters for Benedictine monks, who emerge in the mornings to sing Gregorian chants to accompany morning mass in the church (Mon–Fri 7am, Sat 6am, Sun 10am); Sunday's mass is, unsurprisingly, by far the best attended.

Leading off west from São Bento, the **Viaduto Santa Ifigênia** gives good views of the area looking south, including the new city hall with its rooftop garden. The attractive green area immediately below, the **Vale do Anhangabaú** (or Demon's Valley), stretches between this viaduct and the Viaduto do Chá.

ARAB SÃO PAULO

The area to the west of the Mercado Municipal, particularly around Rua 25 de Março, is where São Paulo's **Lebanese and Syrian community** has traditionally concentrated. Although they're less in evidence than they once were, you'll still find Arabic restaurants and stores selling Middle Eastern food – the Empório Syrio (see page 514), for example, has been going since 1924. The community is fairly evenly divided between Muslims and Christians, and hidden away at Rua Cavalheiro Basilio Jafet 15, you'll find a beautiful Orthodox church.

Mercado Municipal and around

Rua da Cantareira 306 • Mon–Sat 6am–6pm, Sun 6am–4pm • Free • Ⓜ Luz or São Bento

About 1km to the northeast of São Bento you'll find the **Mercado Municipal**, an imposing, vaguely German Neogothic hall, completed in 1933. Apart from the phenomenal display of Brazilian and imported fruit, vegetables, cheese and other produce, the market is most noted for its enormous stained-glass windows depicting scenes of cattle raising, market gardening, and coffee and banana plantations. The food stalls are particularly known for their especially tasty *pastéis de bacalhau* (saltfish pasties), and if you head up to the mezzanine, there's a whole range of patio **restaurants** serving authentic food in a colourful setting.

Museu da Imigração do Estado de São Paulo

Rua Visconde de Parnaíba 1316 • Tues–Sat 9pm–5pm, Sun 10am–5pm • R$10, free on Sat • ⓣ 11 2692 1866, Ⓦ museudaimigracao.org.br • Ⓜ Brás

East of the Mercado Municipal, the run-down neighbourhood of Brás would have little to offer if it wasn't for the superb **Museu da Imigração do Estado de São Paulo**. The old hostel buildings house an immigration research centre, a basic café and one of the best museums in São Paulo.

The museum has a permanent collection of period furniture, documents and photographs, and regularly mounts temporary exhibits relating to individual immigrant nationalities. The main building itself is the most interesting feature of the complex, however, with vast dormitories and its own rail siding and platform that were used for unloading new arrivals and their baggage. Near the entrance, a separate building contained the rooms where they would meet their prospective employers; the government provided interpreters to help the immigrants make sense of work contracts. Designed to hold four thousand people, the hostel housed as many as ten thousand at times, with residents being treated little better than cattle. In its early years, the place was a virtual prison. The exit ticket was securing a contract of employment, and control of potential plantation-workers was considered necessary, since few people actually wanted to work in the fields and there was a large labour leakage to the city of São Paulo itself. The last immigrants were processed here in 1978.

Although the museum is only a five-minute walk from Brás *metrô* station (alongside the rail line and over a pedestrian bridge), the area is a little bit rough and you may feel uncomfortable walking here alone. Taxis are rarely available, but on weekends and holidays (10.30am–4pm) you can take the **Trem do Imigrante**, a wonderful little nineteenth-century steam train, from Brás or Moóca *metrô* stations (Ⓦ abpfsp.com.br/passeio_trem.htm; R$20–25 per ride).

Praça da República

A kilometre west of Praça da Sé, the area around Praça da República is now dominated by office buildings, hotels and shops, but was once full of lavish **mansions** belonging to coffee-plantation owners, who began to take up residence in the city from about 1870. Built out of British iron, Italian marble, Latvian pine, Portuguese tiles and Belgian stained glass, these mansions were soon abandoned as the city centre took on the brash and commercial character of its present-day form. The Praça da República itself – once home to a bullring – has a green area with a small lake where turtles sunbathe and rows of fortune tellers throw shells and cards to part the gullible from their *reaís*.

Theatro Municipal

Praça Ramos de Azevedo • Free guided tours, in Portuguese Tues–Fri 11am, 3pm & 5pm, Sat 2pm & 3pm; in English Tues–Fri 11am, Sat noon • 11 3053 2092, theatromunicipal.org.br • Anhangabaú

Three blocks east of Praça da República, in the direction of Praça da Sé, the **Theatro Municipal** is São Paulo's most distinguished public building, an eclectic mixture of Art Nouveau and Italian Renaissance styles. Work began on it in 1903, when the coffee boom was at its peak and São Paulo at its most confident. The theatre is still the city's main venue for classical music, and the auditorium, lavishly decorated and furnished with Italian marble, velvet, gold leaf and mirrors, can be viewed by attending a performance or on a free guided tour.

Outside, just down the steps leading into the Vale do Anhangabaú (see page 488), a dramatic **sculpture fountain** represents the characters from Carlos Gomes' opera *O Guarani*, based on the book by José de Alencar. (The opera, a story set among the Guaraní, premiered at La Scala in 1870 and was one of the first works by a New World composer to achieve success in Europe.)

Avenida São Luís

Edifício Itália: Av Ipiranga 344 • Terraço Panorâmico Mon–Sat 3–5pm • Free • 11 2189 2929, República

In the 1940s and 1950s, **Avenida São Luís**, the street leading south from the Praça da República, was São Paulo's version of New York's Fifth Avenue, lined with high-class apartment buildings and offices; though no longer fashionable today, it still retains a certain degree of elegance. Among the buildings lining it, the 46-storey **Edifício Itália**, built in 1965 to dwarf the Edifício Martinelli, was for many years Latin America's tallest building. On cloud- and smog-free days, the *Terraço Itália* restaurant on the 41st and 42nd floors is a good vantage point from which to view the city, but unless you want to eat there, viewing is limited to a two-hour slot.

Edifício Copan

Avenida Ipiranga 200 • copansp.com.br • República

Admirers of the Brazilian architect Oscar Niemeyer will immediately recognize the serpentine curves of the 1950 **Edifício Copan**, just to the west of Avenida São Luís, and by far the largest of the apartment and office buildings on the avenue. It's regarded as something of a social experiment in this otherwise sharply divided city, with its residents paying a wide variety of prices for the 1160 apartments that range in size from 26 to 350 square metres.

Luz

The once affluent and still leafy *bairro* of **Luz**, home to both of São Paulo's main train stations, has for many years been one of the city's seediest red-light districts. Recently, though, Luz has slowly been undergoing a renaissance, with city and state government investment aimed at transforming the area into a top-rank cultural centre.

Ascending from Luz *metrô*, you'll immediately notice the imposing **Estação da Luz**. The station was part of the British-owned rail network that contributed to São Paulo's explosive growth in the late nineteenth century. The station was built in 1901 and everything was imported from Britain for its construction – from the design of the project to the smallest of screws. Although fire destroyed the refined decoration of its chambers in 1946, interior details (iron balconies, passageways and grilles) bear witness to the majestic structure's original elegance. Until the 1940s there was a sizeable British community in the area; some of the engineers and their families were housed in the **Vila Inglesa** at Rua Mauá 836, a group of 28 distinctively English-style houses built in 1924 which have long since been used as shops, offices and restaurants.

MERCADO MUNICIPAL, SÃO PAULO

EISENBAHN
Rua

Museu da Língua Portugesa

Praça da Luz • Wed–Sun 10am–6pm, Tues 10am–10pm; last ticket sold an hour before closing • R$6; closed for renovation at time of research • ⓣ 11 3322 0080, ⓦ museudalinguaportuguesa.org.br • Ⓜ Luz

The upper floors of the **Estação da Luz** have been transformed to house the **Museu da Língua Portugesa**, a celebration of the Portuguese language. Opened in 2006, the museum charts the development of the language and explores its global variations through the display of written texts, spoken word, song and images. There are also temporary exhibitions examining individual writers such as Brazil's Machado de Assis and Clarice Lispector, and Portugal's Fernando Pessoa.

Parque da Luz

Praça da Luz • Tues–Sun 9am–6pm • Free • Ⓜ Luz

Located directly across Rua Mauá from the Estação da Luz is **Parque da Luz**. Dating back to 1800, the park was São Paulo's first public garden, and its intricate wrought-iron fencing, Victorian bandstands, ponds and rich foliage attest to its prominent past. Until recently, the park was considered off limits, but security is now excellent and, as one of the few centrally located patches of greenery in the city, it is popular with local residents and visitors to the surrounding cultural centres. The space includes large display panels (in English and Portuguese) on the history of the Luz district and has been developed as a sculpture park.

Pinacoteca do Estado

Praça da Luz 2 • Daily except Tues 10am–6pm (last entry 5.30pm) • R$6; Sat free • ⓣ 11 3324 1000, ⓦ pinacoteca.org.br • Ⓜ Luz

The **Pinacoteca do Estado** is São Paulo's state art gallery. It is housed in an imposing Neoclassical building by the Parque da Luz that was constructed in 1905 and thoroughly renovated in 1998. The gallery is one of the finest in Brazil and has an excellent permanent collection of Brazilian paintings. Pride of place in the nineteenth-century galleries goes to images of rural São Paulo by Almeida Júnior, but the work of other Brazilian landscape, portrait and historical artists of the period is also well represented. The twentieth-century galleries include Cubist-influenced engravings; important paintings by the European expressionist turned Brazilian modernist Lasar Segall (see page 500); and works by other painters, including Emiliano di Cavalcanti, noted for his choice of Afro-Brazilian and urban themes, Cândido Portinari, whose work contained clear social and historical references, and the vibrant paintings of Tarsilla do Amaral. There is also a very pleasant café with a terrace opening onto the Parque da Luz.

Museu de Arte Sacra

Av Tiradentes 676 • Tues–Sun 9am–5pm • R$6, free on Sat • ⓣ 11 3326 3336, ⓦ museuartesacra.org.br • Ⓜ Tiradentes

A short walk north of Praça Luz on Avenida Tiradentes is one of the city's few surviving colonial churches, the **Igreja do Convento da Luz**, a rambling structure of uncharacteristic grandeur built on the site of a sixteenth-century chapel. The former Franciscan monastery and church date back to 1774, but they've been much altered over the years. Today they're home to São Paulo's **Museu de Arte Sacra**, displaying a fine collection of Brazilian seventeenth- and eighteenth-century wooden and terracotta religious art and liturgical pieces.

Memorial da Resistência

Largo General Osório 66 • Daily except Tues 10am–5.30pm • Free • ⓣ 11 3335 4990, ⓦ memorialdaresistenciasp.org.br • Ⓜ Luz

West of Praça da Luz along Rua Mauá stands the infamous Edifício DOPS, a large, anonymous-looking building that was once the headquarters of the Departamento de Ordem Política e Social, and one of the two main torture centres in São Paulo during the 1960s–80s military dictatorships. Now it houses the **Memorial da Resistência**, and serves as an exhibition centre commemorating its ugly past with displays charting

Brazil's history of repression, from the rise of Getúlio Vargas in the 1930s to the more recent struggle for democracy. Temporary art exhibitions administered by the Pinacoteca do Estado (see page 492) are also held here.

Estação Júlio Prestes

Complexo Cultural Júlio Prestes: Rua Mauá 51 • Mon–Fri 12.30–4.30pm, Sat 2–4.30pm • R$5 • ⓣ 11 3337 5414 • Ⓜ Luz

At the intersection of Rua Mauá with Rua Duque de Caxias, you'll find the **Estação Júlio Prestes**, built between 1926 and 1937, and drawing on late nineteenth-century French and Italian architectural forms. The building's most beautiful features are its large stained-glass windows, which depict the role of the railway in the expansion of the Brazilian economy in the early twentieth century. Although part of the building still serves as a train station for the CPTM (metropolitan overground railway), its Great Hall was transformed in the late 1990s into the Sala São Paulo, home of the Orquestra Sinfônica do Estado de São Paulo (ⓦosesp.art.br), and centrepiece of the **Complexo Cultural Júlio Prestes**, a cultural centre mainly devoted to classical music that now occupies most of the building.

Bom Retiro

The *bairro* adjoining Luz to the north is **Bom Retiro**, known for its shops selling cheap clothes and fabric. In the early 1900s the neighbourhood was predominantly Italian, with successive waves of Jewish, Greek, Korean and Bolivian immigrants becoming the most prominent ethnic groups as the century progressed. The main reason for visiting is to sample the food; there remains a fine Jewish deli, a Greek café and a rapidly growing number of Korean restaurants (see page 506).

Bela Vista

Since the early twentieth century, the *bairro* of **Bela Vista**, lying just southwest of downtown, has been known as "Little Italy". It's also commonly called **Bixiga**, and indeed "Bela Vista" has nowadays come to refer to a wider area stretching all the way from Avenida Paulista to the city centre. Calabrian stonemasons built their own modest houses here with leftover materials from the building sites where they worked, and the neighbourhood's narrow streets are still lined with these homes today. Italian **restaurants** exist throughout the city, but the greatest concentration (if not the greatest quality) can be found in Bixiga. This normally quiet neighbourhood springs to life in the evening when people throng to the central Rua 13 de Maio, and to the streets running off it, which are lined with *cantinas*, pizzerias, bars and small theatres. During the day on Sunday there's a lively flea market, Mercado de Antiguidades e Artesanato do Bixiga, at Praça Dom Orione (see page 514).

Liberdade

South of the centre and east of Bixiga, the *bairro* of **Liberdade** is the traditional home of São Paulo's large Japanese community, though in recent years a number of Vietnamese, Chinese and especially Koreans have settled here. Rua Galvão Bueno and its intersecting streets are devoted mostly to Japanese and other East Asian restaurants as well as shops selling semiprecious stones, Japanese food and clothes.

Museu da Imigração Japonesa

Rua São Joaquim 381 (7th, 8th & 9th floors) • Tues–Sun 1.30–5pm • R$10 • ⓣ 11 3209 5465, ⓦ www.museubunkyo.org.br • Ⓜ São Joaquim

The **Museu da Imigração Japonesa** has a Japanese-style rooftop garden and excellent displays honouring the Japanese community in Brazil, from their arrival in 1908 to work on the coffee plantations to their transition to farming and their varied contributions to modern Brazil.

Templo Busshinji

Rua São Joaquim 285 • Mon–Sat 8am–5pm • Free • ⓣ 11 3208 4515, ⓦ sotozen.org.br • Ⓜ São Joaquim

Slightly incongruous among the drab-looking office and apartment buildings of Libertade's Rua São Joaquim is the instantly recognizable **Templo Busshinji**, a Japanese Buddhist temple built in 1995; visitors are welcome to look around the wooden building and attend meditation sessions.

IMMIGRATION AND SÃO PAULO

São Paulo is a city built on **immigrants**, and it was largely thanks to new arrivals that its population grew a hundred-fold in just 75 years to make it, by 1950, the country's second-largest city. Besides sheer numbers, the mass influx of people had a tremendous impact on the character of the city, breaking up the existing social stratification and taking economic and political power away from the traditional elite groups much earlier than in other Brazilian cities.

Despite an attempt to bring over share-croppers from Prussia (Germany) in the 1840s, mass immigration didn't begin until the late 1870s. Initially, conditions on arrival were dire, and many immigrants succumbed to **malaria** or **yellow fever** while waiting in Santos to be transferred inland to work on the coffee plantations. In response to criticisms, the government opened the Hospedaria dos Imigrantes in 1887, a hostel in the eastern suburb of Brás, now converted to a museum (see page 489).

Immigration to São Paulo is most closely associated with the **Italians**, who constituted 46 percent of all arrivals between 1887 and 1930. Soon after arriving in Brazil, they would be transported to a plantation, but most slipped away within a year to seek employment in the city or to continue south to Argentina. The rapidly expanding factories in the districts of Brás, Moóca and Belém, east of the city centre, were desperately short of labour, and well into the twentieth century the population of these *bairros* was largely Italian, but it is **Bela Vista** (Bixiga) where the Italian influence has been most enduring. Originally home to freed slaves, Bela Vista had by the early 1900s established itself as São Paulo's "Little Italy". As immigration from Italy began to slow in the late 1890s, arrivals from other countries increased. From 1901 to 1930 **Spaniards** (especially Galicians) made up 22 percent, and **Portuguese** 23 percent, of immigrants, and their languages (Galician is very similar to Portuguese) allowed them to assimilate quickly; only Tatuapé developed into a specifically Portuguese *bairro*.

The first 830 **Japanese** immigrants arrived in 1908 in Santos to be sent to the coffee plantations. By the mid-1950s a quarter-of-a-million Japanese had emigrated to Brazil, most settling in São Paulo state. Unlike other nationalities, the rate of return migration among them has always been small: many chose to remain in agriculture at the end of their contract, often as market gardeners. The city's large Japanese community is centred on **Liberdade**, a *bairro* just south of the Praça da Sé and home to the excellent **Museu da Imigração Japonesa** (see page 493).

São Paulo's **Arab** community is also substantial. Arabs from Syria and Lebanon started arriving in the early twentieth century and, because they originally travelled on Turkish passports, are still commonly referred to as *turcos*. Typically starting out as itinerant traders, the community was soon associated with small shops, and many Arabs became extremely successful in business. Many boutiques in the city's wealthy *bairros* are still Arab-owned, but it's in the streets around **Rua 25 de Março**, north of Praça da Sé, that the community is concentrated (see page 489).

The **Jewish** community has prospered in São Paulo, too. Mainly of Eastern European origin, many of the city's Jews started out as roaming pedlars before settling in **Bom Retiro**, a *bairro* near Luz train station. As they became richer, they moved to the suburbs to the south of the city, in particular to Higienópolis, but some of the businesses in the streets around Rua Correia de Melo are still Jewish-owned and there's still a synagogue there. As the Jews moved out, **Greeks** started moving in during the 1960s, followed in larger numbers by **Koreans**. The area has long been known as a centre of the rag trade and in Korean-owned sweatshops the latest immigrant arrivals – **Bolivians** and **Chinese** – are employed, often illegally and amid appalling work conditions.

Higienópolis and around

At the end of the nineteenth century, many coffee barons moved from downtown São Paulo to a hilly part of the city named **Higienópolis**, so called because it was supposedly more hygienic than the spit 'n' sawdust Praça da República. While the city centre's mansions have long gone, a few still remain in Higienópolis. Completed in 1902, the Art Nouveau–influenced **Vila Penteado**, at Rua Maranhão 88 (at the intersection of Rua Sabará), is one of the finest examples and one of the last to be built in the area; it now forms part of the University of São Paulo's architecture faculty and visitors can enter the impressive marble-lined lobby.

After the coffee barons came families who'd become rich from the business boom of the twentieth century. Higienópolis remains very wealthy, with attractive tree-lined roads, pleasant parks and large houses and luxury apartment buildings, so very different from the chaos of the city centre just a few blocks away. A high proportion of today's residents are Jewish, and there are several synagogues and Jewish community schools in the neighbourhood.

Estádio do Pacaembu

Praça Charles Miller, Pacaembu • See website for matches and ticket prices • Ⓦ corinthians.com.br • Ⓜ Paulista

Higienópolis merges to the west into **Pacaembu**, best known for the **Estádio do Pacaembu**, the city-owned stadium where the Corinthians football team used to play its home matches (see page 515). It's located in Praça Charles Miller (named after the Anglo-Brazilian credited with introducing the modern game of football to Brazil), and was designed by Lúcio Costa (best known for his work on Brasília), opening in 1940 with a capacity of 60,000, although 72,000 have been squeezed in. With subsequent modernization, including the introduction of seating, the stadium can manage a crowd of 38,000 nowadays. So far as Corinthians are concerned, Pacaembu has now been superseded by the all new, 48,000-capacity Arena Corinthians, located on the eastern edge of town in Itaquera (at the end of *metrô* line 3). Built for the 2014 World Cup, the new stadium then became the club's regular home ground.

Museu do Futebol

Estádio do Pacaembu, Praça Charles Miller, Pacaembu • Tues–Fri 9am–5pm, last entrance 4pm; Sat, Sun & public holidays 9am–6pm, last entrance 5pm; closes early on match days • R$10, Sat free • Ⓣ 11 3664 3848, Ⓦ museudofutebol.org.br • Ⓜ Paulista

Unless attending a match (generally held on Wed & Sat), the best way to see the stadium is to visit the **Museu do Futebol**. Opened in 2008, this is certainly one of São Paulo's best museums and, surprisingly, the only one in the country devoted to the national sport. Although the museum is lodged in the same building that hosts Corinthians, it is careful to be completely neutral when it comes to attention paid to particular teams. While it helps to arrive with at least a mild interest in football, the museum is not merely there to pay simple homage to the sport – although there are plenty of relics, including a football kicked by **Pelé** as a child, on display. Instead, the focus of the museum is the history of twentieth-century Brazil, using football as a vehicle to explore this. Displays ranging from traditional **memorabilia** to high-tech **interactive exhibits** examine issues including the changing face of race in Brazilian football, how dictators co-opted the sport and how football affected a diverse range of writers and artists, including Cândido Portinari, Heitor Villa-Lobos and Jorge Amado. There's a great entertainment area where visitors can test their skills against a (virtual) star goalkeeper, and an excellent shop selling a range of football-related souvenirs.

Avenida Paulista and around

By 1900, the coffee barons had moved on from Higienópolis to flaunt their wealth through new mansions set in spacious gardens stretching along the 3km-long **Avenida**

KOBRA'S MURALS

São Paulo is a city that celebrates its street art – notably in Vila Madalena's **Beca do Batman** (see page 499) – but one street artist whose work stands out from an already excellent crowd is Sampa's own world-famous muralist, **Eduardo Kobra**. Responsible for Rio de Janeiro's *Etnias* (see page 65), Kobra has works dotted around São Paulo, and you can't fail to notice them as you explore the city. Typically his works are portraits in kaleidoscopic bright colours. There's a huge one of Ayrton Senna on Consolação 2608 at Avenida Paulista, one of architect Oscar Niemeyer on Praça Oswaldo Cruz, and one of Einstein on a bicycle at Rua Oscar Freire 944 in Jardins, not to mention several in Vila Madalena. Lately Kobra has been painting murals in places as far afield as Tokyo and Amsterdam, but here in his home city is where you'll find the greatest concentration. For more, check out his website at Ⓦ eduardokobra.com.

Paulista – then a tree-lined avenue set along a ridge 3km southwest of the city centre (look out for old photos, sometimes sold as postcards, showing the startlingly different avenue a century ago.) In the 1960s and 1970s, it became a giant construction site, as banks and other companies competed to erect ever-taller buildings, with little time for creativity – along the entire length of the avenue it would be difficult to single out more than one example of decent modern architecture. However, a handful of Art Nouveau and Art Deco mansions got official protection from the developers' bulldozers; some lie empty, the subjects of legal wrangles over inheritance rights, while others act as prestigious headquarters for banks. The avenue itself has become something of a promenade, especially in the evenings, with buskers and street sellers, and on Sundays the whole road is closed to traffic, and it becomes a pedestrian (and skaters') zone.

Casa das Rosas

Av Paulista 37 • Tues–Sat 10am–10pm, Sun 10am–6pm • Free • Ⓣ 11 3285 6986, Ⓦ casadasrosas.org.br • Ⓜ Brigadeiro

One mansion well worth visiting is the French-style **Casa das Rosas**, near Brigadeiro *mêtro* station at the eastern end of the *avenida*. Constructed in 1935 as a private residence, the building is set in a rose garden and has a beautiful Art Nouveau stained-glass window, making for a stunning contrast with the mirrored-glass-and-steel office building behind it. The state of São Paulo owns the Casa das Rosas, which is now a cultural centre where poetry-related exhibitions are often held.

Museu de Arte de São Paulo (MASP)

Av Paulista 1578 • Tues, Wed & Fri–Sun 10am–6pm, Thurs 10am–8pm (last ticket sold 30min before closing) • R$30; free Tues • Ⓣ 11 3149 5959, Ⓦ masp.art.br • Ⓜ Trianon-Masp

One of the few interesting modern buildings along Avenida Paulista is the **Museu de Arte de São Paulo**. Designed in 1957 by the Italian-born, naturalized-Brazilian architect Lina Bo Bardi and opened in 1968, the monumental concrete structure appears to float above the ground, supported only by remarkably delicate pillars. MASP is the pride of São Paulo's art lovers, and is considered to have the most important collection of Western art in Latin America, featuring the work of great European artists from the last five hundred years on its top floor. For most North American and European visitors, notable though some of the individual works of Bosch, Rembrandt and Degas may be, the highlights of the collection are often the seventeenth- to nineteenth-century landscapes of Brazil by European artists – none more important than the small but detailed paintings by Frans Post, a painter of the Dutch Baroque school whose rich Brazil-inspired works were used as tapestry designs by the French Gobelins factory, some of which are also displayed in the museum. The museum's moderately priced lunchtime restaurant makes for an excellent escape from the crowds, exhaust fumes and heat of Avenida Paulista outside.

Parque Siqueira Campos

Av Paulista (opposite MASP) • Daily 8am–6pm • Free • Ⓜ Trianon-Masp

Almost directly across Avenida Paulista from MASP is one of São Paulo's smallest but most delightful parks, the **Parque Siqueira Campos**, also known as Parque Trianon. Created in 1912 when building in the area began, the park was planned by the French landscape artist Paul Villon and based around local vegetation with some introduced trees and bushes; in 1968 it underwent a thorough renovation, directed by the great designer Roberto Burle Marx. The park now consists of 45,000 square metres of almost pure Atlantic forest with a wealth of different trees, and there's a network of trails as well as shaded benches for escaping the intense summer heat. Wardens patrol the park, but a degree of alertness is still called for – don't doze off.

Jardins

Avenida Paulista marks the southwestern boundary of downtown São Paulo, and beyond that are Jardim Paulista, Jardim America and Jardim Europa – the **Jardins** – which were laid out in 1915 and styled after the British idea of the garden suburb. These exclusive residential neighbourhoods have long since taken over from the city centre as the site of most of São Paulo's **best restaurants** and **shopping streets**, and many residents never stray from their luxurious ghettos – protected from Third World realities by complex alarm systems, guards and fierce dogs.

Jardim Paulista

At the northeastern edge of Jardins, the neighbourhood of **Jardim Paulista** lies within the wider district of Cerqueira César, which straddles both sides of Avenida Paulista. Just a few blocks into Jardins from Avenida Paulista is a mixed bag of hotels, offices and apartment buildings interspersed with shops, restaurants and bars geared towards the city's upper middle class. Wander along Rua Oscar Freire and the intersecting *ruas* Haddock Lobo, Bela Cintra and da Consolação for some of the neighbourhood's most exclusive boutiques and excellent restaurants.

Jardim America and Jardim Europa

Rua Augusta, lined with shops of all sorts, bisects Jardim Paulista and then turns into Rua Colômbia and Avenida Europa in the adjoining **Jardim America** and then **Jardim Europa**. Unfortunately, the winding tree-lined roads of these largely residential neighbourhoods afford only occasional glimpses of the Victorian or Neoclassical houses that are all but hidden behind their gardens' high walls.

Museu da Imagem e do Som

Av Europa 158 • Tues–Sat 10am–9pm, Sun & public holidays 10am–7pm • R$12, Tues free • Ⓣ 11 2117 4777, Ⓦ www.mis.sp.gov.br • Ⓜ Fradique Coutinho

In Jardim Europa, it's worth stopping off near the intersection of Avenida Europa with Rua Groenândia to see what's on at the **Museu da Imagem e do Som**, which draws on its vast film and photography archive to host often fascinating exhibitions of contemporary and historic Brazilian photography and a varied international film programme.

Museu da Casa Brasileira

Av Brigadeiro Faria Lima 2705 • Tues–Sun 10am–6pm • R$10; weekends and public holidays free • Ⓣ 11 3032 3727, Ⓦ mcb.org.br • Ⓜ Cidade Jardim

The **Museu da Casa Brasileira**, located near the junction of Rua Groenândia with Avenida Brigadeiro Faria Lima, boasts a varied collection of seventeenth- to twentieth-century Brazilian furniture and decorative items. The building itself – an imposing ochre-coloured Palladian villa built in the 1940s – is typical of Jardim Europa's mansions.

VILA MADALENA & JARDINS
ACCOMMODATION
Augusta Park 2
Café Hostel 1
Emiliano 9
Fasano 6
Maksoud Plaza 5
Meliã Paulista 4
Pousada Dona Ziláh 3
Regent Park 7
Transamerica Prime International Plaza 8
EATING
Apfel 6
Andrade 12
Arábia 16
Bacio di Latte 9, 22
Bella Paulista 2
Bovinu's 4
Calçadão Urbanidade 1
Capim Santo 13
Company 7
Consulado Mineiro 5
D.O.M. 21
Empanadas 3
Fasano 17
Figueira Rubaiyat 20
Galeto's 8, 18
Gero 19
Le Vin Bistro 11
Rodeio 15
Tordesilhas 10
Z-Deli 14
SHOPPING
Casa Santa Luzia 9
Deposito Kariri 7
FNAC Centro Cultural 8
Galeria Arte Brasileira 4
Havaianas 6
Iandé – Casa das Culturas Indígenas 1
Livraria Cultura 3
Mercado de Antiguidades e Artes 2
Mercado de Antiguidades do MASP 5
Ponto Solidário 10
DRINKING & NIGHTLIFE
A Lanterna 5
Astor 3
Bar do Sacha 2
Bar Samba 6
Cachaçaria Paulista 14
Caixote Bar 1
Canto da Ema 13
Carioca Club 16
Choperia Opção 12
Eagle 4
Filial 7
The L Club 8
Ó do Borogodó 11
Posto 6 9
São Cristóvão 10
Traço de União 15
Metro L2
Metro L4
0 500 metres
Dinho's (350m)
PACAEMBU
Pacaembu Stadium & Museu do Futebol
Cemitério do Araçá
Cemitério São Paulo
JARDIM PAULISTA
JARDINS
PINHEIROS
VILA MADALENA
MASP
Parque Siqueira Compos
Kobra Einstein mural
Beco do Batman
Instituto Tomie Ohtake
PRAÇA BENEDITO CALIXTO
Vila Madalena
Sumaré
Clínicas
Consolação
Paulista
Trianon -Masp
Fradique Coutinho
Faria Lima
AVENIDA PAULISTA
AV. DR. ARNALDO
AVENIDA PAULO VI
AVENIDA HEITOR PENTEADO
AVENIDA REBOUÇAS
AV. NOVE DE JULHO
AV BRIGADEIRO FARIA LIMA
AVENIDA PEDROSO DE MORAIS
R. DA CONSOLAÇÃO
R. AUGUSTA
R. OSCAR FREIRE
R. HENRIQUE SCHAUMANN
RUA TEODORO SAMPAIO
RUA CARDEAL ARCOVERDE
R. ARTUR DE AZEVEDO
R. BELA CINTRA
R. HADDOCK LOBO
AL. SANTOS
ALAMEDA JAÚ
ALAMEDA ITU
ALAMEDA FRANCA
ALAMEDA TIETÊ
ALAMEDA LORENA
ALAMEDA MIN. ROCHA AZEVEDO
ALAMEDA CASA BRANCA
R. PADRE JOÃO MANUEL
R. JOSÉ MARIA LISBOA
R. PEIXOTO GOMIDE
R. PAMPLONA
R. ESTADOS UNIDOS
R. BARÃO DE CAPANEMA
R. DOS PINHEIROS
R. FIDALGA
R. ASPICUELTA
R. LUÍS MURAT
R. MOURATO COELHO
R. FRADIQUE COUTINHO
R. MADALENA
R. SIMPATIA
R. ABEGOARIA
R. HARMONIA
R. RODÉSIA
R. PASCOAL VITA
R. GIRASSOL
R. PURPURINA
R. WISARD
R. JOÃO MOURA
R. CAPOTE VALENTE
R. ALVES GUIMARÃES
R. CRISTIANO VIANA
R. LISBOA
R. MATEUS GROU
R. JOAQUIM ANTUNES
R. CÔNEGO EUGÊNIO LEITE
R. FRANCISCO LEITÃO
R. DR. VIRGÍLIO DE CARVALHO PINTO
R. SÃO CARLOS DO PINHAL
R. ANTÔNIO CARLOS
R. LUÍS COELHO
R. FR. CANECA
R. BARATA RIBEIRO
R. MAJ NATANAEL
AV ANGELI
AV. DR. ENÉAS DE CARVALHO AGUIAR
R. DR. MELO ALVES
AL. GABRIEL MONTEIRO DA SILVA
R. SOMÃO ALVARES
R. BELMIRO BRAGA
R. INÁCIO PEREIRA DA ROCHA

Itaim Bibi and Pinheiros

The traffic-choked Avenida Brigadeiro Faria Lima, with the mixed residential and commercial neighbourhoods of **Itaim Bibi** towards its southern end, and popular after-dark destination **Pinheiros** to the north, is the main artery of São Paulo's newest business expanse. Although the latest buildings around here have generally been constructed at a break-neck speed, leaving little time for architectural reflection, Pinheiros is not without its attractions – although you'll have to go some distance from the main concentration of office development to find them.

Instituto Tomie Ohtake

Av Brigadeiro Faria Lima 201 (entrance on Rua Coropés) • Tues–Sun 11am–8pm • Free • ⓣ 11 2245 1900, ⓦ institutotomieohtake.org.br • ⓜ Faria Lima

One construction you won't fail to notice in Pinheiros is the striking red-and-blue office building at Avenida Brigadeiro Faria Lima 201 designed by **Ruy Ohtake**, one of Brazil's most important contemporary architects. Other buildings of his include hotels such as the *Unique* (see page 505). Opened in 2002, the building is notable for its curved lines and use of colour, both characteristic of Ohtake's work and a deliberate move away from the modernist tradition that has been so dominant in Brazilian architecture.

Housed on the lower floors of the building, the **Instituto Tomie Ohtake** honours the Japanese–Brazilian artist Tomie Ohtake – the architect's mother. The artist's early Brazilian work (notably landscapes) is most closely informed by her Japanese background, but it is still apparent after her shift to abstraction, in which the restrained brushstroke remains the key element. Although only a small portion of the exhibition space features her work – in rotating displays that highlight particular periods or themes – this section is always well worth a look. Otherwise the galleries are devoted to temporary exhibits of contemporary Brazilian artists or influential twentieth-century Brazilian constructivists. There's also a gift shop and a restaurant.

Vila Madalena

The **Vila Madalena** neighbourhood ("Vila Madá" to its aficionados) at the northern end of Pinheiros has been a trendy student hangout since the 1970s. Its resulting high density of bars and nightclubs makes it the best part of town to head for an evening's drinking and entertainment. Shops in the area tend to be small, independent concerns rather than malls and chain stores, and there are quite a few art galleries and bookshops too. Vila Madalena gained nationwide fame in 1999 when a popular soap opera – also *called Vila Madalena* – was set here.

The neighbourhood's main tourist attraction is **Beca do Batman** (Batman Alley, officially Rua Gonçalo Afonso), a small street whose walls are completely covered in colourful street art and murals, one of which originally featured a laughing Batman in flip-flops swinging from the telegraph wires, hence the name.

The Parque do Ibirapuera and around

Av Pedro Álvares Cabra • Daily 5am–midnight • Free • ⓦ parqueibirapuera.org • A 10min walk from the bus stops on Av Brigadeiro Luís Antônio

The **Parque do Ibirapuera**, southeast of Jardins, is the most famous of São Paulo's parks and the main sports centre for the city. Officially opened in 1954, the park was created to mark the 400th anniversary of the founding of the city of São Paulo. Oscar Niemeyer designed most of the buildings and Roberto Burle Marx produced impressive designs for landscaping. Inside the park, attractions include the peaceful and unusual **Bosque de Leitura** (reading woods) – where on Saturdays and Sundays (10am–4pm) you can borrow Portuguese books from a small outdoor library and sit among the trees reading them – and several of the city's museums. The park is also significant as the site where, in 1822, Brazilian independence was declared; in the northern half of the park is a monument celebrating the event – a replica of the Casa do Grito, the simple house where Dom Pedro I slept – and the chapel where he and his wife were later buried

At the park's main north entrance, in Praça Armando Salles de Oliveira, look out for the **Monumento às Bandeiras**, by Victor Brecheret. One of the city's most popular postcard sights, the 1953 sculpture shows a *bandeirante* expedition setting off, led by a Portuguese and a native on horseback. One of the park's main attractions, the **Museu Paulista** (aka Museu do Ipiranga), which houses paintings, furniture and other items that belonged to the Brazilian royal family, is currently closed for repairs and is not expected to reopen until 2022.

Museu de Arte Moderna

Parque do Ibirapuera (near gate #3) • Tues–Sun 10am–6pm (last ticket 5.30pm) • R$6; free Sat • ⓣ 11 5085 1300, ⓦ mam.org.br

On the east side of the park, next door to the Pavilhão da Bienal, the **Museu de Arte Moderna**, or MAM, is a relatively small art gallery that mainly hosts temporary exhibits of the work of Brazilian artists. There's an excellent café serving light meals and snacks, and a good bookshop.

Museu Afro-Brasil

Parque do Ibirapuera (near gate #10) • Tues–Sun 10am–5pm • R$6, free Sat • ⓣ 11 3320 8900, ⓦ museuafrobrasil.org.br

The **Museu Afro-Brasil**, in the northern part of the park near the lake, exhibits photos, artworks and artefacts illustrating the history of Brazil's black community, whose experience has been a neglected subject in this part of the country. The museum's exhibits, displayed in a large, airy space, mostly come from the private collection of its Bahian curator. Pride of place goes to an installation recalling the way people were kidnapped in Africa and brought over to Brazil in horrific conditions.

Museu de Arte Contemporânea

Av Pedro Álvares Cabral 1301 • Tues 10am–9pm, Wed–Sun 10am–6pm • Free • ⓣ 11 2648 0254, ⓦ www.macvirtual.usp.br

The University of São Paulo's **Museu de Arte Contemporânea**, located just outside the Parque do Ibirapuera on Avenida Pedro Álvares Cabra, regularly alters its displays, drawing upon its huge stored collection. The collection includes work by important European artists like Picasso, Modigliani, Léger and Chagall, and Brazilians such as Tarsila do Amaral, Di Cavalcanti and Portinari.

Museu Lasar Segall

Rua Berta 111 • Daily except Tues 11am–7pm • Free • ⓣ 11 2159 0400, ⓦ museusegall.org.br • ⓜ Vila Mariana

The *bairro* due east of the Parque do Ibirapuera, Vila Mariana, contains the wonderful **Museu Lasar Segall**. As most of Lasar Segall's work is contained in this museum (which served as his home and studio from 1932 until his death in 1957), the Latvian-born, naturalized-Brazilian painter is relatively little known outside Brazil. Part of the German Expressionist movement at the beginning of the twentieth century, Segall settled in Brazil in 1923 and became increasingly influenced by the exuberant colours of his adopted homeland. Look out especially for the vibrant jungle green of *Boy with Gecko* and the interracial *Encounter*, an early and sensitive treatment of a complex Brazilian theme.

Butantã and Morumbi

If you've got the time, it's worth making the trek out to the *bairros* of **Butantã** and **Morumbi**, in southwest São Paulo. No houses from the colonial era remain standing in the city centre, but out here in the suburbs a few simple, whitewashed adobe **homesteads** from the time of the *bandeirantes* have been preserved.

Casa do Bandeirante

Praça Monteiro Lobato, Butantã • Tues–Sun 9am–5pm • Free • ⓣ 11 3031 0920, ⓦ www.museudacidade.sp.gov.br/casadobandeirante.php • ⓜ Cidade Universitária

The **Casa do Bandeirante**, near the huge Universidade de São Paulo campus, is the only one of Butantã's *bandeirante* homesteads that is open to the public. It's a typical early eighteenth-century *paulista* dwelling containing period furniture and farm implements. This part of Butantã, where many of the university teaching staff live, is extremely pleasant to wander around – tasteful hammock-slung little houses are set amid lush foliage noisy with birdsong and cicadas.

Fundação Maria Luiza e Oscar Americano

Av Morumbi 4077 • Tues–Sun 10am–5.30pm • R$10, free Sat • ⓣ 11 3742 0077, ⓦ fundacaooscaramericano.org.br • Take a bus to Av Morumbi (bus #5119-10 along Av Brigaadeira Luis António, in Liberdade or at Av Paulista; or #6291-10, which runs along Rua 9 de Julho via Bixig and across Av Paulista

Situated in the elegant suburb of Morumbi, the **Fundação Maria Luiza e Oscar Americano** is a sprawling modernist house full of eighteenth-century furniture, tapestries, religious sculptures and collections of silver, china, coins and tapestry. Among the most valuable works are Brazilian landscapes by the seventeenth-century Dutch artist Frans Post, and drawings and important paintings by Cândido Portinari and Emiliano di Cavalcanti. The hilltop house, designed by Oswaldo Arthur Bratke, is clearly influenced by the work of the American architect Frank Lloyd Wright, and the beautiful wooded estate, which mainly features flora native to Brazil, helps make this spot an excellent escape from the city.

Parque do Estado

Av Miguel Stefano 3687 (near Congonhas airport) • Jardim Botânico: Tues–Sun: winter 9am–5pm;summer 9am–6pm • R$10 • ⓣ 11 5067 6000, ⓦ jardimbotanico.sp.gov.br • Ⓜ Jabaquara, then there is a connecting shuttle bus

South of the city centre is the largest expanse of greenery within the city: the **Parque do Estado**. The park features an extent of Mata Atlântica (the Atlantic rainforest), with trails and picnic areas. The other big attraction of the park is the **Jardim Botânico**, next to the zoo, featuring both native and exotic flora; its "garden of the senses" comprises plants with unusual textures and heavy scents.

Zoológico de São Paulo

Parque do Estado • Tues–Sun 9am–5pm (last ticket 4.30pm) • R$35 • ⓣ 11 5073 0811, ⓦ zoologico.com.br • Ⓜ Jardim

By far the Parque do Estado's biggest draw is the **Zoológico de São Paulo**; one of the largest zoos in the world, it houses an estimated 3200 animals from around the globe – predominantly Brazilian and African species. The reptile and monkey houses have especially important collections of the latter, while the natural habitat of the park draws several thousand migratory birds annually.

ARRIVAL AND DEPARTURE — SÃO PAULO CITY

São Paulo has two airports and three bus stations. Always remember that **thieves** thrive in the confusion of airports and transport terminals – watch your belongings at all times, and beware of phoney distractions.

BY PLANE

GUARULHOS

Most domestic and all international flights use Guarulhos airport (ⓣ 11 2445 2945, ⓦ www.gru.com.br), 25km northeast of the city.

Facilities There are ATMs and money-changing facilities and tourist information desks in arrivals (daily 6am–10pm).

By bus to the city centre There's a 24hr a/c express airport bus service (R$48.80; ⓣ 0800 770 7995, ⓦ www.airportbusservice.com.br) to Praça da República 343, leaving at least once an hour during the day, less frequently at night, with a slightly less frequent service to Tietê bus station. From Praça da República to Guarulhos, there are no buses between 11.40pm and 5.40am. During the day (6am–11pm) there's a service from to the top hotels around Avenida Paulista and Itaim Bibi. A slower but much cheaper option (R$5.95) is city bus #257, which connects Guarulhos airport with Tatuapé *metrô* station (daily 5am–midnight, every 15min weekdays, 20min weekends, occasionally supplemented by bus #299).

By taxi to the city centre There are taxi desks in arrivals halls, and you pay a fixed price depending on your destination. The fare to the centre is around R$120.

By metrô to the city centre CPTM (metropolitan overground) line 13, connecting Guarulhos with Engenheiro Goulart station on line 12, was due for completion in 2015, but has been delayed indefinitely due to technical problems.

CONGONHAS

Congonhas airport, just south of the centre (T 11 5090 9000, W aeroportocongonhas.net) handles services within the state, and to Rio and some other relatively local destinations such as Curitiba and Belo Horizonte. Congonhas is served by the same express airport bus as Guarulhos (see page 501) and is linked by local **buses** with São Judas station on *metrô* line 1, but from the end of 2019, it should be served a new **metrô** monorail line (line 17, originally due to open in 2014). There are fixed-price **taxi** desks in arrivals; a cab to the city centre costs around R$39.

BY BUS

TIETÊ

The main intercity terminal is Tietê in the north of the city (W rodoviariadotiete.com), the second-largest bus terminal in the world. Buses to most destinations run from here. Exits, ticket offices, and so on, are well signposted and there's a helpful information desk (*Informações*). Tietê is served by Portuguesa-Tietê station on *metrô* line 1.

International destinations Asunción (2 daily; 20hr); Buenos Aires (9 weekly; 36hr); Montevideo (2 weekly; 30hr); Santiago de Chile (2 weekly; 53hr).

Domestic destinations Belo Horizonte (30 daily, mostly overnight; 8hr 30min); Brasília (10 daily; 16hr); Campinas (every 20min; 1hr 30min); Campo Grande (9 daily; 14hr); Curitiba (1–2 hourly; 6hr 20min); Florianópolis (11 daily, mostly overnight; 12hr); Foz do Iguaçu (5 daily; 17hr); Paraty (5 daily; 5hr); Recife (1 daily; 40hr); Rio (4–8 hourly; 6hr); Salvador (2 daily; 33hr); Santa Bárbara d'Oeste (hourly; 2hr 10min); São Sebastião (6 daily; 4hr); Ubatuba (8 daily; 4hr).

JABAQUARA

Jabaquara, south of the centre, is for buses to and from the Santos region and São Paulo's southern shore as far as Peruíbe, It's at the southern end of *metrô* line 1.

Destinations Guarujá (every 45min; 1hr 20min); Santos (every 15min; 1hr 15min).

BARRA FUNDA

Barra Funda bus station, northwest of the centre (W www.terminalbarrafunda.com.br), serves destinations in southern São Paulo state. Barra Funda is on *metrô* line 3, and CPTM lines 7 and 8.

Destinations Cananéia (1 daily; 4hr 30min); Iguape (4 daily; 4hr 30min); Registro (9 daily; 4hr).

GETTING AROUND

BY METRÔ

Quiet, comfortable and fast, São Paulo's *metrô* (W www.metro.sp.gov.br) is by far the easiest way to move around the city. Although only five lines of the metropolitan train system (including a partly completed monorail line) are classified as *metrô* lines – there are also overground (CPTM: W cptm.sp.gov.br) lines, plus an underground line run by an independent firm – it matters little because a R$3.80 ticket allows free interchange between all twelve lines. The *metrô* runs every day from 5am until midnight, although the ticket booths close at 10pm. You can buy a bunch of tickets in one go to avoid having to queue each time (but if you start your journey on the CPTM, you need a CPTM ticket – a *metrô* ticket won't work, and vice-versa), and there are integrated bus and *metrô* tickets too.

BY BUS

São Paulo's buses and trolleybuses (R$3.80) have numbers is clearly marked at the front, with cards posted at the front and the entrance (towards the back) to indicate the route. At bus stops you have to flag down the buses you want – be attentive or they'll speed by. Buses run between 4am and midnight, but can be very full during the evening rush hour (around 5–7pm), and traffic congestion can make progress slow. You can check the bus routes from one part of town to another on W onilinhas.com.br.

BY TAXI

Sooner or later you'll find yourself in need of a taxi, especially in the wee hours, when they are pretty much the only public transport. Luckily, they are reliable and abundant but, given the volume of traffic and the often considerable distances, fares can quickly mount. There are two main types. The yellow *comuns*, generally small cars that carry up to three passengers, are the cheapest and are found at taxi ranks or hailed from the street. *Rádiotáxis* are larger and more expensive, and are ordered by phone; try Coopertax (T 11 2095 6000, W coopertax.com.br) or Ligue Táxi (T 11 2101 3030, W liguetaxi.com.br). Both types of taxi have meters with two fare rates, and a flag, or *bandeira*, is displayed on the meter to indicate which fare is in operation: fare "1" is standard (Mon–Sat 6am–9pm); fare "2" costs twenty percent more (after 9pm, plus Sun & public hols).

BY CAR

The main difficulties of driving your own car in São Paulo are the volume of traffic and finding a parking space – you're better off sticking with public transport. Roads are, however, well signposted and it's surprisingly easy to get out of the city.

Car rental Avis, Rua Tito 66, Lapa (T 11 3594 4015); Hertz, Rua da Consolação 419, Centro (T 11 3231 3055); Unidas, Rua Cincinato Braga 388, Bela Vista (T 11 3155 4770).

SOME USEFUL BUS ROUTES

#107T From near Tietê Rodoviária Tietê to metrô Faria Lima (via Avenida Tiradentes and Rua Augusta).
#702U From Praça da Sé to São Paulo University (via Avenida Consolação and Avenida Rebouças).
#875P From Rodoviária Barra Funda to metrô Ana Rosa (via Avenida Paulista).
#930P From Praça da Sé and Praça da República to Avenida Brigadeiro Faria Lima (via Rua Augusta).

INFORMATION

Tourist information São Paulo Turismo (☎11 2226 0400, Ⓦcidadedesaopaulo.com) maintains information booths, located in Praça República (daily 9am–6pm), on Av Paulista at Parque Siqueira Campos (mobile van, usually there Mon–Sat 9am–4pm), in Tietê bus terminal (daily 6am–10pm) and at Congonhas airport arrivals (daily 7am–10pm); there are also tourist information desks at Guarulhos airport, run by the airport authorities. The state tourist office, based on the 8th floor of Rua Bandeira Paulista 716, 8th floor in Itaim Bibi (☎11 3709 1654, Ⓦturismo.sp.gov.br), can answer queries on travel within the state.

Magazines/newspapers For up-to-date listings of what's going on, the São Paulo edition of the weekly magazine *Veja* contains an excellent entertainment guide, and the daily newspaper *Folha de São Paulo* (Ⓦfolha.uol.com.br) lists cultural and sporting events and, on Friday, contains an entertainment guide, the *Guia da Folha* (Ⓦguia.folha.uol.com.br).

Maps Finding a good map of a city as spread out as São Paulo is not easy. The free tourist-office maps are not very detailed. If you're planning on staying more than a day or two in the city, it may be worth buying a copy of the *Guia Quatro Rodas Ruas São Paulo*, an indexed street atlas to the city that's no longer in print (the last edition was in 2007) but still available online.

TOURS

Bem São Paulo Rua Camilo 583, suite 2, Vila Romana ☎11 4272 0895, Ⓦbemsaopaulo.com. Runs seven different 5hr all-inclusive in-depth tours focusing on different aspects of the city, but not exactly cheap, at R$339 per person, although they also offer more economical (R$100) 3–5hr tours and a R$29 walking tour of Parque do Ibirapuera (Ⓦibirawalkingtour.com).

Graffit Rua Joaquim Távora 128, Vila Mariana ☎11 5549 9569, Ⓦgraffit.com.br. Offers a variety of themed tours, such as art, nightlife or religion, in and around São Paulo.

Linha Circular Turismo ☎0800 116566, Ⓦcidadedesaopaulo.com/sp/br/linha-circular-turismo. A hop-on, hop-off circular bus tour of the city's main sights, including Praça República, São Bento monastery, Av Paulista (except on Sundays, when it's diverted around it), the football museum and Parque do Ibirapuera, with R$40 tickets valid for 24hr but currently only three buses a day.

São Paulo Free Walking Tour Ⓦsaopaulofreewalkingtour.com. Does what it says on the tin, offering free walking tours in English: on Mon, Wed, Fri and Sat a 4hr city-centre tour starts at 11.30am by the tourist information booth in Praça República; on Tues, Thurs and Sun a 3hr Vila Madalena tour starts at 11am outside Fradique Coutinho *metrô* station, and a 3hr Rua Augusta and Av Paulista tour begins at 3.30pm at the Banco do Brasil by Consolação *metrô* station. To join a tour, just turn up 15min before it starts. It's free but tips are appreciated, and note that tours don't always run on public holidays.

ACCOMMODATION

Hotel prices of hotels vary enormously throughout the year, with hefty **discounts** offered during the quieter summer months of January and February. **Weekend discounts** of up to fifty percent are often given at hotels that otherwise cater largely to business executives, and conversely, hostels often charge more at weekends. The rates quoted below are for weekday reservations and breakfast is included unless stated otherwise. If making an **online reservation** directly with the hotel, compare the rates on the Portuguese- and the English-language versions of the website – the former may be lower. Many budget and mid-priced places are in the **Centro** (downtown) area, where visitors, especially women, may feel uncomfortable walking alone at night, but by being alert during the day, and taking taxis at night (R$36 or so from Vila Madalena to Centro), you should have no problems. As an alternative to hotels, Oasis (Ⓦoasiscollections.com) offer apartments with hotel services such as cleaning and linen changing, and a concierge to ask for local advice, starting at around R$140 a day.

CENTRO

155 Hotel 13 de Maio 731 ☎11 3150 1555, Ⓦ155hotel.com.br; Ⓜ República; map p.486. They bill this as "the most luxurious low-cost hotel in São Paulo", and that's what they try to be. It's quite stylish in black and white decor, and if the rooms and the breakfasts are on the small side, they're still pretty good for the price. The lower floors get a fair bit of street noise, so go for an upper floor if that bothers you. R$195

Bourbon Av Viera de Carvalho 99 11 3337 9200, bourbon.com.br; República; map p.486. Aimed at budget-oriented business travellers, this is an efficiently run place with smallish but comfortable a/c rooms, and extras such as a sauna, fitness room and business centre, and there are usually big discounts on this rack rate, especially at weekends. R$694

Ferrari Palace Rua Conselheiro Nébias 445 11 3224 8087, ferraripalacehotel.com.br; República; map p.486. While not exactly a palace, this modest hotel, located on a side street near Praça da República that's full of motorbike repair shops, is clean and comfortable, with cheap eating places nearby. F R$120

Marabá Av Ipiranga 757 11 2137 9500, hotelmaraba.com.br; República; map p.486. A decent mid-range city-centre hotel, which has been renovated a few times over the years, and still bears a few of the scars, although not too obtrusively. The beds are good and the staff generally attentive, but it's worth asking for a room high up and at the back if you don't like downtown street sounds . R$330

8

Normandie Design Hotel Av Ipiranga 1187 11 3311 9855, normandiedesign.com.br; República; map p.486. The lobby, currently in blue and turquoise, strives for a designer "look", but the rooms don't bother: they're lino-tiled with some rather hasty paintwork, but they're fine to stay in, everything works, and the staff are friendly. R$250

República Park Av Vieira de Carvalho 32 11 3226 5000; República; map p.486. A nice little haven in this slightly rough city-centre neighbourhood, where you've got a/c rooms, TV, wif-fi and service with a smile, and it's also handy for the airport bus. It's worth asking for a room with a balcony on an upper floor, from which you can see Praça da República. R$185

São Paulo Hostel Rua Barão de Campinas 94 11 3337 3505, hostelsp.com.br; República; map p.486. This is an official HI hostel, and card holders get a discount (dorms R$59, doubles R$159). The large size and relative comfort of the single rooms make them a better deal than at most hotels. The hostel's main drawback is the neighbourhood, which isn't the safest if you're staggering back from a night out. Dorms R$67, doubles R$169

São Paulo Inn Largo Santa Ifigênia 40 11 3614 9970, nacionalinn.com.br/hotel-sao-paulo/sao-paulo-inn; República; map p.486. Across the square from Santa Ifigênia church and there's a slightly religious air to this place (they keep a Bible on the reception desk, for example). It's located in a very grand, early twentieth-century block, and although the rooms aren't huge, they're cosy and clean, most with a small balcony overlooking the square. R$214

LIBERDADE

Akasaka Praça da Liberdade 149 11 3207 1500, akasakahotel.com.br; Liberdade; map p.486. A good budget choice in the heart of Liberdade. The corridors are a bit battered, but the rooms are spacious and in fine nick, with the brightest overlooking the *praça*, but breakfast is not included. R$170

Banri Rua Galvão Bueno 209 11 3207 8877; Liberdade; map p.486. The rooms are small, but well-kept (including some R$75 "economico" single rooms with shared bathroom), and it's handy for great Japanese dining nearby. R$164

Nikkey Palace Rua Galvão Bueno 425 11 3207 8511, nikkeyhotel.com.br; São Joaquim; map p.486. This comfortable hotel markets itself to Japanese businessmen. Choose between standard rooms or larger, minimalist-style ones, and either a Brazilian or Japanese buffet breakfast. R$299.25

BELA VISTA

Augusta Park Rua Augusta 922 11 3124 4400, augustapark.com.br; Paulista; map p.498. All the rooms here are actually suites, with bedroom, sitting room, kitchenette and bathroom, and great value for the price, Rua Augusta can be quite lively so it's a good idea to get a room on one of the top floors (and at the back) if noise from the street bothers you. R$196

Maksoud Plaza Alameda Campinas 150 11 3145 8000, maksoud.com.br; Trianon-Masp; map p.498. For many years São Paulo's most distinguished hotel, the *Maksoud Plaza* and its luxurious rooms now seem somewhat mundane compared to the extravagance of new places like the *Unique*. Nonetheless, the staff are efficient and welcoming, there's a pool and several decent on-site restaurants, and you'll rarely pay the full rack rate. R$614.25

Orione Rua 13 de Maio 731 11 2769 3604, facebook.com/orionehotel; Brigadeiro; map p.486. A simple, no-frills budget hotel, clean, friendly and good value, but the wi-fi signal can be iffy in some rooms, and though all rooms have bathrooms, the door is only slightly frosty glass, so don't be too fussy about privacy with whoever you're sharing a room with. R$115

★ **Pousada Dona Ziláh** Rua Minas Gerais 112 11 3062 1444, zilah.com; Paulista; map p.498. This long-time favourite, the only proper *pousada* in the area, has changed location, and downsized but upgraded, with six rooms in a lovely house with a pleasant garden, in a quiet street, but just a short walk from Av Paulista. There's solar-powered hot water, much of it recycled after use to feed the plants, and most of the rooms have balconies or verandas, some with great views. R$345

Pousada dos Franceses Rua dos Franceses 100 11 3288 1592, pousadadosfranceses.com.br;

Brigadeiro; map p.486. Despite the name, this is a hostel rather than a *pousada*, with most accommodation in (segregated) dorms, although it has some private rooms too (with or without bathroom). It's extremely well run, friendly, clean and secure, in a quiet neighbourhood, with use of kitchen. Dorms R$55, doubles R$198

JARDINS

Emiliano Rua Oscar Freire 384 11 3068 4390, emiliano.com.br; Oscar Freire; map p.498. Ultra-deluxe hotel offering discreet, individual attention for a rich clientele. The light, airy rooms feature soft beds dressed in Italian linen, en-suite marble bathrooms, home cinema systems and hi-tech a/c. For an extra charge you can arrange to be transferred to and from Guarulhos airport by helicopter. US$895 (R$2820)

Fasano Rua Vittório Fasano 88 11 3896 4000, fasano.com.br; Oscar Freire; map p.498. São Paulo's classiest (as opposed to most expensive) hotel, where the decor of the lounge, bar, dining area and guest rooms could hardly be more stylish – modern, but with traditional accents. Service is impeccable, staff super-professional, and the hotel has one of São Paulo's best Italian restaurants (see page 508). Rates do not include breakfast. US$598 (R$1885)

Meliã Paulista Av Paulista 2181 11 2184 1600, meliahotels.com.br; Consolação; map p.498. Comfortable, efficient and friendly, this is an excellent business hotel situated in the heart of Avenida Paulista's banking district, an easy stroll to excellent restaurants and right by the *metrô* station. Rates don't include breakfast, but you'll probably pay rather less than half of this official "rack" rate if you book online. R$919

Regent Park Rua Oscar Freire 533 11 3065 5555, regent.com.br; Oscar Freire; map p.498. A very good apartment-hotel with one of the neighbourhood's best addresses. Accommodation is mainly in one-bedroom units, but there are also a few two- and three-bedroom ones; all include a living room and a small but fully equipped kitchen. There's also a rooftop pool with panoramic views of the city. Rates are substantially lower for stays of a week or longer. R$421.50

Transamerica Prime International Plaza Plaza Alameda Santos 981 11 3262 6000, www.transamericagroup.com.br; Trianion-Masp; map p.498. One- or two-bedroom flats with semi-kitchenettes (microwave but no stove) and more space than the average hotel room. There are a dozen or so *Transamericas* throughout the city, but this one is close to MASP and has a top-floor pool and bar with excellent views. R$289.50

Unique Av Brigadeiro Luís Antônio 4700 11 3055 4700, hotelunique.com.br; map p.484. São Paulo's most fashionable Ruy Ohtake-designed hotel looks rather like an extraterrestrial cruise ship. It's so hip there's no sign outside, nor any reception, and your cash gets you plenty of extra perks, such as a red-lit swimming pool and sliding hatches in rooms to watch a plasma TV from your digitally controlled hydro-bath. For those who just want to check the place out, you can visit the rooftop bar, which is open to non-guests. R$665

ITAIM BIBI

Radisson Blu Av Cidade Jardim 625, Itaim Bibi 11 2133 5960, radissonblu.com; Cidade Jardim; map p.484. The most luxurious hotel in the area (the "Blu" label means it's more deluxe than a plain old Radisson), with a choice of well-equipped standard room, or "royal" rooms with extras such as DVDs and "butler" room service. There's a sauna, fitness centre and attractive pool, and the staff try hard to please. R$613

Tryp Iguatemi Rua Iguatemi 150, Itaim Bibi 11 3704 5100, solmelia.com; Cidade Jardim; map p.484. A typically efficient but rather characterless example of the Meliã chain – which has eleven hotels in São Paulo – this hotel has comfortable rooms, a fine buffet breakfast, a small rooftop pool and pleasant staff who provide helpful and professional service. R$461

VILA MADALENA

Café Hostel Rua Agissé 152, Vila Madalena 11 2649 7217, cafehostel.com.br; Vila Madalena; map p.498. One of a number of small, low-priced hostels opening up in this neighbourhood and around town, it's very friendly, if a bit squashed together, with minimal breakfast, but it's handy for Vila Madalena's nightlife and *metrô*, and among the very cheapest places to stay in São Paulo. Private rooms are a bit cheaper midweek. Dorms R$32, doubles R$150

EATING

Eating out is a major pastime for wealthier *paulistanos*, who take great pride in the vast number of restaurants in the city. With its array of immigrant communities, São Paulo offers an impressive variety of dining, be it Brazilian, ethnic, or fusion. Aside from regional and modern Brazilian cooking, the city is also particularly good for Italian, Japanese, Arabic and Jewish cuisine.

CENTRO

Casa de Mortadela Av São João 633 11 3223 9787; República; map p.486. Big fat mortadella or calabresa sausage sandwiches for R$14 (R$10 Sunday lunchtime) – the city's best – that will seriously plug a gap if you're feeling peckish around town. Daily 9am–9.30pm.

Estadão Viaduto Nove de Julho 193 ☎11 3257 7121, ⓦestadaolanches.com.br; Ⓜ República; map p.486. This busy *lanchonete* (cheap diner) is famous for its *pernil* (pork loin) sandwiches (R$16). More importantly, it's open round the clock, so it could be just the place you need if you're suffering an attack of the munchies, or just need a beer, downtown in the wee hours. Daily 24hr.

★ **Jardim de Napoli** Rua Dr Martinico Prado 463, Higienópolis ☎11 3666 3022, ⓦjardimdenapoli.com.br; Ⓜ Santa Cecilia or Marechal Deodoro; map p.484. A simple *cantina* where some of São Paulo's best Italian food is served at moderate prices. Justifiably famous for its *polpettone* (giant meatballs; R$66), it also does excellent pasta. Mon noon–3pm & 7–11pm, Tues–Fri noon–3pm & 7pm–midnight, Sat noon–4pm & 7pm–midnight, Sun noon–5pm & 7–11pm.

Ponto Chic Largo do Paissandu 27 ☎11 3222 6528, ⓦpontochic.com.br; Ⓜ República; map p.486. This sandwich bar, going since 1922, is where they invented the traditional *baurú* sandwich (roast beef, tomato, pickle and a mix of melted cheeses in a baguette; R$24.90), and it's still the best place in town to try one. Mon–Sat 8am–2am.

8

Raful Rua Abdo Schahin 118, Centro ☎11 3229 8406, ⓦraful.com.br; Ⓜ São Bento; map p.486. This bright Lebanese diner is a great spot for meze (Middle Eastern hors d'oeuvres), or just a coffee, and in case you're hungrier than that, it also offers a big tasting menu for R$65. Mon–Fri 7am–6pm, Sat 7am–4pm.

Rei do Filet Praça Júlio Mesquita 175 (just off Av São João) ☎11 3221 8066, ⓦreidofilet.com; Ⓜ República; map p.486. Serving customers since 1914, the house speciality of this very simple and very traditional restaurant is steak. To show how tender the meat is, the bowtie-wearing waiters cut the steaks using soup-spoons. If a 240g (½lb) chateaubriand for R$63.95 won't do you, try a 490g (1lb) one for R$106.70. There's a second branch at Alameda Santos 1105 in Jardins. Downtown daily 11am–10pm; Jardins Mon–Thurs & Sun 11am–10pm, Fri & Sat 11am–1am.

TOP 4 JEWISH AND ARAB RESTAURANTS

Middle Eastern restaurants in São Paulo are excellent value, typically serving **Lebanese** or **Syrian** food. The city's substantial **Jewish** community also run a handful of authentic and very good restaurants.

Arábia (Lebanese; Cerqueira César) See page 507

Raful (Lebanese/Syrian; Centro) See above

Shoshi Delishop (Jewish; Bom Retiro) See below

Z-Deli (Jewish; Cerqueira César) See page 509

BOM RETIRO

Acrópoles Rua da Graça 364, Bom Retiro ☎11 3223 4386, ⓦrestauranteacropoles.com.br; Ⓜ Tiradentes; map p.484. Traditional Greek food, including moussaka (R$52), is served in this long-established, popular and moderately priced restaurant. Daily 7.30am–8pm.

Seok Joung Rua Correia de Melo 135, Bom Retiro ☎11 3338 0737, ⓦseokjoung.wordpress.com; Ⓜ Tiradentes; map p.484. The most sophisticated of the numerous Korean restaurants appearing in this *bairro*. Very authentic – and inexpensive – dishes (the speciality being *gogi gui*, or Korean barbecue; R$110) are served to largely Korean diners. Mon–Sat 11.30am–2.30pm & 5.30–9pm.

★ **Shoshi Delishop** Rua Correia de Melo 206, Bom Retiro ☎11 3228 4774, ⓦdelishoprestaurante.com.br; Ⓜ Tiradentes; map p.484. Stop in for inexpensive Eastern European Jewish food, cheesecake and dishes incorporating contemporary Italian–Brazilian touches. Adi, the friendly English-speaking Bulgarian-Israeli owner, is a mine of local information. Snack on gefilte fish (R$16), or come on Friday or Saturday for a *cholent* (slow-cooked beef stew, a traditional Sabbath lunch; R$45). Mon–Sat 8.30am–3.30pm.

LIBERDADE

Asia House Rua da Glória 86, Liberdade ☎11 3106 1159, ⓦasiahouse.com.br; Ⓜ Liberdade; map p.486. The excellent-value Japanese *comida por quilo* buffet here (R$67.90/kg) is particularly suitable if you want to make a foray into the country's cuisine but find the thought of a Japanese-Portuguese sushi menu a little daunting. There is also another branch at Rua Augusta 1918 in Jardins. Mon–Sat 11am–3.30pm.

Kisetsu Rua da Glória 234, Liberdade ☎11 3101 1938, ⓦfacebook.com/restaurantekisetsu; Ⓜ Liberdade; map p.486. The unlimited *rodizio* of wonderful sushi, sashimi and other delicious Japanese specialities served here is a bargain at R$56 on weekday lunchtimes (until 3pm), R$60.90 weekday evenings, and R$69.90 weekends. Daily 11am–9pm.

Korea House Rua Galvão Bueno 43 (upstairs) ☎11 3208 3052, Liberdade; Ⓜ Liberdade; map p.486. One of the first Korean restaurants in São Paulo, where the inexpensive, often spicy dishes are very different from the Japanese places in the same neighbourhood – try the Korean beef broth (R$52). Mon, Tues & Thurs–Sun 11.30am–2.30pm & 6–10pm.

Okuyama Rua da Glória 553, Liberdade ☎11 3341 0780, ⓦrestauranteokuyama.com.br; Ⓜ Liberdade;

TOP 5 EAST ASIAN RESTAURANTS

Thanks to the make-up of its immigrant communities, São Paulo's best **East Asian food** tends to be Japanese and Korean rather than Chinese or Thai. **Liberdade**, the city's Japanese quarter, is full of restaurants and sushi bars. More recently, a number of low-priced Korean restaurants have been opening up in **Bom Retiro** to cater for the neighbourhood's large Korean community.

Jun Sakamoto (Japanese; Vila Clementino) See page 509
Kisetsu (Japanese; Liberdade) See page 506
Okuyama (Japanese; Liberdade) See page 506
Seok Joung (Korean; Bom Retiro) See page 506
Sushi-Yassu (Japanese; Liberdade) See below

map p.486. Great-value Japanese food and lots of it: the "festival de sushi" (R$62) – with vast amounts of sushi, sashimi and other dishes too – takes some getting through, and if you're in a singing mood, you can head upstairs to their karaoke bar. Mon–Fri 11.30am–2pm & 6pm–2am, Sat noon–3pm & 6pm–3am, Sun noon–3pm & 6.30–11pm.

Sushi-Yassu Rua Tomás Gonzaga 98A, Liberdade ⓣ11 3209 6622, ⓦsushiyassu.com.br; ⓜLiberdade or São Joaquim; map p.486. Excellent, traditionally presented sushi, sashimi, noodle and other Japanese dishes are offered here. Unusual for Brazil, eel (sautéed with soy sauce and sake; R$110) is regularly served, and sea urchin roll (R$46) is frequently on the menu. Tues–Fri 11.30am–3pm & 6–11pm, Sat noon–4pm & 6–11.5pm, Sun noon–10pm.

BELA VISTA

Bella Paulista Rua Haddock Lobo 354 ⓣ11 3214 3347, ⓦbellapaulista.com; ⓜConsolação; map p.498. A very handy place for a drink, a meal, a coffee and cake or just an ice cream at any time of the day or night, and it's a rare hour of a rare day that it isn't buzzing. The meaty signature dishes are named after local streets, so their "Haddock" isn't a fish but a steak in shitake mushroom sauce with broccoli and mashed manioc (R$51.80). Daily 24hr.

Bovinu's Rua Augusta 1513 ⓣ11 3253 5440, ⓦbovinusaugusta.com.br; ⓜConsolação; map p.498. This excellent-value *churrascaria* (it has branches around town, but this is the best) has a huge selection of salads, Brazilian stews and other dishes, and, of course, lots of meat – various cuts of beef as well as pork, chicken and fish. The best time to go is weekend lunchtimes, when there's an unlimited buffet (Sat R$42.90, Sun R$49.90). Mon–Fri 11.15am–3.30pm, Sat & Sun noon–4pm.

Calçadão Urbanidade Rua Augusta 1291; ⓜConsolação; map p.498. A super-hip and very fine eating and drinking venue and a great place to begin a night out this food court of pop-up catering trucks has food from around the world – anything from pastrami burgers to pad thai, plus craft beers from Brazil and abroad, and caipirinhas, obviously (although you'll get those cheaper elsewhere). Very tasty indeed. Mon, Tues & Sun 6–10pm, Wed–Sat 6pm–midnight.

Company Av Paulista 2073 ⓣ11 3266 3250; ⓜConsolação; map p.498. Popular with nearby office workers at lunchtime, this canteen-like diner offers good-value self-service buffet breakfasts (R$20) and lunches (R$39). Mon–Sat 6am–midnight, Sun 9am–8pm.

Famiglia Mancini Rua Avanhandava 81 (off Rua Augusta) ⓣ11 3256 4320; ⓜRepública; map p.486. Established by a prominent local Italian–Brazilian family who bought up this run-down street and turned it into a popular eating venue with five restaurants, of which this is the flagship: an Italian restaurant specializing in pasta. There's a choice of pastas with a big choice of sauces (pesto, carbonara, *arrabiata* and *palermitana*, for example, all go for R$108), as well as lasagne, risotto and some meat dishes. Mon–Wed 11.30am–1am, Thurs–Sat 11.30am–2.30am. Sun 11.30am–midnight.

Madreperola Rua Avanhandava 30 ⓣ11 3258 4243; ⓜRepública; map p.486. Another restaurant in the *Famiglia Mancini* stable (see above), this one has a slightly maritime feel, and actually it's a good place for just a drink and a sample of the *por quilo* antipasti, but should you be in the mood for a squid and prawn risotto (R$69) or a goat and saffron risotto (R$59), they'll rustle you one up with no trouble. Daily noon–2am.

JARDINS

Apfel Rua Bela Cintra 1343, Jardim Paulista ⓣ11 3062 3727; ⓦapfel.com.br; ⓜConsolação; map p.498. An excellent and largely organic vegetarian buffet – a hundred percent veg, ninety percent organic, they say – features both hot and cold dishes, including salads, soups, sweets and savouries, for R$34.90 on weekdays, R$40.90 at weekends. Mon–Fri 11.30am–3pm, Sat & Sun 11.30am–4pm.

★ **Arábia** Rua Haddock Lobo 1397, Cerqueira César ⓣ11 3061 3234, ⓦarabia.com.br; ⓜOscar Freire; map p.498. Excellent and moderately priced Middle Eastern food, with an emphasis on Lebanese cuisine, is served in very pleasant and spacious surroundings here. The mixed meze is a good way to sample a mixture of Middle Eastern hors d'oeuvres (R$122 for six dishes), or try a tender lamb mechoui (R$79.80). Daily noon–midnight.

Bacio di Latte Rua Oscar Freire 136, Jardim Paulista ⓣ11 3062 0819, ⓦbaciodilatte.com.br; ⓜTrianon-Masp; map p.498. The flagship of São Paulo's very own chain of ice-cream parlours, based on the Italian tradition, but outdoing anything you'll find in Italy. They do a very sleek bitter chocolate ice cream made with cocoa from the island of São Tomé, and if that isn't chocolatey enough, they have a super-intense triple-chocolate flavour. By contrast, refreshing fruit flavours include passion fruit and raspberry. R$11.75 will get you three flavours. There are branches all over town, including two on Av Paulista (at nos.854 & 2001). Oscar Freire Mon–Fri & Sun 10am–midnight, Sat 10am–1am; Av Paulista branches daily 9am–10pm.

Bolinha Av Cidade Jardim 53, Jardim Europa ⓣ11 3061 2010, ⓦbolinha.com.br; ⓜFaria Lima or Cidade Jardim; map p.484. Traditionally, *feijoada* (a black bean, pork and sausage stew) is served in Brazil only on Wednesdays and Saturdays, but here it's the house staple every day, served as a *rodizio* along with *farofa* (toasted manioc), rice, sliced oranges and other trimmings (R$98 weekdays, R$116 weekends). Tues–Sun 11.30am–11.30pm.

8

Capim Santo Alameda Ministro Rocha Azevedo 471, Jardins ⓣ11 3089 9500, ⓦcapimsanto.com.br; ⓜTrianon-Masp; map p.498. Excellent and moderately priced food is served in an attractive patio setting, landscaped with palms and jungle fronds. The lunch buffet (R$68) is a great way to experience the highlights of Bahian food, and in the evening the à la carte offerings provide a similarly wide choice of dishes, or try the shrimp in coconut curry (R$73). Tues–Sat noon–3pm & 7–11.30pm, Sun noon–5pm.

Dinho's Alameda Santos 45, Paraíso ⓣ11 3016 5333, ⓦdinhos.com.br; ⓜBrigadeiro; map p.484. One of the city's oldest *churrascarias*, *Dinho's* is still among the best spots in town for a good steak (R$130 for a T-bone), with a good selection of wines to accompany it. At lunchtime on Wednesdays and Saturdays, they do a *feijoada* buffet (R$152). Mon–Sat 11.30am–3.30pm & 7pm–midnight, Sun 11.30am–6pm.

★ **D.O.M.** Rua Br. De Capanema 549, Jardim Paulista ⓣ11 3088 0761, ⓦdomrestaurante.com.br; ⓜOscar Freire; map p.498. Chef Alex Atala is considered one of the best in Brazil, and his restaurant consistently features in worldwide top tens. The faultless fusion cooking at *D.O.M.* is sublime, but prices, as you'd expect, are high. Most novices go for the tasting menu (R$485 for four courses, R$645 for eight courses, vegetarian versions also available). Mon–Thurs noon–3pm & 7–11pm, Fri noon–3pm & 7pm–midnight, Sat 7pm–midnight.

Fasano Hotel Fasano, Rua Taiarana 78, Cerqueira César ⓣ11 3062 4000, ⓦfasano.com.br; ⓜOscar Freire; map p.498. Serving some of the best Italian food in São Paulo, this elegant hotel restaurant is a good choice for special occasions. Renowned for its top-quality ingredients, the chef adds his own twist to dishes from different Italian regions, with creations such as risotto with parmesan and foie gras (R$185), or duck ravioli in orange sauce (R$125). Mon–Sat 7pm–12.30am.

Figueira Rubaiyat Rua Haddock Lobo 1738, Jardins ⓣ11 3063 3888, ⓦrubaiyat.com.br; ⓜOscar Freire; map p.498. Centred around a massive, golden-lit, 130-year-old majestic fig tree, this place serves the city's very best beef and veal, although it doesn't come cheap. A *bife chorizo* (sirloin strip) steak for example, goes for R$131, "baby beef" (super-tender heart of top sirloin) for R$141. Mon–Fri noon–4pm & 7–11pm, Sat & Sun 11am–midnight.

Galeto's Alameda Santos 2209, Jardim Paulista ⓣ11 3342 5310, ⓦgaletos.com.br; ⓜConsolação; map p.498. Since the 1970s, this fairly inexpensive restaurant has specialized in barbecued chicken, served with salad and polenta (R$54), along the lines of the rustic food commonly found in the areas of Italian settlement in Brazil's southernmost state of Rio Grande do Sul. It has another branch along the street at no.1112. Mon–Thurs & Sun 11.30am–11pm, Fri & Sat 11.30am–midnight.

Gero Rua Haddock Lobo 1629, Cerqueira César ⓣ11 3064 0005, ⓦfasano.com.br; ⓜOscar Freire; map p.498. This relaxed bistro-style restaurant with the same owners as *Fasano* has a smaller but still very good menu. The food is more moderately priced than other places like it (fish of the day is R$104, *tiramisú* R$44), but you may have to wait for a table. Mon–Thurs noon–3pm & 7pm–midnight, Fri & Sat noon–4pm & 7pm–1am, Sun noon–4pm & 7pm–midnight.

Le Vin Bistro Alameda Tietê 184, Jardim Paulista ⓣ11 3081 3924, ⓦlevin.com.br; ⓜConsolação or Oscar Freire; map p.498. Simple but attractively presented food, particularly good as a light lunch (they open in the morning for breakfast, but main meals are served from noon). Well known for its oysters from Cananéia (R$63.80 a dozen), though the salmon is recommended too (R$74.80). Daily 8am–11pm.

Rodeio Rua Haddock Lobo 1498, Jardim Paulista ⓣ11 3474 1333, ⓦrodeiosp.com.br; ⓜOscar Freire; map p.498. Overly elegant, perhaps, and certainly expensive, the quality of the meat is exceptional (T-bone R$128). The relaxed setting and discreet but efficient service has long made this a popular meeting point for politicians, bankers and business executives. Mon–Fri 11.30am–3.30pm & 6.30pm–midnight, Sat 11.30am–midnight, Sun 11.30am–11pm.

★ **Tordesilhas** Alameda Tietê 489 (between Consolação and Bela Cintra), Consolação ⓣ11 3107 7444, ⓦtordesilhas.com; ⓜOscar Freire; map p.498. The trailblazer of new Brazilian cuisine; traditional recipes gathered from throughout the country then adapted with a lighter touch, as evidenced in dishes such as their wonderful prawn *bobó* (R$$79). As well as being extremely tasty, the food is beautifully presented and served in a very attractive rustic-chic setting, and on Tues–Sat you can opt for the R$160 tasting menu. Tues–Fri 6pm–1am, Sat noon–5pm & 7pm–1am, Sun noon–5pm.

Z-Deli Alameda Lorena 1689, Cerqueira César ☎ 11 3088 5644, Ⓦ zdelivery.com.br; Ⓜ Oscar Freire; map p.498. A small Jewish deli-restaurant with an outstanding spread (available noon–4pm) of Ashkenazi Jewish specialities such as gefilte fish, chopped liver and cheesecake, plus Middle Eastern meze items such as hummus and falafel, and the odd Brazilian dish just for good measure. R$49 gets you all you can eat (R$65 on Saturdays, when the selection's bigger). There's another branch at Alameda Gabriel Monteiro da Silva 1350 in Jardim América. Mon–Fri 9am–5pm, Sat 10am–5pm.

VILA MADALENA, ITAIM BIBI AND PINHEIROS

Andrade Rua Artur de Azevedo 874, Pinheiros ☎ 11 3085 0589, Ⓦ restauranteandrade.com.br; Ⓜ Fradique Coutinho; map p.498. Northeastern food is the speciality here, with dishes including *carne do sol* (sun-dried beef) served with pumpkin, sweet potato and manioc (R$90 for a full portion that'll serve two people, or R$61 for a half-portion). Live *forró* music is performed Thursday to Saturday evenings and Sunday lunchtime. Tues–Thurs noon–3pm & 7pm–midnight, Fri & Sat noon–3pm & 7pm–4am, Sun noon–5pm.

Braz Rua Vupabussu 271, Pinheiros ☎ 11 3037 7973, Ⓦ brazpizzaria.com.br; Ⓜ Faria Lima; map p.484. With some of the best pizzas in São Paulo, busy *Braz* strives to live up to expectations. The secret lies in the generosity of their toppings – hunks of mozzarella, roast vegetables and meat, drizzled with olive oil – not to mention a sourdough base made with stoneground wholemeal Italian flour. The house speciality, called a Braz pizza (R$47 or R$79, depending on the size), comes topped with mozzarella, parmesan and courgette (zucchini). They do deliveries, but the downtown and Avenida Paulista areas are covered by their Higienópolis branch (☎ 11 3255 8090). Mon–Wed & Sun 6.30pm–midnight, Thurs 6.30pm–12.30am, Fri & Sat 6.30pm–1.30am.

Consulado Mineiro Praça Benedito Calixto 74, Pinheiros ☎ 11 3064 3882, Ⓦ consuladomineiro.com.br; Ⓜ Oscar Freire or Fradique Coutinho; map p.498. Authentically hearty *mineiro* food makes this a popular spot, but it's particularly bustling on weekends when Praça Benedito Calixto hosts an antiques and crafts market. Dishes are mostly meat served with all the trimmings (*farofa*, sweet potato, etc – *tutu à mineira*), for example, at R$94. Tues–Sun 11.45am–midnight.

Empanadas Rua Wisard 489 ☎ 11 3032 2116, Ⓦ empanadasbar.com.br; Ⓜ Vila Madalena or Fradique Coutinho; map p.498. The simple but effective selling point of this busy bar is that, in addition to beer, it serves *empanadas* (savoury pasties popular throughout South America but usually referred to as *empadas* in Brazil). And very good they are too, with small ones at R$7 each or R$36.30 for half a dozen, big ones at R$8.90. Mon–Thurs noon–1am, Fri & Sat noon–3am, Sun 1pm–1am.

ELSEWHERE

Jun Sakamoto Rua Cel Lisboa 55, Vila Clementino ☎ 11 3088 6019; Ⓜ Vila Mariana; map p.484. São Paulo's top Japanese restaurant, with attractive steel-and-wood setting and a daring chef who adds modern twists to otherwise classic dishes. The emphasis is on sushi, which is creatively presented, but the tempura, in a light batter with sesame seeds, is also excellent. It's wise to book ahead here, particularly on weekends. Mon–Fri 7pm–midnight, Sat 7pm–1am.

TOP 5 ITALIAN RESTAURANTS

Italians are São Paulo's biggest ethnic minority, and the city's **Italian restaurants** range from family-run cantinas and pizzerias to elegant, expensive establishments. For the most part, Italian restaurateurs are the children or grandchildren of immigrants, and they've adapted mainly northern Italian recipes to suit Brazilian tastes as well as the availability of ingredients. São Paulo's "Little Italy", **Bixiga**, has a lot of Italian restaurants as you'd expect, but the food there is nothing special, and you'll find higher-quality dishes in other neighbourhoods.

Braz (Pinheiros) See above
Famiglia Mancini (off Rua Augusta) See page 507
Fasano (Cerqueira César) See page 508
Gero (Cerqueira César) See page 508
Jardim de Napoli (Higienópolis) See page 506

DRINKING AND NIGHTLIFE

The two main areas for drinking and nightlife are **Vila Madalena**, stretching south into **Pinheiros**, which host the lion's share of trendy bars, including some with a slightly bohemian feel, and the area around **Rua Augusta**, which is more downmarket, and is the main centre of LGBT life in the city. Wednesday and Thursday nights are often as popular as

LGBT SÃO PAULO

São Paulo has a large **gay** population but most gay venues tend to be mixed or "GLS" (gays, lesbians and sympathizers). The scene is centred in the **Jardins** area. Since 1997, the city has hosted a Carnaval-style annual **Gay Pride parade** on a Sunday in May or June, along Avenida Paulista. The first parade attracted just two thousand participants but organizers now claim well over three million revellers, making it by far the largest event of its kind in the world. For dates and other information, see ⓦ paradasp.org.br.

Eagle Rua São Miguel 57, Bela Vista ⓣ 11 96446 0260, ⓦ eaglesaopaulo.com.br; Ⓜ Consolação; map p.498. A branch of an NYC gay men's bar, now a worldwide chain, with lots of leather and butchness. Mon–Thurs & Sun 7pm–1am, Fri & Sat 7pm–6am.

The L Club Rua Luiz Murat 370, Vila Madalena ⓣ 11 2604 3393, ⓦ facebook.com/baladathelclub; Ⓜ Fradique Coutinho; map p.498. It's girls' night out every Friday at this easy-going lesbian club, where the music's largely house, with a dab or two of Brazilian "funk" and MPB. Fri 11.30pm–6am.

Vermont Itaim Rua Pedroso Alvarenga 1192, Itaim Bibi ⓣ 11 3071 1320, ⓦ vermontitaim.com.br; Ⓜ Cidade Jardim; map p.484. This classy GLS club plays samba, MPB and house, and there's an on-site restaurant. Thurs 7.30pm–2am, Fri & Sat 9pm–4am, Sun 5pm–midnight.

The Week Rua Guaicurus 324, Lapa ⓣ 11 3868 9944, ⓦ theweek.com.br; Ⓜ Agua Branca; map p.484. São Paulo's biggest and most famous gay and lesbian club attracts top DJs and a fair few VIPs (not necessarily gay). Sat 11.30pm–8am, and sometimes other days.

weekend nights, particularly in the summer when the middle class head out of town on Friday evenings. Bars with live music in particular levy a cover charge, which varies according to the day, time and your sex (men usually pay double the amount women do), but count on an average of about R$20. To see what's on in the way of music, consult the weekly *Veja* magazine, the daily *Folha de São Paulo* newspaper (especially its Friday supplement) and the website ⓦ obaoba.com.br. *Gafieiras* tend to be out of the centre and in poor neighbourhoods, and can be rather disconcerting if you've just arrived in Brazil, although you'll certainly be made to feel welcome in no time. São Paulo's **nightclubs** attract DJs from around the globe, and there's plenty of homegrown talent too; cover charges vary wildly, but expect to pay between R$30 and R$100, sometimes with a drink or two thrown in.

CENTRO AND BELA VISTA

Bar Brahma Av São João 665 (at the corner with Av Ipiranga), Centro ⓣ 11 2039 1250, ⓦ barbrahmacentro.com; Ⓜ República; map p.486. Opened in 1948, this is one of the city's oldest bars, and was formerly a haunt for musicians, intellectuals and politicians. It features live acts – stand-up comedy as well as music – with a cover charge and sometimes obligatory reservations. Mon–Thurs 11am–1am, Fri & Sat 11pm–2am, Sun 11am–midnight.

Cachaçaria do Rancho Praça Dom José Gaspar 86, Centro ⓣ 11 3259 7959, ⓦ bit.ly/CachacariadoRancho; Ⓜ República or Anhgangabaú; map p.486. Open-air eating and – more to the point – drinking in this downtown city square, with, as its name suggests, a huge selection of cachaças on the menu. Best time to come is Thursday and Saturday afternoons (2–8pm), when there's *feijoada*, accompanied by live samba music, washed down with beer or caipirinha, and finished off with a shot or two of good cachaça. Mon–Sat noon–midnight.

Café Piu-Piu Rua 13 de Maio 134, Bela Vista ⓣ 11 3258 8066, ⓦ cafepiupiu.com.br; Ⓜ Brigadeiro; map p.486. Although this dance bar has a nice neighbourhood feel to it, the wide range of Brazilian music – including live samba and MPB – draws a mixed crowd into the early hours of the morning. Tues–Sun, hours vary but typically 9.30pm–late.

Caixote Bar Rua Augusta 914 ⓣ 11 97624 6168, ⓦ facebook.com/pg/caixotebarsp; Ⓜ Consolação; map p.498. A great place to start the night, the *Caixote* ("crate") *Bar* is decorated with plastic beer crates, and serves beer, cocktails and nibbles (such as olives and lupini beans) at sensible prices with no airs, graces or pretensions, to a soundtrack of MFB and indie rock. Mon–Thurs 6pm–midnight, Fri & Sat 6pm–2am, Sun 3–9pm.

Você Vai Se Quiser (aka Bar da Graça) Rua João Guimarães Rosa 281 (at Praça Roosevelt) ⓣ 11 3129 4550; Ⓜ República; map p.486. A very popular traditional-style samba bar where they serve *feijoada* on Saturdays, loads of beer, and a good time is had by all. Fri 6–11pm, Sat 1–9pm.

BOM RETIRO AND BARRA FUNDA

Caos Rua General Júlio Marcondes Salgado 321, Campos Elíseos ⓣ 11 3791 5391; Ⓜ Santa Cecila; map p.484. Relocated from Rua Augusta to larger premises, this bar-cum-antique shop is decorated with old toys and film memorabilia, which are all for sale. The music is eclectic but mainly retro, with anything from Motown to rock'n'roll, but it's always fun. Tues–Sat noon–1am.

D-Edge Alameda Olga 170, Barra Funda ⊕11 3665 9500, ⊕facebook.com/dedgeclub; Ⓜ Palmeiras-Barra Funda; map p.484. Sampa's premier electronica hotspot, with two dancefloors and a roof terrace, and nightly DJs playing anything from techno to *baile* to an up-for-it crowd most nights of the week, but Friday nights tend to be the best. Mon & Wed–Sat from midnight, with an after party on Sun 6am–noon.

Villa Country Av Francisco Matarazzo 774, Agua Branca ⊕11 3868 5858, ⊕villacountry.com.br; Ⓜ Palmeiras-Barra Funda; map p.484. This 1800-capacity venue plays *serteneja* (Brazilian country music) to a crowd clad in cowboy hats and cowgirl hotpants. Thurs–Sun 8pm–5am, dancefloors Fri & Sat from 11pm.

JARDINS AND PARAÍSO

Barnaldo Lucrecia Rua Abilio Soares 207, Paraíso ⊕11 3885 3425, ⊕barnaldolucrecia.com.br; Ⓜ Paraíso; map p.484. Located in an easy-to-spot yellow house, this bar draws a young crowd. There is live music most evenings, but it's especially festive on Fridays. Tues–Fri 7pm–late, Sat 8pm–late.

Choperia Opção Rua Carlos Comenale 97 ⊕11 3288 7823, ⊕choperiaopcao.com.br; Ⓜ Trianon-Masp; map p.498. Just metres from Avenue Paulista and MASP, this is a really popular after-work bar, with an outdoor terrace that's great for watching workhorse Sampa go by. Daily 5pm–2am.

Veloso Rua Conceição Veloso 56, Vila Mariana ⊕11 5572 0254, ⊕velosobar.com.br; Ⓜ Vila Mariana; map p.484. Perennially popular bar, which has been voted as serving Sampa's best caipirinhas and *coxinha* savouries. Inevitably neither comes cheap, but they are worth it. Tues–Fri 5.30pm–12.30am, Sat 12.30pm–12.30am, Sun 4–10.30pm.

VILA MADALENA

BARS

Astor Rua Delfina 163 ⊕11 3815 1364, ⊕barastor.com.br; Ⓜ Vila Madalena; map p.498. This well-established bar done out in Art Deco style, with an impressive stack of Johnny Walker bottles behind the bar, is one of the neighbourhood's trendiest meeting points. Excellent beer and *petiscos* (snacks) make it a great place to start or end a night out in Vila Madalena. Mon 6pm–midnight, Tues & Wed 6pm–2am, Thurs–Sat noon–3am, Sun noon–7pm.

Bar do Sacha Rua Original 45 ⊕11 3815 7665, ⊕bardosacha.com; Ⓜ Vila Madalena; map p.498. Situated on a hillside opposite a pleasant grassy garden, this is a good spot to come for a *chopp* or a caipirinha on a sunny day or a warm evening. Daily 11.30am–1am.

Filial Rua Fidalgo 254 ⊕11 3813 9226, ⊕www.barfilial.com.br; Ⓜ Faria Lima or Vila Madalena; map p.498. Though it looks like a simple local bar, this is actually quite a sophisticated locale with a chequered floor, bow-tie-wearing waiters and wide range of cachaças. Popular with self-consciously bohemian types, 30 and over. Daily 5pm–late.

Posto 6 Rua Aspicuelta 644, Vila Madalena ⊕11 3812 4342, ⊕barposto6.com.br; Ⓜ Faria Lima or Fradique Coutinho; map p.498. This lively Rio-style simple corner bar, in one of the few areas of the city where bars cluster together, is a popular place for friends to meet up at the start of a night. Mon & Tues 4pm–1am, Wed–Fri 4pm–2am, Sat & Sun noon–2am.

São Cristóvão Rua Aspicuelta 533 ⊕11 3097 9904, ⊕facebook.com/pg/barsaocristovao; Ⓜ Fradique Coutinho map p.498. This sports bar is a shrine to Brazilian football, and the walls here are completely covered with football memorabilia – scarves, flags, shirts, stickers, you name it. The beer's always cold, there's a choice of good cachaças and bar snacks, and guess what's showing on the telly. Daily noon–2am.

CLUBS AND MUSIC VENUES

A Lanterna Rua Fidalga 531, Vila Madalena ⊕11 3031 0483, ⊕facebook.com/pg/lanternabar; Ⓜ Vila Madalena or Sumaré; map p.498. A fun place to drop by that's popular with the under-25s, who are entertained by a wide variety of guest acts, Brazilian and foreign, playing poppy rock and MPB (see page 662). Fri & Sat 10pm–4am.

Bar Samba Rua Fidalga 308, Vila Madalena ⊕11 3819 4619, ⊕facebook.com/barsambabr; Ⓜ Vila Madalena; map p.498. As the name suggests, this is the place to head for if you want to listen to Brazil's most famous musical export. It's open daily but the best time to go is for the *roda de samba* (Wed–Fri 9pm, Sat 1pm), when the audience joins in with the musicians. Wed 7pm–1am, Thurs 7pm–2am, Fri 7pm–3am, Sat 1–7pm & 9pm–3am.

PINHEIROS

BARS

Cachaçaria Paulista Rua Mourato Coelho 593 ⊕11 96374 4412, ⊕ bit.ly/CachacariaPaulista; Ⓜ Fradique Coutinho; map p.498. Small and with limited nocturnal hours, this is nonetheless a great place to sample different cachaças, of which they have over 300 from all over Brazil. Fri & Sat 9pm–4am.

EAP (Empório Alto dos Pinheiros) Rua Vupabussu 305 ⊕11 3031 4328, ⊕altodospinheiros.com.br; Ⓜ Faria Lima or Pinheiros map p.484. For serious beer lovers, this is a bar with dozens and dozens of craft beers from around the world, including one or two from São Paulo itself, and others from elsewhere in Brazil. Not the cheapest *chopp* in town, but undoubtedly the finest. Mon–Wed & Sun noon–midnight, Thurs–Sat noon–1am.

Pirajá Av Brigadeiro Faria Lima 64 ⓣ 11 3815 6881, ⓦ piraja.com.br; Ⓜ Faria Lima; map p.484. This attractive, mahogany bar serves tasty Spanish-style tapas (*petiscos* in Portuguese) and is well known for its excellent *chopp* (draught beer). Often gets packed out from around 8pm. Mon–Thurs noon–midnight, Fri & Sat noon–1am, Sun noon–7pm.

CLUBS AND MUSIC VENUES

Canto da Ema Av Brigadeiro Faria Lima 364 ⓣ 11 3813 4708, ⓦ cantodaema.com.br; Ⓜ Faria Lima; map p.498. One of the city's most popular *forró* clubs, where they play both old-school (traditional northeastern) and newfangled (electronic) varieties of the genre. Very friendly but not exactly spacious. Wed & Thurs 10.30pm–2am, Fri & Sat 10.30pm–5am, Sun 7pm–midnight.

Carioca Club Rua Cardeal Arcoverde 2899 ⓣ 11 3813 8598, ⓦ cariocaclub.com.br; Ⓜ Faria Lima, map p.498. Puts on a wide variety of live acts including samba, *pagode* and MPB bands, with some acts starting early (7–11pm), and others late (11pm–5am). Check the website for comprehensive details of what's on when.

Ó do Borogodó Rua Horácio Lane 21 ⓣ 11 3814 4087, ⓦ facebook.com/odoborogodobar; Ⓜ Fradique Coutinho; map p.498. For a taste of the real Brazil, a bit rough round the edges but as authentic as you'll get, leave your pretensions behind and head down to this slightly gritty, old-school samba club, where nobody stands on ceremony and everybody dances with everybody, especially once the caipirinhas start kicking in. Mon 8.15–11pm, Tues 9pm–2am, Wed–Sat 10pm–3am, Sun 7pm–12.30am.

Traço de União Rua Claudio Soares 73 ⓣ 11 3031 8065, ⓦ tracodeuniao.com.br; Ⓜ Faria Lima; map p.498. One of the city's top samba venues, especially busy on Friday nights, but also known for its Saturday *feijoadas*, and always with a good vibe. Thurs & Fri 9pm–3am, Sat 1–9pm, Sun (sometimes) 3–10pm.

ITAIM BIBI AND MOEMA

All of Jazz Rua João Cachoeira 1366, Itaim Bibi ⓣ 11 3849 1345, ⓦ allofjazz.com.br; Ⓜ Vila Olimpia; map p.484. Intimate, laidback pub-style bar with mediocre drinks menu and service, but consistently excellent live jazz. Mon–Sat 8.30pm–4am.

Bourbon Street Music Club Rua dos Chanés 127, Indianópolis ⓣ 11 5095 6100, ⓦ bourbonstreet.com.br; map p.484. This consistently good, though expensive (entry often R$250), cozy little jazz club hosts visiting international artists and frequent festivals. Tues & Wed 8pm–late, Thurs 8.30pm–late, Fri, & Sat 9pm–late, Sun 7.30pm–not so late.

Kia Ora Rua Dr Eduardo de Souza Aranha 377, Itaim Bibi ⓣ 11 3846 8300, ⓦ kiaora.com.br; Ⓜ Vila Olimpia; map p.484. With its live rock bands, Kiwi-owned *Kia Ora* is a popular pub among expats and *paulistanos* alike. On some nights there's a long wait to get in, although you can reserve ahead. Be aware that there's a dress code – no shorts or football shirts, for example. Tues 6pm–1am, Wed & Thurs 6pm–3.30am, Fri 7pm–4am, Sat 8pm–4.30am.

Rey Castro Rua Min. Jesuino Cardoso 181, Vila Olímpica ⓣ 11 3842 5279, ⓦ reycastro.com.br; Ⓜ Vila Olimpia; map p.484. It's debatable what Castro would make of this Cuban-themed bar, but its *mojitos*, cigars and waiters dressed as guerrillas – not to mention the live salsa music – go down well with *paulistanos*. Wed 8pm–3.30am, Thurs 8pm–4am, Fri & Sat 8pm–5am.

ENTERTAINMENT

THEATRES

Teatro Brasileiro de Comédia (TBC) Rua Major Diogo 315, Bixiga ⓣ 11 3104 5523; Ⓜ Liberdade. The country's foremost comedy theatre. Founded in 1948, it closed down in 1964, but was reborn at the end of the 1990s, and reopened yet again in 2013 after a five-year refurbishment.

Teatro Sérgio Cardoso Rua Rui Barbosa 153, Bixiga ⓣ 11 3288 0136, ⓦ teatrosergiocardoso.org.br; Ⓜ Liberdade. Two auditoriums allow this theatre to put on a variety of productions, with a reputation for high-quality performances.

OPERA AND CLASSICAL MUSIC VENUES

Sala São Paulo Praça Júlio Prestes 16, Centro ⓣ 11 3367 9500 ⓦ osesp.art.br; Ⓜ Luz. This 1500-seat concert hall inside the beautifully renovated Estação Júlio Prestes is home to the world-class Orquestra Sinfônica do Estado de São Paulo.

Teatro Municipal Praça Ramos de Azevado, Centro ⓣ 11 3053 2090, ⓦ theatromunicipal.org.br; Ⓜ Anhangabaú. The traditional focal point for São Paulo's opera and classical music season (in the 1920s, Villa-Lobos himself performed here), with a full programme of classical music, opera, theatre and dance.

SHOPPING

For visitors, there are no obvious **souvenirs** of São Paulo as such, but the city is a good place to find the things Brazil generally does well – from cachaça and samba records to bikinis and flip-flops. The main **shopping streets** in the centre of the city are near Praça da República, especially the roads running off Avenida Ipiranga: Rua Barão de Itapetinga, Rua 24 de Maio and Rua do Arouche. South of the Mercado Municipal, Rua 25 de Março is another busy street, lined with hawkers selling everything from pirated CDs to Carnaval costumes.

FESTIVALS IN SÃO PAULO

CARNAVAL IN SÃO PAULO

Although São Paulo's **Carnaval** is not as spectacular or glamorous as its *carioca* sister, neither is it low-key. São Paulo has its own enthusiastically supported samba schools that spend all year preparing for the festival and collectively form the union of *paulistano* samba schools, UESP (T 11 3287 1112, W uesp.com.br or W facebook.com/uespUniaoDasEscolasDeSambaPaulistanas). As in Rio, the samba competition takes the form of a massive parade, held in the Oscar Niemeyer–designed *sambódromo*, a 530m-long stadium that can accommodate around 26,000 and is part of the huge Parque Anhembi leisure complex, near the Tietê bus terminal north of the city centre.

Ticket prices are cheaper than in Rio, starting at around R$30 for a bench seat in the stands on the Sunday, rising to over R$2400 for a seat in a VIP box for the main parade on Saturday. In general, the closer you are to the ground, the better the view and the more you pay. Tickets are sold online by W ingressosligasp.com.br, but you usually need a Brazilian ID number to buy them (your hotel may help). Otherwise try Ticketmaster (W ticketmaster.com.br) or the tourist office (see page 503).

In the weeks leading up to Carnaval, you can attend **rehearsals** at the city's samba schools – one of the best to visit is Rosas de Ouro at Rua Euclides Machado 1066 in Barra Funda (T 11 3931 4555, W sociedaderosasdeouro.com.br).

THE SÃO PAULO BIENAL

The **São Paulo Bienal** (W biennialfoundation.org/biennials/sao-paolo-biennialv) has been held in the Parque do Ibirapuera every two years since 1951. It's widely considered to be the most important exhibition of **contemporary visual art** in Latin America, and São Paulo was the second city in the world to hold one of these Biennial festivals after the original one in Venice (there are now quite a number of them at locations worldwide). At São Paulo's event, each Latin American country sponsors work by its most influential contemporary artists, while a select few artists (living or dead) are also chosen by the Bienal's curators. At best, the Bienal can be an exhilarating venue to see important retrospectives and experience a wealth of innovative art, but at worst it can be little more than an embarrassing – or amusing – showing of fourth-rate global art. The Bienal is now held in October and November in even-numbered years.

MOSTRA

Mostra (aka the São Paulo International Film Festival; W mostra.org) has been held every October since 1977. It has nowadays become quite a prestigious event. It now involves over 300 movies from all over the world being shown in cinemas across town, and has been attended on occasion by the likes of Dennis Hopper, Pedro Almodóvar, Wim Wenders, Satyajit Ray and Quentin Tarantino.

ARTS AND CRAFTS

Deposito Kariri Rua Artur de Azevedo 874, Pinheiros T 11 3064 6586; M Fradique Coutinho; map p.498. A warehouse-style handicrafts emporium that takes a "pile 'em high, flog 'em cheap" attitude to its wares. The emphasis isn't on quality here, but prices are good, for carvings, ceramics, textiles and hammocks among other things. Mon–Fri 9am–6pm, Say 9am–3pm.

Galeria Arte Brasileira Alameda Lorena 2163, Jardim Paulista T 11 3062 9452, W galeriaartebrasileira.com.br; M Oscar Freire; map p.498. A large, museum-like selection of well-chosen artisan products from throughout Brazil, especially the Amazon and the Northeast, including naive-style paintings, and items made from "golden grass" by people from Quilambo (descendants of escaped slaves) communities in Tocatins. Mon–Fri 10am–6.30pm, Sat 10am–2pm.

Galeria Brasiliana Rua Cardoso de Almeida 1297, Perdizes T 11 3086 4273, W galeriabrasiliana.com.br; M Sumaré; map p.484. Popular Brazilian paintings and other artwork – not cheap, but of excellent quality, with the pieces made by top craftspeople. Daily 1.30–6pm, but best to call ahead before visiting.

Iandé – Casa das Culturas Indígenas Rua Augusta 1371, unit 107 T 11 3283 4924, W iande.art.br; M Consolação; map p.498. A small shop showcasing indigenous crafts, including basketware, wooden carvings, ceramics and beadwork. Mon–Fri 10am–7pm, Sat 1–5.30pm.

Ponto Solidário Rua José Maria Lisboa 838, Jardim Paulista T 11 5522 4440 W pontosolidario.org.br; M Trianon-Masp; map p.498. This small NGO outlet for crafts by co-opertives and Indigenous peoples is attached to a small museum (Mon–Fri 10am–4pm, call ahead to arrange a guided tour) housing artifacts collected by the first outsiders to vist the Xingu region of Mato Grosso, and the shop sells identical crafts made by local people there, as well as basketware, wood carvings, seed necklaces and textiles from across Brazil, all fair trade needless to say. Mon–Fri 10am–7pm, Sat 10am–2pm.

BOOKS AND MUSIC

Casa Amadeus Musical Rua Quintino Bocaiuva 22, 1st floor, Centro ⊤11 3101 6790, Ⓦbit.ly/CasaAmadeusMusical; ⓂSé; map p.486. This music store has a good selection of Brazilian sheet music, percussion and stringed instruments. Mon–Fri 9am–6pm, Sat 9am–1pm.

FNAC Centro Cultural Av Pedroso de Moraes 858, Pinheiros ⊤11 3579 2000, Ⓦfnac.com.br; ⓂFaria Lima; map p.498. Good range of CDs and books, including a nice array of English-language titles and high-quality Brazilian art and other coffee-table books. The surrounding area is clustered with independent music and bookshops, too. There's a smaller branch at Av Paulista 901. Mon–Sat 10am–10pm, Sun 11am–8pm.

Galeria do Rock Av São João 439, Centro ⊤11 3337 2361, Ⓦgaleriadorock.com.br; ⓂRepública; map p.486. A shopping mall for music and urban fashions, with 450 different shops, and a good place to find Brazilian music, both past and present, on CD and vinyl, plus clothes and accessories galore. Mon–Sat 10am–6pm.

Livraria Cultura Conjunto Nacional building, Av Paulista 2073; ⓂConsolação; map p.498. By far the best bookshop in São Paulo, spread over three different locales and several floors within the same building (one specializes in language, one in art, and the other – absolutely huge – in everything else, including CDs). There's a great café here too. Mon–Sat 9am–10pm, Sun 11am–8pm.

Sampa Discos Av São João 556 & 572 ⊤11 3337 6474; ⓂRepública; map p.486. This cavernous and chaotic, warehouse-like secondhand record store (in two locations, two doors from each other) is chock-full of Brazilian and foreign vinyl, CDs and DVDs, at rock-bottom prices, but in no particular order. You can find serious bargains here, but you'll need a long browse. They also have other branches around town. Mon–Fri 10am–5.30pm, Sat 10.30am–7pm.

FOOTWEAR

Havaianas Rua Oscar Freire 1116, Jardins ⊤11 3079 3415, Ⓦhavaianas.com.br; ⓂOscar Freire; map p.498. An entire shop devoted to designer flip-flops in all sorts of colours, with lots of snazzy designs, a bin to recycle your old ones and places to check your size (US and European sizes are different from Brazilian ones, but all are printed on the flip-flops). You can even have them custom-made to your specifications. Mon–Sat 10am–8pm, Sun noon–6pm.

FOOD

Casa Santa Luzia Alameda Lorena 1471, Jardim Paulista ⊤11 3897 5000, Ⓦsantaluzia.com.br; ⓂOscar Freire; map p.498. This gourmet supermarket is the perfect place to stock up if you're staying in an apartment-hotel in the area. Otherwise, check out the luxury Brazilian food items that include preserves, wines and liquors. Mon–Sat 8am–8.45pm.

Extra Hipermercado Av Brigadeiro Luís Antônio 2013, Bela Vista ⊤11 3016 8600, Ⓦextra.com.br; ⓂBrigadeiro; map p.484. A large supermarket, handy if you're self-catering (it has a good fish counter, for example) but particularly handy for being open 24/7. Daily 24hr.

Emporio Syrio Rus Abdo Schahin 136, Centro ⊤11 3228 4725, Ⓦemporiosyrio.com.br; ⓂSão Bento; map p.486. The main reason for visiting this Middle Eastern grocery store, fascinating though its shelves full of exotic cans and jars may be, is to sample the sticky delights of its Arabic pastries. Baklava and most other Middle Eastern sweets are R$5 each. Mon–Fri 8.30am–5pm, Sun 8.30am–3.30pm.

MARKETS

Feira das Artes Praça da República, Centro; ⓂRepública; map p.486. Among the tack in this tented street market, there are some interesting handicrafts, vintage records and semiprecious stones. Sun 9am–5pm.

Feira Oriental Praça da Liberdade, Liberdade; ⓂLiberdade; map p.486. Japanese horticulturalists sell house plants here and some stalls sell good Japanese meals and snacks – usually prepared and sold by kimono-clad Afro-Brazilians. Sat & Sun 9am–6pm.

Mercado de Antiguidades e Artes Praça Benedito Calixto, Pinheiros; ⓂOscar Freire or Sumaré; map p.498. Cheaper, livelier and with a larger collection of bric-a-brac than the similar market beneath MASP (see page 496), you may pick up the odd bargain here. Some good restaurants are located around the square and there are food stalls in the market itself. Sat 9am–7pm.

Mercado de Antiguidades e Artesanato do Bixiga Praça Dom Orione, Bixiga; ⓂBrigadeiro; map p.486. This flea market has little worth purchasing, but lots of local atmosphere. Sun 10am–6pm.

Mercado de Antiguidades do MASP Museu de Arte de São Paulo (MASP), Av Paulista 1578; ⓂTrianon-Masp; map p.498. Comprising mostly medals, old letters and ceramics, this is a fun place to browse, but don't expect to find much worth buying. Sun 10am–5pm.

Mercado Municipal Rua da Cantareira 306, Centro; ⓂLuz or São Bento; map p.486. About the most fantastic array of fruit, vegetables, herbs, meat, fish and dairy produce that you're likely to find anywhere in Brazil. For taking home, you'll find interesting jams, preserves, pepper sauces and other packaged items. Excellent meals and snacks are also available. Mon–Sat 6am–6pm, Sun 6am–4pm.

DIRECTORY

Consulates Argentina, Av Paulista 2313 (11 3897 9522); Australia, Alameda Santos 700, 9th floor, suite 92, Cerqueira César (11 2112 6200); Bolivia, Rua Coronel Artur Godói 7, Vila Mariana (11 3289 0443); Canada, Av das Nações Unidas 12901, 16th floor, Itaim Bibi (11 5509 4321); Colombia, Rua Tenente Negrao 140, 7th floor, Itaim Bibi (11 3078 0262); Ireland, see dfa.ie/irish-consulate/sao-paulo; New Zealand, Av Paulista, 2421 (Edifício Bela Paulista), 12th floor (11 3898 7400); Paraguay, Rua Bandeira Paulista 600, 8th floor (11 3167 7793); Peru, Av Paulista 2439 (11 3149 2525); South Africa, Av Paulista 1754, 12th floor (11 3265 0449); UK, Rua Ferreira de Araújo 741, 2nd floor, Pinheiros (11 3094 2700); Uruguay, Rua Estados Unidos 1284, Jardim America (11 2879 6600); US, Rua Henri Dunant 500, Campo Belo (11 3250 7000).

Football There are two major first-division teams based in São Paulo: Corinthians (corinthians.com.br), who play their home games at the new Arena Corinthians in Itaquera (Corinthians-Itaquera); and São Paulo (saopaulofc.net), who play at Morumbi Stadium (bus #7241 from Praça República). Matches are generally held on Wed and Sat. Ticket prices start at R$50; better seats go for R$180–250. Anyone with even the faintest interest in the sport should make time to visit Pacaembu's marvellous Museu do Futebol (see page 495).

Health The private Hospital Albert Einstein, Av Albert Einstein 627, Morumbi (11 2151 1233, einstein.br), is considered to be the best hospital in Brazil. For dentistry, Banatti, Av Paulista 925, 13th floor, Cerqueira César (11 3251 0228, benattiodontologia.com.br), is central and English-speaking.

Money and exchange Branches are concentrated along *avenidas* Paulista and Brigadeiro Faria Lima, and Rua 15 de Novembro. The best exchange rates for cash can be found at *casas da cambio* on *avenidas* São Luís and Paulista.

Police DEATUR, a special police unit for tourists (11 3257 4475), is located at Rua da Cantareira 390 by the Mercado Municipal and has posts at the two airports.

Post office The main post office is downtown at Praça Correio, at the corner of Avenida São João (Mon–Fri 9am–6pm, Sat 9am–1pm). Smaller offices (Mon–Fri 9am–5pm), with their distinctive yellow signage, are scattered throughout the city.

Public holidays In addition to the normal Brazilian public holidays (see page 43), most things close in São Paulo on January 25 (Founding of the City) and on Ash Wednesday (the day after Mardi Gras).

Visas To extend your visa, visit the Polícia Federal, Rua Hugo D'Antola 95, 3rd floor, Lapa de Baixo (Mon–Fri 8am–2pm; 11 3538 5000; Lapa), and make sure you have all the necessary forms and receipts (see page 27).

8

Around São Paulo and upstate

What only a few years ago were clearly identifiable small towns or villages **around São Paulo** are today part of Greater São Paulo. Despite the traffic, escaping from the city is surprisingly easy, and there are even some points on the coast that can make for good excursions. Easy day-trips from town include the arty market at **Embu**, the old train depot of **Paranapiacaba**, the former sugar entrepôt of **Campinas**, and the port of **Santos**. Further afield, you can check out the US Confederate influence at **Santa Bárbara d'Oeste** and the Dutch influence at **Holambra**, or take the mountain air in **Campos do Jordão**.

Embu

Founded in 1554, **EMBU** was a mere village before São Paulo's explosive growth in the twentieth century. Located just 27km west of the city, Embu (often now called Embu das Artes) has now effectively merged with its massive neighbour, and yet, surprisingly, it has managed to retain its colonial feel. Quaint buildings predominate in the town's compact centre, which is traffic-free.

Handicraft market

Largo dos Jesuítas • Sat & Sun 8am–6pm • Free

In the 1970s, Embu was a popular retreat for writers and artists from São Paulo, many of whom eventually set up home here. Today, the **handicraft market** in Largo dos Jesuítas, the main square, makes the town a favourite with *paulistano* day-trippers. The shops around the main square stock a similar selection to what's on offer in the market – pseudo-antiques, rustic furniture, ceramics, leather items, jewellery and home-made jams – but they are also open during the week (although many close on Mon).

Igreja Matriz Nossa Senhora do Rosário

Largo dos Jesuítas 67 • Museum: Tues–Sun 9am–5pm • R$8

Largo dos Jesuítas holds an eighteenth-century church called **Igreja Matriz Nossa Senhora do Rosário**, graced with a typical colonial Baroque exterior. Attached to it, the **Museu de Arte Sacra dos Jesuítas** houses an interesting collection of eighteenth-century religious artefacts, including a life-size statue of Jesus after crucifixion, carved from a single log of wood.

ARRIVAL AND INFORMATION — EMBU

By bus Local bus #033 ("Embu/Eng Velho") runs from Butantã *metrô* station (Linha 4) in São Paulo to the centre of Embu (1hr 10min).

Tourist information The Centro de Atendimento ao Turista (CAT) is on Largo 21 de Abril (daily 8am–7pm; ☎ 11 4704 6565).

EATING

Buenos Aires Latino America Rua da Matriz,62 ☎ 11 4557 0623. This moderately priced but actually quite classy restaurant isn't really as Argentine as all that, but they'll do you a *bife chorizo* (Argentine-style sirloin strip steak) for R$56.20 or, if you're in a less carnivorous mood, a plate of ricotta and walnut ravioli for R$39. Tues–Fri 11.30am–3pm, Sat & Sun noon–5pm.

Nilda Travessa Marechal Isidoro Lopes 21 ☎ 11 4704 5410. A good place for a weekend lunch by Largo dos Jesuítas, with granite-topped tables, although the dark wood decor is a bit heavy. Specialities include house-style *carne de sol* (sun-dried meat), served with kale, beans and *carreteiro* rice (R$85 for two). Sat & Sun noon–6pm.

Paranapiacaba

Forty kilometres southeast of São Paulo, **PARANAPIACABA** is a funny little village of railway cottages associated with the old São Paulo Railway. The 139km rail line was built by a British company in 1867 to carry coffee from the area north of São Paulo down to the coast at Santos, and it remained under British control until 1947. Paranapiacaba was the line's administrative and engineering centre, and at one time housed four thousand workers, many of them British. Neatly laid out in the 1890s in a grid pattern, the village has remained largely unchanged over the years. All that remains of the original train station is the **clocktower**, said to be a replica of London's Big Ben, but the workers' cottages, locomotive sheds (which house old British-built carriages and steam engines) and funicular cable station are in an excellent state of preservation, and some are open to the public.

Museu Castelo

Caminho dos Mendes • Sat & Sun 9am–5pm • R$3

At the top of the village you'll find the **Castelinho**, the 1897 wooden residence of the São Paulo Railway's chief engineer. Today it houses the **Museu Castelo**, open at weekends only, which displays old maps and photographs of the rail line's early years, as well as original furniture, clocks and a scale model of Paranapiacaba.

Parques Nascentes e da Serra do Mar

You don't have to be a railway buff to appreciate Paranapiacaba. The village is set amid one of the best preserved areas of Mata Atlântica in the country and most visitors use it as a starting place for fairly serious hikes into the thickly forested **Parque Nascentes** and **Parque Estadual da Serra do Mar**, notable for their amazing orchids and bromeliads. Employing a guide is strongly advised as trails are unmarked, often very narrow and generally hard going, and venomous snakes are common.

THE OLD TRAIN STATION, PARANAPIACABA

ARRIVAL AND INFORMATION — PARANAPIACABA

By train and bus The easiest way to get to Paranapiacaba is to take the CPTM (metropolitan overground) line 10 from either Brás (on *metrô* line 3) or Tamanduateí (on *metrô* line 2) down to Rio Grande da Serra (about 1hr), and from there take local bus #424 (hourly; 20min) to Largo da Igreja, directly above Paranapiacaba town. Although line 10 is not strictly speaking part of the *metrô*, the transport system is integrated so your *metrô* ticket covers the change onto the CPTM, and vice-versa on the way back. Alternatively, on Saturdays and Sundays, you can take a special Expresso Turistico train all the way, departing from Luz station at 8.30am and returning at 4.30pm (R$45 return; 0800 055 0121, cptm.sp.gov.br/ sua-viagem/ ExpressoTuristico); tickets should be bought a week or two in advance online or at Luz station (ticket office daily 9am–6pm).

Tourist information The Centro de Informações Turisticas (CIT) is on Largo das Padeiros at the bottom of Rua Direita (Sat & Sun 9am–5pm; 11 4439 0109). The Parques Nascentes e da Serra do Mar have a visitors' centre on Rua Direita (a couple of doors up from the tourist office), where you can engage a guide.

Campinas

Around 100km northwest of São Paulo, **CAMPINAS** has been in relative decline compared to its neighbour since the nineteenth century, when it was by far the more important of the two cities. It started life as a sugar-plantation centre, produced coffee from 1870 and later made its money as a hub for agricultural processing. More recently, Campinas has become something of a centre for high-tech industry and education. An attractive city, with a reasonably compact centre, it doesn't have many tourist sights as such, but it's certainly worth a wander, and its city centre, less glitzy than São Paulo's, still hosts a lot of the small, independent shops that its bigger neighbour sometimes seems so short of.

8

The heart of the downtown area is Praça Bento Quirino, with its impressive blue-and-white fin-de-siècle **Jockey Club**. The other main square is Largo do Rosário, overlooked by its 1883 **Catedral**. About 13km from the city centre, **Unicamp** (the Universidade Estadual de São Paulo), founded in 1969 on land belonging to Colonel Zeferino Vaz, became – thanks to the protection afforded by Vaz – a refuge during the worst years of military terror for left-wing teachers who would otherwise have been imprisoned or forced into exile. Campinas has a student population of 100,000 and a reasonably lively cultural life, centred on the **Centro de Convivência Cultural**, at Praça Imprensa Fluminense.

Fazenda Tozan

SP-340, Km 121 • Visits (3hr), by appointment only, for 1–8 people • Mon–Fri R$576 (plus R$72 per extra person), Sat, Sun & public holidays R$664 (plus R$83); plus R$250/group for an English-speaking guide • Book on 19 3257 1236 or by email at osamu@tozan.com.br

If you have a car, one of the most interesting places you can visit near Campinas is the **Fazenda Tozan** (aka Fazenda Monte d'Este), 12km from town, just off the SP-340 (the road leading to Holambra). Built during the nineteenth-century coffee boom, the beautiful *fazenda* house is open to the public and contains a small museum outlining the development of the area's former coffee-based economy.

ARRIVAL AND DEPARTURE — CAMPINAS

By bus The rodoviária (which has a very helpful tourist information desk, Mon–Sat 9am–5pm) is 800m west of the centre, with a municipal bus station right next door, so you can either take a city bus into town or walk (15min) along Av Lix da Cunha to the old train station, turn left onto Av Andrade Neves and then right down Av Dr Campos Sales or Av Benjamin Constante. Buses from the rodoviária serve São Paulo's Tietê terminal (every 20min; 1hr 15min) and Santa Bárbara d'Oeste (roughly hourly; 1hr) as well as many other state and interstate destinations, but local bus #693 for Holambra (12 daily; 1hr) leaves from a stop behind the rodoviária, on Rua Dr Ricardo at Rua Dr Mascarenhas.

ACCOMMODATION

Royal Palm Tower Rua Boaventura do Amaral 1274 (at Praça Carlos Gomes) 19 2117 5900, royalpalm.com.br. A very comfortable business hotel in a tall mustard-and-white tower overlooking a green square, with well-appointed rooms and a whirlpool spa. The actual rate changes daily, and the official rack rate never actually applies. R$917

CONFEDERATES IN SÃO PAULO STATE

In the face of economic devastation following their 1865 defeat in the US Civil War, thousands of former **Confederates** from the American South resolved to "reconstruct" themselves in often distant parts of the world, forcing a wave of emigration without precedent in the history of the United States. Brazil rapidly established itself as one of the main destinations, offering cheap land, a climate suited to familiar crops, political and economic stability, religious freedom and – more sinisterly – the possibility of continued **slave ownership**. Just how many Confederates came is unclear; suggested numbers vary between 2000 and 20,000, and they settled all over Brazil, though it was in São Paulo that they had the greatest impact. While Iguape, on the state's southern stretch of coast, had a large Confederate population, the most concentrated area of settlement was the Santa Bárbara colony, in the area around present-day **Santa Bárbara d'Oeste**.

The region's climate and soil were ideally suited to the growing of **cotton** and the Confederates' expertise soon made Santa Bárbara d'Oeste one of Brazil's biggest producers of the crop. As demand for Brazilian cotton gradually declined, many of the immigrants switched to **sugar cane**, which remains the area's staple crop, though others, unable to adapt, moved into São Paulo city or returned to the United States. Today as many as 100,000 people claim descent from these Confederate exiles.

San Rafael Rua Bernadino de Campos 255 19 3236 0399, hotelsanrafaelcampinas@gmail.com. No frills and no breakfast (but wi-fi, en-suite bathrooms and hot water) at this very simple and very cheap little hotel located halfway between the rodoviária and the centre. R$70

Sonotel Av Francisco Gilcério 1444 19 3234 7688, monrealehotels.com. An efficient hotel where the rooms are all carpeted and those on the top floors give views over the town. The price never actually comes near the official rack rate, especially at weekends, and is usually less than R$200 in practice. R$468

EATING

City Bar Lanches Av Julio de Mesquita 450 (at Rua General Osório) 19 3252 5296. A terrace bar and *lanchonete* on Largo da City Banda, specializing in Portuguese dishes, and particularly *bacalhau* (salt cod). They claim to do the the coldest beer in Campinas and the best *bolinhos de bacalhau* (saltfish croquettes; R$7 each) in the world – a slight exaggeration maybe, but the beer and *bolinhos* certainly go very well together, and they also do a fine saltfish pie for R$80. Mon–Sat 6am–2am.

Eden Rua Barão de Jaguara 1216 (on Praça Visconde de Indaiatuba) 1216 19 3231 2513. On the ground floor of what was once a very grand hotel, this is now a good self-service restaurant (R$24.90 buffet weekdays, R$29.90 weekends), with good à la carte options too. Buffet Mon–Fri 11am–3pm & 6–10pm, Sat 11am–3.30pm & 6–11pm, Sun 11am–4pm; à la carte Mon–Sat 11am–11pm, Sun 11am–4pm.

Modo Mio Rua Sacramento 46 (on Praça Bento Quirino) 48 19 3236 3588, modomiorestaurante.com.br. By day a good little restaurant where you can lunch on salmon steak (R$30.90) or filet mignon (R$33,90), but after 4pm it becomes a lively terrace bar where you can check the comings and goings in the city's main square. Daily 11am–midnight.

Santa Bárbara d'Oeste

When considering Confederate immigration to Brazil the town of Americana tends to spring to mind, but in fact it's **SANTA BÁRBARA D'OESTE**, 13km to the west, which has more Confederate associations. Whereas there are some 25 English-speaking families in Americana, Santa Bárbara, much the smaller of the two cities, is home to about thirty families of Confederate origin – most of whom still speak English, with more than a touch of Dixie in their voice.

Museu da Imigração

Rua João Lino 371 at Praça 9 de Julho • Tues–Sat 8am–2pm • Free • 19 3455 5082, facebook.com/MuseudaImigracaodeSantabarbara

Near the main square, a short walk from the rodoviária, the excellent **Museu da Imigração** has displays on the history of the Confederates in the area, and that of other

FAZENDAS AROUND SÃO CARLOS

During the late nineteenth-century coffee boom, the interior of São Paulo state was known for its coffee, and the area around **São Carlos**, now a bustling university city 140km northwest of Santa Bárbara d'Oeste, was particularly productive. Today the farms around the city are largely given over to sugar cane and oranges, and little evidence remains of the area's coffee-producing past; the following *fazendas* are well worth a visit.

★ **Casa do Pinhal** Rodovia Domingos Innocentini, Km 4.5, São Carlos. At Km 227 of the SP-310 highway take the exit for Riberão Bonito, then turn immediately onto Estrada da Broa; after 4km you'll see a sign marking the entrance ⓣ 16 3377 9191, ⓦ casadopinhal.com.br. One of the oldest surviving and best-preserved rural estates in the state. The *casa grande* was built in 1831 and, typical of the period, it was modelled after the large, comfortable Portuguese city dwellings of the eighteenth century; it still retains its original furnishings and there are numerous outbuildings, including the *senzalas*, or slave quarters. The *fazenda* is an easy day-trip from Campinas – and, at a stretch, São Paulo – but you'll need your own transport. Visits should be arranged in advance by phone or email (ⓔ agendamento@casadopinhal.com.br); R$15 per person (but free for under-21s and over-60s). Visits (2hr) Tues–Fri 9am & 2pm, Sat 2pm.

Fazenda Salto Grande Rua Lilia Eliza Eberli Lupo (off SP-310 Rodovia Washington Luis highway at Km 273), Araraquara ⓣ 16 3301 2160, ⓦ hotelfazendasaltogrande.com.br. A *fazenda* 47km northwest of São Carlos that has been developed into a superb luxury hotel. Constructed to serve as a coffee plantation in the late nineteenth century, today the estate offers two swimming pools, horse riding, very comfortable guest rooms and excellent country cooking; full board available for R$566. R$368

8

nationalities, chiefly Italian. Although you wouldn't think so to look at it now, the 1896 building that houses it was originally the town jail.

Cemitério do Campo

Estrada dos Confederados (access via exit 136 on the SP-304 Rodovia Luiz de Queiroz highway) • Visits to the cemetery (R$20 per group plus R$5 per person) must be arranged at least 48hr in advance with the Fraternidade Descendência Americana (ⓣ 19 99783 8164 or ⓣ 19 99941-3024, ⓦ fdasbo.org.br), and require submission of a form which can be downloaded at ⓦ fdasbo.org.br/site/contato/visitas

About 10km from town, the **Cemitério do Campo** is a cool and shaded cemetery on a hill overlooking endless fields of sugar cane. It dates back to 1910, and all the tombstones, as well as the monument commemorating the Confederate immigrants, bear English inscriptions. There's a small chapel here, too, and a picnic area where, on the third Sunday in April, the Fraternidade Descendência Americana hold an annual Confederate Feast here (ⓦ festaconfederada.com.br) with country music and Dixie food, attended by descendants of Confederate immigrants from across Brazil. There's no politics to this: the right-wing associations of Confederate symbols in the US do not really register with this immigrant community here in Brazil.

ACCOMMODATION — SANTA BÁRBARA D'OESTE

Casablanca Rua General Osório 407 ⓣ 19 3455 7419, ⓦ hotelcasablancasbo.com.br. You'll be well looked after at this welcoming hotel, which has friendly staff, good-sized rooms and a decent restaurant, and is well located in the centre of town. R$160

Nossotel Av de Cillo 445 ⓣ 19 3455 1106, ⓦ nossotel.com.br. A modest hotel with a central location and a range of rooms, and everything you need in the way of TV and DVDs. The master suite even has a jacuzzi. R$175

Holambra

About 143km north of Campinas is the small town of **HOLAMBRA**, established in the nineteenth century by settlers from the Netherlands and retaining to this day a great deal of its Dutch character. Twentieth-century arrivals to Holambra (its name is a contraction of Holândia, América and Brasil) from Holland and Indonesia specialized

FAZENDA CASA DO PINHAL, NEAR SÃO CARLOS

in the cultivation of **flowers**, and today's residents like to boast that their prosperity is based on the work ethic those immigrants brought with them.

The town's origins are played up with a dollop of Dutch kitsch. Many of the buildings have Dutch-style facades, and gardens are neatly tended and filled with flowers, while the sidewalks have windmill motifs and many of the traffic signs have tulip shapes around them. The highlight of the year here is **Expoflora**, the annual spring flower festival, which takes place on most weekends throughout September; the event attracts not only commercial buyers but also ordinary individuals drawn by the colourful displays, Dutch folk-dancing, musical shows and food.

ARRIVAL AND DEPARTURE — HOLAMBRA

By bus Bus #693 to and from Campinas (12 daily; 1hr) stops on Rua Rota dos Imigrantes just east of town; change at Campinas for São Paulo.

ACCOMMODATION

Shellter Av das Tulipas 57 ⓣ 19 3802 1329, ⓦ shellterhotel.com.br. Very central, this homey little hotel is neat as a new pin, with rooms downstairs and upstairs, a/c, ceiling fans, parking space and a lock-up for motorbikes. They even speak a bit of Dutch. R$205

Top Centrum Rua Rota dos Imigrantes 470 ⓣ 19 3802 8555, ⓦ topcentrumhotel.com.br. Does what it says on the tin: it's the top hotel in Holambra, and it's slap-bang in the centre of town – indeed, it could be said to actually mark the centre of town. The staff are efficient, and the large rooms come equipped with a frigo-bar, a microwave and an electric kettle, R$340

8

EATING

Confeitaria Martin Holandesa Rua Doria Vasconcelos 15 ⓣ 19 3802 1295, ⓦ martinholandesa.web2301.uni5.net/site2. You can get a meal here, or even a beer, but what this place really specializes in is coffee and scrumptious Dutch-style cakes, so don't bother with lunch: come here instead for afternoon tea and pig out on the pastries, especially those made with apples (apple ball, apple slice, apple tart, apple turnover – all R$9.50). Mon 9am–4pm, Tues–Thurs 9am–11pm, Fri & Sat 9am–midnight, Sun 9am–10pm.

The Old Dutch Estrada do Fundão 200 ⓣ 19 3802 1290, ⓦ olddutch.com.br. As its name suggests, what you get here is real Old Dutch dishes, with lots of meat and hearty stodge – check out the delicious *stoofpot van lamsvlees* (lamb stew with garlic and apple; R$65). Tues–Fri 11.30am–2.30pm, Sat & Sun 11.30am–4pm.

Sabor e Arte Rua Rua Rota dos Imigrantes 470 ⓣ 19 3802 2122, ⓦ saborearteholambra.com.br. Good solid Brazilian grub, and especially good value at lunchtimes (11am–2pm), when they do an all-you-can-eat buffet for R$26 (R$32 at weekends). Mon 7am–2pm, Tues–Sat 7am–10pm, Sun 10am–4pm.

Campos do Jordão

East of São Paulo, in the direction of Rio, the **Serra da Mantiqueira** highlands boast the lively winter resort of **CAMPOS DO JORDÃO**, 1628m above sea level. Founded by the British in the late nineteenth century, the town lies on the floor of a valley, littered with countless hotels and private homes resembling Swiss chalets. The town has three parts: **Abernéssia**, the commercial centre, where you'll find ordinary shops and cheap eating places; **Juaguaribe** in the middle, where the rodoviária is located; and the monied resort-like area of **Capivari**, where most of the hotels, boutiques and expensive restaurants are concentrated. The three are joined by a single main drag, called variously Avenida Frei Orestes Girardi, Avenida Dr Januário Miraglia or Avenida Emilio Ribas, which consists of two carriageways separated by a tramway.

The novelty of donning sweaters and legwarmers draws the crowds in the southern winter, who spend their days filling in the hours before nightfall when they can light their fires. Day-time temperatures at this time of year are typically very pleasant, the sky is clear and the trails dry. In the summer, the altitude offers relief from the searing heat of the coast – but avoid going after heavy rains, which can make walking unpleasant.

Parque Estadual Campos do Jordão

Horto Florestal: 8am–5pm; closed Wed • R$14 • 12 3663 3762

There's not much in the way of entertainment in the town itself, unless you have a thing for pastiche alpine architecture, but in the surrounding area there are some good walks, with well-signposted trails. The **Parque Estadual Campos do Jordão** is 12km outside the town, and its vegetation, including graceful *araucária* (*Paraná* pine) trees, provides a striking counterpoint to the lower-altitude Mata Atlântica. Its most accessible part, the Horto Florestal, can be reached by hourly buses from the main drag, and has a number of short trails, the nicest being the Cachoeira trail, which leads to a waterfall. A tougher option is to climb the nearby 1950m **Pedra do Baú** peak, for which you must hire a guide (around R$100).

Morro do Elefante teleférico

Rua Dr Marco Antônio Cardoso 240, Capivari • Thurs–Sun 9.30am–5pm • R$16 round trip • 12 3663 1350

From the centre of Capivari, near a small boating lake (*lago de pedalinhos*), you can take a **ski lift** (*teleférico*) up to the **Morro do Elefante**, a high rock overlooking the town. From here you get a view over Campos do Jordão and the surrounding Paraíba Valley, and it's also possible to hire horses.

ARRIVAL AND GETTING AROUND — CAMPOS DO JORDÃO

By bus The rodoviária is off the main drag (Av Dr Januário Miraglia) at the Capivari end of Juaguaribe, with eight daily buses to São Paulo's Tietê terminal (3hr), but only two to Rio (5hr). Buses along the main drag link Abernéssia, Juaguaribe and Capivari.

By tram As well as buses, there's a tram (*bondinho*) along the main drag, but really only for fun, as it isn't frequent enough to be useful as transport.

By bicycle Bicycles can be rented from Desafius, Av Frei Orestes Girardi, Juaguaribe (12 3664 6096, desafius.com.br; R$90/day); although useful for getting around the spread-out town, you probably wouldn't want to take them on the rather bumpy trails.

INFORMATION AND ACTIVITIES

Tourist information The Centro de Informacões Turisticas (Mon–Sat 8am–5pm, Sun 8am–noon; 12 3663 1235) is on Praça João de Sa, on Av Dr Januário Miraglia at the very beginning of Capivari and not far from the rodoviária. It is marked by an old train carriage out front. They can supply a tourist map of the town and there's also an informative website (in Portuguese) at visitecamposdojordao.org.br.

Train rides There are a few train rides you can take, mostly short trips of about forty minutes, such as the one to the tiny village of Pindamonhangaba, surrounded by cattle and rice plantations. Details of all of these can be found on www.efcj.sp.gov.br.

Motorbiking Off-road motorbike excursions are offered by Alemão Motos, Av Frei Orestes Girardi 3257, Juaguaribe (12 3662 5549, alemaomotoracing.com.br).

ACCOMMODATION

Although there are dozens of **hotels**, finding a room at weekends and during June and July can be difficult, especially If you want an affordable one. During this high season some places demand a minimum stay of three or even seven nights; on the other hand, out of season, rates plummet.

Campos do Jordão Hostel Rua Pereira Barreto 22, Abernéssia 12 3662 2341, camposdojordaohostel.com.br. More like a cheap hotel than a traditional youth hostel, with just a couple of small dorms and rather more private rooms, but the staff go out of their way to be of help and it still offers the cheapest beds in town. Dorms R$8, doubles R$220

Geneve Av Dr Januário Miraglia 2022, Abernéssia 12 3662 1711, hotelgeneve.com.br. A small, unpretentious hotel on the main drag, with neat rooms and a communal front room where they get a big roaring fire going of a winter evening. R$200

Nevada Praça Maria de Lourdes Gonçalves 27, Av Macedo Soares, Capivari 12 3663 1611, hotelnevada.com.br. They throw in breakfast and evening "*sopa*" at this good-value mid-range hotel in the centre of Capivari, where rooms at the back are slightly cheaper than those at the front. Midweek prices are roughly fifty percent cheaper. R$460

Pousada Villa Capivary Av Victor Godinho 131, Capivari 12 3663 1736, capivari.com.br. A very comfortable chalet-like hotel, where the rooms are cosy and the salon, with big fireplace, is like the front room in a well-kept house. If you come here at the weekend (Fri & Sat night), you have to take a two-night package, which includes a big brunch on Saturday and Sunday mornings. Midweek rates are roughly a third of the price quoted. Weekend package R$1530

EATING AND DRINKING

Baden Baden Rua Djalma Forjaz 93, Capivari 12 9980 3680, obadenbaden.com.br. Get out your lederhosen for beer, sausage and fondue at this trendy bar, which gets packed out in season. If you don't fancy a cheese fondue for two (R$128.80), the R$38.80 giant steak and cheddar sandwich should fill a gap. Mon–Thurs & 11am–11pm, Fri & Sat 11am–2am.

Fraülein Bierhaus Rua Professora Isola Orsi 33, Capivari 12 3663 1529, facebook.com/Fraulein.Bierhaus. You can get good German food here – a mixed grill with sauerkraut and potatoes costs R$110 for two, for example. But what you really want is at the end of the menu: the beer list, with a huge selection of German, British and microbrewery Brazilian, and even American, brews. Not cheap (R$23.50 for a bottle of Bombardier ale), but a massive step up from a can of Skol or Bavaria. Daily noon–midnight.

Harry Pisek Av Pedro Paulo 857 (3km out of town) 12 3663 4030, pousadaharrypisek.com.br. The eponymous Harry studied sausage-making in Germany, and serves up his own wurst in several varieties at this restaurant and "salsicharia" (sausage shop) on the way to the Horto Florestal, with a big sausage sign outside so you can't miss it. If you're not sure which wurst to plump for, go for a misto (mixed platter; R$130). Mon–Fri & Sun 10am–5.30pm, Sat 10am–11pm; July daily noon–11pm.

Le Foyer Pousada Chateau La Villette, Rua Cantídio Pereira de Castro 100, Vila Everest (1km above Capivari) 12 3663 2767, chateaulavillette.com.br. The best of the town's numerous pseudo-Swiss fondue restaurants, with a Swiss-French rather than Swiss-German emphasis. It's very posh, and advance reservation is obligatory. A cheese fondue for two costs R$134. Daily 7–11pm.

The coast

Despite its proximity to the city, São Paulo's 400km **coast** has sometimes been overlooked in favour of more glamorous Rio. But don't listen to *cariocas* who sniff that the state's beaches aren't up to par: many are fabulous, although foreign visitors are relatively rare. Northeast, towards the border with Rio state, the area is developing rapidly, but still offers great contrasts, ranging from long, wide stretches of sand at the edge of a coastal plain to idyllic-looking coves beneath a mountainous backdrop. A car is an advantage for exploring the more isolated, less spoilt, beaches, but if it's a popular beach resort you're after, public transport can usually take you there from São Paulo in less than half a day. In the other direction – southwest of **Santos** – tourism remains low-key, in part because the roads aren't as good, but also because the beaches simply aren't as beautiful.

Santos

SANTOS, one of Portugal's first New World settlements, was founded in 1535. Today it's home to Latin America's largest port, through which passes a large proportion of the world's coffee, sugar and oranges. The city stands partly on São Vicente island, its docking facilities and old town facing landwards, with ships approaching by a narrow, but deep, channel. In a dilapidated kind of way, the compact centre retains a certain charm that the development of the enormous port complex has not yet extinguished. It's massively popular with local tourists, and, although you may want to skip the rather murky beaches, there is a good deal of historical and maritime interest around the city.

Rua do Comércio and around

Pelé Museum Tues–Sun 10am–6pm (last entry 5pm) • R$10

In the centre you'll find the ruins of some of Santos's most distinguished buildings along **Rua do Comércio**. Although sometimes only the facades remain, some of the

SANTOS'S TOURIST TRAIN

Running right through Santos's historical centre, the **tourist tram** (hourly 11am–5pm; R$7) is a slightly twee but popular way to see the sights. The restored tram (*bonde*), originally brought over from Scotland in 1910, departs regularly from the old railway station in Rua do Comércio (tickets on sale in the Pelé Museum opposite) and takes 40 minutes to do its circuit.

nineteenth-century former **merchants' houses** that line the street are gradually being restored, the elaborate tiling and wrought-iron balconies offering a hint of the old town's lost grandeur.

At the end of Rua do Comércio, in Rua São Bento, you'll find the old **train station**, built between 1860 and 1867, and while the claim that it is a replica of London's Victoria station is a bit difficult to swallow, it is true the building wouldn't look too out of place in a British town. Opposite, some of the street's nicest old houses have been restored to house the **Pelé Museum**, dedicated to Santos's – and Brazil's – greatest footballer, where you can see some of the shirts and boots he wore, balls he played, and trophies he won, as well as some of Pelé's own collected memorabilia.

Igreja de Santo Antônio do Valongo

Rua São Bento 13 • Tues–Sat 8am–7pm • Free

Next to the old train station, the **Igreja de Santo Antônio do Valongo** was built in 1641 in colonial Baroque style, but with its interior greatly altered over the following centuries; few of its original features remain. Another seventeenth-century church, the **Convento do Carmo** on Rua 15 de Novembro, likewise retains its Baroque facade, but no original features inside.

Museu de Café

Rua XV de Novembro 95 • Tues–Sat 9am–6pm, Sun 10am–6pm • R$10 • Ⓦ museudocafe.org.br

The **Museu de Café**, charting the history of the coffee trade, is housed in the former Bolsa de Café (coffee exchange), where coffee prices were once fixed, and the quality of the beans assessed. The 1922 building retains its original fixtures.

Monte Serrat funicular railway

Praça Correia de Mello 33 • Daily 8am–8pm; Mon–Fri every 30min, Sat, Sun & public holidays 20min • R$40 round trip

To get a great view over the whole of Santos, head three blocks south from Rua do Comércio to Praça Correia de Mello, where a very steep funicular railway pulls you 150m up **Monte Serrat**. You could save your cash and climb the steps, but that would be missing half the fun.

Vila Belmiro Stadium

Rua Princesa Isabel 77 • Tues–Sun 9am–7pm • R$8, guided tour R$15 • Ⓦ santosfc.com.br

The local **Santos Futebol Clube** is best known as the club for which the great Pelé played for most of his professional life (from 1956 to 1974); their stadium, the **Vila Belmiro**, is open to the public when there's no game on. In addition to honouring Pelé at the club's small museum, you can take an hour-long guided tour including the players' bar and dressing rooms.

The beaches

Santos's **beaches** are across town from Centro on the south side of the island, twenty minutes by bus from Praça Mauá or around R$30 by taxi. The beaches are huge, stretching around the Atlantic-facing Baía de Santos, and popular in summer, but they're also fairly scruffy. To the east, the huge **port area** is a fascinating place, with its giant elevators pouring grain into ships, and warehouses piled to the roof with sugar, but its sheer size means that you really need transport to get around it.

Gonzaga

Alongside the beach, facing the Baía de Santos, is **Gonzaga**, where the town's hotels are concentrated, as well its shopping malls. A lot less interesting than the town centre, it is nonetheless here that you are most likely to end up staying. The neighbourhood's main landmark – aside from the beach – is a huge statue of Santos's most famous native son, the early nineteenth-century revolutionary politician, Antônio Carlos Ribeiro de Andrada e Silva, which stands in the middle of Praça da Independência.

ARRIVAL AND INFORMATION — SANTOS

By bus The rodoviária is in the Centro on Praça dos Andradas. Coming from São Paulo, remember that buses to Santos (every 15min; 1hr 15min) leave from the Jabaquara rodoviária and not from Tietê. Other destinations served from Santos include Iguape (1 daily; 4hr) and Rio (5 daily; 7hr 30min). Local buses from the municipal terminal by the rodoviária serve Gonzaga (#42, #139, #154, #194) and the ferry.

By boat Regular ferries to Guarujá depart from the Ferry Boat terminal at the southeast end of town (frequent; 10min). The ferry terminal is served by bus #100, #158 and, #191 from the municipal bus terminal by the rodoviária in Centro, or #23, #42, #52, and #152 from Av Presidente Wilson in Gonzaga.

Tourist information The tourist office at the rodoviária (daily 9am–7pm) is extremely friendly and helpful.

ACCOMMODATION

Avenida Palace Av Presidente Wilson 9, Gonzaga ⊕13 3284 9629, ⓦwww.avenidapalace.com.br. This once-grand 1900 seafront hotel has now settled into being a slightly run-down budget place, with an air of faded grandeur, plain rooms (although they have bathrooms, hot water and wi-fi) and friendly staff. R$169

Parque Balneario Av Ana Costa 555 at Av Presidente Wilson ⊕13 3285 6900, ⓦparquebalneario.com.br. Being the first hotel on the seafront, this grand old place bagged the top spot, at its main junction, and although it's no youngster, it's been upgraded and modernized, and remains the best hotel in town. If you just walk in, you'll pay the rack rate, but reserve ahead (online, for example) and you're sure to get a discount (often sizeable). R$693

Ritz Av Marechal Deodoro 24, Gonzaga ⊕13 3284 1171, ⓦhotelritz.com.br. Not as ritzy as its name suggests, but the staff are friendly, the rooms are nice and fresh, with tiled floors, in an Art Deco building that still has hints of its original 1930s style, and it's just a couple of blocks from the beach. R$180

Torre Panorama Rua Euclides da Cunha 15, Gonzaga ⊕13 3208 6400, ⓦmendesplaza.com.br. A rather hideous-looking tower block, but it's the best-value mid-range place around, and the rooms are modern and well equipped. Discounts often apply, and it's cheaper at weekends. R$388

EATING

Café Paulista Praça Rui Barbosa 8, Centro ⊕13 3219 5550. A lovely old café, founded in 1911, with tiled murals of local agriculture on the walls. Nowadays it doubles up as a restaurant specializing in fish, with top billing going to the house-style sole in seafood sauce (R$108). Mon–Sat 7am–6pm.

Casa Velha Boulevard Dr Othon Feliciano 10, Gonzaga ⊕13 3284 1425, ⓦfacebook.com/casavelha.arte.comida.petisco. Down an alley ("Boulevard" is a slight pretension) off Av Ana Costa, this is a good place for an espresso, a cake or even lunch (dishes include fish in prawn sauce, R$29.90), served inside, or out on the street. They also serve beer and cachaça, and there's music on Saturdays from 9pm. Wed–Sat 7.30–10pm, Sun 12.30–3pm.

Nova Mineira Rua Bahia 115, Gonzaga ⊕13 3286 2790, ⓦnovamineira.com.br. Minas-style grub (and other Brazilian dishes) by the kilo (R$42.90 weekdays, R$44.90 weekends), or as daily specials – and in case you can't be bothered to roll up in person, they also deliver. Mon–Fri noon–3.30pm, Sat 11am–3.30pm.

Último Gole Rua Carlos Afonseca 214, Gonzaga ⊕13 3284 0508. A restaurant and *choperia* where you can get good, solid Portuguese food with no pretensions. It's particularly hot on *bacalhau* (salt cod), which comes in *bolinhos* (croquettes) at R$5 apiece – great company for a glass of *chopp* (draught beer) – or in dishes such as *zé do pipo* (baked in a creamy sauce with onion and potato; R$90). Daily 11am–midnight.

Guarujá

The very commercialized **GUARUJÁ** is São Paulo's most popular beach resort, featuring a set of large hotels and apartment buildings alongside lengthy, rather monotonous beaches. In the summer, finding space on the main beach, **Pitangueiras**, can be difficult, and the beaches within walking distance or a short bus ride away to the northeast are little better. In fact, without a car and considerable local knowledge, Guarujá is best avoided unless you really just need a beach within easy striking distance of São Paulo.

ARRIVAL AND INFORMATION — GUARUJÁ

By bus The rodoviária is 1km north of the town centre – a longish walk or short bus hop. Buses depart every 45min for São Paulo's Jabaquara rodoviária (1hr 20min). There are three direct buses a day to the rodoviária in Santos (30min), but it's better to take a local bus (#62) to the ferry terminal, cross on the boat, and take another local bus on the other side.

Tourist information The tourist office is at Av Marechal Deodoro da Fonseca 723, opposite the end of Av Puglisi, in the middle of Pitangueiras (Mon–Fri 8am–5pm; 13 3344 4600).

ACCOMMODATION

Guarujá Hostel Av Guadalajara 646, Praia da Enseada (2km east of Pitangueiras, off Av Dom Pedro I) 13 3878 1439, guarujahostel.com.br. This is about the cheapest accommodation you're going to find in Guarujá, 800m from the beach (Enseada is the next one east from Pitangueiras), but it has a pool, and it's well run and friendly. HI cardholders get a small discount. Dorms R$70, doubles R$250

Hotel Rio Rua Rio de Janeiro 131, Praia da Pitangueiras 13 3355 9281, hotelrioguaruja.com. A small hotel just a block from the beach in the centre of town, with fresh a/c rooms, wi-fi and a friendly welcome. Prices are slightly lower midweek. R$256

Maresias and around

The road east from Guarujá passes through the forested Serra do Mar before descending into **MARESIAS**, a resort drawing surfers and clubbers, and a good place to head if you want to beach it until sunset and then party until dawn. Some 10km or so further on from Maresias you'll find the much quieter and less developed **Praia Toque-Toque Pequeno** and **Praia Toque-Toque Grande**, which can be reached by local bus and are the prettiest beaches in the area.

ARRIVAL AND DEPARTURE — MARESIAS AND AROUND

By bus There are buses to Santos (3 daily; 3hr 30min), São Paolo (12 daily; 4hr) and São Sebastião (8 daily; 35min).

ACCOMMODATION

Pousada Pé da Mata Rua Nova Iguaçu 1992 12 3865 5019, pedamata.com.br. Located 2km from the beach in a pretty forest setting with spacious grounds, its selling point is that by staying here you can be "in direct contact with nature". It also has a nice pool and a choice of rooms or chalets, some of which have their own kitchenettes for self-catering. R$250

Pousada San Sebastian (Maresias Hostel) Rua Sebastião Romão Cesar 406 12 3865 6612, alberguemaresias.com.br. This is the local youth hostel, which has all standard hostel facilities but with the added benefit of a pool. Rates are slightly more expensive on Fridays and Saturdays. Dorms R$48, doubles R$110

NIGHTLIFE

Sirena Rua Sebastião Romão César 418 11 4231 9415, sirena.com.br. This fabled nightclub is the reason many well-heeled partygoers flock to Maresias. As well as the best Brazilian DJs, it plays host to top international names, attracting enthusiastic clubbers from all over the state and beyond. Sat 9pm–late, and sometimes other days too.

São Sebastião

The bustling little town of **SÃO SEBASTIÃO**, directly opposite the island of Ilhabela, was founded in the first years of the seventeenth century. For over a century it relied on its sugar cane and coffee farms before entering a period of decline. This lasted until the growth of a local fishing industry and the development of a large oil refinery helped it emerge from this stagnation in the 1980s, and the upshot is that it still has a lot of colonial and nineteenth-century buildings.

8

The narrow roads that make up the historic centre allow for pleasant wandering among the pastel-coloured colonial-style facades. Praça Major João Fernandes is the heart of São Sebastião and home to a slew of one-storey snack bars and stores, all dominated by the quietly impressive **Igreja Matriz**, built in 1636 and almost as old as the town (although its interior is twentieth-century plaster). The simple white construction, topped with a red-roofed bell tower, is typical of Franciscan-built churches of the period.

On summer evenings, the **waterfront** (Avenida Dr Altino Arantes) becomes the site of a fair selling clothes and bric-a-brac, in addition to hosting free outdoor concerts.

ARRIVAL AND INFORMATION — SÃO SEBASTIÃO

By bus The rodoviária is northwest of the town centre at the junction of Av Antonio Januario do Nascimento with Rua São Geraldo; buses from here serve Rio (3 daily; 7hr) and São Paulo (6 daily; 4hr). Local buses to Caraguátatuba (for Ubatuba) stop along Av Guarda Mór Lobo Viana, the main road through town.

By boat Ferries to Ilhabela (every 30min; 20min; ⓣ 0800 773 3711, ⓦ dersa.sp.gov.br) leave from the dock at the western end of Av Antonio Januario do Nascimento. Pedestrians go free.

Tourist information The very helpful tourist office is in a little building by the Praça de Eventos at Av Dr Altino Arantes 174 (Mon–Fri 8am–6pm, Sat & Sun noon–8pm; ⓣ 12 3892 2206).

ACCOMMODATION

Hotel Porto Grande Av Guarda Mór Lobo Viana 1440 ⓣ 12 3892 1101, ⓦ portograndehotel.com.br. This pretty, whitewashed hotel is just a 10min walk from the centre of town and set in park-like gardens that stretch down to the beach. Rooms are spacious and well equipped, and there's a pool, but it has the disadvantage of being on a busy main road. R$250

Hotel Roma Praça Major João Fernandes ⓣ 12 3892 4622, ⓦ hotelroma.tur.br. A simple but handsome old hotel on the city's main square, where there's a range of rooms, sleeping one to four people, newer ones with private bathrooms around an attractive garden, and older ones without bathrooms in the main building. Breakfasts are good but wi-fi is in the reception area only. R$110

★ **Pousada da Ana Doce** Rua Expedecionário Brasileiro 196 ⓣ 12 3892 1615, ⓦ pousadaanadoce.com.br. This is the prettiest, and one of the friendliest, places to stay in the town's historic centre. The small but perfectly adequate rooms are set around a delightful courtyard garden with a thatched veranda. R$320

Pousada da Sesmaria Rua São Gonçalo 190 ⓣ 12 3892 2347, ⓦ pousadadasesmaria.com.br. A charming, centrally located *pousada* with colonial-style furnishings. They lend out bicycles for their guests to explore São Sebastião and Ilhabela, and rates include afternoon tea as well as an excellent breakfast. R$280

EATING

Caldeirão Caiçara Rua Três Bandeirantes 75 ⓣ 12 3892 4299. A cheap and friendly self-service diner, where a buffet lunch goes for the princely sum of R$12.90. Daily 11am–4.30pm.

Canoa Av Dr Altino Arantes (Rua da Praia) 234 ⓣ 12 3892 1772. Deservedly the most popular seafood restaurant on the town's waterfront. A *caldadeira* (fish in palm oil and coconut milk) here costs R$62.80. Daily 10am–11pm.

Rocha Dr Altino Arantes (Rua da Praia) 200 ⓣ 12 3892 4552, ⓦ sorveteriarocha.com.br. This excellent local ice-cream firm has a huge range of flavours, mostly very Brazilian, including caramelized banana, burnt coconut, ginger, passion fruit (of course), and even *cupuaçu*, all at R$7 a scoop. Daily 9am–late.

Ilhabela

Without a shadow of a doubt, **ILHABELA** is one of the most beautiful spots on the coast between Santos and Rio, though it can get rather crowded in late December and early January. Of volcanic origin, the island's startling mountainous scenery rises to 1370m and is covered in dense tropical foliage. With 83 percent of the island protected within the boundaries of the **Parque Estadual de Ilhabela**, the dozens of waterfalls, beautiful beaches and azure seas have contributed to the island's popularity. Old or new, most of the buildings are in simple Portuguese-colonial styles – as far removed from brash Guarujá as you can get. The island is a haunt of São Paulo's rich who maintain large and discreetly located homes on the coast, many of which have mooring facilities for luxury yachts or helicopter landing-pads.

Vila Ilhabela

Almost all of the island's 30,000 inhabitants live along the sheltered western shore, with the small village of **VILA ILHABELA** (often referred to as "Centro") serving as the main population centre. After about a twenty-minute drive from the ferry landing, look out on the right-hand side of the road for the grand eighteenth-century main house of the **Fazenda Engenho d'Agua**, which is located a few kilometres outside the village. This was one of the largest sugar plantations on the island, famous for its high-quality cachaça. Today there's virtually no agricultural production on Ilhabela, its economy completely geared to tourism.

Vila Ilhabela, which has a few pretty colonial buildings, is dominated by the **Igreja Matriz**, a little church completed in 1806. Situated on a hill, the white-and-blue wedding cake-like building has a Spanish-marble floor and provides both a cool retreat from the sun and a good view over the area. The crucifixion sculpture in front of it is by Gilmar Pinna, whose works dot the island, the most impressive being the stations of the cross, by the beach (and main road) 2km south of Vila Ilhabela.

The beaches

Following the coastal road south from Vila Ilhabela along the mainland-facing shore, the beaches are small, but pleasant enough, the calm waters are popular with windsurfers, and bars and restaurants dot the roadside as far as **Perequê**, the island's second-biggest town, about halfway south along the island and the location of the ferry port.

There are more attractive beaches on the further-flung coasts of the island, most of which can be reached by schooner and/or jeep. Pretty beaches in coves along the northern coast, such as the **Praia do Jabaquara**, can only be reached by boat or by clambering down steep trails hidden from view from the road. It's along this stretch of

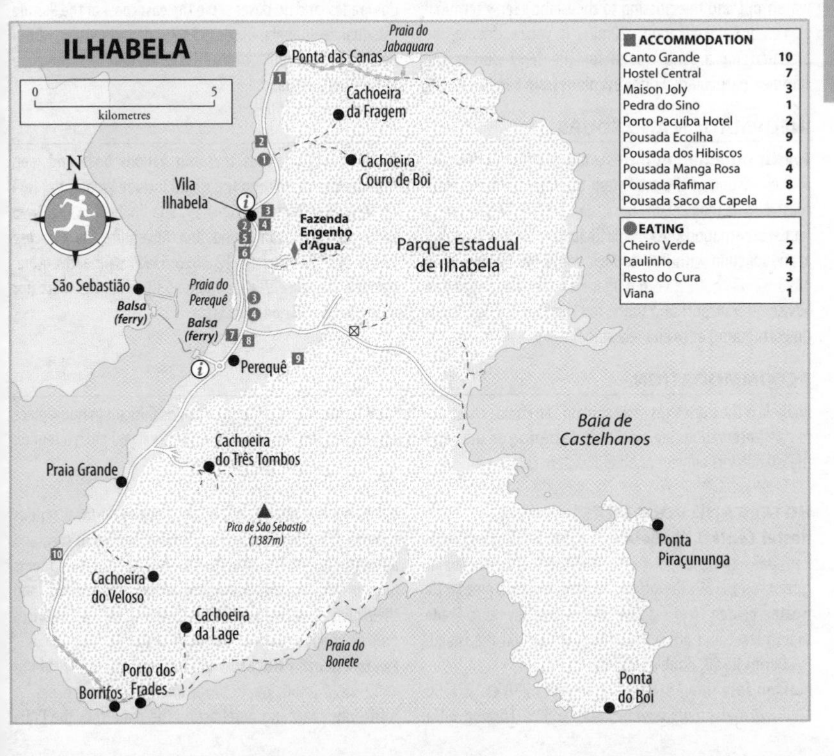

coast that some of the island's most exclusive villas are located, and their owners have an interest in making sure the road remains in bad condition and that the beaches are difficult to reach. The road is also poor along the southern shore, where some of the best beaches are located; after the road ends at Porto dos Frades it's a two-hour walk along an inland trail to the tiny fishing hamlet at **Praia do Bonete**; on the way there you'll pass an impressive waterfall, the **Cachoeira da Lage**, beneath which a natural pool has formed. Just beyond both of these places lie a couple of other fine beaches.

Parque Estadual de Ilhabela

Daily 8am–6pm, entry before 2pm • Free • T 12 3896 2585, W ilhabela.com.br/parque-estadual-de-ilhabela

The interior of the island and much of its east coast falls within the **Parque Estadual de Ilhabela** and is protected from commercial tourist development. The east-coast beaches of the **Baia de Castelhanos**, 25km across the island via a steep mountain road often washed out by heavy rain, have the most surf and are considered by many to be the island's most beautiful. As Castelhanos has no public transport, you'll need a jeep to visit; the easiest way round this is to book an all-day tour (see below), which costs around R$80 per person (wear trainers or walking shoes, and bring a towel and swimming costume).

ARRIVAL AND GETTING AROUND — ILHABELA

By ferry Ferries (24hr; every 30min by day, hourly midnight–6am; pedestrians and bicycles free; motorbikes R$9.20 weekdays, R$13.80 weekends; cars R$18.50 weekdays, R$27.70 weekends; T 0800 773 3711, W dersa.sp.gov.br) depart from São Sebastião's waterfront and the crossing to the island's ferry terminal at Perequê takes about 20min. If you're driving, be prepared for a long queue for the ferry during the summer, particularly Friday evenings from São Sebastião, and Sunday evenings from Perequê, unless you book in advance.

By bus Getting around the island can be a problem. The main bus route is along Ilhabela's western shore north as far as the lighthouse at Ponta das Canas and south to Porto dos Frades, and no buses serve the east coast or the Parque Estadual de Ilhabela. Buses (R$3.75) depart regularly from outside the Perequê terminal to Vila Ilhabela, and there are always taxis on hand.

INFORMATION AND TOURS

Tourist information There's a tourist office in Perequê, at the junction of the road from the ferry with the main coastal road (daily 9am–6pm; T 12 3895 7220), and a tourist information kiosk in Vila Ilhabela on Rua Dr Carvalho at the junction with Rua do Meio (daily 9am–6pm; T 12 3896 3777); both give out maps of the island and can advise on transport and tours. You can find online listings (in Portuguese) at W ilhabela.com.br.

Tours Travel agencies that run various boat and jeep combinations exploring the island include Webtour at Rua do Meio (Rua São Benedito) 59, Vila Ilhabela (T 12 3896 6519, W webtur.com), and Ilha Adventure, Av Princesa Isabel 605, Perequê (T 12 3896 5399, W ilhaadventure.com.br). *Hostel Central* (see page 530) also runs tours (for both guests and non-guests).

ACCOMMODATION

Ilhabela is the most expensive spot on São Paulo's coast, and in **high season** (Dec–March) it can be difficult to find a place to stay (reservations are essential). **Camping** on the beaches is forbidden, but no one seems to care if you pitch a tent on the island's virtually uninhabited eastern side.

HOTELS AND POUSADAS

Hostel Central Ilhabela Rua Irene R. Barbosa 116, Perequê, T 12 3896 6363, W hostelcentralilhabela.com; map p.529. The official HI hostel, with a pleasantly weatherbeaten feel, is on the street by the Frade supermarket and offers the cheapest beds on the island. Dorms R$60, doubles R$180

Maison Joly Rua Antônio Lisboa Alves 278 T 12 3896 1201, W maisonjoly.com.br; map p.529. Located on a hill above the village, this is the place to go for a serious splurge. The king of Sweden has been known to stay, and all of the hotel's luxurious but tastefully furnished rooms have private terraces with spectacular ocean views, and their own jacuzzis in addition to the hotel's pool. Prices drop by about a third midweek. R$715

Porto Pacuíba Hotel Av Leonardo Reale 2392, Viana T 12 3896 2466, W portopacuiba.com.br; map p.529. A friendly, charming hotel across the road from the Praia do Viana and a 20min walk (or hourly bus) into town. The beach is small and a bit rocky but there's a nice pool at the hotel. R$720

Pousada Ecoilha Rua Benedito Garcêz 164, Água Branca 12 3896 3098, ecoilha.com.br; map p.529. This attractive inland option is on the edge of the Parque Estadual, just off the road leading to the Baía de Castelhanos. The rooms are basic but comfortable and the property is entirely surrounded by tropical forest – making a good supply of insect repellent essential. R$384

Pousada dos Hibiscos Av Pedro Paulo de Moraes 720 12 3896 1375, pousadadoshibiscos.com.br; map p.529. A reception and courtyard brimming with flowers make this one of the prettiest *pousadas* to stay in. It also has a pool and the rooms feature cool white linen, tiled floors and wooden furniture. R$352.40

Pousada Manga Rosa Rua Francisco Gomes da Silva Prado 34 12 3896 1118, mangarosailhabela.com.br; map p.529. Three blocks from the centre of Vila Ilhabela, this modern *pousada* is conveniently located and offers simple, clean rooms connected by a series of wooden walkways, plus a small pool. R$445.50

Pousada Rafimar Av Brigadeiro Faria Lima 71, Perequê 12 3896 9999, rafimar.com.br; map p.529. While it's not in the prettiest part of the island, this simple hotel is very reasonably priced and has a pool. The nearby ferry landing at Perequê is convenient for reaching the mainland. R$275

Pousada Saco da Capela Rua Itapema 167 12 3896 8020, sacodacapela.com.br; map p.529. This well-maintained *pousada* at Saco da Capela, just south of Vila Ilhabela, has beautiful rooms with verandas, lush tropical gardens and a pool. Rates are slightly cheaper midweek. R$440

CAMPSITES

Canto Grande Av Riachuelo 5638, Praia Grande 12 3894 1506, cantogrande.com.br; map p.529. A campsite right by the beach at the southern end of the west coast, with hot and cold showers and parking space. . Per person R$50

★ **Pedra do Sino** Av Perimetral Norte 3872 (4km north of Vila Ilhabela) 12 3896 1266, campingpedradosino.com.br; map p.529. A well-kept and well-shaded campsite with lots of trees, good views, a pool and TV room. You can also rent a room or a trailer. The beach is across the main road, but relatively empty and not far away. No wi-fi but it's in the pipeline. Doubles R$160, camping per person R$50

8

EATING

Cheiro Verde Rua da Padroeira 109, Vila Ilhabela 12 3896 3245, bit.ly/CheiroVerde; map p.529. A popular diner in the centre of Vila Ilhabela, with a R$29.80 menu till 5pm, and inexpensive fish dishes (fish and chips R$22.80) Daily 11.30am–11pm.

Paulinho Rua Pedro de Freitas 201 12 3896 2755; map p.529. Simple but good home-style cooking, off the beach road north of Perequê. The fish of the day (R$105 for two) is of course from the day's local catch Wed–Sun noon–11pm.

Resto do Cura Av Princesa Isabel 337 12 3896 1341; map p.529. A good *comida por quilo* joint (R$59.90/kg) on the beach road between Vila Ilhabela and Perequê. Mon–Fri 11.30am–4pm, Sat & Sun 11.30am–6pm.

Viana Av Leonardo Reale 1560, Viana 12 3896 1089, viana.com.br; map p.529. The island's top restaurant, which is rather formal and specializes (unsurprisingly) in seafood. Starters include a seafood bisque for R$36, which you can follow with *peixe a Dom Vasco da Gama* (fish in a white wine sauce) for R$92. The more informal hut on the beach opposite has the same menu. Restaurant April–Nov Fri–Sun 1–10pm; Dec–March daily 1–10pm; beach hut daily 10am–6pm.

Ubatuba and around

UBATUBA is a friendly little town on the Tropic of Capricorn, 50km northeast of São Sebastião. The main draw is the local beaches, 72 in all, on islands and curling around inlets, and reckoned by some to be among the state's best. Ubatuba is centred on Praça 13 de Maio, a couple of blocks from the rodoviária on Rua Conceição. Although there's nothing wrong with the town's own **Praia de Iperoig**, Ubatuba is best used as a base from which to visit some of the numerous other beaches accessible by bus or private boat.

Projeto Tamar

Rua Antônio Athanásio 273, Itaguá • Mon, Tues, Thurs & Sun 10am–6pm, Fri, Sat & school holidays 10am–8pm • R$19 • 12 3832 6202, tamar.org.br

Worth a visit is the local branch of the environmental organization Projeto Tamar, which has display panels (in English and Portuguese) on their work protecting **sea turtles** (mainly loggerheads) that graze offshore, and live turtles on view in pools.

Aquário de Ubatuba

Rua Guarani 859, Itaguá • Sun–Thurs 10am–8pm, Fri, Sat & public holidays 10am–10pm • R$28 • ⓣ 12 3834 1382, ⓦ aquariodeubatuba.com.br

Designed largely with kids in mind, Ubatuba's small aquarium is a fun hour's visit with everything from sharks and piranhas to crustaceans and jellyfish, and a touching tank, where kids can stroke a starfish or two, not to mention exhibits on ecosystems such as coral reefs and mangrove swamps.

Beaches northeast of Ubatuba

The least developed – and the most attractive – beaches are to the **northeast** of town, with the furthest, Camburi, 46km away on the border with Rio state. To get to these beaches, take the **local bus** marked "Prumirim" from the rodoviária and ask the driver to stop at whichever stretch takes your fancy. One possible point to make for is the Bairro do Picinguaba, a fishing village with a couple of bars and simple restaurants set alongside a very pretty beach and connected to the main road by a 3km-long narrow winding road.

Beaches and islands south of Ubatuba

The more popular beaches are to the south of Ubatuba and also easily reached by bus from the town centre, although almost all of them are fringed with hastily built condominiums as well as shopping and entertainment complexes. **Enseada**, 9km from Ubatuba, is lined with expensive beachfront hotels; nestled in a bay protected from the lively surf, its beach is popular with families, and in the summer it's always uncomfortably crowded.

Across the bay is a series of beautiful isolated beaches that draw fewer people. Walk out of Enseada on the main road for about 2km until you reach Ribeira, a yachting centre and colourful fishing port. From here, you can get boats (around R$30/person) over to the **Ilha Anchieta**, a state park on an island where only a few fisherfolk live. Beyond Ribeira are sandy coves you can reach by clambering down from the trail on the cliff above the sea.

Parque Estadual Serra do Mar

Guide around R$150, depending on trail length • ⓣ 12 3832 1397, ⓦ www.parqueestadualserradomar.sp.gov.br

It's easy to arrange hikes inland from Ubatuba to the **Parque Estadual Serra do Mar**, a large state nature reserve north of Ubatuba that is divided into several sections, or "nuclei", and stretches in a band running inland alongside more than half of the state's coastline. Local buses serve the Picinguaba "nucleus" near Ubatuba.

ARRIVAL AND INFORMATION — UBATUBA AND AROUND

By bus The rodoviária is on Rua Thomaz Gallardo in the town centre. Buses serve Paraty (6 daily; 1hr 30min), Rio (2 daily; 5hr) and São Paulo (8 daily; 4hr). The local bus terminal is nearby, just down Bendito Pimenta on Rua Conceição. For São Sebastião, change at Caraguatatuba (local bus from Rua Conceição near the terminal). For Campos do Jordão, change at Taubaté.

Tourist information On the seafront at the end of Rua Conceição (one block north of Rua Thomaz Gallardo) there's a very helpful tourist office (Mon–Fri 8am–6pm, Sat 9am–5pm; ⓣ 12 3833 7300), which supplies maps of the town and surrounding beaches.

ACCOMMODATION

Itamambuca Eco Resort Rodovia Rio-Santos Km 36, Praia de Itamambuca (13km northeast of town) ⓣ 12 3834 3000, ⓦ itamambuca.com.br. Set back between trees near Itamambuca, one of the area's best beaches, this resort has attractive cabins of varying degrees of luxury, with its own on-site restaurants and activities for children. Minimum stay three nights. **R$636**

★ Pousada da Ana Doce Praia do Lázaro (15km southwest of town) ⓣ 12 3842 0102, ⓦ pousadaanadoce.com.br. Sister to the *pousada* of the same name in São Sebastião (see page 528), this is almost as charming, plus it has a pool. **R$320**

Pousada das Artes Praia das Toninhas (5km south of town) ⓣ 12 3842 3679, ⓦ pousadadasartes.com.br. Arty and slightly pretentious, this is nevertheless a comfy place to stay south of town. Themed guest rooms are based on different cultures, including Indian, Arabian, Japanese, and of course Brazilian. **R$300**

Pousada da Praia Praia do Félix (15km northeast of town) ⓣ 12 3845 1196, ⓦ praiadofelix.com.br. Simple bungalow apartments, each with a veranda and a kitchen, situated in beautiful gardens near one of the area's prettiest beaches. Reservations by phone only. No wi-fi. R$450

Pousadinha Rua Guarani 686 ⓣ 12 3832 2136, ⓦ ubatuba.com.br/pousadinha. This small, friendly *pousada* is handy if you want to stay in town. All rooms are a/c, but there's no pool. R$250

Tribo Hostel Rua Amoreira 71, Praia do Lázaro (15km southwest of town) ⓣ 12 3842 0585, ⓦ ubatubahostel.com. A well-equipped youth hostel with beds in small, four-to six-bed dorms and some private rooms. The hostel is linked to town by bus. Minimum stay three nights. Dorms R$70, doubles R$210

EATING AND DRINKING

Alentejano Rua Guarani 612 ⓣ 12 3833 4254, ⓦ pousadaalentejano.com.br/restaurante.html. In among all the fish restaurants, here's one for meat eaters: a *por quilo* hostelry specializing in *churrasco*, at R$45.90. Daily 11.30am–5pm.

Peixe com Banana Rua Guarani 255 ⓣ 12 3832 1712. One of the best beach-side restaurants in town, serving outstanding seafood at low prices, in particular, as its name suggests, fish and banana, including the local speciality, *azul-marinho* (fish stewed with green banana in an iron pot that turns it blue; R$145 for two). Daily noon–10pm.

Rei do Peixe Rua Guarani 480 ⓣ 12 3832 3272, ⓦ reidopeixe.com.br. The first of what's become a small local chain, serving well-cooked super-fresh fish. The *mocequa* is R$124 for two with fish, or R$156 with shellfish. Mon–Fri 11.30am–10.30pm, Sat & Sun 11.30am–11.30pm.

Iguape and around

IGUAPE, roughly 180km west of Santos, was founded in 1538 by the Portuguese to guard against Spanish encroachment. Its poor strategic location at the tip of an estuarine island left it a backwater, so many of its simple colonial buildings survive today in good condition. The greatest concentration of them is around **Largo da Basílica**, Iguape's main square, which is rimmed by whitewashed and brightly coloured buildings constructed in colonial, nineteenth-century and even Art Deco styles.

In summer, Iguape is popular with *paulistanos* seeking a beach vacation away from the sophistication, crowds and expense of resorts further north. The nearest good beach on the mainland is **Barra do Ribeira**, frequented by surfers; it's a fifteen-minute boat ride to get there from Iguape, or a 20km car ride over rough track.

Ilha Comprida

Facing Iguape is another island, the **Ilha Comprida**, 86km long but just 3km wide, with an interior of scattered forest; an uninterrupted beach stretches the entire Atlantic-facing length of the island. In the summer it gets very crowded near the access road that crosses the island, where the beginnings of urban development, including some basic hotels and snackbars, are increasing apace; if you want to be alone, just walk south for a few kilometres. Alternatively, the island can be reached from Cananéia (see page 534).

ARRIVAL AND INFORMATION — IGUAPE AND AROUND

By bus The rodoviária is 1.5km north of the town centre on Rua Professor Bento Pereira Rocha, which you can follow into town (about 20min on foot, or a short taxi ride). To reach the rodoviária from Largo da Basílica, take Rua Jeremias Junior near the Solar Colonial Pousada, and it's pretty much straight ahead past the Igreja de São Bento and up Rua Dom Idílio José Soares. Coming from São Paulo, it's Barra Funda rodoviária you need, not Tietê.

Destinations Curitiba (1 daily; 4hr 30min); Registro (20 daily; 1hr); Santos (1 daily; 4hr); and São Paulo (4 daily; 4hr 30min). For Cananéia you need to change at Pariquera Açu (16 daily; 30min).

ACCOMMODATION

Pousada Casa Grande Rua Major Rebelo 768 ⓣ 13 3841 1920, ⓦ bit.ly/PousadaCasaGrande. A warm, welcoming and rather homely *pousada* in a nineteenth-century house just three blocks from Largo da Basílica, this is the place to stay if you want somewhere quiet. R$160

★ **Solar Colonial** Largo da Basílica 30 ⓣ 13 3841 1591, ⓦ bit.ly/SolarColonial. A charming and atmospheric *pousada* in a lovely nineteenth-century building right on the main square (which is overlooked by the breakfast room and by room #7). It's the top place in town to stay, and not expensive – you certainly won't save much money by staying elsewhere. R$180

8

EATING

Itacurumins Rua Porto do Rosário 2 ⓣ 13 3841 1536. A good fish restaurant, open lunchtime only, when they serve the local catch in various forms – notably paella (R$259 for two). Daily except Tues 11am–4.30pm.

Panela Velha Rua 15 de Novembro 190 ⓣ 13 3841 1869. Iguape's top eating-house, which also functions as a bar. You can eat meat or veg here, but fish is what they excel at: the house speciality is *robalo á Panela Velha* (sea bass stuffed with tapioca; R$149.90), and, like all their dishes, it feeds two. Mon & Sun 11am–5pm, Tues–Sat 11am–11pm.

Cananéia and around

More appealing than Iguape, **CANANÉIA**, 50km further south and also on an island, lies between Ilha Comprida and the mainland, to which it's linked by a short bridge. At the height of summer it gets crowded here, but for the rest of the year, both the town and the beaches are extremely quiet.

In the old centre of Cananéia, in particular along *ruas* Tristão Lobo, Bandeirantes and Dom João II, you'll find a fair few colonial and nineteenth-century buildings, but in many cases only the facade is original. One that's well preserved is the seventeenth-century **Igreja São João Batista** (open daily for Mass), on Praça Martim Afonso de Souza. The **Museu Municipal** (Tues–Sun 9am–6pm; R$8) at Rua Tristão Lobo 78 is also worth a brief look, with pride of place among its exhibits going to a preserved shark that weighed 3500kg.

ARRIVAL AND INFORMATION — CANANÉIA AND AROUND

By bus Buses from São Paulo depart from Barra Funda rodoviária and pull up on Rua Silvino de Araújo, between Av Independência and the seafront.

Destinations Registro (6 daily; 1hr); São Paulo (1 daily; 4hr 30min). For Iguape you have to change at Pariquera Açu (7 daily; locals change buses at the road junction by the cemetery rather than going into the bus station).

By boat Ferries from the dock by Praça Martim Alfonso de Souza in the centre of town (ⓣ 0800 773 3711 or ⓣ 13 3358 2741, ⓦ dersa.sp.gov.br) run between the town centre and Ilha Comprida (1–2 hourly 6am–11.30pm; 20min), from where you can either take a bus (roughly hourly) or follow the road for 3km straight ahead by foot or bicycle to the beach. For Paraná, there are launches (Mon, Wed & Thurs 8am; 3hr; ⓣ 13 3851 2056; R$57.30) that travel via a tranquil inland waterway to Ariri, a small fishing community on the border of Paraná, but there is a risk that there will be no connecting launch on to Guaraqueçaba or Paranaguá.

By car At low tide, cars are permitted to drive along the beach between Iguape and Cananéia on the Atlantic-facing beach, a journey that can be completed in less than an hour, although really you need 4WD; check and double-check tidal times and drive carefully, neither too near the water's edge nor too high up the beach or you risk getting stuck in the sand.

Information There is no tourist office, but maps of the town are posted up on the waterfront in Av Beira Mar.

ACCOMMODATION

Beira-Mar Av Beira Mar 219 ⓣ 13 3851 1115, ⓦ hotelbeiramarcananeia.com.br. A one-storey hotel on the waterfront, which has expanded in recent years, and now has a pool along with fully equipped rooms (cheaper midweek and off-season). R$150

Coqueiro Av Independência 542 ⓣ 13 3851 1255, ⓦ hotelcoqueiro.com.br. The sign here is in Japanese as well as Portuguese, and the owners are Japanese-Brazilian, but there's more of a seaside feel than a Japanese feel about this easy-going low-rise hotel on the main drag with a decent pool and reduced prices off-season. R$180

Golfinho Plaza Av Independência 885 ⓣ 13 3851 1655, ⓦ golfinhoplazahotel.com.br. The best hotel in Cananéia, where the deliciously cool rooms all have a veranda along with the usual a/c and fridge, the pool is on the roof and the price is great value. R$160

Pousada Recanto do Morro Rua Profesor Besnard 420, Morro de São João ⓣ 13 3851 3370, ⓦ pousadarecantodomorro.com.br. Offers good rooms set in attractive gardens and surrounded by lush vegetation, 500m west of the town centre beyond the fishing port. There's also a pool and a lake full of carp. R$220

EATING AND DRINKING

Bacharel Av Independência 835 ⓣ 13 3851 1182. Smart fish and seafood restaurant whose mainstays are either done the Brazilian way (*moquecas* from R$152 for two) or the Japanese-Brazilian way (seafood sukiyaki R$163 for two), with individual portions at sixty percent of the for-two price. Tues–Sat 10.30am–4pm & 6–11pm, Sun 6–11pm.

EXPLORING ILHA CARDOSO

To the south of Cananéia, the island of **Ilha Cardoso** is a protected **nature reserve**, with isolated beaches, fishing villages and some wonderful trails. **Boat excursions** to Cardoso, departing from the wharf by Saidera Bar on Praça Martin Alfonso de Souza in the centre of town, last five or six hours, including a stop at a long beach – deserted except for a small café and rangers' post – and the chance to go for undemanding treks through the reserve. Expect to pay around R$30 per person, with a minimum of four people (most likely at weekends and in the December–February high season). The waters are home to around three thousand Tucuxi dolphins, which can easily be seen from the boat and come in amazingly close to shore.

Ponts Av Beira Mar 71 ⓣ 13 3851 1262. Done out rather like an English pub (even decorated with some British car registration plates), this little place will whip you up a great seafood *caldeirada* (R$75), or a *prato executivo* such as fish fillet with salad, rice and beans (R$29.90), well prepared, well served and well tasty. Tues–Sun 4–11pm.

Porto Camarão Av Independência 884 ⓣ 13 3851 3702. A large and popular seafood restaurant, where the dishes are enough to serve two or three people – a bubbling seafood *caldeirada*, for example, costs R$120. Daily 11am–11pm.

Registro

If travelling south to Paraná, you'll have to change buses in **REGISTRO**, a bustling and rather ugly town an hour inland from both Iguape and Cananéia in the heart of Brazil's main tea-growing region. Registro's once overwhelmingly Japanese character has been greatly diluted in recent years by the arrival of migrants from other parts of the state and with a gradual exodus of young people of Japanese descent drawn to greater opportunities elsewhere.

ARRIVAL AND ACCOMMODATION — REGISTRO

By bus From Registro buses serve Cananéia (6 daily; 1hr), Curitiba (5 daily; 4hr), Iguape (19 daily; 1hr) and São Paulo (9 daily; 4hr).

Lito Palace Av Pref Jonas Banks Leite ⓣ 13 3821 1055, ⓦ litopalacehotel.com.br. The most comfortable hotel in town, mainly business-oriented but hospitable enough, with good rooms, parking space, a pool and a fitness centre. R$170

The South

THE JESUIT MISSION OF SÃO MIGUEL

9

The South

Southern Brazil – the states of Paraná, Santa Catarina and Rio Grande do Sul – is a land of *gaúchos*, sumptuous barbecues and long, sandy beaches. The region's spectacular natural features include the mesmerizing Iguaçu Falls on the Brazilian-Argentine frontier and the mind-bending canyons of the Aparados da Serra, but it's also the most developed region in the country, with more in common culturally with Europe or Argentina than with the rest of Brazil.

The southern **coast** has a subtropical climate that in the summer months (Nov–March) draws Brazilian (and Argentine) holidaymakers who want to avoid the oppressive heat of the northern resorts, and an atmosphere and flora that feel more Mediterranean than Brazilian. Much of Paraná's shore is still unspoilt by the ravages of mass tourism, and building development is essentially forbidden on the beautiful islands of **Paranaguá Bay**. By way of contrast, tourism has encroached along Santa Catarina's coast, but only a few places, such as **Balneário Camburiú**, have been allowed to develop into a concrete jungle. Otherwise, resorts such as most of those on the **Ilha de Santa Catarina** around **Florianópolis** remain fairly small and do not seriously detract from the region's natural beauty.

The **interior** is less frequently visited. Much of it is surprisingly – and spectacularly – mountainous, the home of people whose way of life seems to have altered little since the arrival of the European pioneers in the nineteenth and early twentieth centuries. Cities in the interior that were founded by Germans (such as **Blumenau** in Santa Catarina), Italians (**Bento Gonçalves** in Rio Grande do Sul) and Ukrainians (**Prudentópolis** in Paraná) have lost much of their former ethnic character, but close by are villages and hamlets where time appears to have stood still.

Paraná

Paraná, immediately to the south of São Paulo, is one of Brazil's wealthiest and most dynamic states, but it's also rich in natural and cultural attractions, most

PARQUE NACIONAL DOS APARADOS DA SERRA

Highlights

❶ **Museu Oscar Niemeyer** Stunning contemporary art museum designed by the Brazilian master, located in Curitiba, dynamic capital of Paraná. See page 546

❷ **Serra Verde Express** One of South America's most scintillating train rides, snaking through the Mata Atlântica. See page 549

❸ **Ilha do Mel** Brazil's chilled out island paradise, blissfully undeveloped and car-free. See page 559

❹ **Iguaçu Falls** No trip to the South is complete without a visit to these awe-inspiring waterfalls. See page 562

❺ **Florianópolis beaches** Known as a surfing hot spot, Florianópolis also offers plenty of gorgeous swimming beaches. See page 577

❻ **Churrascarias** Choose from a staggering selection of cuts at these popular barbecue houses – you'll find the best in Porto Alegre. See page 612

❼ **Parque Nacional dos Aparados da Serra** Hike one of the continent's most spectacular canyons, with sensational views. See page 619

❽ **Rota Missões** The fine Jesuit ruins of São Miguel are dramatically sited in the sparsely inhabited interior of Rio Grande do Sul. See page 626

HIGHLIGHTS ARE MARKED ON THE MAP ON PAGE 540

obviously the **Iguaçu Falls** in the far west. Travelling overland from São Paulo, however, the affluent state capital of **Curitiba** makes a good base from which to start exploring the region. **Paranaguá Bay** can be visited as a day-trip, but its islands and colonial towns could also easily take up a week or more of your time – especially the laidback, car-free, beach and surf centre of **Ilha do Mel**. The **Serra Verde Express** between Curitiba and Morretes is one of South America's most thrilling train rides.

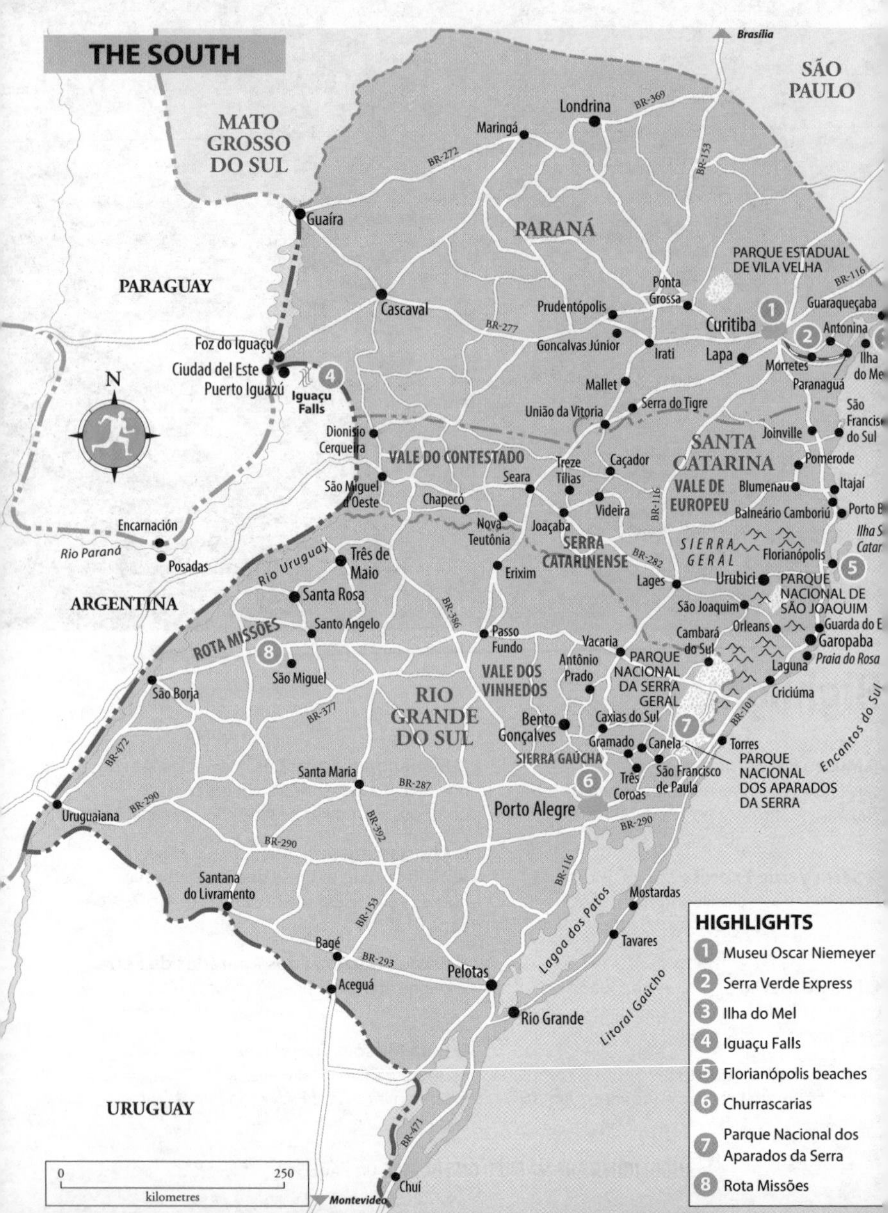

Brief history

Paraná's population is ethnically diverse, but largely comprised of the descendants of immigrants from **Eastern Europe**. Settlement of the coast by the Portuguese began in the sixteenth century, but the inland was largely left to the indigenous Tupi-Guaraní peoples. For several decades after breaking away from São Paulo in 1853, the state of Paraná remained sparsely populated by indigenous peoples, the Portuguese and mixed-race settlers known as *caboclos*, who worked on the *latifúndios* (vast, privately owned estates), scratched a living as semi-nomadic subsistence farmers or, on the coast, fished. Its economy was based on pig-raising, timber extraction and *erva maté* (a bush whose leaves are used to make a tea-like beverage).

Immigration was the key to expanding Paraná's economy. As mainly coffee or soya farmers, Germans moved northwards from Rio Grande do Sul and Santa Catarina in the 1880s; Poles and Italians settled near the capital, Curitiba; Ukrainians centred themselves in the south, especially around Prudentópolis; Japanese spread south from São Paulo, settling around Londrina and Maringá; and a host of smaller groups, including Dutch, Mennonites, Koreans, Russian "Old Believers" and Danube-Swabians, established colonies elsewhere with varying success rates. Thanks to their isolation, the immigrants' descendants have retained many of their cultural traditions, which have only gradually been eroded by the influences of television and radio, the education system and economic pressures. Nevertheless, this multi-ethnic blend still lends Paraná its distinct character and a special fascination. Today Paraná boasts one of the largest state economies in Brazil, largely thanks to a booming **farm sector** (soybeans, corn, sugar cane, cattle, pork, chicken and coffee) and a diversified industrial base around Curitiba that includes a massive **Volvo car factory**.

Curitiba

An ever-expanding sea of high-rises, bike lanes, and artfully landscaped parks, **CURITIBA** ("curi-chiba") offers the chance to experience the wealthier side of Brazil: on average, *Curitibanos* enjoy Brazil's highest standard of living. The city boasts a transport system and facilities that are the envy of other parts of the country and its eco-friendly design is a model that many urban planners try to emulate. The small *centro histórico* (the area around Largo da Ordem and Praça Garibaldi) withstanding, it's not an especially attractive city, but there's a real big-city buzz and Curitiba remains relatively safe and almost Northern Europe-like in its efficiency – an intriguing alternative Brazil to all points north. The only real showstopper is the jaw-dropping **Museu Oscar Niemeyer**, but the *centro histórico* is worth a wander, and you could easily spend an enjoyable day touring the diverse parks and attractions in the city's outskirts via the convenient **Linha Turismo** bus service.

Brief history

Founded by the Portuguese in 1693, Curitiba was of little importance until 1853 when it was made capital of the newly created state of Paraná. Since then, the city's

FUTEBOL CURITIBA

Curitiba is home to two major **football clubs**: Coritiba (aka "Coxa"; ⓦ coritiba.com.br) and Atlético Paranaense ("the Furacão"; ⓦ atleticoparanaense.com), who meet for a frenzied derby known as the **Atletiba**. Coritiba plays at central **Estádio Couto Pereira**, while Atlético play at the hyper-modern **Estádio Joaquim Américo** (aka Arena da Baixada) in the Água Verde neighbourhood (4.5km south of the centre). Your hotel or hostel should be able to help get tickets to a match.

population has grown steadily from a few thousand to 1.8 million, its inhabitants largely descendants of Polish, German, Italian, Ukrainian and other immigrants attracted by the booming logging and agricultural sectors (today the city is a major car manufacturing hub) – the city has also weathered the latest Brazilian economic crisis far better than its peers.

Rua das Flores

Linha Turismo stop #2

The **Rua das Flores** – a pedestrianized section of **Rua XV de Novembro**, lined with carefully restored, pastel-coloured early twentieth-century buildings – is central Curitiba's main late-afternoon and early-evening meeting point, when its bars, tearooms and coffee shops are crammed with customers. Two historic bars on this stretch have become tourist attractions thanks to a rivalry over the humble hot dog: *Bar Mignon* (at no. 42 since 1946), and *Bar Triângulo* (at no. 36 since 1934) both claim to have introduced the snack to Curitiba over seventy years ago, both knock out sumptuous versions of their own – and both are great places to soak up Curitiba street life or grab a cold beer. Just beyond leafy **Praça General Osório**, at the far end of Rua das Flores, there's a small shopping arcade, the **Rua 24 Horas** (between Visconde de Nácar and Rio Branco) an attempt by city planners to keep the centre of Curitiba alive outside of office hours, though it's not open around the clock as its name suggests.

Museu de Arte Contemporânea do Paraná

Rua Westphalen 16 • Tues–Fri 10am–7pm, Sat & Sun 10am–4pm • Free • 41 3323 5328, www.mac.pr.gov.br • Linha Turismo stop #2

Housed in the old Department of Public Health building (a striking pink confection amid all the concrete high-rises, completed in 1928), the **Museu de Arte Contemporânea do Paraná** showcases the work of local and Brazilian contemporary artists in a variety of media through changing exhibitions. The museum owns around 1500 works: quality varies, but aficionados will appreciate the work of Argentine artist Tomás Abal, respected Modernist Alfredo Volpi, leading neo-constructivist sculptor Amílcar de Castro, experimental artist José Bechara and the often bizarre work of multimedia artist and poet Alex Flemming. The list of actual *paranaense* painters is quite small, but includes Miguel Bakun, Theodoro De Bona and Guido Viaro.

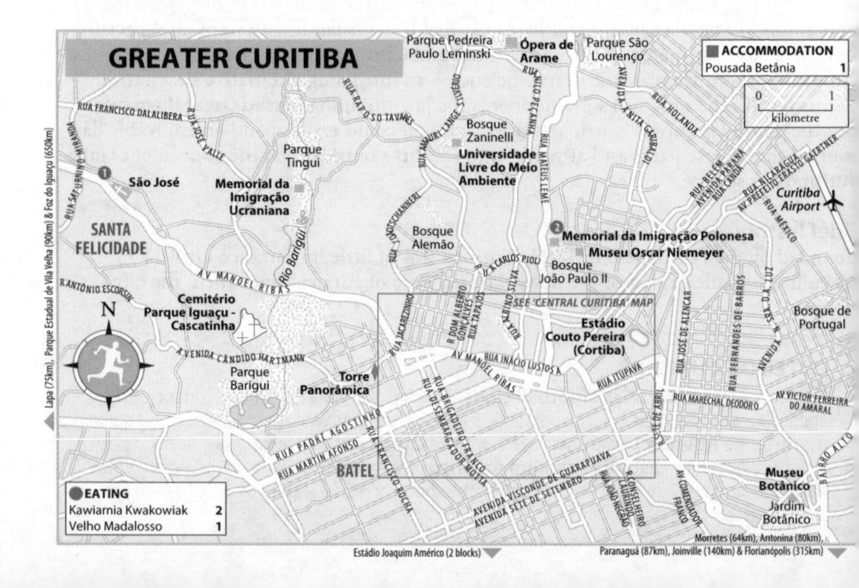

Praça Tiradentes

Catedral Basilica Menor: Daily 6am–7pm • Free • Linha Turismo stop #1

Always busy and slightly worn around the edges, **Praça Tiradentes** remains the traditional heart of the city, invigorated in the spring by the bright yellow blossoms of its *ipê* trees. The plaza is the terminus of the Linha Turismo bus (see page 550), and is also the home of the twin-towered **Catedral Basilica Menor de Nossa Senhora da Luz**, dedicated to the patron of the city (there's a revered statue of this incarnation of Mary inside). Inaugurated in 1893, its unremarkable Neogothic facade gives way to an ornate, richly decorated interior – look for Pope John Paul II's chair, preserved shrine-like to the right of the entrance.

Paço de Libertade

Praça Generoso Marques 189 • Tues–Fri 10am–9pm, Sat 10am–6pm, Sun 11am–5pm • Free • ☎ 41 3234 4200

To the southeast, Praça Tiradentes blends into Praça José Borges – notable as the home of a small **flower market** (daily 9am–6pm) – and further along the **Paço de Libertade** (the former city hall) on Praça Generoso Marques, a magnificent Art Nouveau construction built in 1916 and converted into a cultural centre (it's often closed for events).

Largo da Ordem

Casa Romário Martins Tues–Fri 9am–noon & 1–6pm, Sat & Sun 9am–2pm • Free • ☎ 41 3321 3255

A pedestrian tunnel leads from Praça Tiradentes to Curitiba's **centro histórico**, beginning with the small plaza known as **Largo da Ordem** and leading to the adjoining **Praça Garibaldi** via pedestrianized Claudino dos Santos, an area of charming eighteenth- and nineteenth-century architecture, bars and cafés. On Sundays be sure to check out the **Feira de Artesanato** here (9am–2pm), Curitiba's biggest craft market, with stalls selling handicrafts produced primarily in Paraná. The early eighteenth-century **Casa Romário Martins**, on Largo da Ordem itself, is Curitiba's oldest-surviving house, and now home to a small exhibition area with revolving displays on local history and art.

Igreja da Ordem Terceira de São Francisco das Chagas

Largo da Ordem • Museum: Tues–Fri 9am–noon & 1–6pm, Sat & Sun 9am–2pm • Free • ☎ 41 3321 3265

Dating from 1737 (but rebuilt with a bell tower in the 1880s), the **Igreja da Ordem Terceira de São Francisco das Chagas** is the city's oldest-surviving building. Plain outside, the church is also simple within, its only decoration being some tiny examples of Portuguese blue-and-white tiling and late Baroque altars. Next door a separate entrance leads to the mildly interesting **Museu de Arte Sacra**, with relics such as statuary, calvaries, vestments and chalices gathered from Curitiba's Roman Catholic churches going back to the seventeenth century.

Solar de Rosário

Rua Duque de Caxias 4 • Mon–Fri 10am–8pm, Sat 10am–1pm, Sun 10.30am–2pm • Free • ☎ 41 3225 6232, Ⓦ solardorosario.com.br

Art galleries are a prominent feature around Largo da Ordem; one of the most intriguing is **Solar de Rosário**, which shows local contemporary art in a handsome nineteenth-century mansion and also includes a bookshop (art books, calendars, posters) and a small teahouse.

Memorial de Curitiba

Claudino dos Santos 79 • Tues–Fri 9am–noon & 1–6pm, Sat & Sun 9am–3pm • Free • ☎ 41 3321 3313, Ⓦ fundacaoculturaldecuritiba.com.br

Curitiba is especially well endowed with cultural centres, and the **Memorial de Curitiba** is one of the biggest, a jarringly modern edifice opened in 1996 in the heart of the historic district. In addition to a regular schedule of performances, changing exhibits and lectures, the interior features a series of exuberant murals by local artist Sérgio Ferro and permanent sculptures by Poty Lazzarotto, Ricardo Todd, João Turin and other Brazilian artists.

9

Museu Alfredo Andersen

Rua Mateus Leme 336 • Tues–Fri 9am–6pm, Sat & Sun 10am–4pm • Free • 41 3222 8262, www.maa.pr.gov.br

Dedicated to the work of the eponymous Norwegian-born artist and located in his former home and studio, the **Museu Alfredo Andersen** is an artistic gem. Although a gifted painter, Andersen (1860–1935) is hardly known in his native country, in part because the majority of his artistic output is in Brazil and because his subject matter

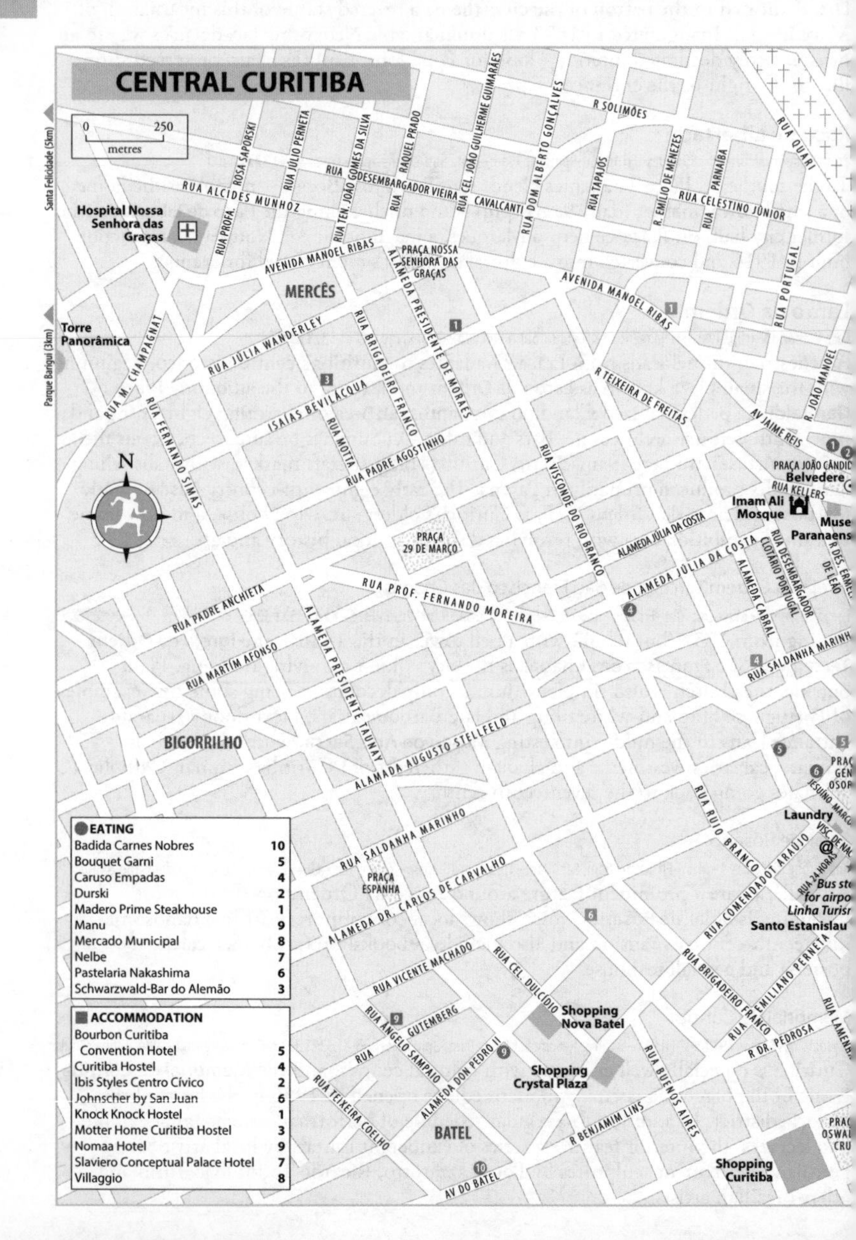

– late nineteenth- and early twentieth-century landscapes and rural people – solely concerned Paraná. The collection is small but gives a decent taster of Andersen's oeuvre (there are also items from his studio and a self-portrait of 1932), while other rooms feature temporary exhibitions of local artists. Andersen came to Paraná in 1902, moving into this house in 1915 and becoming the state's adopted artistic treasure.

Praça Garibaldi and around

Igreja de Nossa Senhora do Rosário: Tues–Fri 1.30–5.30pm, Sat 2–6pm, Sun 8am–noon • Free • Linha Turismo stop #25

Claudino dos Santos ends at **Praça Garibaldi**, dominated by the **Palácio Garibaldi**, the elegant palatial-like headquarters of the local Italian society, which was built in 1900, and the handsome Baroque **Igreja de Nossa Senhora do Rosário**, built by and for Curitiba's slave population in the eighteenth century. However, after falling into total disrepair, the church was demolished and completely reconstructed in the 1940s.

Museu Paranaense and around

Rua Kellers 289 • Tues–Fri 9am–6pm, Sat & Sun 10am–4pm • Free • T 41 3304 3300, W www.museuparanaense.pr.gov.br

The city's best museum is the **Museu Paranaense**, housed in the beautifully renovated Neoclassical-style Palácio São Francisco, completed in 1929 (the mansion served as the state governor's residence from 1938 to 1958). The facade is a little dour, but the rooms inside retain some of their elegance, with period furniture and other rather desultory exhibits – everything from old coins and notes to the history of *yerba mate*, leading families of the city and a pristinely restored bathroom. The modern extension next door (connected by walkway) covers state history in conventional chronological fashion, from prehistoric finds to sections on the Jesuit missions and a scale model of the town in 1876, showing just how explosive its growth has been since then. Labelling throughout is in Portuguese only.

The museum overlooks **Praça João Cândido**, home to the ruins of Igreja de São Francisco de Paula, as well as the 1915 Art Nouveau **Belvedere**, now smothered in ugly graffiti.

Jardim Botânico

Rua Eng. Ostoja Roguski 690 • **Jardim Botânico** Daily 6am–9pm (8pm June–Sept) • Free • T 041 3264 6994 • **Museu Botânico** Mon–Fri 8.30am–noon & 1–5pm, Sat & Sun 9am–6pm • Free • T 041 3264 7365 • Linha Turismo stop #6

Created in 1991 some 4.5km southeast of the city's *centro histórico*, Curitiba's **Jardim Botânico** is a high-profile project promoting the city's green image. Laid out in the formal style of a French garden, its main attractions are its seasonal flowerbeds, gently wooded grounds, **Art Nouveau greenhouse** featuring Brazilian tropical plants and the small **Museu Botânico**, notable for its large herbarium.

Museu Oscar Niemeyer

Rua Marechal Hermes 999 • Tues–Sun 10am–6pm • R$16 • T 41 3350 4400, W museuoscarniemeyer.org.br • Linha Turismo stop #12; bus to Boqueirão/Centro Cívico (#505)

About 3km to the north of Curitiba's *centro histórico* is the **Centro Cívico**, the sprawling complex of state government buildings with park-like surroundings that was created in the 1950s. The Centro Cívico itself has little architectural merit, but alongside it is the stunningly beautiful **Museu Oscar Niemeyer**, by far Curitiba's biggest attraction. Designed by Niemeyer in 1967 but not constructed until 2003, the building has won over even the architect's most bitter critics. Like all Niemeyer buildings, the structure is visually imposing – in this case dominated by a feature that resembles a giant eye (or space ship) – but it also works well as an exhibition space. Consistently excellent **changing exhibitions** of Brazilian or other Latin American art are hosted here. After exploring the main building, you reach the "eye" portion via a 1960s space-age tunnel. There's also a permanent sculpture garden and a gallery dedicated to Niemeyer himself (featuring scale models and photos of his famous creations).

Memorial da Imigração Polonesa

Rua Euclides Bandeira • Bosque João Paulo II: daily 6am–7.30pm; Memorial: Tues–Sun 9am–6pm • Free • T 41 3321 3247 • Linha Turismo stop #13

Adjoining the grounds behind the Museu Oscar Niemeyer is the **Bosque João Paulo II**, a jungly, densely forested, but small, park created to commemorate the papal

POLES AND UKRAINIANS IN PARANÁ

The ethnic group most often associated with Paraná is the **Poles**, who settled in tightly knit farming communities around Curitiba in the late nineteenth and early twentieth centuries. Poles migrated to Brazil in three main waves: the smallest number between 1869 and 1889, the largest during the period of so-called "**Brazil fever**" that swept Poland and the Ukraine between about 1890 and 1898 (when most of current-day Poland and all of Ukraine were part of the Russian Empire), and the next-largest contribution in the years just before World War I. Most of the Poles settling in the vicinity of Curitiba arrived in the 1880s with subsequent immigrants settling further afield in south-central Paraná. Well into the twentieth century, the Polish community was culturally isolated, but as Curitiba expanded, absorbing many of the old farming settlements, assimilation accelerated. Today the lives of most of the approximately one million *paranaenses* of Polish origin are indistinguishable from those of their non-Polish neighbours. In recent years, however, there has been a revival of interest in people's Polish heritage, and, wherever there are large concentrations of Poles, Polish language classes, folk dance and music groups are being established to preserve or revive folk traditions.

THE UKRAINIANS

Ukrainians also came to southern Brazil: between 1895 and 1914, over 35,000 immigrants arrived in the Ukraine's "other America". Today, there are over 300,000 Brazilians of Ukrainian extraction, of whom eighty percent live in Paraná, largely concentrated in the southern centre of the state. As most of the immigrants came from the western Ukraine, it's the Ukrainian Catholic rather than the Orthodox Church that dominates; throughout the areas where Ukrainians and their descendants are gathered, onion-domed churches and chapels abound. **Prudentópolis**, 210km west of Curitiba, is heralded as the capital city of Ukrainian Brazil, though it's typically Brazilian in appearance: visit the **Museu do Milênio**, Rua Cândido de Abreu in Praça Ucrânia (Mon–Fri 9–11.30am & 2–5.30pm; free; ⓣ 42 3446 3327), for the background on Ukrainian settlement in Brazil. To see some of the rural environs, take a local bus or drive around 10km northwest to the small villages of **Nova Galícia**, sporting a beautiful, multi-domed wooden church ("Igreja Ucraniana"), or **Gonçalves Júnior**, about 45km southeast of Prudentópolis. Of this village's four churches (Lutheran, Roman Catholic, Ukrainian Catholic and Ukrainian Orthodox), the only one that merits much attention is the Orthodox one, **Igreja Ortodoxa Dão Pedro e São Paulo**, built in 1934, with an extremely beautiful interior featuring Orthodox icons, plus a ceiling and walls smothered in intricately painted frescoes.

Without any doubt, the most intriguing and most eye-catching Ukrainian church in Paraná is in **Serra do Tigre**, a small settlement another 70km south of Gonçalves Júnior that still retains much of its Ukrainian character. Built in 1904, the **Igreja de São Miguel Arcanjo**, spectacularly positioned high upon a mountain top near the heart of the village, is the oldest Ukrainian Catholic church in Paraná. In traditional fashion, the church was constructed totally of wood – including, even, the roof tiles – and both the exterior and the elaborately painted interior frescoes are carefully maintained as a state monument. Without a car, however, all these villages are awkward and time-consuming to reach.

visit to Curitiba in 1980. On the west side of the park, the **Memorial da Imigração Polonesa** commemorates Polish immigration to Paraná with seven pine log cabins, built by Polish immigrants in the 1870s and 1880s and relocated here from the villages of Tomás Coelho (present-day Araucária) and Muricy (the present-day São José dos Pinhais). The cabins contain displays of typical objects used by pioneer families, with one originally built in 1883 now a **chapel** dedicated to Nossa Senhora de Częstochowa (aka the "Black Madonna of Częstochowa"), the most revered Polish incarnation of the Virgin Mary. Another cabin serves as a **shop** selling Polish handicrafts and books.

Universidade Livre do Meio Ambiente

Rua Victor Benato 210, Pilarzinho • Bosque Zaninelli: daily 8am–8pm; Universidade daily 8am–7pm • Free • T 41 3254 3734, W unilivre.org.br • Bus #169 (JD Kosmos) from Largo da Ordem; Linha Turismo stop #15

One of Curitiba's more bizarre sights is the **Universidade Livre do Meio Ambiente**, just over 4km north of the *centro histórico*, an education centre promoting environmental awareness set within the small but densely forested **Bosque Zaninelli** (a short walk from the bus stop on the road outside). Established in 1992 with the help of legendary conservationist **Jacques Cousteau**, the main building is a crazy spiral of wooden walkways and huts, a bit like a giant treehouse – you can walk to the top to a small viewpoint that looks over a former quarry and muddy lake that is favoured by freshwater turtles, black swans and other birdlife.

Ópera de Arame

Rua João Gava 970, Pilarzinho • Tues–Sun 8am–6pm • Free • T 41 3354 4482 • Linha Turismo stop #17

The **Ópera de Arame** ("wire opera house") is one of the most unusual sights on the Linha Turismo bus route. A huge circular theatre, it was fashioned from tubes and wires in 1992, and is surrounded by trees and a lake in a disused quarry (access is via a footbridge).

Parque Tingüi and the Memorial da Imigração Ucraniana

Rua Dr. Mbá de Ferrante, Parque Tingüi • Tues–Sun 10am–6pm • Free • T 41 3240 1103 • Linha Turismo stop #20; bus marked "Raposo Tavares" (#168) from Praça Tiradentes

Curitiba has many green spaces and **Parque Tingüi** is one of the most attractive, lining the Rio Barigui through the northwest corner of the city. The only real sight here is the **Memorial da Imigração Ucraniana**, 5.5km from the *centro histórico*, a Ukrainian-style onion-domed replica church, built in 1995 in a rustic (and very photogenic) wooden style modelled on the much larger Igreja de São Miguel Acanjo in Serra do Tigre (see page 547). The photographs, icons, *pysanky* (painted eggs) and handicrafts on display inside celebrate Paraná's Ukrainian population, who started coming here in the 1890s – the shop next door sells T-shirts and gifts.

Santa Felicidade

Buses run from Travessa Nestor de Castro, at the intersection of Rua do Rosário, just below Curitiba's *centro histórico* (30min); also Linha Turismo stop #22

Now completely absorbed into Curitiba, about 8km northwest of the centre, **Santa Felicidade** was founded as a farming colony in 1878 by immigrants from northern Italy. Today the neighbourhood's Italian character has virtually disappeared, with only a few buildings surviving from the early decades; it's essentially another affluent northern suburb of the city, with a host of modern development along the main drag **Avenida Manoel Ribas**. The church of **São Jose** retains its Romanesque facade and Italianate campanile, but the main reason to visit Santa Felicidade today is for its kitsch but fun **Italian restaurants** *Velho Madalosso* (see page 551).

Torre Panorâmica

Rua Lycio G. de Castro Vellozo 191, Mercês • Tues–Sun 10am–7pm • R$5 • T 41 3339 7613 • Take the bus marked "Alto-Santa Felicidade" (#307) from Travessa Nestor de Castro; Linha Turismo stop #24

Curitiba's most popular family attraction (lines tend to be longest before sunset), in the posh suburb of Mercês (4km west of the *centro histórico*), the **Torre Panorâmica** (aka Torre Mercês) is the only telecom tower in Brazil with an observation deck (109m), offering sensational views across the city and across to the Serra do Mar mountains. Completed in 1991, inside there's also a mural by famed local artist **Poty Lazzarotto**, and a small **Museu do Telefone** (telephone museum) at the entrance.

ARRIVAL AND DEPARTURE

CURITIBA

By plane The ultramodern Aeroporto Internacional Afonso Pena (41 3381 1153) is about 18km southeast and 30min from the city centre. There are a good range of shops (including several excellent handicraft shops), a tourist information desk (Mon–Fri 7am–11pm, Sat & Sun 7am–6pm; 41 3381 1153), car rental desks, a post office, banks and ATMs. Taxis from the airport to the centre use the meter – reckon on at least R$80. Linha Aeroporto Executivo minibuses (every 15–20min; 45min; R$15; 41 3381 1326, aeroportoexecutivo.com.br) connect the airport with the rodoferroviária, Rua Visconde de Nácar near Rua 24 Horas (which is the name of the stop) and Shopping Estação. City bus #E32 (R$4.30) trundles between the airport and the Terminal do Boqueirão in the suburbs every 20–30min, where you'll have to change to reach the centre.

By bus The rodoferroviária (41 3320 3121) is about ten blocks southeast of the city centre at Rua Presidente Alfonso Camargo 330. It takes about 20min to walk to the centre, or you can a bus at the intersection of Av Presidente Afonso Camargo and Av Sete de Setembro, to the left of the entrance to the station's driveway. A taxi should be around R$13–15 to hotels in the centre. The bus station is divided into two terminals, for state and interstate destinations – tickets are sold at the upper level, with departures from the lower level. Look for Graciosa (viacaograciosa.com.br) for Antonina, Morretes and Paranaguá, Princesa dos Campos (princesadoscampos.com.br) for Prudentopolis and inland destinations, Catarinense (www.catarinense.com.br) for Santa Catarina and Rio Grande do Sul, and Ouro e Prata (viacaoouroeprata.com.br) for buses to Santo Angelo and the Mission Route (lots of companies serve São Paulo and points north).

Destinations Antonina (1hr 30min) via Morretes (7–8 daily; 1hr); Blumenau (6 daily; 4hr); Balneário Camboriú (hourly; 2hr 30min); Florianópolis (hourly; 4–5hr); Foz do Iguaçu (9 daily; 10hr); Joinville (hourly; 2hr 30min); Paranaguá (14 daily; 1hr 30min); Prudentopolis (daily 8.15am, 3.15pm, 6pm; 3–4hr); Porto Alegre (8 daily; 12–13hr); Rio de Janeiro (4–5 daily; 13hr); São Paulo (hourly; 6–7hr).

By train The train station for the Serra Verde Express (see below) is in a separate building on the south side of the rodoferroviária complex.

Destinations Morretes (1 daily; 3hr)

SERRA VERDE EXPRESS

The **Serra Verde Express** (41 3888 3488, serraverdeexpress.com.br) is one of the most scenic train rides in Brazil, winding around mountainsides, slipping through tunnels and traversing one of the largest Atlantic Forest (Mata Atlântica) reserves in the country. Sadly, it no longer runs all the way to Paranaguá, but it is undoubtedly the most atmospheric way to travel between **Curitiba** and the charming colonial town of **Morretes** (see page 554). Ask for a seat on the left-hand side of the train for the best views (or on the right if you're not good with heights) – though in practice seats are usually allocated by computer. Sweeping down from the plateau upon which Curitiba lies, the dramatic mountain range known as the Serra do Mar has long been a formidable barrier separating the coast of Paraná from the interior. Until 1885 only a narrow cobblestone road connected Curitiba to the coast. In 1880, work began on the construction of a rail line – completed five years later, this remains a marvel of late nineteenth-century engineering and the source of much local pride, as it is one of the country's few significant rail lines developed with Brazilian finance and technology. Sufferers of vertigo be warned: the line grips narrow mountain ridges, traverses narrow bridges and viaducts and passes through numerous tunnels as the trains gradually wind their way down to sea level. Passing through the **Parque Estadual de Marumbi** (see page 555) on a clear day, the views are absolutely mesmerizing, and the towering Paraná pines at the higher altitudes and the subtropical foliage at lower levels are unforgettable.

RIDING THE TRAIN

The complete three-hour run to **Morretes** usually departs daily 8.15am, arriving 11.15am; it returns at 3pm, arriving Curitiba at 6pm. There's also a luxury train running Saturday and Sunday only (9.15am–12.15pm; returning 2.30pm, arriving in Curitiba at 5.30pm). A variety of **tickets** is available, from coach class (*economica*) at R$94 one-way (R$72 for the return leg) to R$174 one-way for the special *executivo* service (which includes an English-speaking guide and local beer) and over R$360 for the weekend luxury train. **Buses** back to Curitiba are plentiful from Morretes, if you opt for a one-way ticket.

GETTING AROUND

Municipal buses Curitiba has an efficient municipal bus network (urbs.curitiba.pr.gov.br). In the city centre, the two main bus terminals are at Praça Tiradentes and Praça Rui Barbosa, from where buses (pay as you enter the odd-looking tubular stations, or on the bus if there's no tube; R$3–4.25) head out into the suburbs as well as to neighbouring *municípios*.

Linha Turismo buses The most convenient way to view Curitiba's outer attractions is to take the Linha Turismo buses that depart from Praça Tiradentes every 30min year-round (Tues–Sun; first bus leaves here at 9am, last bus 5.30pm; R$45, cash only) and stop at 25 attractions around the city centre and suburbs. The bus takes around 3hr to complete the itinerary, but tickets allow passengers to get off at four of the stops and rejoin the tour on a later bus. Stops are announced and basic commentary provided on taped loop (if you can hear it). Aim to stop at the furthest points from the centre to make the most of the ticket.

Taxis Easy to come by and, as distances are generally small, they're not too expensive; the meter starts at R$5.40.

INFORMATION

Tourist information The city tourism head office is on Rua da Glória 362 (Mon–Fri 8am–noon & 2–6pm; 41 3352 8000, turismo.curitiba.pr.gov.br); there are more convenient branches in the rodoferroviária (daily 8am–6pm; 41 3320 3121); in Palacete Wolf, Praça Garibaldi 7 (Mon–Sat 9am–6pm, Sun 9am–4pm; 41 3321 3206); and at the Torre Panorâmica (Tues–Sun 10am–7pm; 41 3339 7613).

ACCOMMODATION

Bourbon Curitiba Convention Hotel Rua Cândido Lopes 102 41 3321 4600, bourbon.com.br; map p.544. Widely considered the best hotel in the city, with an atmosphere of traditional elegance combined with every modern facility, including a pool, business centre and excellent restaurants. Parking is R$28/day. R$360

Curitiba Hostel Rua Dr Claudino Santos 49, Largo da Ordem 41 3232 2005, curitibahostel.com.br; map p.544. Fabulous location right in the heart of the old town, with clean dorms featuring triple bunks, cheap single rooms (R$70), buffet breakfasts, hot showers and extra-friendly staff. Dorms R$45, doubles R$145

Ibis Styles Centro Cívico Rua Mateus Leme 358 41 3324 0469, ibis.com; map p.544. This popular chain hotel's reception and dining area is in an attractive, German-style house, with small but well-appointed guest rooms in an interlinked tower block behind. Excellent value, and its central location near the historic centre and Shopping Mueller makes reservations essential. Parking R$17/day. R$175

★ **Johnscher by San Juan Hotéis** Rua Barão do Rio Branco 354 41 3302 9600, sanjuanhoteis.com.br; map p.544. The *Johnscher* opened as a luxury hotel in 1917 and established itself as a meeting point for Curitiba high society. Since then it's been thoroughly renovated, reopening as a 24-room boutique property with a starkly modern lobby and extremely comfortable, traditionally furnished rooms. Unfortunately, only the rooms at the front have a view, and these ones are especially spacious. The hotel also features an excellent restaurant. Parking R$20/day. R$225

Knock Knock Hostel Rua Isaías Bevilácqua 262 41 3152 6259, knockhostel.com; map p.544. Stylish, modern hostel a 10min walk from the centre, featuring six dorms, a fully equipped kitchen, laundry, barbecue area and terrace. No parking. Dorms R$50

★ **Motter Home Curitiba Hostel** Rua Desembargador Motta 3574 41 3209 5649, motterhome.com.br; map p.544. This popular hostel in a stylish 1950s mansion offers four clean dorms, three private rooms, a communal kitchen, TV lounge and pool table, all a short stroll from the centre. Free public parking nearby. Dorms R$53, doubles R$158

★ **Nomaa Hotel** Rua Gutemberg 168 41 3087 9595, nomaa.com.br; map p.544. Justly popular (and pricey) boutique hotel in Batel, currently the best place for a splurge in the city, with an earthy, contemporary theme (using leather, walnut wood and white marble) with lots of plants, green spaces and art put together by local outfit Smolka Arquitetura. Each luxurious room comes with an iPad concierge. Parking R$30/day. R$415

Pousada Betânia Monteiro Tourinho 1335, Bacacheri 41 2118 7900, pousadabetaniacuritiba.com.br; map p.542. Cosy, tranquil accommodation in a sleepy suburb 20min from the bus station (8km from the centre), with compact, modern en-suite rooms. Free parking. R$136

Slaviero Conceptual Palace Hotel Rua Senador Alencar Guimarães 50 41 3017 1000, slavierohoteis.com.br; map p.544. Conveniently located just off Praça Osório, this well-established hotel is popular with business travellers. The rooms are stylish and large with flat-screen TVs and contemporary furnishings. R$195

Villaggio Rua Tibagi 950 41 3074 9100; map p.544. A friendly, extremely efficient modern hotel located just minutes from the rodoferroviária. The standard rooms are simple and very small but some can sleep three people. An excellent breakfast is served and there's a restaurant with a reasonable Italian menu. Parking R$25/day. R$155

EATING

Badida Carnes Nobres Av Sete de Setembro 6045, Seminário ⓣ41 3243 0473, ⓦbadida.com.br; map p.544. Stylish *churrascaria* with a menu extending beyond beef to include other meats and salads. Steak lovers should not miss this – the cuts are some of the best in Brazil (prime rib and T-bone R$60–116). Good lunch specials too. Mon–Thurs 11.30am–3pm & 7–11.30pm, Fri 11.30am–3.30pm & 7–11.30pm, Sat 11.30am–4pm & 7–11.30pm, Sun 11.30am–4pm.

★ **Bouquet Garni** Alameda Doutor Carlos de Carvalho 271 ⓣ41 3223 8490; map p.544. Excellent vegetarian restaurant offering lunch buffets of chickpea stroganoff, spinach lasagne and *feijoada* with onion, turnip and coconut (Mon–Fri R$25; Sat & Sun R$35). Mon–Fri 11am–3pm, Sat & Sun 11am–3.30pm.

Caruso Empadas Rua Visconde do Rio Branco 877 ⓣ41 3029 5411; map p.544. It's surprisingly rare to find a café with style and historic cachet in central Curitiba, but this tiny place delivers, with a few tables inside and on the street since 1954. It's best just for coffee (simple and strong, poured from an antique pot) and its signature treat, the *empada* (small pot pies made with filo pastry), stuffed with cod, sausage, shrimp, heart of palm or chicken, with boiled eggs and olives mixed in ($9–14). Mon–Fri 8.45am–8.30pm, Sat & Sun 8.45am–8pm.

★ **Durski** Av Jaime Reis 254 ⓣ41 3225 7893, ⓦdurski.com.br; map p.544. Curitiba's celebrated Ukrainian restaurant (from celebrity chef Junior Durski), located in an elegant mansion dining room overlooking Praça Garibaldi. The food (including Polish and Brazilian dishes) is attractively presented and very tasty (try the delicious *filet mignon* with mash and sautéed mushrooms in Madeira wine). Mains R$70–130. Wed–Fri 7.30–10.30pm, Sat noon–3pm & 7.30–10.30pm, Sun noon–3pm.

Kawiarnia Krakowiak Rua Wellington de Oliveira Vianna 40 (on the lane between the Memorial da Imigração Polonesa and the Linha Turismo bus stop) ⓣ41 3026 7462; map p.542. This small and very authentic Polish café (decked out in rustic style) is located at the main entrance to the Bosque João Paulo II (see page 546). The menu features items such as *bigos* (R$20) and *pierogi* (R$15), but it's the large assortment of delicious Polish cakes ($5–10) that's the real attraction. Mon 2–9pm, Tues–Sun 10am–9pm.

Madero Prime Steakhouse Av Jaime Reis 262 ⓣ41 3013 2300, ⓦrestaurantemadero.com.br; map p.544. Popular burger and steak chain (also helmed by chef Junior Durski), where the speciality is beef in all its forms (cheeseburgers from R$38 and *filet mignon* from R$56). The Argentine cuts are good, but their claim to serve "the best burgers in the world" is a bit tongue-in-cheek (the burger bar is further down on Praça Garibaldi with slightly longer opening hours). The setting is elegant, and the wine list is outstanding. Mon–Thurs noon–2.30pm & 7–11pm, Fri noon–2.30pm & 7pm–midnight, Sat noon–3.30pm & 7pm–midnight, Sun noon–10pm.

★ **Manu** Alameda Dom Pedro II 317, Batel ⓣ041 3044 4395, ⓦrestaurantemanu.com.br; map p.544. Tiny but acclaimed gourmet restaurant that offers a contemporary Brazilian take on global heavyweights like *Noma* and *Alinea*, where Chef Manu Buffara learnt her trade, with a choice of various tasting menus that change daily – the plates are very small but the flavours are very exotic (for example, wild boar with pickled strawberries, prime rib with banana and manioc). Tasting menus from R$160 (five snacks, four main courses and dessert) to R$235 (with wine pairing), with a vegetarian option at both levels. Reservations essential. Tues–Sat 7–11pm.

Mercado Municipal Av Sete de Setembro 1865 ⓣ41 3363 3764, ⓦmercadomunicipaldecuritiba.com.br; map p.544. Curitiba's main market contains a food court featuring cheap diners such as *Box Curitiba* (Italian; mains R$24–28; Tues–Fri 11am–4pm, Sat 11am–4.30pm, Sun 11am–3pm) and the *Café do Mercado* (Brazilian coffee; Tues–Sat 9am–6pm, Sun 9am–1pm). Mon 7am–2pm, Tues–Sat 7am–6pm, Sun 7am–1pm.

★ **Nelbe** Praça General Osório 175 ⓣ41 3016 1608; map p.544. This beautiful mustard-coloured Neoclassical mansion ("Casa Amarela") hosts a wonderful *por quilo* lunch buffet (Mon–Fri R$46.90/kg, Sat R$48.90/kg), with an amazing spread of desserts. The mansion was built in 1916 by former Paraná president Afonso Camargo and later served as the residence for Governor Bento Munhoz da Rocha Neto. Mon–Sat 11.15am–2.30pm.

Pastelaria Nakashima Praça General Osório 367 ⓣ41 9973 1204; map p.544. This tiny, Japanese–Brazilian owned hole-in-the-wall (with just a row of stools at the counter) has garnered a loyal following thanks to its tasty fried *pastels* stuffed with meat, banana, heart of palm or cheese (R$4–8). Mon–Fri 8.30am–8.30pm, Sat 8.30am–1.30pm

Schwarzwald-Bar do Alemão Rua Claudino dos Santos 63 ⓣ41 3223 2585, ⓦbardoalemaocuritiba.com.br; map p.544. This pub and restaurant has outdoor seating and a spacious, kitsch Bavarian-themed interior. A popular evening meeting point for students in Largo da Ordem, at the heart of the old town, it serves excellent German food with cold beer. Lunch deals for around R$22, while a plate of pork knuckle and sausages for two will set you back R$50. Daily 11am–2am.

Velho Madalosso Av Manoel Ribas 5852 ⓣ41 3273 1014, ⓦvelhomadalosso.com.br; map p.542. Santa Felicidade mainstay since 1963, with a mountainous Italian-inspired buffet (*rodízio*; around R$50), though it's more Rio than Roma. It's a fun place to soak up the Felicidade vibe at the weekends with live Italian classical singing on Sundays. Tues–Sun 11.30am–3pm & 7–11.30pm.

DRINKING AND NIGHTLIFE

During the late afternoon and early evening locals congregate in the pavement cafés at the **Praça Osório** end of Rua das Flores, but as the evening progresses the area of **Novo Batel** (just west of the centre, at Av Batel and Rua Bispo Dom José), and the *centro histórico* come to life, their bars, restaurants and theatres attracting a mainly young and well-heeled crowd. On **Praça Garibaldi**, and the streets extending off it, there are numerous bars – many with live music (typically Brazilian rock music or jazz).

★92 graus Av Manoel Ribas 108 ⊕41 3045 0764, Ⓦ92graus.negocio.site; map p.544. Open since 1991 in an old house on the edge of the historic centre, "92 degrees" remains one of the city's most popular underground and alternative live music venues, with tasty craft beers served. Thurs–Sat 8pm–2am, Sun 4–10pm.

★Bar Stuart Praça General Osório 427 ⊕41 3323 5504; map p.544. This old stalwart has been serving locals, artists and politicos since 1904 (it was a hangout of beloved local poet Paulo Leminski in the 1970s). Festooned with historical photos, it's a cosy place for a Brahma (R$12) or *cachaça*, watch live football and try some exotic bar snacks such as *carne de onça* (steak tartare served with onion and garlic) and *testículos de touro* (they are what they sound like). Mon–Fri 9am–11pm, Sat 9am–4pm, Sun 9am–3pm.

Clube do Malte Rua Desembargador Motta 2200 ⊕41 3014 9313, Ⓦclubedomalte.com.br; map p.544. Great selection of beers and IPAs (including local craft beers), plus live rock and metal at the weekends. Mon–Sat 10am–midnight.

Kapele Bar Rua Saldanha Marinho 670 ⊕41 3225 4927; map p.544. Established in 1974, this legendary dive bar hosts some of the best MPB, rock bands and singers in the city and is popular with the local literati. Daily 8pm–2.30am.

El Mago Rua Dr Muricy 1089 ⊕41 3077 7189; map p.544. This lovely 1927 mansion just off Praça Garibaldi is the unlikely setting for a heaving club and lounge bar ("The Wizard"), featuring live acts and electrofunk/house DJs. Fri & Sat 11pm–6am.

Quintal do Monge Rua Dr Claudino dos Santos 24 (Largo da Ordem) ⊕41 3232 5679; map p.544. The "Monk's Backyard" right on the main drag offers a fabulous beer selection, with indoor or outdoor tables, decent bar food and burgers and occasional live music. Try the "submarine", a huge glass of beer served with a shot of Steinhäger (German gin) inside it (it's a favourite in the south). Tues–Sat 11am–2am, Sun 11am–9pm.

DIRECTORY

Hospitals Hospital Nossa Senhora das Graças at Rua Alcides Munhoz 433 in Mercês has a 24hr hotline: ⊕41 3240 6555 (Ⓦwww.hnsg.org.br).

Internet Try *Get On Lan House*, Rua Visconde de Nácar 1388, open 24hr (R$5/hr).

Laundry Premium Lavanderia at Rua Visconde de Nácar 1371 (Mon–Fri 8am–6.30pm, Sat 8am–noon; wash from R$15; ⊕41 3322 0092), is a good central option.

Money and exchange Main offices of banks are concentrated at the Praça Osório end of Rua das Flores. ATMs are found throughout the city.

Post office The most convenient central office is at Rua Marechal Deodoro 298 (Mon–Fri 9.30am–6pm; Sat 9.30am–1pm; ⊕41 3324 7311).

Lapa

LAPA is a sleepy provincial town that was founded in 1731 on the trail linking Rio Grande do Sul to the once important cattle market in Sorocaba, near São Paulo. As Lapa is one of the very few towns in Paraná's interior that has made any efforts to preserve its late eighteenth- and early nineteenth-century buildings – typical rustic Portuguese-style colonial structures – the town has become a favourite place for Sunday excursions from Curitiba. It's also the chance to sample *paranaense* cooking – rare in Curitiba itself – that makes Lapa really worth a visit.

Igreja Matriz de Santo Antônio

Praça General Carneiro • Tues–Sun 9–11.30am & 1–5pm • Free

Four blocks behind the rodoviária, Lapa's main church, the **Igreja Matriz de Santo Antônio**, dominates the principal square, Praça General Carneiro. Built between 1769 and 1784, the church is a charmingly simple Portuguese colonial structure, but its interior displays – all too typically – no original features.

Casa Lacerda

Rua XV de Novembro 60 • Tues–Fri 9am–noon & 1–5pm, Sat 9–11.30am & 1.30–5pm, Sun 1.30–5pm • R$2 (free Tues) • ⊤ 41 3622 3524

There are several small museums of mild interest near the main church, most notably the **Casa Lacerda**, a townhouse built in 1842 and furnished in period style opposite the Panteon dos Heroes. Local hero Joaquim de Rezende Correia de Lacerda was born here in 1845, the man who defended the city during the Federalist Revolution in 1894, with his troops dubbed *pica-paus* (woodpeckers).

Museu de Armas

Alameda David Carneiro • Tues–Sun 9am–5pm • R$3.50

Housed in the old Casa de Câmara e Cadeia (town hall and jail) of 1868, the **Museu de Armas** contains a collection of primarily nineteenth-century weaponry, mostly used by the Brazilian army during the Imperial period (Nordenfeld and Krupp guns), as well as two engravings by French painter Jean-Baptiste Debret, made after a visit here in 1827.

ARRIVAL AND DEPARTURE — LAPA

By bus There are 7 buses a day between Curitiba and Lapa via Expresso Maringá (7am–7pm; 90min; R$25.81 one-way; ⓦ www.expressomaringa.com.br). The last bus back (R$21.11 one-way) departs at 8pm.

EATING

★ **Panificadora Zeni** Av Dr Manoel Pedro 2078 ⊤ 41 3622 1763, ⓦ padariazeni.com.br. Many Brazilians visit Lapa solely to patronize this venerable bakery, established in 1937 and still knocking out a mouthwatering array of cakes, tarts, pastries and desserts. Daily 7am–8pm.

★ **Restaurante Espaço Único** Praça General Carneiro 326 ⊤ 41 3622 8114, ⓦ lipskirestaurante.com.br. The tasty *Lapeana* cooking featured in this rustic old home is rooted in the early nineteenth century and in the food carried by the cattle drivers who passed through the town en route from Rio Grande do Sul to São Paulo. No meal is complete without a plate of *arroz de carreteiro – charque* (jerked beef) cooked with rice, onion and tomato (Sun buffet R$40; Mon–Sat per kilo, around R$25). Daily 11.30am–3pm.

Parque Estadual de Vila Velha

BR-376 Km 515, Ponta Grossa • Fri–Sun 8.30am–5.30pm (last admission 3.30pm); Mon, Wed & Thurs by appointment only at ⓔ pevilavelha@iap.pr.gov.br • Whole park R$18; craters and lagoon only R$8; rock pillars only R$10 • ⊤ 42 3228 1539, ⓦ pontagrossa.pr.gov.br/parque-estadual-vila-velha

For a taster of Paraná's rugged interior, head 100km northwest of Curitiba to the spectacular **Parque Estadual de Vila Velha**, the site of 23 rock pillars (*arenitos*) carved by time and nature from glacial sandstone deposits, which from a distance look like monumental abstract sculptures or crumbling medieval towers. The formation is a result of sand deposited between 300 and 400 million years ago during the Carboniferous period, when the region was covered by a massive ice sheet. The park also includes series of **craters** (*furnas*) and a tranquil lagoon rich in birdlife (**Lagoa Dourada**). The park has made it mandatory for visitors to **hire a guide** before entering the park; you can do this in advance (ⓔ guiasngtur.pg@gmail.com), or just organize one

TRAVERSING THE ESTRADA DA GRACIOSA

From Curitiba (which sits at 932m above sea level), heading towards the coast means cutting through the jagged, jungle-smothered mountains of the Serra do Mar, often enveloped in mist – even if you are travelling by bus on the main highway (BR-277) be prepared for some spectacular views as the road snakes dramatically through the hills. If you've rented a car, an alternative is the **Estrada da Graciosa** (PR-410), the winding, 30km colonial road connecting Curitiba (from BR-116, north of the city) with Morretes and Paranaguá Bay (it's paved the whole way). Snaking through the Atlantic rainforest, the road features plenty of hiking trails and places to stop to enjoy the fresh air – it also passes the Parque Estadual de Marumbi (see page 555).

9

MORRETES CACHAÇA

If you love **cachaça** you should linger in Morretes, the home of some of the finest distilleries in the country thanks to the high quality of the local sugar cane and water. Legend has it that the tradition began when several Italian families emigrated to the area in the 1870s. The Scucato family started producing *cachaça* in barrels made of local *araribá* wood around 1880, and they maintain the tradition at their distillery outside Morretes, Estrada do Anhaia Km 8, (call ⓣ41 3462 1314 to schedule a visit), where the acclaimed **Engenho São Pedro** brand is produced. Out on Estrada Cruz Alta (4.5km from the centre), the **Porto Morretes** distillery (Mon–Fri 8.30–11.30am & 2–5pm, Sat 8.30–11.30am; ⓣ41 3462 2743, ⓦportomorretes.com.br) cooks up another popular brand of organic *cachaça*. Both places are open to visitors and for tours (free), but call ahead to confirm.

on arrival (though you may have to join another group, and English speakers are rare). On weekends guides charge R$10/person, with rates variable on weekdays.

ARRIVAL AND DEPARTURE — PARQUE ESTADUAL DE VILA VELHA

By bus The best way to reach the park from the Curitiba rodoferroviária is to take a Princesa dos Campos bus (ⓦprincesadoscampos.com.br) straight there (daily 7.45am, 2.30pm & 5pm; 1hr 45min; R$33). Alternatively, you can take any bus (roughly every hour) to Ponta Grossa and ask to be let off at the park's entrance. There are good late-afternoon bus services back to Curitiba, so there's no chance of being left stranded. If you're travelling on to Iguaçu, there's no need to return to Curitiba: instead, take a bus to Ponta Grossa (20km) from where you can catch an overnight service to Foz do Iguaçu.

Morretes

Just 16km inland from the Atlantic, and the terminus of the Serra Verde Express (see page 549), **MORRETES** is a small colonial town founded in 1721 where the Rio Nhundiaquara meets the tidal waters of Paranaguá Bay. It remains a sleepy little place noted mainly for its production of *cachaça* (see above), for its *balas de banana* (chewy sweets typical of the region) and for *fandango*, a local dance introduced into the area during Spanish colonial times. Most people only stay long enough for lunch – the local *barreado* (see page 555) is worth sampling – but the cobbled riverside streets, pretty colonial-era houses and small-town atmosphere make this an attractive spot to wander.

Rua XV de Novembro is the main commercial drag, but the prettiest part of town is quite small, the stretch of pedestrianized waterfront between the Ponte de Ferro ("iron bridge") and the nineteenth-century **Igreja Matriz de Nossa Senhora do Porto**, on the slightly raised Largo da Matriz. The simple, all-white **São Benedito** church, inland from the river at the intersection of Sinimbu and Fernando Amaro has roots in a religious order of slaves and free black population in the 1760s, but was built in the nineteenth century.

ARRIVAL AND DEPARTURE — MORRETES

By train The train station lies in the centre of town on Rua Padre Saviniano, three blocks inland from the river; the Serra Verde Express (see page 549) departs from Morretes daily at 3pm for Vila Marumbi (45min) and Curitiba (3hr; from R$65), plus 2.30pm Sat & Sun.

By bus The bus station lies just outside the centre on Rua Odilon Negrão; head left along Rua XV de Novembro for around 350m, then turn right on Rua Visconde do Rio Branco to reach the main church and river. Buses run to and from Paranaguá every hour or so (1hr; R$6.20), 7–8 times daily to/from Antonina (30min; R$6.20) and 9 times daily to/from Curitiba (1hr 30min; R$21). See ⓦviacaograciosa.com.br for schedules.

ACCOMMODATION AND EATING

Armazém Romanus Rua Visconde do Rio Branco 141 ⓣ41 3462 1500. For the best seafood and *barreado*, head for this unassuming place, where the dish is made traditionally in a clay pot (from R$60). Mon–Fri 10am–4pm, Sat 10am–5.30pm & 7–10pm, Sun 10am–5.30pm.

Casarão Largo Dr José Pereira 25 ⓣ41 3462 1314,

barreado.com.br. Colonial-style, old-fashioned place picturesquely located with a balcony overlooking the river, next to the Casa Rocha Pombo. Another good place to sample *barreado* (R$40–58). Mon & Wed–Fri 11am–3.30pm, Sat & Sun 11am–4pm.

Hotel Nhundiaquara Rua General Carneiro 13 41 3462 1228, nundiaquara.com.br. Picturesquely positioned on the river in the town centre, this hotel occupies a seventeenth-century building and has been managed by the Alpendre family since 1944. Rooms are simple but cosy (the cheapest with shared bathroom) and the restaurant has great views, but the *barreado* is not the best here. R$190

Parque Estadual de Marumbi

Occupying one of the largest and least-spoilt stretches of Mata Atlântica in the country, the **Parque Estadual de Marumbi** features a wealth of flora and fauna and a fine network of trails that, on all too rare clear days, provide stunning views across Paranaguá Bay. From the Vila Marumbi train station trails lead up to the highest peaks of the Serra Marumbi (Olimpo, 1539m), with the **Trilha Noroeste** (marked with red ribbons and arrows) taking at least three to four hours one-way – it's a steep climb with an elevation gain of 1100m, so make sure you leave enough time to catch the 3.45pm train.

The enticing alternative is to hike across the park along the scenic **Caminho do Itupava**, a clearly marked trail constructed between 1625 and 1654 by indigenous peoples and miners. This starts in **Porto de Cima**, just 7km north of Morretes on PR-411, and runs for around 22km through the forest (skirting the big peaks) to **Quatro Barras** (around 8–9hr), where there are buses to Curitiba. Though the path is generally safe, note that armed robberies have occurred here in the past – try to walk in a group. Entrance to the park is free.

ARRIVAL AND INFORMATION — PARQUE ESTADUAL DE MARUMBI

By train From Curitiba, the Serra Verde Express (see page 549) stops at Vila Marumbi at the foot of the park daily at 10.35am, returning at 3.40pm (giving you just 5hr to hike some of the trails – don't miss the train). Near the station there's a small park office (daily 8am–4pm; 41 3432 2072), where you can pick up a trail map.

By bus Most people hike the Caminho do Itupava downhill, which means taking a city bus from Curitiba's Terminal Guadalupe to Quatro Barras, then switching to a taxi or bus to the trailhead at Borda do Campo (final bus stop). Local buses run from Porto de Cima at the other end of the trail to Morretes (7km).

Tourist information There's a small information kiosk at Borda, and the Centro de Visitantes de Prainhas is 1.5km from Cima (both usually manned Sat & Sun only 8am–6pm).

Antonina

An important town until the 1940s, **ANTONINA** has long been superseded as Paraná's main port, though a happy consequence of this decline has been the preservation of many of its eighteenth- and nineteenth-century buildings, leaving the place with

BARREADO

In Paraná's coastal towns (in particular Morretes, Antonina and Paranaguá), **barreado**, the region's equivalent of *feijoada*, appears on most restaurants' menus. This speciality, a convenience dish that can provide food for several days and requires little attention while cooking, used only to be eaten by the poor during Carnaval, but is now enjoyed throughout the year. Traditionally, *barreado* is made of beef, bacon, tomatoes, onion, cumin and other spices, placed in successive layers in a **large clay urn**, covered and then "*barreada*" (sealed) with a paste of ash and *farinha* (manioc flour), and then slowly cooked in a wood-fired oven for twelve to fifteen hours. Today pressure cookers are sometimes used (though not by the better restaurants), and gas or electric ovens almost always substitute for wood-fired ones. *Barreado* is served with *farinha*, which you spread on a plate; place some meat and gravy on top and eat with banana and orange slices. Though tasty enough, *barreado* is very heavy and a rather more appropriate dish for a chilly winter evening than for summer and Carnaval, as originally intended.

a certain backwater charm. The town attracts a weekend crowd from Curitiba, but during the week Antonina makes for a pleasantly sleepy alternative to Paranaguá, only 55km away.

Central **Praça Coronel Macedo** is where you'll find the town's principal church, **Nossa Senhora do Pilar**; set on a small rise with fine views of the surrounding bay and mountains, it dates back to 1714 and is built in typical Portuguese colonial style, all white with yellow trim. Its interior has sadly been completely remodelled and preserves no original features. One block inland on Rua Carlos Gomes da Costa lies the **Teatro Municipal** (Mon–Fri 8–11.30am & 1.30–5pm; ⊕41 3978-1093), a wonderful pink edifice dating from around 1906 that contains the town information desk, and the **Igreja de São Benedito**, a simple white church (usually closed), completed in 1859.

Shady **Praça Dr Romildo Gonçalves Pereira**, along the small, elegantly faded waterfront area (one block from the bus station), features a pier that allows a greater perspective of the surrounding mountains and waterways, plus the old Mercado Municipal, now containing a few shops and restaurants.

The annual town **festa** (climaxing on August 15) honours Nossa Senhora do Pilar and attracts crowds from all over the state, while its annual **carnaval** is also a major street party.

ARRIVAL AND INFORMATION — ANTONINA

By bus The rodoviária is located in the town centre near the waterfront: turn right onto Rua XV de Novembro, the main commercial thoroughfare, and walk two blocks past some rather elegant nineteenth-century merchants' houses, then continue one block along Rua Vale Porto to reach Praça Coronel Macedo.

Destinations Curitiba (7 daily; 2hr); Guaraqueçaba (2 daily; 3hr 30min); Morretes (hourly; 30min); Paranaguá (hourly; 1hr 30min).

Tourist information There's a small desk in the Teatro Municipal (Mon–Sat 9am–6pm, Sun 10am–6pm; ⊕41 3978 1080, ⓦportalantonina.com), Rua Carlos Gomes da Costa 322.

ACCOMMODATION AND EATING

★ **Caçarola do Joca** Praça Dr Romildo Gonçalves Pereira 42 ⊕41 3432 1286. This tiny, long-standing weekend-only favourite, with views across the bay and rustic interior, does an especially good *barreado* that costs R$60 for two, as well as fine seafood such as local crab and giant prawns – try the *casquinha de xiri*, a sort of crab bake. Sat 11.30am–4pm & 7.30–10pm, Sun & holidays 11am–5pm.

Hotel Camboa Rua Valle Porto 208 ⊕41 3432 3267, ⓦhotelcamboa.com.br. The most distinctive hotel in town, built amid the ruins of an eighteenth-century Jesuit mission right on the main square, with cosy rooms and the added attraction of a pool and views of the bay. R$215

Pousada Porto Feliz Rua Daniel Pires 512, Itapema ⊕41 3432 0655, ⓦpousadaportofeliz.com. Gorgeous property on the southern edge of town (3km from the main plaza), featuring spectacular views, small pool and four modern, en-suite chalets with fan (the largest takes five people, from R$495). R$170

Restaurante Buganvil Rua Vale Porto 10 (Praça Coronel Macedo) ⊕41 3432 1434, ⓦrestaurantebuganvil.com.br. Another seafood specialist, right on the main plaza, with especially fresh lobster, crab and shrimp, plus a decent *barreado*. Tues–Thurs & Sun 11.30am–3.30pm, Fri & Sat 11.30am–3.30pm & 7–10pm.

Paranaguá

Brazil's second most important port for exports, **PARANAGUÁ**, 92km east of Curitiba, has lost some of its former character, though the colonial-style pastel-coloured buildings along the waterfront retain a certain charm. Founded in the 1550s on the banks of the Rio Itiberê, it is one of Brazil's oldest cities, but only recently have measures been undertaken to preserve its colonial heritage. Today the appeal of Paranaguá lies in wandering around the cobbled streets and absorbing the faded colonial atmosphere of the town. Almost everything worth seeing is concentrated along **Rua XV de Novembro** a block inland from the waterfront (a short walk from the bus station), which is also a departure point for ferries to Ilha do Mel (see page 559).

Museu de Arqueologia e Etnología

Rua XV de Novembro 575 • Tues–Sun 8am–8pm • Free • 41 3721 1200, www.proec.ufpr.br

Paranaguá's most imposing building, the fortress-like **Colégio dos Jesuítas**, is home to the **Museu de Arqueologia e Etnología**. None of the museum's exhibits relates to the Jesuits, concentrating instead on prehistoric archeology and human evolution, indigenous culture and *paranaense* folk art and crafts (with some mildly interesting exhibits on festival costumes, basketry, lace-making and the like), but you need to read Portuguese to make the most of this (no English labels). The building dates back to 1698, sixteen years after the Jesuits were invited by Paranaguá's citizens to establish a school for their sons. Because it lacked a royal permit, however, the authorities promptly halted work on the college until 1738, when one was at last granted and building recommenced. In 1755 the college finally opened, only to close four years later with the Jesuits' expulsion from Brazil.

Instituto Histórico Geográfico de Paranaguá

Rua XV de Novembro 603 • Mon–Fri 1–5pm • Free • 41 3423 2892

Next to the larger Museu de Arqueologia, the **Instituto Histórico Geográfico de Paranaguá** contains a small but interesting collection of historic artefacts relating to the history of the town, including some rare indigenous relics and a cannon from a

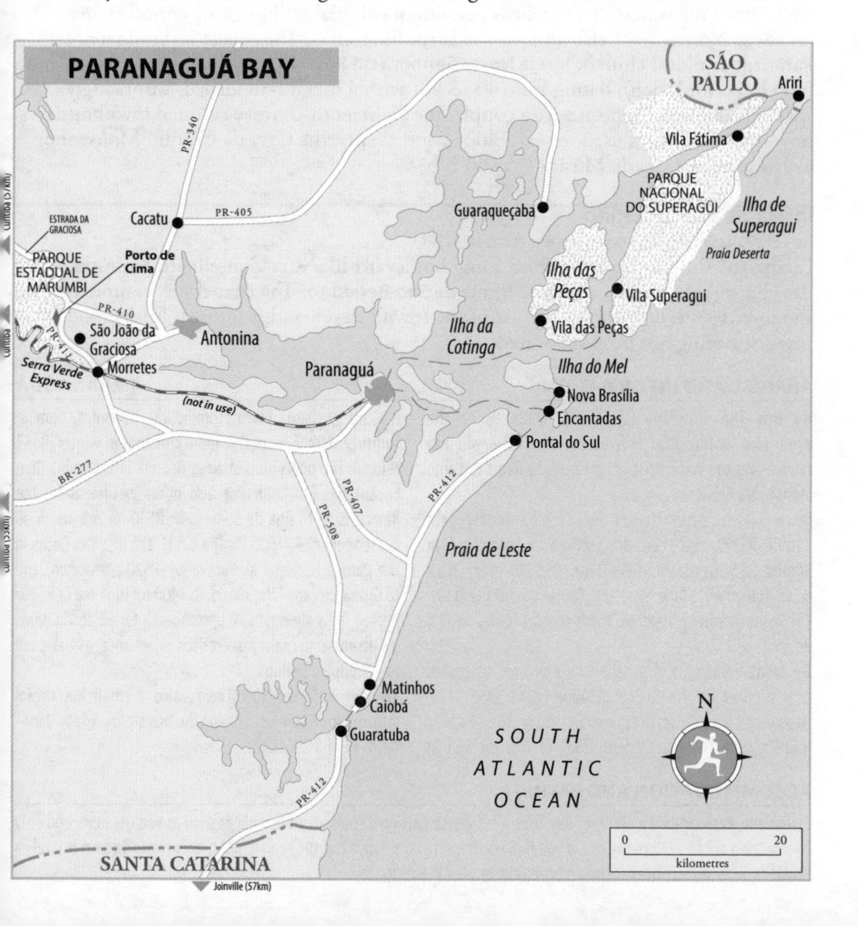

French ship that sank nearby in 1718. The small but elegant premises were built in 1896 as a school.

Mercado Municipal do Café

Rua General Carneiro 458 • Mon–Sat 7am–6pm, Sun 7am–3pm • Free

Paranaguá's **Mercado Municipal do Café** is an early twentieth-century building that once served as the city's coffee market, right on the waterfront. Today the Art Nouveau structure mostly contains restaurants serving excellent, cheap seafood (buffets from R$16) and the famed "*pastel de banana*". The handsome former fish market across the street, built in 1914, is now the **Mercado Artesanato** (Mon–Fri 9am–5pm, Sat & Sun 9am–3pm), home to arts and crafts shops.

Igreja da Ordem Terceira São Francisco das Chagras

Rua XV de Novembro and Rua Presciliano Correa • Daily 9am–5.30pm • Free • ⓣ 41 3422 5224

Completed in 1784, the pretty **Igreja da Ordem Terceira São Francisco das Chagras** is a small and simple all-white church with a tower added in 1841. Inside, it still contains its delicate Baroque altars.

Largo Monsenhor Celso

Away from the waterfront the city's remaining colonial buildings are concentrated on **Largo Monsenhor Celso** and the roads running off it. The square is dominated by Paranaguá's oldest church, **Igreja Nossa Senhora do Rosário** (nominally daily 8am–7pm, but closed for lunch), dating from 1578 but with a much remodelled, surprisingly spacious interior. Opposite are a couple fine eighteenth-century colonial townhouses, now cultural centres used for exhibitions and events, the Casa da Cultura Monsenhor Celso and the Casa da Música Brasílio Itiberê.

Igreja de São Benedito

Rua Conselheiro Sinimbú • Daily 8am–6pm • Free • ⓣ 41 3423 2205

Facing the Rosário church, 300m along boulevard-like Rua Conselheiro Sinimbú, lies the charmingly simple, all-white **Igreja de São Benedito**. The chapel was completed in the seventeenth century for the use of the town's slaves, and is unusual for its modest interior having not been renovated.

ARRIVAL AND INFORMATION — PARANAGUÁ

By bus The rodoviária (ⓣ 41 3420 2925) is on the waterfront at Rua João Estevão 40; from here you can stroll along the waterfront or up Rua João Régis to Largo Monsenhor Celso.

Destinations Buses depart for Curitiba hourly (1hr 30min; R$32), and there are services to Antonina (1hr 30min; R$6.20) via Morretes (1hr; R$6.20) every hour or so, Joinville (2 daily; 3hr) and Pontal do Sul (12 daily; 1hr 15min), where there are more regular ferries to Ilha do Mel.

By boat Paranaguá is a departure point for scheduled boat services to Ilha do Mel. Abaline (ⓣ 41 3455 1129, ⓦ abaline.com.br) services depart from the Estação Nautica (Rua General Carneiro 258) to Ilha do Mel at 8.30am, 9.30am, 11am, 1pm, 3pm, 4.30pm & 6pm in summer, with 9.30am & 3.30pm crossings in winter (R$53 return); the boats stop at Nova Brasília (1hr 30min) then Encantadas (2hr). Abaline also offers excursions for the 3hr crossing to Ilha de Superagüi (R$30 for minimum 40 passengers or R$1600 for the boat), the Ilha das Peças in the Parque Nacional do Superagüi (R$20 per person) and to Guaraqueçaba (2hr 30min; R$1400 for the boat or R$30/person for a minimum 40 passengers); for all destinations it's essential to make reservations in advance, as there are no scheduled sailings.

Tourist information There's also a small but useful information kiosk just outside the bus station (daily 9am–6pm; ⓣ 41 3425 4542).

ACCOMMODATION AND EATING

Essentially, Paranaguá is a place for day-trips – it's worth getting details about leaving as soon as you get here, and only later setting out to explore the city. If you find you have no alternative but to spend a night, **accommodation** is rarely a problem, with several inexpensive and centrally located places to stay.

★**Casa do Barreado** Rua José Antônio da Cruz 78, Ponta do Caju ☎41 3423 1830. As the name suggests, this friendly place at the end of a quiet residential street (10min walk from the bus station), specializes in *barreado* (R$40), but also offers an excellent menu of seafood dishes at reasonable prices (R$45–60). Sat, Sun & holidays noon–4pm.

Hotel San Rafael Rua Júlia da Costa 185 ☎41 3721 9000, ⓦsanrafaelhotel.com.br. The best of a fairly mediocre bunch when it comes to comfort in Paranaguá, with spacious a/c rooms and a pool – some rooms are newer than others, so check first. Free parking. R$300

★**Pastelaria Kubo** Mercado Municipal do Café ☎41 3423 2336. Tucked away in the old coffee market since 1950, this tiny Japanese-Brazilian stall knocks out delicious, crispy *pastels* in just four flavours: meat, cheese, shrimp and banana with cinnamon (R$4–6). Wash them down with some potent black coffee. Tues–Sat 7am–noon & 2–6pm, Sun 7am–noon.

Ilha do Mel

Famed for its golden beaches and tranquil setting, the idyllic **ILHA DO MEL** ("Island of Honey") in the Bay of Paranaguá is a hit with backpackers and surfers looking to enjoy the simpler things in life – and the island's waves. With just over a thousand permanent residents, visitors greatly outnumber locals during the peak summer months. The island is little more than 12km from north to south, but given its rugged topography most trails hug the coast. Bear in mind that there are no cars, no public transport, no banks (or ATMs) and no pharmacies on the island, only basic shops and electricity for just a short period each day – so come prepared.

Nova Brasília and around

The island's bulbous northern half, a protected Atlantic forest ecological station (entry is prohibited), is joined to the south by a bridge of land stretched between two gently curving, sheltered bays where the lively main area **NOVA BRASÍLIA** is located – this is where the bulk of the island's inhabitants live and where most tourist facilities (such as they are) are located. Close to the jetty where the passenger boats land, there's a police post, clinic and post office, and beyond this an immense beach, the **Praia do Farol**, where all the action takes place. For a pleasant and undemanding one-hour stroll, wander 4km north along the beach towards the ruins of **Fortaleza Nossa Senhora dos Prazeres**, the Portuguese fort (completed in 1769 to guard the entrance of Paranaguá

PARQUE NACIONAL DO SUPERAGÜI

The islands north of Ilha do Mel – **Superagüi** and the **Ilha das Peças** – form the **Parque Nacional do Superagüi**, noted for its orchids, frolicking dolphins and Atlantic forest birds (toucans and parakeets are common), as well as rare red-tailed parrots on tiny **Ilha do Pinheiro** (best viewed at sunset). The main sections of park are off limits, but boats can cut close to the shore, and you can visit the main village, Barra de Superagüi, home to around 700 people, location of most of the hostels and restaurants; private operators offer rides from Paranaguá (dock opposite *Restaurante Danúbio*; Mon–Sat from around 2.30pm, returning 7am; 2hr 30min; R$30–35 return; Barcos Megatron ☎41 3482 7131) and Ilha do Mel (on demand; reckon on around R$250–300 for four people for Peças and R$400 and up for Superagüi itself). On the east side of the island, a short walk or bike ride from the village (4km) and also open to visitors, **Praia Deserta** is a wild beach stretching 38km. Here you'll see marine birds such as cormorants and frigates, and in March and April these are joined by thousands of migratory birds from North America.

ACCOMMODATION AND EATING

Pousada Bella Ilha Rua Principal, Ilha do Superagüi ☎41 3422 8805, ⓦbellailha.com. Delightful inn and restaurant, with ten rooms (some with bunks, some with doubles), all spotless with fans and shared bathrooms. R$210

Pousada Sobre as Ondas Ponta da Gaviota (beach), Ilha do Superagüi ☎41 3482 7118. Friendly place with large, slightly faded cottages with room for four to six people. All basic rates include breakfast, but full board is also possible if arranged in advance. The daily lunch buffet here is great value (R$35). R$320

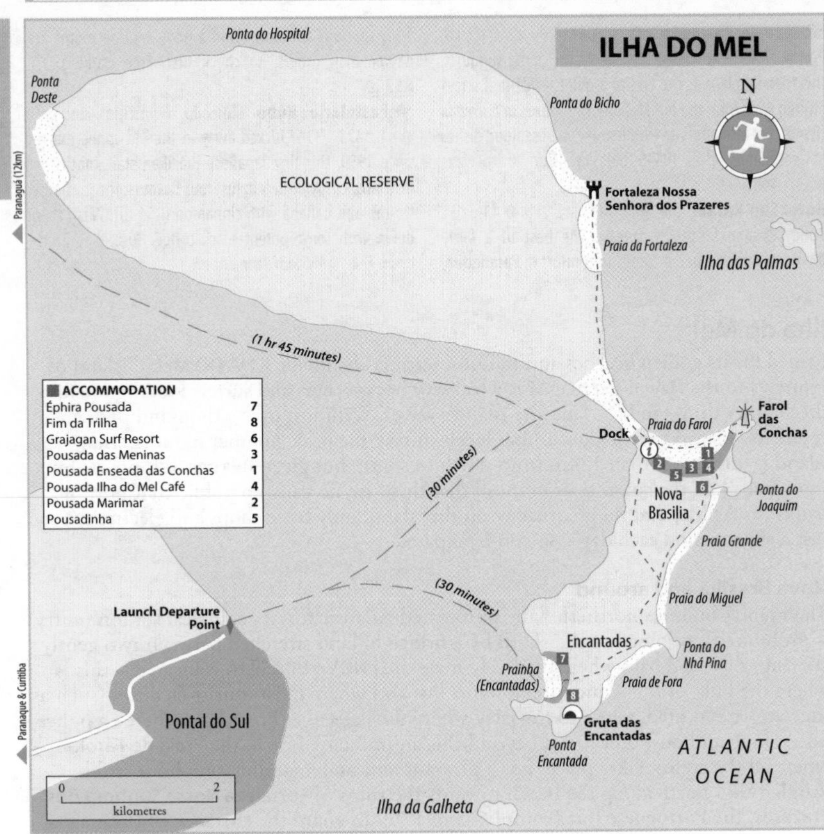

Bay), in the opposite direction from the **Farol das Conchas** (lighthouse) that overlooks Nova Brasília.

Encantadas

The island's other major settlement, **ENCANTADAS**, near the southwest corner, has the atmosphere of a sleepy fishing village and attracts most of the day-trippers. Apart from fishermen's clapboard houses, all there is to Encantadas are a few places to stay and eat, and a police post. In a sheltered position facing the mainland with the mountains all around, it can feel rather claustrophobic, but only a few minutes' walk behind the village on the east side of the island is the **Praia de Fora**, where powerful waves roll in from the South Atlantic.

The southeast beaches

The most beautiful part of the island is the series of **beaches** along its mountainous southeast side, between Praia de Fora and Nova Brasília – an area of quiet coves, rocky promontories and small waterfalls. It takes about two hours to walk the 6km trail between the two settlements via **Praia Grande** but, because of the need to clamber over rocks separating the beaches, the journey should only be undertaken at low tide. Let someone know where you're going, and carry a bottle of water (there's a mountain stream about halfway for a refill) and enough money to be able to return by boat if need be.

The southern tip of the island (beyond Praia da Fora), known as **Ponta Encantada**, is where you will find the **Gruta das Encantadas** (Enchanted Cave), focal point for a number of local legends (10min walk from Encantadas).

ARRIVAL AND DEPARTURE

ILHA DO MEL

By boat The island is reached by direct boat services from Paranaguá (see page 558) or, more frequently, from Pontal do Sul, where Viação Graciosa buses from Curitiba or local buses from Paranaguá terminate (5 daily; 2hr 30min; R$40). If travelling by car, there are private parking areas here where you can safely park for a charge of R$15–20 per day. The crossing to Encantadas or Nova Brasília from Pontal do Sul takes about 20min, with boats departing hourly (Mon–Thurs 8am–4pm Fri & Sat 8am–6pm, Sun 8am–5pm; R$35 return).

GETTING AROUND AND INFORMATION

By boat Local boats ply between Encantadas and Nova Brasília (7–9 daily; 20min; R$10).

Tourist information There is a small tourist information booth at the dock in Nova Brasília (daily 8am–7pm). See also the useful websites Ⓦ ilhadomelonline.com.br and Ⓦ visiteilhadomel.com.br.

ACCOMMODATION AND EATING

If you plan to visit in the height of **summer** without a reservation it's best to arrive during the week and as early as possible in the morning as accommodation is scarce and prices high. The island is always filled to capacity over **New Year** and **Carnaval** when reservations should be made weeks in advance and are accepted only for minimum stays of four or five nights. **Restaurants** on the island pretty much all offer an unsophisticated menu, based on fish, prawns, rice and beans. Summer evenings are always lively, with notices advertising live music and club nights.

NOVA BRASÍLIA AND PRAIA DO FAROL

In Nova Brasília porters will carry your luggage to your hotel for around R$25.

★ **Pousada das Meninas** Praia do Farol Ⓣ 41 3426 8023, Ⓦ pousadadasmeninas.com.br; map p.560. Simple but chic accommodation built from driftwood, local stone and recycled materials, ranging from individual a/c bungalows to more basic options. There's a lovely tree-filled garden, satellite TV and a café (*Café das Meninas*) on site. Café daily 7am–11pm. **R$340**

Pousada Enseada das Conchas Praia do Farol Ⓣ 41 3426 8040, Ⓦ pousadaenseada.com.br; map p.560. Towards the lighthouse, at the quieter end of the beach (800m from the dock), with just four cosy a/c en-suite rooms, arranged according to the principles of Feng Shui. The beach is accessed via a short path across the marsh. **R$306**

Pousada Ilha do Mel Café Praia do Farol Ⓣ 41 3426 8065, Ⓦ pousadailhadomel.com; map p.560. Laidback café (great espressos and crêpes) and hotel, with cosy en-suite double rooms (single rates from R$160) in rustic surroundings with small library. A great source of local information too. Café daily 9am–10pm. **R$330**

Pousadinha Caminho do Farol Ⓣ 41 3426 8026, Ⓦ pousadinha.com.br; map p.560. Popular choice 180m inland from the dock with leafy gardens and relaxing hammocks for chilling out. The en-suite rooms for three to four people are simple but good value (there's satellite TV and fan), and multilingual staff can assist with booking activities. **R$180**

PRAIA GRANDE

Grajagan Surf Resort Ⓣ 41 3426 8043, Ⓦ grajagan.com.br; map p.560. On Praia Grande directly facing the Atlantic, this is the island's largest and most expensive place to stay. The all-wood chalets are relatively plain but a little more chic than usual for the island (with a/c and TV), and most have a terrace with wonderful views of the beach. Restaurant: daily noon–late. **R$540**

ENCANTADAS

Éphira Pousada Praia das Encantadas Ⓣ 41 3426 9056, Ⓦ ephira.com.br; map p.560. Well-appointed rustic-chic cabins (all with private bathrooms and a/c) that sleep up to five people, just 80m from the beach and 300m from the pier. There's also a swimming pool, pool table and communal grill. **R$520**

Fim da Trilha Trilha da Gruta Ⓣ 41 3426 9052, Ⓦ fimdatrilha.com.br; map p.560. Relatively luxurious and tranquil choice, 180m from the pier, with an eco-friendly ethos and very comfy a/c units (with cable TV). The breakfast (included) is especially good here, as is the restaurant. **R$300**

Pousada Marimar Praia das Encantadas Ⓣ 41 3426 9052, Ⓦ pousadamarimar.com.br; map p.560. Right on the beach, with spacious common area, great breakfasts and friendly staff. Rooms (for two to four people) come with a/c, TVs and fridge. **R$220**

9

The Iguaçu Falls and around

The **IGUAÇU FALLS** are, unquestionably, one of the world's great natural wonders. To describe their beauty and power is a tall order, but for starters cast out any ideas that Iguaçu is some kind of Niagara Falls transplanted south of the equator; compared to Iguaçu, with its total of 275 falls that cascade over a precipice 3km wide, Niagara is a mere ripple. But it's not the falls alone that make Iguaçu so special: the vast surrounding subtropical **nature reserve** – in Brazil the Parque Nacional do Iguaçu, in Argentina the Parque Nacional de Iguazú – is a timeless haunt that even the hordes of tourists fail to destroy.

The Iguaçu Falls are a short distance from the city of **Foz do Iguaçu** in Brazil, **Puerto Iguazú** in Argentina and **Ciudad del Este** in Paraguay. Foz do Iguaçu and Puerto Iguazú are both about 20km northwest of the entrances to the Brazilian Parque Nacional do Iguaçu and the Argentine Parque Nacional de Iguazú, while Ciudad del Este is 7km northwest of Foz do Iguaçu. Most tourists choose to stay in Foz do Iguaçu, much the largest and most developed of the three places, though many visitors prefer the relative tranquillity and frontier atmosphere of Puerto Iguazú. Ciudad del Este is a wholly unattractive border town that mostly serves as a cheap shopping trip for Brazilian tourists, and is best avoided.

Foz do Iguaçu

Although one of the largest cities in the south of Brazil, most visitors' experience of **FOZ DO IGUAÇU** is limited to the rodoviária or airport, their sights understandably entirely focused on the falls and park a short distance to the south. With many hotels located alongside the highway connecting Foz do Iguaçu with the park, and with

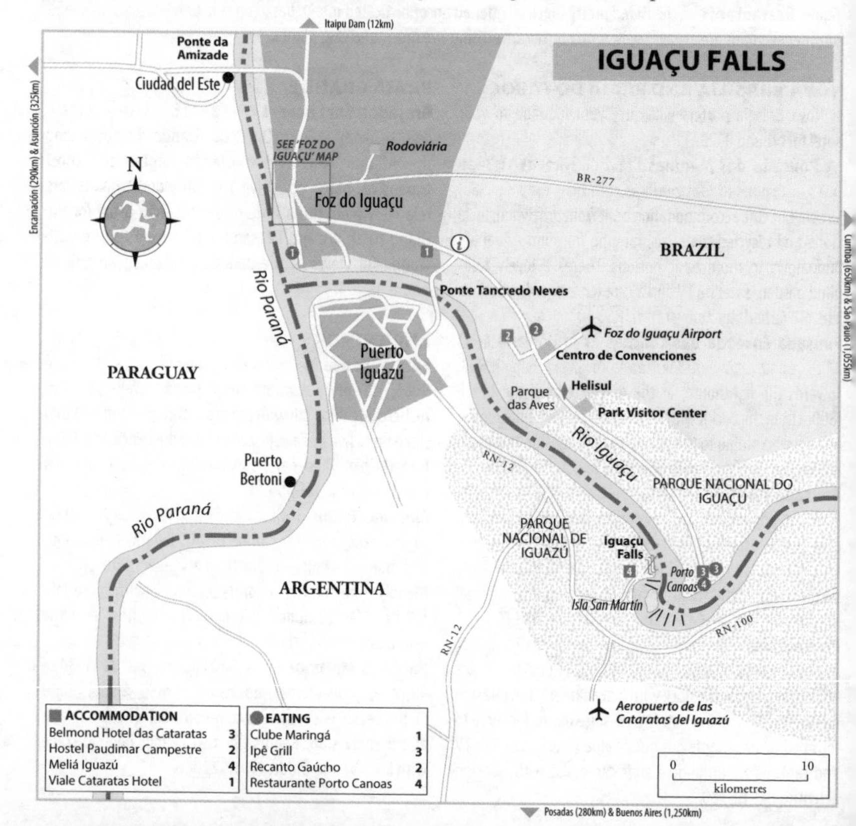

VISITING THE LAND OF WATERFALLS

The **Iguaçu Falls** are formed by the Rio Iguaçu, which has its source near Curitiba. Starting at an altitude of 1300m, the river snakes westward, picking up tributaries and increasing in size and power during its 1200km journey. About 15km before joining the mighty Rio Paraná, the Iguaçu broadens out and then plunges precipitously over an 80m-high cliff, the central point of 275 interlinking cataracts that extend nearly 3km across the river. There is no "best time" to visit since the falls are impressive and spectacularly beautiful whatever the season. That said, the rainy season is during the **winter** months of April to July, and at this time the volume of water is at its greatest – but then the sky is usually overcast and the air, especially near the falls themselves, is quite chilly. By the end of the **summer** dry season, around March, the volume of water crashing over the cliffs is reduced by a third (only once, in 1977, did the falls dry up altogether), but even then there's no reduction in impact, with the added attraction of the rainbow effects from the splashing of falling water and the deep blue sky. The one time to avoid at all costs is **Easter**, when the area attracts vast throngs of Argentine and Brazilian tourists.

Although many people arrive at Iguaçu in the morning and depart the same evening, the falls should really be viewed from both the Brazilian and the Argentine sides of the river: at least **two days** are needed to do them justice and you could easily spend longer. There are good bus services between the two cities and onwards to the falls, but consider renting a car if your time is limited (see below).

nothing in the urban area of particular interest, it's perfectly reasonable to ignore the city completely, though it does boast the best **bars** and **restaurants** in the region.

Founded in 1914, Foz remained a jungle backwater for decades, only really expanding following the inauguration in 1965 of the bridge linking Brazil with Paraguay and the construction of the nearby Itaipu Dam (see page 572): the population leapt from 34,000 in 1970 to 136,000 just ten years later, and is now three times bigger again. In the last few years the city has become a lot safer and more tourist friendly than it once was, with plenty of services and an easy-to-use local bus system.

ARRIVAL AND DEPARTURE — FOZ DO IGUAÇU

BY PLANE

Foz do Iguaçu Airport (Aeroporto Internacional de Foz do Iguaçu/Cataratas; ⓣ45 3521 4200) is 12km southeast of the city, just off the road to the falls. Inside the terminal you'll find an information booth and car rental desks.

Car rental Avis (ⓣ45 3529 6160), Hertz (ⓣ45 3529 8789) and Localiza (ⓣ45 3529 6300) are all represented at the airport (rates from around R$150/day, with cheaper deals for longer rentals). Note that if you are just travelling between Foz do Iguaçu and Puerto Iguazú or the two national parks, then no special car documentation is required to cross the Brazilian/Argentine border. If, however, you intend to take your rental car to the Argentine Jesuit missions (see page 628) or anywhere else south of Puerto Iguazú, you'll need to pay extra for a permit. You are not permitted to take a car into Paraguay.

By bus to the city centre From the airport, bus #120 (Mon–Sat 5.45am–12.40am, every 20min, Sun 5.30am–12.40am every 45min; R$3.45) runs to the Terminal de Transporte Urbano (TTU) in the centre of town on Av Juscelino Kubitschek (30min), and, in the other direction, to the Brazilian falls (40min).

By taxi to the city centre The fixed fare from the airport into Foz is around R$50, R$30 to the falls and R$85–95 to Puerto Iguazú in Argentina (see page 568).

Destinations Curitiba (4 daily; 1hr 10min); Lima (Peru; 1 daily; 4hr 15min); Porto Alegre (1 daily; 1hr 10min); Rio (3–4 daily; 2hr); São Paulo (6 daily; 1hr 30min–1hr 50min).

BY BUS

Foz do Iguaçu's rodoviária (ⓣ45 3522 3633) is located 4km north of the centre on the road to Curitiba (Av Costa e Silva 1601) and is served by buses from throughout southern Brazil, as well as Buenos Aires. Buses #105 and #115 link the rodoviária with the Terminal de Transporte Urbano in town (R$3.45); taxis cost around R$25.

Destinations Blumenau (2 daily; 14hr); Buenos Aires (1 daily; 19hr); Curitiba (10 daily; 9hr); Florianópolis (9 daily; 16hr); Joinville (8 daily; 12hr); Porto Alegre (6 daily; 14hr); Rio (3 daily; 24hr); São Paulo (5 daily; 14–15hr).

GETTING AROUND

Buses and taxis in Foz usually take **currency** from Argentina and Paraguay as well as Brazil, but don't count on it – they are not obliged to, so it depends on the individual driver.

9

Local buses City bus fares are R$3.45, which you pay at the gate at the TTU terminal (Brazilian *reais* only), or on the bus itself.

Destinations (from the TTU terminal) Brazilian falls via the airport and Parque de Aves (#120; Mon–Sat 5.45am–12.40am, every 20min, Sun 5.30am–12.40am every 45min); rodoviária (#105; Mon–Sat 5.40am–7.07pm, Sun 5.35am–5.35pm; #115: Mon–Sat 5.38am–11.35pm).

Taxis Finding taxis is easy; most hotels and restaurants will call them if required. Taxis here are expensive; meters start at R$5.10 and turn over at R$3.45–3.85/km; figure on at least R$50 to the Brazilian park entrance from the city centre (taxis can go no further into the park). Fixed rates apply to Puerto Iguazú (R$60–70 one-way), Ciudad del Este (R$30–50 one-way) and the Argentine Falls (R$120–150 round-trip), but it's worth shopping around and asking at your hotel.

INFORMATION

Tourist information There are tourist offices at the airport (daily 8am–10pm; ☎ 45 3521 4276) and at the rodoviária (daily 7am–6pm; ☎ 45 3522 1027). In town, there are offices at the Terminal de Transporte Urbano (daily 7.30am–6pm; ☎ 45 3523 7901), and on the way to the falls, the Centro Municipal de Turismo, Av das Cataratas 2330, Vila Yolanda (daily 7am–11pm; ☎ 0800 451516, ⓦ pmfi.pr.gov.br/turismo).

Money and exchange Foreign currency can be easily changed in travel agencies and banks along Av Brasil; the latter also have ATMs.

Post office Praça Getúlio Vargas 72, near Rua Barão do Rio Branco (Mon–Fri 9am–5pm).

ACCOMMODATION

Finding somewhere to stay in Foz do Iguaçu is usually easy, and outside the peak tourist months of January, February and July, and over Easter, you are likely to be offered a **discount rate** at all but the top-end establishments. Many of the hotels are located some distance from town on the road leading to the falls – the **Avenida das Cataratas** – though the bigger, more luxurious resorts here are not especially good value for independent travellers. The obvious exception is the magnificent *Hotel das Cataratas* in the Parque Nacional do Iguaçu itself (see page 568). Hotels tend to be a bit cheaper in **Puerto Iguazú** (see page 568).

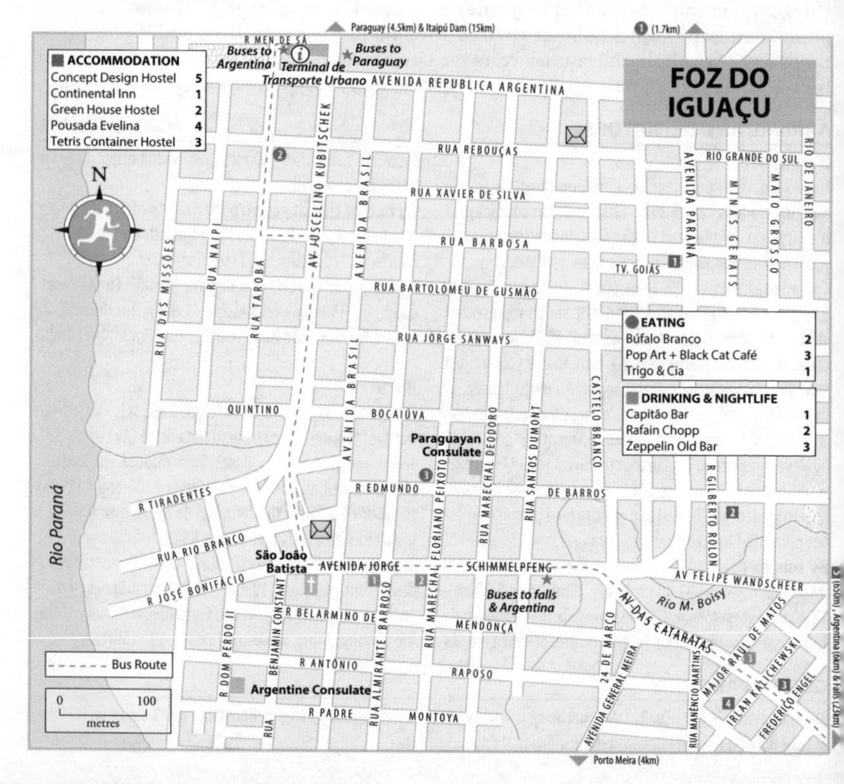

IGUAZÚ BORDER CROSSINGS: ARGENTINA AND PARAGUAY

TO PUERTO IGUAZÚ, ARGENTINA

By bus Puerto Iguazú buses (which should be labelled "Argentina") depart every 40min or so (7am–7pm; hourly Sat & Sun, 45min past the hour; R$7/A$25) from Rua Men de Sá (at Rua Tarobá,), the street just north of the Terminal de Transporte Urbano (you can also flag them down at stops en route), terminating at the bus terminal in the centre of Puerto Iguazú (the trip can take 1hr), where you can transfer to regular buses to the Argentine falls (see page 571). Bus drivers won't wait for you while you clear Brazilian immigration at the border; keep your ticket and take the next one coming through (the bus usually stops at the Argentina side, as everyone has to get off).

By taxi Taxis charge around R$60–70 to Puerto Iguazú, and R$120–150 to the Argentine falls (round-trip). Taxi drivers will wait for you while you clear immigration.

Entry requirements for Brazil You'll have to stop at both the Brazilian and Argentine immigration posts in both directions, but waiting times are rarely more than a few minutes. If you're of a nationality that normally requires a visa to visit Brazil (Australia, Canada, USA etc), don't worry; the Brazilian border guards will re-admit you if it's obvious you've visited the Argentine side for one day (the dates will be in your passport, which you'll still need to bring); you will still need to hand in your entry form at the border when leaving Brazil, and fill in another entry card when you cross back over later on. However, check the current situation before you leave Brazil.

Entry requirements for Argentina Most nations do not need a visa to enter Argentina for up to 90 days. However, one important caveat for Australian and Canadian passport holders: prior to arrival in Argentina you must pay a reciprocity fee (Australia US$100; Canada U$92); by credit card online (ⓦdnm.provincianet.com.ar). You must print out the receipt and present it to the Argentine immigration officer at the time of entry (for Canada it's valid for ten years and for multiple entries; Australians get multiple entries over just one year). Even if you visit Argentina for just a few hours, you must pay this fee.

TO CIUDAD DEL ESTE, PARAGUAY

By bus Buses depart across Av Juscelino Kubitschek from the Terminal de Transporte Urbano every 30min or so (7am–8.50pm; R$6; 40min). The Ciudad del Este bus terminal is just south of the centre, to which it is linked by local buses.

By taxi Taxis to Ciudad del Este charge around R$40–50. Depending on border traffic, it can take between fifteen minutes and two hours to travel between the two cities – it's often faster to walk across the international bridge and pick up a taxi or bus on the other side.

Entry requirements for Paraguay Border controls over the Ponte da Amizade into Paraguay are usually quite lax: if you are visiting Ciuded del Este for the day there's no need to stop at immigration (or to change money – US$ are widely accepted here). However, note that if you are from a nation that officially requires a visa to enter Paraguay and you get stopped randomly by immigration officers, they may expect you to cough up a "fee". Visas are officially required for citizens of the US (US$160), Australia (US$135-equivalent), Canada (US$150-equivalent) and New Zealand (US$140-equivalent); you must apply for visas in advance (visas on arrival are only available at Asunción airport). Heading back into Brazil the same rules apply as with coming back from Argentina (see above).

★ **Concept Design Hostel** Rua Vereador Moacyr Pereira 337, Vila Yolanda ⓣ45 3029 3631, ⓦconceptdesignhostel.com; map p.564. This stylish, budget boutique hotel has spacious doubles with individual colour themes, slick Ikea-like dorms (each bed is equipped with reading lights and power sockets), a central pool, bar and communal kitchen. It's also close to the bus stop for the falls. Dorms R$50, doubles R$155

Continental Inn Av Paraná 1089 ⓣ45 2102 5000, ⓦcontinentalinn.com.br; map p.564. Good value for a high-quality – if somewhat anonymous – downtown hotel. The well-equipped rooms are spacious, breakfasts are ample, the staff are efficient and English-speaking, and there's a good pool. R$313

Green House Hostel Rua Edmundo de Barros 1130 ⓣ45 3572 8668, ⓦhostelgreenhouse.com.br; map p.564. Within walking distance of the bars and restaurants on Jorge Schimmelpfeng, this fun hostel offers spotless dorms and excellent amenities (pool, bar, small but well-equipped kitchen and tranquil garden). Dorms R$40, doubles R$140

9

Hostel Paudimar Campestre Av das Cataratas, Km 12.5 ☎45 3529 6061, paudimar.com.br; map p.562. An excellent hostel with great facilities, including male and female dorms, a large pool and an on-site travel agency offering a range of excursions. Cabins (with private bathrooms) sleep five to eight people (R$23–40 per person) and there are also basic but comfy double rooms. Dorms R$48, doubles R$118, camping/pitch R$30

Pousada Evelina Rua Irlan Kalichewski 171, Vila Yolanda ☎45 3574 3817, pousadaevelinafoz.com.br; map p.564. An extremely friendly family-run place in the city centre that mainly attracts foreign backpackers. Rooms, all of which have en-suite bathrooms, are simple but spotless; breakfasts are adequate, there's free parking and multilingual owner Evelina goes out of her way to be helpful. Well located for buses to the falls. Dorms R$45, doubles R$120

★ **Tetris Container Hostel** Av das Cataratas 639, Vila Yolanda ☎45 3132 0019, tetrishostel.com.br; map p.564. Quirky but very cool sustainable hostel primarily made out of brightly painted shipping containers (water is solar-heated, it has a green roof, rainwater is used for toilets and all the containers, and most of the furniture, is recycled). Choose from female-only or mixed a/c dorms (where the snappy colours continue), or compact doubles, with private bathroom and a/c. There's a bar (one free drink nightly), garden, shared kitchen even a container swimming pool. Dorms R$53, doubles R$150

Viale Cataratas Hotel Av das Cataratas 2420 ☎45 2105 7200, www.vialehoteis.com.br; map p.562. Conveniently located for access to both the Argentine and Brazilian falls, this sparkling place is rather like a high-end airport hotel. Rooms are simple but stylish (with LCD TVs) and there's a fine pool. R$265

EATING

Foz do Iguaçu is certainly no gastronomic paradise, but it's possible to eat fairly well without paying too much. The main drag for restaurants and bars is **Avenida Jorge Schimmelpfeng**, south of the city centre – taxis should be around R$10–15 (on the meter) from most hotels in town.

Búfalo Branco Rua Engenheiro Rebouças 530 ☎45 3523 9744, bufalobranco.com.br; map p.564. Good top-notch *churrascaria* with the all-you-can-eat *rodizio* system and a vast, excellent salad bar. Normally around R$79 per person, but look for lunchtime special offers. Also offers free transfer from your hotel. Daily noon–11pm.

★ **Clube Maringá** Rua Dourado 111, Porto Meira (6km south of the centre) ☎45 3527 9683, restaurantemaringa.com.br; map p.562. Justly popular among locals for its superb *rodizio de peixe* lunch and stunning views of the Rio Paraná. As well as a vast selection of local freshwater fish (golden dorado, pacu, tilapia – mostly fried and battered, but some soups and grilled fish too), there's an excellent salad bar and desserts. The buffet operates lunch and dinner for R$60 per person (à la carte dishes are about the same). Take the "Porto Meira" bus and ask for directions, or take a taxi at night (R$25). Tues–Sat 11.30am–11pm, Sun 11.30am–4pm.

★ **Pop Art + Black Cat Café** Rua Edmundo de Barros 257 ☎45 3029 5939; map p.564. Stylish coffee culture comes to Foz thanks to this cool T-shirt store and café, with really excellent espresso, plus gluten free and/or vegan-friendly snacks (think beetroot panini, zesty bean soup and sublime carrot muffins; R$6–16). Mon 11.30am–6pm, Tues–Fri 11.30am–8pm, Sat 1.30–9pm, Sun 3–8pm.

Recanto Gaúcho Rua Oscar Genehr (800m off Av das Cataratas Km 15, near the airport ☎45 3529 8194; map p.562. A favourite Sunday outing for locals and tourists. The atmosphere's lively, the meat's excellent and cheap (R$50 per person for all you can eat) and the owner (who always dresses in full *gaúcho* regalia) is a real character. Turn up early; food is served up until 3pm. It's advisable to phone ahead. Sun 10.30am–6pm.

Trigo & Cia Av Paraná 1750 (at Av José Maria de Brito) ☎45 3025 3800; map p.564. Ten minutes by bus from the centre of town, this busy café serves tasty savoury snacks, good coffee and the best cakes in Foz (R$6–14), at all hours. Daily 24hr.

DRINKING AND NIGHTLIFE

Capitão Bar Av Jorge Schimmelpfeng 288 ☎45 3572 1512, capitaobar.com; map p.564. One of a series of lively bars on this stretch, this is a particularly popular nightspot with the local youth on account of its loud music, "Torre de Chopp" (2.5l beer towers, R$36), mojitos (R$17.50) and affordable pizzas. Outdoor tables fill quickly so arrive early in summer if you want to sit outside. Daily 11.30am–2am.

Rafain Chopp Av Jorge Schimmelpfeng 450 ☎45 3523 5373; map p.564. Hip and happening bar on the main nightlife strip, with live music, big TV screens and outdoor seating – big range of steaks, pastas and pizzas along with potent *caipirinhas* and towers of draught beer ("Torre Temática"). Mon–Thurs 4pm–2am, Fri–Sun 2pm–2am.

Zeppelin Old Bar Rua Major Raul Mattos 222 ☎45 3523 1804; map p.564. Cool lounge bar and live music venue, hosting everything from jazz and bossa nova to MPB and Brazilian rock bands. Cover charge R$15–20. Tues 7pm–midnight, Wed 8pm–1am, Thurs–Sat 9pm–2am.

Parque das Aves

Av das Cataratas Km 17.1 • Daily 8.30am–5pm • R$40 • ⓣ 45 3529 8282, ⓦ parquedasaves.com.br • Bus #120

The only major attraction on the road to the falls is the **Parque das Aves**, located just 100m from the entrance to the national park on the Brazilian side of the Rio Iguaçu. The bird park maintains both small breeding aviaries and enormous walk-through aviaries, which are still surrounded by dense forest (all birds have been rescued from traffickers and would not survive alone in the wild). There is also a large walk-through butterfly cage – butterflies are bred throughout the year and released when mature. All the butterflies and eighty percent of the eight hundred bird species here are Brazilian, many endemic to the Atlantic forest.

Parque Nacional do Iguaçu

BR-469 Km 22.5 (Av das Cataratas) • Daily 9–5pm • R$63, includes R$10 fee for buses inside the park; parking fee R$22 • ⓦ cataratasdoiguacu.com.br • Bus #120

The finest overall view of the **Iguaçu Falls** is obtained from the **Parque Nacional do Iguaçu** on the Brazilian side, best in the morning when the light is much better for photography. If you skip all the activities on offer, you'll only need about half a day here (longer if you're also visiting the Parque das Aves), since, although the view is mind-blowing and it's from here that you get the clearest idea as to the size of the falls, the area from which to view them is fairly limited.

Buses from Foz terminate at the **visitors' centre** at the park entrance where, after paying the entrance fee, you transfer onto a **park bus** for the ride to the falls: buses make stops along the way, terminating at the tourist complex of shops and restaurants at the top of the falls, **Porto Canoas Square**, which makes a pleasant spot for a snack.

The main event is accessed from bus stop #5 (the one before Canoas), the "**Path of the Falls Stop**" where a stairway leads down to a 1.2km cliffside **path** along the rim of the falls. From spots all along the trail there are mesmerizing views, at first across the lower river at a point where it has narrowed to channel width. At the bottom of the path, where the river widens again, there's a walkway leading out towards the falls

THE SELVA: IGUAÇU WILDLIFE

One of the remarkable aspects of Iguaçu is that visitors can gain access to a **semi-deciduous tropical rainforest** without any difficulty and without posing a threat to people or nature. Even by keeping to the main paths around the falls, you get a taste of the jungle, in particular on the Argentine side. The forest is home to over two thousand plant varieties, four hundred bird species, dozens of types of mammal and innumerable insects and reptiles. Much of this wildlife is spread out over a wide area, often nocturnal and usually extremely timid. However, if you get up early, walk quietly away from other people and look up into the trees as well as towards the ground, you have a chance of seeing something.

One critter you will almost certainly see, especially on the Brazilian side, is the **coatimundi**, the size of a domestic cat but related to the raccoon. Though it's certainly a thrill to see a family of "coatis" for the first time, the novelty soon wears off – they have become a real pest, hoping to scrounge food from tourists (although feeding the animals is strictly forbidden), and can get aggressive. Another common sight is the bizarre basket-like nests of the **red-ruffed fruitcrow** (the birds have bright red breasts), and there are plenty of buzzards and vultures all over the park.

Around the water's edge, you may occasionally see **tapirs**, a large animal shaped rather like a pig with a long snout. Smaller, but also with a pig-like appearance, is the **peccary**, dangerous when cornered, but shy around humans. The *caí*, or **capuchin monkey**, is often seen on the Argentine side and is recognizable by its long legs and tail, small size and the black skullcap mark that gives it its name. These monkeys travel the forest canopy in large groups and emit strange bird-like cries. Far bigger and with a deep voice is the **howler monkey**. You may not see any, but you're likely to hear their powerful voices emanating from the jungle. With a good eye you should also be able to see **toucans**, **parakeets** and **hummingbirds** even without straying from the main paths. Again, their most active hours are soon after dawn when it's cooler.

9

themselves at **Garganta del Diablo** (Devil's Throat) – the point where fourteen separate falls combine to form the world's most powerful single cascade in terms of the volume of water flow per second. Depending on the force of the river, the spray can be quite heavy, so if you have a camera be sure to carry a plastic bag. From here, you can either retrace your steps back up the trail (it's not that steep) or take the **elevator** (daily 9.30am–6.15pm; free) to the top of the cliff and the road leading to Porto Canoas (200m or so further along). If you walk up one level to the terrace beyond the elevator you'll be free of the crowds with perfect views of the falls up close.

ARRIVAL AND DEPARTURE — PARQUE NACIONAL DO IGUAÇU

By bus City buses (R$3.45) run from the TTU terminal in Foz to the Brazilian falls via the airport and Parque de Aves (#120; Mon–Sat 5.45am–12.40am, every 20min; Sun 5.30am–12.40am, every 45min).

By taxi Taxis between Foz and the falls entrance are around R$50.

ACCOMMODATION AND EATING

Belmond Hotel das Cataratas BR-469 Km 32, Parque Nacional do Iguaçu ⓣ45 2102 7000, ⓦbelmond.com; map p.562. The only hotel within the Brazilian national park, located just out of sight from the falls. After years of neglect, the hotel was completely renovated by the Orient Express group, with luxurious guest rooms, posh lounges, superb dining options and beautifully landscaped gardens. The location is perfect for an early-morning view of the falls. R$1005

Ipê Grill Hotel das Cataratas BR-469 Km 32, Parque Nacional do Iguaçu ⓣ45 2102 7000, ⓦbelmond.com; map p.562. The only hotel restaurant worth a splurge, even if you're not staying here. Located by the pool, it offers an extensive but very pricey buffet breakfast and dinner of typical Brazilian dishes and *gaúcho* style barbecue (around R$150 for dinner). Lunch is à la carte, with mains R$65–89. Daily 6.30–10am, 12.30–3pm & 7.30–11pm.

Restaurante Porto Canoas BR-469 Km 30, Parque Nacional do Iguaçu ⓣ45 3521 4443; map p.562. The main park restaurant, overlooking the Rio Iguaçu at the head of the falls, serves a decent – but pricey (R$59/person, plus ten percent) – all-you-can-eat buffet. Otherwise, there's a basic food court nearby. Daily noon–4pm.

Puerto Iguazú (Argentina)

In complete contrast to neighbouring Foz, **PUERTO IGUAZÚ** is sleepier, smaller and visibly less developed than its big brother across the Rio Iguaçu. If you're on a budget, staying here is a better idea: it's less crowded and the cheap hotels are more pleasant on the Argentine side of the border. Note that with the collapse in value of the Argentine peso since the start of 2014 (when US$1 was A$6.50; it was worth A$18 by the end of 2017), prices in pesos have continued to rise fairly regularly – where possible we've used US dollar equivalents (US$ are often accepted in Argentina).

ARRIVAL AND GETTING AROUND — PUERTO IGUAZÚ (ARGENTINA)

By plane Aeropuerto Internacional de las Cataratas del Iguazú lies 7km from the falls and 20km from Puerto Iguazú. Aerolíneas Argentinas (ⓦaerolineas.com.ar) operates regular flights to Buenos Aires (1hr 30min). Buses (A$120) to town meet arriving flights and taxis are available (at least A$350, or US$20-equivalent).

By bus Puerto Iguazú's combined local and long-distance Terminal de Ómnibus, at Av Córdoba and Av Misiones (ⓣ+54 03757 423006), is in the town centre, with several daily departures to Buenos Aires and Posadas, near the Jesuit ruins of San Ignacio Miní (see page 628).

By taxi Taxis charge fixed rates from the centre of town and the bus station, but given the instability of the peso, these are constantly changing – the following is for reference only (US$ are usually accepted): US$15-equivalent to the airport; US$20-equivalent to the airport on the Brazilian side; US$15-equivalent to the Argentine falls (US$20-equivalent to the falls on the Brazilian side); US$19-equivalent to Foz; and US$32-equivalent to Ciudad del Este in Paraguay.

Services There's an ATM near the bus station in Puerto Iguazú (useful if you get stuck without A$); it's open 24hr and should accept foreign cards.

ACCOMMODATION AND EATING

There's a good range of places to stay in Puerto Iguazú for all prices. Unless otherwise indicated, the following places are concentrated within a few blocks of the **bus station**. This being Argentina, food means beef (although most restaurants

9

IGUAÇU ACTIVITIES: THE BRAZILIAN SIDE

Iguaçu Falls has become a major **adventure sports** destination with a bewildering range of activities available. Martin Travel, Travessa Goiás 200 in Foz do Iguaçu (45 3523 4959, www.martintravel.com.br), is a reliable local tour agency that specializes in ecotourism and puts together groups to go canoeing, rafting or mountain biking along forest trails. See also Loumar at Av República Argentina 1700 in Foz (45 3521 4000, loumarturismo.com).

HELICOPTER RIDES

Helisul (45 3529 7474, helisul.com) operates helicopter rides from just outside the park's entrance (Av das Cataratas Km 16.5), across from the Parque das Aves, offering ten-minute flights (daily 8.30am–5.30pm) over the falls for R$430 per person (minimum three people); the views are sensational, but the flights are controversial thanks to the noise pollution (which scares wildlife). The longer (30–35min) ride over the falls and Itaipu Dam is better value if you can afford it (around R$4000 for the whole helicopter, maximum seven people).

JET BOAT

Macuco Safari (daily 9am–5.30pm, every 15min; 45 3529 6262, macucosafari.com.br), at its own dedicated bus stop in the park, operates a crazy jet-boat ride through white water right up to and into the falls for R$215 per person; it's fun, but the crew takes non-stop video and photos of passengers squealing in delight (to sell to them later), and everyone gets absolutely saturated by ice-cold water as the boat passes through the cascade again and again. The boat ride is preceded by a ride and walk through the jungle, but even if you understand Portuguese (no English) the guided commentary is fairly dull, and you are unlikely to see any animals.

HIKING TRAILS

The 9km **Poco Prieto Trail**, accessed from its own dedicated bus stop inside the park, is a generally tranquil and easy path through the jungle to the river. Macuco Safari (see above) runs guided tours for R$107, combined with various excursions on the water. The **Trilha das Bananeiras** provides a similar though shorter (1.6km) jaunt between the main park road and the river.

also serve *surubí*, the local fish, and pasta), accompanied by decent wine. What nightlife there is in Puerto Iguazú takes place in the "downtown" bars on **Avenida Victoria Aguirre**.

Boutique Hotel de la Fonte 1 de Mayo y Corrientes +54 03757 420625, bhfboutiquehotel.com. This Italian-owned hotel offers six well-equipped a/c rooms (all with cable TV) – one of which boasts an oversized jacuzzi – and an attractive garden with a pool. You can dine here too, with beautiful-looking and -tasting dishes that incorporate local flavours. US$120

★ **Casa Yaguarete** Av Posadas and El Dorado, Zona de Granjas +54 03757 450097, casayaguarete@gmail.com. Welcoming B&B with cosy doubles and triples, all with hot showers, cable TV and hearty breakfast included. The friendly owners can help arrange trips and tickets. US$65

Garden Stone Hostel Av Córdoba 441 +54 03757 420425, gardenstonehostel.com. Overall the best hostel in town, this is a friendly, spotless place with four-bed dorms (with a/c) and doubles, with or without private bathroom. There's a communal kitchen, TV room and pool, plus reception is open 24hr. Dorms US$10, doubles US$31

Jasy Hotel San Lorenzo 154 +54 03757 424337, jasyhotel.com. Fabulous accommodation in a series of ten rustic lodges set on a slope, all simply furnished but spacious and stylish (a/c and cable TV included). The restaurant is also great (jasyrestobar.com). (communal areas only) US$78

★ **Secret Garden B&B** Los Lapachos 623 +54 03757 423099, secretgardeniguazu.com. This marvellous B&B has just three small but perfectly maintained rooms set around a small, verdant garden. Simple but excellent breakfasts are provided, while in the evenings *caipirinhas* are offered. John Fernandes, a photojournalist originally from India but long resident in Argentina, could not be a better host. US$125

Parque Nacional de Iguazú (Argentina)

Ruta Nacional 101 • Daily 8am–6pm (last entry 4.30pm; last Tren de la Selva 4pm, return 5.30pm); Centro de Visitantes: daily 7am–8pm • A$500 (pesos cash only); parking A$100 • +54 03757 491469, iguazuargentina.com

For more detailed views of the falls, and greater opportunities to view the local flora and fauna at close range, **Parque Nacional de Iguazú** in Argentina offers by far the best vantage points. The falls on the Argentine side are much more numerous and the viewing area more extensive, though these days both sides tend to be mobbed by tourists in equal numbers.

Buses and taxis drop you at the main entrance, where you'll find the **Centro de Visitantes**, a small exhibition hall focusing on the region's natural and human history (from the Guarani and the Jesuits to nineteenth-century colonists), with English labelling. It's here that you'll see the extremely shy, and mainly nocturnal, forest animals – though they're all stuffed. From the centre you transfer to the grandly named **Tren de la Selva**, a miniature railway that winds its way through the forest between the park's entrance and the falls. The first stop is the Estación Cataratas for the *Sheraton Hotel* and the Circuito Inferior and Circuito Superior trails; the second and final stop is the Estación Garganta del Diablo.

The Circuito Inferior and Superior

The **Circuito Inferior** involves an easy 1.6km walk that, with a few interruptions to admire the scenery, is likely to take a couple of hours. Despite not being as dramatic as the falls upriver, few parts of the park are more beautiful and the path passes by gentler waterfalls and dense vegetation. At the river shore, **boats** (9.30am–3.30pm; free) cross to the **Isla San Martín**, whose beaches are unfortunately marred by the streams of sand flies and mosquitoes. One of the many enchanting spots on the island is **La Ventana**, a rock formation that's framed, as its name suggests, like a window. From here you can continue around the marked circuit, but, if you are at all agile, haul yourself instead across the rocks in front and behind La Ventana where, hidden from view, is a deep natural **pool** fed by a small waterfall, allowing some relaxing swimming.

In stark contrast, the **Circuito Superior** (accessed off the Circuito Inferior) runs straight along the top of the falls for 650m, offering a series of dramatic viewpoints en route, as well as the chance to get up close to the churning waters.

Garganta del Diablo

The Argentine falls embrace a huge area, but the most spectacular spot is the **Garganta del Diablo** (Devil's Throat) at Puerto Canoas, the final *tren* stop opposite its counterpoint in Brazil (see page 568). Catwalks lead 1.1km into the middle of the river to a central viewing platform, from where it's easy to feel that you will be swallowed by the tumbling waters: be prepared to get drenched by the spray, mist and rain. From Puerto Canoas the train will take you back to the park's entrance complex.

ARRIVAL AND INFORMATION PARQUE NACIONAL DE IGUAZÚ (ARGENTINA)

By bus Río Uruguay buses depart from the Terminal de Ómnibus on Av Córdoba and Av Misiones (T +54 03757 423006) in Puerto Iguazú every 30min (daily 7.20am–7.20pm, return 7.50am–8pm; A$65; buy tickets at the terminal booth). They take around 30min to reach the park entrance.

By taxi Taxis charge around US$15–20 or peso-equivalent to get to the park from Puerto Iguazú (you might be able to negotiate a lower rate depending on the currency you intend to use).

Money and exchange Try to get pesos in Foz before you come; there's an ATM near the bus station in Puerto Iguazú.

TOURS

Iguazú Jungle Located at the Circuito Inferior T +54 03757 421 600, W iguazujungle.com. Runs guided tours (daily 8.45am–3.45pm, every 30min) into the jungle on the Argentine side of the falls. A typical trip lasts one and a half hours (A$950; US$54), and involves being driven in the back of a truck along a rough 8km road through the jungle, a walk down a narrow trail to the river, and a wild 6km boat ride down some rapids towards the Garganta del Diablo. Don't expect to see a lot of wildlife (much of which is nocturnal), but guides may point out some of the flora. You can also just opt for the jet-boat ride (A$550; US$31), which is similar to those on the Brazilian side (see page 570).

ACCOMMODATION

Meliá Iguazú Parque Nacional Iguazú +54 03757 491 800, meliahotelsinternational.com; map p.562. The Meliá group bought this former Sheraton concrete (but luxurious) behemoth in 2017, and it remains the sole hotel in the Argentine Parque Nacional. The newly renovated hotel should debut in 2018, offering extreme pampering, excellent food, luxurious rooms with balconies and outstanding views. **US$250**

Itaipu Dam

Av Tancredo Neves 6702 • **Itaipu Dam** panoramic tours: daily 8.30am–5pm (hourly; 2hr); special tours: daily 8.30am, 9.30am, 11am, 1pm, 2.30pm & 3.30pm (2hr 30min) • panoramic pour: R$36; special tour: R$78 • 45 3520 6676, turismoitaipu.com.br • **Ecomuseu** Tues–Sun 8am–5pm • R$12 • Bus #101 from Foz do Iguaçu

Some 12km north of central Foz do Iguaçu, the **Itaipu Dam** harnesses the power of the Rio Paraná in what is supposedly the world's largest operating hydroelectric facility (jointly with China's Three Gorges Dam). It's a stark contrast to the natural wonders of the falls, but mind-bending nevertheless: almost 8km long and 196m high, the dam supplies around ninety percent of the total electricity consumed by Paraguay (and 19 percent consumed by Brazil). In 2009 a temporary disruption at the dam blacked out the whole of Paraguay for fifteen minutes.

Work on the dam began in the early 1970s at a cost of US$25 billion, and its eighteen 700,000-kilowatt generators became fully operational in 1991. The project has been controversial from the start, with some ten thousand families forced off their land, the destruction of the Guaíra Falls and as yet unknown ecological consequences, despite the much-publicized animal rescue operations and financial assistance for displaced farmers.

Buses drop you at the **visitors' centre** where a film about the project, in English and other languages, is shown, and from where illuminating **guided tours** of the complex depart – special tours take you inside the dam itself, while panaromic tours end at the viewpoint on top (English speakers should be available). You can also take a look at the **Ecomuseu** on the edge of the complex, which chronicles the history of the site.

Santa Catarina

Another relatively rich state, **Santa Catarina** is best known for its beaches, especially around the holiday resort of **Ilha Santa Catarina**, the small, beautiful, laidback island that, confusingly, shares the name of the state. The island is sometimes referred to in general as **Florianópolis**, but note that this more specifically refers to the main city and state capital on its west coast (the city now also extends to the mainland) – don't book a hotel in the city and expect to wake up next to a palm-fringed beach. Elsewhere, cities such as **Blumenau** and **Joinville**, established by German immigrants in the nineteenth century, have become wholly Brazilian (with the exception of Blumenau's hearty **Oktoberfest**), but in the surrounding villages such as **Pomerode**, and on isolated farms, many people still speak the language of their forebears in preference to Portuguese; Germans, Austrians and Italians all settled here in numbers between the 1850s and 1910s.

Florianópolis

Founded on the **Ilha Santa Catarina** in 1675 by Portuguese adventurer Francisco Dias Velho, **FLORIANÓPOLIS** – aka "Floripa" – really got going 75 years later thanks to an influx of immigrants from the Azores. Since then, it's gradually developed from sleepy provincial backwater to a middle-sized, fairly affluent **state capital** of just over 400,000. Until 1893, the city was known as Desterro, but it was renamed for Marshal Floriano Peixoto, the second president of Brazil and a republican hero. Florianópolis as a port has all but died, and today the city thrives as an administrative, information technology and tourist centre. Land reclamation for a multi-laned highway and bus terminals has tarnished the character of the old seafront, but despite the changes, the remaining late

9

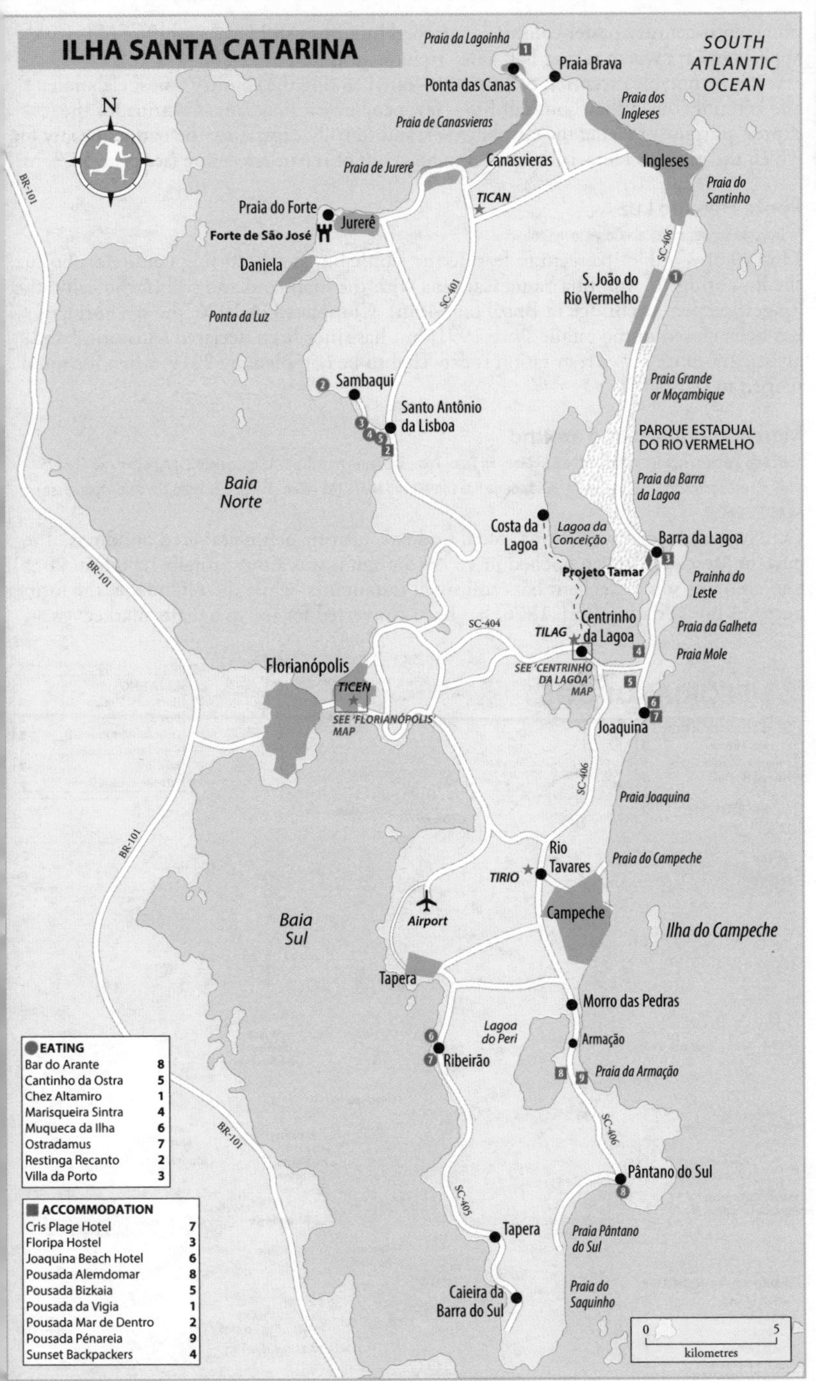

ILHA SANTA CATARINA
N
Praia da Lagoinha
Praia Brava
Ponta das Canas
SOUTH ATLANTIC OCEAN
Praia dos Ingleses
Praia de Canasvieras
Praia de Jurerê
Canasvieras
Ingleses
Praia do Santinho
TICAN
Praia do Forte
Jurerê
Forte de São José
Daniela
S. João do Rio Vermelho
SC-406
SC-401
BR-101
Ponta da Luz
Praia Grande or Moçambique
Sambaqui
Santo Antônio da Lisboa
PARQUE ESTADUAL DO RIO VERMELHO
Baia Norte
Praia da Barra da Lagoa
Costa da Lagoa
Lagoa da Conceição
Barra da Lagoa
Projeto Tamar
Prainha do Leste
SC-404
Centrinho da Lagoa
TILAG
Praia da Galheta
Praia Mole
Florianópolis
TICEN
SEE 'CENTRINHO DA LAGOA' MAP
SEE 'FLORIANÓPOLIS' MAP
Joaquina
Praia Joaquina
Rio Tavares
Praia do Campeche
TIRIO
Campeche
Airport
Baia Sul
Ilha do Campeche
Tapera
Morro das Pedras
Lagoa do Peri
Armação
Ribeirão
Praia da Armação
SC-405
Pântano do Sul
Tapera
Praia Pântano do Sul
Praia do Saquinho
Caieira da Barra do Sul
0 5 kilometres
Garopaba (25km), Praia do Rosa (37km) & Porto Alegre (411km)
EATING
Bar do Arante 8
Cantinho da Ostra 5
Chez Altamiro 1
Marisqueira Sintra 4
Muqueca da Ilha 6
Ostradamus 7
Restinga Recanto 2
Villa da Porto 3
ACCOMMODATION
Cris Plage Hotel 7
Floripa Hostel 3
Joaquina Beach Hotel 6
Pousada Alemdomar 8
Pousada Bizkaia 5
Pousada da Vigia 1
Pousada Mar de Dentro 2
Pousada Pénareia 9
Sunset Backpackers 4

nineteenth-century pastel-coloured, stuccoed buildings still have a whiff of old-world appeal, and it's worth taking half a day to look around.

With the notable exception of **Carnaval** – rated among the country's most elaborate, and certainly the liveliest south of Rio – few people visit Ilha Santa Catarina for the express purpose of seeing the city, however, and to truly experience the natural beauty for which the island is renowned, it's best to head out of the urban centre (see page 577).

Ponte Hercílio Luz

Av Oswaldo Rodrigues Cabral • Closed to the public

Most photos of Floripa seem to feature the iconic but slowly rusting **Ponte Hercílio Luz**, the first bridge to link Ilha Santa Catarina with the mainland and still (technically) the longest suspension bridge in Brazil (at 340m). Completed in 1926, the steel bridge has been closed to the public since 1991, but has since been declared a historical and artistic monument – a restoration is expected to be complete by 2019, when it should reopen to traffic.

Mercado Público and around

Mercado Público Rua Jeronimo Coelho 60 • Mon–Fri 7am–7pm, Sat 7am–2pm (bars can open until 10pm) • Free • T 48 3225 8464, W mercadopublicofloripa.com.br • **Alfândega** Rua Conselheiro Mafra 141 • Mon–Fri 9am–6.30pm, Sat 9am–1pm • Free • T 48 3665 6097

On Floripa's former waterfront, you'll find two historic ochre-coloured buildings. The current **Mercado Público** opened in 1899 (though it was almost totally rebuilt in 2015), and contains some excellent bars and small restaurants, while the **Alfândega**, the former customs house dating from 1876, has been converted for use as a crafts market.

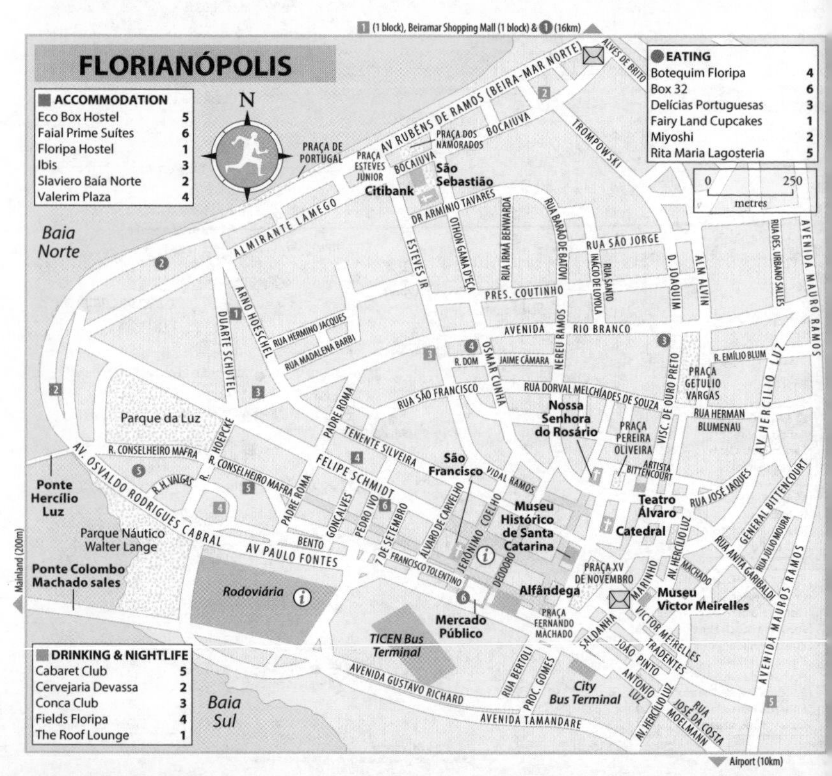

Praça XV de Novembro

Rua Felipe Schmidt is the main, pedestrianized commercial artery of the city, ending at the lush, jungly **Praça XV de Novembro**, at the centre of which is the enormous, gnarled "**Centenary Fig**" tree. According to legend, walking three times around the tree will guarantee you fame and fortune. By the end of 2018 the old Casa de Câmara e Cadeia on the plaza's southeast corner should be open as the **Museu da Cidade**, chronicling the history of the city.

Museu Histórico de Santa Catarina

Praça XV de Novembro 227 • Tues–Fri 10am–6pm, Sat & Sun 10am–4pm • R$5; free on Sun • ⓣ 48 3028 809, ⓦ mhsc.sc.gov.br

Now open to the public as the **Museu Histórico de Santa Catarina**, the Palácio Cruz e Souza is an ornate, pink confection dating back to the eighteenth century, but largely built in its current form in the 1890s. It served as the official governor's palace until 1984, and is named after local Afro-Brazilian poet **João da Cruz e Sousa** (1861–98) – the latter's remains were reinterred here in 2007 (the urn lies in the memorial in the garden next door to the palace). It's worth strolling the upper floor to admire the nineteenth-century decor, parquet floors, touches of Art Nouveau and the Carrera marble staircase, guarded, incongruously, by two fanciful statues of English kings Arthur and Alfred. Rooms here have been restored to their gubernatorial glory *circa* 1898 and are labelled in English, but the exhibits downstairs (on various historical themes) tend to rotate and are labelled in Portuguese only.

Catedral Metropolitana

Praça XV de Novembro • Mon–Fri 6.15am–8pm, Sat 8am–noon & 4–8pm, Sun 7am–noon & 4–9pm • Free • ⓣ 48 3224 3357, ⓦ www.catedralflorianopolis.org.br

Overlooking the Praça XV de Novembro from its highest point is the unremarkable **Catedral Metropolitana**, dedicated to Nossa Senhora do Desterro. It was originally constructed between 1753 and 1773, but was enlarged and totally remodelled in 1922 with a rather awkward twin-tower configuration, and there's little to see inside.

Museu Victor Meirelles

Rua Victor Meirelles 59 • Tues–Fri 10am–6pm, Sat 10am–2pm • R$2 • ⓣ 48 3222 0692, ⓦ museuvictormeirelles.museus.gov.br

A short walk behind the central plaza lies the enlightening **Museu Victor Meirelles**, dedicated to the eponymous painter born in this building in 1832. Meirelles became famous for his historically themed paintings, and the museum displays sixteen of them on the first floor (the most notable being the *Battle of Guararapes*, which celebrates Portugal's acquisition of northeastern Brazil from the Dutch in 1649).

Igreja de Nossa Senhora do Rosário e São Benedito

Rua Marechal Guilherme 60 • Open for services only • Free

The only church in the city centre dating back to the colonial era is the simple but charming **Igreja de Nossa Senhora do Rosário e São Benedito**, built from 1787 to 1830 and approached by a flight of steps at Rua Marechal Guilherme, two blocks north of the Praça XV de Novembro.

ARRIVAL AND DEPARTURE — FLORIANÓPOLIS

By plane Florianópolis-Hercílio Luz International Airport (ⓣ 48 3331 4000) is 12km south of the city centre, with daily flights from Brasília, Buenos Aires, São Paulo, Rio and Porto Alegre. A taxi is around R$50 to the city centre or R$60 to Lagoa; or catch green bus #183 or #186 (every 10–30min and labelled "Corredor do Sudoeste"; R$3.90), which will end up at the Terminal de Integração Centro (TICEN) in the centre (around 45min).

Car rental All major car rental firms have desks in the airport terminal and can arrange delivery in the city centre, including Avis, Av Deputado Diomicio Freitas s/n (ⓣ 48 3331 4176), Hertz (ⓣ 48 3236 1244) and Localiza, Rua Henrique Valgas 112A (ⓣ 48 2107 6464). During the peak summer season advance reservations are essential.

9

By bus Buses arrive at the Terminal Rodoviária Rita María (☎48 3212 3100) at the foot of the road bridge that links the island to the mainland. Cross Av Paulo Fontes and it's a short walk to the centre; the local bus terminal (TICEN) is one long block east at Paulo Fontes 701.

Destinations Blumenau (hourly; 3hr); Buenos Aires (1 daily; 28hr); Curitiba (hourly; 4–5hr); Foz do Iguaçu (14 daily; 14hr 30min–15hr 40min); Joinville (hourly; 2.5–3hr); Porto Alegre (12 daily; 5–7hr); Rio (1 daily; 14hr 40min); São Paulo (hourly; 11–12hr). From Terminal de Integração Centro (TICEN): #311, #330 or #320 to Lagoa Da Conceição (TILAG); #231 or #233 to Canasvieiras (TICAN).

INFORMATION

Tourist information There's a tourist information kiosk (daily 8am– 6pm; ☎48 3228 1095) at the Terminal Rodoviária. Santa Catarina's state tourist board is based at Rua Felipe Schmidt 249, on the 8th floor (Mon–Fri 8am–7pm; ☎48 3212 6328, turismo.sc.gov.br).

ACCOMMODATION

Most tourists choose to stay at nearby beaches and resorts (see page 578), but staying in Florianópolis itself has the benefit of **direct bus services** to other parts of the island. It's not cheap, though, and accommodation is snapped up quickly in high season. **Conferences** – becoming more frequent – can also double prices and sell out rooms.

Eco Box Hostel Rua Conselheiro Mafra 847 ☎48 3025 3945, ecoboxhostel.com.br; map p.574. Hostel near the bus station that features tiny plywood a/c cubicles ensuring a modicum of privacy, and clean, modern bathrooms. The smallest singles are *very* small (two square metres for just R$43), but you can opt for bigger doubles (five square metres). Parking R$20/day. **R$100**

Faial Prime Suítes Rua Felipe Schmidt 603 ☎48 3225 2766, hotelfaial.com.br; map p.574. One of the city centre's oldest business hotels with a traditional-looking lobby and spacious contemporary-style rooms. The staff are helpful and the rates are good value – there's also a pool. Parking R$21/day. **R$275**

Floripa Hostel Rua Duarte Schutel 227 ☎48 3225 3781, floripahostel.com.br; map p.574. Everything you would expect from an HI hostel (linens and lockers, healthy buffet breakfast), though, as in the rest of town, you'll find yourself paying more than elsewhere in the region. It fills rapidly in summer, so get here early. R$10 cheaper for HI members. No parking. Dorms **R$65**, doubles **R$145**

Ibis Av Rio Branco 37 ☎48 3216 0000, ibis.com; map p.574. A typical Ibis package featuring small, well laid-out a/c rooms and friendly, efficient service. Note that breakfast is R$23 extra, and on-site parking is a prohibitive R$21/hr. **R$235**

Slaviero Baía Norte Florianópolis Av Beira Mar Norte 220 ☎48 3229 3144, slavierohoteis.com.br; map p.574. Pleasant rooms, but be sure to ask for one facing the ocean. Though the corridors seem dark and dingy, the rooms are modern, bright and clean, with cable TV, balcony and a/c. Although just a short walk from good bars and restaurants, it's a longer trek into the commercial centre itself. Parking R$18/day. **R$240**

Valerim Plaza Rua Felipe Schmidt 705 ☎48 2106 0200, hotelvalerim.com.br; map p.574. A solid, centrally located business hotel with contemporary, stylish a/c rooms (some sleeping up to six), equipped with LCD TV and *frigobar*. Parking R$20/day. **R$270**

EATING

Come evening, there's very little life in the commercial centre around Praça XV de Novembro. Instead, people head for the **bars and restaurants** that spread out along the **Beira Mar Norte**, a dual carriageway that skirts the north of the city, lined with condo high-rises, and the parallel **Almirante Lamego**, or make for much more fashionable **Lagoa** (see page 582). Where Mauro Ramos meets the Beira Mar, the giant **Beiramar Shopping mall** (Mon–Sat 10am–10pm) contains dozens of chain outlets in the 3/F food court.

Botequim Floripa Av Rio Branco 632 ☎48 3333 1234, www.botequimfloripa.com.br; map p.574. Old-fashioned bar with a lively happy hour and cold beer on tap, which also serves up a great-value set lunch daily (R$15.90). Mon–Sat 11.30am–2.30pm & 5pm–1.30am.

★ **Box 32** Mercado Público ☎48 3224 5588, box32.com.br; map p.574. Seafood specialist and meeting place of the local glitterati who come to slurp oysters and munch prawns (try the *pastel de camarão*). That said, it's not as expensive as you might fear, with most meals setting you back R$30–35. Mon–Fri 10am–8pm, Sat 10am–3pm.

Delícias Portuguesas Rua Visconde de Ouro Preto 559 ☎48 3224 6448; map p.574. An authentic Portuguese restaurant, specializing predictably in fish (lots of cod). Although meals are rather expensive (mains R$62–65), you can just opt for some *petiscos* (snacks) – the *bolinhos de bacalhau* (R$9) are superb. Tues–Sat 11.30am–11.30pm.

Miyoshi Av Beira Mar Norte 1068 ☎48 3225 5050, miyoshi.com.br; map p.574. Florianópolis's best Asian restaurant with a choice of a buffet (including a good

LGBT FLORIPA

Florianópolis has developed a major gay scene over the last few years, with its own annual **Gay Pride** events in September (aka Floripa Gay Carnival) and numerous bars and clubs catering to the LGBT community. Note that most bars in the city are gay-friendly – including *Box 32* (see page 576). The nudist beach at **Praia da Galheta** (north of Mole) is the primary gay beach on the island.

EATING

Fairy Land Cupcakes Caminho dos Açores 1740, Santo Antônio de Lisboa ⓣ48 3209 7462; map p.574. Floripa even has its very own gay-friendly café and cake shop, located north of the city in Santo Antonio. Tues–Sun 2–8pm.

NIGHTLIFE

★ **Bar do Deca** Praia Mole ⓣ48 3232 2052, ⓦbardodeca.com.br. Floripa's most famous gay beach bar is on the east coast of the island (see page 581), hosting major dance parties year-round, especially on Sundays. Daily 9am–midnight.

Cabaret Club Rua Menino Deus 47 ⓣ48 3324 0102; map p.574. The old *Mix Café* was reborn as the *Cabaret Club* in 2017, with wild party nights and a top sound system (cover from R$15). Fri–Sun 9pm–7am.

Conca Club Av Rio Branco 729 ⓣ48 3024 4969, ⓦconca.com.br; map p.574. This is the city's major late-night party house, with resident and guest DJs spinning electro, two dancefloors and five bars. Fri & Sat 11.45pm–8am.

sushi selection; R$50–70) and an à la carte menu featuring mainly Japanese dishes, though also with a few Chinese and Thai options too. Mon–Thurs & Sun 6–11pm, Fri & Sat 6–11.30pm.

★ **Rita Maria Lagosteria** Rua Henrique Valgas 318 ⓣ48 4009 2442; map p.574. One of the city's hottest gourmet restaurants is definitely worth a splurge, with a fabulous spread of seafood from the signature giant lobsters and fresh oysters to sea urchin and fresh fish (mains $70–150). Finish with guava ice cream. It's small, so call ahead or go early. Daily 11.30am–11.30pm.

DRINKING AND NIGHTLIFE

Cervejaria Devassa Rua Bocaiúva 2198 ⓣ48 3304 9800, ⓦcervejariadevassa.com.br; map p.574. Buzzing local outpost of the national beer chain, serving all its prime pours on draught, plus a menu of Brazilian favourites. Wed–Sun 6pm–2am.

★ **Fields Floripa** Av Paulo Fontes 1250 ⓣ048 3025 6646, ⓦfieldsfloripa.com.br; map p.574. Popular club featuring live *sertanejo*, a musical style that has its origins in the Brazilian countryside (it's usually translated as "country") and one of the most popular genres in Brazil today. Cover R$50–100 (parking is R$30). Wed, Fri & Sat 11pm–5am.

The Roof Lounge Av Beira Mar Norte 2746 (Majestic Palace Hotel) ⓣ48 3231 8000, ⓦtheroof.com.br; map p.574. Roof-top hotel lounge bar (with the *Black Sheep* sushi bar), with sensational views along the seafront, plush armchair and couch seating and an expensive cocktail list. Wed–Sat 7.30pm–4am.

DIRECTORY

Money and exchange Banks are located on Rua Felipe Schmidt and by Praça XV de Novembro.

Pharmacies Farmacia Bela Vista, Rua Tenente Silveira 110. For homeopathic remedies try Farmacia Homeopática Jaqueline, Rua Felipe Schmidt 413.

Post office The main post office is at Praça XV de Novembro 242 (Mon–Fri 9am–5pm & Sat 8am–noon).

Ilha Santa Catarina

Beyond the city of Florianópolis, **Ilha Santa Catarina** is noted throughout Brazil for its beaches, Mediterranean-like scenery and traditional fishing villages – the fishing boats, lacemakers, folklore, cuisine and the colonial architecture add to the allure. The island has a subtropical climate, rarely cold in winter and with a summer heat that is tempered by refreshing South Atlantic breezes. Nevertheless, don't expect an untouched paradise. The island is peppered with resorts and holiday condos, and is surprisingly built up, with its mostly narrow roads often clogging up with local traffic regardless of tourists – this is one of the richest parts of Brazil and it looks it. To make the most of the island you need to take your time and get off the roads; there are still some sections of coast that remain wild and untouched, but you'll often need to hike to reach them.

The following account assumes a clockwise route around the island from Florianópolis – note that locals refer to the whole island as Florianópolis, with the city known simply as *centro*.

GETTING AROUND — ILHA SANTA CATARINA

By bus/minibus The island has several local bus terminals, so be prepared to change if travelling extensively by bus (transfers are free). The standard bus fare is R$3.90 – If you buy a stored-value card (*cartão magnético*) the rate drops to R$3.71. Faster, a/c yellow minibuses – called *executivos* (R$6.50–8.50) – also zip between the main beaches.

By taxi Taxi meters start at R$4.60 (airport taxis start at R$7), and are only really economical travelling close to Florianópolis.

By car Despite the existence of a good bus network, this is one place where renting a car (see page 575) should be seriously considered, especially if you have limited time and want to see as much of the island as possible: the roads are all excellent and well signposted, though horribly congested in summer and all year round at rush hour.

Santo Antônio de Lisboa and around

Founded in 1698, picturesque **SANTO ANTÔNIO DE LISBOA** lies just off the main highway (SC-401), some 17km north of Florianópolis. It's one of the island's oldest, most attractive and least-spoilt settlements, the houses almost all painted white with dark blue sash windows – in typical Azorean style. As was the case with most of the island's villages, Santo Antônio has its origins with the arrival of immigrants from the Azores, and the present-day inhabitants – who still refer to themselves as being Azorean – retain many traditions of the islands from which their forefathers came. Fishing, rather than catering to the needs of tourists, remains the principal activity, and the waters offshore are used to farm mussels and oysters.

Coming into the centre, look for the all-white colonial **Igreja Nossa Senhora das Necessidades** on Praça Getulio Vargas, overlooking the water, which dates back to 1750 (open for Mass only; Sat 6.30pm, Sun 9.30am). From here you can wander along waterfront **Rua Quinze de Novembro** (with views back to Floripa), or parallel **Rua Cônego Serpa**.

Around 3km further north along a pretty coast road lies the sleepy fishing village of **SAMBAQUI** – you'll have to retrace your steps back to the main highway to continue north.

ARRIVAL AND DEPARTURE — SANTO ANTÔNIO DE LISBOA AND AROUND

By bus Bus #212, #222, #310, #331 and #332 run from the TICEN in Florianópolis to Terminal de Integração de Santo Antônio de Lisboa (TISAN) on SC-401.

ACCOMMODATION AND EATING

SANTO ANTÔNIO DE LISBOA

★ **Cantinho da Ostra** Rua 15 de Novembro, 280 ⓣ 48 235 2296; map p.573. Shack bar on the beach directly in front of the church, with plastic tables scattered in the sand, serving fried fish, shrimp *pastels* (R$6–7) and the freshest of oysters (dozen from R$18–20). Cash only. Fri–Sun noon–6pm.

Marisqueira Sintra Rua XV de Novembro 147 ⓣ 48 3234 4219, ⓦ marisqueirasintra.com.br; map p.573. Gourmet seafood from lauded chef Andréia de Paula, who is famed for her garlicky shrimp dishes, such as *camarão à guilho* served in a small pan with bread (mains R$45–146). There is also a decent Portuguese wine list. March–Nov Mon & Wed–Sat noon–3.30pm & 7.30–11.30pm, Sun noon–4pm & 7.30–11pm; Dec–Feb Mon & Wed–Sat noon–11.30pm, Sun noon–11pm.

Pousada Mar de Dentro Rua Caminho dos Açores 1929 ⓣ 48 3235 1521, ⓦ pousadamardedentro.com.br; map p.573. Gorgeous setting overlooking the waterfront, with comfy a/c rooms (plus TV and fridge) and a tiny pool. R$320

★ **Villa da Porto** Rua 15 de Novembro 123 ⓣ 48 3234 1000, ⓦ villadoporto.com.br; map p.573. This fine Spanish and Azorean seafood restaurant (think tapas and *paella marinera*) on the waterfront is housed in a mansion dating back to 1750 (Emperor Dom Pedro II allegedly stayed here in 1845). Mains range from R$44 (risotto) to R$149 (panko shrimp on rice for two). Mon, Tues & Thurs–Sat 11.30am–11pm, Sun 11.30am–5pm.

SAMBAQUI

★ **Restinga Recanto** Rodovia Rafael da Rocha Pires 2759 ☎48 3235 2093, restingarestaurante.com.br; map p.573. This restaurant with whimsical papier-mâché decor overlooks the beach outside of Sambaqui on the road from Santo Antônio. It's justly famed for its views and specialities such as *camarão na moranga* (shrimp in pumpkin) and *entrevero do dandão* (a huge plate of seafood). Mains cost R$50–120. March–Nov Tues–Sat 11am–midnight, Sun 11am–6pm; Dec–Feb Tues–Sun 11am–midnight.

Jurerê

The island's booming resort industry kicks into gear at **JURERÊ**, 26km north of Florianópolis, a 4km wedge of plush condos, hotels and holiday homes that lines the entire, sandy curve of **Praia Jurerê**. The beach is fabulous but the resort is rather sedate – it feels a bit like a Florida retirement community.

Fortaleza de São José

Servidão José Cardoso de Oliveira 3547 (end of Av dos Búzios) • Daily 9am–noon & 1–5pm; Jan & Feb till 7pm • R$8 • Buses (#272) terminate at the base of the headland (where the single-lane road begins)

Drive to the far western end of Praia Jurerê and the road becomes a narrow, single lane as it climbs the Ponta Grossa headland to the **Fortaleza de São José**, the island's only major historic remnant. Built in 1740 to guard the northern approaches to the city, this enigmatic stone fortress has been sensitively restored, with several bronze cannons peering out and the main buildings converted into small museums – the views of the coast and across to the mainland are stunning. The Casa do Comandante at the top contains archeological bits and pieces (mostly glass, animal bones and pottery found on the site), while the Paiol da Polvora (storeroom) above charts the history of the fort (in Portuguese). Below, the Quartel da Tropa (barracks) contains an exhibit on local lace-making (with some English labels).

Praia do Forte

Along the road from the Fortaleza de São José, the **Praia do Forte** is a totally undeveloped stretch of white sand below the fort, with just a couple of laidback beach bars and a car park (this is the end of the road). Keep walking south and you'll find a series of coves fringed by luxuriant vegetation between here and Daniela – they can be reached by climbing over the rocks that separate one from another.

Daniela

DANIELA, a few kilometres south of Jurerê, is now similarly developed, though the condos are separated from its great swathe of sand by a thick barrier of vegetation, making this beach a lot more appealing. Another bonus: the beach extends all the way to the tip of the **Ponta da Luz** promontory, where it is almost always deserted.

Canasvieras

Just around the headland to the east of Jurerê, the long, gently curving bay of **CANASVIERAS** is the most crowded of the northern resorts, largely geared towards *paulistanos*, Argentine and Uruguayan families who own or rent houses near to the beach. Most of the bars along the beach (Av das Nações) cater to the tourists, playing Argentine and North American pop music, and serving Argentine snacks accompanied by Brazilian beer. By walking away from the concentration of bars at the centre of the beach, towards the east and **Ponta das Canas**, it's usually possible to find a relatively quiet spot.

ARRIVAL AND DEPARTURE — **CANASVIERAS**

By bus From Canasvieras (TICAN) you can take: #842 to Lagoa Da Conceição (TILAG); #276 to Balneário Canasvieras; #231 or #233 to Floripa (TICEN).

Praia da Lagoinha and around

The bay to the east of Canasvieras is now one long strip of development, through dusty Cachoeira do Bom Jesus and Ponta das Canas to the utterly soulless condo resort of **Praia Brava** on the other side of the headland. Tucked in between, at the extreme northern tip of the island, is the kilometre-long **Praia da Lagoinha** – by far the prettiest beach hereabouts and with the island's warmest water. Seagulls and turkey vultures happily share the sand with sunbathers. Though the beach here is also backed by developments, these are low-key, and separated by a swathe of seagrape and small bushes. The only way to access the beach is via the parking area at the eastern end.

The Bottle House

On the road to Ingleses, Rua Epitacio Bittencourt 120 • casaarteflorianopolis.com

If you're driving, don't miss the spectacular **Casa Arte** – aka "Bottle House" – just south of Praia da Lagoinha, where banks of coloured bottles and sculptures line the road. Created by local artist Jaime Machado Riccio over fifteen years, the installations total around 2.5km in length.

ACCOMMODATION — **PRAIA DA LAGOINHA AND AROUND**

★ **Pousada da Vigia** Rua Conêgo Walmor Castro 291 48 3284 1789, pousadadavigia.com.br; map p.573. Located just metres from the shore, this is one of the most exclusive places to stay on the island. Once the private residence of a former state governor, the property has been turned into a *pousada* of understated luxury. R$360

Ingleses and around

The beaches of the island's east coast are wilder and not as developed as the north – in part because of the heavy surf that pounds them year-round. **INGLESES** is another major resort and traffic bottleneck that lines the wonderful, balmy waters of the 5km-long **Praia dos Ingeles** and sprawls into the Rio Vermelho valley to the south. Like Canasvieras, it's popular with Argentine and Brazilian tourists, but northerners will find it a poor imitation of popular beach resorts in Spain or Florida.

Praia do Santinho, beyond Ingleses, is a relatively tranquil stretch of sand, separated from the rest of the island by an astounding range of **dunes** – sand boarding and hiking are popular activities here.

EATING — **INGLESES AND AROUND**

★ **Chez Altamiro** Rodovia João Gualberto Soares 6065 (SC-406), Ingleses do Rio Vermelho 48 3269 7727, chezaltamiro.com.br; map p.573. Inland from the main Ingleses resort, this is one of the most outstanding, and surprising, restaurants on the island. It's run by chef Altamiro Nunes Filho, who, despite having never set foot in France, cooks extremely good traditional French food (with wine, reckon on at least R$200 a head). The restaurant is in the middle of nowhere, but is easily recognized by the tricolour that adorns the outside of the wooden building. Reservations strongly advised. Daily 8pm–midnight.

Praia da Moçambique

Stretching for 12km along the east coast, **Praia da Moçambique** (also known as Praia Grande) is the longest beach on the island. Good for surfing, it's also one of the least developed, thanks to the **Parque Estadual do Rio Vermelho**, a huge expanse of pine trees that takes up most of its hinterland. The beach is signposted off coastal SC-406 – drive here if you crave seclusion.

Barra da Lagoa and around

BARRA DA LAGOA, the village at the eastern entrance to the inland **Lagoa da Conceição**, has succeeded fairly well in allowing tourism to develop alongside the inhabitants' traditional livelihood – fishing. Indeed, there are no resorts here, with **surfing** the dominant activity – its gentle swells make this a good place to learn and it's also the home of world champion Jacqueline Silva. The village lies just behind the beach (off SC-406), which is itself the southern extension of Praia da Moçambique.

For a bit more seclusion, cross the river at the southeastern end of Barra da Lagoa's beach (via the Ponte Pêncil, a rickety suspended footbridge), and walk across the headland to the very pretty **Prainha do Leste**, a small cove flanked by forbidding rock formations where beach parties are often held in summer.

Projeto TAMAR

Rua Professor Ademir Francisco, Barra da Lagoa • Daily: late Dec–early March 10am–7pm; early March–late Dec 9.30am–5.30pm; turtle feedings at 3.30pm • R$15 • ⓣ 48 3236 2015, ⓦ tamar.org.br • Parking opposite is R$10/day

The southern headquarters of **Projeto TAMAR** (Save the Turtles) is located on the western side of Barra da Lagoa (signposted from SC-406), a small but informative showcase for their conservation work but primarily of interest for the always adorable **turtles** on view (all injured off Brazil's coast). You'll mostly see giant leatherbacks, loggerheads, Olive Ridley and hawksbill turtles here, all lounging in various pools, and while they don't seem entirely happy to be cooped up, at least they are still alive. Labels are in English and Portuguese.

ACCOMMODATION — BARRA DA LAGOA AND AROUND

Floripa Hostel Rua Inelzyr Bauer Bertoli 273 ⓣ 48 3232 4491, ⓦ floripahostel.com.br; map p.573. This laidback outpost of the island's HI-affiliated chain is the best place to crash near the beach, with fan-cooled dorms (four beds), breakfast, 24hr reception and communal kitchen. HI member rates are R$ 10 lower. Dorms **R$75**, doubles **R$250**

Praia Mole

South of Barra da Lagoa, the main road (SC-406) passes **Praia Mole**, one of the most beautiful beaches in Brazil and slightly hidden beneath low-lying cliffs. Mole is extremely popular with young people but, rather surprisingly, commercial activity has remained low-key, probably because there's a deep drop-off right at the water's edge – it's another major surf beach, and the road here can be a real bottleneck in summer. Park where you can – the small official car park charges R$4 per hour or R$10 per day.

ACCOMMODATION AND EATING — PRAIA MOLE

Sunset Backpackers Rodovia Jornalista Manoel de Menezes 631 ⓣ 48 3232 0141, ⓦ sunsetbackpackers.com; map p.573. Chilled-out hostel overlooking the bay from a ridge near Praia Mole, with a mix of private rooms and dorms that have fans and a/c, free *caipirinhas* for residents (daily 7.30–8.30pm), a hearty Brazilian barbecue on Sundays and the friendly *Elementum Temple* bar, specializing in the microbrews of Cervejaria Elementum. Bar Wed–Sun 4pm–1am. Dorms **R$40**, doubles **R$160**

Praia da Joaquina

A short drive south of Praia Mole, on a signposted spur road from SC-406, **Praia da Joaquina** is extremely popular with surfers – particularly so during the Brazilian national surf championships, held annually in the last week of January. The water's cold, however, and the sea rough and only really suitable for strong swimmers. Parking here is R$10 per day.

The road to the beach is dotted with hostels and surf shops, before it climbs to the top of another range of mighty **sand dunes**. If you have the energy, climb to the top where you'll be rewarded with the most spectacular views in all directions. The dunes are also a popular location for paragliding and sandboarding – no skill is required if you sit, rather than stand, on a board as you hurtle down a dune (boards are available to rent at the roadside for R$15/hr).

ACCOMMODATION — PRAIA DA JOAQUINA

Cris Plage Hotel Av Prefeito Acácio Garibaldi São Thiago 2399 ⓣ 48 3232 5104, ⓦ crishotel.com.br; map p.573. Modern hotel with spacious rooms for up to five people overlooking the beach, with a/c, fridge, TV and balcony, plus high-quality art gallery during the summer. **R$220**

9

Joaquina Beach Hotel Av Prefeito Acácio Garibaldi São Thiago 2323 ⊕48 3232 5059, ⊕joaquinabeachhotel.com.br; map p.573. Usually booked solidly in the summer, with simple en-suite a/c rooms that have tiled floors and TVs. (public areas only) R$190

Pousada Bizkaia Av Prefeito Acácio Garibaldi São Thiago 682 ⊕48 3232 5273, ⊕pousadabizkaia.com; map p.573. Some 1.4km from the beach on the road to Lagoa, this rustic choice is a relatively good deal, with hearty buffet breakfasts, clean, a/c rooms and friendly staff. R$239

Centrinho da Lagoa

The serene lagoon in the centre of the island, **Lagoa da Conceição** is very popular among families and others who want to swim, canoe or windsurf. **CENTRINHO DA LAGOA** (usually simply referred to as Lagoa), a bustling little town at the southern end of the lagoon, is a very pleasant place to stay, with frequent bus services from here into Florianópolis and to the east-coast beaches, and a post office (Mon–Fri 9am–5pm), pharmacy, banks and supermarkets.

There are also numerous restaurants and bars on the main road through the town, **Avenida das Rendeiras**, from Praça Pio XII near the bridge over the canal, to the main strip of **Rua Manoel Severino de Oliveira**. Former number one tennis player **Gustavo Kuerten** was born in Floripa and now lives in Lagoa, teaching and playing tennis – you might see him around town.

ACTIVITIES — CENTRINHO DA LAGOA

The highway along the southern lagoon from town is lined with outfits offering "Stand Up" (paddleboarding) for R$20, while cycling is a great way to get around.

Floripa Bike Tours Rua Henrique Veras do Nascimento 240 ⊕48 9996 2031, ⊕floripabiketour.com. Well-established bike rental and tour operator, with a range of sport bikes (R$35/day), mountain bikes (R$60/day) and even electric bikes R$80. Daily tours range across the island ($49–120). Rentals 9am–5pm.

ACCOMMODATION

Hostel Way2Go Rua Rita Lourenço da Silveira 139 ⓣ48 3364 6004; map p.582. Well-located hostel near the bridge in Centrinho, with mixed and female-only dorms. Washing machines available for guests' use, TV room and excellent kitchen space. No curfew. Dorms R$60

Magic Monkey Hostel Rua José Henrique Veras 469 ⓣ48 3065 0075, ⓦmagicmonkeyhostel.com; map p.582. Friendly hostel that's convenient for the local bus station (TILAG) in Centrinho and where staff make you feel part of the extended family. There's a sundeck, jacuzzi, pool table, huge widescreen TV, basic dorms and rooms with a/c. Dorms R$36, doubles R$130

Mama Africa Hostel Rua João Josino da Silva 196 ⓣ48 3030 0396; map p.582. Large modern doubles, shared terrace with hammocks and a/c dorms (mixed and female breakfasts), plus excellent breakfasts. Dorms R$75, doubles R$200

★ **Tucano House Backpackers** Rua das Araras 229 ⓣ48 3207 8287, ⓦtucanohouse.com; map p.582. Popular place with six dorms and five doubles (all with a/c), some of which have lagoon views, though this hostel closes in low season. Serves meals every night in an outside patio area, which makes a great place to meet fellow travellers. There are also half-price drinks at the bar between 5pm and 7pm. Other services include a pool, surfboard rental and bikes (R$40/day). Open Dec to mid-March; cash only. Dorms R$55, doubles R$220

EATING

Books & Beers Rua Senador Ivo D'Aquino 103 ⓣ48 3206 6664, ⓦbooksbeers.com.br; map p.582. Relaxed spot for a cold beer or seafood (mains R$31–60), with a cool terrace overlooking the lake and a cosy interior lined with books. Some of the craft beers are excellent but most are pricey (R$35–50); check before ordering. Tues–Fri 5pm–midnight, Sat 12.30pm–midnight, Sun 12.30–10.30pm.

DNA Natural Rua Manoel Severino de Oliveira 680 ⓣ48 3207 3441, ⓦdnanatural.com.br; map p.582. Chain specializing in natural, healthy foods, including tasty wraps and huge mixed salads. There's also an exhaustive range of tropical juices and shakes (R$6–12). Daily 8am–midnight.

Querubim Av Henrique Veras do Nascimento 255 ⓣ48 3232 8743; map p.582. Arguably the best-value place to have lunch in Centrinho. The delicious buffet includes chicken, beef, shrimp and salads (around R$44/kg or R$26 as much as you like). 11.30am–3.30pm and afterwards for snacks until 4am.

DRINKING AND NIGHTLIFE

Lagoa is one of the liveliest nightspots on the island during the **summer** and at **weekends** throughout the year, with restaurants always crowded and people overflowing into the street from the bars until the small hours of the morning.

Black Swan Rua Manoel Severino de Oliveira 592 ⓣ48 3234 5682, ⓦtheblackswan.com.br; map p.582. Faux-English pub and sports bar run by a British expat, which is popular with Brazilians and an international crowd. There's standard-priced local beer on tap, plus a range of expensive imported beer from Europe. Hosts live music most nights (cover R$10–20) happy hour 5–9.30pm. Mon–Fri 5pm–midnight, Sat & Sun 10.30am–2am.

Costa da Lagoa

There are some attractive beaches on the isolated northwest shore of Lagoa da Conceição – one of the most beautiful parts of the island – around **COSTA DA LAGOA**, a charming fishing village barely touched by tourism. The area is impossible to reach by road and involves either a three-hour walk along a trail skirting the lagoon, or an hour's boat ride. Once at Costa da Lagoa, a ten-minute walk along a rough trail will take you to the 6m-high *cachoeira* (waterfall), where you can take a refreshing dip in the natural pool. Back in the village there are swimming beaches and a couple of places to eat.

ARRIVAL AND DEPARTURE — COSTA DA LAGOA

By boat Boats leave every hour or so (7.10am–11.30pm; returning 5.50am–9.30pm; R$10) from the Passeois de Barco beneath the bridge in Centrinho da Lagoa, stopping off at isolated houses, restaurants and a couple of minor sights: a traditional Azorean flour mill and a ruined mansion.

Campeche

The bustling, fairly unattractive town of **CAMPECHE** lies off the main highway (SC-406) in the south of the island, and if you drive all the way to the end of the main drag

(Av Pequeno Príncipe) you'll come to its exceptional, untrammelled beach, **Praia do Campeche**. With the **Ilha do Campeche** just offshore – but only accessible by dinghy in high season (see below) – it's definitely a contender for the most beautiful stretch of the island's coast, but due to the strong current and often ferocious surf fewer people are attracted here than to the beaches to the north. Consequently, there's been comparatively little construction, and only a few houses and a couple of beach bars are concentrated around the end of the road (where there's free parking).

Armação and around

The fishing village of **ARMAÇÃO** (take Av Antônio Borges de Santos off the main highway, SC-406) boasts a stunning location, backed by hills, and is a traditional place largely untouched by mass tourism. There's an attractive boardwalk and beach – though the waves and currents are unforgiving – and well-marked trails leading to more protected coves to the south. The village centre, some 23km from Floripa, lies around the small chapel of **Sant' Ana e São Joaquin**, built in 1772 but restored since then, and a cluster of simple restaurants.

Ilha do Campeche

Walk across the bridge at the southern end of Armação beach to the small island offshore to take a boat operated by the local fishermen's association to **Ilha do Campeche**. Here the pristine white-sand beach (Praia da Enseada) is protected from any form of development – only four hundred visitors are permitted at any one time, along with a few people selling refreshments. There are around a hundred ancient petroglyphs on the island and several trails, though you officially need to pay for a guide to access these.

ARRIVAL AND DEPARTURE — ARMAÇÃO AND AROUND

By boat The boat service from Armação to Ilha do Campeche costs R$80–90 return/person. It takes about 30–40min to complete the 3km crossing, with boats running 9am–1pm; the latest you can stay is 3.30pm. To explore the inland trails you must pay another R$10–25. In high season (Dec–Feb) rubber dinghies run across to the island from Campeche (see above) but these will be much more expensive (R$120–150).

ACCOMMODATION

★ **Pousada Alemdomar** Rua Tulio de Oliveira 403 ⓣ48 3237 5600, ⓦalemdomar.com.br; map p.573. This enticing B&B, 250m south of the village near the Lagoa do Peri, has brightly coloured rooms (all of which have either a terrace or a balcony, some of which have sea views) and an extremely relaxing atmosphere. R$290

Pousada Pénareia Rua Hermes Guedes da Fonseca 207 ⓣ48 3338 1616, ⓦpousadapenareia.com.br; map p.573. Exclusive accommodation right on the beach, with big, healthy breakfast, kayaks, bikes, cable TV, massages and DVDs. R$320

Pântano do Sul

Practically the end of the road at the southern end of the island, **PÂNTANO DO SUL** is a genuine, no-frills fishing village at the head of a well-protected bay with a mountainous backdrop. The village itself is not that attractive, but you can drive all the way down to the beach and park on the sand among numerous fishing boats, enjoy the views of the prettier houses on the cliffs and sample excellent seafood. Tourism has had only a minimal impact on the inhabitants' lives, and Azorean traditions have remained strong, most visibly during **Carnaval** when brass bands wend their way through the streets and along the beach (the rhythms are very different from the familiar beat of samba drums).

EATING — PÂNTANO DO SUL

★ **Bar do Arante** Rua Abelardo Otácilio Gomes 254 ⓣ48 3237 7022; map p.573. Right at the end of the road and the best of several restaurants right on the beach, *Bar do Arante* is lauded for serving some of the best seafood on the island in a whimsical dining room smothered in tiny bits of paper scribbled on by patrons since 1958. Seafood mains cost R$60–180. Daily 11.30am–midnight.

Ribeirão da Ilha

Some 36km south of Florianópolis, with views across the misty mountains of the mainland, **RIBEIRÃO DA ILHA** is the largest oyster producer in Brazil and vies with Santo Antônio (see page 578) as the most attractive Azorean village on the island – the locals here still speak an Azorean dialect, which even if you understand Portuguese can be difficult to follow.

The main road passes below the lovely bougainvillaea-lined plaza, topped by the **Igreja de Nossa Senhora da Lapa do Ribeirão**, built in 1806, and runs along a picture-perfect waterfront, replete with top-class restaurants, colourful houses and domino tables along the water. Intricately fashioned lace tablecloths, mats and other handicrafts are often displayed for sale outside some of the houses.

ARRIVAL AND EATING — RIBEIRÃO DA ILHA

By bus The village is accessible via route #561.

Muqueca da Ilha Rodovia Baldicero Filomeno 7487 ⓣ48 3232 7676; map p.573. This gorgeous old house and Carvalho family restaurant offers a slightly more affordable experience compared to *Ostradamus* (full meals for two from R$80), though the fresh seafood and tasty house dish (*muqueca* – a rich seafood stew) are almost as good. Tues–Sat 11am–11pm, Sun 11am–6pm.

★ **Ostradamus** Rodovia Baldicero Filomeno 7640 ⓣ48 3337 5711, ⓦostradamus.com.br; map p.573. Justly popular spot serving up creative dishes such as a dozen oysters with martini and lemon, as well as delicious mains. Despite the high prices and long waits for tables (which cover the narrow pier from the main restaurant into the bay), this is easily one of the island's best restaurants. Try the seafood risotto, washed down with local wine (most mains R$110–140). Tues–Sat noon–11pm, Sun noon–4pm.

Costa Verde e Mar

Heading north on Santa Catarina's coastal highway (the BR-101) from Florianópolis is a region dubbed the **Costa Verde e Mar** by the tourism authorities. It's the magnificent **beaches** that take centre stage here, though much of the seafront is lined with ugly development and high-rises. Travelling by bus, the obvious stopover is the free-wheeling party town of **Balneário Camboriú**, though some of the finest bathing and surfing to be found lies on the **Porto Belo** peninsula, closer to Floripa. With a car you'll have a lot more options, though the heavy traffic on the main highway is not for the faint-hearted.

Porto Belo

Less than two hours from Florianópolis, the town of **PORTO BELO** is a fishing community that lies at the hub of a series of idyllic beaches clinging to the adjacent peninsula, and is easily reached by bus. The most enticing stretches of sand and warm, aquamarine waters are at **Bombas** and **Bombinhas**, 5km and 8km east of Porto Belo respectively and separated from one another by a rocky promontory. The bay in which they're found is extremely pretty, with rich vegetation behind the beach, and waves suitable for inexperienced **surfers**. South of Bombinhas, if you're looking for open sea and more powerful waves, the east-facing **Praia do Mariscal** is better, but should be braved by only the most expert of surfers.

ARRIVAL AND GETTING AROUND — PORTO BELO

By bus Viação Navegantes (ⓣ0800 724 1234, ⓦviacaonavegantes.net) runs buses between Florianópolis (65km) and Porto Belo (Mon–Fri 7am, 9am, 11.30am, 2pm, 5pm & 6.30pm; Sat 8.30am, 2pm & 5.30pm, Sun 8.30am & 6.30pm). Praiana (ⓣ0800 647 8400, ⓦpraiana.com.br) runs buses every 20–50min between Balneário Camboriú and Porto Belo (1hr; R$5.85), though services reduce at the weekends. Frequent buses zip between Porto Belo and Bombas (15min; R$4) and Bombinhas (30min; R$4).

ACCOMMODATION

Pousada Gaúcha Rua Castanheira 27, Bombinhas ⓣ47 3369 2472, ⓦpousadagaucha.com.br. The best beach hotel in the area, though it's pricey in high season. Rooms are fairly standard, though the breakfast

9

is excellent, and there's a full gym and jacuzzi, but this is really all about the prime location. R$355

Pousada Villa Verde Rua Domingos Jaques 867, Perequê, Porto Belo 47 3369 8994, pousadavilaverde.tur.br. Right in town on the edge of the beach (with its own beach chairs and umbrellas), with spacious, modern rooms and a heated swimming pool. R$150

Toca Da Moreia Rua Sardinha 51, Bombinhas 47 3393 7470, tocadamoreia.com.br. Best budget digs in the area, which are very close to the beach and offer a choice of spotless a/c dorms or doubles, plus a decent breakfast thrown in. The bar attached offers snacks and cheap booze. Dorms R$60, doubles R$140

Balneário Camboriú

If you are travelling in search of the Santa Catarina party scene, look no further than **BALNEÁRIO CAMBORIÚ**, an effervescent resort town 85km north of Florianópolis with a distinctly hedonistic approach to life often dismissed by *cariocas* as the "poor man's Copacabana". Either way, it's a popular summer destination with young Brazilians, Uruguayans and Argentines, and the town is packed out during the peak season (Dec–Feb) with sunbathers and fun-seekers. Indeed, Camboriú has something of a Mediterranean holiday resort feel to it, with its high-rise buildings and pedestrian streets lined with artists peddling souvenirs. The place is not without its charms – not least its 7km-long **Praia Central**, offering safe swimming and golden sand. **Praia do Pinho**, on the other side of the peninsula west of town, is the site of Brazil's first nudist beach.

Cristo Luz

Rua Indonésia 800, Bairro das Nações • April & Sept Wed–Sat 4pm–midnight; May, Aug & June Thurs–Sat 4pm–midnight; July, Oct & Nov Tues–Sat 4pm–midnight; Dec–March Mon–Sat 4pm–midnight; year-round Sun 10am–midnight • 10am–7pm R$15; after 7pm R$30 • 47 3367 4042, cristoluz.com.br

Camboriú even has its own 33m-high Rio-style Christ statue, the **Cristo Luz** (though this one, rather bizarrely, holds a symbol of the sun), completed in 1997 and illuminated at night, casting a faint greenish glow over the town. On summer evenings the park at the foot of the statue is the site of concerts, theatre and poetry recitals.

Parque Unipraias

Av Atlântica 6006 • Daily 9.30am–6pm (last ride 5pm); later hours Dec–Feb • Cable car and park access R$39; ZipRider R$45; Youhooo! R$34 • 47 3210 4567, unipraias.com.br

The forested hillside of Morro da Aguada in the southern part of town is a nature reserve-cum-theme park – the **Parque Unipraias**. You can reach it via the 3.25km **Bondinho** (cable car) that starts at the **Estação Barra Sul** on the Praia Central before shooting up to the **Estação Mata Atlântica** on the summit (240m), offering glorious views over the town, beaches and out to sea. From here you can stroll the trails in the **Parque Ambiental** (same hours; included in price), enjoy the 750m drop on the **ZipRider** zip-line, or the **Youhooo!** 60km per hour toboggan ride. The cable car continues down to the beach at **Praia Laranjeiras**.

ARRIVAL AND INFORMATION — BALNEÁRIO CAMBORIÚ

By bus Camboriú sits on the main Curitiba–Florianópolis highway (BR-101). Buses arrive at the rodoviária (47 3367 2901) on Av Santa Catarina, at the edge of town close to the highway.

Destinations Buenos Aires (1 daily; 28hr); Curitiba (22 daily; 2hr 30min); Florianópolis (38 daily; 1hr 30min); Joinville (26 daily; 1hr 30min); Porto Alegre (9 daily; 8–9hr); Porto Belo (6 daily; 1hr); São Paulo (13 daily; 8–9hr).

Tourist information There is a tourist information office at Av do Estado 5041 (daily 7am–10pm; 47 3367 8005, visitebalneariocamboriu.com.br), but inconveniently located some 2km inland from the beach, just off the main highway into the city.

ACCOMMODATION

Hostel 325 Rua Panama 325 47 99604 8718, 325hostel@gmail.com. Stylish modern hostel with comfy dorms (mixed, male or female), small outdoor courtyard with barbecue in a quiet residential block, a short walk from the beach. Shared kitchen, pool table and sociable clientele, though staff rarely speak English. Dorms R$60

Hotel Mercure Camboriú Av Atlântica 2010 ⓣ 47 3056 9500, ⓦ mercure.com. If you're looking for a little luxury on the beach this is the obvious choice, with all the amenities you'd expect of a five-star chain; huge breakfast buffet (R$35 extra), posh rooms, ocean views and big outdoor pool. Parking R$35/day. R$335

Little Hostel Balneário Camboriú Rua 1500, no. 1555 ⓣ 47 99927 4558, ⓦ hostelbalneariocamboriu.com. Popular hostel, a 15min walk from the beach, with clean, cheap a/c dorms (mixed, male or female), decent breakfast and free cookies. No parking. Dorms R$45

EATING

In addition to the proliferation of **fast-food joints** and *lanchonetes* that you might expect in a town populated by twenty-somethings, there are also some excellent **restaurants** around, with seafood platters featuring heavily on most menus.

O Pharol Av Atlântica 2554, at Rua 2000 ⓣ 47 3367 3800, ⓦ opharol.com.br. Classy seafood restaurant well worth the extra *reais*. The seafood *rodizio* (R$87/person) is something special and includes prawns, lobster, oysters and more. *Feijoada* is served on Wednesday and Saturday. Daily 11am–1am.

Taj Bar Av Atlântica 5710 ⓣ 47 3264 0464, ⓦ tajbar.com.br. Restaurant and bar that turns into a glamorous club, attracting well-heeled twenty-somethings. The menu is Brazilian/Asian fusion food, though the sushi is usually the best item (rolls R$11–15; plates R$21–22). Tues, Wed & Sun 6pm–1am, Thurs–Sat 6pm–2am.

DRINKING AND NIGHTLIFE

Camboriú has a vibrant nightlife aimed mainly at a young crowd who seek loud music, bare flesh and lots of dancing. Most places are on or around Av Atlântica, especially at the southern end, the **Barra Sul**, where you'll find a huge array of beach bars and discos. Things don't start to get lively until well after midnight, and the action continues until after the sun comes up.

Guacamole Av Normando Tedesco 1122 ⓣ 47 3366 0311, ⓦ guacamolemex.com.br. Charismatic Mexican mini-chain with live music, *mariachis* and "*tequileros*" who are only too happy to wet your whistle. Latin dance shows every Tues night add to the experience. Spicy mains from R$45. Mon–Sat 7pm–3am, Sun 7pm–midnight.

Wood's Av Atlântica 4450 ⓣ 47 3081 2810, ⓦ woodsbar.com.br. This popular *sertanejo*-style (country) pub and club chain features top live acts and cold beers served in a beachfront location. Cover usually ranges around R$50–80. Fri & Sat 11pm–5am.

Joinville and around

The largest city in Santa Catarina state, **JOINVILLE** ('join-VEE-lay') is an ever-growing sea of high-rises and a major centre for conferences that boasts one of the highest standards of living in South America. There's not a lot in the way of sights, but it's a fun and friendly place to stay for a night or two, while remnants of its German heritage provide some historical allure. Shops and services are concentrated along Rua Princesa Isabel, Rua XV de Novembro and Rua IX de Março, running parallel and terminating at the Rio Cachoeira. The main plaza – **Praça Nereu Ramos** – is a rather shabby, modern affair, with just one cheap café, domino tables and lots of concrete.

Brief history

Ironically, the region was originally granted to French royalty: François d'Orléans, aka the **Prince of Joinville** and the son of Louis-Philippe of France, was ceded the area as a dowry for marrying the Emperor Dom Pedro II's sister in 1843. However, there's little evidence the prince ever came here (he spent most of his life in Europe), and he sold the land in 1851 to German senator Mathias Schröder, head of a Hamburg-based colonization society. Soon after, 118 German and Swiss immigrants arrived, followed by 74 Norwegians, to exploit the fifty square kilometres of virgin forest, stake out homesteads and establish the "Colônia Dona Francisca" – soon known as Joinville.

From 1852 to 1888, Joinville absorbed 17,000 more German immigrants, developing from an agricultural backwater into the state's foremost industrial city (GM opened

DANCING JOINVILLE

Every July Joinville is host to the **Festival de Dança de Joinville** (Joinville Dance Festival; Ⓦ festivaldedanca.com.br), which is reputed to be the world's largest dance event. Some 5000 dancers take part, over two weeks, with exhibitions, shows, competitions and street dancing.

Not coincidentally, Joinville is the only city outside of Moscow to have a school of the **Bolshoi Ballet**, the renowned Russian ballet company (Escola de Teatro Bolshoi; Ⓣ 47 3422 4070, Ⓦ escolabolshoi.com.br); established here in 2000, the Bolshoi had been inspired by attending the dance festival in the 1990s. You can visit the school at Av José Vieira 315 for tours (often given by dancers; R$5), but these must be arranged in advance by email. Note that it's unlikely any of the guides will speak English. The school also puts on classical ballet performances at the school throughout the year –check the website for dates.

a massive car factory here in 2012). Today little remains of these Germanic roots – Joinville is a thoroughly Brazilian city, albeit with a handful of German-style buildings and bakeries, and a smattering of blue-eyed, blond-haired citizens.

Museu Nacional de Imigração e Colonização

Rua Rio Branco 229 • Tues–Sun 10am–4pm • Free • Ⓣ 47 3433 3736

Joinville's premier historic site is the **Museu Nacional de Imigração e Colonização**, a grand 1870 mansion built for the Prince of Joinville – though the hapless French royal claimant never lived here (whatever you might be told). The three floors of the main building feature rooms decked out with period furniture and a collection of antique musical instruments, but the museum's most interesting features lie in the garden behind the main building. A replica of an old barn contains an impressive collection of historic carriages (some of which resemble American nineteenth-century wagons), while the typical nineteenth-century *enxaimel* farmhouse opposite contains more humble period furnishings and a workshop full of antique tools at the back.

Museu Arqueológico de Sambaqui

Rua Dona Francisca 600 • Tues–Sun 10am–4pm • Free • Ⓣ 47 3433 0114

If you've more than a passing interest in Joinville's history, make time for the superbly organized **Museu Arqueológico de Sambaqui**, where exhibits throw light on the prehistoric cultures of the region and the numerous shell middens (*sambaqui*) that litter the coast.

Cemitério do Imigrante

Rua XV de Novembro 978 • Casa da Memória Mon–Fri 8am–2pm • Free • Ⓣ 47 3433 3732

Around twenty minutes' walk from the centre, the crumbling **Cemitério do Imigrante** is the atmospheric resting place of many of Joinville's pioneer settlers. Founded in 1851 and covering a hillside from which there are fine views of the city, the cemetery is protected as a national monument (though in dire need of restoration). The tombs and headstones serve as testimony to Joinville's Lutheran origins – some three thousand Protestants are thought to have been buried here between 1851 and 1937. The small Casa da Memória at the entrance provides information (the building was constructed in 1857 to house the grave diggers).

ARRIVAL AND INFORMATION — JOINVILLE

By plane The Aeroporto de Joinville-Lauro Carneiro de Loyola (Ⓣ 47 3467 1000) lies 13km north of the city, with flights to Campinas (Azul) and São Paulo (Gol and LATAM). Take a taxi (Ⓣ 47 3467 3337) from here into the centre (around R$65; 25min).

By bus The rodoviária (Ⓣ 47 3433 2991) is 2km southwest of the city centre, reached in 5min by bus (R$4.50) or in half an hour on foot by walking down Rua Ministro Calógeras and then left along Av Kubitschek. Taxis should be around R$13–14 to the centre from here (meters start at R$5.25). Left luggage costs R$5 per item per day.

Destinations Blumenau (15 daily; 2hr); Curitiba (hourly;

2hr); Florianópolis (hourly; 2hr 30min); Porto Alegre (3 daily; 9hr); Rio (2 daily; 15hr); São Francisco do Sul (hourly; 1hr); São Paulo (12 daily; 8hr).

Tourist information Rua XV de Novembro 4305 (daily 8am–8pm; 0800 643 5015).

Post office Rua Felipe Schmidt 173 (Mon–Fri 9am–6pm).

ACCOMMODATION

★ **Germânia** Rua Ministro Calógeras 612 47 3433 9886, hotelgermania.com.br. Excellent hotel that to all appearances is just another brash tower block, but which has extremely comfortable a/c rooms, helpful staff and very friendly owners. Free parking. R$360

Joinville Hostel Rua Dona Francisca 1376 Saguaçú 47 3424 0844, joinvillehostel.com.br. The local HI hostel offers all the usual amenities: hammocks, rental bikes (R$25/day), comfy male- or female-only dorms and a range of private rooms with or without bathroom. Free parking. Prices for HI members are R$5 lower. Dorms R$65, doubles R$139

Príncipe Rua Jerônimo Coelho 27 47 3433 4555, hprincipe.com.br. Solid budget hotel with simple, clean rooms (a/c and cable TV), friendly staff, central location and decent buffet breakfast included. Parking R$13.50/day. R$136

Tannenhof Rua Visconde de Taunay 340 47 3433 8011, tannenhof.com.br. Large luxury hotel in the guise of a kitsch Alpine high-rise, with great views and tiny balconies, spacious rooms with wooden Bavarian touches and cable TV. It's no longer the best hotel in town, but still the most original. Free parking. R$190

EATING AND DRINKING

The days of kitsch German restaurants are long gone in Joinville, with a growing range of **international bars and restaurants** designed to appeal to its upwardly mobile citizens and the hordes of Brazilian conference attendees. The best **food court** is in the Shopping Mueller mall at Rua Senador Felipe Schmidt 235 (shops: Mon–Sat 10am–10pm, Sun 2–8pm; food court Tues–Sun 10am–10pm; muellerjoinville.com.br); it's clean and relatively good value, with plenty of Asian and Brazilian food and the usual fast-food options.

Churrascaria Chimarrão Rua Visconde de Taunay 343 47 3027 7632, chimarraochurrascaria.com.br. Cosy Brazilian steakhouse offering all the usual barbecue cuts and meats, as well as a *rodízio* buffet (around R$74) of pastas and salads, and a range of wines. Tues–Sat 11.30am–2.30pm & 7–10.30pm, Sun 11.30am–2.30pm.

★ **Delicatesse Viktoria** Rua Felipe Schmidt 400 47 3422 0570, delicatesseviktoria.com.br. This small café is a real treat, operated by an Austro-Brazilian family since 1990 (the friendly Viktoria herself was born in Salzburg), and maintaining the city's Germanic traditions. The main event here is *café colonial*, an afternoon tea buffet of glorious cakes, strudel, savoury pies, tea, juice and

DEUTSCH SANTA CATARINA

German immigrants to Santa Catarina started arriving in the 1850s, and by the end of the nineteenth century complete communities had evolved, with flourishing German cultural organizations and a varied German-language press. After Brazil's entry into World War II, restrictions on the use of German were introduced and many German organizations were proscribed, accused of being Nazi fronts. Later, due to the compulsory use of Portuguese in schools, the influence of media and an influx of migrants from other parts of the state to work in the region's industries, the German language appeared to be dying in Santa Catarina. As a result, in **Joinville** and **Blumenau** German is now rarely heard. However, in outlying villages and farming communities such as **Pomerode**, German remains very much alive, spoken everywhere but in government offices.

Recently, too, the German language and Teuto-Brazilian culture have undergone a renaissance for which the German government has provided financial support. Property developers are encouraged to heed supposedly traditional **German architectural styles**, resulting in a plethora of buildings that look very incongruous in the Brazilian subtropics. A more positive development has been the move to protect and restore the houses of the early settlers, especially those built in the most characteristic local building style, that of **enxaimel** ("Fachwerk" in German) – exposed bricks within an exposed timber frame. These houses are seen throughout the region but concentrated around Pomerode. Keen to reap benefits from this cultural awareness, local authorities have initiated pseudo-**German festivals**, such as Blumenau's Munich-inspired Oktoberfest (see page 592) and Pomerode's more authentic Festa Pomerana (see page 596), both of which have rapidly become major tourist draws.

9

coffee (Tues–Sat 3.30–8pm, Mon & Sun 4–7pm; R$55 or R$9.90/100g), regularly attracting the city's most affluent ladies, but the cakes and coffee are top-notch at any time. Mon & Sun 2–8pm, Tues–Sat 10am–9pm.

Doceria São José Av Getúlio Vargas 328 ⓣ 47 3433 2626, ⓦ doceriasaojose.com.br. Local bakery and café established in 1984, which is popular for coffee and cakes (from 95¢). There is also a branch at 1/F Shopping Mueller (see page 589), open daily 10am–10pm. Mon–Fri 6.15am–9.30pm, Sat 7am–8.30pm, Sun 7.30am–8.30pm.

Zum Schlauch Rua Visconde de Taunay 555 ⓣ 47 3422 2909, ⓦ zumschlauch.com.br. Fun German-themed restaurant, with good draught beer and a hearty buffet R$35 (most à la carte mains R$42–65) plus live music in the evenings (local pop, rock and folk). Daily 11am–12.30am.

Ilha de São Francisco

Just 45km east of Joinville lies the **Ilha de São Francisco**, a low-lying island separated from the mainland by a narrow strait spanned by a causeway. As Joinville's port and the site of a major Petrobras oil refinery, São Francisco may seem like a place to avoid, but both the port and refinery keep a discreet distance from the old colonial town of **São Francisco do Sul**, and the island's enticing beaches. French sailors first visited the island as early as 1504, though the town wasn't established by the Portuguese until the middle of the following century.

São Francisco do Sul

One of the oldest settlements in the south, the gorgeous *centro histórico* of **SÃO FRANCISCO DO SUL** (aka "São Chico") is separated from the main commercial part of town by a ring of small hills, giving it a relaxed, languid air unusual in this part of Brazil – it's also one of the few places in Santa Catarina where a concentration of colonial and nineteenth-century buildings survives. Though it's certainly geared up for tourists (and, increasingly, cruise-ship day-trippers), it retains an authentic, old-world feel. Dominating the city's skyline is the huge yellow-and-white **Igreja Matriz Nossa Senhora da Graça**, the main church, originally built in 1699 by indigenous slaves, but completely reconstructed in 1926.

The waterfront

The São Francisco **waterfront** (Rua Babitonga) is quite short and lined by colourful colonial buildings; the tiny **Mercado Municipal** (Mon–Fri 7.30am–6.30pm, Sat 7.30am–1pm, Sun 8am–2pm) opened in 1900, is an odd sort of place, with a couple of stalls, a café and a handful of ageing domino players inside. Don't miss the Art Deco **Texaco petrol station** (aka Posto Musse & Irmão; Rua Almirante Moraes Rego 1), opened in 1938 and still operating today.

Museu Nacional do Mar

Rua Manoel Lourenço de Andrade 133 • Tues–Fri 9am–5.30pm, Sat & Sun 10am–5.30pm • R$5 • ⓣ 47 3481 2155, ⓦ fcc.sc.gov.br/museudomar

São Francisco's pride and joy is the **Museu Nacional do Mar**, dedicated to the history of ocean travel and the people who make their living from the sea, with an emphasis on Brazil. Housed in a series of enchanting wharf sheds built around 1900, the museum is surprisingly big, and aficionados of boats and all things marine will spend at least two hours here – there are over 200 models of virtually every kind of traditional Brazilian boat, as well as sixty full-size versions, and an excellent café (see page 591). Labels are in Portuguese only.

Museu Histórico Municipal

Rua Coronel Carvalho 1 • Tues–Fri 9am–5pm, Sat & Sun 10am–4pm • R$3 • ⓣ 47 3444 5443

It's a bit of a trek from the main waterfront, but the **Museu Histórico Municipal** is worth a visit if you read Portuguese. Housed in São Francisco's eighteenth-century city hall and prison building (which, incidentally, remained in use until 1968), the old offices and former cells have been converted into small exhibition rooms with a huge range of subjects and artefacts, from the early history of the town, football and President Vargas' visit in 1940, to displays on local worthies such as poet Júlia da Costa (1844–1911), and German-born consul and shipping magnate Carl Hoepcke (1844–1924).

The beaches

The prettiest beaches on Ilha de São Francisco – the bays around **Paulas** and **Praia dos Ingleses** – are also the nearest to town, just a couple of kilometres along the northwest coast (beyond the port on Rua Mascarenhas). Both are small, and have trees to provide shade, and surprisingly few people take advantage of the protected sea, which is ideal for a gentle swim.

Further up the northwest coast, **Praia de Ubatuba**, 16km from the centre, and the adjoining **Praia de Enseada**, about 20km from town, are the island's most popular beaches, with enough surf to have fun in but not enough to be dangerous. On the wilder, ocean-facing east coast (a ten-minute walk across the peninsula from the eastern end of Enseada) lies **Prainha**, where the waves are suitable for only the toughest surfers, and the long, wind-swept stretch of **Praia Grande** to the south.

ARRIVAL AND INFORMATION — ILHA DE SÃO FRANCISCO

By bus The easiest way to reach São Francisco do Sul is by Verdes Mares bus from Joinville's rodoviária (1hr 30min; R$11.85; vmares.com.br) which run regularly along BR-280 through the day. The bus terminates at the rodoviária, inconveniently located outside São Francisco do Sul centre on Rua Dom Fernando Trejo y Sanabria (just off the main highway); most people get off the bus at the junction of Afonso dos Santos and Barão do Rio Branco in the commercial heart of town – from here it's a fairly straightforward 20min walk to the *centro histórico* (ask if you get lost), or R$5–10 by taxi (47 3444 2047). Similarly, heading back to Joinville you can pick up the bus from the bus stop in town (taxi drivers all know it) – no one goes all the way to the rodoviária to catch the bus.

Destinations Curitiba (daily; 3hr); Joinville (hourly; 1hr 30min); São Paulo (daily; 8hr).

By taxi Taxis charge around R$120 (one-way) between Joinville and São Francisco do Sul. Local taxis don't use the meter, so make sure you fix a price before getting in.

GETTING AROUND AND INFORMATION

By bus Local buses to the beaches (R$3.95) depart from the plaza near the church in São Francisco do Sul (Praça da Igreja); bus #5440 runs to Prainha and there are numerous buses to Enseada along the coast road in both directions.

Tourist information On the waterfront at Rua Babitonga 62 (Mon–Fri 7.30am–1.30pm; 47 3444 5380, visitesaofranciscodosul.com.br), and a kiosk on Rua Fernandes Dias, next to the Parque Ecológico Celso Amorim Salazar (Mon–Fri 9am-6pm; 47 3444 6682).

ACCOMMODATION

Hotel Kontiki Rua Babitonga 211 47 3444 2232, hotelkontiki.com.br. Attractive hotel forged from two historic properties: the nineteenth-century Hospital de Caridade and the old police station, dating from 1920. Rooms are fairly basic (with fan or a/c) but clean and comfy, with cable TV. R$190

Zibamba Rua Fernandes Dias 27 47 3444 2020, hotelzibamba.com.br. The town's top digs is a gorgeous old property near the waterfront, with relatively plain rooms, a pool and decent seafood restaurant – try and get a room with a balcony. R$206

EATING AND DRINKING

Bar do Banana Av Brasília at Rua João Pessoa, Prainha (18km from downtown São Francisco) 47 3444 0785, bardobanana.com.br. Popular with twenty-somethings (and cruise-ship passengers) looking for reasonably priced drinks, food and fun by the sea. Daily 11am–11pm.

★ **Café do Museu** Rua Manoel Lourenço de Andrade 133 47 3444 8071. Opposite the main entrance to Museu Nacional do Mar (and attached to the exit), this small café is by far the most atmospheric place to drink or grab a snack in town. It's a mellow, artsy space with old shed walls, part shop, part snack bar, with coffee, beers and light meals on offer. Tues–Fri 9am–6pm, Sat 10am–midnight, Sun 1–6pm.

Container Burger and Buffet Rua Almirante Guilhen 245 47 3444 2236, containerrestaurante.com.br. Best place to eat in town, with a clean, spacious a/c interior (plus outdoor seating), bargain lunch buffet for R$15 and hefty cheeseburgers. Mon 11am–2.30pm, Tues–Sat 11am–2.30pm & 6–11.30pm.

OKTOBERFEST IN BLUMENAU

Blumenau's crazy **Oktoberfest** (T 47 3326 6901, W oktoberfestblumenau.com.br) has been held since 1984, usually over eighteen days in October. Besides vast quantities of beer and German food, the main attractions are the local and visiting German bands and German folk-dance troupes. The festival takes place at the Parque Vila Germânica (entry R$12–40; beers R$5–11), on Rua João Pessoa on the city's outskirts (frequent buses run during the festival period), as well as in the downtown streets. If you intend to visit during Oktoberfest, **advance hotel** reservations are essential.

Blumenau

With Joinville now an international boomtown, **BLUMENAU**, to the south, has succeeded in promoting itself as the "capital" of German Santa Catarina. The distinction is rather moot, however – like Joinville, Blumenau will seem thoroughly Brazilian to anyone who has actually been to Germany, with a dynamic modern economy and commercial centre, albeit with slightly more evidence of its Teutonic roots. Picturesquely located on the banks of the Rio Itajaí, Blumenau was founded in 1850 by Hamburger **Dr Hermann Blumenau**, who served as director of the colony until his return to Germany in 1880 – as late as the 1920s, two-thirds of the population spoke German as their first language. Things changed during World War II (see page 589), however, and now German is virtually extinct in the city, despite domestic tourism revolving around its German heritage – especially **beer** and the madness of **Oktoberfest** (see page 592), established in 1984 to boost visitor numbers.

Rua XV Novembro

The commercial heart of Blumenau lies south of the river along **Rua XV Novembro** (once known as Wurststrasse), sprinkled with a handful of original German-style homes (now shops or banks) in between the concrete, and culminating at the starkly modern **Catedral São Paulo Apóstolo**, built in 1958 with its tall, brick bell tower.

Nearby, the **Havan department store** at Rua XV Novembro 1050 is the most striking Hanseatic-style building in the country (which makes it a major photo op). Known as the Castelinho, it's actually just a skilfully crafted replica, built in 1978 (based, loosely, on the world-famous Michelstadt Town Hall, constructed in 1484).

Mausoléu Dr Blumenau

Rua XV de Novembro 161 • Daily 10am–4pm • Free • T 47 3326 6990

The oldest part of Blumenau lies across a short bridge over the Ribeirão Garcia on the continuation of Rua XV de Novembro, where the **Mausoléu Dr Blumenau** preserves the memory of the city's earnest founder. Inside you'll find the graves of Dr Hermann Blumenau (1819–99) and his immediate family, along with a handful of reverentially displayed personal effects and photos. The bronze statue of the great man outside was created in 1940.

Museu da Cerveja

Praça Hercílio Luz/Rua XV Novembro 160 • Mon–Fri 9am–5pm, Sat & Sun 10am–4pm • Free • T 47 3326 6791

Shady Praça Hercílio Luz contains the small **Museu da Cerveja**, a tribute to the beer-making traditions of Blumenau (and a nod to Oktoberfest, with mugs and posters). Most of the city's beermakers went out of business after World War II, and the museum displays some ageing equipment from the defunct Feldmann Brewery (and a pair of 1930s clodhoppers) dating from the 1890s through to the 1960s.

Museu da Família Colonial

Alameda Duque de Caxias 78 • Tues–Sun 10am–4pm • R$5 • T 47 3322 1676

The city's de facto history museum, the **Museu da Família Colonial** lies on the "avenue of palms" and comprises three historic buildings: the oldest was constructed in red brick and timber *enxaimel*-style in 1858 for the Wendeburg family, while the main house next door was completed in 1864 for the family of Dr Blumenau's nephew, Gaertner (the family also built the third property in 1920). The two oldest houses have been filled with period furniture and photographs of life in the settlement during its early years, but it's in the beautiful forest-like **Parque Edith Gaertner** at the back that you'll find the most curious feature: the tiny **Cemeterio do Gatos**, the final resting place for the much-loved cats – Bum, Musch, Mirko and the rest – of the great-niece of Dr Blumenau.

ARRIVAL AND INFORMATION — BLUMENAU

By bus The rodoviária (**T** 47 3323 0690) is 7km from the city centre in the suburb of Itoupava Norte (the "Cidade Jardim" bus runs into the centre; R$3.90). Taxis into the centre will cost around R$20 (meters start at R$5.35). Volkmann buses to Pomerode depart from Terminal da Fonte, Rua Amazonas 540, around 1km south of the centre (23 daily Mon–Fri 3.55am–10.10pm; 10 daily Sat 6.30am–10.10pm, 7 daily Sun 9am–10.10pm; 35–40min; R$6).
Destinations Curitiba (9 daily; 4.5hr); Florianópolis (hourly; 3hr); Joinville (14 daily; 2hr); Pomerode (hourly; 45min).

Tourist information Rua Itajaí 3435, on the eastern edge of town (Mon–Fri 10am–4pm; **T** 47 3222 3176, **W** turismoblumenau.com.br). They can provide maps and information, though staff are rarely English-speakers (or even German-speakers). The front desk at the more conveniently located Museu da Cerveja (see page 592) also acts as an information centre.

ACCOMMODATION

Hotel Glória Rua 7 de Setembro 954 **T** 47 3326 1988, **W** hotelgloria.com.br; map p.593. Cool boutique hotel, with contemporary, stylish a/c rooms (the exterior is deceiving) and free parking. Top-notch breakfast buffet included. **R$150**

Stamm Hostel Backpackers Rua Pará 569, Itoupava Seca **T** 47 3338 5266, **W** stammhostel.com.br; map p.593. No frills but friendly hostel (with a beer theme), in a quiet neighbourhood 4km northwest of the centre. Large shared lounge and kitchen (with free coffee all day; basic breakfast) and helpful owners. Doubles (some with private bathrooms and a/c) are a great deal. Dorms **R$45**, doubles **R$105**

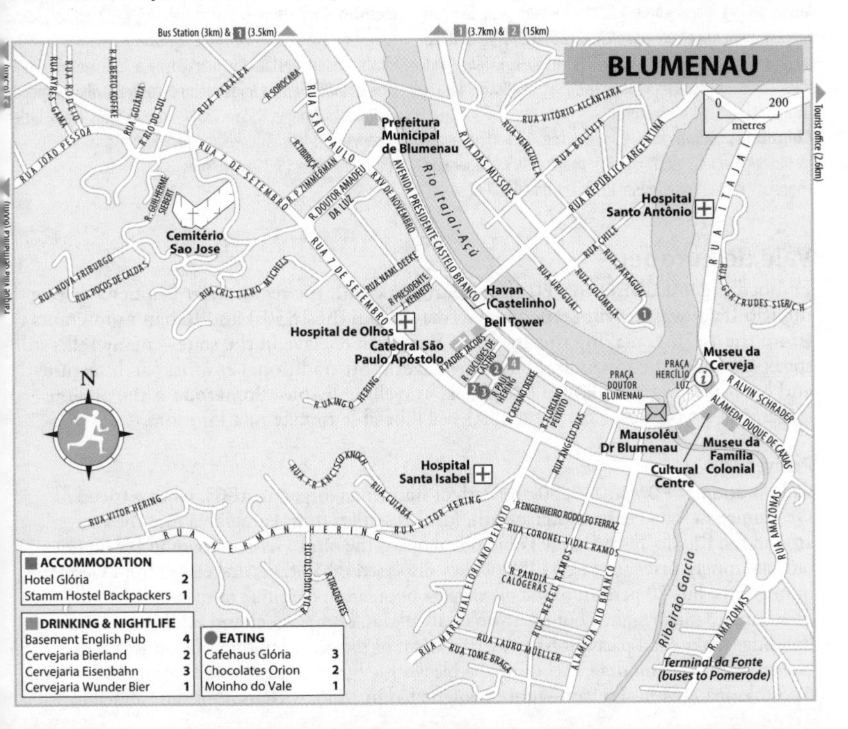

BLUMENAU BEER

Blumenau's **microbreweries** have blossomed in in recent years with several top-notch beer makers adhering to the German Reinheitsgebot laws and offering tours and tastings, plus a fun English pub:

Basement English Pub Rua Paul Hering 35 ⓣ47 3340 0534, ⓦbasementpub.com.br; map p.593. Blumenau's most congenial watering hole, with a great selection of beer on tap (Eisenbahn brews), fish and chips, and cosy sofas and stone walls that do an admirable job of replicating the atmosphere of an olde British pub. Mon–Sat 6pm–midnight.

Cervejaria Bierland Rua Gustavo Zimmerman 5361, Itoupava Central ⓣ47 3337 3100, ⓦbierland.com.br; map p.593. Founded in 2003, with a range of German but also Belgian and North American-style ales. Sample them at the *Bar da Fábrica Bierland*, separated from the brewery by a glass wall. Tues–Fri 4pm–midnight, Sat 10am–midnight.

Cervejaria Eisenbahn Rua Bahia 5181, Salto Weissbach ⓣ47 3488 7307, ⓦeisenbahn.com.br; map p.593. Founded in 2002 and now producing fourteen kinds of beer, including Lust, made by the same method used for French champagne. You can sample the brews at the *Bar da Fábrica* (live music Wed–Sat from 7.30pm); they'll even drive you back to your hotel for free. Tours of the factory are also available if arranged in advance (Mon–Fri 4.30pm; R$10). Mon & Tues 5–11pm, Wed 5pm–midnight, Thurs–Sat 5pm–1am.

Cervejaria Wunder Bier Fritz Spernau 155, Bairro Fortaleza ⓣ47 3339 0001, ⓦwunderbier.com.br; map p.593. Founded in 2007, with a tasty range of *weizen*, *pilsen* and even *wein bier* (wine beer). You can visit the factory but tours must be arranged in advance. Otherwise you can sample the suds in the *Wunder Bar* tap room in front of the factory. Mon–Thurs 6pm–midnight, Fri & Sat 6pm–1am.

EATING

★ **Cafehaus Glória** Rua 7 de Setembro 954 ⓣ47 3321 1945, ⓦcafehaus.com.br; map p.593. Fabulously kitsch dining room where you can indulge your German fantasy, with huge *café colonial* spreads (R$70/kg or R$38 all-you-can-eat) and lunch buffets (R$60/kg). Mon–Sat 8am–8pm; café colonial: Mon–Sat 4–8pm; lunch buffet Mon–Fri 11am–2pm.

Chocolates Orion Rua Curt Hering 226 (Shopping Neumarkt) ⓣ47 3037 1661; map p.593. Venerable chocolate maker founded in 1958, crammed full of sweet temptations in a variety of shapes and sizes. Mon–Fri 8.30am–7pm, Sat 8.30am–1.30pm.

Moinho do Vale Rua Porto Rico 66 ⓣ47 3322 3440, ⓦrestaurantemoinhodovale.com.br; map p.593. Plush modern restaurant marked by a full-size windmill (the *moinho*), with a huge menu of tasty Brazilian seafood and steaks (mains R$55–135) – the risottos are a little cheaper (R$46). Tues–Sat 11.30am–3pm & 7pm–midnight, Sun 11.30am–3pm.

Vale de Europeu

Dubbed the **VALE DE EUROPEU** (ⓦvaleeuropeu.com), the region near Blumenau along the Rio Itajaí was heavily settled by German (from the 1830s) and Italian immigrants (from the 1870s), making this the most European enclave in the state – many folks still speak German, the towns and bucolic villages sport traditional *enxaimel* architecture and beer-brewing is making a comeback. Travelling by bus, **Pomerode** is the obvious target, but if you rent a car (or a bike) you'll be able to take in a lot more.

Pomerode

Colonization of **POMERODE**, 30km north of Blumenau, began in 1863, when a friend of Dr Blumenau, one Ferdinand Hackrath, first led settlers from Pomerania into the area around the Rio do Testo. Today Pomerode remains the most German town in Brazil; not only are ninety percent of its 31,000 widely dispersed inhabitants descended from German immigrants, but 70 percent of the *município*'s population continue to speak the language. There are no major sights, but the town's leafy plazas, beer gardens and traditional *enxaimel* buildings make for a pleasant half-day trip. Most of the older buildings lie on Rua XV Novembro, the main drag, including the Neogothic Igreja Evangélica de Confissão Luterana Apóstolo João (Mon–Fri 9am–4pm), inaugurated in 1885, with its 35m spire added in 1900.

Museu Pomerano and the Osterbaum

Rua Hermann Weege 111 • Tues–Fri 10am–11.30am & 1–5pm, Sat & Sun 10am–4pm • R$6 • ☎ 47 3387 0408

The small **Museu Pomerano** (on the other side of the Rio do Testo from the main church) tells the story of the town, with an array of miscellaneous objects on display, from old glass and porcelain to rare photographs, documents and original items brought from Pomerania (mostly part of Poland today).

Behind the museum, in the courtyard of the Centro Cultural, lies the most popular sight in town – the **Osterbaum** or "Easter egg tree", a pecan tree festooned with thousands of painted eggshells hanging from its branches. The centuries-old German tradition is supposed to commemorate Easter (Osterfest in Pomerode), though this tree tends to remain decorated year-round. In 2017 it officially became the largest Easter tree in the world, with over 80,000 eggs draped over it.

ARRIVAL AND INFORMATION — POMERODE

By bus Volkmann buses (☎ 47 3395 1400, ⓦ turismo volkmann.com.br) to and from Blumenau stop outside the Lutheran church on Rua XV de Novembro, the main street, which sprawls alongside the banks of the Rio do Testo. The buses depart from Blumenau's Terminal da Fonte, Rua Amazonas 540 (23 daily Mon–Fri 4.10am–10.10pm; 10 daily Sat 6.30am–10.10pm, 7 daily Sun 9am–10.10pm; 35–40min; R$6). There are also direct buses to Joinville (5–7 daily; 2hr), Curitiba (5 daily; 4hr–4hr 30min) and Balneário Camboriú (2 daily; 2hr).

Tourist information Inside the Hanseatic-style city gate, the Portal Turístico do Sul, at Rua XV de Novembre 818 (daily 8am–6pm; ☎ 47 3387 2627, ⓦ pomerode.sc.gov.br), provides a good map and details of forthcoming events, and has a small selection of local wooden and ceramic handicrafts for sale.

ACCOMMODATION

Pousada Blauberg Av. 21 de Janeiro 3250 ☎ 47 3387 5064, ⓦ pousadablauberg.com.br. Quiet, cosy accommodation in the centre of town, with simple rooms, cable TV, helpful owners and a hearty breakfast. R$230

Pousada Rural Mundo Antigo Rua Ribeirão Herdt, Km 5 ☎ 47 3387 3143, ⓦ mundoantigo.com.br. By far the prettiest (and most German-like) place to stay, but a half-hour walk from the centre of town, is this rustic B&B housed in several *enxaimel* farm buildings dating from 1924, in a beautiful rural setting. Rates include a big breakfast, with full-board packages starting at R$600 for two. R$300

EATING AND DRINKING

Cervejaria Schornstein Rua Hermann Weege 60 ☎ 47 3387 6655, ⓦ schornstein.com.br. Pomerode's local craft brewery (named after its 30m chimney) makes excellent German-style *pilsen*, *bock* and *weizen* beers (as well as IPA), while its on-site bar and restaurant (*Schornstein Kneipe*) also serves decent food like German-style sausages. Wed–Fri 6pm–midnight, Sat & Sun noon–midnight.

★ **WunderWald** Rua XV de Novembro 8444 ☎ 47 3395 1700, ⓦ wunderwald.com.br. This is, without doubt, Pomerode's best restaurant, serving typical German food like *bockwurst* and *hackepeter*, Schornstein beer and local specialities such as *marreco* (wild duck) in an *enxaimel*-style farmhouse (mains R$45–65). The restaurant lies 5km south of the centre on the main road to Blumenau (SC-418). Mon–Fri 11.30am–4pm & 6–10.30pm, Sat & Sun 11.30am–4pm & 6–11pm.

ROTA DO ENXAIMEL

Pomerode boasts the largest collection of **enxaimel buildings** ("Fachwerk" in German; exposed bricks within an exposed timber frame) outside Germany – some 240 structures scattered throughout the municipality. The highest concentration is located in the Testo Alto neighbourhood (5km north of the centre, signposted off SC-110), where around fifty buildings line a 16km stretch of road (Rua Testo Alto) dubbed "Rota do Enxaimel", beginning with the **Pórtico do Imigrante** "Wolfgang Weege", a replica of a city gate from the old Pomeranian city of Stettin (now Szczecin in Poland), just north of the Rua Testo turn-off. Other highlights include the old church, the **Igreja Luterana de Testo Alto** (at Rua Progresso and Rua Gustav Krahn), and the 1867 *Pousada Casa Wachholz*, now a hotel (at Rua Progreso 2320). You'll need your own transport to make the most of the route.

POMERODE'S FESTIVALS

Pomerode is renowned for its **festivals**, the chief of which is the **Festa Pomerana**, a celebration of local industry and culture held annually for ten days, usually from around January 7. Most of the events take place on the outskirts of town, on Rua XV de Novembro, about 1km from the tourist office, and during the day thousands of people from neighbouring cities descend on Pomerode to sample the local food, attend the song and dance performances and visit the commercial fair. By late afternoon, though, the day-trippers leave and the Festa Pomerana comes alive as the ***colonos*** from the surrounding areas transform the festivities into a truly popular event. Local and visiting bands play German and Brazilian music, and dancing continues long into the night. In July, Pomerode organizes the smaller, though similar, **Winterfest**.

There are more regular festivities too, as every Saturday the local hunting clubs take turns to host **dances**. Visitors are always made to feel welcome, and details of the week's venue are displayed on posters around town, or ask at the tourist office. As many of the clubs are located in the *município*'s outlying reaches, a bus is laid on, leaving from outside the post office on Rua XV de Novembro.

Encantos do Sul

The Santa Catarina coast south of Florianópolis has been dubbed the **ENCANTOS DO SUL** ("southern charm") by those ever-creative tourism folk, with a handful of worthy stopovers off the BR-101 highway. In addition to the beach and surf resorts of **Garopaba**, **Laguna** is an attractive colonial town and the coast is also a favoured spot for **right whales** to breed between June and November.

Guarda do Embaú

The first accessible spot on the Encantos do Sul worth stopping at is **GUARDA DO EMBAÚ**, 50km south of Florianópolis, a fishing village on the southern edge of the town of Pinheira, justly famed for its excellent surf breaks and the gorgeous bank of sand that lies just across the Rio do Madre (it's usually shallow enough to wade through, but local fishermen also charge R$5 to ferry you across). There's not much in the way of services, but it's a mellow place to chill out for a day or so, especially if you're on a budget.

ARRIVAL AND DEPARTURE — GUARDA DO EMBAÚ

By bus Paulotur runs regular buses between Florianópolis and Guarda do Embaú (2hr). Continuing south by bus is a bit of a hassle; you'll need to take the bus back to BR-101 (10min), and try to flag down a (non-express) bus heading to Garopaba (another 30min). Your hotel might be able to arrange a cheap taxi ride instead.

ACCOMMODATION

Pousada Anjo da Guarda Rua Inês Maria de Jesus 156 ⓣ48 3283 2527, ⓦpousadaanjodaguarda.com. Right in the heart of the action, 150m from the beach, with modern brick chalets with a/c or fan, flat-screen TVs and hammocks outside. R$360

ZuluLand Pousada Servidão Emerenciana ⓣ48 3283 2706, ⓦzululand.com.br. Hip boutique hotel designed by model and actor Paulo Zulu, with a series of cottages and apartments furnished in an eclectic, contemporary style with cable TV – there's a pool table and swimming pool on site too. R$290

Garopaba

Some 45km south of Embaú, via the BR-101 highway, **GAROPABA** is an old fishing village inhabited by people of Azorean origin, which, despite attracting more and more people every summer, has not yet been totally overwhelmed by tourism. The main village beach and nearby Praia Silveira (for surfing) are fine, and large enough to take the summer crowds, but try to make it to the outlying beaches if you can. A few kilometres to the north is **Praia Siriú** (you can walk along a trail from the centre), backed by huge dunes, while 16km

north of town (30min by road), **Praia da Gamboa** is a fabulous beach for swimming, with a beautiful mountain backdrop (this eventually runs up to Guarda do Embaú).

ARRIVAL AND ACCOMMODATION — GAROPABA

By bus There are Paulotur buses to Florianópolis (2hr) leaving from Rua Marquês Guimarães, and those destined for points south as far as Porto Alegre from Praça Silveira. There are also frequent local services plying the route between Garopaba and Praia da Rosa for around R$3.80 (30min).

Pousada da Lagoa Rua Rosalina Aguiar Lentz 325 ⓣ48 3254 3201, ⓦpousadadalagoa.com.br. Lovely, modern hotel set in a huge tropical garden, just 400m from the beach, with stylish a/c rooms decorated with contemporary art, a pool and a sauna. R$415

Praia do Rosa

Some 18km south of Garopaba, just to the north of Imbituba, **Praia do Rosa** is a 3km strip of dazzling sand and a major surf destination. Other than lounging on the beach (a 20min walk down the hill from the small town centre), it's a great place to learn to surf, and to organize whale-watching trips in the winter. In the summer the town attracts a fairly boisterous party scene, and hotels near the beach have become expensive.

ARRIVAL AND DEPARTURE — PRAIA DA ROSA

By bus There are frequent local buses that link Garopaba and Praia da Rosa (R$3.80) – you can catch a bus south or north from Garopaba.

ACCOMMODATION AND EATING

Haleakala Hostel Rua Doze (John Lennon) ⓣ48 99678 5763, ⓦfacebook.com/haleakala.hostel.fan. Friendly hostel near the village centre (it's quite a walk from the beach) with a tiny outdoor pool, hammocks on the deck, cosy double rooms with fan and compact mixed dorms with two bunks in each (with fan). Cash only. Dorms R$50, doubles R$100

Hostel Vale do Rosa Rua dos Poncianos ⓣ48 3355 7078, ⓦvaledorosa.com.br. Great-value hostel a 20min walk from the beach, with clean but fairly cramped female-only or mixed dorms (triple bunks) with fans, spotless tiled bathrooms, spacious shared kitchen and fine hill views from the balconies. Dorms R$40

★ **Tigre Asiático** Centrinho da Praia do Rosa (Rod. 434 Km 11) ⓣ48 3355 7045, ⓦtigreasiaticorestaurante.com.br. The menu at this lavish Balinese- and Thai-inspired restaurant blends Thai, Indonesian and Japanese dishes and flavours (mains R$48–76). Daily 7–11pm.

★ **Village Praia do Rosa** Av Porto Novo 1028 ⓣ48 3355 7199, ⓦvillagepraiadorosa.com.br. Luxurious resort with sensational sea views, outdoor and indoor pools and large apartment (two people) or townhouse (6–8 people) accommodation, all with full kitchens and dining area (though breakfast is still included, and there's a restaurant on site). R$304

Laguna

Founded in 1676 some 125km south from Florianópolis, **LAGUNA** is the closest Santa Catarina gets to having a near-complete colonial town, making it one of the most enticing targets in the southern half of the state. Sitting at the end of a narrow peninsula, at the entrance to the Lagoa Santo Antônio, Laguna divides into two distinct sections. Facing west onto the sheltered lagoon is the old port and Laguna's historic centre, protected as a national monument. Two kilometres away, on the far side of a granite outcrop of mountainous proportions that separates the city's two parts, is the new town, facing east onto the Atlantic Ocean. Most of Laguna's hotels and restaurants are in the new town, alongside and parallel to the **Praia do Mar Grosso**, the city's main beach.

Igreja Santo Antônio dos Anjos

Praça Vidal Ramos • Daily 7am–7pm • Free

Not all of Laguna's old town dates from the eighteenth century, but its general aspect is that of a Portuguese colonial settlement. The oldest streets are those extending off **Praça Vidal Ramos**, the square that holds the **Igreja Santo Antônio dos Anjos**. Built in

RIGHT WHALE-WATCHING

Between mid-June and mid-November, the south coast of Santa Catarina is the most popular place in Brazil for **whale watching**. With luck you should be able to spot southern right whales swimming just 30m from the beach, but for near-certain viewing of both adult whales and their calves it's best to take a boat excursion: Vida Sol e Mar (48 3355 6111, vidasolemar.com.br) in Praia do Rosa is the most experienced operator (R$150–R190), with boats especially designed for whale watching.

1694, the church retains its late eighteenth-century Baroque altars and, though rather modest, is considered the most important surviving colonial church in Santa Catarina.

Museu Casa de Anita

Praça Vidal Ramos • Tues–Sun 9am–6pm • R$5

This small colonial home built around 1711 is now the **Museu Casa de Anita**, dedicated to **Anita Garibaldi** (1821–49), the remarkable Brazilian wife of Giuseppe Garibaldi, maverick military leader of the Italian unification movement. Garibaldi was employed as a rebel mercenary in the Brazilian **Guerra dos Farrapos** (1835–45), the war between republicans and monarchists. Anita was born in Laguna, but not in this building; she did prepare for her first marriage here, in 1835 when she was just 14. After a whirlwind romance and having his child, Anita married Garibaldi in Uruguay in 1842, and when she died of malaria in Italy at the age of 29 he was said to have been heartbroken. The museum commemorates the domestic life of the Garibaldis during their brief time together in Laguna, with some period furniture, utensils allegedly used by Anita and her family (scissors and hairbrushes), and an urn containing earth from Anita's grave in Ravenna, Italy.

Museu Histórico Anita Garibaldi

Praça República Juliana • Tues–Sun 9am–6pm • R$5

Housed in the old Câmara e Cadeia (town hall and jail) built in 1735, the **Museu Histórico Anita Garibaldi** is nominally dedicated to the Guerra dos Farrapos – it was in this building that a short-lived republic was declared in 1839. There are some fine photographs of nineteenth-century Laguna on display, but there's actually little on Anita Garibaldi or republican activities; instead there are archeological displays, exhibits on nineteenth-century politician **Jerônimo Francisco Coelho** (born here in 1806) and of **Pedro Raymundo** (1906–1973), the beloved local accordionist, composer and singer (his record collection and accordion are preserved here). A bronze statue of Anita Garibaldi stands in the square outside the museum.

Farol de Santa Marta

Tours of the interior require advance permission from the Delegacia da Capitania dos Portos, Av Engenheiro Machado Salles 72, in Laguna (48 3644 0196, facebook.com/Delegacia.da.Capitania.Portos.Laguna), Portuguese-language only

About 19km south of town (via a short ferry) is the **Farol de Santa Marta**, an unusual square lighthouse erected in 1891 (still in use). It's surrounded by bleak but beautiful scenery offering wild seas (suicidal for even the strongest of swimmers, but popular with local surfers nonetheless) and protected beaches, with several low-key pousadas and restaurants catering to the steady stream of Brazilian visitors. Between June and September this stretch of shore is a popular spot from which to watch the migrating **right whales**, which are clearly visible from the shore with binoculars.

ARRIVAL AND INFORMATION — LAGUNA

By bus The rodoviária (48 3644 0208) is at Rua Arcângelo Bianchini, a couple of minutes' walk from the waterfront and the old town. There are around twelve buses daily to and from Florianópolis (1hr 50min), and at least eight daily to Porto Alegre (5–6hr 30min).

To the Farol Several buses run direct to Farol de Santa

Marta; Alvorada (transportesalvorada.com.br) runs two buses (around R$16) a day between the Farol and Tubarão, where you can change for points north and south; from Laguna itself there's a special bus that runs direct to the Farol (8 daily Mon–Fri, 3 on Sat, 2 on Sun), but you can also take more frequent buses (R$4) to the ferry ("balsa") to Barra, cross as a foot passenger, and take another bus on the other side (R$12–15 total; allow 2hr). The Laguna Navegação ferry to Barra runs from Rua Pedro Rosa 27 (24hr; R$1 pedestrians, R$11 cars; 48 3646 0887).

Tourist information Located at the official entrance to town, 3km from central Laguna on Rua Manoel Américo de Barros in Portinho – this runs parallel to Av Calistralo Muller Salles or SC-436 (Mon–Sat 8am–6pm; 48 3644 2441).In town, the tourism office is on Praça Lauro Muller (Mon–Fri 1–7pm; 48 3644 2542).

ACCOMMODATION

Hotel Mar Grosso Rua Criciúma 36, Bairro Mar Grosso 48 3647 0298, margrossohotel.com.br. The best mid-range choice in town, 50m from the beach with clean, compact, simple en-suite rooms in a great location, with TV and fans. R$140

Pousada Vento & Cia Estrada Geral do Farol (Av Beira Mar) 48 3646 3005, pousadaventoecia.com.br. Most comfortable option near the lighthouse (*farol*), with compact, simply decorated modern doubles (with full kitchens, a/c and TV), right on the Praianha do Farol (beach). R$104

The Serra Catarinese

The region known as the **SERRA CATARINESE** (serracatarinense.com) is the most picturesque part of inland Santa Catarina, well worth exploring if you have your own transport. Until the road-building programme of the 1970s, the mountainous hinterland of the state was pretty much isolated from the rest of the region. Even today it remains well off the beaten path for tourists – the area is time-consuming to access without your own car – despite boasting some scintillating mountain scenery (it sometimes snows here in winter, the major draw for Brazilian tourists).

Urubici and around

The dazzling pine-swathed **Serra Geral** range separates the Serra Catarinese from the coastal regions, with the mountain town of **URUBICI**, 158km west of Florianópolis, the centre of a flourishing trade in adventure tourism. From here mostly unpaved roads run 29km to the peak of the **Morro da Igreja** (1822m), the second-highest mountain in the state, inside the **Parque Nacional de São Joaquim**. The summit is often snow-covered in winter, and from here you can admire the **Pedra Furada**, a remarkle natural arch some 30m wide, just down the slope.

Other attractions near Urubici include the **Cachoeira Rio dos Bugres**, a spectacular 12m-high waterfall (14km from the centre), and the 4000-year-old petroglyphs at **Morro do Avencal**, 5km from town.

ARRIVAL AND TOURS — URUBICI AND AROUND

By bus Reunidas (www.reunidas.com.br) runs buses from Florianópolis to Urubici daily at 6.30pm (arriving 10.10pm; R$61.16), returning daily at 7.15am. Florianópolis to Sao Joaquim buses (1 daily) usually stop in Urubici, but check in advance.

Tours The experienced and friendly folks at Graxaim Ecoturismo e Aventuras, Rodovia SC-110, Km 371.8, Águas Brancas (49 3278 5617, graxaim.com), can help arrange tours and accommodation in the area.

ACCOMMODATION

Pousada Casa da Serra Rua Boanerges Pereira Medeiros 1078 049 3278 4412, reserva@casadaserra-sc.com.br. Rustic but cosy rooms and two spotless wooden chalets (with TV, a/c, heaters and microwaves), plus great breakfasts and super-friendly owners. R$180

São Joaquim

Formerly just a small highland ranching centre, **SÃO JOAQUIM**, 60km beyond Urubici, has only really been on the Brazilian map since the mid-1970s when **apple orchards** were introduced here. Within twenty years, Brazil changed from importing nearly all the apples consumed in the country to becoming a major exporter of the fruit. At an altitude of 1360m (making this one of the highest towns in Brazil), temperatures in the winter occasionally dip to -15°C and, as this is one of the few parts of Brazil that sees regular frost and sometimes snow, there is a surprising amount of tourism, with camping being especially popular among Brazilians as a way of truly experiencing the cold.

Vinícola Villa Francioni

A few kilometres north of town at Rodovia SC-438, Km 70 • Tours (40min) Mon–Fri 10am, 11am 1.30pm, 2.30pm & 3.30pm, Sat & Sun 10.30am, 11.30am, 2pm, 3pm & 4pm • R$30 • 49 3233 8200, villafrancioni.com.br

To sample the local **wines**, a visit to the **Vinícola Villa Francioni** is a must: the production is small but arguably Brazil's finest. Founded in 2004, the winery was constructed from material salvaged from ruined colonial houses in the region, and stained glass from Uruguay.

ARRIVAL AND DEPARTURE — SÃO JOAQUIM

By bus The rodoviária (49 3233 0400) is a couple of minutes' walk from the city centre. Nevatur runs buses on to Lages (Mon–Sat 8.15am, 12.15pm, 4.45pm, 8.15pm). Reunidas (www.reunidas.com.br) runs to Florianópolis daily at 6am (buses leave Floripa daily at 6.30pm; 4hr 45min) via Urubici (1hr 15min; R$20). For the far west, Reunidas runs buses to Chapecó for the Museu Entomológico Fritz Plaumann (see page 604) daily at 7.30pm (7hr 20min) via Joaçaba (5hr 40min).

By car From Florianópolis head to Orleans and take the hair-raising Estrada da Serra do Rio do Rastro (SC-438) across the Serra Geral towards São Joaquim.

ACCOMMODATION AND EATING

★ **Restaurante Pequeno Bosque** Rua Major Jacinto Goulart 212 49 3233 3318. High-end bistro with a creative menu featuring local produce such as pine nuts, apples, lamb and fresh trout in Brazilian and international dishes (the pastas and risottos are very good). Mains from around R$60. Tues–Sun 11.45am–2pm & 6.30pm–midnight.

São Joaquim Park Hotel Praça João Ribeiro 58 49 3233 1444, saojoaquimparkhotel.com.br. The main hotel in town, this tower block next to the central plaza and church has ageing but comfy rooms with heating (no a/c). Check out the views from the roof. R$140

Lages and around

Although founded in 1766, nothing remains in **LAGES** from the days when it was an important pit stop for cowhands herding cattle and mules on the route northwards to the market in Sorocaba. Located 76km northwest of São Joaquim, it's now a collection of anonymous post-1950s buildings, and the main reason to visit is to get a taste of life in the *gaúcho* high country. Several of the surrounding cattle *fazendas* offer accommodation, offering a glimpse of life in outlying parts of the *serra* – otherwise extremely difficult for tourists to experience.

ARRIVAL AND INFORMATION — LAGES AND AROUND

By bus The rodoviária (49 3222 6710) is a half-hour walk southeast of the centre, or you can take a bus marked "Dom Pedro". Reunidas (www.reunidas.com.br) runs 7 daily buses direct to Lages from Florianópolis (4–5hr) and also on to Chapecó (1–2 daily; 6hr 30min) and Joaçaba (1–2 daily; 2hr 30min). Nevatur (nevatur.com.br) runs buses to São Joaquim (Mon–Sat 6.30am, 10am, 1.30pm & 6pm; 2hr).

Tourist information In the centre at Rua Hercílio Luz 573 (Mon–Fri 8am–noon & 2–6pm; 49 3223 6206). Distributes a good map of Lages and can help with booking *fazenda* accommodation.

ACCOMMODATION AND EATING

★ **Fazenda do Barreiro** SC-438, Km 42 (4km off the highway on a dirt road), Urupema 49 3222 3031, fazendadobarreiro.com.br. Lovely old property 35km southeast of Lages that traces its origins to 1782, though its buildings are more recent. Offers simple but cosy rooms, four meals a day, an on-site museum and plenty of activities like horse riding. R$230

★ **Galpão Gaúcho** Av Duque de Caxias 1141 049 3225 2689. Soak up the *gaúcho* atmosphere at this Argentine-style bar and barbecue steakhouse, replete with rustic timber decor, cosy booths and reasonable prices (mains from R$45). There is live music on Fridays and Saturdays. Mon–Sat 7.30pm–midnight.

Hotel Fazenda Pedras Brancas SC-438, Km 10, Pedras Brancas ⊕49 3223 2073, ⊕fazendapedrasbrancas.com.br. Another gorgeous farmhouse hotel with plush, modern suites, rustic cabins and beautiful views of the nearby pond. The food is superb and there's a pool, horse riding and nightly cooking over a wood fire (the *sapecada*). R$240

Ibis Lages Av Duque de Caxias 579 ⊕49 322 14444, ⊕accorhotels.com. The best option in town, this newish outpost of the popular chain offers the usual compact but cosy rooms and amenities, plus free parking. Breakfast is extra (R$21). R$160

The Vale do Contestado and Grande Oeste

Very few foreign tourists make it to the far western reaches of Santa Catarina, regions dubbed the **Vale do Contestado** (named after the bloody Contestado War of 1912–14) and the **Grande Oeste** ("Grand West"). As with the rest of the state, much of the appeal comes from the surviving immigrant communities – typically Italian and Austrian – and the rustic landscapes en route, but as always you'll get a lot more out of the region with your own transport.

Treze Tílias

The claim of the *município* of **TREZE TÍLIAS**, 220km northwest of Lages, to be the "Brazilian Tyrol" is by no means without foundation. In 1933, 82 Tyroleans led by Andreas Thaler, a former Austrian minister of agriculture, arrived in what is now Treze Tílias. As the dense forest around the settlement was gradually cleared, more settlers joined the colony, but after Germany's annexation of Austria in 1938, immigration came to an end – as did funds to help support the pioneers during the difficult first years. The area eventually came to specialize in dairy farming, and today its milk products are sold in supermarkets throughout Santa Catarina. The **Tirolerfest** (⊕tirolerfest.com.br) during the first two weeks of October is a lively display of Austrian folk traditions including singing and dancing.

But for the absence of snowcapped mountain peaks, the general appearance of Treze Tílias is not dissimilar to that of a small Alpine village. **Walking** in any direction, you'll pass through peaceful pastoral landscapes; the gentle 7km walk to the chapel in the hamlet of **Babenberg** is particularly rewarding. If you decide to visit the local **waterfalls** a few kilometres outside town, get very detailed directions before setting out.

In Treze Tílias itself, try to visit some of the **woodcarvers**, several of whom have shops in the centre of the village where items, large and small, are for sale. The best woodcarvers learned their craft in Europe, and their work is in demand from churches throughout Brazil.

Museu Municipal Andreas Thaler

Rua Pedro Nelcido Käfer 115 • Mon & Wed–Sat 9am–noon & 2–5pm, Sun 10am–noon • Nominally R$1 but usually free • ⊕49 3537 0997

On the main street, the grand mansion known as the "Castelinho" is now the **Museu Municipal Andreas Thaler**, featuring a small collection of photographs and paintings of the area in the 1930s and 1940s, as well as items brought with the immigrants from Austria. Completed in 1937, the house was initially the residence of town founder Andreas Thaler (1883–1939) and his family until 1969, serving thereafter as the city hall until 2002.

ARRIVAL AND INFORMATION — TREZE TÍLIAS

By bus All buses stop right in the centre of the village outside the *Hotel Áustria*. Treze Tílias is only an hour or so north of Joaçaba (37km), where you'll have to change coming by bus. To get to Joaçaba, Reunidas (⊕www.reunidas.com.br) runs 5–10 daily buses direct from Lages (3hr) and Florianópolis (8hr 30min–9hr 30min), and on to Chapecó (3hr–3hr 25min); from Joaçaba, Empresa Terci (⊕49 3535 0178) buses run to Treze (Mon–Sat only at

11am & 4.40pm, returning 7.30am & 12.15pm; 1hr; R$21). Reunidas also runs 1 daily bus between Joaçaba and Videira (12.10pm; 2hr).

Tourist information Secretaria do Turismo at Rua Pedro Nelcido Käfer 115 (Mon–Fri 8am–5pm; ⓣ 49 3537 0997, ⓦ trezetilias.com.br).

ACCOMMODATION

Hotel Schneider Rodovia dos Pioneiros, Km 2 (SC-465) ⓣ 49 3537 0184. Traditional Austrian-style lodge 2km southeast of the centre, where even the rooms are decorated with beautiful wood-carvings and come with TV and a/c (rooms at the front tend get some noise from the highway). R$210

Hotel Tirol Rua São Vicente de Paula 111 ⓣ 49 3537 0125, ⓦ hoteltirol.com.br. Typical Tyrolean-style chalet hotel, complete with geraniums hanging from every balcony, very comfortable, modern rooms and a heated pool. Also does decent buffets in its restaurant. Daily 11am–3.30pm. R$250

EATING AND DRINKING

★ **Cervejaria Bierbaum** Rua Dr Gaspar Coutinho 439 ⓣ 49 3537 0531, ⓦ bierbaum.com.br. Top-notch microbrewery attached to *Edelweiss* where you can sample the Reinheitsgebot-sanctioned suds (or buy bottles to take away), with unusual flavours such as pineapple, right next to the factory. Tues–Sun 6pm–midnight.

★ **Edelweiss** Rua Dr Gaspar Coutinho 441 ⓣ 49 3537 0531. Traditional-looking place with excellent craft beers brewed next door, and typical Austrian/German food (mains R$45–65), with especially good sausages and strudel (but also pizza) and live music. Tues–Sun 6pm–midnight.

Videira

Some 40km east of Treze Tílias in the valley of the Rio do Peixe, **VIDEIRA** (ⓦ videira.sc.gov.br) has a population that is mainly of Italian origin, descended from migrants who came from Rio Grande do Sul in the 1940s, their brightly painted wooden houses instantly distinguishable from the Austrians' chalets. Thanks to the Italians, this is Brazil's "Capital do Vinho", and vines dominate the landscape.

Museu do Vinho Mário de Pellegrin

Rua Padre Anchieta 344 (Praça do Coreto) • Tues–Fri 8.30am–noon & 1.30–6pm, Sat & Sun 2–5.30pm • R$2 • ⓣ 49 3566 6133

The only formal attraction in town is the small but well-organized **Museu do Vinho Mário de Pellegrin**, housed in a traditional wooden building dating from 1931 on Praça do Coreto, next to the pretty church, the **Igreja Matriz Imaculada Conceição** (1947). The museum chronicles local wine making in the early years of settlement. There's a *cantina* inside where you can taste the local vintages.

ARRIVAL AND DEPARTURE — VIDEIRA

By bus Reunidas (ⓦ www.reunidas.com.br) runs one daily bus between Joaçaba and Videira (12.10pm; departing Videira 2.30pm; 1hr 35min–2hr) and one daily bus to/from Caçador (1hr 5min). Catarinense runs services daily to/from Blumenau (2 daily; 5hr 25min–6hr 15min); Florianópolis (3 daily; 8hr 30min–9hr 50min); Lages (1 daily; 3hr).

Caçador

Some 35km northeast of Videira along the Rio do Peixe (and SC-303), **CAÇADOR** is very different in character from the largely agricultural settlements to the south, with a workaday atmosphere, a landscape dominated by pine plantations and an engaging museum.

Museu do Contestado

Getúlio Vargas 100 • Tues–Fri 8.30am–noon & 2–6pm, Sat & Sun 9am–5.30pm • Free • ⓣ 49 3567 1582

The one reason to stop in Caçador is to visit the small but illuminating **Museu do Contestado**, housed in the old train station. The museum commemorates the brutal war ("**Guerra do Contestado**") that took place in the Rio do Peixe valley from 1912 to 1916 between the Brazilian government, which was protecting the interests of the American-owned railway company that had been awarded huge land grants in the region, and the displaced native and *caboclo* population led by a charismatic "monk" named José Maria. The war eventually led to the deaths of 20,000 people, and well-presented exhibits in the museum commemorate the lives of the local indigenous peoples and *caboclos* who fought in the conflict. Outside the station is a perfectly preserved 1907 Baldwin locomotive and passenger carriage.

ARRIVAL AND DEPARTURE — CAÇADOR

By bus Reunidas (www.reunidas.com.br) runs 1–2 daily buses here direct from Florianópolis (8hr) and one daily bus to/from Videira (1hr 5min). Buses on to Chapecó (for the Museu Entomológico Fritz Plaumann) depart at 1.30pm (6hr), and to Joaçaba (for Treze Tílias) there are 1–2 daily (2hr 35min).

Museu Entomológico Fritz Plaumann

Nova Teutônia • Mon–Thurs 8.30am–noon & 1–5pm, Sat 9am–4pm • R$3 • 49 3452 1191, museufritzplaumann.ufsc.br

One of the few attractions in the far west of the state, the **Museu Entomológico Fritz Plaumann** lies in **NOVA TEUTÔNIA**, an overwhelmingly German rural community some 20km west of the town of **Seara** (285km northwest of Lages). Housed in a large 1940s wooden house typical of the region, the museum boasts what is quite possibly the most important (if not the biggest) collection of **insects** in Latin America. Plaumann (1902–94) arrived in Nova Teutônia from Germany in 1924 and went on to dedicate his life to entomological studies, collecting 80,000 specimens representing 17,000 species, including 1500 that had previously been unknown. Pride of place goes to the displays of butterflies at every stage of development, but what's truly impressive is that the entire collection is supported by detailed notebooks, correspondence and other documentation representing seventy years of Plaumann's professional and personal life.

ARRIVAL AND DEPARTURE — MUSEU ENTOMOLÓGICO FRITZ PLAUMANN

By bus Nova Teutônia lies 10km south of the main road (SC-283) between Chapecó and Seara; buses stop at the turning, but it's a long walk from there – you'll need to take a taxi from Seara or have your own transport. Reunidas (www.reunidas.com.br) runs 5–6 daily buses direct from Lages, Joaçaba and Florianópolis to Seara and Chapecó (10–12hr).

Rio Grande do Sul

Closer in spirit to the pampas culture of bordering countries Uruguay and Argentina than many parts of Brazil, **Rio Grande do Sul** is at the heart of the south's *gaúcho* traditions, where cowboys still work the *campanha*, the *churrasco* is sublime and even city slickers drink *chimarrão* in special gourd cups. Somewhat removed from the nation's political heart, the state has had its share of movers and shakers nonetheless: ex-president and dictator **Getúlio Vargas** was born here in 1882; impeached former president **Dilma Rousseff** rose to power in Porto Alegre in the 1970s, helping to create the Democratic Labour Party (PDT) here; while the state's (and possibly Brazil's) most idolized superstar, model **Gisele Bündchen**, was born in the small town of Três de Maio in 1980 (she's been living in the US, though, since 1997). Today Rio Grande do Sul is one of the nation's most prosperous states, with plenty of attractions: the capital **Porto Alegre** is the cultural centre of the south, while its hinterland of quaint Italian and German towns provides gastronomic allure. To really appreciate the size and raw beauty of the region, however, you need to visit its sensational **national parks**.

Porto Alegre

The capital of Rio Grande do Sul, **PORTO ALEGRE** lies on the eastern bank of the Rio Guaíba, at the point where five rivers converge to form the **Lagoa dos Patos**, a giant freshwater lagoon navigable by even the largest of ships. In 1752 settlers from the Azores arrived here, but it wasn't until Porto Alegre became the gateway for the export of beef

PORTO ALEGRE'S ART AND BOOK FAIRS

In October or November, Praça da Alfândega is occupied by the **Porto Alegre Book Fair** (Ⓦ feiradolivro-poa.com.br), the largest of its kind in Latin America. Note also that the three galleries/museums (see below) in the *praça* are often closed before and after the **Bienal do Mercosul** (Ⓦ fundacaobienal.art.br), a major contemporary art expo that usually takes place every two years mid-September to mid-November (though in 2018 it ran April–May). During the expo the galleries/museums are open Tues–Sun 9am–7pm.

that it developed into Brazil's leading commercial centre south of São Paulo, with a population today of some 4.5 million. Though it's not especially attractive (like most major Brazilian cities), with a skyline of primarily tired 1960s high-rises, and the recent economic downturn has definitely taken a toll, the **Fundação Iberê Camargo** is a must-see for art lovers (assuming it's open), and the city remains a fun place to eat and drink.

Mercado Público

Largo Glênio Peres (Av Júlio de Castilhos) • Mon–Fri 7.30am–7.30pm, Sat 7.30am–6.30pm • Ⓦ mercadopublico.com.br

Founded in 1869, the vast, elegant **Mercado Público** is at the heart of Porto Alegre's commercial district. It contains an absorbing mix of stalls selling household goods, food, a vast variety of herbs, *erva maté* (*yerba maté* or *chimarrão*) of all grades of quality, items used in *umbanda* rituals and regional handicrafts – and the city's most helpful tourist office (see page 611). It's also an excellent **place to eat** (see page 612).

Just opposite the market, the Bavarian-style *Chalé da Praça XV* – a charming nineteenth-century bar and restaurant (see page 612) that was formerly the meeting place of the city's artists and intellectuals – is an especially good spot from which to watch the world go by.

Paço Municipal

Praça Montevidéu 10 • Mon–Fri 9am–noon & 1.30–6pm • Free

On the other side of Praça Montevidéu from the Mercado Público lies the ornate Neoclassical **Paço Municipal** or "Paço dos Açorianos" (city hall), built between 1898 and 1901, and now home to a small art collection, the **Pinacoteca Aldo Locatelli**, focusing on local *gaúcho* artists such as Pedro Weingärtner, João Fahrion and Carlos Scliar, in addition to the mayor's office. In front of the building lies the **Fonte Talavera de la Reina**, a tiled fountain donated to the city in 1935 by its once considerable Spanish community.

Praça da Alfândega

Porto Alegre's most elegant and vibrant plaza, **Praça da Alfândega** is surrounded by grand high-rises and French-style Neoclassical buildings, studded with palm, kapok, jacaranda and *ipê* trees and always packed out with shoppers, shoe shiners, trinket sellers and market stalls. On the southern side, look for the ornate facade of the Banco Safra building at Andradas 1035; this was completed in 1913 for **Previdência do Sul**, an insurance company. Next door is the equally florid **Clube do Comércio**, a pink Art Deco beauty built in 1939 and still the city's premier social club.

Museu de Arte do Rio Grande do Sul

Praça da Alfândega • Tues–Sun 10am–7pm • Free • Ⓣ 51 3227 2311, Ⓦ margs.rs.gov.br

Housed in a grand edifice built in 1912 for the Revenue Service, the stately **Museu de Arte do Rio Grande do Sul** has been a showcase for *gaúcho* artists since 1979. The nineteenth-century landscapes here deserve particular attention. The permanent collection includes work from neo-realist Cândido Portinari, Emiliano Di Cavalcanti, local boy Iberê Camargo and Austrian-born artist Xico Stockinger (who died here in his adopted city in 2009).

9

Memorial do Rio Grande do Sul

Rua Sete de Setembro 1020 (Praça da Alfândega) • Tues–Sat 10am–6pm, Sun 1–5pm • Free • 51 3224 1724, www.cultura.rs.gov.br

The grand Neoclassical Correios e Telégrafos (post office) building was completed in 1914, and now serves as the **Memorial do Rio Grande do Sul**. Housed here are the state archives, along with an oral history centre and various other artefacts preserving the history of Rio Grande do Sul; galleries host travelling exhibitions and rotating displays from the permanent collection.

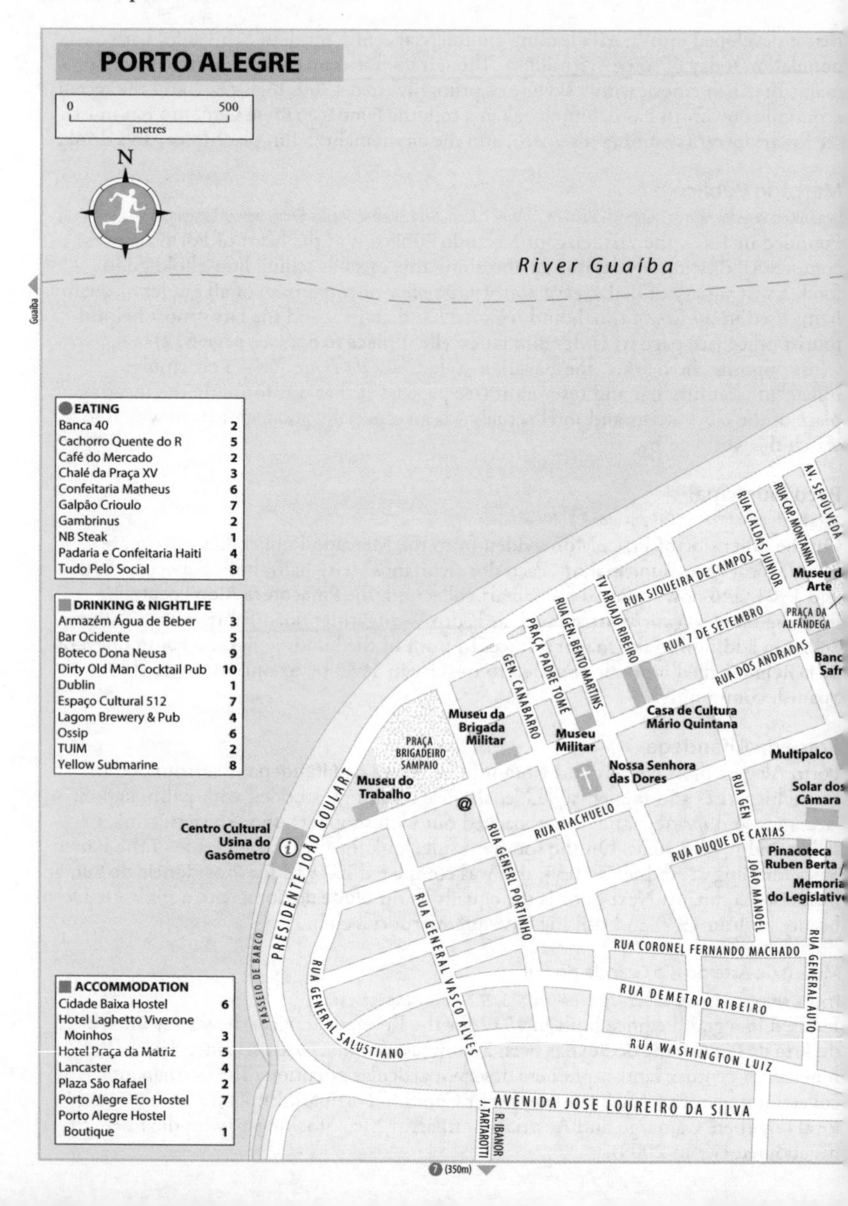

Santander Cultural

Rua Sete de Setembro 1028 (Praça da Alfândega) • Tues–Sat 10am–7pm, Sun 2–7pm • Free (concerts $12, movies $10) • 51 3287 5500, www.santandercultural.com.br

The **Santander Cultural** completes the trio of historic buildings on the north side of Praça da Alfândega that hosts temporary exhibitions of Brazilian art, often major works from galleries in São Paulo, and classical concerts. The building itself, a converted 1932 bank, features some remarkable stained-glass windows, while the basement where the vaults were installed now houses an art movie theatre and café.

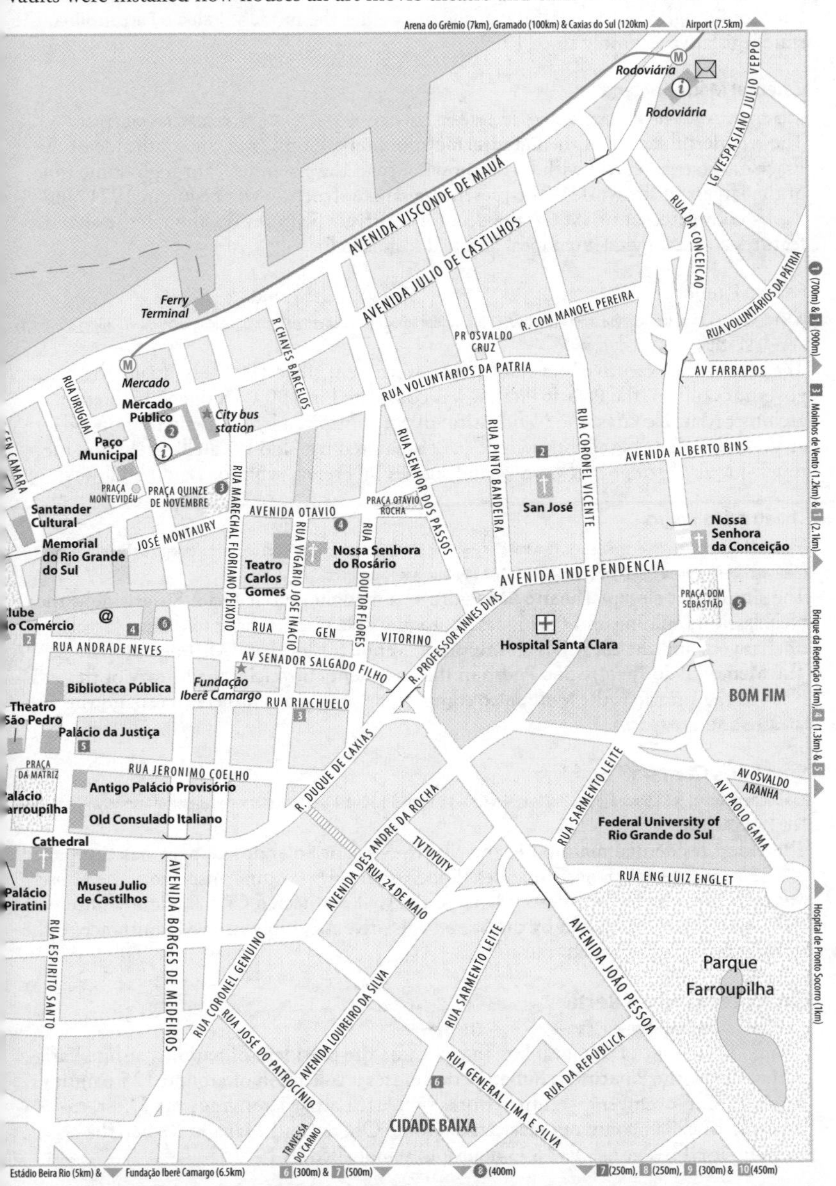

Praça da Matriz

Crowning the hill to the south of Praça da Alfândega is **Praça da Matriz** (officially called Praça Marechal Deodoro), a square of greenery surrounded by a mix of Modernist offices and some of Porto Alegre's oldest buildings. The north side is dominated by the modern **Palácio da Justiça** (courthouse) and **Theatro São Pedro**, while some delicate examples of nineteenth-century architecture grace the east side, including the former **Consulado Italiano** (Italian consulate) at no. 134, whose prominent position reflects the important role Italians once played in Porto Alegre (it's now the Brazilian Progressive Party building). On the west side of the square lies the modern **Palácio Farroupilha**, the state legislative assembly since 1967.

Catedral Metropolitana

Praça da Matriz • Mon–Fri 7am–7pm, Sat 9am–7pm, Sun 8am–7pm • Free • T 51 3228 6001, W catedralportoalegre.com.br

The wonderful facade of the **Catedral Metropolitana** looms over the south side of the Praça da Matriz, replete with lavish mosaics, twin towers and a 75m-high dome (one of the largest in the world). The present Italianate structure was begun in 1921, and wasn't completed until 1986 – the decor is relatively plain inside, though the altar features a mural by talented local artist Aldo Locatelli.

Palácio Piratini

Praça da Matriz • Tours (Portuguese only) every hour (30min), depending on the Governor's schedule; Mon–Fri 9.30–11.30am & 2–5pm • Free • T 51 3210 4170, W estado.rs.gov.br

The seat of the executive branch of state government since 1921 (essentially the governor's office), the **Palácio Piratini** was completed in 1909. Designed by French architect Maurice Grâs, the Neoclassical pile was inspired by the Petit Trianon palace at Versailles. Tour highlights include panels painted by Aldo Locatelli, including the much-loved *Negrinho do Pastoreio*, and statues by French sculptor Raul Landowski.

Theatro São Pedro

Praça da Matriz • Ticket office (on Rua Gen. Câmara) Mon–Fri 1–6.30pm, Sat & Sun 3pm–start of show; Memorial do Theatro São Pedro: check website for current times • Free • T 51 3227 5100, W teatrosaopedro.com.br

The simple but elegant **Theatro São Pedro** was inaugurated in 1858. Surprisingly, the Neoclassical building and Portuguese Baroque-style interior have remained largely unchanged, and the theatre is an important venue for local and visiting companies. The **Memorial do Theatro São Pedro** in the basement chronicles the history of the site. Next to the theatre is the **Multipalco** complex, an ambitious project to expand the city's theatre and art spaces.

Solar dos Câmara

Rua Duque de Caxias 968 • Guided tours (1hr) Mon–Fri 8.30–11.30am & 1.30–6.30pm (enter through Legislative Assembly) • Free • T 51 3210 1148, E visitasguiadas@al.rs.gov.br

The oldest residential mansion in the city, the elegant **Solar dos Câmara** was completed in 1824 for José Feliciano Fernandes Pinheiro, the city customs inspector. The house was later inhabited by the descendants of the well-connected Câmara family until 1975, and it was purchased by the State Legislative Assembly in 1981. Entrance to the lavish interior is by guided tour only.

Pinacoteca Ruben Berta

Rua Duque de Caxias 973 • Mon–Fri 10am–6pm • Free • T 51 3289 8292

Named in honour of the local boy that became the president of national airline Varig in the 1940s, the **Pinacoteca Ruben Berta** houses a collection of around 125 paintings, ranging from seventeenth-century works by Dutch artist Jeronymus van Diest, to Japanese-Brazilian contemporary artists Tomie Ohtake and Manabu Mabe. The building itself is a gorgeous 1893 mansion, remodelled in 1917.

Museu Júlio de Castilhos

Rua Duque de Caxias 1205 • Tues–Sat 10am–5pm • Free • 51 3221 3959, www.museujuliodecastilhos.rs.gov.br

The **Museu Júlio de Castilhos** is Porto Alegre's ramshackle history museum, occupying a graceful old mansion once owned by respected journalist and politician **Júlio de Castilhos** (1860–1903), twice the governor of Rio Grande do Sul in the 1890s. His house (no. 1231), was built in 1887 – Castilhos lived here from 1898 to 1903. No. 1205 next door was built in 1916 and merged with the museum seventy years later. The gallery exploring the link between the Azores and the city is poor, but the prehistoric ("Indígena") exhibit contains some rare **Guaraní** cultural artefacts and a 2000-year-old mummified skull. Other galleries contain religious statuary, displays on the failed **Farroupilha Revolution** (1835–45), still keenly remembered here, Castilhos himself and the history of slavery in the state, but everything is labelled in Portuguese only.

Rua dos Andradas and around

The heart of the *centro histórico*, **Rua dos Andradas** (aka Rua da Praia), is pedestrianized and cobbled for most of its length, and after a period of decline is once again the city's main commercial thoroughfare, crammed with shoppers. Much of the western end is taken up by historic (but still used) military buildings, with a couple of dusty military museums, of interest to hard-core aficionados only.

Igreja Nossa Senhora das Dores

Rua dos Andradas 597 • Daily 8.30am–noon & 1.30–6.30pm • Free • 51 3228 7376

The **Igreja Nossa Senhora das Dores** at no. 597 is the oldest surviving church in Porto Alegre (built from 1807 to 1904). Its grand twin-towered brilliant-white facade is far more impressive than the interior.

Casa de Cultura Mário Quintana

Rua dos Andradas 736 • Tues–Fri 9am–9pm, Sat & Sun noon–9pm • Free • 51 3221 7147, ccmq.com.br

The most beguiling attraction on Andradas is the **Casa de Cultura Mário Quintana**, a warren of beautifully restored art galleries, libraries and theatres. Designed in Neoclassical style by the German architect Theo Wiederspahn and constructed between 1914 and 1929, the elegant rose-coloured building served as the *Hotel Majestic* until 1980 and as such was once a popular meeting point for local artists, intellectuals and politicians, including presidents Vargas and Goulart. The seminal Brazilian poet **Mário Quintana**, the poet of "simple things", was a resident from 1968 to 1980 (hence the name), and his room on the second floor (no. 217, **Quarto do Poeta**) is assiduously maintained, shrine-like behind glass, as if the great man has just walked out (readings of his poems play on a loop in Portuguese only). You could spend a couple of hours exploring the numerous art galleries in the building (mostly temporary exhibits), but highlights include the room dedicated to tragic pop singer **Elis Regina** (2/F; Tues–Fri 9am–6pm, Sat & Sun noon–6pm), born in the city in 1945, the **Museu de Arte Contemporânea** (6/F; Tues–Sun 10am–7pm), the old photos of the hotel on the second floor (**Memorial do Hotel**), and *Café Santo de Casa* on the top (seventh) floor.

Centro Cultural Usina do Gasômetro

Av Presidente João Goulart 551 • Tues–Fri 9am–9pm, Sat & Sun 10am–9pm • Free • 51 3289 8100

At the western tip of the city, the **Centro Cultural Usina do Gasômetro** is a striking post-industrial landmark, an old coal-fired power station in use from 1928 to 1974, with its 117m chimney still looming over the bay. The centre hosts changing contemporary art exhibits and shows, and the giant warehouse-like space itself is worth a quick visit, looking like a mini Tate Modern. The shabby riverside promenade nearby (**Passeio de Barco**) is lined with cheap souvenir and food stalls, but safe enough for a stroll during the day.

BOM FIM'S SUNDAY MARKET

If you're in Porto Alegre on a Sunday, don't despair – while almost everything is closed, locals flock to the Bom Fim neighbourhood for the **Brique da Redenção** (Sun 9am–5pm; ⓦ briquedaredencao.com.br), held on tree-lined Av José Bonifácio on the south side of Redenção Park. The three hundred or so stalls here are part farmers' market, part souvenir and flea market, with plenty of antiques, arts, crafts and jewellery of varying quality on sale. Most stalls take cash and credit cards. The scene is well worth checking out, with lots of cafés nearby and great people-watching as Porto Alegre comes out to play; you'll see plenty of folks sipping *chimarrão* as they wander around.

Fundação Iberê Camargo

Av Padre Cacique 2000 • Sat & Sun 2–7pm • Free • ⓣ 51 3247 8000, ⓦ iberecamargo.org.br • Take any bus towards the Zona Sul (from Av Senador Salgado Filho to Juca Batista, Serraria, Padre Réus or Camaquã); to return you'll have to walk back along the highway to the bus stop, and then take any bus headed to town; a taxi from the bus station should be R$22, from the airport R$40; see also Linha Turismo (see page 611)

Porto Alegre's undervisited crown jewel, the **Fundação Iberê Camargo** lies 5km south of the *centro histórico* along the bay. The fascinating Modernist building, designed by Portuguese architect Álvaro Siza and opened in 2008, is itself part of the attraction, vaguely reminiscent of the Guggenheim in New York, with a gleaming all-white interior and a spiral layout. The contemporary art exhibits here are usually impressive; displays revolve, but there's always work from Rio Grande do Sul artist **Iberê Camargo** (1914–94), whose unsettling, Expressionist images have become some of Brazil's most revered art. The café here is the best place to **watch the sunset** over the Guaíba. Note that the foundation's **opening hours have been cut** drastically since Brazil's current economic crisis began (check the website for the latest).

Moinhos de Vento

To get a taste of upwardly mobile Brazil, spend an afternoon in the fashionable **Moinhos de Vento** district, 4km east of the old centre. Though the cornerstone of the area remains leafy Moinhos de Vento Park (aka *parcão*) and its replica Azorean windmill, it's now studded with hip bars, street cafés and restaurants (see page 614), as well as the deluxe **Moinhos Shopping** mall. The main strip is **Rua Padre Chagas**.

Hidráulica Moinhos de Vento and around

Rua 24 de Outubro 200 • Gardens daily 8am–7pm • Free

The only sight as such in Moinhos de Ventos is the **Hidráulica Moinhos de Vento**, the old city waterworks and its pretty landscaped **gardens**, built in 1928 and modelled on Versailles no less, though the small **gallery** underneath the elegant **water tower** was closed at the time of writing. Not far from here, the "world's most beautiful street" is a stretch, but the **Rua Gonçalo de Carvalho** is pleasant nonetheless, shaded by giant *tipuana tipu* trees.

ARRIVAL AND DEPARTURE — PORTO ALEGRE

By plane The Aeroporto Internacional Salgado Filho (ⓣ 51 3358 2000, ⓦ aeroportoportoalegre.net) is just 6km northeast of downtown Porto Alegre on Av Severo Dulius. Terminal 1 (Avianca, Gol and international flights; Terminal 2 (Azul). Both terminals contain car rental desks and ATMs. Fixed-price Cootaero taxis (pay at the booth before you leave the terminal; ⓣ 51 3342 5000) charge R$34–42 into the centre (reckon on R$40–55 heading back, when taxis use the meter); you can also take the monorail link (Aeromóvel) to the nearest metro station (3min), the Estação Aeroporto, and catch trains into the city (5am–11.20pm; R$1.70; buy ticket before you board the Aeromóvel) in just 10min (the Mercado station). There are also buses direct from the airport to Canela and Gramado (around R$35); buy tickets at the VEPPO kiosk in Terminal 1 arrivals.

By bus The rodoviária (ⓣ 51 3210 0101) is northeast of the centre at Largo Vespasiano Júlio Veppo 11, but within walking distance of most of the *centro histórico*. After dark it's safer, and easier, to ride the metro to the Mercado

Público or take a taxi (R$10–30; ☎51 3221 9371). Local buses also stop constantly just outside the bus station, most going to the Mercado Público (#429, #436, #491, #493 and #495 for example). Inside the rodoviária are plenty of cheap places to eat and a couple of ATMs, though English-speakers are rare at the tourist information centre here. Left luggage is R$5/day.

Destinations Buenos Aires (1 daily; 18hr); Canela (hourly; 2hr); Curitiba (8 daily; 11hr); Florianópolis (14 daily; 7–8hr); Foz do Iguaçu (8 daily; 14–16hr); Gramado (hourly; 2hr); Laguna (5 daily; 7hr); Montevideo (1 daily; 11hr); Pelotas (hourly; 3hr); Rio de Janeiro (1–2 daily; 24–25hr); Rio Grande (hourly; 4hr 30min); Santo Ângelo (13 daily; 6–7hr); São Paulo (4 daily; 18hr).

GETTING AROUND

By metro (Trensurb) Links the Mercado Público all the way to Novo Hamburgo (daily 5am–11.20pm; R$1.70; ⓦtrensurb.gov.br), but its use for visitors is limited to the connection between the bus station, airport and Mercado Público. Buy tickets at the counter at any station.

By bus Public buses are more useful, with most of them charging a flat R$4.05 (commuter minibuses are R$6); you pay the ticket collector when you get on the bus (correct change is appreciated but not required).

By taxi Taxi meters begin at R$5.18, drivers are honest and taxis easy to flag down in the centre (☎51 3342 5000).

By bicycle Porto Alegre has a rental bike scheme dubbed Bike POA (6am–10pm; ☎51 4003 6052, ⓦbikepoa.tembici.com.br); you need a working smartphone to use it. Paying an upfront fee of R$5 allows you to ride bikes for up to 1hr free within a 24hr period; over 1hr you'll be charged an additional R$8/hr. Bike docks are spread all over the city.

INFORMATION AND TOURS

Tourist information The local Secretaria Municipal de Turismo (ⓦportoalegre.travel) has very helpful branches (usually with English speakers) at the airport (see page 610), rodoviária (daily 7am–10pm), the Centro Cultural Usina do Gasômetro (Tues–Sun 9am–6pm; ☎0800 517 686) and at the Mercado Público (Store 99, Ground Floor; Mon–Sat 8am–6pm; also ☎0800 517 686).

Boat tours Excursions (1hr 30min) on the Rio Guaíba with Barco Cisne Branco leave from the tour-boat berth (Cais do Porto) on Av Mauá 1050, near the metro station (daily 10.30am, 3pm & 4.30pm; R$35; ☎51 3224 5222, ⓦbarcocisnebranco.com.br).

City tours The Municipal Tourism department operates "Linha Turismo" (Tues–Fri R$25, Sat & Sun R$30; ☎51 3289 0176), an open-top double-decker bus that takes in the *centro histórico* (Tues–Sun departures from the Mercado Público 9.55am–2.55pm, hourly; 1hr 20min). Buy tickets at the tourist office at the Mercado Público (see page 605).

ACCOMMODATION

There's a good range of hotels scattered around the city centre, and as distances are small it's possible to **walk** to most places, although great care should be taken at night when the area tends to be eerily quiet. There are a handful of budget and more expensive options in **Cidade Baixa** and **Moinhos de Vento**, places that allow for evening walks and offer a choice of bars and restaurants. Hotels here are geared towards **business travellers**, and as a consequence most offer substantial discounts at weekends (the rates quoted here are for weekdays).

FUTEBOL PORTO ALEGRE

Porto Alegre is home to two fiercely competitive football teams: **Grêmio** (ⓦgremio.net), who play in Série A (Brazil's premier league) at Arena do Grêmio (ⓦarenapoa.com.br) north of the centre; and **Sport Club Internacional** (ⓦinternacional.com.br), who play at the Estadio Beira-Rio, south of the city (the team was relegated to Série B in 2016) – this latter stadium is where World Cup 2014 matches took place. Both teams have been the launching pad for world-class players such as **Ronaldinho** (who was born in Porto Alegre), **Alexandre Pato**, **Falcão** and **Luiz Felipe Scolari**, who managed Grêmio in the 1990s. The annual derby between the two teams – dubbed the "Gre-Nal" – is one of the biggest games in Brazil. You can take **tours** of the Arena do Grêmio (Wed–Sun 10am–4pm hourly; R$32) and visit the on-site **Museu do Grêmio** (Wed–Sun 10am–6pm; R$14; with tour R$40) to learn about the history of the club; the **Museu do Sport Club Internacional** at the Beira-Rio (Tues–Sun 10am–6pm; R$40 with tour) offers a similar experience (1hr tours of the stadium are available daily 10am, 1pm, 3pm & 5pm). Tickets for matches usually cost R$30–120; buy tickets at the stadium box office on the day, or ask your hotel.

9

Cidade Baixa Hostel Rua Sarmento Leite 964, Cidade Baixa 51 3398 4648, cidadebaixahostel.com.br; map p.606. Friendly, bright hostel in a great area for nightlife, with a series of comfy but compact dorms (five mixed, one female-only) and spanking new bathrooms – the public spaces here (kitchen, TV room) are a bit cramped, but the staff are super-friendly and the breakfast is good. Dorms R$41

★ **Hotel Laghetto Viverone Moinhos** Rua Dr Vale 579, Moinhos de Vento 51 2102 7272, hotellaghettomoinhos.com.br; map p.606. This stylish modern hotel is attached to an elegant villa, making this one of the more interesting places to stay; the compact rooms feature a slick contemporary style, and there's a gorgeous rooftop pool area and a small bar. Parking R$33/day. R$347

★ **Hotel Praça da Matriz** Largo João de Albuquerque 72 51 3224 8872, pracadamatrizhotel.com.br; map p.606. This beautifully renovated 1927 mansion is a great deal in the heart of the city, with small but stylish rooms that blend contemporary and Art Deco design – much of the original stained glass has been retained, and the central atrium features ornate metalwork. Parking is R$30/day. R$197

Lancaster Travessa Acelino de Carvalho 67 51 3224 4737, hotel-lancaster-poa.com.br; map p.606. Located in one of the liveliest commercial areas downtown, this modern hotel is set behind an imposing 1940s Art Deco facade. Rooms are small but well equipped, and excellent value for money. Parking R$24/day. R$142

Plaza São Rafael Av Alberto Bins 514 51 3220 7000, plazahoteis.com.br/saorafael/br; map p.606. Although there are now several better top-end hotels in Porto Alegre, this has a certain traditional style that's found in none of the newer establishments. Located in the city centre, rooms are all spacious and very comfortable – be sure to ask for one overlooking the lagoon. There's also an indoor pool. Parking R$35/day. R$307

Porto Alegre Eco Hostel Rua Luiz Afonso 276 51 3019 2449, portoalegreecohostel.com.br; map p.606. Justly the most popular hostel in the city, with excellent staff and comfy mixed or female-only dorms right in Cidade Baixa. Extras include a swimming pool, games room, garden and bike rental. Dorms R$40, doubles R$120

Porto Alegre Hostel Boutique Rua São Carlos 545 51 3228 3802, hostel.tur.br; map p.606. Great location, and though not really a "boutique", the rooms here are a step up from a normal HI hostel; all en-suite in a historic mansion, with a/c and TVs. There's a buffet breakfast (usually R$9 extra), with laundry and communal kitchen on site too. Prices for HI members are R$6–10 lower. Dorms R$60, doubles R$135

EATING

As the home of Brazilian **churrasco** (barbecue), Porto Alegre has some enticing places to eat – if you're a meat-eater it's worth splashing out on a steak at least once. **Buffets** are also good value – all over town, there's usually a "livre" price – typically R$15 – or a *por quilo* fee. You'll also see locals everywhere (especially at Bom Fim market) sipping the local **yerba maté tea** – *chimarrão* – with a metal straw (*bomba*) from a special *cuia* (cup), topping up the hot water from flasks. Some of the best places to eat lie beyond the *centro histórico* in the Bom Vim, Moinhos de Vento and Cidade Baixa neighbourhoods.

CENTRO HISTÓRICO

Banca 40 Mercado Público Loja 40 51 3226 3533, banca40.com.br; map p.606. Open since 1927 (it looks modern, however), this local institution in the centre of the market is justly lauded for its *bomba royal* (R$15) ice-cream dessert; regular scoops of ice cream start at R$6, and you can also order sandwiches. Mon–Fri 8am–7.30pm, Sat 8am–6.30pm.

★ **Cachorro Quente do R** Praça Dom Sebastião 51 3019 3436, cachorroquentedor.com.br; map p.606. This legendary cart has been cooking up hot dogs (*cachorro*) in front of Colégio Rosário (the city's grand old catholic school) since 1962 (several imitators have since emerged). Choose your sausage type (*salsicha* is typical hot dog; *linguiça* is a meatier, cured sausage), then what you want on it; mushy peas, parsley, ketchup, mustard or chilli. The gut-busting finished product (R$9.25–14.50) is smothered in their secret sauce and grated cheese. Daily 11am–midnight.

Café do Mercado Mercado Público Loja 73 51 3029 2490, cafedomercado.com.br; map p.606. Best Brazilian coffee in the central market, noted for cappuccinos (R$7.70) and espressos (R$5), with a few tables inside and outside on the plaza. You can also buy freshly roasted coffee beans here. Mon–Fri 8.30am–7.30pm, Sat 9am–5pm.

★ **Chalé da Praça XV** Praça 15 Novembro 51 3225 2667, chaledapracaxv.com.br; map p.606. Porto Alegre institution, opposite the market, in a gorgeous chalet dating back to 1885 (with Art Nouveau alterations in 1911), and a menu of the usual café meals (mains R$18–30) and drinks (large beers R$6.90 during happy hour, Mon–Thurs, Sat & Sun 4–7pm) – grab a chair on the outdoor terrace to soak up the scene. Daily 11am–11.30pm.

Confeitaria Matheus Av Borges de Medeiros 421 51 3224 2179; map p.606. Classic downtown bakery and café founded in 1947, with a bustling interior and an amazing cake selection (R$5–9). Popular for breakfast – order the *dupla café cortado*, coffee with steamed milk, and the calorie-packed *sanduíche farroupilha*, a toasted sandwich with cheese and ham (R$5.20). Coffee from R$5. Mon–Fri 6am–10pm, Sat 7am–9pm.

Galpão Crioulo Parque Maurício Sirotsky Sobrinho ⊙51 3226 8194, ⊚churrascariagalpaocrioulo.com.br; map p.606. A huge and always reliable *churrascaria* in near the Centro Cultural Usina do Gasômetro, with a bewildering selection of meats in its *rodízio* (reckon on around R$100 per person for dinner), and a good range of salad and vegetable offerings (it's the usual all-you-can-eat set-up). In the evenings there's *gaúcho* music and traditional dance performances (Mon–Fri 8.15–11pm, Sat & Sun 12.30–3pm & 8.15–11pm). Daily 11.30am–3pm & 7.30pm–midnight.

★**Gambrinus** Mercado Público Loja 85 ⊙51 3226 6914, ⊚gambrinus.com.br; map p.606. Visit the city's oldest restaurant (founded in 1889 and named for the unofficial patron saint of beer) for a posh, old-fashioned southern Brazil experience where you can sample some real classics: *rabada* (oxtail), a fillet of beef with fried eggs, or salted cod. *Filet mignon* costs from R$39 and the best steaks are R$46–58. Mon–Fri 11am–9pm, Sat 11am–4pm.

Padaria e Confeitaria Haiti Av Otavio Rocha 151 ⊙51 3221 3577, ⊚cafehaiti.com.br; map p.606. This 1955 diner oozes character, with a bar, huge cake selection and tightly packed eating area (get a coupon before you enter), serving classics such as "*a la minuta*" (stew; mains R$6.50–20), or you can walk up to the second floor for the lunch buffet (Mon–Sat 11am–3pm; R$19 "livre" or R$4.80/100g). Mon–Sat 6.30am–10pm, Sun 10am–6.30pm.

OUTSIDE THE CENTRE

★**NB Steak** Av Ramiro Barcelos 389, Floresta ⊙51 3225 2205, ⊚nbsteak.com.br; map p.606. In the opinion of many locals this is Porto Alegre's best *churrascaria* – quite something in a city where people appreciate meat. Located between downtown and Moinhos de Vento, this unpretentious-looking restaurant boasts *rodizio* offerings of the highest quality and an excellent and tremendously varied salad bar. Dinner costs around R$250 per person. Mon–Fri 11.30am–3.30pm & 6.30–11.30pm, Sat 11.30am–11.30pm, Sun 11.30am–10pm.

Tudo Pelo Social Rua João Alfredo 448, Cidade Baixa ⊙51 3226 4405; map p.606. Hugely popular restaurant that serves Brazilian classics like rice, beans and steak. The lunchtime buffet is a bargain at R$13 per person, while the à la carte *picanha* "for two" (R$23; steak R$32) comes with huge portions of chips, rice and salad, and easily feeds three to four people. Mon–Sat 11am–2.45pm & 6–11.45pm, Sun 11am–2.45pm.

DRINKING AND NIGHTLIFE

Porto Alegre has two main centres for nightlife: the more flashy action revolves around **Moinhos de Vento**, and the hub of Rua Padre Chagas, while the **Cidade Baixa** (the rough triangle south of the centre formed by Av Jose Loureiro da Silva, Av João Pessoa and Av Aureliano de Figueiredo Pinto) offers more traditional samba joints and bohemian bars. Try and sample the local **microbrews**; Toca da Coruja (⊚cervejacoruja.com.br) is one of the best in Brazil. The city has also been an important hub for **live music** – "rock rural" and MPB – since the 1970s, with local legends such as Nelson Coelho de Castro (still around) and Carlinhos Hartlieb (who died in 1984), and adopted son Bebeto Alves.

CENTRO HISTÓRICO

Armazém Água de Beber Rua Vigário José Inácio 686 ⊙51 9827 8000, ⊚armazemaguadebeber.blogspot.com; map p.606. Tiny bar on the edge of the old centre, run by two beer aficionados: they claim around a hundred different beers are served ($14–20 for 0.5l), plus beer snacks (rib sandwich from R$11), while DJs spin on Friday nights. Mon–Fri 5–11pm.

TUIM Rua General Câmara 333 ⊙51 9962 8851; map p.606. Just off Praça de Alfândega, this pocket-sized pub in the centre is ideal for a cool, quiet beer. *TUIM* also has an impressive variety of spirits, including quality *cachaça*. Mon–Fri 10am–9pm.

CIDADE BAIXA

Boteco Dona Neusa Rua Lima e Silva 800 ⊙51 3013 8700, ⊚botecodonaneusa.com.br; map p.606. No-frills samba joint, with live bands and dancing most nights, plus plenty of *chopp* (draught beer) and snacks from Northeast Brazil. Mon–Sat 5pm–1am.

Dirty Old Man Cocktail Pub Rua Lima e Silva 956 ⊙51 3085 8227, ⊚dirtyoldman.com.br; map p.606. A tribute to cult American writer Charles Bukowski, in a tiny old house, with a decent range of local microbrews and cocktails. Also does excellent Brazilian food (try the *batata rústica*). Tues–Thurs & Sun 7pm–1am, Fri & Sat 7pm–2am.

★**Espaço Cultural 512** Rua João Alfredo 512 ⊙51 3212 0229, ⊚espaco512.com.br; map p.606. Legendary live music bar with a busy weekly programme of performances and a popular house cocktail, the *maracangalha* (*cachaça*, pineapple, ginger, passion fruit and red pepper). Cover charge R$10–15. Tues, Wed & Sun 7pm–midnight, Thurs 7pm–1am, Fri 7pm–2am, Sat 8pm–2am.

Ossip Rua da República 677 ⊙51 3224 2422; map

p.606. Lively and colourful Cidade Baixa hangout, with samba and bossa nova playing most nights – patrons tend to spill out of the tiny bar and onto the street. Also does good pizza. Daily 6pm–1.30am.

Yellow Submarine Shopping Nova Olaria (Loja 2), Rua Lima e Silva 776 ⓣ51 3226 5201, ⓦbaryellowsubmarine.com.br; map p.606. Buzzy bar and restaurant with live bands in a newish shopping mall, loosely dedicated to the Beatles (including the menu items) and their much-loved song. Good, kitsch fun. Mon 11.30am–2pm, Tues–Fri 11.30am–2pm & 6pm–12.30am, Sat & Sun 6pm–12.30am.

BOM FIM

Bar Ocidente Av Osvaldo Aranha 960, at João Telles ⓣ51 3012 2675, ⓦbarocidente.com.br; map p.606. Legendary former meeting place of dissidents since 1980, now best known for good veggie lunches (R$10–17), its art gallery and lively party nights: Saturday is always a themed club night (cover R$15–50). Mon–Sat 11.45am–2.30pm & 6pm–2am.

MOINHOS DE VENTO

Dublin Rua Padre Chagas 342, Moinhos de Vento ⓣ51 3268 8835, ⓦdublinpub.com.br; map p.606. Every city must have one: this is your standard faux-Irish bar and the current place where well-to-do *gaúchos* look to enjoy themselves. Live bands play daily and an entry fee is charged after 9pm (R$10–20). Mon–Wed & Sun 6pm–3am, Thurs–Sat 6pm–5am.

Lagom Brewery & Pub Rua Bento Figueiredo 72 ⓣ51 3062 5045; map p.606. Porto Alegre's first brew pub serves a range of tasty ales, stouts and IPAs on a seasonal basis – top tipples include the amber ale and oatmeal stout. Tues & Wed 6pm–1am, Thurs–Sat 6pm–2am.

DIRECTORY

Hospital Hospital Municipal de Pronto Socorro (HPS), Largo Teodore Herzl (Av Osvaldo Aranha), ⓣ51 3289 7999.

Internet Free wi-fi is available at the Mercado Público, Praça da Alfândega and Usina do Gasômetro. Internet cafés can still be found in the centre: try *Dreams Lavanderia* at Rua dos Andradas 405 (Mon–Fri 7.30am–9pm, Sat 8am–2pm; R$5/hr), or *Office Lan House* at Galeria Edith, Rua dos Andradas 1273 (walk to the end of the passage; Mon–Fri 8am–7.30pm, Sat 9am–1pm; R$5/hr).

Money and exchange There are banks and *casas de câmbio* (Mon–Fri 10am–4.30pm) along Rua dos Andradas and Av Senador Salgado Filho near Praça da Alfândega, and there are ATMs everywhere. Citibank and HSBC have branches in Moinhos de Vento.

Post office In the *centro histórico* at Rua Siqueira Campos 1100 (Mon–Fri 9am–6pm, Sat 9am–noon; ⓣ51 3220 8800), and inside the rodoviária (Mon–Fri 9am–6pm; ⓣ51 3225 1945).

The Serra Gaúcha

North of Porto Alegre the **Serra Gaúcha** is a range of hills and mountains populated mainly by the descendants of German and Italian immigrants. The Germans, who settled in Rio Grande do Sul between 1824 and 1859, spread out on fairly low-lying land, establishing small farming communities. The Italians, who arrived between 1875 and 1915, settled on more hilly terrain further north and, being mainly from the uplands of Veneto and Trento, they quickly specialized in **wine production**. It is here, in and around the smaller towns of the **Vale dos Vinhedos**, that the region's (and Brazil's) wine production is centred.

To the **east**, and at much higher altitudes, are the resort towns of **Gramado** and **Canela**, where unspoilt landscapes, mountain trails, refreshing temperatures, luxurious hotels and the *café colonial* – a vast selection of cakes, jams, cheeses, meats, wine and other drinks produced by the region's *colonos* – attract visitors from cities throughout Brazil. Beyond here lies some even more rugged terrain, notably the majestic canyons of **Parque Nacional dos Aparados da Serra**, one of southern Brazil's most impressive natural wonders.

Gramado

Some 120km north of Porto Alegre, booming **GRAMADO** is Brazil's best-known mountain resort – famous for its **Natal Luz** (Christmas lights) and its annual **film festival**, held in August (see page 615). Architecturally, Gramado tries hard to appear Swiss, with "alpine" chalets and flower-filled window boxes the norm. It's a mere affectation, though, since hardly any of the inhabitants are of Swiss origin – the town

GRAMADO'S FESTIVALS

For a week in mid-August, Gramado is overrun by the prestigious **Festival de Cinema** (54 3286 1475, festivaldegramado.net), which since 1973 has developed into one of the most important events of its kind in Brazil. In winter the festival **Natal Luz** (mid-Nov to early Jan) also stirs things up, with concerts, an ersatz German Christmas market and Carnaval-style parades in December that end in an (artificial) snowstorm, but unless the kitschness of it all appeals to you, the entire event is something to avoid.

was settled by the Portuguese in 1875 and a small minority is of German extraction (most locals today are of Italian ancestry). Indeed, today the town has become a major Brazilian family resort, with generally expensive hotels (it's primarily a haven for Brazil's wealthy), a host of theme parks and kitsch attractions such as the pretty flower-filled Parque Knorr aka **Aldeia do Papai Noel** at Rua Bela Vista 353, which is home to a whimsical Santa Claus village.

Assuming you're not excited by the prospect of seeing Santa, old cars and Harleys, model villages, paintball and go-karts, Gramado can still make for a pleasant visit, where you can enjoy the clear mountain air, flower-adorned houses and especially the food. The city is centred on tiny **Praça Major Nicoletti** and the fairly plain basalt stone church of **Igreja Sao Pedro**, a mini-version of Canela's, inaugurated in 1942, with streets lined with cafés, shops and hotels in all directions from here.

The most pleasant time to visit is in spring (Oct & Nov) when the parks, gardens and roadsides are full of flowers, though hotels raise prices accordingly. At 825m, Gramado is high enough to be refreshingly cool in summer and positively chilly in winter.

Ecoparque Sperry

Estrada Linha 28, 8km from town; signposted off Av das Hortênsias, the road to Canela • Tues–Sun 9am–5pm • R$15 • 54 9629 8765, ecoparquesperry.com.br

The Vale do Quilombo surrounding Gramado is magnificent, and best appreciated at the **Ecoparque Sperry**. Here you can peruse the conservation park's **Centro de Interpretação** or stroll along forest trails and past waterfalls, taking in the local flora. Roads in the mountainous areas around Gramado are unpaved and can be treacherous after rain, so guided tours are a safer bet – ask at the tourist office for recommendations.

ARRIVAL AND INFORMATION — GRAMADO

By bus Buses (citral.tur.br) from Porto Alegre (2hr 30min) run every 30min to 1hr to the rodoviária (54 3286 1302) on Av Borges de Medeiros 2100, a couple of minutes' walk south from the town centre. Buses to Canela (20min; R$3.45 "Circular"; R$5–8 other buses) leave every 10–15min.

By car Driving to Gramado is fairly straightforward (1hr 30min to 2hr from Porto Alegre), but the town itself can be very busy and parking hard to find. Most street parking requires a ticket (generally R$1/30min), even if it's not obvious – find a machine or an attendant who will issue a ticket.

By taxi Local taxi drivers should shuttle you between Gramado and Canela for around R$40 (one-way).

Tourist information Av Borges de Medeiros 1647, at Av das Hortências in the centre of town (Mon–Thurs 9am–6pm, Fri–Sun 9am–8pm; 54 3286 1475, visitgramado.com.br).

ACCOMMODATION

Casa da Montanha Av Borges de Medeiros 3166 54 3286 2544, casadamontanha.com.br. Rustic-style accommodation with extremely luxurious, pricey rooms with old-world decor (and some with balconies), and an indoor heated pool. In December rates soar to over R$1500. R$575

★ **Estalagem St Hubertus** Rua da Carriere 974 54 3286 1273, sthubertus.com. The place to splurge, this is a gorgeous boutique hotel set in attractive grounds overlooking Lago Negro, with a heated pool and stylish, duplex suites that have cable TV. R$666

Gramado Hostel Av das Hortências 3880 54 3295

1020, gramadohostel.com.br. About 1.5km outside town on the road to Canela (20min walk or R$1.80 on the Canela bus), this HI hostel is decent value with dorm rooms and some doubles – prices in low season can be as low as R$100 for doubles and R$54 for dorms. Prices for HI members are R$10 lower. Dorms R$70, doubles R$200

Pousada Belluno Rua Nilo Dias 50 54 3286 0820, pousadabelluno.com.br. One of the cheaper hotels downtown, with contemporary, heated rooms, cable LCD TVs and floor-to-ceiling windows. The substantial buffet breakfast will set you up for the day. R$210

EATING

Gramado is noted for its **handmade chocolate** and has some good restaurants (especially fondue places), but expect to pay through the nose for anything resembling a good meal; aim for the buffets or *café colonial* places to fill up properly. Note that the best places tend to line the busy main road between Gramado and Canela (Av Das Hortências), or lie in the surrounding countryside – areas more easily accessed with your own transport.

★ **Bela Vista Café Colonial** Av Das Hortências (1.7km from central Gramado, on the right side of the highway heading to Canela) 3500 54 3286 1608, belavista.tur.br. One of Gramado's classic Alpine-style cafés, offering fabulous *café colonial* spreads of cakes, pastries and meats for a hefty R$75. There's another branch further up the road at no. 4665. Mon–Fri 11.30am–11pm, Sat & Sun 10am–11pm.

Chocolate Caseiro Planalto Av Borges de Medeiros 2918 54 3286 2268, chocolateplanalto.com.br. One of several artisan chocolate makers in the centre of town, and while it's not the cheapest it's definitely one of the best, with a range of sweet treats and sublime hot chocolate. Daily 10am–8pm.

ITA Brasil Rua São Pedro 1005 (1km from the centre) 54 3286 3833. Off the main drag and very crowded, but well worth seeking out for the cheap lunch buffets (around R$26 or R$46/kg) of classic Italian-Brazilian food, fresh juices, strong coffee and home-made cachaça. Daily 11.30am–2.30pm.

★ **La Caceria** Av Borges de Medeiros 3166, Hotel Casa da Montanha 54 3295 7575, lacaceria.com.br. An intriguing but expensive hotel restaurant, specializing in game dishes (mains R$98–129) like wild boar, rabbit and "Black Lake crocodile", with unusual tropical fruit sauces that complement the often strong-tasting meat. Tues–Sun 7.30–11.30pm.

St Gallen Av das Hortências 1122 (700m southwest of the centre) 54 3286 2519, stgallen.com.br. Classic place to try a German-style buffet (R$96) or the local *rodízio de fondue* (lunch R$67, dinner R$83), a gut-busting trio of cheese (Emmenthal, Gruyére), meat (*filet mignon*) and superb chocolate (or caramel and marshmallow) fondue courses. Also has live music and provides a free lift back to your hotel. Daily 11.30am–3pm & 6pm–midnight.

Canela

The wealthy resort town of **CANELA** ("cinnamon" in Portuguese), 8km east of Gramado, is slightly smaller and not as brashly commercialized as Gramado, though the distinction lessens each year. Other than the Neogothic **Catedral de Pedra** (dedicated to Nossa Senhora de Lourdes) on central **Praça da Matriz**, nominally completed in 1972 (though work has continued ever since) with an imposing 65m spire, the town offers little of interest other than **eating**, but it is better situated for the **Parque Estadual do Caracol** (see page 617). From Praça da Matriz, Rua Felisberto Soares runs east toward **Praça João Correa** (becoming Av Osvaldo Aranha), where events are held and an artists' market operates (Sun 9am–5pm).

ARRIVAL AND INFORMATION — CANELA

By bus Buses (citral.tur.br) from Porto Alegre (6am–8.15pm; 3hr) run every 30min to 1hr via Porto Alegre airport to Canela's rodoviária (54 3282 1375), just behind, Av Júlio de Castilhos, a short walk from Praça João Corea. Buses to Gramado (20min; R$3.45 "Circular"; R$5–8 other buses) leave every 10–15min. Citral runs buses to São Francisco de Paula, for the Parque Nacional dos Aparados da Serra (8 daily 8am–7.30pm; 1hr). Buses also depart here for Parque Caracol (see page 617).

By car Most street parking in Canela requires a ticket (generally R$1 per 30min), even if it's not obvious – find a machine or an attendant who will issue a ticket.

By taxi Local taxi drivers charge around R$40 (one-way) to Gramado or Parque Caracol.

Tourist information Praça João Correa (daily 8am–7pm; 54 3282 2200).

Tourist bus The Bus Tour (54 3286 7777, bustour.com.br) tourist hop-on hop-off loop service is expensive (from R$69/day) but is a convenient way to see all the major sites around Canela without a car (including Parque Estadual do Caracol, Bondinhos Aéreos and the Castelinho Caracol; admission to sights is extra). Four buses run the loop daily (8.15am–6.30pm; one loop around 3hr), with audio in English, but check the current schedule before boarding.

ACCOMMODATION

Accommodation can be hard to come by during **peak periods** (especially Christmas and New Year), when you should book ahead (the prices quoted below are for peak season, with rates cut by fifty percent at other times). Though hotels in Canela tend to be cheaper than Gramado, it is not cheap per se, and the town can be easily visited on a **day-trip** from Gramado or even Porto Alegre.

Hostel Viajante Rua Ernesto Urbani 132 ⓣ 54 3282 2017, ⓦ pousadadoviajante.com.br. Right next to the rodoviária, this is the best budget choice, with economical rooms with shared bathrooms and neat and tidy en-suite doubles – perfect for travellers winding down after a hard day's bungee jumping. R$160

★ **Pousada Encantos da Terra** Rua Tenente Manoel Corrêa 282 ⓣ 54 3282 2080, ⓦ pousadaencantosdaterra.com.br. Friendly hotel with compact, simple but tastefully furnished a/c rooms, all with LCD cable TVs. The helpful owners can organize car rentals. R$336

Quinta dos Marques Rua Gravataí 200 ⓣ 54 3282 9813, ⓦ www.quintadosmarques.com.br. For luxury and tranquillity, this thirteen-room hotel is the most distinctive choice available, in an imposing 1930s wooden building – in typical highland style – beautifully renovated to offer rustic-chic accommodation. R$520

EATING AND DRINKING

★ **Empório Canela** Rua Felisberto Moraes 258 ⓣ 54 3031 1000, ⓦ emporiocanela.com.br. Lovely old house near the cathedral that doubles as an antique, crafts and book shop. The menu ranges from typical café fare to sandwiches, salads, Italian risottos and pastas. Wed–Mon 11.30am–11pm.

Lá Em Casa Rua José Luís Correa Pinto 346 (1km from the centre) ⓣ 54 3278 1049. Rustic, home-made Brazilian food served buffet style, where around R$50 gets you all the food you can eat. Leave room for the delicious *pudim de leite* (milk pudding). Also does *feijoada* on Saturdays. Tues–Fri 11.30am–2pm, Sat & Sun 11.30am–3pm.

Restaurante da Torre (Cervejaria Farol) Rua Severino Inocente Zini 150 (3.5km from the centre) ⓣ 54 3282 7007, ⓦ cervejariafarol.com.br. Excellent microbrewery (marked by a 32m "lighthouse"), offering the chance to tour the facilities (R$15 with tastings) before sampling the beers (the IPA is especially tasty) – it also serves a decent menu of German dishes and snacks, and offers free lifts to and from your hotel. There's live music on Tuesdays, Fridays and Saturdays. Tues–Fri 5pm–midnight, Sat 11am–midnight, Sun noon–3pm.

★ **Schnitzelstubb** Rua Baden Powell 246 ⓣ 54 3282 9562. This German-inspired restaurant is the best place to sample that schnitzel, wurst and apple strudel. Most mains cost R$40–60. Tues 7.30–11pm, Wed–Sat noon–3pm & 8–11pm, Sun 11.45am–3pm.

Parque Estadual do Caracol

RS-466, Km 0 • **Park** Daily 9am–5.30pm • R$20 • ⓣ 54 3278 3035 • **Observatorio Ecológico** Daily 9am–5.30pm • R$12, in addition to park entry • ⓦ observatorioecologico.com.br • Buses run from Canela's rodoviária to the entrance (Mon–Sat 8.20am, 12.20pm & 5.30pm, returning at 8.35am, 12.25pm & 5.50pm; Sun 8.05am, 1.35pm & 5.35pm, returning 8.20am, 1.50pm & 5.50pm; R$3.25) or you can take a taxi (R$40 one-way)

Just 7km northeast of Canela at the end of RS-466 (aka Estrada do Caracol), the highlight of the **Parque Estadual do Caracol** is the spectacular **Cascata do Caracol**, a stunning waterfall on the Río Caracol that plunges dramatically over a 131m-high cliff of basaltic rock in the middle of dense forest. The main park area (near the entrance) essentially comprises a series of viewpoints on the lip of the canyon overlooking the falls, but you can also take a lift ("*elevador panorâmico*") up the 27m high **Observatorio Ecológico**, which will give you a 360-degree bird's-eye view of the park and falls, across the park's distinctive araucaria pines. The **Centro Historico Ambiental**, a short walk from the car park, contains a small exhibit on the park, while trails fan out along the canyon rim and down to the falls themselves, though this involves over 700 exhausting steps.

STRUDEL AT THE CASTELINHO

Heading to the Parque Estadual do Caracol from Canela, you'll pass the araucaria wood **Castelinho Caracol** (RS-466, Km 3; daily 9am–1pm & 2.20–5.40pm; admission R$10; ⓣ 54 3278 3208, ⓦ castelinhocaracol.com.br), a fairy-tale German-style mansion dating from 1915 and now a memorial to German immigration in the area. It also serves incredible *apfelstrudel* in the tea rooms.

Teleférico de Canela (Bondinhos Aéreos)

Estrada da Ferradura 699 (RS-466) • Daily 9am–5pm, 20min • R$42 • ⓣ 54 3504 1405, ⓦ parquesdaserra.com.br • Tourist bus (see page 616) or taxi

For even more scintillating views of the waterfall, take the 830m **Teleférico de Canela** cable car (500m further along the road from the Parque Estadual do Caracol entrance, and down a short side road), which zips up and down the slopes to two stations with several viewpoints.

Parque da Ferradura

RS-466, Km 15 • Tues–Sat 9am–5pm • R$12 • ⓣ 54 3728 9000 • No public transport

Further still along the main road (now the gravel-surfaced Caminho da Graces), at Km 15 is the entrance to the **Parque da Ferradura**, where three viewpoints cover the dramatic 420m "horseshoe" canyon of the Río Caí and the Arroio Caçador waterfall. It's a lot more rustic here and quieter, with sensational panoramas, a small café and four trails.

Templo Budista Chagdud Khadro Ling

Estrada Linha Águas Brancas 1211, Três Coroas • Wed–Fri 9.30am–11.30am & 2–5pm, Sat & Sun 9am–4.30pm • Free • ⓣ 51 3546 8201, ⓦ chagdud.org • Buses (ⓦ citral.tur.br) from Gramado to Três Coroas run roughly every hour (R$5.90–7.25), where you can get a taxi (R$15–18) up to the temple. Citral also runs buses direct to Três Coroas from Porto Alegre (15 daily)

Just 30km south, but a world away from both Canela and Gramado, is the **Templo Budista Chagdud Khadro Ling**, the only Tibetan Buddhist temple complex in Latin America, attracting devotees from all over Brazil and even North America. Situated on a hilltop outside the traditionally ethnic German village of **Três Coroas**, the temple was founded by **Chagdud Tulku Rinpoche** (1930–2002), a high lama who left Tibet for Nepal following the Chinese invasion in 1959, settling in Brazil in 1995. On a clear day you can see the buildings – red in colour, adorned with yellow details and colourful symbols that sparkle like jewels – from far into the distance. Seen close up, the remarkable site includes a huge statue of Buddha, eight large *stupas* (holy structures representing the enlightened mind), the **temple** itself with colourful murals depicting Buddha's life, and various other buildings erected by devotees, and by artists and craftsmen from Nepal.

Cambará do Sul

The small town of **CAMBARÁ DO SUL**, some 190km northeast of Porto Alegre, is the gateway to two remarkable national parks, Parque Nacional dos Aparados da Serra, and the wilder Parque Nacional da Serra Geral. There's not much to see in town, but you'll likely spend at least one night here.

ARRIVAL AND DEPARTURE — CAMBARÁ DO SUL

By bus The bus station is in the centre of town. Citral (ⓦ citral.tur.br) runs one bus to Cambará from Porto Alegre (Mon–Sat 6am; 5hr 30min). From Gramado (see page 614) or Canela (see page 616) you need to take a bus to São Francisco de Paula; from there you need to take another bus 60km northeast to Cambará (Mon–Sat 9.15am & 5pm, Sun 11am; 1hr). Citral buses return from Cambará for São Francisco daily at 1.30pm, and also 6.30am Mon–Sat, while São Marcos runs direct to Caxias do Sul (Mon–Fri 7.45am & 10.45am, Sat 7.30am, Sun 5.30pm; 3hr) where you can change for the Vale dos Vinhedos. There is no bus service direct to the Parque Nacional dos Aparados da Serra (see page 619) or Parque Nacional da Serra Geral (see page 620).

ACCOMMODATION AND EATING

Pousada João de Barro Rua Padre João Francisco Ritter 631 ⓣ54 3251 1216, ⓦjoaodebarropousada.com.br. This cosy little hotel in the centre of town is superb value, with just five en-suite rooms, TVs and delicious, wholesome breakfasts. The living room and fireplace is popular in winter. **R$150**

Restaurante Galpão Costaneira Rua Dona Úrsula 1069 ⓣ54 3251 1005. Knocks out inexpensive, authentic local dishes served in a rustic, but attractive, setting; the *comida campeira* buffet is a great deal (R$29), and there's a craft shop at the entrance. Mon–Sat 11.30am–3pm & 7.30–10.30pm, Sun 11.30am–3pm.

Vila Ecológica de Cambará do Sul Rua Padre João Pazza 1166 ⓣ54 3251 1351, ⓦvilaecologica.blogspot.com. All three en-suite rooms here feature rustic furnishings and beds made of timber, with wood stoves, cable TV and DVD player. **R$160**

Parque Nacional dos Aparados da Serra

Rodovia RS-427, Km 18 • Tues–Sun 8am–5pm • R$17/person, plus R$15/car • ⓣ54 3251 1277

The largely untouched wilderness of the **PARQUE NACIONAL DOS APARADOS DA SERRA** is one of southern Brazil's great natural wonders, though it attracts a fraction of the visitors to Iguaçu Falls. The park protects just a small section of a truly remarkable phenomenon (one that you can only really appreciate fully from the air); a 700m-high plateau of basalt rock, looming over the coastal plain of Rio Grande do Sul for hundreds of kilometres, which was created around 150 million years ago when lava slowly poured onto the surface of the Brazilian Shield. The edge of the plateau is sheer and crinkled, punctured by vast canyons such as **Itaimbézinho**; some 5.8km in length, between 600m and 2000m wide and 720m deep, Itaimbézinho is a dizzying sight. The canyon and the area immediately surrounding it have two distinct climates and support very different types of vegetation. On the higher levels, with relatively little rainfall, but with fog banks moving in from the nearby Atlantic Ocean, vegetation is typical of a cloud forest, while on the canyon's floor a mass of subtropical plants flourishes. The park has abundant birdlife and is home to over 150 different species.

In the park, there's a **visitors' centre** with a display explaining the region's history and geological structure, and a snack bar. From here, you can hire a guide to lead you down the steep **Trilha do Rio do Boi** (including a 5m vertical incline that you must negotiate by rope; 8hr) to the canyon floor. You'll need to be physically fit, have good hiking boots and be prepared for flash floods. Most visitors, however, follow the well-marked **Trilha do Cotovelo** (6.3km round-trip) keeping to the top of Itaimbézinho, enjoying scintillating views into the canyon (a 2hr 30min walk from the visitors' centre), or the easier **Trilha do Vértice** (1.4km), which affords views of Itaimbézinho and two spectacular waterfalls, Véu da Noiva and Andorinhas.

ARRIVAL AND DEPARTURE — PARQUE NACIONAL DOS APARADOS DA SERRA

Access Getting to the park can be tough – organized tours are worth considering. From Cambará it's a further 18km to the park entrance along dirt road Estrada do Itaimbézinho (RS-427) towards Praia Grande (taxis charge at least R$100 return, but you'll need to negotiate pick-up in advance), and another 2km from there to the edge of the canyon. There is no bus service direct to the park.

ACTIVITIES AND TOURS

Canyons do Sul Abel Esteves de Aguiar, Praia Grande (Santa Catarina) ⓣ48 3532 1085, ⓦcanyonsdosul.com.br. Offers guided hiking tours to Parque Nacional da Serra Geral and the Aparados da Serra, as well as arranging all sort of activities from rappelling and canyoning to horse riding.

Guia Aparados da Serra Av Getulio Vargas 920, Cambará do Sul ⓣ54 3251 1173, ⓦadventure.guiaaparadosdaserra.com.br. Offers vast range of hiking and 4WD tours to Itaimbézinho, trekking in Cânion Fortaleza, rappelling, mountain biking, horse-riding and lots of off-road adventures.

VISITING THE APARADOS DA SERRA

The **Parque Nacional dos Aparados da Serra** can be visited throughout the year, but spring (Oct & Nov) is the best time to see flowers. In the winter, June through to August, it can get very cold, though visibility tends to be clearest. Summers are warm, but heavy rainfall sometimes makes the roads and trails impassable, and fog and low-lying clouds can completely obscure the spectacular views. Avoid April, May and September, the months with the most sustained rain. As only one thousand visitors are permitted to enter the park each day, it's advisable to phone the visitors' centre (T 54 3251 1277) in advance to reserve a place. Bring strong footwear and mosquito repellent.

ACCOMMODATION

Parador Casa da Montanha Estrada do Faxinal 4800 T 54 3504 5302, W paradorcasadamontanha.com.br. By far the most luxurious option in the area, situated at the beginning of the road that leads to the Parque Aparados da Serra (9km). Accommodation is in thermal tents, but they're secure even in the strongest of winds and have every comfort of a good hotel room. In the lodge, there's a sitting and dining area, and a terrace with views out towards a sheep-rearing *fazenda*. The food is superb, based on local beef, mutton, squash and bean dishes, and the restaurant is open to non-guests. There are also bikes (R$50/day) and TV lounge, but no internet access and rarely English speakers. R$530

Parque Nacional da Serra Geral

RS-012 • Daily 8am–5pm • Free • T 54 3251 1277

Encompassing the wild borderlands between Rio Grande do Sul and Santa Catarina north of Aparados da Serra, the **Parque Nacional da Serra Geral** is home to the jaw-dropping **Cânion Fortaleza**, some 8.2km long and more than 900m deep – the views from the rim are mind-blowing. Unfortunately, getting here is not easy – the main access point is 22km from Cambará do Sul on a dirt road, with no public transport (RS-012, a continuation of Rua Getúlio Vargas in Cambará). Without a car your best bet is to contact a tour operator in Cambará or Praia Grande (see page 619).

Vale dos Vinhedos

Over recent years the quality of **Brazilian wine** has improved greatly, with some of the most innovative producers located to the southwest of Bento Gonçalves in the alluring region of Rio Grande do Sul, which has become known as the **Vale dos Vinhedos** ("Valley of the Vineyards"). The economy and way of life here are dominated by wine, with grapes growing on every patch of farmland – in 2010 it was awarded its own Denominação de Origem (DO). It's worth visiting this region where, on the surface at least, the way of life has changed little over the years. The calendar revolves around the grape, with weeding, planting, pruning and the maintenance of characteristic stone walls – the main activities during the year – leading up to the harvest between January and late March.

Bento Gonçalves

Approach **BENTO GONÇALVES**, 125km north of Porto Alegre, from any direction and there's no doubting that this is the heartland of Brazil's wine-producing region. Founded in 1875, the town itself is an undistinguished-looking place today, whose economy, of course, totally revolves around grape and wine production, and it's the obvious base for a tour of the local wineries. There are numerous **cantinas** in the centre of town offering free tours and tastings while the **Museu do Imigrante**, Rua Herny Hugo Dreher 127 (Tues–Sat 8am–11.45am & 1.30–5.45pm; free; T 54 3451 1773), chronicles the history of Italian immigration to the region with all sorts of artefacts and everyday items donated by the community.

ARRIVAL AND DEPARTURE

BENTO GONÇALVES

To make the most of this area you'll need a **car**, or to take a **tour**. Bento Gonçalves is easy to reach by bus, but getting around the area is not easy without transport. You'll get the best deal on car rentals back in **Porto Alegre**, especially at the airport.

By bus Bento Gonçalves bus station is 1km north of the centre of town, at Gomes Carneiro 19. Hourly buses run to and from Porto Alegre (2hr 30min), but for Gramado, Canela and Cambará do Sul you'll need to change in the city of Caxias do Sul (hourly; 1hr 15min). Moving on, Unesul (W unesul.com.br) has 3 daily buses (7hr 5min) to Sant Ângelo (for the Rota Missões).

INFORMATION AND TOURS

Tourist information Rua Marechal Deodoro 70 (Mon–Fri 8–11.45am & 1–7pm, Sat 9am–5pm; T 54 3451 1088). See also W valedosvinhedos.com.br.

Tours Try Vale das Vinhas, Rua Barão do Rio Branco 245, Bento Gonçalves (T 54 3451 4216, W valedasvinhastur.com.br), or Giordani Turismo (W giordaniturismo.com.br).

ACCOMMODATION AND EATING

★ **Borghetto Sant'Anna** Via Trento 868 T 54 3453 2355, W borghettosantanna.com.br. Exquisite accommodation with views across the vineyards; there's a choice of deluxe *casas de pedras* (old stone houses) and modern suites, but all come with cable TV and those stunning views. R$400

★ **Hotel Laghetto Viverone Bento** Rua Carlos Flôres 301, Bento Gonçalves T 54 3449 1919, W laghettoviveronebento.com.br. This bright, newish place is easily the best place to stay in Bento, with slick, contemporary-styled rooms and Japanese bathtubs. R$240

Pousadas Casa Valduga Via Trento 2355 T 54 3453 1154, W casavalduga.com.br. The five *pousadas* attached to the Casa Valduga winery make this a romantic place to stay, with 24 spacious, luxurious rooms altogether that have all the usual amenities. The *Restaurante Maria Valduga* serves good, and reasonably priced, local-style Italian food. Daily noon–3pm & 8–10.30pm. R$250

★ **Restaurante Valle Rustico** Linha Marcílio Dias, 15 da Graciema T 54 3067 1163, W vallerustico.com.br. Highly acclaimed "slow food" restaurant in a typical, Italian-style house, with most of the produce served sourced locally; the menu is primarily Italian. Wed–Sat 7.30–10pm, Sun noon–3pm.

Vinocap Rua Barão do Rio Branco 245, Bento Gonçalves T 54 3451 1566, W vinocap.com.br. This counts as budget in this part of the world, with good, modern rooms (cable TV, some a/c), and basic breakfast in a central location. R$199

The Litoral Gaúcho

The coast of Rio Grande do Sul, or the **Litoral Gaúcho**, is a virtually unbroken 500km-long beach, dotted with a series of popular resorts. In winter the beaches are

BRAZIL'S LITTLE ITALY

If you have your own transport, consider a trip to **Antônio Prado**, 184km north of Porto Alegre, a small town founded in 1886 by a group of northern Italian immigrants. Often regarded as the most Italian of Brazilian towns, the locals still speak Italian, celebrate traditional festivals with fervour and take pride in cooking real Italian food. Antônio Prado also contains the largest ensemble of Italian-style wood and masonry homes in the country (48 at last count). Many of the best-preserved houses are found along Linha 21 de Abril (off the RS-122, 6km in the direction of Flores da Cunha). Especially worth visiting in town are the **Farmácia Palombini** at Av Valdomiro Bocchese 439, whose interior has remained unchanged since it opened in 1930, and the **Casa da Neni** at Rua Luísa Bochese 34 (Praça Garibaldi), constructed in 1910. Today it serves as the **Museu Municipal** (Tues–Fri 8.30–11.30am & 1.30–5pm, Sat, Sun & public holidays 1–5pm; free; T 54 3293 3935) charting the history of the region. See W antonioprado.rs.gov.br for more on the town.

EATING

★ **O Porão** Av Valdomiro Bochese 681 T 54 3293 3131. Serves a blend of typical southern Brazilian food and Italian classics, from *filé a parmegiana* to spaghetti carbonara. Daily 11am–11pm.

TOURING THE VALLEY OF THE VINEYARDS

The main wine route from Bento Gonçalves follows the BR-470 highway, then the RS-444, a county road dubbed the **Estrada da Vinho** (any southbound bus from Bento Gonçalves will drop you off at the intersection). About 400m along the road (at the petrol station) you'll find an excellent **information centre** (daily 9am–6pm; T 54 3451 9601, W valedosvinhedos.com.br) where you can pick up a map indicating wineries and other local businesses open to visitors. You can make a loop by heading back to Bento on a smaller road, the Via Trento – everything is well signposted. The **wineries** vary enormously in character and it's wise to settle on just a few to stop off for tastings – the best time to visit is January through to March when the grapes are harvested, but visitors are welcomed throughout the year for tastings. English-language tours are usually available if reserved in advance.

Casa Valduga Via Trento 2355 T 54 2105 3122, W casavalduga.com.br. The first producer to introduce modern wine-making techniques and European vines, with roots that go back to the arrival of the Valduga family here in 1875. Tour (1hr 15min) and five tastings R$40 (English tours must be arranged in advance). Also has restaurant and accommodation on-site (see page 621). Mon–Sat 9.30am–4.30pm, Sun 9.30am–3.30pm (hourly tours).

★ **Famiglia Tasca** Linha Santo Isidoro, Monte Belo do Sul T 54 3453 2210, W famigliatasca.com.br. This small family wine and grape-juice producer with a shop should not be missed: located on a side road in the extreme west of the Vale dos Vinhedos, the well-maintained wood and stone farm buildings are some of the oldest in the area (they even have a small museum commemorating the arrival of the Tasca family here in 1882), and the views across the neighbouring Aurora valley are breathtaking. Mon–Fri noon–6pm, Sat 10am–6pm, Sun 10am–5pm.

Pizzato Vinhas e Vinhos Via dos Parreirais T 54 3459 1155, W pizzato.net. Still very much a family concern, with a pleasant restaurant on-site, and tours/tastings held throughout the year (R$18). Daily 10am–5pm.

Vinhos Larentis Linha da Leopoldina, Km 6 T 54 3453 6469, W larentis.com.br. An up-and-coming producer of fine wines (the Malbec is exceptional), matured in American oak barrels; treat yourself to a bottle from the shop. Tours and tastings are free. Mon–Fri 9–11.30am & 1–5pm, Sat & Sun 10am–5pm.

Vinícola Miolo RS-444 (Estrada da Vinho), Km 21 T 54 2102 1540, W miolo.com.br. Probably the best of Brazil's large-scale producers. Tours and tastings R$30 (includes R$10 credit in shop). Tours and tastings: Mon–Sat on the hour 9am–4pm & 4.30pm; Sun 10.30am, 11.30am, noon, 1.30pm, 2.30pm & 3.30pm; shop: Mon–Sat 8am–5.45pm, Sun 10am–4.45pm.

deserted and most of the hotels closed, but between mid-November and March it's easy to believe that the state's entire population has migrated to the resorts. Most tend to be crowded, while – because of the powerful Río de la Plata – the water is usually murky, and even in summer Antarctic currents often make for chilly bathing. Of the resorts, the only one really worth visiting is **Torres**, featuring impressive cliffs and rock formations. Further south and towards the Uruguayan border are the ports of **Pelotas** and **Rio Grande**, their grand nineteenth-century buildings testimony to the cities' former prosperity.

Torres

The northernmost point on the Litoral Gaúcho, 197km northeast from Porto Alegre, **TORRES** is the state's one beach town that is actually worth going out of your way for. It's considered Rio Grande do Sul's most sophisticated coastal resort, and the beaches behind which it huddles, **Praia Grande** and **Prainha**, are packed solid in the summer with *gaúcho* and Uruguayan holidaymakers.

Parque da Guarita

Rua Benjamin Constant 154 • Daily 8.30am–5.30pm (Dec–Feb till 8pm) • Free; parking R$8 • T 51 3626 9150

By walking across the Morro do Farol (a hill, identifiable by its lighthouse) and along the crowded Praia da Cal, you come to the **Parque da Guarita**, one of the most beautiful stretches of the southern Brazilian coast. The development of the state preserve was supervised by the landscaper Roberto Burle Marx, together with Brazil's pioneer environmentalist, José Lutzenberger.

The preserve is centred on a huge basalt outcrop, with 35m-high cliffs rising straight up from the sea, from where there are superb views up and down the coast. At several points, steps lead down from the clifftop to basalt pillars and cavern-like formations beaten out of the cliff face over the years. Continue along the clifftop, and you'll eventually reach the **Praia da Guarita**, a fairly small beach that is never as crowded as those nearer town.

ARRIVAL AND INFORMATION — TORRES

By bus From the rodoviária (T 51 3664 1787), served by buses from Porto Alegre (hourly; 3hr) and Florianópolis (2 daily; 4hr 30min–6hr), walk down Av José Bonifácio to Av Barão do Rio Branco, the city's main drag.

Tourist information Av Barão do Rio Branco 315 (Mon–Fri 8am–12.30pm & 1–7pm, Sat 9am–2pm, Sun 2–7pm; T 51 3664 1411, W torres.rs.gov.br).

ACCOMMODATION AND EATING

★ **Cantinho do Pescador** Av Beira Rio 210 T 51 3626 4374, W cantinhodopescador.com.br. This has long been the best restaurant in town (open since 1973); it's a casual place overlooking the river piers near the beach with delicious, no-nonsense seafood (crab and shrimp are always the freshest dishes). Most mains R$70–120. Daily 11am–midnight.

Hotel Bauer Rua Ballino de Freitas 260 T 51 3664 1290, W hotelbauer.com.br. Budget hotel with a choice of doubles and larger apartments with full kitchens; simple but clean and good value, with a hefty breakfast included. R$120

Pousada la Barca Av Beira-Mar 1020 T 51 3664 2925. One of the better major hotels in town, with a heated pool and ageing but comfy rooms right on the beach. Look for a discounted rate online. R$180

★ **Vivenda Da Barra** Rua Egídio Michaelsen 232, Barra do Mampituba T 51 3626 3393, W vivendadabarra.com.br. Pretty chalet-style hotel, with new, cosy a/c rooms (all with TV, DVDs to play and a delicious breakfast) and a friendly owner, Sissa, who is a mine of local information. R$370

Pelotas and around

Rio Grande do Sul's third-largest city, **PELOTAS**, 270km to the south of Porto Alegre, is situated on the left bank of the Canal de São Gonçalo, which connects the massive Lagoa dos Patos with the Lagoa Mirim. Founded in 1812 as a port for the *charque* (jerked beef) producers of the surrounding region, Pelotas rapidly emerged as the wealthiest city in Rio Grande do Sul, becoming a byword for conspicuous consumption – today the remnants of its golden age provide much of the allure.

Praça Coronel Pedro Osório

The main square of Pelotas, **Praça Coronel Pedro Osório**, is the city's heart, and most of its very elegant, stuccoed buildings with wrought-iron balconies date from the nineteenth or early twentieth centuries. The French-built fountain in the centre, "As Nereidas", was erected in 1873 to replace the old whipping post. In the southwest corner, the **Prefeitura Municipal** was completed in 1881 and contains a small history exhibit, the **Memorial dos Ex-Prefeitos** (Mon–Fri 1.30–6pm; free; T 53 3225 7355), commemorating the administrators of city hall over the decades, through documents and faded photographs. Next door the city's **Biblioteca Pública**, a pink Neoclassical confection raised between 1878 and 1881, contains the tiny **Museu Histórico e Bibliográfico** (Mon–Fri 9am–6pm; free; T 53 3222 3856), with miscellaneous bits and pieces relating to the history of Pelotas and the old library. On the south side of the plaza, a city icon, the former **Grande Hotel** was built in Art Nouveau style between 1925 and 1928. Today it's no longer a hotel, but development by its current owner the Universidade Federal de Pelotas has been delayed for several years.

Theatro 7 de Abril

Rua XV de Novembro 560 (Praça Coronel Pedro Osório 160)

The elegant **Theatro 7 de Abril** was inaugurated in 1833, and as such stands as one of the oldest formal buildings in the city (though the Art Deco facade you see today was added in the 1930s). It's been undergoing restoration for several years, and at the time of research was still closed.

Mercado Público

Praça Sete de Julho • Mon–Fri 8am–7pm, Sat 8am–1pm • Free

Adjoining Praça Coronel Pedro Osório, to the south, is the **Mercado Público** on Praça Sete de Julho, a distinguished-looking building dating back to 1853 (re-worked in Art Nouveau style in 1914), with a mix of stalls selling food and general goods.

Catedral da Igreja Episcopal do Redentor

Rua XV de Novembro 472 • Tues–Thurs 2.30–5.30pm, Sun 9.30am–11.30pm • Free • ⓣ 53 3222 5679

As a railhead, port and important commercial centre, late nineteenth-century Pelotas was home to considerable British and American communities. Bearing witness to this is the **Catedral da Igreja Episcopal do Redentor**, a block from the Mercado Público. Opened in 1892, the ivy-smothered Neogothic church (dubbed "Igreja Cabeluda" or "hairy church") would go unnoticed in any English town (it was raised to cathedral status in 1988), but in Brazil it looks completely alien.

Catedral de São Francisco de Paula

Praça José Bonifácio 15 • Mon–Sat 10am–noon & 1.30–7.30pm, Sun 8am–noon & 6–8pm • Free • ⓣ 53 3222 2096

Six blocks to the north of Praça Osório is the grand **Catedral de São Francisco de Paula**, housing a revered image of its namesake saint (the patron of the city) brought from what's now Sacramento in Uruguay. While its interior has undergone some alteration over the years, the exterior, crowned with a majestic dome, has not been fundamentally altered since it was begun in 1846.

Museu da Baronesa

Av Domingos de Almeida 1490 • Tues–Fri 1.30–6pm, Sat & Sun 2–6pm • R$3 • ⓣ 53 3228 4606, ⓦ www.museudabaronesa.com.br • Take a bus marked "Laranjal"

Scattered around the city are numerous mansions that once housed the *pelotense* aristocracy. Many of these are in a state of disrepair, but a fine example survives in the **Museu da Baronesa** in the suburb of Areal, about 1km northeast. The pink and white-stuccoed building was built in 1863 as a wedding present for the son and daughter-in-law of the Antunes Maciel banking family, its grandeur symbolic of the wealth that was generated during the *charque* era. The museum includes a mix of family mementoes (the family owned the house until 1978) and period furniture, and offers a glimpse into the lifestyle of nineteenth-century high society.

Charqueada São João and Charqueada Santa Rita

Estrada da Costa 750 • **Charqueada São João** Mon–Sat 9.30am–6pm, Sun 2–6pm • R$30 • ⓣ 53 3228 2425, ⓦ charqueadasaojoao.com.br • **Museu do Charque** Daily 9am–6pm • R$10 • ⓣ 53 3228 2024, ⓦ charqueadasantarita.com.br • Both *charqueadas* are located about 5km northeast of the centre of Pelotas; a taxi will cost around R$25, or take any bus to "Laranjal" and get off just before the bridge that crosses the Arroio Pelotas

The oldest surviving *charqueada* in Pelotas, the **Charqueada São João**, was established in 1810 by Portuguese settler, Antônio Gonçalves Chaves, and still contains period furniture as well as traditional tools. In 2002 the property served as the location of hit Globo TV series *A Casa das Sete Mulheres*, set during the Guerra dos Farrapos in the 1830s. You can also take a short **boat ride** (40min) along the Arroio Pelotas from here (R$40). Almost next door to São João at Estrada da Costa 200 is the **Charqueada Santa Rita**, another colonial-style house built in 1826. Santa Rita now serves as a *pousada* (see page 625), but its illuminating **Museu do Charque** is open to the public.

THE CHARQUEADA

The first **charqueada** (covered sheds where beef jerky is salted and dried) was established in the Pelotas area in 1780, and by the late 1820s there were two-dozen producers of *charque* in the city. Production was a brutal affair, relying almost wholly on slave labour, and when cattle were being slaughtered the Canal de São Gonçalo was stained bright red from the blood and waste. With the introduction of **refrigeration** in the late nineteenth century, demand for beef increased, and with it Pelotas's importance as a port and commercial centre. However, by the turn of the century, Rio Grande's port, able to take larger ships, had superseded it and the local economy entered a long period of decline. Evidence still remains of the *charqueadas*, however, with several ruins on the banks of the Arroio Pelotas as well as two fine houses built by *charqueadores* that are open to visitors (see page 624).

ARRIVAL AND INFORMATION — PELOTAS AND AROUND

By plane Pelotas's tiny airport is 8km from the centre on Av Zeferino Costa in Bairro Três Vendas. Azul operates flights to and from Porto Alegre (Mon–Fri 1–2 daily; 50min).

By bus The rodoviária (☎53 3284 6700) is 7km out of town at Av Presidente João Goulart 4605 in Fragata, with local buses running into the centre every 10min. Expresso Embaixador (🌐expressoembaixador.com.br) is the primary local carrier.

Destinations Bagé (10 daily; 3hr 15min); Chuí (5 daily; 3hr 45min); Montevideo (2 daily; 8hr); Porto Alegre (hourly; 3hr); Rio Grande (every 30min; 1hr); Santo Ângelo (1 daily; 9–10hr).

Tourist information Praça Coronel Pedro Osório 6 (Mon–Fri 9am–6pm; ☎53 3225 3733).

ACCOMMODATION AND EATING

★ **Charqueada Santa Rita** Estrada da Costa 200 ☎53 3228 2024, 🌐charqueadasantarita.com.br. By far the most distinctive and pleasant place to stay is this former *charqueada* (see page 624), now a *pousada* offering high levels of comfort in a relaxed setting. There's a pool, and the very helpful Anglo-Brazilian owner offers boat trips on the pretty Arroio Pelotas, the natural canal that backs onto the property. R$270

Choperia Cruz de Malta Rua Andrade Neves 4183 ☎53 3283 7702, 🌐choperiacruzdemalta.com.br. The best bar in town, with a decent range of draught beers, snacks (plus mains such as steaks) and an open terrace – it's always busy. Mon–Sat 6pm–1am.

Doceria Márcia Aquino Av Bento Gonçalves 3275 ☎53 3222 7640, 🌐marciaaquino.com.br. Pelotas is famous for its intense Portuguese-style sweets and cakes, and the best place to try them is this buzzing café, serving chocolate, sweets and *tortas* (cakes), sandwiches and hot chocolate with whipped cream. Mon–Sat 10am–8pm.

★ **El Paisano** Rua Marechal Deodoro 1093 ☎53 3227 1507, 🌐elpaisano.com.br. Cosy Uruguayan style *parrilla* (grill), with great steaks and great sides (roasted peppers, roast potatoes), and old-fashioned decor reminiscent of Montevideo. Mains cost R$25–50. Tues–Sat 7–11.30pm, Sun 11am–2pm & 7–11pm.

Jacques Georges Hotel Rua Gonçalves Chaves 512 ☎53 3284 9000, 🌐jghotel.com.br. The best option downtown, with simple (but clean and comfy) rooms that have cable TV and fridge, plus parking (R$18/day). R$250

Rio Grande and around

The city of **RIO GRANDE** was founded on the entrance to the Lagoa dos Patos in 1737, at the very southern fringe of the Portuguese empire. With the growth of the *charque* and chilled-beef economy, Rio Grande's port took on an increasing importance from the mid-nineteenth century. Rather more spread out than Pelotas (60km to the north), it does not share that city's instant charm. However, you'll find some distinguished-looking nineteenth-century buildings in the area around Rua Floriano Peixoto and **Praça Tamandaré** (the main square), which is almost next to Largo Dr Pio and the modest and much-renovated eighteenth-century **Catedral de São Pedro**.

Museu Oceanográfico

Rua Heitor Perdigão 10 • Tues–Sun 9–11.30am & 2–6pm • R$5 • ☎53 3232 9107, 🌐museu.furg.br

Rio Grande's **Museu Oceanográfico**, part of a complex of museums operated by the Universidade Federal do Rio Grande, is perhaps the most important of its kind in Latin America, stuffed with fossils and all manner of preserved sea creatures, including over 51,000 shells. The adjacent **Museu Antártico** (same hours; free) celebrates Brazil's presence on Antarctica, with a replica of some of the facilities at the Comandante Ferraz base, while boats shuttle from here across to the **Museu da Ilha da Pólvora** in the Laguna dos Patos (Fri–Sun 2–6pm; R$5), where there are exhibits on the natural history of the Rio Grande estuary.

Museu Histórico da Cidade do Rio Grande

Rua Riachuelo • Tues–Fri 8.30–11.30am & 1.30–5pm, Sat 10am–3.30pm • Free • ⓣ 53 3232 6111, ⓦ museucrg.com.br

The small **Museu Histórico da Cidade do Rio Grande** traces the city's history through photographic archives and miscellaneous objects. The museum is housed in the old customs house (*alfândega*), a Neoclassical building built in 1879 that's more interesting than the collection. The museum's **Coleção de Arte Sacra** (collection of religious art and arefacts; same hours) is housed in the Capela São Francisco de Assis, completed in 1814 on the other side of nearby Praça Xavier Ferreira (behind the Catedral de São Pedro).

ARRIVAL AND DEPARTURE — RIO GRANDE AND AROUND

By bus A few blocks from Praça Tamandaré is Rio Grande's rodoviária (ⓣ 53 3232 8444), at Vice Alimirante Abreu 737, served by buses from most cities in Rio Grande do Sul and from cities as far north as Rio de Janeiro.

Destinations Chuí, at the Uruguay border (2 daily; 4hr); Pelotas (every 30min; 1hr); Porto Alegre (hourly; 5hr).

ACCOMMODATION AND EATING

Restaurante Marco's Shopping Praça Rio Grande, Rua Rua Jockey Clube 155 ⓣ 53 3036 2144. Still serves excellent seafood (especially shrimp/prawn dishes; R$60–70) despite moving to fairly bland premises in a shopping mall. Also does various lunch buffet options for R$30–60. Daily 11am–2pm & 6–10pm.

★ **Paris Hotel** Rua Marechal Floriano 112 ⓣ 53 3231 3866, ⓦ hotelvillamoura.com.br. Built in 1826 on the waterfront, this was once the place to stay in Rio Grande and, after decades of neglect, much of its former "Grand Hotel" feel has been restored, making it an important sight in its own right. There's a wood-panelled breakfast room and an extremely pretty courtyard with a central fountain, and while most of the bedrooms are fairly basic, some have period furnishings and offer amazing value. R$125

The Rota Missões (Mission Route)

Though less well known than those in Argentina and Paraguay, Rio Grande do Sul is home to several abandoned **Jesuit Missions** (see page 628), the ruins of some of which are in an excellent state of preservation and grouped together on what is called the **Rota Missões** (ⓦ rotamissoes.com.br). The best place to base yourself for the Brazilian ruins is the town of **Santo Ângelo** in the far southwest of Rio Grande do Sul; the best ruins in **Argentina** and **Paraguay** – San Ignacio Miní, Santísima Trinidad del Paraná and Jesús de Tavarangué – are only a relatively short drive away (see page 628).

Brief history

The Jesuits arrived here in 1626 determined to convert the **Guaraní**, with the missions founded between 1682 and 1706 in nominal Spanish territory. With a total population of 150,000, these mini-cities became centres of some importance, with *erva maté* and cattle the mainstays of economic activity, though spinning, weaving and metallurgical cottage industries were also pursued. In fact the region was virtually independent of both Spain and Portugal, a state of affairs ended by the 1750 Treaty of Madrid when the missions became definitively Portuguese; this led to the **Guarani War** of 1756, devastating the region (and dramatized in the 1986 film *The Mission*). The missions themselves were dissolved, either razed to the ground or abandoned to nature, surviving only as ruins. Of the thirty former Guaraní mission towns, sixteen were in present-day Argentina, seven in Paraguay and seven were situated in what is now Brazil.

Santo Ângelo

The city of **SANTO ÂNGELO**, set in a farming region inhabited predominantly by people of German origin, is a good point from which to catch buses to the missions. There's not much to see in the town itself, although the magnificent **Catedral Angelopolitana**, on the main square, Praça Pinheiro Machado, is worth a look as it's a fair replica of São Miguel's church – this version was only started in 1929, however, and completed in the 1970s.

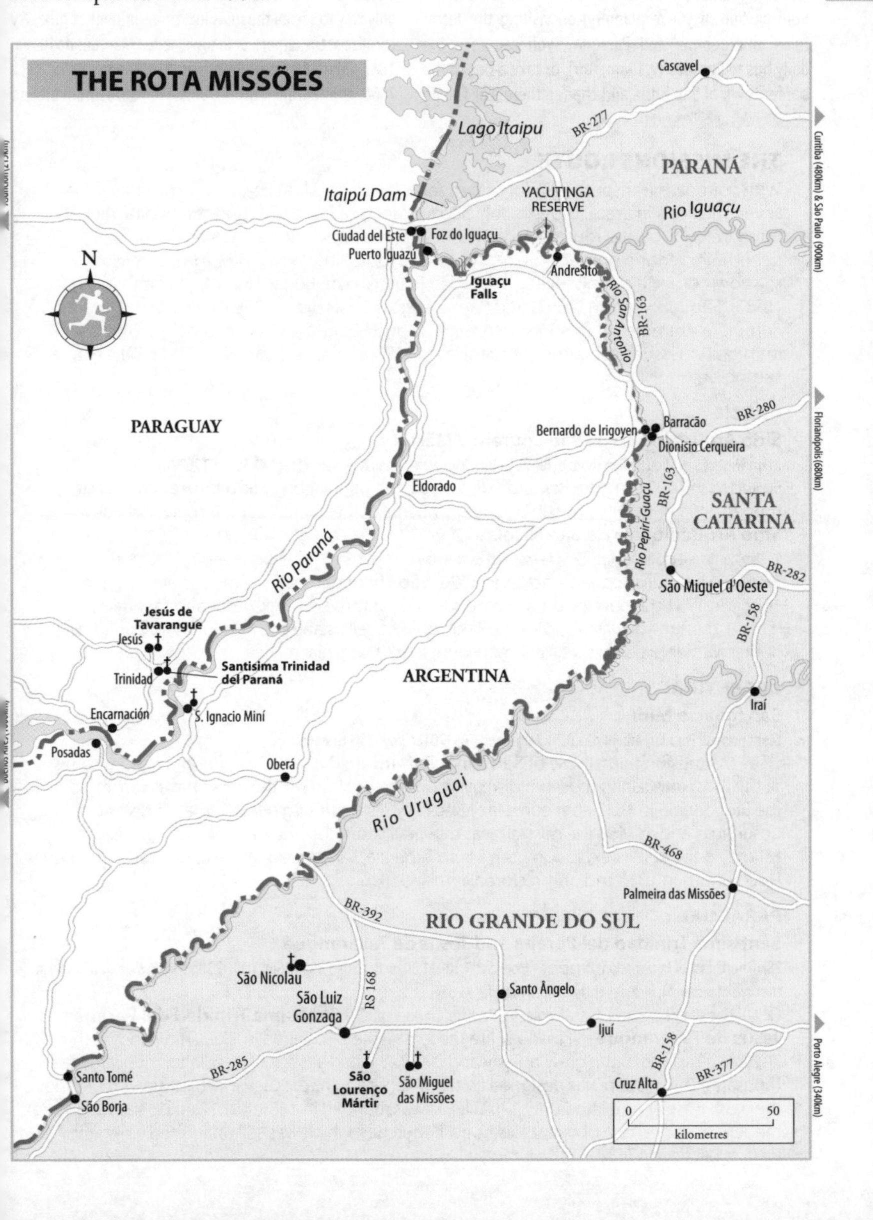

9

ARRIVAL AND TOURS — SANTO ÂNGELO

By bus The rodoviária (☎55 3313 2618) is 1km west of Praça Pinheiro Machado at Rua Sete Povos das Missões 419. Antonello runs buses to São Miguel (Mon–Fri 7.15am, 11am, 3.30pm & 4.45pm, Sat 10am & 3.30pm, Sun 9.30am & 6.20pm; R$10.50; 1hr 20min), with the last bus returning at 5.45pm Mon–Fri, 5.30pm Sat and 5pm on Sun. If you're planning on visiting the Jesuit ruins in Argentina and Paraguay, you can take the daily bus to Posadas (9.15am; 6hr), or take a bus to the border town of São Borja and change there. For Foz do Iguaçu you'll need to take a bus to Santa Rosa (1hr) and change there.

Destinations Bento Gonçalves (3 daily; 7–8hr); Curitiba (1 daily; 13hr); Porto Alegre (10 daily; 6–7hr); Rio (1 daily; 28hr); São Miguel (2–4 daily; 1hr 30min).

By car Getting around by car is a good idea and is the only way to see all the ruins in a short amount of time; try Localiza at the airport, or in town at Rua Marquês do Herval 1867 (Mon–Fri 8am–6pm, Sat 8am–noon; ☎55 3312 7000, localizahertz.com), which rents cars from around

THE MISSIONS ROUTE

With your own transport (or a lot of patience, taking local buses), you can visit all seven missions in Brazil, though only São Miguel (see page 629) and the two others listed below – on the route between São Miguel and São Borja (see page 630), near the Argentine border – are really worth a look. Little remains of the other four missions (portaldasmissoes.com.br): São Francisco de Borja (1666), São Luiz Gonzaga (1687), São João Batista (1697) and Santo Ângelo Custódio (1706). There are also more complete examples of missions in Argentina and Paraguay, also listed below. And check immigration issues concerning Argentina and Paraguay (see page 565 and 630) before setting out.

BRAZIL

Sítio Arqueológico de São Lourenço Mártir

24km west of São Miguel, 9km south of BR-285 • Tues–Sun 9am–noon & 2–6pm • Free • ☎55 3352 2699

Founded in 1690 by Padre Bernardo de la Vega, the population of **São Lourenço Mártir** topped 6400 in 1731. It's possible to see remnants of the church, cemetery and college.

Sítio Arqueológico de São Nicolau

113km northwest of São Miguel, RS-561 • Mon–Fri 8am–noon & 2–6pm, Sat & Sun 2–6pm • Free • ☎55 3363 1441

Founded by Padre Roque Gonzales in 1626, **São Nicolau** moved to the current location in 1687 – in 1731 the population was around 7700. Only the ceramic floors and foundations remain, though you can also visit the original wine cellars and the Museu Municipal (same hours) with displays on the excavation work that's taken place here.

ARGENTINA

San Ignacio Miní

60km north of Posadas, Argentina • Daily 7am–7pm • A$170 (or around U$10-equivalent)

Of all the mission ruins, those of **San Ignacio Miní** are the largest in area and feature some of the most interesting museum displays. Consecrated in 1609, the mission was moved to the Río Yabebirí in 1632 after constant attacks by slave-hunting *bandeirantes*. This site proved unsuitable, and in 1695 the mission was moved a short distance to its present location. Following the Jesuits' expulsion from South America, San Ignacio Miní was destroyed by the Paraguayans in 1817 and only restored in the 1940s.

PARAGUAY

Santísima Trinidad del Paraná and Jesús de Tavarangué

28km northeast of Encarnación, Paraguay • Mon–Sat 7.30–11.30am & 1.30–5.30pm, Sun 1.30–5.30pm • PYG25,000 (US$4.50 at the time of research); includes entry to both ruins for 15 days

Of the best-preserved Jesuit mission ruins, those of the **Santísima Trinidad del Paraná** and **Jesús de Tavarangué** in Paraguay are the least visited. Founded in 1706, Trinidad was the last Jesuit mission, but it grew quickly and by 1728 it had a Guaraní population of over three thousand. The mission was designed by the Milanese architect Giovanni Baptista Prímoli, and the work wasn't completed until 1760. Jesús was founded in 1685, just 12km up the road; here the Jesuits started one of their biggest ever churches, which was still unfinished when they were expelled in 1768.

R$100/day (plus insurance), though there are restrictions/fees for crossing the border.

Tours Caminho das Missões, Rua Antunes Ribas 984, Santo Ângelo (55 3312 9632, caminhodasmissoes.com.br), runs various hiking and biking tours along the Rota Missões.

ACCOMMODATION AND EATING

Arena Grill Rua Marquês do Herval 1780 55 3312 4763. Popular bar and Brazilian restaurant, with a decent lunch buffet (R$30 or R$50/kg), killer happy hour (especially buzzy on Tuesday night) and à la carte dishes with very good pizza (R$28–45) in the evenings. Boasts a surprisingly good line-up of touring bands (Thurs & Fri). You'll find the Arena bowling alley next door. Daily noon–3.30pm & 5.30pm–1am.

Kemper's Haus Rua Marquês do Herval 1763 55 3312 3922, kempershaus.com.br. Enticing café and bakery with a wide range of cakes, desserts, savoury snacks and excellent espresso; try the pink "Torta do General", with strawberry and whipped cream, a local speciality created in 1957. Also has free wi-fi. Mon–Sat 9am–8pm.

Maerkli Hotel Av Brasil 1000 55 3313 2127, versarehoteis.com.br. Centrally located, standard mid-range business hotel with modern, clean a/c rooms that have cable TV. Parking R$7/day. The hotel's website offers the best rates. R$283

Turis Hotel Santo Ângelo Av Antônio Manoel 726 55 3313 5255, turishotelsantoangelo.com.br. Just off the main square, this is the standard "budget" choice in town, though the rooms are rather old and not that cheap considering; a/c included, though. R$120

São Miguel da Missões

São Miguel Arcanjo, Rua São Nicolau • Tues–Sun 9am–noon & 2–6pm; Oct–Feb till 8pm • R$5 • 55 3381 1294

The most accessible and best preserved of the Jesuit missions in Brazil is **São Miguel Arcanjo** in the village of **SÃO MIGUEL DA MISSÕES**, 60km southwest of Santo Ângelo (16km south of BR-285 on RS-536). Despite vandalism and centuries of neglect, São Miguel's ruins offer ample evidence of the sophistication of Guaraní Baroque architecture, and of *redução* life generally. Founded in 1632, to the west of the Rio Uruguai, São Miguel moved only a few years later to escape *Paulista* slavers, and then a few years after that it was destroyed by a violent windstorm. After being rebuilt, its population increased rapidly and in 1687 it was relocated across the river to its present site.

The mission's initial priority was to provide housing, so not until 1700 did work begin on the **church**, designed by the Milanese Jesuit architect Giovanni Baptista Prímoli, the ruins of which still stand; the facade is a handsome example of colonial architecture. One of the church's two towers is missing, but otherwise its stone structure is reasonably complete, the lack of a vault or dome explained by the fact that these would have been finished with wood. Other aspects of the ruins are of less interest, but the outline of the mission's **walls** provides a guide to the former extent of São Miguel, which, at its peak, was home to over four thousand people.

Guided tours are available, and the small **Museu das Missões** (same times; museudasmissoes.blogspot.com.br) has an excellent collection of stone and wood sculptures, which are beautifully displayed in Jesuit-influenced but stylistically modernist buildings designed by Lúcio Costa, the urban planner of Brasília. Every evening a kitschy **sound-and-light show** (Espetáculo de Som e Luz; Feb–April & Aug–Oct 8pm; May–July 7pm; Nov–Jan 9.30pm; 50min; R$15) brings the story of the Jesuits to life, with some shows in English (usually Wed, Fri & Sun).

ARRIVAL AND ACCOMMODATION — SÃO MIGUEL DA MISSÕES

By bus The bus station (515 3381 1457) at Av Antunes Ribas 1525 is within walking distance of the ruins. Antonello runs 3–4 buses daily to and from São Miguel from Santo Ângelo (see page 627).

★ **Pousada das Missões** Rua São Nicolau 601 55 3381 1202, pousadadasmissoes.com.br. Right next to the ruins, this is a smart choice if you intend stay for the sound-and-light show. It's an excellent HI hostel that has clean dorm rooms as well as doubles (with a/c and TV) and a relaxing pool. HI members rates R$10 less for dorms (there is only one rate for doubles). Dorms R$80, doubles R$190

CROSSING INTO URUGUAY AND ARGENTINA

Most overland travellers cross the **southern Brazilian borders** via long-distance bus – in this case formalities are fairly straightforward (everyone gets off the bus to go through immigration). The borders here are generally open, meaning anyone can just walk across – if you are a foreigner travelling independently, however, you need to find the nearest **immigration post** to have your passport stamped; failing to do so will mean that you're likely to have difficulties entering or leaving Brazil later on. The main border crossings in the region are listed below – there is also an additional border crossing to Argentina in **São Borja** (see below).

TO URUGUAY: CHUÍ/CHUY

By far the most travelled route between Brazil and Uruguay passes through **Chuí**, 527km south of Porto Alegre (and 340km northeast of Montevideo). Buses entering and leaving Brazil stop at the 24hr immigration office a short distance north of the town itself (Chuí/Chuy is actually divided by the border, but there's no barrier between the two) on BR-471. The 24hr Uruguayan customs is 3km further south on Rte-9. Regular buses connect Chuí with Pelotas (5 daily; 4hr), Rio Grande (2 daily; 4hr) and Porto Alegre (2 daily; 7hr), while the bus companies in Chuy (mostly along Calle Leonado Oliveira, near Av Brasil, the street running along the border) service Montevideo (5hr). Most nationalities can visit Uruquay visa-free.

TO ARGENTINA: URUGUAIANA

Most travellers heading to Argentina from Brazil cross the frontier at **Foz do Iguaçu** (see page 562), but if you find yourself in the south of the country, **Uruguaiana**, 694km west of Porto Alegre, is the most convenient crossing – with Paso de los Libres on the other side (around 740km north of Buenos Aires). Customs formalities take place at either end of the 1400m-long road bridge across the Rio Uruguai/Río Uruguay. Accommodation and restaurant options are both better on the Argentine side of the border. Bus services from Uruguaiana are excellent, and you can get to or from most of the important centres from Rio southwards. From Paso de los Libres, there are equally good services to points within Argentina, including Buenos Aires, Posadas and Puerto Iguazú. For most nationalities (except Australian and Canadian) no visa is required for Argentina (see page 565).

São Borja

Today a fairly major border crossing point and regional trading centre, **SÃO BORJA** is best known in the rest of Brazil as the birthplace of two of the country's most controversial presidents: **Getúlio Vargas** and **João Goulart**, aka "Jango".

Museu Getúlio Vargas

Av Presidente Vargas 1772 • Mon–Sat 8.30am–noon & 1.30–5pm • Free • 55 9992 8484

In São Borja, if nowhere else in Brazil, the populist Getúlio Vargas remains a venerated figure, and his former home, built in 1910, is now open to the public as the **Museu Getúlio Vargas**, containing his private library, personal objects and furniture. His blood-stained bed sheets – preserved after he committed suicide – are also (rather morbidly) displayed in a funerary urn in the "Sala da Morte".

Museu João Goulart

Av Presidente Vargas 2033 • Tues–Sat 9am–noon & 2–5pm • Free

The hapless João Goulart, whose presidency led to the military's seizure of power in 1964, is commemorated at the **Museu João Goulart**, the former Goulart family home, completed in 1927. Further along the same avenue lies leafy Praça XV de Novembro, the location of the Modernist **Mausoléu Getúlio Vargas**, designed by Oscar Niemeyer (for free) and the final resting place of ex-president Vargas.

Cemitério Jardim da Paz

Rua Eng. Manuel Luís Fagundes • Daily 8am–noon & 2–6pm • Free

João Goulart was reburied in 2013 in the **Cemitério Jardim da Paz** (at a state funeral denied him in 1976), after being exhumed on his family's request (many believe he was poisoned). **Leonel Brizola**, the Vargas protégé and ex-governor of Rio Grande do Sul and Rio de Janeiro, was buried nearby in 2004. The **Vargas family tomb** is also here – president Vargas was buried here in 1954 before his re-interment in the Mausoléu (see above) in 2004. The cemetery is 1.5km west of Praça XV de Novembro.

ARRIVAL AND DEPARTURE — SÃO BORJA

By bus São Borja has good bus connections with Santo Ângelo (for São Miguel; 3–4hr), most other important towns in Rio Grande do Sul (Porto Alegre: 6–7 daily; 10hr), Curitiba (1 daily; 16hr 35min), and São Paulo (1 daily; 24hr).

To Argentina Across the bridge that links São Borja with Argentina lies the Argentine town of Santo Tomé. From Santo Tomé there are several bus services a day to Posadas, Puerto Iguazú, Buenos Aires and other towns in Argentina. For most nationalities (except Australian and Canadian) no visa is required for Argentina (see page 630).

CAVE PAINTINGS AT PARQUE NACIONAL DA SERRA DA CAPIVARA

Contexts

History

Brazil's recorded history begins with the arrival of the Portuguese in 1500, although it had already been settled by human beings for millennia. The importation of millions of African slaves over the next four centuries completed the rich blend of European, indigenous and African influences that formed modern Brazil and its people. Achieving independence from Portugal in 1822, Brazil's enormous wealth in land and natural resources underpinned a boom-and-bust cycle of economic development that continues to the present day.

Early history

Very little is known about the thousands of years during which Brazil was inhabited exclusively by **indigenous tribes**. The most widely accepted theory is that South America was settled by migrant hunters who came from Asia via the Bering Strait around 10,000 years ago, though stone tools discovered in the Serra da Capivara National Park in 2012 have challenged this theory – the tools were made 22,000 years ago. The oldest ceramics yet found in the Americas were discovered near Santarém in the 1990s and date back 8,000 years, suggesting that the Amazon was colonized before the Andes in remote prehistory. Indeed, research in the Amazon Basin – expertly summarized in Charles Mann's *1493* – has uncovered tantalizing evidence of advanced civilizations all along the river, and even suggests that many tropical plants and fruits that appear to be randomly spread throughout the jungle were actively cultivated by prehistoric peoples. But the fragile, material traces these early inhabitants left have for the most part not survived. The few exceptions – such as the exquisitely worked, glazed ceramic jars unearthed on Marajó island in the Amazon – come from cultures that have vanished so completely that not even a name records their passing.

By the time the Portuguese arrived in Brazil in the 1500s, the region was inhabited by hundreds of different native tribes, whom they dubbed "Indians" (*índios*). Linguistically and culturally these tribes were quite homogeneous, broadly divided into **Tupi-Guaraní** (mostly along the coast) and the **Tapuia** (north and inland). Nowhere was stone used for building. There was no use of metal or the wheel, and no centralized, state-like civilizations on the scale of Spanish America. The arrival of the Portuguese was an utter catastrophe for these peoples: measles, smallpox, tuberculosis, gonorrhoea and influenza killed thousands, often spreading along local trade routes long before direct contact with Europeans. In 1500 the total number of indigenous people was probably around five million – by 1800 there were just 250,000. However, the 2010 census revealed that 817,000 Brazilians now classify themselves as indigenous, and given that almost every single Portuguese colonist took a local wife in the early years of settlement, millions of Brazilians are likely to carry indigenous genes today.

6000 BC	1500 AD	1532	1537
Earliest evidence of human habitation in Brazil	Pedro Álvares Cabral lands in Brazil and claims it for the Portuguese crown	Portuguese establish São Vicente (near present-day Santos), and Piratininga (now São Paulo)	Olinda founded

THE FRENCH IN BRAZIL

The greatest threat to Portugal's claims on Brazil in the early years of colonization came not from their Spanish rivals but from the French. The colony of **France Antarctique** was established near present-day Rio in 1555 by Huguenots (French Protestant settlers). In 1560 Mem de Sá, the new Portuguese Governor-General of Brazil, attacked the French, but it wasn't until 1567 that all the colonists were expelled. Similarly, the colony of **France Équinoxiale** was established in 1612 at São Luís in the Northeast, but this was destroyed by the Portuguese in 1615. Though unable to maintain a foothold in Brazil, the French had a decisive impact on its history; in the aftermath of their crackdowns the Portuguese were motivated to establish Rio de Janeiro and their own incarnation of São Luís.

The Portuguese

The Portuguese discovery of Brazil, when **Pedro Alvares Cabral** landed in southern Bahia on April 23, 1500, was officially an accident: Cabral was blown off course as he steered far to the west to avoid the African doldrums on his way to India. After a week exploring the coast he continued to the Philippines, where he drowned in a shipwreck a few months later. King Manuel I sent **Amerigo Vespucci** to explore further in 1501. Reserving the name of the continent for himself, he spent several months sailing along the coast, calendar in hand, baptizing places after the names of saints' days: entering Guanabara Bay on New Year's Day 1502, he called it Rio de Janeiro. The land was called Terra do Brasil, after a tropical redwood that was its first export: the scarlet dye it yielded was called *brasa*, "a glowing coal".

Portugal, preoccupied with the lucrative Far East spice trade, neglected this new addition to its empire for a few decades; apart from some lumber camps, they made no attempt at settlement. Other European countries were not slow to move in, with French (see above) and English privateers in the lead. Finally, in 1532, King João III was provoked into action. He divided up the coastline into fifteen **sesmarias** or "captaincies" fifty leagues wide and extending indefinitely inland, distributing them to aristocrats and courtiers in return for undertakings to found settlements. It was hardly a roaring success: Pernambuco, where sugar took hold, and São Vicente, gateway to the Jesuit mission station of São Paulo, were the only securely held areas.

Settlement and the rise of sugar

Irritated by the lack of progress, King João repossessed the captaincies in 1548 and brought Brazil under direct royal control, sending out the first governor-general, **Tomé de Sousa** (1503–79), to the newly designated **capital** at Salvador in 1549. The first few governors successfully rooted out the European privateers, and – where **sugar** could grow – wiped out indigenous resistance. By the closing decades of the century increasing numbers of Portuguese settlers were flowing in. **Slaves** began to be imported from the Portuguese outposts on the African coast in the 1570s, as **sugar plantations** sprang up around Salvador and Olinda. Brazil, no longer seen merely as a possible staging point on the way to the Far East, became an increasingly important piece of the far-flung Portuguese Empire. When Europe's taste for sugar took off in the early seventeenth century, the northeast of Brazil quickly became very valuable real estate,

1540–1640	**1549**	**1555–67**	**1565**
Sugarcane production booms in the Northeast	Salvador founded by Tomé de Souza, the first Governor-General of Brazil	French colonists establish France Antarctique in the area of present-day Rio	Rio de Janeiro founded by the Portuguese

and a tempting target for the expanding maritime powers of northern Europe, jealous of the Iberian monopoly in the New World.

War with the Dutch

The **Dutch**, with naval bases in the Caribbean and a powerful fleet, were the best placed to move against Brazil. From 1580 to 1640 Portugal was united with Spain, against whom the Dutch had fought a bitter war of independence; the continuing Spanish presence in Flanders still menaced them. In 1624 a Dutch fleet appeared off Salvador and occupied the city within 24 hours. But they were pinned down by enraged settlers and expelled in 1625 by a hastily assembled combined Spanish and Portuguese fleet – the only direct intervention made by either country in the conflict. When a Dutch force was once more repulsed from Salvador in 1627, they shifted their attention further north and found the going much easier. Olinda was taken in 1630, the rich sugar zones of Pernambuco were occupied, and Dutch control extended up to the mouth of the Amazon by 1641. With settlers moving in and a fleet more powerful than Portugal's, Dutch control of the Northeast threatened to become permanent.

John Maurice of Nassau (1604–79) was sent out as governor of the new Dutch possessions in Brazil in 1636, as the Dutch founded a new capital in Pernambuco – Mauritzstaadt, now Recife. His enlightened policies of allowing the Portuguese freedom to practise their religion, and including them in the colonial government, may have resulted in a Dutch Brazil had it not been for the conservatism of the **Dutch West India Company**, his effective employers. They insisted on Calvinism and heavy taxes to pay for his lavish expenditures, and when John Maurice resigned in disgust and returned to Holland in 1644 the settlers rose. After five years of ambushes, plantation burnings and massacres, the Brazilians pushed the Dutch back into an enclave around Recife. The Dutch poured in reinforcements by sea, but two climactic battles in 1648 and 1649 at **Guararapes**, just outside Recife, saw Dutch military power broken. They finally surrendered Recife in 1654 – in the **Treaty of The Hague** (1661) the Dutch gave up all claims to Brazil in exchange for four million reais.

The bandeirantes

The expulsion of the Dutch demonstrated the toughness of the early Brazilians, which was also very evident in the penetration and settlement of **the interior** during the seventeenth and eighteenth centuries. Every few months expeditions set out, following rumours of gold and looking for indigenous peoples to enslave. They carried an identifying banner, a *bandeira*, which gave the name **bandeirantes** to the adventurers; they became the Brazilian version of the Spanish *conquistadores*. São Paulo became the main *bandeirante* centre thanks to its position on the Rio Tietê, one of the few natural highways that flowed east–west into the deep interior.

The average *bandeira* would be made up of a mixed crew of people, reflecting the many – and often conflicting – motives underlying the expedition. None travelled without a priest or two (*bandeirantes* may have been cut-throats, but they were devout Catholic cut-throats); Jesuits and Franciscans – in their drive to found missions and baptize the heathen – backed many *bandeiras*.

The journeys *bandeiras* made were often epic in scale, covering immense distances and overcoming natural obstacles as formidable as the many hostile tribes they

1605–94	**1612–14**	**1624**	**1630–54**
Quilombo dos Palmares, a community of escaped slaves, is governed by quasi-historical leaders Ganga Zumba and Zumbi	Failed French attempt to colonize São Luís region	The Dutch temporarily occupy Salvador	Dutch occupation of Olinda and Recife

encountered. It was the *bandeirantes* who pushed the borders of Brazil far inland, and also supplied the geographical knowledge that now began to fill in the blanks on the maps. But the most important way they shaped the future of Brazil was by locating the Holy Grail of the New World: gold.

The gold rush

Bandeirantes first found **gold** in the 1690s, at the spot that is now Sabará, in Minas Gerais. As towns sprang up around further gold strikes in Minas, gold was also discovered around Cuiabá, in Mato Grosso, adding fresh impetus to the opening-up of the interior. By the mid-eighteenth century, the flow of gold from Brazil was keeping the Portuguese Crown afloat, temporarily halting its long slide down the league table of European powers. In Brazil the rush of migrants to the gold areas changed the regional balance, as the new interior communities drew population away from the Northeast. The gateways to the interior, Rio de Janeiro and São Paulo, grew rapidly. The shift was recognized in 1763, when the capital was transferred to Rio from Salvador, and what was then a filthy, disease-ridden port began its slow transformation into one of the great cities of the world.

The Jesuits

Apart from the *bandeirantes*, the most important agents of the colonization of the interior were the **Jesuits**. The first Jesuit missionaries arrived in Brazil in 1549 and, thanks to the influence they held over successive Portuguese kings, they acquired power in Brazil second only to that of the Crown itself. In Salvador they built the largest Jesuit college outside Rome, and set in motion a crusade to convert the indigenous population. The usual method was to congregate the indigenous tribes in **missions**, where they worked under the supervision of Jesuit fathers. From 1600 onwards, dozens of missions were founded in the interior, especially in the Amazon and in the grasslands of the southeast.

The impact of the Jesuits was complex. Mission Indians were often released to work on plantations, where they died like flies, and the missionaries' intrepid penetration of remote areas resulted in the spread of diseases that wiped out entire tribes. Yet many Jesuits distinguished themselves in protecting tribes against the settlers, a theological as

PADRE ANTÔNIO VIEIRA

The most remarkable defender of the indigenous peoples in colonial Brazil was **Antônio Vieira** (1608–97), who abandoned his privileged position as chief adviser to the king in Lisbon to become a missionary in Brazil in 1653. Basing himself in São Luís, he struggled to implement the more enlightened indigenous laws that his influence over João IV had secured, to the disgust of settlers clamouring for slaves. Vieira denied them for years, preaching a series of sermons along the way that became famous throughout Europe, as well as Brazil. He didn't mince his words: "An Indian will be your slave for the few days he lives, but your soul will be enslaved for as long as God is God. All of you are in mortal sin, all of you live in a state of condemnation, and all of you are going directly to Hell!" he thundered to settlers from the pulpit in 1654. So high did feelings run that in 1661 settlers forced Vieira onto a ship bound for Portugal, standing in the surf and shouting "Out! Out!" Vieira managed to return to Bahia in 1681, where he died sixteen years later, still campaigning for indigenous freedoms.

1632
Jesuit mission of São Miguel Arcanjo founded in the South

1690s
Gold rush in Minas Gerais – the region booms throughout the 1700s

1727
Coffee introduced to Brazil

1756
Guaraní War: the Portuguese and Spanish destroy Jesuit missions in the South

well as a secular struggle, for many Portuguese argued that the native population had no souls and could therefore be treated like animals.

The Guaraní War (1756)

Jesuit influence reached a peak in the remarkable theocracy of the **Guaraní missions**, over a dozen institutions founded by Spanish and Portuguese priests on what is now the borderlands of Brazil, Uruguay and Argentina. Left alone for fifty years, they effectively became a Jesuit state, until the Treaty of Madrid in 1752 divided up the land between Spain and Portugal; the treaty ordered the missions to be abandoned so that settlers could move in. The Guaraní rebelled immediately. The Jesuit hierarchy made half-hearted efforts to get them to move, but most of the priests stayed with their Guaraní flocks. Resistance was heroic but hopeless: the superior fire power of a joint Spanish–Portuguese military expedition decimated both Guaraní and Jesuits in 1756 (the tragedy was dramatized in the 1986 film *The Mission*).

Jesuit involvement in the Guaraní War lent added force to the long-standing settler demands to expel them from the colony. The rise to power of the **Marquês de Pombal** (1699–1782), who became the power behind the Portuguese throne for much of the eighteenth century, helped; he seized upon the war as an excuse to expel the Order from Brazil (and all Portuguese territory) in 1759.

Independence

Brazil – uniquely among South American countries – achieved a peaceful transition to independence, although the odds seemed against it at one point. Brazilian resentment at exclusion from government and at the Portuguese monopoly of foreign trade grew steadily during the eighteenth century. It culminated in 1789 with the **Inconfidência Mineira**, a plot hatched by twelve prominent citizens of Ouro Preto to proclaim Brazilian independence. But the rebels were betrayed before they started; their leader, **Tiradentes** (1746–92), was executed and the rest exiled. Then, just as the tension seemed to be becoming dangerous, events in Europe took a hand in shaping Brazil's future.

The Portuguese exile

In 1807 **Napoleon** invaded Portugal. With the French army poised to take Lisbon, the British navy hurriedly evacuated Queen Dona Maria I and her son the Prince Regent (the effective ruler and future **Dom João VI**) to Rio, which was declared the temporary capital of the Portuguese Empire and seat of the government-in-exile. While **Wellington** set about driving the French from Portugal, the British were able to force the opening-up of Brazil's ports to non-Portuguese shipping, and the economic growth that followed reinforced Brazil's increasing self-confidence (though the British were the chief beneficiaries). Dom João VI became king officially in 1816 but was entranced by his tropical domain, unable to pull himself away even after Napoleon's defeat and the bloody **Pernambucan Revolt** of 1817 (which was utterly crushed). Finally, in 1821, he was faced with a liberal revolt in Portugal and was unable to delay his return any longer. In April 1822 he appointed his son, **Dom Pedro** (1798–1834), as prince regent and governor of Brazil; when he sailed home his last words to his son were, "Get your hands on this kingdom before some adventurer does."

1757	1759	1763	1789
Slavery of indigenous peoples abolished	Jesuits expelled from Brazil	Rio replaces Salvador as capital of Brazil	The Inconfidência Mineira, a failed attempt to gain independence from Portugal. One of the leaders, Tiradentes, is hanged

The Empire of Brazil

Dom Pedro, young and headstrong, grew increasingly irritated by the strident demands of the Cortês (Portuguese parliament) that he return home to his father and allow Brazil to be ruled from Portugal once again. On September 7, 1822, Pedro was out riding on the plain of Ypiranga, near São Paulo. Buttoning himself up after an attack of diarrhoea, he was surprised by a messenger with a bundle of letters from Lisbon. Reading the usual demands for him to return, his patience snapped, and he declared Brazil independent with the cry "Independence or death!". With overwhelming popular support he had himself crowned **Dom Pedro I**, Emperor of Brazil, on December 1, 1822. The Portuguese, preoccupied by political crises at home, put up little resistance. Apart from an ugly massacre of Brazilian patriots in Fortaleza, and some fighting in Bahia and Belém, the Portuguese withdrawal was peaceful and by the end of 1823 none of its forces remained. To seal the deal, the British helped negotiate a treaty in 1825 whereby Brazil paid Portugal two million pounds for the loss of its colony – funded with a loan arranged in London, of course. Indeed, Brazil's viability as an independent nation was largely dependent on British support for several decades.

Imperial Brazil: wars and revolts

The early decades of independence proved much more difficult than the break with Portugal. Dom Pedro became increasingly estranged from his subjects, devoting more attention to scandalous romances than affairs of state. In April 1831 he was forced to abdicate and returned to Portugal (he died three years later). His son and heir, **Dom Pedro II** (1825–91), would later prove an enlightened ruler but, as he was only five at the time, his capacity to influence events was limited. With a power vacuum at the centre of the political system, tensions in the provinces erupted into revolt. There were common threads in all the **rebellions** that ranged in the provinces between the 1820s and 1840s: slaves rebelling against masters, indigenous and mixed-race resentment of white domination, Brazilians settling scores with Portuguese and the poor rising against the rich.

Rebellion

The first and most serious conflagration under Dom Pedro II's rule was the **Cabanada** or **War of Cabanos** (1832–35) in Pernambuco, where insurgents demanded the return of Dom Pedro I, and continued with the **Cabanagem** in Pará, where a mass revolt of the dispossessed began in 1835. The rebels destroyed most of Belém, killing the governor of Pará and many of the town's elite; the uprising spread through the Amazon like wildfire and took five years to put down. Elsewhere the **Sabinada** in Bahia (1837–38)

THE CISPLATINE WAR

In 1816 Brazil invaded the area known as **Banda Oriental** (the land between the Río de la Plata and Rio Grande do Sol), eventually defeating the nascent government of José Gervasio Artigas, and making it Cisplatine Province in 1821. But just four years later a group of local nobles proclaimed independence. The ensuing **Cisplatine War** (1825–28) was a disaster for Brazil; after heavy military defeats the new nation of Uruguay gained its independence in 1828.

1808	1817	1821	1822
The Portuguese court, fleeing Napoleon, relocates to Rio	Pernambucan revolution crushed by Portuguese troops	João VI returns to Portugal, leaving his son Pedro in charge of Brazil	Brazil declares independence from Portugal; Dom Pedro I becomes emperor

saw a brutal struggle for Salvador, while the **War of the Farrapos** (1836–45) in Rio Grande do Sul was essentially a *gaúcho* revolt, aided by Italian fighter **Giuseppe Garibaldi** – unusually, it was ended by peace treaty and the rebels given general amnesty. The **Balaiada** began in Maranhão in 1838, where the rebels took Caxias, the second city of the state, and held out against the army until 1840. The last of the provincial rebellions was the **Praieira** of 1848, also in Pernambuco – it dragged on for two years.

Dom Pedro II

The crisis led to **Dom Pedro II** being declared emperor four years early, in 1840, when he was only fourteen. He was a sensible, scholarly man, completely unlike his father. His instincts were conservative, but he also had a modernizing streak and was respected even by republicans. With government authority restored, the provincial rebellions had by 1850 either blown themselves out or been put down. With **coffee** beginning to be planted on a large scale in Rio, São Paulo and Minas, and the flow of European immigrants rising from a trickle to a flood, the economy of southern Brazil began to take off in earnest.

The War of the Triple Alliance (1864–70)

With the rebellions in Brazil's provinces, the **army** became increasingly important in Brazilian political life. Pedro insisted it stay out of domestic politics, but his policy of diverting the generals by allowing adventures abroad ultimately led to the disaster of the war with Paraguay; although Brazil emerged victorious, it was at dreadful cost. The **War of the Triple Alliance** is one of history's forgotten conflicts, but it was the bloodiest war in South American history, with a casualty list almost as long as that of the American Civil War: Brazil alone suffered over 100,000 casualties. It pitted in unequal struggle the landlocked republic of Paraguay, under the dictator **Francisco Solano López** (1827–70), against the combined forces of Brazil, Argentina and Uruguay. López started the war by invading Mato Grosso in 1864 (historians still disagree about his motives, though in part it was a reaction to Brazilian interference in Uruguay, to the south). The Brazilian army and navy were confident of victory as the Paraguayans were heavily outnumbered and outgunned. Yet under the able leadership of López the Paraguayan army proved disciplined and brave, always defeated by numbers but terribly mauling the opposition. It turned into a war of extermination and six bloody years were only ended when López was killed in 1870; by this time the population of Paraguay was reduced (by disease and starvation as well as war) by some 60 percent – estimates suggest anywhere from 500,000 to 1.2 million people died. Brazil ended the war even deeper in debt to Britain.

The end of slavery

From the seventeenth to the nineteenth century around four million Africans were transported to Brazil as **slaves** – many times more than were shipped to the United States – yet the death rate in Brazil was so great that in 1860 Brazil's slave population was half the size of that in the US. Slavery was always contested. Slaves fled from the cities and plantations to form refugee communities called *quilombos*; the largest was **Palmares** (see page 640).

1825–28	**1830**	**1831**	**1840–1930**
Cisplatine War: Uruguay gains independence from Brazil	Slave trade to Brazil made illegal; law weakly enforced until 1850	Dom Pedro II becomes emperor after his father abdicates	Coffee production booms in Brazil

THE LEGEND OF ZUMBI

The largest and most famous of all Brazil's rebellious *quilombos* (refugee communities) was **Palmares**, a vibrant community of freed slaves in the interior of the northeastern state of Alagoas that remained independent between 1605 and 1694. Not much is known about Palmares, but scholars estimate up to 11,000 fugitives may have lived there at its height, a combination of several *mocambos* or villages. Contemporary accounts of the many Portuguese expeditions sent to crush the community talk of a semi-mythical leader dubbed Ganga Zumba – his successor, Zumbi, waged almost constant war against the Portuguese. **Zumbi** was captured and beheaded in 1695 (Palmares was totally destroyed in 1694), and though almost nothing is known about him, he is revered as a symbol of freedom today. The day of his death – November 20 – has been celebrated as a day of Afro-Brazilian awareness ("Dia da Consciência Negra"), primarily in Rio and Salvador, since 2003.

It was not until the nineteenth century that slavery was seriously challenged. The initial impetus came from Britain, where the slave trade had been abolished in 1807. Large landowners in Brazil regarded abolition with horror, and a combination of racism and fear of economic dislocation led to a determined rearguard action to preserve slavery. A complicated diplomatic waltz began between Britain and Brazil, as slavery laws were tinkered with *para inglês ver* – "for the English to see" – a phrase that survives in Portuguese to this day, meaning to do something merely for show. Brazil made the **slave trade** officially illegal in 1830, but British abolitionists were not deceived, and until the 1850s the Royal Navy maintained a squadron off Brazil, intercepting and confiscating slave ships, and occasionally entering Brazilian ports to seize slavers and burn their vessels – one of history's more positive examples of gunboat diplomacy. In 1850 the Brazilian parliament finally passed a law enforcing the slave trade ban, and after 1851 few African slaves entered the country – but slavery itself remained legal.

Ultimately it was a passionate campaign within Brazil itself, led by the fiery lawyer **Joaquim Nabuco** (1849–1910), that finished slavery off. The growing liberal movement, increasingly republican and anti-monarchist, squared off against the landowners, with Dom Pedro II hovering indecisively somewhere in between. By the time full **emancipation** came, in the "Golden Law" of May 13, 1888, Brazil had achieved the shameful distinction of being the last country in the Americas to abolish slavery.

The first republic (1889–1930)

The end of slavery was also the death knell of the **monarchy**. Since the 1870s the intelligentsia, deeply influenced by French liberalism, had turned against the emperor and agitated for a republic. By the 1880s they had been joined by the officer corps, who blamed Dom Pedro II for lack of backing during the Paraguayan war. When the large landowners withdrew their support, furious that the emperor had not prevented emancipation, the **monarchy collapsed** very suddenly in 1889.

Once again, Brazil managed a bloodless transition. The push came from the army, detachments led by **Deodoro da Fonseca** (1827–92) meeting no resistance when they occupied Rio on November 15, 1889. They invited the royal family to remain,

1864–70	1879–1912	1880s	1888
Paraguayan War: Argentina, Brazil and Uruguay crush Paraguay	The Amazon rubber boom	British railway workers introduce football to Brazil	Slavery abolished; European immigrants flood into Brazil

but Dom Pedro chose exile, boarding a ship to France where he died two years later. Deodoro, meanwhile, began a Brazilian tradition of ham-fisted military autocracy. Ignoring the clamour for a liberal republic he declared himself dictator in 1891, but was forced to resign three weeks later when even the army refused to support him. His deputy, **Floriano de Peixoto** (1839–95), took over, but proved even more incompetent; Rio was actually shelled in 1893 by rebellious warships demanding his resignation. Finally, in 1894, popular pressure led to Peixoto stepping down in favour of the first elected civilian president, **Prudente de Morais** (1841–1902).

Coffee with milk – and sugar

The years from 1890 to 1930 were politically undistinguished but saw large-scale **immigration** from Europe and Japan rapidly transform Brazil. They were decades of swift growth and swelling cities, which saw a very Brazilian combination of a boom-bust-boom economy and corrupt pork-barrel politics. **Coffee** and **rubber**, at opposite ends of the country, led the boom. They had very different labour forces. Millions of *nordestinos* moved into the Amazon to tap rubber, but the coffee workers swarming into São Paulo in their hundreds of thousands came chiefly from Italy. Between 1890 and 1930 over four million migrants arrived from Europe and another two hundred thousand from Japan. Most went to work on the coffee estates of southern Brazil, but enough remained to turn São Paulo into the fastest-growing city in the Americas. Urban industrialization appeared in Brazil for the first time, taking root in São Paulo to supply the voracious markets of the young cities springing up in the *paulista* interior. By 1930 São Paulo had displaced Rio as the leading industrial centre.

More improbable was the transformation of **Manaus** into the largest city of the Amazon. Rubber turned it from a muddy village into a rich trading city within a couple of decades. The peak of the **rubber boom**, from the 1870s to the outbreak of World War I, financed its metamorphosis into a tropical *belle époque* outpost, complete with opera house. Rubber exports were second only to coffee, but proved much more vulnerable to competition. Seeds smuggled out of Amazônia by Victorian adventurer Henry Wickham in 1876 ended up in Sri Lanka and Malaysia, and the resulting plantation rubber pushed wild Amazon rubber out of world markets. The region returned to an isolation it maintained until the late 1960s.

Political development did not accompany economic growth. Power was concentrated in the two most populous states of São Paulo and Minas Gerais, which struck a convenient deal to alternate the presidency between them. This way of ensuring both sets of snouts could slurp away in the trough uninterrupted was called "**café com leite**" by its opponents: coffee from São Paulo and milk from the *mineiro* dairy herds. In fact, it was coffee with milk and sugar: the developing national habit of the sweet *cafézinho* in the burgeoning cities of the south provided a new domestic market for sugar, which ensured support from the plantation oligarchs of the Northeast.

Resistance to the Republic

Not everyone was happy with the new republic. In 1893 the **Federalist Riograndense Revolution** erupted in Rio Grande do Sul, a bloody struggle by monarchists and separatists that lasted two-and-a-half years. In the late 1890s the autonomous community of **Canudos** (see page 247), comprised of landless farmers, former slaves,

1889

Monarchy overthrown by a military coup led by General Deodoro da Fonseca, who becomes Brazil's first president

1894–1930

The *política do café com leite:* the presidency is controlled by coffee oligarchies from São Paulo and Minas Gerais, alternately

1896–97

The community of Canudos is brutally crushed by the government indigenous people and *cangaceiros*, was brutally crushed by the Republican government as well. The **Contestado War** raged in the South between 1912 and 1916 as settlers and landowners fought over land rights (inspired by itinerant preachers), and in the 1920s bandit leader **Lampião** roved the Northeast as (rather tenuously) Brazil's "Robin Hood" (see page 261).

The revolution of 1930

Revolution in 1930 brought **Getúlio Vargas** (1882–1954) to power, the wealthy son of a *gaúcho*, pro-industrial nationalist and anti-communist governor of Rio Grande do Sul. Vargas dominated Brazilian politics for the next quarter-century. He had much in common with his Argentine contemporary, Juan Perón: both were charismatic but also cunning and ruthless, and created new power bases in their countries rooted in the urban working class.

It was the **working class**, combined with disillusion in the junior ranks of the military, which swept Vargas to power. Younger officers, accustomed to seeing the armed forces as the guardian of the national conscience, were disgusted by the corruption of the military hierarchy. When the **Great Depression** hit, the government spent millions protecting coffee growers by buying crops at a guaranteed price; the coffee was then burnt, as the export market had collapsed. Workers in the cities and countryside were appalled, seeing themselves frozen out while vast sums were spent on landowners, and as the economic outlook worsened the pressure started building up from other states to end the São Paulo and Minas grip on power. This time the transition was violent.

In 1926, **Washington Luís** (1869–1957) was made president without a proper election, as the elite contrived an unopposed nomination. When Luís appeared set to do the same thing in 1930, an unstoppable **popular revolution** developed, first in Vargas's home state of Rio Grande do Sul, then in Rio, then in the Northeast. There was some resistance in São Paulo, but the worst fighting was in the Northeast, where street battles left scores dead. Although São Paulo rose briefly against Vargas in 1932, the revolt was swiftly crushed.

Vargas and the Estado Novo (1930–56)

It was not just **Vargas** who took power in 1930, but a new generation of young, energetic administrators who set about transforming the economy and the political system. Vargas nationalized the oil, electricity and steel industries, and set up a health and social welfare system that earned him unwavering working-class support even after his death. Reforms this fundamental could not be carried out under the old constitutional framework. Vargas simplified things by declaring himself **dictator** in 1937 and imprisoning political opponents – most of whom were in the trade union movement, the Communist Party or the *Integralistas* (the Brazilian Fascists). He called his regime the "New State", or **Estado Novo**, and although he cracked down hard on dissent, Vargas was never a totalitarian dictator. He was highly popular and his political talents enabled him to outflank most opponents.

The result was both political and economic success. The ruinous coffee subsidy was abolished, industry encouraged and agriculture diversified; by 1945 São Paulo had

1912–16	1922–38	1930	1938
Contestado War; guerilla revolt in the South	Bandit leader Lampião terrorizes the Northeast	Getúlio Vargas becomes president after military revolt	Lampião killed in shoot-out with police

become the largest industrial centre in South America. With the federal government increasing its powers at the expense of the states, power in the regions was wrested out of the hands of the oligarchs for the first time.

World War II (1939–45)

It took **World War II** to bring Vargas down. At first Brazil stayed neutral, reaping the benefits of increased exports, but when the United States offered massive aid in return for bases and Brazilian entry into the war, Vargas joined the Allies in 1942. Outraged by German submarine attacks on Brazilian shipping, Brazil was the only country in South America to play an active part in the war. A **Brazilian Expeditionary Force** of over 20,000 men fought in Italy from 1944. When it returned, the military High Command was able to exploit the renewed prestige of the army, forcing Vargas to stand down. They argued that the armed forces could hardly fight for democracy abroad and return home to a dictatorship, and, in any case, after fifteen years a leadership change was overdue. In the election that followed in 1945 Vargas grudgingly endorsed army general **Eurico Dutra**, who duly won – but Getúlio, brooding on his ranch, was not yet finished with the presidency.

The return and fall of Vargas (1950–54)

Dutra proved a colourless figure, and when Vargas ran for the presidency in 1950 he won a crushing victory, the old dictator "returning on the arm of the people", as he wrote later. But he had powerful enemies in the armed forces and on the right, and his second stint in power was turbulent. Dutra had allowed inflation to climb, and Vargas proposed to raise the minimum wage and increase taxation of the middle classes. In the charged climate of the Cold War, the right denounced this as veering towards communism, and vitriolic attacks on Vargas and his government were made in the press, notably by a slippery, ambitious Rio journalist named **Carlos Lacerda**.

Vargas's supporters reacted angrily and argument turned into crisis in 1954, when shots were fired at Lacerda, missing their target but killing an air-force officer guarding him. The attempt was traced to one of Vargas's bodyguards, and the press campaign rose to a crescendo. Finally, on August 25, 1954, the military High Command demanded his resignation. Vargas received the news calmly, went into his bedroom in the Palácio de Catete in Rio, and shot himself through the heart.

He left an emotional suicide note to the Brazilian people: "I choose this means to be with you always… I gave you my life; now I offer my death. Nothing remains. Serenely I take the first step on the road to eternity, as I leave life and enter history." When it was published, the initial stunned popular reaction gave way to fury and Vargas's supporters turned on the forces that had hounded him to death, burning the newspaper offices, driving the army back into barracks and forcing Lacerda to flee the country. Eighteen months of tension followed, as an interim government marked time until the next election.

JK and Brasília (1956–61)

Juscelino Kubitschek (1902–76) – "JK" to Brazilians – was president from 1956 to 1961, and proved just the man to fix Brazil's attention on the future rather than the

1940	**1942**	**1945**	**1950**
Pelé (Edson Arantes do Nascimento) born in Minas Gerais	Brazil joins the Allies in World War II	Vargas ousted in military coup	Maracanã stadium opens in Rio

past. He combined energy and imagination with integrity and political skill, acquired in the hard school of Minas Gerais, one of the main nurseries of political talent in Brazil. "Fifty years in five!" was his election slogan, and his economic programme lived up to its ambitious billing. His term saw a spurt in growth rates that was the platform for the "economic miracle" of the next decade, and he left a permanent reminder of the most successful post-war presidency in the form of the country's new capital, **Brasília**, deep in the Planalto Central.

It could so easily have been an expensive disaster: a purpose-built capital miles from anywhere, the personal brainchild of a president anxious to make his mark. But Kubitschek implanted the idea in the national imagination by portraying it as a renewed statement of faith in the interior, a symbol of national integration and a better future for all Brazilians, not just those in the South. He brought it off with great panache, bringing in the extravagantly talented **Lúcio Costa** (1902–98) whose brief was to come up with a revolutionary city layout, and the great architect **Oscar Niemeyer** (1907–2012) to design the buildings to go with it. Kubitschek spent almost every weekend on the huge building site that became the city, consulted on the smallest details, and had the satisfaction of handing over to his successor, **Jânio Quadros** (1917–92), in the newly inaugurated capital.

The road to military rule

At the time, the **military coup of 1964** was considered a temporary hiccup in Brazil's post-war democracy, but it lasted 21 years and left a very bitter taste. The first period of military rule saw the famous **economic miracle**, when the economy grew at an astonishing average annual rate of ten percent for a decade, only to come to a juddering halt after 1974. But most depressing was the effective end of democracy for over a decade, and a time – from 1969 to 1974 – when terror was used against opponents by military hardliners. It was the first time Brazilians experienced systematic brutality by a government, and even in the years of economic success the military governments were loathed across the political spectrum.

The coup was years in the brewing. It had two root causes: a constitutional crisis and the deepening divides in Brazilian society. In the developed South relations between trade unions and employers went from bad to worse, as workers struggled to protect their wages against rising inflation. But it was in the Northeast that tension was greatest, as a result of the **Peasant Leagues** movement. Despite industrial modernization, the rural region was still stuck in a time-warped land-tenure system, moulded in the colonial period and in many ways unchanged since then. Rural labourers, under the charismatic leadership of **Francisco Julião** and the governor of Pernambuco, **Miguel Arrães**, began forming cooperatives and occupying estates to press their claim for agrarian reform; the estate owners cried communism and openly agitated for a military coup.

The presidency of João Goulart (1961–64)

The crisis might still have been avoided by a more skilful president, but Kubitschek's immediate successors were not of his calibre. Quadros resigned after only six months, in August 1961, on the anniversary of Vargas's suicide, and the vice-president, **João**

1951	1953	1954	1956–61
Vargas elected president	Petrobras – still the largest company in Brazil and Latin America – is founded; its oil monopoly is revoked in 1997	Vargas commits suicide after military tells him to resign or be overthrown	Juscelino Kubitschek is president

Goulart (1918–76), aka "Jango", took over. Goulart's accession was viewed with horror by the right. He had a reputation as a leftist firebrand, having been a minister of labour under Vargas, and his position was weakened by the fact that he had not succeeded by direct popular vote. As political infighting began to get out of control, with the country polarizing between left and right, Goulart decided to throw himself behind the trade unions and the Peasant Leagues; his nationalist rhetoric rang alarm bells in Washington and the army began to plot his downfall, with tacit American backing.

The coup was swift and bloodless. On March 31, 1964, troops from Minas Gerais moved on Rio; when the military commanders there refused to oppose them, the game was up for Goulart. After futile efforts to rally resistance in Rio Grande do Sul, he fled into exile in Uruguay (his death by heart attack in 1976 is still regarded as suspicious), and the first in a long line of generals, **Humberto Castelo Branco** (1897–1967), became president.

Military rule (1964–85)

The **military** moved swiftly to dismantle democracy. Congress was dissolved, and those representatives not to military taste were removed. It then reconvened with only two parties, an official government and an official opposition ("The difference," ran a joke at the time, "is that one says 'Yes', and the other, 'Yes Sir!' "). All other parties were banned. The Peasant Leagues and trade unions were repressed, with many of their leaders tortured and imprisoned, and even prominent national politicians like Arrães were thrown into jail. The ferocity of the military took aback even those on the right who had agitated for a coup. Even Lacerda was imprisoned.

The political climate worsened steadily during the 1960s. An **urban guerrilla campaign** took off in the cities – its most spectacular success was the kidnapping of the American ambassador in 1969, released unharmed in return for over a hundred political detainees – but it only served as an excuse for the hardliners to crack down even further. General **Emílio Garrastazú Médici** (1905–85), leader of the hardliners, took over the presidency in 1969 and the worst period of military rule began. Torture became routine, censorship was strict and thousands were driven into exile; this dark chapter in Brazilian history lasted for five agonizing years, until Médici gave way to **Ernesto Geisel** (1907–96) in 1974. The scars Médici left behind him, literally and metaphorically, have still not completely healed.

The economic miracle

Despite the cold winds blowing on the political front, the Brazilian economy forged ahead from the mid-1960s to 1974 – the years of the **economic miracle** – and the combination of high growth and low inflation indeed seemed miraculous to later governments. The military welcomed foreign investment, and the large pool of cheap but skilled labour was irresistible. Investment poured in, both from Brazil and abroad, and the boom was the longest and largest in Brazilian history. Cities swelled, industry grew, and by the mid-1970s Brazil was the economic giant of South America; **São Paulo** state alone had a GNP higher than any South American country, a distinction it maintains to this day. The problem was uneven development. Even miraculous growth rates could not provide enough jobs for the hordes migrating to the cities, and the squalid **favelas** expanded even faster than the economy.

1958	1960	1962	1964
Brazil wins its first World Cup – it wins again in 1962, 1970 and 1994	Kubitschek moves capital to Brasilia	*The Girl from Ipanema* is written by Antônio Jobim and Vinicius de Moraes.	President João Goulart ousted in bloodless coup, flees into exile. Military rule follows

OPENING UP THE AMAZON

Kubitschek, who built a dirt highway linking Brasília to Belém, took the first step towards opening up the vast interior of the **Amazon**. But things really got going in 1970, when General Médici realized that the Amazon could be used as a huge safety valve, releasing the pressure for agrarian reform in the Northeast. "Land without people for people without land!" became the slogan, and an ambitious programme of highway construction began. The main links were the **Transamazônica**, running west to the Peruvian border, the **Cuiabá–Santarém** highway into central Amazônia, and the **Cuiabá–Porto Velho/Rio Branco** highway, opening access to western Amazônia.

For the **military**, the Amazon was empty space, overdue for filling, and a national resource to be developed. They set up an elaborate network of tax breaks and incentives to encourage Brazilian and multinational firms to invest in the region, who also saw it as empty space and proceeded either to speculate with land or cut down forest to graze cattle. The one group that didn't perceive the Amazon this way was, naturally enough, the millions of people who already lived there. The immediate result was a spiralling **land conflict**, as ranchers, rubber tappers, Brazil-nut harvesters, gold-miners, smallholders, indigenous communities, multinationals and Brazilian companies all tried to press their claims. The result was chaos.

By the 1980s the situation in the Amazon was becoming an international controversy, with the uncontrolled **destruction of forest** in huge annual burnings, and the invasion of indigenous lands. Less internationally known was the **land crisis**, although a hundred people or more were dying in land conflicts in Amazônia every year. It took the assassination in 1988 of **Chico Mendes**, leader of the rubber-tappers' union and eloquent defender of the forest, to bring it home (see page 397).

After 1974 petrodollars were sloshing around the world banking system, thanks to oil price rises. Anxious to set this new capital to work, international banks and South American military regimes fell over themselves in their eagerness to organize deals. Brazil had a good credit rating – its wealth of natural resources and jailed labour leaders saw to that. The military needed money for a series of huge development projects central to its trickle-down economic policy, like the **Itaipu dam**, the **Carajás** mining projects in eastern Amazônia, and a **nuclear power programme.** By the end of the 1970s Brazilian debt was at US$50 billion; by 1990 it had risen to US$120 billion, and the interest payments were crippling the economy.

Democracy returns: the abertura

Growing popular resentment of the military could not be contained indefinitely, especially when the economy turned sour. By the late 1970s debt, rising inflation and unemployment were turning the economy from a success story into a joke, and the military were further embarrassed by an unsavoury chain of **corruption scandals**. Geisel was the first military president to plan for a return to civilian rule, in a slow relaxing of the military grip called **abertura**, the "opening-up". Yet again Brazil managed a bloodless – albeit fiendishly complicated – transition. Slow though the process was, the return to democracy would have been delayed even longer had it not been for two events along the way: the **strikes** in São Paulo in 1977 and the mass **campaign for direct elections** in 1983–84.

1968–73	1980s	1984	1985
Economy experiences spectacular growth	Economy stagnates – rampant inflation becomes major problem	Itaipu Dam completed	Tancredo Neves elected first civilian president in 21 years, but dies shortly afterwards. José Sarney

The strikes – led by unions that were still illegal, and the charismatic young factory worker **Lula (Luís Inácio da Silva)** – began in the car industry and soon spread throughout the industrial belt of São Paulo, in a movement bearing many parallels with Solidarity in Poland. There was a tense stand-off between army and strikers, until the military realized that having São Paulo on strike would be worse for the economy than conceding the right to free trade unions. This dramatic re-emergence of organized labour was a sign that the military could not control the situation for much longer.

Reforms in the early 1980s lifted censorship, brought the exiles home and allowed normal political life to resume. But the military came up with an ingenious attempt to determine the succession: their control of Congress allowed them to pass a resolution that the president due to take office in 1985 would be elected not by direct vote, but by an electoral college made up of congressmen and senators, where the military party had the advantage. The democratic opposition responded with a counter-amendment proposing a direct election. It needed a two-thirds majority in Congress to be passed, and a campaign began for **diretas-já**, "direct elections now". Even the opposition was surprised by the response, as the Brazilian people, thoroughly sick of the generals, took to the streets in their millions. The campaign culminated in huge rallies of over a million people in Rio and São Paulo, and opinion polls showed over ninety percent in favour; but when the vote came in March 1984 the amendment just failed. The military still nominated a third of Senate seats, and this proved decisive.

Tancredo Neves

It looked like defeat; in fact it turned into victory. The moment found the man in **Tancredo Neves** (1910–85), ex-minister of justice under Vargas, ex-prime minister, and a wise old *mineiro* fox respected across the political spectrum, who put himself forward as opposition candidate in the electoral college. By now it was clear what the public wanted, and Tancredo's unrivalled political skills enabled him to stitch together an alliance that included dissidents from the military's own party. In January 1985 he romped home in the electoral college, to great national rejoicing, and military rule came to an end. Tancredo proclaimed the civilian **Nova República**, but tragically, the "New Republic" was orphaned at birth. The night before his inauguration Tancredo was rushed to hospital for an emergency operation on a bleeding stomach tumour; it proved benign, but in hospital he picked up an infection and six weeks later died of septicaemia. His funeral was the largest mass event in Brazilian history; a crowd of two million followed his coffin from the hospital where he had died in São Paulo to Guarulhos airport.

The New Republic: crisis and corruption

The vice-president, **José Sarney** (born 1930), a second-league politician from Maranhão who had been fobbed off with a ceremonial post, suddenly found himself serving a full presidential term. His administration was disastrous, though not all of it was his own fault: he was saddled with a ministerial team he had not chosen, and a newly powerful Congress that would have given any president a rough ride. But Sarney

1988	**1989**	**1992**
Rubber-workers' leader Chico Mendes assassinated; Paulo Coelho publishes *The Alchemist*	Fernando Collor de Mello becomes first directly elected president since 1960; inflation out of control	Collor resigns after being accused of corruption and is impeached

made matters worse by a lack of decisiveness, and wasn't helped by the sleaze that hung like a fog around his government, with **corruption** institutionalized on a massive scale. No progress was made on the economic front either. By 1990 inflation accelerated into **hyperinflation** proper, and, despite spending almost US$40 billion repaying interest on the foreign debt, the principal had swollen to US$120 billion. The high hopes of 1985 had evaporated – Sarney had brought the whole notion of civilian politics into disrepute and achieved the near-impossible: making the military look good.

Collor and Franco (1990–94)

Brazil still managed to begin the next decade on a hopeful note, with the inauguration in 1990 of **Fernando Collor de Melo** (born 1949), the first properly elected president for thirty years, after a heated but peaceful campaign had managed to consolidate democracy at a difficult economic moment. The campaign had passed the torch to a new generation of Brazilians, as the young Collor, playboy scion of one of Brazil's oldest and richest families, had squared off against **Lula**. Now a respected – and feared – national politician, head of the Workers' Party that the strike movement had evolved into, Lula took most of the cities, but Collor's conservative rural support was enough to secure a narrow victory.

His presidency began promisingly enough, but the economy resisted all attempts at surgery and inflation began to climb again. Collor became even more unstable than the economy; he was increasingly erratic in public and rumours grew about dark goings-on behind the scenes. Thanks to fine journalism and a denunciation by Collor's own brother (apparently angry that Fernando had made a pass at his wife), it became clear that a web of **corrupt dealings** masterminded by Collor's campaign treasurer, **P.C. Farias**, had set up what was effectively a parallel government. Billions of dollars had been skimmed from the government's coffers in a scam breathtaking even by Brazilian standards.

Impeachment proceedings were begun in Congress but few politicians expected them to get anywhere. But then demonstrations began to take off in the big cities, led initially by students but soon spreading to the rest of the population. In September 1992 Collor was duly impeached and **Itamar Franco** (1930–2011), the vice-president, replaced him. Farias was jailed, dying later in mysterious circumstances – he was allegedly murdered by a girlfriend who then committed suicide, but the full story of his death will never be known. Collor, who probably knows more than most about the murder, is still active in politics (he's the current federal senator for Alagoas). Corruption charges failed and his continued liberty is eloquent testimony to the weakness of the Brazilian legal system.

Franco, like Sarney before him, proved an ineffectual leader. The real power in his government was the finance minister, **Fernando Henrique Cardoso** (born 1931), who staked his claim to the succession by implementing the **Plano Real** in 1994. This finally tamed inflation and stabilized the economy, for the first time in twenty years. A grateful public duly gave him an overwhelming first-round victory against Lula in the presidential election later that year.

Cardoso: stability and reform (1994–2002)

Cardoso, a donnish ex-academic from São Paulo universally known by his initials, FHC, proved able and effective. Ironically, before he became a politician he was one of

1994	1996	2001
Fernando Cardoso elected president; he is re-elected in 1998 and brings some stability to the economy with his Plano Real.	Eldorado dos Carajás massacre; 19 landless farmers shot by police in Pará	Beloved author Jorge Amado dies in Salvador

the world's most respected left-wing theorists of economic development. His political career, however, moved along a different track, as his government opened up the Brazilian economy and pushed through important **political reforms**.

On the economic front he built on the Plano Real by pushing through a privatization programme, cutting tariff barriers, opening up the economy to competition and making Brazil the dominant member of **Mercosul**, a regional trade organization that includes Argentina, Uruguay and Paraguay. During his first term the result was healthy growth, falling unemployment and low inflation, an achievement without precedent in modern Brazilian history. Politically, he steered a skilful middle course between right and left. In a steady if unspectacular process, a series of constitutional amendments was passed, reducing the role of the state and reforming the political system.

The stabilization of the economy Cardoso achieved was not forgotten by the poor, who were the most affected by hyperinflation; he was **re-elected** in 1998, again beating Lula, and providing a much-needed period of stability at the top. His second term proved more difficult, however. The **Asian financial collapse** of 1998 brought down much of Latin America with it, including Brazil. Yet despite devaluations of the *real*, foreign investment kept coming and inflation remained low – an important break with earlier economic patterns, and a sign that at least some of Cardoso's reforms were working.

The Lula era (2003–10)

Historic is an overused word, but there was no question it was the only one to describe the **2002 election of Lula** to the presidency of Brazil, at the fourth attempt. The outcome represented the final consolidation and maturing of Brazilian democracy, as the generation that had been tear-gassed by the military and opted for armed struggle suited up and became ministers (there were four ex-guerrilla ministers in Lula's first government, and its dominant figure, **José Dirceu**, had plastic surgery in Cuba and lived underground for five years). **Lula** (born 1945) himself is a truly historic figure – the first Brazilian president not to be a member of the country's elite. Born in desperate poverty in the Pernambuco *sertão*, like millions of Northeasterners he made the journey as a child to São Paulo on the back of a truck. He worked as a shoeshine boy before becoming a factory worker at a car plant, eventually rising to leadership of the strike movement in the early 1980s and founding the PT (Partido dos Trabalhadores, or Workers' Party), which allied the union movement to the liberal middle class. With FHC's retirement no other Brazilian politician was able to match Lula's charisma.

Lula proved adept at keeping his party happy with tub-thumping rhetoric and playing up his image as a reformist on the international conference circuit, but in fact his first government bore a distinct resemblance to that of his predecessor. **Antonio Palocci**, a quiet but competent finance minister, kept the economy open and inflation down – which was just as well, since politically the government rapidly ran into deep trouble.

Corruption scandals

Lula had been elected in large part because the Brazilian electorate believed his PT was, uniquely among Brazilian political parties, largely untouched by **corruption**. They

2002	**2004**	**2006**	**2010**
Brazil wins the World Cup for the fifth time; Lula (Luís Inácio da Silva) elected president	Brazil launches its first space rocket	Lula is re-elected president	Dilma Rousseff becomes Brazil's first female president

were rapidly disabused. From 2004 Brazilian journalism yet again proved itself the healthiest part of the body politic by revealing a series of large-scale scams and rackets commanded by Lula's political enforcer, **José Dirceu**. Although it was clear Lula was at least aware of what was happening, he managed to avoid impeachment by firing Dirceu and convincing the opposition, by now fancying its chances in the 2006 election, that the national interest would be best served by having the government finish its term.

Brazil booms again

Lula also won the 2006 election as Brazilians credited him for the increasing economic prosperity and stability of his first term. Lula continued to preside over higher economic growth, combined with a continuing reduction of income inequality and improvement in social indicators – most famously in a programme called **Bolsa Família** (the family grant), where poor families receive cash payments in return for keeping children in school, getting them vaccinated, and so forth. It has proven extremely effective and become a model for many parts of the developing world. A series of major **oil discoveries** in the seas off Rio was the icing on the cake, with Brazil becoming self-sufficient in oil in 2006. The **financial crisis of 2008** in some ways showed how far Brazil had come. While it would have led to instant economic collapse prior to the second FHC government, Brazil came through the first phase of the crisis well and maintained large currency reserves, a well-regulated banking sector and an economy driven more by the domestic market than exports to help it weather the storm.

The rise and fall of Dilma

In 2011, **Dilma Roussef** (born 1947), Lula's anointed Workers' Party successor, became Brazil's **first female president**. Roussef, the daughter of a Bulgarian immigrant, has her own long history of struggle in Brazil's democracy movement, tortured and imprisoned by the military in the 1970s and later serving as Lula's chief of staff. As president she largely continued the populist policies of her mentor: reducing the federal taxes on energy and removing regressive taxes on meat, milk, beans, rice, flour, potatoes, bread and other everyday commodities, for example. Roussef narrowly won re-election in 2014, but the economy was failing and her presidency was rocked by a series of **scandals**: the Petrobras scandal involved kickbacks and corruption; her plan to build hydroelectric dam projects in the Amazon River was much criticized; and major events such as the World Cup in 2014 and Rio Olympics in 2016 did little for Brazil's poor. In 2016, Roussef was impeached and removed from office, replaced by her Vice President **Michel Temer**. Temer has been tarnished by his own corruption scandals from the beginning, and is likely to face calls for impeachment before his terms concludes at the end of 2018. In 2017 ex-president Lula was also charged with money laundering and corruption, part of the mammoth "car wash" (lava jato) scandal, Brazil's biggest ever (which is saying something). At the time of writing, his arrest looked set to cause another crisis, and would also bar him from running in the next presidential election. Meanwhile, Brazil's economy began to grow again in 2017 after several years of decline, though huge problems remain. Crime rates remain high, and almost every Brazilian city is still surrounded by *favelas* reminiscent of the world's poorest nations – this despite a controversial "pacification" programme initiated in Rio, which has had mixed results.

2012	2014	2016	2017
Architect and designer of Brasília Oscar Niemeyer dies at the age of 104	Brazil hosts the World Cup for the second time	Rio hosts the Olympics; Roussef is impeached, replaced by Michel Temer.	Brazil's economy starts to recover after three years of recession; Temer charged with taking bribes.

The Amazon: a guide to the issues

The Amazon rainforest is the largest and most biodiverse tropical forest on Earth. It is culturally diverse too: home to over 300,000 indigenous people, some still isolated, speaking over two hundred languages. Many Brazilians react with outrage at being lectured on the preservation of the Amazon and the protection of native peoples by North Americans and Europeans. Justifiable as Brazilian accusations of hypocrisy may be, they cannot hide the fact that there is a real environmental crisis in the Amazon. It has high visibility as an issue inside Brazil as well as abroad, and as climate change moves up political agendas in Brazil as elsewhere, there is momentum for reform – and some grounds for hope.

The Amazon contains one fifth of the world's fresh water, sustaining the world's largest rainforest – over six million square kilometres – which in turn supports millions of animal and plant species, many of them still unknown. At the heart of the forest, the Rio Amazonas is a staggering 6500km from source to mouth. About seventeen percent of the Brazilian Amazon has been deforested, mostly in the last forty years, and at least as much again has been affected by selective cutting of trees and other environmental stresses, like over-hunting. In 2017, President Michel Temer abolished the Renca Amazonian reserve in Brazil's northern states of Pará and Amapá, horrifying conservation groups and raising fears of further damage from mining and timber companies.

Lands and rivers

The Amazon is generally thought of as flat, steamy, equatorial forest. This is misleading – it has mountains, parts of it suffer droughts, and by no means all of it is jungle. Around twenty-five percent of the Amazon is actually savannah, known in Brazil as **cerrado**, and concentrated in a vertical band through the central Amazon from Roraima to southern Mato Grosso, where soil and rain conditions are markedly dry. Between five and ten percent of the Amazon, depending on the time of year, is **várzea** (flood plain), a zone of marshes, lakes, wetlands and annually flooded forest (*igapó*) that is the most varied and among the most biodiverse of the Amazon's ecosystems; it's also one of the most threatened, since for historical reasons all of the Amazon's larger cities and most of its human population are concentrated on the flood plain. But the bulk of Amazonian forests are **terra firme** (upland) that never flood; upland forest topography is typically made up of gentle hills and occasional steep escarpments. The Amazon also has a long **coastline**, where mangroves alternate with sand dunes, and the largest and most ecologically complex river estuary in the world.

Amazonian rivers are equally varied. There are three main river types. The Amazon itself is laced with **sediments** scoured from the Andes giving it the colour of milky tea or coffee; other rivers of this type include the Madeira, Juruá and Purus. **Blackwater** rivers drain granite uplands with few sediments, and are stained black by chemicals released by decomposing vegetation; they are much poorer in nutrients and have much less aquatic biodiversity as a result, but have the side benefit of being blessedly free of insects in general. Rivers of this type in the Amazon include, as the name suggests, the Rio Negro, but many other smaller rivers, like the Arapiuns near Santarém. The third type of river drains areas between these two extremes and is the most beautiful of all, with a blueish-green colour; the Tapajós is the largest river of this type.

Flora and fauna

Over six thousand species of **plants** have been reported from one square kilometre tract of Amazon forest, and there are close to a thousand species of birds spread about the region. The rainforest has enormous structural diversity, with layers of vegetation from the forest floor to the canopy 30m above providing a vast number of habitats. With the rainforest being more stable over longer periods of time than temperate areas (there was no Ice Age here, nor any prolonged period of drought), the fauna has also had freedom to evolve, and to adapt to often very specialized local conditions. This is the foundation of the Amazon's biodiversity.

Most of the **trees** found in the Amazon flood plain are tropical palms, scattered between which are the various species of larger, emergent trees. Those plants which are found growing on the forest floor are mostly tree **saplings**, **herbs** (frequently with medicinal applications) and **woody shrubs**. The best-known of all Amazon trees are concentrated on the upland *terra firme*, which never floods; here you can find the **rubber tree** (*Hevea brasiliensis*), known as *seringueira* in Brazil, and the **Brazil nut tree** (*Bertholletia excelsa*), which grows to 30m and takes over ten years to reach nut-bearing maturity; once this is reached, a single specimen can produce over 450kg of nuts every year.

Deforestation

The amount **deforested** in the Amazon varies from year to year because of a number of factors, especially climate. In **El Niño** years, such as 2015, the Amazon is much drier than usual and fires start more easily; this in turn means bigger areas are denuded of forest, allowing farmers to move in. Thus many models of climate change over the next few decades, which suggest longer dry seasons and a drier forest in many parts of the Amazon, are a cause for concern. What matters is not a deforestation spike in one year or another, but general trends over time. These show deforestation increased alarmingly in the 1970s and 1980s, fell back in the 1990s, and then rose again in the early twenty-first century. Much deforested land is abandoned and regrows over time; although it usually does not return to the level of ecological complexity it had, deforested land can reacquire some of its biodiversity value.

In other words, all is not lost; the bulk of the Amazon is intact, and even the damaged areas need not be written off. The other thing to remember is that the **frontier period** of Amazonian development is largely over. The Amazon's population is stable, and rapidly urbanizing; almost seventy percent of the Amazon's population lives in cities. There are no longer waves of migrants flooding to the region, or a growing rural population putting pressure on the forest. Policy makers and Amazonians themselves are realizing it makes more sense to concentrate development efforts into degraded areas, where there are already roads and people living, intensifying development instead of extending it. This is unfortunate for the environmental integrity of the twenty-five percent or so of the Amazon in this position, but it offers the real prospect that pressure on the remaining 75 percent will diminish.

Threats to the forest

Forest clearance generally follows **road building**. When a road reached into new territories in the glory days of highway building into the Amazon in the 1970s and 1980s, it brought with it the financial backing and interests of big agricultural and industrial companies, plus an onslaught of land-seeking settlers. Historically, the great villain in the deforestation piece has been **ranching** – the latest research suggests that around eighty percent of forest cleared was turned into pasture, dwarfing the deforestation caused by smallholders, commercial agriculture and logging. Although much has been written recently about **soy farming** as a cause of deforestation, most soy planting takes place on land that has already been cleared, and it remains a very minor cause of deforestation. Forest **fires** are a major threat, generally caused by colonizing farmers and ranchers, often exacerbated by the process of selective **logging**, which opens up the forest canopy and leaves debris ripe for lighting. In recent years **mining companies** have also presented a threat, with huge open-cast operations creating havoc in the forest.

Resistance in Acre

Until roads opened up the Amazon, many areas were inhabited and exploited only by **indigenous peoples**. The indigenous tribes and many of the modern forest-dwellers – including rubber-tappers, nut collectors and, increasingly, even peasant settlers – view the forest as something which, like an ocean, can be harvested regularly if it is not overtaxed. **Chico Mendes**, the Brazilian rubber-tappers' union leader, was the best-known voice on the side of those arguing for a more sustainable approach. Hired gunmen killed him outside his house in Acre state in 1988, but his ideas lived on.

In time, Acre became the showpiece state of the Brazilian environmental movement from 1998, when a PT government, led by **Jorge Viana** and dominated by old friends and colleagues of Chico Mendes, implemented an environmental programme, including a rubber subsidy to help rubber-tappers remain in the forest, and a series of innovative initiatives for marketing forest products. Over twenty years, the environmental movement in Acre has moved to the centre of Brazilian political life: Viana was triumphantly re-elected in 2002 and went on to become an adviser to Lula (he's now a Federal senator for Acre); and a close friend, **Marina da Silva**, an ex–rubber-tapper from Acre who had been a colleague of Mendes in the rubber-tapper union movement, was Minister of the Environment from 2003 to 2008, and was the Green Party candidate for president of Brazil in 2010 (she tried again in 2014).

The consequences of deforestation

The most serious effects of the destruction of the Amazon rainforest are related to global warming.

- **Local climate change** There is now hard scientific evidence from the deforested highway corridors that removing forest reduces rainfall, creates dry seasons where there were none, and extends them where they already existed. This has obvious implications for crops, soils, flora and fauna.
- **Global climate change** The Amazon is a vital link in maintaining regional rainfall and it is clear that continuing large-scale deforestation would change weather patterns in the rest of the hemisphere too, including the US. The destruction of the forest has two effects on the earth's atmosphere. The carbon in the smoke released by forest clearances makes a significant direct contribution to the greenhouse effect; tropical deforestation as a whole accounts for around twenty percent of global carbon emissions. The exact percentage contributed by Amazonian deforestation is controversial. Few experts accept a figure of less than five percent of global emissions, but the Brazilian government fiercely contests this. Less immediately, the fewer trees there are to absorb carbon dioxide, the faster the planet will warm.

Forces driving deforestation

The blame for deforestation is often wrongly attributed. The following are some popular, but mistaken, explanations:

- **Population and land pressures** Perhaps the most popular theory of all, certainly in Brazil, is that an unstoppable tide of humanity is swamping the forest. While there was something to this between the 1960s and the early 1990s, the rural Amazon has been losing population for a decade, and the region as a whole has a stable population.
- **Debt** Brazil's foreign debt is another popular scapegoat, but this is even less convincing. The bulk of the capital Brazil borrowed to create the debt was invested in southern Brazil. The need to make interest payments has not been a driver of economic policy in Brazil since the debt was restructured in the early 1990s. Most of

the borrowed capital invested in the Amazon went into the mineral sector and into building dams, neither of which were significant causes of deforestation compared to ranching and agriculture.

- **The logging industry** Virtually no deforestation can be directly attributed to logging. The biodiversity of the Amazon means that economically useful trees are jumbled together with valueless ones. As a result, clearcutting – removing forest tracts for timber – is almost unknown in the Amazon. Logging is more selective, resulting in the fragmentation of forest cover – degradation rather than deforestation. One often hears that logging trails open up areas into which deforesters later move, but just as often it is the loggers who head down the trails made by others.
- **"Big business"** It is certainly true that most of the deforestation in the grim decades of the 1970s and 1980s was driven directly by big business – specifically the tax breaks that attracted large companies to the region, and the ignorance and arrogance that led them to think development projects in the jungle would make money. But when the tax breaks were withdrawn in the early 1990s, most of the large companies left. The big companies remaining in the Amazon – mainly in mining and commercial agriculture – work in areas degraded long ago, and are not drivers of much new deforestation.
- **Soy and biofuels** Despite the headlines, soy is not and never has been an important driver of Amazon deforestation. Only two percent of cleared land in the Amazon is commercially farmed; ranching and smallholder agriculture account for the rest. Although there are grain terminals in the Amazon, almost all the soy they ship is grown outside the Amazon. A ban on buying soy from deforested land has been in place since 2006 and is enforced. Biofuels are equally unimportant as a driver of deforestation. Little sugar cane is grown in the Amazon, and although palm oil may be an important Amazonian product in the near future, it will be grown on land cleared decades ago in the eastern Amazon, where costs are lowest and ports are close.

A number of reasons are now put forward for the continuing destruction of the rainforest. A complete answer would include the following three major factors:

- **The Brazilian economy** Save for minerals and soy, the vast bulk of what the Amazon produces is consumed within the Amazon, or goes elsewhere in Brazil. For every cubic metre of tropical hardwood exported, for example, two cubic metres are consumed in Brazil, largely by the furniture and construction industries. The export of Amazonian timber is highly regulated; educated consumers in the US and EU demand proof that Amazon timber in products they buy has been sustainably produced – non-certified Amazon timber is barred from the EU, for example. There is no such regulation in Brazil and, until there is, the domestic economy will be the single biggest driver of deforestation. Within the domestic economy itself, the biggest problem is ranching, which accounts for four out of every five units of land cleared in the Amazon.
- **Government policy** Regional development policy is one of the most unreconstructed areas of the federal government. Corruption, in the form of loosely monitored federal contracts and regional development funds that operate as slush funds for politicians of every ideological complexion, hangs like a fog over everything the government does in the Amazon.
- **Amazonian state governments** With a couple of exceptions – most notably Acre – Amazonian states tend to be run by old-style oligarchs, ignorant, provincial and deeply hostile to an environmental agenda they feel is threatening to "development". As far as they can – which fortunately is not very far, given their limited resources – they tend to back policies harmful to the forest.

Possible solutions

Deforestation happens because it makes economic sense for the person cutting the tree down; the key to **preserving the forest** is to ensure it makes more economic sense to keep it standing. A perfect example of the latter is the case of Belém; the largest city in the Amazon is surrounded by extensive areas of intact flood-plain forest. This is because there is massive demand for **açaí**, a palm fruit central to Amazonian cuisine, and palm heart. Both are locally consumed in large quantities, but also preserved, packed and exported to the rest of Brazil and the world. Both products come from flood-plain palm forests and, as a result, vast areas of flood-plain forest are preserved. Because gathering these forest products can never be mechanized, tens of thousands of livelihoods are assured, and the industry is sustainable. Overharvesting does not happen because everyone knows the level of production the ecosystem can sustain, and that they would shortly be out of a job if they went beyond it.

But this is only half the story. Gathering palm products is a living, but there is not much money in it – or wasn't. In the early 1990s **DaimlerBenz** was looking for a way to reassure its German shareholders of its environmental responsibility. The R&D department discovered compressed fibres from Amazon palms could be used to stuff upholstery and also to make a material from which sunshields could be manufactured. They hooked up with the local university in Belém, which brokered a series of contracts with cooperatives in Marajó to supply and process palm fibre, creating what by local standards are scores of well-paid jobs. Everybody won: the local people, the local university (which gets a cut of each contract), the foreign corporation, the Brazilian consumer in southern Brazil driving the car, and, most of all, the environment. The Marajó villagers are now going to the university for help in reforesting deforested areas – because it makes economic sense.

So far these are isolated success stories, but they are part of a trend. Other companies looking to the Amazon to source products include Pirelli, which is producing tyres in southern Brazil with Acrean rubber, and Hermès, the French luxury-goods firm, which is using *couro vegetal*, a form of latex treated to look and feel like leather, to make handbags and briefcases. Even big companies investing in the Amazon, like **Cargill** and **Alcoa**, are looking to minimize potential damage to their reputations by setting up compensation funds and managing their supply chains to reduce environmental impact.

The principles underlying this sea change are clear. First, long-term success usually lies in satisfying **local and regional demand**, not the export market. Second, interventions are often necessary: partly the removal of subsidies that reward destruction, now largely accomplished, but also incentives to encourage more environmentally friendly land use. A recent example is the national credit programme for family farms, PRONAF, which established a credit line for small Amazonian farmers who want to do agro-forestry, rather than straight farming, with subsidized rates of repayment. Thousands have so far taken it up. If this can be increased to tens or hundreds of thousands, it could transform the scene in the rural Amazon.

The economics of change

The other principles of change are more controversial. First, it is always going to make economic sense for certain parts of the Amazon to be **dedicated to production**, not conservation. No country refuses to develop rich mineral deposits, or blocks investments in commercial agriculture with high rates of return. The choice is not whether to develop, but where development takes place and whether the environmental movement has any influence in channelling and controlling it. Looking at the broader picture, it makes better political and economic sense to accept the more controllable form of development – capitalism – in areas already degraded, and thus ensure the frontier fills out rather than moves on to new areas where the damage would be much greater.

Finally, it needs to be recognized that many parts of the Amazon, because of their remoteness or lack of marketable resources, are never going to be able to generate income or jobs. These areas do however provide valuable **environmental services**: their forests remove carbon from the atmosphere, reducing global warming, and keeping forests intact also protects watersheds and soil quality beyond the areas themselves. As things stand, neither the Brazilian government nor the inhabitants of these areas receive any compensation for this, although perhaps in the future new markets in carbon and environmental services will fill the gap. In the meantime they should be protected, and the international community should be willing to pay most of the costs toward this, which to an extent is already happening.

The future

It is actually possible to feel **optimistic** about the future of the Amazon, especially when comparing the situation now to that of thirty years ago. Deforestation is at a manageable level (just). Crucial players, like the ministry of the environment, the World Bank and the scientific community inside and outside Brazil, are stressing environmental safeguards and the importance of reconciling conservation with development, the opposite of their positions a generation ago. Despite President Temer's decision to abolish the Renca reserve in 2017, increasing areas of the Amazon are being put under strict or partial protection, and, astonishingly, 22 percent of it has been demarcated and ratified as **indigenous reserves**. Perhaps most encouraging, a state government – **Acre** – running on an explicitly environmentalist platform has been wildly successful in attracting investment and resources to a remote part of the western Amazon.

Still, there is some way to go. The murder of American missionary **Dorothy Stang** in 2005 was a salutary reminder that going up against ranchers and illegal loggers in much of the Amazon is still potentially lethal. Stang was killed because she was trying to protect local smallholders from ranchers by forming them into an association and pressing for the creation of a sustainable development reserve. The international outcry at her murder forced the Brazilian government to act, and her killers, including – unprecedentedly – the rancher who commissioned the murder, were eventually tried and convicted a few months later. But Stang's death was an indication of how far there is still to go when only the international spotlight could make the justice system deliver.

It is still too early to say whether all this will be enough in the long term. Even if Brazil gets its act together, the fate of the Amazon is not only determined within Brazil. Global **climate change** is already having an impact in the Amazon. But if things come as far in the next 25 years as they have in the last 25, and if the pressure is kept up, the satellite images may in the future be showing recovery, as well as loss.

Indigenous peoples

Today, there are around 300,000 indigenous people living in Brazil's **Indigenous Territories** (Terras Indígenas), mostly in the Amazon region, spread between more than two hundred tribes speaking a hundred and eighty languages or dialects. When the Portuguese first arrived in the sixteenth century, there were probably over five million indigenous inhabitants, and today over 800,000 Brazilians claim indigenous ancestry.

The opening up of first the centre-west region in the 1950s with the construction of Brasília, and then the Amazon from the 1960s, was an unmitigated disaster for Brazil's indigenous peoples. They were dispossessed of their lands, and one of the consequences of the chaotic settlement of new frontiers was the spread of diseases, which brought many groups to the verge of extinction. The military regime regarded indigenous peoples with open racism: the "Indian Code" (Estatuto do Índio), which the military drew up in 1973 (and which is still technically in force today, although widely ignored), explicitly said it was a transitional set of legal regulations to be enforced until indigenous tribes were assimilated, and indistinguishable from other Brazilians. In

FURTHER INFORMATION ON AMAZONIAN ISSUES

For more information on issues involving the Amazon contact Survival, 6 Charterhouse Buildings, London EC1M 7ET, UK ⓣ 020 7687 8700, ⓦ survival-international.org. Also check out ⓦ socioambiental.org for information and news on the Amazon, environmental issues, NGOs working in the region, maps and other more general travel and political links.

the Amazon especially, many non-indigenous people in the areas around indigenous reserves are still openly racist – a sad legacy of their forebears who migrated there a generation ago.

Within Brazil indigenous peoples have always had defenders, notably in the Catholic Church, in the universities, and even in more liberal circles in the Brazilian military and FUNAI (the federal agency overseeing indigenous issues), where some individuals were able to make a difference. The best examples were the brothers **Claudio and Orlando Vilas-Boas**, who were able to create the **Parque Indígena do Xingu** in southern Mato Grosso in the 1960s, which turned out to be crucial in assuring the eventual survival of many indigenous groups of the southern Amazon. But these were isolated actions in the midst of what is best described as genocide by negligence.

The beginnings of change came in the darkest days of military repression and unrestrained road building in the late 1960s, when a combination of embarrassing international media coverage, foreign pressure and lobbying by the Catholic Church forced the military to curb the worst excesses of development in indigenous areas, and provide emergency medical assistance – too late in many cases. With the fall of the military regime the situation gradually improved; the **1988 Constitution** guaranteed indigenous land rights and protection of indigenous languages and culture. Although enforcing it has been problematic, it at least provided a legal basis for effective protection of indigenous lands.

The situation now is incomparably better than it was a generation ago. The presidencies of Fernando Henrique Cardoso and Lula were quite sound on indigenous issues. During the 1990s most of the outstanding issues to do with the demarcation and full legalization of indigenous areas were resolved. A remarkable 22 percent of the Brazilian Amazon is now officially indigenous land – an area more than twice the size of France (thirteen percent of the whole country). Though presidents Roussef and Temer seemed to favour the agricultural lobby over indigenous groups, President Temer did establish the 12,000-square-kilometre **Indigenous Territory of Turubaxi-Téa** in Amazonas in 2017.

The indigenous movement

Perhaps the greatest grounds for hope in the future lies in the strength of the **indigenous movement.** Born out of the patient organizational and educational work of the Catholic Church from the 1960s, the movement rapidly outgrew its religious roots to become an important secular force, founding local associations and regional confederations, and learning from their non-indigenous colleagues in the rural-union and rubber-tapper movements. Prominent national leaders like **Mário Juruna**, elected federal deputy for Rio in the 1980s despite being from Mato Grosso, were important in getting the movement off the ground. Juruna died in 2002, but an able new generation of younger indigenous leaders – **Daví Yanomami**, **Escrawen Sompre**, **Ailton Krenak**, **Sonia Guajajara**, Kayapó leader **Chief Raoni Metuktire**, the late **Jorge Terena** and others – have taken up the torch.

Music

Brazil's talent for music is so great it amounts to a national genius. Out of a rich mix of African, European and Indian influences it has produced one of the strongest and most diverse musical cultures in the world. Most people have heard of samba and bossa nova but they are only the tip of a very large iceberg of genres, styles and individual talents. Accompanying the music is some of the most stunning dancing you are ever likely to see. In Brazil, no one looks twice at a couple who would clear any European and most American dancefloors. You don't need to be an expert, or even understand the words, to enjoy Brazilian popular music, but you may appreciate it better – and find it easier to ask for the type of music you want – if you know a little about its history.

The bedrock of Brazilian music is the apparently inexhaustible fund of "traditional" **popular music**. There are dozens of genres, most of them associated with a specific region of the country, which you can find in raw uncut form played on local radio stations, at popular festivals, impromptu recitals in squares and on street corners, and in bars and *dancetarias* (the dance halls Brazilians flock to at the weekend). There's little argument that the best Brazilian music comes from Rio, Salvador, the Northeast and parts of Amazônia, with São Paulo and southern Brazil lagging a little behind.

Samba

Brazil's best-known musical genre, **samba**, began in the early years of the twentieth century, in the poorer parts of Rio as **Carnaval** music. Over the decades it has developed several variations. The deafening **samba de enredo** is the setpiece of Carnaval, with one or two singers declaiming a verse joined by hundreds or even thousands of voices and drums for the chorus, as the *bloco*, the full samba school, backs up the lead singers. A *bloco* in action during Carnaval is the loudest music you'll ever hear, and it's all done without the aid of amplifiers – the massed noise of the drums vibrates every part of your body. No recording technology yet devised comes close to conveying the sound, and songs and music often seem repetitive. Still, every year the main Rio samba schools make a compilation record of the music selected for the parade.

On a more intimate scale, and musically more inventive, is **samba-canção**, which is produced by one singer and a small back-up band, who play around with basic samba rhythms to produce anything from a (relatively) quiet love song to frenetic dance numbers. This style transfers more effectively to recordings than *samba de enredo*, and in Brazil its more laidback pace makes it especially popular with the middle-aged. Reliably high-quality *samba-canção* is anything by **Beth Carvalho**, acknowledged queen of the genre, **Alcione**, the late, great **Clara Nunes**, and the even greater **Paulinho da Viola**, who always puts at least a couple of excellent sambas on every record he makes. **Elza Soares** (born 1937) is a legendary samba artist still going strong, winning a Latin Grammy in 2016 with *A Mulher do Fim do Mundo,* while veteran Ivan Lins won with *América, Brasil* in 2015.

Choro

Much less known, **choro** (literally "crying") appeared in Rio around the time of World War I, and by the 1930s had evolved into one of the most intricate and enjoyable of all Brazilian forms of music. It's one of the few Brazilian genres that owes anything to Spanish-speaking America, as it is clearly related to the Argentine **tango** (the real River Plate versions, that is, rather than the sequined ballroom distortions that get passed off as tango outside South America). *Choro* is mainly instrumental, played by a small group; the backbone of the combo is a guitar, picked quickly and jazzily, with notes sliding all over the place, which is played off against a flute, or occasionally a clarinet or recorder, with drums and/or maracas as an optional extra. It is as quiet and intimate as samba is loud and public, and of all Brazilian popular music is probably the most delicate. You often find it being played as background music in bars and cafés; local papers advertise such places. The loveliest *choros* are by **Paulinho da Viola**, especially on the album *Chorando*. After years of neglect during the post-war decades *choro* is now undergoing something of a revival, and it shouldn't be too difficult to catch a *conjunto de choro* in Rio or São Paulo. The eponymous *Casa de Choro* in Brasília is another outpost. Current bandolinist **Hamilton de Holanda** is known for his blend of *choro* and contemporary jazz, while clarinetist and saxophonist **Nailor Azevedo** also dabbles in *choro*.

North by Northeast

A full list of other "traditional" musical genres would have hundreds of entries and could be elaborated on indefinitely. Some of the best known are **forró**, **maracatú**, **repentismo** and **frevo**; you'll find them all over the Northeast but especially around Recife. **Baião** is a Bahian style that bears a striking resemblance to the hard acoustic blues of the American Deep South, with hoarse vocals over a guitar singing of things like drought and migration. **Axé**, also from Bahia, is a samba-and-reggae mix that is the basis of inescapable and rather repetitive, light Brazilian pop in Salvador and elsewhere. **Carimbó** is an enjoyable, lilting rhythm and dance found all over northern Brazil but especially around Belém; a souped-up and heavily commercialized version of *carimbó* enjoyed a brief international vogue as **lambada** in the 1990s. **Bumba-meu-boi**, the haunting music of Maranhão, is one of the strangest and most powerful of all Brazilian genres.

A good place to start is with works by the late **Luiz Gonzaga**, also known as **Gonzagão**. His version of a beautiful song called *Asa Branca* is one of the best loved of all Brazilian tunes, a national standard, and guaranteed to reduce any homesick Northeasterner to tears immediately.

The golden age: 1930–60 and the radio stars

It was the growth of radio during the 1930s that created the popular-music industry in Brazil, with home-grown stars idolized by millions. The best known was **Carmen Miranda** (1909–55), spotted by a Hollywood producer singing in the famous Urca casino in Rio and whisked off to film stardom in the 1930s. Although her hats made her immortal, she deserves to be remembered more as the fine singer she was. She was one of a number of singers and groups loved by older Brazilians, including **Francisco Alves**, **Ismael Silva**, **Mário Reis**, **Ataulfo Alves**, **Trio de Ouro** and **Joel e Gaúcho**. Two great songwriters, **Ary Barroso** and **Pixinguinha**, provided the raw material.

Brazilians call these early decades *a época de ouro*, and that it really was a golden age is proved by the surviving recordings. It is slower and jazzier than modern Brazilian music, but with similar rhythms and beautiful, crooning vocals. Even in Brazil it used to be difficult to get hold of **records** of this era, but after years of neglect there is now a widely available series of reissues called *Revivendo*.

International success: bossa nova

With this wealth of raw material to work with it was only a matter of time before Brazilian music burst its national boundaries, something that duly happened in the late 1950s with the phenomenon of **bossa nova**. Several factors led to its development. The classically trained **Antônio Carlos ("Tom") Jobim**, equally in love with Brazilian popular music and American jazz, met up with fine Bahian guitarist **João Gilberto** and his wife **Astrud Gilberto** to create the first bossa nova sound. The growth in the Brazilian record and communications industries allowed bossa nova to sweep Brazil and come to the attention of people like **Stan Getz** in the United States; and, above all, there was a new market for a sophisticated urban sound among the newly burgeoning middle class in Rio, who found Jobim's and Gilberto's slowing down and breaking up of what was still basically a samba rhythm an exciting departure. It rapidly became an international craze, and Astrud Gilberto's quavering version of one of the earliest Jobim numbers, *A Garota de Ipanema*, became the most famous of all Brazilian songs, *The Girl from Ipanema* – although the English lyric is considerably less suggestive than the Brazilian original.

Over the next few years the craze eventually peaked and fell away, leaving most people with the entirely wrong impression that bossa nova is a mediocre brand of muzak well suited to lifts and airports. Tom Jobim would later talk of being haunted by innumerable cover versions murdering *The Girl from Ipanema*. In North America, bossa nova sank under the massed strings of studio producers but in Brazil it never lost its much more delicate touch, usually with a single guitar and a crooner holding sway. Early bossa nova still stands as one of the crowning glories of Brazilian music, and all the classics – you may not know the names of tunes like *Corcovado*, *Isaura*, *Chega de Saudade* and *Desafinado* but you'll recognize the melodies – are all easily available on the various Jobim and Gilberto compilation recordings. But for the best bossa-nova album of all time, look for *Elís e Tom*, the incomparable collaboration between Elís Regina and Tom Jobim when both were at their peak in the early 1970s.

The great Brazilian guitarist **Luiz Bonfá** also made some fine bossa-nova records – the ones where he accompanies Stan Getz are superb. The bossa-nova records of **Stan Getz** and **Charlie Byrd** are one of the happiest examples of inter-American cooperation, and as they're easy to find in European and American shops they make a fine introduction to Brazilian music. They had the sense to surround themselves with Brazilian musicians, notably Jobim, the Gilbertos and Bonfá, and the interplay between their jazz and the equally skilful Brazilian response is often brilliant. Brazilian legend **Sérgio Mendes** started out as a bossa nova artist in the 1960s, though his sound was heavily crossed with jazz and funk. The 2006 re-recorded version his *Mas Que Nada* with The Black Eyed Peas gave him a surge of global recognition.

Tropicalismo

The **military coup** in 1964 was a crucial event in Brazil. Just as the shock waves of the cultural upheavals of the 1960s were reaching Brazilian youth, the lid went on in a big way: censorship was introduced for all song lyrics; radio and television were put under military control; and some songwriters and musicians were tortured and imprisoned for speaking and singing out – although fame was at least some insurance against being killed. The result was the opposite of what the generals had intended. A movement known as **tropicalismo** developed, calling itself cultural but in fact almost exclusively a musical movement, led by a young and extravagantly talented group of musicians. Prominent among them were **Caetano Veloso** and **Gilberto Gil** from Bahia and **Chico Buarque** from Rio. They used traditional popular music as a base, picking and mixing genres in a way no one had thought of doing before – stirring in a few outside influences like the Beatles and occasional electric instruments, and topping it all off with lyrics that often stood alone as poetry – and delighted in teasing the censors. Oblique images and comments were ostensibly about one thing, but everyone knew what they really meant.

Caetano, Gilberto and Chico – all of Brazil is on first-name terms with them – spent a few years in exile in the late 1960s and early 1970s, Caetano and Gil in London (both still speak fluent English with immaculate BBC accents) and Chico in Rome, before returning in triumph as the military regime wound down. They have made dozens of records between them and are still, in their seventies, the leading figures of Brazilian music. Gilberto Gil's stint as **Minister of Culture** in Lula's government, while thin on political achievements, at least meant Brazil could boast unquestionably the coolest government minister on the planet. Chico Buarque's dense lyrics and hauntingly beautiful melodies are still flowing, although he produces recordings more rarely now, devoting more of his time to novel-writing and theatre. Pride of place, however, has to go to **Caetano Veloso**. Good though he was in the 1960s and 1970s, he is improving with age, and his records over the last fifteen years have been his best: mature, innovative, lyrical and original as ever. His continuing originality has kept him at the leading edge of Brazilian popular music, acknowledged everywhere from the *favelas* of Rio to Carnegie Hall as the finest modern Brazilian musician.

Female singers

Brazilian music has a strong tradition of producing excellent female singers. The great **Elis Regina** was something of a Brazilian Edith Piaf: her magnificent voice was tragically stilled in 1984, when she was at the peak of her career, by a drug overdose. Two of her songs in particular became classics, *Águas de Março* and *Carinhoso*, the latter being arguably the most beautiful Brazilian song of all. After her death the mantle fell on **Gal Costa**, a very fine singer although without the extraordinary depth of emotion Elis could project. More recently, **Marisa Monte** has emerged as a worthy heir to Elis; the classic *Cor de Rosa e Carvão* is the best introduction to her enormous talent, and she won a Latin Grammy for *Verdade, Uma Ilusão* in 2014.

Other good younger singers include **Maria Rita**, **Silvia Torres**, **Belô Veloso** (a niece of Caetano) and **Fernanda Porto**, whose musical style is a fusion of samba and drum 'n' bass. The talented **Maria Gadú** released her first album in 2009, and her single *Shimbalaiê* went to number one in Italy in 2011.

More recently, younger singers – like Brazilian footballers – have been heading abroad much earlier and carving careers in the US and Europe as much as at home. Rio and New York are developing particularly close musical links, best represented by the eclectic, fusion sound and occasional English lyrics of **Céu**, a superb singer whose ability to mix influences from all over and still remain unmistakeably Brazilian is a sign that Brazilian music will surf globalization rather than be swamped by it – to everyone's benefit.

The Bahian sound

Although Rio is the traditional capital of Brazilian music, for some years now it has been rivalled by **Salvador**, the capital of Bahia. Bahia in general, and Salvador in particular, has always produced a disproportionate number of Brazil's leading musicians including Caetano Veloso and his sister, **Maria Bethânia**. The main reason for this is the extraordinary musical blend provided by deep African roots, Caribbean and Hispanic influences coming in through the city's port, and a local record industry that quickly realized the money-making potential of Bahian music.

The Bahian sound has two dimensions. Bahian pop is, at its best, an enjoyable blend of Brazilian and Caribbean rhythms, exemplified by groups including **Reflexus**, and singers such as **Luis Caldas**, **Margareth Menezes**, **Ivete Sangalo** and **Daniela Mercury**. But Bahia also has a much funkier, rootsy and percussive side, much rougher and rawer than Bahia's more poppy singers. Its guiding light is the percussionist and producer **Carlinhos Brown**; a great performer and songwriter in his own right, he is also the

FIFTY OF THE BEST: A SELECTED DISCOGRAPHY

For **back catalogues**, armed with the names of recommended artists in the sections above, go to a Brazilian music store and look for series called *A Arte de…*, *O Talento de…*, *A Personalidade de…*. Below, we've picked out both the historically essential and our take on the best of the rest. Putumayo (in the US) and Globestyle (in the UK) regularly produce good Brazilian compilations and are a good starting point, given their availability outside Brazil. The list – as in Brazilian music stores – is by first name of the artist.

Belô Veloso
Belô Veloso
Bezerra da Silva
Se Não Fosse o Samba
É Isso Aí o Homem
Caetano Veloso
Velô
Estrangeiro
Circuladô Vivo
Fina Estampa
Um Outro Som
Caetano Veloso and Roberto Carlos
A Música de Tom Jobim
Carlinhos Brown
Timbalada
Cartola
Cartola
Céu
Chico Buarque
Ópera do Malandro
Vida
Para Todos
Uma Palavra
Daniela Mercury
Daniela
Dorival Caymmi
A música de Caymmi
Elís Regina and Tom Jobim
Elís e Tom
Fernanda Porto
Fernanda Porto
Gal Costa
Aquarela do Brasil
Gilberto Gil
Parabolicamera
Unplugged
O Sol de Oslo
Gilberto Gil and Caetano Veloso
Tropicalia 2
João Gilberto
Voz e Violão
Jorge Ben Jor
Acústico
Ao Vivo
Kid Abelha
Acústico
Luiz Gonzaga
Maiores Sucessos
Maria Bethânia
Ambar
Marisa Monte
M
Cor de Rosa e Carvão
Barulhinho Bom
Memórias, Crônicas e Declarações de Amor
Universo Ao Meu Redor
Milton Nascimento
Clube da Esquina
Paulinho da Viola
Cantando
Chorando
Eu canto samba
Bebado samba
Seu Jorge
Cru
América Brasil
Tim Maia
In Concert
Tom Jobim
Wave
Tribalistas
Tribalistas
Various
Eu Tu Eles (film soundtrack)
Velha Guarda da Mangueira
E Convidados
Zeca Baleiro
Por onde andará Stephen Fry?
Líricas

éminence grise behind the rise of other prominent artists like Marisa Monte, with whom he joined forces, together with the punk singer **Arnaldo Antunes**, to create the **Tribalistas** group.

MPB (Música Popular Brasileira)

The number of high-quality singers and musicians in Brazilian music besides these leading figures is enormous, often grouped within the rather nebulous genre of **MPB** traditional Brazilian styles. **Milton Nascimento** has a talent that can only be compared with the founders of *tropicalismo*, with a remarkable soaring voice, a genius for composing stirring anthems and a passion for charting both the experience of blacks in Brazil and the traditions of his native Minas Gerais. **Fagner**, **Morães Moreira**, **Zé Ramalho**, **Elba Ramalho** and **Alceu Valença** are leading modern interpreters of Northeastern music and strikingly original singers. **Renato Borghetti**, from Rio Grande do Sul, has done much to popularize *gaúcho*-influenced music through his skill on the accordion and his adaptations of traditional tunes. **Jorge Ben** is arguably the most danceable of all Brazilian musicians, although the late, great **Tim Maia**, heavily influenced by US funk and soul (although Brazilian to every last centimetre of his enormous girth), runs a close second.

Vinícius de Morães and **Toquinho** are (or were, in the case of Vinícius) a good singer-and-guitarist team, and **Dorival Caymmi**, who died in 2008, was the grand old man of Bahian music. While all these figures have been going strongly for decades now, **Zeca Baleiro** (best known for his hit *Salão de Beleza*) from Maranhão, with a Bumba-meu-boi- and reggae-influenced style, and **Seu Jorge**, born Jorge Mário da Silva and raised in a Rio *favela*, are also popular. Jorge is no mean actor too, and can be seen basically playing himself in the superb film *Cidade de Deus* – "City of God" (see page 666).

More recent stars of the genre have included **Roberta Sá**, **Vanessa da Mata** – her 2004 hit "Ai, Ai, Ai" is still popular – **Comunidade Nin-Jitsu**, electropop outfit **Bonde do Rolê**, and **rock bands** such as **Detonautas Roque Clube**, **NX Zero**, **Fresno** and **Vespas Mandarina**. One of the hottest Brazilian bands right now is **Boogarins**, a psychedelic rock outfit that started out in humble Goiânia, light years away from the scenes in São Paulo and Rio. Their 2013 album *As Plantas Que Curam* garnered a favourable reception not just at home, but also from indie fans in the US and Europe and their follow-up appeared in 2015.

Brazilian hip-hop has also come a long way, from its early beginnings in 1980s São Paulo; **Posse Mente Zulu** and **Racionais MC's** dominated the early 1990s, while contemporary rappers include **Emicida**, **Flora Matos** and **Marcelo D2**.

Cinema

Brazil has a strong tradition of film-making, and the best Brazilian directors often work outside the country on international productions. Brazil has produced excellent films since the 1950s, many of them widely available abroad or online, and a few nights in front of the TV or computer before departure is a good investment in getting the most out of your trip.

Two-way traffic

Brazil, for understandable reasons, has long attracted foreign film-makers looking for exotic scenery. **Orson Welles** spent many months filming in Brazil immediately after *Citizen Kane* had made him a star. Although he was, characteristically, never able to finish the project, the footage was later put together into a documentary film called *It's All True*, an invaluable record of Rio and Carnaval in the early 1940s. Two decades later, French director **Marcel Camus** filmed *Orfeu Negro* ("Black Orpheus") in Rio with a largely amateur cast, resetting the Orpheus myth during the Rio Carnaval and putting it to an unforgettable soundtrack by Tom Jobim. *Pixote*, a searing 1982 film about street children in Rio that also used amateurs, was directed by **Hector Babenco**, an Argentine. Key scenes in the James Bond movie *Moonraker* (1979), and *The Incredible Hulk* (2008), were filmed in and around Rio, while the family blockbusters *Rio* (2011) and Rio 2 (2014) brought the sights and sounds (albeit computer-animated) of the country to a new generation.

Since the 1980s, Brazilians have been moving the other way. **Sônia Braga** traded in success in Brazilian films in the 1970s for a career in US independent cinema from the 1980s on, but the country's most distinguished cinematic exports have been directors, most notably **Walter Salles**, who caught international attention with *Central Station* in 1998, the underestimated, beautifully filmed biopic of Che Guevara's early life, *The Motorcycle Diaries*, and 2012's *On The Road*, based on the Jack Kerouac classic. **Fernando Meirelles**'s brilliant *City of God* in 2003 led to *The Constant Gardener* (2005), the first international Hollywood hit directed by a Brazilian. His success outside Brazil, with four Oscar nominations so far, is an indication of how Brazilian talent can be a shot in the arm for international cinema.

But Brazilian cinema's recent international success was built on decades of hard work, establishing a **national cinema industry** and somehow keeping it going in the face of intense competition from television on the one hand and Hollywood on the other. Along the way Brazil has created a national cinema like no other South American country, returning again and again to its history for inspiration.

The early years: chanchadas and cinema novo

The history of Brazilian cinema goes right back to the earliest years of the medium: the first **cinematograph** arrived in Brazil in 1897 and there were already 22 cinemas registered in Rio by 1910. But the first decades of cinema in Brazil were dominated by American and European silent films, and it was not until the early years of sound that the first Brazilian features were made. The first Brazilian film studio, Cinedia, based in Rio, was making Carnaval films and slapstick comedies, nicknamed *chanchadas*, from the early 1930s – **Carmen Miranda** was the major star of the period, making her film debut in *A Voz do Carnaval* ("The Voice of Carnaval") in 1932. But in an indication of the low quality of the Brazilian film industry in those years it was not her films that led to her discovery by Hollywood, but the fact that a Hollywood producer saw her sing and dance in the legendary Urca casino in the late 1930s and took her home for a screen test.

Serious cinema in Brazil really began in the early 1950s when Assis Chateaubriand, a Brazilian press baron and early media entrepreneur, put up the money to create Vera Cruz Studios and hired director **Lima Barreto** to make *O Cangaçeiro* ("The Outlaw"). The film, shot in luminous black and white, looked fabulous and was a minor sensation in Europe, winning Brazilian cinema's first international award for best adventure film at Cannes in 1952.

O Cangaçeiro was a forerunner of what by the late 1950s was being called *cinema novo*: heavily influenced by the Italian neorealism of masters like Vittorio Da Sica, young Brazilian directors took a hard look at the trials and tribulations of daily life in Brazil. The Northeast loomed large in *cinema novo*; the two classics of the genre, *Vidas Secas* ("Barren Lives"), directed by Nelson Pereira dos Santos in 1963, and *O Pagador de Promessas* ("The Promise Keeper"), directed by **Anselmo Duarte** in 1963, are both set in the region and were both banned by the military after the 1964 coup for their unflinching portrayal of poverty and rural desperation.

Cinema under dictatorship

The **military** had a paradoxical effect on Brazilian cinema. On the surface they were every bit as repressive as one would expect: films and scripts were subject to rigid censorship and regularly banned, and anything that could be considered unpatriotic – such as the portrayal of poverty or social problems – was off limits. On the other hand, the military did believe a flourishing film industry was a form of building national prestige, and in 1969 set up a state film production and financing company, **Embrafilme**, still going today and without which the modern Brazilian film industry would not exist. As a channel for (modest) government subsidy towards the film industry, it allowed a generation of Brazilian film-makers to hone their talents without having to spend all their time chasing commercial work, and with expanding television networks supplying increasing numbers of professional actors to the film industry, the 1960s and 1970s saw a sharp rise in the number of films produced in Brazil.

In cinema, as in music, this was a time of great inventiveness in Brazil. Film-makers reacted to military censorship in a number of ways. One was diverting political comment into genres the authorities usually didn't bother to monitor, such as erotic films, where the usual scenes of rumpy-pumpy would be punctuated by political monologues as the characters smoked cigarettes in bed together afterwards. Another was to make dramas that faithfully portrayed episodes of Brazilian history, but in a way pregnant with meaning for the present. This was a style one of the masters of *cinema novo*, the director **Nelson Pereira dos Santos**, made his own with two superb films during the dictatorship. *Como Era Gostoso o Meu Francês* ("How Delicious Was My Frenchman"), released in 1971, went so far as to be shot largely in Tupi and French instead of Portuguese. It was a faithful historical reconstruction of the earliest days of Brazil but also a hilarious political allegory. *Memórias do Cárcere* ("Memories of Jail"), produced in 1984, was based on Graciliano Ramos's prison diaries during his various incarcerations by Getúlio Vargas in the 1930s and 1940s. Another example of the genre was **Joaquim Pedro de Andrade**'s *Os Inconfidentes* ("The Conspirators"), released in 1974 at the peak of the dictatorship. An uncensorable reconstruction of the national hero Tiradentes' eighteenth-century conspiracy against the Portuguese Crown, so well researched that much of the dialogue is taken from court transcripts of the period, its portrayal of the brutal repression of dissent by the colonial authorities was a brilliantly subversive use of a national myth to make contemporary political points.

The other response was to make films so elliptical and packed with symbolism that nobody outside film schools could understand them. The influence of 1960s French film-makers, especially Godard, was overwhelming in the main exponent of this genre, **Glauber Rocha**. Still widely admired by the Brazilian intelligentsia, his films created a stir on the European art-house circuit of their time, but his best-known works, *Terra* *em Transe* ("Land In Trance", 1967) and *Antônio das Mortes* (1969), are unwatchable today, save for their historical interest.

Modern Brazilian cinema

As the military dictatorship wound down, **realism** returned to Brazilian cinema, notably with Leon Hirszman's portrayal of the São Paulo car-factory strikes in *Eles Não Usam Black Tie* ("They Don't Wear Dinner Jackets", 1981) and Cacá Diegues's excellent *Bye Bye Brazil* (1979), which followed a tawdry group of circus perfomers through the country's hinterland against a marvellous soundtrack by Chico Buarque. Hector Babenco's *Pixote* (1982) became the best-known film abroad from this period, but *Bye Bye Brazil* is the real classic.

The 1990s

It was not until the consolidation of **democracy** in the 1990s that Brazilian film-makers could relax, put politics in its proper place as part of life rather than the crux of everything and start producing the kind of films that could catch the attention of international audiences in a way Brazilian cinema in previous decades – often fascinating but ultimately a little parochial – was never quite capable of doing.

There were indications of new directorial talent well before the hits came. Female directors emerged for the first time, with **Carla Camaruti** producing a highly entertaining take on early Brazilian history in *Carlota Joaquina* (1994), and **Helen Solberg**'s intelligent and thought-provoking exploration of Carmen Miranda's life and myth in the drama-documentary *Carmen Miranda – Bananas Is My Business* (1994). Young directors also emerged; **Andrushka Waddington** was all of 30 when he directed *Eu Tu Eles* ("Me You Them") in 2002, a reworking of the old *cinema novo* theme of life in the northeastern *sertão*, but this time with the central character a woman choosing from a variety of husbands rather than the other way around, and with yet another superb soundtrack, this time by Gilberto Gil.

But three films in particular catapulted Brazilian cinema to international attention. *O Que É Isso Companheiro* (literally "What's Up Comrade", but sensibly renamed "Four Days in September" for English-speaking audiences), released in 1997, is a taut, beautifully done thriller directed by Bruno Barreto, re-creating very accurately the kidnapping of the American ambassador in 1969 and featuring Alan Arkin in a cameo role as the ambassador. It was a hit internationally, but not as big a hit as two later films by the young and extravagantly talented directors **Walter Salles** and **Fernando Meirelles**.

Central Station

Salles's **Estação Central** ("Central Station"), released in 1998, tells the story of the developing relationship between a young boy and an old woman thrown together by chance, as they travel by bus from Rio into, inevitably, the interior of the Northeast, where all Brazilian film-makers seem to head when they need a metaphor for the national condition. The plot, which could easily have turned sentimental and mawkish in less assured hands, is excellently acted and directed and becomes almost unbearably moving at the end.

City of God and beyond

Cidade de Deus ("City of God"), Fernando Meirelles's stunning directorial debut released in 2003, tells the story of a real Rio *favela* from its early days in the 1960s to the mid-1980s. It is a remarkable film. The cast is largely amateur, drawn from Cidade de Deus itself, with a few professional actors thrown in (including the mesmerizing Matheus Nachtergaele as a gunrunning gangster, also to be seen in an almost equally memorable performance as a cold-blooded terrorist in *Four Days in September*). Meirelles came to cinema from shooting mainly commercials and music videos for television, and it shows, with his jumpy editing and distinctive, stylish use of colour and sound. *Cidade dos Homens* ("City of Men") was the less fêted 2007 follow-up directed by Paulo Morelli, but is just as compelling.

Brazil's next international hit, *Tropa de Elite* ("Elite Troop"), directed by **José Padilha** in 2008, had the same theme. Its extremely violent portrayal of Rio's elite anti-narcotics police unit was mistakenly criticized as fascistic by some reviewers, but the film is in fact ethnographically accurate in its portrayal of police corruption, the nexus between violence, politics and organized crime in Rio, and the complex, intimate yet distant relationship between Rio's middle and working classes, sharing the same urban space but in wholly different ways.

In 2010, crime thriller *Elite Squad: The Enemy Within* became the all-time largest box office ticket seller and highest-grossing film in Brazil, though its fictional take on Rio's special police forces failed to generate the same interest internationally. Brazilian indie movies have continued to generate critical acclaim in recent years, though these tend to be strictly arthouse material and light years behind Hollywood (and local comedies) in terms of box office. *Neighboring Sounds* by Kleber Mendonça Filho (a drama set in Recife) and *Father's Chair* by Luciano Moura were both highly acclaimed in 2012, while *The Pilgrim* (2014) dramatized the life of novelist Paulo Coelho and *A Estrada 47* (2013) is a brilliant movie about Brazil's involvement in World War II. In 2016 Kleber Mendonça Filho returned with controversial joint French–Brazilian drama *Aquarius*, starring Sônia Braga as a women under pressure to sell her apartment to a construction company in Recife. Also in 2016, *Mãe Só Há Uma* (*Don't Call Me Son*) dealt with a teenager grappling with his gender identity. In 2017 *Bingo: O Rei das Manhãs* ("Bingo: the king of the mornings") was a well-received biopic of actor Arlindo Barreto, who played the Brazilian version of Bozo the Clown in the 1980s, while Daniela Thomas' startling *Vazante* (shot in black and white), broke barriers with its depiction of slavery in early nineteenth-century Minas Gerais.

Books

Though things are slowly changing, Brazil is spottily covered by books in English. The riches of Brazilian literature lie largely untranslated, and too many books on Brazilian politics tell you more about the political leanings of their authors than Brazil. Still, a large number of foreign visitors, from Charles Darwin to Michael Palin, have generated a rich "impressions of Brazil" genre.

THE BEST INTRODUCTIONS

★ **Elizabeth Bishop** *One Art* (Farrar, Straus and Giroux). One of the best American poets of the twentieth century spent much of her adult life in Brazil, living in the hills behind Petrópolis from 1951 to 1969 but travelling widely. This selection from her letters and diaries is an intimate, sharp-eyed chronicle of Brazil in those years, and much else. Her *Collected Poems* (Farrar, Straus and Giroux) is equally essential – she is one of the greatest poets of place in English, and her talent is unforgettably unleashed on Rio, Minas Gerais and the Amazon.

★ **Fernando Henrique Cardoso** *The Accidental President of Brazil: A Memoir* (PublicAffairs). A well-written, funny, fair-minded and often moving book by Brazil's most urbane and cosmopolitan president. There's material about his fascinating life before he became president, and the usual vignettes of the famous – including a memorable account of being upstaged at Buckingham Palace by the Brazilian football team. Fascinating introduction to the country by somebody who did more than anyone to modernize Brazil.

Charles Darwin *The Beagle Diaries* (Penguin). Although this collection of extracts includes Darwin's travels all over South America, Brazil, where he spent more time on land than anywhere else, figures heavily, especially Rio and what were then the forests around it. Fresh and interesting in his descriptions of the natural world, Darwin was also a shrewd observer of Brazilian society; his contempt for slavery in action is memorably expressed.

Boris Fausto *A Concise History of Brazil* (Cambridge UP). The best single-volume introductory history of Brazil, written by an eminent historian from São Paulo. Fausto shows very effectively how Brazil has changed dramatically over time, despite the temptation to see it as a prisoner of its own history.

★ **Claude Lévi-Strauss** *Tristes Tropiques* (Picador; Penguin). The great French anthropologist describes four years spent in 1930s Brazil – arguably the best book ever written about the country by a foreigner.

Robert M. Levine and John J. Crocitti (eds) *The Brazil Reader: History, Culture, Politics* (Latin America Bureau; Duke UP). The breadth of subject matter in this thoughtful anthology is impressive, covering Brazil from colonial times to the present, using book and article extracts, original documents and historical photographs. If it wasn't for the volume's sheer weight, it would be the perfect travel companion.

Michael Palin *Brazil*. It's easy to knock the ex-Python comedian turned global traveller, but this TV series and inevitable companion tome is a fun, light-hearted look at the up-and-coming superpower, from the Amazon jungles to the Blumenau Oktoberfest.

★ **Larry Rohter** *Brazil on the Rise: The Story of a Country Transformed*. Brazil's recent economic boom and its effects are expertly chronicled by this *New York Times* reporter, tackling, among other things, the myth of Brazil's sexually charged culture and life in the *favelas*.

Thomas E. Skidmore *Brazil: Five Centuries of Change* (Oxford UP). Very readable account of the emergence of Brazilian national identity, from the first European contact to the present day.

HISTORY

Gilberto Freyre *The Mansions and the Shanties* (California UP). Brazil's most famous – and still most controversial historian decades after his death – looks at the origins of Brazilian urbanism and city life; deliberately provocative conclusions and brilliantly written.

Katia M. de Queiros Mattoso *To be a Slave in Brazil, 1550–1888* (Rutgers UP). A history of slavery in Brazil, unusually written from the perspective of the slave. Writing for the general reader, the author divides her excellent study into three themes: the process of enslavement, life in slavery and escape from it.

Joseph A. Page *The Brazilians* (Addison-Wesley). A cultural history of Brazil in a clear if eclectic style, drawing on sources ranging from economics and political psychology to film and literature. The author is a law professor at Georgetown University in Washington, DC.

Patrick Wilcken *Empire Adrift: The Portuguese Court in Rio de Janeiro 1808–1821* (Bloomsbury). In 1807 the Portuguese royal family, accompanied by 10,000 aristocrats, servants, government officials and priests, fled Lisbon in advance of Napoleon's invading army, which was sweeping across the Iberian Peninsula. In this wonderfully lively account, the author brings to life the incredible atmosphere in Lisbon and Rio during this key episode in Brazilian history.

REGIONS: TRAVEL AND HISTORY

THE AMAZON

Colonel P. H. Fawcett *Exploration Fawcett* (o/p). Fawcett carries his stiff upper lip in and out of some of the most disease-infested, dangerous and downright frightening parts of interior Brazil (see page 476). It's a rattling good read, compiled by his son from Fawcett's diaries and letters after his disappearance. Readily available in secondhand bookshops or online.

Candace Millard *The River of Doubt* (Scribner). Historian with a talent for writing for a general audience tells the fascinating and forgotten story of Teddy Roosevelt's journey to the Amazon after renouncing the presidency of the US in the early twentieth century. It was close to being a complete disaster, almost killed him at the time, and Roosevelt's health never recovered.

Hugh Raffles *In Amazonia: A Natural History* (Princeton UP). Superbly written mixture of history, anthropology and geography, exploring the gap between the way outsiders and Amazonians think about the region and its landscapes, and periodically very moving in its interweaving of personal memory with wider concerns.

MINAS GERAIS AND BRASÍLIA

Glenn Alan Cheney *Journey on the Estrada Real: Encounters in the Mountains of Brazil* (Academy Chicago). A beautiful account of a walk tracing the northern section of the Estrada Real (the Royal Road, also known as the Caminho do Ouro) from Mariana to Diamantina. Cheney offers descriptions of hamlets and villages way off the beaten track – where, for better or worse, life appears to have stood still for generations – and meditations on how communities such as these can survive "development" and the impact of globalization.

Alex Shoumatoff *The Capital of Hope: Brasília and its People* (Vintage). The author talked with government officials and settlers – rich and poor – to weave a very readable account of the first 25 years of the Brazilian capital.

THE NORTHEAST

Billy Jaynes Chandler *The Bandit King: Lampião of Brazil* (Texas UP). Compulsive reading that seems like fiction but is well-documented fact. Based on original sources and interviews with participants and witnesses, an American historian with a talent for snappy writing reconstructs the action-packed (and myth-encrusted) life of the famous social bandit, complete with fascinating photographs.

★ **Euclides da Cunha** *Rebellion in the Backlands* (Picador; Chicago UP). Also known by its Portuguese title *Os Sertões*, this remains perhaps Brazil's greatest historical account. An epic tale of Antônio Conselheiro's short-lived holy city, the Canudos Rebellion and its brutal suppression that left some 15,000 dead, the book is also a powerful meditation on Brazilian civilization.

★ **Gilberto Freyre** *The Masters and the Slaves* (California UP). Classic 1933 history of plantation life in the Northeast, with a wealth of detail (includes index headings like "Smutty Stories and Expressions" and "Priests, Bastards of"). Very readable, and there is passionate debate in Brazil over his take on race and national identity to this day.

Robert M. Levine *Vale of Tears: Revisiting the Canudos Massacre in Northeastern Brazil 1893–1897* (California UP). A vivid portrait of backland life and a detailed examination of the myths behind Canudos. Shocking but utterly compelling reading, especially when read in conjunction with da Cunha's classic.

Peter Robb *A Death in Brazil* (Bloomsbury; John Macrae Books). Sporadically vivid travel writing focused mainly on Recife and Alagoas, interspersed with analysis of the corruption of the Collor years. As the title suggests, Robb's take on Brazil is generally depressing – best read after or during a visit, not before.

RIO AND AROUND

Ruy Castro *Rio de Janeiro* (Bloomsbury). Ruy Castro, a renowned journalist, offers a historical and cultural overview of Rio and, far more importantly, captures his fellow *cariocas'* soul. Leaving aside Castro's sometimes irritating generalizations, this book provides an alluring entry into Rio life.

★ **Alma Guillermoprieto** *Samba* (Bloomsbury; Vintage). The author, a trained dancer and a well-known journalist, describes a year she spent in Rio's Mangueira *favela* preparing with its inhabitants for Carnaval. Riveting, superbly written and the best account in English of *favela* life.

THE SOUTH

Todd Diacon *Millennarian Vision, Capitalist Reality: Brazil's Contestado Rebellion 1912–1916* (Duke UP). Fascinating analysis of the Contestado Rebellion in Paraná. The rebels attacked train stations, sawmills and immigrant colonies in Santa Catarina and Paraná but were ultimately outnumbered and outgunned.

NATIONAL POLITICS AND SOCIETY

Tobias Hecht *At Home in the Street* (Cambridge UP). Excellent study of street children and those who deal with them, from death squads to social workers. Based on work in Recife, but equally applicable to any large Brazilian city.

Daniel Linger *No One Home: Brazilian Selves Remade in Japan* (Stanford UP). Brazil has the largest Japanese population outside Japan and many Brazilians move back and forth between the two countries doing the work the Japanese prefer to leave to others. This is a sensitive, accessible study of their lives, problems and dreams.

Thomas Skidmore *Politics in Brazil 1930–1964; The Politics of Military Rule in Brazil 1964–85* (Oxford UP). The former is the standard work on Brazilian politics from the rise of Vargas until the 1964 military takeover. The latter continues the story to the resumption of Brazil's shaky democracy.

HEALTH, GENDER AND SEXUALITY

Herbert Daniel and Richard Parker *Sexuality, Politics and AIDS in Brazil* (Falmer Press). Excellent, clearly written history of AIDS in Brazil, covering the way the epidemic has developed in relation to popular culture at one end and government policy at the other. There are bright spots – Brazilian TV health education slots on AIDS may be the best in the world, completely frank, and often screamingly funny – but this book will help you understand how this coexisted with a scandalous lack of supervision of blood banks.

Richard Parker *Bodies, Pleasures and Passions* (Beacon Press). A provocative analysis of the erotic in Brazilian history and popular culture. Tremendous subject matter and some fascinating insights into sexual behaviour, combining insider and outsider perspectives.

Daphne Patai *Brazilian Women Speak: Contemporary Life Stories* (Rutgers UP). Oral testimony forms the core of this very readable work that lets ordinary women from the Northeast and Rio speak for themselves to describe the struggles, constraints and hopes of their lives.

Nancy Scheper-Hughes *Death Without Weeping: The Violence of Everyday Life in Brazil* (California UP). An often shocking, ultimately depressing anthropological study of *favela* women, and in particular of childbirth, motherhood and infant death. Although over-long – judicious skipping is in order – it is very accessible to the general reader, interesting and often moving.

RACE

Thomas E. Skidmore *Black into White: Race and Nationality in Brazilian Thought* (Duke UP). First published in 1974, this revised edition has a preface that updates the book to the 1990s. A landmark in the intellectual history of Brazilian racial ideology, examining scientific racism and the Brazilian intellectual elite's supposed belief in assimilation and the ideal of whitening.

France W. Twine *Racism in a Racial Democracy* (Rutgers UP). Fascinating ethnography of racism in a small Brazilian town, by a black American sociologist interested in the differences between Brazilian and American racial politics.

AMAZON POLITICS AND SOCIETY

Warren Dean *Brazil and the Struggle for Rubber* (Cambridge UP). Good environmental history of the rubber boom and subsequent failed attempts to set up rubber plantations in the Amazon.

Susanna Hecht and Alexander Cockburn *The Fate of the Forest* (Penguin; Verso). Excellently written and researched, this is as good an introduction to the problem as you will find. Very strong on Amazonian history, too – essential to understanding what's going on, but often ignored by Amazon commentators.

Chico Mendes and Tony Gross *Fight for the Forest: Chico Mendes in His Own Words* (Latin America Bureau; Inland Book Co). Long, moving passages from a series of interviews the rubber-tappers' union leader gave shortly before his assassination in 1988. Well translated and with useful notes giving background to the issues raised.

BIRDWATCHING AND WILDLIFE

David L. Pearson and Les Beletsky *Brazil: Amazon and Pantanal – The Ecotravellers' Wildlife Guide* (Academic Press). The main body of this book examines the regions' ecosystems and the threats they face before moving on to chapters discussing insects, amphibians, reptiles, birds, mammals and fish. Richly illustrated and clearly written, the book will enrich any visit to the Amazon or Pantanal.

Ber van Perlo *A Field Guide to the Birds of Brazil* (Oxford UP). The only single-volume field guide for birding in Brazil that fits easily into a bag (although not a pocket); heavily illustrated, with a special focus on Brazil's 218 endemic species.

ARTS AND LEISURE

ARCHITECTURE

Marta Iris Montero *Burle Marx: The Lyrical Landscape* (Thames & Hudson; California UP). A beautifully illustrated book celebrating the life and work of one of the twentieth century's foremost landscape architects, who designed many of Brazil's prominent parks, gardens and other urban spaces (the most famous of which are probably the flowing mosaics alongside Copacabana and Flamengo beaches).

Styliane Philippou *Oscar Niemeyer: Curves of Irreverence* (Yale UP). Good biography-cum-assessment of Niemeyer, well illustrated and especially strong on the cultural context of Niemeyer's rise to prominence in the 1940s and 1950s.

ART AND PHOTOGRAPHY

Gilberto Ferrez *Photography in Brazil 1840–1900* (New Mexico UP, o/p). One of the little-known facts about Brazil is that the first-ever non-portrait photograph was taken of the Paço da Cidade in Rio in 1840, by a Frenchman hot off a ship with the newfangled Daguerrotype. This is a fascinating compendium of the pioneering work of early photographers in Brazil, including material from all over the country, although the stunning panoramas of Rio from the 1860s onward are the highlight.

Daniel Levine (ed) *The Brazilian Photographs of Genevieve Naylor, 1940–1942* (Duke UP). Recently uncovered photographs by a young American photographer, mainly of Rio, Salvador and the small towns of the interior. They are a revelation: Naylor was a great photographer, interested in people and street scenes, not landscapes, and this is a unique visual record of Brazil and its people during the Vargas years.

MUSIC, DANCE AND CAPOEIRA

Bira Almeida *Capoeira – a Brazilian Art Form* (North Atlantic Books). A *capoeira mestre* (master) explains the history and philosophy behind this African–Brazilian martial art/dance form. The book offers valuable background information for those who practise capoeira and for those who are merely interested.

Ruy Castro *Bossa Nova – The Story of the Brazilian Music That Seduced the World* (A Capella). A welcome translation of an excellent book by a Brazilian journalist and biographer. This is basically an oral history of bossa nova, packed with incidental detail on Rio nightlife and city culture of the 1950s and early 1960s. A very good read.

Chris McGowan and Ricardo Pessanha *The Brazilian Sound: Samba, Bossa Nova and the Popular Music of Brazil* (Temple UP). An easy-to-flick-through and well-written basic manual on modern Brazilian music and musicians. Good to carry with you if you're planning on doing some serious music-buying. There's also a useful bibliography and a good discography.

Caetano Veloso *Tropical Truth: A Story of Music and Revolution in Brazil* (Bloomsbury; Knopf). The maestro's account of *tropicalismo* and his early career, including exile, from the 1960s to the early 1970s. Veloso is as good a writer as you would expect, a little over-anxious to show off his learning sometimes, but this is a fascinating despatch from the culture wars of the 1960s.

CUISINE

Michael Bateman *Street Café Brazil* (Conran Octopus; Contemporary Books). The title is rather deceptive, as you're unlikely to come across many of these recipes on Brazilian street stalls, but they are authentic, and the lavish pictures are enough to inspire you to attempt to reproduce them at home.

Fernando Farah *The Food and Cooking of Brazil Aquamarine*. By far the best book on traditional and contemporary Brazilian cooking, by one of the country's most popular celebrity chefs.

Christopher Idone *Brazil: A Cook's Tour* (Pavilion; Clarkson Potter). A region-by-region look at Brazilian cooking, its origins and influences, with a few recipes thrown in as well. The colour photos of ingredients, markets and dishes are mouthwatering and the text lively and informative. It's good to see São Paulo and the Amazon being discussed separately and at length (when it comes to cookbooks, usually only Rio and Bahia get a look-in), but the South is completely ignored.

FOOTBALL

★ **Alex Bellos** *Futebol: The Brazilian Way of Life* (Bloomsbury). Accessible and engaging analysis of Brazilian football, from its early history to its present compulsive mixture of world-class players on the pitch and equally world-class levels of corruption off it. Written by a journalist with an eye for original stories: homesick Brazilians playing in the Faroe Islands, tactics for transvestites and much more. Essential reading.

Luca Caioli *Neymar: The Making of the World's Greatest New Number 10* (Icon Book Ltd). Brazil's newest great hope is given the star treatment in this fawning biography, but it is a fascinating insight into not just Brazil's contemporary football scene, but the social backgrounds of its top players too.

Josh Lacey *God is Brazilian: Charles Miller, the Man Who Brought Football to Brazil* (Tempus). A well-researched and entertaining account of the life and times of Charles Miller, the Anglo-Brazilian who is credited with introducing modern football to Brazil. Football apart, the book offers fascinating observations regarding late Victorian and Edwardian British society both in England and São Paulo.

Pelé *Pelé The Autobiography* (Simon & Schuster). Published to coincide with the 2006 World Cup, this ghost-written "autobiography" of the world's most famous Brazilian is as wooden and formulaic as this type of book always is, but hey – it's Pelé, and therefore compulsive reading for any football fan.

FICTION

WORKS BY BRAZILIAN AUTHORS

Jorge Amado *Gabriela, Clove and Cinnamon*; *Tereza Batista* (both Abacus, o/p; Avon); *Dona Flor and Her Two Husbands* (Serpent's Tail; Avon); *The Violent Land* (Collins; Avon). Amado is the proverbial rollicking good read, a fine choice for the beach or on long bus journeys. He's by far the best-known Brazilian writer abroad – there is even a French wine named after him. Purists rightly quibble that the local colour is laid on with a trowel, but Amado's blend of the erotic and exotic has him laughing all the way to the bank.

Mário de Andrade *Macunaíma* (Quartet Books). First published in 1928, *Macunaíma* is considered one of the greatest works of Brazilian literature. In this comic tale of the adventures of a popular hero, Macunaíma, a figure from the jungle interior, Andrade presents his typical wealth of exotic images, myths and legends.

★ **Machado de Assis** *Posthumous Memoirs of Brás Cubas* (Oxford UP). The most important work by the finest novelist Brazil has yet produced. Told by one of the most remarkable characters in fiction, this is an often-hilarious tale of absurd schemes to cure the world of melancholy and half-hearted political ambitions unleashed from beyond the grave. For good translations of Machado's great short stories, *The Devil's Church and Other Stories* (Texas UP, US, o/p) and *Helena* (California UP) are worth going to some trouble to get hold of. His cool, ferociously ironic style veers between black comedy and sardonic analysis of the human condition.

Paolo Coelho *The Alchemist* (Harper Collins). Love him or hate him, Coelho is the most successful Brazilian writer by a huge margin, with an oeuvre of simple, pseudo-New Age fables that began in 1988 with this modest tale of a young shepherd on a spiritual journey.

Milton Hatoum *The Brothers* (Bloomsbury). Set in late nineteenth-century Manaus, this is a family saga based on Lebanese twin brothers and their relationship with their mother. Filled with local colour, this is one of the best Brazilian novels in translation to emerge in recent years.

Paulo Lins *City of God* (Bloomsbury; Grove Press). The author, who went on to become a photojournalist, was brought up in Rio's *Cidade de Deus* housing project and uses his knowledge of drug trafficking and gang warfare as the basis of this remarkable novel, the book behind the internationally acclaimed film.

Graciliano Ramos *Barren Lives* (Texas UP). Masterpiece of the Northeastern novelist who introduced social realism into modern Brazilian fiction. The heavy use of regional Northeastern Portuguese in the original makes it fiendishly difficult to translate, but it gives you a sense of his great talent.

João Ubaldo Ribeiro *An Invincible Memory* (Faber; HarperCollins, o/p). A family saga spanning a four-hundred-year period from the arrival of the Portuguese in Brazil to the present day, featuring anecdotes, history and myths narrated through the experiences of two Bahian families, one aristocratic, the other enslaved. The book was wildly popular when published in Brazil and is considered a national epic.

Moacyr Scliar *The Collected Stories of Moacyr Scliar* (New Mexico UP). Scliar, who hails from Porto Alegre, is Brazil's most distinguished Jewish writer. This anthology includes haunting, comic and bleak stories that proclaim Scliar as a master of the short story.

Márcio Souza *Mad Maria* (Avon, o/p). A comic drama set against the backdrop of the absurdity of rail construction in nineteenth-century Amazônia. Souza's excellent *The Emperor of the Amazon* (Abacus, o/p; Avon, o/p) is another humorous and powerful description of the decadence that characterized late nineteenth-century Amazonian society.

Antônio Torres *The Land* (Readers International). Set in a decaying town in the parched interior of the Northeast, this is a grim tale of people trapped and people trying to get away. In *Blues for a Lost Childhood* (Readers International), Torres continues with the same theme, but this time focusing on a journalist who makes it to Rio but finds life there to be a living nightmare.

WORKS SET IN BRAZIL

Mario Vargas Llosa *The War of the End of the World* (Faber; Penguin). Goes well with da Cunha (see page 669). The Peruvian writer produced this haunting novel, based on the events of Canudos, in the 1970s. The translation is good and the book is easy to obtain.

Jean-Christophe Rufin *Brazil Red* (Picador; W.W. Norton). The winner of France's prestigious Goncourt literary award, this action-packed historical novel is set against France's ill-fated attempt to conquer Brazil in the sixteenth century as well as questions about the nature of civilization and culture, religion and freedom.

CHILDREN'S LITERATURE

Josua Doder *Grk and the Pelotti Gang* (Andersen Press). Along with his dog Grk, Tim, a brave (and foolhardy) British child, finds himself in the mean streets of Rio in search of the notorious Pelotti gang. Fast-paced and funny and with lots of local colour, Tim and Grk survive being kidnapped and being held in a Rio *favela* as well as jungle adventures. Suitable for 8- to 12-year-olds.

★ **Eva Ibbotson** *Journey to the River Sea* (Macmillan; Puffin). Set at the turn of the twentieth century in Manaus amid the Amazon rubber boom, this old-fashioned adventure story unfolds in an environment that its host of amusing characters either cherishes or feels nothing but contempt for. A great book to give kids to read.

Football

Far more than just a game, football is a central part of popular culture in Brazil, with all Brazilians fiercely proud of the country's record of being the only country to have qualified for all World Cups, and to have won more of them than any other nation. Brazilian fans are the most demanding in the world; it is not enough to win, Brazilians insist on winning in style, using the untranslatable but self-explanatory *futebol-arte*. Even though the Brazilian leagues are still, by and large, feeder leagues for the high-paying teams of Europe, there are such reserves of talent in the country that very high-quality football is still the rule in most of the big cities. And everywhere you find that compulsive mix of brilliant attack and fragile defending that makes the Brazilian national team the most charismatic side in the world, win or lose.

Early days

British railway engineers introduced football to Brazil in the 1880s, and, as in Argentina, the **British influence** is still visible in football vocabulary (*futebol, pênalti*) and in the names of some of Brazil's oldest teams, like São Paulo's Coríntians (the now defunct Corinthian Football Club was one of London's first teams). By the 1920s the Rio and São Paulo state leagues that still largely dominate Brazilian football were up and running. Brazil became the first South American country to send a team to compete in Europe, to Italy in 1934, and already by then Brazilians had realized that football was far too important for race to get in the way: Brazil's first World Cup star, **Leônidas**, who fascinated Europeans in the 1930s with his outlandish skills, was Afro-Brazilian.

Getúlio Vargas was the first in a long line of Brazilian presidents to make political capital out of the game, building the gorgeous Art Deco Pacaembu stadium in São Paulo in the 1930s, and then bringing the **1950 World Cup** to Brazil by constructing what has become one of the game's great global temples, the **Maracanã** in Rio. In that competition, Brazil had what many of the older generation still think was the greatest Brazilian side ever; the team hammered everyone, then came up against Uruguay in the final, where a draw would have been enough to secure Brazil's first *copa*. Brazil went in at half-time ahead 1-0 but the Uruguayans hadn't read the script and won 2-1, a national trauma that still haunts popular memory sixty years on – most notably in a serious argument over whether to play the final of the **2014 World Cup** in the Maracanã, on the grounds that it may be jinxed.

Greatness: 1958–1970

Success was not long in coming. A series of great teams, all with the incomparable **Pelé** as playmaker, won the World Cup in Sweden in 1958 (still the only World Cup a South American team has won in Europe), and then retained it in Chile in 1962, even with Pelé injured. His place as heart of the team was taken by probably the greatest winger in football history, **Mané Garrincha**, an alcoholic all his adult life, including his footballing years, who died tragically young in a life that transfixed Brazilians then and now. Then, most memorably, Brazil won the **1970 World Cup** in Mexico with what is universally regarded as the greatest team in the history of the game, with Pelé surrounded by such great names as **Gerson**, **Rivelino**, **Tostão** and

Carlos Alberto. Brazil got to keep the **Jules Rimet trophy** as the World Cup's first three-time winners. Embarrassingly, but rather typically, bandits stole the historic cup from the headquarters of the Brazilian football association in Rio in 1983; it was never seen again.

The 1980s

After an interlude during the 1970s, Brazil flirted with greatness again in the 1980s, when a new generation of *craques* (the wonderful Portuguese word for crack players), led by **Zico** in attack but also including an extraordinary midfield made up of **Falcão**, **Sócrates**, **Éder** and **Cerezo**, failed to win the World Cups of 1982 and 1986; they played some of the best football in the tournament's history in the process, losing to Italy in 1982 and France in 1986 in matches that have become legendary.

Good but not great: the 1990s

It took Brazil until **1994** to reclaim the World Cup for the **fourth time**, when they beat Italy on penalties in one of the worst finals on record. This was a triumph built on such un-Brazilian virtues as a combative rather than a creative midfield and a solid defence; a team whose only endearing features were the comically dependable incompetence of its goalkeeper, **Taffarel**, maintaining a great Brazilian tradition of fragility between the sticks, and the quality of the attack, where the brilliance of **Romário** found the perfect foil in **Bebeto**.

But there was uneasiness in Brazil at the workmanlike way they had won – an uneasiness that crystallized into scandal four years later in France when, despite the presence of the young prodigy **Ronaldo** leading the attack, they had an unconvincing campaign. They were lucky to get to the final, where a French side that looked inferior on paper beat them 3-0. There was strong suspicion that Ronaldo, who suffered a seizure before the game, only played at the insistence of the team's sponsor, Nike. This symbolized a widespread feeling in Brazil that the game was on the wrong track: club owners selling out to commercial interests; stars making their living in Europe and forgetting their obligation to the national team; and a duller, more European-style emphasis on fitness and teamwork banishing the individual skill that lies at the heart of *futebol-arte* as a result. There was and is something to this; unprecedented amounts of money flowed into Brazilian football in the 1990s, and it would certainly have been unthinkable to the national sides of 1970 and the 1980s that Brazil could play two finals of a World Cup without scoring a goal in open play.

Into the twenty-first century

Brazil's malaise seemed to deepen in the run-up to the **2002 World Cup**: corruption scandals roiled the game; Ronaldo was sidelined by career-threatening injuries; and the team struggled for the first time ever to qualify for the competition, coming close to the indignity of having to play Australia in a play-off to get there at all. So when Brazil won the competition that year – for a **record fifth time** – it was a heartening surprise. There were several factors behind it, most importantly Ronaldo's recovery from injury and shrewd manager **Felipe Scolari**'s ability to pull together a settled, solid side just when it mattered most. Brazil played some fantastic football on their way to a final with a fairy-tale ending, where Ronaldo crowned his comeback with both goals in a 2-0 victory against Germany.

Though Brazil's record World Cup wins (and eight **Copa América** victories, the last in 2007) makes them the undisputed kings of the sport, tournaments since have been disappointments: in **2006** traditional bugbears France beat an overhyped but underperforming Brazil side, while in **2010** the Brazilians were unceremoniously knocked out in the quarter-finals by the Netherlands. In the 2011 Copa América (South America's regional competition), Brazil also fared poorly, knocked out in the quarter-finals by Paraguay. Brazil was host for the **2014 World Cup**, and hopes were high that star player Neymar and co could make it a record six wins. Yet the campaign ended in disaster, when Brazil were beaten 7–1 in the semi-final by Germany; sports newspaper *Lance!* called it "The Biggest Shame in History".

An embarrassing early exit from the **2015 Copa América** followed. Since those low points Brazil's national team has recovered strongly, easily qualifying for World Cup 2018 in Russian, where they will be eager to make amends.

Language

Learning some Portuguese before you go to Brazil is an extremely good idea. Although many well-educated Brazilians speak English, and it's now the main second language taught in schools, this hasn't filtered through to most of the population. If you know Spanish you're halfway there: there are obvious similarities in the grammar and vocabulary, so you should be able to make yourself understood if you speak slowly, and reading won't present you with too many problems. However, Portuguese pronunciation is utterly different and much less straightforward than Spanish, so unless you take the trouble to learn a bit about it you won't have a clue what Brazilians are talking about. And contrary to what you might expect, very few Brazilians speak Spanish themselves.

Unfortunately, far too many people – especially Spanish-speakers – are put off going to Brazil precisely by the language, but in reality this should be one of your main reasons for going. **Brazilian Portuguese** is a colourful, sensual language full of wonderfully rude and exotic vowel sounds, swooping intonation and hilarious idiomatic expressions. You'll also find that Brazilians will greatly appreciate even your most rudimentary efforts, and every small improvement in your Portuguese will make your stay in Brazil ten times more enjoyable.

People who have learned their Portuguese **in Portugal** or in **Lusophone Africa** won't have any real problems with the language in Brazil, but there are some quite big differences. There are many variations in vocabulary, and Brazilians take more liberties with the language, but the most notable differences are in pronunciation: Brazilian Portuguese is spoken more slowly and clearly; the neutral vowels so characteristic of European Portuguese tend to be sounded in full; in much of Brazil outside Rio the slushy "sh" sound doesn't exist; and the "de" and "te" endings of words like *cidade* and *diferente* are palatalized so they end up sounding like "sidadgee" and "djiferentchee".

Pronunciation

The rules of **pronunciation** are complicated, but the secret is to throw yourself wholeheartedly into this explosive linguistic jacuzzi.

Non-nasal vowels

A shouldn't present you with too many problems. It's usually somewhere between the "**a**" sound of "b**a**t" and that of "f**a**ther".

E has three possible pronunciations. When it occurs at the beginning or in the middle of a word, it will usually sound either a bit like the "**e**" in "b**e**t" – eg *ferro* (iron) and *miséria* (poverty) – or like the "**ay**" in "h**ay**" – eg *mesa* (table) and *pêlo* (hair). However, the difference can be quite subtle and it's not something you should worry about too much at the start. The third pronunciation is radically different from the other two: at the end of a word, "**e**" sounds like "**y**" in "happ**y**", eg *fome* ("fommy", hunger) and *se* (if), which actually sounds like the Spanish "si".

I is straightforward. It's always an "**ee**" sound like the "**i**" in "police" – eg *isto* (this).

O is another letter with three possible pronunciations. At the beginning or in the middle of a word, it normally sounds either the way it does in "d**o**g" – eg *loja* (shop) and *pó* (powder) – or the way it does in "g**o**" – eg *homem* (man) and *pôquer* (poker). At the end of a word "**o**" sounds like the "**oo**" in "b**oo**t", so *obrigado* (thank you) is pronounced "obri-GA-doo". And the definite article "**o**" as in *o homem* (the man) is pronounced "**oo**".

U is always pronounced like "**oo**" in "b**oo**t", eg *cruz* (cross).

There is also a variety of vowel combinations or diphthongs that sound pretty much the way you would expect them to. They are **ai** (pronounced like "i" in "ride"); **au** (pronounced as in "sh**ou**t"); **ei** (pronounced as in "**hay**"); and **oi** (pronounced as in "**boy**"). The only one that has an unexpected pronunciation is **ou**, which sounds like "o" in "**rose**".

Nasal vowels

The fun really starts when you get into the **nasal vowel sounds**. Generally speaking, each "normal" vowel has its nasal equivalent. The trick in pronouncing these is to be completely uninhibited. To take one example, the word **pão** (bread). First of all, just say "pow" to yourself. Then say it again, but this time half close your mouth and shove the vowel really hard through your nose. Try it again, even more vigorously. It should sound something like "powng", but much more nasal and without really sounding the final "g".

There are two main ways in which Portuguese indicates a nasal vowel. One is through the use of the **tilde**, as in *pão*. The other is the use of the letters **m** or **n** after the vowel. As a general rule, whenever you see a vowel followed by "m" or "n" and then another consonant, the vowel will be nasal – eg *gente*. The same thing applies when the vowel is followed by "m" at the end of a word, eg *tem*, *bom* – in these cases, the "m" is not pronounced, it just nasalizes the vowel.

Below are some of the main nasal vowels and examples of words that use them. However, it must be emphasized that the phonetic versions of the nasal sounds we've given are only approximate.

Ã, and **-am** or **-an followed by a consonant** indicate nasal "**a**" – eg *macã* (apple), *campo* (field), *samba*.

-ão or **-am at the end of a word** indicate the "**owng**" sound, as explained above in *pão*. Other examples are in *estação* (station), *mão* (hand), *falam* ("FA-lowng"; they talk).

-em or **-en followed by a consonant** indicate a nasalized "**e**" sound – eg *tempo* (weather), *entre* (between), *gente* (people).

-em or **-ens at the end of a word** indicate an "**eyng**" sound – eg *tem* ("teyng"; you have or there is), *viagens* ("vee-A-zheyngs"; journeys).

-im or **-in at the end of a word** or followed by a consonant are simply a nasal "**ee**" sound, so *capim* (grass) sounds a bit like "ca-PEENG".

-om or **-on at the end of a word** or followed by a consonant indicate nasal "**o**". An obvious example is *bom* (good), which sounds pretty similar to "bon" in French.

-um or **-un at the end of a word** or followed by a consonant indicate nasal "**u**" – eg *um* (one).

-ãe sounds a bit like "**eyeing**" said quickly and explosively – eg *mãe* (mother).

-õe sounds like "**oing**". Most words ending in "-ão" make their plural like this, with an "s" (which is pronounced) at the end – eg *estação* (station) becomes *estações* (stations).

Consonants

Brazilian **consonants** are more straightforward than the vowels, but there are a few little oddities you'll need to learn. We've only listed the consonants where they differ from their English counterparts.

C is generally pronounced hard, as in "**c**at" (eg *campo*). However, when followed by "i" or "e", it's pronounced softly, as in "**c**eiling" (eg *cidade*; city). It's also pronounced softly whenever it's written with a cedilla (eg *estação*).

CH is pronounced like English "**sh**", so *chá* (tea) is said "sha".

D is generally pronounced as in English. However, in most parts of Brazil it's palatalized to sound like "**dj**" whenever it comes before an "i" or final "e". So *difícil* (difficult) is pronounced "djee-FEE-siw", and the ubiquitous preposition *de* (of) sounds like "djee".

G is generally pronounced hard as in English "**g**od" (eg *gusto*; I like). But before "e" or "i" it's pronounced like the "**s**" in English "vision" or "measure" – eg *geral* (general) and *gíria* (slang).

H is always silent (eg *hora*; hour).

J is pronounced like the "s" in English "vision" or "measure" – eg *jogo* (game) and *janeiro* (January).

L is usually pronounced as in English. But at the end of a word, it takes on a peculiar, almost Cockney pronunciation, becoming a bit like a "**w**". So Brasil is pronounced "bra-ZEEW". When followed by "h", it's pronounced "**ly**" as in "million"; so *ilha* (island) comes out as "EE-lya".

N is normally pronounced as in English, but when it's followed by "h" it becomes "**ny**". So *sonho* (dream) sounds like "SON-yoo".

Q always comes before "u" and is pronounced either "**k**" or, more usually, "**kw**". So *cinquenta* (fifty) is pronounced "sin-KWEN-ta", but *quero* (I want) is pronounced "KE-roo".

R is usually as in English. However, at the beginning of a word it's pronounced like an English "**h**". So "Rio" is actually pronounced "HEE-oo", and *rádio* (radio) is pronounced "HA-djee-oo".

RR is always pronounced like an English "**h**". So *ferro* is pronounced "FE-hoo".

S is normally pronounced like an English "**s**", and in São Paulo and the South this never changes. But in Rio and many places to the north, "**s**" sounds like English "**sh**" when it comes before a consonant and at the end of a word (*estação*; "esh-ta-SOWNG").

T is normally pronounced as in English but, like "d", it changes before "i" and final "e". So *sorte* (luck) is pronounced "SOR-chee", and the great hero of Brazilian history, Tiradentes, is pronounced "chee-ra-DEN-chees".

X is pronounced like an English "**sh**" at the beginning of a word, and elsewhere like an English "**x**" or "**z**". So *xadrez* (chess) is pronounced "sha-DREYZ", while *exército* (army) is pronounced "e-ZER-si-too".

Stress

Any word that has an accent of any kind, including a tilde, is stressed on that syllable, so *miséria* (poverty) is pronounced "mi-ZE-ree-a". If there is no accent, the following rules generally apply (the syllables to be stressed are in capitals):

- Words that end with the vowels a, e and o are stressed on the penultimate syllable. So *entre* (between) sounds like "EN-tree", and *compro* (I buy) "KOM-proo". This also applies when these vowels are followed by -m, -s or -ns: *falam* is stressed "FA-lowng".
- Words that end with the vowels i and u are stressed on the final syllable: *abacaxi* (pineapple) is pronounced "a-ba-ka-ZEE". This also applies when i and u are followed by -m, -s or -ns, so *capim* is pronounced "ka-PEENG".
- Words ending in consonants are usually stressed on the final syllable, eg *rapaz* (boy), stressed "ha-PAZ".

Some useful examples:

Rio de Janeiro HEE-oo djee zha-NEY-roo
Belo Horizonte BE-loo o-ri-ZON-chee
Rio Grande do Sul HEE-oo GRAN-djee doo Soow
Recife he-SEE-fee
rodoviária ho-do-vee-A-ree-a
onde (where) ON-djee
não entende (he doesn't understand) now en-TEN-djee
sim (yes) SEENG (but hardly sound the final "g")
ruim (bad) hoo-WEENG (again hardly sound the "g")
vinte (twenty) VEEN-chee
correio (post office) co-HAY-oo

Brazilian Portuguese words and phrases

BASIC EXPRESSIONS

Yes, No Sim, Não
Please Por favor
Thank you Obrigado (men)/Obrigada (women)
Where, When Onde, Quando
What, How much Que, Quanto
This, These Este
That one, Those Aquele
Now, Later Agora, Mais tarde
Open, Closed Aberto/a, Fechado/a
Entrance, Exit Entrada, Saída
Pull, Push Puxe, Empurre
With, Without Com, Sem
For Para
Good, Bad Bom, Ruim
Big, Small Grande, Pequeno
A little, A lot Um pouco, Muito
More, Less Mais, Menos
Another Outro/a
Today, Tomorrow Hoje, Amanhã
Yesterday Ontem
But Mas (pronounced like "mice")
And E (pronounced like "ee" in "seek")
Something, Nothing Alguma coisa, Nada
Sometimes Ás vezes

GREETINGS AND RESPONSES

Hello, Goodbye Oi, Tchau (like the Italian "ciao")
Good morning Bom dia
Good afternoon Boa tarde
Goodnight Boa noite
Sorry Desculpa
Excuse me Com licença
How are you? Como vai?
Fine Bem
Congratulations Parabéns
Cheers Saúde

USEFUL PHRASES AND COLLOQUIAL EXPRESSIONS

Do you speak English? Você fala inglês?
I don't understand Não entendo
I don't speak Portuguese Não falo português
What's the Portuguese for this? Como se diz em português?
What did you say? O que você disse?
My name is… Meu nome é...
What's your name? Como se chama?
I am English Sou inglês/inglesa
…Scottish …escocês/escocesa
…Welsh …galês/galesa
…Irish …irlandês/irlandesa
…American …estaduidense
…Canadian …canadense
…Australian …australiano/a
…New Zealander …neozelandês/neozelandesa
…South African …sul-african/a
Do you have…? Você tem…?
the time? as horas?
Everything's fine Tudo bem
OK Tá bom
I'm hungry Estou com fome
I'm thirsty Estou com sede
I feel ill Me sinto mal
I want to see a doctor Quero ver um medico
What's the matter? Qual é o problema?
There is (is there?) Há…(?)
I want, I'd like… Quero…
I can… Posso...
I can't… Não posso…
I don't know Não sei
It's hot Está quente
It's cold Está frio
It's great Está legal
It's boring É chato
I'm bored/annoyed Estou chateado
I've had it up to here Estou de saco cheio
There's no way Não tem jeito
Crazy Louco/a, maluco/a
Tired Cansado/a

ASKING DIRECTIONS, GETTING AROUND

Where is…? Onde fica…?
the bus station a rodoviária
the bus stop a parada de ônibus
the nearest hotel o hotel mais próximo
the toilet o banheiro/sanitário
Left, right, straight on Esquerda, Direita, Direto
Go straight on and turn left Vai direto edobra à esquerda
Where does the bus to…leave? De onde sai o ônibus para…?
Is this the bus to Rio? É esse o ônibus para Rio?
Do you go to…? Você vai para…?
I'd like a (return) ticket to... Quero uma pasagem (ida e volta) para…
What time does it leave (arrive)? Que horas sai (chega)?
Far, Near Longe, Perto
Slowly, Quickly Devagar, Rápido

ACCOMMODATION

Do you have a room? Você tem um quarto?
with two beds/ com duas camas/
double bed cama de casal
It's for one person/ É para uma pessoa/
two people duas pessoas
It's fine, how much is it? Está bom, quanto é?
It's too expensive É caro demais
Do you have anything cheaper? Tem algo mais barato?
Is there a hotel/ campsite nearby? Tem um hotel/ camping por aqui?

NUMBERS

1 Um, Uma
2 Dois, Duas
3 Três
4 Quatro
5 Cinco
6 Seis
7 Sete
8 Oito

9 Nove
10 Dez
11 Onze
12 Doze
13 Treze
14 Quatorze
15 Quinze
16 Dezesseis
17 Dezessete
18 Dezoito
19 Dezenove
20 Vinte
21 Vinte e um
30 Trinta
40 Quarenta
50 Cinquenta
60 Sesenta
70 Setenta
80 Oitenta
90 Noventa
100 Cem
200 Duzentos
300 Trezentos
500 Quinhentos
1000 Mil
2000 Dois mil
5000 Cinco mil
Million/s Milhão/milhões

DAYS AND MONTHS

Monday Segunda-feira (or Segunda)
Tuesday Terça-feira (or Terça)
Wednesday Quarta-Feira (or Quarta)
Thursday Quinta-feira (or Quinta)
Friday Sexta-feira (or Sexta)
Saturday Sábado
Sunday Domingo
January Janeiro
February Fevereiro
March Março
April Abril
May Maio
June Junho
July Julho
August Agosto
September Setembro
October Outubro
November Novembro
December Dezembro

A Brazilian menu reader

BASICS

Açúcar Sugar
Alho e óleo Garlic and olive-oil sauce
Almoço Lunch
Arroz Rice
Azeite Olive oil
Café colonial High tea
Café de manhã Breakfast
Cardápio Menu
Carne Meat
Colher Spoon
Conta/Nota Bill
Copo Glass
Entrada Hors d'oeuvre
Faca Knife
Farinha Dried manioc flour
Garçom Waiter
Garfo Fork
Garrafa Bottle
Jantar Dinner, to have dinner
Legumes/Verduras Vegetables
Manteiga Butter
Mariscos Seafood
Molho Sauce
Ovos Eggs
Pão Bread
Peixe Fish
Pimenta Pepper
Prato Plate
Queijo Cheese
Sal Salt
Sobremesa Dessert
Sopa/Caldo Soup
Sorvete Ice cream
Taxa de serviço Service charge
Tucupi Fermented manioc and chicory sauce used in Amazonian cuisine

COOKING TERMS

Assado Roasted
Bem gelado Well chilled
Churrasco Barbecue
Cozido Boiled, Steamed
Cozinhar To cook
Grelhado Grilled

Mal passado/Bem passado Rare/Well done (Meat)
Médio Medium grilled
Milanesa Breaded
Na chapa/Na brasa Charcoal grilled

SEAFOOD (FRUTOS DO MAR)

Acarajé Fried bean cake stuffed with *vatapá* (see below)
Agulha Needle fish
Atum Tuna
Camarão Prawn/Shrimp
Caranguejo Large crab
Filhote Amazon river fish
Lagosta Lobster
Lula Squid
Mariscos Shellfish
Moqueca Seafood stewed in palm oil and coconut sauce
Ostra Oyster
Pescada Seafood stew, or hake
Pirarucu Amazon river fish
Pitu Crayfish
Polvo Octopus
Siri Small crab
Sururu A type of mussel
Vatapá Bahian shrimp dish, cooked with palm oil, skinned tomato and coconut milk, served with fresh coriander and hot peppers

MEAT AND POULTRY (CARNE E AVES)

Bife Steak
Bife a cavalo Steak with egg and *farinha*
Cabrito Kid
Carne de porco Pork
Carneiro Lamb
Costela Ribs
Costeleta Chop
Feijoada Black bean, pork and sausage stew
Fígado Liver
Frango Chicken
Leitão Suckling pig
Lingüíça Sausage
Pato Duck
Peru Turkey
Peito Breast
Perna Leg
Picadinha Stew
Salsicha Hot dog
Veado Venison
Vitela Veal

FRUIT (FRUTAS)

Abacate Avocado
Abacaxi Pineapple
Ameixa Plum, Prune
Caju Cashew fruit
Carambola Star fruit
Cerejas Cherries
Côco Coconut
Fruta do conde Custard apple (also *ata*)
Goiaba Guava
Graviola Soursop
Laranja Orange
Limão Lime
Maçã Apple
Mamão Papaya
Manga Mango
Maracujá Passion fruit
Melancia Watermelon
Melão Melon
Morango Strawberry
Pera Pear
Pêssego Peach
Uvas Grapes

VEGETABLES AND SPICES (LEGUMES E TEMPEROS)

Alface Lettuce
Alho Garlic
Arroz e feijão Rice and beans
Azeitonas Olives
Batatas Potatoes
Canela Cinnamon
Cebola Onion
Cenoura Carrot
Cheiro verde Fresh coriander/*cilantro*
Coentro Parsley
Cravo Clove
Dendê Palm oil
Ervilhas Peas
Espinafre Spinach
Macaxeira Roasted manioc
Malagueta Very hot pepper, looks like red or yellow cherry
Mandioca Manioc/cassava/yuca
Milho Corn
Palmito Palm heart
Pepinho Cucumber
Repolho Cabbage
Tomate Tomato

DRINKS

Água mineral Mineral water
Batida Fresh fruit juice with *cachaça*
Cachaça Sugar-cane rum
Café com leite Coffee with hot milk
Cafézinho Small black coffee
Caipirinha Rum and lime cocktail
Cerveja Bottled beer
Chopp Draught beer
Com gás/Sem gás Sparkling/Still
Suco Fruit juice
Vinho Wine
Vitamina Fruit juice made with milk

Glossary

Agreste In the Northeast, the intermediate zone between the coast and the *sertão*
Aldeia Originally a mission where indigenous peoples were converted, now any isolated hamlet
Alfândega Customs
Artesanato Craft goods
Azulejo Decorative glazed tiling
Baile funk Afro-Brazilian hip-hop rhythms
Bairro Neighbourhood within town or city
Bandeirante Member of a group that marched under a *bandeira* (banner or flag) in early missions to open up the interior; Brazilian conquistador
Barraca Beach hut; in resorts it usually means a bar or restaurant on the beach
Batucada Literally, a drumming session – music-making in general, especially impromptu
Bolsa Ferry
Bosque Wood
Bossa nova Literally "new trend"; a jazz form that evolved from samba
Caatinga Scrub vegetation of the interior of the Northeast
Caboclo A person of mixed indigenous Brazilian and European heritage
Candomblé African-Brazilian religion
Cangaceiro Outlaws from the interior of the Northeast who flourished in the early twentieth century; the most famous was Lampião
Capoeira African-Brazilian martial art/dance form
Carimbó Music and dance style from the north
Carioca Someone or something from Rio de Janeiro
Cerrado Scrubland
Choro Musical style, largely instrumental
Correio Postal service/post office
Correio electrónico Email
CUT/CGT Brazilian trades union organizations
Engenho Sugar mill or plantation
Ex voto Offering of thanks to a saint for intercession
Favela Shantytown, slum
Fazenda Country estate, ranch house
Feira Country market
Ferroviária Train station
Forró Dance and type of music from the Northeast
Frescão Air-conditioned bus
Frevo Frenetic musical style and dance from Recife
FUNAI Government organization intended to protect the interests of indigenous Brazilians; seriously underfunded and with a history of corruption
Garimpeiro Prospector or miner
Gaúcho Person or thing from Rio Grande do Sul; also southern cowboy
Gringo/a Foreigner, Westerner (not derogatory)
Ibama Government organization for preservation of the environment; runs national parks and nature reserves
Iemanjá Goddess of the sea in candomblé
Jangada Raft
Largo Small square
Latifúndios Large agricultural estates
Leito Luxury express bus
Literatura de cordel Literally "string literature" – printed ballads, most common in the Northeast but also found elsewhere, named after the string they are suspended from in country markets
Litoral Coast, coastal zone
Louro/a Fair-haired/blonde – Westerners in general
Macumba African-Brazilian religion, usually thought of as more authentically "African" than candomblé; most common in the North
Marginal Petty thief, outlaw
Mata Jungle, remote interior
Mata Atlântica Atlantic forest – the native jungle that once covered most of coastal Brazil and its immediate hinterland, but is now restricted to the South
Mineiro Person or thing from Minas Gerais
Mirante Viewing point
MPB Música Popular Brasileira, common shorthand for Brazilian music
Nordeste Northeastern Brazil
Nordestino/a Inhabitant thereof
Paulista Person or thing from São Paulo state
Paulistano Inhabitant of the city of São Paulo
Pelourinho Pillory or whipping post, common in colonial town squares
Planalto Central Vast interior tablelands of central Brazil
Posto Highway service station, often with basic accommodation popular with truckers
Pousada Inn
Praça Square
Praia Beach
Quebrado Out of order
Selva Jungle
Senzala Slave quarters
Sertanejo Inhabitant of *sertão*
Sertão Arid, drought-ridden interior of the Northeast
Sesmaria Royal Portuguese land grant to early settlers
Sobrado Two-storey colonial mansion
Umbanda African-Brazilian religion especially common in urban areas of the South and Southeast
Vaqueiro Cowboy in the North
Visto Visa

Small print and index

A ROUGH GUIDE TO ROUGH GUIDES

Published in 1982, the first Rough Guide – to Greece – was a student scheme that became a publishing phenomenon. Mark Ellingham, a recent graduate in English from Bristol University, had been travelling in Greece the previous summer and couldn't find the right guidebook. With a small group of friends he wrote his own guide, combining a contemporary, journalistic style with a thoroughly practical approach to travellers' needs.

The immediate success of the book spawned a series that rapidly covered dozens of destinations. And, in addition to impecunious backpackers, Rough Guides soon acquired a much broader readership that relished the guides' wit and inquisitiveness as much as their enthusiastic, critical approach and value-for-money ethos. These days, Rough Guides include recommendations from budget to luxury and cover more than 120 destinations around the globe, from Amsterdam to Zanzibar, all regularly updated by our team of roaming writers.

Browse all our latest guides, read inspirational features and book your trip at **roughguides.com**.

Rough Guide credits

Editor: Alice Park
Commissioning editor: Edward Aves
Cartography: Carte, Katie Bennett
Picture editor: Aude Vauconsant
Cover photo research: Phoebe Lowndes
Senior DTP coordinator: Dan May
Head of DTP and Pre-Press: Rebeka Davies

Publishing information

This ninth edition published in 2018 by
Rough Guides Ltd

Distribution
UK, Ireland and Europe
Apa Publications (UK) Ltd; sales@roughguides.com
United States and Canada
Ingram Publisher Services; ips@ingramcontent.com
Australia and New Zealand
Woodslane; info@woodslane.com.au
Southeast Asia
Apa Publications (SN) Pte; sales@roughguides.com
Worldwide
Apa Publications (UK) Ltd; sales@roughguides.com
Special Sales, Content Licensing and CoPublishing
Rough Guides can be purchased in bulk quantities at discounted prices. We can create special editions, personalised jackets and corporate imprints tailored to your needs. sales@roughguides.com.

roughguides.com
Printed in China by CTPS

A catalogue record for this book is available from the British Library

Help us update

We've gone to a lot of effort to ensure that the ninth edition of **The Rough Guide to Brazil** is accurate and up-to-date. However, things change – places get "discovered", opening hours are notoriously fickle, restaurants and rooms raise prices or lower standards. If you feel we've got it wrong or left something out, we'd like to know, and if you can remember the address, the price, the hours, the phone number, so much the better.

Please send your comments with the subject line "**Rough Guide Brazil Update**" to mail@uk.roughguides.com. We'll credit all contributions and send a copy of the next edition (or any other Rough Guide if you prefer) for the very best emails.

Readers' updates

Thanks to all the readers who have taken the time to write in with comments and suggestions (and apologies if we've inadvertently omitted or misspelt anyone's name):
Magda Bulska, José Luís da Silva, Gabriel Del'escaille, Jamila Douhaibi, Luiz Leitão, Anna Letts, Gabriela Marinho, Sara Nicoly, Emma Maev O'Connell, Eun Jin Song.

ABOUT THE AUTHORS

Daniel Jacobs, from London, has worked on Rough Guides to Morocco, Egypt, Israel/Palestine, Kenya, West Africa, India, the Philippines, Colombia and Bolivia.

Stephen Keeling has been travelling to Brazil since 1999. He worked as a financial journalist for seven years before writing his first travel guide and has written several titles for Rough Guides, including books on Puerto Rico, Florida and Mexico, and *The Rough Guide to South America on a Budget*. Stephen lives in New York City.

Madelaine Triebe developed her passion for South America in her early twenties while studying Spanish in Argentina. It later led her to numerous travel adventures in the southern hemisphere, one of the highlights being searching for jaguars in Pantanal. She writes for various travel publications and about her whereabouts on mymaddytravel.com.

Acknowledgements

Daniel Jacobs would like to thank Bob Nadkarni and everyone at *The Maze* in Rio, Patrick, Shane, Edge, Marcelo Armstrong (Favela Tour, Rio), Liliana Ferrarese (Oasis, São Paulo), Marianne Soisalo (Alto Residency, Alto Paraíso de Goiás), and special thanks to Teri Oliveira and Ernesto Klotzel.

Stephen Keeling would like to thank: Constancia Wu and Isabel Liu for laughs on the road and "happy hour"; Harry Maurer for Brazilian maps, books and Minas Gerais tips; editor Alice Park for doing such a thorough job; and Tiffany Wu, the world's greatest travel partner.

Madelaine Triebe Many thanks to Edward Aves for the initial commission, Alice Park for always being a pleasure to work with and to my family and friends. A very special thanks to Larissa and her invaluable guidance in Pantanal, to Naomi McKee at Senderos for arranging my stay at *Cristalino Lodge* and Refúgio Ecológico Caiman and for Tatiana, Vagner and Matheus for showing me the best (and sometimes worse!) of Campo Grande and Corumbá. Muitos beijos!

Photo credits

(Key: t-top; c-centre; b-bottom; l-left; r-right)

Getty Images 9, 11T, 17TR, 17BR, 17BL, 19T, 20TR, 223, 326/327, 436/437
Guido Cozzi/4Corners Images 2
iStock 4, 5, 11B, 12, 13TL, 13TR, 13C, 13B, 14B, 14T, 14C, 15, 15B, 16/17, 19B, 20BL, 22, 26, 55, 83, 109, 136/137, 149, 173, 202/203, 205, 215, 248/249, 251, 269, 313, 353, 385, 439, 473, 478/479, 481, 491, 517, 536/537, 539, 569, 597

Shutterstock 18B, 19C, 20TL, 20/21, 52/53, 139, 329, 400/401, 403, 423, 521, 632

Cover: Beach, Fernando de Noronha **Alex Robinson/ AWL Images**
1: Paraty harbour **Alex Robinson/AWL Images Ltd**

Index

N

O

P

Q

R

S

T

Map symbols

The symbols below are used on maps throughout the book

Listings key

- Accommodation
- Eating
- Drinking/Nightlife
- Shopping